solutions@syngress.com

With more than 1,500,000 copies of our MCSE, MCSD, CompTIA, and Cisco study guides in print, we continue to look for ways we can better serve the information needs of our readers. One way we do that is by listening.

Readers like yourself have been telling us they want an Internet-based service that would extend and enhance the value of our books. Based on reader feedback and our own strategic plan, we have created a Web site that we hope will exceed your expectations.

Solutions@syngress.com is an interactive treasure trove of useful information focusing on our book topics and related technologies. The site offers the following features:

- One-year warranty against content obsolescence due to vendor product upgrades. You can access online updates for any affected chapters.

- "Ask the Author" customer query forms that enable you to post questions to our authors and editors.

- Exclusive monthly mailings in which our experts provide answers to reader queries and clear explanations of complex material.

- Regularly updated links to sites specially selected by our editors for readers desiring additional reliable information on key topics.

Best of all, the book you're now holding is your key to this amazing site. Just go to **www.syngress.com/solutions**, and keep this book handy when you register to verify your purchase.

Thank you for giving us the opportunity to serve your needs. And be sure to let us know if there's anything else we can do to help you get the maximum value from your investment. We're listening.

www.syngress.com/solutions

SYNGRESS®

D1534573

about itfaqnet.com

Syngress Publishing is a proud sponsor of **itfaqnet.com**, one of the web's most comprehensive FAQ sites for IT professionals. This is a free service that allows users to query over 10,000 FAQs pertaining to Cisco networking, Microsoft networking. Network security tools, .NET development, Wireless technology, IP Telephony, Storage Area Networking, Java development and much more. The content on itfaqnet.com is all derived from our hundreds of market proven books, written and reviewed by content experts.

So bookmark **ITFAQnet.com** as your first stop for mission critical advice from the industry's leading experts.

www.itfaqnet.com

SYNGRESS®

SYNGRESS®

BEST DAMN FIREWALL BOOK PERIOD

Anne Carasik-Henmi, Technical Editor

Dr. Thomas W. Shinder | **Cherie Amon** | **Robert J. Shimonski** | **Debra Littlejohn Shinder**

KEY	SERIAL NUMBER
001	PK9ST3V343
002	KATHYT6CVF
003	8J9HFJASQN
004	Z2B4NDREAY
005	U8J3N5R33S
006	X6B7MATTY6
007	G8TR2SH2AK
008	9BKTHQM4S7
009	SW4KP7V6FH
010	5BVF7UM39Z

PUBLISHED BY
Syngress Publishing, Inc.
800 Hingham Street
Rockland, MA 02370

The Best Damn Firewall Book Period

Copyright © 2003 by Syngress Publishing, Inc. All rights reserved. Printed in the United States of America. Except as permitted under the Copyright Act of 1976, no part of this publication may be reproduced or distributed in any form or by any means, or stored in a database or retrieval system, without the prior written permission of the publisher, with the exception that the program listings may be entered, stored, and executed in a computer system, but they may not be reproduced for publication.

Printed in the United States of America

1 2 3 4 5 6 7 8 9 0

ISBN: 1-931836-90-6

Technical Editor: Anne Carasik-Henmi
Acquisitions Editor: Catherine B. Nolan
Indexer: J. Edmund Rush

Cover Designer: Michael Kavish
Page Layout and Art by: Patricia Lupien & John Vickers
Copy Editor: Beth A. Roberts & Amy Thomson

Distributed by Publishers Group West in the United States and Jaguar Book Group in Canada.

Contributor andTechnical Editor

Anne Carasik-Henmi is a System Administrator at the Center for Advanced Computational Research (CACR) at the California Institute of Technology. She is in charge of information security at CACR, which includes every aspect of information security including intrusion detection (running Snort, of course), network security, system security, internal IT auditing, and network security policy. Her specialties include Linux, Secure Shell, public key technologies, penetration testing, and network security architectures. Anne's background includes positions as a Principal Security Consultant at SSH Communications Security, and as an Information Security Analyst at VeriSign, Inc.

Contributors

Debra Littlejohn Shinder (MCSE) is a technology consultant, trainer, and writer who has authored a number of books on networking, including: *Scene of the Cybercrime: Computer Forensics Handbook* published by Syngress Publishing (ISBN: 1-931836-65-5), and *Computer Networking Essentials,* published by Cisco Press. She is co-author, with her husband Dr. Thomas Shinder, of *Troubleshooting Windows 2000 TCP/IP* (ISBN: 1-928994-11-3), the best-selling *Configuring ISA Server 2000* (ISBN: 1-928994-29-6), and *ISA Server and Beyond* (ISBN: 1-931836-66-3). Deb is also a technical editor and contributor to books on subjects such as the Windows 2000 MCSE exams, the CompTIA Security+ exam, and TruSecure's ICSA certification. She edits the Brainbuzz A+ Hardware News and Sunbelt Software's WinXP News and is regularly published in TechRepublic's TechProGuild and Windowsecurity.com. Deb specializes in security issues and Microsoft products. She lives and works in the Dallas-Fort Worth area and can be contacted at deb@shinder.net or via the website at www.shinder.net.

Thomas W. Shinder M.D. (MVP, MCSE) is a computing industry veteran who has worked as a trainer, writer, and a consultant for Fortune 500 companies including FINA Oil, Lucent Technologies, and Sealand Container Corporation. Tom was a Series Editor of the Syngress/Osborne Series of Windows 2000 Certification Study Guides and is author of the best selling books *Configuring ISA Server 2000: Building Firewalls with Windows 2000* (Syngress Publishing, ISBN: 1-928994-29-6) and *Dr. Tom Shinder's ISA Server and Beyond* (ISBN: 1-931836-66-3). Tom is the editor of the Brainbuzz.com *Win2k News* newsletter and is a regular contributor to TechProGuild. He is also content editor, contributor, and moderator for the World's leading site on ISA Server 2000, www.isaserver.org. Microsoft recognized Tom's leadership in the ISA Server community and awarded him their Most Valued Professional (MVP) award in December of 2001.

Robert J. Shimonski (TruSecure TICSA, Cisco CCDP, CCNP, Symantec SPS, NAI Sniffer SCP, Nortel NNCSS, Microsoft MCSE, MCP+I, Novell Master CNE, CIP, CIBS, CNS, IWA CWP, DCSE, Prosoft MCIW, SANS.org GSEC, GCIH, CompTIA Server+, Network+, Inet+, A+, e-Biz+, Security+, HTI+) is a Lead Network and Security Engineer for a leading manufacturing company, Danaher Corporation. At Danaher, Robert is responsible for leading the IT department within his division into implementing new technologies, standardization, upgrades, migrations, high-end project planning and designing infrastructure architecture. Robert is also part of the corporate security team responsible for setting guidelines and policy for the entire corporation worldwide. In his role as a Lead Network Engineer, Robert has designed, migrated, and implemented very large-scale Cisco and Nortel based networks. Robert has held positions as a Network Architect for Cendant Information Technology and worked on accounts ranging from the IRS to AVIS Rent a Car, and was part of the team that rebuilt the entire Avis worldwide network infrastructure to include the Core and all remote locations. Robert maintains a role as a part time technical trainer at a local computer school, teaching classes on networking and systems administration whenever possible.

Robert is also a part-time author who has worked on over 25 book projects as both an author and technical editor. He has written and edited books on a plethora of topics with a strong emphasis on network security. Robert has designed and worked on several projects dealing with cutting edge technologies for Syngress Publishing, including the only book dedicated to the Sniffer Pro protocol analyzer. Robert has worked on the following Syngress Publishing titles: *Building DMZs for Enterprise Networks* (ISBN: 1-931836-88-4), *Security+ Study Guide & DVD Training System* (ISBN: 1-931836-72-8), *Sniffer Pro Network Optimization & Troubleshooting Handbook* (ISBN: 1-931836-57-4), *Configuring and Troubleshooting Windows XP Professional* (ISBN: 1-928994-80-6), *SSCP Study Guide & DVD Training System* (ISBN: 1-931836-80-9), *Nokia Network Security Solutions Handbook* (ISBN: 1-931836-70-1) and the *MCSE Implementing and Administering Security in a Windows 2000 Network Study Guide & DVD Training System* (ISBN: 1-931836-84-1).

Robert's specialties include network infrastructure design with the Cisco product line, systems engineering with Windows 2000/2003 Server, NetWare 6, Red Hat Linux and Apple OSX. Robert's true love is network security design and management utilizing products from the Nokia, Cisco, and Check Point arsenal. Robert is also an advocate of Network Management and loves to 'sniff' networks with Sniffer-based technologies. When not doing something with computer related technology, Robert enjoys spending time with Erika, or snowboarding wherever the snow may fall and stick.

Cherie Amon (CCSA, CCSE, CCSI, NSA) is technical editor of and contributor to the best selling *Check Point Next Generation Security Administration* (Syngress Publishing, ISBN: 1-928994-74-1), as well as the *Nokia Network Security Solutions Handbook* (Syngress, ISBN: 1-931836-70-1). Cherie is a Senior Professional Security Engineer at Integralis, a systems integrator specializing in IT and e-commerce security solutions. She is both a Check Point and Nokia Certified Security Instructor and has been installing, configuring, and supporting Check Point products since 1997. Cherie currently provides third-tier technical support to Integralis clients and acts as Technical Lead for many managed firewall accounts. Cherie is a member of USENIX and SAGE.

Kyle X. Hourihan (NSA) is the Course Development Manager and a Senior Technical Trainer for Nokia Internet Communications in Mountain View, CA. He designs, writes, and teaches Nokia Internet Division's internal and external training material. He conducts Train-the-Trainer sessions for Nokia Authorized Training Partners as well as high-end training for Nokia's internal R&D and TACs (Telephone Assistance Centers). Kyle has been working in Network Security since 1999, and previously worked for 3Com as a Senior Instructor and Developer for their Carrier Systems Division (Commworks). He began his career working as a programmer writing code for Cisco IOS implementing minor routing protocols and performing software QA on their routers. Kyle earned a bachelor's of Science in Computer Science from the University of Maryland, College Park. He was a co-author of the highly acclaimed *Nokia Network Security Solutions Handbook* (Syngress Publishing, ISBN: 1-931836-70-1), and he is also a co-author of Freesoft.org (www.freesoft.org), a comprehensive source of Internet engineering information. Kyle resides in Palo Alto, CA.

James Stanger (Ph.D., Symantec Technology Architect (STA), Convergence Technology Professional, CIW Master Administrator, MCP, Linux+, A+) is co-author of Syngress Publishing's *E-mail Virus Protection Handbook* (ISBN: 1-928994-23-7) and *Hack Proofing Linux: A Guide to Open Source Security* (ISBN: 1-928994-34-2). A network security consultant and writer, James' specialties include virus management, mail server administration, intrusion detection, and network auditing. Currently Senior Course Director for ProsoftTraining, James consults with Symantec to enable security professionals to deploy virus protection, vulnerability management, and firewall/VPN solutions in enterprise networks. James has also consulted for companies and organizations such as IBM, Securify, Brigham Young University, ITM Technology, and the William Blake Archive. James is the Chairperson of the Linux Professional Institute (LPI) Advisory Council and sits on the CompTIA Linux+ and Server+ cornerstone committees. In addition to authoring books for Syngress, James has also authored security books and courses for Sybex, Osborne/McGraw-Hill, and ComputerPREP. James resides in Washington.

Randy Cook (SCSA) is a Senior Engineer with BayMountain (www.baymountain.com) a local IT services company. Randy was the co-author and technical editor of the *Sun Certified System Administrator for Solaris 8.0 Study Guide* (ISBN: 0-07-212369-9), and Syngress Publishing's *Hack Proofing Sun Solaris 8.0* (ISBN: 1-928994-34-2) and has written technical articles for industry publications. He has also hosted a syndicated radio program, *Technically News*, which provided news and information for IT professionals.

Contents

Chapter 9 Passing Traffic   277

Chapter 10 Advanced PIX Configurations   309

Chapter 13 Using the Graphical Interface   491

Part V ISA Server 811
Chapter 22 ISA Server Deployment Planning and Design 813

Chapter 25 Optimizing, Customizing, Integrating, and Backing Up ISA Server   **941**

Foreword

Foreword

In the beginning, there were router access lists…

Then the next firewalls evolved into application proxies. The best definition of a firewall in its simplest form is by Steven Bellovin a co-author of *Firewalls and Internet Security: Repeling the Wily Hacker*. In this book Steven wrote "Firewalls are barriers between *us* and *them* for arbitrary values of 'them'."

With firewalls becoming a chokepoint of the network, they define what is to be trusted and what is not. The untrusted elements range from the standard hackers, spammers, and crackers, to a Human Resources department of an organization deeming the rest of the company "untrusted", to even the conventional chokepoint of a company trusting only itself, and not deeming the Internet "trustworthy or safe". Today firewalls have evolved into more than just a simple chokepoint. Firewalls include all sorts of different solutions: hardware, software, intrusion detection, desktop solutions, and so forth. As technology has evolved, the number of options that users have to choose from has increased exponentially. *The Best Damn Firewall Book Period* provides readers with a guide to the most popular firewall technology implementations.

Before you dive into the various firewall implementations, we recommend that you spend some time reading "Part I: Introduction to Network Security & Firewalls". Part I delves into network security basics, the different types of firewalls, and provides a brief introduction to intrusion detection systems (which should be part of any efficient and effective defense in depth security strategy).

After the Part I, the book is broken down into the following:

- Part II Linux & Solaris Firewalls
- Part III PIX Firewalls
- Part IV: Check Point NG and Nokia IP Series Appliances
- Part V ISA Server
- Part VI Intrusion Detection

This is not a "best of the marketing documentation" for various solutions and vendors. If you need marketing documentation, that's always available from the vendor's Web site. This book is about implementing various solutions on a technical level. This book is great for those system administrators, network administrators, and security administrators who are looking for how various firewall systems work, and how they can help secure your network. Each section provides detailed information with regards to the technical implementations of each firewall, in order to assist you in determining the strengths of each solution, and deciding which implementation would be best for your network.

Before you do pick a firewall, make sure you know that:

1. A firewall is not the end-all, be-all of network security.

2. Your firewall is only as strong as your security policy.

3. Make sure you educate your system administrators, management, and users regularly

Audience

The Best Damn Firewall Book Period is written for the system administrators and network administrators as these are the individuals who are going to be offering the recommendations and implementing the security solutions. Most of this book is quite technical, however this book could be considered a great overview of the variety of security concepts, exploits, and solutions for network security engineers. It provides some basic information about firewalls, as well as plenty of technical details that give you the nuts and bolts of how the various firewalls work.

Acknowledgments

I want to thank my husband Russ Henmi, who has been supportive and loving through all my endeavors (including this one). I also want to thank my colleagues at the Center for Advanced Computing Research (CACR) at Caltech for supporting me in my publications. I particularly want to thank Mark Bartelt, Chip Chapman, and John McCorquodale at CACR who are encouraging and supportive about keeping the network secure. Also thanks to my editor Catherine Nolan, whose comments have kept me on my toes, yet made this a fun book, and a better one, to produce.

Anne Carasik-Henmi
September 2003

Part I

Introduction to Network Security & Firewalls

Chapter 1

Introduction to Information Security

Solutions in this Chapter:

- Insecurity and the Internet
- Threats and Attacks
- Security Policies
- Creating A Security Policy
- Protecting Information Technology
- Using SSL and Secure Shell
- Other Hardware Security Devices

Introduction

In an age where our society relies so heavily on electronic communication, the need for information security is constantly increasing. Given the value and confidential nature of the information that exists on today's networks, CIOs are finding that an investment in security is extremely beneficial. Without security, a company can suffer from theft or alteration of data, legal ramifications, and other issues that all result in monetary losses.

In this chapter, we look at the big picture: what we mean by network security in general and Internet security in particular; why it's necessary and how we can create a comprehensive security policy to protect our networks from unauthorized access.

Network security is a hot topic and is growing into a high-profile (and often highly-paid) IT specialty area. Security-related Web sites such as Net-Security (www.net-security.org), SecurityFocus (www.securityfocus.com), and Packetstorm Security (www.packetstormsecurity.org) are tremendously popular with savvy Internet users. Esoteric security measures such as biometric identification and authentication—formerly the province of science fiction writers and perhaps a few ultrasecretive government agencies—have become almost commonplace in corporate America.

Yet with all this focus on security, many organizations implement security measures in an almost haphazard way, with no well-considered plan for making all the parts fit together. Computer security involves many aspects of safekeeping, from protection of the physical equipment to protection of the electronic bits and bytes that make up the information that resides on the network.

In the next section, we provide a brief overview of what we mean by *security* in general and how the concept applies to your computer network. This chapter focuses on generic computer and Internet security concepts and the way to develop a comprehensive security plan for your organization. In order to understand how firewalls are used in a network, you need to understand the basics of network security. A firewall is not a "security solution" per se; instead, it is part of your security solution.

However, a firewall is a big part of most network security solutions. A firewall is the guardian to the castle at the moat: the firewall decides what is let in and what is let out. This is done through your firewall rules, which are policy-defined. A firewall can be various devices, from a Solaris system to a separate hardware appliance. No matter what type of package a firewall comes in, its job is the same: be the guardian of your network.

Insecurity and the Internet

The federation of networks that became the Internet consisted of a relatively small community of users by the 1980s, primarily in the research and academic communities. Because it was rather difficult to get access to these systems and the user communities were rather closely knit, security was not much of a concern in this environment. The main objective of connecting these various networks together was to share information, not keep it locked away. Technologies such as the UNIX operating system and the Transmission Control Protocol/Internet Protocol (TCP/IP) networking protocols that were designed for this environment reflected this lack of security concern. Security was simply viewed as unnecessary.

By the early 1990s, however, commercial interest in the Internet grew. These commercial interests had very different perspectives on security, ones often in opposition to those of academia. Commercial information had value, and access to it had to be limited to specifically authorized people. UNIX, TCP/IP, and connections to the Internet became avenues of attack and did not have much capability to implement and enforce confidentiality, integrity, and availability. As the Internet grew in commercial importance, with numerous companies connecting to it and even building entire business models around it, the need for increased security became quite acute. Connected organizations now faced threats that they had never had to consider before.

When the corporate computing environment was a closed and limited-access system, threats mostly came from inside the organizations. These *internal threats* came from disgruntled employees with privileged access who could cause a lot of damage. Attacks from the outside were not much of an issue since there were typically only a few, if any, private connections to trusted entities. Potential attackers were few in number, since the combination of necessary skills and malicious intent were not at all widespread.

With the growth of the Internet, *external threats* grew as well. There are now millions of hosts on the Internet as potential attack targets, which entice the now large numbers of attackers. This group has grown in size and skill over the years as its members share information on how to break into systems for both fun and profit. Geography no longer serves as an obstacle, either. You can be attacked from another continent thousands of miles away just as easily as from your own town.

Threats can be classified as structured or unstructured. *Unstructured threats* are from people with low skill and perseverance. These usually come from people called *script kiddies*—attackers who have little to no programming skill and very little system knowledge. Script kiddies tend to conduct attacks just for bragging rights among their groups, which are often linked only by an Internet Relay Chat (IRC) channel. They obtain attack tools that have been built by others with more skill and use them, often indiscriminately, to attempt to exploit a vulnerability in their target. If their attack fails, they will likely go elsewhere and keep trying. Additional risk comes from the fact that they often use these tools with little to no knowledge of the target environment, so attacks can wind up causing unintended results. Unstructured threats can cause significant damage or disruption, despite the attacker's lack of sophistication. These attacks are usually detectable with current security tools.

Structured attacks are more worrisome because they are conducted by hackers with significant skill. If the existing tools do not work for them, they are likely to modify them or write their own. They are able to discover new vulnerabilities in systems by executing complex actions that the system designers did not protect against. Structured attackers often use so-called *zero-day exploits*, which are exploits that target vulnerabilities that the system vendor has not yet issued a patch for or does not even know about. Structured attacks often have stronger motivations behind them than simple mischief. These motivations or goals can include theft of source code, theft of credit card numbers for resale or fraud, retribution, or destruction or disruption of a competitor. A structured attack might not be blocked by traditional methods such as firewall rules or detected by an Intrusion Detection System (IDS). It could even use non–computer methods such as social engineering.

> **NOTE**
>
> *Social engineering,* also known as *people hacking,* is a means for obtaining security information from people by tricking them. The classic example is calling up a user and pretending to be a system administrator. The hacker asks the user for his or her password to ostensibly perform some important maintenance task. To avoid being hacked via social engineering, educate your user community that they should always confirm the identity of any person calling them and that passwords should never be given to *anyone* over e-mail, instant messaging, or the phone.

Another key task in securing your systems is closing vulnerabilities by turning off unneeded services and bringing them up to date on patches. Services that have no defined business need present an additional possible avenue of attack and are just another component that needs patch attention. Keeping patches current is actually one of the most important activities you can perform to protect yourself, yet it is one that many organizations neglect.

The Code Red and Nimda worms of 2001 were successful primarily because so many systems had not been patched for the vulnerabilities they exploited, including multiple Microsoft Internet Information Server (IIS) and Microsoft Outlook vulnerabilities. Patching, especially when you have hundreds or even thousands of systems, can be a monumental task. However, by defining and documenting processes, using tools to assist in configuration management, subscribing to multiple vulnerability alert mailing lists, and prioritizing patches according to criticality, you can get a better handle on the job.

One useful document to assist in this process has been published by the U.S. National Institute of Standards and Technology (NIST), which can be found at http://csrc.nist.gov/publications/nistpubs/800-40/sp800-40.pdf (800-40 is the document number).

Also important is having a complete understanding of your network topology and some of the key information flows within it as well as in and out of it. This understanding helps you define different zones of trust and highlights where re-architecting the network in places might improve security—for example, by deploying additional firewalls internally or on your network perimeter.

Defining Information Security

Over the last couple of decades, many companies began to realize that their most valuable assets were not only their buildings or factories but also the intellectual property and other information that flowed internally as well as outwardly to suppliers and customers. Company managers, used to dealing with risk in their business activities, started to think about what might happen if their key business information fell into the wrong hands, perhaps a competitor's.

For a while, this risk was not too large, due to how and where that information was stored. *Closed systems* was the operative phrase. Key business information, for the most part, was stored on servers accessed via terminals or terminal emulators and had few interconnections with other systems. Any interconnections tended to be over private leased lines to a select few locations, either internal to the company or to a trusted business partner.

However, over the last five to seven years, the Internet has changed how businesses operate, and there has been a huge acceleration in the interconnectedness of organizations, systems, and networks. Entire corporate networks have access to the Internet, often at multiple points. This proliferation has created risks to sensitive information and business-critical systems where they had barely existed before. The importance of information security in the business environment has now been underscored, as has the need for skilled, dedicated practitioners of this specialty.

We have traditionally thought of security as consisting of people, sometimes with guns, watching over and guarding tangible assets such as a stack of money or a research lab. Maybe they sat at a desk and watched via closed-circuit cameras installed around the property. These people usually had minimal training and sometimes did not understand much about what they were guarding or why it was important. However, they did their jobs (and continue to do so) according to established processes, such as walking around the facility on a regular basis and looking for suspicious activity or people who do not appear to belong there.

Information security moves that model into the intangible realm. Fundamentally, information security involves making sure that only authorized people (and systems) have access to information. Information security professionals sometimes have different views on the role and definition of information security

The three primary areas of concern in information security have traditionally been defined as follows:

- **Confidentiality** Ensuring that only authorized parties have access to information. Encryption is a commonly used tool to achieve confidentiality. Authentication and authorization, treated separately in the following discussion, also help with confidentiality.

- **Integrity** Ensuring that information is not modified by unauthorized parties (or even improperly modified by authorized ones!) and that it can be relied on. Checksums and hashes are used to validate data integrity, as are transaction-logging systems.

- **Availability** Ensuring that information is accessible when it is needed. In addition to simple backups of data, availability includes ensuring that systems remain accessible in the event of a denial of service (DoS) attack. Availability also means that critical data should be protected from erasure—for example, preventing the wipeout of data on your company's external Web site.

Often referred to simply by the acronym *CIA*, these three areas serve well as a security foundation. To fully scope the role of information security, however, we also need to add a few more areas of concern to the list. Some security practitioners include the following within the three areas described above, but by getting more granular, we can get a better sense of the challenges that must be addressed:

- **Authentication** Ensuring that users are, in fact, who they say they are. Passwords, of course, are the longstanding way to authenticate users, but other methods such as cryptographic tokens and biometrics are also used.

- **Authorization/access control** Ensuring that a user, once authenticated, is only able to access information to which he or she has been granted permission by the owner of the information. This can be accomplished at the operating system level using file system access controls or at the network level using access controls on routers or firewalls.

- **Auditability** Ensuring that activity and transactions on a system or network can be monitored and logged in order to maintain system availability and detect unauthorized use. This process can take various forms: logging by the operating system, logging by a network device such as a router or firewall, or logging by an intrusion detection system (IDS) or packet-capture device.

- **Nonrepudiation** Ensuring that a person initiating a transaction is authenticated sufficiently such that he or she cannot reasonably deny that they were the initiating party. Public key cryptography is often used to support this effort.

You can say that your information is secure when all seven of these areas have been adequately addressed. The definition of *adequately* depends, however, on how much risk exists in each area. Some areas may present greater risk in a particular environment than in others.

Common Information Security Concepts

A generic dictionary definition of *security* (taken from the American Heritage Dictionary) is "freedom from risk or danger; safety." This definition is perhaps a little misleading when it comes to computer and networking security, because it implies a degree of protection that is inherently impossible to achieve in the modern connectivity-oriented computing environment.

For this reason, the same dictionary provides another definition specific to computer science: "The *level to which* a program or device is safe from unauthorized use" (emphasis added). Implicit in this definition is the caveat that the objectives of security and accessibility—the two top priorities on the minds of many network administrators—are, by their very nature, diametrically opposed. The more accessible your data, the less secure it is. Likewise, the more tightly you secure your data, the more you impede accessibility. Any security plan is an attempt to strike the proper balance between the two.

Knowledge Is Power

The preceding heading is a famous hacker's motto (along with such other gems as "Information wants to be free" and the simplistic but optimistic "Hack the world!"). "Knowledge is power" is a truism that applies not only to people attempting to gain access to data they aren't supposed to see, but also to those who are trying to protect themselves from such intruders. The first step in winning any battle—and network security *is* a battle, a battle for the ownership and control of your computer files—is the same as it's always been: "Know thine enemy."

To protect your network resources from theft, damage, or unwanted exposure, you must understand who initiates these events, why they do it, and how they do it. This knowledge will make *you* powerful, too—and better able to prevent unauthorized intrusions into your network. The section "Preventing Unauthorized External Intrusions and Attacks" discusses the various motivations that drive network intruders and the types of people who make a practice of "breaking and entering" networks.

The very best place to learn is from hackers themselves. Even so, many network administrators and even some security specialists eschew the books and Web sites that are written to a hacker audience or from the hacker's point of view. This might be because they fear "guilt by association" or believe that they would be somehow lowering themselves to "hang out" with hackers. Although possibly based on high moral ground, this attitude is, strategically, a mistake. Whether you take a more formal route, such as the SANS GIAC or CISSP certification courses, or opt to learn on your own, you'll need to understand who the hackers are, what they do, and how and why they do it if you want to effectively protect your network from unwanted intrusions.

Think Like a Thief

It is well known in law enforcement circles that the best criminal investigators are those who are best able to "get inside the mind" of the lawbreaker. Network intrusion detectives will find that the same is true: to prevent your network from falling prey to hackers or to catch data thieves when they do get in requires you to be able to adopt a mindset emulating theirs.

This means learning to anticipate the intruder's actions. First, you must determine *what* needs to be protected, and to what degree. A wealthy person not only establishes a general security perimeter by building fences around his or her house and locking doors and windows, but the wise person also places the most valuable items in a wall or floor safe. This action provides multiple *layers* of protection.

Removing Intrusion Opportunities

The term *computer security* encompasses many related but separate topics. These topics can be stated as security objectives:

- Control of physical accessibility to the computer(s) and/or network
- Prevention of accidental erasure, modification, or compromise of data
- Detection and prevention of intentional internal security breaches
- Detection and prevention of unauthorized external intrusions (hacking)

Network security solutions can be loosely divided into three categories:

- Hardware
- Software
- Human

This chapter provides an overview of basic security concepts, then examines all four security objectives and takes a look at each of the three categories of security solution. A good network security system will help you easily remove the temptations (open ports, exploitable applications) and will be as transparent to your users as possible.

Crime prevention officers tell members of the community that they probably can't keep a potential burglar from wanting to steal, and they certainly can't keep the potential burglar from obtaining burglary tools or learning the "tricks of the trade." What community members *can* do is take away, as much as possible, the opportunity for the burglar to target their own homes.

This means putting dead-bolt locks on the doors (and using them); getting a big, loud, unfriendly dog; installing an alarm system, and the like. In other words, the homeowner's goal is not to prevent the burglar from burglarizing (that's the job of the police) but to make his or her home a less desirable target. Similarly, as a network "owner," your objective is to "harden" your own network so that all those hackers out there who already have the motive and the means will look for a more likely victim.

If you don't use them, the best and most expensive locks in the world won't keep intruders out of your house. And if those locks are difficult to use and cause you inconvenience in your everyday comings and goings, you probably *won't* use them—at least, not all the time. A poorly implemented network security system that is difficult to administer or that unduly inconveniences network users could end up similarly; eventually you will throw your hands up in frustration and just turn the darn thing off. And that will leave your network wide open to intruders.

For example, a network administrator would add Intrusion Detection Systems, router access lists, Tripwire to the local systems to check for changed system binaries, and public key or digital certificate authentication to allow him or herself a substitute for a password. However, if you've implemented this and not used it, you're wasting your resources.

It is not the job of the homeowners to prevent burglars from burglarizing—only to protect *themselves* from being victimized. Likewise, it is not the job of a network administrator or network security manager to keep hackers from hacking. You can only take steps to protect your network and its resources from those who "break and enter" networks for fun or profit.

Threats and Attacks

Ensuring a physically secure network environment is the first step in controlling access to your network's important data and system files, but it is only part of a good security plan. This is truer today than in the past because networks have more ways in than they once did. A medium-sized or large network can have multiple dial-in servers, virtual private network (VPN) servers, and a dedicated full-time Internet connection. Even a small network is likely to be connected to the Internet part of the time.

Physical Security

One of the most important and at the same time most overlooked aspects of a comprehensive network security plan is physical access control. This matter is often left up to facilities managers and plant security departments or outsourced to security guard companies. Network administrators concern themselves with sophisticated software and hardware solutions that prevent intruders from accessing internal computers remotely while doing nothing to protect the servers, routers, cable, and other physical components of the network from direct access. In far too many supposedly security-conscious organizations, computers are locked away from employees and visitors all day, only to be left open at night to the janitorial staff, who have keys to all offices. It is not at all uncommon for computer espionage experts to pose as members of cleaning crews to gain physical access to machines that hold sensitive data. This is a favorite ploy for several reasons:

- Cleaning services are often contracted out, and workers in the industry are often transient, so your company employees might not be easily aware of who is or isn't a legitimate member of the cleaning company staff.

- Cleaning is usually done late at night, when all or most company employees are gone, making it easier to surreptitiously steal data.

- The cleaning crew members are often paid little or no attention by company employees, who take their presence for granted and think nothing of their being in areas where the presence of others would normally be questioned.

Physically breaking into the server room and stealing the hard disk on which sensitive data resides might be a crude method of breaching security; nonetheless, it happens. In some organizations, it could be the easiest way to gain unauthorized access, especially for an intruder who has help "on the inside."

It is beyond the scope of this book to go into great detail about how to physically secure your network, but it is important for you to make physical access control the outer perimeter of your security plan. This means:

- Controlling physical access to the servers
- Controlling physical access to networked workstations
- Controlling physical access to network devices
- Controlling physical access to the cable
- Being aware of security considerations with wireless media
- Being aware of security considerations related to portable computers
- Recognizing the security risk of allowing data to be printed
- Recognizing the security risks involving floppy disks, CDs, tapes, and other removable media

There is also a special type of external intruder who *physically* breaks into your facility to gain access to your network. Although not a true "insider" because he or she is not authorized to be there and does not have a valid account on the network, this person has many of the advantages of those discussed in the section on internal security breaches. Your security policy should take into account the threats posed by these "hybrid" types of intruders.

Network Security

Virtual intruders never set foot on your organization's property and never touch your computers. They can access your network from across the street or from halfway across the world. But they can do as much damage as the thief who breaks into your company headquarters to steal or destroy your data—and they are much harder to catch. In the following sections, we examine specific network security risks and ways to prevent them.

With the growth of the Internet, many organizations focused their security efforts on defending against outside attackers (that is, those originating from an external network) who are not authorized to access the systems. Firewalls were the primary focus of these efforts. Money was spent on building a strong perimeter defense, resulting in what Bill Cheswick from Bell Labs famously described years ago as "a crunchy shell around a soft, chewy center." Any attacker who succeeded in getting through (or around) the perimeter defenses would then have a relatively easy time compromising internal systems. This situation is analogous to the enemy parachuting into the castle keep instead of breaking through the walls (the technology is off by a few centuries, but you get the idea!). Perimeter defense is still vitally important, given the increased threat level from outside the network. However, it is simply no longer adequate by itself.

Various information security studies and surveys have found that the majority of attacks actually come from inside the organization. The internal threat can include authorized users attempting to exceed their permissions or unauthorized users trying to go where they should not be at all. The insider is potentially more dangerous than outsiders because he or she has a level of access that the outsider does not—to both facilities and systems. Many organizations lack the internal preventive controls and other countermeasures to adequately defend against this threat. Networks are wide open, servers could be sitting in unsecured areas, system patches might be out of date, and system administrators might not review security logs.

The greatest threat, however, arises when an insider colludes with a structured outside attacker. The outsider's skills, combined with the insider's access, could result in substantial damage or loss to the organization.

Attacks can be divided into three main categories:

- **Reconnaissance attacks** Hackers attempt to discover systems and gather information. In most cases, these attacks are used to gather information to set up an access or a DoS attack. A typical reconnaissance attack might consist of a hacker pinging IP addresses to discover what is alive on a network. The hacker might then perform a port scan on the systems to see which applications are running as well as try to determine the operating system and version on a target machine.

- **Access attacks** An access attack is one in which an intruder attempts to gain unauthorized access to a system to retrieve information. Sometimes the attacker needs to gain access to a system by cracking passwords or using an exploit. At other times, the attacker already has access to the system but needs to escalate his or her privileges.

- **DoS attacks** Hackers use DoS attacks to disable or corrupt access to networks, systems, or services. The intent is to deny authorized or valid users access to these resources. DoS attacks typically involve running a script or a tool, and the attacker does not require access to the target system, only a means to reach it. In a distributed DoS (DDoS) attack, the source consists of many computers that are usually spread across a large geographic boundary.

Recognizing Network Security Threats

In order to effectively protect your network, you must consider the following question: from *who* or *what* are you protecting it? In this section, we approach the answer to that question from two perspectives:

- **Who** Types of network intruders and their motivations
- **What** Types of network attackers and how they work

First we look at intruder motivations and classify the various types of people who have the skill and desire to hack into others' computers and networks.

Understanding Intruder Motivations

There are probably as many different specific motives as there are hackers, but we can break the most common intruder motivations into a few broad categories:

- **Recreation** Those who hack into networks "just for fun" or to prove their technical prowess; often young people or "antiestablishment" types.

- **Remuneration** People who invade the network for personal gain, such as those who attempt to transfer funds to their own bank accounts or erase records of their debts; "hackers for hire" who are paid by others to break into the network. Corporate espionage is included in this category.

- **Revenge** Dissatisfied customers, disgruntled former employees, angry competitors, or people who have a personal grudge against someone in the organization.

The scope of damage and extent of the intrusion is often—although by no means always—tied to the intruder's motivation.

Recreational Hackers

Teen hackers who hack primarily for the thrill of accomplishment often do little or no permanent damage, perhaps only leaving "I was here" messages to "stake their claims" and prove to their peers that they were able to penetrate your network's security.

There are more malevolent versions of the fun-seeking hacker, however. These are the cyber-vandals who get their kicks out of destroying as much of your data as possible or causing your systems to crash.

Profit-Motivated Hackers

Hackers who break into your network for remuneration of some kind—either directly or indirectly—are more dangerous. Because money is at stake, they are more motivated than other hackers to accomplish their objective. Furthermore, because many of them are "professionals" of a sort, their hacking techniques could be more sophisticated than those of the average teenage recreational hacker.

Monetary motivations include:

- Personal financial gain
- Third-party payment
- Corporate espionage

Those motivated by the last goal are almost always the most sophisticated and the most dangerous. Often *big* money is involved in theft of trade secrets. Corporate espionage agents could be employees who have been approached by your competitors and offered money or merchandise or even threatened with blackmail or physical harm.

In some instances, hackers working for competitors will go "undercover" and seek a job with your company in order to steal data that they can take back to their own organizations. To add insult to injury, these "stealth spies" are then paid by your company at the same time they're working against you to the benefit of your competitor.

There are also "professional" freelance corporate spies. They can be contacted and contracted to obtain your company secrets, or they might do it on their own and auction the data off to your competitors.

These corporate espionage agents are often highly skilled. They are technically savvy and intelligent enough to avoid being caught or detected. Fields that are especially vulnerable to the threat of corporate espionage include:

- Oil and energy
- Engineering
- Computer technology
- Research medicine
- Law

Any company that is on the verge of a breakthrough that could result in large monetary rewards or worldwide recognition, especially if the company's involvement is high profile, should be aware of the possibility of espionage and take steps to guard against it.

Vengeful Hackers

Hackers motivated by the desire for revenge are dangerous as well. Vengeance seeking is usually based on strong emotions, which means that these hackers could go all-out in their efforts to sabotage your network.

Examples of hackers or security saboteurs acting out of revenge include:

- Former employees who are bitter about being fired or laid off or who quit their jobs under unpleasant circumstances
- Current employees who feel mistreated by the company, especially those who are planning to leave soon
- Current employees who aim to sabotage the work of other employees due to internal political battles, rivalry over promotions, and the like
- Outsiders who have grudges against the company, such as dissatisfied customers or employees of competing companies who want to harm or embarrass the company
- Outsiders who have personal grudges against someone who works for the company, such as employees' former girlfriends or boyfriends, spouses going through a divorce, and other relationship-related problems

Luckily, the intruders in this category are generally less technically talented than those in the other two groups, and their emotional involvement could cause them to be careless and take outrageous chances, which makes them easier to catch.

Hybrid Hackers

Of course, the three categories of hacker can overlap in some cases. A recreational hacker who perceives himself as having been mistreated by an employer or in a personal relationship could use his otherwise benign hacking skills to impose "justice" for the wrongs done to him, or a vengeful ex-employee or ex-spouse might pay someone else to do the hacking.

It is beneficial to understand the common motivations of network intruders because, although we might not be able to predict which type of hacker will decide to attack our networks, we can recognize how each operates and take steps to protect our networks from all of them.

Even more important than the type of *hacker* in planning our security strategy, however, is the type of *attack*. In the next section, we examine specific types of network attacks and ways in which you can protect against them.

Categorizing Security Solutions

A multi-layer security plan incorporates multiple security solutions. Security is not a "one size fits all" issue, so the options that work best for one organization are not necessarily the best choices for another. Security solutions can be generally broken down into two categories: hardware solutions and software solutions.

Back to Basics: TCP/UDP Well-Known Ports

The official well-known port assignments are documented in RFC 1700, available on the Web at www.freesoft.org/CIE/RFC/1700/index.htm. The port assignments are made by the Internet Assigned Numbers Authority (IANA). In general, a service uses the same port number with User Datagram Packet (UDP) as with TCP, although there are some exceptions. The assigned ports were originally numbered from 0–255, but the numbers were later expanded to 0–1023.

Some of the most used well-known ports are:

- TCP/UDP port 20: FTP (data)
- TCP/UDP port 21: FTP (control)
- TCP/UDP port23: Telnet
- TCP/UDP port 25: SMTP
- TCP/UDP port 53: DNS
- TCP/UDP port 67: BOOTP server
- TCP/UDP port 68: BOOTP client
- TCP/UDP port 69: TFTP
- TCP/UDP port 80: HTTP
- TCP/UDP port 88: Kerberos

- TCP/UDP port 110: POP3

- TCP/UDP port 119: NNTP

- TCP/UDP port 137: NetBIOS name service

- TCP/UDP port 138: NetBIOS datagram service

- TCP/UDP port 139: NetBIOS session service

- TCP/UDP port 194: IRC

- TCP/UDP port 220: IMAPv3

- TCP/UDP port 389: LDAP

Ports 1024–65,535 are called *registered ports;* these numbers are not controlled by IANA and can be used by user processes or applications. However, that does not mean that they, too, are not vulnerable to attack. For example, port 1433 is used by SQL, which might be of interest to hackers.

There are a total of 65,535 TCP ports (and the same number of UDP ports); they are used for various services and applications. If a port is open, it responds when another computer attempts to contact it over the network. Port-scanning programs such as Nmap are used to determine which ports are open on a particular machine. The program sends packets for a wide variety of protocols and, by examining which messages receive responses and which don't, creates a map of the computer's listening ports.

Port scanning in itself does no harm to your network or system, but it provides hackers with information they can use to penetrate a network. Potential attackers use port scans in much the same way that a car thief might try the doors of parked vehicles to determine which ones are unlocked. Although this activity does not, in itself, constitute a serious offense, what the person conducting the scan does with the information can present a big problem.

> **NOTE**
>
> The intrusion and attack reporting center at www.doshelp.com/PC/trojanports.htm is an excellent resource for information on ports that should be closed, filtered, or monitored because they are commonly used for Trojan and intrusion programs.

IP Half-Scan Attack

Half scans (also called *half-open scans* or *FIN scans*) attempt to avoid detection by sending only initial or final packets rather than establishing a connection. A half scan starts the SYN/ACK process with a targeted computer but does not complete it. Software that conducts half scans, such as Jakal, is called a *stealth scanner.* Many port-scanning detectors are unable to detect half scans.

IP Spoofing

IP spoofing involves changing the packet headers of a message to indicate that it came from an IP address other than the true source. The spoofed address is normally a trusted port, which allows a hacker to get a message through a firewall or router that would otherwise be filtered out. Modern firewalls protect against IP spoofing.

Spoofing is used whenever it is beneficial for one machine to impersonate another. It is often used in combination with one of the other types of attacks. For example, a spoofed address is used in the SYN flood attack to create a "half-open" connection, in which the client never responds to the SYN/ACK message because the spoofed address is that of a computer that is down or doesn't exist. Spoofing is also used to hide the true IP address of the attacker in ping of death, teardrop, and other attacks. IP spoofing can be prevented using source address verification on your router, if it is supported.

Source-Routing Attack

TCP/IP supports *source routing,* which is a means to permit the sender of network data to route the packets through a specific point on the network. There are two types of source routing:

- **Strict source routing** The sender of the data can specify the exact route (rarely used).
- **Loose source record route (LSRR)** The sender can specify certain routers (hops) through which the packet must pass.

The source route is an option in the IP header that allows the sender to override routing decisions that are normally made by the routers between the source and destination machines. Source routing is used by network administrators to map the network or to troubleshoot routing and communications problems. It can also be used to force traffic through a route that will provide the best performance. Unfortunately, source routing can also be exploited by hackers.

If the system allows source routing, an intruder can use it to reach private internal addresses on the Local Area Network (LAN) that normally would not be reachable from the Internet, by routing the traffic through another machine that is reachable from both the Internet and the internal machine. Source routing can be disabled on most routers to prevent this type of attack.

Other Protocol Exploits

The attacks we have discussed so far involve exploiting some feature or weakness of the TCP/IP protocols. Hackers can also exploit vulnerabilities of other common protocols, such as HTTP, DNS, Common Gateway Interface (CGI), and other common protocols.

Active-X controls, JavaScript, and VBScript can be used to add animations or applets to Web sites, or even to HTML e-mail messages, but hackers can exploit these to write controls or scripts that allow them to remotely plant viruses, access data, or change or delete files on the hard disks of unaware users who visit the page and run the script. Both Web browsers and e-mail client programs that support HTML mail are vulnerable.

System and Software Exploits

System and software exploits allow hackers to take advantage of weaknesses of particular operating systems and applications (often called *bugs*). Like protocol exploits, they are used by intruders to gain unauthorized access to computers or networks or to crash or clog up the systems to deny service to others.

Common "bugs" can be categorized as follows:

- **Buffer overflows** Many common security holes are based on buffer overflow problems. Buffer overflows occur when the number of bytes or characters input exceeds the maximum number allowed by the programmer in writing the program.

- **Unexpected input** Programmers might not take steps to define what happens if invalid input (input that doesn't match program specifications) is entered. Such input could cause the program to crash or open up a way into the system.

- **System configuration bugs** These are not really "bugs" per se; rather, they are ways of configuring the operating system or software that leaves it vulnerable to penetration.

Popular software such as Microsoft's Internet Information Server (IIS), Internet Explorer (MSIE), and Outlook Express (MSOE) are popular targets of hackers looking for software security holes that can be exploited.

Major operating system and software vendors regularly release security patches to fix exploitable bugs. It is very important for network administrators to stay up to date in applying these fixes and/or service packs to ensure that their systems are as secure as possible.

NOTE

Microsoft issues *security bulletins* and makes security patches available as part of TechNet. See the Web site (www.microsoft.com/technet/treeview/default.asp?url=/technet/security/default.asp).

Trojans, Viruses, and Worms

Intruders who access your systems without authorization or inside attackers with malicious motives could plant various types of programs to cause damage to your network. There are three broad categories of *malicious code*:

- Trojans
- Viruses
- Worms

Trojans

The name, short for *Trojan horse*, refers to a software program that appears to perform a useful function but in fact performs actions that the program user did not intend or was not aware of. Trojan horses are often written by hackers to circumvent the security of a system. Once the Trojan is installed, the hacker can exploit the security holes it creates to gain unauthorized access, or the Trojan program could perform some action such as:

- Deleting or modifying files
- Transmitting files across the network to the intruder
- Installing other programs or viruses

Basically, the Trojan can perform any action that the user has privileges and permissions to perform on the system. This means that a Trojan is especially dangerous if the unsuspecting user who installs it is an administrator and has access to the system files.

Trojans can be very cleverly disguised as innocuous programs, utilities, screensavers, or the like. A Trojan can also be installed by an executable script (JavaScript, a Java applet, Active-X control, etc.) on a Web site. Accessing the site can initiate the installation of the program if the Web browser is configured to allow scripts to run automatically.

Viruses

Viruses include any programs that are usually installed without the user's awareness and perform undesired actions (often harmful, although sometimes merely annoying). Viruses can also replicate themselves, infecting other systems by writing themselves to any floppy disk that is used in the computer or sending themselves across the network. Viruses are often distributed as attachments to e-mail or as macros in word processing documents. Some viruses activate immediately on installation; others lie dormant until a specific date or time or when a particular system event triggers them.

Viruses come in thousands of varieties. They can do anything from popping up a message that says "Hi!" to erasing the computer's entire hard disk. The proliferation of computer viruses has also led to the phenomenon of the *virus hoax,* which is a warning—generally circulated via e-mail or Web sites—about a virus that does not exist or that does not do what the warning claims it will do.

Real viruses, however, present a real threat to your network. Companies such as Symantec and McAfee make anti-virus software that is aimed at detecting and removing virus programs. Because new viruses are created daily, it is important to download new *virus definition files,* which contain information required to detect each virus type, on a regular basis to ensure that your virus protection stays up to date.

Worms

A *worm* is a program that can travel across the network from one computer to another. Sometimes different parts of a worm run on different computers. Worms make multiple copies of themselves and spread throughout a network. The distinction between viruses and worms has become blurred. Originally the term *worm* was used to describe code that attacked multi-user systems (networks) and *virus* was used to describe programs that replicated on individual computers.

The primary purpose of the worm is to replicate. Worm programs were initially used for legitimate purposes in performing network management duties, but their ability to multiply quickly has been exploited by hackers who create malicious worms that replicate wildly and might also exploit operating system weaknesses and perform other harmful actions.

Classifying Specific Types of Attacks

The *attack type* refers to *how* an attacker gains entry to your computer or network and *what he does* once he has gained entry. In this section, we discuss some of the more common types of hack attacks, including:

- Social engineering attacks
- DoS attacks
- Scanning and spoofing
- Source routing and other protocol exploits
- Software and system exploits
- Trojans, viruses, and worms

When you have a basic understanding of how each type of attack works, you will be better armed to guard against them.

> **NOTE**
>
> In this chapter, we use the words *attacker*, *intruder*, or *hacker* to refer to a person who compromises the security of a network by gaining unauthorized access or who compromises the accessibility of a network by preventing authorized access.

Social Engineering Attacks

Unlike the other attack types, *social engineering* does not refer to a technological manipulation of computer hardware or software vulnerabilities and does not require much in the way of technical skills. Instead, this type of attack exploits *human* weaknesses—such as carelessness or the desire to be cooperative—to gain access to legitimate network credentials. The talents that are most useful to the intruder who relies on this technique are so-called "people skills," such as a charming or persuasive personality or a commanding, authoritative presence.

What Is Social Engineering?

Social engineering is defined as obtaining confidential information by means of human interaction (*Business Wire,* August 4, 1998). You can think of social engineering attackers as specialized con artists. They gain the trust of users (or even better, administrators) and then take advantage of the relationship to find out the user's account name and password, or they have the unsuspecting users log them on to the system. Because this type of attack is based on convincing a valid network user to "open the door," social engineering can successfully get an intruder into a network that is protected by high-security measures such as biometric scanners.

Social engineering is, in many cases, the easiest way to gain unauthorized access to a computer network. The social engineering competition at a Defcon annual hackers' convention in Las Vegas attracted hundreds of attendants eager to practice their manipulative techniques. Even hackers who are famous for their technical abilities know that *people* make up the biggest security vulnerability on most networks. Kevin Mitnick, convicted computer crimes felon and celebrity hacker extraordinaire, tells in his lectures how he used social engineering to gain access to systems during his hacking career.

> **NOTE**
>
> For more information on Mitnick's lectures, see "Mitnick Teaches Social Engineering," at www.zdnet.com/filters/printerfriendly/0,6061,2604480-2,00.html.

These "engineers" often pose as technical support personnel, either in-house or pretending to work for outside entities such as the telephone company, the Internet service provider, the network's hardware vendor, or even the government. They often contact their victims by phone, and they usually spin a complex and plausible tale of why they need the user to divulge his or her passwords or other information (such as the IP address of the user's machine or the computer name of the network's authentication server).

Protecting Your Network Against Social Engineers

Protecting against social engineering attacks is especially challenging. Adopting strongly worded policies that prohibit divulging passwords and other network information to anyone over the telephone and educating your users about the phenomenon are obvious steps you can take to reduce the likelihood of this type of security breach. Human nature being what it is, however, some users on every network will always be vulnerable to the social engineer's con game. A talented social engineer is a master at making users doubt their own doubts about his legitimacy.

The "wannabe" intruder could regale the user with woeful stories of the extra cost the company will incur if he spends extra time verifying his identity. He could pose as a member of the company's top management and take a stern approach, threatening the employee with disciplinary action or even loss of job if he doesn't get the user's cooperation. Or he might try to make the employee feel guilty by pretending to be a low-level employee who is just trying to do his job and who will be fired if he doesn't get access to the network and get the problem taken care of right away. A really good social engineer is patient and thorough. He will do his homework, and he will know enough about your company, or the organization he claims to represent, to be convincing.

Because social engineering is a human problem, not a technical problem, prevention must come primarily through education rather than technological solutions.

> **NOTE**
>
> For more information about social engineering and how to tell when someone is attempting to pull a social engineering scam, see the preview chapter "Everything You Wanted to Know about Social Engineering—But Were Afraid to Ask" at the Happy Hacker Web site, located at www.happyhacker.org/uberhacker/se.shtml.

Denial-of-Service Attacks

In February 2000, massive DoS attacks brought down several of the biggest Web sites, including Yahoo.com and Buy.com. DoS attacks are one of the most popular choices for Internet hackers who want to disrupt a network's operations. Although they do not destroy or steal data as some other types of attacks do, the objective of DoS attackers is to bring down the network, denying service to its legitimate users. DoS attacks are easy to initiate; software is readily available from hacker Web sites and *warez* newsgroups that will allow anyone to launch a DoS attack with little or no technical expertise.

NOTE

Warez is a term used by hackers and crackers to describe bootlegged software that has been "cracked" to remove copy protections and made available by software pirates on the Internet, or in its broader definition, to describe any illegally distributed software.

The purpose of a DoS attack is to render a network inaccessible by generating a type or amount of network traffic that will crash the servers, overwhelm the routers, or otherwise prevent the network's devices from functioning properly. Denial of service can be accomplished by tying up the server's resources—for example, by overwhelming the CPU and memory resources. In other cases, a particular user or machine can be the target of DoS attacks that hang up the client machine and require it to be rebooted.

NOTE

DoS attacks are sometimes referred to in the security community as *nuke attacks*.

Distributed Denial-of-Service Attack

Distributed DoS (DDoS) attacks use intermediary computers, called *agents,* on which programs called *zombies* have previously been surreptitiously installed. The hacker activates these zombie programs remotely, causing the intermediary computers (which can number in the hundreds or even thousands) to simultaneously launch the actual attack. Because the attack comes from the computers running the zombie programs, which could be on networks anywhere in the world, the hacker is able to conceal the true origin of the attack.

Examples of DDoS tools used by hackers are Tribe FloodNet (TFN), TFN2K, Trinoo, and Stacheldraht (German for *barbed wire*). Early versions of DDoS tools targeted UNIX and Solaris systems, but TFN2K can run on both UNIX and Windows systems.

NOTE

An excellent article that provides details on how TFN, TFN2K, Trinoo, and Stacheldraht work is available on the NetworkMagazine.com Web site. You'll find the article, *Distributed Denial of Service Attacks,* at www.networkmagazine.com/article/ NMG20000512S0041.

It is important to note that DDoS attacks pose a two-layer threat. Not only could your network be the target of a DoS attack that crashes your servers and prevents incoming and outgoing traffic, but your computers could be used as the "innocent middlemen" to launch a DoS attack against another network or site.

DNS DoS Attack

The *DNS DoS attack* exploits the difference in size between a DNS query and a DNS response, in which all the network's bandwidth is tied up by bogus DNS queries. The attacker uses the DNS servers as "amplifiers" to multiply the DNS traffic.

The attacker begins by sending small DNS queries to each DNS server, which contain the spoofed IP address of the intended victim (see "IP Spoofing" in this chapter). The responses returned to the small queries are much larger in size, so if there are a large number of responses returned at the same time, the link will become congested and denial of service will take place.

One solution to this problem is for administrators to configure DNS servers to answer with a "refused" response, which is much smaller in size than a name resolution response, when they receive DNS queries from suspicious or unexpected sources.

NOTE

Detailed information on configuring DNS servers to prevent this problem are contained in the U.S. Department of Energy's Computer Incident Advisory Capability information bulletin J-063, available at www.ciac.org/ciac/bulletins/j-063.shtml.

SYN and LAND Attack

Synchronization request (SYN) attacks exploit the TCP *three-way handshake*, the process by which a communications session is established between two computers. Because TCP (unlike UDP) is connection-oriented, a *session*, or direct one-to-one communication link, must be created prior to sending data. The client computer initiates the communication with the server (the computer that has the resources it wants to access).

The *handshake* includes the following steps:

1. The client machine sends a SYN segment.

2. The server sends an acknowledge (ACK) message and a SYN, which acknowledges the client machine's request that was sent in Step 1 and sends the client a synchronization request of its own. The client and server machines must synchronize each other's sequence numbers.

3. The client sends an ACK back to the server, acknowledging the server's request for synchronization. When the two machines have acknowledged each other's requests, the handshake has been successfully completed and a connection is established between the two computers.

Figure 1.1 illustrates how the process works.

Figure 1.1 TCP Uses a "Three-Way Handshake" to Establish a Connection between Client and Server

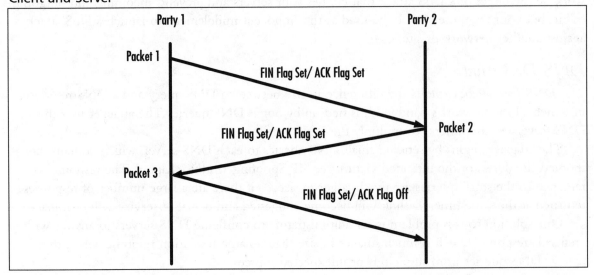

This is how the process normally works: a SYN attack uses the handshake process to flood the system targeted as the victim of the attack with multiple SYN packets that have bad source IP addresses, which causes the system to respond with SYN/ACK messages. The problem comes in when the system, waiting for the ACK message from the client that normally comes in response to its SYN/ACK, puts the waiting SYN/ACK messages into a queue. This is a problem because the queue is limited in the number of messages it can handle. When the queue is full, all subsequent incoming SYN packets will be ignored. In order for a SYN/ACK to be removed from the queue, an ACK must be returned from the client or an interval timer must run out and terminate the three-way handshake process.

Because the source IP addresses for the SYN packets sent by the attacker are no good, the ACKs for which the server is waiting never come. The queue stays full, and there is no room for valid SYN requests to be processed. Thus service is denied to legitimate clients attempting to establish communications with the server.

The LAND attack is a variation on the SYN attack. In the LAND attack, instead of sending SYN packets with IP addresses that do not exist, the flood of SYN packets all have the same spoof IP address—that of the targeted computer. The LAND attack can be prevented by filtering out incoming packets for which source IP addresses appear to be from computers on the internal network.

Ping of Death

Another type of DoS attack is the *ping of death* (also known as the *large packet ping*). The ping of death attack is launched by creating an IP packet (sometimes referred to as a *killer packet*) larger than 65,536 bytes, which is the maximum allowed by the IP specification. This can cause the target system to crash, hang, or reboot.

Teardrop

The *teardrop attack* works a little differently from the ping of death but with similar results. The teardrop program creates IP fragments, which are pieces of an IP packet into which an original packet can be divided as it travels through the Internet. The problem is that the offset fields on these fragments, which are supposed to indicate the portion (in bytes) of the original packet that is contained in the fragment, overlap.

For example, normally two fragments' offset fields might appear as shown here:

Fragment 1: (offset) 100 − 300

Fragment 2: (offset) 301 − 600

This indicates that the first fragment contains bytes 100 through 300 of the original packet, and the second fragment contains bytes 301 through 600.

Overlapping offset fields would appear something like this:

Fragment 1: (offset) 100 − 300

Fragment 2: (offset) 200 − 400

When the destination computer tries to reassemble these packets, it is unable to do so and could crash, hang, or reboot.

Variations on the teardrop include:

- NewTear
- Teardrop2
- SynDrop
- Boink

All these programs generate some sort of fragment overlap.

Ping or ICMP Flood

The *ping flood* or *ICMP flood* is a means of tying up a specific client machine. It is caused by an attacker sending a large number of ping packets (ICMP echo request packets) to the Winsock or dialer software. This action prevents the software from responding to server ping activity requests, which causes the server to eventually time out the connection. A symptom of a ping flood is a huge amount of modem activity, as indicated by the modem lights. This attack is also referred to as a *ping storm*.

The *fraggle attack* is related to the ping storm. Using a spoofed IP address (which is the address of the targeted victim), an attacker sends ping packets to a subnet, causing all computers on the subnet to respond to the spoofed address and flood it with echo reply messages.

NOTE

During the Kosovo crisis in Eastern Europe, the fraggle attack was frequently used by pro-Serbian hackers against U.S. and NATO sites to overload and bring down their networks.

You can use programs such as NetXray or other IP tracing software to record and display a log of the flood packets. Firewalls can be configured to block ping packets and prevent these attacks.

Smurf Attack

The *Smurf attack* is a form of "brute force" attack that uses the same method as the ping flood but that directs the flood of ICMP echo request packets at the network's router. The destination address of the ping packets is the broadcast address of the network, which causes the router to broadcast the packet to every computer on the network or segment. This can result in a very large amount of network traffic if there are many host computers, creating congestion that causes a denial of service to legitimate users.

NOTE

The broadcast address is normally represented by all 1s in the host ID. This means, for example, that on class C network 192.168.1.0, the broadcast address is 192.168.1.255 (255 in decimal represents 11111111 in binary), and in a class C network, the last or z octet represents the host ID. A message sent to the broadcast address is sent simultaneously to all hosts on the network.

In its most insidious form, the Smurf attack spoofs the source IP address of ping packet. Then both the network to which the packets are sent *and* the network of the spoofed source IP address become overwhelmed with traffic. The network to which the spoofed source address belongs is deluged with responses to the ping when all the hosts to which the ping was sent answer the echo request with an echo reply.

Smurf attacks can generally do more damage than some other forms of DoS, such as SYN floods. The SYN flood affects only the ability of other computers to establish a TCP connection to the flooded server, but a Smurf attack can bring an entire ISP down for minutes or hours. This is because a single attacker can easily send 40 to 50 ping packets per second, even using a slow modem connection. Because each packet is broadcast to every computer on the destination network, the number of responses per second is 40 to 50 times the number of computers on the network, which could be hundreds or thousands. This is enough data to congest even a T-1 link.

One way to prevent a Smurf attack from using your network as the broadcast target is to turn off the capability to transmit broadcast traffic on the router. Most routers allow you to turn off this option. To prevent your network from being the victim of the spoofed IP address, you need to configure your firewall to filter out incoming ping packets.

UDP Bomb or Flood

An attacker can use the UDP and one of several services that echo packets on receipt to create service-denying network congestion by generating a flood of UDP packets between two target systems. For example, the UDP chargen service on the first computer (which is a testing tool that generates a series of characters for every packet that it receives) sends packets to another system's UDP echo service, which echoes every character it receives. By exploiting these testing tools, an endless flow of echoes goes back and forth between the two systems, congesting the network. This is sometimes called a *UDP packet storm*.

In addition to port 7, the echo port, an attacker can use port 17, the quote-of-the-day service (quotd), or the daytime service on port 13. These services also echo packets they receive. UDP chargen is on port 19. Disabling unnecessary UDP services on each computer (especially those mentioned) or using a firewall to filter those ports and services will protect you from this type of attack.

UDP Snork Attack

The *snork attack* is similar to the UDP bomb. It uses a UDP frame that has a source port of either 7 (echo) or 9 (chargen), with a destination port of 135 (Microsoft location service). The result is the same as that of the UDP bomb: a flood of unnecessary transmissions that can slow performance or crash the systems that are involved.

Mail Bomb Attack

A *mail bomb* is a means of overwhelming a mail server, causing it to stop functioning and thus denying service to users. This is a relatively simple form of attack, accomplished by sending a massive quantity of e-mail to a specific user or system. Programs available on hacking sites on the Internet allow a user to easily launch a mail bomb attack, automatically sending floods of e-mail to a specified address while protecting the attacker's identity.

A variation on the mail bomb program automatically subscribes a targeted user to hundreds or thousands of high-volume Internet mailing lists, subsequently filling the user's mailbox and/or the mail server. Bombers call this attack *list linking*. Examples of these mail bomb programs include Unabomber, Extreme Mail, Avalanche, and Kaboom.

The solution to repeated mail bomb attacks is to block traffic from the originating network using packet filters. Unfortunately, this solution does not work with list linking, because the originator's address is obscured; the deluge of traffic comes from the mailing lists to which the victim has been subscribed.

Scanning and Spoofing

The term *scanner*, in the context of network security, refers to a software program that hackers use to remotely determine the TCP/UDP ports that are open on a given system and thus vulnerable to attack. Scanners are also used by administrators to detect vulnerabilities in their own systems in order to correct them before an intruder finds them. Network diagnostic tools such as the famous Security Administrator's Tool for Analyzing Networks (SATAN), a UNIX utility, include sophisticated port-scanning capabilities.

A good scanning program can locate a target computer on the Internet (one that is vulnerable to attack), determine the TCP/IP services running on the machine, and probe those services for security weaknesses.

NOTE

A common saying among hackers is, "A good port scanner is worth a thousand passwords."

You can find excellent resources for information about the history of scanning, how scanners work, and some popular scanning programs available as freeware on the Internet.

Port Scanning

Port scanning refers to a means of locating "listening" TCP or UDP ports on a computer or router and obtaining as much information as possible about the device from the listening ports. TCP and UDP services and applications use a number of *well-known ports*, which are widely published. The hacker uses his knowledge of these commonly used ports to extrapolate information.

For example, Telnet normally uses port 23. If the hacker finds that port open and listening, she knows that Telnet is probably enabled on the machine. She can then try to infiltrate the system by, for example, guessing the appropriate password in a brute force attack.

For example, a traditional Ethernet hub sends all data out every port on the hub. An intruder who has access to the hub can plug a packet-sniffing device (or a laptop computer with sniffer software) that operates in "promiscuous mode" (in which packets can be captured and read regardless of their source or destination) into a spare port and capture data sent to any computer on the segment, as shown in Figure 1.2.

Figure 1.2 An Intruder with Access to the Hub Can Easily Intercept Data

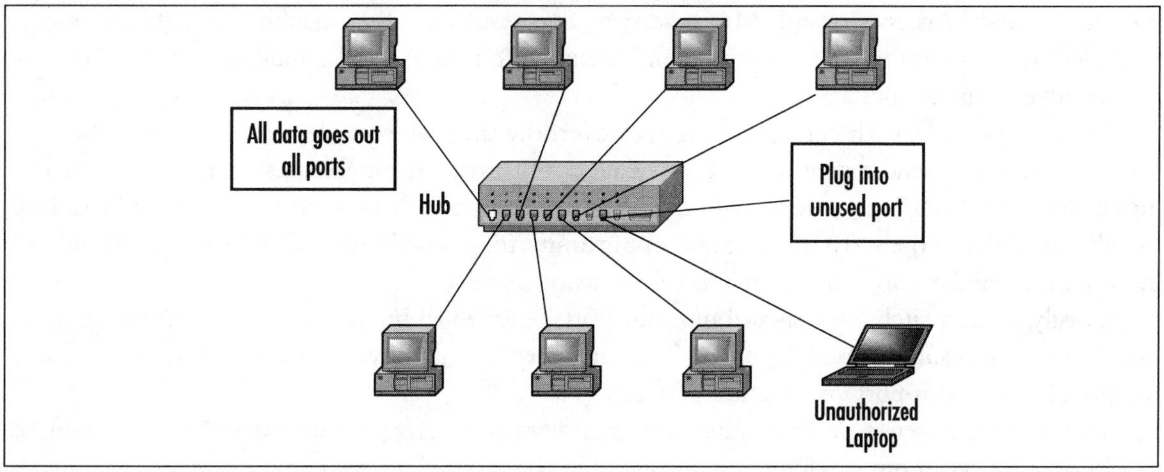

NOTE

Packet sniffers are also called *protocol analyzers* or *network analyzers*. Sniffer and Sniffer Pro are two packet-sniffer products marketed by Network Associates.

Although switches and routers are somewhat more secure than hubs, any device through which the data passes is a point of vulnerability. Replacing hubs with switches and routers makes it more difficult for an intruder to "sniff" on your network, but it is still possible to use techniques such as *Address Resolution Protocol (ARP) spoofing*. This technique is also sometimes called *router redirection*, in which nearby machines are redirected to forward traffic through an intruder's machine by sending ARP packets that contain the router's IP address mapped to the intruder's machine's Media Access Control (MAC) address. This results in other machines believing the intruder's machine is the router, so they send their traffic to it. A similar method uses ICMP router advertisement messages.

It is also possible, with certain switches, to overflow the address tables with multiple false MAC addresses or send a continuous flow of random garbage through the switch and trigger it to change from bridging mode to repeating mode. This means that all frames would be broadcast on all ports, giving the intruder the same opportunity to access the data that he or she would have with a regular hub. This practice is called *switch jamming*.

Finally, if the switch has a special monitor port designed to be used with a sniffer for legitimate (network troubleshooting) purposes, an intruder who has physical access to the switch can simply plug into this port and capture network data.

Due to the existence of devices like the ones described here, your network devices should be placed in a locked room or closet and protected in the same manner as your servers.

How Packet Sniffers Work

Packet sniffer and protocol analyzer devices and programs are not used solely for nefarious purposes, although intruders use them to capture unencrypted data and clear-text passwords that will allow them to break into systems. Despite the fact that these devices can be used to "steal" data as it travels across the network, they are also invaluable troubleshooting tools for network administrators. The sniffer captures individual data packets and allows you to view and analyze the message contents and packet headers. This can be useful in diagnosing network communications problems and uncovering network bottlenecks that are impacting performance. Packet sniffers can also be turned against hackers and crackers and used to discover unauthorized intruders.

The most important part of the sniffer is the capture driver. This is the component that captures the network traffic, filters it (according to criteria set by the user), and stores the data in a buffer. The packets can then be analyzed and decoded to display the contents.

It is often possible to detect an unauthorized packet sniffer on the wire using a device called a time domain reflectometer (TDR), which sends a pulse down the cable and creates a graph of the reflections that are returned. Those who know how to read the graph can tell whether and where unauthorized devices are attached to the cable.

Other ways of detecting unauthorized connections include monitoring hub or switch lights, using Simple Network Monitoring Protocol (SNMP) managers that log connections and disconnections, or using one of the many tools designed for the specific purpose of detecting sniffers on the network. These include the following:

- Antisniff (www.l0pht.com/antisniff)
- neped (www.apostols.org/projectz/neped)
- Sentinel (www.packetfactory.net/Projects/sentinel)

In addition, several techniques using PING, ARP, and DNS could help you catch unauthorized sniffers. The use of these techniques is beyond the scope of this book, but you can find instructions for using them (and much more excellent information on packet sniffing) at Robert

Graham's Sniffing FAQ Web site, located at www.secinf.net/info/misc/sniffingfaq.html. You can even automate the sending of alerts (messages of notification to the administrator) when the presence of a packet sniffer is detected.

Security Policies

Before even trying to decide how to write your firewall rules, you need to establish a security policy. A security policy does not have to be very complicated (however, due to the nature of organizations, they tend to be complicated and political). However, a security policy should define this: who has access to which network resources.

A firewall is an enforcement of your security policy. Your security policy should be designed to prevent intentional internal security breaches, as well as making it something supportive of your system administrators and your users.

Preventing Intentional Internal Security Breaches

According to most computer security studies, as documented in RFC 2196, actual loss (in terms of money, productivity, computer reputation, and other tangible and intangible harm) is greater for internal security breaches than for those from the outside. Internal attackers are more dangerous for several reasons:

- They generally know more about the company, the network, the layout of the building(s), normal operating procedure, and other information that will make it easier for them to gain access without detection.

- They usually have at least some degree of legitimate access and might find it easy to discover passwords and holes in the current security system.

- They know what information is on the network and what actions will cause the most damage.

To a large extent, unintended breaches can be prevented through education. This obviously will not have the same effect on network users who intend to breach security as it has on "innocent" employees. The best way to prevent such breaches depends, in part, on the motivations of the employee(s) concerned.

Tactical Planning

In dealing with network intruders, you should practice what police officers in defensive tactics training call *if/then thinking*. This means considering every possible outcome of a given situation and then asking yourself, "*If* this happens, *then* what could be done to protect us from the consequences?" The answers to these questions will form the basis of your security policy.

This tactic requires that you be able to plan your responses in detail, which means that you must think in specifics rather than generalities. Your security threat must be based in part on understanding the motivations of those initiating the attack and in part on the technical aspects of the type of attack that is initiated. In the next section, we discuss common intruder motivations and specific types of network attacks.

Designating Responsibility for Network Security

In any undertaking as complex as the development and implementation of a comprehensive corporate security plan and accompanying policies, it is vital that areas of responsibility be clearly designated.

Best practices dictate that no one person should have complete authority or control. Besides, in an enterprise-level network, it would be difficult for any single person to handle all facets of developing and implementing the security plan.

Responsibility for Developing the Security Plan and Policies

The initial creation of a good security plan requires a great deal of thought and effort. The policy will impact employees at all levels of the organization, and you should soliciting input from as many representatives of different departments and job descriptions as is practical. An effective approach is to form a committee consisting of people from several areas of the organization to be involved in creating and reviewing the security plan and policies.

Your security planning committee might include some or all of the following:

- The network administrator and one or more assistant administrators

- The site's security administrator

- Heads of various company departments or their representatives

- Representatives of user groups that will be impacted by the security policies (for example, the secretarial staff, the data processing center, etc.)

- A member of the legal department who specializes in computer and technology law

- A member of the finance or budget department

Responsibility for Implementing and Enforcing the Security Plan and Policies

Security policies are generally implemented and enforced by network administrators and members of the IT staff. Job descriptions and policies should designate exactly who is responsible for the implementation of which parts of the plan. A clear-cut chain of command should specify whose decision prevails in case of conflict.

In some cases—such as physical penetration of the network—the company security staff will become involved. There should be written, clearly formulated policies that stipulate which department has responsibility for particular tasks in such situations.

The security plan should also address the procedures for reporting security breaches, both internally and if the police or other outside agencies are to be brought in (as well as who is responsible for or has the authority to call in outside agents).

One of the most important factors in a good security policy is that it must be enforceable. If the policy can be enforced through security tools, this method is preferred. If the policies must be enforced through reprimand or other actions against employees who violate them, there should be clearly worded, universally distributed written documentation indicating what constitutes a violation and the sanctions that will result, as well as who is responsible for imposing such sanctions.

Designing the Corporate Security Policy

The process of designing a good corporate network security policy will differ from organization to organization. However, common elements should be addressed, including (but not limited to) the following:

- Developing an effective password and authentication policy

- Developing a privacy policy that sets forth reasonable expectations of privacy as to employees' e-mail, monitoring access to Web sites, access to users' directories and files, and so forth

- Developing an accountability policy that defines responsibility in regard to security issues, including policies regarding users' obligation to report security violations and the process for doing so

- A network use statement that defines users' responsibilities in regard to accessing network resources, protecting password confidentiality, reporting problems, and expectations as to availability of network resources

- A disaster protection and recovery policy that specifies policies for fault tolerance, scheduling data backups and storing backed-up data, fail-over plans for critical systems, and other related matters

It is beyond the scope of this chapter to provide detailed examples of all these elements. We do, however, address the first issue: how to go about developing an effective password policy and some of the factors that should be considered. The other policy areas should be addressed in similar depth and detail in your plan. Also refer to Chapter 13 for an additional discussion of security policies that encompass some of these other elements.

Developing an Effective Password Policy

In the networking world, passwords (in combination with user account names) are normally the "keys to the kingdom" that provide access to network resources and data. It might seem simplistic to say that your comprehensive security plan should include an effective password policy, but it is a basic component that is more difficult to implement than it might appear at first glance.

In order to be effective, your password policy must require users to select passwords that are difficult to "crack" yet easy for them to remember so that they don't commit the common security breach of writing the password on a sticky note that will end up stuck to the monitor or sitting prominently in the top desk drawer.

A good password policy is the first line of defense in protecting your network from intruders. Careless password practices (choosing common passwords such as "god" or "love" or the user's spouse's name; choosing short, all-alpha, one-case passwords, writing passwords down or sending them across the network in plain text) are like leaving your car doors unlocked with the keys in the ignition. Although some intruders might target a specific system, many others simply "browse" for a network that's easy to break into. Lack of a good password policy is an open invitation them.

NOTE

Expensive, sophisticated firewalls and other strict security measures (short of biometric scanning devices that recognize fingerprints or retinal images) will not protect you if an intruder has knowledge of a valid username and password. It is particularly important to use strong passwords for administrative accounts.

Best practices for password creation require that you address the following:

- Password length and complexity
- Who creates the password?
- Forced changing of passwords

Password Length and Complexity

It's easy to define a "bad" password: It's one that can be easily guessed by someone other than the authorized user.

One way in which "crackers" (hackers who specialize in defeating passwords to break into systems) do their work is called the *brute force attack*. In this kind of attack, the cracker manually or, more often, using a script or specially written software program, simply tries every possible combination of characters until he or she finally hits on the right one. These programs can utilize huge dictionaries that contain many thousands of words and character combinations. Using this method, it is easier to guess a short password than a longer one because there are more possible combinations. For this reason, most security experts recommend that passwords have a minimum required length (for example, eight characters). Modern network operating systems such as Windows 2000 allow domain administrators to impose such rules so that if a user attempts to set a password that doesn't meet the minimum length requirement, the password change will be rejected.

Physical security is critical in thwarting brute force attacks, since they are more likely to succeed when the hacker has physical access to the machine than when they are launched across the network.

NOTE

In addition to the accounts assigned to individual users, services use accounts to perform their functions. Because the passwords on these service accounts are often static, they present a special point of vulnerability.

Who Creates the Password?

Network administrators might be tempted to institute a policy whereby they create all passwords and "issue" them to users. This method has the advantage of ensuring that all passwords meet the administrator's criteria in regard to length and complexity. However, it has a few big disadvantages as well:

- It places a heavy burden on administrators, who must handle all password changes and be responsible for letting users know what their passwords are. Of course, you would not want to notify the user of his or her password via e-mail or other insecure channels. In fact, the best way is to personally deliver the password information. In a large organization, this becomes particularly taxing if you have a policy requiring that passwords be changed on a regular basis (as you should; we discuss this rule in the next section).

- Users have more difficulty remembering passwords that they didn't choose themselves. This means that they are more likely to write the passwords down, resulting in security compromises. Otherwise, users might have to contact the administrator frequently to be reminded of their passwords.

- If the administrator creates all passwords, the administrator *knows* everyone's password. This might or might not be acceptable under your overall security policy. Some users (including management) could be uncomfortable with the idea that the administrator knows their passwords. Even though an administrator can generally access a user's account and/or files without knowing the password anyway, that fact is less obvious to users and thus of less concern.

Allowing users to create their own passwords within set parameters (length and complexity requirements) is usually the best option. The user is less likely to forget the password because he or she can create a complex password that is meaningless to anyone but the user.

For example, it would be difficult for others to guess the password "Mft2doSmis." It has 10 characters, combines alpha and numeric characters, and combines upper and lower case in a seemingly random manner. To the user, it would be easy to remember because it means "My favorite thing to do on Sunday morning is sleep."

Password Change Policy

Best practices dictate that users change their passwords at regular intervals and after any suspected security breach. Windows 2000 allows the administrator to set a maximum password age, forcing users to change their passwords at the end of the specified period (in days). Password expiration periods can be set from 1 to 999 days. The default is 42 days.

NOTE

Individual user accounts that need to keep the same passwords can be configured so that their passwords never expire. This configuration overrides the general password expiration setting.

Because it is the nature of most users to make their passwords as easy to remember as possible, you must institute policies to prevent the following practices, all of which can present security risks:

- Changing the password to a variation of the same password (for example, changing from Tag2mB to Tag3mB)

- Changing the password back and forth between two favored passwords each time a change is required (that is, changing from Tag2mB to VERoh9 and back again continuously)

- "Changing" the password to the same password (entering the same password for the new password as what was already being used)

Administrators can use operating system features to prevent these practices. For example, in Windows 2000, you can configure the operating system to remember the user's password history so that up to a maximum of the last 24 passwords will be recorded. This way, the user will not be able to change the password to one that has been used during that time.

Summary of Best Password Practices

Keep these best practices in mind:

- Passwords should have a minimum of eight characters.
- Passwords should not be "dictionary" words.
- Passwords should consist of a mixture of alpha, numeric, and symbol characters.
- Passwords should be created by their users.
- Passwords should be easy for users to remember.
- Passwords should never be written down.
- Passwords should be changed on a regular basis.
- Passwords should be changed any time compromise is suspected.
- Password change policies should prevent users from making only slight changes.

Designing a Comprehensive Security Plan

Now that you have some understanding of basic security concepts and terminology, general security objectives, common motivation of network intruders, various types of specific attacks and how they are used, and an overview of available hardware and software solutions, you can begin to design a comprehensive security policy for your organization.

A widely accepted method for developing your network security plan is laid out in RFC 2196, *Site Security Handbook,* and attributed to Fites, et al (1989). It consists of the following steps:

- Identify what you are trying to protect.
- Determine what you are trying to protect it from.
- Determine how likely the anticipated threats are.

- Implement measures that will protect your assets in a cost-effective manner.

- Review the process continually and make improvements each time a weakness is discovered.

NOTE

The entire text of RFC 2196, which provides many excellent suggestions that focus primarily on the implementation phase, can be found on the Web at www.faqs.org/rfcs/rfc2196.html.

It is important to understand that a security *plan* is not the same thing as a security *policy*, although the two words are sometimes used interchangeably. Your security policies (and there are likely to be many of them) grow out of your security plan. Think of policy as "law" or "rules," whereas the security plan is procedural; it lays out *how* the rules will be implemented.

Your security plan will generally address three different aspects of protecting your network:

- **Prevention** The measures that are implemented to keep your information from being modified, destroyed, or compromised.

- **Detection** The measures that are implemented to recognize when a security breach has occurred or has been attempted, and if possible, the origin of the breach.

- **Reaction** The measures that are implemented to recover from a security breach, to recover lost or altered data, to restore system or network operations, and to prevent future occurrences.

These can be divided into two types of actions: *proactive* and *reactive*. The first, prevention, is proactive because it takes place *before* any breach has occurred and involves actions that will, if successful, make further actions unnecessary. Unfortunately, our proactive measures don't always work. Reactive measures such as detection and reaction do, however, help us develop additional proactive measures that will prevent future intrusions.

Regardless of how good your prevention and detection methods, it is essential that you have in place a reaction plan in case attackers do get through your line of defense and damage your data or disrupt your network operations. As the old saying goes, "Hope for the best, and plan for the worst."

NOTE

For a concise commentary that is useful to keep in mind during security planning, see the Ten Immutable Laws of Security Administration on Microsoft's TechNet Web site at www.microsoft.com/technet/security/10salaws.asp.

Evaluating Security Needs

Before you can develop a security plan and policies for your organization, you must assess the security needs, which will generally be based on the following broad considerations:

- Type of business in which the organization engages
- Type of data that is stored on the network
- Type of connection(s) of the network to other networks
- Philosophy of the organization's management

Each of these factors will play a part in determining the level of security that is desirable or necessary for your network.

Assessing the Type of Business

Certain fields have inherently high security requirements. An obvious example is the military or other government agencies that deal with defense or national security issues. Private companies with government defense contracts also fall into this category. Others might be less obvious:

- Law firms, bound by law and ethics to protect client confidentiality
- Medical offices, which must protect patient records and confidentiality
- Law enforcement agencies, courts, and other governmental bodies
- Educational institutions that have student records stored on their networks
- Any company that gathers information from individuals or organizations under guarantee that the data will be kept confidential

The competitive nature of a business is also a consideration. In a field such as biogenetic research, which is a "hot" market in which new developments—any of which could involve huge profits for the company that patents the idea—occur on a daily basis, protecting trade secrets becomes vitally important.

Most businesses have *some* data of a confidential nature on the network's computer systems, but the security requirements in some fields are much higher than in others. The confidentiality needs of the business should be considered as you begin to develop your security plan.

Assessing the Type of Data

The second question to consider involves the type of data stored on your network and where it is stored. You could find that a higher level of security is needed in one department or division than another. You might, in fact, want to divide the network physically, into separate subnets, to allow better control of access to various parts of the company network independently.

Generally, payroll and human resource records (personnel files, insurance claim documents, and the like), company financial records (accounting documents, financial statements, tax documents), and a variety of other common business records need to be protected. Even in cases in which these documents must be made public, you will want to take steps to ensure that they can't be modified or destroyed. Remember that *data integrity* as well as *data confidentiality* are protected by a good security plan.

Assessing the Network Connections

Your business's exposure to outside intruders is another consideration in planning how security will be implemented on your network. A LAN that is self-contained and has no Internet connectivity nor any modems or other outside connections does not require the degree of protection (other than physical security) that is necessary when an intruder can take many avenues "in."

Dial-up modem connections merit special consideration. A dial-up connection is less open to intrusion than a full-time dedicated connection—both because it is connected to the outside for a shorter time period, reducing the window of opportunity for intrusion, and because it usually has a dynamic IP address, making it harder for an intruder to locate it on multiple occasions—allowing workstations on your network to have modems and phone lines can create a huge security risk.

If improperly configured, a computer with a dial-up connection to the Internet that is also cabled to the internal network can act as a router, allowing outside intruders to access not only the workstation connected to the modem but other computers on the LAN as well.

One reason for allowing modems at individual workstations is to allow users to dial up connections to other private networks. A more secure way to do this is to remove the modems and have the users establish a VPN connection with the other private network through the LAN's Internet connection.

The best security policy is to have as few connections from the internal network to the outside as possible and control access at those entry points (collectively called the *network perimeter*).

Assessing Management Philosophy

This last criterion is the most subjective but can have a tremendous influence on the security level that is appropriate for your organization. Most companies are based on one (or a combination of more than one) management model.

Understanding Management Models

Some companies institute a highly structured, formal management style. Employees are expected to respect a strict chain of command, and information is generally disseminated on a "need to know" basis. Governmental agencies, especially those that are law enforcement-related such as police departments and investigative agencies, often follow this philosophy. This model is sometimes referred to as the *paramilitary model*.

Other companies, particularly those in the IT industry and other fields that are subject to little state regulation, are built on the opposite premise: that all employees should have as much information and input as possible, that managers should function as "team leaders" rather than authoritarian supervisors, and that restrictions on employee actions should be imposed only when necessary for the efficiency and productivity of the organization. This is sometimes called the *one big happy family model*. Creativity is valued more than "going by the book," and job satisfaction is considered an important aspect of enhancing employee performance and productivity.

In business management circles, these two diametrically opposed models are called *Theory X* (traditional paramilitary style) and *Theory Y* (the modern, team-oriented approach). Although numerous other management models such as management by objective (MBO) and total quality management (TQM) have been popularized in recent years, each company's management style falls somewhere on the continuum between Theory X and Theory Y. The management model is based on the personal philosophies of the company's top decision makers regarding the relationship between management and employees.

An organization's management model can have a profound influence on what is or isn't acceptable in planning security for the network. A "deny all access" security policy that is viewed as appropriate in a Theory X organization could meet with so much resentment and employee dissatisfaction in a Theory Y company that it disrupts business operations. Always consider the company "atmosphere" as part of your security planning. If you have good reasons to implement strict security in a Theory Y atmosphere, realize that you will probably have to justify the restrictions to management and "sell" them to employees, whereas those same restrictions might be accepted without question in a more traditional organization.

Understanding Security Ratings

Security ratings could be of interest as you develop your company's security policy, although they are not likely to be important unless your organization works under government contract, requiring a specified level of security.

The U.S. government provides specifications for rating network security implementations in a publication often referred to as the *Orange Book*, formally called the *Department of Defense Trusted Computer System Evaluation Criteria*, or *TCSEC*. The *Red Book*, or *Trusted Network Interpretation of the TCSEC (TNI)*, explains how the TCSEC evaluation criteria are applied to computer networks.

Other countries have security rating systems that work in a similar way. For example:

- CTPEC (Canada)

- AISEP (Australia)

- ITSEC (Western Europe)

To obtain a government contract in the United States, companies are often required to obtain a C2 rating. A C2 rating has several requirements:

- That the operating system in use be capable of tracking access to data, including both who accessed it and when it was accessed (as is done by the auditing function of Windows NT/2000)

- That users' access to objects be subject to control (access permissions)

- That users be uniquely identified on the system (via user account names and passwords)

- That security-related events be traceable and permanently recorded for auditing (audit log)

In order to receive certification, a company must implement these requirements in particular ways. If your organization needs C2 rating for its systems, you should consult the National Computer Security Center (NCSC) publications to ensure that they meet all the requirements.

> **NOTE**
>
> The Department of Defense (DoD) Trusted Computer System Evaluation Criteria (the *Orange Book*) can be accessed online at www.radium.ncsc.mil/tpep/library/rainbow/ 5200.28-STD.html.

Legal Considerations

Another important step in preparing to design your network security plan is to consider legal aspects that could affect your network. It is a good idea to have a member of your company's legal department who specializes in computer law be involved in the development of your security plan and policies. If this is not possible, the written policies should be submitted for legal review before you put them into practice.

Addressing Security Objectives

If your security goal is to have complete control over the data that comes into and goes out of your networks, you must define objectives that will help you reach that goal. We listed some general security objectives related to computer networks—especially those connected to an outside internetwork such as the Internet—as controlling physical access, preventing accidental compromise of data, detecting and preventing intentional internal security breaches, and detecting and preventing unauthorized external intrusions. In the following sections, we examine each of these objectives in detail.

Know Your Users

To prevent accidental compromise of data, you should first know your users and their skill levels. Those with few technical skills should be given as little access as possible; allow them the access required to do their jobs, and no more. Too many network users have, in all innocence, destroyed or changed important files while attempting to clear space on their hard disks or troubleshoot a computer problem on their own.

Control Your Users

In some cases, establishing clear-cut policies and making staffers and other users aware of them will be enough. In other cases, you will find that users are unable or unwilling to follow the rules, and you will have to take steps to enforce them—including locking down desktops with system or group policies and implementing access rules and filtering to prevent unauthorized packets from being sent or received over the network.

Luckily, most users will at least attempt to comply with the rules. A more serious problem is the "insider" who is looking to intentionally breach network security. This person could be simply a maverick employee who doesn't like being told what to do, or he or she could be someone with a darker motive.

Hiring and Human Resource Policies

In many cases, prevention starts with good human resources practices. That means that management should institute hiring policies aimed at recruiting people of good character. Background investigations should be conducted, especially for key positions that will have greater than usual user network access.

The work environment should encourage high employee morale; in many cases, internal security breaches are committed as "revenge" by employees who feel underpaid, under-appreciated, or even mistreated. Employees who are enthusiastic about their jobs and feel valued by the organization will be much more likely to comply with company rules in general and network security policies in particular.

Another motivation for internal breaches is money. If your company engages in a highly competitive business, competitors could approach employees with lucrative offers for trade secrets or other confidential data. If you are in a field that is vulnerable to corporate espionage, your security policies should lean toward the *deny all access* model, in which access for a particular network user starts at nothing and access is added on the basis of the user's need to know.

> **NOTE**
>
> The "deny all access" policy model is one of two basic starting points in creating a security policy. The other is *allow all access*, in which all resources are open to a user unless there are specific reasons to deny access. Neither of these is "right" or "wrong," although the "deny all access" model is undisputedly more secure and the "allow all access" model is easier to implement. From which of these starting points you work depends on the *security philosophy* of your organization.

Creating a Security Policy

A comprehensive security policy is fundamental to an effective information security program, providing a firm basis for all activities related to the protection of information assets. In creating their policies, organizations take one of two basic approaches: that which is not expressly prohibited is allowed, or that which is not explicitly allowed is prohibited. The chosen approach is usually reflective of the organization's overall culture.

Educating Network Users on Security Issues

The best security policies in the world will be ineffective if the network users are unaware of them or if the policies are so restrictive and place so many inconveniences on users that they go out of their way to attempt to circumvent them.

The security plan itself should contain a program for educating network users—not only regarding what the policies are but *why* they are important and how users benefit from them.

Users should also be instructed in the best ways to comply with the policies and what to do if they are unable to comply or if they observe a deliberate violation of the policies on the part of other users.

If you involve users in the planning and policy-making stages, you will find it must easier to educate them and gain their support for the policies at the implementation and enforcement stages

Educating your users is one of the most important factors in eliminating or reducing internal incidents. This does not necessarily mean upgrading the users' technical skills (although it can). Turning all your users into power users might not be cost effective or otherwise desirable. What *is* essential is to train all your network users in the proper procedures and rules of use for the network.

Every person who accesses your company network should be aware of your user policies and should agree to adhere to them. This includes notifying technical support personnel immediately of any hardware or software problems, refraining from installing any unauthorized software on their machines or downloading files from the Internet without authorization, and never dialing their personal ISPs or other networks or services from company machines without permission.

NOTE

A good security policy addresses the following areas:
- Defines roles and responsibilities
- Defines acceptable use of the organization's computing resources
- Serves as a foundation for more specific procedures and standards
- Defines data sensitivity classifications
- Helps prevent security incidents by making clear management's expectations for protecting information
- Provides guidance in the event of a security incident
- Specifies results of noncompliance

Figure 1.3 shows a hierarchical security model. Each layer builds on the ones beneath it, with security policies serving as the foundation. An organization that implements security tools without defining good policies and architecture is likely to encounter difficulties.

Figure 1.3 Security Hierarchy

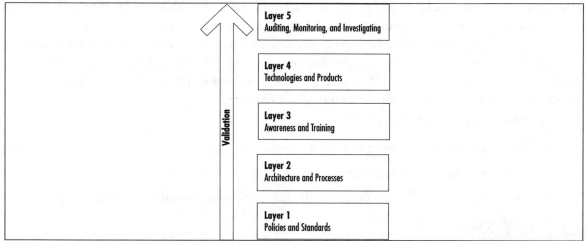

Creation of the security policy is guided by management's level of trust in the organization's people, de facto processes, and technology. Many organizations resist formalizing their policies and enforcing them, since they do not want to risk damaging their familial and trusting culture. When a security incident occurs, however, these organizations discover that they might have little or no guidance on how to handle it or that they do not have a legal foundation to prosecute or even terminate an employee who breaches security. Others follow a command-and-control model and find that defining policies fits right into their culture. These organizations, however, could wind up spending a great deal of money to enforce controls that provide little incremental reduction in risk and create an oppressive atmosphere that is not conducive to productivity. For most organizations, a middle approach is best, following the dictum "Trust, but verify."

The policy creation process might not be easy. People have very different ideas about what the policies represent and why they are needed. The process should strive to achieve a compromise among the various stakeholders:

- Executive managers
- Internal auditors
- Human resources
- IT staff
- Security staff
- Legal staff
- Employee groups

As you can see, some level of buy-in from each of these stakeholder groups is necessary to create a successful policy. Particularly important is full support from executive management. Without it, a security policy will become just another manual gathering dust on the shelf. Employees need to see that management is behind the policy, leading by example.

Once a representative policy development team has been put together, its members should begin a risk-assessment process. The result of this effort is a document that defines how the organization approaches risk, how risk is mitigated, and the assets that are to be protected and their worth. The policy should also broadly define the potential threats that the organization faces. This information will be a guideline to the amount of effort and money that will be expended to address the threats and the level of risk that the organization will accept.

The next step is to perform a business needs analysis that defines information flows within the organization as well as information flowing into and out of it. These flows should each have a business need defined; this need is then matched with the level of risk to determine whether it will be allowed, allowed with additional controls, or restricted.

A good policy has these characteristics:

- States its purpose and what or who it covers
- Is realistic and easy to implement
- Has a long-term focus—in other words, does not contain specifics that will change often
- Is clear and concise

- Is up to date, with provisions for regular review

- Is communicated effectively to all affected parties, including regular awareness training

- Is balanced between security of assets and ease of use

Probably the most important component of a security policy is the definition of acceptable use. It covers how systems are to be used, user password practices, what users can and cannot do, user responsibility in maintaining security, and disciplinary action if users engage in improper activity. It is essential that all users sign this policy, acknowledging that they have read and understood it. Ideally, users should review the acceptable use policy on an annual basis. This practice helps reinforce the message that security is important.

Finally, an organization's security policy guides the creation of a perimeter security policy (including firewalls), which we cover in a later section.

NOTE

You'll find examples of security policies, including a sample acceptable use policy, on the *SANS Security Policy Resource* page located at www.sans.org/newlook/resources/policies.

Protecting Information Technology

Once you have your security policy in place, you should be able to protect your information technology. One way of doing this is improving your security—staying on top of the day-to-day security issues. As information technology is never stagnant, your maintenance should not be either. In addition to basic maintenance, encrypting your network connections and even your data can make your information technology secure.

Also, it is important to regularly test your network security. You can do this through various tools to make sure your defenses are sufficient. In order to do this, make sure you have a clear understanding of how the tools work as well as their possible adverse effects.

Improving Security

The fourth phase in the Security Wheel is that of improving security. In addition to securing your network, setting up monitoring, and performing vulnerability testing, you need to stay abreast, on a weekly or even daily basis, of current security news, primarily consisting of new vulnerability reports. Waiting for a particular vendor to alert you to new vulnerabilities is not enough; you also need to subscribe to third-party mailing lists such as Bugtraq (www.securityfocus.com) or Security Wire Digest (www.infosecuritymag.com). Also important is verifying configurations on key security systems on a regular basis to ensure that they continue to represent your current policy. Most important of all, the four steps of the Security Wheel must be repeated continuously.

Protecting the Servers

File servers on which sensitive data is stored and infrastructure servers that provide mission-critical services such as logon authentication and access control should be placed in a highly secure location. At a minimum, servers should be in a locked room to which only those who need to work directly with the servers have access. Keys should be distributed sparingly, and records should be kept of issuance and return.

If security needs are high due to the nature of the business or the nature of the data, access to the server room could be controlled by magnetic card, electronic locks requiring entry of a numerical code, or even biometric access control devices such as fingerprint or retinal scanners.

Other security measures include monitor detectors or other alarm systems, activated during non-business hours, and security cameras. A security guard or company should monitor these devices.

Keeping Workstations Secure

Many network security plans focus on the servers but ignore the risk posed by workstations that have network access to those servers. It is not uncommon for employees to leave their computers unsecured when they leave their offices for lunch or even when they leave for the evening. Often a workstation in the receptionist area is open to visitors who walk in off the street. If the receptionist manning the station must leave briefly, the computer—and the network to which it is connected—is vulnerable unless steps have been taken to ensure that it is secure.

A good security plan includes protection of all unmanned workstations. A secure client operating system such as Windows NT or Windows 2000 (unlike Windows 9x) requires an interactive logon with a valid account name and password in order to access the operating system. In addition, it allows a user to "lock" the workstation when he or she will be away from it, so someone else can't simply step up and start using the computer. Some degree of security can be provided for Windows 9x clients by using password-enabled screensavers, although savvy intruders can bypass this form of security by rebooting the computer.

Don't depend on access permissions and other software security methods alone to protect your network. If a potential intruder can gain physical access to a networked computer, he or she is that much closer to accessing your valuable data or introducing a virus onto your network.

Ensure that all workstation users adhere to a good password policy, as discussed in the section "Designing a Comprehensive Security Plan" later in this chapter.

Many modern PC cases come with some type of locking mechanism that will help prevent an unauthorized person from opening the case and stealing the hard disk. Locks are also available to prevent use of the floppy drive, to prevent copying of data to a diskette, or to prevent rebooting the computer with a floppy.

Protecting Network Devices

Hubs, routers, switches, and other network devices should be physically secured from unauthorized access. It is easy to forget that merely because a device doesn't have a monitor on which you can *see* data, that doesn't mean the data can't be captured or destroyed at that access point.

Securing the Cable

The next step in protecting your network data is to secure the cable across which it travels. Twisted-pair and coaxial cable are both vulnerable to data capture; an intruder who has access to the cable can tap into it and eavesdrop on messages sent across it. A number of companies make such "tapping" devices.

Fiber optic cable is more difficult to tap into because it does not produce electrical pulses but instead uses pulses of light to represent the 0s and 1s of binary data. It is possible, however, for a sophisticated intruder to use an optical splitter and tap into the signal on fiber optic media.

Compromise of security at the physical level is a special threat when network cables are not contained in one facility but span a distance between buildings. There is even a name for this risk: *manhole manipulation,* a term that refers to the easy access intruders often have to cabling that runs through underground conduits.

Cable taps can sometimes be detected using a TDR or optical TDR to measure the strength of the signal and determine where the tap is located.

Using SSL and Secure Shell

Secure Sockets Layer (SSL) is a protocol that can be used to manage the security of Internet communications. SSL operates between HTTP at the Application layer and TCP at the Transport layer. Although it was originally developed by Netscape for secure communications with their browser, SSL is now included in both Netscape Communicator and Microsoft Internet Explorer browser software. SSL uses public key encryption and digital certificates to ensure secure communications.

SSL is used not only for Web services, but you can also use it for mail services (POP3 and IMAP) as well as other TCP based applications. Stunnel is a universal SSL wrapper, and can be used with applications like Telnet and FTP. Stunnel can be found at www.stunnel.org

However, many UNIX systems use Secure Shell (SSH) instead of Telnet or FTP over SSL to encrypt network logins. The most common version of Secure Shell in use is OpenSSH, but there are commercial solutions available. OpenSSH is available at www.openssh.org.

NOTE

By default, SSL tunneling is used for outbound client requests to port 443. Secure Shell uses port 22.

Testing Security

It is far, far better to test your own security and find holes than for a hacker to find them for you. An effective security program includes regular vulnerability assessments and penetration testing as well as updates to your risk assessment when there are significant changes to the business or the technology. For example, initiating extranet links to business partners or starting to provide remote broadband access to employees should be accompanied by an updated risk profile that identifies the risks of the new activity and the component threats, prioritized by probability and severity. This testing identifies the components that have to be better secured and the level of effort required.

Things that have to be tested or checked include:

- Security policy compliance, including things like password strength
- System patch levels
- Services running on systems
- Custom applications, particularly public-facing Web applications
- New servers added to the network
- Active modems that accept incoming calls

A multitude of tools, both freeware and commercial off-the-shelf tools, are available to perform security testing. Some freeware tools include:

- **Nmap (www.insecure.org/nmap/)** Nmap is one of the most commonly used network and port scanning tools, used by hackers and security professionals alike. It has the ability to "fingerprint" the operating system of the target host by analyzing the responses to different types of probes.

- **Nessus (www.nessus.org)** Nessus is a powerful, flexible vulnerability-scanning tool that can test different target platforms for known holes. It consists of a server process that is controlled by a separate graphical user interface (GUI). Each point of vulnerability is coded via a plug-in to the Nessus system, so new vulnerabilities can be added and tested.

- **whisker (http://sourceforge.net/projects/whisker/)** whisker is a collection of PERL scripts used to test Web server CGI scripts for vulnerabilities, a common point of attack in the Web environment.

- **Security Auditor's Research Assistant (www-arc.com/sara/)** SARA is a third-generation UNIX-based security assessment tool based on the original SATAN. SARA interfaces with other tools such as nmap and Samba for enhanced functionality.

- **L0phtCrack (www.atstake.com/research/lc/)** L0phtCrack is used to test (crack) Windows NT passwords. It is a good tool to look for weak passwords.

Commercial tools include:

- **ISS Internet Scanner (www.iss.net)** Internet Scanner is used to scan networks for vulnerabilities. ISS also makes scanners specifically for databases, host systems, and wireless networks.

- **Symantec Enterprise Security Manager (www.symantec.com)** ESM helps monitor for security policy compliance.

- **PentaSafe VigilEnt Security Manager (www.pentasafe.com)** VigilEnt assesses for vulnerabilities across an enterprise with easy-to-use reporting.

In addition to testing security yourself, it is good practice to bring in security experts that are skilled in vulnerability assessments and penetration testing. These experts (sometimes known as *ethical hackers*) conduct attacks in the same manner as a hacker would, looking for any holes accessible from the outside. They are also able to conduct internal assessments to validate your security posture against industry best practices or standards such as the Common Criteria (http://csrc.nist.gov/cc/) or ISO17799. Internal assessments include interviews with key staff and management, reviews of documentation, and testing of technical controls. A third-party review potentially provides a much more objective view of the state of your security environment and can even be useful in convincing upper management to increase IT security funding.

Other Hardware Security Devices

Other hardware-based components of your network security plan could include devices that provide extra security for authentication, such as:

- Smart card readers

- Fingerprint scanners

- Retinal scanners

- Voice analysis devices

These devices can be used in environments that require a high level of security for secure and reliable network authentication. Microsoft has acquired Biometric API (BAPI) technology from I/O Software and plans to incorporate support for biometric authentication devices into future versions of its operating systems. Windows 2000 already supports smart card authentication.

Monitoring Activity

As you make efforts to secure your environment, you move into the next phase of information security: establishing better mechanisms for monitoring activity on your network and systems. Adequate monitoring is essential so that you can be alerted, for example, when a security breach has occurred, when internal users are trying to exceed their authority, or when hardware or software failures are having an impact on system availability. Effective monitoring has two components: turning on capabilities already present on your systems and implementing tools for additional visibility. The first component includes use of the auditing function built into:

- Operating systems such as administrator account access.

- Network devices, as in login failures and configuration changes.

- Applications, including auditing capability in the application as created by the vendor (for commercial software), as well as auditing added within a custom-developed application. Monitored events tend to be more transactional in nature, such as users trying to perform functions they are not authorized to perform.

Most systems have such auditing turned off by default, however, and require you to specifically enable it. Be careful not to turn on too much, since you will be overwhelmed with data and will wind up ignoring it. This "turn on and tune" methodology flows into the second component, which also includes deployment of tools such as IDS on networks and hosts.

In any environment that contains more than a few systems, performing manual reviews of system and audit logs, firewall logs, and IDS logs becomes an impossible and overwhelming task. Various tools (such as Swatch, at www.oit.ucsb.edu/~eta/swatch) can perform log reduction and alert only on important events.

Detecting Internal Breaches

Implementing auditing will help you detect internal breaches of security by recording specified security events. You will be able to track when objects (such as files or folders) are accessed, what user account was used to access them, when users exercise user rights, and when users log on or off the computer or network. Modern network operating systems include built-in auditing functionality.

Preventing Intentional Internal Breaches

Firewalls are helpful in keeping basically compliant employees from accidentally (or out of ignorance of security considerations) visiting dangerous Web sites or sending specific types of packets outside the local network. However, firewalls are of more limited use in preventing intentional internal security breaches. Simply limiting user access to the external network cannot thwart insiders who are determined to destroy, modify, or copy your data. Because they have physical access, they can copy data to removable media or a portable computer (including tiny handheld machines) or perhaps even print it on paper and remove it from the premises that way. They could change the format of the data to disguise it, or they could upload files to Web-based data storage services.

In a high security environment, computers without floppy drives—or even completely diskless workstations—might be warranted. System or group policy can be applied to prevent users from installing software (such as that needed for a desktop computer to communicate with a Pocket PC or Palm Pilot). Cases can be locked; physical access to serial ports, USB ports, and other connection points can be covered so that removable media devices can't be attached.

Intentional internal breaches of security constitute a serious problem, and company policies should treat them as such.

Preventing Unauthorized External Intrusions and Attacks

External intrusions (or "hacking into the system") from outside the LAN have received a good deal of attention in the media and thus are the major concern of many companies when it comes to network security issues. In recent years, there have been a number of high-profile cases in which the Web servers of prominent organizations (such as Yahoo! and Microsoft) have been hacked. Attempts to penetrate sensitive government networks, such as the Pentagon's systems, occur on a regular basis. DDoS attacks—although not technically "intrusions" because only access to the system, not security of data, is affected—are still looked on as hacks by the media and the public, and these events make front-page news when they crash servers and prevent Internet users from accessing popular sites.

Psychological factors are involved as well. Internal breaches are usually seen by companies as personnel problems and are handled administratively. External breaches could seem more like a "violation" and are more often prosecuted in criminal actions. Because the external intruder could come from anywhere at any time, the sense of uncertainty and fear of the unknown could cause organizations to react in a much stronger way to this type of threat.

The good news about external intrusions is that the area(s) that must be controlled are much more focused. There are usually only a limited number of points of entry to the network from the outside. This is where a properly configured firewall can be invaluable, allowing authorized traffic into the network while keeping unauthorized traffic out. On the other hand, the popularity of firewalls ensures that dedicated hackers know how they work and spend a great deal of time and effort devising ways to defeat them.

Never depend on the firewall to provide 100 percent protection, even against outside intruders. Remember that in order to be effective, a security plan must be a multifaceted, multilayered one. We hope the firewall will keep intruders out of your network completely—but if they *do* get in, what is your contingency plan? How will you reduce the amount of damage they can do and protect your most sensitive or valuable data?

Summary

In this chapter, we looked at the big picture of network security and why it's necessary to have a comprehensive security policy to protect our networks from unauthorized access. Network security has generated jobs and security-related Web sites such as Net-Security (www.net-security.org), SecurityFocus (www.securityfocus.com), and Packetstorm Security (www.packetstormsecurity.org). Many aspects are important, including authentication, authorization, and confidentiality. In addition to the basic concepts, it's important to understand how each component of security fits into physical security, application security, and network security. It's also important that both management and users agree to work with you on enforcing security policies.

## Chapter 2

Firewall Concepts

Best Damn Topics in this Chapter

- Defining a Firewall
- Networking and Firewalls
- Popular Firewalls

Introduction

When you take a shower, you'll notice that everything goes down the drain, whether you want it to or not. If you don't put a drain cover over, you'll end up letting water, hair, and soap scum go down, even if you only want water to drain through. This is how a firewall works: it's a drain filter for your network. A firewall enables you to permit traffic that you want (like water in our shower analogy) and keep out the things you don't (like hair).

Anyone who has been running a network has dealt with chatty protocols, including AppleTalk and IPX (Novell NetWare's base network protocol). These protocols are constantly (approximately every five seconds) asking who's here and announcing what they do. This is a type of "hair" we want out of our drain to keep it from clogging. Another hair we want to keep out is various unwanted attacks, such as Denial of Service (DoS) attacks and intrusion through insecure protocols (Telnet, Remote Shell [RSH], and NetBIOS).

Defining a Firewall

The term *firewall* comes from the bricks-and-mortar architectural world. In buildings, a firewall is a wall built from heat- or fire-resistant material such as concrete that is intended to slow the spread of fire through a structure. In the same way, a network firewall is intended to stop unauthorized traffic from traveling from one network to another. The most common deployment of firewalls occurs between a trusted network and an untrusted one, typically the Internet.

In the past, it was actually rather common for Internet-connected organizations to have no firewalls, instead simply relying on the security of their host systems to protect their data. As networks got larger, it became unwieldy and risky to try to adequately secure each and every host, especially given the ever-increasing hacker threat.

Regardless of what type of firewall you're using, a firewall provides several services. The most essential firewall functions include:

- **IP address conservation and traffic forwarding** Many firewalls act as routers so that different networks (i.e., the 192.168.1.1/24 and 10.100.100.0/24 networks) can communicate with each other. Many network administrators use this function to help create additional subnets. This feature is included as a firewall element simply because it is accomplished using either Ipchains or Iptables. Thus, anyone with only one IP address can create a local area network (LAN) or wide area network (WAN) that has full access to the Internet. You should understand, however, that a firewall does not necessarily have to provide Network Address Translation (NAT). Still, many firewalls (including those provided by Linux and Ipchains/Iptables) allow you to choose this feature.

- **Network differentiation** A firewall is the primary means of creating a boundary between your network and any other network. Because it creates a clear distinction between networks, a firewall helps you manage traffic. A firewall does not necessarily have to be deployed between a trusted, private network and the Internet. Many times, a firewall is deployed within a company network to further differentiate certain company divisions (such as research and development or accounting) from the rest of the network.

- **Protection against DoS, scanning, and sniffing attacks** A firewall acts as a single point that monitors incoming and outgoing traffic. It is possible for this firewall to limit any traffic that you choose.

- **IP and port filtering** The ability to allow or reject a connection based on IP address and port. Such filtering is likely the most understood function of a firewall. Generally, this type of filtering is accomplished using packet filters (i.e., Linux systems that use either Ipchains or Iptables). Packet filtering can become quite complex, because you must always consider that traffic can be filtered according to the source of the packet, as well as the packet's destination. For example, a packet filter can block traffic to your network if it originates from a particular IP address and port.

- **Content filtering** Proxy servers are generally the only types of firewall that manage and control traffic by inspecting URL and page content. If configured properly, a proxy-oriented firewall can identify and block content that you consider objectionable.

- **Packet redirection** Sometimes, it is necessary for a firewall to send traffic to another port or another host altogether. For example, suppose that you have installed Squid proxy server on a separate host than your firewall. It is likely that you will want to have your firewall automatically forward all traffic sent to ports 80 and 443 (the standard HTTP and HTTPS ports) to your proxy server for additional processing.

- **Enhanced authentication and encryption** A firewall has the ability to authenticate users, and encrypt transmissions between itself and the firewall of another network.

- **Supplemented logging** One of the most important—though commonly ignored—benefits of a firewall is that it allows you to examine all details about network packets that pass through it. You can learn, for example, about port scans and various connections to your system.

Firewalls, by definition, do not provide you with all of your network's security functions, nor should they. Other systems should provide you with authentication mechanisms (passwords, public key, or digital certificates), intrusion detection, or remote access (Virtual Private Networks or dial-up). These are separate functions of your network, and your firewall should not be taxed with other functions.

Types of Firewalls

Although the original Firewall Toolkit (sometimes referred to as an fwtk) used a proxy-type design, other types of firewalls use a much different approach. Before we look at these, recall the Open Systems Interconnect (OSI) model (see Figure 2.1).

Figure 2.1 The OSI Model

Application	FTP, Telnet, HTTP, etc.
Presentation	
Session	
Transport	TCP, UDP, etc.
Network	IP, ICMP, etc.
Data link	Ethernet, Token Ring, etc.
Physical	Copper or optical media, or wireless

Using this model as a reference, we can compare how the types of firewalls operate and make informed decisions about which type of firewall is appropriate for a particular need.

Packet Filters

In its most basic form, a *packet filter* makes decisions about whether to forward a packet based only on information found at the IP or Transmission Control Protocol (TCP)/User Datagram Packet (UDP) layers; in effect, a packet filter is a router with some intelligence. However, a packet filter only handles individual packets; it does not keep track of TCP sessions. Thus, it is poorly equipped to detect spoofed packets that come in through an outside interface, pretending to be part of an existing session by setting the Acknowledge (ACK) flag in the TCP header. Packet filters are configured to allow or block traffic according to source and destination IP addresses, source and destination ports, and type of protocol (TCP, UDP, (Internet Control Message Protocol [ICMP], and so on).

So why would you use a packet filter if spoofing is so easy? The primary benefit is speed. Since it does not have to do any inspection of application data, a packet filter can operate nearly as fast as a router that is performing only packet routing and forwarding. As we will see, however, the packet filter concept has been improved.

Stateful Inspection Packet Filters

The concept of *stateful inspection* came about in an effort to improve on the capability and security of regular packet filters while still capitalizing on their inherent speed. A packet filter with stateful inspection is able to keep track of network sessions, so when it receives an ACK packet, it can determine its legitimacy by matching the packet to the corresponding entry in the connection table. An entry is created in the connection table when the firewall sees the first Synchronize (SYN) packet that begins the TCP session. This entry is then referenced for succeeding packets in the session. Entries are automatically timed out after some configurable timeout period.

Statefulness can also be applied to UDP communication in a pseudo fashion, which normally has no concept of state. In this case, the firewall creates an entry in the connection table when the first UDP packet is transmitted. A UDP packet from a less secure network (a response) will only be accepted if a corresponding entry is found in the connection table. If we move up to the application layer, we can see further use for statefulness for protocols such as File Transfer Protocol (FTP). FTP is a bit different in that the server that the user connects to on port 21 will initiate a data connection back on port 20 when a file download is requested. If the firewall has not kept track of the FTP control connection that was initially established, it will not allow the data connection back in. This concept also applies to many of the newer multimedia protocols such as RealAudio and NetMeeting.

Stateful inspection packet filters remain the speed kings of firewalls and are the most flexible where new protocols are concerned, but they are sometimes less secure than application proxies. Check Point FireWall-1 (FW-1) and the Cisco PIX are the leading examples of this type of firewall.

Application Proxies

As the name implies, application proxy firewalls act as intermediaries in network sessions. The user's connection terminates at the proxy, and a corresponding separate connection is initiated from the proxy to the destination host. Connections are analyzed all the way up to the application layer to determine if they are allowed. It is this characteristic that gives proxies a higher level of security than packet filters, stateful or otherwise. However, as you might imagine, this additional processing extracts a toll on performance. Figure 2.2 shows how packet processing is handled at the application layer before it is passed on or blocked.

Figure 2.2 Application Proxy Data Flow

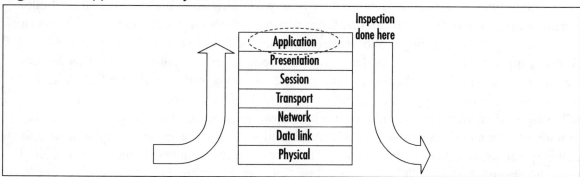

One potentially significant limitation of application proxies is that as new application protocols are implemented, corresponding proxies must be developed to handle them. This means that you could be at the mercy of your vendor if there is a hot new video multicasting technology, for example, but there is no proxy for it.

NOTE

Modern proxy-based firewalls often provide the ability to configure generic proxies for IP, TCP, and UDP. Although not as secure as proxies that work at the application layer, these configurable proxies often allow for passing of newer protocols.

Examples of proxy-based firewalls include Gauntlet from Secure Computing (acquired from Network Associates) and Symantec Raptor (also known as Enterprise Firewall).

Networking and Firewalls

For quite some time, it was common for companies to think that once they deployed a firewall, they were secure. However, firewalls are just one component in an enterprise security strategy. They are generally good at what they do (filtering traffic), but they cannot do everything. The nature of perimeter security has also changed; many companies no longer need outbound-only traffic. Many enterprises now deal with much more complex environments that include business partner connections, Virtual Private Networks (VPNs), and complicated e-commerce infrastructures. This complexity has driven huge increases in firewall functionality. Most firewalls now support multiple network interfaces and can control traffic between them, support VPNs, and enable secure use of complicated application protocols such as H.323 for videoconferencing. The risk, however, is that as more and more functionality is added to the firewall, holes might arise in these features, compromising integrity and security. Another risk is that these features will exact a performance penalty, reducing the firewall's ability to focus on traffic filtering.

So the message is this: Try to use your firewall to the minimum extent possible so it can focus on its core function, and you can better manage the security risk of the other functions by shifting them to other systems to handle the load.

Firewall systems have certainly evolved over the years. Originally, firewalls were hand-built systems with two network interfaces that forwarded traffic between them. However, this was an area for experts only, requiring significant programming skills and system administration talent. Recognizing a need in this area, the first somewhat commercial firewall was written by Marcus Ranum (working for TIS at the time) in the early 1990s. It was called the Firewall Toolkit, or fwtk for short. It was an application proxy design (definitions are given for firewall types in the following section) that intermediated network connections from users to servers. The goal was to simplify development and deployment of firewalls and minimize the amount of custom firewall building that would otherwise be necessary. The now familiar Gauntlet firewall product evolved from the original fwtk, and TIS was acquired by Network Associates, Inc. Other vendors got into the firewall market, including Check Point, Secure Computing, Symantec, and of course, Cisco.

RBC Capital Markets estimated in a 2002 study that in 2000 the firewall market globally represented US$736 million, with an annual growth rate of 16 percent over the following five years. This shows that not everyone has deployed a firewall yet, that more companies are deploying them internally, and that there is ongoing replacement activity.

Next, let's look at the types of firewalls and compare their functionalities.

Firewall Interfaces: Inside, Outside, and DMZ

In its most basic form, a firewall has just two network interfaces: inside and outside. These labels refer to the level of trust in the attached network, where the outside interface is connected to the untrusted network (often the Internet) and the inside interface is connected to the trusted network. In an internal deployment, the interface referred to as outside may be connected to the company backbone, which is probably not as untrusted as the Internet but just the same is trusted somewhat less than the inside. Recall the previous example of a firewall deployed to protect a payroll department.

As a company's Internet business needs become more complex, the limitations of having only two interfaces becomes apparent. For example, where would you put a Web server for your customers? If you place it on the outside of the firewall, as in Figure 2.3, the Web server is fully exposed to attacks, with only a screening router for minimal protection. You must rely on the security of the host system in this instance.

Figure 2.3 A Web Server Located Outside the Firewall

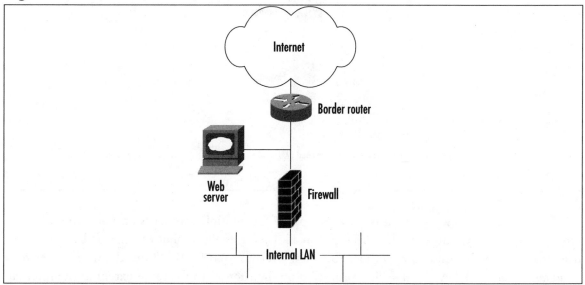

The other possibility in the two-interface firewall scenario is to put the Web server inside the firewall, on an internal segment (see Figure 2.4). The firewall would be configured to allow Web traffic on port 80, and maybe 443 for Secure Sockets Layer (SSL), through to the IP address of the Web server. This prevents any direct probing of your internal network by an attacker, but what if he or she is able to compromise your Web server through port 80 and gain remote superuser access? Then he or she is free to launch attacks from the Web server to anywhere else in your internal network, with no restrictions.

Figure 2.4 A Web Server Located Inside the Firewall

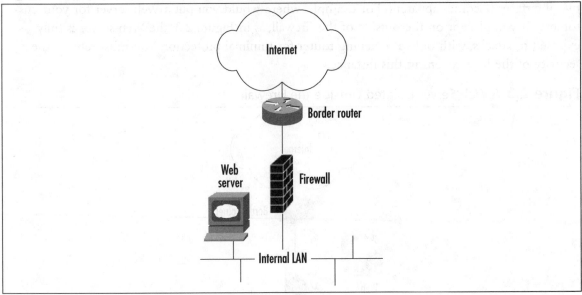

The answer to these problems is to have support for multiple interfaces on your firewall, as most commercial systems now do. This solution allows for establishment of intermediate zones of trust that are neither inside nor outside. These are referred to as DMZs (from the military term *demilitarized zone*). A DMZ network is protected by the firewall to the same extent as the internal network but is separated so that access from the DMZ to the internal network is filtered as well. Figure 2.5 shows this layout.

Figure 2.5 A DMZ Network

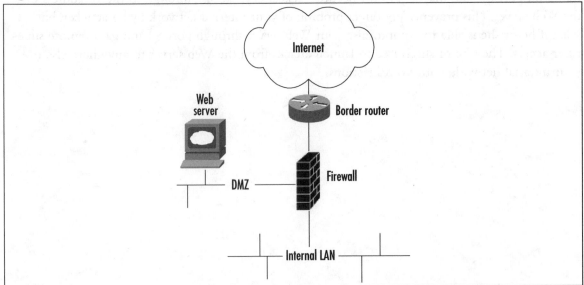

Another design that is sometimes deployed uses two firewalls: an outer one and an inner one, with the DMZ lying between them (see Figure 2.6). Sometimes firewalls from two different vendors are used in this design, with the belief that a security hole in one firewall would be blocked by the other firewall. However, evidence shows that nearly all firewall breaches come from misconfiguration, not from errors in the firewall code itself. Thus, such a design only increases expense and management overhead, without providing much additional security, if any.

Figure 2.6 A Two-Firewall Architecture

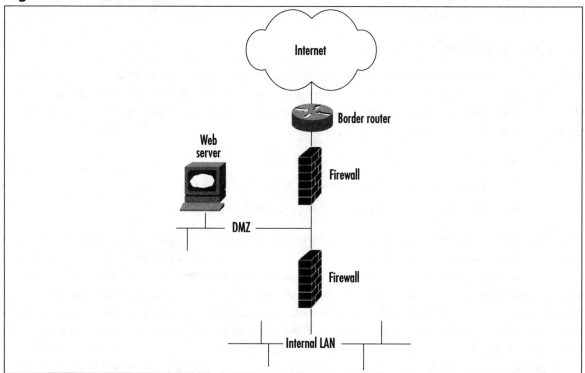

Some sites have even implemented multiple DMZs, each with a different business purpose and corresponding level of trust. For example, one DMZ segment could contain only servers for public access, whereas another could host servers just for business partners or customers. This approach enables a more granular level of control and simplifies administration.

In a more complex e-commerce environment, the Web server might require access to customer data from a backend database server on the internal LAN. In this case, the firewall would be configured to allow Hypertext Transfer Protocol (HTTP) connections from the outside to the Web server and then specific connections to the appropriate IP addresses and ports as needed from the Web server to the inside database server.

Firewall Policies

As part of your security assessment process, you should have a clear idea of the various business reasons for the different communications allowed through your firewall. Each protocol carries with it certain risks, some far more than others. These risks must be balanced with business benefits. For example, one person needing X Windows access (a notoriously difficult protocol to secure properly) through the firewall for a university class she is taking is unlikely to satisfy this requirement. On the other hand, a drop-box FTP server for sharing of files with customers might satisfy the business requirement. It often happens that the firewall rule base grows organically over time and reaches a point where the administrator no longer fully understands the reasons for everything in there. For that reason, it is essential that the firewall policy be well documented, with the business justification for each rule clearly articulated in this documentation. Changes to the firewall policy should be made sparingly and cautiously, only with management approval, and through standard system maintenance and change control processes.

Address Translation

RFC1918, "Address Allocation for Private Internets," specifies certain non-registered IP address ranges that are to be used only on private networks and are not to be routed across the Internet. The RFC uses the term *ambiguous* to refer to these private addresses, meaning that they are not globally unique. The reserved ranges are:

- 10.0.0.0 – 10.255.255.255 (10/8 prefix)

- 172.16.0.0 – 172.31.255.255 (172.16/12 prefix)

- 192.168.0.0 – 192.168.255.255 (192.168/16 prefix)

The primary motivation for setting aside these private address ranges was the fear in 1996 that the 32-bit address space of IP version 4 was becoming rapidly depleted due to inefficient allocation. Organizations that had at most a few thousand hosts, most of which did not have to be accessible from the Internet, had been allocated huge blocks of IP addresses that had gone mostly unused. By renumbering their private networks with these reserved address ranges, companies could potentially return their allocated public blocks for use elsewhere, thus extending the useful life of IP v4.

The sharp reader, however, will point out that if these addresses are not routable on the Internet, how does one on a private network access the Web? The source IP of such a connection would be a private address, and the user's connection attempt would just be dropped before it got very far. This is where Network Address Translation (NAT), defined in RFC 1631, comes into play. Most organizations connected to the Internet use NAT to hide their internal addresses from the global Internet. This serves as a basic security measure that can make it a bit more difficult for an external attacker to map out the internal network. NAT is typically performed on the Internet firewall and takes two forms, static or dynamic. When NAT is performed, the firewall rewrites the source and/or the destination addresses in the IP header, replacing them with translated addresses. This process is configurable.

In the context of address translation, *inside* refers to the internal, private network. *Outside* is the greater network to which the private network connects (typically the Internet). Within the inside address space, addresses are referred to as *inside local* (typically RFC 1918 ranges) and are translated to *inside global* addresses that are visible on the outside. *Global* addresses are registered and assigned in blocks by an Internet Service Provider (ISP). For translations of *outside* addresses coming to the *inside*, distinction is made also between *local*, part of the private address pool, and *global* registered addresses. *Outside local*, as the name might imply, is the reverse of inside global. These are addresses of outside hosts that are translated for access internally. *Outside global* addresses are owned by and assigned to hosts on the external network.

To keep these terms straight, just keep in mind the direction in which the traffic is going—in other words, from where it is initiated. This direction determines which translation will be applied.

Static Translation

In static NAT, a permanent one-to-one mapping is established between inside local and inside global addresses. This method is useful when you have a small number of inside hosts that require access to the Internet and have adequate globally unique addresses to translate to. When a NAT router or firewall receives a packet from an inside host, it looks to see if there is a matching source address entry in its static NAT table. If there is, it replaces the local source address with a global source address and forwards the packet. Replies from the outside destination host are simply translated in reverse and routed onto the inside network. Static translation is also useful for outside communication initiated to an inside host. In this situation, the destination (not the source) address is translated. Figure 2.7 shows an example of static NAT. Each local inside address (192.168.0.10, 192.168.0.11, and 192.168.0.12) has a matching global inside address (10.0.1.10, 10.0.1.11, and 10.0.1.12, respectively).

Figure 2.7 Static Address Translation

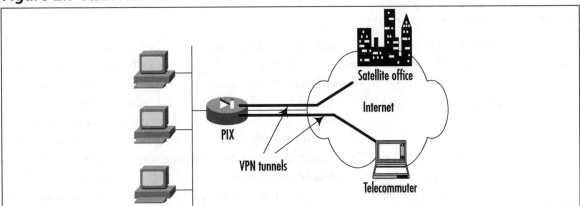

Dynamic Translation

When dynamic NAT is set up, a pool of inside global addresses is defined for use in outbound translation. When the NAT router or firewall receives a packet from an inside host and dynamic NAT is configured, it selects the next available address from the global address pool that was set up and replaces the source address in the IP header. Dynamic NAT differs from static NAT because address mappings can change for each new conversation that is set up between two given endpoints. Figure 2.8 shows how dynamic translation might work. The global address pool (for example purposes only) is 10.0.1.10 through 10.0.1.12, using a 24-bit subnet mask (255.255.255.0). The local address 192.168.0.10 is mapped directly to the first address in the global pool (10.0.1.10). The next system needing access (local address 192.168.0.12 in this example) is mapped to the next available global address of 10.0.1.11. The local host 192.168.0.11 never initiated a connection to the Internet, and therefore a dynamic translation entry was never created for it.

Figure 2.8 Dynamic Address Translation

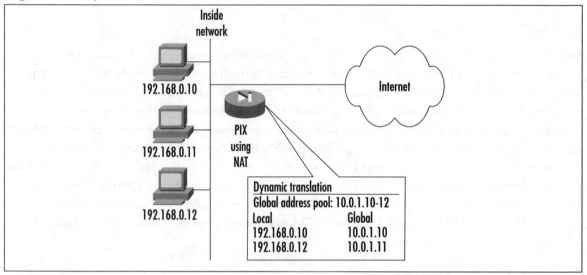

Port Address Translation

What happens when there are more internal hosts initiating sessions than there are global addresses in the pool? This is called *overloading*, a configurable parameter in NAT, also referred to as *Port Address Translation,* or *PAT*. In this situation, you have the possibility of multiple inside hosts being assigned to the same global source address. The NAT/PAT box must have a way to keep track of which local address to send replies back to. This is done by using unique source port numbers as the tracking mechanism and involves possibly rewriting of the source port in the packet header. You should recall that TCP/UDP uses 16 bits to encode port numbers, which allows for 65,536 different services or sources to be identified. When performing translation, PAT tries to use the original source port number if it is not already used. If it is, the next available port number from the appropriate group is used. Once the available port numbers are exhausted, the process starts again using the next available IP address from the pool.

Virtual Private Networking

The concept of VPN developed as a solution to the high cost of dedicated lines between sites that had to exchange sensitive information. As the name indicates, it is not quite private networking, but "virtually private." This privacy of communication over a public network such as the Internet is typically achieved using encryption technology and usually addresses the issues of confidentiality, integrity, and authentication.

In the past, organizations that had to enable data communication between multiple sites used a variety of pricey WAN technologies such as point-to-point leased lines, Frame Relay, X.25, and

Integrated Services Digital Network (ISDN). These were especially expensive for companies that had international locations. However, whether circuit-switched or packet-switched, these technologies carried an inherent decent measure of security. A hacker would typically need to get access to the underlying telecom infrastructure to be able to snoop on communications. This was, and still is, a nontrivial task, since carriers have typically done a good job on physical security. Even so, organizations such as banks that had extreme requirements for WAN security would deploy link encryption devices to scramble all data traveling across these connections.

Another benefit to having dedicated links has been that there is a solid baseline of bandwidth that you could count on. Applications that had critical network throughput requirements would drive the specification of the size of WAN pipe that was needed to support them. VPNs experienced slow initial adoption due to the lack of throughput and reliability guarantees on the Internet as well as the complexity of configuration and management.

Now that the Internet has proven its reliability for critical tasks and many of the management hurdles have been overcome, VPN adopters are now focusing their attention on issues of interoperability and security. The interoperability question has mostly been answered as VPN vendors are implementing industry-standard protocols such as IPsec for their products. The IPsec standards provide for confidentiality, integrity, and optionally, authentication.

Because of these improvements, organizations are now able to deploy VPNs in a rather straightforward manner, enabling secure access to the enterprise network for remote offices and/or telecommuters. Figure 2.9 shows the two main reasons for setting up VPNs. The first is to provide site-to-site connectivity to remote offices. The second is for telecommuters, adding flexibility by enabling enterprise access not only via dial-up to any ISP but also through a broadband connection via a home or hotel, for example. VPNs are used for many other reasons nowadays, including setting up connectivity to customers, vendors, and partners.

Figure 2.9 VPN Deployment

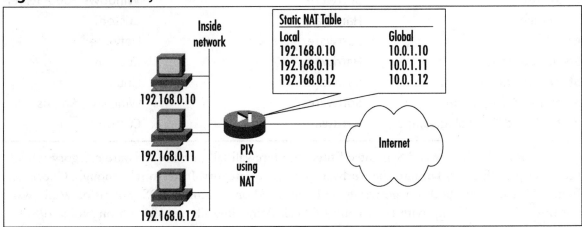

Many organizations have gone through the trouble of setting up VPN links for their remote users but have not taken the extra step of validating or improving the security of the computers that these workers are using to access the VPN. The most secure VPN tunnel offers no protection if the user's PC has been compromised by a Trojan horse program that allows a hacker to ride through the VPN tunnel right alongside legitimate, authorized traffic.

The solution is to deploy cost-effective firewall and intrusion detection software or hardware for each client that will be accessing the VPN, as well as continuous monitoring of the datastream coming out of the tunnel. Combined with real-time antivirus scanning and regular security scans, this solution helps ensure that the VPN does not become an avenue for attack into the enterprise.

Popular Firewalls

There are many players in the firewall market. Naming and describing them all could easily turn into a chapter in and of itself. Firewalls usually take the form of either a computer running a common operating system (OS) with the firewall software installed on top, or a purpose-built hardware appliance that the manufacturer intended as a firewall from the ground up. Those that fall into the latter category either run on pre-hardened versions of a common, general-purpose OS (such as NetBSD or Solaris), or they run a customized, real-time OS that was only intended to run the firewall. Table 2.1 introduces the major vendors and where their products line up in the marketplace:

Table 2.1 Firewall Vendors and Types

Firewall Vendor	Form	OS
3Com Corporation & SonicWALL	Hardware	Custom
Check Point Software Technologies	Both	Windows, Solaris, IPSO
Cisco Systems, Inc.	Hardware	Custom
CyberGuard	Hardware	Custom
Microsoft	Software	Windows 2000 Server
NetScreen	Hardware	Custom
Novell	Software	Netware
Secure Computing	Hardware	Custom
Stonesoft, Inc.	Software	Linux
Symantec Corporation	Software	Windows, Solaris
WatchGuard Technologies, Inc.	Hardware	Custom

Microsoft ISA Server and Symantec Enterprise Firewall fall into the software category while the Cisco PIX firewalls fall into the hardware appliance category. Interestingly enough, Check Point FW-1 falls into both categories: it can be installed on a common OS (Solaris or Windows), but through a partnership with Nokia, most Check Point firewalls actually run on Nokia IPSO appliances.

The vendors that do run as pure software installed on a common, general-purpose OS usually employ some form of hardening process so that hackers do not compromise the security of the underlying OS. Rather than try to subvert the firewall, hackers could just attack the OS that is hosting the firewall and cause that machine to route packets before the firewall sees them. They might also simply obtain a remote terminal session with the desktop and change the security policy altogether.

Axent Raptor, the predecessor to Symantec's Enterprise Firewall, runs a service called Vulture to kill any rogue processes that attempt to start (such as viruses, Trojans, or other malicious applications). Rather than lock the Windows OS down such that outside programs can't infect the server, the Vulture "watchdog" process just makes sure that no new processes start up once the firewall is installed. Similarly, Novell's BorderManager, which runs on NetWare, requires a special version of the Netware core server.exe file to prevent access to the console before authenticating to the machine.

Manufacturers that specialize in hardware appliances will often flaunt the security holes in general-purpose OSs as a weakness of products that run on those platforms. Furthermore, they'll usually state that hardware appliances have better security since the firmware that runs them has no other function. The argument seems to make sense, but it doesn't cover every situation. Check Point FW-1 and Symantec Enterprise Firewall easily exceed the minimum ICSA requirements, while numerous hardware appliances require firmware upgrades to fix security holes. Therefore, you cannot make a judgment about a firewall's security based entirely on whether it is hardware- or software-based. You do, however, need to know into which category your firewall falls because each type presents a different challenge to hackers.

In the end, the decision on which firewall type to use is more of a personal preference. You should select your firewall according primarily to which features you need. Only as a secondary or tertiary criteria should you consider the delivery format—hardware or software. For many, the ease of a plug-and-play hardware appliance is very attractive. If something goes wrong, just slide in a new appliance and off you go. Others may not want to pay the extra money for a purpose-built custom appliance, and instead would like to repurpose some of their old servers that can be converted to use as a firewall. Depending on your organization and the budget you have for your firewall, you will naturally gravitate to either the hardware types of firewall.

Hardware-Based Firewalls

Packet filtering is the basis of the typical firewall. The functions performed by packet filters are similar to those performed by routers, and the languages used to program them are often based on router interface-type rule sets. Many firewall vendors provide hardware-based solutions. Some of the most popular hardware firewalls include the Cisco PIX firewall, SonicWall, the Webramp 1700, the Firebox from WatchGuard Technologies, and the OfficeConnect firewalls from 3Com.

Hardware solutions are available for networks of all sizes. For example, the 3Com products focus on small business and home office users, while the Cisco PIX comes in configurations that support up to 250,000 connections.

Hardware-based firewalls are often referred to as *firewall appliances*. A disadvantage of hardware-based firewalls is the proprietary nature of the software they run. Another disadvantage of many of these products, such as Cisco's highly respected PIX, is the high cost.

The Cisco PIX Firewall

The Cisco PIX firewall is designed to meet the needs of small or home networks to enterprise-sized networks. The PIX provides various types of users with the same security level and features, but performance is increased with the larger PIX appliance. The PIX can support many users, and most PIX models have VPN support. Depending on the model, the PIX may have a fixed chassis that cannot be upgraded to support additional interfaces, where other PIX models may support many network interfaces.

Key items of the PIX firewall include the following:

- A user license that supports either a limited amount of internal IP addresses to access the Internet simultaneously, and the DHCP server feature supports up to a fixed number of DHCP address assignments. Depending on the model, this may be unlimited.

- Various levels of clear-text throughput, from 10Mbps to 1Gbps.

- Various types of hardware, including rack-mountable. Also has many different types of network card support to fixed for a small office.

- Optional encryption licenses, which are required if 168-bit 3DES or 56-bit DES VPN tunnels are used.

- An unlimited number of VPN peers.

The PIX OS is a feature-filled OS that provides a high level of security and performance. Because it is designed solely for the purpose of securing your network infrastructure, it doesn't have the weaknesses inherent to general OSs such as Windows or UNIX. However, the PIX OS's lack of a general OS does not mean that the PIX has fewer features than its competitors. The PIX has a full set of security features and with its streamlined OS and specially designed hardware it has the ability to outperform many of its competitors.

Features include:

- **Purpose-built operating system** Eliminates the weaknesses found in most general OSs.

- **Adaptive security algorithm (ASA)** Method the PIX uses to provide stateful packet filtering, which analyzes each packet to ensure only legitimate traffic traverses the PIX.

- **URL filtering** Can limit URLs accessed by the user's base on a policy defined by the network administrator or a security policy. Requires an external Netpartner's WebSense server or N2H2 server.

- **Content filtering** Can block ActiveX or Java applets.

- **NAT and PAT** Hides internal addressing from the Internet and makes more efficient use of private address space.

- **Cut-through proxy** Authenticates users accessing resources through the PIX.

- **VPN** Capable of handling mobile user access and site-to-site VPNs utilizing DES, 3DES, and AES encryption methods.

- **Intrusion detection** Enables the PIX to protect against various forms of malicious attack with features such as DNSGuard, FloodGuard, MailGuard, and IPVerify as well as the ability to identify attacks via attack "signatures."

- **DHCP** Can act as a DHCP Client and/or Server.

- **Routing functionality** Can support static routes, RIP, and OSPF.

- **Support for RADIUS or TACACS+** Authenticating, authorizing, and accounting for users passing through the PIX or to enabled authentication for those connecting to the PIX's management interfaces.

- **Failover** Provides a resilient, high-availability solution in case of failure.

- **Point to Point Protocol over Ethernet (PPPoE) support** Compatible with xDSL and cable modems.

- **Common Criteria EAL4 Certification** Certain PIX OS versions have achieved the highest level of certification handed out by Common Criteria, an independent international security organization. You can find more information about Common Criteria at www.commoncriteria.org.

It is very important to security because stateful inspection provides a deeper level of filtering than ACLs found in routers, which may only filter based on header information. Firewalls that perform stateful inspection analyze individual data packets as they traverse the firewall. In addition to the packet header, stateful inspection also assesses the packet's payload and looks at the application protocol. It can filter based on the source, destination, and service requested by the packet. The term stateful inspection refers to the firewall's ability to remember the status of a connection and thereby build a context for each data stream in its memory. With this information available to it, the firewall is able to make more informed policy decisions.

Nokia Firewall

The Nokia hardware platform comes with a hardened FreeBSD operating system out-of-the-box. The hardware is rack-mountable, and it is easily maintained by using a common firewall software package—Checkpoint FW-1. The Checkpoint FW-1 software is covered in the next section.

Firewall Software

In addition to firewall appliances, there are various firewall software applications you can use on a standard OS such as Solaris, Windows, or Linux. Many of these software packages do not strictly run at the OSI TCP/IP application level; rather, they use stateful inspection which runs through the entire OSI stack.

Check Point FW-1

Though the statistics are a few years old, at one point it was estimated that FW-1 was deployed on one of every four firewall implementations. FW-1's feature set and complexity have made it quite popular with enterprises. The complexity of the software has also led to the creation of several levels of certifications for use of the product itself. This says little about the product but more about its wide use.

Check Point includes most features that one would expect from a standard firewall package. It uses stateful packet filtering, works with multiple interfaces, and can perform NAT services. Some deployments can be configured to provide fail-over services in the event of loss of one firewall.

Prior to using FW-1 for a DMZ implementation, it is recommended that people using the software familiarize themselves with the package. Although the slick GUI for configuration could put some users at ease, inexperience with the software can lead to a very frustrating experience. In addition to vendor documentation, you can obtain useful information at www.phoneboy.com.

Darren Reed's IPFilter

IPFilter is a firewall software implementation developed and maintained by Darren Reed. This personal project has turned into an industrial-strength firewall software implementation that rivals many commercial packages. It also plays on a field on which commercial firewall software packages can't compete—it's free.

IPFilter provides stateful traffic inspection, much like any standard firewall software implementation. It also provides NAT functionality and can handle multiple network interfaces. These features are critical to the implementation of any DMZ.

The IPFilter software package can be downloaded from http://coombs.anu.edu.au/~avalon/ip-filter.html. The package supports both 32- and 64-bit Sparc architectures. A 32-bit implementation can be easily compiled using the freely available GNU C Compiler and will essentially compile right out of the box. A 64-bit build requires a little more work, including obtaining a compiler capable of building binaries for the architecture. This particular situation is one in which the trial version of Sun Forte C Compiler comes handy.

Microsoft ISA Server

Microsoft ISA Server is meant to be used as an all-in-one security package—firewall, intrusion detection, Active Directory, encryption, and policy manager.

Because the ISA Server is designed to be the central connection between your network and the Internet (or any untrusted network that you're connected to), you should consider running the other services that the ISA provides (e.g. intrusion detection, Active Directory) on other servers.

Summary

Before investing time and money into a firewall, you need to make sure you understand where the firewall will be in your network and which will be the best solution for your organization. There are many different types of firewalls, including hardware and software, freeware or commercial, and application proxy or packet filtering. Various solutions will be covered throughout this book. They include Linux Iptables and Ipchains, Solaris built-in firewalling, Cisco PIX, Microsoft ISA Server, and Check Point FW-1. Firewalls not only depend on where you put them on your network, but how they are configured and what you use them for. Just remember that a firewall is only as good as its rule set.

## Chapter 3

DMZ Concepts, Layout, and Conceptual Design

Best Damn Topics in this Chapter:

- DMZ Basics

- DMZ Design Fundamentals

- Advanced Risks

- Advanced Design Strategies

Introduction

During the course of the last few years, it has become increasingly evident that there is a pronounced need for protection of internal networks from the outside world. As machine technologies have improved and extensive shifts in the functions that a user can accomplish through more user-friendly interfaces have occurred, many more attacks have been mounted against enterprise and nonenterprise systems. Unlike the patterns in the past, when networks were primarily attacked and probed by "professional" attackers, the systems you protect are now routinely scanned by individuals and groups ranging from pre-teens "just trying it out" to organized groups of criminals seeking to abridge your systems or use information that is stored within your enterprise that can give them identities, disclose trade information, allow them access to funds, or disrupt critical services that your organization provides.

This chapter is designed for your use in understanding the concepts of protection, the terminology and pieces of the demilitarized zone (DMZ) structure, and design of the DMZ for the enterprise. A DMZ is a method of providing segregation of networks and services that need to be provided to users, visitors, or partners through the use of firewalls and multiple layers of filtering and control to protect internal systems.

There are two very important things to remember when planning your DMZ:

- **Least privilege** This concept is used by the security planner and team to define the levels of access to resources and the network that should be allowed. From a security standpoint, it is always preferable to be too restrictive with the capability to relax the access levels than to be too loose and have a breach occur.

- **Trusted users** An important cog in maintaining the integrity of our security efforts.

DMZ Basics

Before we get into an in-depth discussion of DMZs and firewalls, we need to go over some definitions of the components and a brief history of the DMZ and the philosophy that has led to the implementation of the technologies for protection. To begin, we define some common terms that we will use throughout the book as we discuss DMZs. Table 3.1 details and defines these terms.

Table 3.1 DMZ Definitions

Term	Definition or Description
DMZ	In computer networks, a demilitarized zone, or DMZ, is a computer host or small network inserted as a "neutral zone" between a company's private network and the outside public network. The DMZ prevents outside users from getting direct access to a server that has company data. (The term comes from the geographic buffer zone that was set up between North Korea and South Korea following the United Nations "police action" in the early 1950s.) A DMZ is an optional and more secure approach to a firewall and effectively acts as a proxy server.

Continued

Table 3.1 DMZ Definitions

Term	Definition or Description
Bastion host (untrusted host)	A machine (usually a server) located in the DMZ with strong host-level protection and minimal services. It is used as a gateway between the inside and the outside of networks. The bastion host is normally *not* the firewall but a separate machine that will probably be sacrificial in the design and expected to be compromised. The notation "untrusted host" may be used because the bastion host is always considered to be potentially compromised and therefore should not be fully trusted by internal network clients.
Firewall	A hardware device or software package that provides filtering and/or provision of rules to allow or deny specific types of network traffic to flow between internal and external networks.
Proxy server	An application-based translation of network access requests. Provision for local user authentication for access to untrusted network. Logging and control of port/protocol access may be possible. Normally used to connect two networks.
Network Address Translation (NAT)	Application-based translation of requests for service or connection to an external network. No user authentication is possible, and port/protocol filtering is not usually performed here. Used to redirect requests through one interface. Requests for connection at outside interface must have originated from inside host or they are dropped.
Packet filtering	The use of a set of rules to open or close ports to specific protocols (such as allowing Transmission Control Protocol (TCP) or User Datagram Protocol (UDP) packets) or protocol ID(s) such as allowing or blocking Internet Control Message Protocol (ICMP).
Stateful packet filtering	The use of a process to inspect packets as they reach the firewall and maintain the state of the connection by allowing or disallowing packets to pass based on the access policy.
Screened subnet	An isolated network containing hosts that need to be accessible from both the untrusted external network and the internal network. An example is the placement of a bastion host in a dual-firewall network, with the bastion host in the network between the firewalls. A screened subnet is often a part of a DMZ implementation.
Screening router	An often-used initial screening method to limit traffic to and from a protected network. It may employ various methods of packet filtering and protocol limitation and act as a limited initial firewall device.

DMZ use has become a necessary method of providing the multilayer approach to security that has become a popular method of providing security. The use of DMZ structures was developed as evolving business environments required the provision of increasing numbers of services and connectivity to accomplish the desired tasks for the particular business. New technologies and designs have provided a higher level of protection for the data and services we are charged with protecting.

Planning for network security requires an evaluation of the risks involved with loss of data, unauthorized access to data, and information compromise. The plan must also consider cost factors, staff knowledge and training, and the hardware and platforms currently in use, as well as helping with the estimations of future need. As we will see, the DMZ plan and concept provide a multilayered security capability, but as with anything that involves multiple components, administration costs and equipment costs increase with the complexity of the system.

It should be understood that no security plan is ever a final plan. Instead, we work continuously to revise and update the plan in an ongoing effort to provide the best possible coverage that minimizes the risk of intrusion and damage. Of course, before we can provide a meaningful and effective evaluation of the areas we need to protect, we must understand the components that have to be protected.

Originally, firewalls were used to divide a network into two: the trusted network (your enterprise network) and the untrusted network (usually the Internet or some other public network). Figure 3.1 shows the original firewall concept.

Figure 3.1 Original Basic Firewall Configuration

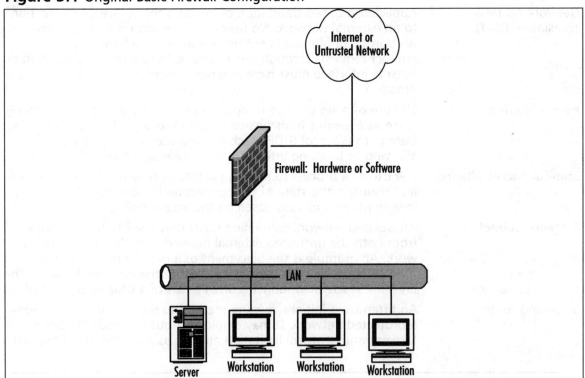

Since then, we've greatly expanded the role of our network infrastructure and our resources to provide information in response to both public requests and those of our employees and customers or partners. Additionally, the freely available tools and relative ease with which spoofing attacks and other attacks can be mounted against us have increased the requirements that we isolate our networks and protect the information that is contained on them. This is where we begin to consider the use of the DMZ concept, allowing us to better segregate and divide our networks. Figure 3.2 demonstrates a generic DMZ configuration.

Figure 3.2 Generic DMZ Configuration

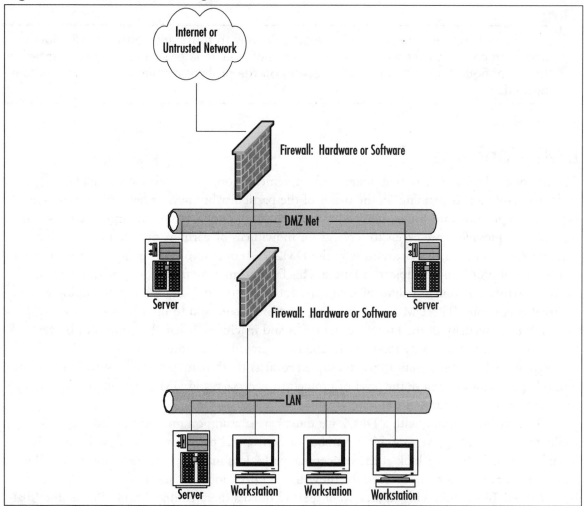

One of the reasons for this shift in coverage is our need to provide services to some employees and others outside of the local area network (LAN) environment when we might not want to allow those services to be available to everyone. A single-method protection option (firewall, NAT, packet filtering) requires the administrator to completely allow or block a service or protocol to all connections and doesn't have granularity or flexibility in its operation. This inflexible arrangement meant that the third part of the triad, *availability*, was not always possible.

The addition of the extra layer of filtering provided by the second firewall (or more) in the control environment allows us to more finely control access to the data and servers hosting that data. This in turn allows us to more fully implement the second part of the triad, *integrity*. If we can control these access points more closely through access control lists (ACLs) and user accounts, for example, it is much more likely that we will succeed in maintaining the integrity of the data and keeping it in a protected and undamaged state. This gives the DMZ design flexibility and contributes greatly to the administrator's ability to provide good security and still provide services to those who need them.

> **NOTE**
>
> The firewall configurations we will use act primarily to route and restrict traffic flow to and from particular network segments. As we will see in later sections of the chapter, those configurations are varied and depend on the protections we have determined are needed.

DMZ Concepts

The use of a DMZ and its overall design and implementation can be relatively simple or extremely complex, depending on the needs of the particular business or network system. The DMZ concept came into use as the need for separation of networks became more acute when we began to provide more access to services for individuals or partners outside the LAN infrastructure. One of the primary reasons why the DMZ has come into favor is the realization that a single type of protection is subject to failure. This failure can arise from configuration errors, planning errors, equipment failure, or deliberate action on the part of an internal employee or external attack force. The DMZ has proven to be more secure and to offer multiple layers of protection for the security of the protected networks and machines. It has also proven to be very flexible, scalable, and relatively robust in its ability to provide the protection we need. DMZ design now includes the ability to use multiple products (both hardware- and software-based) on multiple platforms to achieve the level of protection necessary, and DMZs are often designed to provide failover capabilities as well.

When we are working with a DMZ, we must have a common ground to work from. To facilitate understanding, we examine a number of conceptual paths for traffic flow in the following section. Before we look at the conceptual paths, let's make sure that we understand the basic configurations that can be used for firewall and DMZ location and how each of them can be visualized. In the following figures, we'll see and discuss these configurations. Please note that each of these configurations is useful on internal networks needing protection as well as protecting your resources from networks such as the Internet. Our first configuration is shown in Figure 3.3.

Figure 3.3 A Basic Network with a Single Firewall

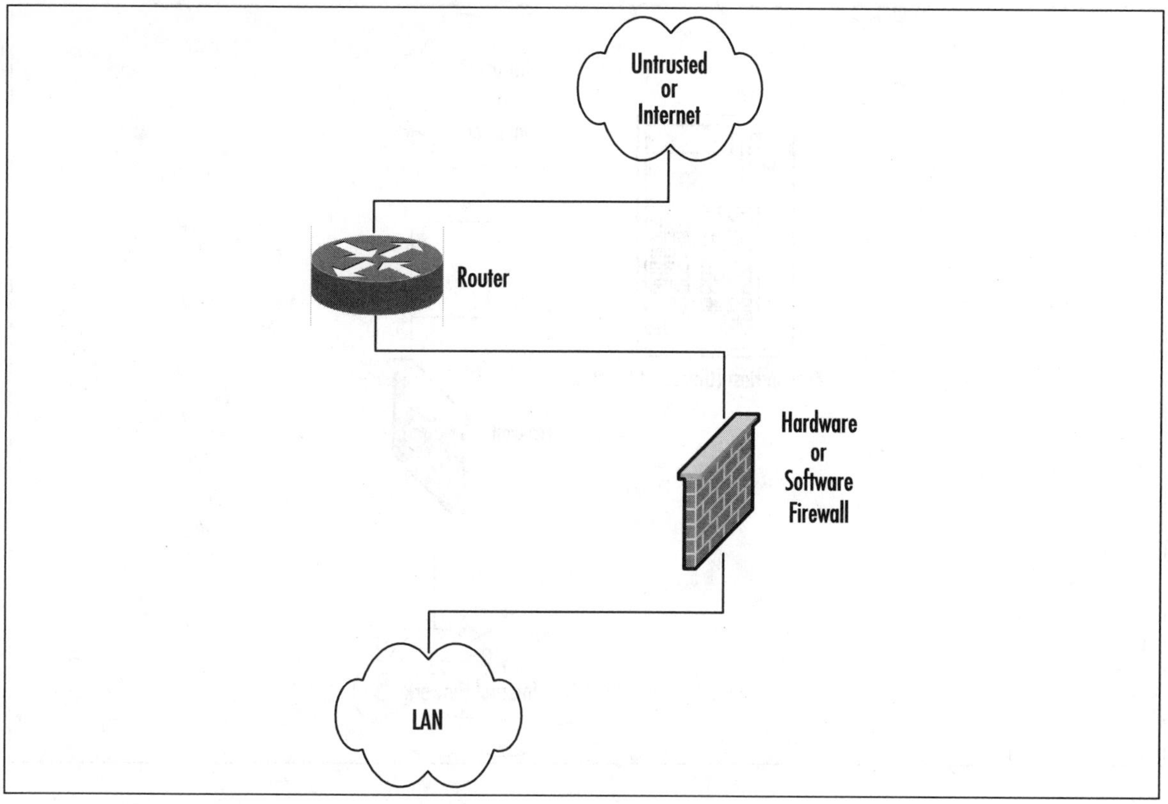

In Figure 3.3, we can see the basic configuration that would be used in a simple network situation in which there was no need to provide external services. This configuration would typically be used to begin to protect a small business or home network. It could also be used within an internal network to protect an inner network that needed to be divided and isolated from the main network. This situation could include payroll, finance, or development divisions that need to protect their information and keep it away from general network use and view.

Figure 3.4 details a protection design that would allow for the implementation and provision of services outside the protected network. In this design, it would be absolutely imperative that rules be enacted to not allow the untrusted host to access the internal network. Security of the bastion host machine would be accomplished on the machine itself, and only minimal and absolutely necessary services would be enabled or installed on that machine. In this design, we might be providing a Web presence that did not involve e-commerce or the necessity to dynamically update content. This design would not be used for provision of virtual private network (VPN) connections, FTP services, or other services that required other content updates to be performed regularly.

Figure 3.4 Basic Network, Single Firewall and Bastion Host (Untrusted Host)

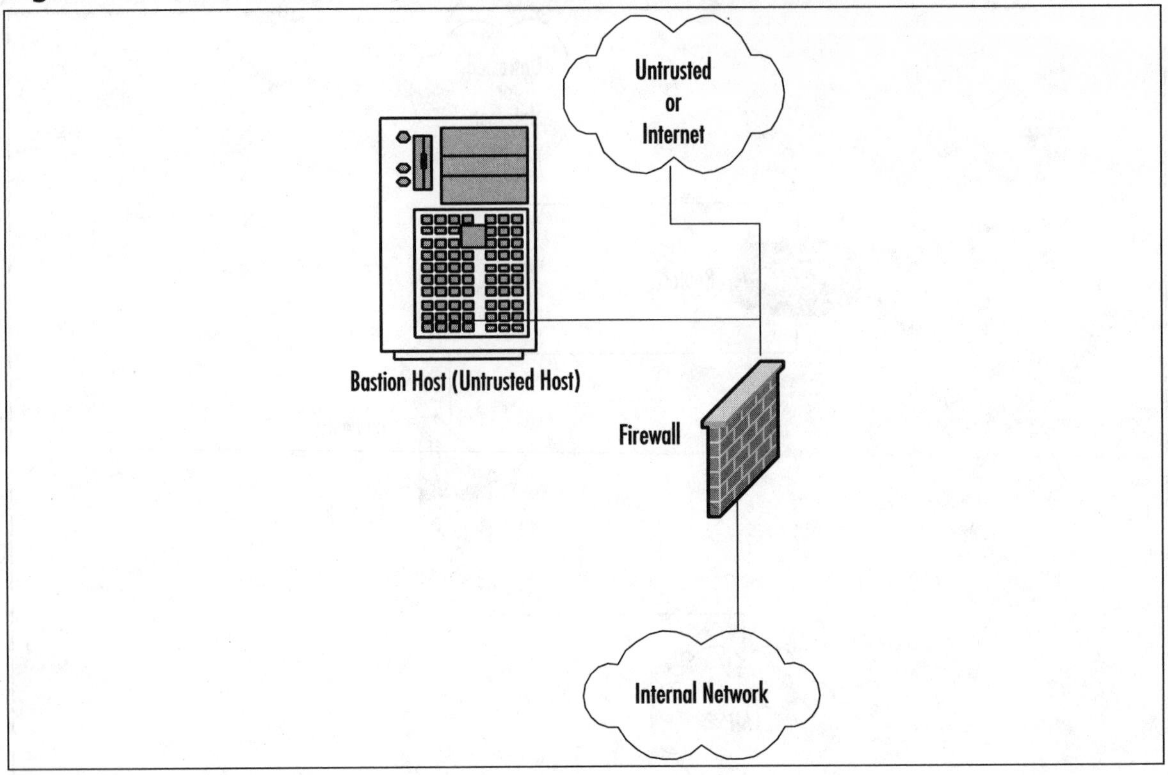

Figure 3.5 shows a basic DMZ structure. In this design, the bastion host is partially protected by the firewall. Rather than the full exposure that would result to the bastion host in Figure 3.4, this setup would allow us to specify that the bastion host in Figure 3.5 could be allowed full outbound connection, but the firewall could be configured to allow only port 80 traffic inbound to the bastion host (assuming it was a Web server) or others as necessary for connection from outside. This design would allow connection from the internal network to the bastion host if necessary. This design would potentially allow updating of Web server content from the internal network if allowed by firewall rule, which could allow traffic to and from the bastion host on specific ports as designated. (There is more on that topic later in the chapter.)

Figure 3.5 A Basic Firewall with a DMZ

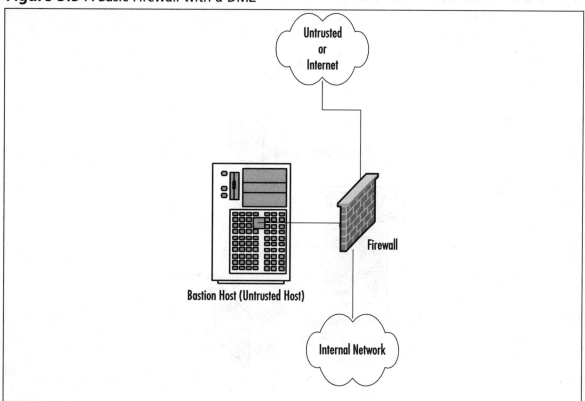

Figure 3.6 shows a generic dual-firewall DMZ configuration. In this arrangement, the bastion host can be protected from the outside and allowed to connect to or from the internal network. In this arrangement, like the conditions in Figure 3.5, flow can be controlled to and from both of the networks away from the DMZ. This configuration and method is more likely to be used if more than one bastion host is needed for the operations or services being provided.

Figure 3.6 A Dual Firewall with a DMZ

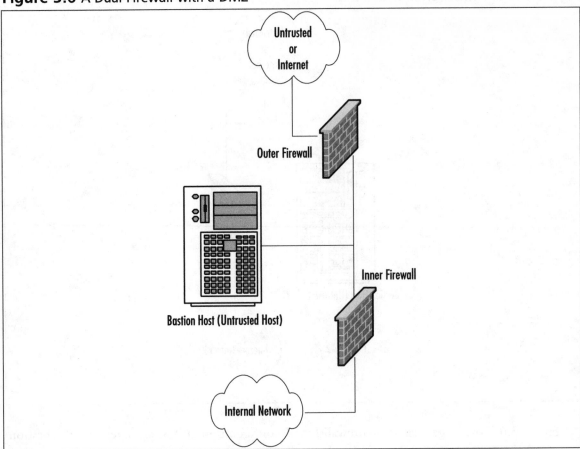

> **NOTE**
>
> Although in this example we use the Cisco PIX, this design can be implemented with any firewall.

For example, Figure 3.7 shows a multiple DMZ environment with Web servers, e-mail relays, and FTP servers on the first DMZ leg (DMZ 1), and services such as VPN and dial-in user access on a second DMZ leg (DMZ 2). This setup separates the functions of the DMZs. DMZ 1 supports services that are publicly available over the Internet, such as the company's Web site. DMZ 2 supports remote users accessing resources on the internal LAN via a dial-in or VPN. By making remote users traverse the firewall, we make the internal LAN environment secure because rules can be set up to restrict remote user access. Adding DMZ legs helps keep the firewall rule sets manageable, especially when each DMZ has different access requirements. It also isolates any errors in configuration because a change on an ACL for one DMZ will not affect the ACL of another DMZ interface. You can add redundancy by adding a secondary firewall, similar to the redundant traditional "three-legged" firewall design.

Figure 3.7 Multi-DMZ Infrastructure

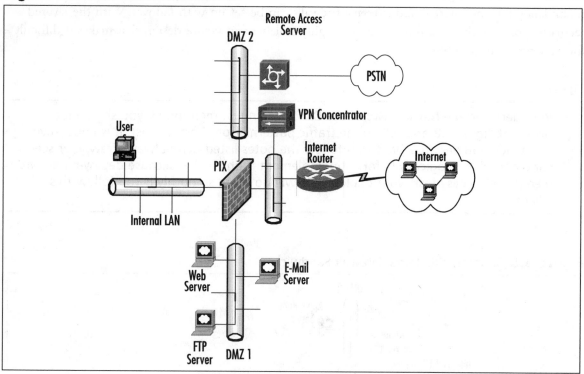

The previous designs are ideal for standard, multipurpose DMZ environments, but the internal/external firewall design (see Figure 3.8) is intended for the specific purpose of supporting an e-commerce site for which various levels of security are required. Large e-commerce sites separate the servers' functions into three components, consisting of a Web server cluster, an application server cluster, and a database cluster, which is most commonly known as a three-tier design. In this design, Internet users accessing an e-commerce site only interact with the Web servers on DMZ 1. The job of the Web server is to be the front-end GUI for the e-commerce site. The Web servers will in turn call upon the application servers on DMZ 2 to provide content. The application server's job is to collect the information the user is requesting and provide content back to the Web server for the user to view.

The application server requests information by making SQL calls to the database servers on DMZ 3, which houses the site's data. Each component has different security requirements, which only allows necessary communication between DMZ 1, 2, and 3. The external firewall will only allow users to access the Web site on DMZ 1 via HTTP or HTTPS (SSL-enabled HTTP). The user community will not need to access any other part of the site, because the Web server will serve all the necessary content to the users; therefore, access is restricted to DMZ 1. The external firewall will allow the Web servers to make requests only to the application servers on DMZ 2 for content. DMZ 2 is located between the internal and external firewall sets with a Layer 3 switch acting as the default gateway for DMZ 2 as well as routing traffic though this environment. The internal firewall only allows the application servers to send SQL requests to the database servers located on DMZ 3. The internal firewall also allows administrators on the internal LAN to manage the e-commerce environment. For simplicity, Figure 3.8 does not show redundancy, but the internal and external firewalls can be set up with failover. With the layered security approach, this solution provides a highly scalable and secure design that makes it difficult for hackers to compromise.

NOTE

To understand the traffic flows of the DMZ design just mentioned, you should look closely at Figure 3.8 and follow the traffic patterns from host to host. It is imperative that when you design a DMZ, you follow the notes listed here; always draw your scenario and plan it logically before you implement it physically. Because deploying a DMZ scenario is no easy task, your deployment will go more smoothly if you follow this advice.

Figure 3.8 An Internal/External Firewall Sandwich

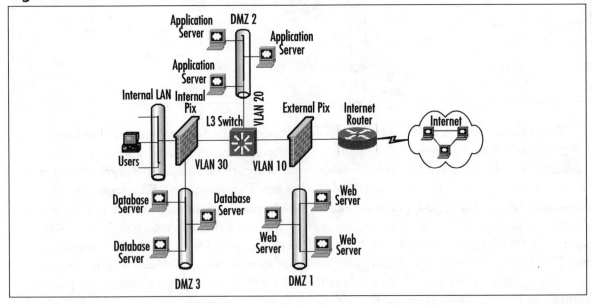

Traffic Flow Concepts

Now that we've had a quick tour of some generic designs, let's take a look at the way network communications traffic typically flows through them. Be sure to note the differences between the levels and the flow of traffic and protections offered in each.

Figure 3.9 illustrates the flow pattern for information through a basic single-firewall setup. This type of traffic control can be achieved through hardware or software and is the basis for familiar products such as Internet Connection Sharing (ICS) and the NAT functionality provided by digital subscriber line (DSL) and cable modems used for connection to the Internet. Note that flow is unrestricted outbound, but the basic configuration will drop all inbound connections that did not originate from the internal network.

Figure 3.9 Basic Single-Firewall Flow

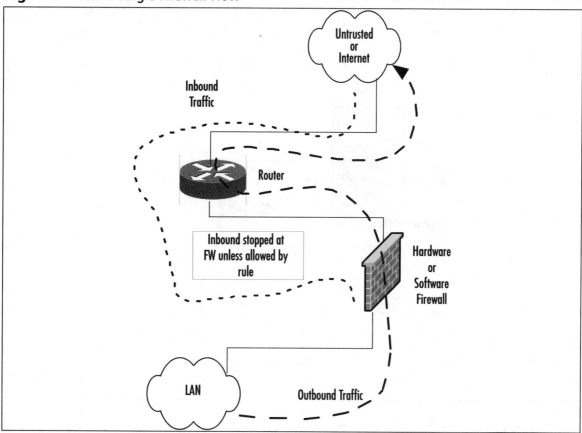

Figure 3.10 reviews the traffic flow in a network containing a bastion host and a single firewall. This network configuration does not produce a DMZ; the protection of the bastion host is configured individually on the host and requires extreme care in setup. Inbound traffic from the untrusted network or the bastion host is dropped at the firewall, providing protection to the internal network. Outbound traffic from the internal network is allowed.

> **NOTE**
>
> *Bastion hosts* must be individually secured and hardened because they are always in a position that could be attacked or probed. This means that before placement, a bastion host must be stripped of unnecessary services, fully updated with the latest service packs, hot fixes, and updates, and isolated from other trusted machines and networks to eliminate the possibility that its compromise would allow connection to (and potential compromise of) the protected networks and resources. This also means that a machine being used for this purpose should have no user accounts relative to the protected network or directory services structure, which could lead to enumeration of your internal network.

Figure 3.10 A Basic Firewall with Bastion Host Flow

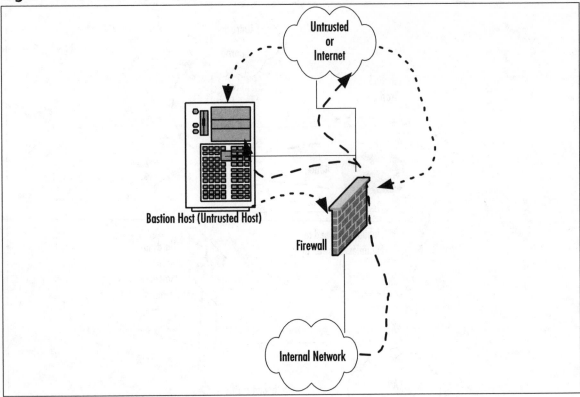

Figure 3.11 shows the patterns of traffic as we implement a DMZ design. In this form, inbound traffic flows through to the bastion host if allowed through the firewall and is dropped if destined for the internal network. Two-way traffic is permitted as specified between the internal network and the bastion host, and outbound traffic from the internal network flows through the firewall and out, generally without restriction.

Figure 3.11 A Basic Single Firewall with DMZ Flow

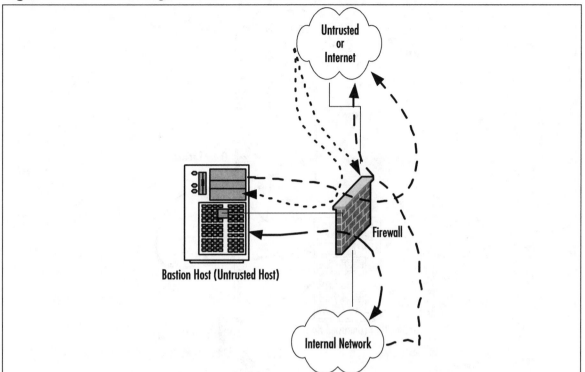

Figure 3.12 contains a more complex path of flow for information but provides the most capability in these basic designs to allow for configuration and provision of services to the outside. In this case, we have truly established a DMZ, separated and protected from both the internal and external networks. This type of configuration is used quite often when there is a need to provide more than one type of service to the public or outside world, such as e-mail, Web servers, DNS, and so forth. Traffic to the bastion host can be allowed or denied as necessary from both the external and internal networks, and incoming traffic to the internal network can be dropped at the external firewall. Outbound traffic from the internal network can be allowed or restricted either to the bastion host (DMZ network) or the external network.

Figure 3.12 A Dual Firewall with DMZ Flow

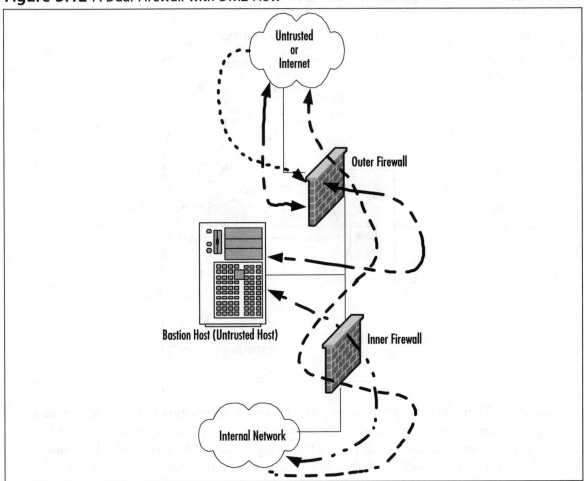

As you can see, there is a great amount of flexibility in the design and function of your protection mechanisms. In the sections that follow, we expand further on conditions for the use of different configurations and on the planning that it done to implement them.

Networks with and without DMZs

As we pursue our discussions about the creation of DMZ structures, it is appropriate to also take a look at the reasoning behind the various structures of the DMZ and when and where we'd want to implement a DMZ or perhaps use some other alternative.

During our preview of the concepts of DMZs, we saw some examples of potential design for network protection and access. Your design may incorporate any or all of these types of configuration, depending on your organization's needs; for example, a simple firewall configuration that may occur in the case of a home network installation or perhaps with a small business environment that is isolated from the Internet and does not share information or needs to provide services or information to outside customers or partners. This design would be suitable under these conditions, provided configuration is correct and monitored for change.

In the network design where a bastion host is located outside the firewall, the bastion host must be stripped of all unnecessary functionality and services and protected locally with appropriate file permissions and access control mechanisms. This design would be used when an organization needs to provide minimal services to an external network, such as a Web server. Access to the internal network from the bastion host is generally not allowed, because this host is subject to compromise.

A screened subnet incorporates the first of the actual DMZ designs. In this type of design, the firewall controls the flow of information from network to network and provides more protection to the bastion host from external flows. This design might be used when it is necessary to be able to regularly update the content of a Web server, or provide a front end for mail services or other services that need contact from both the internal and external networks. Although better for security purposes than Figure 3.2, this design still produces an untrusted relationship in the bastion host in relation to the internal network.

In the next section, we profile some of the advantages and disadvantages of the common approaches to DMZ architecture and provide a checklist to help you to make a decision about the appropriate use (or not) of the DMZ for protection.

Pros and Cons of DMZ Basic Designs

Table 3.2 details the advantages and disadvantages of the various types of basic design discussed in the preceding section.

Table 3.2 Pros and Cons of Basic DMZ Designs

Basic Design	Advantages	Disadvantages	Appropriate Utilization
Single firewall	Inexpensive, fairly easy configuration, low maintenance	Much lower security capabilities, no growth or expansion potential	Home, small office/home office (SOHO), small business without need to provide services to others
Single firewall with bastion host	Lower cost than more robust alternatives	Bastion host extremely vulnerable to compromise, inconvenient to update content, loss of functionality other than for absolutely required services; not scalable	Small business without resources for more robust implementation or static content being provided that doesn't require frequent updates
Single firewall with screened subnet and bastion host	Firewall provides protection to both internal network and bastion host, limiting some of the potential breach possibilities of an unprotected bastion host	Single point of failure; some products limit network addressing to DMZ in this configuration to public addresses, which might not be economic or possible in your network	Networks requiring access to the bastion host for updating of information

DMZ Design Fundamentals

DMZ design, like security design, is always a work in progress. As in security planning and analysis, we find that a DMZ design carries great flexibility and change potential to keep the protection levels we put in place in an effective state. The ongoing work is required so that the system's security is always as high as we can make it within the constraints of time and budget, while still allowing appropriate users and visitors to access the information and services we provide for their use. You will find that the time and funds spent in the design process and preparation for the implementation are very good investments if the process is focused and effective; this will lead to a high level of success and a good level of protection for the network you are protecting. In this section of the chapter, we explore the fundamentals of the design process. We incorporate the information we discussed in relation to security and traffic flow to make decisions about how our initial design should look. Additionally, we'll build on that information and review some other areas of concern that could affect the way we design our DMZ structure.

NOTE

In this section, we look at design of a DMZ from a logical point of view. Physical design and configuration are covered in following chapters, based on the firewall solution you are interested in deploying.

Why Design Is So Important

Design of the DMZ is critically important to the overall protection of your internal network—and the success of your firewall and DMZ deployment. The DMZ design can incorporate sections that isolate incoming VPN traffic, Web traffic, partner connections, employee connections, and public access to information provided by your organization. Design of the DMZ structure throughout the organization can protect internal resources from internal attack. As we discussed in the security section, it has been well documented that much of the risk of data loss, corruption, and breach actually exists *inside* the network perimeter. Our tendency is to protect assets from external harm but to disregard the dangers that come from our own internal equipment, policies, and employees.

These attacks or disruptions do not arise solely from disgruntled employees, either. Many of the most damaging conditions that occur are because of inadvertent mistakes made by well-intentioned employees. Each and all of these entry points is a potential source of loss for your organization and ultimately can provide an attack point to defeat your other defenses.

Additionally, the design of your DMZ will allow you to implement a multilayered approach to securing your resources that does not leave a single point of failure in your plan. This minimizes the problems and loss of protection that can occur because of misconfiguration of rule sets or ACL lists, as well as reducing the problems that can occur due to hardware configuration errors. In the last chapters of this book, we look at how to mitigate risk through testing of your network infrastructure to make sure your firewalls, routers, switches, and hosts are thoroughly hardened so that when you do deploy your DMZ segment, you can see for yourself that it is in fact secure from both internal as well as external threats.

Putting It All Together: A Business Case Study

If a DMZ is correctly planned and designed, it will make simple the tasks of implementing, maintaining, and supporting the DMZ infrastructure. It is important to note that a DMZ cannot be properly designed without a clear vision of what the DMZ will support. Will the DMZ environment contain a handful of servers that provide the enterprise with basic services, and therefore does not require much performance or resiliency? Or will the DMZ environment contain major services that the enterprise needs to be productive and profitable and therefore will need to be in operation at all times? Alternatively, will it be somewhere between these two scenarios? There is only one way to determine the category your DMZ infrastructure will fit into: You need to understand the business, the role the DMZ will play, the type of traffic the DMZ will support, the performance required, and plans for future growth.

As the network architect for the company, you are given the task of supplying the infrastructure to support the new Web site. The company already has Internet connectivity via a broadband connection, and you are protecting your network using a low-end firewall that was easy to install and worked well but does not have the ability to support a DMZ. Now you realize that you must upgrade the entire Internet infrastructure in order to host the new Web site. It is now time to gather the information and requirements so you can design and build a DMZ infrastructure that will be able to support the new Web site for its launch and into the future.

You need to begin gathering information, starting with the facts and requirements:

- The facts are that the company is making a strategic move to offer its customers a new method to purchase auto parts as well as to attract new customers.

- The site is important to the growth of the business.

- The Web site will start out small but could grow as sales over the Internet increase.

- The site will be a scalable server environment with a single Web/application server and a database server.

- A DMZ will need to be built on site to support the new web site.

- The infrastructure currently in place is not capable of supporting the new Web site.

- The site is estimated to reach 10,000 hits and 1000 transactions a day at first, and then grow steadily.

You next ask questions so you can be informed of data that was missing so you can move on to designing a solution:

- How much Internet bandwidth is required to support the site?

- What kind of security is needed? Will there be a need for both Web traffic and SSL traffic?

- Does the site require high availability?

- What are the connectivity requirements among the internal network, the Web/application server, and the database server?

- What is the budget for the DMZ infrastructure?

After you asked the questions, the developers and business managers come back to you with their answers. They tell you that since the site will only receive 10,000 hits and 1000 transactions a day, they initially need two T1s; as the site grows, they will add bandwidth. Since the site will be processing credit card transactions, both Web traffic (TCP port 80) and SSL (TCP port 443) need to be allowed to access the Web/application server from the Internet. The database should only be accessed by the internal LAN and should respond to Web/application server requests for information.

All Web servers and switches are 100Mbps full-duplex capable devices. Even though the servers can be a single point of failure, the DMZ infrastructure should be built with redundancy. The DMZ infrastructure should be built with scalability in mind, with close attention to the budget—in other words, do not over-engineer the infrastructure.

From this information, you can now start to develop your solution. Analyzing the requirements, you decide that the multileg DMZ with redundant firewalls offers you the most secure and scalable solution that fits your budget. The multileg DMZ allows you to separate the Web/application server into separate DMZs to allow for greater security.

DMZ 1 will contain the Web/application server, and DMZ 2 will contain the database servers. Because users will only access the Web/application server, the firewall rules will be configured so it only accesses the server on DMZ 1 via the Web port (TCP port 80) and SSL port (TCP port 443). DMZ 2 will allow no connectivity from the Internet; it will only respond to requests made for data by the Web/application server or by the internal LAN for management. Separating the Web/application server and the database servers into different DMZs allows for greater security in the event the Web/application server is compromised by an intruder. Since the Web/application server is directly accessible by the Internet, it is always the most vulnerable. Furthermore, the design allows for the addition of a redundant firewall that will take over for the primary should the primary go offline.

Designing End-to-End Security for Data Transmission between Hosts on the Network

Proper DMZ design, in conjunction with the security policy and plan developed previously, allows for end-to-end protection of the information being transmitted on the network. The importance of this capability is explored more fully later in the chapter, when we review some of the security problems inherent in the current implementation of TCP/IPv4 and the transmission of data. The use of one or more of the many firewall products or appliances currently available will most often afford the opportunity not only to block or filter specific protocols but also to protect the data as it is being transmitted. This protection may take the form of encryption and can use the available transports to protect data as well. Additionally, proper use of the technologies available within this design can provide for the necessary functions previously detailed in the concepts of AAA and CIA, using the multilayer approach to protection that we discussed in earlier sections. This need to provide end-to-end security requires that we are conversant with and remember basic network traffic patterns and protocols. The next few sections help remind us about these and further illustrate the need to design the DMZ with this capability in mind.

Traffic Flow and Protocol Fundamentals

Another of the benefits of using a DMZ design that includes one or more firewalls is the opportunity to control traffic flow into and out of the DMZ much more cohesively and with much more granularity and flexibility. When the firewall product in use (either hardware or software) is a product designed above the home-use level, the capability usually exists to control traffic that is flowing in and out of the network or DMZ through packet filtering based on port, and often to allow or deny the use of entire protocols. For example, the rule set might include a statement that blocks communication via ICMP, which would block protocol 1. A statement that allowed IPsec traffic where it was desired to allow traffic using ESP or AH would be written allowing protocol 50 for ESP or 51 for AH. (For a listing of the protocol IDs, visit www.iana.org/assignments/protocol-numbers.) Remember that like the rule of security that follows the principle of least privilege, we must include in our design the capability to allow only absolutely necessary traffic into and out of the various portions of the DMZ structure.

DMZ Protocols

Protocol use within a DMZ environment is always problematic. We should be well aware of the potential risks associated with protocol use in various implementations and those that are frequently and actively attacked because of the vulnerabilities that exist. Table 3.3 briefly overviews some of the known issues with various protocols. This table is not intended to be all-inclusive; rather, it is indicative of the fact that the DMZ designer must be aware of these limitations when designing a plan for DMZ structure and access both into and out of the DMZ.

Table 3.3 Protocols with Known Weaknesses

Protocol	Basic Weakness
Asynchronous Transfer Mode (ATM)	No authentication or encryption, subject to spoofing and interception
Internetwork Packet Exchange (IPX)	Designed for LAN use, doesn't scale well for wide area network (WAN) operations, high bandwidth usage with SAP broadcasts, aging protocol
Internet Protocol (IP)	No default data protection of packets, subject to many attacks, needed for connection to Internet
Kerberos	Vulnerable to buffer overflow attacks, replay, and spoofing to gain privilege and discover passwords, allowing potential for breach of service
Lightweight Directory Access Protocol (LDAP)	Some implementations are subject to buffer overflow and DoS attacks, with possibility of privilege elevation
Simple Network Management Protocol (SNMP)	DoS and buffer overflow attacks are possible, as are security risks posed by administrators who leave the community names and other information in default configurations; some conditions can result in privilege escalation and compromise
Secure Shell (SSH)	Privilege escalation, system compromise when code run under SSH credential, DoS attacks

Designing for Protection in Relation to the Inherent Flaws of TCP/IPv4

The current implementation of TCP/IPv4 contains a number of well-documented flaws that affect the design of both your security plan and your DMZ. Some of these problems were corrected in IPv6, but since implementation of this technology isn't on the immediate horizon, we must accommodate the weaknesses of the existing protocols when implementing the design of our DMZ. We must therefore plan for certain known problems:

- Data, including passwords not protected by the operating system, are sent in clear-text in TCP/IP packets
- SYN attacks, a DoS condition resulting from overflow of the wait buffer
- IP spoofing, allowing the attacker to pretend it is another host
- Sequence guessing, allowing reassembly or delivery of forged packets
- Connection hijacking, allowing man-in-the-middle attacks
- Lack of authentication capability in the protocol

You can find a good discussion of the problems with TCP/IPv4 and a more complete discussion of the flaws and improvements made in TCP/IPv6 at www.linuxsecurity.com/resource_files/documentation/tcpip-security.html. The design that we create for our DMZ structure will accommodate the weaknesses of the TCP/IP protocol and will provide the protection that is needed to stymie these types of attacks and their resulting potential for breach. To accomplish that goal, as we design we need to consider the various problems and design the working protections into the configuration of rules and ACL settings and consider the use of other protocols such as IPsec and L2TP to protect the data on the wire.

Public and Private IP Addressing

One of the primary reasons why the DMZ concepts have been so useful is that network administrators have a greatly expanded capability to use public and private addressing. As you will recall, the initial TCP/IPv4 implementations were based on class, with default subnet masks that limited to some degree the ability of network administrators to achieve true flexibility in their network designs. With the advent of classless addressing and improvements provided with the acceptance of that concept, much greater utilization has been made of functions such as NAT to provide addressing for the internal network without exposing that network to the dangers of the public network. The DMZ design must incorporate the methods and equipment being used for address translation and routing, and it becomes a method of hiding internal addresses from unwanted contact.

We also must plan for and use the ability to subnet within the private IP addressing ranges, which are shown in Table 3.4.

Table 3.4 Private IP Address Ranges

Private IP Range	CIDR Mask	Decimal Mask
10.0.0.0–10.255.255.255	/8	255.0.0.0
172.16.0.0–172.31.255.255	/16	255.255.255.0
192.168.0.0–192.168.255.255	/24	255.255.255.0

This allows us much greater flexibility in the segregation of the DMZ and assuring that the network addressing and contact between the protected network, the buffer (DMZ), and the outside world are more difficult for would-be attackers to penetrate.

Ports

Ports used in network communication become an extremely important tool in our ability to filter access levels and establish ACL functions on devices and in software implementations used to protect our assets. Recall that ports 0 through 1023 are reserved for specific uses and that all other ports are functionally available for use by applications. Registered ports include those from 1024 through 49151, and dynamic and/or private ports (used by applications for communication and session maintenance) are those from 49152 through 65535. The entire port list can be found at www.iana.org/port-numbers.

That means, of course, that the DMZ design must incorporate rules that block all traffic that is not necessary for the function of the DMZ or communications that must be carried through that area. Generally, this involves creating a rule set for the ACL that restricts or blocks all unused ports on a per-protocol basis to assure that the traffic is actually stopped. These rules become an integral part of the DMZ defense. The design is often started from two "all or nothing" configurations: all ports open, closing as problems occur (bad), and all ports closed, opening as required (good, but requiring a great deal of administration and learning in a new network that has not been fully documented). Either method can be considered in your design, although the latter provides much more security as you begin your quest to shut down intrusion.

The SANS Institute (www.sans.org) recommends the following port actions at a minimum as you design your DMZ and firewall blocking rules from external networks, as shown in Table 3.5. (The table is adapted from Appendix A of the SANS Top 20 list, which can be found at www.sans.org/top20.)

Table 3.5 Common Ports to Block

Service Type	TCP Port(s)	UDP Port(s)
Login Services	Telnet: 23, ; SSH: 22, ; FTP: 21, ; NetBIOS: f139, ; rlogin: 512, 513, 514	N/A
RPC and NFS	Portmap/rpcbind: 111, ; NFS: 2049, ; lockd: 4045	Portmap/rpcbind: 111, ; NFS: 2049, ; lockd: 4045
NetBIOS in Windows NT and W2K and XP	135, 139, 445(W2K and XP)	135, 137, 138, 445 (W2K and XP)
X Windows	6000 through 6255	N/A

Continued

Table 3.5 Common Ports to Block

Service Type	TCP Port(s)	UDP Port(s)
Naming Services	DNS: Block zone transfers (TCP 53) except from external secondaries	
LDAP: 389	DNS: Block UDP 53 to all machines that are not DNS servers	
LDAP: 389		
Mail	SMTP: 25 to all machines that are not external mail relays	
POP: 109, 110		
IMAP: 143	N/A	
Web	HTTP: 80; SSL: 443, except to external Web servers. Also consider common high-order HTTP port choices, such as 8000, 8080, 8888	N/A
Small Services	Ports below 20, time: 37	Ports below 20, ; time: 37
Miscellaneous	Finger: 79; NNTP: 119; LPD: 515; SNMP: 161, 162; BGP: 179: ; SOCKS: 1080	TFTP: 69; NTP: 123; syslog: 514; SNMP: 161, 162
ICMP	Blocks incoming echo request (ping and traceroute), out-going echo replies, time exceeded, and destination unreachable messages, *except* "packet too big" messages (Type 3, Code 4)	*Note:* This setting will block known malicious uses, but it also will restrict your legitimate use of the ICMP echo request

Using Firewalls to Protect Network Resources

Firewalls have been and continue to be an integral part in the planning process for DMZ deployments. The design can include any or all of the basic designs we looked at earlier in the chapter and may very well incorporate multiple types of configuration, depending on your organization's needs to protect data and resources from different threat areas. Firewalls are not the only component of the design that is important, but they do play a major part in allowing the administrator to control traffic more completely, thus providing a higher level of protection.

Part of the design process includes evaluating and checking the performance of different hardware- and software-based firewall products. This book discusses some of the most-used technologies in later chapters, such as Check Point and Check Point NG, PIX, Nokia, and Microsoft's ISA Server. Additionally, firewall considerations are explored during discussions of protection of wireless networks and methods of protecting networks using Sun and Microsoft network operating system (NOS) software.

Using Screened Subnets to Protect Network Resources

As you proceed to a more advance design for your DMZ, conditions could drive a decision to employ screened subnets for protection or provision of services. The screened subnet, in some designs, actually becomes synonymous with DMZ in usage. However, the screened subnet is actually a security enhanced version of the multihomed screened host configurations that were used in the past. It involves the use of more hardware but provides a more secure basis for configuration and blocking unauthorized access.

The screened subnet that we looked at earlier in the chapter can be configured in a number of different configurations dependent on need. The simplest of the constructions involves a multiple-interface firewall with the capability to filter traffic to more than one network. Although simpler, this design might not be appropriate to use in your environment if you plan to offer services such as Web, e-mail, FTP, or VPN connections from the public network to your private network. In these situations, a good case could be made for the dual-firewall approach, perhaps with multiple screened subnets that provide different services or access based on some criteria that you have identified during your planning process. Certainly, if offering services that involve e-commerce or access to confidential records (such as being HIPAA compliant in an enterprise involved with any type of patient records), your plan will most likely need to include multiple screened subnets, following the earlier suggestions that a multilayer approach be used to restrict access and retard attacks from outside.

Securing Public Access to a Screened Subnet

Public access to screened subnets is secured and restricted through a multilayer process, using a screening router to begin providing protection and a firewall in the next layer to protect the access point coming into the screened subnet. Figure 3.13 shows a possible configuration to begin this protection process.

Figure 3.13 A Basic Screened Subnet

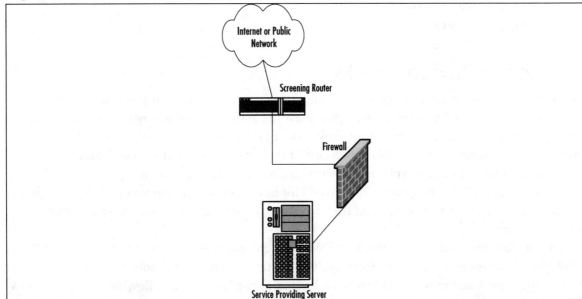

Internet or Public Network

Screening Router

Firewall

Service Providing Server

In this configuration, it is possible to limit the inbound traffic initially by configuring a rule set on the router; this piece might be provided by an Internet service provider (ISP), for example. Further levels of security can be developed as needed in your plan to protect assets on the screened subnet by firewall rule sets and hardening of the server providing services. Additionally, this design could be expanded or used for services or administration of screened subnets, providing greater security to the internal network as well.

Know What You Want to Secure First

As you begin your DMZ design process, you must first be clear about what your design is intended for. A design that is only intended to superficially limit internal users' access to the Internet, for example, requires much less planning and design work than a system protecting resources from multiple access points or providing multiple services to the public network or users from remote locations. An appropriate path to follow for your predesign path might look like this:

- Perform baseline security analysis of existing infrastructure, including OS and application analysis
- Perform baseline network mapping and performance monitoring
- Identify risk to resources and appropriate mitigation processes
- Identify potential security threats, both external and internal
- Identify needed access points from external sources
    - Public networks
    - VPN access
    - Extranets
    - Remote access services
- Identify critical services
- Plan your DMZ

Traffic and Security Risks

After beginning to research the necessary components for designing your protection plan, you will reach a point at which you are trying to assess the actual risks to security from which you are trying to protect your enterprise network. One of the first tools you might consider in this part of your evaluation is the SANS Top 20 list of the current most critical vulnerabilities to find out if there is something that you are not aware of. You can view this list at www.sans.org/top20/; it is updated frequently. This information can help you to at least begin to identify some of the risks involved and then to design a more effective plan to secure what you need to secure.

As we continue with our overview of DMZ design principles, we also need to discuss the management of resources and the challenges that occur in designing for administration and control of equipment and resources that may be located in the DMZ. The following sections detail a number of the areas that we must be aware of during our consideration of the design and its implementation.

Application Servers in the DMZ

Application server placement in the DMZ must be designed with tight control in mind. As in other screened subnet configurations, the basic security of the operating system must first be assured on the local machine, with all applicable patches and service packs applied and unused services disabled or removed if possible.

We spend a great deal of time in this book covering the hardening of your systems (Windows 2000, Sun Solaris, and the like) within the DMZ. Additionally, functionality of the application servers located in the DMZ should be limited to specific tasks that do not involve critical corporate data or information. Therefore, although it is acceptable to place a Web server in the DMZ with a supporting database server, neither of those servers should contain confidential or critical corporate information, because they are still located in an area in which they are considered untrusted.

Critical or confidential information should not be accessible from or stored in the DMZ. For example, as discussed in the following section, it is not acceptable to store any type of internal network authentication information on machines in the DMZ. Likewise, front-end servers or application proxy servers can be placed in the DMZ for other needs, such as an e-mail server front end or a DNS forwarder. In these instances, neither the e-mail front end nor the DNS server should store any information about the internal network or allow general communication to pass unchecked to or from the internal network. Traffic to these servers from the internal network should pass through a firewall restricting traffic to individual machines in both directions using specific port and address information.

Domain Controllers in the DMZ

Domain controllers for Windows networks or other directory services authentication servers should never have those services located within the DMZ if it's possible to keep them out. It is feasible in some configurations to provide a front end to these critical servers from within the DMZ, but it is not recommended, because compromise of the bastion host being allowed to communicate with the internal network through the firewall while requesting service could lead to compromise of the entire internal system. Access to your internal network that requires authentication should instead be handled in your design by the use of VPN solutions, including RADIUS and TACACS/TACACS+, discussed in the next section. It is possible, however, that domain controllers need to be placed within the DMZ depending on what services you plan to provide in the DMZ. For example, if you were running a cluster that is highly available from the Internet on Windows 2000 servers, the cluster will not operate correctly without a domain controller present. For that reason, you have to accurately assess what you will need and analyze how to implement it and secure it.

RADIUS-Based Authentication Servers in the DMZ

Remote Authentication Dial-In User Service (RADIUS) servers, by definition and usage, are required to have full access to the authentication information provided by the Directory Services system in the enterprise, whether Windows, Novell, UNIX, Sun, or another OS. For this reason, the RADIUS server must be fully protected from attack and patched completely to avoid DoS conditions such as those detailed by CERT in advisories issued in 2002. The preferred option would have the RADIUS server located in the internal network, with proxied requests coming from a Routing and Remote Access Services (RRAS) server and restricted communication that would be allowed through the firewall to the RADIUS server only from the specified RRAS servers. Additionally, it would make sense to plan for the use of IPsec to further protect that traffic. Regardless, understand that you will need to analyze the need and deploy it based on a proper design that provides the service that is needed but still remains secure.

VPN DMZ Design Concepts

VPN usage has grown during the past few years. Many organizations embraced the possibility of VPN use as a method to communicate securely from remote offices. This led to a surge of connectivity that was requested in order to allow home "teleworkers" to perform their job functions without entering the secured environs of the actual workplace and its network.

A number of changes have been implemented in VPN technology in the recent past, and these have modified the thought process that we must undertake as we design our DMZ infrastructure. To begin with, VPN solutions should be created in a separate DMZ space, away from the other parts of the Internet-facing infrastructure, as well as your back-end private LAN. The VPN technologies now may incorporate the capability to enter your network space through public switched telephone network (PSTN) connections, Frame Relay connections, modem banks, and the public Internet as well as dedicated connections from customers and business partners that may use any of these access methods. Each of these connection types must be included in the plan, and entry points must be carefully controlled to allow the required access and protection of information while not allowing a back-door entry to our internal networks.

A number of these plans are discussed in subsequent chapters of this book as different firewall configurations and designs are considered and discussed. When we're looking at the possibilities for VPN implementation and protection, it is extremely important to use all potential security tools available, including IPsec and its authentication and encryption possibilities. It is also important to evaluate the actual network design, in order to use RFC1918 (private) addressing in the internal network and properly secure the addressing within the VPN, which should be registered addresses. This is called NAT—Network Address Translation.

Private addressing is one of the basic features of most firewalls. NAT converts private, internal IP addresses into publicly routable addresses. You might want to translate or *to NAT* (using the term as a verb to describe this process) your internal addresses because they are nonroutable private addresses or to discourage attacks from the Internet. RFC1918 lists the addresses that are available for private use on the internal network. The Internet Assigned Numbers Authority (IANA) has reserved the following three blocks of the IP address space for private networks:

- 10.0.0.0 through 10.255.255.255 (10 /8 prefix)

- 172.16.0.0 through 172.31.255.255 (172.16 /12 prefix)

- 192.168.0.0 through 192.168.255.255 (192.168 /16 prefix)

> **NOTE**
>
> You can learn more about RFC1918 by visiting the RFC document online: www.cis.ohio-state.edu/cgi-bin/rfc/rfc1918.html

If you are using these addresses on your internal LAN and clients on the internal LAN need to communicate to Internet resources, you need to NAT these addresses to public addresses in order to be routed throughout the Internet. Public addresses are typically IP addresses assigned to your organization by the Network Information Center (NIC) or by your ISP.

The problem facing IPv4 is that the public address pool has been depleted, so network administrators may no longer be able to assign public addresses to all clients on their internal LANs and have them access Internet resources without the use of NAT. Therefore, administrators are forced to assign private addresses to internal clients and use their allocated public addresses for NAT address pools and for services provided by the DMZ directly accessible by the Internet, such as Web and e-mail relays. NAT makes it possible for a small number of public IP addresses to provide Internet connectivity for a large range of hosts. NAT can provide a static one-to-one IP mapping between private and public addresses or dynamically map a large number of internal private addresses to a pool of public addresses. This can extend a network with only one IP address.

Advanced Risks

After you have considered the basic issues for connectivity to your infrastructure, it is appropriate to begin to explore and plan for other areas that might need protection through your DMZ design. There are nearly infinite possibilities for incorporation into your overall design, including the ability to protect not only the internal network but e-commerce, business partner, and extranet connections. Additionally, your enterprise may be involved in the creation of hosted services, in which you are providing protection to Web, FTP, or other servers that require unique protections and the ability to provide management capabilities as well. This section visits a number of those potential areas that may be appropriate for coverage in the overall DMZ design.

Business Partner Connections

Business partner connections can provide a unique challenge to the DMZ designer. In the case of business partners, there is often a requirement to provide access to and from enterprise resource planning (ERP) packages such as those from Oracle, PeopleSoft, Microsoft's Great Plains software, and others that are currently in use to provide project management, packaging, and collaboration tools to members of multiple organizations. One of the challenges that can arise rather quickly is the question of how to appropriately allow connectivity between organizations with proper authentication and protection of information for all parties. Many of the basic designs that we discussed previously, including the use of specifically screened subnets for VPN access, provide partial solutions to these issues, but each case also requires an in-depth evaluation and most certainly collaboration between the DMZ designers involved to appropriately channel the access entry points, remote access if needed, and authentication of the users from various entities to maintain your security requirements.

Extranets

Of the possibilities that can be explored in relation to business partner connections, extranets provide a great flexibility in their implementation and use by an enterprise. Extranets can be Web browser-based information stores, can allow contact by customers seeking catalog information, and can allow real-time or close to real-time tracking capabilities of shipments and the supply chain. Additionally, the extranet can be configured for collaborative efforts and used between business partners for the ultimate capability to share information and processes while working on joint projects. Extranets, much like the discussion earlier of VPN accesses, will usually be placed on isolated DMZ segments to segregate them from the hosting network's operations. These DMZ segments will house and host machines that will allow for the use of ERP software and the warehousing of information in common to the project. The use of extranet applications is most often Web browser based for the client that is seeking the information and not normally for storing highly sensitive data, although the data should still be protected.

Web and FTP Sites

Customer-based Web and FTP sites that are provided or hosted by your organization can again cause the DMZ design to change in some way. Hosting the information on customer-based sites requires the same processes that we looked at in relation to hosting our own Web and FTP servers in the DMZ, with an additional requirement that some sort of remote management capability be provided for the customer to administer and monitor the sites. This hosting can lead to a plan that involves use of modems or other devices not protected by the DMZ design and must be carefully explored. Ensure that your DMZ design will not be compromised by the methods used to allow remote access to these servers and their administration by the client customer. It may be appropriate to host customer-based operations in a separate DMZ segment, away from your operation altogether.

E-Commerce Services

Among the possibilities that we may include in our overall DMZ design scheme is hosting or supporting e-commerce services. As with other DMZ design considerations, the DMZ segment hosting e-commerce services must provide a level of isolation that protects such things as credit card information and transactions. It can include restrictions that block access from noncustomer address ranges, and it can also include restrictions on traffic to limit it to ports for Web services and Secure Sockets Layer (SSL) to protect the internal records being generated by the action of the services. E-commerce activities should also include restrictions that disable IP forwarding between servers and segregation of services such as noncritical database information among different servers for load balancing and to distribute security to a higher degree. No contact should be allowed between the e-commerce DMZ servers inbound to the internal network.

E-Mail Services

E-mail services are among the most used (and abused) services that are provided through a combination of access points, both external and internal. E-mail server front ends should be located in segregated DMZ subnets, and the firewalls allowing access into and out of the e-mail subnet should incorporate strong ACL rule sets that only allow communication on appropriate ports internally and externally. This construction should also include mail relay settings on the DMZ mail server that do not allow relaying of mail from any network other than the internal network, which limits the potential that your front-end server might be used for spamming. The external firewall that allows access to the e-mail front end should be configured to block outbound SMTP traffic that did not originate at the front-end server, and the front-end server should be configured to only relay mail to accepted internal addresses while rejecting all other communications. Great care must be used in the proper configuration of mail servers from all vendors when access is granted in any fashion from the external networks.

Advanced Design Strategies

Up to this point, the discussion of design has been directed at the access path design and the methods of securing access to the internal network from the external network. In most cases, the DMZ is used to block incoming traffic and control it more completely through the multiple layers that are placed in the design, thus offering tighter control that stops access to the internal network. Standard DMZ designs almost always default to a condition in which the internal network's access to the external public network is unrestricted.

Before we finish our discussion of basic designs, it is appropriate to explore briefly some of the ways we might consider blocking access from the internal network to the external network, either wholly or in part, if the security design we created earlier indicates a need to do so. In the next section, we visit some of the common conditions that your organization might want to block or limit in your efforts to protect your assets and information.

Advanced DMZ Design Concepts

Intranet users have often been allowed full and unrestricted access to public network resources via the DMZ structure. Often, the protection for the internal network involves using NAT or some proxied connectivity to allow outward flow while restricting inbound flow to requests originated within the internal network. You should think about some special considerations while you are working in this area. Let's list some of them and consider them as an addition to the overall design:

- General FTP use that is unrestricted may lead to security breach. Outbound FTP should not be allowed from the internal network.

- DMZ design lends itself to allowing control of unnecessary services that may be present on the external network. For example, the DMZ design may incorporate outbound blocking of ports to services providing instant messaging, nonbusiness–related networks, and other restrictions as appropriate to your system.

- Known management ports for externally located devices and services should be blocked from the internal network.

Additionally, we must look at the applications that are in use from the internal network to determine the appropriate level of outbound access to accommodate those applications. When you're given the task of building a DMZ in a large DMZ environment or when you need to support multiple service types, it might be desirable to separate them by adding additional "legs" to the DMZ. There are two reasons why you might want to use a DMZ leg:

- An additional leg might be necessary if the number of servers has exceeded the number of available IP addresses for hosts on the DMZ subnet. By adding a DMZ interface, you can assign another IP range and add more servers.
- It's a good idea to separate service types. Service types are Web, FTP, e-mail, DNS, VPN, and remote access.

As we continue, a number of other considerations must be taken into account as we create the design plan. For example, although many DMZ configurations are allowing access to a Web server that we are operating, there must be a method in place to advise us of the presence of potential hackers working within our borders.

To this end, the DMZ design will also most often create a provision for some type of IDS system placement in the various levels of the DMZ structure to evaluate and report on intrusion attempts. As with all services that we provide, the Web services servers must be continually evaluated and kept up to date in their levels of security and service packs.

Another conceptual area that must be visited is the difference between a DMZ that is established for the purpose of isolating or segregating the public network from your private network, and a DMZ that is used for the purpose of isolating or segregating a portion of your internal network. The design you create should include the capability to establish internal DMZ structures to protect confidential information from the general LAN operation. This could include segregation of financials or provision for VPN access to the internal network that does not originate from the public network (such as Frame Relay PVC channels or PSTN modem access). Again, when dealing with these special cases, the designer must make sure that the design does not introduce a back-door situation that allows public network bypass of the DMZ structure through compromise of a host machine.

Remote Administration Concepts

Remote management and administration of the various pieces of hardware within the DMZ design you implement provide another challenge for the designer. Although it is extremely tempting to use the built-in capabilities of the various operating systems and the management software provided for many of our hardware devices, it is very important to give the alternatives a good long look. Use of these tools for normal management from within the internal network is almost certainly a quick recipe for breach and disaster.

It is certainly technologically possible to access the equipment in the DMZ through use of SSH, Telnet, or Microsoft's Terminal Services and to create firewall rules allowing traffic on the necessary ports to accomplish this task. So, what's the problem with using the built-in tools? *In-band* versus *out-of-band management* of your systems is the problem we need to work on. In-band management tools, including SNMP-based traps and management agents, rely on the integrity of the network they are mounted on to provide the reports and management capabilities we use to control the various hardware and configuration of hardware and servers. What happens when the underlying network capability is degraded, reduced, or overloaded through an equipment failure or a DoS attack? No management is possible, because we now can't reach the equipment. The other alternative is to provide some type of out-of-band management capability. This can be accomplished in a number of ways, including serial connections to secured management ports on the devices to be managed or a separate management screened subnet, such as illustrated in Figure 3.14.

Figure 3.14 A Method to Provide Out-of-Band Management in the DMZ

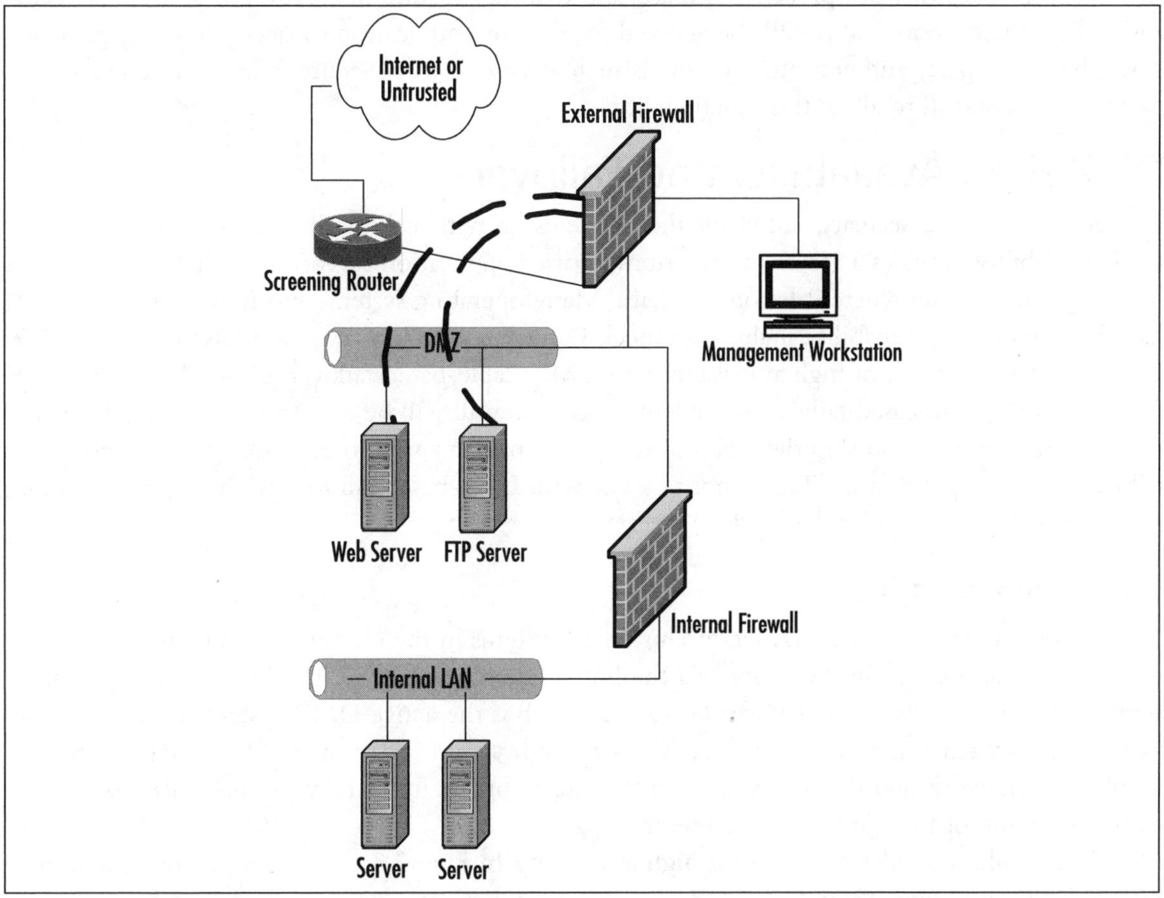

In this simplified design, the servers located in the DMZ are each configured as a multihomed machine, with the additional adapters (represented in the figure by dark dashed lines) configured to accept communications only from the designated management workstation(s), if your security policy allows multiple administrative units. The outside firewall is configured to allow specific port-based traffic to flow from the management workstation to the servers, and the management workstation is not accessible from either the untrusted network or the protected LAN. This eliminates much of the security vulnerability that is presented when management options only include in-band tools.

Authentication Design

Earlier in the chapter, we mentioned that it is generally inappropriate to locate a RADIUS server in a DMZ segment because it creates a condition in which the authentication information is potentially accessible to the public network, with a potential for breach of your DMZ. In some environments, it might be necessary to implement a plan to accommodate the authentication of users entering the DMZ from a public network. In this case, the DMZ design should include a separate authentication DMZ segment, and the equipment in that segment should be hardened, as we previously detailed in our discussion of placement. At this point, it is possible to provide an RRAS server in the DMZ with no account information and use ACLs and packet filtering at the firewall to restrict and encrypt the traffic between the two machines to the authentication traffic. It is recommended that this process use IPsec, and it would require that Protocol ID 51 for IPsec and IKE traffic on port 500 (UDP) be allowed for the communication to occur. It is also possible that other third-party authentication products such as Cisco's CiscoSecure ACS could provide a gateway and controls to allow this functionality.

DMZ High Availability and Failover

The enterprise wants security, and wants their systems up with as little downtime as possible. High availability provides a server (be it a firewall or an application server) with the ability to have a system pick up where it let off if it fails. Many operating systems and firewall appliances have high availability capability, including Check Point Firewall-1, Solaris, and Cisco PIX.

There are two types of high availability in a DMZ: cable-based failover and LAN-based failover. When cable-based failover is implemented, a firewall will be able to immediately fail over to the secondary unit and skip the series of tests if the primary unit loses power due to a power failure or it is simply shut off. This is not possible with LAN-based failover, where a power failure of the primary unit must be detected via a series of tests.

DMZ Server Cluster

This configuration shows a DMZ server cluster. All systems in the cluster maintain an active connection to other systems in the cluster via the hub. The only system in the cluster that maintains active connections outside the failover information hub is the active DMZ system. When the primary DMZ system fails, it deactivates (or is deactivated) via information over the failover communication network, and the next system in the cluster brings up its network interfaces to perform the job of the primary DMZ server.

We must also consider the need for high availability. In Figure 3.15, we have a configuration that differs slightly from a standard DMZ.

Figure 3.15 DMZ Servers in a Conceptual Highly Available Configuration

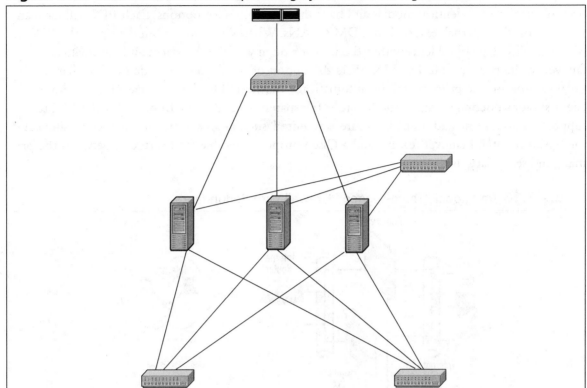

Figure 3.15 contains many features similar to those in a typical DMZ. However, what is different is that rather than one DMZ system connected to the external network switch, three DMZs are connected to the external network switch. Additionally, there are several connections from these DMZ systems to the same public and private networks. We also see a connection between the DMZ systems.

The PIX Failover Services

When your DMZ design calls for a highly available firewall solution because downtime due to a problem with the firewall hardware will not be tolerated, consider using the PIX's failover feature. The failover feature allows you to set up a second PIX in Standby mode, and if the primary, or active, PIX should go offline, the secondary PIX will switch to Active mode and take over for the failed PIX. If the optional stateful failover feature is configured, the secondary PIX can maintain operating state for active TCP connections during failover, so users will not lose their sessions as the PIX fails over to its backup unit. In order to enable failover, the primary and secondary PIX firewalls need to be identical in terms of chassis, OS version, and hardware options.

If high availability is required, the DMZ architect can consider adding a second PIX in conjunction with the PIX's failover feature, which allows the secondary PIX firewall to back up the primary PIX in the event of a failure. Figure 3.16 shows how redundancy can be added to the traditional "three-legged" firewall design. This design is ideal for corporations of all sizes, where the Internet/DMZ infrastructure is essential to the business and therefore they cannot afford downtime and require a resilient, highly available solution. Both the primary and secondary PIX firewalls need to be identical models and have the same interface options. Each PIX will have an interface on the internal, external, and DMZ LANs. When set up as a redundant pair, the PIX has the ability detect problems within the units or on any of the interfaces and automatically failover to the backup unit. The PIX offers the option of *stateful failover*, which means that any open sessions on the primary will be automatically transferred to the secondary unit without client sessions disconnecting, so the failure is transparent to end users. In order for the PIX to support failover, some additional hardware is required, such as an additional interface to support the optional stateful failover feature, and a Cisco proprietary cable for heartbeats between the primary and secondary units. .

Figure 3.16 Traditional "Three-Legged" Firewall with Redundancy

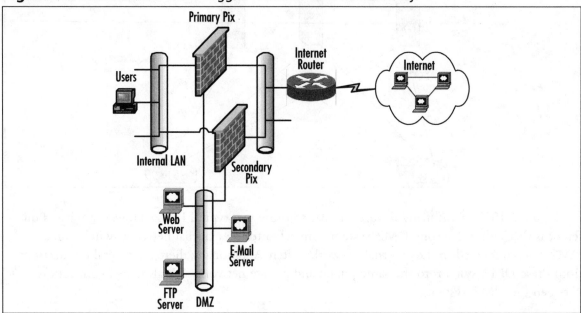

The PIX offers two options that provide connectivity for the primary and secondary PIX firewalls to exchange heartbeats and configuration information. The first option is a Cisco proprietary high-speed serial cable connected to a special serial failover port on the PIX. The second option is to use one of the PIX LAN interfaces to carry heartbeat and configuration traffic. The advantage of using the Cisco proprietary high-speed serial cable to send heartbeat and configuration traffic is that it will not waste a LAN interface for a rather small amount of traffic. Instead, it uses a serial port specifically designed for failover. The disadvantage is that the high-speed serial cable is rather short (six feet long), and if the PIX firewalls are not physically located close together, you cannot use the cable-based solution because the cable cannot be extended. If you have a situation in which the PIX firewalls are not physically located together, you can consider the second option, a LAN-based failover, which uses interfaces on each PIX to provide dedicated media for heartbeat and configuration traffic. The disadvantage of this option is that an interface on each PIX will be wasted just for heartbeat and configuration traffic. It is important to note that heartbeat and configuration traffic should not be confused with state traffic used for the stateful failover option, which the active PIX uses to send the standby PIX TCP state information. Although you can configure the PIX to carry heartbeat, configuration, and state traffic all on one interface on each PIX using the LAN-based failover option, doing so is not recommended.

When failover occurs, the standby PIX assumes all the IP addresses and MAC addresses on all interfaces of the failed PIX. Because there is no change to the IP address or MAC address information, other devices on the network will not be aware of a failure and that they are now communicating through a different device. Another feature of failover is that when a configuration change is made to the primary, it is automatically copied to the secondary PIX, and when a *write memory* command to save the configuration to Flash is issued on the primary, it also copies the configuration to the secondary's Flash.

What Causes Failover to Occur

To determine the health status of each PIX, the primary and secondary PIX poll each other. The poll interval is set using the *failover poll* command; the default is 15 seconds. Polls, also called *heartbeats*, are sent over all interfaces, including the failover cable. If either PIX misses two consecutive heartbeats, each PIX will go through a series of tests to determine which PIX is in trouble. Each unit goes through four tests to determine its health: a Link Up/Down test, a Network Activity test, an ARP test, and a Broadcast Ping test. Each PIX firewall performs one test at a time. If a unit passes a test and the other unit does not, the PIX that passed will take over. If both PIX units fail, they move on to the next test. At the default poll interval (15 seconds), the PIX units can take up to 45 seconds to run through all the tests and determine if failover should take place.

Summary

DMZ design includes a number of important steps that make the overall design process smoother and less subject to breach. These steps include the capability and duty to perform a complete physical and logical security analysis of the systems to be protected, followed by the adoption of an enterprise security policy to detail the path of management, monitoring, enforcement, and responsibility for various areas of the enterprise's security. Once we have completed a security analysis and have a security policy that has been supported and is in place, we can begin to think about the design of the DMZ structure.

Generically, we create the basic DMZ structure after we have identified the assets and resources that need protection. This generic plan is followed by an evaluation of how the information currently flows in the organization and how it should be handled in a secure sense to isolate and protect the systems from compromise.

When the generic tasks have been completed, the design begins to take shape as we configure and define the various levels of the DMZ structure to provide necessary services to customers, employees, and partners. There are nearly infinite possibilities in the use of various equipment and configurations, and we're charged with creating a design that is functional and economically feasible in the reduction of risk. Here we begin to consider not only the best logical design but also the design that might be the most feasible to protect our data.

We find as we proceed that the level of service that we are providing and the connectivity needs of the various partners and operations greatly affect the level of configuration within the DMZ structure. We also find that it is possible to allow connectivity in multiple levels for various services while always striving to protect the internal network from harm.

## Chapter 4

Introduction to Intrusion Detection Systems

Best Damn Topics in this Chapter:

- What Is Intrusion Detection?

- What Is an Intrusion?

- Why Are Intrusion Detection Systems Important?

- What Else Can Be Done with Intrusion Detection Systems

Introduction

"Intruder Alert! Intruder Alert! Warning, Will Robinson!" When we heard that ominous announcement emanating from a robot as it twisted and turned with arms thrashing and head spinning, we sat galvanized to our televisions waiting for the intruder to reveal itself. Would this be the end of Will Robinson, as we knew him?

All right, this might be a bit dramatic for a prelude to a discussion of intrusion detection, but with most security administrators, when a beeper goes off there is a moment of anxiety. Is this the big one? Did they get in? Do they own my network? Do they own my data?

These and many other questions flood the mind of the well-prepared security administrator. Conversely, the ill-prepared security administrator, being totally unaware of the intrusion, experiences little anxiety. For him, the anxiety comes later.

Okay, so how can a security-minded administrator protect his network from intrusions? The answer to that question is quite simple, with an intrusion detection system.

NOTE

Intrusion detection works in conjunction with firewalls in various ways. One of the ways is to use intrusion detection is to test your firewall rules to make sure they are working properly. One of the other ways is to use intrusion detection and firewalls to set rules for a firewall. For more information on integrating an IDS with a firewall, refer to Chapter 31 of this book, "Combining Firewalls and IDS."

What Is Intrusion Detection?

Webster's dictionary defines an intrusion as "the act of thrusting in, or of entering into a place or state without invitation, right, or welcome." When we speak of intrusion detection, we are referring to the act of detecting an unauthorized intrusion by a *computer* on a *network*. This unauthorized access, or intrusion, is an attempt to compromise, or otherwise do harm, to other network devices.

An Intrusion Detection System (IDS) is the high-tech equivalent of a burglar alarm—a burglar alarm configured to monitor access points, hostile activities, and known intruders. The simplest way to define an IDS might be to describe it as a specialized tool that knows how to read and interpret the contents of log files from routers, firewalls, servers, and other network devices. Furthermore, an IDS often stores a database of known attack signatures and can compare patterns of activity, traffic, or behavior it sees in the logs it is monitoring against those signatures to recognize when a close match between a signature and current or recent behavior occurs. At that point, the IDS can issue alarms or alerts, take various kinds of automatic action ranging from shutting down Internet links or specific servers to launching backtraces, and make other active attempts to identify attackers and actively collect evidence of their nefarious activities.

By analogy, an IDS does for a network what an antivirus software package does for files that enter a system: It inspects the contents of network traffic to look for and deflect possible attacks, just as an antivirus software package inspects the contents of incoming files, e-mail attachments, active Web content, and so forth to look for virus signatures (patterns that match known malware) or for possible malicious actions (patterns of behavior that are at least suspicious, if not downright unacceptable).

To be more specific, intrusion detection means detecting unauthorized use of or attacks on a system or network. An IDS is designed and used to detect and then to deflect or deter (if possible) such attacks or unauthorized use of systems, networks, and related resources. Like firewalls, IDSs can be software based or can combine hardware and software (in the form of preinstalled and preconfigured stand-alone IDS devices). Often, IDS software runs on the same devices or servers where firewalls, proxies, or other boundary services operate; an IDS *not* running on the same device or server where the firewall or other services are installed will monitor those devices closely and carefully. Although such devices tend to operate at network peripheries, IDSs can detect and deal with insider attacks as well as external attacks.

IDSs vary according to a number of criteria. By explaining those criteria, we can explain what kinds of IDSs you are likely to encounter and how they do their jobs. First and foremost, it is possible to distinguish IDSs by the kinds of activities, traffic, transactions, or systems they monitor. IDSs can be divided into network-based, host-based, and distributed. IDSs that monitor network backbones and look for attack signatures are called *network-based IDSs*, whereas those that operate on hosts defend and monitor the operating and file systems for signs of intrusion and are called *host-based IDSs.* Groups of IDSs functioning as remote sensors and reporting to a central management station are known as Distributed IDS (DIDS).

In practice, most commercial environments use some combination of network, and host, and/or application-based IDS systems to observe what is happening on the network while also monitoring key hosts and applications more closely. IDSs can also be distinguished by their differing approaches to event analysis. Some IDSs primarily use a technique called *signature detection*. This resembles the way many antivirus programs use virus signatures to recognize and block infected files, programs, or active Web content from entering a computer system, except that it uses a database of traffic or activity patterns related to known attacks, called *attack signatures*. Indeed, signature detection is the most widely used approach in commercial IDS technology today. Another approach is called *anomaly detection*. It uses rules or predefined concepts about "normal" and "abnormal" system activity (called *heuristics*) to distinguish anomalies from normal system behavior and to monitor, report on, or block anomalies as they occur. Some anomaly detection IDSs implement user profiles. These profiles are baselines of normal activity and can be constructed using statistical sampling, rule-base approach or neural networks.

Literally hundreds of vendors offer various forms of commercial IDS implementations. Most effective solutions combine network- and host-based IDS implementations. Likewise, the majority of implementations are primarily signature based, with only limited anomaly-based detection capabilities present in certain specific products or solutions. Finally, most modern IDSs include some limited automatic response capabilities, but these usually concentrate on automated traffic filtering, blocking, or disconnects as a last resort. Although some systems claim to be able to launch counterstrikes against attacks, best practices indicate that automated identification and backtrace facilities are the most useful aspects that such facilities provide and are therefore those most likely to be used.

IDSs are classified by their functionality and are loosely grouped into the following three main categories:

- Network–Based Intrusion Detection System (NIDS)
- Host–Based Intrusion Detection System (HIDS)
- Distributed Intrusion Detection System (DIDS)

Network IDS

The NIDS derives its name from the fact that it monitors the entire network. More accurately, it monitors an entire network segment. Normally, a computer network interface card (NIC) operates in nonpromiscuous mode. In this mode of operation, only packets destined for the NICs specific media access control (MAC) address are forwarded up the stack for analysis. The NIDS must operate in promiscuous mode to monitor network traffic not destined for its own MAC address. In promiscuous mode, the NIDS can eavesdrop on all communications on the network segment. Operation in promiscuous mode is necessary to protect your network. However, in view of emerging privacy regulations, monitoring network communications is a responsibility that must be considered carefully.

In Figure 4.1, we see a network using three NIDS. The units have been placed on strategic network segments and can monitor network traffic for all devices on the segment. This configuration represents a standard perimeter security network topology where the screened subnets on the DMZ housing the public servers are protected by NIDSs. When a public server is compromised on a screened subnet, the server can become a launching platform for additional exploits. Careful monitoring is necessary to prevent further damage.

The internal host systems inside the firewall are protected by an additional NIDS to mitigate exposure to internal compromise. The use of multiple NIDS within a network is an example of a defense–in–depth security architecture.

Figure 4.1 NIDS Network

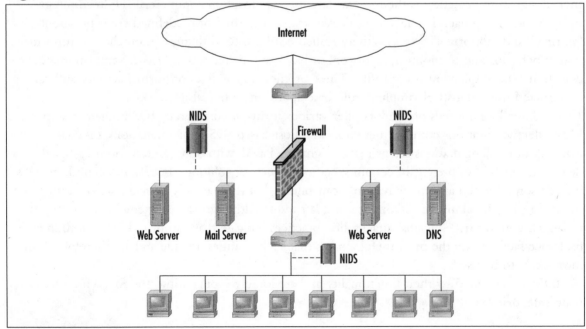

Host-Based IDS

HIDS differ from NIDS in two ways. HIDS protects only the host system on which it resides, and its network card operates in nonpromiscuous mode. Nonpromiscuous mode of operation can be an advantage in some cases, because not all NICs are capable of promiscuous mode. In addition, promiscuous mode can be CPU intensive for a slow host machine. HIDS can be run directly on the firewall as well, to help keep the firewall secure.

Another advantage of HIDS is the ability to tailor the ruleset to a specific need. For example, there is no need to interrogate multiple rules designed to detect DNS exploits on a host that is not running Domain Name Services. Consequently, the reduction in the number of pertinent rules enhances performance and reduces processor overhead.

Figure 4.2 depicts a network using HIDS on specific servers and host computers. As previously mentioned, the ruleset for the HIDS on the mail server is customized to protect it from mail server exploits, while the Web server rules are tailored for Web exploits. During installation, individual host machines can be configured with a common set of rules. New rules can be loaded periodically to account for new vulnerabilities.

Figure 4.2 HIDS Network

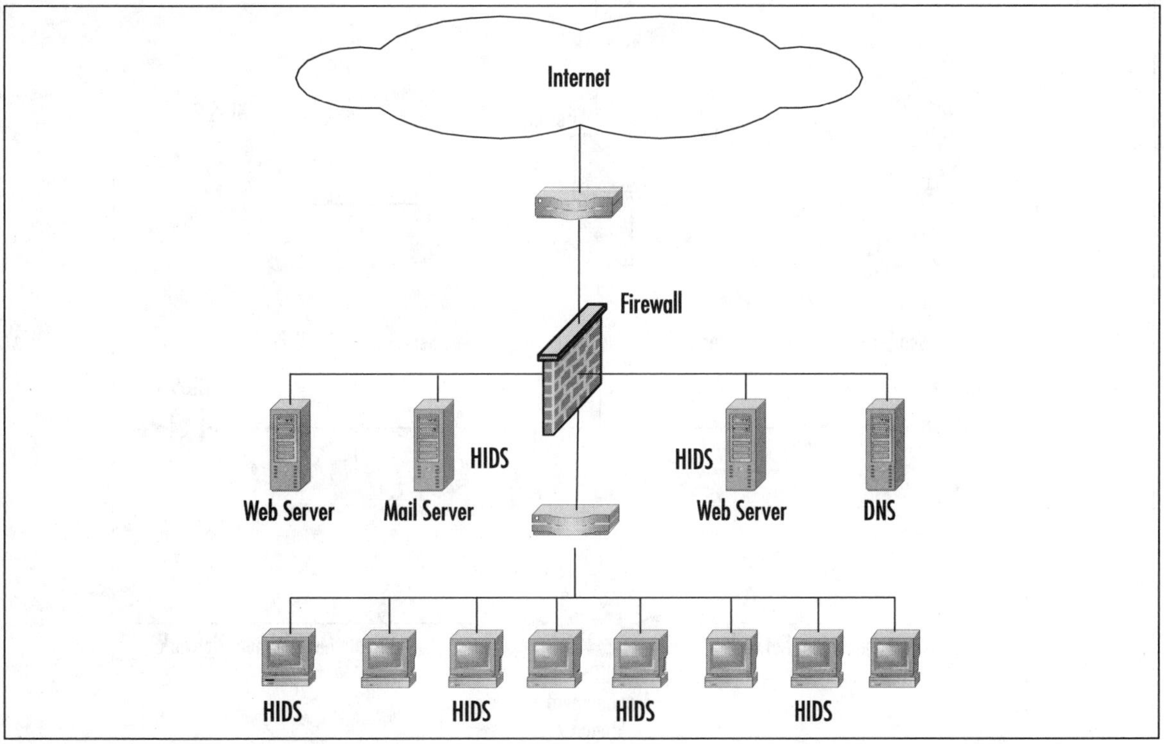

Distributed IDS

The standard DIDS functions in a Manager/Probe architecture. NIDS detection sensors are remotely located and report to a centralized management station. Attack logs are periodically uploaded to the management station and can be stored in a central database; new attack signatures can be downloaded to the sensors on an as-needed basis. The rules for each sensor can be tailored to meet its individual needs. Alerts can be forwarded to a messaging system located on the management station and used to notify the IDS administrator.

In Figure 4.3, we see a DIDS system comprised of four sensors and a centralized management station. Sensors NIDS 1 and NIDS 2 are operating in stealth promiscuous mode and are protecting the public servers. Sensors NIDS 3 and NIDS 4 are protecting the host systems in the trusted computing base. The DIDS are on the outside of the firewall, usually on the DMZ or outside.

The network transactions between sensor and manager can be on a private network, as depicted, or the network traffic can use the existing infrastructure. When using the existing network for management data, the additional security afforded by encryption, or VPN technology, is highly recommended.

Figure 4.3 DIDS Network

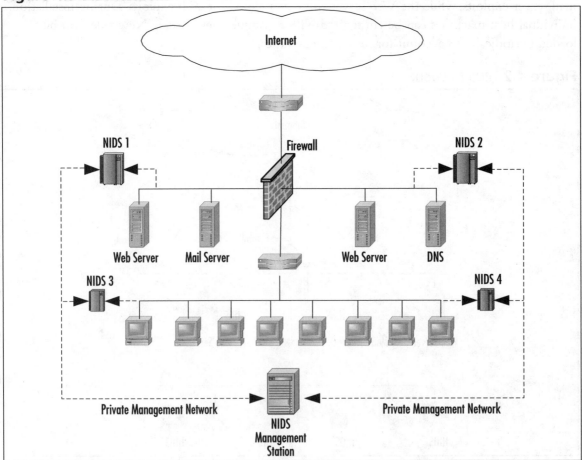

In a DIDS, complexity abounds. The scope and functionality varies greatly from manufacturer to manufacturer, and the definition blurs accordingly. In a DIDS, the individual sensors can be NIDS, HIDS, or a combination of both. The sensor can function in promiscuous mode or non-promiscuous mode. However, in all cases, the DIDS' single defining feature requires that the distributed sensors report to a centralized management station.

What Is an Intrusion?

At the scene of a crime, one of the first tasks of the forensic evidence technician is the gathering of fingerprints. These fingerprints can be used to determine the identity of the criminal. Just as in criminal forensics, network forensics technicians gather fingerprints at the scene of a computer crime. The fingerprints are extracted from the victim computer's log and are known as *signatures* or *footprints*. Almost all exploits have a unique signature. Let's look at the signatures of our three: Directory Traversal, CodeRed, and Nimda.

- **Directory Traversal footprint** The Directory Traversal exploit or dot "../" could be used against IIS 4.0 and 5.0 if extended Unicode characters were used to represent the "/" and "\". For example, if a hacker entered the string in Figure 4.4 into his browser, the contents of a directory on the victim's computer would be displayed on the hacker's system. The important part of this example is the uniqueness of the pattern /..%c1. The pattern can be used as a digital fingerprint or signature/footprint in an IDS.

Figure 4.4 Directory Traversal Footprint

```
http://Victim.com/scripts/..%c1%1c../winnt/system32/cmd.exe?/c+dir
```

- **CodeRed footprint** For the CodeRed exploit, the system footprint was provided by *Advisory CA-2001-19* and stated that the CodeRed worm activity can be identified on a machine by the presence of the entry in the Web server log files (Figure 4.5). The footprint of Figure 4.5 is extremely important from an intrusion detection point of view. It represents the information necessary to detect the intrusion before it can do damage to your network.

Figure 4.5 CodeRed Footprint

```
/default.ida?NNNNNNNNNNNNNNNNNNNNNNNNNNNNNNNNNNNNNNNNNNNNNNNNNNNNNNNNNNNNNNNNNNNNNNNN
NNNNNNNNNNNNNNNNNNNNNNNNNNNNNNNNNNNNNNNNNNNNNNNNNNNNNNNNNNNNNNNNNNNNNNNNNNNNNNNNNNNNNN
NNNNNNNNNNNNNNNNNNNNNNNNNNNNNNNNNNNNNNNNN%u9090%u6858%ucbd3%u7801%u9090%u6805%ucbd3%  u7801
etc.
```

- **Nimda footprint** The numerous footprints described in the *CERT Advisory CA-2001-26* read like a dictionary of exploits. Within Figure 4.6 are displayed a few of the exploits delivered in its payload. When one is building an *intrusion detection rule*, Nimda's system footprints offer many signatures from which to choose. Furthermore, because the zombie machines or hacker scripts cycle through the complete list, any entry could be used to detect the intrusion. The most obvious one to use (from a security administrator's point of view) is GET /scripts/root.exe. GET root.exe in an HTML request is very suspicious, especially on a Windows machine.

Figure 4.6 Nimda Footprint

```
GET /scripts/root.exe?/c+dir
GET /c/winnt/system32/cmd.exe?/c+dir
GET /d/ winnt/system32/cmd.exe?/c+dir
GET /scripts/..%5c../..%5c../winnt/system32/cmd.exe?/c+dir
GET /_mem_bin/..%5c….%5c../winnt/system32/cmd.exe?/c+dir
GET /_vti_bin/..%5c….%5c../winnt/system32/cmd.exe?/c+dir
```

Why Are Intrusion Detection Systems Important?

Everyone is familiar with the oft-used saying, "What you don't know can't hurt you." However, anyone who has ever bought a used automobile has learned, first hand, the absurdity of this statement. In the world of network security, the ability to know when an intruder is engaged in reconnaissance, or other malicious activity, can mean the difference between being compromised and not being compromised. In addition, in some environments, what you don't know can directly affect employment—yours.

IDSs can detect ICMP and other types of network reconnaissance scans that might indicate an impending attack. In addition, the IDS can alert the admin of a successful compromise, which allows him the opportunity to implement mitigating actions before further damage is caused.

IDSs provide the security administrator with a window into the inner workings of the network, analogous to an x-ray or a blood test in the medical field. The ability to analyze the internal network traffic and to determine the existence of network viruses and worms is not altogether different from techniques used by the medical profession. The similarity of network viruses and worms to their biological counterparts has resulted in their medical monikers. IDSs provide the microscope necessary to detect these invaders. Without the aid of intrusion detection, a security administrator is vulnerable to exploits and will become aware of the presence of exploits only after a system crashes or a database is corrupted.

Why Are Attackers Interested in Me?

"The Attack of the Zombies"—sounds a lot like an old B-grade movie, doesn't it? Unfortunately, in this case, it is not cinema magic. Zombie attacks are real and cost corporations and consumers billions. Zombies are computerized soldiers under the control of nefarious hackers, and in the process of performing distributed denial-of-service (DDoS) attacks, they blindly carry out the will of their masters.

In February 2000, a major DDoS attack blocked access to eBay, Amazon.com, AOL-TimeWarner, CNN, Dell Computers, Excite, Yahoo!, and other e-commerce giants. The damage done by this DDoS ranged from slowdown to complete system outages. The U.S. Attorney General instructed the FBI to launch a criminal investigation. This historical attack was perpetrated by a large group of compromised computers operating in concert.

The lesson to be learned from this event is that no network is too small to be left unprotected. If a hacker can use your computer, he will. The main purpose of the CodeRed exploit was to perform a DDoS on the White House Web site. It failed, due only to the author's oversight in using a hard-coded IP address instead of Domain Name Services. The exploit compromised over a million computers, ranging from corporate networks to home users.

In light of the recent virus activity, the growth of the information security industry, and taking into account government-sponsored hacking, the use of an IDS such can prove crucial in the protection of the world's network infrastructure.

Where Does an IDS Fit with the Rest of My Security Plan?

IDSs are a great addition to a network's defense-in-depth architecture. They can be used to identify vulnerabilities and weaknesses in your perimeter protection devices; for example, firewalls and routers. The firewall rules and router access lists can be verified regularly for functionality. In the event these devices are reconfigured, the IDS can provide auditing for change management control.

IDS logs can be used to enforce security policy and are a great source of forensic evidence. Inline IDSs can halt active attacks on your network while alerting administrators to their presence.

Properly placed IDSs can alert you to the presence of internal attacks. Industry analysis of percentages varies. However, the consensus is that the majority of attacks occur from within.

An IDS can detect failed administrator login attempts and recognize password-guessing programs. Configured with the proper ruleset, it can monitor critical application access and immediately notify the system administrator of possible breaches in security.

Doesn't My Firewall Serve as an IDS?

At this point, you may hazard the question, "doesn't my firewall serve as an IDS?" Absolutely Not! Having said that, we shall try to stop the deluge of scorn from firewall administrators who might take exception to the statement. Admittedly, a firewall can be configured to detect certain types of intrusions, such as an attempt to access the Trojan backdoor SubSeven's port 27374. In addition, it could be configured to generate an alert for any attempt to penetrate your network. In the strictest sense this would be an IDS function.

However, it is asking enough of the technology to simply determine what should and shouldn't be allowed into or out of your network without expecting it to analyze the internal contents of every packet. Even a proxy firewall is not designed to examine the contents of all packets; the function would be enormously CPU intensive. Nevertheless, a firewall should be an integral part of your defense-in-depth, with its main function being a gatekeeper and a filter (see Table 4.1).

Table 4.1 Comparing Firewalls and IDS

Functionality	Firewall	IDS
Detects unauthorized and malicious access by a computer	Yes	Yes
Uses signatures to identify malicious intrusions	No	Yes
Defines borders on a trusted network from an untrusted network	Yes	No
Enforces Network Security Policies	Yes	Yes
Can detect failed administrator login attempts and recognize password-guessing programs	No	Yes
Used to identify vulnerabilities and weaknesses in your perimeter protection	No	Yes
Defines network traffic flow	Yes	No
Detects Trojan horses and Backdoors	No	Yes

Firewalls and IDS do both enforce network policy, but how they implement it is completely different. An IDS is a reconnaissance system: It collects information and will notify you of what it's found. An IDS can find any type of packet it's designed to find by a defined signature.

A firewall, on the other hand, is a like a dragon protecting the castle. It keeps out the untrusted network traffic, and only allows in what it has defined as being acceptable. For example, if an attacker has managed to compromise a Web server and uses it to store contraband (for example, pornographic materials, pirated software), your firewall will not detect this. However, if your Web server is being used for inappropriate content, this can be discovered through your IDS.

Both firewall logs and IDS logs can provide you with information to help with computer forensics or any incident handling efforts. If a system is compromised, you will have some logs on what has been going on—through both the firewall and the IDS.

What makes an IDS necessary for a defense in depth is that it can be used to identify vulnerabilities and weaknesses in your perimeter protection devices; in other words, firewalls and routers. Firewall rules and router access lists can be verified regularly for functionality. You can set up various IDS signatures to test your firewall to make sure it's not letting some undesired network traffic through the filter. This is covered in greater detail in Part VI of this book.

Where Else Should I Be Looking for Intrusions?

When computers that have been otherwise stable and functioning properly begin to perform erratically and periodically hang or show the Blue Screen of Death, a watchful security administrator should consider the possibility of a *buffer overflow attack*.

Buffer overflow attacks represent a large percentage of today's computer exploits. Failure of programmers to check input code has led to some of the most destructive and costly vulnerabilities to date.

Exploits that are designed to overflow buffers are usually operating system (OS) and application software specific. Without going into detail, the input to the application software is manipulated in such a manner as to cause a system error or "smash the stack" as it is referred to by some security professionals. At this point in the exploit, malicious code is inserted into the computer's process stack and the hacker gains control of the system.

In some cases, for the exploit to be successful, the payload, or malicious code, must access OS functions located at specific memory addresses. If the application is running on an OS other than that for which the exploit was designed, the results of overflowing the buffer will be simply a system crash and not a compromise; the system will appear to be unstable with frequent resets. Interestingly, in this situation the definition of the exploit changes from a system compromise to a DoS attack.

IDSs can alert you to buffer overflow attacks. Snort has a large arsenal of rules designed to detect these attacks; the following are just a few:

- Red Hat lprd overflow
- Linux samba overflow
- IMAP login overflow
- Linux mountd overflow

Backdoors and Trojans

Backdoors and Trojans come in many flavors. However, they all have one thing in common—they are remote control programs. Some are malicious code designed to "zombiefy" your computer, drafting it into a hacker's army for further exploits. Others are designed to eavesdrop on your keystrokes and send your most private data to their authors. Programs such as Netbus, SubSeven, and BO2k are designed to perform these tasks with minimal training on the part of the hacker.

Remote control programs can have legitimate purposes, such as *remote system administration*. PCAnywhere, Citrix, and VNC are examples of commercial and free remote control programs. However, it should be pointed out that commercial products, in the hands of hackers, could just as easily be used for compromise. The legitimate use of these tools should be monitored, especially in sensitive environments.

Snort has many rules to aid the security administrator in detecting unauthorized use of these programs.

Case Study: The Unpatriotic Computer

Being alerted when an attempt to compromise your network is taking place provides valuable information. Such information allows you to take proactive steps to mitigate vulnerabilities, and then to take steps to secure your perimeter from further attempts. Equally valuable information, and perhaps even more important, is confirmation that you have been compromised. In other words, while the knowledge of an attempt might be useful, the knowledge of a successful compromise is crucial.

In the early hours of the CodeRed attack, the information available to construct an attack signature was sketchy. The global Internet community was reeling from the sheer volume of attacks and trying to cope with the network destruction. During those initial hours, we became aware of the intent of CodeRed. One of its main purposes was to perform a DoS attack on the White House Web site. Thousands of computer zombies operating in concert would have flooded www.whitehouse.gov with 410MB of data every four and a half hours per instance of the worm. The amount of data would quickly have overwhelmed the government computer and rendered it useless.

Armed with this knowledge, at our site we immediately built an attack signature using the White House's IP address of 198.137.240.91 and configured Snort to monitor the egress to the Internet. Any attempt to access this address would generate an alert, plus the log provided us with the source address of the attacking computer. Essentially, what we accomplished was a method of remotely detecting the presence of compromised systems on our internal network.

The author of CodeRed hard-coded the Internet address into the payload, thereby allowing the White House networking administrators to simply change the Internet address and thwart the attack. We continued to use our signature that was built on the old IP address and it proved to be invaluable on many occasions, alerting us to newly compromised systems.

What Else Can Be Done with Intrusion Detection?

The name "Intrusion Detection System" conjures up a vision of a device that sits on the perimeter of your network alerting you to the presence of intruders. While this is a valid application, it is by no means the only one. IDS can also play an important role in a defense-in-depth architecture by protecting internal assets, in addition to acting as a perimeter defense. Many internal functions of your network can be monitored for security and compliance.

In this section, we look at various internal IDS applications and reveal how an IDS can be used to protect your most valuable resources.

Monitoring Database Access

When pondering the selection of a candidate for the "Crown Jewels" of a company, there is no better choice than the company's database. Many times, an organization's most valuable assets are stored in that database. Consider the importance of data to a pharmaceutical research company or to a high-tech software developer. Think the unthinkable—the theft of the U.S. military's launch codes for the nation's Intercontinental Ballistic Missile System. The importance of data confidentially, integrity, and availability in such situations cannot be stressed strongly enough.

Admittedly, database servers are usually located deep within a network and are only accessible by internal resources. However, if one considers the FBI's statistics for internal compromise, this location is not as safe as one might assume. A NIDS, when properly configured on the same segment with your database server, can go a long way in preventing internal compromise.

Snort includes a comprehensive ruleset designed to protect from database exploits. The following are a few examples:

- ORACLE drop table attempt
- ORACLE EXECUTE_SYSTEM attempt
- MYSQL root login attempt
- MYSQL show databases attempt

Monitoring DNS Functions

What's in a name? For our discussion, the important question is, "What's in a name server?" The answer is, "Your network's configuration." The entries in your domain name server might include internal network component names, IP addresses, and other private information about your network. The only information a hacker requires to map your network can be gleaned from a DNS zone transfer. The first step in a DNS reconnaissance probe is to determine the version of your DNS server. An IDS detects this intrusion by invoking the rule "DNS Name Version Attempt." The second step in the exploit will be detected by the rule "DNS Zone Transfer Attempt."

IDSs placed at key locations within your network can guard against DNS exploits. An IDS offers many rules to protect your namespace.

E-Mail Server Protection

When taking into account e-mail protection, we often resort to e-mail virus-scanning software to mitigate exposure. These programs have matured over the years and have become a formidable defense against attacks stemming from e-mail. Snort has many rules that can detect e-mail viruses such as the QAZ worm, NAVIDAD worm, and the newest versions of the ExploreZip. In response to a brand new threat or a revision of an existing virus, Snort rules can be modified immediately. Viruses are often in the wild for a considerable amount of time before virus-scanning companies respond with updates; this delay can prove to be a costly one.

In addition, one should develop a comprehensive approach to e-mail security by considering the possibility of an attack on the server itself. Snort has the ability to detect viral e-mail content while simultaneously protecting the e-mail server from attack. It is this added functionality that makes Snort stand out. An IDS can be configured to detect and block e-mail bombers, as well as other exploits that might disable your e-mail services.

Using an IDS to Monitor My Company Policy

In today's litigious society, given the enormous legal interest in subjects such as downstream litigation and intellectual property rights, it would be prudent to consider monitoring for compliance with your company's security policy. Major motion picture companies have employed law firms specializing in Internet theft of intellectual property. Recently, many companies were sued because their employees illegally downloaded the motion picture *Spiderman*. Some of the employees involved were not aware that their computers were taking part in a crime. Nevertheless, the fines for damages were stiff—up to $100,000 in some cases.

Many file-sharing programs, such as Kazaa and Gnutella, are often used to share content that is federally prohibited. Computers are networked with computers in other countries that have differing laws. In the United States, the possession of child pornography is a federal offense. One is liable under the law simply for possessing it and can be held accountable whether one deliberately downloaded the content or not.

Summary

IDSs can serve many purposes in a defense-in-depth architecture. In addition to identifying attacks and suspicious activity, you can use IDS data to identify security vulnerabilities and weaknesses. IDSs work well with firewall, either as a complement to the firewall, or directly in conjunction with it.

IDSs can enforce security policy. For example, if your security policy prohibits the use of file-sharing applications such as KaZaA, Gnutella, or messaging services such as Internet Relay Chat (IRC) or Instant Messenger, you could configure your IDS to detect and report this breach of policy.

IDSs are an invaluable source of evidence. Logs from an IDS can become an important part of computer forensics and incident-handling efforts. Detection systems are used to detect insider attacks by monitoring outbound traffic from Trojans or tunneling and can be used as incident management tools to track an attack.

A NIDS can be used to record and correlate malicious network activities. The NIDS is stealthy and can be implemented to passively monitor or to react to an intrusion.

The HIDS plays a vital role in a defense-in-depth posture; it represents the last bastion of hope in an attack. If the attacker has bypassed all of the perimeter defenses, the HIDS might be the only thing preventing total compromise. The HIDS resides on the host machine and is responsible for packet inspection to and from that host only. It can monitor encrypted traffic at the host level, and is useful for correlating attacks that are detected by different network sensors. Used in this manner it can determine whether the attack was successful. The logs from an HIDS are a vital resource in reconstructing an attack or determining the severity of an incident.

Part II

Solaris & Linux Firewalls

## Chapter 5

Implementing a Firewall with Ipchains and Iptables

Best Damn Topics in this Chapter:

- **Understanding the Need for a Firewall**

- **Deploying IP Forwarding and Masquerading**

- **Configuring Your Firewall to Filter Network Packets**

- **Understanding Tables and Chains in a Linux Firewall**

- **Logging Packets at the Firewall**

- **Configuring a Firewall**

- **Counting Bandwidth Usage**

- **Using and Obtaining Automated Firewall Scripts and Graphical Firewall Utilities**

Introduction

Over the years, the open source community has excelled in creating firewall software that is ideally suited for networks of any size. Linux natively supports the ability to route and/or filter packets. Modern Linux systems use either Ipchains or Iptables to do this.

Iptables supports Linux kernel 2.4 and higher (it was first implemented in Linux kernel 2.3). For those still using Linux kernel 2.2, use Ipchains instead. The Iptables package supports packet masquerading and filtering functionality as found in the 2.3 kernel and later. This functionality is known as *netfilter*, which is what Iptables is based on. Therefore, in order to use Iptables, you must recompile the kernel so that netfilter is installed, and you must also install the Iptables package. This is found by clicking **Networking Options | IP: NetFilter Configuration**.

> **NOTE**
>
> Ipfwadm is the precursor to both Ipchains and Iptables. Because it is used in older Linux kernels, this chapter does not consider it.

Depending on your kernel version, you can use these applications to configure your Linux system to act as a router, which means that it ensures that packets are sent from one network to another. At this level, a Linux router does not examine or filter any traffic. It simply ensures that all traffic addressed to a remote network gets sent to it.

Ipchains and Iptables also allow you to configure your Linux router to masquerade traffic (in other words, to rewrite IP headers so that a packet appears to originate from a certain host), or to examine and block traffic. It is even possible to configure your Linux router to do both. The practice of examining and blocking traffic is often called *packet filtering*. In this chapter, you will learn how to invoke packet filtering on your Linux system.

A packet filter works at the network layer of the Open System Interconnection Reference Model (OSI/RM). Daemons such as Squid (www.squid-cache.org) also allow you to examine and block traffic. However, Squid is not a packet filter; it is a proxy server that is designed to operate at the application layer of the OSI/RM. The primary difference between a packet filtering router (for example, one created by using Ipchains or Iptables) and a proxy server (for example, one enabled by Squid) is that a packet filtering router does not inspect network packets as deeply as a proxy server does.

However, proxy servers require more system resources in order to process network packets. As a result, a proxy server can sometimes be slow when honoring requests, especially if the machine is not powerful enough. This is why packet filters and proxy servers are both necessary in a network: one (the packet filter) blocks and filters the majority of network traffic, and the proxy server inspects only certain traffic types.

In this chapter, you will learn how to configure a system as a simple router and how to implement complex packet filtering so that you can protect your network from various attacks.

Understanding the Need for a Firewall

Regardless of whether you are implementing a packet filter or a proxy server, a firewall provides several services. The most essential Linux firewall functions include:

- **IP address conservation and traffic forwarding** Many firewalls first act as routers so that different networks (the 192.168.1.1/24 and 10.100.100.0/24 networks) can communicate with each other. Many network administrators use only this function to help create additional subnets. This feature is included as a firewall element simply because it is accomplished using either Ipchains or Iptables. Thus, anyone with only one IP address can create a local area network (LAN) or wide area network (WAN) that has full access to the Internet. You should understand, however, that a firewall does not necessarily have to provide Network Address Translation (NAT). Still, many firewalls (including those provided by Linux and Ipchains/Iptables) allow you to choose this feature.

- **Network differentiation** A firewall is the primary means of creating a boundary between your network and any other network. Because it creates a clear distinction between networks, a firewall helps you manage traffic. A firewall does not necessarily need to be deployed between a trusted, private network and the Internet. Many times, a firewall is deployed within a company network to further differentiate certain company divisions (such as research and development or accounting) from the rest of the network.

- **Protection against denial-of-service (DoS), scanning, and sniffing attacks** A firewall acts as a single point that monitors incoming and outgoing traffic. It is possible for this firewall to limit any traffic you choose.

- **IP and port filtering** The ability to allow or reject a connection based on IP address and port. Such filtering is likely the most understood function of a firewall. Generally, this type of filtering is usually accomplished by packet filters (in other words, Linux systems that use either Ipchains or Iptables). Packet filtering can become quite complex, because you must always consider that traffic can be filtered according to the source of the packet, as well as the packet's destination. For example, a packet filter can block traffic to your network if it originates from a particular IP address and port.

- **Content filtering** Proxy servers are generally the only types of firewall that manages and controls traffic by inspecting URL and page content. If configured properly, a proxy-oriented firewall can identify and block content that you consider objectionable.

- **Packet redirection** Sometimes, it is necessary for a firewall to send traffic to another port or another host altogether. For example, suppose you have installed Squid proxy server on a separate host than your firewall. It is likely that you will want to have your firewall automatically forward all traffic sent to ports 80 and 443 (the standard HTTP and HTTPS ports) to your proxy server for additional processing.

- **Enhanced authentication and encryption** A firewall has the ability to authenticate users, and encrypt transmissions between itself and the firewall of another network.

- **Supplemented logging** One of the most important—although commonly ignored—benefits of a firewall is that it allows you to examine all details about network packets that pass through it. You can learn, for example, about port scans and various connections to your system.

Building a Personal Firewall

It is possible to use Iptables or Ipchains on a standard client system. A personal firewall can be helpful in the following situations:

- You have only one system directly connected to the Internet, and don't want to create a router or a firewall as an intervening host.

- You want to log all blocked (or even allowed) traffic, and then read the entries in the /var/log/messages file.

- You want to block certain ports, such as those belonging to X (177 tcp and 177 udp, and tcp ports 6000 and 7100).

- You want to disable all pinging on the host. If you don't want to use Iptables or Ipchains, you can change the value of /proc/sys/net/ipv4/icmp_echo_ignore_all to 1 using

  - echo "1" > /proc/sys/net/ipv4/icmp_echo_ignore_all.

When it comes to building any type of firewall, it is important to consider your own situation. The commands you learn in the next section will help you implement the proper solution.

Understanding Packet Filtering Terminology

Generally, whenever a packet passes through a firewall, it is compared to its rules. If a packet matches a rule, then the firewall processes the packet.

Whenever a packet enters a chain in Ipchains, it must pass all the way through before the kernel allows it to pass on to the operating system, or pass through to another host. Iptables uses a similar principle, except that it allows you to create specific tables that can be either processed or ignored, making the packet-filtering process quicker and more efficient. Iptables will likely become the standard for some time. Now that you understand some of the basic firewall terms, it is time to learn more about the most common uses of a Linux system in regard to routing and firewalling.

Many times, a router can be a completely separate host from the firewall. This is especially the case in medium to large networks, where it is necessary to balance the load between the two. However, routers commonly have features that allow you to program them as a packet filter. Linux is a particularly handy tool because it allows you to do both simple routing and packet filtering.

> **NOTE**
>
> Ipchains gets its name from the fact that it connects each of its rules in an order, much like connecting links in a chain.

Choosing a Linux Firewall Machine

Contrary to what you may think, a firewall does not necessarily have to be the most powerful system on your network. It should, however, be a dedicated host, which means that you should not run any other services. The last thing you want to do is configure your firewall to also be a Samba server or print server. Additional services may cause a performance drain, and may open up vulnerabilities as well.

Ideally, a small network would be well served by a typical Pentium III or Pentium IV system with 128MB of RAM and a 500MHz processor. Depending on the amount of traffic the network generates, however, you could get by with a much less powerful system. It is not uncommon to see a network with 25 systems accessing the Internet using a Linux router that is no more powerful than a low-end 300MHz system. A good NIC is vital for firewalls and routers.

Larger businesses, say, those with demands for Web surfing, e-mail retrieval, and additional protocols, may require a more powerful system. Considerations for more powerful systems might include:

- A 1GHZ processor.

- At least 256MB of RAM (512MB of RAM or more may be preferable).

- Quality network interfaces and I/O cards, and possibly RAID 0 for faster data processing. RAID 0 does not provide data redundancy. It does, however, provide you with faster read/write time, which is helpful in regard to a firewall. Although a firewall does not store data as would a database application server, fast I/O is important, because you want the machine to process data as quickly as possible. Fast I/O is especially important if you plan to log extensive amounts of data.

- SCSI hard drives. SCSI systems tend to be faster and longer lasting than their IDE counterparts, thus allowing you a more powerful firewall.

Protecting the Firewall

One of the benefits of having a firewall is that it provides a single point that processes incoming and outgoing traffic. However, consider that a firewall can also provide a central point of attack or failure. A firewall does inform a hacker that a series of networks does exist behind it. If a hacker is able to defeat this one firewall, the entire network would be open to attack. Furthermore, if a hacker were able to somehow disable this host, the entire network would be denied all Internet services. It is important, therefore, that you take measures to protect your firewall. Consider the following options:

- Limit router and firewall access to interactive login only, and physically secure the system. This way, your firewall is much less susceptible to remote attack. It is still possible, however, that problems in the kernel (for example, buffer overflows and other programming problems) may occur. Such problems can lead to compromise of the system, even if you have no other services running.

- If remote access is necessary, access the firewall only via Secure Shell (SSH) or Stunnel, properly configured to use public keys to authenticate. Although SSH is not immune to security threats, it is one of the most popular and secure remote administration tools for Linux firewalls. Stunnel is also another viable option. You can get Stunnel from www.stunnel.org.

- Create a backup host: If your host crashes due to an attack, or simply because of a hard drive failure, you should have an identical system available as a replacement. If that is not possible, make sure you have a copy of the kernel configuration, the Iptables configuration, and most everything in the /etc directory.

- Monitor the host: Use an IDS application to listen in on connections made to your router. Usually, installing an IDS application on a separate host on the network is best. This is called *passive monitoring*, because the remote host does not consume the system resources of the firewall. The IDS application can, for example, send a random ping to the firewall to test whether it is up, and can then inform you if the host is down. Consider using an application such as Cheops, for example.

- Watch for bug reports concerning Ipchains, Iptables, the Linux kernel, and any applications such as SSH that you have installed. Keeping current about such changes can help you quickly upgrade your system in case a problem is discovered.

Deploying IP Forwarding and Masquerading

IP forwarding is the ability for a Linux system to act as a router. Packets enter the Linux kernel, and are then processed by the operating system. Follow these steps to make your Linux operating system act as a simple IP forwarder:

1. Install at least two NICs into your system. This is necessary, because your Linux system will then be able to service two different networks. You must, of course, have all of the required cables and hubs to allow systems to use all of the available network hosts.

2. Issue the following command at a terminal:

```
echo "1" > /proc/sys/net/ipv4/ip_forward
```

   This command enables IP forwarding on your Linux router. Entering the preceding command into some sort of file that runs whenever the system boots up. This way, if you restart your system, IP forwarding will be enabled by default. You can create your own file, or you can enter it at the bottom of the /etc/rc.d/rc.local file.

3. You can verify whether your system is acting as a router (in other words, IP forwarder) by issuing the following command:

```
cat /proc/sys/net/ipv4/ip_forward
1
 host #
```

4. If it reads 1, then your system is now acting as a router. A value of 0 means that your Linux system is not routing.

The main thing to remember is that a Linux system with simple IP forwarding enabled can route any network address to another. If you are allotted a range of IP addresses from a local or regional Internet registry, you can use a multihomed Linux system to route this set of addresses to another network. For example, if you are allotted the 128.187.22.0/24 block of IP addresses, you can use a Linux router to route this network to the 221.9.3.0 network, or to any other.

However, Internet routers will not forward traffic from private IP addresses (in other words, any network address of 10.0.0.0/8, 172.16.0.0/12, or 192.168.0.0/16). Figure 5.1, for example, shows how traffic from the 10.1.2.0 network and the 192.168.1.0 network can reach all networks, including the 128.187.22.0 network. However, only traffic from the 128.187.22.0 can reach the Internet.

Figure 5.1 A Linux System Configured as a Forwarding Router

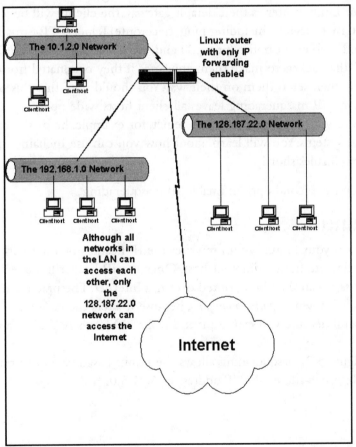

Figure 5.1 shows that traffic from the 10.1.2.0 and 192.168.1.0 networks cannot reach hosts across the Internet, only because the Internet routers will simply drop the traffic. To allow private network addresses to reach the Internet, you need to invoke Ipchains/Iptables-based IP masquerading. However, you have at least two solutions available to you:

- **Place a proxy server on the network that has at least two NICs** This proxy server can be configured to accept requests from the internal network and forward them to the outside network. The first NIC must be internal, because it will receive traffic passing from inside the network. The second NIC must be external, and will pass internal traffic to the outside world, and will also receive outside traffic so that it can be routed to the internal network. Another way of explaining this concept is that the proxy server receives egress traffic (in other words, traffic passing outside of the private IP address networks) and uses an Internet-routable IP address to forward the packets. The proxy server can also receive ingress traffic and translate it so that internal systems can receive it. This option requires the use of an additional software daemon, such as Squid.

- **Enable IP masquerading** In a Linux router, you can use either Ipchains or Iptables to forward and/or alter the IP headers of packets originating from private IP address networks to pass through Internet routers. Both Ipchains and Iptables do this by processing IP packets through the Linux kernel. As long as the client hosts are configured to use your Linux router as their default gateway, the clients will be able to access any and all Internet services, including ping, traceroute, Telnet, FTP, e-mail (SMTP and POP3), and Web client traffic (ports 80 and 443). This is because the Linux system "mangles" the packets to make them appear as if they originated from a legitimate IP address, and then sends them on their way. You should note that this option is not necessarily secure—IP masquerading leaves all client hosts wide open to attack. If a hacker can attach to your Linux router using Telnet, for example, he or she can then directly access your systems. You will learn about how you can use Ipchains and Iptables to create firewall rules shortly.

We will focus on the second option: Enable IP masquerading.

Masquerading

Masquerading is when your Linux system rewrites the IP headers of a network packet so that the packet appears to originate from a different host. Once the IP header has been rewritten to a nonprivate IP address, it can then be rerouted over the Internet. The practice of rewriting IP packets is colloquially known as *packet mangling*, because it alters the contents of the packet. Masquerading is useful because you can use it to invoke NAT, where one IP address can stand in for several.

As shown in Figure 5.2, masquerading allows the Linux-based system to translate the 10.1.2.0 network in to the Internet-addressable IP address of 66.1.5.0.

Figure 5.2 Masquerading the 10.1.2.0 Network as the 66.1.5.1 IP Address

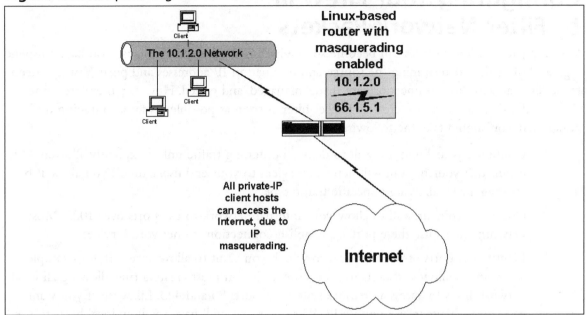

Once the private network of 10.1.2.0 is masqueraded as the IP address of 66.1.5.1, all hosts on this network can access the Internet. Depending on the subnet mask used for the 10.1.2.0 network, this means that hundreds and perhaps even thousands of client hosts can be masqueraded under this one IP address.

Translating the private to routable Internet address is accomplished by a database stored on the Ipchains/Iptables-based Linux router. The Linux masquerading router keeps this database so that it knows how to "untranslate," as it were, the packets that have been mangled so that they can then be addressed to the local, private network. This process occurs very quickly, although it is important that you have the proper amount of system power to enable the translation database to do its jobs.

Simple masquerading leaves the network "wide open," meaning that anyone who enters your firewall or router as a default gateway can have full access to all attached networks. Packet filtering is the answer to locking down access to your network. You can learn more about masquerading by reading the NAT-HOWTO file, which can be found at www.netfilter.org/documentation/HOWTO/NAT-HOWTO.html.

> **NOTE**
>
> Ipchains-based NAT is not compatible with Microsoft Point-to-Point Tunneling Protocol (PPTP) VPN clients. Not surprisingly, Microsoft did not follow RFC-defined standards. Not only did they not follow RFCs, but their PPTP is also plagued by a number of design vulnerabilities that affect security. You can, if you want, find workarounds to provide IPsec and VPN support between your Linux system and Microsoft VPN-enabled systems at www.impsec.org/linux/masquerade/ip_masq_vpn.html.

Configuring Your Firewall to Filter Network Packets

Creating packet-filtering rules can become somewhat involved, mainly because you have to spend a great deal of time determining the source and destination IP addresses and ports. You also need to be familiar with how connections are made, managed, and ended. However, there are some simple rules that can help you create a packet filter as soon as possible. As far as outgoing traffic is concerned, you should take the following steps:

1. Configure your Linux firewall to deny all outgoing traffic unless explicitly allowed. This means that your firewall will deny all services to your end users, unless you allow it by creating a rule allowing a specific traffic type.

2. Configure your firewall to allow your internal network to use ports over 1023. Most network clients use these ports to establish connections to network services.

3. Identify the ports of your services to which you want to allow access. If, for example, you want to allow end users to access the Web, you must create a rule allowing all local network hosts to access all remote systems at ports 80 and 443. Likewise, if you want your local clients to use remote POP3 servers, you will have to allow local hosts to use access remote systems at port 110.

As far as incoming traffic is concerned, you have many options. Many systems administrators want to create a firewall that forbids all incoming traffic, except for the TCP and UDP packets necessary when building up and tearing down a network connection. For example, if you want to allow internal clients to allow access to the Web, you will need to allow remote hosts to make connections to your firewall. This involves allowing remote hosts to open their local ports above 1023 to access your systems at ports above 1023. Therefore, you should take the following steps:

1. Configure your firewall to prohibit all incoming traffic from accessing any services below port 1023. The most secure firewall will not allow any connections to these ports.

2. Forbid all incoming traffic unless it is part of an already established session. In Ipchains, the -y option will do this. In Iptables, you would use the —SYN option. Each of these options will have the firewall match and discard any incoming packet with the SYN bit set. All other packets with the FIN or ACK bit set will be allowed, because the firewall assumes that these packets are part of an already established session (for example, an internal user is closing an SMTP or POP3 session with a remote host on the Internet). If you do not add this rule, then it is easier for malicious users to get around your firewall.

3. Disable all incoming ICMP traffic to protect yourself against DoS attacks. This step is optional, of course, because disabling this feature often makes network troubleshooting quite difficult.

4. Disable all forwarding except for networks that require it. The *Ipchains* and *Iptables* commands allow you to masquerade private IP networks. You want to, however, masquerade only certain networks.

5. To enable logging, use the -l option in Ipchains, or the -j LOG *target* in Iptables.

Customized Packet Filtering

Your firewall configuration needs will be specific to your situation. You need to consider the design of your network, and the services you need to provide. If, for example, you want to allow remote clients to access certain internal hosts, such as a Web server, you can place the Web server outside the firewall, or you can allow incoming traffic to access port 80. Consider, however, that if you place your Web server behind your firewall, you will have to ensure that this request is then forwarded to a specific internal host. Later in this chapter, you will see how you can manipulate the default INPUT, FORWARD, and OUTPUT chains using Ipchains and Iptables.

It is common practice to use packet filtering to block the following:

- Incoming and outgoing ICMP packets

- Access to remote POP3 servers

- Access to remote SMTP servers

- Access to the Web, or to certain sites (unproductive or offensive sites)

- Access to additional remote TCP/IP services, such as Telnet, FTP, finger, and so forth

Configuring the Kernel

Most Linux operating systems, such as Red Hat, Slackware, SuSE, and Caldera, support IP forwarding, masquerading, and firewalling by default. However, you may have to reconfigure your kernel in order to provide full functionality. When recompiling the kernel, choose the **Network packet filtering (replaces Ipchains)** option in the Networking section. In the 2.2 and earlier kernels, check the following Networking options:

- Network firewalls
- TCP/IP networking
- IP accounting

Packet Accounting

Packet accounting is the ability to summarize protocol usage on an IP network. For example, you can use this feature to list the amount of TCP, ICMP, and IP traffic that passes through your interfaces. Once you have recompiled the kernel and restarted your system, find out if the following file is present in the /proc virtual file system:

```
/proc/net/ip_acct
```

If the file exists, then your kernel supports IP accounting, in addition to all other features. Of course, you may want to check to see if this file exists before taking the time to recompile the kernel.

Understanding Tables and Chains in a Linux Firewall

Iptables derives its name from the three default tables it uses, which are listed in Table 5.2. Each interface on your system can have its packets managed and modified by the chains contained in each of these tables.

Table 5.1 Default Tables and Chains

Table Name	Default Chains	Description
Filter	INPUT FORWARD OUTPUT	Enables you to filter out packets.
Nat	PREROUTING OUTPUT POSTROUTING	Enables masquerading.
Mangle	PREROUTING OUTPUT	Allows you to further "mangle" packets by changing their contents. This feature, for example, allows you to shape packets so that they are ready for certain VPN clients, such as Microsoft PPTP.

Iptables is an extension of Ipchains, because Iptables adds the *nat* and *mangle* tables. Ipchains uses only the three chains listed in the filter table in Table 5.1. Thus, with Ipchains, you have access to only the INPUT, FORWARD, and OUTPUT options. If you want to masquerade using Ipchains, you will use the —*masquerading* option for the FORWARD chain. In Iptables, if you want to filter out packets using, you will use the *filter* table, and if you want to masquerade packets, you will use the *nat* table. In Iptables, if you do not specify a table, it will default to the filter table. Now that you understand tables, it is important to understand the specific chains.

A chain is a series of actions to take on a packet. Whenever you use Ipchains or Iptables to configure a firewall, the proper perspective to adopt is to view all packets from the firewall itself. Even more specifically, you should consider all packets from the perspective of the network interface, the table used, and the specific chains. For example, if you are using the filter table, each interface on your network has three different default chains:

- **INPUT** Contains rules that determine what will be done with all packets that enter this specific interface (for example, eth0).

- **FORWARD** For the purposes of this chapter, contains rules that determine if a packet will be masqueraded.

- **OUTPUT** Contains rules that determine filtering for packets leaving the interface.

The nat and mangle tables contain two additional chain types. The PREROUTING chain alters packets when they enter the interface. The POSTROUTING chain is used for altering packets when they are ready to leave the host. The POSTROUTING chain is essential to masquerading connections.

Built-In Targets and User-Defined Chains

Ipchains and Iptables use built-in targets to specify the destination of a packet. By far, the most common built-in targets are DROP and ACCEPT. Table 5.2 describes each of these in detail. (Additional targets exist. You can read about them by consulting the Ipchains or Iptables man page.)

Table 5.2 Common Ipchains and Iptables Targets

Target	Description
DROP	The packet is immediately discarded. The target of REJECT is also used.
ACCEPT	Allows the packet to pass through the rest of the chain. By default, all default chains are configured to allow any and all connections.

User-defined chains are often useful if you want to create a large number of rule entries, but do not want a chain to become too long. Chains that become too long can slow down the packet, and are difficult to read and organize. The following is a sequence where a user defined chain is created, modified, and then invoked:

```
ipchains -N custom
ipchains -A custom -s 0/0 -d 0/0 -p icmp -j REJECT
ipchains -A input -s 0/0 -d 0/0 -j custom
```

This is a trivial example, of course. The –A option "appends" a rule, meaning that it is placed at the beginning of a chain. The –I option adds the rule to the end of a chain. The user-defined rule of james is created, and then a rule dropping all ICMP packets is added to this custom chain. Then, a rule is added to the default input chain that all packets are processed by the custom chain. As a result, any and all ICMP packets will be dropped. If you were to make the mistake of forgetting to have the input chain refer to the chain named custom, then the custom chain would never be read.

In Iptables, the equivalent of the preceding command sequence would be very similar (it is possible, of course, to create user-defined chains that are much more ambitious).

```
ipchains -N custom
ipchains -A custom -s 0/0 -d 0/0 -p icmp -j DROP
ipchains -A input -s 0/0 -d 0/0 -j custom
```

Iptables would look like this:

```
iptables -N custom
iptables -A custom -s 0/0/ -d 0/0 -protocol icmp -j DROP
iptables -A input -s 0/0 -d 0/0/ -j custom
```

Specifying Interfaces

If no interface is specified, the first interface (usually eth0) is assumed. If you have multiple interfaces, you must specify the interface you want to be added to the chain. Thus, in a multiple-NIC system, when you use the INPUT chain to deny all ICMP traffic, you must specify the interface.

If, for example, you have a system with two interfaces that allowed all traffic, you would have to issue the following commands:

```
ipchains -A input -i eth0 -s 0/0 -d 0/0 -p icmp -j REJECT
ipchains -A input -i eth1 -s 0/0 -d 0/0 -p icmp -j REJECT
```

Now, this system will not forward ICMP packets on either the eth0 or the eth1 interface. For Iptables, the commands would be as follows:

```
iptables -A INPUT -i eth0 -s 0/0 -d 0/0 --protocl icmp --icmp-type
    echo-reply -j REJECT
iptables -A INPUT -i eth1 -s 0/0 -d 0/0 --protocl icmp --icmp-type
    echo-reply -j REJECT
```

In both Iptables and Ipchains, the *FORWARD* chain allows you to specify a source and destination interface. This is because the *FORWARD* chain is used to masquerade connections. Thus, the *-i* and *-o* options allow you mark packets passing between interfaces.

Setting Policies

Both Ipchains and Iptables default to accepting all connections. The safest option is to set the default policy to first deny all traffic. You can then create rules to explicitly allow certain traffic types. You can change this default stance using the *-P* option. For example, the following Ipchains command changes the default policy of the *input* chain to deny:

```
ipchains -P input DENY
```

The following command does the same thing in Iptables:

```
iptables -P input DROP
```

To reset the policy to accept, you simply use the ACCEPT target.

Listing Tables and Chains

Once you generate Ipchains or Iptables rules, you can then list them. For example, the following Ipchains command would list all chains and rules:

```
ipchains -L
```

Iptables uses the same command:

```
iptables -L
```

You can, if you want, list specific chains:

```
ipchains -L output
```

Because Iptables allows you to modify three different tables, you can also list specific tables. To list all nat chains, you would issue the following command:

```
iptables -t nat -L
```

The following command would view only the *POSTROUTING* chain in the nat table:

```
iptables -t nat -L POSTROUTING
```

Consider the following output from the *-L* option in Iptables:

```
iptables -L
Chain INPUT (policy ACCEPT)
target       prot opt source               destination
custom         icmp --  anywhere             anywhere


Chain FORWARD (policy ACCEPT)
target      prot opt source                destination


Chain OUTPUT (policy ACCEPT)
target      prot opt source                destination


Chain LD (0 references)
target      prot opt source                destination


Chain custom (1 references)
target      prot opt source                destination
DROP         icmp --  anywhere             anywhere
```

This output shows that the *INPUT* chain of the filter table contains one rule. This rule does not block ICMP traffic. Rather, it specifies that all ICMP traffic will be handled by the custom chain. The custom chain, listed last, does the actual dropping of all ICMP packets sent to this host.

The following commands allow you to list all of the rules by number:

```
ipchains --line-numbers -L
iptables --line-numbers -L
```

Saving, Flushing, and Restoring Rules

Once you have created rules in Ipchains or Iptables, you can save them using the following commands:

```
/sbin/ipchains-save
/sbin/iptables-save
```

These commands are helpful for two reasons. First, you can save the tables and rules to a text file in order to study them. Second, backing up your rules is important, as it generally takes considerable time to create the "perfect" firewall for your situation, and you should keep a backup in case your firewall configuration somehow gets lost. To save your Iptables information to a text file, for example, you would issue the following command:

```
/sbin/iptables-save > iptables.txt
```

To flush any existing rules, you can use the $-F$ option:

```
ipchains -F
iptables -F
```

Used without arguments, this command will erase the contents of all rules in Ipchains, and all rules in the filter table of Iptables. To flush a specific chain, you would issue the following command(s):

```
ipchains -F input
iptables -F INPUT
```

The *-F* option does not delete rules from either the nat or mangle tables in Ipchains, however. To delete information from a specific table, you have to specify the table as follows:

```
iptables -t nat -F
```

The $-F$ function does not change a policy from *DROP* to *ACCEPT*, either. You must use the $-P$ option, discussed earlier.

In case you need to restore your backup information, you can use the following commands:

```
ipchains-restore
iptables-restore
```

For example, to restore the Iptables rules database using the iptables.txt file created earlier, you would issue the following command:

```
/sbin/iptables-restore iptables.txt
```

By default, *Ipchains-restore* will append any restore information to any existing rules. You can use the *-f* option to flush out any existing rules, if you want.

However, the *Iptables-restore* command automatically erases any existing Iptables rules whenever it is used. However, you can use the *–n* option, which appends the contents of the restore file to any existing rules.

Using Ipchains to Masquerade Connections

The Ipchains command has only one table, and three chains (*INPUT*, *FORWARD*, and *OUTPUT*). Using the *FORWARD* chain and the MASQ target, you can masquerade any IP address you want. Suppose, for example, that you have a router that connects the 192.168.1.0/24 network and the 10.100.100.0/24 network. Suppose further that this firewall's eth0 interface contains the Internet-addressable IP address of 66.1.5.1/8. The following Ipchains command issued on the router would enable both private-IP networks to communicate via the Internet:

```
ipchains –A forward –I eth0 –s 192.168.1.0/24 –j MASQUERADE
ipchains –A forward –I eth0 –s 10.100.100.0/24 –j MASQUERADE
```

This rule specifies that any connection from the 192.168.1.0/24 and 10.100.100.0/24 networks will be masqueraded as 66.1.5.1/8 on eth0. The *–A* option adds the rule to the forward chain, and the *–I* option specifies the eth0 interface. The *–s* option specifies the networks in question.

This particular configuration actually exposes the network. Any remote host would be able to use your masquerading firewall to access your host. The following additions to the *FORWARD* chain of the filter table ensures that your masquerading router masquerades only for your internal network:

```
ipchains –A forward –s 192.168.1.0/24 –j ACCEPT
ipchains –A forward –d 192.168.1.0/24 –j ACCEPT
ipchains –A forward –s 10.100.100.0/24 –j ACCEPT
ipchains –A forward –d 10.100.100.0/24 –j ACCEPT
ipchains –A forward –j DROP
```

Iptables Masquerading Modules

Many of the protocols you want to use on the Internet, such as FTP or RealAudio, require additional support. Iptables provides several modules that allow masqueraded clients to access these resources. Some of these are described in Table 5.3.

Table 5.3 Ipchains Masquerading Modules

Module	Description
ip_masq_ftp	Module for masquerading FTP connections
ip_masq_raudio	RealAudio
ip_masq_irc	IRC
ip_masq_vdolive	For VDO Live
ip_masq_cuseeme	CU-See-Me

Enabling these options requires that you use the */sbin/insmod* command. For example, to enable the *ip_masq_ftp* and *ip_masq_raudio* modules, you would issue the following command:

```
/sbin/insmod ip_masq_ftp
/sbin/insmod ip_masq_raudio
```

To automate this process, you can place these entries into a script, or into /etc/rc.local.

Using Iptables to Masquerade Connections

Using the same example of the 192.168.1.0/24 network and the 10.100.100.0/24 network connected by the firewall with the IP address of 66.1.5.1/8, you would use the following command:

```
iptables -t nat -A POSTROUTING -d ! 192.168.1.0/22 -j MASQUERADE
iptables -t nat -A POSTROUTING -d ! 10.100.100.0/24 -j MASQUERADE
```

This rule is added to the nat table (-t), and is added to the *POSTROUTING* chain (-*a*). The *!* mark tells netfilter/Iptables to masquerade all packets not destined for the internal networks. Specifically, it stipulates that if the packet is not sent to either the 192.168.1.0/22 or 10.100.100.0/24 network, then the packet needs to be modified so that it masquerades as the 66.1.5.1/8 IP address. Consequently, any packet that leaves the interface will be rewritten with the 66.1.5.1/8 address, but packets that stay on the internal network will not be rewritten. The eth0 interface is assumed by default. If, for some reason, you had to specify a different interface that has the Internet-routable address, you would use the *–o* option:

```
iptables -t nat -o eth1 -A POSTROUTING -d ! 192.168.1.0/22 -j MASQUERADE
iptables -t nat -o eth1 -A POSTROUTING -d ! 10.100.100.0/24
    -j MASQUERADE
```

As with Ipchains, this particular configuration leaves the network wide open. The following additions to the *FORWARD* chain of the filter table ensure that your masquerading router masquerades only for your internal network:

```
iptables -A FORWARD -s 192.168.1.0/24 -j ACCEPT
iptables -A FORWARD -d 192.168.1.0/24 -j ACCEPT
iptables -A FORWARD -s 10.100.100.0/24 -j ACCEPT
iptables -A FORWARD -d 10.100.100.0/24 -j ACCEPT
iptables -A FORWARD -j DROP
```

Notice the order of these entries. Both Ipchains and Iptables consider rules in strict order, which is why the preceding rules first accept certain packets and then drop the rest. If the final entry (*iptables –A FORWARD –j DROP*) were listed first, then all packets would be denied.

> **NOTE**
>
> Because both Ipchains and Iptables default to allowing any and all input, it is quite easy to create rules that inadvertently allow unwanted traffic to pass through. Some systems

administrators prefer to first change the policy of all rules in all tables to deny. Doing so, however, will require you to add explicit rules to all affected chains so that your masquerading will work properly.

WARNING

One of the easiest ways to avoid a firewall is to find and exploit improperly configured modem banks. Many times, modems are configured to allow access to all areas of the network, and are often not protected or monitored very closely. As you establish your firewall, consider inspecting any and all systems for modems. You should approach your modem bank with the same care and consideration as you would your firewall.

Even modems not configured to receive incoming calls can be a danger. Consider also that an end user who connects to another network through a modem may be opening up a security breach. For example, suppose that a user has mapped several drives mapped to a file server that contains sensitive information. If an end user connects regularly to a remote dial-up server, it is possible for a malicious user to discover this connection and gain access to the mapped drives, and hence to the sensitive information.

Iptables Modules

Table 5.4 lists some of the most commonly used modules for Iptables.

Table 5.4 Iptables Masquerading Modules

Module	Description
ipt_tables	The module for Iptables support. As with all of these modules, it is possible to compile the kernel so that all of these modules are included.
ipt_LOG	Support for advanced logging, which includes the ability to log only initial bursts of traffic, and capture an certain amount of traffic over a period of time.
ipt_mangle	The IP masquerading module.
ipt_nat	The NAT module.

You can load these modules using *insmod*. Iptables masquerades the FTP, RealAudio, and IRC protocols by default.

Exercise: Masquerading Connections Using Ipchains or Iptables

1. Configure your Linux system with at least two NICs.

2. Enable IP forwarding using the instructions given earlier in this chapter.

3. Using either Ipchains or Iptables, invoke masquerading for your IP addresses using the instructions given earlier in this chapter.

4. Now, configure the *FORWARD* chain in the filter table (or just the *FORWARD* chain in Ipchains) so that it will masquerade only your internal hosts.

5. If necessary, load the modules necessary to support FTP, IRC, and additional protocols.

6. You will likely have to adjust your masquerading settings. Make sure that you save your settings using the */sbin/ipchains-save* command.

Logging Packets at the Firewall

As discussed earlier, the Iptables *–l* option allows you to log matching packets. You can insert *–l* into any rule, as long as you do not interrupt a particular option. For example, the following command logs all matching TCP packets that are rejected:

```
ipchains -I input -i eth0 -p tcp -s 0.0.0.0/0 -y -l -j REJECT
```

However, the following command would be a mistake, because Ipchains would think that *–l* is an argument for the source of a packet:

```
ipchains -I input -i eth0 -p tcp -s -l 0.0.0.0/0 -y -j REJECT
```

Once you establish logging, you can view Ipchains output in the /var/log/messages file.

Iptables allows you to log packets, as well, but in a much more sophisticated way. This is because Iptables uses the *LOG* target, which you specify just like *DROP* or *ACCEPT*. For example, to reject and also log all initial TCP traffic, you would issue the following two commands:

```
iptables -A INPUT -i eth0 -p tcp -s 0.0.0.0/0 -syn -j LOG
iptables -A INPUT -i eth0 -p tcp -s 0.0.0.0/0 -syn -j DROP
```

As with Iptables, you can view the results of your logging in the /var/log/messages file.

Setting Log Limits

By default, Iptables will limit logging of packets. The default limit rate is three logging instances an hour. Each time a logging instance starts, only the first five packets will be logged by default. This behavior is meant to ensure that log files do not get too large. You can change the default logging rate by specifying the –limit and –limit-burst flags. The –limit flag allows you to determine the limit rate by second, minute, hour, or day. The –limit-burst figure allows you to determine how many initial packets will be logged. For example, to log ICMP packets at a rate of two per minute, you would issue the following command:

```
iptables -A INPUT -i eth0 -p icmp -s 0.0.0.0/0 -limit 2/min
   -limit-burst 2 -j LOG
```

Notice also that the limit-burst value is set to 2.

> **NOTE**
>
> Be careful not to log too many packets. You will quickly consume hard drive space if you log all packets passing through your firewall interfaces.

Adding and Removing Packet Filtering Rules

Thus far, you have created a masquerading router. However, you have not yet invoked any packet filtering. Following are some examples of packet-filtering rules you may want to create on your system. First, consider the following Ipchains and Iptables commands:

```
ipchains –P input DENY
ipchains –A input –I eth0 –p tcp  –s 0/0 –d 0/0 22 –j ACCEPT
```

Now, consider the equivalent series of Iptables commands:

```
iptables –P INPUT DROP
iptables –P FORWARD DROP
iptables –A FORWARD –i eth0 –p tcp –dport 22 –j ACCEPT
```

These commands effectively prohibit every service from entering your firewall, except for SSH, which uses port 22. No other service can access your network. Notice that Ipchains refers to the input chain in lowercase, whereas Iptables uses the *FORWARD* chain in uppercase. Iptables always refers to chains in uppercase. In addition, Iptables does not use the *INPUT* chain for packets destined for the internal network. In Iptables, the *INPUT* chain refers only to packets destined for the local system. Thus, in Iptables, you should explicitly drop all packets to the *INPUT* interface, unless you want to allow access to your firewall, say by SSH or another relatively secure administration method. Your firewall will still forward packets on the nat table using the *FORWARD, POSTROUTING*, and *PREROUTING* chains.

Notice also that Ipchains uses *DENY* as a target name, whereas Iptables uses *DROP*. The difference is in the way source and destination are specified. This difference is actually not necessary; both Ipchains and Iptables can use –*s* and –*d*, or the –*dport* option. When using –*dport* or –*sport*, if you do not specify a source or destination, both Iptables and Ipchains assume the first local interface. The –*I* option in Ipchains specifies a particular interface (in this case, the eth0 interface), whereas in Iptables, the –*I* option specifies the incoming interface.

The preceding configuration is both extremely simple and restrictive. It allows outside hosts to access SSH users to access only SSH, and will not allow any user interactively logged in to the system to check e-mail or any other Internet-based service. This is because the rule is designed to lock down the firewall as much as possible.

ICMP Types

Notice that with Iptables, you can reject specific ICMP types. Table 5.5 explains some of the additional types, including the numbers assigned in RFC792, which is the document that defines the parameters for all ICMP messages.

Table 5.5 Common ICMP Names and Numbers

Iptables/Ipchains ICMP Message Name	RFC Name and Number	Description
echo-request	8 Echo	The packet sent out by the common *ping* command.
echo-reply	0 Echo Reply	The reply a host gives to the *ping* command.
destination-unreachable	3 Destination Unreachable	Informs an echo request packet that there is a problem reaching the intended host.
source-quence	4 Source Quench	If a router is too busy and cannot fulfill a client request, it will send back this message to a client.
Redirect	5 Redirect	Sent by a router that has, essentially, discovered a more direct route to the destination than originally found in the network packet sent by the network host.
time-exceeded	11 Time Exceeded	If a datagram is held too long by a router, its Time-To-Live (TTL) field expires. When this occurs, the router is supposed to send a message back to the host informing it of the drop.
parameter-problem	12 Parameter Problem	Sent by either standard hosts or routers, this message informs other hosts that a packet cannot be processed.

You can learn about additional arguments by typing **iptables –p icmp –h** at any terminal.

A Personal Firewall Example

Suppose that you want to create a personal firewall for a system that you use as a desktop. You would modify the previous Ipchains commands as follows:

```
ipchains -P input DENY
ipchains -A input -I eth0 -p tcp  -s 0/0 -d 0/0 22 -j ACCEPT
```

To create a personal firewall system using Iptables, you would issue the following commands:

```
iptables -P INPUT DROP
iptables -A INPUT -I eth0 -p tcp -dport 22 -j ACCEPT
iptables -A INPUT -I eth0 -p tcp -dport 1023 -j ACCEPT
iptables -A INPUT -I eth0 -p udp -dport 1023 -j ACCEPT
```

The preceding commands allow SSH, but no other service. However, now a user can browse the Web, contact DNS servers, and so forth, and use the system with a reasonable degree of security. This system now cannot even be pinged, which helps to protect it against distributed DoS and ping scanning attacks.

Exercise: Creating a Personal Firewall and Creating a User-Defined Chain

1. Using either Ipchains or Iptables, add the following rules to your INPUT table to create a personal firewall:

   ■ Deny all incoming ICMP traffic, and make sure the denial is logged

   ■ Deny all incoming FTP traffic

   ■ Deny all incoming DNS traffic

   ■ Deny Telnet

   ■ Deny SMTP and POP3

2. If you are using Iptables on a standard system with one interface, you would issue the following commands:

```
iptables -A INPUT -s 0/0 -d 0/0 -p icmp -j DROP
iptables -A INPUT -s 0/0 -d 0/0 -p icmp -j LOG
iptables -A INPUT -s 0/0 -d 0/0 -p tcp -dport 20 -j DROP
iptables -A INPUT -s 0/0 -d 0/0 -p tcp -dport 21 -j DROP
iptables -A INPUT -s 0/0 -d 0/0 -p tcp -dport 53 -j DROP
iptables -A INPUT -s 0/0 -d 0/0 -p udp -dport 53 -j DROP
iptables -A INPUT -s 0/0 -d 0/0 -p tcp -dport 21 -j DROP
iptables -A INPUT -s 0/0 -d 0/0 -p tcp -dport 25 -j DROP
iptables -A INPUT -s 0/0 -d 0/0 -p tcp -dport 110 -j DROP
```

   Of course, there is more than one way to do this. For example, you could create a user-defined chain and handle all SMTP and POP3 there:

```
iptables -N icmptraffic
iptables -A icmptraffic -s 0/0 -d 0/0 -p icmp -j DROP
iptables -A icmptraffic -s 0/0 -d 0/0 -p icmp -j LOG
iptables -A INPUT -s 0/0 -d 0/0 -p icmp -j icmp
```

3. List the *INPUT* chain. If you created a user-defined chain, list this as well.

4. Save your configuration for the sake of backup. If you are using Iptables, use the following command:

```
iptables-save > iptables.txt
```

5. Flush all of the rules you created. If you are using Iptables, issue the following command:

```
iptables -F
```

6. List the *INPUT* chain (and any other) to verify that you have in fact flushed this chain.

7. Use the *iptables-restore* (or *ipchains-restore*) command along with the text file you created to restore your Iptables chains:

```
iptables-restore iptables.txt
```

8. List your tables and chains again to verify that your rules have been restored.

9. Thus far, you have created a personal firewall that starts with a "wide open" policy, and then proceeds to lock down ports. Now, use the *−P* option to block all traffic, and then allow only SSH, or any other protocol(s) of your choice. If, for example, you are using Iptables, issue the following commands:

```
iptables -P INPUT DROP
iptables -A INPUT-p tcp --dport 22 -j ACCEPT
iptables -A INPUT-p tcp --dport 1023: -j ACCEPT
iptables -A INPUT-p udp --dport 1023: -j ACCEPT
```

You can specify *−i eth0*, if you wish. However, if you only have one interface, both Ipchains and Iptables will default to using this interface. Remember, you should open up the ephemeral TCP and UDP ports so that you can still do things like checking your e-mail, and so forth. If, of course, you do not want any services open on your network, you could omit the *—dport 22* line altogether.

10. Now, log all traffic that attempts to connect to your system. If you are using Iptables, issue the following command:

```
iptables -A INPUT-p udp --dport 1023: -j LOG
iptables -A INPUT-p tcp --dport 1023: -j LOG
```

This feature may log too much information for your server, depending on your system's activity. Make sure you check your log files regularly.

11. Log all attempts to scan the standard ports for Microsoft networking. If you are using Iptables, issue the following command:

```
iptables -A INPUT-p tcp --multiport  --destination-port
    135,137,138,139 -j LOG
iptables -A INPUT-p udp --multiport  --destination-port
    137,138,139 -j LOG
```

The *—multiport —destination-port* option allows you to specify a range of ports. You can read more about these options in the Iptables man page.

12. If your server needs to support additional protocols, experiment with adding them.

Redirecting Ports in Ipchains and Iptables

Port redirection is where a packet destined for a certain port (say, port 80) is received by an interface, and is then sent to another port. Redirecting ports is common in networks that use proxy servers. To redirect a port in Ipchains to the local system's eth0 interface, you could issue the following command:

```
ipchains -A input -i eth1 -s 0/0 -d 0/0 -p tcp 80 -j REDIRECT 8080
ipchains -A input -i eth1 -s 0/0 -d 0/0 -p tcp 443 -j REDIRECT 8080
```

In Iptables, you must use the *REDIRECT* target from the nat table:

```
iptables -t nat -A PREROUTING -i eth1 -s 0/0 -d 0/0 -p
    tcp 80 -j REDIRECT /
--to-ports 8080


iptables -t nat -A PREROUTING -i eth1 -s 0/0 -d 0/0 -p
    tcp 443 -j REDIRECT /
--to-ports 8080
```

These rules ensure that any hosts that try to bypass your proxy server by specifying your firewall are redirected to a proxy server on the firewall. Another strategy is to deny all requests to ports 80 and 443, and then make sure that all Web clients are configured to access your proxy server.

Configuring a Firewall

Because your situation will be unique, it is impossible to provide a "cookbook" firewall for you. However, the following is a beginning firewall for a system with three NICs. The NICs have the following IP addresses:

- **Eth0** 207.1.2.3/24
- **Eth1** 192.168.1.1/24
- **Eth2** 10.100.100.1/24

Thus, Eth0 represents the 207.1.2.0/24 network, Eth1 represents the 192.168.1.0/24 network, and Eth2 represents the 10.100.100.0/24 network. The intention is to create a firewall that allows the Eth1 and Eth2 networks to communicate freely with each other, as well as get on to the Internet and use any services (Web, e-mail, FTP, and so forth). However, no one from the Internet should be able to access internal ports below port 1023. Again, this configuration does not spend much time limiting egress (outbound) traffic. Rather, it focuses on trying to limit ingress (inbound) traffic. Any of the Ipchains or Iptables commands given in the following sections can be entered into any script, or into a directory or file such as /etc/rc.d/init.d/ or /etc/rc.d/rc.local. This way, your rules will be loaded automatically when you reboot your system.

Setting a Proper Foundation

Regardless of whether you are using Ipchains or Iptables, the first thing you will have to do for your firewall is to flush all existing rules using the *–F* option. Then, you need to use the *–P* option to set the firewall policies to deny all connections by default. The subsequent rules you create will then allow the protocols you really want. Then, use the necessary commands to enable forwarding and masquerading, as shown earlier in this chapter. Without this foundation, you will not be able to forward packets at all, and thus firewalling them would be superfluous.

Creating Anti-Spoofing Rules

Many times, a hacker will try to use your firewall as a default gateway and try to spoof internal packets. If a firewall's "Internet interface" (the one that is responsible for addressing packets to the Internet) is not configured to explicitly deny packets from the network, then you are susceptible to this attack. To deny spoofing, you would issue the following commands, depending on what kernel you are using:

```
ipchains -A input -s 192.168.1.0/24 -i eth0 -j deny
ipchains -A input -s 10.100.100.0/24 -i eth0 -j deny


iptables -A FORWARD -s 192.168.1.0/24 -i eth0 -j DROP
iptables -A FORWARD -s 10.100.100.0/24 -i eth0 -j DROP
```

You may want to log all of the attempts, just so you know how often you are attacked:

```
ipchains -A input -s 192.168.1.0/24 -i eth0 -l -j deny
ipchains -A input -s 10.100.100.0/24 -i eth0 -l -j deny
```

The preceding rules are different only in that they specify the *–l* option. In Iptables, create two additional entries to log the traffic:

```
iptables -A FORWARD -s 192.168.1.0/24 -i eth0 -j LOG
iptables -A FORWARD -s 10.100.100.0/24 -i eth0 -j LOG
```

Remember, if you have additional interfaces, you have to add a rule for each. Do not leave one interface open to a spoofing attack. You will be surprised how quickly a hacker can discover this vulnerability.

Allowing TCP

The following is an example of what you can do with your network when it comes to allowing inbound and outbound TCP connections. If you are using Ipchains, issue the following commands to allow TCP connections:

```
ipchains-A input -p tcp -d 192.16.1.0/24 ! 80 -y -b -j ACCEPT
ipchains-A input -p tcp -d 10.100.100.0/24 ! 80 -y -b -j ACCEPT
```

The *–y* option prohibits remote hosts from initiating a connection to any port except port 80. This is because the *!* character reverses the meaning of anything that is immediately in front of it. In this case, only connections meant for port 80 will be allowed; all others will be denied. This may seem strange, but remember, this rule is for the input chain, and many times these rules seem to be the reverse of common sense. The *-b* option "mirrors" the rule, which means that the rule applies to packets going in both directions. This rule allows one rule to do the same thing as repeating the command and reversing the source and destination flags (-s and −d).

If you are using Iptables, issue the following commands:

```
iptables −A FORWARD −m multiport −p tcp −d 192.168.1.0\24
    --dports 25,110, 80, 443, 53 /
! −tcp flags SYN, ACK ACK −j ACCEPT


iptables −A FORWARD −m multiport −p tcp −s 192.168. 1.0\24
    --sports 25,110, 80, 443,53 /
 ! −tcp  flags SYN, ACK ACK −j ACCEPT


iptables −A FORWARD −m multiport −p tcp −d 10.100.100.0\24
    --dports 25,110, 80, 443, 53 ! /
−tcp  flags SYN, ACK ACK −j ACCEPT


iptables −A FORWARD −m multiport −p tcp −s 10.100.100.0\24
    --sports 25,110, 80, 443, 53 ! /
−tcp  flags SYN, ACK ACK −j ACCEPT
```

The preceding rules allow ports to be opened above 1023, as long as they are continuing a connection that has first been established by a host inside the firewall. You can, of course, add additional ports, according to your needs. The / character is a simple line continuation character that you may have to specify in a script. As with Ipchains, the ! character reverses the meaning of anything that is in front of it. In this case, it means that any packet that does not have the SYN, SYN ACK, or ACK bit set is accepted.

TCP Connections Initiated from Outside the Firewall

You may want to allow certain outside hosts to initiate a connection to your firewall. If you do, you can issue the following commands.

For Ipchains, you would issue the following:

```
ipchains −A input −p tcp −I eth0 −d 192.168.1.0/24 80 −y −j ACCEPT
```

The difference between this command and those given previously is that this one specifies the interface, as opposed to the IP address.

For outgoing connections, you would issue the following:

```
ipchains −A input −p tcp −i eth0 −d 0/0 −j ACCEPT
```

For Iptables, you would do the following for standard TCP connections:

```
iptables −A FORWARD −m multiport −p tcp −i eth0 −d 192.168.
```

```
      1.0/24 80--syn /
--syn -j  ACCEPT


iptables -A FORWARD -m multiport -p tcp -i eth0
    -d 10.100.100.0/24 80--syn /
--syn -j ACCEPT
```

To allow for outgoing connections, you would issue the following:

```
iptables -A FORWARD -m multiport -p tcp -i eth0 -d 0/0 --syn  -j ACCEPT
iptables -A FORWARD -m multiport -p tcp -i eth1 -d 0/0 --syn -j ACCEPT
iptables -A FORWARD -m multiport -p tcp -i eth2 -d 0/0 --syn -j ACCEPT
```

All other TCP traffic will be locked out.

Firewalling UDP

To filter incoming and outgoing UDP, you would follow many of the same procedures as outlined earlier. However, you should allow both TCP port 53 and UDP port 53, at least at first. Most of the time, DNS uses UDP port 53. However, DNS can use TCP when a request grows too large, so you should account for this by creating explicit rules. For Ipchains, you would do the following to allow incoming connections:

```
ipchains-A input -p udp -i eth0 -d 192.168.1.0/24 53 -j ACCEPT
ipchains-A input -p udp -i eth0 -d 10.100.100.0/24 -j ACCEPT
```

The preceding rule is necessary only if you plan to allow outside users to access your DNS server.

```
ipchains-A input -p udp -i eth0 -d 0/0 -j ACCEPT
```

For Iptables, you would issue the following commands:

```
iptables -A FORWARD -m multiport -p udp -i eth0 -d 192.168.1.0/24 /
--dports  53-j ACCEPT
iptables -A FORWARD -m multiport -p udp -i eth0 -s 192.168.1.0/24 /
--dports  53-j ACCEPT
```

Outgoing UDP usually requires that you enable DNS lookups, which are usually at UDP port 53:

```
iptables -A FORWARD -m multiport -p udp -i eth0 -d 0/0 -dports
    53-j ACCEPT
iptables -A FORWARD -m multiport -p udp -i eth0 -s 0/0 -dports
    53-j ACCEPT
```

It is possible that your network requires additional ports. For example, if you are running SNMP, you would have to open ports 160 and 161.

Enhancing Firewall Logs

If you want to log these connections, do the following using Ipchains:

```
ipchains -A input -p tcp -l -j REJECT
ipchains -A input -p udp -l -j REJECT
ipchains -A input -p icmp -l -j REJECT
```

The preceding commands will log any packet that is matched. If you are using Iptables, the equivalent commands are:

```
iptables -A FORWARD -m tcp -p tcp -j LOG
iptables -A FORWARD -m udp -p udp -j LOG
iptables -A FORWARD -m udp -p icmp -j LOG
```

Usually, creating the ideal packet-filtering rules requires some trial and error, as well as research specific to your own situation. For more information about using Ipchains, consult the Ipchains man page, and the Ipchains-HOWTO available at www.linuxdoc.org/HOWTO/IPCHAINS-HOWTO.html#toc1.

For more information about using Iptables, consult the Iptables man page, and the Iptables-HOWTO available at various sites, including www.guenthers.net/doc/howto/en/html/IP-Masquerade-HOWTO.html#toc2. Using the information in this chapter and additional resources, you will be able to create a firewall that blocks known attacks.

Counting Bandwidth Usage

A Linux firewall can inform you about the number of packets it has processed, in addition to blocking and logging attacks. The process of counting packets is often called *packet accounting*. Many companies are very interested in determining how much traffic a department or network has generated. This can help them determine the type of equipment necessary to support the department further. Such information can also help a company determine how much it can bill a client or department. In many situations, the firewall is an ideal place to gather such statistics. If you have the following two networks, these rules will count packets that pass between the two:

```
ipchains -A forward -p icmp -s 192.168.1.0/24 -d 10.100.100.0/24
```

The preceding rule will identify all of the traffic passing from the 192.168.1.0/24 network to the 10.100.100.0/24 network.

If you are using Iptables, you have many additional options. For example, you can identify specific ICMP packets that are forwarded by the firewall:

```
iptables -A FORWARD -m icmp -p icmp -f -j LOG
```

To gather information about a more specific element of ICMP, you could issue the following command:

```
iptables -A FORWARD -m icmp -p icmp --sports echo-request -j LOG
```

This rule will count all icmp echo-request packets (icmp 0). The following command discovers all of the icmp-reply packets that have been forwarded:

```
iptables -A FORWARD -m icmp -p icmp --sports echo-reply -j LOG
```

You are not limited to ICMP packets. If, for example, you wanted to gather information about the HTTP packets being forwarded, you would enter the following:

```
iptables -A FORWARD -p tcp --sports 80,443 -j LOG
```

To determine the amount of HTTP traffic passing between two networks, you would issue the following command:

```
iptables -A FORWARD s 192.168.1.0/24 -d 10.100.100.0/24 -p tcp
   --sports 80,443 /
-j LOG
```

Listing and Resetting Counters

To list the counter information, you can issue either of the following commands from a terminal:

```
ipchains -L -v
iptables -L -v
```

You can save this information using the *ipchains-save* and *iptables-save* commands. The following commands reset the counters:

```
ipchains -L -Z
iptables -L -Z
```

Setting Type of Service (ToS) in a Linux Router

Many routers, including Linux routers using Ipchains or Iptables, are capable of shaping traffic as it passes through. The IP header for all packets has a special field called the Type of Service (ToS) field, which allows you to prioritize traffic as it passes through the router. Using the ToS field, you can make certain types of traffic (for example, SMTP and POP3) take precedence over others (for example, SSH and Telnet). Packets that are marked will be treated differently at the router. Setting the ToS field occurs at the network layer (Layer 3 of the OSI/RM). You can learn more about how ToS works by consulting RFC1349.

Usually, assigning priority for packets is a secondary concern when configuring a firewall. In some situations, however, you will find it useful for a firewall to "double up" and offer both services. The main reason why you would set the ToS field in network traffic is to cut down on network congestion, especially in networks that have high amounts of traffic.

NOTE

Do not confuse Type of Service (ToS) with Quality of Service (QoS). QoS refers to the ability of physical devices (switches, routers) to transmit packets according to ToS values found in IP packets. QoS concerns might include whether the packet is delivered via

Frame Relay, Asynchronous Transfer Mode (ATM), Ethernet, Synchronous Optical Network (SONET), and so forth. Because ToS refers to the ability to mark certain packets so that they have a higher priority than others do, these markings determine whether they are available for QoS routing.

Service Values

The normal-service value is 0 (or, 0x00 in the actual packet). Table 5.6 lists the four different options available to you when marking a packet.

Table 5.6 ToS Field Options

Service Value	Description
Minimum delay	The minimum delay field reduces the time a datagram takes to get from the router to the host. The minimum delay option is ideal for protocols that require speed when building initial connections, or when transferring control data. Traffic such as the ftp-control port (20), Telnet, and SSH benefits from this setting. Marking this traffic will reduce latency (the time interval between a request and a reply) at the router. The ToS field bit is 10 (0x10 in the actual packet).
Maximum throughput	This value is appropriate for the ftp-data port (20) and for large file transfers via HTTP. Networks that use the X Windows system to export displays between systems should consider using this bit as well. The ToS field bit is 8 (0x08 in the actual packet). If you anticipate large volume transfers via POP3, you could consider this option as well.
Maximum reliability	Used in an attempt to reduce retransmissions. Sometimes, UDP protocols such as DNS (port 53) and SNMP (ports 161 and 162) receive this option. However, TCP-based protocols such as SMTP also benefit from this ToS option, because systems can waste bandwidth to keep retransmitting this protocol. The ToS bit value is 4 (0x04 in the actual packet).
Minimum cost	This option is often only implemented by commercial products. The ToS field bit is 2 (0x02 in the actual packet).

It may be useful to consider these four options in terms of common network tasks. Client hosts (hosts that use X, SSH, FTP, HTTP, and other protocols) may benefit from either maximum throughput or minimum delay settings. Servers generally benefit from maximum throughput, depending on the traffic they generate.

Setting ToS Values in Ipchains and Iptables

To set ToS values in Ipchains, add the following values to the end of any rule:

```
-t andmask xormask
```

The *andmask* value is usually 01, because this value compares, or "ands" the original TOS value, and then allows you to make a change to the packet. The xormask value can be any of the service values found in Table 5.6 (for example, 08 for maximizing throughput). This second field is evaluated as an "or" value, meaning that if the value you specify is different from the original value, the one you specify will be set.

For example, to mark the ToS field for maximum throughput for HTTP (port 80) for all packets being sent out to all remote systems, you would do the following:

```
ipchains -A output -s 0.0.0.0/0.0.0.0 -d 0.0.0.0/0.0.0.0 80
   -p 6 -t 01 08
```

The *–p 6* option specifies TCP as the protocol. You would never set a ToS value on a packet that will eventually be dropped. Following are some additional examples of the ToS value being set on additional protocols:

```
ipchains-A output -s 0.0.0.0/0.0.0.0-d 0.0.0.0/0.0.0.0 21 -p 6 -t 01 04
ipchains-A output -s 0.0.0.0/0.0.0.0-d 0.0.0.0/0.0.0.0 20 -p 6 -t 01 08
ipchains-A output-s 0.0.0.0/0.0.0.0-d 0.0.0.0/0.0.0.0 22:22-p 6 -t 01 10
ipchains-A output-s 0.0.0.0/0.0.0.0-d 0.0.0.0/0.0.0.0 25:25-p 6 -t 01 04
ipchains-A output-s 0.0.0.0/0.0.0.0-d 0.0.0.0/0.0.0.0 53:53-p 6 -t 01 04
ipchains-A output-s 0.0.0.0/0.0.0.0-d 0.0.0.0/0.0.0.0 80:80 -p 6-t 01 08
ipchains-A output-s0.0.0.0/0.0.0.0-d 0.0.0.0/0.0.0.0 110:110-p 6-t 01 08
ipchains-A output-s0.0.0.0/0.0.0.0-d 0.0.0.0/0.0.0.0 143:143-p 6-t 01 04
ipchains-A output-s0.0.0.0/0.0.0.0-d 0.0.0.0/0.0.0.0 443:443-p 6-t 01 04
```

Additional ToS Options in Iptables

Iptables, as you might suspect, adds several options and uses some different terminology. First, you can set your router to either match packets with certain ToS options set, or you can have the router set the actual ToS options. These are two very different things. One allows the router to handle packets with the ToS value already set, whereas the other actually sets the values. To create a rule that matches a ToS field, you would use the *-m* option, complete with its arguments:

```
-m tos --TOS tos_value -j TARGET
```

In the preceding syntax, the tos_value number is any ToS bit found in Table 5.6 (for example, 08 for maximum throughput). As far as target value is concerned, you can specify any target you want (ACCEPT, a user-defined chain, and so forth). For example, the following rule accepts packets from port 80 with the ToS value set to 08:

```
iptables -A INPUT -p tcp -m tos 0x08 -j ACCEPT
```

As far as setting ToS values is concerned, you can only set them in the FORWARD and OUTPUT chains. The syntax is as follows:

```
-j TOS --set-tos tos_value
```

For example, to set the ToS value to maximum throughput for all outgoing Web traffic, you would do the following:

```
iptables -A OUTPUT -p tcp -m tcp --dport 80 -j TOS --set-tos 0x08
```

Following are some additional examples where Iptables has been used to set ToS fields for various traffic:

```
iptables A OUTPUT -p tcp -m tcp --dport 21 -j TOS --set-tos 0x04

iptables A OUTPUT -p tcp -m tcp --dport 20 -j TOS --set-tos 0x08

iptables -A OUTPUT -p tcp -m tcp --dport 22 -j TOS --set-tos 0x010

iptables -A OUTPUT -p tcp -m tcp --dport 25 -j TOS --set-tos 0x04

iptables -A OUTPUT -p tcp -m tcp --dport 53 -j TOS --set-tos 0x04

iptables -A OUTPUT -p tcp -m tcp --dport 80 -j TOS --set-tos 0x08

iptables -A OUTPUT -p tcp -m tcp --dport 110 -j TOS --set-tos 0x08

iptables -A OUTPUT -p tcp -m tcp --dport 143 -j TOS --set-tos 0x04

iptables -A OUTPUT -p tcp -m tcp --dport 443 -j TOS --set-tos 0x04
```

Using and Obtaining Automated Firewall Scripts and Graphical Firewall Utilities

Several attempts have been made to automate the process of creating a firewall in Linux. Similarly, developers are also busy creating GUI applications that make the job easier. Many of these utilities are quite useful, although they are mostly effective in beginning your firewall configuration; you will likely have to customize the rules these applications generate.

The more effective firewall scripts and GUI tools include the following:

- **Firestarter** A fairly sophisticated graphical tool that supports both Ipchains and Iptables. It can be used to create a personal firewall, but also supports multihomed systems. Like many automated firewalls, it creates multiple rules to filter out known and expected attacks. You may need to adjust some of these automatic settings. Although Firestarter does support multiple interfaces, it, like most of the open-source GUI firewall applications, is best used only as a beginning to a firewall on a multihomed system. You can obtain Firestarter at http://sourceforge.net/projects/firestarter.

- **Mason** A unique product, Mason is designed to first listen in on traffic passing through your firewall, and then generate Ipchains or ipfwadm (the precursor to ipchains and Iptables) rules. As of this writing, Mason does not support Iptables. In spite of this, Mason's approach to rules creation is both unique and sound, as it attempts to create rules based on your network traffic about your firewall needs. You can download this binary at http://users.dhp.com/~whisper/mason. Do not confuse this product with the HTML Mason utilities meant to dynamically generate HTML for Apache Server.

- **Knetfilter** A GUI firewall designed to work with the KDE desktop environment. Although it purports to be stable, it appears to have problems working with common versions of KDE. You can learn more about Knetfilter at http://expansa.sns.it:8080/knetfilter.

- **Firewall Builder** Firewall Builder is in many ways the most ambitious open-source GUI tool. It allows you to create rules for multiple interfaces, networks, and hosts. It is also quite unstable on most versions of Red Hat Linux through version 7.1. Learn more about Firewall Builder at http://sourceforge.net/projects/fwbuilder.

- **EasyChains** EasyChains has a ncurses-based GUI, and supports Ipchains and Iptables. You can download it at http://sourceforge.net/projects/easychains.

Weighing the Benefits of a Graphical Firewall Utility

As you consider using any of the GUI applications covered in this section, keep in mind the following issues:

- Often, these downloads do not provide public keys or hash values for their code; therefore, before using any of the applications, make sure that you review the source code. If you cannot review the source code yourself, then employ someone to check it, especially if you plan to use it in an enterprise environment.

- Most of these applications are still in beta form, so remember that they often provide limited functionality. Although some, such as Mason, are quite impressive, limitations still persist: As of this writing, Mason does not support Iptables.

- The more advanced GUI applications often require you to upgrade to either the very latest version of a particular window manager, such as KDE or Gnome, or to use an idiosyncratic version or configuration. Consequently, you may have to spend a great deal of time configuring your window manager. Generally, this time could be better spent learning how to use Iptables or Ipchains commands.

Firewall Works in Progress

The following is a partial list of applications being developed at the current time:

- **jb dynFW** (http://sourceforge.net/projects/jbdfw) This project appears to be interested in creating a personal firewall product, as opposed to a multihomed firewall.

- **Heimdall Linuxconf Firewall** (http://sourceforge.net/projects/heimdall) A promising effort, mainly because it proposes to be an add-on to the Linuxconf application.

- **NetFilter-1** (http://sourceforge.net/projects/netfilter-1) If it lives up to its promise, this particular project could produce a truly useful piece of software, because it is trying to mimic the Check Point Firewall-1 product. Its "secure logging" feature will employ encryption so that the firewall can log to remote systems without the fear of sniffing attacks.

- **PHP Ipchains project** (http://sourceforge.net/projects/phpchains) The primary strength of this product is that it is based on PHP, which is a truly portable language, and is well supported by Apache Server. Because many other security applications use PHP, this product may allow you to apply skills you have already learned.

- **Positive Control** (http://sourceforge.net/projects/positivecontrol) Not only does this project plan on releasing a GUI, it also plans on creating a firewall that can detect port scans through *stateful inspection*, which is basically a way for the firewall to maintain and scan its own dynamic database. If this database senses a number of ports that have been scanned in a row, the firewall can take action. Some actions the firewall can take may include automatic firewall reconfiguration and automatic alerts.

Exercise: Using Firestarter to Create a Personal Firewall

1. Make the necessary preparations for your firewall. If you are creating a personal firewall, then you can simply move on to step 2. If you want to use your firewall to masquerade connections, you should understand that Firestarter may not do the best job creating forwarding and nat/masquerading rules, so you may want to create them first. You will see later in this exercise how you can configure Firestarter to enable masquerading for you.

2. Once you have verified and tested your masquerading (if necessary), download the latest Firestarter RPM or tarball from http://sourceforge.net/projects/firestarter. The RPM and tarball packages are equivalent. They do not require any special libraries; if you have installed either the Gnome or KDE window managers, you will have no problem.

3. Install Firestarter. If you are using the RPM, you would issue the following command:

```
rpm –ivh firestarter-0.7.0-1.i386.rpm
```

4. Now, start X and enter the following in a terminal:

```
firestarter
```

5. If an existing Ipchains or Iptables configuration exists, you may see the warning shown in Figure 5.3.

Figure 5.3 Firestarter Warning

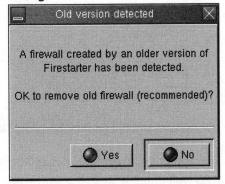

If necessary, click **Yes**. You should note that this warning will also appear if you restart Firestarter. If you are using this wizard on a system that already has masquerading configured, you would click **No** to save this configuration. Firestarter will simply append its configuration to yours.

6. When you first launch Firestarter, the configuration wizard, shown in Figure 5.4, should appear automatically.

Figure 5.4 The Firestarter Configuration Wizard Initial Screen

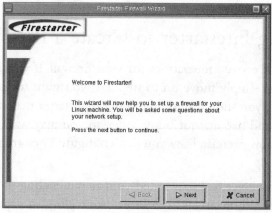

If the wizard does not appear, maximize the main interface and go to **Firewall | Run firewall wizard**.

7. Once the wizard begins, click **Next**.

8. The Network Device Configuration screen will appear, as shown in Figure 5.5. Select the interface you want to protect, and click **Next**.

Figure 5.5 The Network Device Configuration Screen

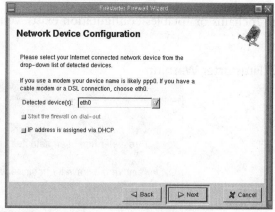

You will notice that in this particular example, the eth0 interface is selected. Firestarter is written well enough so that it will automatically detect all of your interfaces.

9. The Services Configuration window, shown in Figure 5.6, will appear.

Figure 5.6 The Services Configuration Window

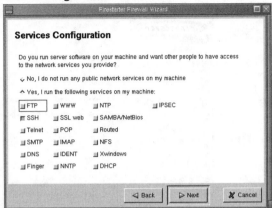

10. Configure the services that you want. Figure 5.6 shows that only SSH will be allowed to connect to the firewall. Your settings will differ according to your needs. When you are finished selecting the services you want to provide on this interface, click **Next**.

11. The ICMP Configuration screen will appear, as shown in Figure 5.7. By default, Firestarter disables all ICMP filtering, which means that all ICMP packets will be allowed to pass through the firewall. Select **Enable ICMP Filtering**, and then select the ICMP packet types that you want to filter. You will notice that in this particular example, no ICMP packets will be allowed to traverse the firewall.

Figure 5.7 The ICMP Configuration Screen

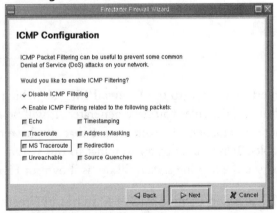

12. When you have selected the ICMP packets you want to block, click **Next**. Firestarter will inform you that it is ready to generate the firewall, as shown in Figure 5.8. Click **Finish** to do so.

Figure 5.8 Completing the Firewall Generation Process in Firestarter

13.   The wizard will disappear, and you will see the Firestarter main interface, shown in Figure 5.9.

Figure 5.9 The Firestarter Main Interface

14.   The main interface defaults to the **Firewall hits** tab, which is a graphical logging device. If a packet matches the rules you have generated, it will be instantaneously logged here. From a remote system, generate some traffic that you have blocked. For example, if you have not enabled Telnet support, try to telnet to this system. After enough traffic is generated, you will see the logging screen fill up, as shown in Figure 5.10.

Figure 5.10 Viewing Logged Packet Matches in Firestarter

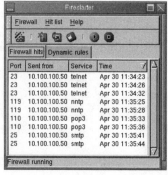

15. Now, select the **Dynamic Rules** tab. From here, you can add rules to those that Firestarter has automatically generated. It is important to understand that Firestarter imposes a fairly strict series of rules. You may need to open some ports to suit your needs. Following is a brief overview of your options:

- **Deny all connections from** Allows you to block a specific host. If, for example, you have left the SSH port open to all systems, you can specify a host or range of IP addresses here. As with any of the dynamic options, the rules you enter here will override any settings established by either Firestarter or the Firestarter wizard.

- **Allow all connections from** Enables you to allow a host or range of IP addresses full access to your system. Be careful when using this option, because it can expose your firewall to IP spoofing. Remember, it opens all ports on your interface to a remote system.

- **Open service to machine** Allows you to open a specific port or range of ports to a specific host or range of IP addresses.

- **Open service to anyone** Opens a port to all hosts on the network, and any other network. Like the **Allow all connections from** setting, this option is quite powerful, and can reduce your firewall's security. Specifying this option allows any host on your network or on any other to access the port you specify.

  You can also add and remove all rules in a particular group, or you can remove all of the dynamic rules you have created.

16. Right-click in the **Allow all connections from** field, and then select **Add new rule**. You will see a dialog box, shown in Figure 5.11, where you can enter either an IP address or a host name. Enter the IP address of a remote host here. Although you can enter a DNS name, it is best if you use an IP address. When you are finished, click **OK**.

Figure 5.11 The Add New Rule Dialog Box

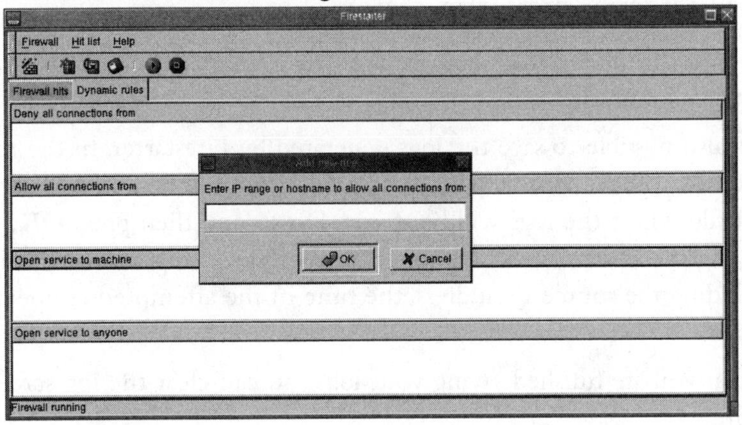

17. You will see that the IP address or host name (if this is what you entered) is entered in the **Allow all connections from** dialog box (Figure 5.12). Test this setting by using the remote client you have specified.

Figure 5.12 Allowing SSH and Telnet Service to a System Named "keats"

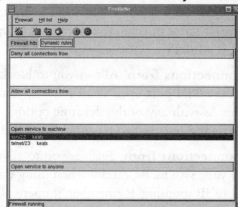

18. Experiment with the additional settings to see how well Firestarter is able to configure the interface to suit your needs.

     When you have configured Firestarter, open a second terminal and list the chains. If, for example, you are using Iptables, issue the following command:

     ```
     iptables -L
     ```

19. You will see a list of many different rules, most of which have been added by Firestarter. Consider that some of these rules may not be necessary for your particular situation. Use the **–D** option to delete the rules you do not need. Make sure you test your firewall each time you delete a rule.

20. When you are finished, use the **iptables-save** or **ipchains-save** command to save your rules:

     ```
     ipchains-save > firestarter.chains
     iptables-save > firestarter.chains
     ```

     You can then restore your firewall by using the **ipchains-restore** or **iptables-restore** command.

21. It is also possible to save the logs generated by Firestarter. In the main interface, go to **Hit List | Save firewall hit list to file**. You will be asked to enter the name of the text file where the logs will be stored. Do so, and then press **OK**. When you have saved the log file, open it in a text editor. You will see a report that details the connection, including the source IP address, the time of the attempted connection, and the protocol used.

22. When you are finished saving your log, you can clear the log screen and begin logging again.

Exercise: Using Advanced Firestarter Features

1. Go to **Firewall | Preferences** and examine the additional options offered by Firestarter. These include the ability for Firestarter to play a sound whenever a packet matches a rule, starting Firestarter "hidden," so that you do not see the interface, and, the most interesting feature, the one that shows every page in the configuration wizard. You can access this feature by selecting the **Advanced** icon, and then clicking **Show every page in wizard**.

2. When you have done this, restart the wizard. You will then be given additional options, including the ability to create masquerading rules, as shown in Figure 5.13, and the ability to create ToS associations, shown in Figure 5.14.

Figure 5.13 The IP Masquerade Configuration Screen

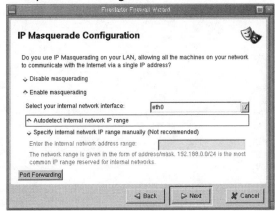

This particular page allows you to have Firestarter automatically discover the internal network IP range, which works rather sporadically. In addition, notice that you can also enable specific port forwarding rules. If you do not want to rely on the Autodetect feature, you can specify your own range.

Figure 5.14 The ToS Configuration Screen

The ToS configuration feature is effective if you want to give certain services, such as e-mail or the X Windows system, more priority than others have. In this particular example, the choice was made to give priority to server applications, such as FTP, Squid, SSH, SMTP, and POP3. You will, of course, choose the option that best suits you. You can choose these settings according to your needs.

3. When you are finished using the wizard, you can then re-edit your settings to create the best firewall for your situation.

Summary

In this chapter, you learned about IP forwarding, as well as masquerading and packet filtering. You then used Ipchains and Iptables to create firewall rules. The Iptables package supports packet masquerading and filtering functionality as found in the 2.3 kernel and later. This functionality is known as *netfilter*. Therefore, in order to use Iptables, you must recompile the kernel so that netfilter is installed, and you must install the Iptables package.

This chapter also showed you how to enable logging and ToS bits on network traffic, ands how to save, edit, and restore Ipchains and Iptables entries. You were provided with practical advice concerning commands to take, and saw how GUI and automated applications have been created to help build firewalls.

With this information, you now have all of the tools necessary to begin creating your own firewall using either Ipchains or Iptables.

Summary

## Chapter 6

Maintaining Open Source Firewalls

Best Damn Topics in this Chapter:

- **Testing Firewalls**

- **Using Telnet, Ipchains, Netcat, and SendIP to Probe Your Firewall**

- **Understanding Firewall Logging, Blocking, and Alert Options**

- **Obtaining Additional Firewall Logging Tools**

Introduction

Regardless of the type of firewall you deploy, you will have to test and maintain it carefully. You need to actively monitor your firewall so that you can discover scanning attacks, connection attempts, and general weaknesses. Of course, you will have to scan your firewall to ensure that all extraneous ports and daemons are closed. You can use a scanner such as Nessus (www.nessus.org) to do this. However, even an application such as Nessus cannot implement the specific attacks necessary to truly test your firewall. In this chapter, you will learn about how to properly test and log activity. You will be able to verify that the firewall is working, make intelligent changes on demand, and generate useful reports.

In this chapter, you will use applications such as Telnet, Netcat, and SendIP, and Nmap to query the firewall. Doing so will help you determine if your firewall is truly protecting your network. Just one accidental omission of a rule can open a hole that could allow a hacker into your network.

You may never know that a hacker has entered your network unless you carefully monitor your firewall logs. Doing so is sometimes an unglamorous, thankless job. However, using applications such as Firedaemon and fwlogwatch, both of which are profiled in this chapter, you can receive automatic alerts. fwlogwatch can even automatically reconfigure your firewall for you in case of a scanning attack. Even if you choose to not automatically block traffic, using the testing and logging tools discussed in this chapter you can maintain your firewall so that it is blocking and allowing the right traffic for your business.

Testing Firewalls

Before you can start logging access to your firewall, you need to ensure that you have configured it correctly. Even if you have extensive experience configuring firewalls, you will have to test your implementation when you first install it. In fact, experienced professionals know that they have to continually test a firewall to ensure that it is properly configured, and that its current configuration protects the network. It is not enough to just check or read the Ipchains/Iptables rules and then think that you have properly tested the firewall. You need to actively send packets and monitor your firewall and internal network to be sure.

Before you learn about applications that can help you test your firewall, you first need to consider some of the actual attacks, problems, and issues to look for. When testing your firewall, consider the following:

- **Internet Protocol (IP) spoofing** Many hackers outside of the firewall try to imitate internal network hosts in order to bypass authentication.

- **Open ports/daemons** Many firewalls and/or routers allow unnecessary ports to remain open, which can expose your firewall to threats unnecessarily.

- **Monitoring system hard drives, RAM, and processors** If your firewall runs out of disk space, or begins to run low on memory, your network may become incapacitated. Check your server's performance regularly using standard tools (*df*, *vmstat*, *top*, and so forth).

- **Suspicious users, logins, and login times** Even if you allow only interactive login at your firewall, monitor it carefully to determine who has logged on. It is vital that you know exactly who is controlling the flow of packets on your network.

- **Check the rules database** One of the common moves by a hacker is to alter the rules database in subtle ways that make it easier for the hacker to gain access to the network. Check your rules and compare them carefully to ensure that no unauthorized changes have occurred.

- **Verify connectivity** After you have configured or reconfigured your firewall, make sure that these changes do not cause problems for management and employees.

- **Remain informed concerning the operating system** Bugs may be discovered in the kernel and/or daemons that you are using. If you do not keep current concerning the tools you are using, you may end up exposing yourself to hackers.

- **Port scans** If you are relatively new to securing firewalls, you will be amazed to find out how many times your firewall will be scanned. Logging all scans can consume an unnecessary amount of hard drive space and processor time. Still, the proper amount of logging will help you remain informed and will help you document scans that may be preludes to an attack.

Following is a more detailed discussion concerning each of these issues.

IP Spoofing

Your firewall should not allow any packets to pass from outside the network into your internal network if the source address is the same as any host in your internal network. Suppose, for example, that your external network interface card (NIC) has the IP address of 128.1.2.3.4/16, and your internal NIC has the address of 192.168.1.0/24. You then need to find a way to test your firewall to see if any traffic is passing through the external interface from, say, the 192.168.1.1 IP address.

If such packets are able to traverse your firewall, then a hacker can configure his or her system to use your firewall as a default gateway and participate on your network. Leaving your packet-filtering firewall open to spoofing attacks largely obviates the reason for having a firewall, so you should take every step to test exactly what your firewall drops and allows. If you require, for example, your end users to have access to the World Wide Web, you will find that it is necessary to allow ephemeral ports (any port over 1023) to access the Internet. However, if you are using private IP addresses (for example, the 192.168.45.0 network), no system outside of the firewall should ever be able to assume this IP address and access your internal network's ephemeral ports.

Open Ports/Daemons

Your firewall should be as secure as possible. Disable all unused services and configure the used ones with security in mind. If you are running Squid or another proxy server on the firewall, make sure that only this port is open. Daemons such as Telnet, File Transfer Protocol (FTP), Hypertext Transfer Protocol (HTTP) and others should be shut down in almost all situations. In many situations, you may require the ability to remotely administer your firewall. Still, consider disabling all login to the outside interface.

In many situations, it is best to allow only interactive logins at your firewall. This way, you need only secure the firewall's physical security. If you must, use only a relatively secure login application, such as Secure Shell (SSH). You could also consider Kerberos, although this requires you to open several additional ports. Even using one-time passwords (OTP) at the firewall is a solution, although the use of OTP does not encrypt the data that subsequently passes from your system to the router. If you do need to leave certain ports open, be prepared to conduct regular scans of your firewall to test the daemons listening on these ports. As suggested earlier, applications such as Nessus (www.nessus.org) are ideal in this type of situation.

Monitoring System Hard Drives, RAM, and Processors

Firewall logs can consume hard drive space, especially in busy networks. If you configured your firewall to log both accepted incoming and outgoing access, you will find that your log files will grow very large in a short period of time. You may need to cut back on your log settings. However, if you cannot do this, regularly use the *df -h* command to discover the total amount of hard drive space you have left. You could, for example, create a simple crontab entry that sends you this information automatically every Monday at 8:05:

```
5  8  *  *  mon  df -h | mail -s "HDRIVE" jstanger@prosofttraining.com
```

Of course, keeping the cron daemon enabled on your firewall can present its own problems, because it will require you to ensure that this daemon is not subject to bugs that can cause a security problem. Any daemon, such as cron, that acts automatically can cause problems if misconfigured, so carefully review all default scripts, and you will be in good shape. It is an additional service, after all. You will have to make the decision yourself.

Following is a quick overview of standard Linux tools that can help you determine if your system is becoming overburdened:

- **vmstat** Informs you about the amount of random RAM and virtual RAM used on the system.

- **top** Used to inform you about the processes that occupy the largest percentage of CPU time. The busiest processes rise to the top of the display. The Gtop and Ktop applications, both available from www.rpmfind.net, are graphical versions that are somewhat easier to use than the original.

Suspicious Users, Logins, and Login Times

Use the *who* and *last* commands to learn about who has logged in to the firewall. In addition, manually check the /etc/passwd and /etc/shadow files to determine if any users have been added. An application such as Tripwire can be extremely helpful if you want to remain informed about any changes to such files.

Check the Rules Database

Determine if any unauthorized changes have been made to your database. When you first created your firewall, you should have created a backup using either the *ipchains-save* or *iptables-save* commands. Use the *diff* command to compare the two files to see if any changes have occurred. You can also use *md5* to generate fingerprints of the configuration files to see whether any unauthorized changes have been made to them.

Truly talented hackers are interested in entering a network and then controlling it without your knowledge. Accordingly, many will deactivate certain logging rules on your firewall, and then activate them again. If you leave the *ipchains* or *iptables* commands on your system, this will be very easy. To at least slow down the hacker, try removing these applications from the system. This way, the hacker will at least be forced to install these applications on your system before he or she can manipulate it. If you have Tripwire installed, you will then be informed of massive changes to the hard drive.

Verify Connectivity with Company Management and End Users

After you install and configure your firewall according to your security policy, check with various managers and employees to ensure that your firewall rules are working properly. You may have to further adjust your firewall to ensure that the right services are available to the company. You may have to inform people about certain services that are no longer available by design. Otherwise, you will receive help desk calls informing you that service has been interrupted.

Employee education is often necessary whenever you make any changes to the firewall. Otherwise, you will receive complaints that the network is "down," when in fact it is behaving according to your design. In order to cut down on ill will and employee frustration, find ways to carefully and tactfully inform employees concerning changes. Consider the following suggestions:

- Contact management and make sure that they understand and agree with the changes you are making.

- Many times, upper management will ask for certain changes and not quite understand how this will affect the end user. Decisions to cut off certain services (for example, Web traffic, or access to outside Post Office Protocol v3 [POP3] accounts) may negatively affect the company's ability to conduct business, or may cause unnecessary problems with employee morale. Make sure that upper management understands the ramifications of any suggestions they make.

- Warn employees before any changes to the security policy/firewall rules will occur.

- Remind employees that changes have occurred.

- Use e-mail, word of mouth, and employee area bulletin boards to remind people about changes.

Port Scans

Ipchains/Iptables-based firewalls are classic examples of packet-filtering firewalls. This type of firewall has traditionally been vulnerable to scanning attacks; they can simply allow scans to occur without informing anyone, because packet filters generally do not pay attention to Transmission Control Protocol (TCP)-based connections. They are interested, rather, in filtering out IP addresses and ports (they pay attention to the network layer of the Open System Interconnection Reference Model OSI/RM).

The introduction of log analysis software such as firelogd and Fwlogdaemon have made it possible to detect and block such scans, all the while sending an alert to the systems administrator. This type of software can help reduce a firewall's exposure to distributed denial-of-service (DDoS) attacks, because it helps the firewall completely drop certain hosts. However, this strategy introduces new problems, because it is possible for attackers to spoof source IP addresses and assume the identity of hosts you trust. The result is that hackers can use your own strategies against you and make your own software conduct a DoS attack against you by blocking your network from its own Domain Name System (DNS) servers, default gateways, and other hosts that you trust implicitly. However, most adjunct software, such as fwlogwatch, provides ways to exclude trusted hosts from being blocked. You will learn more about this later in this chapter.

NOTE

As long as unencrypted, non-IPsec versions of IPv4 remain the most commonly used version of IP, spoofing will remain a fact of life. If you find that spoofing attacks keep occurring against your network, you can take the following actions:

- Edit the configuration files of your log-watching software and increase thresholds to eliminate false positives.
- Carefully manage any Ipchains/Iptables entries created by your log-scanning software so that sensitive hosts are not blocked.

These strategies are ways that you can mitigate and manage spoofing attacks, as opposed to eliminating them, because until all systems use IPsec or move to IPv6, there is really no way to completely eliminate them. Even when IPsec and/or IPv6 become common, it is likely that hackers will find newer and cleverer ways to spoof these protocols as well.

Using Telnet, Ipchains, Netcat, and SendIP to Probe Your Firewall

Now that you understand what to look for, you can use the following tools to help you:

- **Rule checkers** Although Iptables does not support rule checking, the *ipchains -C* command allows you to check how your existing rule set operates. It will return information as to whether the packet is dropped or accepted. It is up to you to act on this information.

- **Port scanners** A simple port scan can help you determine which ports are left open on your firewall. Using applications such as Telnet and Netcat, you can then determine what daemon is listening behind that port.
- **Packet generators** Using applications such as SendIP, you can generate packets designed to test whether your firewall rules are working properly.

Following is a discussion of some tools that allow you to quickly test your firewall rules.

Ipchains

The *ipchains -C* option allows you to send packets to test whether the rules you have created work properly. Iptables does not have the equivalent, as of this writing. When checking Ipchains rules, you simply place *-C* (make sure you use the uppercase C) in front of the rule. The *—check* and *-C* options, by the way, are equivalent. You will be informed if the packet is blocked. For example, suppose you create the following rule in Ipchains:

```
ipchains -I input -i eth0 -s 0/0 -d 0/0 -p icmp -j DENY
```

To test this rule, you would issue the following command on the same system:

```
ipchains -C input -i eth0 -p icmp -s 0/0 1 -d 0/0 1
```

Ipchains will then inform you that the packet is denied. This tool is handy if you are logged in to the same system as you are testing, and you are becoming familiar with the existing rules and want to send out packets that test how the rules are working.

Telnet

More universal testing methods exist. The humble Telnet application is still useful when testing a firewall. Do not use it for logging on, however. You can use it to test whether a certain firewall rule is running the way you think it should. For example, suppose that you allow all access but that which is explicitly denied by a rule, and that you have configured the following firewall rule in Iptables:

```
iptables -A INPUT -i eth0 -s 0/0-p tcp --dport 80 -j LOG
iptables -A INPUT -i eth0 -s 0/0-p tcp --dport 80 -j REJECT
```

You can use your Telnet client to see whether it is working properly by specifying the port you are blocking and logging:

```
prompt$ telnet firewall.yournetwork.com 80
```

You can then view the log by using the *tail* command to read the file where your system stores kernel messages. For the sake of convenience, use tail's *–f* option so that you can view results as they happen:

```
tail -f /var/log/messages
```

Using Multiple Terminals

If you have logged in to the firewall interactively, it is often useful to open two terminals. You can use the first terminal to issue the *telnet* command, and you can use the second terminal to view the results in the /var/log/messages file. Remember that if you specify more complex logging options, and then send too many packets, the kernel will stop logging traffic after a certain period of time (three logging instances an hour, with only the first five packets logged). If you do not remember this, you may make the mistake of thinking that a certain rule is not working, when in fact it really is.

Netcat

You are not limited to using Telnet. Netcat is a great tool for socket creations, especially for firewall testing, which is available at http://freshmeat.net/redir/netcat/7041/url_tgz/nc110.tgz. Netcat is quite versatile, and is the self-described "Network Swiss Army Knife." Hackers and systems administrators alike use it as a tool to conduct scans, communicate with open ports, and even transfer information between hosts. Because it is so versatile, it can also be used against you, so if possible, you should install this application only on a client system, rather than on the router. This is because it can be used to open a back door on your system. Still, careful use of the application can allow you to quickly audit your firewall.

Used in the simplest way, Netcat is much like a Telnet client, because it can be used to access any remote host at any port. To connect to the host named firewall.yournetwork.com at port 80, you would issue the following command:

```
./nc firewall.yournetwork.com 80
```

You will then have to press **Ctrl-c** to exit the program. If the port is open, you can then enter any command you want. As far as port 80 is concerned, you can just enter some gibberish once a connection is made, and the Web server will return an error message, which usually includes the name of the Web server. Chances are, the port will not recognize your command, but for the purposes of testing a firewall, you usually want to just see if a port is open and listening. The *netcat -h* command provides a list of all available options, which are listed in Table 6.1 for your reference.

Table 6.1 Netcat Options

Option	Description
-i *value*	Tells Netcat to delay sending packets for a certain number of seconds. For example, to have Netcat wait five seconds between scanning ports, you would specify **–i 5**.
-n	Has Netcat report information using only IP addresses. This option is helpful when conducting ping scans, or if you do not have any DNS support.
-p *value*	A port spoofing option. Allows you to specify the port number of the packet being sent. For example, to have a packet appear as it were sent from port 53 of a host, you would enter **–p 53. –p.**

Continued

Table 6.1 Netcat Options

Option	Description
-r	Allows you to have Netcat scan ports at random, instead of simply one after the other.
-s *value*	Spoofs the source address of a packet. This option does not work on all systems, however.
-u	Netcat defaults to sending TCP packets. This option allows you to send User Datagram Protocol (UDP) packets, instead.
-v	Verbose mode. Reports additional information about the connections you are making. If you specify **-v** twice (**-v -v**), you will receive twice the amount of information.
-w *value*	Sets the time (in seconds) that Netcat will wait at a responding port. This option is often combined with **-z**.
-z	Called "zero-I/O mode," this option has Netcat forbid any i/o from the source system. If you do not use this option, Netcat will "hang" indefinitely at a port that responds. This option is mostly applicable when using Netcat as a scanner.
-l	Has Netcat open a listening port. Used with additional options, it is possible to bind a root shell to this listening portlisten mode, which can lead to security problems.

Sample Netcat Commands

To use Netcat in a more sophisticated and helpful way, you must use the following syntax:

```
nc [-options] hostname port[s] [ports]
```

For example, if you want to scan ports 1 through 1023 of your firewall and ensure that Netcat will not "hang" at any ports, you could issue the following command:

```
./nc -z -w 2 -v -v firewall.yournetwork.com 1-1023
```

The *-z* and *-w 2* options tell Netcat to not bind a port, and to wait only two seconds in case a connection is accidentally made. The two *-v* options place Netcat into ultra verbose mode. It is likely, though, that only certain groups of ports will be open on an unsecured firewall. For example, the following command scans only certain ports and groups of ports:

```
./nc -z -w 2 -v -v firewall.yournetwork.com 20-30, 53, 80, 100-112, 443,
    6000-6050
```

Analysis of Netcat Scan

The preceding scan searches for ports associated with several protocols, including:

- FTP (20 and 21)
- SSH (22)
- Telnet (23)

- DNS (53)
- WWW (both 80 and 443)
- X (ports in the 6000 range)

Figure 6.1 shows the results of a scan against a router that has left several ports open.

Figure 6.1 Scanning an Open Router

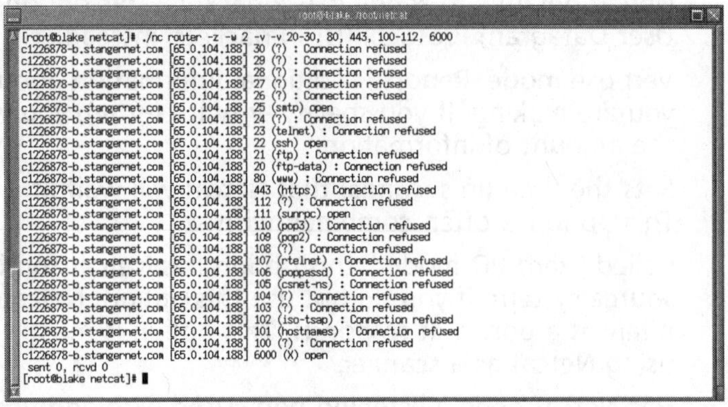

```
[root@blake netcat]# ./nc router -z -w 2 -v -v 20-30, 80, 443, 100-112, 6000
c1226878-b.stangernet.com [65.0.104.188] 30 (?) : Connection refused
c1226878-b.stangernet.com [65.0.104.188] 29 (?) : Connection refused
c1226878-b.stangernet.com [65.0.104.188] 28 (?) : Connection refused
c1226878-b.stangernet.com [65.0.104.188] 27 (?) : Connection refused
c1226878-b.stangernet.com [65.0.104.188] 26 (?) : Connection refused
c1226878-b.stangernet.com [65.0.104.188] 25 (smtp) open
c1226878-b.stangernet.com [65.0.104.188] 24 (?) : Connection refused
c1226878-b.stangernet.com [65.0.104.188] 23 (telnet) : Connection refused
c1226878-b.stangernet.com [65.0.104.188] 22 (ssh) open
c1226878-b.stangernet.com [65.0.104.188] 21 (ftp) : Connection refused
c1226878-b.stangernet.com [65.0.104.188] 20 (ftp-data) : Connection refused
c1226878-b.stangernet.com [65.0.104.188] 80 (www) : Connection refused
c1226878-b.stangernet.com [65.0.104.188] 443 (https) : Connection refused
c1226878-b.stangernet.com [65.0.104.188] 112 (?) : Connection refused
c1226878-b.stangernet.com [65.0.104.188] 111 (sunrpc) open
c1226878-b.stangernet.com [65.0.104.188] 110 (pop3) : Connection refused
c1226878-b.stangernet.com [65.0.104.188] 109 (pop2) : Connection refused
c1226878-b.stangernet.com [65.0.104.188] 108 (?) : Connection refused
c1226878-b.stangernet.com [65.0.104.188] 107 (rtelnet) : Connection refused
c1226878-b.stangernet.com [65.0.104.188] 106 (poppassd) : Connection refused
c1226878-b.stangernet.com [65.0.104.188] 105 (csnet-ns) : Connection refused
c1226878-b.stangernet.com [65.0.104.188] 104 (?) : Connection refused
c1226878-b.stangernet.com [65.0.104.188] 103 (?) : Connection refused
c1226878-b.stangernet.com [65.0.104.188] 102 (iso-tsap) : Connection refused
c1226878-b.stangernet.com [65.0.104.188] 101 (hostnames) : Connection refused
c1226878-b.stangernet.com [65.0.104.188] 100 (?) : Connection refused
c1226878-b.stangernet.com [65.0.104.188] 6000 (X) open
sent 0, rcvd 0
[root@blake netcat]#
```

This firewall, for example, still allows connections to Simple Mail Transfer Protocol (SMTP), the sunrpc portmapper service (port 111), and X. You can, of course, specify additional ports. For example, the ranges of 20 through 00 and 5900 through 7000 can reveal commonly used ports. Consult your /etc/services file for more ideas.

Additional Netcat Commands

When compiled properly, Netcat can also spoof IP addresses. If you want to spoof the source IP address, you would use the *-s* option:

```
./nc -s 10.100.100.1 -z -w 2 -v -v firewall.yournetwork.com 20-30, 53,
    80, 100-112, 443, 6000-6050
```

However, you should note that the *-s* option does not work well on some operating systems. Because Netcat defaults to TCP, you can use the *-u* option to send a UDP packet to a port:

UDP Scans

```
./nc -u -w 2 firewall.yournetwork.com 80, 443
```

You will have to press **Enter** twice to finish the command. Depending on the rules you have set (you will have to explicitly log UDP using either the *-l* option in Ipchains or the *-j LOG* target in Iptables), your firewall will log this traffic.

Testing Source Ports

If you have set a firewall rule to deny a particular source port, you can test it with Netcat. For example, if you have prohibited all hosts from accessing ports 1 through 1023 of an interface, you can test this by issuing the following command:

```
./nc -p 80 -w 2 -v -v firewall.yournetwork.com 1-1023
```

Testing DNS Connectivity

Many times, you will want to allow UDP and TCP access from and to port 53, in case a domain zone transfer needs to be made. To test whether this port is open, you would issue the following commands:

```
./nc -p 53 -w 2 -v -v firewall.yournetwork.com 53
./nc -u -p 53 -w 2 -v -v firewall.yournetwork.com 53
```

You can also scan a range of ports using Netcat. If, for example, you wanted to scan ports 1 through 1023, you would issue the following command:

```
./nc firewall firewall.yournetwork.com 1-1023
```

Additional Netcat Features

If you want to have Netcat open a shell and listen for inbound connections (this is definitely not recommended in most circumstances), you would use the following syntax:

```
nc -l -p port [-options] [hostname] [port]
```

In addition, Netcat ships with several scripts and applications. Some of these are geared toward the hacker community, while others offer quick solutions to common problems. Most of them are less practical than they are interesting. For example, if you want to test port redirection, you can use the webproxy and webrelay applications found in the scripts directory.

You can learn more about using Netcat in this way by reading the README file that comes with the source code. For those who are truly curious about using Netcat to open listening connections, a patch exists that allows you to authenticate and encrypt traffic that streams between versions of Netcat running on opposite servers. Called *aes-netcat*, you can download it from packetstorm.security.com and other sites.

Using Netcat

1. Create a new directory named netcat and change into it. This step is necessary, because the tarball will deposit many different files into the destination directory.

2. Obtain Netcat version 1.10 from http://freshmeat.net/redir/netcat/7041/url_tgz/nc110.tgz.

3. Once you have obtained Netcat and saved it to the netcat directory, untar and unzip it:

   ```
   tar -zxvf nc110.tgz
   ```

4. Most versions of Linux do well with the following compile option:

   ```
   make generic
   ```

   However, you may want to read the file named Makefile and see if your operating system is specifically listed.

5. Once you have compiled Netcat, the nc binary will be created in the present directory. Copy it to the /bin/ directory. Or, if you prefer, you can just leave it in the present directory and use **./** in front of the command while it is in the same directory. Now that Netcat is ready to be used, create several firewall rules that log port scans.

6. Open a terminal on your firewall and view the /var/log/messages file:

```
tail -f /var/log/messages
```

7. Now, conduct a sample portscan against your firewall:

```
./nc-w 2 -v -v firewall 1-1023
```

You can now use Netcat to conduct tests against your firewall.

SendIP: The Packet Forger

Although Netcat does have the ability to create some packets in certain instances, it is not a true packet generator. SendIP is designed to allow you to create packets of your own choosing. This practice is often called "arbitrary packet generation." SendIP allows you to create your own IP, Internet Control Message Protocol (ICMP), TCP, and UDP packets. For example, you can generate TCP packets with the FIN, ACK, and SYN bits set according to your testing needs. You can obtain SendIP from several sites, including www.earth.li/projectpurple/progs/sendip.html.

SendIP Syntax

Although there are many options, SendIP syntax is relatively straightforward:

```
sendip [hostname] -p <type> -d <data> <options>
```

SendIP Options

The *-p* option specifies the protocol you want to generate, and the *-d* option allows you to enter a random text string. The options, many of which are listed in Table 6.2, allow you to customize the contents of the packets you generate.

Table 6.2 SendIP Options

Option	Description
-p *value*	The option that determines which type of packet SendIP will create. Values include *ip, icmp, tcp,* and *udp*.
-is	Specifies a source IP address of your own choosing. By default, the "true" IP address of the local host is used.
-id	Specifies the destination IP address for the packet you are generating.
-ih	For customizing the length of the IP header.
-iy	Sets the Type of Service (ToS) field for the packet. Consult the previous chapter for values that you can enter. The default value is to leave all fields blank.
-il	Sets the length of the packet.

Continued

Table 6.2 SendIP Options

Option	Description
-it	Sets the Time-To-Live (TTL) for the packet you generate. The default value is 255 bytes.
-ip	Tells SendIP to create an IP packet.
-ct *value*	For generating ICMP packet types. The default is echo-request (8), but you can specify any other type by entering **-ct 03**, for example
-us	Specifies the source port for UDP packets. The default is the random port assigned to the packet when it is sent out.
-ud	The destination port of a UDP packet. You must specify a destination port.
-ts	Specifies the source port of a TCP packet. The default is the random port assigned to the packet when it is sent out.
-td	Sets the destination port for the TCP packet. You must specify a destination port.
-tn	Allows you to specify the TCP sequence number. By default, the number will be random.
-tfa	Sets the ACK bit on a TCP packet. By default, the value is not set, unless you use the -*ta* option along with -*tfa*. This is because an ACK packet is used to finish the process of tearing down a connection.
-ta	Allows you to request an acknowledgment packet, which is used to acknowledge that the TCP connection is ready to end.
-tfr	Creates a RESET packet.
-tfs	Alters the packet so that the SYN bit is set.
-tu	Creates a packet with the URGENT pointer set. This pointer begins the process of prioritizing traffic.
-tfu	Sets the URGENT bit in a TCP packet. The default is 0 unless you use the -*tu* option along with -*tfu*. For more information, consult RFC1122.
-tff	Sets the FIN bit.
-r	Randomizes all options. For example, if you specify IP as the protocol, the -*r* option automatically creates a random sending IP address.

The SendIP man page contains additional options. As you can see, SendIP allows you to forge any part of a TCP session, as well as any element of an IP, UDP, or ICMP packet. SendIP also allows you to forge all elements of IPv6 addresses, and also allows you to forge Routing Information Protocol (RIP) packets.

This tool is useful in regard to firewalls because it allows you to simulate any situation. The *ipchains -C* command has similar functionality. However, you can install SendIP anywhere, whereas many newer kernels do not support Ipchains. Besides, using SendIP, you can spend your time learning only one application.

Using SendIP to Probe a Firewall

1. The source files do not differ from the RPM. Download SendIP RPM from www.earth.li/projectpurple/progs/sendip.html.

2. As root, type the following:

```
rpm -ivh sendip-1.5-1.i386.rpm
```

3. Now that you have installed SendIP on this system, it will be known as the "attacking host." You are now going to use SendIP on this attacking host to check your firewall's ability to block spoofed packets coming in from the outside interface. To check your firewall's configuration, set up a machine outside of your firewall, and then give your firewall's IP address as the default gateway.

4. Suppose that you have only the internal networks of 192.168.2.0/24 and 10.100.100.0/24, and a simple Linux client using the IP address of 192.168.2.37. You want to test your firewall to see if spoofed traffic from outside the network can get through your firewall to your Linux client. To test this, configure a system on your internal network (say, with the IP address of 192.168.2.37) to use a packet sniffer such as Tcpdump or Ethereal to view all packets on the 192.168.2.0 network. This will be the internal host.

5. Put the NIC of the internal host into promiscuous mode so that it can capture the spoofed packet you are about to send. Hopefully, the spoofed packet won't get through.

6. Issue the following command from the attacking host to the internal host:

```
sendip 192.168.2.37 -p icmp -is 192.168.2.36
```

7. You have just issued a spoofing attack against your firewall and internal network. Now, stop your capture of packets on your internal host. Were you able to see an echo request from 192.168.2.36? Did the 192.168.2.37 system issue an echo reply? Did you see any DNS traffic that appears to be an attempt to resolve the 192.168.2.37 IP address? If you did, then review your spoofing rules. If you did not, chances are that you have properly configured anti-spoofing on your firewall.

Remember, if you are on a switched network, you will have to configure a packet sniffer on the victim host, and then ping that victim host directly. This is because a switched network does not use broadcasting as does a standard hub-based network.

8. If you have enabled logging for such packets, use the *tail -f* command on your firewall to see if the kernel records capturing the packet.

9. Now, try spoofing with another protocol:

```
sendip 192.168.2.37 -p tcp -ts 2 -td 80 -tn -is 192.168.2.36
```

This command sends a tcp packet with the source port of 2 to the 192.168.2.37 host at port 80. Your firewall should block this packet, because it should not allow packets to privileged ports (ports below 1023) to go into the internal network.

10. When you are reasonably sure that your firewall is blocking spoofed packets, issue the following command from your attacking host:

```
sendip 192.168.2.37 -p tcp -ts 2 -td 80 -tn -is 45.2.5.6
```

11. This command does much the same thing, but instead, it creates a packet that has a stronger chance of passing through your firewall. Why? Because this packet apparently originates from the 45.2.5.6 host, which is an IP address that could plausibly originate from the Internet. In addition, at least for the purposes of this exercise, this address does not exist inside your network. However, this packet should not be passed through, either, because it originates from a privileged port and is directed at a privileged port (80) on the destination. Finally, issue the following command:

```
sendip 192.168.2.37 -p tcp -ta 1 -ts 4356 -td 6450 -tn -is 45.2.5.6
```

12. Depending on your firewall configuration, this packet may be allowed to pass through. This is because the ACK bit has been set using the *-ta* option. As a result, the firewall rules may allow it through because it is part of an already-established session. In addition, notice that the source and destination ports are ephemeral, and not well known (below 1023). Consider using additional commands to further test your firewall. Make the necessary changes, without affecting the services that you want to provide.

NOTE

Applications such as SendIP and Netcat are often used in the hacker community. Take care that you do not allow all users on your network to access such applications. In fact, even using Telnet in the way shown previously is not recommended unless you own the systems you are scanning, or you have explicit permission from the operator of the system you are going to scan. Educate your IT personnel that they should use this software very carefully, and that they should never assume that they are allowed to scan or otherwise issue packets to a system that is not their responsibility.

To guard against illicit use of such applications, consider placing a note in your security policy to the effect that only certain users are allowed to access scanning and IP spoofing software for security auditing purposes.

Understanding Firewall Logging, Blocking, and Alert Options

You have already seen how you can check the kernel messages for log entries using the *tail –f /var/log/messages* command. However, more elegant ways to capture and view firewall logs exist. Third-party logging applications such as Firewall Log Daemon (firelogd) and fwlogwatch are available to help you sort and act on the information gathered by the firewall.

Firewall Log Daemon

firelogd (Firewall Log Daemon) is a relatively simple program that can either be run as an application or (you might have guessed) as a daemon. It does two things:

- It reads the kernel log entries and passes them into a "first in, first out" (FIFO) pipe, which firelogd can then process.

- Once its buffer is full, it e-mails a report of suspicious traffic to an account of your choosing. You can have it mailed to a local account, or to a remote system of your choice.

The application supports both Ipchains and Iptables. Older versions required you to edit the dmn.h file, and then use the *make* command to compile the application. Now, however, firelogd supports command-line arguments. You have various options, which are listed in the following sections.

Obtaining firelogd

You can download the most recent version of firelogd from http://rouxdoo.freeshell.org/dmn. The RPM file is best for Red Hat systems. As of this writing, the tarball format does not have any special features.

Syntax and Configuration Options

The syntax for using firelogd is as follows:

```
/usr/sbin/firelogd [-dmskh] [-b buffersize] [-e email] [-l log]
    [-t template] [-]
```

If you install firelogd using the available RPM, you can also start firelogd by using its startup script (/etc/rc.d/init.d/firelogd). You will have to edit this script to customize it if you want to change or add any of the options.

Commonly Used Options

Following is a list of the most often-used options.

- **Daemon mode** If used without any options at all, fwlogwatch runs as a simple application. The *-d* option has firelogd "fork off" and run as a daemon.

- **E-mail destination** The person who receives the e-mail messages. You can specify this either by using the *-e* option, or by editing the /etc/rc.d/init.d/firelogd script that comes with the RPM.

- **Log file** The location of the log file that firelogd reads from. On Red Hat Linux, for example, this is usually /var/log/messages. You can specify a log file by either using the *-l* option, or by modifying the /etc/rc.d/init.d/firelogd script.

- **Buffer size** Tells firelogd to wait for x number of entries before mailing them. The default is 10, which means a single e-mail will contain 10 entries. A value of 100 may be a more reasonable number. Using the default, you will receive dozens of e-mails in the case of a simple Nmap scanning attack. Experiment with these settings. If 100 gives you too little information about the nature of traffic at your firewall, then decrease the setting.

- **Template** firelogd allows you to customize the alert messages. You can have firelogd send you a great deal of information, or you can configure it to be as sparse as possible. The /etc/firelog.conf file contains the default template.

You can learn more about the additional options by consulting the firelogd man page.

Message Format

The e-mail message you receive will include multiple packet hits giving you the following information:

1. The date and time of the rejected or logged packet.

2. The name of the chain responsible for dropping or logging the packet.

3. The input interface.

4. The packet's TTL.

5. The IP of the firewall host and the number of the port to which the packet was sent (the destination port).

6. The origin of the IP address. Remember, it is possible to spoof IP addresses.

Here is an example of a default firelogd log entry:

```
01:28:37/May-5 ****S* TCP *D* REJECT/input-9 eth0 ***|***** ttl:64
badguy.hackerz.com -> hems(151)
128.37.08.43:4218 -> firewall.goodguys.com:151
```

Here is output from a more detailed example:

```
prompt# /usr/sbin/firelogd


LOG ENTRY:
April  5 09:53:37 firewall kernel: Packet log: input REJECT eth0 PROTO=6
    45.128.2.3:2748 128.1.2.3.4:3049 L=60 S=0x00 I=0 F=0x4000 T=64 SYN
    (#9)
CONTEXT INFORMATION:
  Time:   April 5 09:53:37
  Msg:    REJECT/input-9
  In:     eth0
  Out:
  Mac:


IP DATAGRAM INFORMATION:
```

```
Source:   45.128.2.3 badguy.badguy.com

Dest.:    128.1.2.3.4   firewall.goodguys.com

IPlen:   60

TOS:   TOS-0x00, PREC-0x00 -> ***|*****

TTL:   64

FRAG:   0x4000 -> *D*


ICMP SPECIFIC DATA:

  Type:

  Code:

  Info:

  Triggering Packet:


TCP SPECIFIC DATA:

  Window:

  Reserved Bits:

  Flags:   SYN -> ****S*


UDP SPECIFIC DATA:

  UDP Datagram length:


TCP/UDP SERVICE PORTS:

  Source Port: 2748(fjippol-polsvr) -> 3049(nsws)
```

In the preceding output, the attacking host's IP address is 45.128.2.3, and the firewall's IP address is 128.1.2.3.4. In this particular example, ICMP logging is not activated on the kernel. However, you can gather information about the nature of the attack by viewing the logs. This is an example of a simple, full TCP scan.

Customizing Messages

You can customize firelogd messages by editing the /etc/firelogd.conf file and changing the values to suit your own situation. The default file comes with several suggested templates, which are commented out by using the following two words:

```
startcomment
endcomment
```

firelogd will not read anything within these lines. firelogd contains three entries. The first, discussed previously, is moderately verbose. The second is described as a "one-liner," and gives information about the time of the scan, as well as the source and destination IP addresses and ports. The final option is quite verbose, informing you about the details of the connection. You can, of course, create your own entry using the syntax described in the /etc/firelogd file. For example, the following sample code records the source IP address and the destination port address, as well as the interface where the traffic occurred. The text "From the firewall at the company" acts as a header for the information.

```
tab From the firewall at the company. nl
tab srcip sp r_dstpt sp in sp
```

The tab, space, and nl entries create tabs, single space, and new lines, respectively. The char srcip field has firelogd inform you of the source IP address of the packet. The r_dspt field provides the destination port for the packet. Finally, the char in field has firelogd report the interface. You can, of course, specify your own text and other options. The /etc/firelog.conf file shows you all of the options. Figure 6.2 shows an example of the configuration file.

Figure 6.2 The /etc/firelog.conf File

> **NOTE**
>
> firelogd simply parses the log files generated by either Ipchains or Iptables. It does not generate the log files themselves. Therefore, you must have logging enabled through Iptables or Ipchains in order for firelogd to operate properly.

Reading Log Files Generated by Other Firewalls

You can read log files generated by other systems, as well. For example, if you downloaded the /var/log/messages file from a remote system, you can read it with the following command:

```
cat messages | firelogd -
```

The hyphen allows the application to read the command directly from standard input.

Configuring and Compiling firelogd

1. Obtain firelogd from http://rouxdoo.freeshell.org/dmn/. The RPM file is best for Red Hat systems. The tarball does not provide any special configuration options.

2. Install the RPM. Once you install the RPM, the firelogd will automatically begin running. Stop firelogd by issuing the following command:

   ```
   /etc/rc.d/init.d/firelogd stop
   ```

3. Issue the following command:

   ```
   /usr/sbin/firelogd
   ```

4. Use a port scanner such as Gnome Service Scan or Nmap to scan your firewall. Remember that the firewall must have logging enabled at the interface you are scanning.

5. You should see output on your screen. You will not receive any e-mail message, because you have not supplied any arguments.

6. Stop firelogd by pressing **CTRL + C**.

7. Now, prepare firelogd to run as a daemon. Make a copy of the /etc/rc.d/init.d/firelogd initialization script file and name it firelogd.bak. Edit the original so that the entries are as follows:

   ```
   QSIZE=30
   # Who is the administrator
   MAIL=your_address@yourcompany.com
   # Where is the output template
   ```

   You may have to adjust the QSIZE settings to fit your own situation.

8. Make a copy of the /etc/firelogd.conf in case anything goes wrong, and then edit the original file so that verbose logging is enabled. To do this, first comment out the default log entries, which are immediately below the text that reads "I like the look of the one below." Use the *startcomment* and *endcomment* keywords. Then, uncomment the entry that begins with the text that reads "This one is very verbose," and save the file.

9. Start firelogd:

   ```
   /etc/rc.d/init.d/firelogd start
   ```

10. Use Gnome ServiceScan or Nmap to conduct an attack that scans multiple ports of your firewall.

11. View the message using your e-mail client.

12. Re-edit the /etc/firelogd file and comment out the verbose entries and uncomment the entries that are beneath the text that reads "This one is a one-liner." This entry will send terse messages. If you want, set the QSIZE value to 100, which means that each e-mail

firelogd sends will have 100 entries in it. It also means that firelogd will not send you alerts as often; the larger the buffer value, the longer it will take to receive a message. Consequently, firelogd will be less responsive to attacks, and will not inform you as often. However, one longer message is likely easier to read than several shorter messages.

fwlogwatch

fwlogwatch, written by Boris Wesslowski, is a logging and reporting mechanism that also allows you to automatically block all traffic that is identified as an attack. Used in conjunction with firelogd, it helps create a system that continuously keeps you informed concerning port scans and other network events that surpass the thresholds you set. fwlogwatch is available at the CERT-RUS Web site (http://cert.uni-stuttgart.de/projects/fwlogwatch) and Wesslowski's personal Web site (www.kyb.uni-stuttgart.de/boris/software.shtml). It is available in both tarball and RPM format, and there is no significant difference between the two. Although fwlogwatch is similar to firelogd, it is far more versatile. You can configure fwlogwatch to do the following:

- Parse the firewall log file and generate user-friendly HTML reports, which you can read with any Web browser. fwlogwatch can read log files from any Ipchains or Iptables-enabled system, as well as Cisco firewalls and routers.

- E-mail an alert to you when suspicious activity occurs (for example, when numerous connection attempts—usually port scans—surpass the threshold you set in /etc/firelog-watch.config, the fwlogwatch configuration file). As with fwlogwatch, this option will work only on packets that you decide to log.

- Issue a Windows Messenger Service alert that creates a "pop up" message to a Windows NT or 2000 server of your choice.

- Deliver summary-based e-mail messages informing management of the scans that have occurred.

- Insert Ipchains or Iptables-based rules that block hosts from connecting to your firewall and/or internal network hosts.

- Execute custom-created commands. You can have fwlogwatch run any script that you want to create.

fwlogwatch Modes

fwlogwatch operates in one of three modes. Table 6.3 describes each.

Table 6.3 fwlogwatch Modes

Mode	Description
Realtime	fwlogwatch operates as a daemon and reads the kernel messages file (usually /var/log/messages), waiting for Ipchains/Iptables-generated packets to occur. When the packets surpass the threshold, fwlogwatch generates an alert. This mode is generally not for generating reports. Several Common Gateway Interface (CGI) scripts are available to help you generate HTML reports.
Interactive	Allows you to have fwlogwatch read the /var/log/messages file and issue e-mail messages to various destinations. To use this mode, you must uncomment various lines, such as at least one e-mail account, in fwlog-watch.conf (or whatever name you are using). The e-mail messages are formatted according to the information found in the /etc/fwlogwatch. template file. When you start fwlogwatch in interactive mode, it will parse the /var/log/messages file and then ask you if you want to send an e-mail message to your recipient.
Log Time	Has fwlogwatch inform you concerning the total number of entries in the /var/log/messages file. It also includes the first and last entries the kernel makes.

You can also manually generate HTML reports. You can generate the help menu, which shows all your command line options, by entering **fwlogwatch –h**.

You can also consult the fwlogwatch man page for additional details. This chapter will focus on generating reports and configuring fwlogwatch to send real-time alerts.

fwlogwatch Options and Generating Reports

Table 6.4 is a list of the more relevant options, if you choose not to use the /etc/fwlogwatch.config file.

Table 6.4 fwlogwatch Options

Option	Description
-c <file>	Allows you to specify your own configuration file. The default is /etc/fwlogwatch.config. If you leave this filename at its default, you will not be able to manually use fwlogwatch or use CGI scripts to generate automatic reports.
-f <file>	Allows you to read a different kernel log file, rather than the default of /var/log/messages.
-L	Has fwlogwatch give the time of the first and last log entry.
-l <time>	Allows you to specify only certain events in terms of time. Arguments to the -*l* option include seconds (s), hours (h), minutes (m), days (d), weeks (w), months (m), and years (y). The default is to not have any limit at all, which can result in huge HTML log entries. If, for example, you wanted to generate a log file for only the last two days, you would specify **-l 2** at the command line.
-n	Resolves host names in the log file. This can slow performance considerably.

Continued

Table 6.4 fwlogwatch Options

Option	Description
-v	Places fwlogwatch into verbose mode. Use it twice to obtain more information.
-z	Shows the amount of time between the start of a perceived attack and the end.
-m *value*	Has fwlogwatch ignore all identical packets that number less than the value. The result is that you will receive entries that have a higher uniqueness value. As far as alerting is concerned, you will probably want to ignore the receipt of multiple packets if they are of only one type. For example, if you want to ignore all identical packets unless the firewall receives 15 of them, you would specify -**m 15** in the command line.
-s, -d,	Informs you concerning the source and destination ports.
-t	If more than one of the same type of packet is logged, then show the start and end times that they entered the system.
-z	Show the total amount of time that elapses between a series of entries. The series is determined by the threshold.
-y	List all elements of the TCP session.
-p	Informs you concerning all logged protocols (TCP, ICMP, and so forth).
-o	Allows you to specify the location of an output file.
-w	Tells fwlogwatch that the output file should be in HTML.

Generating Reports

As of this writing, if the /etc/fwlogwatch.config file is present, the fwlogwatch binary automatically ignores any options you specify at the command line. This poses a problem, because if you want to manually generate a report, you need to specify command-line options.

> **NOTE**
>
> You will need to rename the /etc/fwlogwatch.conf file to some other name if you want to use fwlogwatch to generate HTML reports via CGI or cron.

To solve this problem, rename the /etc/fwlogwatch.config to /etc/fwlogwatch.config.alert. This way, you can still use this file to generate alerts, as discussed later, and still generate manual reports, when necessary. Although many different combinations are available to you, the following command is quite useful:

```
prompt$./fwlogwatch -v -v -s -d -t -z -y -n -p -w -l 2d -o firewall.html -f
/var/log/messages
     Resolving firewall-linux.goodguys.com
     Resolving 10.100.100.1.1 from cache
     Resolving 192.168.2.2 from cache
```

```
Resolving sl-gw8-sj-0-3.sprintlink.net
Resolving 217.0.54.100
Resolving pD9003664.dip.t-dialin.net
Resolving 192.168.2.2 from cache
Resolving 194.91.224.19
Resolving 10.46.247.251
Resolving pD9003664.dip.t-dialin.net
Resolving adsl-63-206-155-186.dsl.lsan03.pacbell.net
Resolving cpe-24-221-58-193.az.sprintbbd.net
Resolving www.cnn.com
Resolving www.abcnews.com from cache
```
prompt$

The preceding command has fwlogwatch read the –f /var/log/messages file and generate a report named firewall.html. The "Resolving . . ." lines indicate that fwlogwatch has found log entries and is finding the IP address or DNS name for the hosts. Notice that the preceding command reads the firewall entries for the last two days (*–l 2d*), and that it uses the *-w* option to generate an HTML file, instead of a plain text file. Figure 6.3 shows an example of the HTML file, which can be viewed with any Web browser.

Figure 6.3 Viewing an fwlogwatch HTML File

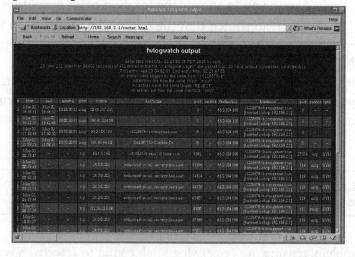

Using fwlogwatch manually is especially useful if you plan to view log file entries from a remote host, such as another Linux system or a Cisco router. You can obtain the log file, copy it to your home directory, and then issue the preceding command, specifying the log file you want to read.

As long as you have renamed the /etc/fwlogwatch.config file, you can use cron to have fwlogwatch automatically create HTML reports and place them in your Apache Server home directory (or any other properly aliased directory).

Generating an HTML-Based Firewall Log with fwlogwatch

1. Make sure that your system is using either Ipchains or Iptables to log packets.

2. Create a user and a group named bw. These groups are necessary to enable fwlogwatch to run additional processes as a nonroot user.

3. Install the fwlogwatch RPM or tar ball.

4. Rename the /etc/fwlogwatch.config file to /etc/fwlogwatch.config.alert.

5. Issue the following command to create a simple HTML report:

    ```
    fwlogwatch -v -v -s -d -t -z -y -n -p -w -l 2d -o firewallreport.html -f
    /var/log/messages
    ```

6. Open the firewallreport.html file in any browser. This report is, of course, portable, allowing anyone (even Windows users) to view it (see Figure 6.4).

Figure 6.4 Viewing a Report in Microsoft Internet Explorer

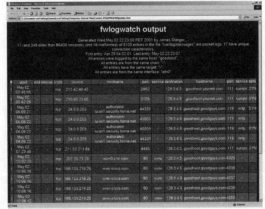

Automating fwlogwatch

Perhaps the most intriguing feature of fwlogwatch is its ability to automatically configure Ipchains/Iptables and issue alerts. The best way to do this is to edit the three configuration files to suit your needs. The three files you will use are:

- **/etc/fwlogwatch.config (or whatever you rename it to)** The primary configuration file. If you change this filename, then you must use the -c option to specify it when starting fwlogwatch.

- **/usr/sbin/fwlw_notify** A script that allows you to configure all alerting options, including where e-mail and Samba/Windows "pop up" messages will be sent. Do not confuse these options with the interactive options, which are mutually exclusive. In other words, if you want to have fwlogwatch send you alerts, do not configure the interactive mode, which will ask you if you want to send each report that fwlogwatch generates.

- **/usr/sbin/fwlw_respond** This script determines Ipchains and Iptables behavior. You do not have to edit this file.

The fwlogwatch Configuration File

You can customize all fwlogwatch features by editing the /etc/fwlogwatch.config file (or /etc/fwlogwatch.config.alert, if you have renamed it in order to use the manual option). Figure 6.5 shows the configuration file.

Figure 6.5 The fwlogwatch Configuration File

This file allows you to automatically invoke the options listed earlier in Table 6.4. For example, this file allows you to:

- Set verbose logging options.
- Create HTML files
- Customize the alert threshold.
- Specify a different input file from /var/log/messages.
- Exclude hosts and ports.
- Sort host, protocol, port, and IP entries in the HTML files, as well as configure the files to inform you concerning the time the packets were generated, and the duration of a perceived attack.
- Determine how much of the kernel log file to read (for example, only two minutes, three days, and so forth).
- Set realtime, interactive, and log times mode options.
- Create a proprietary Web server (not recommended).

If you change any of these values, you will have to restart fwlogwatch so that it rereads this file.

Setting the Alert Threshold in fwlogwatch.config

It is likely that you will have to experiment with the ideal alert threshold for your firewall. The default value is 10, and you may find it necessary to increase this value significantly (say, to 100) so that you are not overwhelmed by the data you generate.

Understand, however, that if you receive too much data, you may also need to adjust the logging in Iptables/Ipchains.

Excluding Hosts

fwlogwatch will monitor all entries that pass through the kernel log file (usually /var/log/messages). fwlogwatch will block any interface—including its own—that violates the alert threshold value. One of the features found in fwlogwatch is the ability to exclude certain IP addresses and address ranges from alerts and Ipchains/Iptables rules. This is necessary, because anyone with a port scanner that can spoof IP addresses can conduct a port scan on your firewall and specify an IP address important to your network. Such addresses might include the DNS and e-mail servers necessary to keep your business on a paying basis. It is possible to exclude these addresses from fwlogwatch by opening the configuration file and finding the following lines:

```
known_host =
known_host =
```

fwlogwatch allows you to get much more granular by using the additional entries shown here:

```
#exclude_src_host      =
#exclude_src_port      =
#exclude_dst_host      =
#exclude_dst_port      =
#include_src_host      =
#include_src_port      =
#include_dst_host      =
#include_dst_port      =
```

These entries allow you to exclude certain source and destination ports, as well as source and destination IP addresses.

Notification Options

To configure fwlogwatch to notify you about attacks, you must first edit the /etc/fwlogwatch.config file and uncomment the following values:

```
realtime_response
notify
```

Once these values are uncommented, and once you have restarted fwlogwatch, it will automatically call the /usr/sbin/fwlw_notify file. These files determine who will be informed, and what will be done, respectively. You will have to restart the fwlogwatch binary for these changes to take effect.

Thankfully, both the fwlw_notify and fwlw_respond files are even easier to understand than fwlogwatch.config. The /usr/sbin/fwlw_notify script, shown in Figure 6.6, allows you to determine who will receive notification messages, and allows you to determine how this notification will occur.

Figure 6.6 The /usr/sbin/fwlw_notify File

E-Mail Settings

All you have to do is uncomment the lines for any function you want to enable. Then, enter your own e-mail address in the EMAIL= field. The default setting is for fwlogwatch to send e-mail to root@localhost. If you are happy with this setting, you don't have to edit this line. The next entry to edit determines the actual contents of the e-mail message. By default, the message will contain the following information:

- Number of packets (as indicated by the $1 value)
- The source IP address (as indicated by the $2 value)
- The destination IP address (as indicated by the $2 value)

You can, of course, edit any aspect of the e-mail configuration settings. If, for example, you want to change the subject heading, edit the quoted line after the –s field. Just make sure that you retain the quotation marks, as they allow you to enter multiple words into one subject line. Figure 6.7 shows an example of an e-mail alert.

Figure 6.7 Viewing E-Mail Alerts Generated by fwlogwatch

Note that Figure 6.7 actually shows two e-mail messages. The first e-mail message is a result of a log entry that blocks and logs all ICMP traffic. The second message has been generated at the same time. It is an alert informing the systems administrator that the loopback interface (127.0.0.1) has generated an attack. As a result, the loopback interface will be added to the Iptables fwlw user-defined chain, and no traffic will be allowed to pass through it. In many cases, this is not a problem, although it is a false positive. This systems administrator needs to add a rule excluding the local host being blocked.

Windows Pop-Up Messages

fwlogwatch uses the smbclient application to send messages to remote Windows hosts. All you have to do is uncomment and edit the SMBHOST= line so that a message is sent to a real host, and then uncomment the next line so that a message is sent. For example, to send a pop-up message to a host named *sandi*, you would change the SMBHOST= entry and uncomment the following line:

```
SMBHOST=sandi
/bin/echo "fwlogwatch ALERT on $HOSTNAME: $1 packet(s) from $2" |
    /usr/bin/smbclient -M $SMBHOST
```

You can alter the second line at will. Read the script for additional values to enter. For example, if you want to be informed of the protocol, you could use the $4 value.

This file also supports the creation of custom log entries through the use of the *logger* command, as well as the creation of a custom log file. fwlogwatch also allows you to create your own alerting options. If, for example, your Linux system has a paging application installed, you can have your message sent directly to you. Figure 6.8 shows an example of a pop-up message received by a Windows 2000 Advanced Server system.

Figure 6.8 A Windows 2000 Advanced Server "Pop Up" Message

Response Options

To configure fwlogwatch to actually respond to attacks, edit the /etc/fwlogwatch.config file and uncomment the following values:

```
realtime_response
respond
```

Then, restart fwlogwatch. The /usr/sbin/fwlw_respond file is straightforward. As with /usr/sbin/fwlw_notify, you can edit this file to enter custom commands. You can, for example, have this script load additional scripts and applications that can reconfigure the local system, as well as remote systems (see Figure 6.9).

Figure 6.9 The fwlw_Respond File

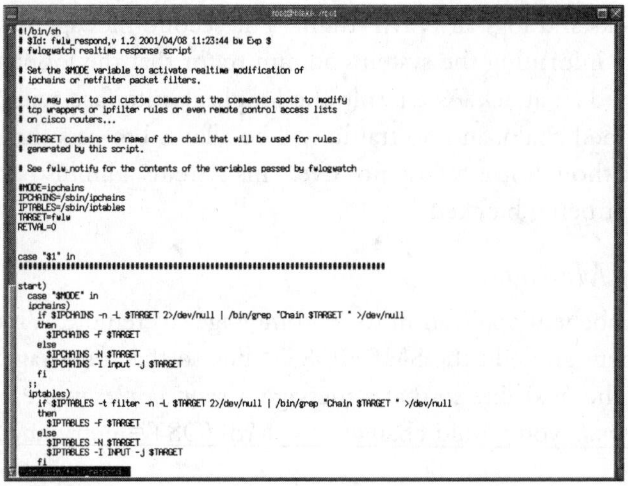

```
#!/bin/sh
# $Id: fwlw_respond.v 1.2 2001/04/08 11:23:44 bw Exp $
# fwlogwatch realtime response script

# Set the $MODE variable to activate realtime modification of
# ipchains or netfilter packet filters.

# You may want to add custom commands at the commented spots to modify
# tcp wrappers or ipfilter rules or even remote control access lists
# on cisco routers...

# $TARGET contains the name of the chain that will be used for rules
# generated by this script.

# See fwlw_notify for the contents of the variables passed by fwlogwatch

$MODE=ipchains
IPCHAINS=/sbin/ipchains
IPTABLES=/sbin/iptables
TARGET=fwlw
RETVAL=0

case "$1" in
########################################################################
start)
    case "$MODE" in
    ipchains)
        if $IPCHAINS -n -L $TARGET 2>/dev/null | /bin/grep "Chain $TARGET " >/dev/null
        then
            $IPCHAINS -F $TARGET
        else
            $IPCHAINS -N $TARGET
            $IPCHAINS -I input -j $TARGET
        fi
        ;;
    iptables)
        if $IPTABLES -t filter -n -L $TARGET 2>/dev/null | /bin/grep "Chain $TARGET " >/dev/null
        then
            $IPTABLES -F $TARGET
        else
            $IPTABLES -N $TARGET
            $IPTABLES -I INPUT -j $TARGET
        fi
```

How Hosts Are Blocked

By default, fwlogwatch creates a user-defined Ipchains or Iptables entry for the specific table and/or chain receiving the traffic. You can, of course, edit the script to alter this behavior, although it works quite efficiently as written.

fwlogwatch and Root Privileges

Real-time response is protected. Only root can initiate fwlogwatch to use Ipchains/Iptables blockings or e-mail and Samba-based alerts. Once initiated, fwlogwatch will then run as the user bw. However, if you only require fwlogwatch to generate reports, you do not need to run it as root. You must still ensure that fwlogwatch can read the /var/log/messages file. You can do this by placing the user who will execute fwlogwatch in the same group as the log file.

> **NOTE**
>
> In regard to fwlogwatch, alerting and reporting are always two separate things. Do not be surprised that the e-mail message you receive is quite terse. You will learn how to automate reports using CGI scripts later in this chapter.

> **NOTE**
>
> In order to send pop-up messages, your system must have the samba-client package installed. If you are using RPM, the following command will tell you if you have the samba-client package installed:
>
>   rpm -qa | grep samba
>
> Otherwise, search for the smbclient application. The Samba server is not necessary, and should not be activated at your firewall.

Configuring fwlogwatch to Send Automatic Alerts and Block Users

1. Make sure that you have Iptables/Ipchains entries that your kernel can log. You must have either the –l or –j LOG entries activated on at least one rule.

2. If you have not already, rename your /etc/fwlogwatch.config file to /etc/fwlogwatch.config.alert. The file named /etc/fwlogwatch.config should no longer exist.

    If you do not do this, you will not be able to issue command-line options, nor will you be able to issue alerts.

3. Edit the /etc/fwlogwatch.config.alert file and adjust the following parameters:

    ■ Enable verbose logging by simply uncommenting both lines that read verbose.

    ■ Uncomment the resolve option.

    ■ Enable the times and duration options. The former gives the times of the connections, while the latter gives the entire duration of the session.

    ■ Uncomment the known_host lines, and enter the IP addresses of your DNS and e-mail servers, as well as others that you do not want to block.

    ■ Enable the html line so that the daemon generates HTML pages.

    ■ Uncomment the recent value and change it from three days (3d) to one day (1d).

    ■ Uncomment the at_least value to 10 may have to change lower.

    ■ Enable and change the alert_threshold setting to 15.

    ■ Activate the notify and respond values by simply uncommenting them.

4. Edit the /usr/sbin/fwlw_notify file and adjust the following parameters:

    ■ Activate the e-mail and Samba settings.

    ■ Enter an e-mail address that you can check.

    ■ In the Samba settings, alter the HOST=line so that fwlogwatch sends a message to the correct system. Make sure that your Windows NT/2000 system is configured to receive messages.

5. Review the /usr/sbin/fwlw_respond file, but do not make any changes unless you have a very good idea of what to do.

6. Start fwlogwatch, making sure you tell it where the configuration file is:

```
/usr/sbin/fwlogwatch -c /etc/fwlogwatch.config.alert
```

7. Now, using Nmap or Gnome ServiceScan, conduct a scan of your firewall so that your activity matches some of the Ipchains/Iptables rules you have created.

8. You will receive e-mail and Samba "pop up" messages informing you that activity has surpassed established thresholds.

Using fwlogwatch with CGI Scripts

fwlogwatch ships with two CGI scripts that, with minor modifications, can allow you to check your logs via a Web server. Although it is often important to shut down all services, activating Apache Web Server may be a useful and relatively safe exception to this rule. If you have installed the scripts using the RPMP, you can obtain the raw scripts in the /usr/share/doc/fwlogwatch-0.3/ directory. If you have installed the files using a tarball, they will be in the source directory.

The first CGI script is quite simple. It creates an HTML page and tells fwlogwatch to place all of the events that have occurred within the last hour inside of it. With some modifications, it can create an HTML file in your Apache Server directory (see Figure 6.10).

Figure 6.10 The fwlogsummary.small.cgi File

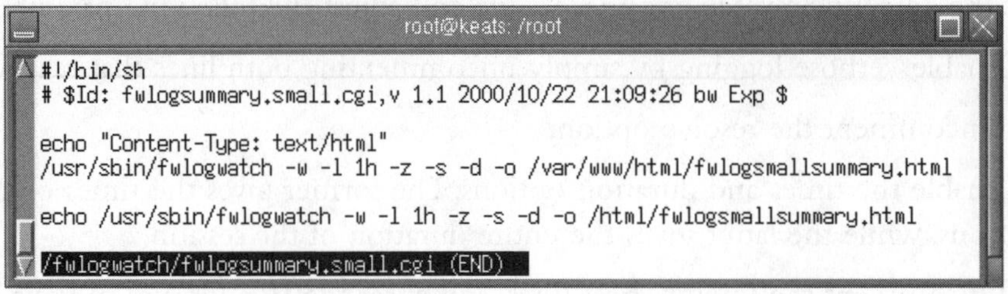

```
root@keats: /root                               □ ⊠

#!/bin/sh
# $Id: fwlogsummary.small.cgi,v 1.1 2000/10/22 21:09:26 bw Exp $

echo "Content-Type: text/html"
/usr/sbin/fwlogwatch -w -l 1h -z -s -d -o /var/www/html/fwlogsmallsummary.html

echo /usr/sbin/fwlogwatch -w -l 1h -z -s -d -o /html/fwlogsmallsummary.html

/fwlogwatch/fwlogsummary.small.cgi (END)
```

This file first has the command echoed so that if it is run by cron, a message will be sent to the systems administrator via e-mail, informing him or her that the command has been executed. The actual command is shown here:

```
/usr/sbin/fwlogwatch -w -l 1h -z -s -d -o /var/www/html/fwlogsmallsummary.html
```

You can, of course, alter this script as you wish. For example, if your Web server's HTML directory is located at /home/httpd/html/, you can edit the file accordingly. If you want to have a more verbose log entry, you can specify -v -v. However, this file is meant specifically for a quick rundown of the last hour's traffic.

To automate this file, place the script in the /etc/cron.hourly directory, or create the following crontab owned by root:

```
1 * * * * /fwlogsummary/fwlogsummary.small.cgi
```

When this script executes, you will be able to view the HTML file, as long as you have activated Apache Server (see Figure 6.11).

Figure 6.11 Viewing the Results of the fwlogsummary.small.cgi Script

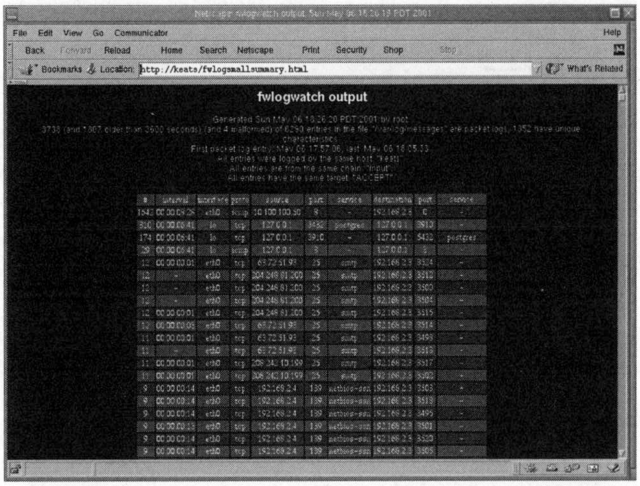

Obtaining More Information

For a more detailed view of the file, use the fwlogsummary.cgi file. Before you use this file, however, edit it so that it has the following characteristics:

- The file should point to a directory supported by your Web server. As of this writing, the fwlogsummary.cgi file defaults to using the /home/httpd/html/ directory, so make sure you specify the correct directory for your Web server. Red Hat 7.1 uses the /var/www/html/ directory, so create a subdirectory named /var/www/html/fwlogdaemon/. Or, you can create an entirely different directory and use an alias. It is up to you. It is important, however, that you create a dedicated directory, because the fwlogsummary.cgi script will create several files inside of it. The most important file is index.html, which contains several links that allow you to view all log entries as defined by the $RECENT value (the default, which you can change, is one hour).

- The file should specify the full path of the fwlogwatch binary.

- Remove the line that reads <a href="/cgi-bin/fwlogwatch.cgi">Regenerate summaries now</a>. As of this writing, this feature is not yet supported sufficiently. The edited file is shown in Figure 6.12.

Figure 6.12 The fwlogsummary.cgi File

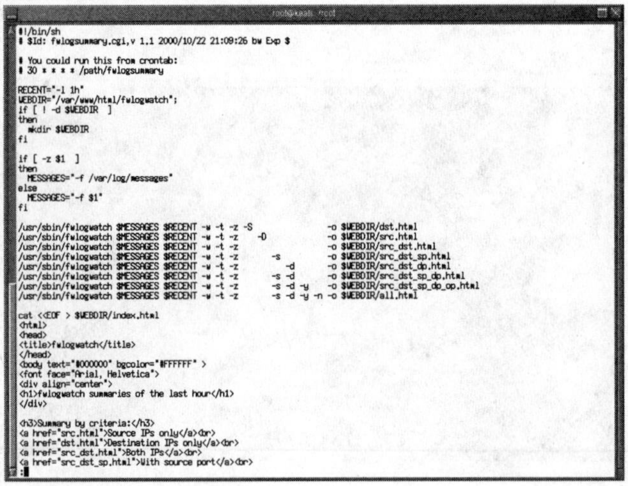

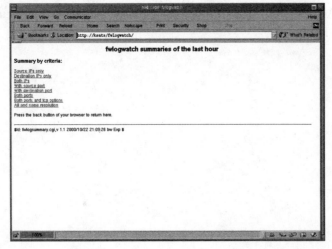

You can make additional trivial changes, such as altering the colors used in the HTML file. Once you have edited the file to your liking, you can place a script in the /etc/cron.hourly file, or create a crontab similar to the one discussed for the fwlogsummary.small.cgi script.

```
1 * * * * /fwlogsummary/fwlogsummary.cgi
```

Viewing the Results

Once you have edited the necessary files, created the necessary directories, and started the daemons (Apache Server and cron), you can use your Web browser to view the index.html file generated by fwlogwatch.cgi. You will have to specify a directory or alias, but you will not have to specify a filename, because most Web servers present index.html by default. Thus, if your firewall Web server's root directory for HTML pages is /var/www/html/, and you have created a directory named /var/www/html/fwlogwatch/, then you would enter the following URL: http://firewall.goodguys. com/fwlogwatch. Figure 6.13 shows an example for the system named "keats."

Figure 6.13 Viewing the Index Page Generated by fwlogsummary.cgi

If you click on the **All and name resolution** link, for example, you will see a report summary similar to that shown in Figure 6.14.

Figure 6.14 Viewing the All and Name Resolution Page

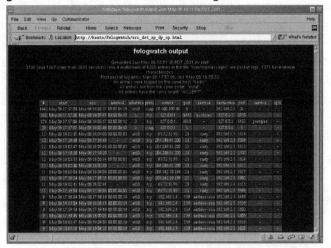

You will see that this particular HTML page is similar to the results of the Fwlogsummary.small.cgi file, except that you will see more hosts listed. The additional links will help you determine what has happened at your firewall.

> **NOTE**
>
> When you capture traffic using the Linux Netscape browser, you may find that it will "hang" for some time before rendering the HTML. You may have to wait for a few minutes to see the Fwlog output. At other times, you may find that the browser has crashed. Lynx, a text-based Web browser, and Windows-based browsers usually do not exhibit this behavior.

Using cron and fwlogwatch CGI Scripts to Generate an Automatic HTML Report

1. Create the /fwlogsummary directory. This directory will hold your CGI scripts.

2. Find and copy the fwlogsummary.small.cgi and fwlogsummary.cgi scripts to the /fwlogsummary directory.

3. Find the directory that contains your Web server's HTML documents. Create a new subdirectory off this directory named fwlogwatch. This directory will contain all of the files generated by the fwlogsummary.cgi file.

4. Create another subdirectory off your Web server's HTML document directory named fwlogwatchshort. This directory will contain the results of the fwlogsummary.small.cgi script.

5. Edit the fwlogsummary.small.cgi and fwlogsummary.cgi scripts so that they reflect your environment. For example, make sure that the both scripts refer to the fwlogwatch subdirectory. The fwlogsummary.small.cgi script should specify the fwlogsmallsummary.html file as an output file. This file should go into the fwlogwatchshort directory. Be especially careful to edit the fwlogsummary.cgi file so that it refers to the correct Web server directory, and that it no longer has the <a href="/cgi-bin/fwlogwatch.cgi">Regenerate summaries now</a> link. Read earlier in this chapter for more details.

6. Now, create crontab entries for each script. Make sure that you specify the correct path of the CGI scripts. For example, if you have created the /fwlogsummary directory, you would create the following crontab entries:

```
1 * * * * /fwlogsummary/fwlogsummary.small.cgi
1 * * * * /fwlogsummary/fwlogsummary.cgi
```

You can create these entries by issuing the following command as root:

```
crontab -e
```

You can also create scripts in the /etc/cron.hourly directory, if you wish.

7. Now, after 30 minutes, you will see that these scripts have generated several files. Point your Web browser to your firewall's /fwlogsummary subdirectory, and view the links generated by the fwlogsummary.cgi script.

8. For a more succinct description of the last hour's activities, point your browser at the /fwlogwatchshort directory. You will have to specify the fwlogsmallsummary.html file, because it is doubtful that your Web browser uses this as a default document. If you want, you can edit the CGI script to create an index.html file. For the purposes of this exercise, a different name was used to eliminate confusion with the /fwlogsummary directory.

9. Finally, consider the following options:

   ■ If you are using Apache Server, use .htaccess files and htpasswd so that this information is password protected.

   ■ Further secure this directory with Secure Sockets Layer (SSL). You can learn about enabling SSL support with Apache Server at www.openssl.org.

Additional fwlogwatch Features

fwlogwatch contains the following features not discussed in this chapter:

- **Sorting** By editing the /etc/fwlogwatch.conf file, you can determine which events are listed first. This is a very useful feature, which allows you to emphasize information that it is important to you.

- **Web server** The Web server offered by fwlogwatch is not as robust as Apache Server, nor is it as well documented. It is advised that you use Apache Server if you want to use CGI at all.

Obtaining Additional Firewall Logging Tools

Table 6.5 contains an all-too-brief discussion of additional tools available to you.

Table 6.5 Additional Logging Tools

Tool	Description
Ipchains logger	A logging enhancer similar to Fwlogd, but limited to Ipchains. It is especially strong in its ability to log masqueraded connections. Its home page is at http://ipchainslog.sourceforge.net.
LogGrep	This daemon uses the grep utility to read and sort log files. It is limited, as of this writing, to Ipchains. With this utility, you can sort protocol, date, IP port firewall log entries to generate custom log files. Currently, it can also discover port scans, and generate HTML pages. The project's home page is at http://loggrep. sourceforge.net/.
Open Correlation	Although this project has not produced any files as of this writing, this project hopes to create an all-purpose logging daemon that can scan as many different types of log files as possible. Although it is dangerous to mention the word *universal* when discussing anything concerning Linux, this promises to be a helpful tool. The project's home page is at http://sourceforge.net/ projects/opencorrelation/.
Fwlogsum	This application generates HTML-based reports. The developers aim to create a logging utility that is powerful, yet easy to configure. HTML reports are meant to emulate those created by the popular, commercial Check Point FW-1 log firewall. The project's home page is at http://fwlogsum.sourceforge.net/.
IP Firewall Accounting (IPFA)	This logging software is meant to enhance IP accounting log information. It allows you to gather the following information: ■ Per month protocol usage ■ User monitoring, as long as identd is enabled on client hosts ■ Binding of IP addresses to MAC addresses

Continued

Table 6.5 Additional Logging Tools

Tool	Description
	You can obtain this software at www.tucows.com, or at http://linuxberg.eunet.fi/conhtml/adm_firewall.html.
Appsend	An application similar to SendIP. However, this application also allows you to simulate additional attacks, such as SYN floods and additional denial-of-service (DoS) attacks. http://www.tucows.com, or at http://linuxberg.eunet.fi/conhtml/adnload/58289_31510.html.
Ipmeter	IPmeter monitors network usage, and is designed to help you bill clients for usage. It generates HTML reports with embedded graphics. You can download it at www.ipmeter.com.
Mrtg	A traffic load monitor that generates HTML reports with embedded graphics. Similar to IPmeter, Mrtg is intended as a network management and monitoring tool, but it can also be very helpful as a security tool, because network management and security management concerns and tools are closely related. You can obtain Mrtg at www.mrtg.org, or at http://ee-staff.ethz.ch/~oetiker/webtools/mrtg/.
Ntop	Ntop is a powerful tool that allows you to identify the nature of all egress and ingress traffic. The latest version is available at www.ntop.org. It is much like the standard top application, in that it gathers information about hosts, and then places the most active hosts at the top of the display. It can be run on a terminal just like the standard top application; you can run it in Web server mode, or as a Web server. This mode supports authentication, thus it allows you to easily limit access to only specific users.

Summary

This chapter focused on ways for you to gain information from your firewall and take action. You read about ways that you can make your firewall aware of port scans, and enhance its reporting and blocking capacity.

It is vital that you make it as easy as possible to read your firewall log files and respond to new threats. Although the premier reason to create a firewall is to selectively allow traffic in and out of a network, the second most important benefit of a firewall is its ability to log traffic. In this chapter, you learned how to test your firewall by conducting limited attacks against it. You also learned how to remain informed concerning scanning attacks and others designed to crash your firewall. You now have the tools and skills required to receive automatic alerts, and have your firewall automatically drop connections to scanning hosts.

It is vital that you maintain your firewall, and with the tools presented in this chapter, you can gather the information required to maintain it intelligently. You now can receive informative alerts, and comprehensive information concerning your firewall. In regard to logging, both firelogd and fwlogwatch can be used together to create a comprehensive information system. Of course, new tools are being developed all the time, and you should work to remain informed about new projects, as well as updates to the tools presented in this chapter.

## Chapter 7

Configuring Solaris as a Secure Router and Firewall

Best Damn Topics in this Chapter:

- Configuring Solaris as a Secure Router

- Routing IP Version 6

- IPV 6 Hosts

- Configuring Solaris as a Firewall

Introduction

With its foundations in Berkley Software Distribution (BSD) UNIX, Solaris—much like its predecessors—is a multifaceted operating system. It is perfectly suited to running on a 124-processor E15000 that acts as the foundation of a multinational banking firm or reproducing seismographs of the earthquakes along the San Andreas fault over the last 10,000 years within the period of a few minutes, but its performance and reliability as a secure router, secure gateway, and firewall are equally valuable. Although it will not outperform a hardware-based solution such as a Cisco router or a NetScreen firewall, it does offer reliable, stable service. Solaris is the operating system of choice for many commercial packages that provide firewall services.

Our first exposure to using Solaris for such a task was at a small Internet service provider (ISP) in eastern North Carolina. In the first year of operation, the ISP had anticipated no more than 1000 clients from the small coastal town. The end of the year came—with a total of 7000 clients, new service offerings in five additional towns along the Carolina coast, and lots of problems. Not only was this growth not anticipated; worse yet, it wasn't budgeted. Faced with the problem of an internal network and server pool both in need of access control, we faced the dilemma of making do with what we had. This type of dilemma often inspires the kind of panic that proves the resourcefulness of systems administrators.

In this chapter, we first examine the use of Solaris as a secure router and gateway. Next, we look at using Solaris as an Internet firewall, and we discuss using host-based firewalls on Solaris. Finally, we talk about guarding Internet access. We highlight the reasons for using Solaris for these types of tasks and talk about some of the security implications involved with using the OS in each scenario. We also examine implementations of these types and discuss some of the steps required in implementation.

Configuring Solaris as a Secure Router

To differentiate between a host and router, let's first define the functions of each. A *host* is typically a system with any number of interfaces that may or may not be connected on the same network. A host does not allow traffic to enter in one interface and out another. A typical server in a high-availability configuration has multiple interfaces, with each interface connected to a different network segment to prevent a single point of failure.

A *router* is a system with a minimum of two interfaces connected to at least two segments of different networks. The router allows traffic to reach its destination by entering one interface and passing out through another. An *interface* is loosely defined as a physical connection that allows other systems to communicate with the system via Ethernet, serial port, point-to-point link, or some other method. We will not get into a discussion of how the decision is made for the traffic to reach its destination; that issue is outside the scope of this chapter. A good reference on traffic routing and TCP/IP is *TCP/IP Illustrated, Volume 1: The Protocols*, by W. Richard Stevens.

Reasoning and Rationale

Let's attempt to answer the inevitable question, "Why use Solaris?" There are numerous platforms and designs available to use as a low-cost router, all of which are viable solutions. Some key factors in selecting one over others are the availability of hardware, the amount of time allotted to deploy the solution, and business needs. Solaris is a good choice as a router because it is stable, easily secured, and easily deployed.

Solaris is a stable operating system, capable of months and even years of continuous uptime without the need for rebooting. Solaris is scalable, able to run in both small and large environments on systems from workstation size to enterprise class. Additionally, Solaris is an easily secured operating system. The ability to shut down all services on the system, make configuration changes to a running kernel, and create multiple layers and access control on the system without bouncing the system make Solaris the perfect choice for a network with a 110-percent uptime requirement.

Finally, Solaris is easily deployed as a router or gateway. The stock install of Solaris provides connectivity between the divided portions of the same network or even different networks altogether by simply turning up the system with the interfaces configured to communicate with connected networks. This feature of simplicity is a double-edged sword. It can lead to easily deploying a system to perform the important job of routing network traffic. It can also result in an unintended and unrestricted path between two networks that could be exploited to leverage an attack.

Routing Conditions

In a default installation, Solaris routes traffic if a specific set of conditions are met:

- The system has at least two interfaces.
- The /etc directory contains at least two hostname.interface files that configure the interfaces when the system is booted.
- The stock /etc/r2.d/S69inet file exists.

The first condition refers to any two interfaces and is not limited by a difference in types of card, such as one 10Base card and one 100Base card, or types, such as Ethernet and point-to-point. The second condition refers to the hostname.interface file. For example, in the case of the previously mentioned cards, one hostname.le0 file and one hostname.hme0 file would represent the 10Mbit, or le0 interface, and the 100Mbit, or hme0 card.

The third condition refers to the init file executed when the system enters run-level 2. This is important because it's common for a systems administrator to make alterations to the S69inet script in an effort to secure the system. If a system is to be used as a router, it is recommended that an initial install be performed on the system to ensure the integrity of the machine. If such an install is not possible, it is at least recommended that these two scripts be replaced with known unaltered copies or those verified against the Solaris Fingerprint Database. We discuss using new installs and existing installs as routers later in this chapter.

When the system bootstraps, it first executes the script /etc/rcS.d/S30network.sh. This script is responsible for configuring the loopback and other interfaces. It brings up any interfaces on the system that have a hostname.interface file in /etc. When the system enters run-level 2, it executes the S69inet script, which handles all the necessary functions of bringing up network connectivity. This script is designed to bring up a system with multiple network configuration options. However, here we review only the details pertinent to our discussion.

The S30network.sh Script

To get a better understanding of how network connectivity is initialized on a system, let's first look at the S30network.sh script internals. The S30network.sh is an inode-level link to the master script network, located in /etc/init.d. This script is the preliminary phase of network initialization. It is executed early in the bootstrap process to service the needs of any other systems that might be relying on the host to provide some service. Diskless clients are an example of such hosts.

Let's look at some of the snippets of code from this script. Typically, a host that is going to act as a router does not rely on things such as DHCP or NIS, because these are added risks and could result in a higher probability of vulnerability exposure and potential compromise. This could allow an attacker to compromise the Achilles' heel of a network. Therefore, we examine the sections of code that are pertinent to our discussion. Suffice it to say that a router should not rely on other systems for anything.

In our first sample from the script, we have the following code on line 22:

```
/sbin/ifconfig lo0 plumb 127.0.0.1 up 2>&1 >/dev/null
```

This command is responsible for bringing up the loopback interface when the system bootstraps. This is the first initialization of an interface by the system. Shortly thereafter, we have this piece of code beginning on line 71:

```
interface_names="'echo /etc/hostname.*[0-9] 2>/dev/null'"
if [ "$interface_names" != "/etc/hostname.*[0-9]" ]; then
```

This section of code begins the parsing of hostname.interface files, putting them into the $interface_names environment variable. The interface name is placed into environment variable $1 later, and on line 106 the interface is plumbed:

```
/sbin/ifconfig $1 plumb
```

Finally, when line 123 of the script is reached, the interfaces are configured by the following code:

```
/sbin/ifconfig $1 inet $ifcmds \
    2>&1 >/dev/null
```

When this script completes, all network interfaces with a hostname.interface configuration file in the /etc directory are configured and ready for communication. The system completes its execution of the init scripts in the /etc/rcS.d directory and, under normal circumstances, continues to multiuser mode. The init program moves on to /etc/rc2.d and eventually executes S69inet, which begins the second phase of network initialization.

The S69inet Script

S69inet is executed by init when the system reaches run-level 2, or multiuser mode. S69inet is an inode link to master configuration file /etc/init.d/inetinit. At this stage, the necessary routing functions are configured, and if a machine is configured with two or more interfaces, the system begins routing traffic between interfaces. If this is the intended configuration, this can be a good thing. However, if the system's intention is to function as a multihomed host in a high-availability configuration, this configuration can have unexpected results.

To get a better understanding of why Solaris automatically routes traffic when two interfaces are present, let's look at some of the code in the S69inet script. We'll look only at the code pertinent to our discussion. On line 93, we have the following block:

```
if [ "$_INIT_NET_STRATEGY" = "dhcp" ] && [ -n "'/sbin/dhcpinfo Router'" ]; then
        defrouters=`/sbin/dhcpinfo Router`
elif [ -f /etc/defaultrouter ]; then
        defrouters='/usr/bin/grep -v \^\# /etc/defaultrouter | \
             /usr/bin/awk '{print $1}''
        if [ -n "$defrouters" ]; then
```

This code first checks DHCP for routing information. If the system does not return routing information from the program dhcpinfo, it next checks for the existence of the file /etc/defaultrouter, which is used for static default route entries. The last line in the block checks the variable *$defrouters* for a nonzero value. If the variable length is greater than zero, some further checking of routing information is performed. If the check on the last line of the block yields a nonzero value, the system sets the default routes contained in /etc/defaultrouter on line 124. Otherwise, it flushes the routing table. If neither of the first two tests is true, the script sets the *$defrouters* variable to a null value.

The decision of whether to run the system as an IPv4 router is made on line 186. The script first checks for the existence of the /etc/notrouter file. Following this check, the script checks the configured interfaces to count the number that were configured via DHCP. The script then checks for a number of interfaces greater than two (loopback plus one interface) or if any point-to-point interfaces are configured. Finally, the script checks to see if the /etc/gateways file exists. If:

- The /etc/notrouter file does not exist, the number of interfaces configured by DHCP is equal to zero, and the number of interfaces configured, including the loopback device, is greater than two

- There are one or more point-to-point connections, or

- The /etc/gateways file exists

the script executes ndd to manipulate the IP kernel module and sets the *ip_forwarding* variable to 1. The script then launches in.routed and forces in.routed to supply routing information. The in.rdisc daemon is started next, launched in router mode. Otherwise, *ip_forwarding* is set to 0, in.rdisc is launched in solicitation mode to discover routers on the network, and in.routed is launched in quiet mode.

Configuring for Routing

A default installation of Solaris with more than two interfaces (including the loopback interface) that aren't configured by DHCP will route traffic by default. This process, of course, depends on the system having not been altered by administrative staff. In some situations, however, it might be impossible to reinstall an operating system on a machine that will be routing traffic. In this situation, we need to be able to configure the system to route traffic manually.

Let's walk through a check of an already configured and functioning system to ensure that it's ready to route traffic. First, we make a list of items to check and, if necessary, alter. We'll do this in step-by-step fashion, in order to pay due attention to detail and ensure that we don't miss a step that could result in failure of our objective. Following the step-by-step account, we briefly discuss each step and any possible caveats.

A Seven-Point Checklist

Here's our checklist:

1. Check for interfaces configured via DHCP.
2. Ensure that each interface to be configured has a corresponding hostname.interface file in /etc and that the contents of the files are valid.
3. Check the /etc/rcS.d/S30network.sh file (inode link to /etc/init.d/network) for signs of alteration.
4. Check the /etc/rc2.d/S69inet file (inode link to /etc/init.d/inetinit).
5. Check for the /etc/notrouter file, and if it exists, remove it.
6. After the system has booted, poll /dev/ip for the status of the ip_forwarding variable.
7. Test the system in an isolated environment to ensure traffic routing.

Each step is covered in more detail in the following sections.

Step 1: Check for Interfaces Configured via DHCP

In the first step, we verify that all the interfaces are being configured with static information. As previously mentioned, a system using interfaces configured by DHCP will not be configured as a router. The easiest way to check for this configuration is by using the *ifconfig* command on a running system and then examining the output. Using the *all* flag with *ifconfig* typically displays the pertinent information, as we see in Figure 7.1.

Figure 7.1 A hme0 Interface That Has Been Configured with DHCP

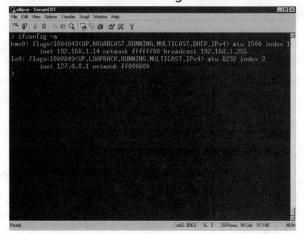

Step 2: Ensure Each Interface Has Corresponding File

Ensure that each interface to be configured has a corresponding hostname.interface file in /etc and that the contents of the files are valid. It is necessary to have a hostname.interface file for each interface to be configured when the system is bootstrapped. A nonexistent hostname.interface file will result in a nonexistent interface. Similarly, an incorrectly formatted hostname.interface file will result in an incorrectly configured interface.

For each interface to be configured by the system, create a hostname.interface file. For example, if there were two 100Mbit interfaces on a system, there would have to be a hostname.hme0 and hostname.hme1 file in the /etc directory. The device names can be discovered by reviewing the output of command, as we see in Figure 7.2.

Figure 7.2 Browsing dmesg for Interfaces Detected during Bootstrap

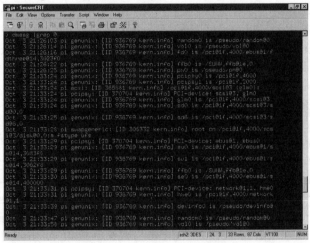

Ensure that the hostname.interface files contain one of two things: an IP address or a host name with an entry in the /etc/hosts file. In a standard configuration, the host name is placed in the hostname.interface file with an entry for the host name in the /etc/hosts file. When the system boots, it resolves this host name against the /etc/hosts file and configures the interface with the corresponding IP address. Although it's possible to place an IP address directly in the hostname.interface file, it is recommended that, for consistency, you follow the standard procedure. The file must contain either an IP address or a host name; it can't contain both.

Steps 3 and 4: Check the /etc/rcS.d/S30network.sh and /etc/rc2.d/S69inet Files

Check the /etc/rcS.d/S30network.sh file (inode link to /etc/init.d/network) for signs of alteration. In addition, check the /etc/rc2.d/S69inet file (inode link to /etc/init.d/inetinit). It is common practice for a systems administrator to alter boot scripts in order to create a more secure system. This practice can lead to problems for those who inherit such a system, however, because problems can occur that are not immediately traceable. Two scripts commonly modified are the /etc/rcS.d/S30network.sh and /etc/rc2.d/S69inet scripts.

Often, documents that discuss the hardening of systems instruct administrators to alter these files and change or comment out sections of code to create a more secure configuration. Some automated system-hardening tools alter these scripts as well. These scenarios can result in unpredictable behavior and abundant frustration when a system's mission and configuration change.

In the third and fourth steps, we verify the integrity of these two files. We can do this via one of three methods. The first method, and the most unreliable one, is to visually inspect the file for signs of alteration by using an editor and examining the change time of the file. The second and more reliable method is to compare the file against a known unaltered copy of the file. The third and most secure method is to compare the file md5 sum of the file against the known sum in the Sun Fingerprints Database. When in doubt, restore from the CD-ROM.

Step 5: Check for the /etc/notrouter File and, If It Exists, Remove It

Check for the /etc/notrouter file; if it exists, remove it. The /etc/notrouter file is used to keep the system from being configured as a router. A typical system on which this file will exist is a correctly configured multihomed host. This file is not created by default, nor is there a configuration option in the install process to create it. Therefore, a freshly installed system will not have this file and so this situation won't be a concern. However, you should manually check previously installed hosts. If this file exists, remove it.

Step 6: Poll /dev/ip for the Status of the ip_forwarding Variable

After the system bootstrap, poll /dev/ip for the status of the *ip_forwarding* variable. The system will not route traffic if IP forwarding is not turned on. Therefore, after you've taken the previous configuration steps, reboot the system, and the *ip_forwarding* variable of the IP kernel module will be polled to ensure that the system is prepared to route traffic. The result is a Boolean. If the variable returns 1, the configuration was successful and the system is ready to route traffic. If the variable returns 0, there was an error somewhere in procedure and the system will not route traffic.

Step 7: Test the System

Test the system in an isolated environment to ensure traffic routing. In the final step, testing should be conducted to ensure that the system is functional. A private, isolated segment of network should be created to test the router's functionality and ensure proper configuration, reliability, and performance.

Security Optimization

A number of parameters associated with TCP/IP on a Solaris system can be modified to provide enhanced security. The configuration of ARP, IP, TCP, UDP, and ICMP in their default state might not provide the greatest level of security. For the sake of brevity, we don't delve deeply into this topic nor discuss it in brief. This would not do the topic justice. This topic has been covered comprehensively in a document, "Solaris Operating Environment Network Settings for Security," by Keith Watson and Alex Noordergraaf of Sun Microsystems Blueprints. Their documents are available from Sun Blueprints at www.sun.com/blueprints.

Security Implications

You don't have a hope of security or integrity for your network without first having a secure router. Therefore, the implementation of a system as a router must be secure by design. This consideration must be made at the very beginning of system design and observed diligently through deployment and afterward in maintenance. The intricacies of designing a secure router are covered in detail elsewhere in this book. Here we give some general guidelines to enhance security. From these guidelines, we'll repeat the minimalism mantra.

Minimal Installation

A secure router should include a minimal, functional installation of the operating system. However, this is more a management issue than a security issue. Simply put, smaller software installations make machines that are more easily managed and monitored for intrusion.

A system with a smaller installation is more easily managed because only the necessary pieces are in place. What constitutes *necessary* is the software to achieve your mission and business needs. A system with a minimal installation also removes a number of unnecessary services and makes it easier to monitor the system for intrusion.

There are two camps on the types of software that should be installed on a system. One side is against having a C compiler on the system; the other is for it. Neither side is right or wrong, but both have valid lines of reasoning to take into account.

The side against an accessible local C compiler fears a local user compiling exploits or other programs and using the system for unauthorized activities. Such violations could lead to a local user gaining elevated privileges or unauthorized network access. The other side of the argument believes that having a C compiler on the local system is a necessary utility. Without a C compiler, they believe, it's impossible to build programs from source.

We're happy to announce that we're proud members of both camps. We're against local users having unlimited free reign of a system through some goody built with a C compiler, but not against having the C compiler. This risk can be eliminated through proper permissions and access control such as RBAC or simple access control lists (ACLs).

Minimal Services

A router needs very little in terms of services. Since the system has one purpose, there isn't a necessity for things such as NFS, NIS, RPC, and sendmail. By eliminating these services, you enhance overall system performance.

Additionally, eliminating these services closes entry points for possible intruders. By limiting the channels that allow an intruder potential access to the system, we've mitigated the risk of opening a system to future compromise by a new vulnerability. Shutting down all services or using the system solely as a router isn't always possible. This is, however, the recommended practice.

Many of these services are started via the Internet daemon (inetd). Commenting out the services is a good practice. Commenting out the services and not starting inetd at all is the best methodology. The inetd is started in the /etc/rc2.d/S69inet script.

Another good practice is checking the rc directories in /etc for programs that might be started. For example, the rc3.d directory starts a number of services that, in addition to being unnecessary, also have a history of security risks. Services such as the NFS server and the DMI compatibility programs are started at run-level 3.

If you are interested we urge you to check out the article *Back to the Basics: Solaris and init* available at www.securityfocus.com/infocus/1359. This document describes the services started on a stock install of Solaris and where they're started. Through the ps and netstat programs, it's possible to narrow down the majority of undesired services and disable them. If the use of these programs fails to yield the port number on which a particular service is running, the lsof utility can be a saving grace.

Minimal Users

A Solaris system is a multiuser system. However, a router should not be a multiuser system. Giving general users access to a system through which the traffic of the entire network flows is not only dangerous, it's reckless. Shell access to the router should be limited to administrative staff and strictly regulated. A router shouldn't bring unnecessary attention to itself by handling e-mail or other such services. It's unnecessary to state that the system is critical.

Minimal Dynamic Information

One feature that can turn into a problem on any network is dynamic information. Such information includes routing protocols, name services, and the like. These services are designed to make network management easier, but the design of such services often isn't the most secure.

A router should be limited in the amount of dynamic information on which it relies. Solaris routers typically start the in.routed and in.rdisc daemons when launching and gain routing information through UDP and ICMP. With any service that relies on dynamic data updates, it's possible to generate fictitious data and send it to the host, which could result in a denial-of-service (DoS) or other attack. Therefore, it is a best practice to eliminate all services on the router that rely on dynamic data, including in.rdisc and in.routed.

Minimal Cleartext Communication

One final note on minimalism: It is a best practice to communicate with this system using the minimal amount of cleartext possible. Although we can build the most armored host on Earth and surround it with armed guards, if we're communicating with the system via a channel that can be intercepted by a potential intruder, our efforts are in vain.

The best policy is to use one of the available implementations of the Secure Shell (SSH) protocol. If you want to add other means of communication and administration to the system, such as a Web-based configuration interface or perhaps a Web-based intrusion detection log analyzer, do so via a cryptographically secure channel. Any services that provide remote interactive communication are vulnerable to sniffing or connection hijacking. The only way to ensure communication integrity is via cryptography.

Unconfiguring Solaris Routing

We previously discussed the process of configuring Solaris as a router. We talked about some of the caveats involved with configuration and implementation. We also discussed the steps necessary to make Solaris function as a router from a default install as well as a previously implemented install.

In this section, we take a look at taking a Solaris router and returning it to host stage. As always, it's a best practice to do an initial install on a system before changing the system's purpose and mission. However, this isn't always an option. We discussed in a step-by-step scenario the process of changing an existing system to a router. In this section, we discuss in a step-by-step list of procedures the process of changing a system from a router to a multihomed host.

A Three-Point Checklist

Let's look at the steps necessary to ensure that the system isn't routing traffic. As we did previously, we create a step-by-step list of procedures to configure and check the system. We follow the list with a brief discussion of the steps:

1.   Check for the /etc/notrouter file. If it does not exist, create it.

2.   Check the value of *ip_forwarding* in the IP kernel module after the system has been rebooted.

3.   Test the system by attempting to reach one interface of the system through the other.

Each step in this checklist is covered in further detail in the sections that follow.

Step 1: Check for the /etc/notrouter File

Check for the /etc/notrouter file. If it does not exist, create it. As previously mentioned, the system checks a number of things when booting and before making the determination that it will be a router. When /etc/rc2.d/S69inet executes, it tests for the existence of the /etc/notrouter file. If this file is not found, it acts as a router. However, if this file is found, it acts as a host. You can create this file by simply using the *touch* command.

Step 2: Check the Value of ip_forwarding

Check the value of *ip_forwarding* in the IP kernel module after the system has been rebooted. After the /etc/notrouter file has been created and the system has been rebooted, check the *ip_forwarding* variable. As /etc/rc2.d/S69inet executes and discovers the notrouter file, the code that sets the *ip_forwarding* variable to 1 should not execute.

Step 3: Test the System

Test the system by attempting to reach one interface of the system through the other. The purpose of this test is to confirm that one interface on the system is not reachable via the other interface. In a typical multihomed host configuration, the system has at least two interfaces connected to different segments of network and incapable of communicating with one another without first sending traffic to a router. You can perform this test using one of any number of network debugging tools. One way to run the test is to use the source-routing functionality of the traceroute program.

In this example, we see that traceroute is executed on Solaris machine, and the traffic is directed at another Solaris machine with two interfaces. The –*g* flag specifies the IP to use as a gateway, which is the Solaris system with two interfaces. The end point is the other interface of the system. A successful configuration of a multihomed host results in the failure of this test.

Routing IP Version 6

Beginning with versions distributed from February 2000 and later, Solaris 8 is IP version 6 capable. It is not possible to configure Solaris 8 as a solely IPv6 system from the installation menu. It is possible, however, to configure an interface to communicate with any IPv6 host on the network and still retain IPv4 communications. This process is known as *running a dual stack*. A Solaris system can be configured to run strictly IPv6 by removing the hostname.interface file, although this configuration could cause problems when communicating with IPv4 hosts that do not currently support IPv6. This makes it possible for Solaris to function in any IPv6 environment as a host, gateway, or router.

In this section, we discuss setting up a Solaris IPv6 router. We talk about the file configurations necessary to make IPv6 functional. We also discuss the programs necessary to IPv6. However, we do not discuss the protocol, since there are better documents that do so. It is recommended that a user interested in setting up IPv6 for the first time reference the appropriate RFCs.

Configuration Files

Putting everything in place to make IPv6 functional on a Solaris 8 system is relatively easy. One prerequisite is having the system to route traffic configured for regular IPv4 traffic. Once we have completed the steps for configuring an IPv4 router, we can proceed with the setup of an IPv6. In this section, we talk about the files necessary to get an IPv6 router working. These files include the hostname6.interface file, the ndpd.conf file, and the ipnodes file.

The hostname6.interface File

This file is similar to the previously discussed hostname.interface for IPv4. The syntax of items contained in the hostname6.interface file is different from that of the IPv4 version, however.

Previously, the only thing needed in this file was either an IP address or a host name with an entry in the /etc/hosts directory. Now additional parameters must be entered in the hostname6.interface file. These parameters are parsed by the S30network.sh script in /etc/rcS.d when the system boots and are then passed to ifconfig. In the following example, we see a hostname6.interface entry for our IPv6 router:

```
addif sturgeon.mydomain.com/64 up
```

The first parameter we see is *addif*. The *addif* parameter is an extension of the Solaris *ifconfig* command, which tells *ifconfig* to add the address to the next available interface. Since we are seeing this file in the /etc/hostname6.hme0 file, *ifconfig* searches the interface table for the next available virtual interface on the hme0 device. The address resolving to sturgeon.mydomain.com will be configured to this interface. At the end of the line, we see the *up* command, which makes the interface network accessible. As we can see in Figure 7.3, this address was configured to the hme0:1 device.

As we can see, the address is now configured with the ROUTER flag and is ready to handle traffic from other hosts. However, additional configuration steps have been taken prior the interface being brought up. We'll talk about these steps shortly, in addition to the configuration steps necessary for *ifconfig* to resolve the address for sturgeon.

Figure 7.3 A Configured IPv6 Address Attached to the hme0:1 Interface after a Reboot

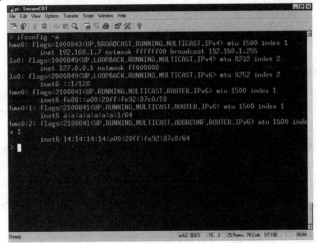

One subtle point we have not mentioned is that we're configuring this interface with a static address. There is a good reason to do so. With IPv6, it's possible to autoconfigure hosts when they boot. These systems poll the network during bootstrap to get information necessary to communicate with the rest of the network. If we do this with a router, we're forced to remember that the link-local address in.ndpd assigns to the interface at bootstrap. This address is usually easily remembered because it's typically composed of our network information and the Media Access Control (MAC) address of the interface. Whether or not we configure Solaris 8 with a static IPv6 address, the link-local address is configured by design.

In most cases, it is much easier to remember an address we've specifically assigned to the system. If there is ever a problem on the network, we'll know the address we have given to the router. This knowledge makes the router a little more accessible, a little easier to remember, and a little easier to name with a host name. This process does not take into account DNS, which will be mentioned later.

The ndpd.conf File

The ndpd.conf file is the configuration file for the in.ndpd program, or the Internet Network Discovery Protocol Daemon. This configuration file is supposed to reside in the /etc/inet directory and is read by the daemon when it is launched by the S69inet script when the system enters run-level 2, typically during the bootstrap process. It is worth mentioning that the ndpd.conf file does not exist by default. To understand why this configuration file is significant, we should talk about the in.ndpd program and the purpose it serves.

The in.ndpd program, when implemented on a router, must be configured to act as a router for the IPv6 network. This configuration involves making some entries in ndpd.conf to make the daemon the known router for the network. When other systems bootstrap and send a request for routing information via Neighbor Discovery Protocol, in.ndpd responds as the router for the network.

Minimal configuration of ndpd.conf that provides IPv6 functionality on a Solaris system consists of the following two entries:

```
ifdefault AdvSendAdvertisements true
prefix 0A:0A:0A:0A:0A:0A:0A:0/64 hme0
```

To understand these entries, let's examine them in a little more detail. On the first line, we see the *ifdefault* command. The *ifdefault* and *if* commands are used to set interface configuration parameters. The *ifdefault* command must precede any *if* commands, because *ifdefault* is used to specify any default operations of the interface.

The next variable we see is the *AdvSendAdvertisements* parameter. This parameter designates whether or not the system will function as an IPv6 router. By default, this option is set to *false* on systems, which causes in.ndpd to run in host mode. When *AdvSendAdvertisements* is set to *true*, in.ndpd initiates itself as a router on the interface on which it is being configured to operate, sending periodic router advertisements via multicast and responding to router solicitations.

On the next line, we see the *prefix* entry. The *prefix* command controls the configuration variables for each prefix, or network. There is also a *prefixdefault* variable, which is similar to the *prefix* variable, except that the *prefixdefault* variable specifies configuration parameters for all prefixes. The *prefixdefault* variables must precede any prefix variables in ndpd.conf.

Next on the prefix line we see the network address. This is the 128-bit address, divided into eight blocks of 16 bits. At the end of the address we have the netmask. It is worth mentioning that this is a classless interdomain routing address block, also known as CIDR. We should also mention that this address is strictly for educational purposes and should not be used. At the end of the string, we have the name of the physical network interface.

Additional configuration options are supported in this ndpd.conf file. The preceding configurations will get the daemon functioning as the IPv6 router for the 0A:0A:0A:0A:0A:0A:0A:0 network. For more information on other supported options, see the ndpd.conf(4) man page.

The ipnodes File

With IPv4, Solaris uses the /etc/inet/hosts file to resolve known hosts. This process is controlled by the nsswitch.conf file in the /etc directory. When a process from the local system attempts to connect by host name to another system via IPv4, the nsswitch.conf forces the process to check the /etc/inet/hosts for name resolution. With IPv6, Solaris now uses the /etc/inet/ipnodes file to resolve known hosts. This is controlled by the ipnodes entry in nsswitch.conf. The ipnodes configuration file structure is similar to that of the hosts file. In Figure 7.4, we see two entries in the ipnodes file of sturgeon.

On the first line, we see the entry for our router, sturgeon.mydomain.com. Much like the hosts file, this entry assigns the pictured address to the host name and gives it a canonical name of *sturgeon*. Following this entry, we see an entry for one of the nodes on the network, barracuda.mydomain.com. This address allows us to reach the system barracuda without the necessity for DNS.

Figure 7.4 IPv6 Addresses Specified via the ipnodes File

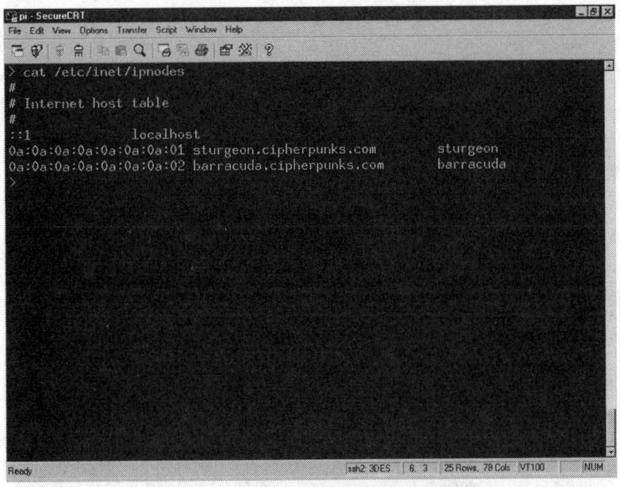

The nsswitch.conf File

As we mentioned previously, the nsswitch.conf files in /etc references local files by default. These files are /etc/inet/hosts for IPv4 and /etc/inet/ipnodes for IPv6. If our systems are on a network with a name server that supports IPv6, we might want to change the entries in nsswitch.conf to use DNS.

Enabling DNS can do one of two things on our network. If it is properly configured, it can make our network easier to maintain and smoother running. If configured incorrectly, it can create all kinds of headaches, mysterious problems, and, perhaps, security issues.

In order for DNS to work with an IPv6 network, we need a DNS server that is IPv6 compatible. Currently, the only name service daemon available with IPv6 support is the Berkley Internet Name Daemon (BIND). The series 9 BIND is currently the only version with IPv6 support. If we are going to use DNS with the IPv6 network, we should migrate to BIND9. The current implementation included with Solaris 8 is version 8.1.2.

IPv6 Programs

In this section, we talk about the programs necessary for IPv6 to function. We look at programs that have been designed specifically for IPv6 and their role in ensuring that the network operates smoothly. We also look at programs that have been adapted for the coming of IPv6 in the Solaris operating system and speak briefly about their new features.

The in.ndpd Program

The in.ndpd program is the Neighbor Discovery Protocol Daemon. This program is responsible for the majority of the operations on an IPv6 network in terms of configuration, routing information, and IP addressing. We mentioned the configuration file previously; now we talk specifically about the daemon.

The in.ndpd program is started in the S69inet file when the system enters run-level 2. The script executes a test to determine whether or not the /etc/inet/ndpd.conf script exists. Figure

7.5 contains the code from the S69inet script that determines the system is a router if the ndpd.conf file is found.

Figure 7.5 Code from the S69inet Script That Determines the System Is a Router if the ndpd.conf File Is Found

If this test returns *true*, the variables *ip6_forwarding*, *ip6_send_redirects*, and *ip6_ignore_redirect* are set to 1. The daemon is launched in router mode, and the in.ripngd program is started. If the test for the configuration file fails, the previously mentioned variables are set to 0, and the in.ndpd program is launched in host mode.

By examining the code, we can see that we can easily determine whether the system is running as an IPv6 router or an IPv6 host. If the system is running as an IPv6 router, the message "Machine is an IPv6 router" is printed to standard output (stdout) when the system bootstraps. If the system is functioning as an IPv6 host, the message "Starting IPv6 neighbor discovery" is printed to stdout. We can therefore determine whether the system thinks it is an IPv6 router by watching the system bootstrap or reviewing the contents of dmesg.

After the in.ndpd program has been configured to act as an IPv6 router, when a system is set up to autoconfigure via IPv6 bootstraps and polls the network, in.ndpd on the router will respond. The host sends a router solicitation via ICMPv6, the ICMP implementation in IPv6, to the network via the multicast address space. The router then responds with an ICMPv6 packet to the multicast address space, advertising itself as a router. The host receives this packet and configures itself to interact with the advertised router.

The in.ripngd Program

The in.ripngd program is the Routing Information Protocol, New Generation Daemon. This is the Routing Information Protocol (RIP) implementation for IPv6. When the system is bootstrapped and configured as a router, this daemon is launched to manage network routing information.

This daemon is to IPv6 what in.routed is to IPv4. The in.routed program listens on port 520 via UDP, and the in.ripngd program communicates via UDP on port 521. On a router, this daemon multicasts request packets on all functioning IPv6 interfaces and waits for replies from IPv6 hosts. When the daemon receives response packets, it places information about the responding host into RIP tables. This information is later used to update system routing tables.

We will not delve into deep discussion about this program, since it is simply a means to get the job done. It is not essential to our mission, although it can be helpful. More information about this program is available via the in.ripngd(1M) man page.

The *ifconfig* Command

At one point or another, you will need to manually configure an interface. This is life as a systems administrator or in any other position responsible for the operation, maintenance, and availability of systems. The standard UNIX *ifconfig* command has been adapted to function with IPv6, providing expanded functionality at the expense of learning the new features.

The differences in syntax for the IPv6 functions of Solaris are relatively minute. It is possible to add addresses to a single interface without worrying which virtual interface will host the address. This is done simply by using the *addif* flag, as demonstrated here:

```
ifconfig hme0 inet6 addif 0A:0A:0A:0A:0A:0A:0A:05/64
```

This code allows us to add the :05 address to the hme0 interface and let the system decide which virtual interface the address will reside on. Executing *the ifconfig –a* command, we see that the address now resides on the hme0:3 virtual interface.

Accordingly, we can also remove the address, letting the system find and remove it for us. This can be done with the removeif flag. Observe the following example:

```
ifconfig hme0 inet6 removeif 0A:0A:0A:0A:0A:0A:0A:05
```

This code allows the system to do our dirty work, removing the :05 address. After executing the command, we can see that the address and virtual interface have been removed.

IPv6 Router Procedure

Let's now take a look at setting up an IPv6 router. As we have previously, we will do this step by step, to ensure that we observe attention to detail. This section can also be made into a checklist for the implementation of any IPv6 routers that you deploy:

1. **Gather all necessary documentation.** This information includes RFCs, checklists, and technical documents. We might include RFCs detailing things such as the IPv6 Specification RFC (RFC2460) and the autoconfiguration of hosts on IPv6 networks RFC (RFC2462).

2. **Decide on a design for our network.** The design includes addressing, services that will be offered to the IPv6 network such as DNS, names of systems, whether the systems will also support IPv4, and how the systems will be configured for IPv6.

3. **Deploy services we will need for the IPv6 Network.** If we are planning to use DNS or anything else that needs to be configured especially for IPv6, we should do this ahead of the transition to assure a smooth change of protocol.

4. **Design the IPv6 router.** The router's design should conform to the specifications we decided on in Step 2. This includes security concerns, any host-based intrusion detection systems we will use, and necessary software. It also includes deciding whether the router will be created from an initial install of Solaris 8 or whether an existing Solaris 8 system will be used.

5. **Implement the router.** Build the router according to the specifications previously established.

6. **Configure the necessary files for IPv6.** These files include the /etc/inet/ipnodes file, the /etc/inet/ndpd.conf file, the /etc/hostname6.interface file(s), and the /etc/nss-witch.conf file.

7. **Reboot and test.** Reboot the router after the configuration changes have been made. After the router reboots, we need an IPv6 host to test the router functionality. This test can be performed a number of ways. One way is to take down the IPv4 interface and attempt to reach the hosts outside the IPv6 network solely over IPv6. Another is to perform a *traceroute* outside the IPv6 network, specifying that the IPv6 router as a gateway with the −*g* flag.

Stopping IPv6 Routing

The process of stopping IPv6 routing is simple. To stop an IPv6 system from routing traffic, there are two methods we can use.

Method 1: Rebooting the System

This method requires a reboot of the system:

1. **Remove or move the /etc/inet/ndpd.conf file.** If we want to save the ndpd.conf file, we must move it to a different location, or change the name to something like NOndpd.conf. When the system boots and does not find this file, in.ndpd will start in host mode.

2. **Reboot and test.** After the system has been rebooted, check the bootstrap output for the string "Starting IPv6 neighbor discovery." Additionally, check *the ip6_forwarding, ip6_send_redirects*, and *ip6_ignore_redirect* variables via ndd to ensure they are set to 0.

Method 2: Not Rebooting the System

This method does not require reboot of the system. It requires no downtime on the part of the interfaces, and the system will continue to be reachable while these actions are performed:

1. **Remove or move the /etc/inet/ndpd.conf file.** If we want to save the ndpd.conf file, we must move it to a different location or change the name to something like NOndpd.conf. When the system boots and does not find this file, in.ndpd will start in host mode.

2. **Send the HUP signal to in.ndpd.** This can be done via the command *pkill -1 in.ndpd*. Performing this action will restart in.ndpd, and it will attempt to reload the /etc/inet/ndpd.conf file. When it does not find the file, it will enter host mode.

3. **Check local interfaces to ensure that the ROUTER flag is no longer present.** In Figure 7.6, we see that the interfaces are designated as routing interfaces. Note the differences between Figures 7.6 and 7.3. Notice the change in the Router flag in the output of an *ifconfig −a*. The system in Figure 7.6 is in a multihomed state.

Figure 7.6 System in a Multihomed State

4. **Disable the IPv6 kernel module routing parameters.** This can be done via ndd. We need to set the parameters *ip6_forwarding*, *ip6_forwarding*, *ip6_send_redirects*, and *ip6_ignore_redirect* to 0. Refer to the ndd(1M) man page for more information on the use of ndd.

5. **Test the configuration.** As always, test the configuration to assure that the system is no longer routing traffic.

IP Version 6 Hosts

We've discussed the configuration and implementation of an IPv6 router. However, what good does an IPv6 router do without IPv6 hosts? In the interest of providing complete documentation on an IPv6 network deployment, here we talk about configuring a Solaris 8 system to interact with an IPv6 network.

Automatic Configuration

One feature of IPv6 is the ability to autoconfigure systems with an IP address when they boot-strap. This feature, built into the IPv6 protocol, is seamlessly supported by Solaris 8. This can be an advantage in networks with a large number of hosts that might not need connectivity with one another or a known accessible address. The steps to take advantage of this feature are minimal.

A Solaris 8 system depends on the /etc/hostname6.interface file for IPv6. When the system boots, if it finds this file, it attempts to configure itself to the information contained in the file. To create a Solaris 8 host that is configured via the network, the only necessity is having a hostname6.interface file with no information. This causes the system to use the data attained from the network via in.ndpd and configure itself for communication using the network information and MAC address of the interface.

Manual Configuration

Interfaces on a Solaris 8 system using IPv6 can be manually configured using data on the system or via data attained from DNS. This configuration is beneficial in that it gives systems a known address at which they can be reached. This is an ideal configuration for servers on an IPv6 network.

The ipnodes File

One of a few ways a Solaris 8 host can be configured manually is by using the /etc/inet/ipnodes file. This method is ideal in a situation in which IPv6 DNS is not available. To take advantage of this feature, our first step is to make an entry in the ipnodes file for the address we want the system to configure and a host name. Take a look at Figure 7.7. It is an ipnodes file entry for a host that will boot with IPv6 configured.

Figure 7.7 An ipnodes File Entry for a Host That Will Boot with IPv6 Configured

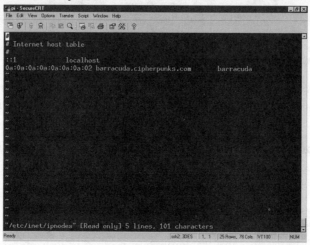

In this example, we see that our host has an entry for 0A:0A:0A:0A:0A:0A:0A:02 in the ipnodes file, with the host name barracuda and on mydomain.com. This entry is referenced when the system bootstraps. To give the system the address we desire, we need to place the address in the hostname6.interface file. We use the following entry to force the system to configure an interface using this address:

```
addif barracuda.mydomain.com/64 up
```

When the system is next rebooted, this code instructs the system to place the address resolving to barracuda.mydomain.com in the ipnodes file on the next available virtual interface, bound to the physical interface denoted at the end of the hostname6.interface file.

DNS

Another of a few ways Solaris 8 can be configured to attain a desired IP address is via DNS. The benefit of this method is that it allows systems to attain their IP addresses from one centrally managed server. This can be helpful in a large network in which systems need awareness of one another and users need to be able to access systems within the network via a known address or name.

This configuration option depends entirely on a network with support for IPv6 DNS. To configure a host to use DNS, the /etc/nsswitch.conf file must be edited. The ipnodes line within /etc/nsswitch.conf by default uses files to resolve host names. Edit the /etc/nsswitch.conf, and make the ipnodes line look like the following example:

```
ipnodes:    files dns
```

Under this configuration, when the host attempts to resolve an IPv6 address or an IPv6 host name, it first consults the /etc/inet/ipnodes file. If it cannot find an entry for the host in the ipnodes file, it then turns to DNS. When the host receives a response from the name server, it configures this response to the interface on which the hostname6.interface file ends. This address is configured to the next available virtual interface on the physical network interface.

Configuring Solaris as a Secure Gateway

In this section we talked about using Solaris as a router between different networks. Solaris is capable of functioning as a gateway as well. In implementation, there is little difference between the two functions. The main difference is in their placement on networks and the way in which they interact with hosts.

A *gateway* is a system that connects two or more segments of the same network via two or more interfaces. The reasons for this configuration are typically situations such as dial-up users who don't need dedicated connections or segments of the same network that are divided by some physical obstacle in which an additional outbound link to the Internet either isn't needed or isn't wanted.

Solaris is suited for this type of use. As mentioned previously, a default installation of Solaris will work for this purpose. The only requirement for a Solaris gateway is two or more interfaces, and the system will automatically configure itself to pass traffic between the two networks. By observing our discussion about minimalism, it's possible to create a system that will, in most cases, provide secure, reliable service.

One key configuration difference we should mention is the changing of the IP kernel module variables. In our previous discussion, we recommended the disabling of the *ip_forward_directed_broadcasts* and the *ip_forward_src_routed* variables. In a gateway environment in which systems are on the same subnet, we do not want to disable these options. These options, in a gateway situation, are helpful in terms of network management. A correctly designed network will not let broadcast into or out of the subnet.

Configuring Solaris as a Firewall

We've talked about using Solaris as both a router and a gateway. Implementations of such systems using Solaris are reliable, stable, and secure. However, using Solaris in such an environment has many drawbacks in terms of security. Unlike hardware solutions, Solaris offers nothing in terms of network access control in a stock install.

In the interest of providing a more secure network, in this section we discuss various methods and packages available for providing firewall services to networks and systems. The benefit of doing so lies in allowing us to control the traffic that flows from one side of our router to the other. We also discuss design of networks using these packages and deployment of the systems. Additionally, we discuss the benefits and the drawbacks of using such systems.

There are many free commercial implementations of firewalls that run on Solaris. Gauntlet and Firewall-1 are two examples. Additionally, free firewall packages such as Sun's SunScreen Lite and IP Filter by Darren Reed are available. We focus our discussion on SunScreen Lite and IP Filter.

General Firewall Theory

What is the idea behind a firewall? The concept, in basic terms, is to keep the bad guys out while letting the good guys continue to have access to the outside (or at least the things that they are allowed to access on the outside) and letting in the people that need access. Although this sounds easy enough at first blush, implementing a firewall system is far more complicated in reality.

Most enterprises use multiple layers of firewalls to accomplish their mission. This multilayering has the benefit of distributing the load of access control, which prevents any one system from being a bottleneck. It also has the benefit of providing several layers of access control before reaching the final destination. The overall benefit is that network security and performance are enhanced.

There are also drawbacks to this design. One drawback is that it creates multiple systems to maintain. This can result in additional labor expenditure and more man hours. Another drawback to this design is the added complexity of multiple firewall rule sets. One change on any of the systems can easily result in a network nightmare.

So, what is the best solution? Opinions vary, and the armies of the "bigger firewalls" and the "more firewalls" camps continue to wage war over this issue. Our suggestion is to create an infrastructure that meets your business needs, provides security to hosts on the network, and does not restrict user access to the point of being unusable. The key to providing good network security is continuous planning.

Deploying security infrastructure is not a silver bullet, nor is it a permanent fix. You will continually discover problems with software; operating systems, applications, even firewall packages themselves are affected and in need of continuous update. Additionally, network needs and network sizes change. What works for your network today could be a burden on the network tomorrow. It is essential that you continuously monitor the security infrastructure placed on a network for performance and security.

It is impossible to dictate in this book the best firewall design for a network. All networks have their own sets of needs and requirements. In the next section, we discuss general firewall design. We approach this topic from an objective standpoint and mention only the concepts we can apply to all networks.

General Firewall Design

Each firewall differs in configuration commands, administrative interfaces, and various features. All firewalls, however, are designed to do basically the same thing, which is filter traffic. The two types of firewalls available are stateless and stateful. Let's take a closer look at these two terms.

Stateless firewalls are firewalls designed to enforce firewall rule set, without keeping track of traffic. These types of firewall are generally referred to as *packet filters*. In this type of firewall, there is no tracking of connection activity, or the "state" of connections. Stateless firewalls are comparable to software packages such as TCP Wrappers except that they work on a broader range of services and ports. Stateless firewalls are, in most cases, easily bypassed.

Stateful firewalls are firewalls designed to enforce firewall rule sets and keep track of connections to and from the system. Unlike packet filters, these firewalls watch the state of connections between hosts and permit further connectivity based on the state of current connections. This type of firewall is more granular and configurable than that of the stateless variety and offers more security.

Previously, we mentioned that it is impossible to dictate in this text the best firewall rules for a network. This noble truth has not changed. However, we can establish some guidelines that can be generally applied to any network. Let's gather some of these extrapolations into a list.

- **Use multiple layers of access control.** This means filtering untrusted traffic from the border routers of the network, all the way to the firewall. This method has two benefits. The first is that a connection is scrutinized at multiple places on the network. The second is that it distributes the load of access control, preventing any one system from being a bottleneck as decisions are made about traffic.

- **Block all unnecessary traffic.** A firewall should be implemented to block everything unless otherwise specified. This means blocking everything that is not mission critical. E-mail, for example, is mission critical. Any services that are required should be passed through a proxy, if possible. This is not possible on every network, but the closer we get to this type of implementation, the better. This system has the benefit of restricting access from not only the outside, where an attacker can get into our network, but also from the inside, where an unwitting user could execute a Trojan horse program that connects to hosts across the Internet and gives an intruder the ability to execute commands on the system locally.

- **Use stateful rules.** Having a stateful firewall can greatly enhance overall network security. However, a stateful firewall does us no good if we do not use the stateful connection inspection features. When implementing rules, ensure that they check the state of connections.

It is outside the scope of this book to address network design issues such as private networks and the demilitarized zone, but it is worth noting that these concepts can be applied to networks of any type.

Let's move on and talk about some of the tools necessary to get the job done. Many firewall implementations are available for Solaris in the commercial arena, such as Gauntlet and Check

Point Firewall-1. We discuss only the freely available tools here. We will not dig deeply into the use of these tools but merely mention them as part of the decision-making process in further securing our network.

SunScreen Lite

SunScreen Lite is a free version of the SunScreen Secure Net firewall package. SunScreen Lite is designed to operate in routing mode. This means that the filter only filters traffic that the Solaris router is routing. This is perfect for our needs. SunScreen Lite can be used in VPNs and supports Simple Key Management for Internet Protocol (SKIP).

Some drawbacks are associated with this package as well. First, it has a number of package dependency issues that could require the addition of packages, depending on how your system was designed. Next, it will not support high-availability clustering. This means that a SunScreen packet filter is a single point of failure. In a situation in which the system fails for one reason or another, the entire network screened by the firewall becomes unavailable.

Another drawback is that it does not support proxies. If we decide to allow some services from within the confines of a draconian network and these services require a proxy to communicate with the outside network, we can't use SunScreen Lite. This could limit the use of some application proxies.

Finally, SunScreen Lite is limited in the number of interfaces supported and in the number of IP addresses that can be used for Network Address Translation (NAT). The package supports a maximum of two interfaces on a system. This is undesirable if we would like to place our systems on a private network and allow only certain traffic from the outside to a predetermined IP address to reach the port of a system inside the private network. SunScreen Lite supports only 10 private address and two NAT rules. Additionally, SunScreen Lite has no IPv6 support.

The commercial SunScreen package supports all these features. Additionally, it provides some advanced features such as stealth firewalling, multiple interfaces, and time-based access control. If the constrains of this product do not prohibit its use on your network, SunScreen Lite might be your best option. SunScreen is available from the Sun Download Center. Documentation regarding the installation and administration of SunScreen is also freely available from Sun.

IP Filter

The IP Filter package is one of the older firewall implementations available on the Internet, originally released in 1993. Written by Darren Reed, the program remains popular as a stateful firewall for UNIX hosts. It is freely available, open-source software. It can be implemented both as a network firewall and a host-based firewall. It supports both IPv4 and IPv6 networks.

The mail IP Filter site is http://coombs.anu.edu.au/ipfilter/index.html. There is documentation in the form of FAQs linked on the site. Two other documents about IP Filter are a two-part document written by Jeremy Rauch in July 2000, "Introduction to IP Filter," and one written by Kristy Westphal, "Solaris and IP Filter: How to Make Them Your NAT Solution," both available via SecurityFocus at www.securityfocus.com.

With the many benefits of IP Filter, it suffers the same high-availability problems as SunScreen. There is no high availability, so the software introduces a single point of failure into the network. Additionally, IP Filter is not cryptographically aware. The latter issue is more easily solved than the former, but it is something to take into account in the decision process.

Using NAT

Another method that can be used to secure traffic is placing information systems on a private network and using NAT. NAT is defined in RFC3022. The term *private* means that the addresses contained within the network are not routable over the Internet. Systems on the network managed by the router pass traffic out through the router, which performs the address translation to make the packets appear as though they originated at the router.

The systems behind the NAT router are not directly accessible from the router's outside interface. Therefore, users outside the local network cannot access systems behind the NAT router unless either a specific port on the NAT router has been mapped to a specific port on a host or a specific IP address on the NAT router has been mapped to a specific IP address on the private network. This restriction provides the network with a limited amount of security.

Solaris 8 does not include utilities to provide NAT infrastructure in the default software installation. The previously mentioned firewall packages all have NAT capabilities and can be used for this purpose. The drawback of this type of implementation is that by relying solely on NAT and no access control, it is still possible for hosts inside the network to communicate with hosts outside, either on a voluntary or involuntary basis. As we mentioned previously, an unwitting user who executes a Trojan horse program could give a remote attacker access to the system across the NAT router; this is just one of many risks. This could result in the attacker compromising the system and, potentially, other network resources.

NAT is, however, an extremely useful infrastructure and is the saving grace of networks with limited public IP address space. If NAT is to be used, it is recommended that you use the firewall capabilities of the previously mentioned software packages also to provide a more secure network posture.

Summary

In this chapter, we discussed implementing Solaris as a secure IPv4 router and described a host as a system with any number of interfaces connected to the same or different networks. We described a router as a system with a minimum of two interfaces, connected to different segments of network and asserted that Solaris is a good choice as a router because of its stability, the ease of securing the operating system for production network use, and the ease of deployment.

Next, we discussed the way Solaris identifies itself as a router and mentioned that Solaris will route traffic by default if the system has two interfaces, at least two /etc/hostname.interface files, and a stock /etc/rc.d/S69inet is installed. We demonstrated that /etc/rcS.d/S30network.sh configures interfaces on the system and that /etc/rc2.d/S69inet makes the decision to route traffic based on the system having two or more interfaces, the existence of the /etc/gateways file, and the nonexistence of the /etc/notrouter file.

Later, we gave the seven steps for configuring a Solaris router and discussed a policy of minimalism and deploying a system with minimal installation, services, users, dynamic information, and cleartext communication. We then detailed the three steps of unconfiguring a Solaris router, returning it to multihomed host state.

Next, we covered implementing Solaris 8 as an IPv6 router. We examined the entry in the /etc/hostname6.interface file, described the ifdefault and prefix entries in the /etc/inet/ndpd .conf file, talked about making entries for IPv6 addresses to be configured on the system in the /etc/inet/ipnodes file, and described adding dns to the ipnodes entry line in /etc/nsswitch.conf to make the system resolve its IP addresses via DNS. We also described in.ndpd and its use both on routers to configure IPv6 hosts, the in.ripngd that manages routing information on IPv6 networks, and the IPv6 functionality additions with the inet6 flag to ifconfig. We ended our IPv6 router discussion with the seven steps to implementing an IPv6 router and described turning an IPv6 router into a multihomed IPv6 host, both by removing the ndpd.conf file and rebooting, and by removing the ndpd.conf file, sending the HUP signal to in.ndpd, checking our interfaces, and disabling IP forwarding in the IP6 kernel module.

We next rounded out our IPv6 discussion with details of designing an IPv6 host. We described auto-configuring an IPv6 host by simply using touch to create an /etc/hostname6 .interface file. We also discussed making an entry in the /etc/inet/ipnodes file for a static address, and placing an *addif* command in the hostname6.interface file to configure the IPv6 address to the host. We ended our discussion about IPv6 hosts by mentioning the necessity of IPv6-compatible DNS if we desire configuring our system through resolution of its host name in the /etc/hostname6.interface file against a nameserver.

We followed up our discussion about routers with a brief talk about Solaris gateways. We defined a Solaris gateway as a system that connects two segments of the same network. We additionally talked about leaving the kernel module variables *ip_forward_directed_broadcasts* and *ip_forward_src_routed* untouched in a Solaris gateway implementation.

Following up to our discussion of gateways, we covered the topic of using Solaris as a firewall. We described general firewall theory as keeping the bad guys out while letting the good guys still have the access they need. We described the benefits of using distributed firewalls and multiple layers of access control, such as better network performance. We highlighted the fact that security infrastructure is not a one-time fix and requires planning and continuous monitoring for the best performance and security.

We segued into an ideal design situation of firewalls. The stateless firewall does not track connection state, and the stateful firewall maintains records of current connections. We listed our general firewall design best practices as multiple layers of access control, firewalls that block all unnecessary traffic, and are implemented with stateful rules.

Later, we covered SunScreen Lite and IP Filter. We talked about the benefits of SunScreen Lite, such as SKIP. We also described the drawbacks of SunScreen Lite, such as the lack of high availability, the limitation of 10 private addresses, its lack of functionality on IPv6 networks, and the limitation of two Network Address Translation (NAT) rules. We described the benefits of IP Filter, such as its support of both IPv4 and IPv6. We also described the drawbacks of IP Filter, such as its lack of support for high availability, and no support for cryptography.

Part III

PIX Firewalls

Chapter 8

Introduction to PIX Firewalls

Best Damn Topics in this Chapter:

- **PIX Firewall Features**
- **PIX Hardware**
- **PIX Licensing and Upgrades**
- **The Command-Line Interface**

Introduction

Good security administration is labor-intensive, and therefore organizations often find it difficult to maintain the security of a large number of internal machines. Increasingly, firewalls provide additional security or performance services; since they sit at a point in the network that mediates all communication with the end host, various types of service extensions can naturally be integrated into them.

Even in high-security environments, where the resources to harden and provide ongoing security support for the end application are available, firewalls can play an important role. In addition to the features described previously, firewalls can support the concept of defense in depth: multiple protective technologies support higher levels of trust in case of error or omission at one layer. Having multiple controls also supports the concept of separation of duties: different groups can support application layer and network layer securities, ensuring that no single person or group can compromise the system.

Cisco's PIX firewalls are a series of appliances that offer world-class security and high levels of performance and reliability. They are a mature product, having been a part of enterprise and service provider networks since 1995. Cisco PIX firewalls fit into a wide range of environments, from small office/home office (SOHO) environments to large enterprises and service providers. With support for complex protocols, the latest VPN technologies, and intrusion detection features, the PIX is one of the leading firewalls in the market.

In this chapter, you will learn about some of the main features that Cisco PIX firewalls have to offer. We will look at the different models of PIX and the types of environment in which they fit. We will then perform basic configuration on a PIX firewall through the command-line interface.

PIX Firewall Features

The PIX 500 series firewalls are a market-leading security appliance, and for good reason. They provide robust performance in a firewall while providing a highly scalable architecture ranging from plug-and-play SOHO devices to carrier-class firewalls with gigabit connections. They provide protective services that define what a firewall should do. From stateful packet inspection to content filtering, VPN termination to address translation, support for PKI applications, and providing security to multimedia applications, the PIX does it all.

With such flexibility comes the requirement to configure the devices correctly. Luckily, for those who are already comfortable with a router prompt, the PIX is based on a familiar command prompt. Of course, the PIX fits into standard Cisco management tools such as CiscoWorks, so it will seamlessly integrate into your LAN/WAN environment.

Embedded Operating System

Many firewalls are based on general-purpose operating systems (OSs). This means that maintenance is required to ensure not only correct configuration but that the base OS is patched and secured. This requirement offers both a higher long-term cost as well as the potential for security weaknesses.

An embedded OS is one in which the OS is self-contained in the device and resident in ROM. This involves reduced maintenance costs, since no customizations or OS configurations are required; a single image is downloaded and stored to flash. It means that there is little that can go wrong; you cannot accidentally leave an unnecessary service running, since the firewall has all its services tuned to only those features appropriate for a security device.

Unlike some appliances that are based on a general kernel such as Linux or Windows CE, the PIX is based on a hardened, specialized OS specific to security services. This OS allows for kernel simplification, which supports explicit certification and validation: The PIX OS has been tested for vendor certification such as ICSA Labs' firewall product certification criteria and the very difficult-to-obtain International Standards Organization (ISO) Common Criteria EAL4 certification. This testing allows for maximum assurance in deployment from Cisco's positive security engineering based on good commercial development practices. Kernel simplification has advantages in throughput as well; the PIX 535 will support up to 256,000 simultaneous connections, far exceeding the capabilities of a UNIX- or Windows-based OS on equivalent hardware.

One key advantage to the software on a PIX firewall is its similarity to Cisco IOS. This means that internetworkers have the ability to rapidly master management of the PIX, reducing deployment costs and supporting management by network operations center (NOC) personnel. You should not have to be an expert in UNIX or Windows 2000 to be able to deploy a VPN or firewall!

The Adaptive Security Algorithm

The heart of the PIX is the Adaptive Security Algorithm, or ASA. The ASA is a mechanism to determine if packets should be passed through the firewall, consistent with the information flow control policy as implemented in the access control list (ACL) table. The PIX evaluates packet information against developed state and decides whether to pass the packet.

Let's go through this process one step at a time. First, there is the concept of a *datastream*. Packets that are flowing across a wire have identifying characteristics: IP address of source and destination, sometimes numbers associated with the type of communication (ports) of source and destination, and numbers such as IP identifiers or synchronization and acknowledgment numbers that identify where a packet belongs in a particular connection. When you open a Web page—say, to www.cisco.com/index.html—you establish a connection between your browser and the Web server. One piece of HTML is transferred; if it has not been cached, this page represents about 90K of text. That text might then open up additional connections for all the embedded pictures. The process involves a "dance" between browser and server—a "handshake" to initialize the connection, a "get" to specify the data being requested, a "response" to say if the data is available, and the actual data itself. Since the file is so large, these steps all occur in multiple packets between browser and Web server, with data flowing down from the server and acknowledgment of receipt of data flowing up from the browser.

The information flow control policy is an expression of the information that is allowed to flow through the network. A sample policy might be, "If the datastream was initiated by someone on the inside, let it pass; if the datastream was initiated by someone from the outside, block it."

An ACL table is a mechanism via which you can try to implement this policy. It compares those distinguishing numbers against a database to see if the packet is consistent with policy. If it is not allowed by the database, the packet is dropped and perhaps logged.

The earliest routers used fixed ACLs to determine if a packet should be routed; they compared fundamental information about the packet, such as the IP address of the source or destination or the type of service requested or, for some services such as TCP, individual flags on the packets. Then, based on fixed rules, they decided to route the traffic or to drop it. For example, the fixed rules might allow any packet that might possibly be a "return" packet, since under certain circumstances such a packet would be valid. This isn't too much of a problem, since a "return" packet, if it hasn't been requested by the original host, should be dropped by the host. However, that can cause some information to leak out, so it is helpful to get rid of such packets if we can.

The concept of *state* is the idea that ACLs should probably change over time. A stateful packet filter allows for dynamic rule bases—for example, if the packet is coming from the outside toward the inside, you should check to see if this packet was part of a previously opened datastream. Now, we only allow packets back in if they were previously authorized; that Cisco Web server can't decide to send us data unless we previously requested it.

The biggest problem with fixed rules is that in order to allow certain kinds of traffic—FTP, for example—overly permissive ACLs would need to be implemented. In FTP, two TCP data flows are developed. One, the command channel, runs from the client out to the user—from the inside to the outside. Routers would generally be able to determine the direction of this flow and allow that traffic, as described previously. The second, the data channel, is negotiated by the FTP server and flows from the server back into the client—from the outside to the inside. Moreover, the TCP port—a service identifier telling you an identifier for the port—varies depending on how many files the server has transferred since reboot; thus the ACL would have to allow *all* inbound traffic in a wide range of TCP ports. This means that a malicious user would have free run of the network in those ranges. Consequently, router ACL-based firewalls are little more than Swiss cheese enforcement points!

The smart idea is to watch for the negotiation between the FTP server and client. That's part of the concept of state. Armed with that piece of information, the firewall can open only the necessary port for the inbound data flow, and open it only while the transfer is active—dynamically changing the ACLs over time. This allows the firewall to permit authorized traffic and disallow inappropriate traffic with far more sophistication than a static rule.

State

More deeply, *state* is a way of saying that the firewall is maintaining a history of the traffic that has passed and will compare the new packet against previous history to see if the packet is allowed by the information flow control policy rules. There is also a performance benefit of maintaining state: If a packet can be determined to be similar to those already passed, a full analysis against the firewall policy rules does not need to be followed, it can be passed based on the existing state. This allows the PIX to perform at line rate where static access lists might bog down.

One key piece of state is to record active connections. If we can add something to a connection table when it first starts and remove that thing from a connection table when the connection is (gracefully) closed, we have a leg up for that concept of "similar to those already passed." This data is stored in the connections table (CONN).

The PIX has the ability to rewrite the characteristic information described previously, such as IP address and port data. Thus, another piece of state is to remember what IP address and port data the PIX has seen lately as well as remembering what it did with them before. It needs to remember how it translated something from a protected net into the outside world. This data is stored in the translations table (XLATE).

Here are the XLATE and CONN tables' output as displayed by PIXOS on a quiet firewall:

```
PIX1# show xlate
3 in use, 112 most used
PAT Global 63.110.38.230(1225) Local 10.10.10.11(32775)
PAT Global 63.110.38.230(22451) Local 10.10.10.11(4025)
PAT Global 63.110.38.230(22450) Local 10.10.10.11(32778)
PIX1# show conn
1 in use, 26 most used
TCP out 63.122.40.140:21 in 10.10.10.11:32775 idle 0:00:10 Bytes 154
     flags UIO
```

This code shows that someone on machine 10.10.10.11 has connected to 63.122.40.140 on port 21 (FTP). The translation maps between socket 63.110.38.230, 1225 on the outside and socket 10.10.10.11, 32775 on the inside. The flags from the connection table are showing that the connection is up and that there is inbound and outbound data. A little while later:

```
PIX1# show conn
1 in use, 26 most used
TCP out 63.122.40.140:21 in 10.10.10.11:32775 idle 0:06:48 Bytes 216
     flags UFRIO
```

Notice that the idle counter is larger (the traffic flow has been idle, no packets have been received), a few more bytes have passed, and the flags now have *F*, for *outside FIN*, and *R*, for *outside acknowledged FIN*.

This indicates that the firewall has taken notice of the transfer. In addition to the basic housekeeping of passing traffic appropriately (there is address translation going on, so that must be addressed), the PIX is keeping an eye on the transported traffic. Port 21 is FTP, so it knows that there might be an inbound connection. It knows from the first output that traffic between those two machines on those socket pairs is expected and should be passed. It knows from the second output that traffic between those two machines should no longer occur, because the sides have reset each other, and that any stray packets are now either lost retransmissions or someone doing something he or she should not. The firewall has "learned" about the transfer over time and is able to change its rules in response to past traffic.

Security Levels

When firewalls were first implemented, they typically had only two interfaces: the outside, or "black," network, and the inside, or "red," network. These interfaces corresponded to degrees of trust: Because the inside was controlled and was "us," we could allow pretty much anything originating in the red network to travel to the black network. Furthermore, because the outside was "them," we limited pretty much anything originating in the black network to come inside the firewall.

The modern style is to have a DMZ, or multiple service networks. This makes the idea of "us vs. them" much more complex. The PIX 535 has a modular chassis with support for up to 10 interfaces! Using the *nameif* command, you can assign a security level, an integer between 0 and 100. Make sure that each interface has a different value. When you are designing your security zones, the idea should be to order the zones by degrees of trust and then assign integers to the levels, corresponding to how much you trust the network—0 for the outside (untrusted network), 100 for the inside (trusted network), and values between 0 and 100 for relative trust.

How ASA Works

Informally, ASA allows traffic to flow from a higher security level to a lower security level, unless modified by the *conduit* or *access-list* commands. More formally, the manual notes:

- No packets can traverse the PIX firewall without a connection and state.

- Outbound connections or states are allowed, except those specifically denied by ACLs. An outbound connection is one in which the originator or client is on a higher security interface than the receiver or server. The highest security interface is always the inside interface, and the lowest is the outside interface. Any perimeter interfaces can have security levels between the inside and outside values.

- Inbound connections or states, except those specifically allowed, are denied. An inbound connection or state is one in which the originator or client is on a lower security interface or network than the receiver or server. You can apply multiple exceptions to a single *xlate* (translation). This lets you permit access from an arbitrary machine, network, or any host on the Internet to the host defined by the *xlate*.

- All ICMP packets are denied unless specifically permitted.

- All attempts to circumvent the previous rules are dropped and a message is generated. It is sent to a management device (local buffer, SNMP trap, syslog, console), depending on the severity of the attempt and local configuration. (Note that normal traffic might also trigger logging, again depending on configuration. At the highest debugging mode, every packet generates an alert!)

Technical Details for ASA

The PIX is an Internet Protocol (IP) firewall. It accepts and passes only IP packets; all others are dropped. It is worth taking a moment to look at the details of the protocols to see what the PIX is looking at and how it uses that information.

Internet Protocol

IP is an unreliable, routable packet delivery protocol. All upper-layer protocols use IP to send and receive packets. IP receives segments from the transport layer, fragments them into packets, and passes them to the network layer.

The IP address is a logical address assigned to each node on a TCP/IP network. IP addressing is designed to allow routing of packets across internetworks. Since IP addresses are easy to change or spoof, they should not be relied on to provide identification in untrusted environments. As shown in Figure 8.1, the source and destination addresses are included in the IP header.

Figure 8.1 The IP Header

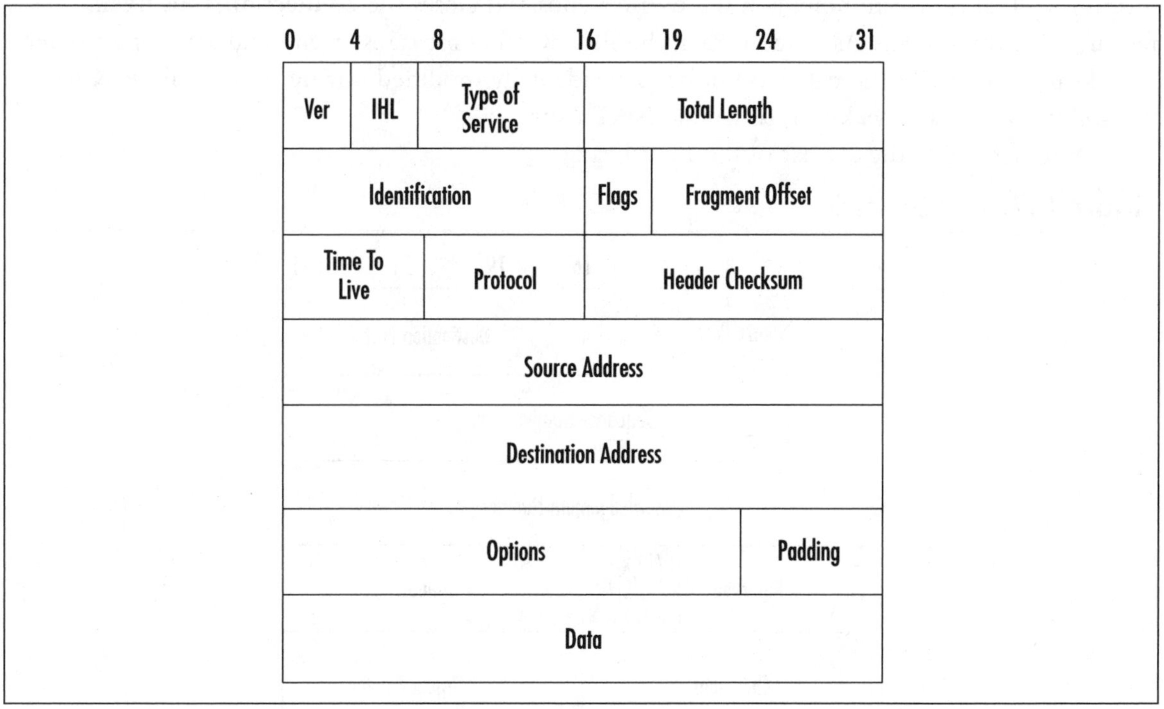

Let's quickly review the meaning of key fields in Figure 8.1. Most are not specifically part of the review exam, but it helps to put what the PIX does in context:

■ The *protocol* parameter indicates the upper-level protocol that is using IP. The decimal value for TCP is 6, and UDP is 17. The list of assigned numbers for this field is available at www.iana.org/assignments/protocol-numbers. Note that this field is important for *access-list* commands. The command syntax is:

```
access-list <acl_ID> {deny | permit} <protocol>…
```

The protocol number here corresponds to this field. Note that you can specify the keyword *tcp* for type 6 or *udp* for type 17.

■ The *source address* and *destination address* fields are filled with the IP addresses of the respective devices; note that an IP address is four octets, so this can be viewed as a 32-bit number. You will see these numbers in the XLATE table.

Transmission Control Protocol

Many Internet services, such as HTTP, SMTP, or SSH, are based on TCP. This protocol provides reliable service by being connection-oriented and includes error detection and correction. The connection must be established before a data transfer can occur, and transfers are acknowledged throughout the process. Firewalls can identify the connection establishment and often interrupt that establishment as part of the protective mechanism. Acknowledgments assure that data is being received properly. The acknowledgment process provides robustness in the face of network congestion or communication unreliability. The acknowledgment has also been used to penetrate stateless firewalls; the PIX can identify packets that are not part of valid streams and block transmission. TCP also determines when the transfer ends and closes the connection, thus freeing resources on the systems. As noted earlier, the PIX watches for transfer end and acts appropriately. Checksums assure that the data has not been accidentally modified during transit. The PIX has the ability to rewrite checksums to handle NAT issues.

Figure 8.2 shows the format of the TCP header.

Figure 8.2 The TCP Header

The PIX inspects TCP packets for several fields, notably source port, destination port, sequence and acknowledgment numbers, and TCP flags. Notice that source and destination ports and information about the flags are listed in the CONN connections table.

The concept of *port* is common to both TCP and UDP (discussed in the following section). The idea is that for these types of protocols, we can identify an ordered pair (IP address and port), called a *socket*, with each side of the communication flow. Multiple communications from the same host (same IP) can be distinguished by different port numbers—thus different sockets.

Sockets on the server generally have a "well-known port" number. The PIX has a mapping between well-known ports and their English equivalents.

We have enough background to see how ASA works for TCP connections. A TCP datastream begins with the "three-way handshake." The idea is for each side to set up the *initial sequence number*, a pointer that will describe the position in the datastream for each packet sent. The TCP flag that indicates a request to start that datastream is the SYN flag. The first three packets are an initial SYN request from the client to the server; then back from the server to the client with acknowledgment of the client's request (by setting the ACK flag) and the server's need to initialize as well (by setting the SYN flag); and finally the client back to the server, acknowledging the server's synchronization request. Therefore, from the TCP level, the path is SYN, SYN/ACK, ACK.

At the PIX, a little more goes on. Figure 8.3 provides a diagram for how information flows through the PIX. Let's follow the first two network packets.

Figure 8.3 Basic ASA Operations

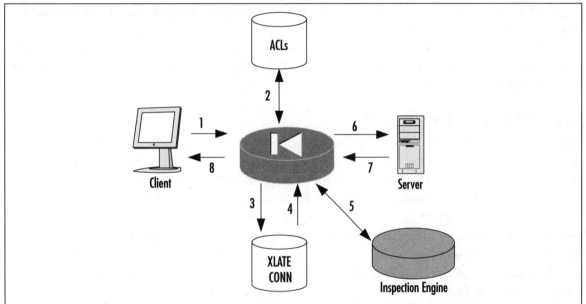

1. The client generates a SYN packet, headed toward the server, to establish a new connection.

2. The PIX investigates the ACL to determine if the information flow control policy should permit the new connection.

3. Assuming the connection is valid, the PIX updates the connections table.

4. The XLATE table is updated as necessary.

5. The stream is processed by the Application Inspection Engine, if necessary, which could involve rewriting the packet.

6. The packet is sent on to the server.

7. On the reverse path, the server responds with its SYN/ACK.

8. However, since this is not an initialization request, inspection of the rule base is not required; it looks the packet up in the connections table and then forwards it back to the client.

TCP Sequence Number Randomization

All that SYN and SYN/ACK work is designed so that both sides will agree on an initial sequence number (ISN) for each side of their communication. This adds a layer of security protection; in theory, one would have to be able to "hear" the TCP SYN request to know what ISN to use, and thus the IP address of the host in the datastream must be able to receive the packet, and therefore, for example, hosts on the Internet can't masquerade as local hosts.

Unfortunately, many servers use an easily guessed ISN generation function. One famous break-in, Kevin Mitnick's raid on Tsunomo Shinomura's data, chronicled in the book *Takedown*, was based on this flaw. The PIX provides protection against this type of attack by using TCP sequence number randomization. As the packets pass through the firewall, they are rewritten so that the ISNs cannot be predicted.

This system is not perfect; you should still use authentication and authorization at the server where available. However, it should provide an extra layer of protection that will let your security officers sleep better at night.

User Datagram Protocol

Several Internet applications, notably Domain Name Service (DNS) and many streaming audio and video protocols, are based on User Datagram Protocol (UDP). The UDP protocol is a simple, unreliable transport service. It is connectionless, so delivery is not assured. Look at the simple design of the UDP header in Figure 8.4 and you will understand this protocol's efficiency. Since connections aren't set up and torn down, there is very little overhead. Lost, damaged, or out-of-order segments will not be retransmitted unless the application layer requests it. UDP is used for fast, simple messages sent from one host to another. Due to its simplicity, UDP packets are more easily spoofed than TCP packets. If reliable or ordered delivery of data is needed, applications should use TCP.

Figure 8.4 The UDP Header

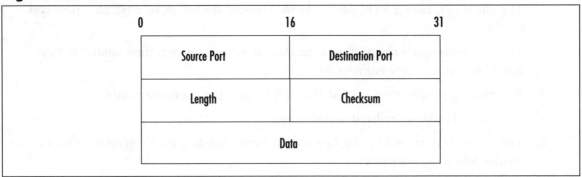

There is usually a trade-off between simplicity and security, and this is true with UDP. Because TCP is connection oriented, we can identify the start of the session by unique flags—but as you can see in Figure 8.4, there aren't any flags here. All you have to work with is the UDP socket pairs.

This is where the firewall state comes in. The PIX has the ability to recognize the first UDP packet in a datastream. When the first packet is permitted by the information flow control policy (either because it is coming from a trusted net toward a less trusted one or because of an explicit exception in the ACL), the same sort of process shown in Figure 8.3 occurs. If permitted, an entry is made in the connections table, and further packets with the same socket pairs are associated with that authorized datastream until an idle timeout occurs. (The idle timeout is set with the *timeout* command and defaults to two minutes.)

Note that other protocols besides TCP and UDP are permitted. Most common is ICMP, the Internet Control Message Protocol. ICMP provides diagnostic functions and error reporting for IP. For example, ICMP can provide feedback to a sending host when a destination is unreachable or time is exceeded (TTL=0). A ping is an ICMP echo request message, and the response is an ICMP echo reply.

Other types of protocols are filtered by the PIX, although the concept of socket does not apply (and so you cannot specify extra parameters on the access list beyond filtering on the source and destination addresses). The special protocol 0 refers to any IP packet, and you can specify any value between 0 and 255. You can also use literals; you have already seen the literals TCP (which is 17), UDP (which is 6), and ICMP (which is 1).

These other protocols are handled similarly to the UDP approach, with idle timeouts removing entries from the connection table when they are no longer valid.

Advanced Protocol Handling

The PIX has taken elements from both camps in an example of a hybrid firewall, combining stateful packet filtering with advanced protocol handling with proxies via the *fixup* command. For common applications, the PIX provides advanced protocol handling, not only dealing with embedded IP addresses (the scourge of NAT functionality) but improving overall security handling.

Providing support for complex protocols is a distinguishing characteristic of the PIX. The "fixup" proxies include ftp, http, h323, ils, rsh, rtsp, smtp, sip, skinny, and SQL. Some protocols, such as DNS Guard (which prevents multiple DNS responses from penetrating to the host), are supported in the native PIX services and do not need to be configured.

Application support of this type is where the real power of a firewall shines. The PIX is more than just a gatekeeper, passing or blocking packets; it understands the underlying protocol and actively rewrites the communications—enforcing RFCs, eliminating dangerous commands, and preventing the leakage of information—to provide the highest level of security available, consistent with application functionality.

VPN Support

An important aspect of network security is confidentiality of information. Packets flowing along a network are much like postcards sent through the mail; if you don't want the world reading your messages, you have to take additional care.

To achieve the kind of confidentiality offered on a private network, several approaches have been followed. One is to use encryption to conceal the information. An early standard, followed by Microsoft, is the Point-to-Point Tunneling Protocol (PPTP). Much like putting a letter inside a sealed envelope, this standard allows encapsulating (and concealing) network traffic inside a transport header. A similar but more comprehensive approach is to use the Layer 2 Tunneling Protocol (L2TP). This protocol is native to many Microsoft deployments, and so the PIX's support for PPTP and L2TP is an important element of the feature set.

In the fall of 1998, the Security Architecture for IP (IPsec) was published in RFC2401. Cisco has provided a leadership position in IPsec implementation, having co-authored many of the IPsec RFCs as well as providing solutions for some of the stickier IPsec issues, such as NAT traversal. It should be no surprise that the PIX is an excellent IPsec tunnel terminator. It has a wide range of interoperable standards and is straightforward to configure with pre-shared keys or with a certificate authority (CA). Many companies are using the PIX as an integrated firewall/VPN terminator, particularly in SOHO environments, as well as a stand-alone VPN terminator in conjunction with another (dedicated) firewall.

One of the PIX's best features is VPN performance. The models are designed to produce essentially wire-speed performance under heavy IPsec load. Because of the simplicity of the appliance's maintenance, VPN termination on a PIX is a sound choice for many enterprise or carrier-class environments.

URL Filtering

A uniform resource locator, or URL, is the way we identify addresses for information on the World Wide Web (WWW). The PIX firewall supports URL filtering by capturing a request and querying a database located on an N2H2 or Websense server. The N2H2 server can be running Linux (see www.n2h2.com/products/bess.php?os=lnx&device=pix) or Microsoft Windows (see www.n2h2.com/products/bess.php?os=win&device=pix); the Websense server can use these platforms or be installed on a Solaris server (www.websense.com/products/integrations/ciscoPIX.cfm).

URL filtering provides you with a way to apply an acceptable use policy for Internet browsing as well as to capture and analyze how your personnel are using the Internet. The servers themselves provide reporting capabilities so that you can determine how well your policy is being followed.

NAT and PAT

Another key strength of the Cisco PIX is its ability to translate addresses. Historically, an insider note is that the PIX comes from equipment created by a company called Network Translations Inc., and the PIX's first role was simply to perform address translation. (The name *PIX* comes from *Private Internet Exchange*, reflecting its purpose: to exchange traffic between private networks and the Internet.)

Network Address Translation, or NAT, encapsulates the idea that we can remap IP addresses (or sockets) where desirable in order to provide efficiencies or security. In the late 1990s, there was a great concern that we would run out of IP addresses; every host needed its own IP, and there are only 2^{32} to go around. Once we hit that number of computers, we'd be out of addresses. Worse, when you changed service providers, you generally had to give up your IP addresses and renumber all your machines—an expensive, time-consuming task that often ended up missing some machines, leaving them unable to communicate.

An idea was developed to use "private" addresses internally and, at the perimeter of our control, remap them into "public" addresses given to us by our service provider. Now we do not have to spend a lot of time renumbering our IP addresses; if we change providers, we only have to change the value of the IP addresses on the external firewalls and we are done. In February 1996, Cisco co-authored RFC1918, which established ranges for "private" addresses—all of the 10 network (10.0.0.0 through 10.255.255.255), part of the 172 network (172.16.0.0 through 172.31.255.255), and the 192.168 network (192.168.0.0 through 192.168.255.255). This RFC is followed nearly universally by enterprises today, with IP address schemes chosen from these private networks to simplify the structure of the internal network.

NAT also provides a form of *security through obscurity*. Since the private addresses are not advertised, an outside attacker does not necessarily know how the machine refers to itself; this structure adds an extra layer of work the attacker needs to perform to understand how to connect to an internal host.

There are several different ways to perform the address translation. The simplest form of NAT provides a one-to-one map between internal host IP addresses and external addresses—for example, a map between 10.1.1.1 and 198.133.219.25. Then, any reference, say 198.133.219.25 port 80, gets translated to 10.1.1.1 port 80, and vice versa. This form of NAT has two different flavors: static NAT, in which the translation is set up once and is permanent, and dynamic NAT, in which a translation is set up from a pool of available addresses and is torn down when an idle timeout occurs. The former is perfect for remapping servers that need to provide consistent access to the outside world; because the translated address is fixed, it can be put into public DNSs and readily accessed by outside clients. The latter is perfect for remapping users who need public services and IP addresses for a short time, which can then can be released for other users when the services and addresses are no longer needed. This system allows for, say, 100 people to hide behind 30 addresses, as long as no more than 30 of those people need external access at any one time.

The idea of dynamic NAT can be extended even further. Most IP services are based on sockets, such as IP address/port number pairs. Rather than remapping on IP address, we can remap on sockets. Now 10.1.1.1,80 might get mapped to 198.133.219.25,3125 while 10.1.3.42,80 gets mapped to 198.133.219.25,4176—the same IP address in both cases, but because the port numbers are different, the sockets are different. Therefore, the other side of the conversation would be able to distinguish between these two datastreams.

This concept is called *Port Address Translation (PAT)* and allows for stacking over 30,000 TCP sessions on a single IP address. The good news is that now when you want to hide your 100 users, you can hide them behind a single IP address. The bad news is that certain protocols—ones that expect fixed port addresses—are broken by this translation. The PIX can be configured to use static addresses for fixed servers and dynamic addresses for users with an overflow pool of PAT (or even multiple PAT to give a better chance of being able to preserve port address). You can see that the PIX is a very flexible and highly effective network address translation device.

High Availability

The three fundamental concepts of information security are confidentiality, integrity, and availability. The PIX addresses the availability idea by providing a robust, fault-tolerant environment. *Fault-tolerant* means that if something goes wrong, alarms are set off and something is done to ameliorate the problem.

The term *high availability* usually refers to hardware fault tolerance. Obviously, a firewall is a critical piece of equipment: By its very nature, it has to stand in the center of the traffic flow. Cisco hardware is of very high quality, and the PIX has no moving parts, but sometimes equipment does fail. High availability is a device configuration so that isolated failure of the hardware will not bring down your network.

To achieve this goal, of course, you must have multiple pieces of hardware. In this case, two PIXs are configured similarly, and they communicate between each other. If one piece of hardware dies, the other transparently picks up the traffic, and alarm messages are sent to the network management console.

High availability can be configured in several ways. Naturally, you need a second PIX that will be configured in a hot standby fashion. The simplest and least expensive way is through a serial cable, provided when you purchase the failover license. Alternately, a LAN interface can be dedicated to the failover process. With the failover cable, hello packets containing the number of bytes seen by the interfaces are transmitted between the two boxes, and if the values differ, failover can occur. With the LAN interface, full state information is transmitted so that in the event of a failover, the TCP sessions can keep running without reinitialization.

PIX Hardware

The PIX has many different configuration models to ensure that the product will be suited to different environments. Obviously, the requirements of a SOHO user will be different from those of a service provider. Cisco has provided various classes with different price points to ensure optimum product placement.

Models

Five models are currently supported: the 501, the 506E, the 515E, the 525, and the 535. However, there are three models that you might see deployed in enterprise environments: the 506, the 515, and the 520. At a glance, Table 8.1 shows the vital characteristics of each of the models.

PIX 501

The 501 is the basic entry model for the PIX and has a fixed configuration. It has a four-port 10/100Mbps switch for inside connectivity and a single 10Mbps interface for connecting to the Internet upstream device (such as cable modem or DSL router). It will provide 3Mbps throughput on a 3DES IPsec connection, which should exceed a SOHO user's requirements. The base license is a 10-user license with DES IPsec; optional is a 50-user upgrade and/or 3DES VPN support.

Table 8.1 PIX Model Characteristics

Model	End of Life?	VAC Available?	Processor Type	3DES Throughput	Maximum Interfaces	RAM Memory	Failover Support	Clear-Text Throughput
501	No	No	133MHz AMD SC520	3Mbps	2	16Mb	No	8Mbps
506	Yes	No	200MHz Intel Pentium MMX	6Mbps	2	32MB	No	8Mbps
506E	No	No	300MHz Intel Celeron	16Mbps	2	32MB	No	20Mbps
515	Yes	Yes	200MHz Intel Pentium MMX	10Mbps	6**	64MB**	No	170Mbps
515E	No	Yes	443MHz Intel Celeron	63Mbps*	6**	64MB**	Yes	188Mbps
520	Yes	Yes	233MHz Intel Pentium MMX	60Mbps*	6	128MB	Yes	170Mbps
525	No	Yes	600MHz Intel Pentium III	70Mbps*	8	256MB**	Yes	360Mbps
535	No	Yes	1GHz Intel Pentium III	100Mbps*	10	1GB**	Yes	1Gbps

* Maximum 3DES throughput is achieved with the VAC; ** maximum requires the unrestricted license.

The 501 is based on a 133MHz AMD SC520 processor with 16MB of RAM and 8MB of flash. There is a console port, a half-duplex RJ45 10BaseT port for the outside, and an integrated, autosensing, auto-MDIX 4 port RJ45 10/100 switch for the inside.

PIX 506

The 506 is the basic remote office/branch office device. Once again, the appliance is not hardware configurable, with one console port and two autonegotiate RJ45 10BaseT ports, one for inside and one for outside. Performance is greatly increased; the 506 supports 8Mbps clear-text throughput, with 6Mbps 3DES IPsec, which should permit supporting hundreds of branch office users in a VPN tunnel back to corporate.

The hardware is based on a 200MHz Intel Pentium MMX, with 32MB of RAM and 8MB of flash.

PIX 506E

The 506E product, an enhanced version of the 506, has replaced it on the product sheets. The chassis are similar, but the 506E has a beefier CPU, a quieter fan, and a new power supply. The CPU is the 300MHz Intel Celeron, while the RAM and flash are of the same capacity. Clear-text throughput has been increased to 20Mbps (wire speed), while 3DES throughput increased to 16Mbps. Licensing on the 506E (and 506) is easier than the 501; it is provided in a single, unlimited-user mode. The only extra license you might need is the 3DES license.

PIX 515

The next step up the scale is the PIX 515, intended for the enterprise core of small to medium-sized businesses. Again, this product has wirespeed performance, but this time the pipe is a bit fatter and carries the ability to handle up to 170Mbps of clear-text throughput.

The chassis is a 1U pizza box, intended for rack mounting. Probably the most important difference between the 506 and the 515 is that the chassis is configurable; it comes with a slot for an additional single-port or four-port Fast Ethernet interface, allowing the inside, outside, and up to four additional service networks. The base unit is based on the same 200MHz Intel Pentium MMX with 32MB of RAM and 8MB of flash as the 506E.

The licensing is flexible, so enterprises can purchase only what they need. The restricted license limits the number of interfaces to three and does not support high availability. The unrestricted license allows for an increase in RAM (from 32MB to 64MB) and up to six interfaces, together with failover capability.

PIX 515E

The 515E replaced the 515 in May 2002. It has a higher-performing 433MHz Intel Celeron, increasing base firewall performance. Another new option is the ability to offload the arithmetic load of DES computation from the OS to a dedicated VPN accelerator card (VAC), delivering up to 63Mbps 3DES throughput and 2,000 IPsec tunnels. Licensing is similar: the restricted license limits you to three interfaces and no failover, whereas the unrestricted license has the memory upgrade, the VAC, and up to six interfaces.

PIX 520

The PIX 520 is an odd bird. It was designed as the high-end PIX platform, with the PC-style rack-mount chassis and a wide mix of available media cards, including Token Ring and fiber. Like the earlier PIXs, the 520 comes with a DB9 console port and a diskette drive; it is based on the 200MHz Intel Pentium MMX but with 128MB of RAM. Also unusual is the licensing: Like the 501, the 520's license is based on the number of users. For an entry PIX, you would purchase PIX-CONN-128, which would allow 128 simultaneous users. There were license upgrades to 1024 users or unlimited users.

Having the diskette drive is especially convenient. Although it uses up real estate in the rack, it allows you to have a handy boot medium in case the network goes down or is otherwise inaccessible; TFTP servers are not required. It also allows you to readily reset the password (by booting the appropriate password-clearing binary) or restore to a known good condition. Of course, these features are now achieved through appropriate network management tools, such as CiscoWorks or the PIX Firewall Manager.

PIX 525

The PIX 525 replaced the PIX 520 in June 2001. It is designed for large enterprise or small service provider environments. The diskette drive is gone; however, the 525 still supports single- or four-port 10/100 Fast Ethernet, 4/16 Token Ring, and dual-attached multimode FDDI cards, but now also picks up Gigabit Ethernet. Performance tells the story here: Based on the 600MHz Intel Pentium III, the 525 boasts 360Mbps clear-text throughput and, with the accelerator card, 70Mbps of 3DES IPsec tunnel traffic.

Licensing is based on interface counts and failover, as with the earlier models. The restricted license limits the PIX 525 to 128MB of RAM and six interfaces. The unrestricted bumps RAM to 256MB, allows up to eight interfaces, and supports failover. As before, 3DES licensing is separate, if desired.

PIX 535

The PIX 535 is the top-of-the-line model, suitable for service provider environments. Performance is the key: up to 1Gbps clear-text throughput, half a million simultaneous connections, and 7000 connection initialization/teardowns per second. With the VAC, you can get 100Mbps 3DES throughput, with up to 2000 simultaneous security associations (VPN tunnels).

In terms of hardware, the PIX 535 is based on a 1GHz Intel Pentium III, with up to 1GB of RAM. It has a 16MB flash and 256K cache running at 1GHz, as well as a dual 64-bit 66MHz PCI system bus. Cards available are the one- or four-port 10/100 Ethernet NICs or 1GB Ethernet multimode "stick and click" fiber connectors.

The Console Port

The primary mechanism for talking to a PIX is via the console port. Some devices have the old DB9 connectors—nine-pin D-subminiature connectors similar to those found on the back of many PCs. The newer devices use the Cisco standard RJ45 connector, similar to those found on their routers and switches. In each case, an appropriate cable is provided with your equipment.

The communication is via null-modem and uses communications set to 8-N-1. If you are using Windows, a good program to communicate with a PIX is Hyperterm, which is provided with most Windows-based installations, under Accessories/Communications. When launching Hyperterm, configure your connection to direct-connect to COM 1, as shown in Figure 8.5.

Figure 8.5 Configuring Hyperterm

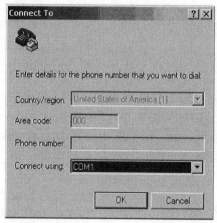

The communications parameters then need to be set, as shown in Figure 8.6.

Figure 8.6 Port Communication Properties for Hyperterm

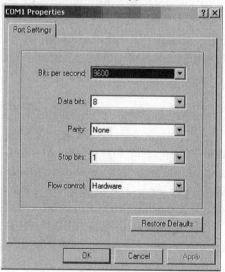

At this point, you should be connected. Power on your PIX, and you will see the boot process taking place, as shown in Figure 8.7. Your output will differ slightly.

Figure 8.7 Sample Output from Boot Sequence

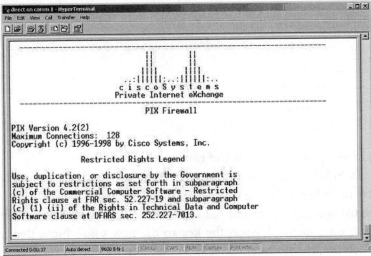

Figure 8.7 shows an older flash version, but they all are similar. If you do not see output or the output is garbled, it usually means your parameters are not set correctly. If you are not using the provided cable, make sure it is null-modem and that your parameters are set as shown in Figure 8.6.

Software Licensing and Upgrades

In order to have a flexible product, the PIX uses software licensing to enable or disable features within the PIX OS. Although the hardware is common to all platforms (except that certain licenses can ship with additional memory or hardware accelerators) and the software is common, features differ depending on the activation key.

The activation key allows you to upgrade features without acquiring new software, although the process is similar. The activation key is computed by Cisco depending on what you have ordered and your serial number, so it's different for each piece of PIX hardware you own. The serial number is based on the flash, so if you replace the flash, you have to replace the activation key.

The activation key enables feature-specific information such as interfaces, high availability, and type of encryption. More specific information is found in the section "PIX Licensing and Upgrades."

To get information about the activation key, use the *show version* command. The command provides information about the code version, hardware information, and activation key information. Alternately, the command *show activation-key* provides something like this:

```
Serial Number: 480090153 (0x1c9d9829)


Running Activation Key: 0x75fe7c49 0xc08b4082 0x08979930 0xe4b4c4b0
Licensed Features:
Failover:          Enabled
VPN-DES:           Enabled
```

```
VPN-3DES:              Disabled
Maximum Interfaces: 6
Cut-through Proxy:    Enabled
Guards:                Enabled
URL-filtering:        Enabled
Inside Hosts:          Unlimited
Throughput:            Unlimited
IKE peers:             Unlimited
```

The *flash activation key* is the *same* as the running key.

This machine is a PIX 515 and has an unrestricted license, with the maximum number of interfaces permitted, including failover.

Updating the activation key in version 6.2 of the PIX OS couldn't be simpler. The command *activation-key <activation-key-four-tuple>* sets the key to the new value. Note that activation four-tuples are in hexadecimal, are case insensitive, and don't require you to start the numbers with 0x. Thus the previously mentioned machine could be set with:

```
PIX1(config)# activation-key 75fe7c49 c08b4082 08979930 e4b4c4b0
```

Updating the activation keys in prior versions is not much more complicated. Power-cycle the PIX, and send an Esc or Break to enter monitor mode. This will present you with a prompt:

```
monitor>
```

Type **a ?** to see the options. Sample output is listed here:

```
Use ? for help.
monitor> ?
? this help message
address    [addr]    set IP address
file       [name]    set boot file name
gateway    [addr]    set IP gateway
help                 this help message
interface  [num]     select TFTP interface
ping       <addr>    send ICMP echo
reload               halt and reload system
server     [addr]    set server IP address
tftp       TFTP      download
timeout    TFTP      timeout
trace                toggle packet tracing
```

It would be a good idea to upgrade your software at this time, but in any event, the PIX will ask you if you want to update your activation key at the end of the TFTP process.

Licensing

Generally, the licensing falls into one of three types, plus an additional factor for crypto constraints. The three main categories are unrestricted, restricted, and failover. If you have a single PIX, you'll want unrestricted or restricted licensing, depending on the number of interfaces you want to support. If you have two PIX appliances and want high availability, you'll want one machine with an unrestricted license and another machine with a failover license.

Upgrading Software

The traditional way of managing images is via TFTP. This is a UDP-based transport protocol—fast and efficient. Unfortunately, it is not authenticated, so you have to be a bit careful to ensure that your data gets saved when you write to a TFTP server and that the data downloaded doesn't get corrupted.

By tradition, UNIX hosts have TFTP software preinstalled. If you do have a UNIX laptop, try *man tftpd* to see how to turn it on. If you have a Windows laptop, the server is not installed (although a client might well be—it's standard on most NT and Win2K environments).

Luckily, a TFTP server for a Windows environment is easy to acquire and install. Perhaps one of the best is the Solar Winds server, part of the Solar Winds suite. The full tool set is an invaluable aid to security professionals, and some pieces of it, like the TFTP server, are free. Installation is via the WISE installation wizard.

Another excellent TFTP server is the one Cisco provides. It is available at www.cisco.com/cgi-bin/tablebuild.pl/tftp and is also free. Simply provide your Cisco user ID when you download, and launch the installer executable.

Running the Cisco TFTP server is straightforward. The server, by default, is not running. (This mode is recommended, since there is no authentication; you don't want anyone uploading or downloading files without your knowledge.) The first time you run it, you will want to press **O** for Options (under the **View** menu) to set the log file, if desired, and set the TFTP root directory. This is where you want to store the images. If you are going to be upgrading the PIX software, FTP the binary image down from the Web into that directory, and you are ready for the transfer.

If you have a very old version of the software (pre 5.1(*x*)), you must upgrade using monitor mode. You can follow the preceding notes or the following step-by-step procedure:

1. Enter monitor mode. Remember, this requires that you get a console session running, power-cycle the box, and press **Escape** within 10 seconds of the boot.

2. The PIX is currently unconfigured. Set up your download interface by doing the following:

    ■ Use **interface <*number*>** to set the TFTP interface. The default is 1, so you don't have to set it if the TFTP server is on the inside.

    ■ Use **address <*IP address*>** to set the IP address of the PIX.

    ■ Hopefully, your server is on the same network as the TFTP interface. If not, you can set a default gateway with **gateway <*IP address*>**.

3. Next prepare the transfer information:

- Use **server** *<IP address>* to set the IP address of your TFTP server.

- Use **file** *<filename>* to set the name of the image to upload.

4. Finally, execute the transfer. Use **tftp** to start the file.

This process loads a new image in place, and when you reboot, you will come up under the new image.

Luckily, this process should not apply—unless you accidentally upload the wrong file or your TFTP transfer fails. Monitor mode is primarily used in the event of disaster.

The process of updating your software on a reasonably new version of code is straightforward. You can avoid monitor mode and do everything from the PIX enable command line. Log in to the PIX and get into enable mode. It is a good idea to ping your TFTP server to verify connectivity—for example:

```
PIX1# ping inside 10.1.1.1
```

Get the version of the software onto your TFTP server, and copy the file to flash:

```
pixfirewall# copy tftp flash
Address or name of remote host [127.0.0.1]? 10.1.1.1
Source file name [cdisk]? pix621.bin
copying tftp://10.1.1.1/pix621.bin to flash
[yes|no|again]? yes
!!!!!!!!!!!!!!!!!!!!!!!!!!!!!!!!!!!!!!!!!!!!!!!!!!!!!!!!!!
Received 1640448 bytes.
Erasing current image.
Writing 1640448 bytes of image.
!!!!!!!!!!!!!!!!!!!!!!!!!!!!!!!!!!!!!!!!!!!!!!!!!!!!!!!!!!
Image installed.
```

On the next reload, the new image is available.

Password Recovery

Passwords are stored on the PIX using an MD5 hash. This is good; you are probably aware that Cisco type 7 passwords can be instantly decrypted using a simple personal digital assistant (PDA). MD5 hash is harder: a hacker essentially has to try out all the combinations. Unfortunately, the MD5 hash used on the PIX is significantly weaker than the Cisco type 5 hash used on Cisco routers. Programs such as Cain & Abel (www.oxid.it) can, with time, discover a password. This weakness has been assigned CVE vulnerability CAN-2002-0954. So, if all you have is a printout, you can recover your password. This can be helpful for machines that are in production environments. (However, the caveat is that others can do the same. Be careful about leaving configuration files on TFTP servers or printouts where others can get to them.)

If your environment can tolerate a little downtime, you can reset your PIX password. You download a program, depending on your OS version, that will execute on the PIX and reset the password to the default, *cisco*. You can then get in and use enable mode to set the password to a known value.

Earlier you saw that monitor mode was used for emergencies. Forgetting the password is a pretty good emergency. Here is what you do:

1. Pick the correct version of the software from Table 8.2.

Table 8.2 PIX Password Recovery Binaries

Version	Filename	URL
4.3 and earlier releases	nppix.bin	www.cisco.com/warp/public/110/nppix.bin
4.4 release	np44.bin	www.cisco.com/warp/public/110/np44.bin
5.0 release	np50.bin	www.cisco.com/warp/public/110/np50.bin
5.1 release	np51.bin	www.cisco.com/warp/public/110/np51.bin
5.2 release	np52.bin	www.cisco.com/warp/public/110/np52.bin
5.3 release	np53.bin	www.cisco.com/warp/public/110/np53.bin
6.0 release	np60.bin	www.cisco.com/warp/public/110/np60.bin
6.1 release	np61.bin	www.cisco.com/warp/public/110/np61.bin
6.2 release	np62.bin	www.cisco.com/warp/public/110/np62.bin

2. Place this software on a TFTP server accessible to the PIX.

3. Connect to the PIX on the console port. Verify connectivity. (You should get a password prompt, which you can't answer.)

4. Reboot the PIX.

5. Within 10 seconds of the reboot, press **Esc** to enter monitor mode.

6. Use the *interface* command to set the interface to that of the TFTP server.

7. Use the *address* command to specify the IP address of that interface.

8. Use the *server* command to specify the IP address of the TFTP server.

9. Use the *gateway* command to specify the default route to the TFTP server, if needed. (This is not recommended; if at all possible, try to have the TFTP server on the same network as the PIX interface to minimize the likelihood of file corruption.)

10. Use the *file* command to specify the filename of the recovery file you chose in Step 1.

11. Use the *ping* command to verify that you can connect to the TFTP server.

12. Use the *tftp* command to start the download.

At this point, you should be prompted to erase the passwords, and you will be in. The default password has now been set to *cisco*, with no enable password.

The Command-Line Interface

Like a Cisco router, the configuration of the PIX is contained in a text file. The job of a PIX administrator is to create the text file. There are many ways to achieve this goal: working offline and uploading configurations, working through an intermediary such as the PIX Device Manager (PDM), or working at the command prompt. Because most maintenance tasks are fairly simple, most of your time will be spent at the command prompt, so it is helpful to spend some time with that.

Factory Default Configurations

There are two basic factory default configurations. Because the PIX 501 and PIX 506 have fairly specific purposes, the default configurations for those devices are suited to their market. Because the PIX 515, 525, and 535 are more general-purpose firewalls, they have correspondingly less configuration.

PIX 501 and 506E

The PIX 501 and 506E are intended to be dropped into a traditional DSL environment. Cisco makes the following assumptions:

1. The default information flow control policy will be anything permitted from the inside allowed out, nothing in.
2. The external interface will have its IP set via DHCP. Both interfaces are set fixed to 10Mbps Ethernet.
3. DHCP will be provided to inside users, with the default route set to the PIX.

The internal network that the PIX provides is the 192.168.1.0 network. (Remember, this is one of the choices allowed by RFC1918.) The PIX will be the default gateway for the network, at 192.168.1.1. This is convenient since many other vendors (such as wireless AP vendors) also use the 192.168.1.0 network and assume that the gate is at 192.168.1.1—so the 501 and 506E can be transparently dropped into most home nets. Limiting the interfaces to 10Mbps is not a problem, since the outside interface is going to be connected to a digital subscriber line (DSL) or cable environment, which will typically be functioning at less than 1Mbps, and fixing the connection to 10Mbps avoids some of the Fast Ethernet duplex handshaking problems that can occur on older switches.

For most users, this solution is reasonable. If this device is part of an enterprise deployment, a little more thought is required; this solution does not support centralized maintenance, for example, or VPN tunnels. If you are rolling out a large number of clients, you will want to determine a template and preconfigure the PIX before sending it to the end users.

PIX 515E, 525, and 535

The PIX 515E and up arrive with essentially blank factory configurations. Interfaces are set to autoconfigure but are disabled, and configuration via the console is required.

Administrative Access Modes

An administrative access mode is a state in which the administrator is able to issue commands, potentially to change the configuration of the PIX. Monitor mode, described earlier, is an administrative access mode, but it is contained in ROM rather than in the binary image, and hopefully you will never have to use it.

When you first log in, you are in an unprivileged mode. You can identify the mode you are in from the prompt: If the prompt looks like the hostname followed by a right-angle bracket (>), you are in unprivileged mode. Few commands are available:

```
PIX1> ?
enable          Turn on privileged commands
help            Help list
login           Log in as a particular user
logout          Exit from current user profile, and to unprivileged mode
pager           Control page length for pagination
quit            Quit from the current mode, end configuration or logout
```

This is not a complete list of the available commands. For example, when you are in unprivileged mode:

```
PIX1> show ?
checksum        View configuration information cryptochecksum
curpriv         Display current privilege level
history         Display the session command history
pager           Control page length for pagination
version         Display PIX system software version
PIX1> show version

Cisco PIX Firewall Version 6.2(1)
Cisco PIX Device Manager Version 1.0(1)


Compiled on Wed 17-Apr-02 21:18 by morlee


pix1 up 160 days 23 hours


Hardware:   PIX-515, 64 MB RAM, CPU Pentium 200 MHz
...
```

The most important of these is enable mode, which turns on the privileged commands. At this point, your prompt will change; now it ends in a pound sign. To show your new privilege:

```
PIX1# ?
arp          Change or view the arp table, and set the arp timeout value
capture      Capture inbound and outbound packets on one or more interfaces
```

```
configure   Configure from terminal
copy        Copy image or PDM file from TFTP server into flash.
debug       Debug packets or ICMP tracings through the PIX Firewall.
disable     Exit from privileged mode
eeprom      Show or reprogram the 525 onboard i82559 devices
flashfs     Show, destroy, or preserve filesystem information
help        Help list
kill        Terminate a telnet session
logout      Exit from current user profile, and to unprivileged mode
logging     Clear syslog entries from the internal buffer
pager       Control page length for pagination
passwd      Change Telnet console access password
ping        Test connectivity from specified interface to <ip>
quit        Quit from the current mode, end configuration or logout
reload      Halt and reload system
session     Access an internal AccessPro router console
shun        Manages the filtering of packets from undesired hosts
terminal    Set terminal line parameters
who         Show active administration sessions on PIX
write       Write config to net, flash, floppy, or terminal, or erase flash
```

At this point, you are more or less protected from accidentally harming the system: you can erase the configuration in total, but it will not make small changes until you enter configuration mode. Use the *configure terminal* command to get into configuration mode. Again, your prompt will change to show privilege:

```
PIX1(config)#
```

There are approximately 100 lines of commands, so it is not appropriate to show them all here. Unlike a Cisco router, for which there are additional modes, these are all the modes that occur: you have no rights, you are somewhat protected, or you are changing the configuration. However, note that if you are in configuration mode, your *show* commands are still available.

The PIX also stores previous commands you've executed. Use the *show history* command to see what you've executed. This feature is helpful in two ways: One, if you are unsure what you have executed so far, is to look at the *show history* command to see what you've done to date. A more common use is when you have lots of similar commands. You can use the Up-arrow key to see the previous line in your history and then use the basic commands (covered in the following section) to edit the line and resubmit it.

> **NOTE**
>
> The PIX firewall provides help functionality built into the command-line interface. Use the question mark key (?)—it is your friend. At any point, pressing **?** will help you complete your commands. In addition, a "man page" functionality is built in. For example, if you want to ping something and forgot the syntax, try *ping ?*. If you don't remember what the ping command does, try *help ping*. This provides usage, and description and syntax issues.

Basic Commands

The environment at the command prompt is similar to that of a Cisco router and uses "emacs"-style commands, shown in Table 8.3.

Table 8.3 Basic Keystroke Shortcuts

Command	Result
Tab	Command-line completion.
Ctrl + A	Moves the cursor to the start of a line.
Ctrl + B	Moves the cursor one character left (nondestructive).
Alt + B	Moves the cursor one word left.
Ctrl + D	Deletes the character under the cursor.
Ctrl + E	Moves the cursor to the end of the line.
Ctrl + F	Moves the cursor one character right.
Alt + F	Moves the cursor one word right.
Ctrl + H or Rubout	Erases the previous character.
Ctrl + R	Reprints a line.
Up Arrow or Ctrl + P	Displays the previous line.
Up Arrow or Ctrl + N	Displays the next line.
Help or ?	Displays help.

To see additional editing commands, try searching the Web for *emacs style commands*. However, the list shown in Table 8.3 is very useful. For example, if you are setting up multiple ACL statements, you can save a great deal of effort by changing only a port number, then pressing **Ctrl + P** to get the previous line, **Alt + F** to move right a few words, **Ctrl + D** to delete the old port, and then typing the new port.

In addition, you don't have to type the full command—you only have to provide enough of the command to establish a unique initial segment. For example, the command *configure terminal* can be abbreviated; the first three letters aren't enough (both *conduit* and *configure* start with *con*), and only one option from the *configure* command starts with *t*. Therefore, to get into configuration mode, just type **conf** *t*. Such shortcuts can save a bit of typing, particularly on long commands.

Hostname and Domain Name

Two useful commands are the *hostname* and *domain-name* commands. These set the hostname (which appears in the prompt) and the domain name of the PIX. The syntax is *hostname* <name> and *domain-name* <name>—for example:

```
PIX1 (config)# hostname PIX1
PIX1(config)# domain-name secret.com
```

Configuring Interfaces

The most important aspect of a network device is the network interface. In the PIX, configuring the network interface is a fairly straightforward process. You need to specify a few parameters to put the security in context and a few parameters to put connectivity in context, and then the default information flow policy takes over.

The nameif Command

The *nameif* command is used to give an interface a logical name and assign it a security level. The name should be memorable, since it will be used in all other commands. The format of the *nameif* command is:

```
nameif <hardware_id> <interface> <security_level>
```

hardware_id corresponds to the hardware associated with the interface, such as ethernet0. *interface* corresponds to a descriptive name, such as *dmz*, and *security_level* corresponds to the level of trust, an integer between 100 (trusted) and 0 (untrusted).

The tradition is to put ethernet0 (the first card from the left) as the outside interface, with a security level of 0—for example:

```
PIX1(config)# nameif ethernet0 outside security0
```

To assign ethernet1 (the second card from the left) as the inside interface with a security level of 100, the command is:

```
PIX1(config)# nameif ethernet1 inside security100
```

The remaining cards, if any, are assigned values between 0 and 100. An example for a DMZ network might resemble the following:

```
PIX1(config)# nameif ethernet2 dmz security50
```

The interface Command

The *interface* command is used to set the physical layer properties of the interface. The syntax of the command is:

```
interface <hardware_id> <hardware_speed> [shutdown]
```

In this command, *hardware_id* corresponds to the value from the *nameif* command, and *hardware_speed* is chosen from Table 8.4.

Table 8.4 Hardware Speed Types for the *interface* Command

Value	Description
10baset	10Mbps Ethernet, half duplex.
100basetx	Fast Ethernet, half duplex.
100full	Fast Ethernet, full duplex.
1000sxfull	Gigabit Ethernet, full duplex.
1000basesx	Gigabit Ethernet, half duplex.
1000auto	Gigabit Ethernet to autonegotiate full or half duplex.
aui	10Mbps Ethernet, half duplex, for an AUI cable interface.
bnc	10Mbps Ethernet, half duplex, for a BNC cable interface.
auto	Sets Ethernet speed automatically. Generally, it is better to hardcode the cable type, since autonegotiation has failed with some hardware devices.

The optional *shutdown* keyword disables the interface; *shutdown* is useful to rapidly terminate a connection on a network that is at hazard or to ensure that unused networks are not accidentally added. An example of the *interface* command is:

```
PIX1(config)# interface ethernet0 100full
```

The ip address Command

The *ip address* command sets the IP address of the particular interface. The syntax of the command is as follows:

```
ip address <interface> <ip_address> <netmask>
```

In the *ip address* command, *interface* corresponds to the same parameter as in the *nameif* command, a descriptive term for the network, and *ip_address* and *netmask* correspond to the usual properties for the interface. An example of this command might look something like this:

```
PIX1(config)# ip address dmz 192.168.0.1 255.255.255.0
```

> **NOTE**
>
> The PIX can also obtain an IP address through DHCP client or PPPoE functionality.

Static Routes

The PIX is not a router and so does not have a wide selection of routing protocols. The PIX supports static routes and RIP. Specifying a static route is done with the following syntax:

```
route <if_name> <ip_address> <netmask> <gateway_ip> [metric]
```

Translating this syntax into English, it reads "If packets destined for interface *if_name* on the network specified by network address *ip_address* are bounded by mask *netmask*, then route it via a next hop at *gateway_ip*." The optional *metric* command is used to give an indication of distance.

A particularly important route is the default route. This is the "route of last resort"—the route used when no other direction is known for the packet. Only one default route is allowed on the PIX. This route is indicated by the *0 route* with *netmask 0*; for example:

```
PIX1(config)# route outside 0 0 63.122.40.140 1
```

Password Configuration

Two passwords need to be set: a password for access to the PIX and an *enable* password to get into privileged (enable) mode. The PIX is limited to 16-byte passwords and is case sensitive. A basic *password* will assign a password, such as:

```
PIX1(config)# passwd cisco
```

```
PIX1(config)# enable password cisco
```

In the configuration, the password is stored in an encrypted fashion. The command then looks like this:

```
enable password 2KFQnbNIdI.2KYOU encrypted
passwd 2KFQnbNIdI.2KYOU encrypted
```

When first connecting to the PIX, you will see a password prompt:

```
Connected to 10.10.10.1.
Escape character is '^]'.


User Access Verification


Password:
Type help or '?' for a list of available commands.
pix1> en
Password: *****
```

You should note that to preserve security, the password is not echoed to the screen, and the previous sequence will get you into enable mode.

> **NOTE**
>
> The PIX also supports local user accounts with individual passwords. Alternatively, you can use RADIUS or TACACS+ for console authentication.

Managing Configurations

Just as with any network device, the most important task related to your PIX is ongoing management. It is important that you be comfortable not just manipulating the configuration with configuration mode but also pushing configurations out to storage and in from backup systems. Key commands here are *write*, which allows you to store a command; *copy*, which allows you to manage the underlying PIX application software; and *configure*, which allows you to update the configuration.

The *write* Command

The *write* command allows you to write the configuration to various types of media. Allowed variants are *write net*, *write memory*, *write standby*, *write terminal*, *write erase*, and *write floppy*.

```
write net [[server_ip] : [filename] ]
```

The *write* command writes the configuration to a TFTP server. The IP address of the server can be specified on the command line or preset with the TFTP server command, *tftp-server [if_name] ip_address path*. Specifying a value on this line supercedes the value on the TFTP server line, but if the TFTP-server information is set, you can provide just a colon (or no parameters at all).

The next command allows you to store the configuration to flash. The *uncompressed* parameter specifies storing the configuration as an uncompressed string and is generally not necessary.

```
write memory [uncompressed]
```

If you want to print the configuration to the terminal (screen), use this command:

```
write terminal
```

Note that this command prints out the running configuration. In version 6.2, two new *show* commands were added: *show running-config*, which gives the same output as *write terminal*, and *show startup-config*, which shows the configuration that is written to flash. If the pager variable is set, the screen will pause after a fixed number of lines. To store the configuration via an ASCII capture, set the pager to 0, and then type **write terminal**.

Similarly to the *write memory* command, on devices that have a diskette drive, the *write floppy* command stores the configuration in a proprietary format. This allows the PIX to readily read the configuration. If you write the configuration to a PIX boot disk, the appliance will come up with the desired configuration. Unfortunately, it is not easily readable on other devices.

```
write floppy [uncompressed]
```

There is one other *write* command: *write erase*. This command clears the flash configuration to a known good state and allows you to reconfigure.

The *copy* Command

The *copy* command is a similar way of managing images. The most common use of the command is in the *copy tftp* command—for example:

```
copy tftp[:[[//location] [/tftp_pathname]]] flash[:[image | pdm]]
```

The first couple of parameters are straightforward: They deal with specifying the location and filename of the TFTP server and, as previously mentioned, can be set with the *TFTP-server* command. The keyword *flash* indicates that the information is being stored to flash. The files can be conventional images, in which case they are available on the next reload, or PDM images, in which case they are available immediately.

Images can also be downloaded from a Web server via conventional HTTP or over SSL. This is specified by the following command:

```
copy http[s]://[user:password@] location [:port ] / http_pathname flash [: [image |
pdm] ]
```

You can probably figure out the parameters. The first part is the standard URI notation: *http* for clear-text Web use or *https* for SSL service. The *user:password@location* portion allows you to encode user information; if you are working via a Web browser, this portion triggers a pop-up window asking you to fill in your username and password. Since the PIX does not have a pop-up, you can specify it on the command line by inserting it before the @ sign. If the Web server is running on a nonstandard port, you can also specify it here by putting the port after a colon, similar to this:

```
copy http://fwadmin:cisco@10.10.10.1:99/pix_image flash
```

This solution is convenient if you do not have a TFTP server handy and can safely store the image files on a Web server.

The *configure* Command

You can manage configurations via the *configure* command. This is often the dual to the *write* commands. For example, just as *write terminal* dumps the configuration to the terminal, *configure terminal* allows you to change the configuration from the terminal.

These commands generally merge the configuration from the media with the existing configuration. You will often want to *clear configure* to wipe out the existing configuration so you can pull a complete stored config. The other choices are:

```
configure [terminal|floppy|memory]
```

You've used this one already, in the *conf t* command. It allows you to add commands from the terminal, from a diskette (if the PIX has a diskette drive), or from flash (memory).

Analogous to the *copy* command, the following command

```
configure http[s]://[<user>:<password>@]<location>[:<port>]/<pathname>
```

merges a configuration that is stored on a Web server with the running configuration.

```
configure net [<location>]:[<pathname>]
```
```
configure factory-default [<inside_ip> [<mask>]]
```

Resetting the System

Generally, after fetching a new image, you will want to have the PIX start under the new image. Similarly, it is helpful to occasionally restore the configuration to what is running on the flash—if, for example, you have been exploring commands and have gotten to an uncertain state. You can always power-cycle the device; this solution has no moving parts, and configurations and images are fully flushed to flash, so you do not have to worry about corruption. However, there is a better way: the *reload* command.

The *reload* Command

You can restart the PIX gracefully using the *reload* command. This command prompts you, to ensure that you really mean what you are saying; it can only be executed from privileged mode:

```
pix1# reload
Proceed with reload? [confirm]
```

At this point, there is a brief pause while the PIX reboots, and then you will be working under the new system. Note: If you want to bypass pressing the second carriage return, you can type **reload noconfirm**, but when you are executing a potentially dangerous command such as a reboot, it is generally good to have an "Are you really sure you want to do this?" checkpoint.

Summary

The PIX is a dedicated firewall appliance based on a special-purpose, hardened operating system. The simplified kernel and reduced command structure (compared with firewalls based on general-purpose operating systems) means that all other things being equal, the PIX will have higher throughput and more reduced maintenance costs than the general-purpose device. In addition, the similarity to IOS provides an edge to security administrators who are familiar with the Cisco environment.

The PIX is a hybrid firewall based on stateful packet filtering with the use of proxies for specific applications. The stateful packet filter is known as the *Adaptive Security Algorithm, or ASA,* and uses two databases: a table of translations and a table of known connections, to maintain state of the traffic transiting the network and to dynamically allow packets through the filter. The ASA inspects both packet header information, including source address, destination address, and TCP and UDP socket information, as well as packet contents for certain protocols, to make intelligent decisions on routing the packets. ASA has additional features: It will rewrite packets where necessary, as part of its inspection engine, where the protocols are well known.

About a dozen proxies are associated with the PIX. Some, such as the FTP proxy, augment the ASA process by permitting the passing of packets associated with an allowed communication—for FTP, while the command channel follows the normal three-way handshake initiated by the client and directed at a well-known socket, the data channels have the handshake initiated by the server (in the opposite direction of the usual security policy) and directed at a port defined during the transaction. Others, such as the SMTP proxy, are designed to enforce a limited subset of protocol commands and, by enforcing the RFC, provide additional security to potentially buggy applications. Still others, such as the multimedia proxies, provide the intelligence to extract IP addresses from the body of the packets and handle the complex rewriting and authorization for these interrelated protocols.

In addition to its native packet-filtering and access control features, the PIX provides additional common firewall services. Again, a key advantage of an appliance is performance, and the PIX makes an excellent VPN terminator, with the ability to pass encrypted traffic at wire speed, when an accelerator card is installed. It can provide content logging and filtering to help control Web surfing and provides address translation to allow for either "sewing together" networks seamlessly at the perimeter or consolidating (and concealing) internal networks to present to the outside world a limited number of addresses.

Modern environments depend on firewalls, and so the PIX provides high resiliency through its failover mechanism. This mechanism provides for a *hot spare*—a second PIX with an equivalent configuration that will automatically press itself into service should the primary device fail.

The PIX's extensive capabilities are matched by hardware flexibility. As of this writing, five different models are shipping, designed to match almost any environment. The PIX 501 is designed for the SOHO user, with a small switch built in for basic use. The PIX 506E, designed for the small or branch office, supports better performance for connecting back to the corporate hub. The PIX 515E is designed for the enterprise core of small to medium-sized business, with a rack-mount chassis and corresponding enterprise-class performance. The PIX 525 is designed for large enterprise or small service provider environments and has a slot-based configuration to allow for multiple interface configurations. The PIX 535 is the top-of-the-line model, designed for service provider environments, with the best possible throughput of the PIX appliances.

Communicating with an unconfigured PIX is most easily achieved through the console cable. This is provided with each firewall kit. Use a communications program such as Hyperterm, set your parameters to 8-N-1, and during the boot sequence you will see characters on your screen.

Licensing for the PIX features is set via an activation key. You should have received information about your activation key when you purchased the PIX; additional features can be purchased and new activation keys applied. The activation keys are dependent on a (hardware) serial number based on your flash. You can add new keys through either monitor mode or the *activation-key* command, new to version 6.2. Licensing usually falls into three types: unrestricted (all features enabled), restricted (limited features and interfaces), or failover (used for hot standby machines).

Password recovery is achieved by running a special program (different for each version of the operating system) on the PIX itself. The process requires either a dedicated boot diskette or the use of monitor mode and a TFTP download of a temporary image.

The normal configuration of the PIX is achieved through a command-line interface. This interface uses the "emacs" editing commands and is very similar to that provided in the Cisco IOS. The command structure is modal, with three major modes: unprivileged, which has very few available commands; privileged, where all commands are available (subject to your privilege level, which can be set in a local database); and configuration mode, by which changes are made to the running configuration.

Things that you will want to set up in every configuration include host and domain name, which configures the prompt and controls fields in the digital certificates used in VPN traffic, and the properties of the interfaces. You control a name—an association between a distinctive identifier for the interface and its default security characteristics—physical properties, and IP properties. You will also probably want to set up some basic routing, particularly the default route.

Passwords on any security device are very important. There are passwords for access to the device (unprivileged mode) and for escalation to privileged mode. They can be shared passwords, one per box, or passwords on a per-user basis. Cisco recommends the latter method, which requires setting up AAA services, either remote or local.

Managing configuration information is also important. Once you have built the perfect configuration, you do not want to have to retype it all in case of an emergency. Configurations can be stored in human-readable format via an ASCII capture (via *write terminal*) or as a text file on a TFTP server (via *write net*). Images can also be brought onto the system with the *copy* command, either from a TFTP server (*copy tftp*) or from a Web server URL (*copy https://servername/pix_image flash*). The system can then be restarted with the *reload* command and is ready to run under the new configuration.

## Chapter 9

Passing Traffic

Best Damn Topics in This Chapter:

- Allowing Outbound Traffic
- Allowing Inbound Traffic
- TurboACLs
- Object Grouping
- Case Study

Introduction

A firewall would not serve any purpose if it blocked all traffic. To properly protect a network environment, network traffic must be filtered both outbound and inbound. The key to configuring a firewall is to ensure that it only allows the traffic you want allowed and only blocks the traffic you want blocked. In some cases, this is not an easy task.

In this chapter, you will learn how to pass traffic through the PIX firewall. To pass traffic through a PIX firewall, some form of address translation must be configured. You will learn how to set up both static and dynamic translations. Once translation has been configured, the PIX will automatically allow all connections from a higher security-level interface to a lower security-level interface and deny all connections from a lower security-level interface to a higher security-level interface. To configure more granular access, you can permit or deny specific traffic. Depending on whether you are configuring inbound or outbound access, different commands are available to accomplish this task. We discuss these different commands in this chapter.

Object grouping is a new feature in PIX firewalls that simplifies access list configuration and maintenance. Here we discuss how to create and use object groups.

Throughout the chapter, we use examples to describe the various commands. We provide a complex case study to review what you have learned. By the end of this chapter, you will be an expert on passing traffic through PIX firewalls.

Allowing Outbound Traffic

Once the initial configuration of the PIX firewall is complete, the first step to passing traffic is to configure the PIX to allow outbound access. Outbound connections on the PIX are defined as connections from a higher security-level interface to a lower security-level interface. Allowing outbound traffic to traverse the PIX requires either configuring address translation or explicitly disabling it. Once address translation is configured, by default, if no access lists or apply/outbound statements are applied, all outbound traffic is allowed. This is a primary feature of the Adaptive Security Algorithm (ASA) and is the reason why security levels are so critical. Since the PIX is stateful, when an outbound connection is initiated, traffic returning to that connection is allowed to traverse back from the lower security-level interface to the higher security-level interface.

Configuring Dynamic Address Translation

Configuring address translation is the first step to pass outbound traffic. Address translation (through NAT and/or PAT) is used to map local IP addresses to global IP addresses. Once NAT and/or PAT are configured, the ASA automatically allows traffic to traverse from a higher security-level interface to a lower security-level interface on the PIX firewall (also known as *outbound connections*). The ASA also permits any return traffic related to these outbound connections.

Configuration of NAT/PAT is a two-step process:

1. Use the *nat* command to identify the local addresses that will be translated.
2. Use the *global* command to define the global addresses to translate to.

On the PIX firewall, address translation records are known as *translation slots* (or *xlate*) and are stored in a table known as the *translation table*. To view the contents of this table, use the *show xlate* command. The *xlate* timer monitors the translation table and removes records that have been idle longer than the defined timeout. By default, this timeout is set to three hours, and the current settings can be verified by using the *show timeout* command. The syntax of the *nat* command is as follows:

```
nat [(<if_name>)] <id> <local_address> [<netmask> [outside] [dns] [norandomseq]
[timeout <hh:mm:ss>] [<connection_limit> [<embryonic_limit>]]
```

The *if_name* parameter is used to apply the *nat* command to the interface where the traffic to be translated enters the PIX. This parameter must match the name used to describe an interface with the *nameif* command. If this parameter is not specified, the inside interface is assumed.

The *id* parameter is an integer between 0 and 2,000,000,000 that is used to establish a mapping between the local IP addresses (*local_address*) identified by the *nat* command and the global IP addresses specified by the *global* command. The *id* 0 is special and is used to specify that you do not want the specified local addresses translated. In other words, the local addresses and the global addresses will be the same.

The *netmask* parameter is used with *local_address* to be more specific about the IP addresses to translate. The *outside* keyword allows for external addresses to be translated. The *dns* keyword configures the PIX to translate the IP address included in DNS responses using active entries in the translation table. By default, when performing address translation, the PIX firewall also randomizes the sequence numbers in TCP segments. The *norandomseq* keyword tells the PIX not to randomize the sequence numbers. This is useful when you will be performing address translation twice (for example, when you have two PIX firewalls in the path) and do not require the sequence numbers to be randomized twice. The *timeout* parameter defines how long to allow an entry in the translation table to stay idle.

The *connection_limit* parameter defines how many total concurrent active connections are allowed, and the *embryonic_limit* parameter defines how many concurrent half-open connections are allowed. Both of these parameters default to 0, which indicates unlimited connections. Too many half-open connections can result from a DoS attack, and tuning the *embryonic_limit* parameter can help reduce the impact of these attacks.

The syntax for the *global* command is as follows:

```
global [(<if_name>)] <id> { {<global_ip> [-<global_ip>] [netmask <global_mask>]} |
interface}
```

The *if_name* parameter defines the interface on which traffic will exit after being translated. If the *if_name* parameter is not specified, the outside interface is assumed. The *id* parameter matches one or more *nat* statements to a global statement. The *global_ip* parameter defines the global IP addresses to be used in translation. If a single IP address is specified, port address translation is performed. If a range is specified, network address translation is used until no more global addresses are available. Once all global addresses have been exhausted, port address translation is performed. The *netmask* keyword is associated with the *global_ip* range, so the PIX will not use broadcast or network addresses in its translation. If the global IP address to be used is assigned to an interface, the *interface* keyword can be used to instead of *global_ip* to specify this.

Let's look at an example of Secure Corporation, a company that has decided to wire three buildings in London and provide Internet access to its employees. This company does not own any Internet address space. One of the company's requirements is to use private address space, because it does not want to readdress the entire network if it has to change ISPs. By using a private IP address scheme, the company can change public IP addresses whenever circumstances require, and all it will have to do is associate the new IP address range to the private IP addresses. Figure 9.1 shows the network layout. (*Note:* Even though it is a private address range, the 10.0.0.0/8 network is being used to represent the public IP address space in this chapter. Keep this in mind as you read the rest of the chapter.)

Figure 9.1 A Network Address Translation Example

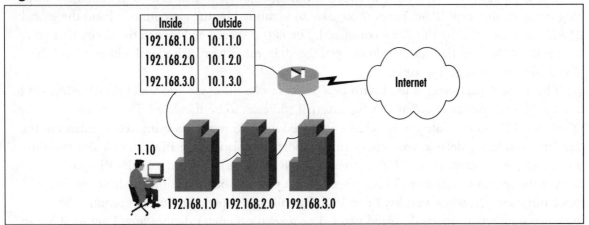

In Figure 9.1, you can see that each of the three buildings has been assigned a 24-bit network from a range specified in RFC1918. These ranges are 192.168.1.0/24, 192.168.2.0/24, and 192.168.3.0/24, respectively. Each ISP-assigned 24-bit subnet (10.1.1.0/24, 10.1.2.0/24, and 10.1.3.0/24) has been mapped to a private address range. This configuration allows each node to have a unique public IP address dynamically mapped from a pool associated with the originating building. This setup allows the system administrators to track down employees very quickly. The configuration in this example is fairly straightforward. Traffic to be translated must be identified using the *nat* command and then mapped to a pool of public IP addresses defined by the *global* command. The commands to configure this are as follows:

```
PIX1(config)# nat (inside) 1 192.168.1.0 255.255.255.0
PIX1(config)# global 1 10.1.1.1-10.1.1.254 netmask 255.255.255.0
PIX1(config)# nat (inside) 2 192.168.2.0 255.255.255.0
PIX1(config)# global 2 10.1.2.1-10.1.2.254 netmask 255.255.255.0
PIX1(config)# nat (inside) 3 192.168.3.0 255.255.255.0
PIX1(config)# global 3 10.1.3.1-10.1.3.254 netmask 255.255.255.0
PIX1(config)# exit
PIX1# clear xlate
```

> **NOTE**
>
> The *clear xlate* command is used to clear contents in the translation table. This command should be executed after any translation configuration changes are made; otherwise, there is a danger of stale entries sticking around in the translation table.

To make sure that everything was typed in correctly, use the *show nat* and *show global* commands:

```
PIX1# show nat
nat (inside) 1 192.168.1.0 255.255.255.0 0 0
nat (inside) 2 192.168.1.0 255.255.255.0 0 0
nat (inside) 3 192.168.1.0 255.255.255.0 0 0
PIX1# show global
global (outside) 1 10.1.1.1-10.1.1.254 netmask 255.255.255.0
global (outside) 2 10.1.2.1-10.1.2.254 netmask 255.255.255.0
global (outside) 3 10.1.3.1-10.1.3.254 netmask 255.255.255.0
```

In the example we just discussed, the ISP provided enough public addresses that Secure Corp. was able to create a one-to-one mapping between local and global addresses. What would happen if the ISP did not allocate enough public address space? Let's assume that the ISP provided a single 24–bit public address range (10.1.1.0/24). Instead of using separate global pools, the company could use one global pool for all buildings and use PAT. PAT allows many IP addresses to be translated to fewer IP addresses by translating both the IP address and the source port. The configuration would be as follows:

```
PIX1(config)# nat (inside) 1 192.168.1.0 255.255.255.0
PIX1(config)# nat (inside) 1 192.168.2.0 255.255.255.0
PIX1(config)# nat (inside) 1 192.168.3.0 255.255.255.0
PIX1(config)# global (outside) 1 10.1.1.1-10.1.1.254 netmask 255.255.255.0
PIX1(config)# exit
PIX1# clear xlate
```

> **NOTE**
>
> PAT works with DNS, FTP, HTTP, mail, RPC, RSH, Telnet, URL filtering, and outbound *traceroute*. PAT does not work with H.323, caching name servers, and PPTP.

To enable NAT to work on multiple interfaces, separate *global* commands are needed for each interface to translate to. The key is making sure you use the same *id* on all the *global* commands. Doing so allows one set of *nat* commands on the inside interface to translate a private IP address to one of many different global address ranges based on destination. For example, the following commands would configure the PIX to NAT the 192.168.1.0/24 network to either a

10.1.1.0/24 address or PAT to the DMZ interface IP address, depending on the interface the packet was going to exit:

```
PIX1(config)# nat (inside) 1 192.168.1.0 255.255.255.0
PIX1(config)# global (outside) 1 10.1.1.1-10.1.1.254 netmask 255.255.255.0
PIX1(config)# global (dmz) 1 interface
PIX1(config)# exit
PIX1# clear xlate
```

As with most commands on the PIX firewall, use the *no* keyword with the *nat* and *global* commands to remove them from the configuration.

Identity NAT and NAT Bypass

Using our Secure Corp. example, consider that instead of using private IP addresses inside the PIX, the company decided to use public IP addresses. Secure Corp. has been assigned a block of portable IP space from the American Registry for Internet Numbers (ARIN) in the form of three 24-bit networks. The corporation chooses, as shown in Figure 9.2, not to use private addressing within its network.

Figure 9.2 An Identity Network Address Translation Example

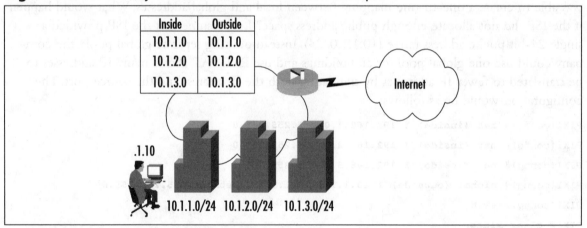

Looking at Figure 9.2, you can see that each of the three ARIN-assigned 24-bit subnets has been allocated to a building. In this example, public addresses will be used both inside and outside the PIX firewall, and no address translation will be performed. There are two ways to accomplish this task: using identity NAT or using NAT bypass.

In identity NAT, instead of using an associated *global* command to define the global address, the internal address is mapped to itself when translating. To configure identity NAT, use the *nat* command with an *id* of 0, and do not define an associated *global* command. The commands to configure the PIX in Figure 9.2 would be as follows:

```
PIX1(config)# nat (inside) 0 10.1.1.0 255.255.255.0
nat 0 10.1.1.0 will be non-translated
PIX1(config)# nat (inside) 0 10.1.2.0 255.255.255.0
```

```
nat 0 10.1.2.0 will be non-translated
PIX1(config)# nat (inside) 0 10.1.3.0 255.255.255.0
nat 0 10.1.3.0 will be non-translated
PIX1(config)# exit
PIX1# clear xlate
```

To verify the configuration, use the *show nat* command to view the current NAT configuration:

```
PIX1# show nat
nat (inside) 0 10.1.1.0 255.255.255.0 0 0
nat (inside) 0 10.1.2.0 255.255.255.0 0 0
nat (inside) 0 10.1.3.0 255.255.255.0 0 0
```

Let's examine the example in Figure 9.2. The client opens a connection to a Web server on the Internet. Since the ASA defines that, by default, higher security-level interfaces can send traffic to lower security-level interfaces, the traffic should traverse the PIX and be listed in the *xlate* table. The *show xlate debug* command should show a mapping for this connection, and it should be flagged with an *I*, or identity flag.

```
PIX1# show xlate debug
1 in use, 1 most used
Flags: D - DNS, d - dump, I - identity, i - inside, n - no random,
    o - outside, r - portmap, s - static
NAT from inside:10.1.1.10 to outside:10.1.1.10 flags iI idle 0:01:27
    timeout 3:00:00
```

The other way to configure the PIX to keep local and global addresses the same is to bypass NAT altogether using *nat 0* with an access list. First, you must define an access list that identifies the traffic to be translated (access lists are discussed in detail in the next section). Then, use the *nat* command with an *id* of 0 and the access list name to bypass the NAT process. The syntax to configure this is:

```
access-list <acl_name> permit ip <source_addr> <source_mask> <dest_addr> <dest_mask>
nat (<if_name>) 0 access-list <acl_name>
```

Using Figure 9.1 as an example, the commands to configure the PIX to bypass NAT using an access list would be as follows:

```
PIX1(config)# access-list inside_public permit ip 10.1.1.0 255.255.255.0 any
PIX1(config)# access-list inside_public permit ip 10.1.2.0 255.255.255.0 any
PIX1(config)# access-list inside_public permit ip 10.1.3.0 255.255.255.0 any
PIX1(config)# nat (inside) 0 access-list inside_public
PIX1(config)# exit
PIX1# clear xlate
```

To verify the configuration, use the *show nat* and *show access-list* commands:

```
PIX1# show nat
nat (inside) 0 access-list inside_public
PIX1# show access-list
access-list inside_public; 3 elements
access-list inside_public permit ip 10.1.1.0 255.255.255.0 any (hitcnt=0)
access-list inside_public permit ip 10.1.2.0 255.255.255.0 any (hitcnt=0)
access-list inside_public permit ip 10.1.3.0 255.255.255.0 any (hitcnt=0)
```

Returning to our example in Figure 9.2, when the client opens a connection to a Web server on the Internet, the *show xlate debug* command should not show a mapping for this connection since it bypasses NAT. Instead, the *show access-list* command should show an incremented *hitcnt* counter on the appropriate access list entry.

```
PIX1# show xlate
0 in use, 1 most used
PIX1# show access-list inside_public
access-list inside_public; 3 elements
access-list inside_public permit ip 10.1.1.0 255.255.255.0 any (hitcnt=10)
access-list inside_public permit ip 10.1.2.0 255.255.255.0 any (hitcnt=0)
access-list inside_public permit ip 10.1.3.0 255.255.255.0 any (hitcnt=0)
```

Although identity NAT and NAT bypass provide similar functionality, using NAT bypass provides some advantages over identity NAT. These advantages include saving resources by bypassing the NAT process as well as allowing for greater flexibility in configuration by including the option to specify destination addresses in the access list.

Blocking Outbound Traffic

As discussed previously, without any configuration the PIX ASA allows all higher security-level interfaces to send traffic to lower security-level interfaces. If certain outbound traffic needs to be blocked, this must be done explicitly. Although the practice is not required, controlling the outbound traffic that is allowed to traverse the PIX firewall is always a part of a well-designed security policy. There are two ways to accomplish this task: using access lists or using outbound/apply statements. Access lists, introduced in PIX firewall software v5.0, are the newer and recommended method for controlling outbound access on the PIX firewall. Only use outbound/apply statements if you have to (for example, if you have an older version of the PIX software).

Access Lists

Access lists on the PIX firewall are very similar to those used on Cisco routers and can be used to limit the traffic allowed to traverse the PIX based on several criteria, including source address, destination address, source TCP/UDP ports, and destination TCP/UDP ports. Access list configuration is a two-step process:

1. The access list itself is defined by creating permit and deny statements using the *access-list* command.

2. The access list is applied to an interface using the *access-group* command.

There are two different syntaxes for the *access-list* command. The first is used for any protocol other than Internet Control Message Protocol (ICMP), and the second is used for ICMP:

```
access-list <acl_name> {deny | permit} <protocol> <src_addr> <src_mask>
[<dest_operator> <dest_port>] <dest_addr> <dest_mask> [<dest_operator> <dest_port>]
access-list <acl_name> {deny | permit} icmp <src_addr> <src_mask> <dest_addr>
<dest_mask> <icmp_type>
```

The *acl_name* parameter is the name of an access list and can be either a name or a number. The *permit* and *deny* keywords are self-explanatory. The *protocol* parameter specifies the IP protocol. You can either enter the numerical value or specify a literal name. Possible literal names are listed in Table 9.1.

Table 9.1 Literal Protocol Names and Values

Literal	Value	Description
ah	51	Authentication header for IPv6, RFC 1826
eigrp	88	Enhanced Interior Gateway Routing Protocol
esp	50	Encapsulated Security Payload for IPv6, RFC 1827
gre	47	General Routing Encapsulation
icmp	1	Internet Control Message Protocol, RFC 792
igmp	2	Internet Group Management Protocol, RFC 1112
igrp	9	Interior Gateway Routing Protocol
ip	0	Internet Protocol
ipinip	4	IP-in-IP encapsulation
nos	94	Network Operating System (Novell's NetWare)
ospf	89	Open Shortest Path First routing protocol, RFC 1247
pcp	108	Payload Compression Protocol
snp	109	Sitara Networks Protocol
tcp	6	Transmission Control Protocol, RFC 793
udp	17	User Datagram Protocol, RFC 768

The address of the network or host from which the packet originated is specified using the *src_addr* parameter. The *src_mask* parameter specifies the netmask bits to apply to *src_addr*. To specify all networks or hosts, use the *any* keyword, which is equivalent to a source network and mask of 0.0.0.0 0.0.0.0. Use the *host* keyword followed by an IP address to specify a single host. The *dest_addr* and *dest_mask* are similar to the *src_addr* and *src_mask* parameters, except that they apply to destination addresses.

NOTE

The syntax for access lists on the PIX firewall is very similar to that of Cisco routers. The key difference is that access lists on PIX firewalls use standard wildcard masks, whereas on routers they use inverse wildcard masks. For example, when blocking a 24-bit subnet, you would use a mask of 255.255.255.0 on a PIX firewall and a mask of 0.0.0.255 on a Cisco router.

An operator comparison lets you specify a port or port range and is used in combination with the *tcp* or *udp* protocol keywords. To specify all ports, do not specify an operator and port. Use *eq* to specify a single port. Use *gt* to specify all ports greater than the specified port. Use *neq* to specify all ports except a given number. Finally, use *range* to define a specific range of ports. The port can be specified using either a number or a literal name. A list of literal port names is presented in Table 9.2.

Table 9.2 Literal Port Names and Values

Name	Port	Protocol	Name	Port	Protocol	Name	Port	Protocol
bgp	179	tcp	http	80	tcp	radius	1645, 1646	udp
biff	512	udp	hostname	101	tcp	rip	520	udp
bootpc	68	udp	ident	113	tcp	smtp	25	tcp
bootps	67	udp	irc	194	tcp	snmp	161	udp
chargen	19	tcp	isakmp	500	udp	snmptrap	162	udp
citrix-ica	1494	tcp	klogin	543	tcp	sqlnet	1521	tcp
cmd	514	tcp	kshell	544	tcp	sunrpc	111	tcp/udp
daytime	13	tcp	login	513	tcp	syslog	514	udp
discard	9	tcp/udp	lpd	515	tcp	tacacs	49	tcp/udp
dnsix	195	udp	mobile-ip	434	udp	talk	517	tcp/udp
domain	53	tcp/udp	nameserver	42	udp	telnet	23	tcp
echo	7	tcp/udp	netbios-dgm	138	udp	tftp	69	udp
exec	512	tcp	netbios-ns	137	udp	time	37	udp
finger	79	tcp	nntp	119	tcp	uucp	540	tcp
ftp	21	tcp	ntp	123	udp	who	513	udp
ftp-data	20	tcp	pim-auto-rp	496	tcp/udp	whois	43	tcp
gopher	70	tcp	pop2	109	tcp	www	80	tcp
h323	1720	tcp	pop3	110	tcp	xdmcp	177	tcp

Note that the system-defined port mapping of *http* is the same as *www* and is silently translated in the configuration. The *icmp_type* parameter allows you to permit or deny access to ICMP message types. A list of ICMP message types can be found in Table 9.3.

Table 9.3 ICMP Message Types

ICMP Type	Literal
0	echo-reply
3	unreachable
4	source-quench
5	redirect
6	alternate-address
8	echo
9	router-advertisement
10	router-solicitation
11	time-exceeded
12	parameter-problem
13	timestamp-reply
14	timestamp-request
15	information-request
16	information-reply
17	mask-request
18	mask-reply
31	conversion-error
32	mobile-redirect

After configuring an access list, you must apply it to an interface using the following command:

```
access-group <acl_name> in interface <if_name>
```

The name associated with an access list is specified as *acl_name,* whereas the name of the interface that the access list will use to monitor inbound traffic is specified by *if_name.* An access list, once applied to an interface using the *access-group* command, denies or permits traffic as it enters the PIX on the specified interface.

NOTE

Access lists on the PIX firewall can only be applied to traffic *entering* an interface, not traffic that is exiting an interface. This is unlike Cisco routers, on which access lists can be applied in either direction.

Access lists on the PIX firewall have an implicit *deny all* attached to the end of the access list. This means that unless traffic has been specifically permitted within the access list, it will be denied by a phantom entry that follows the last entry in every access list. This feature helps ensure that security will be maintained even in the face of configuration errors. Coupling this feature with the fact that access lists are processed sequentially from the first entry to the last, a

PIX administrator can create very complex access lists simply by following the flow of what should and should not be allowed. Only one access list at a time can be applied to an interface.

Let's now look at an example of Secure Corp., which has just purchased a new PIX firewall for its network in New York, as shown in Figure 9.3. All the servers that the company hosts at the site, as well as all the clients within the network, are located on the inside interface of the PIX. The site uses a single network with the address space of 192.168.0.0/22. The ISP has assigned the 10.1.1.0/24 public network to use.

Figure 9.3 The Secure Corporation Access List Example

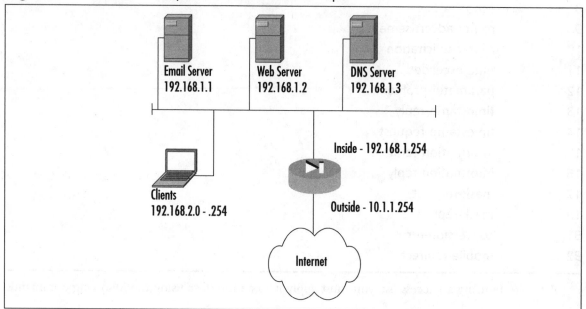

The company's requirements are that the clients only be able to access the Internet with their Web browsers and that the company servers have unrestricted access to the Internet. The design of an access list should start with a definition of what is going to be allowed and then proceed to what is going to be denied. In this example, the access list will have to allow clients in the 192.168.2.0/24 range to access any Internet server on TCP port 80. Second, the access list will have to allow the three listed servers unfettered access to the Internet. The following commands accomplish this result:

```
PIX1(config)# access-list inside_in permit tcp 192.168.2.0 255.255.255.0 any eq 80
PIX1(config)# access-list inside_in permit ip 192.168.1.1 255.255.255.255 any
PIX1(config)# access-list inside_in permit ip 192.168.1.2 255.255.255.255 any
PIX1(config)# access-list inside_in permit ip 192.168.1.3 255.255.255.255 any
PIX1(config)# access-group inside_in in interface inside
```

A good practice is to add an explicit *deny all* statement to the end of an access list so you remember it is there when you do a *show access-list* command and so you can see how many packets have been dropped using the *hitcnt* counter:

```
PIX1(config)# access-list inside_in deny ip any any
PIX1(config)# exit
PIX1# show access-list
access-list inside_in; 4 elements
access-list inside_in permit tcp 192.168.2.0 255.255.255.0 any eq www
    (hitcnt=2)
access-list inside_in permit ip host 192.168.1.1 any (hitcnt=0)
access-list inside_in permit ip host 192.168.1.2 any (hitcnt=0)
access-list inside_in permit ip host 192.168.1.3 any (hitcnt=0)
access-list inside_in deny ip any any (hitcnt=40)
```

Best security practices dictate that publicly accessible servers should not be located on the inside network; instead, they should be located on a DMZ network. The DMZ provides an extra layer of security and helps control the risks associated with a publicly accessible server. If the server becomes compromised, because it is in a DMZ with separate security settings it is possible to contain the compromise to the DMZ and still protect inside clients. However, if the network is set up as in the previous example and the server becomes compromised, there is very little that can be done to stop that server from compromising the entire internal network. Keeping this design practice in mind, Figure 9.4 shows a revised network layout.

Figure 9.4 Secure Corporation Revised Network Layout

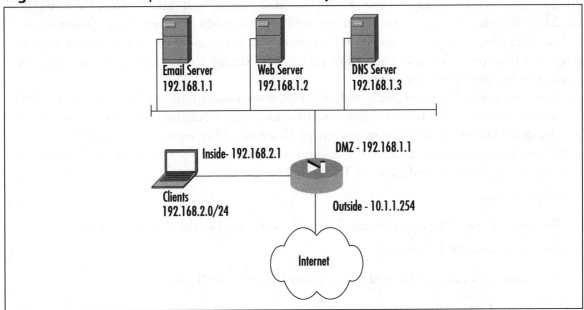

From the diagram, it is apparent that the network requirements have changed, because services the clients used to be able to get to without going through the firewall now need to be added to the access lists. Unlike the access list created before, the servers should not be allowed to access any IP address without restriction. A DMZ access list should be created that locks down the services that the servers are able to use, because if these servers become compromised, you want to limit their ability to infect your network or even someone else's. The commands to create and apply these access lists are:

```
PIX1(config)# access-list inside_in permit tcp 192.168.2.0 255.255.255.0 any eq www
PIX1(config)# access-list inside_in permit tcp 192.168.2.0 255.255.255.0 192.168.1.1 eq smtp
PIX1(config)# access-list inside_in permit tcp 192.168.2.0 255.255.255.0 192.168.1.1 eq pop3
PIX1(config)# access-list inside_in permit udp 192.168.2.0 255.255.255.0 192.168.1.3 eq domain
PIX1(config)# access-list inside_in permit tcp 192.168.2.0 255.255.255.0 192.168.1.3 eq domain
PIX1(config)# access-list inside_in deny ip any any
PIX1(config)# access-group inside_in in interface inside
PIX1(config)# access-list dmz_in permit tcp 192.168.1.1 255.255.255.255 any eq smtp
PIX1(config)# access-list dmz_in permit udp 192.168.1.3 255.255.255.255 any eq domain
PIX1(config)# access-list dmz_in permit tcp 192.168.1.3 255.255.255.255 any eq domain
PIX1(config)# access-list dmz_in deny ip any any
PIX1(config)# access-group dmz_in in interface dmz
```

It is important to note that we have not yet covered how to configure inbound access. The preceding access list only allows these servers to initiate contact with other servers—as a client would do. For example, the e-mail server can send mail to another domain, but it cannot receive it. The DNS server can resolve domain information from another domain, but it cannot respond to queries from other domains. The "Allowing Inbound Traffic" section of this chapter covers in detail how inbound access is enabled.

One very useful feature in configuring the PIX is the *name* command. This command allows you to define a name alias to an IP address so that during configuration, instead of referencing a host by its IP address, the host can be referenced by a name. This feature is very useful for configuring complex configurations, because a descriptive name can be very helpful in configuring and troubleshooting the PIX configuration. The syntax for the command is:

```
name <ip_address> <name>
```

For example, the following command maps the name *mail* to the IP address 10.1.1.10:

```
PIX1(config)# name 10.1.1.10 mail
```

The name *mail* can now be used in access lists instead of an IP address.

Outbound/Apply

The *outbound* and *apply* commands can also be used to control which traffic is allowed to exit the network. The *outbound* command by itself only identifies traffic to be permitted or denied. The *apply* command applies the outbound list to an interface and actually causes packets to be dropped. The first step to controlling outbound traffic is to configure the *outbound* command to identify the traffic to be filtered. The syntax for the *outbound* command is:

```
outbound <list_id> permit | deny <ip_address> [<netmask> [<port>[-<port>]] [<protocol>]
```

The *list_id* is an identifier that maps the traffic identified by the *outbound* command to the *apply* command; *list_id* must be a number between 1 and 99. The *permit* or *deny* keywords specify whether the traffic identified by the *outbound* command will be permitted or denied, respectively. The *ip_address* parameter specifies the traffic to be identified by the *outbound* command. The *netmask* parameter is used in conjunction with the *ip_address* parameter to identify traffic from an entire network. The *port* parameter specifies a specific port number or range to be identified by the *outbound* command. The *protocol* parameter specifies a specific protocol to be identified (*tcp*, *udp*, etc.) and is assumed to be *ip* if it is not specified.

The second step to controlling outbound traffic is to apply the *outbound* list to an interface using the *apply* command. Once the *apply* command is committed to an interface, any incoming traffic to that interface that is denied by the associated *outbound* list will be dropped. The syntax for the *apply* command is as follows:

```
apply [(<if_name>)] <list_id> outgoing_src | outgoing_dest
```

The *interface_name* parameter specifies the interface on which traffic will be filtered using the associated *outbound* list, and if not specified is assumed to be the outside interface. The *list_id* parameter associates the *outbound* list to use to filter outbound traffic. Unlike access lists, multiple outbound lists can be applied to an interface, and the lists are processed starting at the lowest number and working toward the highest.

The *outgoing_src* or *outgoing_dest* keywords are parameters that define how the *apply* command uses the associated *outbound* list to filter traffic. If *outgoing_src* is used, the *ip_address* parameter in the *outbound* list is a source address. If *outgoing_dest* is used, the *ip_address* parameter in the outbound list is a destination address.

Secure Corp. has decided to implement access restrictions from its networks to the Internet. To control what employees can access, the company systems administrators decide to deny all packets sourced from within the company destined to *echo, chargen*, and *discard* ports on the Internet. They choose these ports because they are common ports for attacking Internet servers and there is no reason why an employee should need access to these services on an outside host.

To accomplish this task, it will be helpful to create an outbound list. The first step to configure this list is to allow all traffic through. The next step is defining the rules that deny access to the specific services. Finally, the *outbound* list needs to be applied to an interface. The commands to do these tasks are as follows:

```
PIX1(config)# outbound 20 permit 0.0.0.0 0.0.0.0 0
PIX1(config)# outbound 20 deny 0.0.0.0 0.0.0.0 echo
PIX1(config)# outbound 20 deny 0.0.0.0 0.0.0.0 discard
PIX1(config)# outbound 20 deny 0.0.0.0 0.0.0.0 chargen
PIX1(config)# apply (inside) 20 outgoing_src
```

Unfortunately, even after taking all the precautions we've described, the company gets a phone call that someone in the company is attempting to access a server on the Internet that he should not. The IP address of the Internet server that is being attacked is 10.10.1.10. Therefore, a new outbound rule needs to be created. Since the company has yet to figure out who is causing the trouble, instead of identifying traffic on the source address, administrators need to use the *apply* command to match on the destination:

```
PIX1(config)# outbound 30 permit 0.0.0.0 0.0.0.0 0
PIX1(config)# outbound 30 deny 10.10.1.10 255.255.255.255 0
PIX1(config)# apply (inside) 30 outgoing_dest
```

Another way to accomplish this task is to use the *outbound* command with the *except* keyword. The *except* keyword causes the normal behavior of the outbound list to be exactly opposite for the specified IP address. For example, if the normal behavior of a rule is to allow all source addresses to access all services, an *except* parameter would make a specific destination be denied. Therefore, in the preceding example, instead of creating a new outbound list, we could add an *except* parameter to outbound list 20:

```
PIX1(config)# outbound 20 except 10.10.1.10 255.255.255.255 0
```

To verify your configuration, use the *show outbound [list_id]* command.

> **NOTE**
>
> It might be desirable to block Java applets or ActiveX code coming in from the Internet. The PIX supports this functionality.

Allowing Inbound Traffic

Up to this point in the chapter, we have not discussed how to allow traffic from an untrusted host, such as one on the Internet, to contact a server protected by the PIX. The PIX would not be entirely functional to most organizations if it did not allow traffic from an untrusted source to contact servers within the organization, such as a corporate Web server. The PIX ASA treats traffic entering a lower security-level interface and exiting a higher security-level interface, defined as *inbound traffic*, very differently than outbound traffic.

Unlike outbound traffic, inbound traffic is denied by default. This is to ensure that the security domains defined by the security levels of the interfaces are valid and not bypassed. Much as with outbound traffic, allowing inbound traffic to traverse the PIX is a two-step process. The first is configuration of a static translation. The second is to configure an access list or conduit that will specifically enable the required traffic to enter the PIX. Similar to the *outbound/apply* commands, the functionality provided by the *conduit* command has been replaced by access lists.

Static Address Translation

When a publicly accessible server (hopefully located in a DMZ) is protected by a PIX firewall, it becomes a requirement to allow connections initiated on a lower security-level interface to a higher security-level interface. The first step in accomplishing this task is creating a static address translation. The *static* command creates a permanent map in the PIX translation table for the global-to-local IP address mapping. The syntax for the command is as follows:

```
static [(<internal_if_name>, <external_if_name>)] {<global_ip> | interface} <local_ip>
[netmask <mask>] [<max_conns> [<em_limit>]] [norandomseq]
```

The *static* command requires two interface arguments: the internal interface, which is the interface name to which the server being translated is connected, and the external interface, which is where the global IP address will sit. The *global_ip* and *local_ip* parameters are self-explanatory. The *netmask* parameter is used when you are statically translating more than one IP address at a time. The default value for both *max_conns* and *em_limit* is 0 (unlimited), and these parameters are the same as in the *nat* command.

For example, Secure Corp. has added a DMZ interface to its PIX. It has decided to move its Internet Web server to the PIX DMZ and to allow access to it from the Internet. Figure 9.4 shows the network layout. The format for the *static* command, in this case, is as follows:

```
PIX1(config)# static (dmz, outside) 10.1.5.10 192.168.1.2 netmask 255.255.255.255 0 0
```

If the company had more than one Web server, instead of configuring a separate static entry for each, you could configure a single *static* command with the correct netmask. For example, for 14 Web servers that had the IP addresses of 192.168.1.1 through 192.168.1.15, you would use the following command:

```
PIX1(config)# static (dmz, outside) 10.1.5.0 192.168.1.0 netmask 255.255.255.240 0 0
```

Now consider the fact that the Web server located in the DMZ needs to access a database server located on the inside interface of the PIX. The process is the same: Whenever a lower security-level interface needs to access a higher security-level interface, a static translation needs to be created. The database server IP address does not need to be translated, since the Web servers on the DMZ are a part of the private address network. The following *static* command simply translates the IP address to itself. This is very similar to *nat 0*:

```
PIX1(config)# static (inside, dmz) 192.168.1.2 192.168.1.2 netmask 255.255.255.255 0 0
```

We are now halfway to allowing inbound traffic access to a protected server. The *static* command only creates a static address mapping between global and local IP addresses. Since the default action for inbound traffic is to drop it, the next step is to create an access list or conduit to allow the traffic to enter the PIX. Like the *outbound/apply* commands, the *conduit* command became a legacy command in favor of access lists when version 5.0 of the PIX software was released.

Access Lists

The process of creating an access list to allow inbound access is very similar to creating an access list for outbound access, which was discussed earlier in this chapter. The command syntax is the same, as are all the parameters. The key difference between an access list applied to a lower security-level interface and an access list applied to a higher security-level interface is that static translation must be configured to enable the traffic to traverse up to the higher security-level interface.

Conduits

Conduits, another method for allowing inbound access, have the following syntax:

```
conduit permit | deny <protocol> <global_ip> <global_mask> [<operator> <port>
[<port>]] <foreign_ip> <foreign_mask> [<operator> <port> [<port>]]
```

By default, all inbound traffic is denied unless explicitly permitted. The purposes of the *deny* and *permit* keywords are obvious. The *protocol, operator*, and *port* parameters are the same as access lists. The *global_ip* parameter defines the global IP addresses of the host to allow access to, and the *foreign_ip* parameter defines the IP address to allow access from. The *global_mask* and *foreign_mask* parameters are the subnet masks applied to *global_ip* and *foreign_ip*, respectively.

The PIX processes the *conduit* commands in the order they are typed into the PIX. Once conduits have been created, nothing more has to be done to enable them. Conduits are not explicitly applied to an interface. However, based on the *global_ip* used with the command, it could be said that conduits are applied to an interface in reality.

For example, if a Web server with an internal IP address of 172.16.1.10 resides off the DMZ interface of a PIX, the following commands would allow access to the Web server from any foreign IP address:

```
PIX1(config)# static (dmz, outside) 10.1.5.10 172.16.1.10 netmask 255.255.255.255 0 0
PIX1(config)# conduit permit tcp host 10.1.5.10 eq www any
```

Since the Web server is using a private IP address, the foreign client would use the public address to access the server. The conduit created would only work between the outside and DMZ interfaces because the *static* command defines these interfaces in the translation.

Another example of conduit commands is as follows. This command enables domain lookups to occur from anywhere outside the network to the DNS server of 10.1.5.11:

```
PIX1(config)# static (dmz, outside) 10.1.5.11 172.16.1.11 netmask 255.255.255.255 0 0
PIX1(config)# conduit permit udp host 10.1.5.11 eq domain any
PIX1(config)# conduit permit tcp host 10.1.5.11 eq domain any
```

This command enables an e-mail server (172.16.1.12) to receive e-mail from outside the network as 10.1.5.12:

```
PIX1(config)# static (dmz, outside) 10.1.5.12 172.16.1.12 netmask 255.255.255.255 0 0
PIX1(config)# conduit permit tcp host 10.1.5.12 eq smtp any
```

The *show conduit* command, as illustrated next, can be used to show all the conduits currently configured on the PIX:

```
PIX1# show conduit
conduit permit tcp host 10.1.5.10 eq www any (hitcnt=0)
conduit permit udp host 10.1.5.11 eq domain any (hitcnt=0)
conduit permit tcp host 10.1.5.11 eq domain any (hitcnt=0)
conduit permit tcp host 10.1.5.12 eq smtp any (hitcnt=0)
```

ICMP

Inbound ICMP traffic to the PIX firewall can be controlled using the *icmp* command, which only filters ICMP traffic that is terminating on one of the PIX interfaces, not traversing the PIX. The command has the following syntax:

```
icmp {permit|deny} <ip_address> <netmask> [<icmp_type>] <if_name>
```

The ip_*address* parameter is the source address of the ICMP packet that will be denied or permitted with this command. The *netmask* parameter is the network mask associated with the *ip_address* parameter. The *icmp_type* parameter specifies the ICMP type that is being denied or permitted. A list of the ICMP type values is presented in Table 9.3. The *if_name* parameter is the name of the interface to which this ICMP filter will be applied.

For example, the following command permits the DMZ interface to respond to pings from the private network 172.16.0.0 255.255.240.0:

```
PIX1(config)# icmp permit 172.16.0.0 255.240.0.0 echo dmz
```

Port Redirection

Port redirection allows one public IP address to serve as the public IP address for more than one server. Port redirection allows you to define a mapping between a port on a public IP address and a port on a private IP address. To enable redirection, an access list or conduit still must be created, since the traffic is traversing from a lower security-level interface to a higher security-level interface.

Because the mapping can be set at the port level, one IP address can serve as the gateway to many servers behind the PIX. For example, Secure Corp. has set up a network at its Toronto site and has been assigned only a single public IP address from the ISP. At this site, Secure Corp. has two Web servers, one Telnet server, and one FTP server. How can it make all these services accessible publicly with a single IP address? This is accomplished using the *static* command to perform port redirection:

```
static [(<prenat_if_name>, <postnat_if_name>)] {tcp | udp} {<global_ip> | interface}
<global_port> <local_ip> <local_port> [netmask <mask>] [<max_conns> [<em_limit>]]
[norandomseq]
```

We discussed the *static* command earlier in the chapter, so we will not go through all the parameters again. However, we introduce some new parameters here, including *global_port* and *local_port*. A protocol (*tcp* or *udp*) must also be specified so that the PIX knows the protocol port pair to accept and forward. Instead of using a *global_ip*, you can use the *interface* option to specify the IP address of the PIX interface specified in *postnat_if_name*. This option is important if you do not have any additional usable public IP address.

To configure port redirection for the first Web server using the PIX public IP address as the Web server's public address, the command is as follows:

```
PIX1(config)# static (dmz, outside) tcp interface 80 172.16.1.1 80
```

If the company also wanted to host Telnet, FTP, and another Web server, three more *static* commands would have to be added to map the global ports to the correct servers. Since the Web port is already taken, a high port (8080) is chosen for access to the second Web server. This example is shown in Figure 9.5. The additional commands are as follows:

```
PIX1(config)# static (dmz, outside) tcp interface 23 172.16.1.2 23
PIX1(config)# static (dmz, outside) tcp interface 8080 172.16.1.3 80
PIX1(config)# static (dmz, outside) tcp interface 21 172.16.1.4 21
```

Figure 9.5 A Port Redirection Example

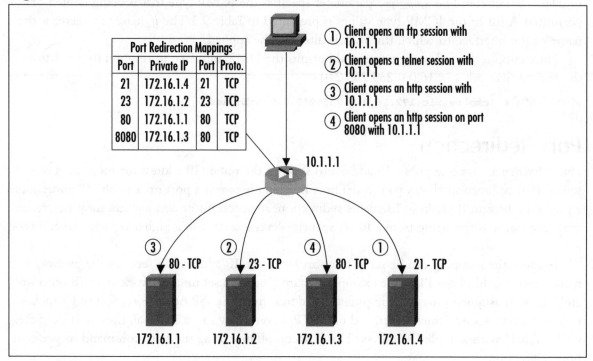

TurboACLs

TurboACLs are a new feature in PIX firewall software version 6.2. The general principal behind TurboACLs is that a long or complex access list is *compiled,* or indexed, to enable faster processing of traffic through the access list.

TurboACLs do not speed up short access lists; in fact, even if configured, the PIX will not enable this feature on an access list unless it is over 18 lines. With longer access lists, the TurboACL feature creates something similar to an index in a book that enables the PIX to read through and process the long access list at a fast rate.

The index created by a TurboACL takes up a fair amount of resources. For this reason, Cisco recommends that TurboACLs should not be configured on anything lower than a 525 series firewall. To enable the TurboACL feature on all access lists of the PIX, use the *access-list compiled* command, as shown:

```
PIX1(config)# access-list compiled
```

To verify that the TurboACLs are indeed turned on, issue a *show access-list* command:

```
PIX1(config)# show access-list
access-list compiled
access-list inside_public turbo-configured; 3 elements
access-list inside_public permit ip 10.1.1.0 255.255.255.0 any (hitcnt=0)
access-list inside_public permit ip 10.1.2.0 255.255.255.0 any (hitcnt=0)
access-list inside_public permit ip 10.1.3.0 255.255.255.0 any (hitcnt=0)
```

If you choose not to enable them at a global level, TurboACLs can be turned on and off for individual access lists. This feature can be very useful if you only have a few access lists that need to be optimized. To configure a single access list to use the TurboACL feature, the syntax is:

```
access-list <acl-name> compiled
```

If a PIX has more than one access list and only the access list applied to the outside interface needs to use the TurboACL feature, the commands to turn off all TurboACLs except the one on the outside interface are:

```
PIX1(config)# no access-list compiled
PIX1(config)# access-list outside_in compiled
```

Object Grouping

Introduced in PIX software v6.2, *object grouping* is a major advancement toward making very complex access lists much simpler to configure on the PIX. Before the object-grouping feature was available, each unique network, node, service, and protocol combination that needed to be defined in an access list had to be configured with a separate *access-list* statement. However, in most organizational security policies, groups of entries have similar access rights. Object groups allow groups of network addresses, services, protocols, and ICMP types to be defined, thereby reducing the number of access list entries needed.

For example, say that an organization wants to deny inside users access to a number of external FTP servers because they are known to be sources of illegal software and viruses. Without object groups, an access list entry has to be defined for each individual FTP server. However, using object groups, we can define a network object group containing a list of hosts that contains all the IP addresses of the banned FTP servers. IP addresses can easily be added and removed from this group at will. Now, only one access list entry has to be created denying access to the object group from the inside. The access list does not need to be modified if entries are added or removed from the object group. As you can see, object groups allow for simplification of access list configuration and maintenance.

Configuring and Using Object Groups

There are four types of object groups: *icmp-type*, *protocol*, *network*, and *service*. Each object group type corresponds to a field in the *access-list* or *conduit* command. Once an object group has been created, a subconfiguration mode is entered so the group can be populated. Each object group type has different subconfiguration options, so we will look at each separately. Once an object group has been configured, it can be used in an *access-list* or *conduit* command.

ICMP-Type Object Groups

An *ICMP-type object group* is a group of ICMP-type numerical or literal values. ICMP-type object groups can be used in place of the *icmp-type* parameter in an access list or conduit. To create an ICMP-type object group, the syntax is:

```
object-group icmp-type <grp_id>
```

Once an object group has been defined, the subconfiguration mode enables the object group to be populated. At this stage, an optional description can be specified using the *description* subcommand. To populate the ICMP-type object group, the syntax is as follows:

```
icmp-object <icmp_type>
```

For example, the following object group defines ICMP-type values that will be used later with an access list or conduit:

```
PIX1(config)# object-group icmp-type icmp-grp
PIX1(config-icmp-type)# description ICMP Type allowed into the PIX
PIX1(config-icmp-type)# icmp-object echo-reply
PIX1(config-icmp-type)# icmp-object unreachable
PIX1(config-icmp-type)# exit
PIX1(config)# exit
```

Network Object Groups

A *network object group* is a group of host IP addresses or networks. Network object groups can be used in place of a *src_addr* or *dst_addr* parameter in an access list or conduit statement. To create a network object group, the syntax is as follows:

```
object-group network <grp_id>
```

Network object groups have two subcommands for defining the group of hosts and networks. The syntax for defining a host entry in the object group is:

```
network-object host <host_addr | host_name>
```

The *host_addr* parameter is the IP address of the host being added to the object-group. Alternatively, the *host_name* parameter specifies the hostname of a host defined using the *name* command.

The syntax for defining a network entry in the object group is:

```
network-object <net_addr> <netmask>
```

For example, the following object group defines host and network values to be used later with an access list or conduit:

```
PIX1(config)# object-group network net-grp
```

```
PIX1(config-network)# description List of Public HTTP Servers
PIX1(config-network)# network-object host 192.168.1.10
PIX1(config-network)# network-object host 172.16.10.1
PIX1(config-network)# network-object 172.16.2.0 255.255.255.0
PIX1(config-network)# exit
PIX1(config)# exit
```

Protocol Object Groups

A *protocol object group* is a group of protocol numbers or literal values. Protocol object groups can be used in place of the *protocol* parameter in an access list or conduit. To create a protocol object group, the syntax is as follows:

```
object-group protocol <grp_id>
```

Once an object group has been defined, the subconfiguration mode enables the object group to be populated. To populate the protocol object group, the syntax is:

```
protocol-object <protocol>
```

The *protocol* parameter is a protocol number or literal value. For example, the following object group defines a group of protocols that will be used later with an access list or conduit to provide VPN access:

```
PIX1(config)# object-group protocol vpn-grp
PIX1(config-protocol)# description Protocols allowed for VPN Access
PIX1(config-protocol)# protocol-object ah
PIX1(config-protocol)# protocol-object esp
PIX1(config-protocol)# protocol-object gre
PIX1(config-protocol)# exit
PIX1(config)# exit
```

Service Object Groups

A *service object group* is a group of TCP and/or UDP port numbers or port number ranges. Service object groups can be used in place of the *port* parameter in an access list or a conduit. The syntax to create a service object group is as follows:

```
object-group service <grp_id> tcp|udp|tcp-udp
```

Since a service object group is a listing of ports and port ranges, the ports defined need to be configured as TCP, UDP, or both TCP and UDP. The *tcp, udp,* and *tcp-udp* keywords define the common IP protocol for all ports listed in the object group. The subconfiguration command syntax to populate the service object group with a single port is:

```
port-object eq <port>
```

The subconfiguration command syntax to populate the service object group with a range of ports is:

```
port-object range <begin-port> <end-port>
```

For example, the following object group defines a group of ports that all Web servers within in organization need to have opened on the firewall:

```
PIX1(config)# object-group service websrv-grp tcp
PIX1(config-service)# description Ports needed on public web servers
PIX1(config-service)# port-object eq 80
PIX1(config-service)# port-object eq 8080
PIX1(config-service)# port-object range 9000 9010
```

To verify that an object group was created and populated with the correct information, we can view the current object group configuration using the *show object-group* command:

```
PIX1# show object-group
object-group icmp-type icmp-grp
  description: ICMP Type allowed into the PIX
  icmp-object echo-reply
  icmp-object unreachable
object-group network net-grp
  description: List of Public HTTP Servers
  network-object host 192.168.1.10
  network-object host 172.16.10.1
  network-object 172.16.2.0 255.255.255.0
object-group protocol vpn-grp
  description: Protocols allowed for VPN Access
  protocol-object ah
  protocol-object gre
  protocol-object esp
object-group service websrv-grp tcp
  description: Ports needed on public web servers
  port-object eq www
  port-object eq 8080
  port-object range 9000 9010
```

If one of the object groups does not look correct or is not needed, it can be removed using the *no object-group <grp_id>* command.

Object groups can be used in place of their respective values in access lists or conduits, but they must be preceded by the *object-group* keyword. For example, to allow the ICMP type values defined in the *icmp-grp* object group to enter the PIX's outside interface, the *access-list* command is:

```
PIX1(config)# access-list icmp_in permit icmp any any object-group icmp-grp
```

To allow access to the Web servers defined in the *net-grp* on the ports defined in *websrv-grp*, the command is:

```
PIX1(config)# access-list outside_in permit tcp any object-group net-grp object-group
websrv-grp
```

One nice feature of object groups is the ability to nest object groups of the same type together. For example:

```
PIX1(config)# object-group network all-servers
PIX1(config-network)# group-object net-grp
PIX1(config-network)# network-object 172.16.3.0 255.255.255.0
```

Case Study

We've covered many important topics in this chapter. Sometimes it is difficult to grasp a topic without actually seeing it in use, so let's look at a complex case study and see how the topics discussed in this chapter can be applied in real-life situations.

Figure 9.6 shows the network layout of the Los Angeles site at Secure Corp. The company has just bought the PIX and needs to configure it. Secure Corp. has already defined a security policy as a precursor to purchasing the PIX so they would know how many interfaces they would need. The site administrators decided that they need four different security domains to ensure the integrity and security of the network.

Figure 9.6 A Complex Configuration Example

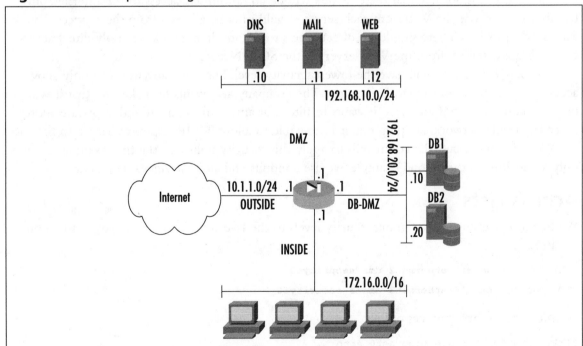

The *inside* interface will be the highest security interface. All corporate users as well as the private and internal servers will be located behind this interface. Private addressing is being used for the nodes located behind this interface, and the PIX needs to use PAT to translate the IP addresses when the nodes send traffic to the Internet. The PIX should not NAT any traffic from the nodes behind this interface when they access any other interface. There should be no direct access from the Internet to any server located behind this interface. Because there is no business case for having Internet POP3 and IMAP4 servers available to nodes on the inside network and because these services are common venues through which viruses are transmitted, no access is allowed to Internet POP3 or IMAP4 servers from the inside network. All other traffic from the inside network is allowed.

The *db-dmz* interface will have the second highest security level and is being used to host database servers that enable the public Web server to build dynamic HTML pages. No private or confidential information is stored on these database servers. The database servers use private addressing and are the only nodes located behind this interface. The database servers do not need access to the Internet, and no direct connections from the Internet should be allowed to the database servers. The database servers are using SQL*Net as the communication protocol between the Web server and the database; therefore, they need to be accessible from the Web server on the DMZ interface. The database servers do not need direct access to any hosts on the inside network.

The *dmz* interface will have the third highest security level. Publicly accessible services, including Web, mail, and DNS servers, will be located behind this interface. The servers will use private addressing and will require static translations so that they can be accessed directly from the Internet. Since it is possible that these servers will be compromised, access to the Internet, plus the ability to browse the Web from each server, should only be allowed from the services that each server provides. There should no direct access to the inside network and only direct access to the database servers from the Web server on the SQL*Net service.

The *outside* interface will have the lowest security level. The company wants to only allow access to the services in the DMZ interface. The company also wants to make sure that it will not be the victim of a spoof attack, so it wants to filter out any traffic sourced with a private address. Since the inside network can ping out, it is desirable to allow ICMP responses back into the PIX.

We will now discuss the commands to apply this security policy. In the first example, we use only access lists. In the second example, we use conduits and *outbound/apply* statements.

Access Lists

We begin by naming and assigning security levels to the two interfaces not already defined on the PIX:

```
PIX1(config)# nameif ethernet2 dmz security40
PIX1(config)# nameif ethernet3 dbdmz security60
```

Now bring the interfaces online:

```
PIX1(config)# interface ethernet0 auto
PIX1(config)# interface ethernet1 auto
```

```
PIX1(config)# interface ethernet2 auto
PIX1(config)# interface ethernet3 auto
```

Assign an IP address to each interface:

```
PIX1(config)# ip address inside 172.16.0.1 255.240.0.0
PIX1(config)# ip address outside 10.1.1.1 255.255.255.0
PIX1(config)# ip address dmz 192.168.10.1 255.255.255.0
PIX1(config)# ip address dbdmz 192.168.20.1 255.255.255.0
```

Assign a default route to the PIX:

```
PIX1(config)# route outside 0.0.0.0 0.0.0.0 10.1.1.254
```

Create access lists to be used later to bypass NAT:

```
PIX1(config)# access-list nonatinside permit ip 172.16.0.0 255.240.0.0 192.168.10.0
255.255.255.0
PIX1(config)# access-list nonatinside permit ip 172.16.0.0 255.240.0.0 192.168.20.0
255.255.255.0
PIX1(config)# access-list nonatdbdmz permit ip 192.168.20.0 255.255.255.0 192.168.10.0
255.255.255.0
```

Create a global pool using PAT for the inside network:

```
PIX1(config)# global (outside) 1 10.1.1.2
Global 10.1.1.2 will be Port Address Translated
```

Bypass NAT where needed:

```
PIX1(config)# nat (inside) 0 access-list nonatinside
PIX1(config)# nat (dbdmz) 0 access-list nonatdbdmz
```

Enable NAT on the inside interface and have it mapped to the global *id*:

```
PIX1(config)# nat (inside) 1 0 0
```

Create static translations for access from the lower-level security interfaces:

```
PIX1(config)# static (dmz, outside) 10.1.1.10 192.168.10.10
PIX1(config)# static (dmz, outside) 10.1.1.11 192.168.10.11
PIX1(config)# static (dmz, outside) 10.1.1.12 192.168.10.12
PIX1(config)# static (dbdmz, dmz) 192.168.20.0 192.168.20.0 netmask 255
    .255.255.0
```

Configure names for the public addresses of the DMZ servers:

```
PIX1(config)# names
PIX1(config)# name 10.1.1.10 dns
PIX1(config)# name 10.1.1.11 mail
PIX1(config)# name 10.1.1.12 web
```

Configure object groups:

```
PIX1(config)# object-group network dbhosts
PIX1(config-network)# network-object host 192.168.20.10
PIX1(config-network)# network-object host 192.168.20.20
PIX1(config-network)# exit
PIX1(config)# object-group network dmzhosts
PIX1(config-network)# network-object host 192.168.10.1
PIX1(config-network)# network-object host 192.168.10.11
PIX1(config-network)# network-object host 192.168.10.12
PIX1(config-network)# exit
PIX1(config)# object-group icmp-type icmp-outside-in
PIX1(config-icmp-type)# icmp-object echo-reply
PIX1(config-icmp-type)# icmp-object time-exceed
PIX1(config-icmp-type)# icmp-object unreachable
PIX1(config-icmp-type)# exit
```

Configure the access lists for each interface:

```
PIX1(config)# access-list inside_in deny tcp 172.16.0.0 255.240.0.0 any eq pop3
PIX1(config)# access-list inside_in deny tcp 172.16.0.0 255.240.0.0 any eq 143
PIX1(config)# access-list inside_in permit ip 172.16.0.0 255.240.0.0 any
PIX1(config)# access-list inside_in permit icmp 172.16.0.0 255.240.0.0 any
PIX1(config)# access-list dbdmz_in permit tcp object-group dbhosts eq
    sqlnet 192.168.10.0 255.255.255.0
PIX1(config)# access-list dbdmz_in permit icmp 192.168.20.0 255.255.255.0 172.16.0.0
255.255.0.0
PIX1(config)# access-list dbdmz_in deny ip any any
PIX1(config)# access-list dmz_in permit tcp host 192.168.10.11 any eq smtp
PIX1(config)# access-list dmz_in permit tcp host 192.168.10.10 any eq domain
PIX1(config)# access-list dmz_in permit udp host 192.168.10.10 any eq domain
PIX1(config)# access-list dmz_in permit tcp object-group dmzhosts any eq http
PIX1(config)# access-list dmz_in permit tcp host 192.168.10.12 object- group dbhosts eq
sqlnet
PIX1(config)# access-list dmz_in permit icmp object-group dmzhosts 172.16.0.0
255.255.0.0
PIX1(config)# access-list outside_in deny ip 0.0.0.0 255.0.0.0 any
PIX1(config)# access-list outside_in deny ip 10.0.0.0 255.0.0.0 any
PIX1(config)# access-list outside_in deny ip 127.0.0.0 255.0.0.0 any
PIX1(config)# access-list outside_in deny ip 172.16.0.0 255.240.0.0 any
PIX1(config)# access-list outside_in deny ip 192.168.0.0 255.255.0.0 any
PIX1(config)# access-list outside_in deny ip 224.0.0.0 224.0.0.0 any
PIX1(config)# access-list outside_in permit tcp any host web eq http
```

```
PIX1(config)# access-list outside_in permit tcp any host mail eq smtp
PIX1(config)# access-list outside_in permit tcp any host dns eq domain
PIX1(config)# access-list outside_in permit udp any host dns eq domain
PIX1(config)# access-list outside_in permit icmp any 10.1.1.0 255.255.255.0 object-group
icmp-outside-in
PIX1(config)# access-list outside_in deny icmp any 10.1.1.0 255.255.255.0
PIX1(config)# access-list outside_in deny ip any any
```

Apply the access lists to the appropriate interfaces:

```
PIX1(config)# access-group outside_in in interface outside
PIX1(config)# access-group inside_in in interface inside
PIX1(config)# access-group dmz_in in interface dmz
PIX1(config)# access-group dbdmz_in in interface dbdmz
```

Conduits and Outbound/Apply

Name and assign security levels to the two interfaces not already defined on the PIX:

```
PIX1(config)# nameif ethernet2 dmz security40
PIX1(config)# nameif ethernet3 dbdmz security60
```

Bring the interfaces online:

```
PIX1(config)# interface ethernet0 auto
PIX1(config)# interface ethernet1 auto
PIX1(config)# interface ethernet2 auto
PIX1(config)# interface ethernet3 auto
```

Assign an IP address to each interface:

```
PIX1(config)# ip address inside 172.16.0.1 255.240.0.0
PIX1(config)# ip address outside 10.1.1.1 255.255.255.0
PIX1(config)# ip address dmz 192.168.10.1 255.255.255.0
PIX1(config)# ip address dbdmz 192.168.20.1 255.255.255.0
```

Assign a default route to the PIX:

```
PIX1(config)# route outside 0.0.0.0 0.0.0.0 10.1.1.254
```

Create access lists to be used later to bypass NAT:

```
PIX1(config)# access-list nonatinside permit ip 172.16.0.0 255.240.0.0 192.168.10.0
255.255.255.0
PIX1(config)# access-list nonatinside permit ip 172.16.0.0 255.240.0.0 192.168.20.0
255.255.255.0
PIX1(config)# access-list nonatdbdmz permit ip 192.168.20.0 255.255.255.0 192.168.10.0
255.255.255.0
```

Create a global pool using PAT for the inside network:

```
PIX1(config)# global (outside) 1 10.1.1.2
Global 10.1.1.2 will be Port Address Translated
```

Bypass NAT where needed:

```
PIX1(config)# nat (inside) 0 access-list nonatinside
PIX1(config)# nat (dbdmz) 0 access-list nonatdbdmz
```

Enable NAT on the inside interface and have it mapped to the global *id*:

```
PIX1(config)# nat (inside) 1 0 0
```

Create static translations for access from the lower-level security interfaces:

```
PIX1(config)# static (dmz, outside) 10.1.1.10 192.168.10.10
PIX1(config)# static (dmz, outside) 10.1.1.11 192.168.10.11
PIX1(config)# static (dmz, outside) 10.1.1.12 192.168.10.12
PIX1(config)# static (dbdmz, dmz) 192.168.20.0 192.168.20.0 netmask 255.255.255.0
```

Configure names for the public addresses of the DMZ servers:

```
PIX1(config)# names
PIX1(config)# name 10.1.1.10 dns
PIX1(config)# name 10.1.1.11 mail
PIX1(config)# name 10.1.1.12 web
```

Configure conduits:

```
PIX1(config)# conduit deny ip any 0.0.0.0 255.0.0.0
PIX1(config)# conduit deny ip any 10.0.0.0 255.0.0.0
PIX1(config)# conduit deny ip any 127.0.0.0 255.0.0.0
PIX1(config)# conduit deny ip any 172.16.0.0 255.240.0.0
PIX1(config)# conduit deny ip any 224.0.0.0 224.0.0.0
PIX1(config)# conduit permit tcp object-group dbhosts eq sqlnet 192.168.10.12
PIX1(config)# conduit deny ip any 192.168.0.0 255.255.0.0
PIX1(config)# conduit permit tcp host web eq http any
PIX1(config)# conduit permit tcp host mail eq smtp any
PIX1(config)# conduit permit tcp host dns eq domain any
PIX1(config)# conduit permit udp host dns eq domain any
PIX1(config)# conduit permit icmp 172.16.0.0 255.255.0.0 object-group dmzhosts
PIX1(config)# conduit permit icmp 172.16.0.0 255.255.0.0 object-group dbhosts
PIX1(config)# conduit permit icmp 10.1.1.0 255.255.255.0 any object-group icmp-outside-in
PIX1(config)# conduit deny icmp any any
PIX1(config)# conduit deny ip any any
```

Configure *outbound* statements:

```
PIX1(config)# outbound 10 deny 0 0 0
PIX1(config)# outbound 10 permit 172.16.0.0 255.240.0.0
PIX1(config)# outbound 10 deny 172.16.0.0 255.240.0.0 pop3
PIX1(config)# outbound 10 deny 172.16.0.0 255.240.0.0 143
PIX1(config)# outbound 20 deny 0 0 0
PIX1(config)# outbound 20 except 192.168.10.0 255.255.255.0 sqlnet
PIX1(config)# outbound 30 deny 0 0 0
PIX1(config)# outbound 30 permit 192.168.10.11 255.255.255.255 smtp
PIX1(config)# outbound 30 permit 192.168.10.10 255.255.255.255 domain
PIX1(config)# outbound 30 permit 192.168.10.0 255.255.255.0 http
```

Apply the *outbound* statements to the appropriate interfaces:

```
PIX1(config)# apply (inside) 10 outgoing_src
PIX1(config)# apply (dbdmz) 20 outgoing_src
PIX1(config)# apply (dmz) 30 outgoing_src
```

Summary

Configuring the PIX to pass inbound or outbound traffic requires multiple steps. Basic connectivity allows users on a higher security-level interface of the PIX to transmit traffic to a lower security-level interface using NAT or PAT. This is accomplished using the *nat* command in conjunction with a *global* command. Because the PIX ASA allows higher security-level interfaces to transmit traffic to lower security-level interfaces, and because the PIX is stateful, users on the inside of the PIX should be able to run almost any application without extra configuration on the PIX.

Controlling outbound traffic is an important part of a comprehensive security policy; this control can be accomplished using the *access-list* command or the *outbound* command applied to a specific interface using the *apply* command. If it is available on the version of PIX you are running, the *access-list* command should be used instead of the *outbound* command to filter traffic. The *access-group* command applies an access list to an interface, much like the *apply* command.

Once outbound access is secure, moving on to allowing inbound access is relatively easy. By default, all inbound access (connections from a lower security-level interface to a higher security-level interface) is denied. Access lists or conduits can be used to allow inbound traffic. Conduits are not tied to a particular interface, and the rules defined in a conduit are applied to all inbound traffic. The fundamentals of the *access-list* command are no different between controlling inbound or outbound traffic. For inbound traffic, configuring a static translation (using the *static* command) is required for each publicly accessible server in addition to *access-list* or *conduit*.

Chapter 10

Advanced PIX Configurations

Best Damn Topics in this Chapter:

- **Handling Advanced Protocols**

- **Filtering Web Traffic**

- **Configuring Intrusion Detection**

- **DHCP Functionality**

- **Other Advanced Features**

Introduction

Now that you have learned how to pass simple traffic through the PIX firewall, we are ready to dive in and deal with configurations that are more complex. In this chapter, we discuss some of the more advanced features that the PIX firewall has to offer. You will learn how the PIX can be configured to handle complex protocols that operate over multiple or dynamic ports. In some cases, these protocols embed IP addresses and port information inside the payload of data packets, creating a challenge for performing NAT/PAT. The PIX firewall also has the ability to block Web traffic, including Java and ActiveX applications. The PIX firewall provides integrated intrusion detection features for common information-gathering stacks and network attacks. We will look at how to use the integrated IDS signature in the PIX firewall to detect patterns of network misuse. In small office/home office (SOHO) environments, it might be beneficial to use the DHCP client and server functionality provided by the PIX firewall. In this chapter, we examine both of these features in detail and show how to use them. Finally, we complete this chapter by discussing unicast and multicast routing, Point to Point Protocol over Ethernet (PPPoE), and reverse-path forwarding.

Handling Advanced Protocols

One of the most important features of all firewalls is their ability to intelligently handle many different protocols and applications. If all our needs were satisfied by devices that simply allow, say, outgoing connections to port 80 (HTTP) and deny incoming connections to port 139 (NetBIOS), the life of a security engineer would be much simpler. Unfortunately, many applications, some of which were developed even before the idea of a firewall emerged, act in a much more complicated manner than Telnet or HTTP. One of earliest examples is File Transfer Protocol, or FTP (which we discuss in detail in the next section). The general problem these applications pose is that they use more than one connection to operate and only one of these connections occurs on a well-known port, while the others use dynamically assigned port numbers, which are negotiated in the process of communication. Figure 10.1 shows an example of what happens when this situation occurs and no special measures are in place. (This is a simplified example of SQL*net session negotiation.)

Thus, any firewall that wants to handle these negotiations well needs the ability to monitor them, understand them, and adjust its rules accordingly. This situation becomes even more complicated when NAT or PAT are involved; the firewall might need to change the data portion of a packet that carries embedded address information in order for the packet to be correctly processed by a client or server on the other side of PIX. There are many implementations of this feature for various firewalls—for example, Stateful Inspection in the Check Point product family or the Adaptive Security Algorithm (ASA) of Cisco PIX devices.

Figure 10.1 Client Redirection without Application Inspection

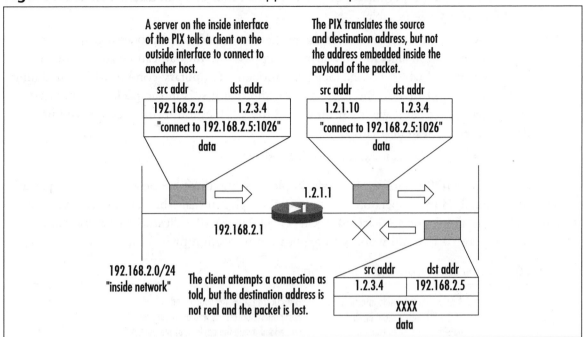

The ASA uses several sources of information during its operation:

- Access control lists (ACLs), which allow or deny traffic based on hosts, networks, and the TCP or UDP ports involved.

- Internal translation (xlate) and connection (xlate) tables, which store information about the state of the established connections and are used for fast processing of the traffic that belongs to these connections.

- Embedded rules for application inspection, which allow automatic processing of most of the complicated cases mentioned. Although some of these rules are configurable, others are fixed.

Here we look at the processing of a TCP packet by ASA, including application-level intelligence (not considering address translation):

1. If the packet is not the first one in a connection (with the SYN bit set), it is checked against internal tables to decide if it is a reply to an established connection. If it is not, the packet is denied.

2. If it is a SYN packet, it is checked against internal tables to decide if it is a part of another established connection. If it is, the packet is permitted and internal tables are adjusted in order to permit return traffic for this connection.

3. If this SYN packet is not a part of any established communication, it is checked against ACLs.

4. If the SYN packet is permitted, the PIX creates a new entry in internal tables (the XLAT and/or CONN table).

5. The firewall checks to see whether the packet needs additional processing by application-level inspection algorithms. During this phase, the firewall can create additional entries in internal tables. For example, it can open a temporary conduit for an incoming FTP connection based on the *PORT* command that it sees in the packet. "Temporary" means that this conduit will exist only until the FTP session terminates and will be deleted after the session is closed.

6. The inspected packet is forwarded to the destination.

The situation for UDP is similar, although simpler because there are no distinct initial packets in the UDP protocol, so the inspection simply goes through internal tables and ACLs and then through application inspection for each packet received. Figure 10.2 illustrates how the same example from Figure 10.1 would work with application inspection turned on.

Figure 10.2 Application Inspection in Action

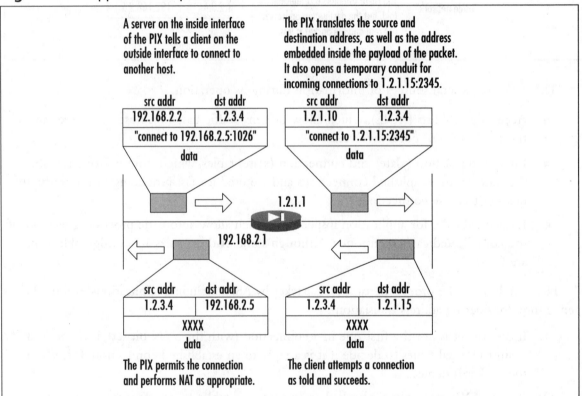

The PIX uses source/destination port numbers to decide if application inspection is needed for a particular packet. Some of these ports are configurable and others are not. Table 10.1 summarizes the application inspection functions provided by PIX firewall software v6.2.

Table 10.1 Application Inspection Features of Cisco PIX Firewall v6.2

Application	PAT Support	NAT 1-1 Support	Configurable?	Default Port	Related Standards
H.323	Yes	Yes	Yes No	UDP/1718 TCP/1720	H.323, H.245, H.225.0, Q.931, Q.932
H.323 RAS	Yes	Yes	Yes	UDP/1719	N/A
SIP	Yes	Yes	Yes No	UDP/5060 TCP/5060	RFC2543
FTP	Yes	Yes	Yes	TCP/21	RFC1123
LDAP (ILS)	Yes	No outside NAT	Yes	TCP/389	N/A
SMTP	Yes	Yes	Yes	TCP/25	RFC821, 1123
SQL*Net v.1, v.2	Yes	Yes	Yes	TCP/1521 (v.1)	N/A
HTTP	Yes	Yes	Yes	TCP/80	RFC2616
RSH	Yes	Yes	Yes	TCP/514	Berkeley UNIX
SCCP	No	Yes	Yes	TCP/2000	N/A
DNS	Yes	Yes	No	UDP/53	RFC1123
NetBIOS over IP	See next two entries				
NBNS/UDP	No	No	No	UDP/137	N/A
NBDS/UDP	Yes	Yes	No	UDP/138	N/A
Sun RPC	No	No	No	UDP/111 TCP/111	N/A
XDCMP	No	No	No	UDP/117	N/A
RTSP	No	No	Yes	TCP/554	RFC2326, 2327, 1889
CU-SeeMe	No	No	No	UDP/7648	N/A
ICMP	Yes	Yes	No	N/A	N/A
VDO Live	No	Yes	No	TCP/7000	N/A
Windows Media (NetShow)	No	Yes	No	TCP/1755	N/A

The main command that is used to configure the services stated as "configurable" in Table 10.1 (FTP, H.323, HTTP, ILS, RSH, RTSP, SIP, SSCP, SMTP, and SQL*Net) is the *fixup* command. Its basic syntax is:

```
[no] fixup protocol [protocol] [port]
```

The following sections describe how this command is used for each protocol. Depending on the protocol it is used with, application inspection (fixup) provides the following functionality for complex protocols:

■ Securely and dynamically open and close temporary conduits for legitimate traffic

- Network Address Translation
- Port Address Translation
- Inspect traffic for malicious behavior

File Transfer Protocol

One of the first application-level protocols that posed problems for simple packet-filtering devices was FTP, which is documented in RFC959. FTP always uses two connections for operation. The first one, known as the *control connection*, is a connection from the client FTP program to the server's FTP port (TCP port 21 by default). This connection is used for sending commands to the server and receiving informational replies. These commands and replies are a little different from what you enter on the keyboard. For example, when you log in to an FTP server and enter your username, your FTP client sends the *USER username* command to the server and probably receives a reply *331 User name okay, need password*. It then asks you for your password, and the login process completes.

The second connection is opened for the actual file transfer operation and can behave differently depending on the mode in which the client is operating; it can be initiated either by the client or by the server. The main difference is whether the client tells the server to operate in *passive* or *active* mode.

Active vs. Passive Mode

The first FTP servers and clients used *active* mode, where a file transfer happens as shown in Figure 10.3 and described here:

1. When the client (already connected to the server's FTP control port and logged in) needs to receive a file from the server, it sends a *PORT A1,A2,A3,A4,a1,a2* command, where A1, A2, A3, and A4 are the four octets of the client's IP address, and *a1* and *a2* are the port numbers on which it will listen for connections. This port number is an arbitrary value and is calculated as a1*256+a2.

2. After receiving a *200 OK* reply from the server, the client sends the *RETR* command to start the transfer.

3. The server opens a connection to the port that the client specified and pipes the file's contents into this connection. After the file is transferred, this data connection is closed, while the control connection stays open until the client disconnects from the server. The source port of this connection is "ftp-data," TCP port 20.

Now, if the client is behind a firewall (or, in PIX terms, is on a higher security-level interface than the server), the connection from the server is likely to be refused unless the firewall permits inbound connections to all high ports on the client side, which is of course not good. The PIX firewall can monitor FTP control connections, so when it discovers a *PORT* command issued by the client, it temporarily permits inbound connections to the port requested by the client in this command.

Figure 10.3 Active FTP Connection Flow

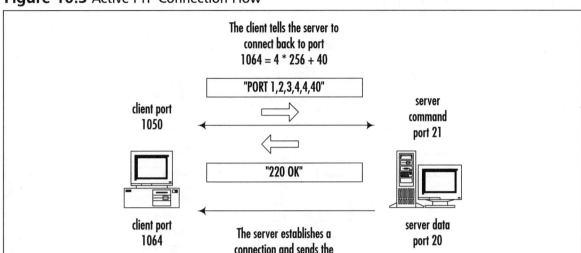

The other issue here is that when NAT or PAT are used, the PIX also translates the address and port number (A1.A2.A3.A4:a1a2) inside this command to the NATed IP and port. For example, if the client's address is 10.0.0.1 and it is translated to 1.2.3.4, the *PORT 10,0,0,1,4,10* command the client issued (which says that the client is ready to receive connections to 10.0.0.1:1034) during its transit through the PIX will be translated to something like *PORT 1,2,3,4,8,10*, so that the server will open the data connection to 1.2.3.4:2058. This destination will be properly translated by the PIX to 10.0.0.1:1034 using its internal tables.

The second mode of FTP operation is *passive* mode. In this mode, a file transfer happens as shown in Figure 10.4 and described here:

1. Soon after connecting to the server's FTP control port and logging in, the client sends the *PASV* command, requesting the server to enter the passive mode of operation.

2. The server responds with "227 Entering Passive Mode A1,A2,A3,A4,a1,a2." This response means that the server is now listening for data connections on the IP address and port it has specified in the reply.

3. The client connects to the specified port and sends the *RETR* command to start the transfer.

4. The server sends the file's contents over this second (data) connection.

This mode of operation does not cause a problem when the client is on a more secure interface, since by default the client is permitted to initiate any outbound connections. Unfortunately, there is a problem when the server is on a more secure interface than the client; the firewall will generally not allow the client to open an inbound connection on an arbitrary port. To overcome this problem, the PIX firewall monitors *PASV* commands and "227" replies, temporarily permits an inbound connection to the specified port, and modifies IP addresses and port numbers to correspond with NATed ones.

Figure 10.4 Passive FTP Connection Flow

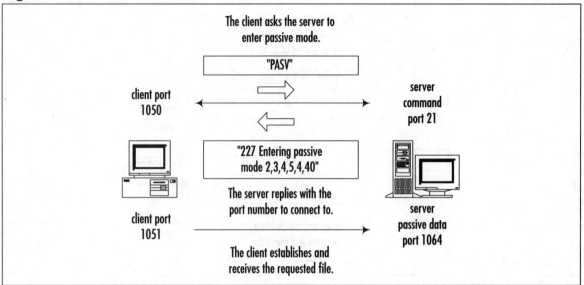

The client asks the server to
enter passive mode.

"PASV"

client port
1050

server
command
port 21

"227 Entering passive
mode 2,3,4,5,4,40"

The server replies with the
port number to connect to.

client port
1051

server
passive data
port 1064

The client establishes and
receives the requested file.

The described behavior of the PIX firewall is turned on by default; it inspects inbound and outbound connections to FTP control port 21. To turn it off or modify the port numbers on which it should perform inspection, use the *fixup protocol ftp* command in configuration mode. The syntax of this command is as follows:

```
[no] fixup protocol ftp [strict] [<port>]
```

Here, *port* is the port number used for control connections, *PORT* commands, and "227" replies. The default state of FTP inspection is equal to:

```
fixup protocol ftp 21
```

If you enter extra *fixup* commands, the ports specified in them are inspected simultaneously for incoming and outgoing FTP control connections. For example, if you enter *fixup protocol ftp 2100*, both default the default port (21) as well as port 2100 will be inspected. The command *no fixup protocol ftp [port]* disables the previously entered *fixup* command. For example, to enable processing of only connections to port 2100, you need to configure the following:

```
PIX1(config)# fixup protocol ftp 2100
PIX1(config)# no fixup protocol ftp 21
```

It is possible to disable inspection of FTP connections using *no fixup protocol ftp*. The result will be that inside users are able to initiate FTP connections to outside hosts only in passive mode, not active mode. Outside clients will be able to initiate FTP connections to inside servers in active mode only (assuming there is a static NAT entry and an access list or conduit in place), not passive mode. To reset application inspection to the standard port settings for all protocols at the same time, use the *clear fixup* command.

The full functionality of FTP application inspection consists of the following tasks:

1. Tracking of FTP command and response sequence (*PORT* and *PASV* commands and "227" replies).

2. Creating a temporary conduit for the data connections based on the result of this tracking (if necessary).

3. NATing of IP addresses inside the commands and replies.

4. Generating an audit trail.

An audit trail is generated in the following cases:

■ An audit record 302002 is generated for each uploaded or downloaded file.

■ Each download (*RETR*) or upload (*STOR*) command is logged.

■ File operations are logged together with the FTP username, source and destination IP addresses, and NAT address.

■ An audit record 201005 is generated if the firewall failed to allocate a secondary channel due to memory shortage.

In the first implementations of FTP inspection, the process of looking for the relevant commands/replies in IP packets was very simple: The PIX only looked for a string such as *PORT* inside the packet and tried to interpret it as a corresponding command. Of course, various attacks were designed to fool the firewall into opening an extra port by sending bogus commands and replies from the client or the server (see www.cisco.com/warp/public/707/pixftp-pub.shtml).

Since then, the inspection process has been greatly improved, and another option, *strict*, has been introduced to perform much more rigorous checks on the command/response stream. If you use this option in configuration of FTP inspection—for example, *fixup protocol ftp strict 21*—the firewall imposes much more rigorous restrictions on the command/response flow. These restrictions can sometimes break applications that are not fully RFC compliant. If one of the following problems is encountered, the connection is denied or dropped:

■ Clients are prevented from sending embedded commands. The connection that tries to use these commands is closed. This action is performed by checking how many characters are present in the *PORT* or *PASV* command after the IP address and port number. If there are more than eight characters, it is assumed that it is an attempt to add another command at the end of the line, and the connection is dropped.

■ Before a new command is allowed, the server should send a reply to each command received.

■ Only servers can generate "227" messages (protection against reply spoofing), and only clients can generate *PASV* and *PORT* commands (protection against command spoofing). The reason here is that without *strict*, a client can send any garbage to the server, including fake "227" messages—for example, *227 foobar A1, A2, A3, A4, a1, a2,* and although the server replies with an error message, the firewall could be fooled into permitting the connection with the parameters specified.

- Extra checking of "227" and *PORT* commands is performed to ensure that they are really commands/replies, not a part of some error message.

- Truncated commands; *PORT* and *PASV* commands are checked for the correct number of commas in them. Each should contain only five commas (see previous examples).

- Size of *RETR* and *STORE* commands; their length (including the filename for download/upload) should not be greater than an embedded constant. This is done to provide protection against possible buffer overflows.

- Invalid port negotiation; the port number used for the data connection must be a high port (that is, a port with number greater than 1024).

- Every FTP command sent by the client must end with *<cr><lf>* characters, as specified by RFC959.

Domain Name Service

The main task of application inspection for DNS (known as *DNS Guard*) is to impose specific restrictions on DNS requests over UDP that pass through the firewall (compared with the generic processing of all UDP communications). Roughly speaking, the data part of each DNS request contains a serial number (ID) and the body of the request. For example, requests for "A-records" (address records) include the DNS name for which an IP address is sought. The reply to this request should contain the same ID and an IP address.

DNS Guard ensures the following:

- Only replies with the correct ID are accepted.

- Only one reply is accepted. In the case of multiple replies, all but the first one are ignored.

- The UDP connection associated with the DNS connection is destroyed as soon as a DNS reply is received, not after the UDP timeout has expired.

- IP addresses in A-record replies are translated if necessary. This process is controlled by the *alias* command. It also translates addresses to be consistent with NAT statements, including outside NAT, which was introduced in v6.2. Generally, the *alias* command is not needed because of this outside NAT feature.

As an example for the last case, consider the configuration in which a client (192.168.0.1) and a Web server (web.company.com, IP address 192.168.0.5) are located on the inside interface of PIX and have nonroutable addresses. A DNS server is on the outside. The PIX is configured to translate both the client and the server addresses via PAT to a single IP of 1.2.3.4. This address is recorded on the DNS server as an address for web.company.com. When a client requests an IP address (an A-record) for the server, the PIX forwards the request to the DNS server, translating the source IP. When it receives the DNS server's reply, it not only translates the packet's destination IP address (changing 1.2.3.4 to 192.168.0.1), but it also changes the address of the Web server contained in the reply's data field (that is, 1.2.3.4 contained in the reply is changed to 192.168.0.5). As a result, the internal client will use the internal address 192.168.0.5 of the Web server to directly connect to it. Figure 10.5 illustrates how the DNS request and reply pass through the PIX.

Figure 10.5 The DNS Guard Operation

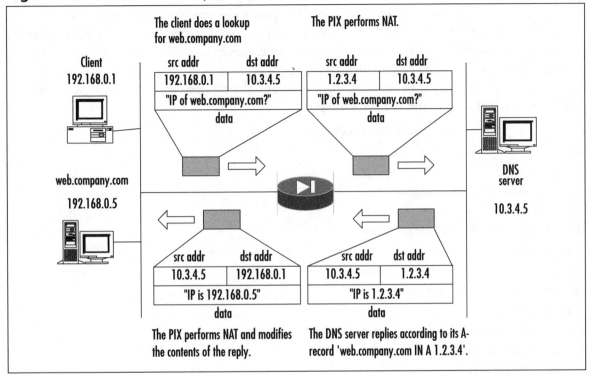

When the DNS server is on a more secure interface than the Web server and/or client, either outside NAT (preferred in v6.2) or *alias* commands are used. Outside NAT is very similar to the previous situation. Before v6.2, you needed to use the *alias* command *alias internal_server_address external_server_address* in order to process A-record replies properly in this case.

> **NOTE**
>
> When using *alias* commands for DNS fixups, you need to turn off proxy ARP on the internal interface, using the *sysopt noproxyarp inside_interface* command. It is also possible to turn off processing of DNS replies for addresses stated in the *alias* commands by using the *sysopt nodnsalias* command.

It is not possible to disable application inspection of DNS or change the DNS port from the default of 53.

Simple Mail Transfer Protocol

Similar to FTP and DNS inspection, application inspection of Simple Mail Transfer Protocol (SMTP), also known as *Mail Guard*, is designed to restrict what servers and clients can do and see while not harming the essential functionality of the protocol—sending electronic mail.

SMTP is described in RFC821 as a Telnet-based protocol designed for transferring electronic mail between servers. The client sends commands to the server, and the server replies with status messages and probably some extra information. In essence, it is very simple: There are commands for specifying a recipient of the message, the sender, and the message itself. An example of an SMTP session is shown in the following output.

```
Server: 220 Simple Mail Transfer Service Ready
Client: HELO example1.com
Server: 250 OK
Client: MAIL FROM:<Alice@example1.com>
Server: 250 OK
Client: RCPT TO:<Bob@example2.com>
Server: 250 OK
Client: RCPT TO:<John@example2.com>
Server: 550 No such user here
Client: DATA
Server: 354 Start mail input; end with <CRLF>.<CRLF>
Client: Blah blah blah...
Client: ...foobar.
Client: <CRLF>.<CRLF>
Server: 250 OK
Client: QUIT
Server: 250 OK
```

This transcript shows the session in which the client tried to send e-mail from Alice@example1.com to Bob@example2.com, which was accepted, and to John@example2.com, which was rejected because a user was not found.

These commands (*HELO MAIL, RCPT, DATA,* and *QUIT*), together with a couple of control commands (*NOOP*, do nothing, and *RSET*, reset state) make up a minimal set required by RFC821, section 4.5.1.

Mail Guard is turned on by default on port 25 and can be reconfigured using the following command:

```
[no] fixup protocol smtp [<port>[-<port>]]
```

This command functions in the same way as *fixup protocol ftp*, except that it is possible to specify a range of TCP ports instead of only one.

The main goal of Mail Guard is to restrict commands clients use to the minimal set described, while monitoring the entire command/response sequence and generating a specific audit trail. In detail:

- Mail Guard monitors commands sent by a client, and if a command does not belong to the minimal set, it is replaced with the *NOOP* command.

- If Mail Guard encounters an unknown command, the whole data portion of a TCP/IP packet is filled with the *X* symbol, which, when received by a server, causes the server to produce an error.

- *MAIL* and *RCPT* commands are monitored for correct usage of <, >, and | characters. The pipeline character | is replaced with a space, and < and > are allowed only when they appear as delimiters of an e-mail address. When an invalid character is replaced in the e-mail address, audit record 108002 is generated.

- Mail Guard checks for truncated or incorrectly terminated commands (ones that do not end with *<cr><lf>*).

- In a banner message—for example, "220 foobar email server ready"—all symbols except "220" are changed to *X*. This is done in order to hide details about the server platform or operating system, which are often reported in these banners.

! WARNING

When enforcing a minimal command set, the PIX causes some problems with Microsoft Exchange servers and Outlook clients. The problem here is that Microsoft's implementation of SMTP is not strictly RFC821 compliant and uses the *EHLO* command instead of *HELO* to start a connection. The PIX changes this command to *NOOP*, so the server simply returns a "250 OK" reply, which is interpreted as a confirmation that the server supports SMTP extensions. Consequently, clients do not fall back to the *HELO* command and continue using extended features (see RFC2821), which are blocked by the PIX. Most non-Microsoft clients, though, after receiving a simple "250 OK" reply instead of a more informative *EHLO* response, do fall back to the *HELO* style of operations and everything works well.

Hypertext Transfer Protocol

With HTTP application inspection active, all traffic to and from the specified ports is subject to the following:

- Logging of all HTTP GET requests

- Screening of URLs by either a Websense or an N2H2 server

- Filtering of ActiveX and Java content

The command for using application inspection for HTTP is shown here:

```
[no] fixup protocol http [<port>[-<port>]]
```

As with SMTP, it is possible to state a range of ports. The default port is 80. URL screening and active content filtering are described later in the chapter, in the "Filtering Web Traffic" section, and is configured using the *filter* command. Note that when you turn HTTP inspection off using *no fixup protocol http*, all HTTP inspection is disabled, even if URL screening rules are configured.

Remote Shell

The *r-utilities* (*rsh*, *rcp*, *rexec*, and *rlogin*) were developed to be convenient tools for remote command executions on UNIX machines, without the need for logging in as in Telnet. These utilities are inherently very insecure and are being phased out everywhere and replaced by SSH-based tools. Most applications that still use these utilities can be changed to use SSH-based means of authentication and file transfer.

Having said that, let's consider how this protocol works and why it poses problems for firewalls. When you try to connect to a remote host via Remote Shell (rsh), the following happens:

1. The rshd server on the remote host listens on a specified port (TCP port 514, by default) for incoming connections. The client establishes a connection to this port.

2. Immediately after the connection is established, the client sends an ASCII-coded number to the server. This is the port number that the server should use for establishing a secondary connection back to the client. This secondary connection is established so that the server can send any error output to the client. (More precisely, the server will pipe a stderr stream to this secondary connection.) This port number is not fixed, so if the firewall does not allow arbitrary connections to the client—for example, when the client is on a more secure interface)—this secondary connection from the server to the client will fail. In this case, the server closes the first connection and generates an error message, "Can't make pipe." See Figure 10.6 for an example of connection flow.

3. After an inbound connection to the client is established, the server performs client authentication. The client sends the server a command to be run on the server and receives the results of its execution (stdout stream) on the first connection, plus any errors that occurred on the second connection.

4. Both connections are closed.

Figure 10.6 RSH Connection Establishment

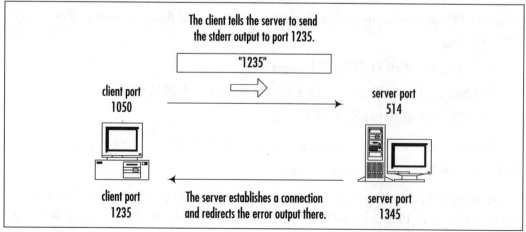

In order to process outbound rsh connections, the PIX monitors the initial connection, notes the port number the client requested, and opens a temporary conduit for the incoming connection by the server. The PIX is also able to perform PAT for this port if it is needed. The command to enable or disable application inspection for rsh is:

```
[no] fixup protocol rsh <port>
```

Inbound rsh connections do no need any special processing, only an access-list entry or conduit for an outside client to reach port 514 (default port for rsh) on the inside server.

NOTE

The r-utilities are inherently very insecure. Please consider using SSH instead.

Remote Procedure Call

Remote procedure call (RPC) is a very general mechanism for client-server applications developed by Sun Microsystems. Many applications are built on top of this system, the most important of which are Network File System (NFS) and Network Information System (NIS), which are used in many UNIX networks.

The RPC server is a collection of procedures, each of which can be called by a client sending an RPC request to the server, possibly passing some parameters. The server runs the required procedure and sends the results to the client. This data exchange is platform-independent and is encoded using External Data Representation (XDR) format. Each procedure is identified by an assigned program number, which the client indicates in the request. The default correspondence between program numbers and procedures is stored on UNIX hosts in the /etc/rpc file. To further complicate things, an RPC server can run various versions of each program at the same time. In this case, the version numbers are added to the request.

On TCP/IP networks, each version of a program running on the server is assigned a TCP and a UDP port (both ports have the same number). In order for this service to be generic (and because RPC programs do not use reserved port numbers), there is no fixed correspondence between program names (or numbers) and the ports they are running on. The ports are assigned dynamically by a separate daemon called *portmapper*, which functions as a multiplexing service. Each program has to register with portmapper in order to be available for RPC calls. Portmapper then reserves a TCP and a UDP port for it. When a client wants to make a call to a remote procedure, it first queries the portmapper daemon (which runs on port 111 by default), sending it a program number and receiving the number of a port it runs on. The client then connects to this port and interacts directly with the required program. Figure 10.7 illustrates this process.

Figure 10.7 RPC Connection Flow

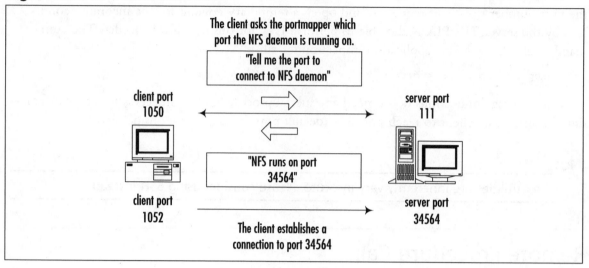

Here, the problem for a firewall arises when the RPC server is on a more secure interface; it is simple to set up a conduit permitting incoming connections to the portmapper port 111, but it is not possible to know beforehand which extra ports need to be opened for incoming RPC requests to specific programs. The PIX does the following:

1. It inspects all outgoing packets that have a source port of 111.

2. When it notices a portmapper reply with some port number, the PIX opens embryonic TCP and UDP connections on this port.

3. The PIX does not inspect RPC packets for anything else. For example, it does not attempt to translate embedded IP addresses.

This feature is not configurable.

Real-Time Streaming Protocol, NetShow, and VDO Live

In this section, we examine streaming applications and the problems they pose to firewalls. Streaming is a form of communication in which the client requests that the server send data at a certain speed. In some implementations, the client needs to confirm each portion of data received. In others, the server just sends data until the client tells it to stop. Major protocols widely used in this area are Real-Time Streaming Protocol, or RTSP (used by RealPlayer, Cisco IP/TV, and Apple QuickTime 4), NetShow (used by Microsoft Media Player), and VDO Live.

The RTSP, defined in RFC2326, is used for session setup and teardown as well as for controlling data flow (stop, play, pause). The RFC allows RTSP to run over both TCP and UDP, but all commercial implementations use only TCP, so Cisco supports application inspection for TCP-based RTSP sessions only. RTSP is a text-based, HTTP-like protocol by which the client sends requests and obtains replies from the server. Requests may be used to negotiate the transport that will be used for streaming data transmission, the options that are supported, asking the server to start or stop streaming, and the like. Embedded in RTSP is Session Description Protocol (SDP, described in RFC2327), which is used to provide the client with some extra information about the source of a datastream, including its physical location (in terms of IP addresses). The following is an example of an RTSP/SDP session (with nonrelevant parts skipped):

```
C> OPTIONS rtsp://www.play.com:554 RTSP/1.0
C> CSeq: 1
S> RTSP/1.0 200 OK
S> CSeq: 1
S> Server: RealMedia Server Version 6.0.3.354 (win32
S> Public: OPTIONS, DESCRIBE, ANNOUNCE, SETUP, GET_PARAMETER,
     SET_PARAMETER, TEARDOWN
S> RealChallenge1: 15d67d72b49fd4895774cfbb585af460
<skipped>
C> SETUP rtsp://www.play.com:554/g2audio.rm/streamid=0 RTSP/1.0
C> CSeq: 3
C> RealChallenge2: 319cd1020892093a7b7290ef22b6f41101d0a8e3, sd=3d00792f
C> Transport: x-real-rdt/mcast;client_port=6970;mode=play,x-real-
    dt/udp;client_port=6970;mode=play,x-pn-tng/udp;client_port=6970;
        mode=play,rtp/avp;unicast;client_port=6970-6971;
            mode=play
S> RTSP/1.0 200 OK
S> CSeq: 3
S> Session: 22660-2
S> RealChallenge3: 9521b5d0fcff7ab0ea7f407f89c5f3584f213d09,sdr=9bf7e48f
S> Transport: x-real-rdt/udp;client_port=6970;server_port=28344
<skipped>
C> PLAY rtsp://www.play.com:554/g2audio.rm RTSP/1.0
C> CSeq: 5
C> Session: 22660-2
S> RTSP/1.0 200 OK
S> CSeq: 5
S> Session: 22660-2
C> TEARDOWN rtsp://www.play.com:554/g2audio.rm RTSP/1.0
C> CSeq: 6
C> Session: 22660-2
S> RTSP/1.0 200 OK
S> CSeq: 6
S> Session: 22660-2
```

The session starts by negotiating client and server capabilities. Then comes the *SETUP* command, in which the transport mode (RDT or RTP) and port are negotiated (highlighted in italics in the preceding code). The client then commands the server to start transmission, and it finally tears the connection down after all data has been received.

Real Data Transport (RDT) is a RealNetworks proprietary protocol for data delivery. It uses two one-way UDP connections: one from the server to the client for data delivery and another from the client to the server for requests to retransmit lost packets. This is the default mode for the RealNetworks G2 server. In the exchange that appears in the preceding code, the client has chosen to receive data on port 6970 and the server has chosen to receive requests on port 28334.

Real-Time Transport Protocol (RTP), described in RFC1889, uses a one-way UDP connection for sending data from the server to the client and another two-way UDP connection for transmission control with RTP Control Protocol (RTCP). RTP/RTCP connections occur on two consecutive ports: the RTP channel is an even number port and RTCP is the next consecutive port. This is the default mode for Apple QuickTime and Cisco IP/TV.

To further complicate matters, there is one more mode of operation, interleaved mode, in which all RDT and RTP communications are embedded into the initial RTSP connection. This is the simplest mode from the firewall's point of view because it requires no extra processing.

RTSP connections occur on the default port of 554. Cisco IP/TV also uses port 8554, which is not enabled by default on the PIX. The command for enabling and disabling RTSP inspection is:

```
[no] fixup protocol rtsp [<port>]
```

For example, in order to enable correct processing of Cisco IP/TV streams, you need to add the following command to the default configuration:

```
PIX1(config)# fixup protocol rtsp 8554
```

When they perform application inspection for the RTSP protocol, the PIX monitors all *SETUP* replies with a code of "200." If the message is inbound and the server is a less secure interface, the firewall needs to open a temporary conduit for the incoming connection from the server to the client on a port stated in the reply. If the message is outbound, no extra actions are needed. The inspection process has the following restrictions:

- The PIX monitors only TCP-based RTSP exchange. RTSP over UDP is not inspected.

- RealNetworks RDT multicast mode is not supported (x-real-rdt/mcast content type).

- Proprietary RealNetworks PNA mode is not supported.

- The PIX is unable to recognize RTSP embedded in HTTP.

- RealPlayer needs to be set up to use only TCP to connect to the server (that is, to use RTSP over TCP only). This is done via **Options | Preferences | Transport | RTSP Settings**. The relevant setting here is Use TCP to Connect to Server. You can further configure it to work in interleaved mode (which needs no application inspection) by selecting **Attempt to use TCP for all content**. You can also configure it to use RDP by selecting **Attempt to use UDP for all content**.

- Supported RDP transports are rtp/avp, rtp/avp/udp, x-real-rdt, x-real-rdt/udp, and x-pn-tng/udp.

Even if the PIX tries its best to fix addresses inside RTSP/SDP packets, many NAT/PAT restrictions apply:

- PAT is not supported.

- NAT of contents of SDP messages inside RTSP is generally also not supported because these messages could be long enough to be split into several packets and the firewall has no means of reconstructing the original message. On the other hand, NAT usually works with Cisco IP/TV RTSP messages.

- NAT of datastream-related connections can be performed for RealNetworks server and Apple QuickTime. For Cisco IP/TV it can only be done when the viewer and the content manager are on the outside interface and the server is on the inside.

Microsoft's NetShow, used by Media Player, is a less complex streaming protocol. Like the other streaming protocols, it has a control channel, which is used to negotiate setup and teardown of a data delivery channel. The data channel can be either TCP- or UDP-based. When UDP streams are used, the following process occurs:

1. The client connects to the server on TCP port 1755.

2. After a connection is established, the client sends a message to the server, proposing a UDP port on which it is going to receive a datastream.

3. After the negotiation is complete, the server starts sending data to the client.

4. The session ends by tearing down the control connection.

As shown here, the firewall needs to open a temporary conduit only when the client is on a less secure interface than the server. The port and IP addresses are extracted from the negotiation process. When TCP datastreams are used, after the initial connection to port 1755 is established, the client simply informs the server that it wants to use the same TCP connection for streaming, and the server starts sending data over the already established connection. There is no need for any extra processing by the firewall in this case (provided that access lists are set up correctly). NetShow application inspection is not configurable.

The VDO Live streaming protocol always uses two connections. The first is a TCP control connection established from the client to port 7000 on the server. The second is a UDP datastream from the server to the client. It always has a source port of 7001 and the destination port (the client-side port) is negotiated over the control connection during initial setup. The PIX monitors the VDO Live control connection and opens a temporary conduit for incoming traffic from port 7001 on the server to the negotiated port on the client. When the control connection is closed, the PIX closes the data connection as well. (There is no separate teardown message in this protocol, so this is the only way for the firewall to notice that communication has finished.) When NAT is involved, the PIX modifies the IP address and port number in the process of its negotiation correspondingly. Application inspection for VDO Live is not configurable and cannot be disabled.

SQL*Net

SQL*Net, which is used to query SQL databases, is another firewall-unfriendly protocol. There are three versions of SQL*Net: SQL*Net v1 (an old version used in Oracle 7), SQL*Net v2, and Net8/Net9 (newer versions of Oracle, such as 8i). Versions 1 and 2 are incompatible, whereas Net8/Net9 is just a small improvement on v2. All these protocols have common behavior: When a client wants to connect to an Oracle server, it first establishes a connection to the dedicated Oracle port (port 1525 by default in SQL*Net v1, port 1521 in v2 and later) and then is redirected by this server to another instance of Oracle running on this machine or even another server. The client now has to establish a connection to the IP address and port it was told. In SQL*Net v2 and later, even after that the client can be redirected again.

The only case in which all communications happen only on one port without any redirection is when Oracle runs in Dedicated Server mode. This might need some extra configuration to function; refer to Oracle documentation if you are interested in this feature.

The problem with firewalls arises when the server is on a more secure interface than the client. Generally, the client will not be able to establish inbound connections to arbitrary ports and IP addresses. In order to process this correctly, the PIX needs to monitor the information exchange between the server and the client to notice which address/port number is negotiated and open a temporary conduit for inbound connections. The command for controlling application inspection of the SQL*Net protocol is:

```
[no] fixup protocol sqlnet [<port>[-<port>]]
```

The default port is 1521. In case of SQL*Net v1, the PIX scans all messages from the server to the client, checks the address and port negotiation, performs NAT on the embedded address if necessary, and forwards the resulting packets to the client. The inbound connections from the client are also de-NATted correctly and permitted by a temporary conduit.

SQL*Netv2 communications are much more complicated than v1, so the inspection process is also more complex. Messages used in this protocol can be of the following types: Data, Redirect, Connect, Accept, Refuse, Resend, and Marker. When the PIX firewall notices a Redirect packet with zero data length, it sets an internal flag for this connection to expect the relevant address/port information. This information should arrive in the next message, which must be only of Data or Redirect type. The relevant part of the message resembles the following:

```
(ADDRESS=(PROTOCOL=tcp)(DEV=6)(HOST=a.b.c.d)(PORT=p))
```

The PIX then needs to NAT this a.b.c.d:p pair inside the message and permit inbound connections on the corresponding IP address/port pair. If anything other than a Redirect or Data packet arrives after the initial null Redirect packet, the internal flag is reset.

H.323 and Related Applications

Voice over IP, or VoIP (including H.323 protocol set, SCCP, SIP, and others), is a real nightmare from both NAT and access control perspectives. VoIP applications use not one but many connections between the server and the client, initiate them in both directions, switch these connections, and embed address and port information in upper layers of communication that firewalls generally do not inspect. Here we look at various VoIP protocols and the degree to which they are supported by PIX application inspection features. All VoIP systems use two or three layers of application protocols, many protocols at the same time:

- **Signaling protocols (for system control and user information exchange)** SIP, MGCP, H.225 and RAS in H.323, SCCP.

- **Protocols for capabilities exchange** SDP, H.245.

- **Audio/media protocols (used for delivering speech and video)** RTP/RTCP.

H.323 can use up to two TCP connections and up to six UDP connections for a single call. Most of these are negotiated dynamically and do not use fixed ports. A basic H.323 call has the following sequence:

1. H.225 is used to initiate and terminate sessions between remote points (at least this connection has a fixed port number—TCP port 1720 by default) and probably uses Registration, Admission and Status (RAS) protocol for some authorization features (UDP ports 1718 and 1719).

2. During this process, a port for H.245 connection is negotiated.

3. The H.245 connection is used for negotiating port numbers for RTP/RTCP datastreams. (These ports can change during the call flow.)

H.323v2 provides a Fast Connect process, which, if used, eliminates the extra connection of H.245. H.245 messages, including RTP port negotiation, are transmitted over the same channel as initial H.225 connection.

NOTE

Support for H.323v2 was introduced in PIX firewall software v5.3.

As with other application protocols, the PIX has the ability to inspect the negotiation process (for H.225, RAS, and H.245), remember the ports required for connection between parties, and perform NAT or PAT on the data portion of the packet. The two commands for controlling H.323 application inspection are:

```
[no] fixup protocol h323 h225 [<port>[-<port>]]
[no] fixup protocol h323 ras [<port>[-<port>]]
```

The first command is used for configuring ports that are monitored for H.225 messages (mainly for H.245 port negotiation), and the second is for ports on which RAS messages are intercepted. The default settings are:

```
fixup protocol h323 h225 1720
fixup protocol h323 ras 1718-1719
```

In PIX terms, "H.323 protocol inspection" means inspection of all protocols used in H.323 VoIP calls. The inspection of H.323 v2 was first implemented in PIX v5.3. This was mainly the support of H.225 and H.245 inspection, including static or dynamic NAT on packet contents. RAS support was introduced in PIX firewall software v6.2. This version also adds PAT support. Two major tasks performed by the PIX are:

- Monitoring and fixing of IP addresses and ports embedded in H.225, H.245, and RAS messages. These messages are encoded in PER format, so ASN.1 decoder is used internally.

- Opening the connections required for normal operations based on the preceding information.

Note that the first task is performed correctly even if messages are split into two or more packets—they are actually generally split in two packets, the first being a so-called TPKT header. When the PIX receives such a packet, it stores the information in an internal table, proxy ACKs this packet to the sender, and after receiving the next packet with IP address information, modifies necessary fields and sends out the modified message together with the new TPKT header. The PIX proxy feature does not support TCP options in the TPKT header.

UDP datastream connections are closed after the timeout period. This works in the same way as with general UDP packets, but you can use the following command to configure the timeout for datastreams separately from the general timeout:

```
timeout h323 <hh:mm:ss>
```

The default timeout is five minutes (this is the minimal setting), which is equivalent to:

```
PIX1(config)# timeout h323 0:5:0
```

> **NOTE**
>
> When RAS and gatekeepers are used, the initial setup is different. The client first sends an "Admission Request" (ARQ) UDP message, and the gatekeeper replies with an "Admission Confirmation" (ACF) message and provides the IP address and port number for a H.225 connection. There is no need to permit inbound traffic over port 1720 in this case; the PIX will open the necessary port based on inspection of the ACF message. Without gatekeepers, you need to enable incoming traffic to H.225 ports (1720 by default).

Besides hardware-based VoIP solutions, the H.323 set of protocols is also used by Intel Internet Phone, CU-SeeMe, CU-SeeMe Pro, MeetingPoint, and Microsoft NetMeeting.

CU-SeeMe is able to work in two different modes: H.323-compliant and native mode. Native mode is used when connecting to another CU-SeeMe client or CU-SeeMe conference server. The main difference here is that it uses a native control stream on UDP port 7648. The PIX performs inspection and NAT on this stream. CU-SeeMe support (other than support for H.323) is not configurable.

Skinny Client Control Protocol

Skinny Client Control Protocol (SSCP), as implied by its name, is a simplified protocol for use in VoIP networks. It is used by Cisco IP Phones. The main difference from full H.323 communications is that the whole session establishment is done not directly between clients but between a client and a Cisco Call Manager. After RTP ports are negotiated, datastreams are directly connected between clients. Thus, the PIX firewall needs to inspect SCCP signaling packets in order to note ports negotiated for RTP and possibly perform NAT on embedded addresses. The PIX firewall is able to recognize and inspect SCCPv3.1.1. The relevant command is:

```
[no] fixup protocol skinny [<port>[-<port>]]
```

The default port number is 2000. NAT of SCCP messages is supported, whereas PAT is not. When the Cisco Call Manager is on a more secure interface than the phones, the IP phones can be configured to use TFTP to download the information used to connect to the Call Manager. (In most cases, the TFTP server runs on the same machine as the Call Manager.) The problem here is that the clients need to initiate an inbound TFTP connection (UDP port 69) to the server. To permit this connection, you need to either allow incoming traffic on port 69 to the TFTP server or create a static entry for this server without NAT, allowing external connections to its IP address. After clients download the configuration they need to contact the Call Manager, the rest of the traffic is controlled using SCCP application inspection.

Currently, the PIX firewall does not support fragmented SCCP messages because the application inspection process checks each received message for consistency and drops any messages with incorrect internal checksums. This usually happens when a single message is split into several TCP packets.

Session Initiation Protocol

Session Initiation Protocol (SIP), defined in RFC2543, is another protocol used for session control in VoIP. It also uses SDP, mentioned previously, to describe each session being established. Each call is started with an *INVITE* message, which contains some of the session parameters, including IP addresses/ports for the next connections, which may use other ports. SDP messages then are used to establish RTP datastreams. The initial SIP session can use UDP or TCP as a channel. The default port for this connection is 5060. Application inspection of SIP over UDP is always on in the PIX and cannot be reconfigured. To change the default port for TCP SIP connections, use the following command:

```
[no] fixup protocol sip [<port>[-<port>]]
```

Application inspection for SIP includes monitoring of SIP and SDP messages, changing the IP addresses of endpoints embedded inside these messages (NAT and PAT), and opening temporary conduits for all negotiated control connections and datastreams based on the information obtained. The PIX maintains an internal database indexed by caller ID, sources, and destinations of each call. Included in this database are IP addresses and ports provided inside an SDP message. For example, a SIP message may look like the following (embedded address negotiation is in italics; these are the most important ones, although it includes much more IP information):

```
INVITE sip:23198@192.168.2.10:5060 SIP/2.0
Expires: 180
Content-Type: application/sdp
Via: SIP/2.0/UDP 192.168.2.10:5060;branch=1FV1xhfvxGJOK9rWcKdAKOA
Via:  SIP/2.0/UDP 10.0.1.134:5060
To:   <sip:23198@192.168.2.10>
From:  sip:15691@10.0.1.134
Call-ID:  c2943000-50405d-6af10a-382e3031@10.0.1.134
CSeq:  100 INVITE
Contact:  sip:15691@10.0.1.134:5060
Content-Length: 219
User-Agent:  Cisco IP Phone/ Rev. 1/ SIP enabled
Accept:  application/sdp
Record-Route: <sip:23198@192.168.2.10:5060;maddr=172.18.192.232>
```

The SDP message looks like the following:

```
v=0
o=CiscoSystemsSIP-IPPhone-UserAgent 17045 11864 IN IP4 10.0.1.134
s=SIP Call
c=IN IP4 10.0.1.134
t=0 0
m=audio 29118 RTP/AVP 0 101
a=rtpmap:0 pcmu/8000
a=rtpmap:101 telephone-event/8000
```

When the session setup starts, the SIP session is considered in a "transient" state until an RTP port has been negotiated for the datastream. If this does not happen within one minute, the session is discarded. After the RTP datastream ports are negotiated, the session is considered active and the SIP connection will remain established until the parties explicitly finish the call or an inactivity timeout expires. This timeout can be configured using the *timeout sip <hh:mm:ss>* command. The default state of this timeout is 30 minutes, which is equivalent to the following setting:

```
PIX1(config)# timeout sip 0:30:0
```

RTP media connections are subject to a default timeout of two minutes, although this setting can be changed using the *timeout sip_media <hh:mm:ss>* command.

You can view the status of SIP, RTP, and any of the connections subject to application inspection by PIX using the command *show conn state*.

You can also specify the type of connections you want to view (for example, *sip, h323, rpc*) with the *show conn state sip* command.

NOTE

The PIX firewall supports PAT of SIP messages since v6.2. NAT support has been available since v5.3.

One issue that could require extra configuration with SIP occurs when a phone on a less secure interface tries to place on hold a phone on a more secure interface. This action is performed by the outside phone sending an extra *INVITE* message to the inside phone. If UDP is used as transport, the PIX will drop the incoming packet after the general UDP timeout has expired. This situation can be overcome either by configuring an access list on the outside interface that permits packets to port 5060/UDP on the inside gateway or by using the following command:

```
PIX1(config)# established udp 5060 permitto udp 5060 permitfrom udp 0
```

This command tells the PIX to allow inbound UDP packets to port 5060 on a client if it had outgoing communication from UDP port 5060.

Internet Locator Service and Lightweight Directory Access Protocol

Microsoft developed the Internet Locator Service (ILS) protocol for use in products such as NetMeeting, SiteServer, and Active Directory services. It is based on Lightweight Directory Access Protocol (LDAP) v2. The main purpose of ILS application inspection is to let internal users communicate locally, even while registered to outside LDAP servers. This is done by inspecting LDAP messages traversing the firewall and performing NAT when necessary. There is no PAT support, because only IP addresses are stored on the server. When attempting translation of an IP address, the PIX searches its internal XLATE table first, then DNAT tables. If neither contains the required address, it is left unchanged.

NOTE

If you use only *nat 0* (that is, you do not use NAT) and do not have DNAT communications, ILS fixup can be turned off safely. Turning it off will also improve the firewall's performance.

The command to configure application inspection for ILS is as follows:

```
[no] fixup protocol ils [<port>[-<port>]]
```

The default port is 389 (standard LDAP port). As with all other configurable inspection features, you can see the current configuration using the *show fixup* command.

ILS/LDAP communications occur on a client/server model over TCP, so there is no need for any temporary conduits to be opened by the PIX. During client/server communications, the PIX monitors for ADD requests and SEARCH responses, decoding them with BER decode functions; parses the message for IP addresses; translates them as necessary; encodes the message back, and sends the received packet to its destination.

Filtering Web Traffic

Although often the most attention is paid to the protection of internal servers or clients from external malicious attempts (the main purpose of ACLs), it is sometimes important to monitor and filter outbound connections made by users. One reason for content inspection is if you want to use your firewall to enforce security policies such as an acceptable use policy, which could specify that internal users may not use the company's Internet connection to browse certain categories of Web sites. There are many solutions for achieving this goal, but the most general one is URL filtering, in which the firewall hands each request for HTTP content to a filtering server, which can approve the request or deny access to it. The firewall then acts accordingly: If the request is approved, it is forwarded to the outside server and the client receives the asked-for content; if not, either the request is silently dropped or the user is redirected to a page telling him or her that the request breaches company policy.

Another reason for filtering is to deal with "active content" such as ActiveX or Java applets. This could be important in order to protect internal users from malicious Web servers that embed these executable applets in their Web pages, because such executable content can contain viruses or Trojan horses. The most general solution is content filtering, which scans incoming applets for viruses and denies them when something wrong is found. Unfortunately, the PIX does not support this general solution, and the only thing you can do with it is to strip all active content from incoming Web pages.

Filtering URLs

It is possible to use access lists to permit or deny access to specific Web sites, but if the list of sites grows long, this solution will affect firewall performance. In addition, access lists do not provide a flexible way of controlling access in this case; it is not possible, for example, to permit or deny access to specific pages on a Web site, only to the whole site identified by its IP address. Access lists will also not work for Web sites that are virtually hosted; in this case, there are many Web sites located on the same server and all of them have the same IP address, so it is only possible to deny or permit access to all of them at the same time.

As stated, one general solution moves most of the work to a dedicated URL filtering server, offloading the PIX's CPU and allowing for fine-tuning of Web access controls. The sequence of events is as follows:

1. A client establishes a TCP connection to a Web server.
2. The client sends an HTTP request for a page on this server.
3. The PIX intercepts this request and hands it over to the filtering server.
4. The filtering server decides if the client should be allowed access to the requested page.
5. If the decision is positive, the PIX forwards the request to the server and the client receives the requested content.

6. If the decision is negative, the client's request is dropped.

Figure 10.8 demonstrates this process.

Figure 10.8 Interaction Among a Client, a Web Server, PIX, and a Filtering Server

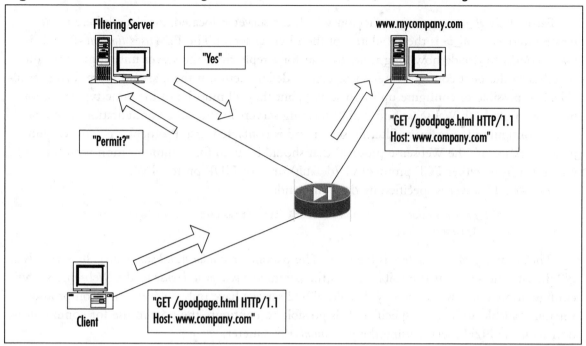

Websense and N2H2

The PIX can interact with two types of filtering servers: Websense (www.websense.com) and N2H2 (www.n2h2.com). Websense is supported in PIX v5.3 and later, and N2H2 support was added in v6.2. PIX URL filtering is applied only to HTTP requests; for example, it does not perform any inspections of FTP links. (Although a URL of type ftp://ftp.somedomain.com can be entered in a Web browser, it uses the FTP protocol, not HTTP.) The PIX also does not inspect HTTPS connections.

The steps to configure URL filtering are:

1. Specify the server to use for URL processing.
2. Tell the firewall the traffic to inspect—ports and IP addresses.
3. Optionally configure some server-specific parameters.
4. Configure filtering rules on the filtering server.

The command for specifying a filtering server for Websense is:

```
url-server (<if_name>) host <local_ip> [timeout <seconds>] [protocol <tcp> | <udp>
[version 1|4]]
```

For example, the following code specifies that the PIX should use a server with IP address 10.0.0.1, which is located on the interface inside, and connect to it using TCP Websense protocol v4:

```
PIX1(config)# url-server (inside) host 10.0.0.1 protocol tcp version 4
```

Particularly, *if_name* is an interface on which the server is located, the default here is the inside interface. *local_ip* is the IP address of the filtering server. The PIX uses *timeout* (default is five seconds) to decide how long it has to wait for a reply from the server until it gives up and switches to the next configured server or takes a default action if there are no more servers available. It is possible to configure up to 16 servers, but they all must be of the same type; it is not possible to use both Websense and N2H2 filtering servers in the same configuration. The first server configured is a primary filtering server and is contacted first. Protocol type and version parameters specify the Websense protocol that should be used for communication with the server. It can be either TCP protocol v1 (default) or 4, or UDP protocol v4.

The N2H2 server is specified by the command:

```
url-server (if_name) vendor n2h2 host <local_ip> [timeout <seconds>]   [port
<port_number>] [protocol tcp | udp]
```

The meaning of parameters is the same. The parameter *vendor n2h2* states that the server is an N2H2 filtering server. It is possible to add the parameter *vendor websense* to the Websense server configuration, but it is assumed by default. N2H2 servers have only a communication protocol version available, so it is not specified. It is possible to configure the port to use for communication with the N2H2 server using the *port_number* parameter.

> **NOTE**
>
> If you switch the application type (that is, change from N2H2 server to Websense or vice versa), all configuration of URL filtering is lost and will need to be re-entered.

The next task is to configure the filtering policy itself. The relevant command is:

```
filter url <port>[-<port>] <local_ip> <local_mask> <foreign_ip> <foreign_mask> [allow]
[proxy-block]
```

This command specifies port numbers on which HTTP connections should be inspected (with the default of port 80). *local_ip* and *local_mask* specify which local clients are subject to monitoring (that is, the requests by the machines from this network will be checked with URL filtering server). The *foreign_ip* and *foreign_mask* parameters specify that only requests to a specific set of servers be checked. The *allow* parameter defines that the PIX should permit traffic through if it is unable to contact the primary URL filtering server. Finally, the *proxy-block* parameter specifies that all requests from any clients to proxy servers will be denied. For example, the following command defines that all HTTP requests to port 80 will be inspected:

```
PIX1(config)# filter url http 0 0 0 0
```

The following command configures inspection of all HTTP requests to port 8080 from clients on network 10.100.1.0/24 to any server and allows the request to pass through in case a filtering server is unavailable:

```
PIX1(config)# filter url 8080 10.100.1.0 255.255.255.0 0 0 allow
```

Another variant of the *filter* command allows specifying that some traffic should be exempt from filtering. The format in this case is:

```
filter url except <local_ip> <local_mask> <foreign_ip> <foreign_mask>
```

When entered after the *filter* command, this command excludes specified traffic from the policy. For example, the following sequence of commands means that all HTTP traffic to port 8080 will be inspected, excluding traffic from network 10.100.1.0/24:

```
PIX1(config)# filter url 8080 0 0 0 0
PIX1(config)# filter url except 10.100.1.0 255.255.255.0 0 0 allow
```

Fine-Tuning and Monitoring the Filtering Process

The two commands we just looked at, *url-server* and *filter url*, constitute a basic configuration for URL filtering, but some extra parameters might need to be configured. One of these is required to deal with the problem of long URLs, which are common nowadays to store session and other information in the URL itself. A typical long URL could look like this:

```
http://www.somebettingcompany.com/?action=GoEv&class_id=1&type_id=2&ev_id=4288&class_na
me=%7CFootball%7C&type_name=%7CChampions+League%7C+%7CQualifying+Matches%7C&ev_name=%7C
Genk%7C+v+%7CSparta+Prague%7C
```

Until v6.2, the PIXs maximum supported URL length was 1159 bytes (for Websense only; N2H2 was not supported at all). In v6.2, the maximum URL length for Websense filtering is 6KB and 1159 bytes for N2H2. Version 6.2 introduced new options to the *filter* command to configure the firewalls behavior when the URL exceeds 1159 bytes with a Websense server. This syntax of this command is as follows:

```
filter url [longurl-truncate | longurl-deny] [cgi-truncate]
```

The *longurl-truncate* parameter specifies that when the URL length exceeds the maximum, only the IP address or hostname from the request, instead of the full URL, is sent to the filtering server. The *longurl-deny* parameter specifies that all long URL requests should be dropped. The *cgi-truncate* parameter specifies that only the CGI script name and its location (the part of the URL before the ? sign) should be passed as the URL to the Websense server. This skips the CGI parameter list, which can be quite long. Without this option enabled, the entire URL, including the parameter list, is passed.

NOTE

Even in PIX 6.2, the default URL size passed to a Websense filtering server for processing is 2KB. In order to increase this size, use the command *url-block url-size <size_in_kb>*, where *size_in_kb* can be from 2 to 6.

There are also commands for fine-tuning performance. The most important is the *url-cache* command which has the following syntax:

```
url-cache {dst | src_dst} size <kbytes>
```

This command is used for tuning the process of caching replies from the filtering servers. By default, the PIX sends requests to the URL filtering server for a decision and to the Web server for content at the same time, and if the Web server replies faster than the filtering server, the Web server's reply is dropped. The Web server is then contacted again if the filtering server permits the connection. In order to prevent these double requests, you might want to store the filtering server replies locally instead of contacting the server every time. The *url-cache* command enables a cache of *kbytes* kilobytes for replies of filtering servers based either on destination (that is, Web server address) when the *dst* option is specified or on both source and destination when *src_dst* is specified. The first option is recommended when all users have the same access privileges (so there is no need to identify clients), and the second is recommended when different users have different access privileges. The statistics of the caching process, including the hit ratio, can be viewed by executing the *show url-cache stat* command. For example, the following command enables a cache of 32KB for all outgoing HTTP requests:

```
PIX1(config)# url-cache dst size 32
```

The following are cache statistics:

```
PIX1# show url-cache stat
URL Filter Cache Stats
_____

Size : 32KB
Entries : 360
In Use : 200
Lookups : 2000
Hits : 1000
```

Another option for overcoming slow filtering server response is to cache Web server replies in advance and pass these replies to the client after the filtering server permits it. This feature is configured on the PIX using the following command:

```
url-block block <block_buffer_limit>
```

This command configures the size of the reply cache. The *block_buffer_limit* parameter can be any number between 1 and 128 and defines how many blocks of memory will be used. Usage statistics for this memory pool can be viewed by using the *show url-block block stat* command. For example:

```
pix(config)# show url-block block stat

URL Pending Packet Buffer Stats with max block          1
_____
```

Cumulative number of packets held: 0

Maximum number of packets held (per URL):   0

Current number of packets held (global):   0

Packets dropped due to exceeding url-block buffer limit: 0

Packet drop due to retransmission: 0

The total amount of memory used for storing URLs and pending URLs (the ones for which no response from the filtering server has yet been received) is configured with the command:

```
url-block url-mempool <memory_pool_size>
```

The size of the allocated memory pool is defined by a number from 2 to 10240, the number in KB. Other commands for viewing the configuration of URL filtering are *show filter, show url-server*, and *show url-server stats*. Here is some example output from these commands:

```
PIX1# show url-server
url-server (outside) vendor n2h2 host 192.168.2.17 port 4005 timeout 5
protocol TCP
url-server (outside) vendor n2h2 host 192.168.2.10 port 4005 timeout 5
protocol TCP
PIX1# show filter
filter url http 0.0.0.0 0.0.0.0 0.0.0.0 0.0.0.0
PIX1# show url-server stats
URL Server Statistics:
_____

Vendor n2h2
URLs total/allowed/denied 2556/2000/556
URL Server Status:
_____

192.168.2.17 UP
192.168.2.10 DOWN
```

show perfmon, show memory, and *show chunks* can also be used for monitoring the performance of the URL filtering process:

Active Code Filtering

As mentioned, active content in Web pages could be considered undesirable from a security point of view. Fortunately, there is a rather easy and effective way to prevent this content from reaching clients. In HTML, active content is denoted by two types of tags. The first is:

```
<object>
...
</object>
```

These tags are more common for ActiveX content, but they also can be used by Java applets. There are also Java-only tags:

```
<applet>
...
</applet>
```

When configured to look for active content, the PIX simply comments out both of these tags inside a TCP packet and the content between them, so they are simply skipped by the client's browser and embedded code is not run. The only problem with this approach is when the first tag is in one packet and the closing tag is in another packet, the PIX cannot perform this operation and the Web page is passed as is. For example, the HTML code inside an incoming packet might be as follows:

```
<td width="185" height="68" valign="top">
  <applet codebase="/classes/" code="tscroll.class" align="absbottom"
      width="185" height="68">
    <param name="bgcolor" value="8,51,128">
    <param name="enddelay" value="4000">
    <param name="scrolldelay" value="25">
    <param name="scrolljump" value="5">
    <param name="speed" value="2">
    <param name="size" value="11">
    <param name="hlcolor" value="255,0,0">
    <param name="centertext" value="false">
  </applet>
</td>
```

After being transformed by PIX, it becomes the code in the following output.

```
<td width="185" height="68" valign="top">
  <!-- <applet codebase="/classes/" code="tscroll.class" align="absbottom"
      width="185" height="68">
    <param name="bgcolor" value="8,51,128">
    <param name="enddelay" value="4000">
    <param name="scrolldelay" value="25">
    <param name="scrolljump" value="5">
    <param name="speed" value="2">
    <param name="size" value="11">
    <param name="hlcolor" value="255,0,0">
    <param name="centertext" value="false">
  </applet> -->
</td>
```

Now the Web browser ignores everything between the *<td>* and *</td>* tags.

Filtering Java Applets

To configure filtering of Java applets, use the following command:

```
filter java <port>[-<port>]  <local_ip> <mask> <foreign_ip> <mask>
```

Here is an example:

```
PIX1(config)# filter java 80 0 0 0 0
PIX1(config)# filter java 80 192.168.2.17 255.255.255.255 0 0
```

The first command configures the PIX to drop all Java applets from incoming Web pages; the second prohibits only one host 192.168.2.17 to download Java applets. The *port* parameter, as usual, specifies the TCP port on which to perform the inspection.

Filtering ActiveX Objects

Java has a more or less robust security model for its active code (there has been only one big security issue with it, and that was due to the poor implementation of this model in some versions of Netscape), but ActiveX objects have almost unrestricted access to the client's machine.

The command to configure filtering of ActiveX code (and all active content that is embedded in "object" tags) is very similar to Java filtering:

```
filter activex <port>[-<port>]  <local_ip> <mask> <foreign_ip> <mask>
```

Here is an example:

```
PIX1(config)# filter activex 80 0 0 0 0
```

This command configures the PIX to comment out all pairs of object tags from all incoming Web pages, disabling ActiveX and some Java applets.

DHCP Functionality

As more Cisco devices are used in SOHO environments, it becomes more important that they support features such as Dynamic Host Configuration Protocol (DHCP). Hosts use DHCP to dynamically obtain their Internet configuration instead of being configured with a static IP address and other parameters. The operation is very simple: Upon connection, a client sends a UDP broadcast, and if receives a specific reply, it configures itself correspondingly. Of course, this works only on the directly connected LAN segment or on the segments that are connected through bridges or routers, which forward broadcasts. This method can be used, for example, to simplify workstation management; all reconfigurations will be carried on only on the DHCP server, which will provide the new configuration to the workstations.

The Cisco PIX firewall can act both as a DHCP server and a client. In the first case, it will probably be a gateway for a small network of workstations and provide them all the information they need in order to connect to the Internet. In its client role, it may be a gateway for a network connected through a dial-up line, acquiring its outside interface address from the ISP's DHCP server.

Although DHCP functionality on the PIX firewall is available on all models of hardware, it was specifically designed for PIX 501, 506, and 506E, which are used primarily in SOHO environments. This is why the DHCP features the PIX firewall offers have some limitations. For example, the DHCP server can only support a maximum of 256 clients (or even fewer, depending on the firewall model, version, and license). There is also no BOOTP support and no failover support; the current state of DHCP server or client is not replicated over failover link.

DHCP Clients

When configured as a DHCP client, the PIX firewall can obtain the configuration of its outside interface from a designated DHCP server—for example, a server located at an ISP. This configuration includes the IP address, the subnet mask, and optionally, the default route.

> **NOTE**
>
> The DHCP client feature can only be configured on the "outside" interface of the PIX firewall.

This address can be used, for example, as a PAT address for all outgoing communications. This is configured in the following way (assuming that the DHCP client is already configured):

```
nat (inside) 1 0 0
global (outside) 1 interface
```

This configuration will work with any IP address assigned to the outside interface by DHCP. The configuration of the DHCP client is rather simple, and all you need to use is the following command:

```
ip address outside dhcp [setroute] [retry <retry_cnt>]
```

You do this instead of specifying a fixed IP address for an outside interface. The optional *setroute* keyword forces the PIX firewall to pick up not only the IP address and the subnet mask but the default route as well. Do not configure a static default route on the firewall if you use the *setroute* option. The *retry* option tells the PIX firewall to try to contact a DHCP server a specified number of times before giving up. If this keyword is not specified, no retries are attempted. If this keyword is specified but no retry count is given, the default number of retries is four. For example, the following command configures a DHCP client on the outside interface to obtain an IP address, subnet mask, and default route from the DHCP server, and only one attempt will be made:

```
PIX1(config)# ip address outside dhcp setroute
```

The following command configures the DHCP client to obtain an IP address and subnet mask only and tries at least five times before giving up if no DHCP servers are available:

```
PIX1(config)# ip address outside dhcp retry 5
```

There are no special commands for renewing and releasing DHCP lease; simply issue the same command again and the lease will be renewed. The address obtained can be viewed using:

```
PIX1# show ip address outside dhcp
```

This produces output similar to the following:

```
Temp IP Addr:123.1.2.3 for peer on interface:outside
Temp sub net mask:255.255.255.0
DHCP Lease server:123.1.2.31, state:3 Bound
DHCP Transaction id:0x4567
Lease:259200 secs, Renewal:129600 secs, Rebind:226800 secs
Temp default-gateway addr:123.1.2.1
Next timer fires after:100432 secs
Retry count:0, Client-ID:cisco-0000.0000.0000-outside
```

This output means that PIX has obtained an IP address of 123.1.2.3 and a subnet mask of 255.255.255.0 from the DHCP server 123.1.2.31. This DHCP lease is granted for 259200 seconds with renewal time of 129600 seconds. Time left until the next renewal is 100432 seconds, and there were no retries in contacting the server.

In case there are any issues with the DHCP client, you can troubleshoot using *debug* commands, including *debug dhpc packet, debug dhcpc detail, debug dhcpc error.* The commands are self-explanatory. *debug dhcpc packet* displays all DHCP traffic between the PIX client and a remote server, the *detail* option shows details of negotiation, and the *error* option displays all errors in this communication.

DHCP Servers

The server part of PIX DHCP support is more complicated. Let's look at the server's abilities and limitations. The most important issue is the number of DHCP clients the server can support and the specific protocol options supported. The number of clients supported on the various versions of PIX firewalls is shown in Table 10.2.

Table 10.2 Number of Clients Supported by the PIX DHCP Server

PIX Firewall Version	PIX Firewall Platform	Client Addresses (Active Hosts)
v5.2 and before	All platforms	10
v5.3 to v6.0	PIX 506/506E	32
	All other platforms	256
v6.1 and after	PIX 501 with 10-user license	32
	PIX 501 with 50-user license	128
	All other platforms	256

Note that the numbers quoted in Table 10.2 are for active hosts. A host is *active* if it has passed any traffic through the PIX, established a connection through the firewall, established a NAT or PAT translation entry, or authenticated itself to the firewall during the last 30 seconds.

> **NOTE**
>
> The DHCP server can be configured only on the inside interface of the PIX firewall and supports only clients on a network directly connected to this interface.

A minimal configuration of the DHCP server requires only two commands: one for specifying a range of IP addresses that can be provided to clients and another for actually turning the feature on. For example:

```
PIX1(config)# dhcpd address 192.168.2.1-192.168.2.127 inside
PIX1(config)# dhcpd enable inside
```

The only parameter that can be changed here is the address pool. Although currently the interface is always *inside*, it is possible that future releases of the PIX will have the ability to run a DHCP server on other interfaces. However, at the time of this writing (v6.2), it does not. It is possible to configure only one pool. Now when a client sends a DHCP request, the PIX provides it with the next IP address available in the pool of 192.168.2.1–192.168.2.127, the same subnet mask that is set for the inside interface of the firewall, and a default route pointing to PIX itself.

Some other configuration parameters are concerned with so-called "DHCP options"— optional information that can be provided to the client by its request. RFC2132, "DHCP Options and BOOTP Vendor Extensions," describes about 100 of these options and provides a mechanism for vendors to specify their own options. Very few of these options are really needed, especially in a SOHO environment, so the PIX supports only a few of them; nevertheless, this does not make it unable to operate as a full-strength server. The options that can be configured are the default domain name, the DNS server, the WINS server, and two TFTP-related options (number 66 and 150). The domain name provided to a client is configured with the following command syntax:

```
dhcpd domain <domain_name>
```

For example:

```
PIX1(config)# dhcpd domain syngress.com
```

The DNS servers that a client should use are configured with the command syntax:

```
dhcpd dns <dns1> [<dns2>]
```

Up to two DNS servers can be configured, using IP addresses:

```
PIX1(config)# dhcpd dns 1.2.3.4 1.2.4.10
```

WINS servers are configured using the following command, with the same restrictions as DNS servers up to two servers, configured using IP addresses:

```
dhcpd wins <wins1> [<wins2>]
```

Options 66 and 150 are used mostly by Cisco IP Phones and are considered later in this chapter. Other DHCP-related commands allow specifying some internal parameters for the server. It is possible to change the default lease time (the amount of time for which an IP address is provided to the client):

```
dhcpd lease <lease_time>
```

This command specifies the time in seconds. The default value is 3600, and possible values are from 300 seconds to 2,147,483,647 seconds. The following command syntax sets a maximum ping timeout in milliseconds (1/1000th of a second):

```
dhcpd ping_timeout <ping_time>
```

The PIX uses *ping* to ensure that another host on the network does not already have the IP address it is about to grant. If no host with this IP replies during this timeout, the IP is considered free. The *ping* timeout specifies how long the PIX will wait for a *ping* response to ensure that a host with the same IP address does not already exist on the network.

Finally, the following command allows the DHCP server to automatically obtain DNS, WINS, and domain parameters from a DHCP client configured on the outside interface:

```
PIX1(config)# dhcpd auto_config outside
```

An example of a SOHO configuration follows. It includes a DHCP client on the outside interface and a DHCP server on the inside interface, and it passes parameters from the client to the server:

```
ip address outside dhcp setroute
PIX1(config)# ip address inside 192.168.2.1 255.255.255.0
PIX1(config)# dhcpd address 192.168.2.201-192.168.2.210
PIX1(config)# dhcpd lease 3000
PIX1(config)# dhcpd auth_config outside
PIX1(config)# dhcpd enable
PIX1(config)# nat (inside) 1 0 0
PIX1(config)# global (outside) 1 interface
```

Without auto configuration, the example may look like this:

```
PIX1(config)# ip address outside dhcp setroute
PIX1(config)# ip address inside 192.168.2.1 255.255.255.0
PIX1(config)# dhcpd address 192.168.2.201-192.168.2.210
PIX1(config)# dhcpd lease 3000
PIX1(config)# dhcpd dns 1.2.3.4 1.2.3.31
PIX1(config)# dhcpd wins 192.168.2.20
PIX1(config)# dhcpd domain example.com
PIX1(config)# dhcpd enable
PIX1(config)# nat (inside) 1 0 0
```

```
PIX1(config)# global (outside) 1 interface
```

Commands are available for checking the state of the server. For example:

```
PIX1(config)# show dhcpd
dhcpd address 192.168.2.201-192.168.2.210 inside
dhcpd lease 3000
dhcpd ping_timeout 750
dhcpd dns 1.2.3.4 1.2.3.31
dhcpd enable inside
```

Other commands show the current state of IP bindings (which client has been assigned which IP address) and general server statistics:

```
PIX1(config)# show dhcpd binding
IP Address Hardware Address Lease Expiration Type
192.168.2.210 0100.a0c9.777e 84985 seconds automatic
```

Here, a client with MAC address 0100.a0c9.777e has obtained IP address 192.168.2.210, and this lease will expire in 84,985 seconds:

```
PIX1(config)# show dhcpd statistics
Address Pools 1
Automatic Bindings 1
Expired Bindings 1
Malformed messages 0
Message Received
BOOTREQUEST 0
DHCPDISCOVER 1
DHCPREQUEST 2
DHCPDECLINE 0
DHCPRELEASE 0
DHCPINFORM 0
Message Sent
BOOTREPLY 0
DHCPOFFER 1
DHCPACK 1
DHCPNAK 1
```

These statistics show the number of IP address pools configured, the number of active leases (bindings), expired bindings, messages received with errors, and a detailed breakdown on message type for correctly received and sent messages.

Cisco IP Phone-Related Options

As described in the "Skinny Client Control Protocol" section, Cisco IP Phones use a TFTP server for obtaining most of their configuration. This address can be configured statically, but it is also possible to use special DHCP options in order to provide phones with the location of the TFTP server. Clients can send to DHCP servers messages with options of two types: number 66, which causes the server to send a name of one TFTP server, and option 150, which results in a list of IP addresses of one or two TFTP servers. These options are supported starting from v6.2 of PIX software and are configured with the following commands:

```
dhcpd option 66 ascii <server_name>
dhcpd option 150 ip <server1_ip> [<server2_ip>]
```

For example:

```
PIX1(config)# dhcpd option 66 ascii tftp.example.com
PIX1(config)# dhcpd option 150 ip 1.2.3.4 2.3.4.5
```

Because the server runs only on the inside interface, IP Phones should be placed on the network directly connected to this interface.

Other Advanced Features

The Cisco PIX firewall has many other security features. Some of these features can be used to protect the network against various DoS attacks. Some of them are related to the processing of routing information—both unicast and multicast.

Fragmentation Guard

Fragmented packets are a challenge to firewalls. For example, nothing in the current Internet standards prevents a person from sending IP packets so fragmented that IP addresses of source and destination and TCP port information are located in different fragments or even in overlapping fragments. The firewall cannot decide on what to do with the packet until it sees the entire TCP/IP header. Some firewalls simply pass the fragments without trying to reassemble the original packets, whereas others try to perform this reassembly. Reassembly can be a dangerous process—for example, it is very easy to send fragments that will cause the reassembled packet to be of illegal size, possibly crashing internal buffers of the IP stack implementation.

The PIX always performs reassembly of fragmented packets before they are checked against access lists and can impose some restrictions on the fragmented traffic that passes through it. The FragGuard feature, when turned on, ensures that:

- Each noninitial IP fragment is associated with an already seen initial fragment (teardrop attack prevention).

- The rate of IP fragments is limited to 100 fragments per second to each internal host.

This feature theoretically breaks some rules of processing fragmented packets, but the current state of the Internet is such that heavy fragmentation usually does not occur naturally and almost always is the result of a malicious hacker trying to circumvent firewall rules or flood an Internet host. Therefore, in general, it is much better to have this feature on, unless you are connected via some strange link that does have a lot of fragmentation—but again, in this case there might be something wrong with the link itself.

This feature is disabled by default and can be turned on or off on all interfaces simultaneously only. The command for enabling it is *sysopt security fragguard*.

The corresponding *no* command turns the feature off. The status of various settings, including FragGuard, can be checked with the *show sysopt* command.

> **NOTE**
>
> The most important side effect of FragGuard is that you could lose the communication with hosts running some versions of Linux if they do fragment IP packets. These versions do not always send the initial fragment first, so the PIX firewall will discard the received sequence of fragments. Although this rarely occurs, you should still watch out for it.

FragGuard settings can be too restrictive at times. It is possible to manually tune the process of virtual reassembly with the *fragment* set of commands. Their syntax is as follows:

```
fragment size <database-limit> [<interface>]
fragment chain <chain-limit> [<interface>]
fragment timeout <seconds> [<interface>]
clear fragment
```

The first command sets the maximum number of blocks that can be used for fragment reassembly. If an interface is not specified, the setting is global; otherwise, this setting is for the specific interface. The default number of blocks is 200 and should never be greater than the total number of available blocks of 1550 bytes' size. In general, a bigger database makes PIX more vulnerable to a DoS attack by flooding it with fragments and exhausting its memory.

The second command sets the maximum allowed number of fragments into which one IP packet is split. The default setting is 24 fragments; the maximum is 8200. Further fragments will be discarded and the packet will not be reassembled. The timeout setting specifies the time frame in which all fragments of one IP packet should be received. The default timeout is 5 seconds and can be up to 30 seconds.

The last command, *clear fragment*, resets all three settings to their default values. The state of fragments database can be displayed with the *show fragment* command:

```
pix(config)# show fragment outside
Interface:outside
Size:200, Chain:24, Timeout:5
Queue:150, Assemble:300, Fail:0, Overflow:0
```

This output shows that the database has default settings: the size of 200 blocks, 24 fragments in a chain, 5-second timeout. There are 150 packets waiting to be reassembled, 300 were already successfully reassembled, and there were no failures or database overflows.

AAA Floodguard

Another flood-related problem is that somebody can abuse the PIX AAA authentication mechanism simply by making a large number of login attempts without providing any login information, leaving the connections open. The PIX firewall will then wait until a timeout expires. By making enough attempts, it is possible to exhaust AAA resources so that no further login attempts will be answered—a DoS on login resources. In order to prevent this situation, the PIX firewall has an internal mechanism for reclaiming AAA resources. It is called Floodguard and is enabled by default. When enabled, Floodguard causes the PIX firewall to monitor resource usage and send a syslog message when these resources are exhausted. When in need of additional resources, the PIX firewall will reclaim the ones that are not in active state. This is done in the following order (by priority):

1. Resources that are in the Timewait state are reclaimed.

2. Resources in the Finwait state are reclaimed.

3. Embryonic resources are reclaimed.

4. Idle resources are reclaimed.

Commands (Configuration mode) related to this feature are *floodguard enable, floodguard disable,* and *show floodguard.* As these commands are relatively self-explanatory, we will not delve into them here.

SYN Floodguard

Another well-known DoS attack is SYN flooding, which occurs when an attacker sends large numbers of initial SYN packets to the host and neither closes nor confirms these half-open connections. This causes some TCP/IP implementations to use a great deal of resources while waiting for connection confirmation, preventing them from accepting any new connections before the backlog of these half-open connections is cleared. The easiest way to prevent this from happening is to control the rate at which new connections are opened or the number of connections that are half-open (other names for this are *SYN Received* or *embryonic*) at any given time. The latter can be performed by specifying a limit on the number of embryonic connections in the *static* and *nat* configuration commands. For example:

```
PIX1(config)# static (dmz, outside) 123.4.5.6 10.1.1.0 netmask 255.255.255.255 100 50
```

This creates a static NAT entry for the DMZ server 10.1.1.0 with an external IP address of 123.4.5.6. The number 100 means that only 100 connections to this server from outside can be in an open state at any given time, and the number 50 is the number of half-open or embryonic connections to this server that can exist at any given time. The *nat* command is similar: Two numbers at the end specify the number of open and embryonic connections that can exist at any given time to each translated host:

```
nat (inside) 1 10.0.0.0 255.0.0.0 100 50
```

When any of these numbers is zero, the number of connections is not limited. The actual behavior of PIX when the number of embryonic connections is reached for a host is different in v5.2 and later (since 5.3).

The TCP Intercept Feature in PIX v5.3 and Later

The implementation of SYN Floodguard in versions before 5.3 was not quite good. When the maximum number of embryonic connections for a host was reached, the PIX firewall simply discarded any further SYN packets directed to the affected host. Thus, while protecting the host against overloading, the PIX firewall prevented any traffic from passing to or from the host in the case of a SYN flood. Similarly, when the maximum number of embryonic connections was not specified, the PIX did not restrict the number of half-open connections, which could lead to a successful SYN flood attack against the host.

Version 5.3 implements a new feature called *TCP Intercept*. Since v5.3, the PIX firewall behaves differently when the number of embryonic connections for a host is reached. If this happens, until the number of embryonic connections falls below threshold, each new SYN packet to the affected host is intercepted instead of being discarded. Then PIX itself replies to the sender instead of the destination server with SYN/ACK. If the client finally replies with a legitimate ACK, the PIX firewall sends the original SYN to its destination (the server), performs a correct three-way handshake between the PIX and the server, and the connection is resumed between a client and a server.

Figure 10.09 illustrates how the TCP Intercept feature works.

Figure 10.09 TCP Intercept in PIX v5.3 and Later

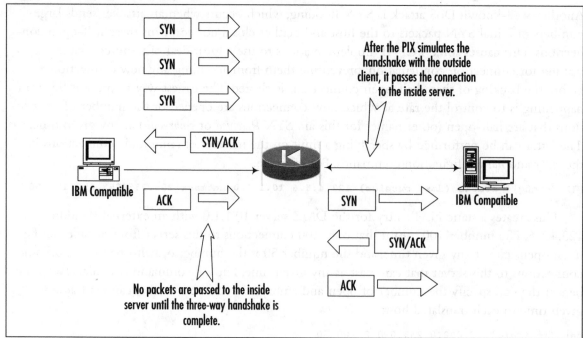

Reverse-Path Forwarding

The concept of reverse-path forwarding (RPF) is rarely understood well, although it is rather simple. The basic idea is to have an extensive routing table and, for each packet arrived, check its *source* address against this table. This is why it is called "reverse" lookup. When a route to this source is found (that is, when there is a reverse path to the source), it is ensured that the packet has arrived on the same interface that is listed in the corresponding route entry (so the packet has arrived on the best path back to its origin). If the interface is correct, the packet has arrived from a verifiable source and is legitimate. If a reverse route is not found or the packet arrived on a wrong interface, it is presumed that the packet is spoofed, and it is discarded.

This feature is used for implementing ingress and egress filtering as specified in RFC2267. It is turned off by default and can be enabled on a specific interface using the following configuration command:

```
ip verify reverse-path interface <interface_name>
```

Ingress filtering is used for checking that outside hosts really have outside addresses, but because the PIX firewall cannot maintain the table of all possible routes on the Internet, most configurations check that packets arriving to the outside interface from the Internet do not have an "inside" source address. Egress filtering does exactly the opposite: It checks that the packets going to the Internet actually have internal source addresses. This filtering makes tracing any packet back to its origin much easier and prevents most spoofing attacks. Although this can all be accomplished using access lists, the RPF feature provides a much easier and more elegant solution.

Let's consider the following example:

```
PIX1(config)# ip address inside 192.168.1.254 255.255.0.0
PIX1(config)# route inside 192.168.2.0 255.255.255.0 192.168.1.254 1
PIX1(config)# route inside 192.168.3.0 255.255.255.0 192.168.1.254 1
PIX1(config)# ip address outside 1.2.3.1 255.255.255.0 2
PIX1(config)# route outside 0.0.0.0 0.0.0.0 1.2.3.127
PIX1(config)# ip verify reverse-path interface outside
PIX1(config)# ip verify reverse-path interface inside
```

Here, two networks—192.168.2.0/24 and 192.168.3.0/24—are connected to the inside interface, and corresponding entries are created in the routing table. The outside interface has a default route to 1.2.3.127. The RPF feature is enabled on both interfaces. Now, when a packet arrives from the network attached to the inside interface, its source address is checked against the routing table. If this address belongs to one of the two networks 192.168.2.0/24 or 192.168.3.0/24, the route lookup succeeds and the packet is allowed to pass through the firewall. If the address is not from either of these networks, no route will be found, and the packet will be discarded.

If a packet arrives from the Internet to the outside interface, its source is also checked because RPF is active on the outside interface. If this address belongs to one of the networks 192.168.2.0/24 or 192.168.3.0.24, route lookup succeeds, but it is noted that this packet has not arrived on the best path to its origin. (The best path goes through the inside interface.) The packet is obviously a spoofed one and it is dropped. In all other cases, the route lookup also succeeds because there is a default route on the outside interface and the packet is permitted to pass through. Thus, *ip verify reverse-path interface inside* provides egress filtering, whereas *ip verify reverse-path interface outside* provides ingress filtering.

> **NOTE**
>
> There are several limitations on using RPF verification. If there is no default route on the outside interface, only the networks mentioned in the routing table are able to send packets to the hosts behind the firewall. In addition, do not turn on RPF verification before routing is fully specified, for the same reason. If your network has asymmetric routing, RPF verification will not work correctly.

If in this configuration we omit RPF verification on the outside interface, only egress filtering on the inside interface will be performed, and spoofed packets from the Internet will be allowed to pass through, whereas any spoofing attempts by inside hosts will be stopped. If RPF verification is enabled only on the outside interface and routes to internal networks are provided, only ingress routing will be performed; outside packets with source IPs belonging to internal networks will be dropped.

RPF-related statistics can be viewed with the following command:

```
pix(config)# show ip verify statistics
interface outside: 5 unicast rpf drops
interface inside: 2 unicast rpf drops
```

Counters here show the number of packets dropped by unicast RPF. The number of RPF drops can also be seen in *show interface* results:

```
pix(config)# show interface
interface ethernet0 "outside" is up, line protocol is up
Hardware is i82559 ethernet, address is 00aa.0000.003b
IP address 1.2.3.4, subnet mask 255.255.255.224
MTU 1500 bytes, BW 100000 Kbit half duplex
1183242 packets input, 1222000001 bytes, 0 no buffer
Received 210 broadcasts, 23 runts, 0 giants
4 input errors, 0 CRC, 4 frame, 0 overrun, 0 ignored, 0 abort
1311231 packets output, 565432270 bytes, 0 underruns, 0 unicast rpf drops
0 output errors, 12332 collisions, 0 interface resets
0 babbles, 0 late collisions, 12342 deferred
0 lost carrier, 0 no carrier
input queue (curr/max blocks): hardware (128/128) software (0/1)
output queue (curr/max blocks): hardware (0/2) software (0/1)
```

Line 8 of this output contains a message *0 unicast rpf drops*; this means there were no drops on this interface.

Not all packets are checked with RPF. What actually happens is:

- ICMP packets are all checked because there is no session state for these types of communication.

- TCP and UDP communications have session information maintained by PIX, so only an initial packet is checked against the routing table. All subsequent packets are checked only for the interface they arrived on. This interface should be the interface on which an initial packet arrived.

The *clear ip verify reverse-path*, and *clear ip verify statistics* commands respectively delete *ip verify* commands from the configuration and clear packet counts,.

Unicast Routing

In this section, we describe some more advanced topics related to unicast routing as performed by the PIX firewall.

Static and Connected Routes

You have already learned how to configure static routes on the PIX firewall using the *route* command:

```
route <interface> <ip_address> <netmask> <gateway_address> [<metric>]
```

For example:

```
PIX1(config)# route outside 0.0.0.0 0.0.0.0 1.2.3.4
```

This command configures a static default route on the outside interface to the gateway 1.2.3.4—a default gateway to be used for network traffic. If you issue a *show route* command, the output will include the following line:

```
route outside 0.0.0.0 0.0.0.0 1.2.3.4 1 OTHER static
```

The keyword *OTHER* simply means that this route is a manually entered static route. There is one interesting variation to the *route* command: It is possible to specify an IP address of PIX's own interface instead of a gateway address. This might seem strange from the point of view of the classic static routing, but this is sometimes very useful, especially in a Cisco infrastructure. The PIX itself automatically creates routes of this type when you enter an IP address for an interface.

So, what happens when a route is set to the PIX interface? The simple answer is that the PIX firewall considers the network directly connected and sends an ARP request for the destination address itself instead of requesting for gateway's destination and forwarding the packet to the gateway. The destination host does not really have to be directly connected; if it is connected via a router that has a *proxy-arp* feature turned on, the router will reply on behalf of the host, the PIX will forward the packet to this router, and the router in turn will forward the packet to the host. Cisco routers and PIX firewalls have proxy ARP turned on by default. For example, if the inside interface has an IP address of 192.168.1.254/24 and two networks, 192.168.2.0/24 and 192.168.3.0/24, are connected to this interface via a router, the following two statements will configure correct routes to these networks (note that the router's IP is not used anywhere; it just has to be in the same network as the inside interface of the PIX):

```
PIX1(config)# route inside 192.168.2.0 255.255.255.0 192.168.1.254
PIX1(config)# route inside 192.168.3.0 255.255.255.0 192.168.1.254
```

The *show route* command displays the corresponding entries in the routing table as:

```
route inside 192.168.1.0 255.255.255.0 192.168.1.254 1 CONNECT static
route inside 192.168.2.0 255.255.255.0 192.168.1.254 1 OTHER static
route inside 192.168.3.0 255.255.255.0 192.168.1.254 1 OTHER static
```

The first entry here was created automatically by the PIX firewall when an IP address was configured on the inside interface. The other two are the result of our two static route entries.

What exactly happens when the default route (outside interface) on the PIX is set to itself? The sequence of steps PIX performs to correctly forward the packet is as follows:

1. The PIX receives a packet on the inside interface destined for the Internet host with IP a.b.c.d.

2. The default route on the outside interface is set to the interface itself. If a separate default gateway was specified, the PIX would simply ARP for the gateway's address and forward the packet there. If not, the PIX sends an ARP request for IP a.b.c.d.

3. Any router (assuming it has proxy ARP turned on) that has a route to a.b.c.d replies with its MAC address on behalf of the host a.b.c.d.

4. The PIX forwards the packet to this router, which will handle it from there.

5. The PIX also adds an entry to its ARP table for IP address a.b.c.d with the MAC address of the router.

The PIX firewall also has the proxy ARP feature turned on by default, so it can act in the same way as the router in the previous example. It is possible to turn the feature off on a specific interface using:

```
sysopt noproxyarp <interface>
```

NOTE

In case you have not heard the phrase, *"one-armed" routing* means that the router has only one interface (with more than one IP address on it). All it does is receive a packet from the network and redirect it to another router/host on the same LAN but maybe on another IP network. This is sometimes useful, but PIX cannot do this, because its Adaptive Security Algorithm does not allow any packet to exit on the same interface as it arrived.

Combined with the default proxy ARP feature, this feature can play tricks on your routing. For example, if a router is behind an inside interface and some host sends an

ARP request for this router's IP, PIX will reply instead (or together with the router) and the packet is forwarded to the PIX. Here comes the problem: The packet needs to be forwarded to the real router, but PIX cannot do this; the packet cannot exit on the same interface.

So, if you prefer to completely control your static routing and you have created all static routes with correct gateways, it is always better to turn off proxy ARP on all interfaces; it has a nasty habit of getting in the way.

Routing Information Protocol

Beside static routes, the PIX firewall also supports Routing Information Protocol (RIP) v1 and v2. This protocol is the simplest dynamic routing protocol and is described in RFCs 1058, 1388, and 2082. Roughly speaking, a router broadcasts (or it may use multicast in v2) its entire routing table to its neighbors, and they update their tables.

Each PIX interface can be configured either to broadcast (multicast) itself as a default route for the network or to passively listen for routing updates from other routers on the LAN. The simple syntax of the RIP configuration command is as follows:

```
rip <if_name> [default | passive] version [1 | 2]
```

The *default* and *passive* keywords define the mode RIP runs on the interface *if_name*. The *default* parameter specifies that a default route should be advertised, and *passive* means listening for updates from other routers. The *version* parameter specifies the version of RIP to use on the interface. If a version is not specified, version 1 is assumed. The major differences between RIPv1 and RIPv2 are that RIPv2 can use multicast to the address 224.0.0.9 instead of broadcasts and that it can use authentication. RIPv1 uses broadcasts only and no authentication of updates. RIPv2 is also a classless routing protocol, which means that it can exchange routing information for networks such as 172.16.1.0/24, whereas RIP v1 uses only networks of A, B, and C classes—for example, Class B network 171.16.0.0/16. Generally, it is better to use RIPv2 if there is no need to interact with older RIPv1 devices.

NOTE

Before PIX v5.3, the PIX firewall was capable of using only broadcasts for RIPv2. Versions 5.3 and later use multicast to the address 224.0.0.9. By default, when you use RIPv2 on the PIX, it sends updates to 224.0.0.9. If passive mode is configured with RIPv2, the PIX accepts multicast updates with the address of 224.0.0.9, and this multicast address is registered on the corresponding interface. Only Intel 10/100 and Gigabit interfaces support multicasting. When RIP configuration commands are removed from the configuration, this multicast address is unregistered from the interface.

If you have a router that talks multicast RIPv2 to an older PIX (before v5.3), the PIX will not receive any updates. It is possible to switch the router into unicast mode using a command *neighbor <pix_address>* in its RIP configuration section. The PIX is capable of receiving unicast updates in any version that supports RIP.

Here is an example of RIP v1 configuration:

```
PIX1(config)# show rip
rip outside passive
no rip outside default
rip inside passive
no rip inside default
PIX1(config)# rip inside default
PIX1(config)# show rip
rip outside passive
no rip outside default
rip inside passive
rip inside default
```

The first *show rip* command displays the default state of configuration: all interfaces listen passively. Then the inside interface is configured to broadcast itself as a default route. Note that the passive listening mode was not turned off by this mode; you would need to disable it separately with *no rip inside passive* if you wanted to turn it off.

RIP v2 also supports two types of authentication: clear-text passwords and MD5 hashes. This feature of RIPv2 protocol adds one more field to the transmitted routing update—an authentication field. It can contain either a cleartext password (not recommended) or a keyed MD5 hash of the whole message. *Keyed* means that there is a key that is used to compute a hash value of the message. PIX configuration is very simple in both cases: An extra parameter needs to be added to the basic configuration command:

```
rip <if_name> [default | passive] version 2 authentication [text | md5] <key_string>
<key_id>
```

For example, the following command uses a clear-text password of *mysecretkey* while broadcasting the default gateway on the inside interface:

```
rip inside default version 2 authentication text mysecretkey 1
```

The following command lists only the messages with a correct MD5 hash keyed by a key *anothersecretkey*:

```
rip outside passive version 2 authentication md5 anothersecretkey 2
```

The *key_id* parameter (a number at the end of the line) is a key identification value and must be the same on all routers with which the PIX communicates.

RIP authentication on routers is more complicated. You need to set up a key chain with some keys (these keys are numbered and are exactly the *key_id* you need to provide in configuring PIX) and turn the authentication on. A sample partial router configuration corresponding to our case of MD5 authentication is:

```
interface ethernet 0
 ip rip authentication key-chain mykeys
```

```
    ip rip authentication mode md5
!
router rip
    network 172.16.0.0
    version 2
!
key chain mykeys
    key 2
    key-string anothersecretkey
```

The *clear rip* configuration mode command removes all RIP configuration statements from the PIX firewall.

Stub Multicast Routing

IP multicasting is becoming increasingly popular, especially in SOHO environments, where hosts are connected via fast links. Multicasting was introduced as a method of packet delivery to multiple hosts. In broadcasting, each host receives all packets sent by a server. In multicasting, a host must join one or more *multicast groups*, represented by a specific IP address (these addresses are 224.0.0.0–239.255.255.255) and then it will listen only for packets destined for this group. Of course, the nature of broadcasting and multicasting implies that it can be used only for UDP transmission, because TCP always requires two endpoints.

So how exactly does multicasting work? As noted, there is a set of multicast group addresses (Class D IP addresses, 224.0.0.0 through 239.255.255.255). A group of hosts listening to a particular multicast group address is called a *host group*. A host group is not limited to one network and can include hosts from many networks at the same time. Membership in a group is dynamic; hosts can enter and leave a group at will. The number of hosts in a group is not limited, and a host does not have to be a member of the group to send a message to this group.

When a host sends a message to a specific group address, this address is not subject to the ARP resolution process. It is simply converted into an Ethernet address by special rules, and an Ethernet frame is sent out with the resulting destination MAC address. If all recipients are on the same physical network, everything else is very simple: Listening hosts decide if the packet is sent to them by looking at the MAC address and its correspondence with the group addresses they are listening on. However, multicast groups are not limited to one network by definition, so there is a need for some means of passing these messages through routers and a means of informing routers if there are any hosts from a specific multicast group on a given physical network. This is done using Internet Group Management Protocol (IGMP).

IGMP is similar to ICMP in that it is also considered part of the IP layer. It is IP protocol number 2. Its basic functionality is as follows:

- When a host joins a multicast group, it informs the router by sending it an IGMP message.

- When a host leaves the group, it does not send any reports about this event (see the next two points).

- A multicast router regularly sends IGMP requests out each of its interfaces requesting connected hosts to report to the multicast groups to which they belong.

- A host responds to the request by sending one IGMP report for each group to which it belongs.

Figure 10.10 illustrates this IGMP exchange.

Figure 10.10 IGMP Used to Report Membership in a Multicast Group

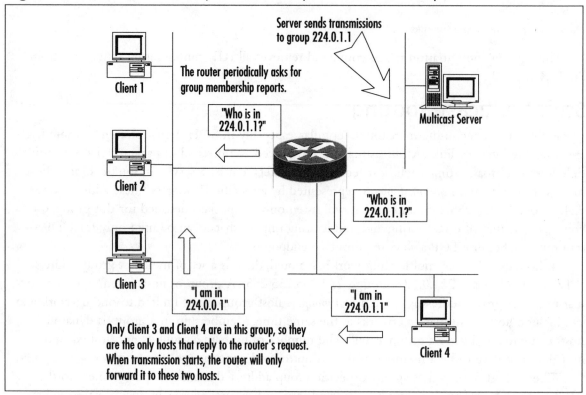

Since v6.2, the PIX can process multicast and IGMP messages. It does not have full capabilities of a multicast router, but it can act as a "stub router" or IGMP proxy agent. An IGMP proxy agent is a device that is able to forward IGMP requests and replies between multicast routers and hosts. When the source and destination of multicast transmissions are divided by a PIX firewall, two obvious cases are possible: when the source of a transmission (or a multicast router) is on a lower security-level interface than the destination and when the source (router) is on a higher security-level interface than the destination. Let's look at these two cases separately.

SMR Configuration with Clients on a More Secure Interface

In this case, a multicast router and a server are on the outside interface of the PIX firewall, and clients are on the inside. The PIX needs to be able to pass multicast traffic from the server and IGMP requests from the router to the inside hosts. It also needs to pass IGMP messages from the internal hosts to the outside router.

All SMR configurations start with the following configuration mode command:

```
multicast interface <interface> [max-groups <number>]
```

This command enables multicast features on the specified interface. The interface is placed into multicast promiscuous mode, and it enters a submode of multicast configuration for a specific interface. (This is a rare case with the PIX because there are very few submodes in configuration mode.) An optional *max-groups* parameter defines the number of multicast groups that can appear on the interface at any given time. The default setting is 500; the number can be up to 2000. This mode has subcommands like *igmp <command>*.

> **NOTE**
>
> To set the version of IGMP used, use the *igmp version {1 | 2}* subcommand under the *multicast* command.

In our case, the PIX needs at least to be able to receive multicast transmissions on its outside interface, so we need to configure:

```
PIX(config)# multicast interface outside
```

Actually, there is not much more to configure on the outside interface. We can optionally configure some counters and protocol options or access control, but this is not specific for a case and is described later. After exiting this multicast configuration mode (but while we're still in configuration mode), we need to configure multicast on the inside interface:

```
PIX1(config)# multicast interface inside
```

The inside interface requires additional configuration. After we enter this mode, we need to configure the interface to which the PIX should forward all IGMP messages from clients. This is the less secure interface where the router is located:

```
PIX1(config-multicast)# igmp forward interface outside
```

Don't forget that this command is entered while we are in the interface multicast configuration mode. *Outside* is the interface name to forward IGMP messages to from the interface being configured. If you have a multicast router on an interface named *dmz1*, the command will look like:

```
PIX1(config-multicast)# igmp forward dmz1
```

If any clients on the inside network are not IGMP-capable, but we still want them to receive multicast traffic from some group, we need to configure the inside interface to join this multicast group statically with the command:

```
igmp join-group <multicast_address>
```

For example:

```
PIX1(config-multicast)# igmp join-group 224.1.1.1
```

With this interface configured, the PIX outside interface acts as a host interested in receiving transmissions for this group, and then the received data will be forwarded to the inside network. Here is an example of the simplest multicast configuration:

```
PIX1(config)# multicast interface outside
PIX1(config-multicast)# exit
PIX1(config)# multicast interface inside
PIX1(config-multicast)# igmp forward interface outside
```

Here is a more complicated example with non-IGMP capable multicast clients who want to receive transmissions for group 224.10.0.9:

```
PIX1(config)# multicast interface outside
PIX1(config-multicast)# exit
PIX1(config)# multicast interface inside
PIX1(config-multicast)# igmp forward interface outside
PIX1(config-multicast)# igmp join-group 224.10.0.9
```

Clients on two interfaces, *inside* and *dmz*:

```
PIX1(config)# multicast interface outside
PIX1(config-multicast)# exit
PIX1(config)# multicast interface inside
PIX1(config-multicast)# igmp forward interface outside
PIX1(config-multicast)# exit
PIX1(config)# multicast interface dmz
PIX1(config-multicast)# igmp forward interface outside
```

SMR Configuration with Clients on a Less Secure Interface

This case is simpler. All you need to do is enable multicast processing on both interfaces and create static multicast routes for passing traffic between the clients and the servers (and routers). Multicast processing is enabled with:

```
PIX1(config)# multicast interface outside
PIX1(config-multicast)# exit
PIX1(config)# multicast interface inside
```

Multicast routes are created using the *mroute* command (which is not a subcommand of the multicast command):

```
mroute <src> <srcmask> <in-if-name> <dst> <dstmask> <out-if-name>
```

The *src* and *srcmask* parameters are the IP address and subnet mask of a multicast source host/router (just normal IP addresses, not multicast addresses.). The *in-if-name* parameter specifies the interface connected to the source. *dst* and *dstmask* are the multicast group address and subnet mask to which the server is sending its transmission. Finally, *out-if-name* is the interface connected to the multicast clients. For example:

```
PIX1(config)# mroute 192.168.2.25 255.255.255.255 inside 224.0.1.1 255.
    255.255.255 outside
```

Here is an example configuration in the case of two servers: 192.168.2.25 on the inside interface multicasting to group 224.1.1.1, and 10.2.3.4 on the dmz interface multicasting to the group 230.1.1.1 and no internal clients:

```
PIX1(config)# multicast interface outside
PIX1(config-multicast)# exit
PIX1(config)# multicast interface inside
PIX1(config-multicast)# exit
PIX1(config)# multicast interface dmz1
PIX1(config-multicast)# exit
PIX1(config)# mroute 192.168.2.25 255.255.255.255 inside 224.1.1.1 255.
    255.255.255 outside
PIX1(config)# mroute 10.2.3.4 255.255.255.255 dmz 230.1.1.1 255.255.255.
    255 outside
```

Access Control and Other Options

It is possible to restrict access to multicast transmissions using the usual PIX means: access lists. In the preceding case with hosts on the inside interface, we could restrict the groups from which the internal hosts can receive transmissions. For example, to allow only multicast transmissions to a group address 224.1.1.1, you should create an access list similar to this:

```
PXI1(config)# access-list 10 permit igmp any 224.1.1.1 255.255.255.255
```

Then apply it to the outside interface:

```
PIX1(config)# multicast interface outside
PIX1(config-multicast)# igmp access-group 10
```

Now only IGMP polls for group 224.1.1.1 will be able to pass through PIX, and thus only members of this group will be known to a multicast router. This prevents the router from sending traffic destined for any other group address in this direction.

Other subcommands of the *multicast* command include *igmp query-interval ,seconds>*. This command sets the interval at which IGMP messages will be sent out this interface. The default interval is 60 seconds. The maximum timeout for response (for IGMPv2 only) can be set usingthe *igmp query-max-response-time <seconds>* command. The default setting is 10 seconds.

Configured settings can be cleared using corresponding *clear* commands. The following command clears the IGMP cache either for a specific group address or the whole cache on the specified interface:

```
clear igmp group [<group-addr> | interface <interface-name>]
```

The following command clears multicast routes for specified transmission source, for a group address, or all routes on the interface:

```
clear mroute [<src-addr> | <group-addr> | interface <interface-name>]
```

Another set of commands (*show igmp, show multicast [interface <interface-name>], show igmp group [grou<p-addr> | interface <interface-name>],* and *show mroute [<src-addr> | <group-addr> | interface <interface-name>])*allows viewing of multicast configuration for the interface, multicast group, routes, and so on.

An example output of the *show igmp* command is:

```
pix(config)# show igmp
IGMP is enabled on interface inside
Current IGMP version is 2
IGMP query interval is 60 seconds
IGMP query timeout is 125 seconds
IGMP max query response time is 10 seconds
Last member query response interval is 1 seconds
Inbound IGMP access group is
IGMP activity: 0 joins, 0 leaves
IGMP querying router is 10.0.1.1 (this system)
IGMP Connected Group Membership
Group Address Interface Uptime Expires Last Reported
```

Two *debug* commands allow monitoring of multicast-related events. The *debug igmp* command monitors all IGMP messages passing through the PIX. Whereas the *debug mfwd* command monitors all events related to multicast forwarding.

PPPoE

Point-to-Point Protocol over Ethernet (PPPoE), documented in RFC2516, is an encapsulation of Point-to-Point Protocol (PPP, RFC1661) for Ethernet networks (which include DSL modems and cable connections). PPPoE is often used in SOHO environments because it allows ISPs to use their existing remote access infrastructure and, as its most important feature, allows authenticated IP address assignment. PPPoE links are established in two main phases:

- **Active discovery phase** During this first phase, a PPPoE client attempts discovery of the PPPoE server, also called the *address concentrator* (AC). The PPPoE layer is established and a session ID is assigned.

- **PPP session phase** A PPP link is established (encapsulated in Ethernet) by the usual means: options and link layer protocols are negotiated, etc. PPP authentication (PAP, CHAP, or MS-CHAP) is performed.

After the session is established, data travels between endpoints encapsulated in PPPoE headers.

The PIX firewall supports PPPoE since software v6.2. Most of the PPPoE configuration is performed using the *vpdn* command. PPPoE configuration starts with configuring the username and password to be used by the PIX in establishing a link to the server.

> **NOTE**
>
> The PIX only supports PPPoE client functionality. PPPoE clients can be enabled only on the outside interface at this time (v6.2).

First, a VPDN group needs to be created:

vpdn group <group_name> request dialout pppoe

The *group_name* parameter can be anything you like. It is used to group all PPPoE settings together. For example:

PIX1(config)# **vpdn group my-pppoe-group request dialout pppoe**

Then the authentication type needs to be selected (if required by an ISP):

vpdn group <group_name ppp> authentication pap | chap | mschap

PAP is Password Authentication Protocol, CHAP is Challenge-Handshake Authentication Protocol, and MS-CHAP is Microsoft's version of CHAP. With the same group name, this command selects an authentication protocol for this specific PPPoE group—for example, with CHAP authentication:

PIX1(config)# **vpdn group my-pppoe-group ppp authentication chap**

Your ISP assigns the username and password to your system, and they are configured on PIX with the following commands:

vpdn group <group_name> localname <username>
vpdn username <username> password <pass>

The second of these commands associates a username with the password, and the first command assigns the username to be used for a specific group, for example:

PIX1(config)# **vpdn group my-ppoe-group localname witt**
PIX1(config)# **vpdn username witt password cruelmail**

These commands assign the username *witt* and password *cruelmail* to be used for the PPPoE dial-out group *my-pppoe-group*. After configuring authentication, the next task is to enable the PPPoE client on the PIX. This is done in the configuration of the outside interface with the *ip address outside pppoe [setroute]* command. After this command is entered, the current PPPoE session is terminated and a new one is established. The *setroute* parameter allows automatically setting the default route for the outside interface. The MTU on the outside interface is automatically set to 1492, which is the correct setting to provide PPPoE encapsulation. It is also possible to designate a fixed IP address for the outside interface. The PIX still has to provide the ISP with the correct username and password in order to establish the session:

```
PIX1(config)# ip address outside 1.2.3.4 255.255.255.0 pppoe
```

It is possible to use the *dhcp auto_config* command if you run the DHCP server on PIX in order to pick up DNS and WINS settings from your provider via the PPPoE client:

```
PIX1(config)# dhcpd auto_config outside
```

To monitor and troubleshoot the PPPoE client, use the following commands:

```
show ip address outside pppoe
debug pppoe event | error | packet
show vpdn session pppoe [id <sess_id>|packets|state|window]
```

Examples of output are as follows:

```
PIX1(config)# show vpdn
Tunnel id 0, 1 active sessions
time since change 10240 secs
Remote Internet Address 10.0.1.1
Local Internet Address 192.168.2.254
1006 packets sent, 1236 received, 98761 bytes sent, 123765 received
Remote Internet Address is 10.0.1.1
Session state is SESSION_UP
Time since event change 10237 secs, interface outside
PPP interface id is 1
1006 packets sent, 1236 received, 98761 bytes sent, 123765 received
PIX1(config)# show vpdn tunnel
PPPoE Tunnel Information (Total tunnels=1 sessions=1)
Tunnel id 0, 1 active sessions
time since change 10240 secs
Remote Internet Address 10.0.1.1
Local Internet Address 192.168.2.254
1006 packets sent, 1236 received, 98761 bytes sent, 123765 received
PIX1(config)# show vpdn session
PPPoE Session Information (Total tunnels=1 sessions=1)
Remote Internet Address is 10.0.1.1
Session state is SESSION_UP
Time since event change 100238 secs, interface outside
PPP interface id is 1
1006 packets sent, 1236 received, 98761 bytes sent, 123765 received
```

Summary

The Cisco PIX firewall is an advanced product and has many different options for supporting various application-layer protocols as well as protecting against network-layer attacks. It also supports content filtering for outbound Web access, intrusion detection, various routing options such as RIP and stub multicast routing, and DHCP server and client functionality.

Many protocols embed extra IP address information inside the exchanged packets or negotiate additional connections on nonfixed ports in order to function properly. These functions are handled by the PIX application inspection feature (also known as *fixup*). PIX supports FTP clients and servers in active and passive modes, DNS, RSH, RPC, SQL*Net, and LDAP protocols. It also supports various streaming protocols such as Real-Time Streaming Protocol, NetShow, and VDO Live. Another set of supported protocols includes all H.323, SCCP, and SIP—all used in VoIP applications. The PIX monitors passing packets for the embedded information and updates its tables or permits embryonic connections according to this information. It is also able to NAT these embedded addresses in several cases.

Content filtering features on the PIX can be used to enforce a company's acceptable use policy. The PIX can interface with Websense (www.websense.com) or N2H2 (www.n2h2.com) servers and deny or allow internal clients to access specific Web sites. The PIX is also able to filter out Java applets and ActiveX code from incoming Web pages to protect clients against malicious code.

For SOHO environments, the PIX firewall provides DHCP server and client functionality, although server capabilities are rather limited. DHCP server supports a couple of specific options that are used by Cisco IP Phones. Other useful PIX features include support of stub multicast routing and PPP over Ethernet client capabilities. It also supports RIPv1 and v2, including authentication and multicast updates for v2.

Finally, the PIX has embedded protection against various DoS attacks, such as SYN floods, attacks on AAA mechanisms, and excessive fragmentation. Antispoofing is supported by the reverse-path forwarding feature.

## Chapter 11

Troubleshooting and Performance Monitoring

Best Damn Topics in This Chapter:

- Troubleshooting Hardware and Cabling
- Troubleshooting Connectivity
- Troubleshooting IPsec
- Capturing Traffic
- Monitoring and Troubleshooting Performance

Introduction

This chapter focuses on troubleshooting PIX firewalls. Once you have mastered its command syntax and basic firewall operations, the PIX is a relatively simple device to configure. Its library of commands is small compared to that of Cisco routers and switches. In previous chapters, we covered the PIX firewall in detail, from the various models in the product line to simple and advanced configurations. This book contains information on how to integrate the PIX firewall into your existing network. As good as your PIX configuration is, problems will still crop up, and you need to know how to resolve them. The purpose of this chapter is to present a methodology that you can use to attack these problems and avoid missing critical troubleshooting steps.

Hardware and cabling problems can be a bane to an otherwise well-functioning network. A hardware problem becomes apparent if you know which indicators to monitor. The limited number of cable types that the PIX supports eases our cable troubleshooting considerably. This chapter provides technical information about these cables so you can validate them.

The PIX firewall is an IP device. Granted, it is a highly specialized device that performs vital security functions, but it is still an IP device. As such, it needs to know where to send traffic. We highlight some common connectivity problems and how you can address them. A valuable function of the PIX firewall is its ability to conserve IP address space and hide network details via Network Address Translation (NAT). If you have problems with NAT, you must be able to isolate and eliminate them.

The PIX firewall provides several access control mechanisms, from simple access lists to complex conduit statements. These access mechanisms have simultaneous loose/tight properties in that certain traffic is allowed while other traffic is denied. Your troubleshooting will not only seek to resolve access problems, but also find the right balance between permitting and denying traffic.

Entire books have been written on IPsec, and for good reason. IPsec can protect your traffic from end to end without having to be implemented at every hop along the way. IPsec configuration can be complex. You must be intimately familiar with IPsec operations in order to support and troubleshoot it. This chapter covers several key aspects of IKE and IPsec to aid your monitoring and support.

Capturing network packets on the PIX firewall can enable you to troubleshoot more effectively. The PIX firewall offers several features that you can use to capture traffic for analysis and problem isolation. Available tools include native PIX commands as well as third-party tools for network capture and packet decode.

How do you know if your PIX firewall is performing as well as it should? How would you know if it was overloaded? You need to monitor firewall performance and health proactively. The goal of monitoring is to prevent minor glitches from turning into major problems. The output of your monitoring efforts can be quite dense and arcane, so you need to know how to interpret what you are monitoring.

Troubleshooting Hardware and Cabling

The most important thing to remember in troubleshooting is to tackle your problems logically so you don't miss any important components or steps. You must confirm the health of all the components that make up the firewall. When addressing PIX firewall problems, you would be best served using the OSI model to guide your efforts. This model was created to guide development efforts in networking by dividing functions and services into individual layers. Per the OSI model, peer layers communicate with each other. For example, the network layer at one host communicates with the network layer at another host.

The approach advocated in this chapter is based on the OSI model shown in Figure 11.1. Problems are tackled starting at the lowest layer, such as validating hardware and cabling at the physical layer. Only when the components at the lower layer have been validated do you turn your attention to components at a higher layer.

Figure 11.1 The OSI Model

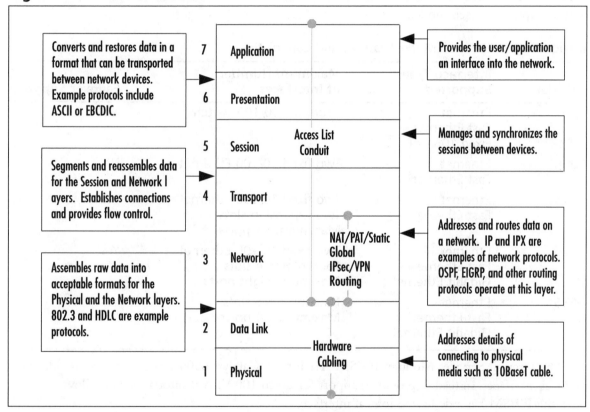

This chapter organizes troubleshooting efforts by the OSI model. Initial troubleshooting starts at Layer 1, the physical layer. Once all physical components have been validated, the troubleshooting focus is shifted to the data link layer components, and so on, up the OSI stack. This controlled approach ensures that we do not miss any facet of our security configuration where the problem could be.

Our first steps in troubleshooting start with physical layer issues. In the context of the PIX firewall, physical components include the firewall hardware and cabling. We start our discussion with a quick overview of the PIX firewall hardware architecture and cabling.

Troubleshooting PIX Hardware

Knowing the details of each PIX firewall model can be helpful in validating your configuration and troubleshooting. Such knowledge can quicken your problem-solving process from the onset by enabling you to determine how to interpret the symptoms you are witnessing. If you use the wrong firewall model for the wrong function, no amount of troubleshooting is going to make it work.

It can be said that your troubleshooting actually starts with your network design and security planning. There are several models of the PIX firewall, each capable of supporting certain numbers and types of network interfaces. Each model has its own upper limit on the number of maximum simultaneous connections, as shown in Figure 11.1. Therefore in Table 11.1 we provide only a snapshot of each model.

Table 11.1 PIX Firewall Model Features and Capabilities

Model	Interface Types Supported	Maximum Number of Interfaces	Failover Support
501	Ethernet Fast Ethernet Fixed 10BaseT	Four-port 10/100 switch	No
506E	Ethernet Fast Ethernet	Two fixed 10/100 Ethernet	No
515E	Ethernet Fast Ethernet	Two fixed 10/100 Ethernet Two expansion slots Maximum: Six ports	Yes
525	Ethernet Fast Ethernet Gigabit Ethernet	Two fixed 10/100 Ethernet Four interface slots Maximum: Eight ports	Yes
535	Ethernet Fast Ethernet Gigabit Ethernet	Nine interface slots Maximum: 10 ports	Yes

The Firewall Services Module (FWSM) 1.1 for the Catalyst 6500 series switches provides no physical interfaces. Instead, it provides support for up to 100 VLAN interfaces. For failover support, the FWSM has a dedicated logical interface.

It is important to know whether the PIX firewall you are using is adequate for the demands planned for it. For example, if you have a network on which 100,000 simultaneous connections will be requested through the firewall and you are using a PIX 501, the firewall will immediately become congested and be virtually unusable. In this scenario, no amount of troubleshooting and configuration will enable the PIX 501 to support the load. The capacity of each firewall model is important because it determines the load that can be placed on that firewall. Overloading your firewall is an invitation to crashes or congestion. Underloading a PIX firewall, although great for performance, can be wasteful in terms of unused capacity and monetary return on investment. For example, if you have a network on which there will never be more than 200 simultaneous connections, installing a PIX 535 means that you will not recoup your hardware or software investment, although performance will be fantastic.

The different models support different types of interfaces and in specific quantities, as shown in Table 11.1. Not shown in the table is the fact that Token Ring and FDDI are also supported by several of the models. Cisco ceased PIX firewall support for Token Ring and FDDI networks, starting with PIX software v5.3. As a rule of thumb, do not mix and match interfaces: Configure the PIX firewall as all Token Ring, all Ethernet, or all FDDI. Maintaining such network purity reduces the burden on the PIX firewall since it will not have to translate between the different LAN formats. Only models 515 and up support interfaces other than Ethernet.

The PIX firewall has a system for identifying its network interfaces, which you need to understand in order to troubleshoot the right piece of hardware. Not knowing how interfaces are enumerated and identified can consume valuable time that could otherwise be used for troubleshooting. Figure 11.2 shows how to "read" the network interface identification scheme. Interface card numbering starts with 0 at the right, with card slot numbers increasing as you go left. The slot in which the card is installed determines the number that is given to that card. Ports are numbered top to bottom, starting with 0 for the port at the top of the card.

Figure 11.2 PIX Firewall Interface Numbering

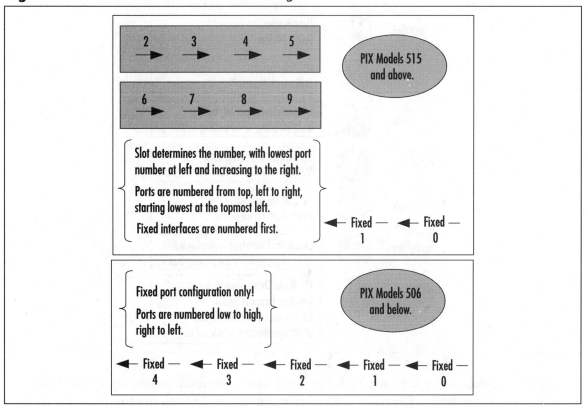

For example, the topmost port on an Ethernet interface card installed in Slot 3 would be identified as Ethernet 3/0. Fixed interfaces are first numerically starting on the right at 0, then the next fixed interface to the left is 1. The first installed network interface card would be 2 (as in

Slot 2) and its topmost interface is 0. It is important that you learn this scheme not only to identify the specific cards but to also ensure that your configuration and troubleshooting efforts focus on the correct interface.

The memory architecture of the PIX firewall is somewhat similar to that of Cisco routers with the exception that there is no NVRAM memory. The PIX uses flash memory to store the firewall operating system (image) as well as the configuration file. Main memory is used to handle data being processed. As a rule of thumb, the flash memory should be big enough to hold the software image and the configuration. Of all the memory types, main memory can potentially have the most significant impact on performance since it is the working space of the firewall. Main memory is used to store data that is waiting to be processed or forwarded. You can never have too much, and you will definitely notice when you have too little, because packet loss will increase or IPsec traffic will become lossy or laggardly.

Each firewall has visual indicators of operation in the form of light-emitting diodes (LEDs). These LEDs vary by model, but some are common to all. Figure 11.3 shows several PIX firewall LEDs and their meanings. Nurturing your knowledge of these LEDs will enable you to start your Layer 1 troubleshooting from the outside.

Figure 11.3 PIX Firewall LED Indicators

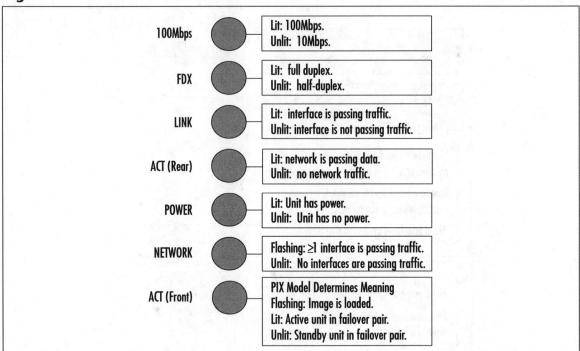

Study the information in Figure 11.3. The LEDs can be lit, unlit, or flashing, all of which indicate specific conditions. The ACT LED, since it can appear on both the front and rear of the PIX, deserves special attention. On certain models, such as the PIX 506 and 506E, the front LED flashes to indicate that the PIX software image has been loaded. When you're troubleshooting, this indicator would be sufficient to tell you if your software image has been loaded correctly or not at all. On higher-end models such as the 515 and up, the same LED indicates which PIX firewall is active and which is standby in a failover pair. This information can be very useful in determining if your failover configuration is cabled correctly.

During the PIX boot sequence, the power-on self-test (POST) can provide a wealth of information to help determine from the onset whether the PIX firewall is healthy or ill. We use an example boot sequence (which can be seen in the following output) to guide our discussion.

```
CISCO SYSTEMS PIX-501
Embedded BIOS Version 4.3.200 07/31/01 15:58:22.08
Compiled by morlee
16 MB RAM

PCI Device Table.
Bus Dev Func VendID DevID Class                Irq
 00  00  00   1022   3000  Host Bridge
 00  11  00   8086   1209  Ethernet              9
 00  12  00   8086   1209  Ethernet             10


Cisco Secure PIX Firewall BIOS (4.2) #6: Mon Aug 27 15:09:54 PDT 2001
Platform PIX-501
Flash=E28F640J3 @ 0x3000000

Use BREAK or ESC to interrupt flash boot.
Use SPACE to begin flash boot immediately.
Reading 1536512 bytes of image from flash.
######################################################################
16MB RAM
Flash=E28F640J3 @ 0x3000000
BIOS Flash=E28F640J3 @ 0xD8000
mcwa i82559 Ethernet at irq  9  MAC: 0008.e317.ba6b
mcwa i82559 Ethernet at irq 10  MAC: 0008.e317.ba6c
----------------------------------------------------------------------
                    ||          ||
                    ||          ||
                   ||||        ||||
               ..:||||||:..:||||||:..
                c i s c o S y s t e m s
                Private Internet eXchange
----------------------------------------------------------------------
              Cisco PIX Firewall
```

```
Cisco PIX Firewall Version 6.2(2)

Licensed Features:

Failover:          Disabled

VPN-DES:           Enabled

VPN-3DES:          Disabled

Maximum Interfaces: 2

Cut-through Proxy: Enabled

Guards:            Enabled

URL-filtering:     Enabled

Inside Hosts:      10

Throughput:        Limited

IKE peers:         5

***************************** Warning *****************************

  Compliance with U.S. Export Laws and Regulations - Encryption.


<<  output omitted  >>

***************************** Warning *****************************


Copyright (c) 1996-2002 by Cisco Systems, Inc.


                    Restricted Rights Legend


<<  output omitted  >>

Cryptochecksum(unchanged): 38a9d953 0ee64510 cb324148 b87bdd42


Warning: Start and End addresses overlap with broadcast address.

outside interface address added to PAT pool

Address range subnet is not the same as inside interface
```

The boot sequence identifies the version of the PIX operating system loaded on firmware used to initially boot. In this example, it is 4.3.200. This is important to know because this is the OS that will be used if there is no software image in flash memory. Notice that the first line identifies the model of firewall—information that can be useful if you are checking the firewall remotely.

After the POST is complete, the software image installed in flash is loaded and takes over from that point, as indicated by the "Reading 1536512 bytes of image from flash" line. The PIX firewall runs its checksum calculations on the image to validate it. The OS in the firmware is also validated. This is a layer of protection against running a corrupted operating system. In our example, the image loaded from flash memory recognizes two Ethernet interfaces present on this unit and displays the MAC addresses associated with them.

The boot display provides information about the PIX firewall hardware. The example shows that this particular unit has 16MB of main memory, something that can be a performance factor, as previously discussed. Other types of hardware such as interfaces (quantity and type) and associated IRQ information are identified as well.

Some very useful information about the features supported by this firewall can save you countless hours of frustration. For starters, the exact version of the operating system is identified—v6.2(2), in this case. More important, the features supported by this firewall are clearly enumerated. For example, VPN-DES is supported, whereas VPN-3DES is not. This makes sense since we are looking at a low-end PIX 501 with a limited license for 11 hosts and 5 IKE peers. This firewall supports cut-through proxy and URL filtering.

The last few lines of the boot screen can highlight errors that the operating system encountered when it parsed the configuration file. You should study these messages and determine if and how you must fix them. In our example, we have several problems with the way we have allocated our IP addresses. We also know that the outside interface address is now part of the PAT pool, which is something that we might or might not want, depending on our particular situation.

Once the firewall has completed booting, you can continue your hardware verification efforts using commands provided by Cisco. These are several commonly used commands to check the composition and health of your PIX firewall at Layer 1. The following output illustrates the *show version* command, which provides a quick snapshot of your PIX firewall. Information provided by this command includes interface information, serial numbers, and so on, as shown in the command output. Use this command when you need information about your firewall's software and hardware. Some of the output is similar to what you saw during the boot sequence.

```
PIX1> show version

Cisco PIX Firewall Version 6.2(2)
Cisco PIX Device Manager Version 2.1(1)


Compiled on Fri 07-Jun-02 17:49 by morlee


PIX1 up 23 secs


Hardware:   PIX-501, 16 MB RAM, CPU Am5x86 133 MHz
Flash E28F640J3 @ 0x3000000, 8MB
BIOS Flash E28F640J3 @ 0xfffd8000, 128KB
0: ethernet0: address is 0008.e317.ba6b, irq 9
1: ethernet1: address is 0008.e317.ba6c, irq 10


Licensed Features:
Failover:          Disabled
VPN-DES:           Enabled
```

```
VPN-3DES:            Disabled
Maximum Interfaces: 2
Cut-through Proxy:   Enabled
Guards:              Enabled
URL-filtering:       Enabled
Inside Hosts:        10
Throughput:          Limited
IKE peers:           5


Serial Number: 406053729 (0x1833e361)
Running Activation Key: 0xc598dce8 0xf775fc1c 0xbd76cee8 0x3f41e74b
Configuration last modified by  at 06:28:16.000 UTC Thu Feb 7 2036
```

The first part of this command identifies the version of OS that is loaded and being used as well as the version of PIX Device Manager (PDM). Next in the output you see the amount of time that has elapsed since the unit was powered on. This information is useful because it can show if your PIX firewall was rebooted or power-cycled recently. The *show version* command gives additional details such as the model, amount of available memory, and CPU speed and type. It also tells you the amount of flash and BIOS memory. When troubleshooting, you should know this information in order to determine if the demands placed on the unit are reasonable. This unit has two Ethernet interfaces; notice that their MAC addresses are enumerated. The last part of the output provides the serial number of this unit as well as the activation key used to activate the image. Although it is not critical to troubleshooting, it might be necessary to provide this information to Cisco TAC should you need to call them for assistance.

When you're troubleshooting, the *show version* command should be one of the first (if not *the* first) commands that you execute to obtain a component inventory of the PIX firewall. It is especially vital that you know which features are supported by the firewall before you begin troubleshooting; otherwise, you could squander valuable time trying to determine why an unsupported featured is not working. When looking at the output of the *show version* command, ensure that you note the MAC addresses of the interfaces; this information can be useful in resolving Layer 2 to Layer 3 address-mapping issues.

The *show interface* command shown in the following output is a tool that can provide information applicable to different layers of the troubleshooting process. It provides details on the network interfaces. As with Cisco routers, this command enables you to check the state of an interface and determine if it is operational. You can also see what each interface is labeled. This command and its associated output are discussed later in the chapter.

```
interface ethernet1 "inside" is up, line protocol is up
  Hardware is i82559 ethernet, address is 0008.e317.ba6c
  IP address 10.10.2.1, subnet mask 255.255.255.0
  MTU 1500 bytes, BW 10000 Kbit full duplex
  4 packets input, 282 bytes, 0 no buffer
  Received 0 broadcasts, 0 runts, 0 giants
```

```
0 input errors, 0 CRC, 0 frame, 0 overrun, 0 ignored, 0 abort
4 packets output, 282 bytes, 0 underruns
0 output errors, 0 collisions, 0 interface resets
0 babbles, 0 late collisions, 0 deferred
0 lost carrier, 0 no carrier
input queue (curr/max blocks): hardware (128/128) software (0/1)
output queue (curr/max blocks): hardware (0/1) software (0/1)
```

The output of the *show interface* command has useful applicability to the troubleshooting process. However, if you do not know how to read the output, the plethora of information presented will be of little value. One of the first things you need to determine with this command is if you want a particular interface to serve a particular network. In our example, Ethernet 1 is considered the "inside" network. As a part of our troubleshooting, we would ensure that Ethernet 1 is indeed connected to our "inside" network. The MAC address assigned to this interface is listed, as is the type of interface (Ethernet).

The maximum transmission unit (MTU) specifies the maximum packet size that this interface can pass without having to fragment it. Anything larger will be broken into the appropriate number of frames to enable passage through this interface. This can be an issue if you have devices that send large frames. This command also verifies the duplex operation of the interface; recall that the interface also has a full-duplex LED that you can use. Duplex mismatches between the PIX and LAN switches are a common problem and can be a headache. Ensure that the speed and duplex settings match on the PIX firewall and the switch.

There is a packet counter for inbound and outbound packets. This indicator tracks how many packets have transited this interface and the total number of bytes that these packets constituted. The "no buffer" counter is especially important to troubleshooting because it indicates the number of times that there were no buffers to store incoming packets until they could be processed by the CPU. If this counter increments, the interface is receiving more packets than it can handle. In this case, you need to upgrade to a higher-capacity interface or throttle back the incoming traffic. Each interface also has counters for tracking broadcasts and errors:

- **broadcasts** Packets sent to the Layer 2 broadcast address of this interface.

- **runts** Packets received that were less than Ethernet's 64-byte minimum packet size.

- **giants** Packets received that were greater than Ethernet's 1518-byte maximum packet size.

- **CRC** Packets that failed the CRC error check. Test your cables and also ensure there is no crosstalk or interference.

- **frame** Framing errors in which an incorrect Ethernet frame type was detected. Make sure you have the appropriate frame type configured on all your hosts.

- **overrun** Input rate exceeded the interface's ability to buffer.

- **ignored/abort** These counters are for future use. The PIX does not currently ignore or abort frames.

- **collisions** Number of transmitted packets that resulted in a collision. On a half-duplex interface, collisions do not necessarily indicate a problem, since they are a fact of Ethernet life.

- **underrun** Indicates that the PIX was too overwhelmed to get data fast enough to the network interface.

- **babbles** This is an unused counter. Babbles indicate that the transmitter has been on the interface longer than the time taken to transmit the largest frame.

- **late collisions** Collisions that occurred after the first 64 bytes of transmission. Unlike normal collisions, these indicate a problem. Usually, late collisions are caused by faulty cabling, long cables exceeding specification, or an excessive number of repeaters.

- **deferred** Packets that had to be deferred because of activity on the link. This generally indicates a congested network since the interface has to keep backing off to find an available transmit window to send; this can become a perpetuating problem that consumes buffer space as outgoing packets have to be stored until a transmit windows opens.

- **lost carrier** The number of times the signal was lost. This can be caused by issues such as a switch being shut off or a loose cable.

- **no carrier** This is an unused counter.

> **NOTE**
>
> On a full-duplex interface, you should never see collisions, late collisions, or deferred packets.

The queue counters refer to the amount of data (measured in bytes) queued for reception and transmission. These counters provide a snapshot of what is currently queued at the time the command is issued. The queues will be depleted if the firewall receives more traffic than it can handle. When a packet is first received at an interface, it is placed in the input hardware queue. If the hardware queue is full, the packet is placed in the input software queue. The packet is then placed into a 1550-byte block (a 16384-byte block on 66MHz Gigabit Ethernet interfaces) and passed to the operating system. Once the firewall has determined the output interface, the packet is placed in the appropriate output hardware queue. If the hardware queue is full, the packet is placed in the output software queue.

In either the input or output software queue, if the maximum blocks are large, the interface is being overrun. If you notice this situation, the only way to resolve it is to reduce the amount of traffic or to upgrade to a faster interface.

Troubleshooting PIX Cabling

After you have ascertained that the PIX hardware is functional, your next step in troubleshooting should be to corroborate cabling. Unlike routers, which use a wide variety of cables, the PIX firewall has a relatively limited number of cable types that we care about in the context of troubleshooting: Ethernet and failover cables.

Certain models of the PIX firewall support Token Ring and FDDI networks in older software versions (up to v5.3). Cisco has discontinued the sale of Token Ring and FDDI for PIX firewalls starting August 2001 and June 2001, respectively. Support is slated to cease in August 2006 and June 2006, respectively. We do not discuss Token Ring or FDDI cables in this book.

Regardless of the cables you are troubleshooting, you should adopt a structured approach. Table 11.2 summarizes some steps you should first take to check your cabling. Ensure that you perform these steps to avoid missing a minor cabling glitch that could be causing a major problem.

Table 11.2 Cable Troubleshooting Checklist

Problem	Troubleshooting Step
Correct cable connected to the correct interface?	Check cable and verify slot and port number.
Correct end of cable connected to correct interface?	*Failover cable only:* Primary end to the primary firewall and secondary end to the secondary firewall.
Correct cable type connected to equipment?	Cross cables, rollover cables, and so on to the correct ports.
Cable pinouts correct?	Visually inspect and check with cable tester.
Cable verified as good?	Test with a cable tester or swap with known good equipment and test.

All PIX firewalls support 10Mbps or 100Mbps Ethernet, but only the high-end models such as 525 and 535 support Gigabit Ethernet. This makes sense when you consider the capacity available on each model: The lower-end models would be overwhelmed by the addition of even a single Gigabit Ethernet interface. As of this writing, the PIX 535 provides 9Gbps of clear-text throughput, the 525 provides 360Mbps, the 515 provides 188Mbps, the 506 provides 20Mbps, and the 501 provides 10Mbps. At the physical layer, the primary issue you will face is to ensure that the correct Ethernet cables are being used and that they are wired correctly. Figure 11.4 shows the pinouts that you should be using for Ethernet and Fast Ethernet cables.

Two wiring schemes for the RJ45 standard are used for 10/100 Ethernet: TA568A and TA568B shown in Figure 11.4. It is important that your cable adhere to one of these standards to prevent interference (crosstalk). If you were to dismantle a RJ45 cable, you would see that there are four pairs of wires. In each pair, the two wires are twisted around each other to minimize crosstalk. If you were to pick wires at random and crimp them into the RJ45 connector to make an Ethernet cable, chances are you would experience problems with your cables. The wiring scheme of the TA568A/B standard is optimized to prevent such interference.

The process of troubleshooting cabling is relatively easy because there are numerous cable testers on the market, ranging from simple pin-checking devices to expensive, full-featured testers. The time that these devices save well justifies their initial cost.

Figure 11.4 Ethernet Cable Pinouts

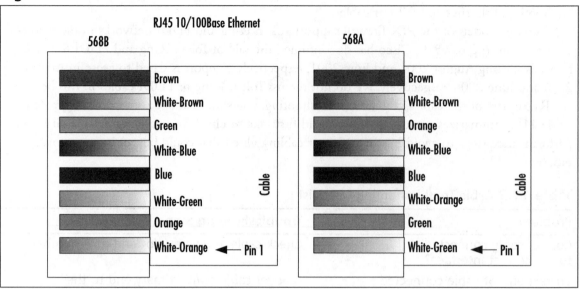

The first step in verifying 10/100 Ethernet copper cable is to visually inspect the cable for breaks. Check the wiring pinouts against Figure 11.4. If they match and appear to be in good physical shape, the next step is to test the cable using a cable tester. Most cable testers will allow you to map the wiring; pin mismatches are a common problem. If you still have problems with the cable after it passes the cable tester, try using a different cable. Chances are, you have a rare bad mix of plastic and metal composition that went into the making of that cable and it is interfering with the cable's ability to transport electrons. If you do not have a cable tester and are not sure of the cable, replace it.

PIX firewall models 525 and 535 support full-duplex Gigabit Ethernet (GE). The GE interfaces use SC multimode fiber optic cables: one strand for receive and the other for transmit, as shown in Figure 11.5. It is important that you cable the wire with the correct cable to the correct connector.

Fortunately, the SC connector Cisco uses prevents us from inserting the cable incorrectly. The connector on the cable is notched to fit the slotted jack on the interface card. You need to understand a little about fiber optic cables to effectively use them with your PIX firewall. Fiber optic is either single mode or multimode. The PIX firewall GE interfaces use multimode fiber, which refracts light, as shown in Figure 11.6.

The fiber optic industry adheres very strictly to its standards. As a result, usually you can visually determine whether you have a multimode or single-mode fiber optic cable attached by its color. Single-mode cables are yellow and have markings down their sides indicating their width in microns. Multimode fiber optic cable used by PIX firewalls is orange and is numerated with either 50 or 62.5 microns, indicating the size of its glass core down which light is sent. The cladding packed in the glass core is the same size for both cables: 125 microns. This is a general rule of thumb only; some manufacturers offer custom colors or do not adhere to the standard color scheme.

Figure 11.5 Gigabit Ethernet SC Fiber Optic Connector

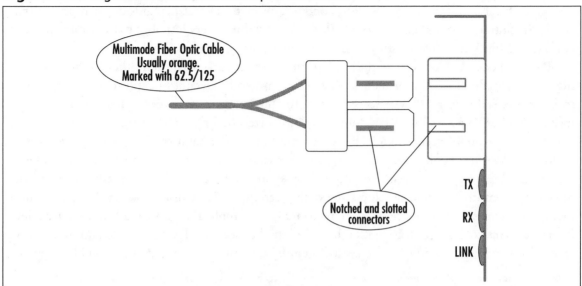

Figure 11.6 Multimode Fiber Optic Cable

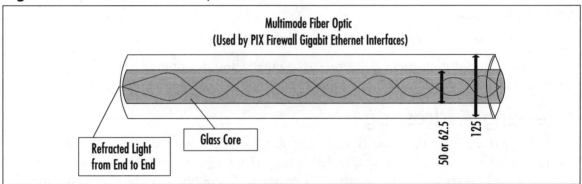

As with twisted-pair cable for Ethernet and Fast Ethernet, you can use a cable tester to verify your fiber optic cable. Unlike copper cables, fiber optic cables are very unforgiving of failure to adhere to tight specifications. If you made the cable that you are using and it is not working, odds are very good that you made an error (poor crimping, insufficient polishing, or the like). It is in such situations that the value of a good cable tester becomes apparent. Unless you are a certified fiber optic technician, it is a good idea to leave the fiber optic cable making to the professionals who specialize in it.

Troubleshooting Connectivity

In order to perform its duties, a PIX firewall must be able to reach its destinations. Its ability to pass traffic from source to destination is affected by factors such as routing, address translation, access lists, and so on. Translation can be particularly critical since all addresses must be translated in order for internal and external networks to communicate with each other.

Get in the habit of executing *clear xlate* to clear any current translations whenever you make a change to NAT, global, static, access lists, conduits, or anything that depends on or is part of translation. Since translation is mandatory on PIX firewalls, this covers just about any feature you can configure. Failure to delete existing translations will cause unexpected behavior.

Remember how interfaces of different security levels work with each other. Traffic from a higher security level to a lower security level is permitted by default but still requires translations to be set up. Traffic from a lower security level to a higher security level (such as outside to inside) requires an access list or conduit, as well as corresponding translations.

It cannot be reinforced enough that you should get in the habit of checking log messages. Syslog provides an ongoing, real-time report of activities and errors—information that can be vital to troubleshooting success. The information syslog provides can help you take your first or next step, so ensure that you develop your syslog reading habits. This can be particularly useful in identifying errors with access lists and translation. For example, if a host on a lower security-level interface wants to communicate with a host on a higher security-level interface and translation is enabled for it, but no conduit or access list is configured, the following message will be logged:

```
106001: Inbound TCP connection denied from x.x.x.x/x to x.x.x.x/x
```

This is your first clue that you need an access list or conduit to permit this access. If the reverse is the case (access list or conduit is present, but no translation is configured), the following message will be logged:

```
305005: No translation group found for...
```

For more information about syslog message numbers and descriptions, see www.cisco.com/univercd/cc/td/doc/product/iaabu/pix/pix_61/syslog/pixemsgs.htm.

Checking Addressing

As with any IP device, unless basic IP addressing and operation are configured correctly and working, none of your PIX firewall troubleshooting efforts regarding routing, access lists, and translation will matter. This point cannot be overstressed: Addressing must be correct in order for the PIX firewall to function. Figure 11.7 shows PIX1 and PIX2 connected to each other.

Figure 11.7 IP Addressing Problem

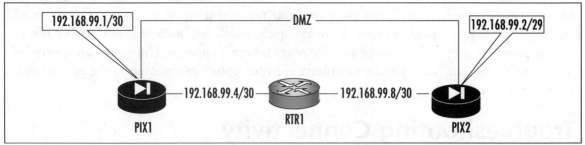

In Figure 11.7, there is an addressing problem on the LAN connecting the two firewalls (which is labeled DMZ in the configuration). For starters, PIX1 has a subnet mask of /30, while FW2 has a mask of /29 for the DMZ network (192.168.99.0), a common network between them. This is confirmed using the *show ip address* command on both firewalls. Notice the differences highlighted in the following command output:

```
PIX1# show ip address
System IP Addresses:
        ip address outside 192.168.99.5 255.255.255.252
        ip address DMZ 192.168.99.1 255.255.255.252
Current IP Addresses:
        ip address outside 192.168.99.5 255.255.255.252
        ip address DMZ 192.168.99.1 255.255.255.252


PIX2# show ip address
System IP Addresses:
        ip address outside 192.168.99.9 255.255.255.252
        ip address DMZ 192.168.99.2 255.255.255.248
Current IP Addresses:
        ip address outside 192.168.99.9 255.255.255.252
        ip address DMZ 192.168.99.2 255.255.255.248
```

The fix here is simply to correct the mask on PIX2. As on Cisco routers, the *show interface* command can also be used to check addressing on your PIX firewall, as shown in the following command output:

```
PIX1# show interface
interface ethernet0 "DMZ" is up, line protocol is up
 Hardware is i82559 ethernet, address is 0008.e317.ba6b
 IP address 192.168.99.1, subnet mask 255.255.255.252
 MTU 1500 bytes, BW 100000 Kbit half duplex
        2 packets input, 258 bytes, 0 no buffer
        Received 0 broadcasts, 0 runts, 0 giants
        0 input errors, 0 CRC, 0 frame, 0 overrun, 0 ignored, 0 abort
        11 packets output, 170 bytes, 0 underruns, 0 unicast rpf drops
        0 output errors, 0 collisions, 0 interface resets
        0 babbles, 0 late collisions, 0 deferred
        0 lost carrier, 0 no carrier
        input queue (curr/max blocks): hardware (128/128) software (0/1)
        output queue (curr/max blocks): hardware (0/2) software (0/1)
```

Regardless of the method you use, verify that all interface IP addresses are correct before proceeding any further in your troubleshooting efforts. Incorrect addressing will prevent advanced features of the PIX firewall from working, even if you configure them correctly. After all, all traffic must pass through at least two interfaces, and the interfaces must be addressed correctly.

Checking Routing

The inability to reach a destination is a prime indicator of routing problems. Such problems can be complex to troubleshoot, but using a structured approach to isolate the cause can ease troubleshooting. The PIX firewall uses both static and dynamic routing. For dynamic routing, the PIX supports only RIP as a routing protocol; otherwise, the routing information it has is manually entered in the form of static routes. We open our routing verification discussion with a review of the various routing options available on the PIX firewall and how they interact.

> **NOTE**
>
> The FWSM 1.1 for the Catalyst 6500 series switches also supports OSPF for dynamic routing. OSPF is not discussed in this chapter.

First, let's review the techniques you use to configure routing on your PIX, starting with the simplest (default route) and onward to using RIP to learn routes. In the simplest configuration, the PIX firewall is configured only with a static default route. For example:

```
route outside 0.0.0.0 0.0.0.0 192.168.99.2 metric 1
```

This command states that all traffic that does not match any of the local interfaces will be sent to the next hop of 192.168.99.2. Assuming this is the only static route configured on the firewall in Figure 11.8, all traffic destined for a nonlocal interface on the PIX firewall will be forwarded to RTR1 to reach its final destination. A single static route such as this one works well for the simple configuration in Figure 11.8, but what happens if we have a more complex architecture, such as the one shown in Figure 11.19?

Figure 11.8 Default Route Example

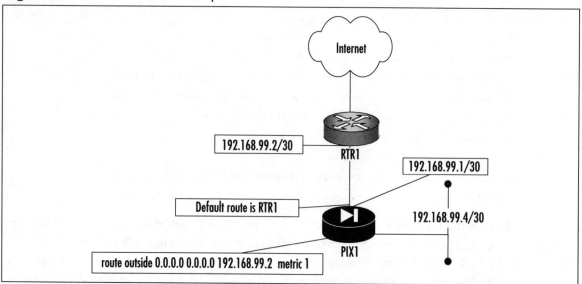

Figure 11.9 shows that the traffic from PIX1 must be forwarded to R2 to reach 192.168.200.0/24. If we used only a default route, any traffic for 192.168.200.0/24 would be sent to RTR1 and would never reach its destination. We can resolve this issue by adding a static route on PIX1 so it knows where to forward traffic destined to 192.168.200.0/24. This is accomplished by adding another (more specific) route to the PIX1 configuration:

```
route inside 192.168.200.0 255.255.255.0 192.168.100.2 metric 2
```

Figure 11.9 Static Routes

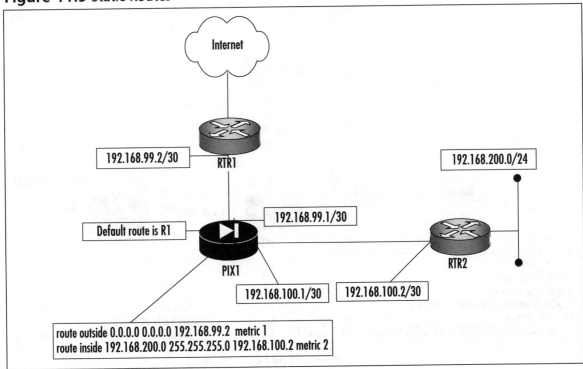

In addition to using these static methods for routing, the PIX firewall supports dynamic routing using RIP v1 or v2. Unlike the wide range of options available for RIP on Cisco routers, the RIP commands on the PIX firewall are sparse.

```
[no] rip <if_name> default
[no] rip <if_name> passive
[no] rip <if_name> version {1 | 2}
[no] rip <if_name> authentication [text | md5] key <key_id>
```

We will not spend an inordinate amount of time debating the merits of RIP as a routing protocol. Suffice to say, the *default* keyword means that the PIX firewall advertises a default route out that interface. The *passive* keyword configures RIP to listen on, but not advertise out, a particular interface. The *version* keyword is used to set the version of RIP that the PIX firewall will use. RIP peers can authenticate each other to ensure that they send and receive updates from legitimate peers. RIP is enabled on a per-interface basis.

In Figure 11.10, we have replaced our statically routed network with RIPv2. Notice how this replacement has changed the routing picture, enabling the PIX firewall to better adapt to network changes.

Figure 11.10 RIP Routing

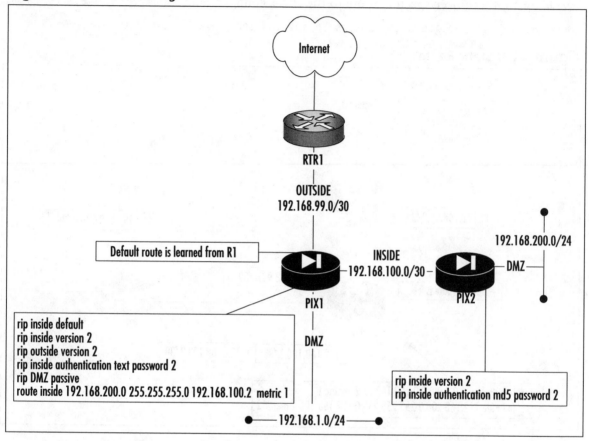

On PIX firewalls, RIP does not advertise from interface to interface. In Figure 11.10, PIX1 is listening for updates on its DMZ network and is learning any routes that might be present behind that network. As a result, PIX1 will know how to reach those networks. Since the *passive* keyword is used, PIX1 will not advertise any RIP routes out its DMZ interface. However, PIX1 will *not* advertise those routes to PIX2 or RTR1. This is a limitation of RIP in the PIX firewall that needs to be resolved by adding a default route to PIX2 (which our configuration has) and a static route on R1 to reach any networks behind PIX1's DMZ interface. What PIX1 will advertise is any of its directly connected interfaces and default routes, so R1 and PIX2 will be able to reach any directly connected network on PIX1. PIX2 will be able to reach the networks behind PIX1's DMZ interface since PIX1 is the default route for PIX2.

This limitation of RIP might not be such a limitation. In actual practice, any addresses that leave or enter PIX1 related to the outside interface would actually be translated. In the case of RTR1, it does not need to know about the networks behind PIX1's DMZ network since those addresses would be translated to a public address, which RTR1 would know to send to PIX1 for processing.

One problem is quite apparent in our configuration in Figure 11.10. There is an authentication mismatch between PIX1 and PIX2. PIX1 is using a clear-text password for authentication, while PIX2 is using MD5. Although the password is the same on both sides, the encryption technique is different. The result is that RIP routing will not work between them, as disagreement on the password encryption technique will prevent the peers from authenticating to each other, which will prevent the exchange and acceptance of routing updates.

Another potential showstopper that you need to be alert for is conflicting versions of RIP. The most significant difference is that RIPv1 broadcasts to an all-hosts broadcast address of 255.255.255.255. RIPv2 generally multicasts to the reserved IP multicast address of 224.0.0.9. Additionally, v2 supports authentication, whereas v1 does not. When troubleshooting routing problems with RIP, look at the configuration of the devices where routing is not working, and check to make sure that all your routing peers agree on the version. If you are using RIPv2 with authentication, ensure that the same password and the same encryption method are used on both. Support for RIPv2 was introduced in PIX software v5.1. Prior versions cannot interoperate with RIPv2 speakers, so keep the RIP version differences in your mind as you troubleshoot. Support for RIPv2 multicast was introduced in v5.3. Prior versions could only handle broadcasts.

Having reviewed how the PIX gets it routes, we now turn our attention to troubleshooting when the PIX is unable to reach a particular destination or when it does not have a route to a particular destination. Your tools of choice for troubleshooting routing issues on the PIX are primarily *show route*, *show rip*, and *ping*. Determine if there is a reachability problem by attempting to ping the destination. If that fails, use *show route* to determine if there is a route (static or RIP) to reach the network. You can use the *show rip* command to confirm your dynamic routing configuration. The *ping* command should be a litmus test to verify that the destination cannot be reached. The syntax of the *ping* command is as follows:

```
ping [<if_name>] <ip_address>
```

For example:

```
PIX1# ping 192.168.99.2
        192.168.99.2 response received -- 20ms
        192.168.99.2 response received -- 20ms
        192.168.99.2 response received -- 20ms
```

Does the PIX have a default route, a static route, or even a dynamically learned route? Check your routing table with the *show route* command. For example:

```
PIX1# show route
    outside 192.168.99.0 255.255.255.252 192.168.99.1 1 CONNECT static
    inside 192.168.100.0 255.255.255.252 192.168.100.1 1 CONNECT static
    DMZ 192.168.1.0 255.255.255.0 192.168.1.1 1 CONNECT static
```

In our case, 192.168.99.2 is on our directly connected outside network. To perform a side-by-side comparison of RIP peers, use the *show rip* command. In the following output, we are looking at the RIP configuration of PIX1 and PIX2; notice how the mismatches between the versions and authentication technique are readily apparent.

```
PIX1# show rip
rip inside default
rip inside version 1
rip outside version 2
rip inside authentication text cisco1 2
rip DMZ passive

PIX2# show rip
rip inside version 1
rip outside version 1
rip inside authentication md5 cisco2 2
rip DMZ passive
```

The result of this configuration is that RIP will *not* work between PIX1 and PIX2 since they do not agree on any of the parameters. A corrected configuration that will work is provided in the following output.

```
PIX1# show rip
rip inside default
rip inside version 2
rip outside version 2
rip inside authentication md5 cisco2 2
rip DMZ passive

PIX2# show rip
rip inside version 2
rip outside version 2
rip inside authentication md5 cisco2 2
rip DMZ passive
```

We conclude our discussion of RIP with the *clear rip* command, which should only be used when you have made a definite decision that you no longer need to use RIP. This command removes all existing RIP commands and parameters from the configuration.

Failover Cable

Cisco provides a wonderful feature called *failover*, wherein the configuration and operations of one firewall are mirrored to a backup firewall. When using standard failover with the failover cable, it is the cable that determines which firewall is the primary and which is the secondary unit in a pairing. The cable makes this determination based on which end is plugged into which firewall.

As part of your PIX firewall troubleshooting knowledge, you need to know the pinout scheme used by this cable. To that end, we have provided a detailed schematic in Figure 11.11. If failover is not working, you need to know what your cable configuration should look like when you analyze it with a cable tester.

Figure 11.11 Failover Cable Pinout

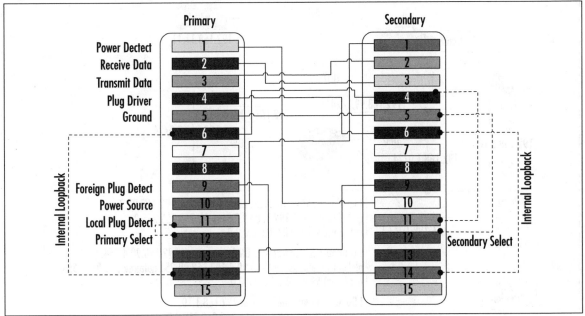

Although all the wires in the DB15 connector at each end are important, you can see that certain wires are cross-connected at each end to distinguish the primary end from the secondary end. The primary firewall is configured by cross-connecting wire 11 (local plug detect) to wire 12 (primary select). The secondary firewall is determined by cross-connecting wire 12 (secondary select) to wire 5 (ground). Knowing the wiring scheme can enable you to not only to check your failover cable, but to also build one from scratch if necessary.

Checking Translation

The PIX firewall performs address translation. In order for internal networks to communicate with external networks, and vice versa, addresses must be translated. Translation is *not* optional. The translation is the act of translating one IP address to another, which can be configured as one to one (NAT) or many to one (PAT).

> **NOTE**
>
> To pass traffic through the PIX traffic, you must translate it, even if this means you will translate IP addresses to themselves.

In this chapter, we quickly review some key concepts using Figure 11.12, which shows all the possible translation scenarios that you can have on your PIX firewall.

Figure 11.12 Translation in Action

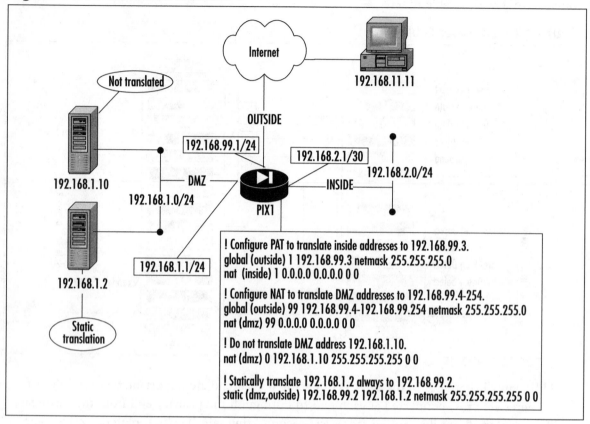

Figure 11.12 shows a PIX firewall, PIX1, connected to three networks: inside, DMZ, and outside. The addresses on the inside network are serviced using PAT. The DMZ has two hosts on it: one that is not translated (in reality, it is just translated to itself) and one that is statically translated. All remaining addresses on the DMZ are dynamically translated using a range of IP addresses associated with the outside network.

In the PIX world, translation is necessary to provide connectivity. When translation does not work, you need to know where to start and finish your troubleshooting. Cisco provides several commands that you can use to validate various aspects of translation. We start with a review of the various translation configuration commands and how to effectively institute them. Let's review the configuration in Figure 11.12.

First, look at which private addresses are being translated to which public addresses. This information will determine if the translation parameters have been configured correctly. Two commands used to perform this task are *show nat* and *show global*:

```
PIX1# show nat
nat (dmz) 0 192.168.1.10 255.255.255.255 0 0
nat (inside) 1 0.0.0.0 0.0.0.0 0 0
```

```
nat (dmz) 99 0.0.0.0 0.0.0.0 0 0
PIX1# show global
global (outside) 99 192.168.99.4-192.168.99.254 netmask 255.255.255.0
global (outside) 1 192.168.99.3 netmask 255.255.255.0
```

Our NAT configuration specifies a nontranslation for the DMZ server at address 192.168.1.10 network (as evidenced by the *nat 0* command). The *nat 99* specifies that all remaining addresses in the DMZ should be translated. The *global* command defines two pools of addresses to be used for translation purposes. The numerical ID is referenced by the NAT command to perform the actual translation. The *global 99* command is used for NAT, whereas *global 1* with its single IP address is used for PAT. In actual practice, you would know at this point if you had configured the translation parameters correctly. Both of these commands provide enough data for you to make this determination. Once you have corrected any errors (the most common being typos or incorrect IP addresses), you can then check to see if connections are being made and translated. The next step is to determine if connections have been made by using the *show conn detail* command:

```
PIX1# show conn detail
1 in use, 1 most used
Flags: A - awaiting inside ACK to SYN, a - awaiting outside ACK to SYN,
       B - initial SYN from outside, D - DNS, d - dump,
       E - outside back connection, f - inside FIN, F - outside FIN,
       G - group, H - H.323, I - inbound data, M - SMTP data,
       O - outbound data, P - inside back connection,
       q - SQL*Net data, R - outside acknowledged FIN,
       R - UDP RPC, r - inside acknowledged FIN, S - awaiting inside SYN,
       s - awaiting outside SYN, U - up
TCP outside:192.168.11.11/24 dmz:192.168.99.2/80 flags UIO
```

The workstation has established a connection to our HTTP server on the DMZ network (as confirmed by its destination port, 80). Notice that the workstation established the connection to the public address of this server rather than to its internal DMZ address (192.168.1.2), which it cannot reach. Now we have a valid connection attempt, but has the translation taken place as it should? To determine that, we must use the next command in our toolbox, *show xlate detail*:

```
PIX1# show xlate detail
1 in use, 1 most used
Flags: D - DNS, d - dump, I - identity, i - inside, n - no random,
       o - outside, r - portmap, s - static
TCP NAT from DMZ:192.168.1.2/80 to outside:192.168.99.2/80 flags ri
```

This command displays a current listing of active translation slots. The output of this command confirms that our host's attempt to access the Web server at 192.168.99.2 has resulted in the correct translation to 192.168.99.2. Such verification is particularly important if you are providing services that must be accessible by outside users.

There is one more command that we can use to gather information about our translation operations. It is a *debug* command and, as such, should be used sparingly to conserve firewall resources. This command can serve two functions: tracking and decoding packet-level activity between hosts (such as the traffic between our workstation and the Web server), or it can be used if you need to determine exactly which addresses need to be translated and granted access. The latter part of this statement needs to be explained more fully. Assuming that we did not know exactly what the source address of our workstation was going to be, it would be helpful to capture information on its attempts to connect to the DMZ Web server. The command that can provide us with the copious information we need is the *debug packet* command. The syntax of the command is as follows:

```
debug packet <if_name> [src <source_ip> [netmask <mask>]] [dst <dest_ip> [netmask
<mask>]] [[proto icmp] | [proto tcp [sport <src_port>] [dport <dest_port>]] | [[proto
udp [sport <src_port>] [dport <dest_port>]] [rx | tx | both]
```

In our case, the command we would actually enter to find out which addresses are attempting to use our Web server is:

```
PIX1(config)# debug packet outside src 0.0.0.0 netmask 0.0.0.0 dst 192.168.99.2 netmask
255.255.255.0 rx
```

This command captures packet data that comes into the outside interface destined for the Web server's public IP address. Since we do not know exactly which protocols (TCP, UDP, or ICMP) will be used, we have opted not to specify one. After we have captured our data, we can then determine which translation parameters we need to enter.

Checking Access

The PIX firewall provides several mechanisms for controlling access through it. In this section, we cover several of these mechanisms and discuss some ways to monitor and verify their functionality. The default state of the PIX firewall is to permit access to sessions originated from a higher security-level interface to a lower security-level interface, as long as a translation is configured. Traffic that originates from a low security-level interface to a high security-level interface has to be specifically permitted using conduits or access lists (and of course, translations).

The *conduit* command is a special form of an access list. It is used to permit traffic from a lower security-level interface to a higher security-level interface. Figure 11.13 shows several common access scenarios with various hosts needing access to each other. The Web client (security level 0) will be accessing the Web server (security level 50); the default behavior of the PIX firewall is to forbid such traffic. The workstation (security level 100) needs to access Internet resources using the outside network. Figure 11.13 also provides the configuration necessary to enable the access needed by the various hosts and servers, which are denoted *A*, *B*, and *C* for ease of discussion. The assumption is that all translation parameters have been configured and are working correctly, which enables us to focus on specific access issues. The addresses shown are used for discussion, but in your mind, assume that they have been translated.

Figure 11.13 Access Scenario

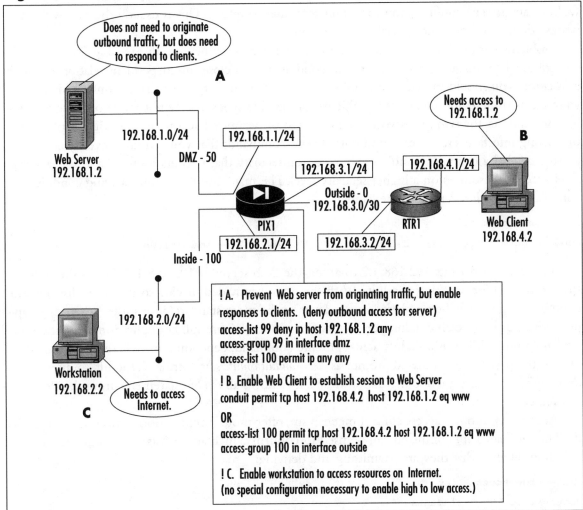

The Web server needs to be prevented from originating sessions to networks located off the DMZ network, but must be able to respond to service requests from the Web client located on the outside network. To accomplish this goal, we created an access list to deny 192.168.1.2 from accessing anything and applied it to the DMZ interface. Then we created a conduit to permit 192.168.4.2 to access Web services (TCP port 80) on 192.168.1.2. Alternatively, we could have used an access list to accomplish the same thing, as shown in Figure 11.13. The option to use access lists instead of conduits is available only on PIX firewall software v5.1 and later. It is important to note that Cisco recommends that you avoid mixing access lists and conduits. Additionally, access lists take precedence over conduits. In the PIX environment, access lists have one and only one direction: in. The *access-group* command applies the access list to traffic coming into the designated interface.

The inside workstation (denoted by *C*) needs to be able to access resources on the Internet. The inside interface has a security level of 100, the highest possible security level. Recall that hosts on higher security-level interfaces can access hosts on lower security-level interfaces without any special configuration to permit responses to return. This is exactly the case with this workstation, so we need no special configuration.

Problems with lack of access become apparent when machines are unreachable. Since access control mechanisms such as access lists and conduits have a close interdependent relationship with translation, you should validate the translation configuration first. Once that is confirmed, begin your access troubleshooting. Access problems can include typos, overly restrictive or loose access lists or conduits, the wrong networks being denied or permitted access, or access lists applied to the wrong interface. Here we demonstrate several commands that you can use to verify access.

Recall that a conduit is a hole in your firewall security that permits hosts on a lower security level access to resources on a higher security level. The main command for verifying conduit configuration is *show conduit*. For example:

```
PIX1# show conduit
conduit permit tcp host 192.168.4.2 host 192.168.1.2 eq www (hitcnt=3)
```

This conduit permits 192.168.4.2 to access the Web server at 192.168.1.2. This is the only PIX command for checking conduits. With the option provided in v5.1 to use access lists instead, conduits are gradually being phased out in favor of the more standard access lists. When that happens, you can remove all conduit parameters from your PIX firewall configuration using the *clear conduit* command. This is a slightly schizophrenic command, depending on where it is it used. If used at the privileged command prompt as *clear conduit counters*, it "zeroizes" the hit counter. If *clear conduit* is used in the Configuration mode, it removes all *conduit* statements from the PIX firewall configuration.

Access lists, another access control mechanism, offer more troubleshooting tools than conduits do. The *show access-list* command can be used to confirm which access lists are configured on the PIX firewall and what they are permitting and denying:

```
PIX1# show access-list
access-list 99; 2 elements
access-list 99 deny ip host 192.168.1.2 any (hitcnt=1)
access-list 99 permit ip any any (hitcnt=0)
access-list 100 permit tcp host 192.168.4.2 host 192.168.1.2 eq www  (hitcnt=5)
```

This command was executed on the firewall in Figure 11.13. Recall that an access list only affects incoming traffic to an interface. Once you have confirmed that the access list is configured as it should be, the next troubleshooting step is to verify that it has been applied to the correct interface. Cisco provides the *show access-group* command for this purpose. For example:

```
PIX1# show access-group
access-group 99 in interface dmz
access-group 100 in interface outside
```

The *in* keyword is mandatory and serves as a reminder that the access list is applied *only* to traffic coming into the interface. Cisco provides a *debug* command for troubleshooting access list events as they occur. Beware that when you use this command, it debugs all access lists. There is no option to do real-time monitoring of a particular access list. This can generate copious amounts of data, especially if you execute it on a high-traffic PIX firewall. As with any *debug* command, use it sparingly and only if you know what you are searching for. The *debug access-list* command can provide feedback on your access list and whether it is permitting or denying the traffic that it should. The command syntax is as follows:

```
debug access-list {all | standard | turbo}
```

Another access control mechanism is *outbound/apply*, but Cisco recommends that it not be used. Cisco recommends that you use the access list features of the PIX firewall instead. The *outbound/apply* commands were the precursor to the access list feature and are still available and supported by the PIX firewall software. However, these commands suffer from a very awkward syntax, are fairly limited, and can be frustrating to troubleshoot. The *outbound* command was designed to control access of inside users to outside resources. Having said all that, a working familiarity with the command is handy for when you encounter situations in which it is still used. The syntax for the *outbound* command is as follows:

```
outbound <ID> {permit | deny | except} <ip_address> [<netmask>] [<port> [-<port>]]
[tcp | udp| icmp]
```

The *ID* parameter specifies a unique identifier for the outbound list. You can either configure a *permit* rule, a *deny* rule, or an *except* rule (which creates an exception to a previous outbound command). Unlike access lists, outbound lists are not processed from top to bottom. Each line is parsed regardless of whether there is a match or not. Cisco recommends that all outbound lists start with a deny all (*deny 0 0 0*), followed by specific statements allowing access. The net effect is cumulative. How the PIX firewall uses the outbound list depends on the syntax of the *apply* command:

```
apply [<interface>] <OUTBOUND_LIST_ID> {outgoing_src | outgoing_dest}
```

When the *outgoing_src* parameter is used, the source IP address, destination port, and protocol are filtered. When the *outgoing_dst* parameter is used, the destination IP address, port, and protocol are filtered. It is vital that you understand that the outbound list does not determine whether the IP address it uses is either a source or a destination; the *apply* command does that. This can be a major troubleshooting headache because an outbound list could be configured correctly but might not work because the *apply* command is configured incorrectly. When troubleshooting *outbound*, ensure that you check the *apply* configuration as well. When multiple rules match the same packet, the rule with the best match is used. The best-match rule is based on the netmask and port range. The stricter the IP address and the smaller the port range, the better a match it is. If there is a tie, a *permit* option takes precedence over a *deny* option.

Here is an example of *outbound/apply*:

```
PIX1(config)# outbound 99 deny 0 0 0
PIX1(config)# outbound 99 permit 0.0.0.0 0.0.0.0 1-1024 tcp
PIX1(config)# outbound 99 except 192.168.2.0 255.255.255.0
PIX1(config)# apply (inside) 99 outgoing_src
```

In this example, the first statement denies all traffic, the second line permits any host access to TCP ports 1–1024 on any host, and the third line denies the 192.168.2.0/24 network from access to any TCP ports permitted by the second line. We are using the *outgoing_src* keyword, meaning that the IP addresses referenced are source addresses.

Cisco only provides a few commands for checking *outbound/apply* parameters. First, do not forget to do a *clear xlate* after configuring *outbound/apply*. Use *show outbound* to view the outbound lists that are configured. The *show apply* command identifies the interfaces and direction to which the outbound lists have been applied. No *debug* commands are associated with *outbound/apply*. Given that access lists have now superseded *outbound/apply*, you would be better served in terms of both configuration and support to use them instead. Not only do access lists conform to the standard Cisco syntax, they also offer better and easier-to-understand filtering.

One feature does not seem to be access related, but since it curtails the operations of selected protocols, one can argue that access to certain features of the "protected" protocol have been negated. The PIX firewall software provides application inspection features through the *fixup* command. There is a standard set of protocols for which the *fixup* capability is enabled automatically, such as HTTP, SMTP, FTP, and so on. This protocol sometimes disables certain commands or features in the target protocols to prevent malicious misuse. To determine for which protocols *fixup* is enabled, run the *show fixup* command. For example:

```
PIX1# show fixup
fixup protocol ftp 21
fixup protocol http 80
fixup protocol h323 h225 1720
fixup protocol h323 ras 1718-1719
fixup protocol ils 389
fixup protocol rsh 514
fixup protocol rtsp 554
fixup protocol smtp 25
fixup protocol sqlnet 1521
fixup protocol sip 5060
fixup protocol skinny 2000
```

Troubleshooting IPsec

IPsec is used on the PIX firewall for the establishment of a secure VPN tunnel between two endpoints for the purpose of securely exchanging data over IP. IPsec can be configured using IKE with RSA key exchange, IKE with CA certificates, IKE with preshared keys, or using preshared keys sans IKE (called *manual IPsec*). When using manual key exchange, you simply create a shared secret that is the same on both endpoints; this technique is not only a security risk, but it has scalability issues.

We focus our efforts on using the tools Cisco provides to troubleshoot IPsec problems using an IPsec with IKE preshared key configuration. Misconfigurations, mismatched parameters, keys, routing, IP addressing issues, and other problems can conspire to make IPsec fail. You need to be able to isolate and resolve these issues by first recognizing the symptoms and then using the correct tools to pinpoint the cause.

Figure 11.14 shows a simple point-to-point IPsec tunnel configured between PIX1 and PIX2. IPsec is a complicated technology and very unforgiving of errors. A single error can prevent your IPsec configuration from working at all. Therefore, you will find that the bulk of your labors will be focused on setting IPsec correctly in the first place.

Figure 11.14 IPsec Configuration

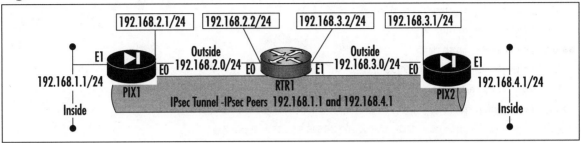

Here we introduce several commands and procedures that you can use to check your configuration:

```
! PIX1 Configuration snippets
nat 99 0.0.0.0 0.0.0.0
global (outside) 99  192.168.2.10-192.168.2.254 netmask 255.255.255.0
route outside 0.0.0.0 0.0.0.0 192.168.2.2
static (inside, outside) 192.168.2.10 192.168.1.1 netmask 255.255.255.255
conduit permit ip 192.168.3.0 255.255.255.0 any
isakmp enable outside
isakmp policy 99 authen  pre-share
isakmp policy 99 encryption des
isakmp policy 99 group 1
isakmp policy 99 hash md5
isakmp policy 99 lifetime 9999
isakmp identity address
isakmp key cisco address 192.168.3.1
access-list 99 permit ip 192.168.0.0 255.255.252.0 any
crypto ipsec transform-set FW1 ah-md5-hmac esp-des esp-md5-hmac
crypto map FW1 1 ipsec-isakmp
crypto map FW1 2 set peer 192.168.3.1
crypto map FW1 3 match address 99
crypto map FW1 2 set peer 192.168.3.1
crypto map FW1 interface outside

! PIX2 Configuration snippets
```

```
nat 99 0.0.0.0 0.0.0.0

global (outside) 99  192.168.3.10-192.168.2.254 netmask 255.255.255.0

route outside 0.0.0.0 0.0.0.0 192.168.3.2

static (inside, outside) 192.168.3.10 192.168.4.1 netmask 255.255.255.255

conduit permit ip 192.168.3.0 255.255.255.0 any

isakmp enable outside

isakmp policy 99 authen  pre-share

isakmp policy 99 encryption des

isakmp policy 99 group 1

isakmp policy 99 hash md5

isakmp policy 99 lifetime 9999

isakmp identity address

isakmp key cisco address 192.168.2.1

access-list 99 permit ip 192.168.0.0 255.255.252.0 any

crypto ipsec transform-set FW1 ah-md5-hmac esp-des esp-md5-hmac

crypto map FW1 1 ipsec-isakmp

crypto map FW1 2 set peer 192.168.2.1

crypto map FW1 3 match address 99

crypto map FW1 interface outside
```

There are several issues with this configuration. For starters, the IPsec peering between PIX1 and PIX2 is to their inside addresses rather than their outside addresses. Although this might work, Cisco does not recommend it as a method to deploy IPsec. Additionally, the addresses for the peering have been statically translated to an outside address. This presents a problem in that the actual source address of IPsec traffic will not match when it reaches the distant end, and the hash values will also be incorrect. Solving this problem involves disabling translation for the addresses used for establish peering (*nat 0*), adding a route to the internal addresses on each firewall, and permitting the addresses to enter the firewall.

IKE

The chief mission of IKE is to negotiate parameters for IPsec by establishing a secure channel over which IPsec will establish its peering. In other words, IKE does the necessary preconfiguration by establishing the security associations to protect IPsec during its negotiations and operations.

IKE peers create the necessary security association if they both agree on a common security policy, which includes using the same encryption, authentication, Diffie-Hellman settings, and hash parameters. Without this agreement, IKE peering will not take place, and IPsec peering will be unable to proceed. IKE authenticates IPsec peers, determines the encryption methods that will be used, and negotiates the various parameters to be used by IPsec, such as encryption, authentication, and keys. In order for IPsec to proceed, IKE must be configured perfectly and working.

IKE works in two phases. In Phase I (main mode), it establishes the security association necessary for two firewalls to become IKE peers. This includes the exchange and search for common security policies until both peers come to an agreement. During Phase II (quick mode), IKE establishes the security association necessary to protect IPsec during its negotiations and operations. Once Phase II is complete, IPsec can then complete its peering.

Before deploying IKE on your PIX firewall, ensure that each peer can reach the IP address of the other side. If an underlying hardware, network, or translation issue prevents the peers from reaching each other, fix it using the structured methodology presented earlier in this chapter. You can verify reachability using *ping*.

Cisco provides several commands that you can use to check your IKE configuration and operation; let's look at those commands. The *show isakmp* command shows how IKE is configured on the PIX firewall. For example:

```
PIX1# show isakmp
isakmp enable outside
isakmp key ******** address 192.168.3.1 netmask 255.255.255.255
isakmp identity address
isakmp policy 99 authentication pre-share
isakmp policy 99 encryption des
isakmp policy 99 hash md5
isakmp policy 99 group 1
isakmp policy 99 lifetime 9999
```

The *show isakmp* or *show crypto isakmp* commands display the current IKE parameters configured on a PIX firewall. Notice how the key is hidden to protect its security. You should run this command on both peers and compare the resulting output to ensure that there will be agreement on at least one security policy. If you desire more detail or need more information about exactly what each parameter does, use the *show isakmp policy* command. This command expands on the previous command by spelling out each parameter and its current settings:

```
PIX1# show crypto isakmp policy
Protection suite of priority 99
    encryption algorithm:   DES - Data Encryption Standard (56 bit
keys).
    hash algorithm:         Message Digest 5
    authentication method:  Pre-Shared Key
    Diffie-Hellman group:   #1 (768 bit)
    lifetime:               9999 seconds, no volume limit
Default protection suite
    encryption algorithm:   DES - Data Encryption Standard (56 bit
keys).
    hash algorithm:         Secure Hash Standard
    authentication method:  Rivest-Shamir-Adleman Signature
    Diffie-Hellman group:   #1 (768 bit)
    lifetime:               86400 seconds, no volume limit
```

Another useful aspect of the *show crypto isakmp policy* command is that it shows you the default values that will be used if you do not specify any values. This information can be useful if you need to determine what a particular unspecified parameter would be if you do not configure it specifically.

IPsec cannot proceed unless IKE is working. The only exception is if you are not using IKE for IPsec—that is, you are using manually generated keys with IPsec.

If you want to watch the ISAKMP negotiation process between two IPsec peers, use the *debug crypto isakmp* command. This command generates a copious amount of output, so use it sparingly. You can use *debug crypto isakmp* to watch the IKE negotiation process and the exchange of session keys. The *debug crypto isakmp* command shows IKE going through Phases I and II. The entire process is triggered when interesting traffic (traffic that matches the applied crypto map) transits the IPsec protected interface. Once that happens, IKE contacts its peer, as shown in Figure 11.15. (Its source port and destination port will be UDP port 500, so you need to ensure that this port is allowed through.)

Figure 11.15 IKE Process

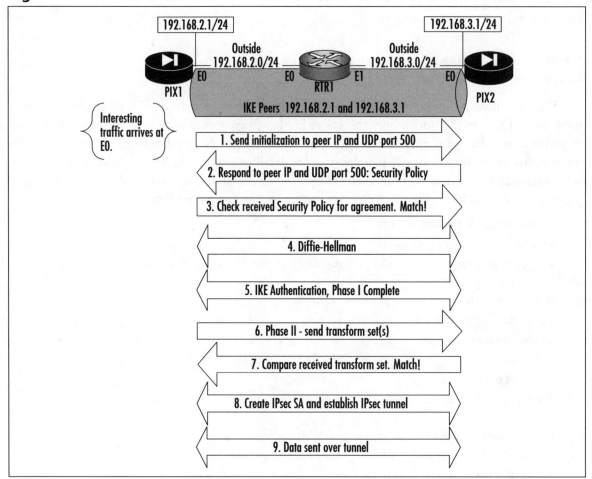

The first thing the peers do is validate that the hostname or IP address and key pair matches their configuration. The initiator sends its security policy parameters to the receiver, which then sends back parameters that match from its policy. Having agreed on the security policy, the IKE peers commence Phase I in earnest, completing the Diffie-Hellman and generating session keys. From there, IKE peer authentication is completed, finishing the Phase I security association. Phase II proceeds relatively quickly (hence the reason it is called "quick" mode) by negotiating the security policy that will be used to protect IPsec peer operations. Once Phase II is complete, IPsec then establishes the tunnel, and data transmission begins.

The most common problems that occur during the IKE phases are mismatched preshared keys and mismatched security policy parameters. The first step in troubleshooting IKE is to compare the configurations of each peer. You can do this with the commands we discussed previously. After you have ascertained that you have an IKE policy that will work on each firewall, initiate the IKE process after executing the appropriate *debug* command. That way, you can monitor its progress or lack thereof.

If you do not define an IKE security policy common to both peers or if you neglect to define a security policy at all, IKE will try the defaults for the various values. This means using DES for encryption, SHA for calculating the hash values, RSA for authentication, and Diffie-Hellman Group 1 (768 bits) with a lifetime of 86,400 seconds. Policy mismatches will be apparent when the output of the *show crypto isakmp sa* command shows "no state," meaning that the peers did not and could not negotiate main mode successfully due to the mismatch. The "no state" error also appears if there is key (password) disagreement between the two peers. Hash calculations will also fail, and this is something you can watch with the *debug crypto isakmp* command.

Cisco provides a *clear crypto isakmp sa* command that you can use to delete existing security associations and force a reinitialization. This command can be useful not only to clear an invalid security association, but it's also helpful in monitoring the IKE negotiation process with *debug*.

IPsec

After IKE successfully negotiates the parameters such as the method to be used for encryption, authentication, and the size key to use, IPsec is then ready to perform its mission of creating a VPN. IPsec requires that IKE already have negotiated the various previously identified parameters. IPsec peers compare transform sets to determine what each can support. They negotiate the authentication, encryption, and hash methods until they find agreement. If they do not find agreement, they do not become peers, and the tunnel will not be established.

To check which transform sets you have configured, use the *show crypto ipsec transform-set* command. Notice that this command tells you if IPsec will negotiate AH, ESP, or a combination of both. Here is an example:

```
PIX1# show crypto ipsec transform-set

Transform set FW1: { ah-md5-hmac  }
   will negotiate = { Tunnel,  },
   { esp-des esp-md5-hmac  }
```

```
           will negotiate = { Tunnel,  },
```

It is important for IPsec peers to have in their transform sets common parameters on which they can agree. Crypto maps are used to specify the traffic to be encrypted. Execute the *show crypto map* command to confirm your maps. For example:

```
PIX2# show crypto map

Crypto Map: "pixola" interfaces: {outside }

Crypto Map "pixola" 1 ipsec-isakmp
        Peer = 192.168.2.1
        access-list 100 permit ip 192.168.2.0 255.255.255.0 any (hitcnt=1)
        Current peer: 192.168.2.1
        Security association lifetime: 4608000 kilobytes/28800 seconds
        PFS (Y/N): N
        Transform sets={ pix, }
```

This command also identifies the IPsec peer and the interface to which the map is applied. In this example, PIX2 has the crypto map *"pixola"* applied to its outside interface. It is peering with PIX1 (at IP address 192.168.2.1) and will encrypt traffic that matches access list 100. It even tells you how many matches have been made against that access list—a quick way to determine if anything is being checked for IPsec processing.

After verifying that there is agreement in the transform sets and the crypto maps are defined correctly, confirm that data is actually being protected. To verify, use the *show crypto ipsec sa* command shown in the following output:

```
PIX1# show crypto ipsec sa
interface: outside
Crypto map tag: pixola, local addr. 192.168.2.1

local ident (addr/mask/prot/port): (192.168.2.1/255.255.255.0/0/0)
remote ident (addr/mask/prot/port): (192.168.3.1/255.255.255.0/0/0)
current_peer: 192.168.3.1
PERMIT, flags={origin_is_acl,}

#pkts encaps: 5, #pkts encrypt: 5, #pkts digest 5
#pkts decaps: 5, #pkts decrypt: 5, #pkts verify 5
#pkts compressed: 0, #pkts decompressed: 0
#pkts not compressed: 0, #pkts compr. failed: 0, #pkts decompress
     failed: 0
#send errors 0, #recv errors 0
```

```
local crypto endpt.: 192.168.2.1, remote crypto endpt.: 192.168.3.1
path mtu 1500, ipsec overhead 56, media mtu 1500
current outbound spi: 3a18fca2
inbound esp sas:
spi: 0x61af4121(2451330208)


transform: esp-des esp-md5-hmac
in use settings ={Tunnel, }
slot: 0, conn id: 1, crypto map: pixola
sa timing: remaining key lifetime (k/sec): (4000159/9460)
IV size: 8 bytes
replay detection support: Y


inbound ah sas:
inbound pcp sas:


outbound ESP sas:
spi: 0x61af4121(2451330208)
transform: esp-des esp-md5-hmac
in use settings ={Tunnel, }
slot: 0, conn id: 1, crypto map: pixola
sa timing: remaining key lifetime (k/sec): (4000159/9460)
IV size: 8 bytes
replay detection support: Y


outbound ah sas:
outbound PCP sas:
```

The output of this command can be very abundant. The *crypto map* tag identifies the crypto map being used, whereas *local* and *remote ident* show the IP addresses of the local and remote peers. The *pkts* counters track how many packets have been encrypted, decrypted, and compressed. So far, five packets have been sent and received encrypted. This is an earmark of successful IPsec operation.

The *crypto endpt* section identifies the IPsec peers. Notice that the path MTU as well as the media MTU are shown, which can be useful in determining if fragmentation will occur. The SPI is a unique identification for this tunnel. We can also view the transform set parameters being used and whether it is operating in tunnel or transport mode. The *lifetime* indicates the amount of time left before the SA will be renegotiated. The last section, *outbound sas*, verifies that both inbound and outbound SA have been established. It also indicates how many seconds and kilobits are left before the SA must be renegotiated.

Check the SA lifetime with the *show crypto ipsec security-association* command. For example:

```
PIX1# show crypto ipsec security-association lifetime
Security association lifetime: 4608000 kilobytes/28800 seconds
```

You can use the *debug crypto ipsec* command to monitor IPsec negotiations, which will start once IKE is fully initialized between the peers. For ease of troubleshooting, run the two commands separately. Otherwise, you will be overwhelmed by the amount of data they produce. First perform IKE troubleshooting (which has to occur before IPsec can proceed), and then move on to IPsec troubleshooting.

If you want to reinitialize IPsec, you can do so. This is useful when you want to clear corrupted or invalid sessions or if you want IPsec to establish a new tunnel. It can also be useful if you want to monitor IPsec operations from the onset using *debug* commands. At any time, you can manually force an SA negotiation to occur with the *clear crypto ipsec sa* command. The *clear crypto ipsec sa* command deletes existing security associations (all of them) and forces the establishment of new associations if there is an active trigger such as a crypto map. You can get very specific with this command, such as specifying a particular peer with *clear crypto ipsec sa 192.168.2.1*.

Capturing Traffic

Cisco has provided an excellent tool for capturing and analyzing network traffic with the introduction of PIX software v6.2. When the *capture* command is used, the PIX can act as a packet sniffer on the target interface, capturing packets for later analysis. This command captures both inbound and outbound traffic.

Capturing packets that transit an interface is very useful for troubleshooting, because it enables you to determine exactly what traffic is being passed. When you're troubleshooting connectivity issues, it is often useful to capture packets from the incoming and outgoing interfaces. You can analyze the captured packets to determine if there are any problems with your configuration, such as IP address disagreement, or problems with IKE or IPsec, such as mismatched or expect parameters that are not being passed. Before this feature, the only recourse an engineer had was to install a packet capture device. The packet capture feature was introduced in PIX firewall v6.2 and is only available for Ethernet interfaces. The syntax of the command is as follows.

```
capture <capture-name> [access-list <ID>] [buffer <bytes>] [ethernet-type <type>]
[interface <if_name>] [packet-length <bytes>]
```

The first parameter, *capture-name*, defines a name for this particular capture session. All other parameters are optional. The *access-list* parameter specifies an access list to limit the source and destination of the traffic captured. By default, all IP packets are matched. The *buffer* parameter specifies the size of the buffer (in bytes) used to store captured packets. The maximum value is based on the amount of available memory on the PIX firewall. The default buffer size is 512K, and once the buffer fills up, the packet capture stops. The *ethernet-type* parameter specifies the protocols to capture. You can specify *ip*, *arp*, *rarp*, *ip6*, or any protocol number between 1 and 65535. By default, all Ethernet types are captured. (Setting the *ethernet-type* parameter to 0 specifies capturing all types.) The *interface* parameter specifies the interface on which to capture packets. The *packet-length* parameter specifies how much of each packet to capture. Usually for troubleshooting, only the first few bytes of a packet are necessary, and the PIX captures up to 68 bytes. For example:

```
PIX1# capture inside-traffic access-list 100 buffer 20000 interface inside packet-
length 200
```

In this example, we are capturing the first 200 bytes of traffic matching access list 100 on the inside interface. We have allocated 20,000 bytes for buffer storage of these captured packets.

Multiple traffic captures can be run simultaneously. To view the list of captures, use the *show capture* command. For example, the following command shows two simultaneous captures, *cap1* and *cap2*, being performed:

```
PIX1# show capture
capture cap1 interface inside
capture cap2 interface outside
```

To clear a capture buffer without stopping the capture, use the *clear capture <capture-name>* command. For example:

```
PIX1# clear capture cap1
```

To stop a capture and clear the associated buffer, use the *no capture <capture-name>* command. For example:

```
PIX1# no capture cap2
```

To stop a capture and save the associated buffer, use the *no capture <capture-name> interface <if_name>* command. For example:

```
PIX1# no capture cap1 interface inside
```

Displaying Captured Traffic

Cisco provides several options via which we can display our captured data. We can display it on the console, which provides for rudimentary viewing, or we can view it using a Web browser. We can even download our captured data and use third-party software such as Ethereal (www.ethereal.com) or tcpdump (www.tcpdump.org) to view them.

Display on the Console

In the course of troubleshooting a PIX firewall problem by capturing data, viewing the capture on the console is probably the most sensible option. If you opt to use the console for this purpose, it is best if you keep the packet length short enough to get the primary headers (IP, TCP, and so forth), because you can easily become confused scrolling through voluminous amounts of data on the simple textual console. To view a capture on the console, use the *show capture* command:

```
show capture <capture-name> [access-list <ID>] [count <number>] [detail] [dump]
```

If you have captured a great deal of data, you can filter it out by specifying an *access-list* in this command, which acts as a display filter. The *count* parameter is used to limit the number of packets displayed on the screen. The *detail* parameter increases the level of detail displayed. The *dump* parameter specifies that the data should be displayed in hex (this does not display MAC information). An example packet capture is shown in the following output:

```
PIX1# show capture inside-traffic count 6
71 packets captured
17:29:35.648434 192.168.2.1.23 > 192.168.2.2.11002: P 942178590:942178597
    (7) ack  2099017897 win 4096(fragment-packet)
17:29:35.848207 192.168.2.2.11002 > 192.168.2.1.23: . ack 942178597 win
    3531(fragment-packet)
17:29:37.610258 192.168.2.2.11002 > 192.168.2.1.23: P 2099017897:
    2099017898(1) ack 942178597 win 3531(fragment-packet)
17:29:37.610442 192.168.2.1.23 > 192.168.2.2.11002: . ack 2099017898 win
    4095(fragment-packet)
17:29:37.610686 192.168.2.1.23 > 192.168.2.2.11002: P 942178597:942178598
    (1) ack 2099017898 win 4096(fragment-packet)
17:29:37.808155 192.168.2.2.11002 > 192.168.2.1.23: . ack 942178598 win
    3530(fragment-packet)
```

Notice how the acknowledgments (ACKs) are incrementing. This particular capture was part of a Telnet session between 192.168.2.1 and 192.168.2.2; the 23 at the end of 192.168.2.1 tells you that it is the Telnet server. At this point, you should have a good idea just how useful *capture* can be in the troubleshooting process.

Display to a Web Browser

Cisco also makes it very easy to securely view packet captures (the packet headers in ASCII format) using a Web browser. To view the contents using your Web browser, enter the appropriate URL to the PIX firewall. The syntax is as follows:

```
https://pix_ip_address/capture/<capture-name>/
```

For example:

```
https://192.168.1.1/capture/inside-traffic/
```

Downloading Captured Traffic

The PIX firewall saves packet capture buffers in PCAP format, which can be downloaded and viewed with third-party software such as Ethereal or tcpdump. The capture can be downloaded either using HTTPS or TFTP. To download the file using HTTPS, enter the appropriate URL to the PIX firewall. The syntax is as follows:

```
https://pix_ip_address/capture/<capture-name>/pcap
```

For example:

```
https://192.168.1.1/capture/inside/pcap
```

This syntax downloads the packet capture to your client in PCAP format. Alternatively, you can download the file using TFTP. This is accomplished using the *copy* command on the PIX firewall. The syntax is as follows:

```
copy capture:<capture-name> tftp://<location>/<filename> [pcap]
```

Without the *pcap* keyword, the ASCII packet headers will be copied. With the *pcap* keyword, the binary file in PCAP format will be copied. For example:

```
PIX1# copy capture:inside-traffic tftp://192.168.99.99/pix-capture pcap
copying Capture to tftp://192.168.99.99/pix-capture:
```

In our example, we are copying the *inside-traffic* capture (in PCAP format) to the TFTP server at 192.168.99.99 to the *pix-capture* filename. Once the file has been copied, you can use any of the aforementioned software packages to open and analyze the captured packets.

Support Options as Troubleshooting Tools

The PIX firewall can be a very critical device on your network. Network architecture planning needs to consider various support options to handle the loss or failure of your PIX firewall. Consider this troubleshooting by prevention, if you will. You can do it all yourself, farm out support to a third-party vendor (reseller), or purchase support from Cisco. Let's examine each option:

- In the "do it yourself" approach, you simply purchase the software and hardware, with no warranty or support other than what was provided as standard. If anything goes wrong, you need the knowledge and resources to fix it yourself.

- In the third-party option, you have a special arrangement with your vendor (reseller) to provide whatever you need to fix your problem, whether software or hardware. Although your reseller might not have the depth and breadth of knowledge that Cisco does, as a reseller, it might be able to offer you a substantial discount on support.

- Using Cisco via the SMARTnet program can ensure that you always have access to a large pool of expert knowledge and the "latest and greatest" information regarding configuration, troubleshooting, and bug fixes. The Cisco Web site offers a wealth of tools and information that you can use to aid your troubleshooting. You can also opt to acquire the Cisco Connection Online (CCO) membership to gain access to even more support such as the ability to open or browse TAC cases online. SMARTnet also provides hardware replacement and software upgrades.

Two things can break on your PIX firewall: the software or the hardware. To protect against hardware failures, you have the option of stockpiling spares. Depending on the ratio of active to stock units, this choice could be cost prohibitive. Software can be plagued with bugs that you discover after you have deployed the perfect configuration. Certain commands or features might not work as you want them to or not work at all. In any case, you will require information from

Cisco to work around the problem or access to the latest release of software that fixes your problem. In general, you are better off putting your firewall under a SMARTnet maintenance contract with Cisco to ensure that you always have access to the latest releases of software. Software is generally much more difficult to fix on your own than hardware, which you can easily replace in case of a failure. You definitely cannot rewrite the software code to fix a problem, and you'll end up spending an excessive amount of time developing a workaround to a problem caused by a buggy software release.

Monitoring and Troubleshooting Performance

We mentioned previously the importance of matching the model of PIX firewall you deploy to the demands you place on it. You need to consider several factors in addition to the amount of traffic you are passing. Table 11.3 summarizes the loads that each model can handle, including information about encryption. Ensure that your design considers these load limits.

Table 11.3 PIX Firewall Model Features and Capabilities

Model	Hardware Maximums (CPU/SDRAM/FLASH)	Clear-text Throughput	DES IPsec Throughput	3DES IPsec Throughput	Simultaneous VPN Tunnels
501	133MHz AMD SC520 16MB RAM 8MB Flash	10Mbps	6Mbps	3Mbps	5 peers
506E	300MHz Intel Celeron 32MB RAM 8MB Flash	20Mbps	20Mbps	16Mbps	25 peers
515E	433MHz Intel Celeron 64MB RAM 16MB Flash	188Mbps	33–120Mbps	63Mbps UR 22Mbps R	2000
525	600MHz Intel Pentium III 256MB RAM 16MB Flash	360Mbps	120–140Mbps	70Mbps	2000
535	1GHz Intel Pentium III 1GB PC133 RAM 16MB Flash	1Gbps	200Mbps	100Mbps	2000

The FWSM 1.1 for the Catalyst 6500 series switches is a high-performance device with support for 5Gbps of aggregated traffic. It does not support IPsec VPN connections.

Three key components of the PIX firewall that affect performance are the CPU, memory, and network interfaces. You need to understand how to monitor these components and ensure that their load is not reaching the limits. We discuss the monitoring of these three components in the following sections. The ultimate question is, can your firewall handle the loads you will place on it?

CPU Performance Monitoring

Your CPU does it all: passes traffic, creates VPN tunnels, and performs encryption on demand. The rule of thumb is that during normal operational mode, the CPU load should stay below 30 percent, on average. During peak traffic hours and attacks, you will see the CPU surge up higher, but that is normal. However, if the CPU utilization consistently stays above 30 percent with normal network activity, consider upgrading to a more powerful model.

Many functions can tax CPU, but encryption (DES and 3DES) has the biggest potential to consume your CPU's precious time. If you are going to deploy a large number of encrypted tunnels (VPNs), we recommend you monitor the processor carefully. If utilization goes high, consider adding a card to the PIX to handle VPN functions (the VPN Accelerator Card). Alternatively, you can think about offloading VPN functions from the PIX to a dedicated VPN concentrator (such as the VPN 3000 series from Cisco). The amount of traffic passing through the firewall is also a factor. If you are seeing high traffic utilization, monitor the CPU utilization on a regular basis to ensure that it is not peaking. The best way to do this is to use a tool such as MRTG or HP OpenView to monitor the CPU through SNMP.

Logging and the excessive use of *debug* commands also affect CPU utilization. To avoid consuming precious CPU cycles, you should set logging to the minimum level of information that you actually need. Table 11.4 displays the logging levels you have at your disposal. If there is a reason you need high logging levels, consider turning off log messages that you do not need using the *no logging message*.

Table 11.4 Logging Levels

Description	Numerical Value
Emergency	0
Alert	1
Critical	2
Error	3
Warning	4
Notification	5
Informational	6
Debugging	7

You can determine the logging options and levels that are enabled on a PIX firewall using the *show logging* command. For example, on this firewall, all logging is disabled:

```
PIX1# show logging
Syslog logging: disabled
    Facility: 20
    Timestamp logging: disabled
    Standby logging: disabled
    Console logging: disabled
    Monitor logging: disabled
    Buffer logging: disabled
    Trap logging: disabled
    History logging: disabled
```

The *show cpu usage* Command

The *show cpu usage* command provides a snapshot of the short-term CPU utilization statistics. Although this information is not useful for history or trending purposes, it can immediately inform you if the CPU is overloaded at the time the command is executed. This command does allow you to check in real time if the CPU is the cause of any performance degradations. For example:

```
PIX1# show cpu usage
CPU utilization for 5 seconds = 2%; 1 minute: 1%; 5 minutes: 1%
```

If you suspect that IPsec encryption is causing performance degradation, use this command before turning on encryption to take a baseline of CPU utilization. Then enable IPsec and run the command again. Compare the CPU utilization. Run the command a few times over a time interval to ensure that the data you gathered is accurate.

The *show processes* Command

If CPU utilization is high, you will often need much more detail than the *show cpu usage* command provides. This is where the *show processes* command comes in. This command identifies every process running on the PIX firewall, how much memory is it using, and CPU cycles. This information is collected from the time the PIX firewall was started. As shown in Figure 11.16, the output of this command is voluminous; in fact, this is an abbreviated listing of the actual output from a PIX 501 firewall, the lowest end of the PIX firewalls. Here we do not explain every row of this of the display, but we do discuss how to interpret what you see in the columns. A detailed analysis of this command is available on Cisco's Web site at www.cisco.com/warp/public/110/pix_shproc.html.

Figure 11.16 Output of the *show processes* Command

```
PIX1# show processes

      PC       SP       STATE     Runtime    SBASE      Stack Process
Hsi 800b0e09 80759798 8052ddd8        0   80758810 3532/4096 arp_timer
Lsi 800b5271 8077c880 8052ddd8        0   8077b908 3912/4096 FragDBGC
Lwe 8020685d 808b8e20 80507300        0   808b6ed8 7644/8192 Logger
Hwe 8020a550 808bbee8 805075b0        0   808b9f70 8008/8192 tcp_fast
Lsi 80137edd 809400f0 8052ddd8        0   8093f168 3928/4096 xlate clean
Lsi 80256f4d 8096c430 8052ddd8        0   8096b4a8 3900/4096 route_process
Mwe 800d2671 809b19e0 8052ddd8        0   809afa68 6940/8192 IPsec timer
Lwe 8012ff5a 809daac8 80539908        0   809d9c50 3704/4096 pix/trace
Lwe 8013016a 809dbb58 80539fd0        0   809dace0 3704/4096 pix/tconsole
Hwe 800b2dd0 809ddbe8 80753b9c        0   809dbd70 7196/8192 pix/intf1
H*  80015207 7ffffe2c 8052ddc0      200   809e1ea0 12652/16384 ci/console
Csi 801299b3 809e6e88 8052ddd8       10   809e5f30 3440/4096 update_cpu_usag

 A    B        C        D       E       F        G     H
```

The first character of the first column refers to the priority of the process, which (ranked highest to lowest) can be: Critical, High, Medium, or Low. The next two characters refer to the current operating state of the process, which can be any of the values shown in Table 11.5.

Table 11.5 Process Operating States

Value	Description
*	The process is currently running.
E	The process is waiting for an event to occur.
S	The process is ready to run—gave up processor time slice (idle).
rd	The process is ready to run—conditions for activation have occurred.
we	The process is waiting for an event.
sa	The process is sleeping until an absolute time.
si	The process is sleeping for a given time interval.
sp	The process is sleeping for a given time interval (alternate).
st	The process is sleeping until a timer expires.
hg	The process is hung and will never run again.
xx	The process has terminated but has not been deleted.

The next column (PC) is the program counter, and the one after it (SP) is the stack pointer. Column D (STATE) identifies the thread queue used by the process. The thread queue may be shared with other processes. The fifth column (Runtime) is how much CPU time in milliseconds the process has consumed since it started. The Stack Base Address (SBASE) column shows the starting address space for the process, and the Stack column shows the ratio of used and total stack space in bytes allocated to the process. Bad processes will attempt to invade the space used by other processes. The last column (Process) identifies the process name.

This command is very useful to determine the processes that are taking up too many CPU cycles. To figure this out, issue the *show processes* command twice, waiting about one minute in between. For the process that you suspect to be a problem, subtract the Runtime value from the second command from the Runtime value from the first command. The result indicates the amount of CPU time (in milliseconds) the processed has received during that one minute. It is important to understand that some processes are scheduled to run at certain times, and others only run when they have information to process. The 577 poll process typically has the largest runtime of all processes because this is the one that polls Ethernet interfaces to see if they have any data that needs to be processed.

The *show perfmon* Command

One extremely useful command for performance monitoring on the PIX firewall is the *show perfmon* command. It shows details a number of statistics, including translations, connections, fixup, and AAA. This is the only command that you can use to view the "average" values for the number of translations and connections on the firewall. The nice thing about this command is that it breaks the connections down by protocol, as shown in the following output. This breakdown can help you determine if a particular connection is using up too much CPU or memory. Table 11.6 lists the values in the *show perfmon* command.

```
PIX1# show perfmon
```

```
PERFMON STATS:        Current        Average

  Xlates                0/s            0/s

  Connections           0/s            0/s

  TCP Conns             0/s            0/s

  UDP Conns             0/s            0/s

  URL Access            0/s            0/s

  URL Server Req        0/s            0/s

  TCP Fixup             0/s            0/s

  TCPIntercept          0/s            0/s

  HTTP Fixup            0/s            0/s

  FTP Fixup             0/s            0/s

  AAA Authen            0/s            0/s

  AAA Author            0/s            0/s

  AAA Account           0/s            0/s
```

Table 11.6 Values in the *show perfmon* Command

Parameter	Description
Xlates	Translations built up per second.
Connections	Connections established per second.
TCP Conns	TCP connections per second.
UDP Conns	UDP connections per second.
URL Access	URLs (Web sites) accessed per second.
URL Server Req	Requests sent to Websense/N2H2 per second (requires the *filter* command).
TCP Fixup	Number of TCP packets that the PIX forwarded per second.
TCP Intercept	Number of SYN packets per second that have exceeded the configured embryonic limit.
HTTP Fixup	Number of packets destined to port 80 per second (requires the *fixup protocol http* command).
FTP Fixup	FTP commands inspected per second.
AAA Authen	Authentication requests per second.
AAA Author	Authorization requests per second.
AAA Account	Accounting requests per second.

As with any measurement, if you do not have a baseline, this type of information is useless. Execute the command on a regular basis over time to build a baseline. You can then compare values to this baseline to find anomalies.

Memory Performance Monitoring

Memory utilization can be as important in determining performance as the CPU. Flash memory is used to hold the PIX operating system and configuration. Unless you have a very large software image, allocation issues with flash memory are not a concern.

Main memory, the focus of this section, is the working space of the PIX firewall. When the PIX firewall first boots, it loads the OS by copying it from flash to main memory. The memory is also used for all processes as well as buffering incoming and outgoing traffic. Because it is used by so many different aspects of the firewall, it is critical to ensure that you have enough memory. You can run several commands to help with this task. In addition, similar to CPU utilization, we recommend using an SNMP tool such as MRTG or HP OpenView to monitor the amount of available memory on the PIX firewall.

The *show memory* Command

The *show memory* command provides an easily comprehensible overview of how much memory is installed and how much is currently being used. This command simply shows you the amount of total and free memory at the time that you run the command. Here is an example of the *show memory* command:

```
PIX1# show memory
16777216 bytes total, 4517888 bytes free
```

To optimize the usefulness of this command, run it on a PIX firewall that has a very basic configuration. That is, run it on a PIX firewall that is not running encryption or other functions and record that information. Then as you add features, execute the command and compare the output. Doing so enables you to record approximately how much memory is consumed by each process.

The *show xlate* Command

One process that consumes memory is address translation. Each translation requires approximately 56 bytes of memory. Knowing this, you can run the *show xlate* command. For example:

```
PIX1# show xlate
100 in use, 341 most used
```

Multiply the number of translations by 56 bytes to determine how much memory has been consumed for translations. In our example, we have 100 translations in use, which means we have 5600 bytes of memory allocated for translation alone.

The *show conn* Command

Each connection made to the firewall also consumes memory. The amount of memory consumed depends on the type of connection. A UDP connection consumes 120 bytes; a TCP connection requires 200 bytes. This memory consumption is necessary to build the connection and maintain state information. Here is an example of the *show conn* command:

```
PIX1# show conn
2 in use, 2 most used
```

If we have 100 TCP connections made through this PIX firewall, that will require 20K of main memory. Of course, this is a transitory number and will fluctuate depending on the time of day.

The *show block* Command

The PIX firewall reserves certain amounts of memory to handle special traffic after the configuration is loaded and running and before any other memory allocation occurs. Certain amounts of memory are allocated into variable byte-sized blocks. Predefining such set-sized blocks relieves the firewall from having to carve memory on the fly. You can use the *show blocks* command to view the currently set block sizes. For example:

```
PIX1# show blocks
   SIZE     MAX    LOW     CNT
      4    1600   1563    1600
     80     400    386     400
    256     500    143     500
   1550    1700   1102    1315
  16384       8      8       8
```

We need to clarify the output of this command starting with the SIZE column, which is measured in bytes. The 4-byte blocks are reserved for certain traffic types such as DNS, IKE, TFTP (traffic that is small and bursty). The 80-byte blocks are used to store failover hellos and TCP intercept acknowledgments. The 256-byte blocks store stateful failover messages. The 1550-byte blocks support Ethernet (10 and 100) packets as they pass through the firewall. The 16384-byte blocks will never be used unless you have Gigabit Ethernet interfaces, something you will only see on high-end firewalls.

The MAX column identifies the maximum number of each type of memory blocks available. The LOW column indicates the lowest number of blocks that have been available since the firewall booted. Stated mathematically, subtract LOW from MAX to get the maximum number of blocks that were used at any particular time. The CNT column shows the available number of blocks. Use the *clear blocks* command to reset the LOW and CNT counters.

Network Performance Monitoring

Congested network interfaces can degrade overall performance. You need to ensure that the interfaces on your PIX firewall can handle the demands placed on them. Cisco offers several commands to check the status of your interfaces.

The *show interface* Command

One such command is *show interface*. You can check how much bandwidth is being consumed and check a myriad of error counters. We discussed *show interface* previously in the chapter, and will not rehash what has already been covered.

The *show traffic* Command

You can narrow your focus to capture the specific number of packets and bytes that are transiting each interface on the PIX firewall. The *show interface* command provides similar information, but you have to make it a specific point to zoom in on that information to determine exactly the amount of traffic being passed on a per-interface basis.

The *show traffic* command provides statistics on the number of packets and bytes passed through each interface. As you can see in the following output, *show traffic* tells you how long the interface has been in operation (either the firewall below has been in operation almost three hours or that much time has elapsed since the clearing of the statistics). The command output displays the amount of traffic transmitted and received in that amount of time.

```
PIX1# show traffic
outside:
        received (in 10035.150 secs):
                2 packets            678 bytes
                0 pkts/sec           0 bytes/sec
        transmitted (in 10035.150 secs):
                14 packets           1026 bytes
                0 pkts/sec           0 bytes/sec
inside:
        received (in 10035.150 secs):
                0 packets            0 bytes
                0 pkts/sec           0 bytes/sec
        transmitted (in 10035.150 secs):
                15 packets           900 bytes
                0 pkts/sec           0 bytes/sec
```

You can reset the traffic counters using the *clear traffic* command, which resets the counters to 0.

Identification (IDENT) Protocol and PIX Performance

There is one particular protocol that we need to address because it affects PIX performance. This is the identification protocol specified in RFC1413. The purpose of this protocol is to enable HTTP, FTP, or POP servers to confirm the identity of clients. When a client connects to one of these ports, a server running IDENT will attempt to connect to TCP port 113 on the client. If successful, the server will read certain identifying data from the client machine. In theory, this process would reduce spam or illegitimate usage by forcing users to connect from legitimate sources. In practice, the IDENT protocol can be circumvented easily.

Users behind a PIX firewall are protected from IDENT by default. Since the IDENT protocol provides information about the user, it can provide details about the internal network, which can be a violation of your security policy. The PIX firewall, like any good firewall, prevents this passage of internal details to the outside. However, the downside of this protection is that users could perceive a very noticeable delay in the server responding to their requests as it attempts to check their identities, or they could even experience a total lack of response.

To identify IDENT issues, set logging to the debugging level. Once that is turned on, you will see denied TCP attempts to port 113 attempts. To get around this issue, you have the following choices:

1. You can contact the administrator of the server running IDENTD and have it turned off. However, you will have to do this for *each* server that has this problem.

2. You can pass IDENT traffic through your firewall unmolested by permitting it with access lists or conduits. This would pass internal network details to the outside, which can compromise security.

3. Another (the recommended) solution is to use the *service resetinbound* command. This command sends a TCP reset (RST) to the IDENT server, which essentially tells it that the client does not support IDENT. Upon receiving that reset, the server provides the requested service to the user. Once this command is entered, the PIX firewall starts sending resets to traffic not permitted by the security policy rather than dropping it silently and causing the user to incur a time penalty.

Summary

This chapter introduced a troubleshooting methodology based on the OSI model. Using this approach, you start at the lowest layers and work up the stack. Doing this enables you to eliminate lower (and typically simpler) layer causes before focusing efforts on higher (and typically more complex) layer aspects of PIX firewall troubleshooting.

Knowledge is power! Knowing the various models of PIX firewalls and their capabilities is extremely important to troubleshooting. Certain models of the PIX firewall, such as models 501 and 506, do not support failover. Knowing such details would prevent you from wasting your time attempting to solve problems with features not supported on a particular model. Other useful information to know about the PIX firewall includes the number of supported connections as well as the number and types of NICs supported (such as Token Ring and Ethernet).

Although the PIX firewall supports a limited number of network types, familiarity with the cables used to connect to those networks can be a useful asset to troubleshooting. The PIX firewall uses standard TA586A/B wiring schemes for 10/100 Ethernet, and SC multimode fiber optic cables for Gigabit Ethernet. The failover cable is an instance of a specialized function made possible by adhering to a stringent Cisco proprietary wiring scheme.

In order for the PIX firewall to perform its function, it must be able to service its internal networks as well as know how to forward traffic to the appropriate destination. This is made possible using a static route or RIP. You need to be able to troubleshoot and resolve reachability issues to enable the PIX firewall to perform its job.

Translation is required for providing connectivity through the PIX firewall. Your troubleshooting toolbox includes many Cisco commands such as *show xlate*, *show nat*, and *show global*, all used to check translation configurations and operations. Ensure that you make *clear xlate* a regularly executed step in your troubleshooting, especially after making configuration changes.

Other connectivity issues you need to troubleshoot involve ensuring that only the proper access is granted to certain external networks. You can use commands such as *show conduit*, *show access-list*, and *show access-group* to validate what access is granted.

IPsec is probably one of the most complex features you will ever configure on the PIX firewall. The troubleshooting is equally complex. In this chapter, we covered several of the most critical commands available for validating IPsec operation. When troubleshooting, divide your efforts to enable better focus by first troubleshooting and resolving IKE issues, and then focusing on IPsec. IPsec depends on IKE, but IKE does not need IPsec to perform its functions.

With the introduction of PIX v6.2, Cisco has provided a useful packet capture and analysis tool in the form of the *capture* command. This command allows you to troubleshoot networks remotely by enabling the capture and analysis of networks connected to the PIX firewall. This reduces the need to install a third-party device on the target network to obtain information about it.

The best troubleshooting practice is proactive monitoring to detect problems before they become unmanageable. You can accomplish this proactive state by gathering performance data about various aspects of your PIX firewall such as CPU performance, memory consumption, and network bandwidth utilization statistics.

Part IV

Check Point NG and Nokia IP Series Appliances

## Chapter 12

Installing and Configuring VPN-1/FireWall-1 Next Generation

Best Damn Topics in this Chapter:

- **Before You Begin**

- **Installing Check Point VPN-1/FireWall-1 NG on Windows**

- **Uninstalling Check Point VPN-1/FireWall-1 NG on Windows**

- **Installing Check Point VPN-1/FireWall-1 NG on Solaris**

- **Uninstalling Check Point VPN-1/FireWall-1 NG on Solaris**

- **Installing Check Point VPN-1/FireWall-1 NG on Nokia**

Introduction

It's important to familiarize yourself with the installation and configuration options available in the Check Point Next Generation (NG) Enterprise Suite of Products. Specifically, we will be installing and configuring VPN-1/FireWall-1 NG on the Windows, Solaris, and Nokia Platforms. The installation process is pretty straightforward. We will focus on installing a Management Module and Enforcement Module on each platform, and will point out the subtle differences you will encounter if you choose to install these components in a distributed environment instead. After installing and configuring each platform, we will walk you through the uninstall process so you will know what to do in case you need to remove the software from your system.

Prior to starting the installation procedure of VPN-1/FireWall-1 NG, there are several steps that you should take to prepare the system and get ready for the installation screens you will be presented with. Most systems are not secure out-of-the-box, and we will help you to secure the host computer before you turn it into a firewall. We will also advise you on some good techniques you can use when preparing for your firewall installation.

Before You Begin

This section will prepare you to install the Next Generation product. We will discuss each step of the installation process so that you understand its importance, and we will guide you in your endeavor to secure your network. The list of minimum system requirements (as defined by Check Point) is outlined in Table 12.1. You can find these online at www.checkpoint.com/products/supported_platforms/index.html.

Table 12.1 Minimum System Requirements

System Requirement	Primary Management & Enforcement Module	GUI Clients (Policy Editor, Log Viewer, etc)
Operating Systems	Microsoft Win2k Server and Advanced Server SP0 and SP1 Windows NT 4.0 SP6a Sun Solaris 7 (32-bit mode only)* Sun Solaris 8 (32- or 64-bit mode)** RedHat Linux 6.2, 7.0 and 7.2	Microsoft Win2k Sun Solaris SPARC Windows 98/ME Windows NT 4.0 SP4, SP5 and SP6a
Disk Space	40 MB	40 MB
CPU	300+ MHz	No minimum specified
Memory	128 MB	32 MB
Network Interfaces	ATM, Ethernet, Fast Ethernet, Gigabit Ethernet, FDDI, Token Ring	Any supported by the operating system
Media	CD-ROM	CD-ROM

★ You must have patch 106327 on Solaris 2.7.

★★ You must have patches 108434 and 108435 on Solaris 2.8.

Solaris patches can be obtained from http://sunsolve.sun.com.

NOTE

To check whether your Solaris machine is in 32- or 64-bit mode, use the following commands:

- *isainfo –b*
- *isainfo –vk*

To change from 64- to 32-bit mode in Solaris 2.7 or 2.8, perform the following actions:

1   Enter EEPROM mode using the **STOP-A** keyboard combination.

2. Type **setenv boot-file kernel/unix** and press **Enter**.

3. Reboot.

4   If the machine has difficulty booting, use the **set-defaults** command to return to 64-bit mode.

To change from 32- to 64-bit mode, do the following:

1   Enter EEPROM mode using the **STOP-A** keyboard combination.

2. Type **setenv boot-file /platform/sun4u/kernel/sparcv9/unix** and press **Enter**.

3   Reboot.

Performance of your firewall software will rely in large part on the hardware you choose. It is highly recommended that you increase your hardware requirements above the minimum listed in Table 12.1 in real-world environments. Keep in mind that your management station will be handling logs from each module it controls, so you should ensure that you have adequate disk space, memory, and CPU to handle these connections.

Before you start your installation, make sure that you complete the items listed as follows:

- Get your licenses.

- Secure the Host.

- Configure routing and test network interface cards.

- Enable IP forwarding.

- Configure Domain Name Service (DNS).

- Prepare for the Check Point Installation and Configuration Screens.

Obtaining Licenses

Check Point licenses have changed (again) with the Next Generation release. You can obtain a license through your Check Point Value Added Reseller (VAR) or you can use the Check Point User Center to license your products at https://usercenter.checkpoint.com/UserCenter/index.jsp (see Figure 12.1). There are two options when it comes to licensing your firewall modules. You can either have them tied to their individual IP addresses (external interface recommended) as with previous versions, or you can tie them all to the management station's IP address. These licenses are called *local* and *central*, respectively. All licenses are maintained on the management console, and administrators can add or remove licenses using the SecureUpdate management tool.

The Management Module itself must have a local license based on its own IP address. The nice thing about using central licenses for the Enforcement Modules is that you can change their IP addresses without having to replace the license, and you can easily move a license from one module to another.

It is always best to obtain your licenses before you install the firewall software. The program will ask you for your license details during the install procedure. If you cannot obtain your permanent license prior to the install, then you should ask for an evaluation license. Check Point's evaluation licenses have full functionality for all VPN-1/FireWall-1 features. They are usually valid for one month, and the product is not adversely affected in any way while running with an evaluation license.

Figure 12.1 Check Point's User Center

Securing the Host

With any firewall installation, it is important to consider the security of the host computer on which you are installing the firewall software. There are some guidelines available on the Internet for securing the various operating systems. The following is a list of some good guides:

- **WinNT**
  http://support.checkpoint.com/kb/docs/public/os/winnt/pdf/Securing_NT.pdf
- **Solaris** http://support.checkpoint.com/kb/docs/public/os/solaris/pdf/strip-sun-server.pdf
- **Solaris** www.spitzner.net/armoring2.html
- **Linux** www.ibiblio.org/pub/Linux/docs/HOWTO/other-formats/html_single/Security-HOWTO.html

Lance Spitzner also has several great papers at www.spitzner.net, which you might want to check out.

When installing the firewall, you should start out by installing the base operating system (OS) without any bells or whistles, and then apply any necessary OS patches. You should not install any additional Internet servers on your firewall host, either. For example, you should not have Internet Information Server (IIS) or a File Transfer Protocol (FTP) server running on your firewall since these services could be vulnerable to attack.

Disabling Services

Probably the most important step in any of these guides is the process of disabling services on the firewall host. Almost any OS installation enables various services out-of-the-box that are not needed for the operation of a firewall. Your firewall should have as few services running as possible. If you are installing on a Windows machine, you should disable NETBEUI or any other non-IP protocols. The kernel processes of the NG product do not inspect traffic on non-IP protocols, so your NETBEUI and IPX traffic would not be protected, therefore it should not be installed on the firewall.

> **NOTE**
>
> By default, the Nokia hardware platform comes with a hardened FreeBSD operating system out of the box. Nothing has to be done to secure a Nokia platform prior to installing the NG product when starting with a default install.

If you are installing the firewall on a Unix system, the most common method of disabling services is through the /etc/inetd.conf file. This file tells the system which services/protocols are enabled, and therefore which ports the system will be listening to. The following code is the beginning of a typical inetd.conf file as installed in Solaris 2.7. As you can see, there are several services running that do not have to be enabled. Most things in the inetd.conf file can be disabled. If you want to leave FTP or Telnet open temporarily, then that is your option.

```
# more inetd.conf
#
#ident   "@(#)inetd.conf 1.33    98/06/02 SMI"   /* SVr4.0 1.5   */
#
#
# Configuration file for inetd(1M).  See inetd.conf(4).
#
# To reconfigure the running inetd process, edit this file, then
# send the inetd process a SIGHUP.
#
# Syntax for socket-based Internet services:
#   <service_name> <socket_type> <proto> <flags> <user> <server_pathname> <args>
#
# Syntax for TLI-based Internet services:
```

```
#
#   <service_name> tli <proto> <flags> <user> <server_pathname> <args>
#
# Ftp and telnet are standard Internet services.
#
ftp       stream  tcp     nowait  root    /usr/sbin/in.ftpd       in.ftpd
telnet    stream  tcp     nowait  root    /usr/sbin/in.telnetd    in.telnetd
#
# Tnamed serves the obsolete IEN-116 name server protocol.
#
#
name      dgram   udp     wait    root    /usr/sbin/in.tnamed     in.tnamed
#
# Shell, login, exec, comsat and talk are BSD protocols.
#
shell     stream  tcp     nowait  root    /usr/sbin/in.rshd       in.rshd
login     stream  tcp     nowait  root    /usr/sbin/in.rlogind    in.rlogind
exec      stream  tcp     nowait  root    /usr/sbin/in.rexecd     in.rexecd
comsat    dgram   udp     wait    root    /usr/sbin/in.comsat     in.comsat
talk      dgram   udp     wait    root    /usr/sbin/in.talkd      in.talkd
```

To disable services in this file, simply edit it, and insert a pound sign or hash mark in front of the line that you wish to disable. When completed, send a *HUP* signal to the inetd process running on the system as shown in the following output:

```
# ps -ef | grep inet
    root   229    1  0   Nov 06 ?         0:00 /usr/sbin/inetd -s
# kill -HUP 229
```

You can verify that the processes are no longer listening on the system by running the *netstat −an* command. Because there are fewer services running on the firewall, the system is more secure. You can think of each of those listening ports as holes into your operating system. Although the firewall software will protect the operating system from direct attack if you have the security policy defined properly, it is better to stay on the safe side and reduce the number of possible ingresses.

Routing and Network Interfaces

We recommend that before you install the Check Point product, first configure and test the networks that the firewall will be communicating on. When you install VPN-1/FireWall-1, the product binds to the interface adapters, and even begins configuring the firewall at this early stage. Regardless of the platform you are installing on, it is recommended that you configure the first interface on your firewall as the external interface, and that this IP address resolves to the name of the host computer in the hosts files. On Windows systems, this means that the external

IP address of the enforcement firewall should go on the network interface that is displayed first in the interface pull-down list under the IP Address tab on the Microsoft TCP/IP Properties window. If this is not defined properly, then several problems may occur with Secure Internal Communications (SIC) and Virtual Private Network (VPN) configurations.

Prior to installation, configure your firewall interfaces with the correct IP addresses and subnet masks. Ideally, you can plug your system into a test network so that you are not putting your unprotected system on the live network before installing the firewall software. It is always best to install a firewall in an isolated environment so that it cannot be compromised before it has been protected. You should test routing and IP forwarding first. Once Check Point VPN-1/FW-1 NG is installed, it will control IP forwarding, but you must first enable IP forwarding in the OS and test that your network adapters and routing are functioning properly. Just imagine if you didn't perform this test before installing the software, and then found that you had a faulty Network Interface Card (NIC). It would have saved you a lot of blood, sweat, and tears if you had determined this first.

> **NOTE**
>
> When you are configuring your interfaces on a Windows system, be sure that you only configure one interface with a gateway. This is a common mistake since each interface gives you the option of filling in a gateway. You should never have more than one default gateway configured on your firewall.

Next, make sure you understand the wide area network (WAN) connections that will be coming into your firewall, and configure routing accordingly. You may decide to set up a dynamic routing protocol on your firewall to maintain its routing table, or you may decide that static routes are the way to go. If you add a route on a Windows system, then you should provide the $-p$ switch so that the route will still be there after a reboot. This switch permanently adds the route into the system registry. For example, the following command will route the 10.1.1.0/24 network to the next hop router of 10.2.2.1 on a WinNT system:

```
route add -p 10.1.1.0 mask 255.255.255.0 10.2.2.1
```

In Solaris, you need to set up your route statements in a file that will be run at startup (for example the /etc/rc2.d directory). The file name must begin with a capital S for the system to run it (e.g. S99local), and you should set the file modes to allow execution. The previous route command can be written in Solaris as follows:

```
route add 10.1.1.0 -netmask 255.255.255.0 10.2.2.1
```

If your firewall will be on the boarder of your network, connecting your LANs and WANs to the Internet, you will need to ensure that default routes are configured throughout on all your workstations and routers so that they are routed to the next hop closest to the Internet. It may prove helpful if you create a network diagram that shows how your network looks prior to having a firewall, and another to show the network after the firewall is in place. This will help you to visualize which connections will be changing so that you can prepare accordingly.

Enabling IP Forwarding

To test your routing and interfaces, you must enable IP forwarding in your OS. To do this on WinNT 4.0, access the **TCP/IP properties** window and select **Enable IP Forwarding** from the **Routing** tab (shown in Figure 12.2). To enable IP forwarding in Win2k, you must edit the registry as outlined in Microsoft's KB article Q230082 as follows:

1. Open the registry by running regedt32.exe.

2. Find the following registry key:
   HKEY_LOCAL_MACHINE\SYSTEM\CurrentControlSet\Services\Tcpip\Parameters

3. Add the following value to this key:

   - Value Name: IPEnableRouter

   - Value type: REG_DWORD

   - Value Data: 1

Figure 12.2 Enable IP Forwarding in WinNT 4.0

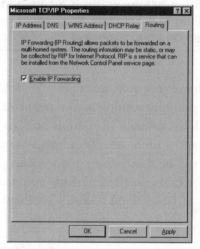

In Solaris, IP forwarding is usually enabled by default. You can switch it off and on with the following command: *ndd -set /dev/ip ip_forwarding 1*. The settings for this command are as follows:

- 0 disables IP forwarding
- 1 enables IP forwarding

Configuring DNS

Since it is suggested that you install your firewall while it is not plugged into any untrusted networks, it will be best to start with DNS disabled on the firewall. If you have DNS enabled and the system cannot reach its name servers, then the system may become sluggish and system performance will be affected. It is important that when you do configure DNS, you configure it properly.

The firewall should be able to resolve its own external IP address to the name of the host computer. This could be set up in advance by creating an A record in your domain for the firewall, and you should enter it into the firewall's hosts file. In Unix, this file is located in /etc/hosts, and in Windows it is located in c:\winnt\system32\drivers\etc\hosts. The Nokia platform also must have the host name associated with its external IP address, and this is done through the **Host Address Assignment** link found under the **System Configuration** heading in the Voyager GUI. You can use this interface to configure host entries instead of editing a host's file.

You should also include IP addresses in the host's file that your firewall may communicate with frequently, like a management server and/or Enforcement Module. Policy installation performance can be increased on a management server by having all network objects (which are defined later) resolvable.

Another DNS record that you should create is a pointer (PTR) record for your firewall's external IP address or any other address(es) that you will be using for Network Address Translation (NAT). Some Web sites and FTP servers require that you have a reverse resolvable IP address before they will grant you or your users access to download their files. If you have obtained a block of IP addresses from your Internet Service Provider (ISP), then chances are that they control the PTR records for your addresses. Sometimes they will provide you with a Web site where you can administer these yourself. Other times, you will need to find the right person who can make the changes for you. If you have your own abstract syntax notation (ASN), then you can set up your own in-addr.arpa domain and create your own PTR records.

Preparing for VPN-1/FireWall-1 NG

During the install process, you will be asked which components you want to install and then you will be required to fill in the configuration screens at the end of the installation procedure. The Check Point Next Generation CD gives you the following options for installation:

- **Server/Gateway Components** Choose this option if you wish to install one or more of the following components from the Next Generation Suite:
  - **VPN-1 & FW-1** This includes FW-1 Management Module and enforcement point software along with the VPN-1 encryption component.
  - **FloodGate-1** Provides an integrated Quality of Service (QoS) solution for VPN-1/FW-1.
  - **Meta IP** Integrated IP Management with DNS and Dynamic Host Configuration Protocol (DHCP) servers.
  - **Management Clients** The GUI for Check Point including the Policy Editor, Log Viewer, and System Status GUI.
  - **UserAuthority** A user authentication tool that integrates with FW-1, FloodGate-1, and other e-business applications.
  - **VPN-1 SecureClient Policy Server** Allows an Enforcement Module to install Granular Desktop Policies on mobile users' SecureClient personal firewalls.

- **Reporting Module** An integrated reporting tool that can generate reports, graphs, and pie charts to display information obtained from the VPN-1/FW-1 logs.

- **Real-Time Monitor** Allows an organization to monitor their VPN connections, Internet connections, etc.

■ **Mobile/Desktop Components (Windows Only)** If you just want to install client software on your mobile users or desktops in the office as described in the following options, then choose this option.

- **VPN-1 SecuRemote** Client Encryption software loaded on your mobile clients.

- **VPN-1 SecureClient** Client Encryption software with Desktop Security (personal firewall) features.

- **Session Authentication Agent** This agent is installed on desktop computers where your users will need to authenticate with Session Authentication.

If you are installing from files, be sure that you download and install the Check Point SVN Foundation first. This package is the base of the entire Check Point Next Generation software suite as its name suggests. It's this program that allows the easy integration of all other NG components. The only VPN-1/FW-1 applications that don't rely on the SVN Foundation are the management clients.

The next important question that the installation process will ask you (if you are installing a management server on your firewall) is whether you want to enable backward compatibility. If you choose *not* to enable backward compatibility, then you will only be able to manage other NG modules. If you do choose to enable backward compatibility, then you will be able to manage NG, 4.1, and 4.0 modules from this management station.

The default folder installation in Windows is c:\winnt\fw1\5.0 and Check Point installs files on Solaris in /opt and /var/opt. Make sure that you have partitioned your disk properly to accept the default installation folder, or be prepared to give a custom location for the installation (Windows only). If you don't accept the defaults, you should verify that the install program configures the firewall's environment variables properly.

> **NOTE**
>
> You will see the use of the FW-1 Environment Variables or the *$FWDIR* environment variable throughout this book. It is the nature of an environment variable to contain some value (similar to a variable used to represent a number in algebra). The *$FWDIR* variable contains the value of your firewall's installation directory, and it is configured upon install. If you install on Windows, this variable is set to *c:\winnt\fw1\5.0*. In Solaris the *$FWDIR* environment variable is set to */opt/CPfw1-50*.
>
> There is also a *$CPDIR* variable, which contains the installation directory of the CPShared (SVN) components. In Windows, the *$CPDIR* variable is set to *c:\Program Files\CheckPoint\CPShared\5.0*, and in Solaris it is set to */opt/CPshared/5.0*.
>
> So, whenever you see these terms used, $FWDIR or $CPDIR, substitute the appropriate directory for your firewall installation in their place. On a Unix system, you can type **echo $FWDIR** to see the value of the variable, or type **set** to see a list of all envi-

ronment variables and their associated values. To be technically accurate, we should probably use *%FWDIR%* when talking about the Windows environment, but we are going to stick to the Unix method of describing variables in this book.

The VPN-1/FW-1 component options are as follows:

- **Enterprise Primary Management** To install a management server only, which will be acting in a primary capacity.

- **Enterprise Secondary Management** To install a management server only, which will be acting in a backup capacity.

- **Enforcement Module & Primary Management** To install both a Primary Management Module and VPN-1/FW-1 Enforcement Module (this is the default option).

- **Enforcement Module** To install an Enforcement Module only, the management server will be installed on a separate host.

The Management Client options are as follows:

- **Policy Editor** Used to connect to your management server to configure your rule base, NAT, FloodGate-1 QoS policy, and SecureClient Desktop Security Policies.

- **Log Viewer** Used to view your VPN-1/FW-1 security logs, accounting logs, and audit logs on the management server.

- **System Status** Used to view the status of the remote enforcement points connected to the management server.

- **SecureClient Packaging Tool** Used to create custom packages for SecuRemote/SecureClient mobile users.

- **Traffic Monitoring** Used to monitor an interface, QoS rule, or virtual link in real time. The display is in the form of a line or bar graph.

- **SecureUpdate** Used for managing licenses and doing remote software updates of the remote enforcement points connected to you're the management server.

- **Reporting Tool** Used to generate reports with graphs and pie charts from the data in the VPN-1/FW-1 logs.

After the Check Point installation wizard copies files, it will run through a number of configuration screens. These will be identical if you are installing a Management Module with or without an Enforcement Module with the exception of the SNMP option in Solaris, which is only configured if you are installing an Enforcement Module. The screens that you can prepare for in advance are the following:

- **Licenses** You should read the section on Licenses if you need help getting licenses. You will be required to fill in the following fields:

- **Host/IP Address** The IP address associated with this license or "eval."

- **Expiration Date** The date that the license expires, which may be "never."

- **SKU/Features** These are the features that this license will enable (e.g. Management or 3DES).

- **String/Signature Key** The license string provided by Check Point to validate the license. This key will be unique for each license and IP address.

- **Administrators** You will need to configure at least one administrator during install. Subsequent sections in the chapter provide additional details for more on adding Administrators.

  - **Administrator Name** Choose a login name. This field is case- sensitive.

  - **Password** Choose a good alphanumeric password. It must be at least four characters long.

  - **Confirm Password** Repeat the same password entered previously.

- **GUI Clients** These are the IP addresses of the management clients that your administrators will use when connecting to this Management Module. You may need to configure static IP addresses for your administrators. You may add as many GUI clients as you'd like or you may enter none; it's up to you. Subsequent details for additional details regarding the GUI client options can be found elsewhere in the chapter.

- **SNMP extension (Unix only)** If you wish to utilize external network management tools such as HP OpenView, then you can install the Check Point FW-1 SNMP daemon. With the daemon installed and activated, you will be able to query the firewall status. You could use a network management tool to monitor the firewall's health and generate alerts based on certain criteria.

- **Group Permissions (Unix only)** If you choose to set group permissions on your VPN-1/FW-1 installation on Solaris, enter the group name at this prompt (from /etc/group). If you do not want to set group permissions, only root will be able to execute all FW-1 commands. You might want to set group permissions so that you can enable a number of firewall operators to execute FW-1 commands without having to grant them superuser privileges on the system.

WARNING

Around mid-February 2002 a CERT Advisory was posted, warning about various vulnerabilities that have been found and exploited in many SNMP implementations. These vulnerabilities could lead to Denial of Service attacks or unauthorized access. Please ensure that you have applied any applicable security patches to your systems prior to accepting SNMP through your firewall. For more information, and links to patches visit the CERT Web site: www.cert.org/advisories/CA-2002-03.html. Nokia IPSO 3.4.2 and above already have the SNMP fix integrated.

Administrators

It is best to use individual administrator usernames instead of a generic username like fwadmin. The problem with using a generic login ID is that you cannot properly audit the activities of the firewall administrators. It may be important for you to know who installed the last security policy when you are troubleshooting a problem. This becomes more and more important when there are several people administering a firewall system. The fields that you need to fill in follow:

- **Administrator Name** Choose a login name for your administrator. This field is case-sensitive.

- **Password** Choose a good alphanumeric password. It must be at least four characters long.

> **NOTE**
>
> If you are installing just an Enforcement Module, then you will not have any administrators or GUI clients to configure.

There is a section labeled Permissions that enables you to define the access level you will require on an individual basis for each administrator. If you select **Read/Write All** or **Read Only All**, then your administrator will have access to all the available GUI client features with the ability to either make changes and updates or view the configuration and logs (perhaps for troubleshooting purposes) accordingly. You may also choose to customize their access so that they may be able to update some things and not others. To do this, select **Customized** and configure each of these options:

- **SecureUpdate** This GUI tool enables you to manage licenses and update remote modules.

- **Objects Database** This tool is used to create new objects to be used in the security policy rule bases.

- **Check Point Users Database** This tool is used to manage users for firewall authentication purposes.

- **LDAP Users Database** This tool is used to manage Lightweight Directory Access Protocol (LDAP) users.

- **Security Policy** This tool is used to create and manage rule bases using the Policy Editor GUI.

- **Monitoring** This option enables access to the Log Viewer, System Status, and Traffic Monitoring GUI clients.

GUI Clients

When you enter GUI clients, you type their hostnames or IP addresses into the **Remote hostname:** field and add them to the list of clients allowed to connect to your Management Module. You are allowed to use wildcards as follows:

- **Any** If you type in the word **Any**, anyone will be allowed to connect without restriction (not recommended).

- **Asterisks** You may use asterisks in the hostname. For example, 10.10.20.* means any host in the 10.10.20.0/24 network, and *.domainname.com means any hostname within the domainname.com domain.

- **Ranges** You may use a dash (-) to represent a range of IP addresses. For example, 1.1.1.3-1.1.1.7 means the 5 hosts including 1.1.1.3 and 1.1.1.7 and every one in between.

- **DNS or WINS resolvable hostnames**

It is recommended that you stay away from using hostnames or domain names, however, since this requires DNS to be configured and working on the firewall. Using IP addresses are the best method since it doesn't rely on name resolving, and will continue to work even if you cannot reach your name servers from the firewall.

Upgrading from a Previous Version

Although this chapter describes how to perform a fresh install of NG, you may be interested in upgrading from your existing versions of FW-1. You can install or upgrade to NG from version 4.0 or 4.1, and it can manage v4.*x* firewalls if you choose the **Backward Compatibility** option during the install. Although NG utilizes Secure Internal Communication (SIC) for other NG modules, it can also use the *fw putkey* command to communicate with previous versions of the product. FW-1 NG is not compatible with versions earlier than 4.0.

It's very important that you upgrade your management console prior to upgrading any of your firewall Enforcement Modules to NG. A 4.1 management station cannot control an NG module. When you do upgrade your enforcement points, you will need to edit their workstation objects in the Policy Editor, and change their version to NG before you will be able to push or fetch a policy.

Read the release notes before you begin. This is very important since there is a list of limitations in the NG release notes that you will need to consider ahead of time. Some of these include, but are not limited to, your resources, VPNs, and external interface settings. NG does not support more than one resource in a rule. If you have rules configured with multiple resources, NG will copy this rule into the new format with only one resource, and will not create new rules for the others. NG does not support Manual IPSec or SKIP VPNs any longer. If you have these types of VPNs in your rule base before the upgrade, they will be converted to IKE VPNs without notification during the upgrade to NG. If you have a limited license on your VPN-1/FW-1 v4.*x* firewall, your *$FWDIR\conf\external.if* settings will not be preserved during the upgrade. You will need to define your firewall's external interface in the workstation properties window under the **Topology** tab after the upgrade. You may also need to run the *confmerge* command to manually merge your objects.C file with the new objects in NG. These things and more are laid out for you in the product release notes.

It is also highly recommended that you have a back-out plan in place if your upgrade to NG does not go as smoothly as planned. Check Point recommends upgrading on a new piece of hardware; that way you will minimize downtime. If you do it this way, remember that you may need to redo SIC or putkeys, and your Internet router or any routers directly connected to the firewall may have to have their ARP cache cleared after putting the new hardware in place.

Last, but certainly not least, make sure that you have a backup of the entire system prior to an upgrade. It is especially important to save the $FWDIR/conf directory and any files that may have been edited from $FWDIR/state (like local.arp in Windows), $FWDIR/database, and $FWDIR/lib (for files like base.def and table.def that may have been modified).

Installing Check Point VPN-1/FireWall-1 NG on Windows

Finally, all of your hard work in preparing for the firewall installation is about to pay off. This section is dedicated to installing the Check Point VPN-1/FW-1 NG on Windows. Hopefully you have read the previous section "Before you Begin" and are prepared to start with the Check Point software installation. If you did not read the "Before you Begin" section, we suggest that you go back to the beginning of this chapter and read this section before you continue.

Although this section describes a standalone installation, different options are pointed out that allow you to install the firewall on Windows in a distributed environment. In other words, you will be installing the Management and Enforcement Modules as well as the GUI all on one machine; however, you could install each piece on separate machines (and use different operating systems) if that is what your network design calls for. The distributed installation is not much different from the distributed installation, and you should feel just as comfortable with the latter as you do with the former after reading this section.

Installing from CD

You can obtain a copy of the Check Point Next Generation CD from Check Point by going to www.checkpoint.com/getsecure.html and requesting an evaluation of the software. If you have a login set up with Check Point, you can download the software and updates from Check Point here: www.checkpoint.com/techsupport/downloadsng/ngfp1.html.

The screenshots throughout this section depict a new installation via CD on a Windows 2000 Professional server. If you are installing on Windows NT, the procedure is the same.

1. Insert the Check Point Next Generation CD into the CD-ROM drive on your firewall system. The Check Point NG Welcome Screen will appear (Figure 12.3). If the Welcome screen does not appear after inserting the CD, then you may start it manually from the CD's wrappers\windows folder by running *demo32.exe*. From this screen you may choose to read the important information regarding evaluation licenses, purchased products, and the contents of the CD.

Figure 12.3 Welcome Screen

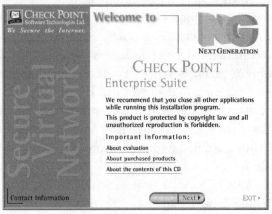

2. If you are ready to continue the installation, select **Next** to start the installation wizard. You will be presented with the License Agreement shown in Figure 12.4.

Figure 12.4 License Agreement

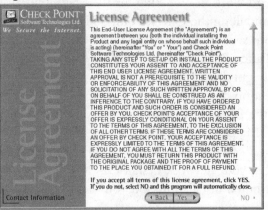

3. You must accept the license agreement in order to continue with installation. Select **Yes** when you are ready to continue. Otherwise, select **No** to exit the installation wizard.

4. The next screen, displayed in Figure 12.5, provides you with the Product Menu so that you can choose which Check Point products to install. You have two options:

    ■   **Server/Gateway Components (Default)** Choose this option if you wish to install one or more of the following components from the Next Generation Suite:

        ■   **VPN-1 & FireWall-1** This includes FW-1 Management Module and enforcement point software along with the VPN-1 encryption component.

        ■   **FloodGate-1** Provides an integrated QoS solution for VPN-1/FW-1.

        ■   **Meta IP** Integrated IP Management with DNS and DHCP servers.

        ■   **Management Clients** The Graphical User Interface for Check Point including the Policy Editor, Log Viewer, and System Status GUI.

- **UserAuthority** A user-authentication tool that integrates with FW-1, FloodGate-1, and other e-business applications.

- **VPN-1 SecureClient Policy Server** Allows an Enforcement Module to install Granular Desktop Policies on mobile users' SecureClient personal firewalls.

- **Reporting Module** An integrated reporting tool that can generate reports, graphs, and pie charts to display information obtained from the VPN-1/FW-1 logs.

- **Real-Time Monitor** Allows an organization to monitor their VPN connections, Internet connections, etc.

- **Mobile/Desktop Components** If you just want to install client software on your mobile users or desktops in the office as described in the following list, then choose this option.

  - **VPN-1 SecuRemote** Client Encryption software loaded on your mobile clients.

  - **VPN-1 SecureClient** Client Encryption software with Desktop Security (personal firewall) features.

  - **Session Authentication Agent** This agent is installed on desktop computers where your users will need to authenticate with Session Authentication.

5. Make sure that the **Server/Gateway Components** option is selected, and click **Next**.

Figure 12.5 Product Menu

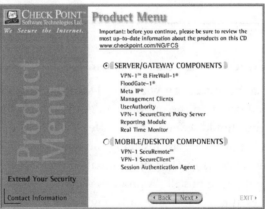

> **NOTE**
>
> During the installation process, use the **Back** button at any time to move to the previous screen, use the **Next** button to advance to the next screen, use the **Exit** option to exit the installation at any time, and use the elevator buttons along the side of the page to scroll up and down.

6. The next screen is the Server/Gateway Components (see Figure 12.6), which provides you with the various options for the individual Check Point components you can

install. We will select **VPN-1 & FireWall-1** and **Management Clients** to install the Management and Enforcement Modules as well as the Graphical User Interface. If you place your mouse pointer over each item (without clicking), you will see a detailed description displayed on the right-hand side.

Figure 12.6 Server/Gateway Components

7. Click **Next** when you are ready to begin the install process.

8. The Check Point installation wizard will start the InstallShield Wizard program to begin the installation based on the options you've chosen thus far. Figure 12.7 illustrates the screen that you should see next. Select **Next** when you are ready to continue. The InstallShield Wizard will start installing the Check Point SVN Foundation. You should note that this is always the first piece installed on a Next Generation system. It will also be the last piece if you uninstall. A progress window will pop up, as shown in Figure 12.8. You should see the window similar to Figure 12.9 when the SVN installation is complete.

Figure 12.7 Selected Products

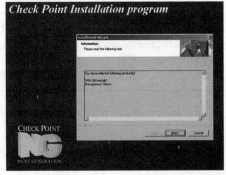

Figure 12.8 Progress Window

Figure 12.9 VPN-1 & FW-1 Installation

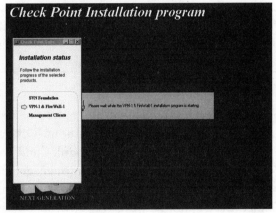

9. Immediately following this screen, another window will pop up prompting you to choose specific components of VPN-1/FW-1 to install:

■   **Enterprise Primary Management** To install a Management server only that will be acting in a primary capacity.

■   **Enterprise Secondary Management** To install a Management server only that will be acting in a backup capacity.

■   **Enforcement Module & Primary Management (Default)** To install both a Primary Management server and VPN-1/FW-1 Enforcement Module.

■   **Enforcement Module** To install an Enforcement Module only, the Management server will be installed on separate hardware.

Select **Enforcement Module & Primary Management**, as shown in Figure 12.10, and click **Next**.

Figure 12.10 VPN-1/FW-1 Product Specification

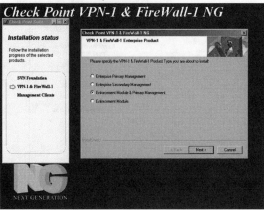

10. The next screen (Figure 12.11) gives you the option of installing with or without back-ward compatibility. If you choose to install without backward compatibility, you will only be able to manage NG Enforcement Modules, and you will not be able to manage VPN-1/FW-1 v4.0 nor v4.1 firewalls from this management station. Choosing to install with backward compatibility support will enable you to manage these older versions of the product. Since we will not be managing any older versions of the product with this management server, choose the default option to **Install without backward compatibility**, and click **Next**.

Figure 12.11 Backward Compatibility Screen

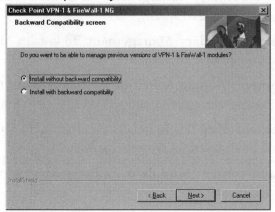

11. Next, Check Point will ask you where you want to install the product files. The default folder location in Windows is c:\winnt\fw1\5.0. If you wish to install to a different folder, choose **Browse**; otherwise, select **Next** to accept the default location and continue. Whatever value you choose for the firewall's installation directory will be the value of the $FWDIR environment variable, which will be used throughout this book when referencing this directory. This is the last screen before VPN-1/FW-1 files are copied to your hard drive (Figure 12.12). Now the system copies files and installs the software. You should see a screen similar to the one in Figure 12.13 as the install program shows you its progress. You may click the **Cancel** button on the bottom right-hand side of this screen if you wish to stop the installation at this point.

Figure 12.12 Choose Destination Location

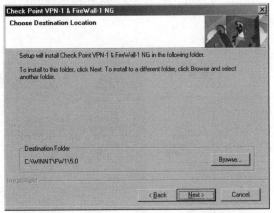

Figure 12.13 Copying Files

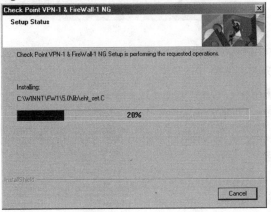

12. Once the system has finished copying files, you may see some messages pop up such as "Installing FW-1 kernel," "Installing FW-1 Service," "Setting Permissions" (NTFS only), and "Register product add-ons…." These windows appear whenever you are installing an enforcement module. The installation wizard will then display a final pop-up window from VPN-1/FW-1 explaining that the installation will complete upon reboot (as shown in Figure 12.14). Click **OK**.

Figure 12.14 Setup Information

13. The system will not reboot after you select **OK**. Instead, it will begin installing the Check Point management clients. You will see a window like the one in Figure 12.15 asking if you wish to install the management clients in the default folder C:\Program Files\CheckPoint\Management Clients. You can either accept the default or click on **Browse...** to choose a new target for the files. Accept the default folder location and click **Next** to continue.

Figure 12.15 Management Client Location

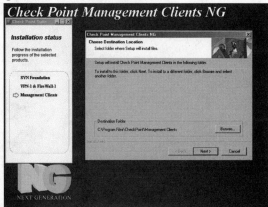

14. Now you will need to choose which of the management clients you will install. Figure 12.16 displays the window you will see with the available options, which are as follows:

- **Policy Editor** Used to configure the rule base, Network Address Translation, FloodGate-1 QoS policy, and SecureClient Desktop Security Policies.

- **Log Viewer** Used to view your VPN-1/FW-1 security logs, accounting logs, and audit logs.

- **System Status** Used to view the status of the remote enforcement points connected to your management server.

- **SecureClient Packaging Tool** Used to create custom packages for SecuRemote/SecureClient mobile users.

- **Traffic Monitoring** Used to monitor an interface, QoS rule, or virtual link in real time. The display is in the form of a line or bar graph.

- **SecureUpdate** Used for managing licenses and doing remote software updates of the remote enforcement points connected to your management server.

- **Reporting Tool** Used to generate reports with graphs and pie charts from the data in the VPN-1/FW-1 logs.
  Accept the default values (Policy Editor, Log Viewer, System Status, and SecureUpdate) and click **Next**. This is the last screen before the Check Point installation wizard begins copying files to your system (Figure 12.17).

Figure 12.16 Select Management Clients to Install

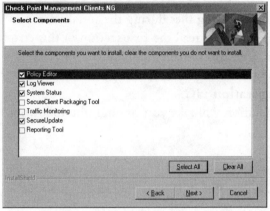

Figure 12.17 Management Clients Copying Files

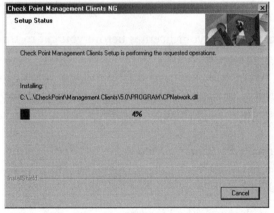

15. When the system is done copying files, the installation process is nearly complete. You can now click on any of the icons in the Check Point Management Clients folder. You can also open the management clients by selecting **Start | Programs | Check Point Management Clients**. Click **OK** to finish the installation (Figure 12.18) and begin the configuration process.

Figure 12.18 Setup Complete

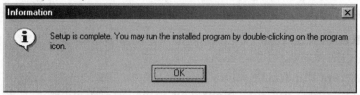

Configuring Check Point VPN-1/FireWall-1 NG on Windows

Once the system is done copying files during the installation procedure, it will begin to display the configuration screens. If you read the first section of this chapter, you should be prepared to configure the firewall. After this initial configuration, you can always come back to any of these configuration screens by selecting **Start | Programs | Check Point Management Clients | Check Point Configuration NG**.

The initial configuration will take you through the following screens:

- Licenses
- Administrators
- GUI Clients
- Certificate Authority Configuration

Licenses

You should have obtained all of your licenses before you get to this step. If you didn't, don't worry. There is even a link to the Check Point User Center, where you can get your licenses, right in the Licenses window. If you need help with your license, read the first part of this chapter, entitled "Before you Begin." If you don't have any permanent licenses to install at this time, you can always request an evaluation license from either Check Point or your Check Point reseller.

Since you have installed a Primary Management Module, you should be installing a local license that was registered with the local management station's IP address. Follow this step-by-step procedure for adding your license(s).

1. Click **Add**, as shown in the Licenses configuration window in Figure 12.19.

Figure 12.19 Licenses

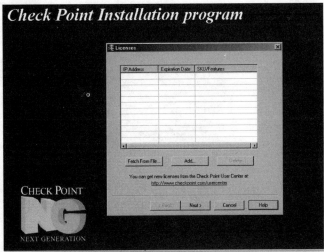

2. Once you click **Add,** you will see a pop-up window like the one illustrated in Figure 12.20. In this window you can either select **Paste License** or enter the license details into the appropriate fields. Figure 12.20 shows the following license installed: cplic putlic eval 01Mar2002 aoMJFd63k-pLdmKQMwZ-aELBqjeVX-pJxZJJCAy CPMP-EVAL-1-3DES-NG CK-CP. In addition you will see the following fields:

- **IP Address** The IP address associated with this license or "eval."

- **Expiration Date** The date that the license expires, which may be "never."

- **SKU/Features** These are the features that this license will enable (e.g. Management or 3DES).

- **Signature Key** The license string provided by Check Point to validate the license. This key will be unique for each license and IP address.

  Enter the license details in the Add License window, and click **Calculate** to verify that the information you entered is correct. Match the Validation Code that you receive in this field to the Validation Code on the license obtained from the Check Point User Center. You can also copy the entire *cplic putlic* command into your clipboard, and then click the **Paste License** button at the top of the screen to fill in all the fields. Click **OK** to continue, and if you entered everything correctly you should see the license entered into the main Licenses window (Figure 12.21).

NOTE

The license configuration window will be displayed when you are installing the Management or the Enforcement Module in a distributed install as well.

Figure 12.20 Adding a License

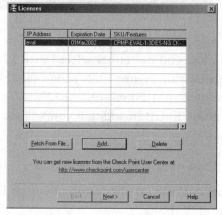

Figure 12.21 License Added Successfully

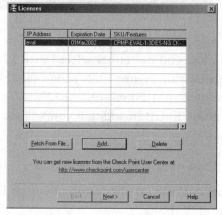

3. Click **Next** to continue. The next screen deals with the Check Point configuration of the Management Module.

Administrators

After installing your licenses, you will be presented with another configuration window (see Figure 12.22) in which you need to configure your firewall administrators. You will need to define at least one administrator during this time. You can always come back to this window later to add, edit, or delete your administrator(s).

Figure 12.22 Configuring Administrators

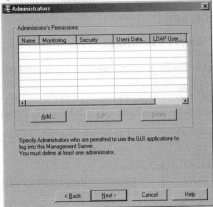

1. The first step to configuring your administrators is to click **Add...**

2. You will be presented with another window similar to the one in Figure 12.23, where you can define the attributes for one administrator. It is best to use individual admin usernames instead of a generic username like fwadmin. The problem with using a generic login ID is that you cannot properly audit the activities of the firewall administrators. It may be important for you to know who installed the last security policy when you are troubleshooting a problem. This becomes more and more important when there are several people administering a firewall system. The fields that you need to fill in are listed as follows. Fill in the required fields in the Add Administrator Window and select **Read/Write All** for the permissions. Click on **OK** to finish adding the administrator.

   - **Administrator Name** Choose a login name for your admin. This field is case sensitive.

   - **Password** Choose a good alphanumeric password. It must be at least four characters long and is also case-sensitive.

   - **Confirm Password** Repeat the same password entered previously.

   The section labeled Permissions enables you to define the access level that you will require on an individual basis for each administrator. If you select **Read/Write All** or **Read Only All**, your administrator will have access to all the available GUI client features with the ability to either make changes and updates or view the configuration and logs (perhaps for troubleshooting purposes), respectively. You may also choose to customize each administrator's access so that he or she may be able to update some things and not others. To do this, select **Customized** and configure each of these options:

   - **SecureUpdate** This GUI tool allows administrators to manage licenses and update remote modules.

   - **Objects Database** This tool is used to create new objects to be used in the security policy.

- **Check Point Users Database** This tool is used to manage users for firewall authentication purposes.

- **LDAP Users Database** This tool is used to manage LDAP users.

- **Security Policy** This tool is used to create and manage a rule base using the Policy Editor GUI.

- **Monitoring** This option enables access to the Log Viewer, System Status, and Traffic Monitoring GUI clients.

Figure 12.23 Adding an Administrator

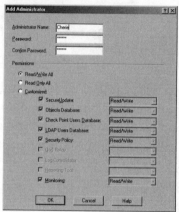

3. When you finish adding an administrator, you will be brought back to the main Administrators configuration window. The administrator should now be listed in the Administrator's Permissions window. From here you may choose to **Add...**, **Edit...**, or **Delete administrators** from this list (see Figure 12.24). When you are done adding administrators, click **Next** to continue with the configuration of the Check Point Management Module.

Figure 12.24 Administrators

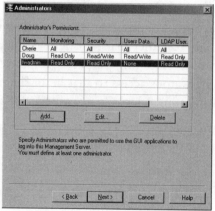

GUI Clients

The GUI Clients are the management clients installed earlier. These clients could also be installed on as many desktops as you wish, but before they can connect to the management server, you need to enter their IP addresses into the GUI Clients configuration window shown in Figure 12.25. You can use this feature, for example, if you install the GUI clients on your own workstation to enable you to control the management server from your PC. This will enable you to connect remotely to manage the security policy and view your logs and system status. You do not need to configure any clients at all during the install, but if you are already prepared for this step, you may enter as many clients into this window as necessary. This client information will be saved in a file on your firewall under $FWDIR/conf and will be named gui-clients. This file can be edited directly, or you can bring up this GUI Clients window at any time in the future.

> **NOTE**
>
> If you have installed an Enforcement Module only, you will not configure GUI clients.

For our example installation, we are not going to enter any GUI Clients. Select **Next** to continue on with the Check Point Management Module installation and read the next section. When you enter GUI Clients, you type their hostnames or IP addresses into the **Remote hostname:** field, then click **Add** to insert the clients to the window on the right. You are allowed to use wildcards as follows:

- **Any** If you type in the word "Any," this will allow anyone to connect without restriction (not recommended).

- **Asterisks** You may use asterisks in the hostname, e.g. 10.10.20.* means any host in the 10.10.20.0/24 network, or *.domainname.com means any hostname within the domainname.com domain.

- **Ranges** You may use a dash (-) to represent a range of IP addresses, e.g. 1.1.1.3–1.1.1.7 means the 5 hosts including 1.1.1.3 and 1.1.1.7 and every one in between.

- **DNS** or **WINS resolvable hostnames**

Figure 12.26 displays an example of the configured GUI Clients window with various options that you can use for your GUI client entries. We recommend staying away from using hostnames or domain names, however, since it requires DNS to be configured and working on the firewall. Using IP addresses are the best method since it doesn't rely on resolving, and will continue to work even if you cannot reach your name servers from the firewall.

Figure 12.25 GUI Clients Configuration Window

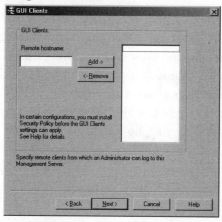

Figure 12.26 GUI Clients Configuration Window Sample Configuration

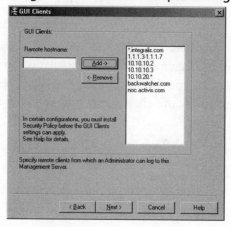

Certificate Authority Initialization

Your Management server will be a Certificate Authority (CA) for your firewall Enforcement Modules, and will use certificates for SIC. This is the step in the installation process where the Management Server's CA is configured, and a certificate is generated for the server itself.

You will be presented with a Key Hit Session window where you will be prompted to enter random text until you hear a beep. The data you enter will be used to generate the certificate, and it is recommended that you also enter the data at a random pace; some keystrokes may be close together and others could have a longer pause in between them. The more random the data, the more unlikely that the input could be duplicated. If the system determines that the keystrokes are not random enough, it will not take them as input, and will display a bomb icon under Random Characters, but if the input is good, then it will display a yellow light bulb.

NOTE

The Key Hit Session screen will also be presented to you if you have installed an Enforcement Module so that you can generate an internal certificate for SIC.

1. Type random characters at random intervals in the Key Hit Session window until the progress bar is full, and the message "Thank you!" appears at the bottom of the window, as seen in Figure 12.27.

2. Click **Next** to continue with the CA configuration.

Figure 12.27 Key Hit Session

3. You will be presented with a window titled Certificate Authority (Figure 12.28). This window simply informs you that the CA is not yet configured and that it will be initialized when you select **Next**. Click **Next** to initialize the Management Module's Certificate Authority. You should receive a message that the initialization completed successfully, as shown in Figure 12.29.

Figure 12.28 Certificate Authority Initialization

Figure 12.29 CA Initialized Successfully

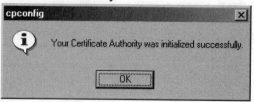

4. Click **OK**.

5. Click **Finish** on the Fingerprint window (shown in Figure 12.30) to exit the configuration. This window will be the last one in the set of configuration screens during the install process. This window displays the fingerprint of the Management Server's CA. You will be able to bring this window up again after the installation through the Check Point Configuration NG Tool, described later in the section titled "Getting Back to Configuration." When a GUI client first connects to the management server, it will be asked to verify the fingerprint to ensure that the client connecting to the right machine. After that, the client software will compare the management server's fingerprints at each connect. If the fingerprints do not match, the client will be warned and asked if to the session should continue. The fingerprint can also be exported to a file also that the GUI clients would have access to.

Figure 12.30 Management Server Fingerprint

Installation Complete

Congratulations! You have now successfully installed and configured a Check Point VPN-1/FW-1 firewall on a Windows system. All you need to do now is navigate your way out of the Check Point Installation program and reboot your computer. Check Point will thank you for using their SVN Integrated installation suite (see Figure 12.31) and ask you if you wish to reboot now or reboot later (Figure 12.32).

Figure 12.31 NG Configuration Complete

1. To finish the installation process, click **OK**.

2. From the InstallShield Wizard dialog box illustrated in Figure 12.32, choose **Yes, I want to restart my computer now** and click **Finish**. Your computer will be shut down and restarted.

Figure 12.32 Reboot Computer

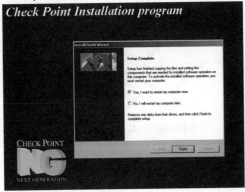

Getting Back to Configuration

Now that installation is complete, you may need to get back into the Configuration screens that you ran through at the end of the install. You can add, modify, or delete any of the previous configuration settings by running the Check Point Configuration NG GUI.

1. Select **Start | Programs | Check Point Management Clients | Check Point Configuration NG**. This will bring up the Configuration Tool displayed in Figure 12.33. As you can see, all of the configuration options that were displayed during the installation are available through the various tabs at the top of the Configuration Tool window. The tabs you can configure using this tool are listed :

   ■ Licenses

   ■ Administrators

   ■ GUI Clients

- PKCS#11 Token—Used to configure an add-on card, like a VPN accelerator card, for example.

- Key Hit Session

- Fingerprint

If you are just reading the chapter at this point, see the top of this section "Configuring the Management Module" to get a walk-through of each of these screens and your options.

2. When you have completed making changes to the firewall configuration, click **OK** to exit the tool.

Figure 12.33 Check Point Configuration Tool

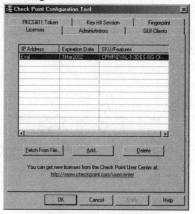

If you installed the Primary Management Module only, the tabs on the Configuration Tool NG will be exactly the same as in Figure 12.33 without the tab for PKCS#11 Token. If you installed an Enforcement Module only, the Configuration Tool screens will be a little different (see Figure 12.34). The two new tabs are as follows:

- **Secure Internal Communication** Enables you to initialize an Enforcement Module for communication. You must enter the same password here as you entered in the Policy Editor GUI (Figure 12.35).

- **High Availability** Enables this Enforcement Module to participate in a Check Point High Availability (CPHA) configuration with one or more other Enforcement Modules. This tab, illustrated in Figure 12.36, will not show up in your installation since you cannot have a Management Module installed on an Enforcement Module in a CPHA cluster.

Figure 12.34 Enforcement Module Configuration Tool

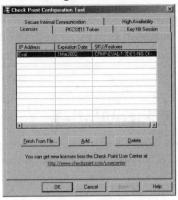

Figure 12.35 Secure Internal Communication

Figure 12.36 High Availability

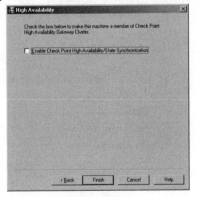

Uninstalling Check Point VPN-1/FireWall-1 NG on Windows

When you uninstall VPN-1/FW-1, it is recommended that you make a full system backup before you begin. If you only need to back up the firewall configuration, you should make a backup of the $FWDIR directory and all of its subdirectories. The default $FWDIR directory in Windows is c:\winnt\fw1\5.0.

Uninstalling VPN-1 & FireWall-1

When you uninstall the firewall, you should remove the Check Point installed components from the Add/Remove Programs in your system's Control Panel. The components should be removed in the following order:

1. Check Point VPN-1 & FireWall-1 NG
2. Check Point SVN Foundation NG

You can remove the Management Clients package at any time, but the order in which you remove these two packages is important.

The following steps are used to completely uninstall all Check Point products from your Windows platform:

1. Exit all GUI client windows that you may have open.
2. Open you're the Windows Control Panel by selecting **Start | Settings | Control Panel**.
3. Select the **Add/Remove Programs** icon. If you are using Windows 2000, you should see a window similar to the window displayed in Figure 12.37.

Figure 12.37 Add/Remove Check Point VPN-1/FW-1 NG

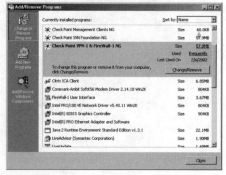

4. Select **Check Point VPN-1 & FireWall-1 NG** and click on **Change/Remove** to uninstall this program.
5. You will receive a message asking if you are sure that you want to remove this program (Figure 12.38). Click **OK** to continue and remove the VPN-1/FW-1 components.

Figure 12.38 Confirm Program Removal

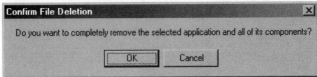

6. You will receive a Question/Warning message from Check Point (see Figure 12.39) asking if it is OK to continue with the uninstallation of the primary management server. Click **Yes** to continue. This is your last chance to change your mind. After you have confirmed that you really do wish to remove the management server VPN-1/FW-1 component, the uninstall process will then stop any running Check Point services before starting to remove files. You will see the message displayed in Figure 12.40.

Figure 12.39 Check Point Warning

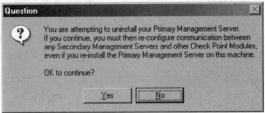

Figure 12.40 Stopping Services

7. Next, you will see a window that displays the progress of the uninstall process (Figure 12.41). Select **Yes, I want to restart my computer now** and click **Finish** to reboot your computer (Figure 12.42).

Figure 12.41 Removing VPN-1/FW-1 Files

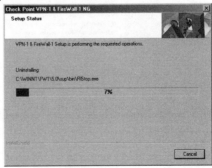

Figure 12.42 VPN-1/FW-1 Uninstall Complete

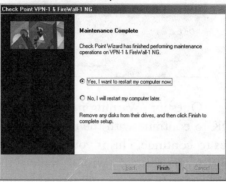

Uninstalling SVN Foundation

You have already uninstalled the VPN-1/FW-1 software, but now you must remove the SVN Foundation. This should always be removed after all other Check Point components, which are built on top of this foundation. If you had installed FloodGate-1 or the Policy Server, for example, these should be removed prior to removing the SVN program files.

1. Log into your computer

2. Choose **Start | Settings | Control Panel**.

3. Select the **Add/Remove Programs** Icon. You should see a window similar to the one in Figure 12.43. Select **Check Point SVN Foundation NG** and click **Change/Remove** to completely remove the SVN Foundation from your system.

Figure 12.43 Add/Remove Check Point SVN Foundation NG

4. Click **OK** to confirm the removal of the selected application (see Figure 12.44). The InstallShield Wizard will then start up and begin uninstalling the SVN Foundation.

5. Click **Finish** when you receive the message **Maintenance Complete** (Figure 12.44). If you are prompted to reboot, select **Yes, I want to restart my computer now** and click **Finish** to reboot your computer. Once the machine reboots, log in again and open the Control Panel to remove the GUI clients (described next).

Figure 12.44 SVN Foundation Maintenance Complete

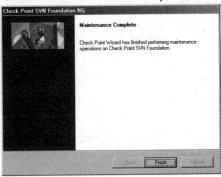

Uninstalling Management Clients

The Management Clients do not really depend on the SVN foundation installation; therefore, you could really remove them at any time without any difficulty.

1. After removing the SVN Foundation, access the **Add/Remove Programs** window. You will see a screen similar to that in Figure 12.45. Highlight **Check Point Management Clients NG** and click **Change/Remove** to uninstall all of the NG Management Clients (e.g. Policy Editor, Log Viewer, etc).

Figure 12.45 Add/Remove Management Clients NG

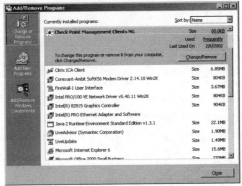

2. Choose to uninstall the GUI clients.

3. Click **OK** when you see the Maintenance Finished window displayed in Figure 12.46.

4. Click **Close** to exit the Control Panel, and you are done uninstalling all Check Point components.

Figure 12.46 Maintenance Finished

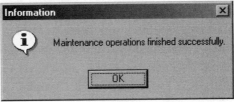

Installing Check Point VPN-1/FireWall-1 NG on Solaris

Finally, all of your hard work at preparing for the firewall installation is about to pay off. This section is dedicated to installing the Check Point VPN-1/FW-1 NG on Solaris. Hopefully you have read the first section of this chapter "Before you Begin" and are prepared to start with the Check Point software installation. If you did not read the "Before you Begin" section, we suggest that you go back to the beginning of this chapter and read this section before you continue.

Although this section describes a standalone installation, different options are pointed out that allow you to install the firewall on Solaris in a distributed environment. In other words, you will be installing the Management and Enforcement Modules as well as the GUI all on one machine; however, you could install each piece on separate machines (and use different operating systems) if that is what your network design calls for. The distributed installation is not much different from the distributed installation, and you should feel just as comfortable with the latter as you do with the former after reading this section. This section assumes that you are already familiar with the Unix operating system, and know how to navigate the file system and list directories within Solaris.

If you are installing on Solaris 2.7, you need to ensure that it is in 32-bit mode and that you have patch 106327 applied before you start. If you are installing on Solaris 2.8, you can install in either 32- or 64-bit modes, and you must have patches 108434 and 108435 applied before you start installing VPN-1/FW-1 NG. Solaris patches can be obtained from http://sunsolve.sun.com.

Installing from CD

You can obtain a copy of the Check Point Next Generation CD from Check Point by going to www.checkpoint.com/getsecure.html and requesting an evaluation of the software. If you have a login setup with Check Point, then you can download the software and updates from Check Point here www.checkpoint.com/techsupport/downloadsng/ngfp1.html.

The following screenshots depict a new install via CD on a Solaris 2.7 (32-bit mode) system. If you are installing on other versions of Solaris, the procedure is the same.

1. Insert the Check Point Next Generation CD into your computer's CD-ROM drive. If you have the automount daemon running on your Solaris system, the drive will be mounted automatically. If not, mount the CD-ROM drive. using the following syntax. You will need to determine which disk to mount before you type this command. Replace the Xs with the appropriate drive numbers for your system.

   ```
   mount -o ro -F hsfs <device> <mount point>
   ```

2. Move into the CD-ROM mount point directory by typing **cd /cdrom/cpsuite_ng_hf1** and press **Enter**. The directory name that you are using may be different depending on the version of the CD that you have. For this installation, you are using the Check Point NG HotFix1 CD. There is a file in this directory titled ReadmeUnix.txt, which explains the contents of the CD and how to begin the install process.

> **NOTE**
>
> If you have downloaded the packages to install on Solaris, you must first unzip and untar them to a temporary directory. Once the files are extracted, use *pkgadd –d <directory>* to install the Check Point VPN-1/FW-1 packages. Problems have been known to occur if these temporary directories are several subdirectories away from the root of the file system. It would be best to extract these packages to /opt or directly to / instead of burying them too far down in the file system hierarchy. If you are in the same directory as the package, type **pkgadd –d .** to begin the installation.
>
> You must install the SVN Foundation package prior to installing any other modules on your system. Make sure you download this package, too, if you want to install VPN-1/FW-1. You can install management clients without the SVN Foundation.

3. When you are ready to start with the installation, type **./UnixInstallScript Enter** to initiate the Check Point installation wizard (see Figure 12.47). If you are in the Common Desktop Environment (CDE), you can also use a file manager and double-click the **UnixInstallScript** file to begin.

   After you press **Enter**, you will be presented with Check Point's welcome screen.

> **NOTE**
>
> If you are installing Check Point NG on Linux, you use the same UnixInstallScript to begin the install process.

Figure 12.47 UnixInstallScript

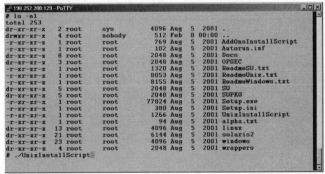

4. The Welcome Screen (Figure 12.48) will present you with the options listed. Type **n** to advance to the next screen.

   - **V – Evaluation Product** Informational page on running this software on an evaluation license.

- **U – Purchased Product** Informational page on installing this software if it is a purchased product.

- **N – Next** Proceed to the next screen.

- **H – Help** To get help with navigating the installation screens.

- **E – Exit** To quit the installation and exit.

The installation will proceed the same, whether you are installing a purchased product or an evaluation version. The only difference between the two is the license you apply during configuration. You can always apply a permanent license to an evaluation system at any time to turn it into a production firewall.

Figure 12.48 Welcome to Check Point NG

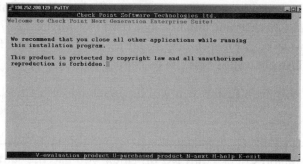

NOTE

While running the UnixInstallScript, keep your eye at the bottom of the screen to see your navigation options. You will enter the letter associated with the menu item to perform the requested action. For example, to exit the system, you see E – exit at the bottom of the screen. Simply press **e** to exit and end the installation at any time.

5. You will see a message at the top of the screen that says, "Checking the OS Version" and then you will see the license agreement shown in Figure 12.49. Press the **spacebar** until you reach the end of the agreement. When you reach the end, the program will prompt you to indicate whether you accept the terms in the license agreement, "Do you accept all the terms of this license agreement (y/n) ?" Enter **y** and press **Enter**.

Figure 12.49 License Agreement

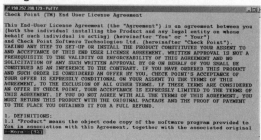

6. You should now be presented with a screen while the system installs the SVN Foundation. This may take a couple of minutes. This screen reads as follows, "Please wait while installing Check Point SVN Foundation...." Once the SVN installation is complete, you will need to select the products that you want to install from this CD (Figure 12.50). The options are explained in the following list:

- **VPN-1 & FireWall-1** This includes FW-1 Management Module and enforcement point software along with the VPN-1 encryption component.

- **FloodGate-1** Provides an integrated QoS solution for VPN-1/FW-1.

- **Meta IP** Integrated IP Management with DNS and DHCP servers.

- **Management Clients** The GUI for Check Point including the Policy Editor, Log Viewer, and System Status GUI. Using the Management Clients feature on Solaris requires a Motif license, and you may need to tweak your environment to get them to run, but you can connect with as many remote Windows GUI clients to a Solaris management server as you wish without any additional licenses.

- **UserAuthority** A user authentication tool that integrates with FW-1, FloodGate-1, and other e-business applications.

- **VPN-1 SecureClient Policy Server** Allows an Enforcement Module to install Granular Desktop Policies on mobile users' SecureClient personal firewalls.

- **Reporting Module** An integrated reporting tool that can generate reports, graphs, and pie charts to display information obtained from the VPN-1/FW-1 logs.

- **Real Time Monitor** Allows an organization to monitor VPN connections, Internet connections, etc.

Type in the number of each package you wish to select. Type the number again to deselect it. If you enter **r** for Review, you will see a new screen in which to select a product by entering its number, and then pressing **r** again to get a description of the product. For this installation exercise, enter **1** and **4** to select **VPN-1 & FireWall-1** and **Management Clients,** respectively. Enter **n** to advance to the next screen.

Figure 12.50 Select Products to Install

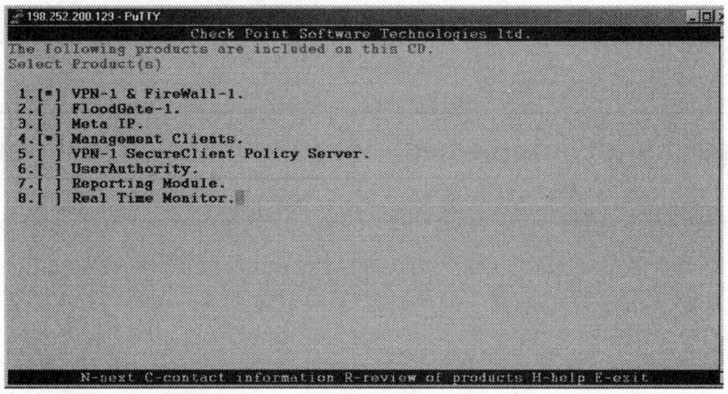

NOTE

If you are installing the Enforcement Module only, select **VPN-1 & FireWall-1**.

7. Next, you will need to select the type of firewall installation you want to perform on this server (Figure 12.51). The options are listed next. Use the keyboard to enter the number of the option you want. To change your selection, simply enter the number of the new option. For this installation, enter **1** to select **Enterprise Primary Management and Enforcement Module**, then press **n** to continue.

   - **Enterprise Primary Management and Enforcement Module** To install both a Primary Management server and VPN-1/FW-1 Enforcement Module.

   - **Enforcement Module** To install an Enforcement Module only, the management server will be installed on separate hardware.

   - **Enterprise Primary Management** To install a management server that will be acting in a primary capacity.

   - **Enterprise Secondary Management** To install a Management server that will be acting in a backup capacity.

Figure 12.51 Choose the Type of Installation

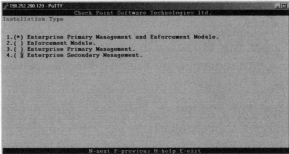

8. If you are installing a Management Module, you will be asked if you want to install with or without backward compatibility (Figure 12.52). If you select **No,** you will only be able to manage other NG modules with this management server. If you select **Yes,** you will be able to manage version 4.0, 4.1 and NG modules with this management server. Enter **2** for No and press **n** to continue.

NOTE

If you are installing an Enforcement Module only, you will not configure backward compatibility.

Figure 12.52 Backward Compatibility

9. On the next screen (Figure 12.53) press **n** to continue. This will be the last screen where you can exit the configuration before the install script will start copying files. While the install script is installing the package and copying files, you will see a progress screen similar to the one in Figure 12.54. The installation could take a few minutes. Next, the firewall will install the VPN-1/FW-1 kernel module and begin the configuration process.

Figure 12.53 Validation Screen

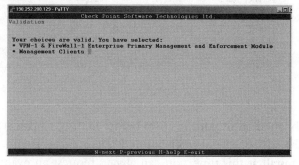

Figure 12.54 Installation Progress

Configuring Check Point VPN-1/FireWall-1 NG on Solaris

Once the required files have been copied by the installation wizard, the system it will begin the configuration process (Figure 12.55). If you have already read the first section of this chapter, you should be prepared to configure the firewall. After this initial configuration, you can always come back to any of these screens by running *cpconfig* from the root shell. We recommend that you go through all of these screens during the install without canceling; you can always go back in to change your initial configuration settings.

The initial configuration will take you through the following screens:

- Licenses
- Administrators
- GUI Clients
- SNMP Extension
- Group Permissions
- Certificate Authority Configuration

Figure 12.55 Welcome to Check Point Configuration Screen

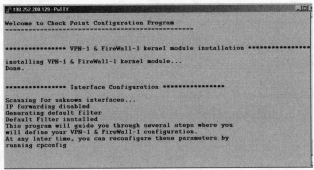

Licenses

You should have obtained all of your licenses before getting to this step. If you need help getting your license, read the part of this chapter entitled "Before you Begin." If you don't have any permanent licenses to install at this time, you can always request an evaluation license from either Check Point or your Check Point reseller.

> **NOTE**
>
> The license configuration option will be displayed regardless of which modules you have installed.

Since you have installed a Primary Management Module, you should be installing a local license that was registered with the local management station's IP address. Follow this step-by-step procedure for adding your license(s). You can see the license configuration input and output outlined in the following output.

1. When prompted to add licenses, enter **y** for yes and press **Enter**.
2. Enter **M** to add the license manually and press **Enter**. Now you will be prompted for each field of the license. The following output shows the following license installed: cplic putlic eval 01Mar2002 aoMJFd63k-pLdmKQMwZ-aELBqjeVX-pJxZJJCAy CPMP-EVAL-1-3DES-NG CK-CP

- **Host** The IP address or hostid associated with this license or the word "eval."

- **Date** The date that the license expires, which may be "never."

- **String** The license string provided by Check Point to validate the license. This key will be unique for each license and IP Address/Host.

- **Features** These are the features which this license will enable (e.g. Management and/or 3DES).

As you can see in the following output, you also have the option of choosing **f** (Fetch from file). If you select this option, the configuration will prompt you to enter the file name of the file.

3. Enter the values for Host, Date, String, and Features pressing **Enter** after each entry.

```
Configuring Licenses...
========================
The following licenses are installed on this host:


Host              Expiration Features




Do you want to add licenses (y/n) [n] ? y

Do you want to add licenses [M]anually or [F]etch from file?: M
Host:eval
Date:01Mar2002
String:aoMJFd63k-pLdmKQMwZ-aELBqjeVX-pJxZJJCAy
            Features:CPMP-EVAL-1-3DES-NG CK-CP
```

Administrators

If you have installed a Management Module, as soon as you enter a license into the configuration program, you will be prompted to add an administrator. You must define at least one administrator at this time. You can always come back later to add, edit, or delete your administrators.

NOTE

If you have installed an Enforcement Module only, then you will not configure Administrators.

It is best to use individual admin usernames instead of a generic username like fwadmin. The problem with using a generic login ID is that you cannot properly audit the activities of the firewall administrators. It may be important for you to know who installed the last security policy when you are troubleshooting a problem. This becomes more and more important when there are several people administering a firewall system. The fields that you need to fill in are asfollows:

- **Administrator Name** Choose a login name for your administrator. This field is case-sensitive.

- **Password** Choose a good alphanumeric password. It must be at least four characters long and is also case-sensitive.

- **Verify Password** Repeat the same password entered previously.

- **Permissions for all Management Clients** (Read/[W]rite All, [R]ead Only All, [C]ustomized)

The following output illustrates the screen for adding an administrator.

```
Configuring Administrators...

==============================
No VPN-1 & FireWall-1 Administrators are currently
defined for this Management Station.
Administrator name: Cherie
Password:
Verify Password:
Permissions for all Management Clients (Read/[W]rite All, [R]ead Only All,
[C]ustomized) w


Administrator Cherie was added successfully and has
Read/Write permission to all management clients


             Add another one (y/n) [n] ? n
```

To add an administrator, follow these steps:

1. Enter the login ID for your Administrator and press **Enter**. **Cherie** is used in the previous example.

2. Enter the password for the administrator (Cherie in our example) and press **Enter**.

3. Confirm the password entered in step 2 and press **Enter**.

4. Enter **w** for Read/Write All to give this administrator full permissions to access and make changes to all management clients.

   Setting permissions enables you to define the access level that you will require on an individual basis for each administrator. If you select **Read/[W]rite All** or **[R]ead Only All,** then your administrators will have access to all the available GUI client features with the ability to either make changes and updates or to view the configuration and logs (perhaps for troubleshooting purposes). You may also choose to customize each administrator's access so that he or she may be able to update some things and not others. To do this, enter **C** for Customized and configure each of the following options (see output directly following the bullet list):

- **SecureUpdate** This GUI tool enables you to manage licenses and update remote modules.

- **Monitoring** This option enables access to the Log Viewer, System Status, and Traffic Monitoring GUI clients.

```
Permissions for all Management Clients (Read/[W]rite All, [R]ead Only All,
[C]ustomized) c
        Permission for SecureUpdate (Read/[W]rite, [R]ead Only, [N]one) w
        Permission for Monitoring (Read/[W]rite, [R]ead Only, [N]one) w


Administrator Doug was added successfully and has
Read/Write permission for SecureUpdate
        Read/Write permission for Monitoring
```

GUI Clients

The GUI clients are the management clients you installed earlier. These clients could also be installed on as many desktops as you wish, but before they can connect to the management server, you need to enter their IP addresses into the GUI Clients configuration, as shown in the next set of output. You can use this feature, for example, if you install the GUI clients on your own workstation to enable you to control the management server from your PC. This will enable you to connect remotely to manage the security policy and view your logs and system status. You do not need to configure any clients at all during the install, but if you are already prepared for this step, you may enter as many clients into this window as necessary. This client info will be saved in a file on your firewall under $FWDIR/conf and will be named gui-clients. This file can be edited directly, or you can bring up this GUI Clients window at any time in the future by running *cpconfig*.

NOTE

If you have installed an Enforcement Module only, then you will not configure GUI clients.

1. Press **c** to create a new list of GUI clients.
2. Type in a GUI client IP address and press **Enter**.
3. Repeat step two for each GUI client you want to add to the list.
4. Press **Crtl + D** to complete the list.
5. Verify that the list is correct, enter **y** for yes and press **Enter** to continue.

```
Configuring GUI clients...
```

```
===========================
GUI clients are trusted hosts from which
Administrators are allowed to log on to this Management Station
using Windows/X-Motif GUI.

Do you want to [C]reate a new list, [A]dd or [D]elete one?: c
Please enter the list hosts that will be GUI clients.
Enter hostname or IP address, one per line, terminating with CTRL-D or your EOF
        character.
```

When creating the GUI clients list, you may use wildcards as follows:

- **Any** This will allow anyone to connect without restriction (not recommended).
- **Asterisks** You may use asterisks in the hostname, e.g. 10.10.20.* means any host in the 10.10.20.0/24 network, or *.domainname.com means any hostname within the domainname.com domain.
- **Ranges** You may use a dash (-) to represent a range of IP addresses, e.g. 1.1.1.3-1.1.1.7 means the 5 hosts including 1.1.1.3 and 1.1.1.7 and every one in between.
- **DNS or WINS resolvable hostnames**

The following displays a configured GUI Clients window. It is recommended that you stay away from using hostnames or domain names, however, since this requires DNS to be configured and working on the firewall. Using IP addresses is the best method since it doesn't rely on resolving, and will continue to work even if you cannot reach your name servers from the firewall.

```
Please enter the list hosts that will be GUI clients.
Enter hostname or IP address, one per line, terminating with CTRL-D or your EOF
character.
*.integralis.com
1.1.1.3-1.1.1.7
10.10.10.2
10.10.10.3
10.10.20.*
backwatcher.com
noc.activis.com
            Is this correct (y/n) [y] ? y
```

SNMP Extension

If you wish to utilize external network management tools such as HP OpenView, you can install the Check Point FW-1 SNMP daemon. With the daemon installed and activated, you will be able to query the firewall status. Additionally, you could use a network management tool to monitor the firewall's health and to generate alerts based on certain criteria. The MIB files are located in $CPDIR/lib/snmp. If you will not be using SNMP, then you should not enable it at this time. You can always come back and activate it by running *cpconfig* in the future. Enter **y** to activate the SNMP daemon as shown in the following output.

```
Configuring SNMP Extension...

===============================

The SNMP daemon enables VPN-1 & FireWall-1 module

to export its status to external network management tools.

                Would you like to activate VPN-1 & FireWall-1 SNMP daemon ? (y/n) [n] ?
y
```

Group Permission

During configuration, you will be prompted to configure groups on your VPN-1/FW-1 module as shown in Figure 12.56. You can either press **Enter** to accept the default setting of no group permissions, or you can enter the name of a group (defined in the file /etc/group) that you would like to have set on the Check Point directories. You might want to set group permissions so that you can enable a number of firewall operators to execute FW-1 commands without having to grant them superuser privileges to the system. Only one user should have superuser privileges on a Unix system, and that is the root account. Press **Enter** to set no group permissions. Press **Enter** again to accept this configuration option.

Figure 12.56 Setting Group Permissions

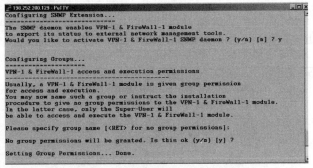

Certificate Authority Initialization

The management server will be a Certificate Authority for your firewall Enforcement Modules, and will use certificates for SIC. This is the step in the installation process where the management server's CA is configured, and a certificate is generated for the server and its components.

You will be presented with the Key Hit Session configuration option where you are asked to input random text until you hear a beep. The data you enter will be used to generate the certificate, and it is recommended that you also enter the data at a random pace; some keystrokes may be close together and others could have a longer pause between them. The more random the data, the more unlikely that the input could be duplicated. If the system determines that the keystrokes are not random enough, it will not take them as input, and will display an asterisk to the right of the progression bar.

> **NOTE**
>
> The Key Hit Session screen will also be presented to you if you have installed an Enforcement Module, so that you can generate an internal certificate for SIC.

1. Type random characters at random intervals in the Key Hit Session window until the progress bar is full, and the message "Thank you" appears at the bottom of the window (Figure 12.57).

   Figure 12.57 Random Pool

   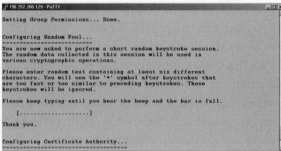

2. The next step is to initialize the internal CA for SIC. It may take a minute for the CA to initialize. Figure 12.58 displays the messages you will receive on the console while configuring the CA. Press **Enter** to initialize the CA.

   Figure 12.58 Configuring Certificate Authority

   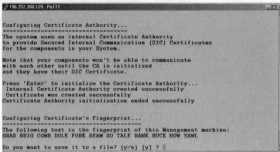

3. Once the CA is initialized successfully, you will be presented with the fingerprint of the management server. This fingerprint is unique to your CA and the certificate on your server. The first time your GUI clients connect to the management server, they will receive the fingerprint so that they can match it to the string listed here and verify that they are connecting to the correct manager. After the first connection, every time the clients connect to the management server, the fingerprint is verified. If the fingerprints

don't match, a warning message will be displayed, and the administrator can decide whether or not to continue with the connection. Type **y** and press **Enter** to save the fingerprint to a file.

4. Enter the filename and press **Enter**. The file will be saved in $CPDIR/conf.

Installation Complete

The configuration program will end, and you may see a few messages on the screen, such as "generating GUI-clients INSPECT code," as the system finishes up the installation of the VPN-1/FW-1 package. Finally, you will receive the following question, "Would You like to reboot the machine [y/n]:" (Figure 12.59). If you select not to reboot, you will exit the installation and go back to a shell prompt. If you choose to reboot, then the system will be restarted.

Figure 12.59 Installation Complete

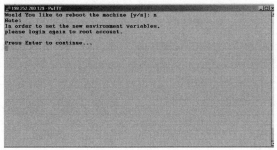

> **WARNING**
>
> If you are connected to this firewall remotely, you will not have access after rebooting. The firewall loads a policy named defaultfilter, which will prevent all access after an install.

1. Enter **n** for no and press **Enter**
2. Press **Enter** again to exit the installation script.

    Once you press **Enter**, you will be put back to the shell. The last message you received on the console was concerning new environment variables. Let's address these environment variables for a moment. The firewall will create a .profile in root's home directory, which runs the Check Point environment script located at /opt/CPshared/5.0/tmp/.CPprofile.sh (for bourne shell) or .CPprofile.csh (for c shell). This script sets the Check Point variables such as $FWDIR and $CPDIR, among others. See Figure 12.60 for a list of environment variables that are set on an install machine.

    Without setting these variables, various firewall commands will fail. For example, if you log in to the system as the standard user and type **su** to root instead of **su –**, you will maintain the standard user's environment; then when you try to run **fw unload localhost** to unload the defaultfilter, for example, you will receive the following error message: "ld.so.1: /etc/fw/bin/fw: fatal: libkeydb.so: open failed: No such file or directory Killed."

3. When you are ready to restart the server, type **sync; sync; reboot** and press **Enter**.

Figure 12.60 Environment Variables

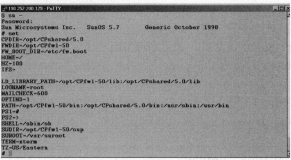

Unload defaultfilter Script

If you are performing a remote upgrade or install, you may run into trouble when you reboot at the end of the installation. Before a security policy is loaded, the system will install a default policy, called defaultfilter, which will block all access to the VPN-1/FW-1 host computer. You can log in to the console and verify that the filter is loaded with the 'fw stat' command:

```
# fw stat
HOST         POLICY      DATE
localhost defaultfilter  8Feb2002 16:51:48 :  [>hme1] [<hme1]
```

If you have access to the console, log in as root and unload the filter with the following command:

```
# fw unload localhost
Uninstalling Security Policy from all.all@NGtest
Done.
```

If you do not have access to the console, you could write a shell script to unload the filter and enable it in cron. Here's a sample unload.sh script that can be used for v4.1 firewalls:

```
#!/bin/sh
/etc/fw/bin/fw unload localhost
```

Unfortunately, this isn't enough in NG. The various environment variables in the $CPDIR/tmp/.CPprofile.sh have to be defined. To do this, simply copy the contents of the .CPprofile.sh file into the middle of the unload.sh script. Even before you reboot, you can test that the script works.

1. To enter the script in cron, first verify that you have enabled execute permissions on the file:

```
chmod +x unload.sh
```

2. Set your EDITOR environment variable to vi:

```
EDITOR=vi; export EDITOR
```

3. Edit cron with the following command:

```
crontab -e
```

4. Finally, enter the following line into your crontab file:

```
0,5,10,15,20,25,30,35,40,45,50,55 * * * * /usr/local/bin/unload.sh > /dev/null
2>&1
```

This command tells the system to run the unload.sh script every five minutes and redirect all output to /dev/null.

Now you can safely reboot the system and log back into it within a five-minute period from the time it is booted. Don't forget to remove (or at least comment out) the crontab entry once you are back in the firewall.

Getting Back to Configuration

Now that the installation is complete, you may need to get back into the Configuration screens that you ran through at the end of the installation. You can add, modify, or delete any of the previous configuration settings by running *cpconfig*.

If you did not log in as root or login and type **su –** to gain root access, your Check Point environment variables may not be set, and you could receive the following errors displayed as follows:

```
# /opt/CPshared/5.0/bin/cpconfig
You must setenv CPDIR before running this program
# CPDIR=/opt/CPshared/5.0; export CPDIR
# /opt/CPshared/5.0/bin/cpconfig
ld.so.1: /opt/CPshared/5.0/bin/cpconfig_ex: fatal: libcpconfca.so: open failed:
No such file or directory
        Can not execute cpconfig
```

If this happens, simply login with **su –**. The dash is an optional argument to su, which provides you with the environment that you would have, had you logged in directly as root. See Figure 12.61 for the output of cpconfig on Solaris.

Figure 12.61 cpconfig

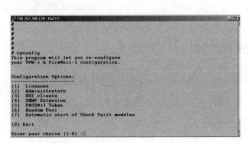

There are two options listed here that did not come up during the initial installation process. Number 5 configures a PKCS#11 Token, which enables you to install an add-on card such as an accelerator card, and number 7 enables you to configure the automatic start of Check Point modules at boot time.

If you installed Enforcement Module Only, the cpconfig screens will be a little different (see Figure 12.62). The two new choices are as follows:

- **Secure Internal Communication** Enables a one-time password that will be used for authentication between this Enforcement Module and its management server as well as any other remote modules that it might communicate with.

- **High Availability** Allows Enables this Enforcement Module to participate in a Check Point High Availability configuration with one or more other Enforcement Modules. This tab will not show up in this chapter's exercise installation since you cannot have a Management Module installed on an Enforcement Module in a CPHA cluster.

Figure 12.62 Secure Internal Communication Configuration

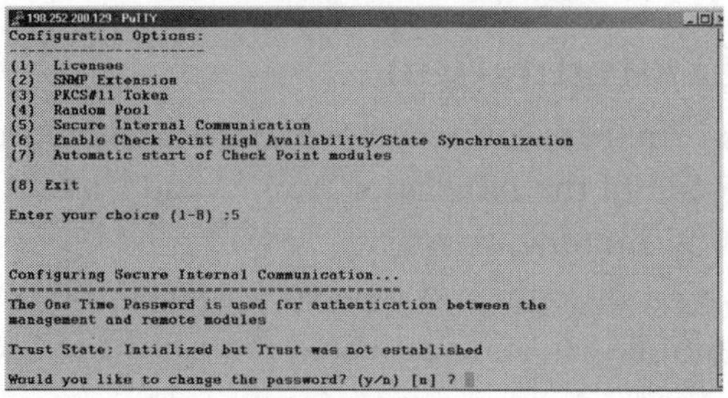

Figure 12.63 illustrates the High Availability option available from the *cpconfig* menu. If you enable high availability here, you will need to set up state synchronization between the firewalls that will be participating in the CPHA cluster.

Figure 12.63 High Availability Configuration

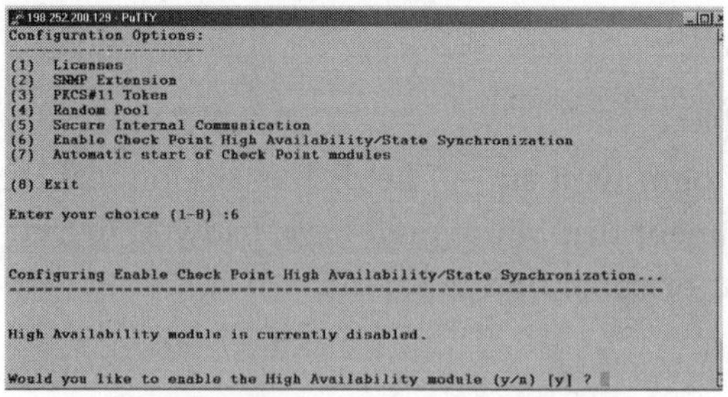

Uninstalling Check Point VPN-1/FireWall-1 NG on Solaris

When you uninstall Check Point VPN-1/FW-1 NG on Solaris, it is recommended that you make a full system backup before you begin. If you only need to back up the firewall configuration, then you should make a backup of /opt/ CP★ and /var/opt/CP★ directories. If you are removing a Primary Management Server, the first time you run *pkgrm*, the removal will fail. Check Point does this intentionally to ensure that you do not accidentally delete your Management Module without understanding that you will not be able to restore SIC to its current state after you remove it.

> **WARNING**
>
> When you remove the Check Point VPN-1/FW-1 software on your system, you will lose all configuration data. The uninstall process deletes all files and directories.

Uninstalling VPN-1 & FireWall-1

When you uninstall the firewall, you should remove the Check Point installed packages using the pkgrm program available on your Solaris system. The components should be removed in the following order:

1. Check Point VPN-1 & FireWall-1 NG
2. Check Point SVN Foundation NG

You can remove the Management Clients package at any time, but the order in which you remove the previously-listed packages is important. The following steps illustrate how to completely uninstall all Check Point products from your Solaris platform. You may wish to run the command *pkginfo* to see which Check Point packages you have installed before you start. The packages you are going to uninstall are listed in the following output.

```
# pkginfo | more
application CPclnt-50      Check Point Managment Clients NG
application CPfw1-50       Check Point VPN-1/FireWall-1 NG
         application CPshrd-50       Check Point SVN Foundation
```

1. Exit all GUI Client windows.
2. Log in to the firewall and su to root by entering **su** and pressing **Enter**.
3. Type **pkgrm** and press **Enter**. You will see a list of installed packages available for removal (as shown in Figure 12.64). In this example, you will choose the Check Point VPN-1/FW-1 NG package CPfw1-50, which is number two in the list.

Figure 12.64 Package Removal Choices

4. Type **CTRL + D**. You will then be presented with the following:

```
Select package(s) you wish to process (or 'all' to process all packages).
(default: all) [?,??,q]:
```

5. Type **2** and press **Enter** to uninstall the CPfw1-50 package.

6. Next, the system will ask you if you are sure you want to remove this package, as shown here. Type **y** for yes and press **Enter**.

```
Select package(s) you wish to process (or 'all' to process all packages).
(default: all) [?,??,q]: 2

The following package is currently installed:
   CPfw1-50         Check Point VPN-1/FireWall-1 NG
                    (sparc) 5.0


Do you want to remove this package? y
```

7. Next, the pkgrm program notifies you that the uninstall process will require the use of superuser privileges, and asks you if you want to continue (as shown next). Enter **y** for yes and press **Enter**.

```
## Removing installed package instance <CPfw1-50>
This package contains scripts which will be executed with super--user
permission during the process of removing this package.


Do you want to continue with the removal of this package [y,n,?,q] y
```

8. Next, the package removal will fail. Check Point has done this on purpose so that you can receive the WARNING notification that is displayed in the following output. This message informs you that if you uninstall VPN-1/FireWall-1, you will lose all configured SIC, and you will not be able to restore SIC to its current state by reinstalling the Primary Management Server. Run **pkgrm** again to uninstall the CPfw1-50 package.

```
## Verifying package dependencies.
## Processing package information.
## Executing preremove script.


There are no packages dependent on VPN-1/FireWall-1 NG installed.


******************************************************************


                    WARNING:
You are attempting to uninstall your Primary Management Server.r.
If you continue, you must then re-configure communication between
any Secondary Management Servers and other Check Point Modules,
```

even if you re-install the Primary Management Server on this machine.
Un-installation is aborting, if you still wish to uninstall
VPN-1/FireWall-50 primary management. Please run un-install again.

****

Please disregard the following error message:
pkgrm: ERROR: preremove script did not complete successfully.

Removal of <CPfw1-50> failed.
    #

9.   Press **CTRL + D**.

10.   Type **2** and press **Enter** to select the CPfw1-50 package.

11.   Type **y** for yes and press **Enter**.

12.   Type **y** for yes and press **Enter**. This time the package removal will be successful. Figures 2.65 and 2.66 show you some of the messages you will see on your console as the package is removed from the system.

Figure 12.65 Uninstall of VPN-1/FW-1

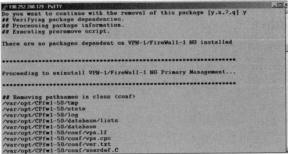

Figure 12.66 Uninstall of VPN-1/FW-1 Continued

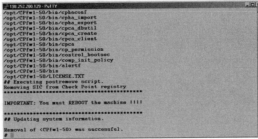

13.   Type **sync; sync; reboot** and press **Enter** to reboot the system.

Uninstalling SVN Foundation

You have already uninstalled the VPN-1/FW-1 software, but now you must remove the SVN Foundation. This should always be removed after all other Check Point components, which are built on top of this foundation (as the name suggests). If you had installed FloodGate-1 or the Policy Server, for example, these should also be removed prior to removing the SVN CPshrd-50 package.

1. Once the machine has rebooted, log back into the console.

2. Type **su -** and press **Enter** to become the superuser (root).

3. Type **pkgrm** and press **Enter**. Now your choices to uninstall are the Check Point Management Clients NG and the Check Point SVN Foundation (see the following output).

```
The following packages are available:
  1  CPclnt-50      Check Point Managment Clients NG
                    (sparc) 5.0

  2  CPshrd-50      Check Point SVN Foundation
                    (sparc) 5.0
```

4. Press **CTRL+ D**.

5. Type **2** and press **Enter** to select the SVN Foundation CPshrd-50 package.

6. When the pkgrm program asks you if you want to remove this program, enter **y** for yes and press **Enter**.

7. Again, pkgrm will print, "This package contains scripts that will be executed with super-user permission during the process of removing this package. Do you want to continue with the removal of this package [y,n,?,q]." Enter **y** for yes and press **Enter** to continue.

The following is a complete view of the uninstall process of the Check Point SVN Foundation on Solaris. You do not need to reboot after uninstalling the SVN package.

```
$ su -
Password:
Sun Microsystems Inc.    SunOS 5.7      Generic October 1998
# pkgrm


The following packages are available:
  1  CPclnt-50      Check Point Managment Clients NG
                    (sparc) 5.0

  2  CPshrd-50      Check Point SVN Foundation
                    (sparc) 5.0

  3  GNUbash        bash
                    (sparc) 2.03
```

```
  4  NOKIjre11       JAVA Runtime Environment V1.3.1 for Solaris
                        (SPARC) 1.3.1
  5  NOKInhm11       Nokia Horizon Manager
                        (sparc) 1.1
  6  NOKIssh11       F-SECURE SSH & SCP client for Nokia NHM
                        (SPARC) 1.3.7
  7  SMCgzip         gzip
                        (sparc) 1.3
  8  SUNWab2m        Solaris Documentation Server Lookup
                        (sparc) 2.00,REV=19980819
  9  SUNWadmap       System administration applications
                        (sparc) 11.7,REV=1998.09.10.20.16
 10  SUNWadmc        System administration core libraries
                        (sparc) 11.7,REV=1998.09.10.19.57


... 142 more menu choices to follow;
<RETURN> for more choices, <CTRL-D> to stop display:^D


Select package(s) you wish to process (or 'all' to process
all packages). (default: all) [?,??,q]: 2


The following package is currently installed:
    CPshrd-50       Check Point SVN Foundation
                        (sparc) 5.0


Do you want to remove this package? y


## Removing installed package instance <CPshrd-50>


This package contains scripts thatwhich will be executed with super-user
permission during the process of removing this package.


Do you want to continue with the removal of this package [y,n,?,q] y
## Verifying package dependencies.
## Processing package information.
## Executing preremove script.
There are no packages dependent on Check Point SVN Foundation NG installed.
rm: /opt/CPshared/5.0/tmp/fg_tmp is a directory
## Removing pathnames in class <conf>
/var/opt/CPshared/registry
```

```
/var/opt/CPshared/5.0/conf/sic_policy.conf

/var/opt/CPshared/5.0/conf/os.cps

/var/opt/CPshared/5.0/conf/cp.macro

...

/opt/CPshared/5.0/LICENSE.TXT

/opt/CPshared/5.0/../registry

## Executing postremove script.

## Updating system information.


Removal of <CPshrd-50> was successful.

#
```

Uninstalling Management Clients

The management clients do not really depend on the SVN foundation installation; therefore, you could really remove them at any time without any difficulty.

1. Run **pkgrm** again to remove the Management Clients package.

2. Press **CTRL + D**.

3. At the prompt, "Select package(s) you wish to process (or 'all' to process all packages). (default: all) [?,??,q]:", enter **1** and press **Enter** to select the Check Point Management Clients NG package (CPclnt-50).

4. Enter **y** for yes and press **Enter** when the pkgrm utility asks you, "Do you want to remove this package?"

5. Enter **y** for yes and press **Enter** when the pkgrm utility presents you with the following prompt, "This package contains scripts that will be executed with super-user permission during the process of removing this package. Do you want to continue with the removal of this package [y,n,?,q]."

The package will be removed. Figure 12.67 illustrates the end of the uninstall process for the management clients.

Figure 12.67 Management Clients Package Removal

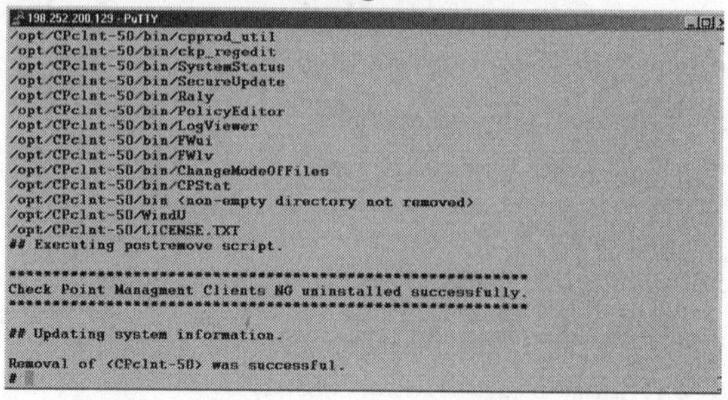

Installing Check Point VPN-1/FireWall-1 NG on Nokia

Check Point's Next Generation Enterprise Suite on the Nokia IPSO appliance is a popular combination. Mike Urban, a Professional Services Engineer at Integralis, explained it best when he said, "Nokia gateways are designed using a hardened UNIX OS specifically tuned for firewall performance and security. As such, they outperform general-purpose OS platforms like Solaris or NT when measuring maximum gateway throughput." Nokia provides a Web front-end, which they call Voyager (see Figure 12.68), for easy package management and system configuration, and they have one of the fastest fail-over mechanisms utilizing VRRP and Check Point's state synchronization, with an average fail-over time of just four seconds.

The first version of Check Point VPN-1/FW-1 NG to run on the Nokia platform was Feature Pack 1. NG FP1 requires Nokia IPSO 3.4.2 for installation. You can either order a Nokia box with Check Point preinstalled, or you can download the installation package from Check Point (with appropriate login ID) and install it yourself. If you need to upgrade your IPSO, you will need to obtain the IPSO image from Nokia support. It may be necessary to upgrade your boot manager prior to upgrading your IPSO image. Please read all release notes prior to installing new packages or images. It is not recommended to upgrade from 4.1 to NG if you have less than 128MB of memory; instead, do a fresh installation.

Figure 12.68 Nokia's Voyager GUI

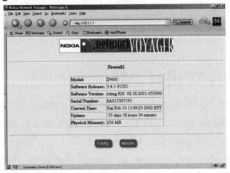

Installing the VPN-1/FireWall-1 NG Package

Since the Nokia appliance is already hardened, there is very little you need to do to prepare it for firewall installation. You must configure and test networking and DNS, set up the Host Address Assignment through the Voyager GUI, and you may need to upgrade your IPSO and boot manager.

Upgrading IPSO Images

If you are on an IPSO version prior to 3.3, it is recommended that you upgrade to 3.3 prior to upgrading to IPSO 3.4.2. You can downgrade from IPSO 3.4.2 to IPSO 3.2.1, 3.3, and 3.3.1 and 3.4. If you are upgrading your IPSO from 3.3 or 3.3.1, then you do not need to upgrade your boot manager prior to installing the new image. The *newimage* command will automatically upgrade the boot manager on IP300, IP600, IP500, IP100, and IP700 series appliances. You can download the 3.4.2 image from https://support.nokia.com (login required). Once you have the image in /var/admin, you can run newimage to install it. The options for *newimage* are given in Table 12.2.

Table 12.2 newimage Command Line Arguments

Switch for newimage	Description
-k	Enables you to upgrade the IPSO image and keep all currently active packages so they will be started upon reboot.
-R	Sets the new image to be used upon the next reboot.
-l <path to image>	Tells the newimage command where to find the ipso.tgz file, which contains the new image.
-T	Enables you to perform a test boot with the new image.
-I	Sets the newimage command in interactive mode. Use this if you need to FTP the file or use the CD-ROM drive (IP440 only) to upgrade the IPSO image.
-b	Forces upgrade of bootmgr.

Assuming that you have the ipso.tgz file downloaded to /var/admin, and your system is on IPSO 3.3 or 3.3.1, the recommended command to upgrade your IPSO image is as follows:

```
newimage -k -R -l /var/admin
```

After updating the image, reboot your system:

```
sync; sync; reboot
```

Installing VPN-1/FireWall-1 NG

To install the VPN-1/FW-1 NG package, you must first install the SVN Foundation and then the VPN-1/FW-1 package. You will need to get the software from Check Point or from a Check Point reseller, since Nokia does not provide VPN-1/FW-1 packages on their support Web site any longer. Follow the step-by-step procedure to install the new package. See Table 12.3 for available arguments to the *newpkg* command.

Table 12.3 newpkg Command Line Arguments

Switch for newpkg	Description
-i	Installs the package, but does not activate it. Prompts you for media type, new packages and old packages that you wish to install or upgrade.
-s <server>	Specifies the FTP server IP address.
-l <username>	Enter the FTP user name (you don't need to enter a username if you will be using anonymous FTP).
-p <password>	Enter the FTP user's password.
-m <CDROM | AFTP | FTP | LOCAL>	Choose the media type. Available options are CDROM, AFTP, FTP or LOCAL.

Continued

Table 12.3 newpkg Command Line Arguments

Switch for newpkg	Description
-d	Prints debug messages.
-v	Verbose mode for FTP.
-n <new package>	Enter the full pathname of the new package you are installing.
-o <old package>	Enter the full pathname of the package you are upgrading from.
-S	This sets the newpkg to install the package silently. If you enable silent mode, you must specify the following arguments: -o, -m, -n and possibly –s and -l, –p if the media type is not LOCAL.
-h	Prints the usage for newpkg (help).

1. Put the following package files in /var/admin. This example will be using the NG FP1 packages since they are the most recent as of this writing.

   - SVN Foundation – cpshared_NG_FP1_0022_1_nokia_packages.tgz

   - VPN-1/FW-1 – fw1_NG_FP1_51012_5_nokia_packages.tgz

NOTE

Do not unzip or untar the Nokia packages. When you run the *newpkg* command, it will do that for you.

2. From the /var/admin directory, type **newpkg –i** and press **Enter**. The newpkg installation program will begin, and will ask you where to install the new package, as shown.

```
fwlab1[admin]# newpkg -i


Load new package from the following:

1. Install from CD-ROM.

2. Install from anonymous FTP server.

3. Install from FTP server with user and password.

4. Install from local filesystem.

5. Exit new package installation.


Choose an installation method (1-5):  4


Enter pathname to the packages [ or 'exit' to exit ]: .
```

```
Loading Package List

Processing package cpshared_NG_FP1_0022_1_nokia_package.tgz ...
Package Description: Check Point SVN Foundation NG Feature Pack 1 (Sun Dec 23
19
:05:20 IST 2001 Build 0022)


Would you like to  :

1. Install this as a new package

2. Upgrade from an old package

3. Skip this package

4. Exit new package installation


            Choose (1-4): 1
```

3. Choose the option for local filesystem (number **4)** and press **Enter**.

4. When you are prompted for the pathname to the package, type a period (**.**) for your current directory (which is /var/admin) and press **Enter**.

5. The newpkg program will locate any packages located in this directory and begin processing them one by one. The Check Point SVN Foundation NG package will be presented to you. Choose **1** to install this as a new package and press **Enter**.

    Once the newpkg program has begun, it will process each package in the current directory until it has run through them all. If a package comes up that is already installed, or if you don't want to install it, choose option 3 to skip the package and continue on with the others. You should reboot your Nokia appliance after each new Check Point package that you install; do not install them all simultaneously.

6. When the installation of SVN is finished, exit the newpkg installation and reboot with the command **sync; sync; reboot**.

7. When the system boots up, log in to Voyager and enable the SVN package.

    - Click **Manage Installed Packages.**

    - Turn on the new NG SVN package.

    - Click **Apply** then **Save**.

8. When done in Voyager, type **newpkg –i** from the /var/admin directory and press **Enter**.

9. Choose the option for localfile system (number **4**) and press **Enter**.

10. Type a period (**.**) for your current directory (/var/admin) and press **Enter**.

11. If you have an earlier version of VPN-1/FW-1 installed, choose to number **2** to upgrade this package from an old package.

12. Choose the package you are upgrading from the available choices.

13. Verify that you want to continue and that the correct packages are being processed by pressing **Enter**.

14. When the installation is complete, exit the newpkg installation and reboot by typing: **sync; sync; reboot**.

Configuring VPN-1/FireWall-1 NG on Nokia

If VPN-1/FW-1 NG is installed on your Nokia appliance, but it hasn't been configured, you must run *cpconfig* before attempting to start the new package. If you just received your Nokia fresh from the factory, and NG is installed, then you will still need to run cpconfig before the package will run properly. This is because you must accept the license agreement, choose what components you want to run (Management and/or Enforcement Module), and configure licenses, administrators, GUI clients, etc. The configuration options are the same as the options on the Solaris platform. See Figure 12.69 for the output of cpconfig on an NG FP1 Nokia appliance.

Figure 12.69 cpconfig on Nokia

After the NG package is installed on your system, you must run cpconfig to configure the package. Follow these steps to configure and activate your VPN-1/FW-1 NG package.

1. Run *cpconfig* and go through each screen. It is recommended that you do not enter **CTRL + C** at any time during the initial cpconfig configuration screens.

2. When finished with *cpconfig*, log in to Voyager and enable your NG package (see Figure 12.70).

   - Click **Manage Installed Packages**.

   - Turn off the old FW-1 package.

   - Turn on the new NG FP1 package.

   - Click on **Apply** then **Save**.
     The Nokia package management makes it simple to back out of an upgrade. As you can see in Figure 12.70, it is easy to toggle back and forth between installed packages. You can also switch back and forth between IPSO images from Voyager's Manage IPSO Images page. After enabling or disabling a package or IPSO image, you must reboot your firewall.

Figure 12.70 Managing Installed Packages

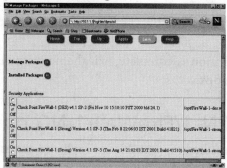

> **NOTE**
>
> Remember to always click **Apply** and then **Save** when making changes in the Voyager GUI. If you don't save your changes, they will not be retained on a reboot.

3. After making changes to the FW-1 packages, you must reboot the system again. You can either restart the system from the Voyager GUI, or exit Voyager and type **sync; sync; reboot** to restart the box.

Summary

The beginning of this chapter started by preparing you to install the Check Point VPN-1/FW-1 NG product on a computer. There are several steps you can take to prepare your host computer prior to turning it into a firewall. First, make sure that your hardware meets and/or exceeds the minimum system requirements provided by Check Point. You will then need to install a base operating system, apply OS patches, configure and test your network interface cards and DNS, enable IP forwarding, disable any unnecessary services, and populate your host's file with at least the external IP address of your firewall, which is configured on the first interface card in your computer.

Next, you will need to prepare for the various Check Point installation screens, you should know in advance which server/gateway components to choose and you should be prepared for the initial configuration options by obtaining a license in advance, deciding on administrator usernames, passwords, and privileges, and statically assigning IP addresses to your administrator's workstations so that you can add them as GUI clients.

If you are installing the VPN-1/FW-1 NG software on a Windows server, you can start the installation wizard by inserting the CD or running windows\wrapper\demo32.exe. The SVN Foundation will be installed before any other Check Point components. After the installation wizard has finished copying files, it will run through the initial configuration screens of Licenses, Administrators, GUI Clients, and the CA initialization screens. Once the configuration is complete, you will need to reboot your firewall. To run the Configuration tool again, go to **Start | Programs | Check Point Management Clients | Check Point Configuration NG.**

To uninstall the VPN-1/FW-1 NG software from a Windows System, you must uninstall the SVN Foundation last. As the name suggests, this is the base of the VPN-1/FW-1 install, and it cannot be removed prior to removing any components that depend on it. After uninstalling VPN-1/FW-1 you must reboot.

If you are installing the VPN-1/FW-1 NG software on Solaris 2.7 or 2.8, make sure you have the correct patches applied and that you are in either 32- or 64-bit mode according to the system requirements in Table 12.1 in the beginning of the chapter. If you are installing from files, then you should unzip and untar the package, and then run *pkgadd −d.* from the directory where the package is located. The SVN Foundation package must be installed prior to installing VPN-1/FW-1; the UnixInstallScript will take care of this for you. After the installation program has finished copying files, you will go through the initial configuration screens, which are Licenses, Administrators, GUI Clients, SNMP Extension, Group Permissions, and CA initialization. You can configure the firewall again at any time by running the *cpconfig* command. After installing VPN-1/FW-1, you must reboot.

After rebooting your firewall, a defaultfilter policy will be installed that prohibits all connections to the firewall server. You can unload the defaultfilter with the command *fw unload localhost.* Keep in mind that you must su to root with the dash (*su -*) in order to obtain the right environment variables to run the *fw unload* and most other FW-1 commands, including *cpconfig.*

To uninstall VPN-1/FW-1 on Solaris, use the *pkgrm* command. The first time you try to remove a Primary Management Server, the uninstall will fail. Simply run *pkgrm* a second time to successfully remove the package. Reboot your computer after uninstalling the VPN-1/FW-1 NG package.

If you are installing the VPN-1/FW-1 NG package on a Nokia appliance, make sure that you are using IPSO 3.4.2 before you begin. Like all the other platforms, you must install the SVN Foundation prior to installing the VPN-1/FW-1 package. Also, you should reboot after each new package you install. You can toggle between installed packages in the Voyager GUI under the Manage Installed Packages link. Be sure to click **Apply** and **Save** after making any changes in Voyager. After the Check Point VPN-1/FW-1 package is installed, you must run *cpconfig* in order to finish the installation procedure.

## Chapter 13

Using the Graphical Interface

Best Damn Topics in this Chapter:

- Managing Objects

- Adding Rules

- Global Properties

- SecureUpdate

- Log Viewer

- System Status

Introduction

Once you have the VPN-1/FW-1 software installed and configured, you are ready to log into the graphical user interface (GUI) and start composing your objects and rule bases. In this chapter we will walk you through all the options you have for creating various objects and we will show you some of the nice features that you can use in the policy editor to manipulate your rules.

We will show you how to access the firewall's implied rules, and we will explain the global properties that affect every security policy you create. It's important to know why your firewall is allowing pings, if you have not explicitly defined them in your rule base.

After paying a lot of attention to your policy options, we will then show you how to access your firewall logs and system status. The Track options you choose in your policy will affect the outcome of your logs. You may choose to log some rules and not others. We will also describe ways to make certain selections in your Log Viewer so that you can view only logs for a specific source IP address, or logs for a specific user. The Check Point Log Viewer has a really high quality interface, and is easy to understand.

Managing Objects

Managing objects is probably the thing you'll be doing most often as a firewall administrator. Luckily for you, Check Point has made this task much easier than you might think. While there is still a lot of information needed to set the foundation for your rule base, you needn't put forth a great deal of effort to get that information into a useable format.

Your first task is to log into the FW-1 GUI management client. On a Windows system, simply start the Policy Editor or your GUI client by double-clicking its icon. On a Unix system such as Solaris or AIX, execute the *fwpolicy* command found in $FWDIR/bin. You'll be presented with a login window, as displayed in Figure 13.1. Note that if this is the initial connection from a GUI client, FW-1 will present the management server fingerprint. This is used as a security measure to enable you to validate the identity of that management server.

Once you have logged into the GUI, you'll see a lot of information. Don't worry; you can easily customize this default view to show you just what you need. You can also add or subtract from this view as needed. A couple of changes have been made from previous versions of the policy editor. Figure 13.1 shows you the new default view.

Figure 13.1 Policy Editor

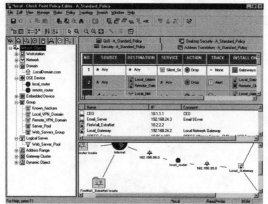

The windowpanes are called (from left moving clockwise) the Objects Tree, Rule Base, Objects List, and Topology Map. You can toggle which one is displayed by selecting **View** from the Policy Editor menu, as displayed in Figure 13.2.

Figure 13.2 View Selection

The Objects Tree gives you a concise and orderly view of the defined objects of each available type. If your manager asks which networks are defined, here's the place that will give you the quickest answer. Next is the rule base. This enables you to instantly sum up the totality of what your firewall is enforcing, but it also enables you to quickly view Network Address Translation (NAT), Quality of Service (QoS) and Desktop Security rule information. Below the rule base you'll find the Objects List, which presents a little more detail than the Objects Tree about your defined objects. The final pane in this window is our "belle of the ball," as it were. New in FireWall-1 NG (assuming you've purchased the Visual Policy Editor) is the Topology Map. This gives you a handsome network map showing the interconnections of all your defined objects. Figure 13.3 shows the Topology Map pane enlarged to full screen.

Figure 13.3 Topology Map

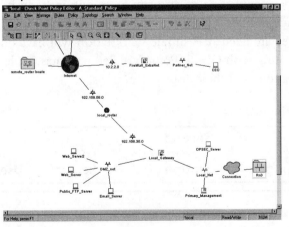

The neat thing is that this map is completely interactive. You can rearrange the placement of the objects and even query them for information, and alter their configuration.

Network Objects

Network objects are, as the name states, simply the objects within your network. An object can be a network range, a group of users, or a single workstation, as examples. Objects can also be groups of other objects, allowing a hierarchical layering and a more concise rule base. More importantly, you must have properly defined the objects of interest within your network before using them in a FW-1 rule.

Network objects can be defined in any of several ways, with the most common method being through the Network Objects Manager, which is shown in Figure 13.4. This GUI window enables you to create, delete, and alter all of the various types of network entities. To access this screen, select **Manage | Network Objects** from the Policy Editor GUI.

Figure 13.4 Network Objects Manager

Workstation

The workstation object defines a single computer, and contains many options. This computer may be a simple workstation, a VPN-1/Firewall-1 system, a third-party VPN device, a gateway, a host, or any combination of these. This flexibility comes with a slight increase in complexity. The Workstation properties page contains a great many more options than its counterpart in previous versions of FW-1, but luckily there is intelligence built in to the window. The branches on the left become visible as they are needed. A simple workstation will have limited options, but the choices expand when dealing with Check Point installed products. Table 13.1 defines some of the more common configurations and their displayed options.

Table 13.1 Configuration Matrix

VPN-1/ FireWall-1	Floodgate-1	Second Management Station	Log Server	UserAuthority	Web Plugin
General	X	X	X	X	X
Topology	X	X	X	X	X
NAT	X	X		X	X
VPN	X			X	
Authentication	X				X
Management	X	X		X	X
Advanced	X	X	X	X	X

The General configuration window, as shown in Figure 13.5, enables you to associate a system name and an IP address with this object. If the name is resolvable via something like DNS, then you can use the **Get Address** button to retrieve the IP address, or else you can type it in manually. The comment field is optional. In common with all FireWall-1 objects, you can assign a color to the object. The remaining fields have special meanings when selected, which impact the way VPN-1/FireWall-1 interacts with them.

Figure 13.5 Workstation Properties, General Window

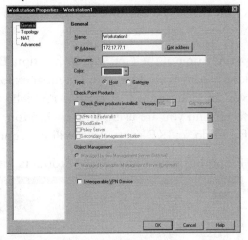

- **Type** Select if this device is a gateway or a host. Note the caution in the sidebar relating to gateway address specification. If this device is a gateway, then rules selected as installed on gateways will be enforced on this system.

- **Check Point Products** This enables you to identify the workstation device as running Check Point software. If the checkbox is selected, the options in Object Management will become active, as will the **Get Version** button. **Interoperable VPN Device** is an exclusive selection, thus it will become grayed out. Also, the **Management, Authentication** and **VPN** branches will become visible, and sub-menus will become available under the **Advanced** branch. You will also see the **Secure Internal Communication** option, which enables you to establish the link between Check Point installed products. Figure 13.6 illustrates the properties window as it appears when this option is selected.

- **Object Management** Here you specify whether the Check Point product specified on the workstation object is internal (managed) or external (not managed) to the management server.

- **Interoperable VPN Device** This enables you to denote this object as an interoperable VPN unit. This means that, while no Check Point software is installed on the device, it is still capable of performing IKE encryption for the purpose of establishing a VPN. If this option is checked, you'll have access to the VPN branch of the Workstation Properties. Interoperable VPN devices are only allowed to use IKE encryption, unlike VPN-1/FW-1 VPN setups.

What's in a Name?

The only requirement for the **Name** field is that it must be unique. However, it is strongly recommended that you use an actual resolvable name. It is also strongly recommended that you include the hostname to address mappings in your systems host files. These files can be found in the following locations:

■ For Unix systems, edit the /etc/hosts and /etc/networks files

■ For Win32 systems, edit the %SYSTEMDIR%\system32\drivers\etc\hosts and %SYSTEMDIR%\system32\drivers\etc\networks

This will ensure the proper function of the Get Address function. Be wary, however, to maintain these files. Hostname and address changes could lead to potential exposure if not done properly.

Also, if the workstation you are defining is a gateway (a multi-homed system that is able to pass traffic between its interfaces), and you are using IKE encryption, be sure to include specify the **outside** address. If you fail to do so, IKE encryption will not function properly!

Figure 13.6 Workstation Properties with Check Point Products Installed

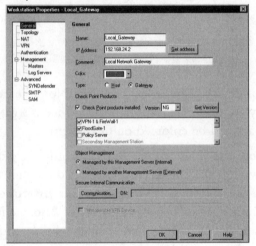

Network

The network object defines a group of hosts or, more specifically, a network range such as a subnet. When defining individual systems as Workstations becomes too tedious or otherwise untenable, it is quite easy to arrange them with the network object type. To create a new Network object, select **New | Network** from the Network Objects management window. This will present you with the panel as shown in Figure 13.7.

The General window allows some simple configuration information to be entered, such as IP address, netmask, and a comment. Note that the portion of the IP address that specifies the host is ignored. We're assuming you are already familiar (at least slightly) with IP subnetting. In the example panel, the network is 10.3.4.X, with a 24-bit subnet, producing a mask of 255.255.255.0. In this case, you enter the host portion as a zero. Keep in mind, though, that the host portion might not always be set as zero, and might not always fall on a tidy boundary. For example, you might have a network address of 10.3.4.128, with a subnet of 255.255.255.128. When in doubt, consult your local networking expert. As with all object types, a color can be assigned as well. The last field, **Broadcast address:**, is used to specify whether the broadcast address will be included within the defined network. The broadcast address is defined as the last possible IP within that range.

The NAT panel is the familiar one, which includes the option to establish automatic translation rules. Nothing extraordinary here.

Figure 13.7 Network Properties—General Window

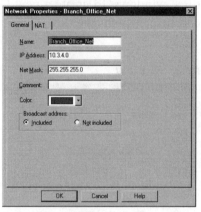

Domain

Another method to group hosts by commonly used techniques is to use the domain object. A machine is determined to be within the domain if a reverse DNS lookup on the machine's IP address yields the proper domain information. Figure 13.8 illustrates this panel, which is accessed by selecting **New | Domain** from the Network Objects management window.

Figure 13.8 Domain Properties

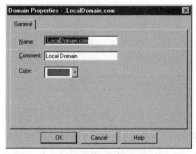

Notice that in the above example the domain name begins with a period. You may be wondering how FW-1 knows what to do with a domain object. When a domain object is used in the rule base as a source or destination, FW-1 will attempt to do a reverse DNS lookup (that is, getting the name for a specified IP) on the appropriate portion of the incoming packet. If the lookup yields the domain information, then you have a match. It is probably obvious that if there is no reverse record, the object will be useless. It is also possible that, through DNS poisoning, this sort of object could lead to a security breach. For these reasons and others, Check Point does not recommend the use of domain objects in your rule base. If you decide to use them, use them as close to the bottom of the rule base as possible.

OSE Device

Open Security Extension technology allows FW-1 to manage third-party devices that support these extensions. Most notable among these devices are Cisco routers running IOS v9 and later. The number of devices that you may manage depends on your license. The configuration for an OSE compliant device features three windows. To create a new OSE Device, select **New | OSE Device** from the Network Objects management window. Figure 13.9 illustrates the General window.

Figure 13.9 OSE Device—General Window

This window enables you to specify some of the basic information about the device, specifically the IP address, name, comment, and device type. The device type may be any of the following:

- BayRS
- Cisco
- 3Com

When a device from this category is managed by the firewall, access control lists are generated based on the security policy and downloaded to the firewall. As with other object types, the **Get address** button will attempt to resolve the specified name to an IP address, saving you that one step.

The topology window is identical to that of its counterpart for the other devices. The main caveat is that at least one interface must be defined (as opposed to, say, a simple workstation) or the ACL entries will not be created successfully. Anti-spoofing and its kin are also defined by editing the interface properties, just as with a workstation. However, there are some additional steps to take, which are accomplished by editing the information on the Setup window.

The Setup window varies depending on the OSE Type specified on the General window. The window as displayed with a Cisco router is displayed in Figure 13.10.

Figure 13.10 Cisco OSE Setup Window

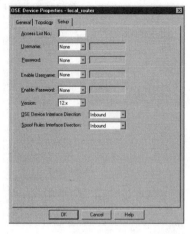

The fields displayed on this window have the following meanings:

- **Access List No.** The number of the ACL that will be applied.

- **Username** This is the exec mode username that will be used for initial access to the device. It, along with the remaining drop-down lists, can be set to **None**, **Known**, or **Prompt**. If set to **Known**, the gray box to the right will become active and allow the entry of a username.

- **Password** Enter the password associated with the exec mode username.

- **Enable Username** The name, if any, of a user with privileged exec access.

- **Enable Password** The password associated with the privileged username.

- **Version** IOS version installed on this router.

- **OSE Device Interface Direction** The direction in which to enforce the security policy. This can be **Inbound**, **Outbound**, or **Eitherbound**.

- **Spoof Rules Interface Direction** The direction in which to enforce anti-spoofing behavior. This can be **Inbound**, **Outbound**, or **Eitherbound**.

The fields for the 3Com and Bay devices are similar in their requirements, and the security policy is enforced in an identical manner.

Embedded Device

An embedded device is defined as a device on which a VPN/FW-1 module or Inspection module is installed. This type of object is restricted to two types (as defined in the **Type** field) with those being Nokia IP5*x* and Xylan with the supported platforms being Ramp and Xylan.

The configuration is pretty straightforward, with the common rules applying. Define the name, IP address, and an optional comment. Then specify the type, and select **VPN-1 &**

FireWall-1 installed if applicable. You must also define your license type. Figure 13.11 illustrates the configuration panel. To open this panel, select **New | Embedded Device**.

Figure 13.11 Embedded Device General Properties

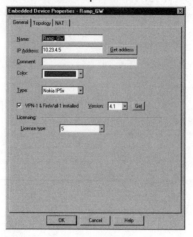

Group

The Group object can be used to manage other objects of dissimilar types. There are three types of groups that you may define within FW-1. To create a new group, select **New | Group** from the Network Objects management window. The group types are as follows:

- Simple Group
- Group with Exclusion
- UAS High Availability group

A simple group is just that. Simple. It is a collection of network devices. The second group type, Group with Exclusion, allows you some granular control over the contents of a group. If you are working in a network with a flat topology, for example, you may be in a situation where there isn't much physical separation within this network. A group of this type enables you to force some structure here. Figure 13.12 illustrates a simple group.

Figure 13.12 Group Properties

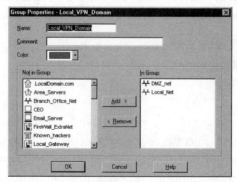

A Group with Exclusion is slightly different than a Simple group, with the difference being that you specify a major group, defined by Check Point as an "outer group." This will be the group that is included for this definition. You then specify minor, or inner, groups. These will be the groups culled out and excluded from the major group.

Logical Server

The logical server group (available by selecting **New | Logical Server** from the Network Objects window) enables you to group like servers (FTP, HTTP, SMTP, etc) to be treated as one and used in a sort of resource sharing, or server pooling. Note that this is an optional feature and may not be included with your FW-1 installation. Workload is distributed among these servers in a user-configurable manner. Figure 13.13 shows the configuration options for this object type.

Figure 13.13 Logical Server Properties Window

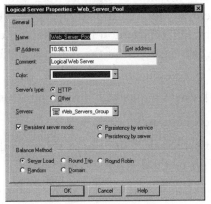

As usual, the name must be entered, and, if resolvable, the **Get address** button can be used to gather the associated IP address. A special note is in order here, specifically regarding the IP you'll select. This address should be that of a non-existent server located on the same network as the destination servers, but can also be that of the FireWall-1 module. Think of this IP as a virtual IP address. It will be used by the clients to connect to the Logical Server group, and therefore cannot belong to any one member of that group.

The **Server's Type** feature really is poorly named. This actually defines the method of load balancing, or even more specifically, the type of algorithm used. The two methods behave very differently. For example, with HTTP selected, only the initial connection will be handled by the logical server address. A redirection is sent to the client informing his or her browser of the new IP (that of the selected destination server), and the remainder of the conversation goes forth without the intervention of the firewall module. If **Other** is selected as the type, address translation is performed and the conversation is balanced per connection, with the firewall module constantly involved, unless **Persistent Server mode** is checked.

The **Servers** section enables you to select the server group that will make up this logical group. If selected, **Persistent server mode** allows some fine-tuning of the balancing mechanism. When enabled, you can enforce connection persistence, meaning you can force packets from an established flow to continue to a single destination. This is very useful for something like an

HTTP conversation when using **Other** as the server type. You can select between two modes here, **Persistency by service** and **Persistency by server**. The main difference between the two is that, when the former is selected, only connections to a single server for a single service will have persistency enforced, while in the latter any service on a specific server will be impacted.

The final settings define the type of balancing to be performed. The Balance Method has several possible options.

- **Server Load** FW-1 sends a query, using port 18212/UDP, to determine the load of each server. There must consequently be a load-measuring agent on each server to support this method.

- **Round Trip** FW-1 sends a simple ICMP ping to each server. The fastest round-trip time is chosen as the preferred server. This lacks somewhat, in that the ping is from the firewall to the server, and may not be optimal from a remote client (remember, the servers need not be centrally located to participate in a server group). Also, a ping doesn't tell you that the HTTP daemon has crashed on the server. As long as the server is up and on the network, regardless of the status of any of its services, traffic will be sent to it.

- **Round Robin** FW-1 selects sequentially from a list. This is among the simplest methods.

- **Random** FW-1 selects randomly from a list.

- **Domain** FW-1 attempts to select the closest server to the client, based on domain naming convention. This method is not recommended.

Address Range

An address range defines a sequential range of IP addresses for inclusion with your rule base. An address range is similar in use to a network object, with the major difference being that you specify a starting and ending IP address instead of a network number and subnet mask. Figure 13.14 illustrates the General panel for this object type, which is available by selecting **New | Address Range** from the Network Objects management window. As usual, the NAT panel features no special information and is the same as that found on most other object types.

Figure 13.14 Address Range Properties Window

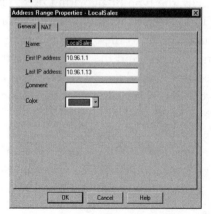

Gateway Cluster

A gateway cluster is a grouping of machines running VPN-1/FW-1 that is grouped together as a means of fail-over support. Clustering is a complex subject, and configuring it is much more detailed than the majority of other object types. First, you have to visit the **Global Properties** and, under the **Gateway High Availability** branch, place a checkmark in the setting to **Enable gateway clusters**.

The next step is to create your workstation objects. In order to support clustering, you must have at least three objects, two of which must be firewall modules, and one a manager. The work-station object should be created as normal for a machine with FW-1 installed. It is important that the interfaces are properly defined, as anti-spoofing is required for proper high-availability func-tion. Next, you create a new gateway cluster object. The General panel is illustrated in Figure 13.15. You'll access this panel by selecting **New | Gateway** Cluster from the Network Objects management window.

Figure 13.15 Gateway Cluster—General Panel

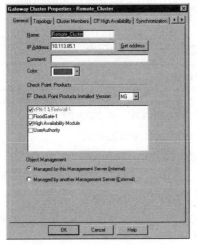

This panel allows the initial configuration for the cluster. The name and IP address are defined here, as are the specific Check Point products that will reside within this cluster. Also, you can specify whether you or another party manage the cluster. You also can specify, on the topology panel, which addresses reside behind this cluster. This is similar to the features on a workstation object's interface properties topology panel.

Dynamic Object

A dynamic object is perhaps the most interesting object type supported on FW-1. It is also one of the most useful in a large enterprise. This object type enables you to define a logical server type, one in which the actual IP address will resolve differently on each FW-1 machine. This enables you to create rules referencing "mail server" and distribute that policy to several different FW-1 machines, all of which will resolve "mail server" as the proper machine within their realm. Figure 13.16 shows you the basic configuration window, which you can see by selecting **New | Dynamic Object** from the Network Objects management window.

Figure 13.16 Dynamic Object Properties Window

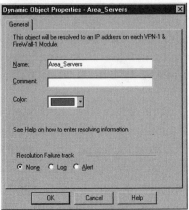

The real key to a dynamic object is the *dynamic_objects* command. This command is run on the firewall module where the name will be resolved, and enables you to specify the values to which it will resolve. Table 13.2 describes this command and its options.

Table 13.2 Dynamic_Objects Command Options

Option	Explanation
-o <object name>	Specify the object name to work with. This option is often used with operators such as –a to add addresses to an existing object.
-r <address range>	Specify an address range.
-a <address range>	Add address of <range> to object.
-d <address range>	Delete addresses from the object.
-l	List all dynamic objects.
-n <object name>	Create a new dynamic object; assuming the VPN-1/FW-1 process has been stopped.
-c	Compare the defined dynamic objects to those defined in the objects.C file.
-do <object name>	Delete the specified object.

Services

The services objects give you a finer level of access control as compared to exclusive use of network entities. With the service object, you can define protocol specific information, like protocol in use (TCP, UDP, and so forth), and port numbers. FW-1 comes preconfigured with many of the more common services in use today, and further enables you to create custom services based on your unique needs.

To add, modify, or delete services, access the Services window by clicking **Manage | Services**. From here, you will be able to act on the following service types.

TCP

The TCP service object enables you to define a basic TCP service. Figure 13.17 illustrates this service type, using the domain-tcp (DNS) service as an example. To bring up this window, select **New | TCP** from the Services management window.

Figure 13.17 TCP Service Properties

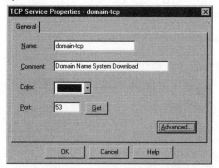

The information required for this service is very limited (which is nice when you have to define a lot of them!). Besides a name and comment, all you have to enter is the destination port number. This can be a specific port, as in Figure 13.17, a range (e.g. 1024-1028), or a greater-than/less-than definition (e.g. <56). There is also an **Advanced** button, which displays the window as shown in Figure 13.18.

Figure 13.18 Advanced TCP Service Properties

The Advanced settings enable you to specify a source port, and allow for the same modifiers as in the General panel's port specification. You can also specify the protocol type, which impacts which security server will provide things like content security for this service. The checkbox marked **Enable for TCP resource**, if checked, enforces screening using a UFP server, mitigating the intervention of a security server. The next item, **Match for 'Any'** allows connections using this service to be matched when a rule is crafted with 'Any' as the service. The **Session Timeout** is a local setting meant to allow override of the global session timeout. The inclusion of the timeout in the GUI is a nice change for FW-1 NG. In previous versions, setting a per-service timeout required manual editing of the base.def file, which is obviously a bit more involved.

UDP

The UDP service object enables you to define a basic UDP service. An example of this is the TFTP service. UDP tracking poses a problem for many firewalls, especially circuit level gateways. Since UDP is connectionless, it's generally an all-or-nothing approach to security. Whole port ranges are often opened to allow UDP traffic, which is not a very nice notion. With FW-1, a second mechanism has been designed to keep track of a virtual "connection."

The General properties are identical to those for TCP, as seen in Figure 13.17. The Advanced options are slightly different, and are shown in Figure 13.19.

Figure 13.19 Advanced UDP Service Properties

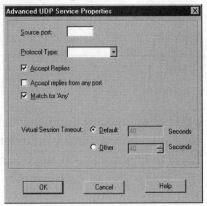

As with the TCP settings, we are able to specify a source port and a protocol type. Additionally, we have the familiar checkboxes, but this time with slightly different values. These are as follows:

- **Accept Replies**   If checked, allows for a bi-directional communication to take place.

- **Accept replies from any port**   Allows the server to reply from any port. An example of the need for this is the TFTP service.

- **Match for 'Any'**   Allows connections using this service to be matched when a rule is crafted with 'Any' as the service.

RPC

RPC services are usually tricky for a firewall administrator. RPC-based connections do not use a fixed port number, so allowing these types of connections is either an all-or-nothing exercise. Usually, administrators choose to block all RPC connections on their external firewalls, while being far more permissive within their network boundaries.

To alleviate this potential risk, FW-1 transparently tracks RPC ports. Application information is extracted from the packet in order to identify the program used. FW-1 also maintains a cache that maps RPC program numbers to the assigned port numbers. The configuration panel, viewed by selecting **New | RPC** from the Service management window, is shown in Figure 13.20.

Figure 13.20 RPC Service Properties

ICMP

ICMP is used for things like network troubleshooting and discovery. Unfortunately, attackers looking to gain information about you can also use it. For this reason, many sites decide to block all ICMP traffic. This isn't really necessary, and may cause more problems than it solves. You can, using FW-1, pick and choose the specific ICMP types (and even sub types, or "codes") allowed. Table 13.3 details some of the more useful ICMP types, their associated codes, and their meanings, as defined by the IANA (www.iana.org/assignments/icmp-parameters).

Table 13.3 ICMP Codes

ICMP Type	ICMP Code	Explanation
0		Echo (ping) reply
3		Destination unreachable:
	0	-network unreachable
	1	-host unreachable
	2	-protocol unreachable
	3	-port unreachable
	4	Dropped because DF (do not fragment) bit was set, fragmentation needed
	5	Source routing not allowed or otherwise failed
4		Slow transmission rate
5		Better network path available:
	0	-for entire network
	1	-for specific host
	2	-for tos and entire network
	3	-for tos and specific host
8		Echo (ping) request
11		Time exceeded for reason:
	0	-TTL reached 0 in transit
	1	-fragment reassembly time exceeded
12		Bad IP header

Figure 13.21 shows us the configuration panel for an ICMP service. Using Table 13.3, you can see how simple it would be to create services, and thus rules, to allow the beneficial types of ICMP while excluding those that may do you harm.

Figure 13.21 ICMP Service Properties

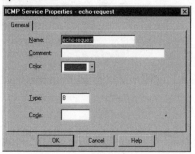

Other

Often called *user-defined* services, this is a catchall for whatever is missing. Its presence gives you a great deal of flexibility, but requires at least a familiarity with the inspect language. The General panel is similar to that found in its cousin objects, allowing you to define a name, add a comment, and assign a color. It also enables you to define the protocol identifier. This is a very important field, as it is the key to matching against the incoming traffic. Figure 13.22 shows you the General panel for this service type.

Figure 13.22 User-Defined Service Properties—General Panel

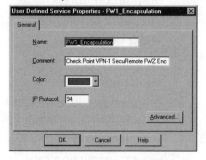

Clicking the **Advanced** button brings up a screen that allows the entry of the most crucial part of this object, the **Match** field. This field is a snippet of inspect code that will be used to check the incoming packets. It can, therefore, be as complex as you can imagine. This makes the user-defined object a truly powerful tool for the enforcement of very specific requirements.

Group

The group object enables you to combine different protocols. This can be used, for example, to define a service whose individual parts must also be separately defined. Ping is a good example. It consists of an echo request and an echo reply. These can be defined and then combined into a group, and that group used in your rule base. Figure 13.23 displays the configuration window, which is accessed by selecting **New | Group** from the Services management window.

Figure 13.23 Group Properties

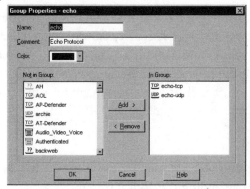

DCE-RPC

This service type works in a similar fashion to the RPC service, in that it tracks DCE-RPC based connections, extracting the information from the packet and creating a virtual session whose information is stored in a local cache. When you define the DCE-RPC service, you will be asked for the UUID for the specific interface as well as the protocol type. Figure 13.24 illustrates this panel.

Figure 13.24 DCE-RPC Properties

Resources

Resource objects are used to configure Content Security on FW-1. Content security includes support for the HTTP, FTP, and SMTP protocols. FW-1 provides this support by using the FW-1 Security Servers. For each connection established through the FW-1 Security Servers, you are able to control access on a granular level according to protocol specific information unique to a specific service. This includes URLs, file names, FTP commands, and so on.

Uniform Resource Identifier

A Uniform Resource Identifier (URI) defines how to access resources on the Internet. Most of us are familiar with the URI by another name: URL. Which term you use is often a matter of tossing the dice, as there is dispute even among the standards developers as to which is more proper.

URI for QoS

Another type of URI object is the **URI for QoS**, which is used when defining a rulebase for FloodGate-1. This resource type allows the security administrator to classify certain URIs as part of a QoS policy. This object type is fairly simple to create. You'll need to define a name, comment, and select the color for the object. Additionally, you will need to define a **Search for URL**. This specifies the URL that will trigger a match, and it can be as specific as a complete URL, or as general as *.jpg, which would match any JPEG file.

SMTP

The SMTP resource defines the methods used by the FW-1 to handle incoming or outgoing e-mail. There are many options, including the ability to remove active scripting components, rewriting fields in the envelope (such as To: or From:) or filtering based on content. The configuration of this resource type is similar to that of the URI, including the ability to use a CVP server.

FTP

An FTP resource is defined in order to enforce content security for FTP connections. We like to use this resource to define the verbs or methods that will be allowed through my firewall. For example, if we have an FTP server that is publicly available for downloading, we can back up the system administrator and deny the ability to PUT.

Open Platform for Security Applications

The Open Platform for Security (OPSEC) object defines for you a means of interacting with a third-party developed security application. These applications add extended functionality to the FW-1 installation. Some examples include virus scanning, content filtering, and intrusion detection. OPSEC allows FW-1 to send its data stream to other applications, and it also allows those applications to send data to the firewall, for example, log entries via the ELA or status via AMON interfaces.

Servers

A server is a host computer running a specific application or service. The server object is the representation of that relationship.

Radius

A RADIUS server is used to provide authentication services. While originally used for remote access services, it is also now commonly used for things like routers and firewalls. To define a radius server, select **Manage | Servers** from the policy editor drop-down menu and then select **New | RADIUS**. The configuration appears as in Figure 13.25.

The RADIUS server object is configured in a way that is fairly common with the other server types. After defining the name, adding a comment, and selecting the associated color, you'll need to specify the **Host** that this RADIUS server is running on. You'll also need to assign a **Priority**. The priority is used to determine the preference for an individual server when more than one is available for contact, for example, when the server is assigned to a RADIUS group.

The next step is to define the **Service**, which is the obvious choice of RADIUS. The **Shared Secret** must be entered in order to establish communication between the firewalled object and the RADIUS server. Consequently, it must be the same on both devices. The final step is to select the proper version from the **Version** drop-down menu.

Figure 13.25 RADIUS Server Properties

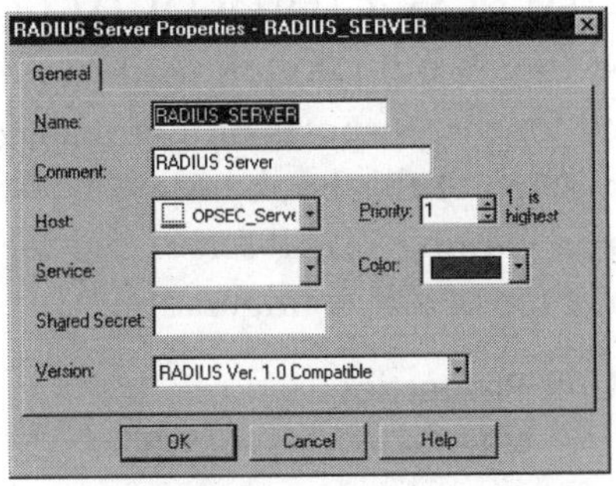

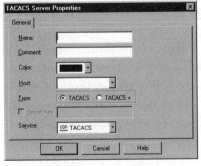

Radius Group

A RADIUS group is used to form a group of RADIUS servers. These servers are then available for use as a single object, with authentication services being performed by the server with the highest priority (e.g. the lowest number). Unlike most other groups, server groups such as this may not contain any dissimilar entities.

TACACS

A Terminal Access Control Access Control Server (TACACS) server is another one of your handy access control methods. The definition of this object shares the same generalities of the other server entities, those being name, comment, color, and host. Once these are defined, you have only to specify if the server is running TACACS or a TACACS+, enter a secret key, if necessary, for TACACS+, and select the appropriate **Service** from the drop-down menu. (Note that you won't have to select a service with TACACS+.) This panel is illustrated in Figure 13.26.

Figure 13.26 TACACS Server Properties

Defender

The Defender server type defines an object running AXENTs Pathways Defender server. This is another authentication method available to you as a FW-1 administrator, and is very easy to incorporate. Besides your four familiar fields of Name, Comment, Color, and Host, you are also able to specify a backup host. Then all that remains is to enter the **Agent ID**, as defined on the Defender server, and the **Agent Key**, which is used to encrypt the communication with the Defender server, and is also specified in the Defender server's configuration.

Lightweight Database Access Protocol Account Unit

The Lightweight Database Access Protocol (LDAP), is used for a bevy of purposes. With regards to FW-1, this server object is used for the purposes of user management. A full discussion of the workings of LDAP is beyond the scope of this book but we'll assume if you are configuring an LDAP object, you have access to an existing LDAP server and the necessary information. Figure 13.27 illustrates the **General** panel for LDAP configuration.

Figure 13.27 LDAP Account Unit Properties

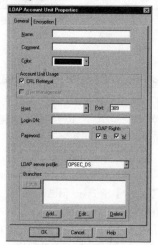

Certificate Authority

We've all heard the buzz about PKI, now here's your chance to jump on the bandwagon. The inclusion of a certificate authority in your security infrastructure enables you to use certificate-based authentication and encryption that eases (or perhaps shifts) the administrative burden of VPN development.

There are three tabs for the Certificate Authority object, with the first being the very simple **General** tab. The associated panel allows the standard configuration information of Name, Comment, and Color, as well as the ability to specify the Certificate Authority via a drop-down menu. You'll have a few choices in this drop-down, with your selection determined by what is available to you. The contents of the second panel depend on the selection in this drop-down box.

The contents of the second panel vary, but generally allow for the importing of a configuration from the PKI server and the importing of the actual certificate. You may also be able to specify the source of the Certificate Revocation List (CRL).

The **Advanced** panel deals with the CRL for this server; specifically, it configures the desire to cache the CRL and when to fetch a new CRL. You can also assign what branches are to be allowed.

SecuRemote DNS

SecuRemote DNS is an internal server type that is used to resolve private addresses to names. SecuRemote DNS replaces the need to create a dnsinfo.C file on the management server's $FWDIR/conf directory. This is a nice change. You will, however, still need to edit $FWDIR/lib/crypt.def though, adding the line *#define ENCDNS* to enable SecuRemote users to download this information along with their topology.

Configuration of this server type is fairly straightforward. You have two tabs: **General** and **Domains**. The **General** panel allows the configuration of the Name, Comment, Color, and Host. As usual, the host must have previously been defined as a workstation object.

The **Domains** panel lists the domains that are included for resolution, as well as something called a **Maximum Label Prefix Count**. This count defines the number of prefixes that will be allowed for the specific domain. For example, if the domain is .edu, then troll.gatech.edu has two prefixes. If the maximum prefix count was one, this domain would not resolve.

Internal Users

The ability to define users on the firewall is a nice feature, but it is also rather administratively intensive. The benefit is that you can select specific users as the source for traffic in a rule. The downside is you have to define these users. Fortunately, Check Point has simplified this process somewhat with the ability to define generic user templates. The use of LDAP as an external source of user information is also supported, which greatly decreases the workload redundancy of a firewall administrator.

The first step is to bring up the Users interface. This is accessed by selecting **Manage | Users** from the policy editor menu. This window is used to define and modify users, and also to install the user database to the VPN-1/FW-1 systems on which this policy is installed.

Time

Time objects are just that. These objects enable you to schedule events, restrict connections, or simply quantify a time period. For example, you can restrict Web browsing not only to specific sites, but also to specific times. There are three possible object types to select from. You can specify a time, a scheduled event, or a group of one or more of these types. To create a new time object, simply select **Manage | Time** from your policy editor window.

The time object is used to restrict the application of rules to specified times. There are two panels to this object: **General** and **Days.** The General panel allows the standard settings, as well as up to three time ranges. These ranges specify the time spans in which this object would be applicable. The second panel, Days, enables you to enforce a finer-grained access control on the time object. We can specify days of a week, or a specific date, or a numbered day in each month. Figure 13.28 illustrates the Days panel.

Figure 13.28 Time Object—Days Panel

Group

A group is formed by the combination of several time object types, and can be used to simplify time-based rules. Instead of using multiple rules, you can create a group of time objects and assign this to a single rule. Creating a time group is similar to the other group types, and consists of assigning a name, comment, and color and then moving time objects from the **Not in Group** list to the **In Group** list.

Scheduled Event

A scheduled event is most often used for administrative purposes, such as scheduling log changes. Configuration is simple, with the only interesting field being the specification of the time at which the event will be triggered. You can also, as with the time object, schedule the repetition frequency of the object. For example, when you define your Management machine, you have access to the Management branch of the Workstation properties. One of the fields, **Schedule log switch to:**, requires the use of a time object as its option.

Virtual Link

A Virtual Link is a path between two VPN-1/FW-1 modules or FloodGate-1 Modules. Virtual Links are defined in the Policy Editor, and can be given Service Level Agreement (SLA) parameters. They can then be monitored using Check Point Traffic Monitoring. To add a new Virtual Link, select **Virtual Links** from the **Manage** menu in the Policy Editor.

There are two panels to be configured. The **General** panel defines the name, etc., for the link, and also enables you to define the endpoints and to optionally activate the link.

The SLA Parameters panel, shown in Figure 13.29, enables you to specify the criteria that will be used to measure the integrity of the link. Thresholds are defined in three directions of traffic. You can specify the Committed Information Rate (CIR) for traffic point A to point B, and the reverse as well. You can also specify a maximum round trip time (RTT) for bi-directional communication, and optionally log the SLA statistics.

Figure 13.29 Virtual Link Properties—SLA Parameters

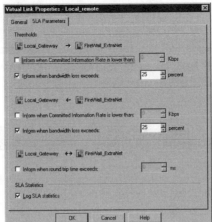

Adding Rules

The Policy Editor is the main interface for all your firewall needs. This is where we have been working to add objects, but it is also the interface to define rules. In the next few sections, we'll show briefly how the Policy Editor can be used to put your network objects into play in the form of firewall rules.

Rules

FW-1, like most firewalls, is designed to enforce a set of rules, known as a rule base. This rule base defines the behavior of the firewall, and is configured by you, the firewall administrator. It is dreadfully important that you carefully consider the underlying needs, related to both security and functionality, and make a measured application of both. You'll probably never be able to strike a perfect balance, but the closer you come, the easier your life will be. Fundamentally, there are two models of firewall configuration. The first considers all traffic to be suspect, and only allows what is necessary (blocking all not explicitly allowed). The second model is far more permissive, allowing all traffic that has not proven to be risky (allowing everything except what is explicitly denied). Which model you subscribe to is a decision that must be made at the policy level. Your firewall will be a technical implementation of that policy.

A rule is made up by the combination of source, destination, action, tracking information, enforcement location, enforcement time, and an optional (but highly recommended) time fields. These fields are explained in the next few sections, along with the methods used to create them.

Adding Rules

Adding rules in FW-1 is very straightforward. There are a few choices about rule placement you have to decide upon when adding a new rule. When you select **Rules | Add Rule** you'll see a submenu with the following choices.

- **Bottom** After the last rule in the rulebase.

- **Top** Before the first rule in the rulebase.

- **After**   After the currently selected rule.
- **Before**   Before the currently selected rule.

After you insert the new rule, it will resemble the one shown in Figure 13.30. You will need to configure the specifics of each rule. In each field of the new rule, right-click to enter the necessary information.

Figure 13.30 New Rule

NO.	SOURCE	DESTINATION	SERVICE	ACTION	TRACK	INSTALL ON	TIME	COMMENT
1	✳ Any	✳ Any	✳ Any	◉ Drop	− None	▥ Gateways	✳ Any	

Source

The source field defines the IP address or hostname that is initiating the data stream. For the sake of your rule base, the source can be any of the properly defined network objects, as well as users or groups of users. When adding a source, you have the choice of adding an object or adding user access. You are not restricted in the number of sources for a rule.

Destination

The destination can be any defined network object. When you right-click in the **Destination** field and select **Add**, you'll see a window similar to that shown in Figure 13.31. Note that a rule can support multiple destinations.

Figure 13.31 Add Object

Service

The service field defines the service that must be present in order to generate a match. To add a service, right-click in the **Service** field and select **Add**. You will have the choice of adding a service, or a service with a resource. You can define any number of services for a rule.

Action

The action is the way that FW-1 reacts when a rule is matched. You have a couple of choices when selecting an action, but only one selection is allowed. The available options are the following:

- **Accept** Accept the packet; allow the connection.

- **Reject** Reject the connection and notify the sender of the condition.

- **Drop** Reject the connection, but do not notify the sender.

- **User Authentication** Use User Authentication for this connection.

- **Client Authentication** Use Client Authentication for this connection.

- **Session Authentication** Use Session Authentication for this connection.

- **Encrypt** Encrypt outgoing packets; decrypt incoming packets.

- **Client Encryption** Accept only if this connection originates from a SecuRemote client.

Track

The Track column defines how information about this session will be recorded. There are several options in the menu when you right-click on this field.

- **Log** Write a log entry regarding this connection.

- **Account** Write an accounting log entry regarding this connection.

- **Alert** Generate a pop-up alert regarding this connection.

- **Mail** Send a mail regarding this connection.

- **SnmpTrap** Generate an SNMP trap based on this connection.

- **User-Defined** Execute the user-defined script as a result of this connection.

Install On

The **Install On** field defines which defined objects will have this policy installed on them. Although the entire policy is installed on each selected object, these objects only enforce the part of the policy that is relevant to them. If no rules are relevant, then no communication will be allowed.

- Enforce on all network objects defined as gateways.

- Enforce on the specified target object(s) only, in the inbound and outbound directions.

- Enforce in the inbound direction on the firewalled network objects defined as Destination in this rule.

- Enforce in the outbound direction on the firewalled network objects defined as Source in this rule.

- Enforce on all OSE devices.

- Enforce on all embedded devices.

Time

In this field, use a time object to restrict the connection to certain specified intervals, or leave the default of **Any**.

Comment

This field is used to describe the rule, its purpose, and its functionality. It is highly recommended that you do not leave this field blank!

Global Properties

While the brunt of your security policy will reside in the rule base, there are other places you have to pay attention to. In order to fully secure your enterprise, you will need to at least be familiar with the Global Properties, and most likely you will need to alter them. You do this by accessing the **Global Properties** from the Policy menu. We'll spend the next few sections discussing these properties. Figure 13.32 displays the initial panel of the Global Properties.

Figure 13.32 Global Properties

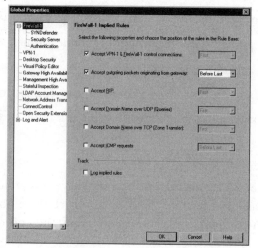

FW-1 Implied Rules

FW-1 has a feature that many find mysterious at first blush. That feature is the *implied* rule base. This rule base is made up of settings in the Global Properties, as opposed to the one explicitly created by you, the firewall administrator. Once you understand this, the mystery is removed, and you'll see that they are actually pretty simple. They are shown, by the way, in Figure 13.32. What you select is up to your security policy, but we highly recommend that you enable the logging of these rules.

One important thing to understand is the implication of the option values. If you select a rule to be included within the implied rule base, you'll need to decide where to place that rule. You have three choices here.

■ First

- Last

- Before Last

You'll need to select the location in the rule base where the selected rule will be placed. This is a critical decision, and you should understand how a packet passes through the rule base in order to assist your decision. Furthermore, not all implied rules are as simple as they may seem. The first implied rule, Accept VPN-1 and FW-1 control connections, for example, enables a service group containing 17 services. You probably don't need to worry about this too much, but it is a good thing to be aware of.

Viewing Implied Rules

There are two methods of viewing implied rules. Certainly, you can view them within the Global Properties window, but this is often cumbersome and difficult to do in a cohesive flow. When you want access to these rules while editing the rest of your rule base, the easiest way is to select the **View** menu and then select **Implied Rules**. You'll see something like what is displayed in Figure 13.33. Note that the implied rules are unnumbered and are highlighted by their different color.

Figure 13.33 Implied Rules

NO.	SOURCE	DESTINATION	SERVICE	ACTION	TRACK	INSTALL ON	TIME	COMMENT
-	Trusted hosts	FW1 host	FireWall1	accept	None	Gateways	Any	Enable FW1 control conne
-	ftp server	local client	expected	accept	None	Gateways	Any	Enable Response of FTP
-	Any	Any	passive f	accept	None	Gateways	Any	Enable ftppasv connectio
-	Any	Any	rpc contr	accept	None	Gateways	Any	Enable RPC Control
1	Any	Any	Silent_Se	Drop	None	Gateways	Any	Silent drop for broadcast

SYNDefender

SYNDefender is a feature used to guard your network from the dreaded SYN flood. Note that this isn't really designed to prevent such an attack against your firewall, but for what it is intended to do it is very handy. It has two modes of operation: SYNGateway and passive SYNGateway. In SYNGateway mode, the firewall actively intercepts SYN packets, completes the three-way handshake, and only then forwards the connection to the true destination. In passive mode, the firewall monitors the connection. If the timeout period is reached, a RST (reset) packet is sent to both the originator and the destination.

Configuring SYNDefender is simple. Simply navigate to the proper sub-menu and select the method, timeout, and maximum connections.

Using SYNDefender to Defend the SYN Attack

The SYN attack is one of the simplest Denial of Service (DoS) attacks to initiate. Unfortunately, it is also one of the most difficult to defend against. The reasons for these truths are identical. The basic operation of a SYN flood is to send hundreds of thousands of connection requests (SYN, or synchronize, packets) to the target server. The target server will send an acknowledgment of that

SYN packet, allocate a bit of memory in a pending connection queue, and then wait, for a predefined timeout period, for the final part of the connection process to complete. Herein lies the rub.

There are two problems here. The first is that the sending of a SYN packet is completely normal. A high-volume server might see thousands of SYN packets in any given time period. The second problem is that the server tends to be too generous in its timeout period, giving the client plenty of time to complete the connection. For example, default configuration of Microsoft Windows 2000 will wait 189 seconds. That's over three minutes *per connection* of resource consumption. While the memory allocated is small, the cumulative impact can be severe enough to gobble up all the resources on the target server.

While firewall tools like SYNDefender can help you keep the bogus SYN packets from reaching the server, you need (and have available) a better method. Since most SYN attacks use spoofed IP addresses, ingress and egress filtering by large ISPs could go a long way to mitigate the dangers of SYN attacks.

Security Server

The Security Server panel allows the entry of welcome messages for many of the most common Internet services. This is accomplished by pointing to the appropriate file containing the message. You can also configure the HTTP Next Proxy, although this is better done in the workstation object, assuming a version of FireWall-1 of NG. Earlier versions still require entry in this field.

Authentication

The Authentication panel enables you to specify the tolerance for failed login attempts. There are parameters for rlogin, telnet, client authentication and session authentication. There is also a section for configuring session timeout, wait mode and logging/alerting for back level modules.

VPN-1

The VPN panel controls the configuration of items like security association (SA) renegotiation, as well CRL and SecuRemote grace periods.

Desktop Security

The Desktop Security panel contains a lot of information regarding the behavior of your firewall with regard to SecuRemote client requests. The settings you select here are highly dependant on your own security policy, but again, WE strongly recommend that you log violation notifications and *not* respond to unauthenticated topology requests.

Visual Policy Editor

The Visual Policy Editor (VPE) provides a very slick interface to view your objects and their interrelations, as mentioned in the beginning of this chapter. This panel enables you to display the VPE or conceal it from view. Note that if you disable the VPE, no topology calculations will take place within the firewall inner workings.

Gateway High Availability

Gateway High Availability is the process in which multiple modules can act as one for the sake of redundancy. This panel lets you enable or disable the feature.

Management High Availability

Management High Availability is similar to that for gateways, except that it allows the management modules to exhibit some redundancy. This panel allows for you to select the synchronization time of the management servers participating in the HA configuration.

Stateful Inspection

Stateful Inspection is the heart of FW-1. This panel does not allow you to change that, but instead enables you to specify some timeout settings for the TCP sessions and to configure stateful UDP and ICMP behavior.

LDAP Account Management

The LDAP account management panel allows the enabling of LDAP for account management. Here you can also set some session timeouts and password rules.

Network Address Translation

The NAT panel configures some general NAT behavior such for the Automatic NAT rules and NAT pools for SecuRemote connections.

ConnectControl

The ConnectControl panel allows the configuration of this very handy feature. On this panel, we can set the interval that VPN-1/FW-1 will wait between server checks (commonly known as heartbeat checks) and the number of retries before a server is considered unreachable. We can also set the persistency timeout. This is the time within which all connections from the same source IP will be forwarded to the same server. Finally, you configure the listening address of the server agent used to measure server load and the pooling interval for that.

Open Security Extension

The Open Security Extension (OSE) panel allows configuration for implied rules that are applied only to OSE compliant routers.

Log and Alert

The Log and Alert panel enables you to configure the responses taken when a packet matches a rule.

SecureUpdate

SecureUpdate is a tool for the easy management of both versioning and licensing for both Check Point and OPSEC products. This component can be a real lifesaver, as you'll understand if you've ever had to manually upgrade several dozens of licenses.

The GUI interface features two panels, one for Products and one for Licenses. These can be selected by clicking on the appropriate tab within the window. Figure 13.34 illustrates this GUI panel.

Figure 13.34 SecureUpdate GUI

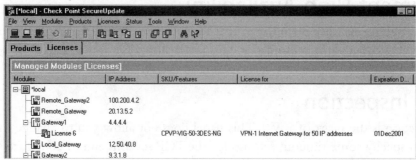

The real blessing of the SecureUpdate tool is that of centralized management and authority. Using this product, you can apply updates to your Check Point modules in a timelier manner, update licenses, and modify the currently licensed machines. Before you begin doing this, however, you should know about a new feature of FireWall-1 NG. This feature is called Central Licensing and uses what is known as a license repository.

In previous versions of FireWall-1, you had only one licensing option, that of a local license. Local licensing mandated that the license be tied to the IP address of the module. This model wasn't very flexible and made upgrades very difficult and migrations nearly impossible. Central licensing binds the license to the address of the management server and allows several benefits.

- When you change the IP address of the firewall module, the license remains useable. This has not always been the case.

- All licenses are bound to only one IP address. This allows great flexibility in your FW-1 deployment. Imagine the scenario where your network boundaries are migrated from one provider to another, and with that comes a new network block. Using central licensing makes that address change a piece of cake. Licenses can be taken from one module and given to another and managed from this central location.

Note that while local licenses can still be used with FW-1 NG, you won't be able to use them like central licenses. This means that they can't be detached from their module after they have been installed.

Before you can begin using the functionality of SecureUpdate product, some common-sense things have to be in place. Obviously, there needs to be connectivity between the management module and the modules that are being maintained. For your purposes, connectivity implies both IP connectivity and FW-1 connectivity (SIC). Once this is all in place, you are on your way to licensing bliss.

Licenses can be added to the license repository in one of two ways. The first, more tedious method is to copy the license details by hand. This is annoying and can lead to typographical errors, (although support exists to paste the license details from the clipboard, obviating the need to hand-type) so you probably will not want to add licenses in this way. The second method is to import a file created by the Check Point User Center. To begin, select **Licenses | New License** from the SecureUpdate tool bar. This will allow you the choice of adding manually or importing from a file. Figure 13.35 illustrates this menu option.

Figure 13.35 Adding a License

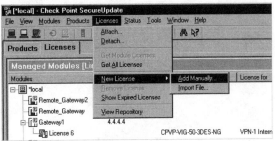

If you opt to add the license manually, you'll see a window with a slew of fields that you'll need to fill out, or as mentioned previously, you can paste the values from the clipboard. If you select **Import File**, you'll see the standard file browse window. Also under this menu option is the ability to view the License Repository. The Repository is a listing of all installed licenses and allows a filtered view. It can show you all licenses, all attached licenses, or all unattached licenses. This is a handy way to get a feel for what spare licenses you have, as well as enabling you to attach and detach central licenses. Remember that the old style licenses can't be detached once they are installed (SecureUpdate automatically attaches them to the proper module when they are imported). Figure 13.36 shows us the license repository.

Figure 13.36 License Repository—View All Licenses

Name	SKU/Features	License for	IP Address	Expiration D...	Type	Attached to
License 6	CPVP-VIG-5...	VPN-1 Inter...	1.1.1.1	01Dec2001	central	Gateway1
License 7	CPVP-VIG-5...	VPN-1 Inter...	1.1.1.1	08Oct2001	central	
License 1	CPVP-VIG-5...	VPN-1 Inter...	1.1.1.1	05Oct2001	central	
License 2	CPFW-FIG-...	FireWall-1 In...	1.1.1.1	05Oct2001	central	Gateway3
License 3	CPTC-FGG-...	FloodGate-1...	9.3.1.8	05Oct2001	local	Gateway2
License 4	CPFW-ENC-...	Add-on VPN...	9.3.1.8	23Dec2001	local	Gateway2
License 5	CPFW-FIG-...	FireWall-1 In...	9.3.1.8	10Nov2001	local	Gateway2

Using the Repository, license administration is as easy as right-clicking. In the Figure 13.36, you'll see all licenses. Notice that several of them are not attached to a specific module. To use these licenses, simply right-click on its entry and select **Attach**. At this point, you'll see a listing of the defined workstations with Check Point modules. Select the desired system and select **OK**.

One other very helpful feature is the ability to view expired licenses. To do this, right-click anywhere within the **Repository** window and select **Show Expired Licenses**. This presents a window (shown in Figure 13.37) listing the licenses that are no longer valid. Selecting an expired license entry and clicking on **Properties** shows you what module the expired license is attached to.

Figure 13.37 Expired Licenses

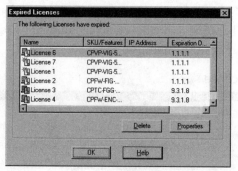

Log Viewer

The Log Viewer is your interface to the log data recorded by VPN-1/FW-1. Log data is created by your rule base, by firewall activities, by your own actions (accounting log), and by several other sources. Viewing this data regularly is a key to good security enforcement, and this GUI will make the task of observing the log data much more pleasant.

Upon startup, the Log Viewer begins display of the active security log. You can also use the GUI to view older logs, which may have been rotated out and placed into archive for later review. Note that the name of the log file being viewed is displayed in the upper-left portion of window title bar, as shown in Figure 13.38. This is helpful in the aforementioned case where you are viewing archived data.

The log viewer has three modes of operation, which are accessed by the drop-down menu shown in the figure, or alternatively, via the **Mode** menu option. These modes are **Log**, **Active**, and **Audit**.

- **Active** mode displays currently active connections being tracked by the firewall. The active mode is most often used when performing real–time monitoring of traffic, or when you wish to block a connection via SAM.

- **Audit** mode is very handy for keeping track of who did what on your firewall. The "who," in this case, is your group of firewall administrators, and the "what" are administrative actions. Examples of these are logging in, creating or deleting objects, and so on. You can also view specific details for any log entry by right-clicking that entry and selecting **Show Details**. Note that the audit data is stored in a separate file, fw.adtlog stored in the $FWDIR/log directory of the firewall installation.

- **Log** mode is the most common method of interacting with the log data, and is the most comprehensive way to view the security events. You can select events to view using the **Selection Criteria**. These criteria define which data is extracted from the log data and displayed to you. You can save your favorite selections and reuse them frequently, or you may opt to use one of the built-in views.

The default views are available via the toolbar or via the **View** menu. These views select some of the more commonly accessed information for display. For example, there is a predefined selection for VPN-1 data, which shows you such entries as Key IDs, encryption method, VPN peer gateway, and so forth. But the real power of the Log Viewer is in its ability for customization. We see the log viewer GUI in Figure 13.38.

Figure 13.38 Check Point Log Viewer

Column Selections

In order to alter the data displayed, click **Selection | Customize**. You will be presented with the window shown in Figure 13.39. Using this window enables you to select or deselect any of the available data fields. You can also change the column width using this window. By clicking the **Selection** button, you have access to very granular methods of defining information. We highly recommend that you spend a few minutes exploring this feature on your firewall.

Figure 13.39 Column Options Window

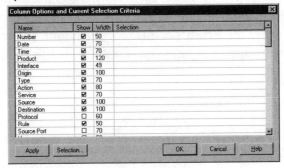

Of course, you probably are looking at the Log Viewer and noticing some familiarity to most common spreadsheet applications. If you feel comfortable with that, then you should feel instantly comfortable interacting with the Log Viewer itself. You can resize columns not only from the options window, but also directly from the viewer main menu.

Right-clicking anywhere within the column you want to modify will bring up a context menu, which enables you to do things like hide that column and resize the width. You can also resize the width by dragging the border of the title header. Once you have tailored the view to your liking, you can begin gathering the information.

The Log Viewer features a very handy search utility, accessed by selecting **Edit | Find**. This enables you to specify the column or columns you want to search through, and the entry of the search criteria. You can also specify a search direction.

System Status

The System Status GUI allows a quick peek at the overall health of your security infrastructure. Real time monitoring, along with status alerting, is featured to assist in the integrity of your enterprise. The System Status viewer is a friendly, lightweight interface. You are presented with a three-pane window, with two of those shown in Figure 13.40.

Figure 13.40 System Status GUI

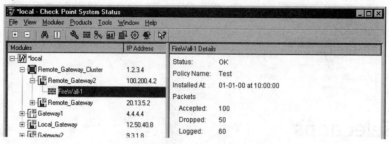

The left-hand pane, known as the **Modules View**, lists the installed and monitored modules. These modules can be either Check Point or third-party OPSEC modules. The right-hand pane, known as the **Details View**, lists the status for the module selected in the **Modules View**. Finally, there is a **Critical Notifications** pane (not shown in Figure 13.40) that keeps you updated on any status alerts generated.

The **Modules View** window is further broken down into three columns: Modules, IP Address, and Status. Their meanings are self-explanatory. You can also select specific components to query for status using either the **Products** menu or the button bar across the top of the window. You can query the following components for status (left to right on the button bar).

- SVN Foundation Details
- FireWall-1 Details
- VPN-1 Details
- FloodGate-1 Details
- High Availability Module Details
- OPSEC Application Details
- Management Details

Summary

We've just completed a marathon look at the GUI provided for access to VPN-1/FW-1. We looked at the process to create each of the possible object types available for use within your enterprise security policy. This includes network objects, as well as servers and resources. You should now feel comfortable creating objects to support your own implementations.

We also looked at the Policy Editor, and saw how to use these newly created objects to create rules. These rules will be the embodiment of your written security policy, and are the definitions that FW-1 enforces. We also saw how FW-1 has included something called an *implied rule*, how to edit them, and how to view them. Speaking of editing, we covered the various methods of editing our rule base, including adding new rules, deleting existing ones, and rearranging the rule base with cut/paste functions.

We also looked briefly at the Global Properties, and learned a little about how these settings impact the behavior of the firewall. We finished with a peek into some of the additional tools provided with VPN-1/FW-1. We saw the Log Viewer and the System Status view, as well as the SecureUpdate tool.

We hope that you feel more at ease with what can often be a daunting and complex task, specifically the representation of your network and the creation of rules to protect it.

## Chapter 14

Creating a Security Policy

Solutions in this chapter:

- Reasons for a Security Policy
- How to Write a Security Policy
- Implementing a Security Policy
- Installing a Security Policy
- Policy Files

Introduction

This chapter covers an important topic, which is how to define a security policy. This is something you need to do early on so that you can find the right solution for your specific environment. Once you determine how you want to enforce security in your company, then you will know whether you really need to spend the time and effort involved in setting up user authentication, or whether you'd rather use your existing Lightweight Directory Access Protocol (LDAP) server, which would save you a lot of trouble. Once you have created a security policy for your company and have planned to introduce security into your network, choosing your implementation strategy should be fairly straightforward.

We will also discuss how to implement your policy into the FW-1 Policy Editor. Of course, if you are using private IP addresses inside your firewall, then you may need to run Network Address Translation (NAT) before you can put your firewall in place, but this chapter will get your firewall ready to enforce your policy and start passing packets in your network.

We will walk you through the setup of a Firewall object, and a step-by-step procedure of adding the services outlined in your information security policy into the FW-1 Policy Editor interface. Then we'll discuss some additional ways in which to manipulate your rules as well as how to finally install your policy so that it is enforced.

Reasons for a Security Policy

You are probably deploying Check Point NG to protect something. Do you know what you are protecting, what you are protecting it from, and how you are protecting it? Before you can effectively deploy any security control, especially a powerful tool like Check Point NG, you need to have an information security policy. This is not to be confused with the Check Point Security Policy, which, according to Check Point is "Defined in terms of a Rule Base and [FW-1 NG] Properties." No, we are talking about an enterprise-wide information security policy that includes an Executive Security Policy, accompanied by standards, guidelines, and procedures for implementing and maintaining an information security program.

Many organizations are now seeing the need to have an articulated information security policy. Having such a policy is making organizations more effective in their preventative, detective, and responsive security measures. Moreover, as a result of government regulations, organizations in certain vertical industries are required to have formally documented information security policies.

In addition, an information security policy is also extremely beneficial to the security manager because it provides, at an executive level, a mandated framework for ensuring the confidentiality, integrity, and availability of an organization's information assets. What this means is that the security manager has some weight in his or her corner for budget requests when he or she has an approved information security policy.

Finally, for the security administrator, having a written and approved policy can ensure that you are able to deploy Check Point NG in a way that minimizes disruption to business. Think of the written policy as a recipe to ensure that you configure everything correctly. Not to mention that a policy is the best way to ensure you will keep your job, should something happen.

How to Write a Security Policy

To completely write an entire information security policy could take months of work with involvement from the legal department, and the various business units. However, in order to implement Check Point NG, you need at a minimum an executive security policy and a perimeter network security policy. Typically, the executive security policy is a high-level document of about three to five pages that points to relevant standards, procedures, and guidelines. Because the highest levels of management or the board of directors must adopt the executive security policy, it should be written without details about technologies, people, or methods. This will ensure that as technology changes or as people change, the document will not become obsolete. Think of the executive security policy as a declaration of the importance of security to your organization. However, choose your words carefully because it is a legal document in many respects.

The executive security policy is important because without an executive endorsement of your security policy, enforcement may become difficult. In order to write an effective executive security policy you must identify early on the departments with an interest in maintaining information assets like research and development, finance, and IT. Approach the managers and request their involvement in drafting an executive-level security document. In addition, you will want to include the legal department and an executive sponsor.

NOTE

Executive support and approval is critical to the success of your Information Security Policy. When the CEO has to follow the same rules as everyone else, it makes policy enforcement much simpler.

The final document should have language such as: "Because of the nature of our business, customer non-public information is frequently transmitted or stored on our information systems. As a result, we will employ appropriate controls and safeguards including encryption to ensure that non-public information is adequately protected against unauthorized disclosure while in storage or transit." We know at this point that our policy seems rather vague and legal. However, resist the impulse to say, "We must use Triple DES encryption on all private data that is stored or transmitted." This is important because technology changes and this document will eventually be presented to management for approval. Management doesn't want to see you once a month asking for changes to the security policy. As a guiding principle, the executive security policy should address why security is important and delegate the further implementation of appropriate standards, guidelines, and procedures to the appropriate individuals or groups.

NOTE

Use the security policy to help you do your job better and get the things you need. For example, use the policy to ensure that you get security training. Include a statement in the policy that says, "To ensure that we are adequately controlling and anticipating current and new threats, the security manager and his or her team must attend security training on a semi-annual basis in the form of conferences, seminars, symposiums, and workshops." As you can see, the security policy can be your friend.

Drafting the second part of your overall information security policy, the perimeter network security policy, is somewhat different. The perimeter network security policy is a document that includes specific standards, procedures, and guidelines for implementing and maintaining perimeter network security. The first step in drafting a perimeter network security policy is to obtain a network map. The network map will help you to better identify resources that need protecting and how to architect your security solution. Depending on the size of your organization, you may elect to do this yourself or to obtain the assistance of individuals with specific knowledge regarding their environment. Although there are a number of software tools to assist you in automatically mapping the network, it will still be necessary to conduct manual validation.

After mapping the network, determine once again the departments or business units with a specific interest in network perimeter security, and assemble the representatives for a meeting. The best approach in this meeting is to identify what is needed and then, by default, disallow everything else. It is at this point that successful security managers recognize the purpose of security to meet business needs. Although it would be great from a security perspective to disconnect the business from the Internet, to stay in business the connection must be maintained. In this meeting you need to specifically ask the representatives if you were to put up a firewall today and block everything, what would need to be changed and configured to allow the business to continue. This step is called defining requirements. For example, some of the requirements that might be voiced include the following:

- We **need** a Web site that has dynamic content.
- We **need** to have an e-Commerce storefront.
- We **need** to be able to get and send e-mail.
- We **need** to secure all of our internal information from external attacks.
- We **need** to be able to access the Internet securely using HTTP, HTTPS, and FTP from the LAN.
- We **need** to secure our critical information from internal attacks or destruction.

In addition, you will also want to identify any wishes the representatives have. This could be your opportunity to look like a hero when you say, "Yes, we can do that." Examples of wishes are as follows:

- We **would like** to have Instant Messaging.
- We **would like** to be able to have Sales reps connect remotely to download order status.

You may find that most needs are simple and can use further refinement. For example, the requirement to send and receive e-mail begs the questions, "From where do you need to send e-mail? Do remote users need to send and receive e-mail? Should there be any additional restrictions on e-mail?" In addition, you should ask questions about what types of communication to log.

> **NOTE**
>
> Make sure that everyone who has an interest in the implementation and maintenance of a security policy is involved in its creation. This may involve representatives from HR or even the custodial staff. Involvement from these departments will ease acceptance of the new policy and make the actual implementation much smoother.

The next stage in the drafting of the perimeter network security policy is risk assessment. Every requirement and wish has a risk attached to it. As a security professional you must be able to identify those risks and communicate them to the involved parties so they can be weighed against the benefits.

Security Design

After identifying the requirements and risks you are willing to accept, you must design security solutions. Having knowledge of the features and abilities of FW-1 NG will help you to determine what you can and cannot do. In addition, be aware of the other types of controls that can be used to maintain perimeter network security. There are three main categories of controls: technical controls, physical controls, and administrative controls. Each category of controls has three functions that include preventative, detective, and responsive, as shown in Table 14.1. The firewall is primarily a technical control of a preventative and detective nature. That is to say, the firewall prevents unauthorized access and can be used to detect unauthorized access. However, do not dismiss addressing physical and administrative controls in your perimeter network security policy.

Table 14.1 Categories of Security Controls

	Technical	Physical	Administrative
Preventative	Check Point NG VPN-1	Locked data centers Identification badges	User ID/Password policy Change management
Detective	Check Point NG	CCTV	Log and report review Rule base audits
Responsive	Check Point NG	High availability	Incident response procedures

Other policies that FW-1 NG can help you enforce are the following:

- NAT Security
- QoS Security
- Desktop security
- Monitoring

Firewall Architecture

Before writing the policy, one thing you need to explore is whether you will need to have different policies for different locations or if you will have only one. If you have one security policy,

Check Point can enforce the same policy on all firewall modules from a central management station. Otherwise, you will have to maintain a different policy for different locations. Although for business reasons this might be necessary, it can add a level of complexity to your environment that could decrease your overall effective security. If it is necessary, then make sure that it is thoroughly documented.

Writing the Policy

Now that you know what is necessary, you can write your perimeter network security policy. As you can see in Figure 14.1, writing a security policy is a logical progression of steps.

Figure 14.1 Steps to Writing a Security Policy

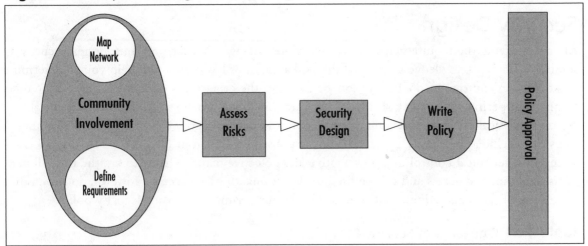

Briefly, the structure of the policy should include the following:

- **Introduction** In this section, you should state the purpose of this policy. What is the objective of the policy? Why it is important to the organization?

- **Guidelines** In this section you should detail guidelines for choosing controls to meet the objectives of the policy. These are the basic requirements. Typically you will see the word *should* in these statements.

- **Standards** In this section you should detail the standards for implementing and deploying the selected controls. For example, this section will state the initial configuration or firewall architecture. This section tends to detail the requirements given in the meeting with the interested departments and business units. This section is written with the words such as, "It is the policy that..."

- **Procedures** In this section you should detail the procedures for maintaining the security solution, such as how often the logs should be reviewed and who is authorized to make changes.

- **Deployment:** The purpose of the deployment section is to assign responsibilities and specific steps for the implementation of the policy. Think of it as a mini project plan. In a perimeter network Ssecurity policy, this is the section that translates the standards and guidelines into language that the security administrator can enforce on the firewall.

- **Enforcement** Although many policies lack this component, all policies require a method for enforcement. A popular and effective method for enforcement is auditing. In this section you could state that the firewall rule base would be subject to an external audit yearly. In addition, this section should detail the enforcement and consequences if someone was to circumvent the firewall or its rules.

- **Modification or exceptions** No policy is perfect, and the policy may require modifications or exceptions. In this section you should detail the methods for obtaining modifications to the policy or exceptions.

The following series of headings could be considered a sample of a perimeter network security policy

Introduction

Due to Company X's required connection and access to the public Internet, it is essential that a strong perimeter firewall exist that sufficiently separates the internal private LAN of CompanyX and the public Internet. The firewall should provide preventative and detective technical controls for access between the two networks.

Guidelines

The implementation of any firewall technology should follow these basic rules:

- The firewall should allow for filtering of communication protocols based on complex rule sets.

- The firewall should provide extensive logging of traffic passed and blocked.

- The firewall should be the only entry and exit point to the public Internet from the CompanyX LAN.

- The firewall operating system should be sufficiently hardened to resist attack both internal and external.

- The firewall should fail closed.

- The firewall should not disclose the internal nature, names, or addressing of the CompanyX LAN.

- The firewall should only provide firewall services. No other service or application should be running on the firewall.

Standards

The implementation of any firewall must follow these basic rules:

- It is the policy that only the identified firewall administrator is allowed to make changes to the configuration of the firewall.

■ It is the policy that all firewalls must follow the default rule: That which is not expressly permitted is denied.

In addition, the following standards for perimeter networks are as follows:

■ The deployment of public services and resources shall be positioned behind the firewall in a protected service net.

■ The firewall shall be configured to disallow traffic that originates in the service net to the general LAN.

■ Any application or network resource residing outside of the firewall and accessible by unauthorized users requires a banner similar to the following:

A T T E N T I O N! PLEASE READ CAREFULLY.

This system is the property of CompanyX. It is for authorized use only. Users (authorized or unauthorized) have no explicit or implicit expectation of privacy. Any or all uses of this system and all files on this system will be intercepted, monitored, recorded, copied, audited, inspected, and disclosed to CompanyX management, and law enforcement personnel, as well as authorized officials of other agencies, both domestic and foreign. By using this system, the user consents to such interception, monitoring, recording, copying, auditing, inspection, and disclosure at the discretion of CompanyX. Unauthorized or improper use of this system may result in administrative disciplinary action and civil and criminal penalties. By continuing to use this system, you indicate your awareness of and consent to these terms and conditions of use. LOG OFF IMMEDIATELY if you do not agree to the conditions stated in this warning.

Procedures

Firewall will be configured to allow traffic as defined below:

■ TCP/IP suite of protocols allowed through the firewall from the inside LAN to the public Internet is as follows:

  ■ HTTP to anywhere

  ■ HTTPS to anywhere

■ TCP/IP suite of protocols allowed through the firewall from the inside LAN to the Service Net is as follows:

  ■ HTTP to Web Server

  ■ SMTP to Mail Server

  ■ POP3 to Mail Server

  ■ DNS to DNS server

■ TCP/IP suite of protocols allowed through the firewall from the Service Net to the public Internet is as follows:

  ■ DNS from DNS server to anywhere

- TCP/IP suite of protocols allowed through the firewall from the public Internet to the LAN is as follows:

    - None

- TCP/IP suite of protocols allowed through the firewall from the public Internet with specific source, destination, and protocols is as follows:

    - SMTP to Mail Server

    - HTTP to Web Server

    - FTP to Web Server

Deployment

The security administrator will define the rule base and configure the firewall as defined above, in addition to other industry standard properties as appropriate.

Enforcement

Traffic patterns will be enforced by the firewall's technical controls as defined by the firewall administrator. Periodically, an external vulnerability assessment will be performed to assure the proper configuration of the firewall. Additionally, an independent third party will annually audit the configured firewall.

Modifications or Exceptions

Request for modification to the firewall configuration must be submitted via e-mail to the security manager and firewall administrator, accompanied by justification and the duration of the requested change.

Implementing a Security Policy

Now that you have a written information security policy and a perimeter security policy, you can begin configuring and deploying Check Point NG by translating your organization's policies into a policy that can be enforced by Check Point NG.

Default and Initial Policies

Let's start by understanding the default and initial policies in FW-1 NG. The default and initial policies taken together comprise boot security for FW-1 NG. Unlike previous versions of FW-1, FW-1 NG automatically applies the default policy upon restart. The default policy is intended to protect the firewall and the networks behind it by blocking all traffic while it is loading the firewall services. Additionally, boot security will disable IP forwarding to keep the operating system (OS) from routing traffic while the firewall is booting. However, there are some things that the default filter will allow. Specifically, the default filter will allow the following:

- Outgoing communication from the firewall itself.

- Incoming communications that are a response to communications initiated by the firewall.

- Broadcasts.

Because the firewall is allowing something, the firewall also enforces anti-spoofing measures to ensure that the allowed FW-1 NG communications are not spoofed on any of its interfaces.

As FW-1 NG boots up and the default filter takes effect, the interfaces are configured and the FW-1 services are started. At this point, FW-1 applies an initial policy made up of implicit rules. The purpose of the initial policy is to add rules that will allow a graphical user interface (GUI) to be trusted and connect to the firewall. After the GUI is able to connect to the firewall, a new security policy can be installed. The initial policy is only installed on a module after *cpconfig* is executed and there is no security policy. The initial policy is replaced after a regular policy is written and installed by the administrator to the module. Thereafter, the enterprise security policy will follow the default filter and interface configuration. The enterprise security policy will be composed of the defined rule base and implicit rules. This process is illustrated in Figure 14.2.

Boot security ensures that at no time is the firewall left unprotected. Ensuring that FW-1 starts at boot will allow boot security to be enforced. It is possible to alter boot security and enable IP forwarding and disable the default filter. However, this is not recommended.

Figure 14.2 Boot Security

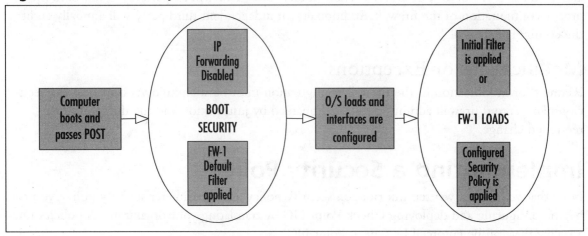

Translating Your Policy into Rules

At this point you can take your written policy and your network map and start translating your documented security policy into a policy that Check Point FW-1 NG can enforce. Remember that the FW-1 NG policy is composed of global properties (which are implicit, as shown in Figure 14.3) and an explicit rule base. Now let's begin translating and building a security policy.

The first thing you have to do is to create a new policy. To create a new policy, choose from the **File** menu in **Policy Editor** and select **New**.

Figure 14.3 Global Properties Implied Rules

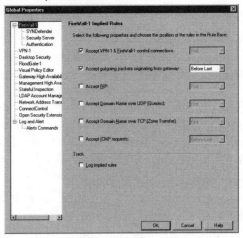

In the new policy dialog as shown if Figure 14.4, you can see that you have a few options. First type a name for the policy. Now select **Security and Address Translation** as your Policy Type. This will now enable the Helpers portion of the dialog. In Check Point NG there are three ways to begin defining your new policy: wizard, Template, and empty policy.

Figure 14.4 New Security Policy Dialog

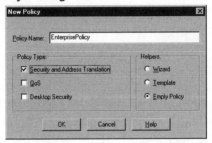

The wizard method is based on four template networks:

- **Starter network** Dual-homed firewall with one connection to the external network. SMTP mail server is on the internal network. The wizard will walk you through allowing SMTP traffic from the Internet to your mail server.

- **Publisher network** Dual-homed firewall with one connection to the external network. Mail server, FTP, and Web servers are located on the internal network. The wizard will walk you through allowing SMTP traffic in to the mail server, allowing FTP traffic to the FTP server with or without authentication, and allowing HTTP or HTTPS traffic to the Web server with or without authentication.

- **DMZ network** Three-homed firewall with one connection to an external network, one to a service net, and one to an internal network. In this template you can configure permitted services from the internal network to the external network. The wizard will walk you through allowing SMTP traffic in to the mail server, allowing FTP traffic to the FTP server with or without authentication, and allowing HTTP or HTTPS traffic to the Web server with or without authentication.

■ **Secure mail network** Three-homed firewall with one connection to an external network, one to a service net, and one to an internal network. In this template you can provide for secure access to the mail server by SecuRemote users.

Using the template method, in contrast to the wizard method, creates an incomplete rule set. Although the rule base gets created, the objects remain undefined until you edit each one individually. In fact, all objects will require definition before you can install the policy. The wizard and template are very similar. However, the wizard walks you through the entire setup and makes you define all of the objects up front.

The wizards and templates are an easy way to get things configured to support basic services, or for new administrator with small networks. However, having a security policy that is fine-tuned for your organization is going to require that you do some manual definitions and ordering of objects and rules. So, let's start with an empty policy and begin building the policy from scratch.

Defining a Firewall Object

The first step in translating the written policy into an enforceable policy is to define the relevant network objects. After creating the network objects, you can create and/or modify the firewall workstation object. Having the networks defined first will enable you to configure anti-spoofing on the firewall object. The firewall object is something you must define before you can install your FW-1 security policy.

If you have initially installed the FW-1 Module, Management Server, and GUI on the same box, then the firewall object will be created and partially configured. If the components are installed in a distributed environment, however, you will have to create the firewall workstation object. You will start by logging into your management server via the Policy Editor GUI. If you haven't opened the Workstation Properties yet, as shown in Figure 14.5, you may do so by selecting the firewall object from the Objects List at the bottom of the window, right-clicking, and choosing **Edit** by double-clicking the firewall object from the Objects List, or by going through the **Manage | Network Objects** menu. You will need to create one firewall object for each firewall module that will be enforcing a security policy and that will be managed by this management server.

If you are creating the firewall object for the first time, then you can right-click **Network Objects** in the Objects Tree and choose **New | Workstation**. The first field you will be challenged with is the name of the firewall. This field should be the firewall module's TCP/IP host name. For better performance, it is recommended that DNS (Domain Name System) be configured to resolve this name to the firewall's external IP address, or at least have it set up in the host's file on the firewall. The next field should contain the external IP address of the firewall. If DNS is configured and you click **Get address**, DNS will be queried and the address will be filled in for you. Otherwise you can just type in the value. In the next field, the **Comment** field, be as descriptive as possible. Using comments is a good way to document what you are doing so that others can understand more quickly and easily. The next decision is what color to give the object. This should be based on a scheme that will help you to read the rules and logs more easily.

Figure 14.5 Workstation Properties with Check Point Products Installed

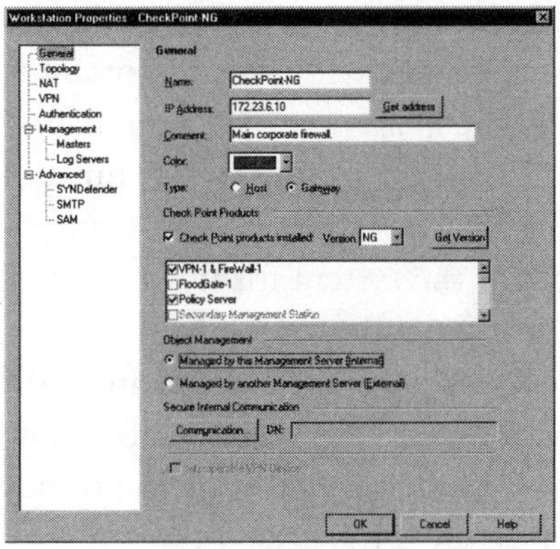

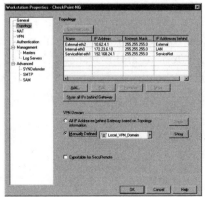

Now let's make this workstation a firewall. If it hasn't been checked already, check the box that reads **Check Point products installed** and select the version **NG**. This will enable the next list of product modules. Choose from the list the modules that are installed on this host. Next, in the section Object Management, you must select whether the Management Server for this firewall is Internal or External. Basically, by checking **Internal**, you signify that this Management Server will be able to install policies on this FW-1 module, and when you view the System Status GUI, this firewall object will be displayed. If the Management Server and firewall module are on different hosts, then you will need to configure Secure Internal Communication (SIC) to establish communication between these two machines. To do so, click on the **Communication** button and enter a shared password. If this object was created for you, Check Point already knows what products you have installed and has made the selection for you. Please double-check that the selection is correct before you continue. Finally, if an external management server manages this firewall module, then you will be able to use this external firewall in the rule base and configure it as a VPN endpoint, but you will not be able to install policies to it (another management server will do that), and it will not be displayed in the System Status Viewer. In short, you do not manage external firewall objects from this management server.

The second branch on the Workstation Properties is the **Topology** window. This enables you to define the networks reachable behind the internal and external interfaces that exist on your firewall object. Figure 14.6 illustrates this configuration window.

Figure 14.6 Topology Window

To define the interface, make sure that you have selected the right one. After selecting an interface to define in Figure 14.6, click **Edit**. This will open up the dialog box shown in Figure 14.7.

If you are configuring an interface manually, it is important to use the proper name, for example, the name as displayed by the *ifconfig -a* Unix command. Failure to properly define the interfaces may cause features such as anti-spoofing to not function, and may leave the network open to attack. If you are running SNMP on the object, then you have access to the **Get Interfaces** feature, which will query the system for its interface information (this is the recommended method of gathering this information).

Not only will you be able to specify this interface as internal or external, but you can also specify the range of addresses that reside behind the interface for enforcing anti-spoofing and generating NAT rules. This is done while manually adding or editing interface information from the Topology tab, as illustrated in Figure 14.7.

Figure 14.7 Topology Definition

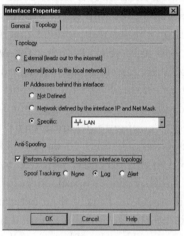

If the interface is internal, then it is very important to define the addresses that reside behind the interface. The first option, **Not Defined**, generally should not be used. If selected, anti-spoofing will be disabled on this interface. Generally speaking, it only makes sense to have anti-spoofing configured either for all or none of the interfaces. If you select the second option, then these addresses will be calculated based on the address and subnet mask for this interface. Finally, you can specify an explicit range of addresses or groups of networks. Anti-spoof tracking can also be defined on a per-interface basis.

The **Management** branch is quite important for your FW-1 configuration. The Management window enables you to specify logging options. These options are broken down into two varieties: Local Logging Options and Advanced Settings.

The **Advanced** window allows the configuration of SNMP settings. If you expand the **Advanced** branch, you will see the following three sub-menus:

- SYNDefender
- SMTP
- SAM

The SYNDefender branch is used to configure the firewall options to defend and respond to SYN attacks. Attackers may try to create a Denial of Service (DoS) by initiating a SYN Flood attack. Taking advantage of the connection-oriented nature and initial three-way handshake of TCP/IP, an attacker can keep requesting connections that a server will accept until it is out of resources. FW-1's SYNDefender option is disabled by default. To enable it, select SYN relay, SYN gateway, or Passive SYN gateway. These options are displayed in Figure 14.8.

Figure 14.8 SYNDefender Options

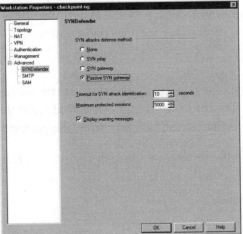

SYN relay monitors all connection attempts, and verifies that the attempt is valid before sending the initial SYN to the server. SYN gateway monitors all connection attempts as well as after the server responds with a SYN-ACK; the firewall also sends an ACK to the server and opens the connection so that the server's backlog queue is available to accept more connection requests. The timeout setting determines how long the firewall will wait before either receiving a response from the client and allowing the connection or closing the connection with the server by sending a RST (reset) packet. Finally, the Passive SYN gateway monitors all connection attempts like the gateway option, but it does not send an ACK to open the connection to the server. Instead, the passive method waits the allotted timeout period, and if the connection is not valid, it will send an RST to the server. For firewall modules prior to NG, the SYNDefender setting is configured under the Global Properties, FW-1 branch. Check Point recommends using the SYN gateway method if your network is susceptible to these types of attacks.

WARNING

A TCP/IP connection is established when a client requests the connection by sending a SYN packet to the server. Once the server receives the request, it will respond with a SYN-ACK acknowledging the client's SYN packet. Finally, the connection is established when the client sends an ACK back to the server completing the three-way handshake. When a SYN Flood attack is underway, a malicious client is sending multiple SYN packets to a server with spoofed source IP addresses so that when the server responds with a SYN-ACK, it does not receive a response in return to complete the connection. The server will save these initial sessions in its backlog queue and wait for a response. A SYN Flood attack works by filling up this backlog queue with bogus requests, which causes any valid connection attempts to fail, thereby creating a DoS.

The SMTP page enables you to set local options on how the SMTP security server handles mail. Typically, the defaults on this page are appropriate, although you may have to define the post-master name. These values are stored in the firewall's $FWDIR/conf/smtp.conf configuration file.

On the final page, you will not need to modify anything unless your SAM server is external to your management server. In most cases, you will skip this section. Changing these values will affect the firewall's $FWDIR/conf/fwopsec.conf configuration file.

Define Rule Base

Now let's use our perimeter network security policy to create a Check Point FireWall-1 NG enforceable policy. The first step is to map things out and identify the objects that will compose the rule base. The following is the relevant excerpt from the policy.

- TCP/IP suite of protocols allowed through the firewall from the inside LAN to the public Internet is as follows:
    - HTTP to anywhere
    - HTTPS to anywhere
- TCP/IP suite of protocols allowed through the firewall from the inside LAN to the Service Net is as follows:
    - HTTP to Web Server
    - SMTP to Mail Server
    - POP3 to Mail Server
    - DNS to DNS server
- TCP/IP suite of protocols allowed through the firewall from the Service Net to the public Internet is as follows:
    - DNS from DNS server to anywhere
- TCP/IP suite of protocols allowed through the firewall from the public Internet to the LAN is as follows:
    - None
- TCP/IP suite of protocols allowed through the firewall from the public Internet with specific source, destination, and protocols is as follows:

    - SMTP to Mail Server
    - HTTP to Web Server
    - FTP to Web Server

Reading through your policy, it refers to the LAN, the Internet, and a Service Net. These are all network objects, which will have to be defined before you can continue. Next, traffic is flowing anywhere, to the Web server, mail server, DNS server, and through the firewall. These three servers on the Service Net will be defined as hosts or workstations. Now that you know what objects are needed, you can create them. Based on the work you did earlier, you should be able to create these on your own.

Now that you have all of the objects defined, it's time to create the rule base. For your first rule, it is best to create the *Clean-up rule*. By default, anything that is not explicitly permitted is dropped. However, it would be nice to log those events, and the only way to accomplish that is to define an explicit drop rule in the policy and enable tracking. For your first rule, select **Rules | Add rule** in Policy Editor. This is your first rule, so bottom or top does not matter, although eventually this rule will be the last rule in the policy. From the rule that appears, confirm the following: source **Any**, destination **Any**, service **Any**, action **Drop**, and **Log.** The only thing you will need to change is the track cell from **none** to **Log**, and add a comment in the **Comment** field such as "Clean-Up Rule". At this point, your rule base should consist of one rule and look like the example in Figure 14.9.

Figure 14.9 The Clean-Up Rule

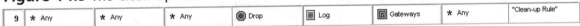

| 9 | ✳ Any | ✳ Any | ✳ Any | ⊙ Drop | ▤ Log | ▥ Gateways | ✳ Any | "Clean-up Rule" |

Another good rule to have in your rule base is the *Stealth Rule*. This rule is defined to protect the firewall and alert you of traffic that is directed to the firewall itself. This time, create the rule by clicking **Rules | Add rule** and choose **Above**. From the newly created rule, change the destination field by right-clicking and selecting **Add** from the context menu. From within the Add dialog, select your firewall object. Next, in the **Track** field select **Alert**. This rule should read **Any**, **Firewall**, **Any**, **Drop**, **Alert** as illustrated in Figure 14.10. Add a comment such as "Stealth Rule" in the **Comment** field.

Figure 14.10 The Stealth Rule

NO.	SOURCE	DESTINATION	SERVICE	ACTION	TRACK	INSTALL ON	TIME	COMMENT
1	✳ Any	▤ checkpoint-ng	✳ Any	⊙ drop	⚠ Alert	▥ Gateways	✳ Any	"Stealth Rule"

Now you have the beginnings of a good rule base. Let's start adding some rules that are based on your policy. The first element in the security policy states that you allow HTTP and HTTPS to anywhere. Because your policy doesn't call for any user authentication, you can leave your Stealth Rule at the top. Let's place this next rule beneath the Stealth Rule. Click on the icon in the toolbar that represents **Add Rule below Current**. The current rule will always be the rule that is highlighted in white, instead of gray like all the other rules. You should see a new rule sandwiched between your two previous rules. There are many ways to create this rule. However, the best way is to select **LAN** as the Source. For the Destination, select the **Service Net** (we'll explain why in a minute). Under the Service field, add **HTTP** and then **HTTPS**. Make sure you select **Accept** in the Action field. The Track field can be left at **None** for this rule. Now right-click on the **Destination Service Net** and choose **Negate**. A red "X" should now appear on the Service Net object in your rule base. What you have done is created a rule that allows LAN users the use of HTTP and HTTPS to everywhere *but* the Service Net. The reason you had to do this is because the policy doesn't allow HTTPS from the LAN to the Service Net, as you will see in the next couple rules. Use the Comment field to enter a comment such as **Permits LAN access to http and https on the Internet**.

Next, you must define what is allowed to the Service Net from the LAN. In these rules, you will allow the LAN access to the mail server for POP3, and the DNS server for DNS queries. Let's leave SMTP and FTP for later. Start creating the next rule by right-clicking on the number two from the previous rule and choosing **Add Rule below**. Just like the previous rule, the Source is the **LAN**; however, the Destination is now the **Email_Server**. In the Services field, add **Pop-3** and select **Accept** in the Action field. As far as the Track field is concerned, there are no requirements to log this traffic, and it might make the logs pretty large anyway, so leave Track as **None**. In the Comments field, write in "Permits LAN access to retrieve email via pop-3." Since the next rule will probably generate a lot of traffic (DNS queries), place it just below your stealth rule. So, add a new rule below rule one, and enter **LAN** in the Source field, **DNS_Server** in the Destination, **domain-udp** as the Service, and **accept** in the Action field. Again, let's not log this traffic because domain queries can be quite numerous and we don't need to log it. Enter **Permit LAN access to DNS server for DNS name resolving** in the Comment field.

Next, let's create a rule that allows your DNS server in the Service Net to perform queries to the Internet for domain name resolution. Add this rule beneath the rule you just finished. Set the rule to read Source-**DNS_Server**, Destination-**LAN** (Negate), Service-**dns**, Action-**accept**, Track-**None**, and Comment, "Permits DNS server access to Internet for domain name resolving."

Now for your final rules, what will you allow in from the Internet? According to the policy you will allow SMTP to the mail server and HTTP and FTP to the Web server. Create a new rule beneath the current rule. This new rule (number four) should be defined as Source-**Any**, Destination-**Email_Server**, Service-**smtp**, Action-**accept**, Track-**Log,** and Comment, " Permit anyone to send e-mail to the e-mail server via SMTP." Notice that this rule also permits your LAN users to connect to the mail server for SMTP. The next rule, Rule number five should be defined as Source-**Any**, Destination-**Web_Server**, Service-**http**, Action-**accept**, Track-**Log,** and Comment, "Permit anyone access to web pages via http on the web server." This rule also allows access for your LAN. Add one more rule below 5, and define it as Source-**LAN** (negated), Destination-**Web_Server**, Service-**ftp**, Action-**accept**, Track-**Log**, and Comment, "Permit anyone on the Internet access to FTP on the Web server." Since your policy doesn't allow your LAN to connect to the Web server for FTP, you had to negate it in the source.

Now you are pretty much done. Your rule base will have nine rules and should look like the FireWall-1 Rule Base shown in Figure 14.11. You should select **File | Save** or click the Floppy Disk Icon to save your finished policy.

Now, with these rules, the ordering is critical. Keep in mind that the firewall matches packets on the first three columns (Source, Destination, and Service) by using top-down processing. Each packet starts at the top rule and moves down until a rule matches. When a packet is matched, no further processing is performed. This is called top-down processing. If you wrote your rule base directly from a piece of paper, then there may be a few problems to sort out. There will always be more than one way to define your policy; the trick is finding the best method for your organization.

As you fine-tune your policy, you can try to simplify the way you say things. By moving rules, consolidating rules, or just by stating rules differently, you can improve the effectiveness and performance of your rule base. You will also need to install your rule base when you are satisfied that is it set up properly. Any changes that are made through the Policy Editor do not take effect on the firewall module until the security policy is installed. The Policy menu will be explained later in this chapter.

Figure 14.11 Rule Base from Security Policy

NO.	SOURCE	DESTINATION	SERVICE	ACTION	TRACK	INSTALL ON	TIME	COMMENT
1	✱ Any	FireWall-1_NG	✱ Any	Drop	Alert	Gateways	✱ Any	"Stealth Rule"
2	LAN	DNS_Server	UDP domain-udp	accept	None	Gateways	✱ Any	Allow DNS Queries from LAN to DNS Server.
3	DNS_Server	LAN	dns	accept	None	Gateways	✱ Any	Allow DNS server to perform lookups and zone tr
4	✱ Any	Email_Server	TCP smtp	accept	Log	Gateways	✱ Any	Allow any SMTP to Email Server.
5	✱ Any	Web_Server	TCP http	accept	Log	Gateways	✱ Any	Allow any HTTP to Web Server.
6	LAN	Web_Server	TCP ftp	accept	Log	Gateways	✱ Any	Allow all except the LAN to FTP to Web Server.
7	LAN	DMZ_net	TCP http TCP https	accept	None	Gateways	✱ Any	Allow the LAN HTTP and HTTPS access everywh
8	LAN	Email_Server	TCP pop-3	accept	None	Gateways	✱ Any	Allow the LAN POP-3 access to Email Server.
9	✱ Any	✱ Any	✱ Any	Drop	Log	Gateways	✱ Any	"Clean-up Rule"

Manipulating Rules

FW-1 features a very flexible rule base. It provides the ability to alter both content and context very simply. The next few sections focus on manipulating the rule base.

Cut and Paste Rules

Rules can be cut and paste in a way that will be instantly familiar to anyone. You simply select the rule (by clicking on its number), and either copy or right-click and select **Cut** from the menu. The menu is shown in Figure 14.12. Alternatively, you can select from the Edit menu. Pasting a rule is just as easy, but there is one additional selection to make. When you select **Paste** from the Edit menu, you'll also have to decide on the placement of the rule. Your choices are top, bottom, above, or below, with the choices indicating a relation to the currently selected rule.

Figure 14.12 Context Menu for Manipulating Rules

Disable Rules

Disabled rules are one step from being deleted. They are not part of your security policy and are not installed when you install the policy. They are, however, displayed in the rule base window. Disabling rules is a handy method of troubleshooting, providing an easy way of recovering the rule's functionality. To disable a rule, simply right-click on that rule's number and select **Disable Rule** from the menu. To reenable the rule, right-click the rule's number and deselect **Disable Rule.**

Notice the big red "X" in Figure 14.13 signifying a disabled rule.

Figure 14.13 Disabled Rule

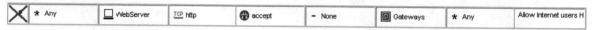

Delete Rules

Deleting a rule eliminates it from both the security policy and your rule base view. To delete a rule, simply click the rule's number and select **Cut** from the Edit menu. You can also select **Cut** from the right-click menu. While it is true that you can delete a rule outright, we recommend getting into the habit of cutting rules, since if you mistakenly remove the wrong rule, you can recover it quickly by pasting it back in.

Hiding Rules

Sometimes, especially with a large rule base, you don't really need to see every rule all the time. Luckily, FW1 allows you the ability to hide rules. These rules are still part of the security policy and are still installed when that policy is loaded, but they are not shown in the rule base window.

To hide a rule, select the rule by clicking its number. Next, right-click and select **Hide** from the menu, or select **Rule | Hide** from the Rules menu. A hidden rule is replaced with a thick, gray divider line, giving you an easy visual indication that a hidden rule exists.

In Figure 14.14 you can see the thick, gray line between rules four and six. Notice how the rule numbers stay the same. Rule five still exists; you just don't see it.

Figure 14.14 Hidden Rules

NO.	SOURCE	DESTINATION	SERVICE	ACTION	TRACK	INSTALL ON	TIME	COMMENT
1	✱ Any	FireWall-1_NG	✱ Any	Drop	Alert	Gateways	✱ Any	"Stealth Rule"
2	LAN	DNS_Server	UDP domain-udp	accept	– None	Gateways	✱ Any	Allow DNS Queries from LAN to DNS Server.
3	DNS_Server	LAN	dns	accept	– None	Gateways	✱ Any	Allow DNS server to perform lookups and zone tr
4	✱ Any	Email_Server	TCP smtp	accept	Log	Gateways	✱ Any	Allow any SMTP to Email Server.
5	✱ Any	Web_Server	TCP http	accept	Log	Gateways	✱ Any	Allow any HTTP to Web Server
7	LAN	DMZ_net	TCP http TCP https	accept	– None	Gateways	✱ Any	Allow the LAN HTTP and HTTPS access everywh
8	LAN	Email_Server	TCP pop-3	accept	– None	Gateways	✱ Any	Allow the LAN POP-3 access to Email Server.
9	✱ Any	✱ Any	✱ Any	Drop	Log	Gateways	✱ Any	"Clean-up Rule"

You also have the ability to both view and manage hidden rules. To view hidden rules, select **View Hidden** from the Rules menu. Managing hidden rules is even more flexible, as it enables you to create and apply masks to the rule base. These masks can be applied or removed to alter the view of the rule base. For example, suppose you have hidden all of the rules with a specific destination. You can store this view as a mask by selecting **Rules | Hide | Manage hidden** and then storing this view. Later, if you choose **Unhide All** from the Rules menu, you can easily reapply the filters via the same menu options. The options for working with hidden rules are in Figure 14.15.

Figure 14.15 Hidden Rules Options

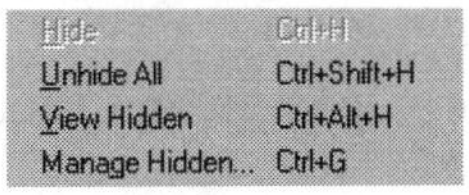

Hide	Ctrl+H
Unhide All	Ctrl+Shift+H
View Hidden	Ctrl+Alt+H
Manage Hidden...	Ctrl+G

Drag and Drop

There are several ways in which you can manipulate the rules by dragging and dropping within the Policy Editor. You can move a rule to a new location in the rule base by simply clicking its rule number and dragging it to the new position. You can also drag network objects and services into your rules from the Object List pane and drop them in the appropriate fields. You can even drag an object from one rule into another. This could save you some time when adding new rules or editing your existing rule base. It's worth your time to play around with this feature a little and start to get the hang of it.

Querying the Rule Base

The rule base can be viewed in many different ways. Sometimes it is beneficial to view it in its entirety, while at other times you may need to see only specific items. This is especially true when dealing with a very large rule base on a very complex network. One way to achieve this narrower view is through the ability to query the rule base.

To query the rule base, select **Query Rules** from the Search menu. A query builder will appear. This window lists defined queries and allows the addition, deletion, or modification of queries. Select **New** to define a new query. A window will appear that enables you to strictly define the criteria to query against. Enter a name for your query, and then click **New** again to begin entering search clauses. This window, the **Rule Base Queries Clause** window, is similar to that presented when creating a group. Simply select the column you wish to query, add the objects you wish to include in the query to the **In List** box, and you're done. You also have the ability to create a negation, that is, a query that will match only if the specified criteria are not present. The final option is to enforce the query explicitly. What this means is that the match must be exact. For example, if you select **Explicit**, then a query that contained a workstation object would not match a rule that used a group containing that workstation.

Policy Options

Once you have created your security policy, you are ready to put it into action. The next few sections describe the options available for working with the policy you have built. Access to these options is available by selecting **Policy** from the Policy Editor menu.

Verify

The Verify option is used to test the policy. It compiles the objects and prepares them for installation, but it does not actually perform the install. This is useful when you are in the process of editing and modifying your security policy, and wish to make sure that you aren't doing something wrong; for example, if you have a rule on top that accepts Telnet to anywhere, and then below that you create a rule to allow Telnet to a specific host. Selecting **Verify** from the Policy menu would tell you that "rule 1 blocks rule 2 for service Telnet." This means that rule 2 is redundant, and will never be matched on a packet, and therefore it is misplaced.

Install

The Install option actually performs the install. You'll be presented with a list of possible firewall objects and can select the proper firewall or firewalls to install on from this list. The policy is then compiled and pushed out to the selected modules. You have a choice as to how these modules are treated:

- **Install on each selected Module independently** This is useful when you are dealing with a large number of gateways. With this option, each module is treated as a single entity, and failure to install policy on one will not impact the others negatively.

- **Install on all selected Modules** This is an all-or-nothing proposition. If you are concerned with configuration integrity, this is the option for you. Failure on any single module will preclude the installation on any other module.

- **Install on all the modules of the selected Gateway Cluster** This applies to Gateway Clusters and is identical in behavior to the above **Install on all selected Modules** option.

You will need to install your security policy whenever you make changes through the Policy Editor and wish for those changes to be enforced. Nothing you do in the Policy Editor will take effect until you push the policy to the appropriate firewalls.

Uninstall

The Uninstall option removes the policy from the objects that you select. The object selection method is identical to that used when installing a policy.

View

The View option enables you to view the compiled security policy; that is, it enables you to view the inspect statements, which allows you to view and save the actual inspect scripts. Saved files can be manually altered and loaded with the command-line interface (CLI) of FW-1.

Access Lists

The Access Lists option is used to incorporate rules into an OSE compliant device, such as a router. When a rule is installed on a router, the firewall actually is generating an access control list (ACL) for that router and applying it as needed. You can also import the existing ACL entries for the OSE device and verify and edit them. This menu option allows for all three functions. When selected, the **OSE Device Access List Operations** window is displayed. This window enables you to select the OSE device you want to interact with and perform the specified operation. When fetching an ACL, you can further specify the direction you are interested in, and the format you wish the ACLs to be presented in (ASCII or GUI). This requires additional licensing.

Install Users Database

The Install Users Database option, available from both the Policy menu and the User Management function, propagates the user database defined on the management server to the selected modules. Note that the user database is also loaded when a security policy is published (pushed/installed) to the modules, but this manual process allows the updating of user information without interfering with the firewall operations.

Management High Availability

The Management High Availability option of the Policy menu enables you to modify the behavior of your Management High Availability groups. This feature allows multiple management modules to synchronize and support each other, just as with highly available FW-1 modules. This option loads a maintenance panel, which allows for both manual synchronization and preempting of the primary management server.

When performing a manual synchronization, you have two modes of behavior to select from:

- **Synchronize Configuration Files Only** If this is selected, only the database and configuration files will be synchronized between management modules.

- **Synchronize Fetch, Install and Configuration files** This mode also synchronizes the fetch and install files, allowing the interaction with a standby management server.

You can also change the current state of the management module, from primary to standby and vice versa.

Installing a Security Policy

After you have defined all objects and composed the rule base, it is time to install the policy on your chosen modules so that it can be enforced. Remember that anytime you modify network objects, rules, or global properties, you need to install the policy for the changes to take effect. The install policy process does a few things before your rules get enforced.

When you select **Install** from the Policy menu, Check Point first saves your objects and rules. Next, Check Point verifies your rule base to ensure that you don't have any conflicting rules, redundant rules, or rules with objects that require definition. Alternatively, before you install, you can verify the policy by choosing **Policy** and then selecting **Verify**. Check Point NG will then parse your rule set. After the verify process returns the results that "Rules Verified OK!" Check Point NG asks you to select on which network object and module to install the compiled policy.

Select the object that you wish to install this policy on, and an installation window will open. The progress of the compile and install will be displayed here. When the policy install is completed, you can click the **Close** button at the bottom of the window as shown in Figure 14.16. If you wish to cancel the installation in progress, click the **Abort** button.

Figure 14.16 Install Policy Progress Window

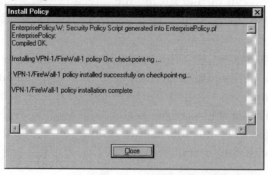

Alternatively, you can install the policy on the firewall modules at the command prompt with the use of *$FWDIR/bin/fw load*. For example, if you want to install the policy named Standard.W on a firewall module defined with an object named Gatekeeper, then you would run the following load command from the Management server's $FWDIR/conf directory:

```
$FWDIR/bin/fw load Standard.W all.all@Gatekeeper
```

To confirm the installation of your policy at the command line, execute *$FWDIR\bin\fw stat*. This will display the host, policy, and time of install.

Policy Files

In the process of compiling your security policy, Check Point NG uses the contents of the rule base file ★.W (which you created through the Policy Editor GUI) to create an INSPECT script with the same name adding a .pf extension. The ★.pf file is compiled into INSPECT code designated as a file called ★.fc (where the ★ represents the name given to your policy in the initial dialog). The INSPECT code is then applied to the network objects (firewalls) specified in the install. Keep in mind that when you install a policy on a module that has no rules to enforce, the default implicit *deny all* will be in effect for that host and module.

To back up your policy, you should make and keep a separate copy of the files listed below:

- $FWDIR\conf\objects_5_0.C
- $FWDIR\conf\★.W
- $FWDIR\conf\rulebases_5_0.fws
- $FWDIR\database\fwauth.NDB★

The objects_5_0.C file stores all the network objects, resources, servers, services, and so on. The ★.W files are each individual policy file that you named via the Policy Editor. The rulebases_5_0.fws file is the master rule base file that holds each of the individual ★.W policies in one place. If you needed to restore your policies, then you would not necessarily have to replace each .W file, but just the rulebases_5_0.fws. When you log into the Policy Editor, this file will open and create the .W files that were not already in the conf directory. This fws file gets called whenever you select **File | Open** in the Policy Editor, and you can rename or delete policies from this file via the **Open** window. Deleting a policy from here does not remove it from the hard drive; it just simply removes it from the rulebases_5_0.fws file. The fwauth.NDB★ files contain the user database.

NOTE

The *.W file can be edited with a text editor. Editing this code does not affect the GUI representation of rules. However, it will be used to create the INSPECT script and may introduce inconsistencies between the GUI interface and the installed policy. As an alternative, the *.def file can be edited instead.

Summary

In this chapter we have discussed the importance of a security policy and how to write one for your organization. Remember that the most important aspect of defining a security policy is involvement. Because the default policy of Check Point NG is to deny everything, with community involvement you can better define the requirements, and as a result, only permit communication that is necessary for business activities while denying all others.

As you implement and translate your written policy into something that can be enforced by Check Point NG, you will have to define network objects. Much of this information should have been gathered during the design of your policy and includes items like workstations, gateways, users, and services. Eventually, the rules you write will use these objects to match packets for processing and applying actions.

A firewall object must be defined for each firewall you are installing a policy on. In a simple, standalone installation where the management server and firewall module reside on the same machine, the firewall object is created for you during software installation. You will need to configure the interfaces topology and anti-spoofing and possibly SYNDefender within your firewall object definition.

FW-1 provides several tools to manipulate the security policy. There are several different methods of adding a rule to the rule base, disabling rules, cutting and pasting rules, and querying the rule base. Once you have the policy defined and you are ready to start the firewall enforcing the policy, you must install the policy onto the firewall objects that you have previously defined.

The installation of a policy is a process that converts the GUI rule base, which is represented as the ★.W file, into an INSPECT script language ★.pf file. The ★.pf file is then compiled into INSPECT code, and is represented as a ★.fc file that can be understood and enforced by the specified Check Point NG modules.

Chapter 15

Advanced Configurations

Best Damn Topics in this Chapter:

- **Check Point High Availability (CPHA)**

- **Single Entry Point VPN Configurations (SEP)**

- **Multiple Entry Point VPN Configurations (MEP)**

- **Other High Availability Methods**

Introduction

The Internet and Internet services have become increasingly important to businesses over time, and several organizations are choosing to implement measures to keep these services highly available to their staff or to their customers. The first task is identifying which services are business-critical, and then determining the best solution to keep that service available 99.9 percent of the time. The reason that keeping a service available is an issue at all is because the Internet and networking technology are not fail-proof. Your ISP connection could be down or slow, your internal router could lose its routing table and stop passing packets, or you could have a hardware failure or power failure at any point in the network infrastructure, which could cause any number of service interruptions.

So, what can you do to prevent these outages from happening? Well, you probably can't control them 100 percent of the time, regardless of how much time, money, and effort you put into the project, but you can make a considerable dent in downtime by setting up some redundant systems and configuring them to failover in the event of a failure.

For example, suppose your company prints a well-known newspaper on the East Coast, and having the Internet available to your reporters is business-critical, since they use this source of information for many of their articles. Therefore, it's your job to have a redundant Internet connection with fail-over abilities. You could contract two ISPs, have two routers set up at each end of each ISP connection, have two or four firewalls set up to fail-over, and have two routers inside each firewall, all plugged into various uninterruptible power supplies (UPSs). This is a complicated configuration, but it can be an operational means to have a high availability (HA) connection to the Internet.

In this chapter, we will discuss the Check Point High Availability module, and discuss a few network configuration models in which Check Point will allow VPNs to fail over. And we'll discuss some of the other options you can utilize with VPN-1/FW-1 in order to have a high availability system.

Check Point High Availability (CPHA)

High availability can be your best friend, both from a network performance and from a security perspective. Many enterprises are concerned about the firewall being their single point of failure, and we've seen more than one contingency plan allowing for the redirection of traffic around a firewall, should it fail. With a highly available solution, this won't be needed.

One of the first questions we are often asked when dealing with high availability concerns the definition of available. What makes a system available? Is it that the operating system is…for lack of a better term…operating? Is it defined by a daemon on the system, or, like a server group discussed earlier in the book, does it require some sort of agent installed to monitor "upness"? To answer these questions, we'll delve into the mechanics of Check Point High Availability.

Enabling High Availability

Before you can begin using HA or define and join clusters, you have to do some preparatory work. Primarily, you need to make sure that you have the proper licensing in place in order to run the High Availability module, and that HA is enabled. Then you must define the configuration and the IP addresses on the future cluster members. The cluster members must have three interfaces, with four interfaces being preferred if you opt to use synchronization. All of the internally facing IP addresses must be the same, as must all of the externally facing addresses. The Check Point High Availability module will make sure that the MAC addresses are identical, so there's no need to play around with Address Resolution Protocol (ARP) entries. Figure 15.1 illustrates what a sample network layout for High Availability might look like. Note that all of the external facing IP addresses are the same in the diagram (noted as .101 to indicate the final octet) as are the Internal IP addresses. Also, while we indicate that a hub or switch can be used, Check Point is, at the time of this writing, reported to be addressing a problem whereby only a hub can be used for a HA cluster. The interfaces on the management segment must each use a unique IP address. Also, if state synchronization is opted for, you'll probably want to connect the firewall machines on another interface, one used exclusively for synchronization. We'll discuss synchronization later in the chapter.

Figure 15.1 An HA Cluster

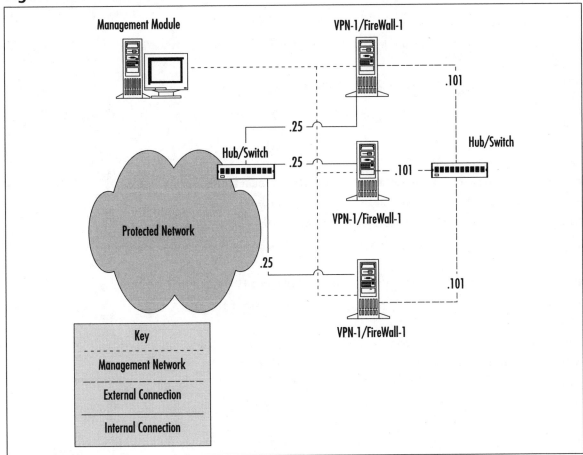

The next step toward gaining the benefits of Check Point High Availability is to enable it on the enforcement module. This is a really easy step, and only involves running the *cpconfig* command. An example of the *cpconfig* command run on a Solaris machine that is running the enforcement module is shown in the output below and in Figure 15.2.

Figure 15.2 Enabling High Availability

```
# cpconfig
This program will let you re-configure
your VPN-1 & FireWall-1 configuration.


Configuration Options:
----------------------
(1)   Licenses
(2)   SNMP Extension
(3)   PKCS#11 Token
(4)   Random Pool
(5)   Secure Internal Communication
(6)   Enable Check Point High Availability/State
 Synchronization
(7)   Automatic start of Check Point modules

(8) Exit


Enter your choice (1-8) :6
Configuring Enable Check Point High Availability/State Synchronization...
===========================================================
High Availability module is currently disabled.


Would you like to enable the High Availability module (y/n) [y] ? y
-----------------------------------------------------------


You have changed the High Availability configuration.
Would you like to restart High Availability Module now
so that your changes will take effect? (y/n) [y] ? y



*************************************************************
The High Availability module is now enabled.
cpconfig will now end. To continue, please run cpconfig again.
```

Enabling Check Point High Availability in Windows is even easier, since the Windows version of *cpconfig* is GUI based. Access the High Availability tab by selecting **Start | Programs | Check Point Management Clients | Check Point Configuration NG | High Availability tab**. Place a checkmark in the checkbox, indicating that you are enabling High Availability.

NOTE

There are two distinct types of bootups for a HA member. Initially, at the first boot, there are no real elements of the cluster associated with that machine. The policy has not yet been installed, no priority is associated with the machine, and no gateway priority has been defined. In this case, the gateway begins to look for information by listening on UDP port 8116, from an already configured cluster member. If it can't determine information from a configured cluster member, then it looks for information from other machines with its shared IP address. Once it sees that traffic, it will select the MAC address from the machine with the lowest Random ID and use it for its own.

After that initial boot, and after the remaining cluster information has been assigned, the CPHA module looks for packets coming from the Primary cluster machine, compares that machine's MAC to its own, and changes its own, if necessary.

There are some restrictions when implementing a High Availability solution. The gateways must be running the same version of VPN-1/FW-1, and they must be on the same platform (e.g., you cannot synchronize a Solaris firewall with a Windows NT firewall). Also, you must have a separate management server; the management module cannot reside on a cluster member.

Another wise bit of advice is to configure each cluster member offline, that is, off of the network. While it is good security practice to build machines disconnected from the network anyway, there is a different reason here. Since each machine will be sharing IP addresses, it's nice to avoid address conflicts that might be present if the machines were active on the network segment. Finally, if you are configuring a Single Entry Point (SEP) Virtual Private Network (VPN) HA solution, the VPN domain for the cluster should be a group object containing the cluster member gateways and their respective VPN domains. We'll discuss SEP later in this chapter.

Failing Over

Now that we've seen how to enable Check Point's High Availability, your next question most likely harkens back to our earlier wonderings about what classifies a system as "up." When dealing with Check Point FW-1, the answer to this question is up to you.

When using the Check Point High Availability module, you gain access to the functionality of the *cphaprob* command. This command enables you to define services that are considered critical to the operation of the VPN-1/FW-1 system. There are also some default conditions that must be met for the system to be considered available. These are as follows:

- The fwd process must be running, and must not report any problems (for example, the un-installation of the security policy is considered a problem).

- The network connection must be active.
- The machine must be running.

These are, of course, the most basic of conditions. As you've come to expect, (and, we hope, appreciate) Check Point enables you to enhance the granularity of the checking. This is done using the aforementioned *cphaprob* command. This command is used to register additional devices within the firewall machine as critical, so that their failure will cause the preemption of cluster control. The options to this command are displayed in Table 15.1.

Table 15.1 *cphaprob* Command Options

Command Option	Command Explanation
-d <device name>	Specify a device to be monitored.
-s <status>	The state of the device. Status can be either "ok," "init," or "problem." If the value is anything besides "ok", the device is not considered active.
-t <timeout>	Define a timeout value. If the device doesn't report its status before the timeout expires, the device is considered to be failed.
-f <filename> register	Allow the specification of a file containing multiple device definitions.
[-I[a]][-e] list	Display the current state of CPHA devices.
Register	Register the device as a critical process.
Unregister	Remove the registration of this device as a critical process.
Report	Display the status of the HA modules.
If	Display the status of interfaces.
Init	Instruct the firewall to reacquire the shared MAC address.

You can also use the *cphaprob* command with the *state* argument to see the status of the HA cluster. Example output for a two-member cluster might resemble this:

```
$ cphaprob state


Number      Unique Address    State


1 (local)   192.168.10.1      active
2           192.168.10.2      standby
```

You can also check your log files for information about both synchronization and failover.

Firewall Synchronization

State Synchronization allows the firewall or VPN module to be really highly available, in the truest sense. Without synchronization, when a fail-over occurs, the connections that are currently active will be dropped. This may not be that important when dealing with a firewall, for example, when the majority of the traffic through your firewall is destined for the Web, but can be disastrous in a VPN context. You probably never want to be without synchronization when dealing with a VPN.

Synchronization maintains an identical state table on all of the machines involved in the gateway cluster. This, obviously, uses resources. The synchronization process consumes memory, CPU, and network resources, and depending on the size of the state table, this could be significant.

How does it work? The first thing to grasp is that the entire state table is not copied from machine to machine all the time. Obviously, the first synchronization involves the entire state table, but subsequent updates only involve the changes since the last update. The updates occur by default every 100 milliseconds, and while this can be changed, the process isn't easy and you'll probably never want to try. Another thing to consider is that processing the updates takes a minimum of 55 milliseconds. If you are maintaining a particularly busy site, one with a lot of HTTP traffic, for example, your state table may have a larger number of changes, and processing may require more time than the minimum. When we say that synchronization consumes resources, we mean it.

Also, synchronization is not available when using a Multiple Entry Point (MEP) VPN solution. This is because, as we will discuss later in this chapter, MEP is designed for use with a disperse VPN solution. Synchronization is most often used with a SEP VPN solution, and you can see a screen shot of the Synchronization panel in the section on SEP. In a truly user-friendly manner, enabling synchronization is as easy as placing a checkmark in the box labeled **Use State Synchronization** on the **Synchronization** tab of the cluster object. Next, you'll need to define the synchronization network by clicking on **Add** on the **Synchronization** panel. Clicking **Add** will show you a panel similar to the one shown in Figure 15.3.

Figure 15.3 Add Synchronization Network

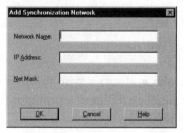

There's a caveat here: Make sure that the synchronization network is trusted. The way we do this is to segment the synchronization traffic from any general-use traffic (for example, by using a crossover cable when dealing with a two-member cluster). Next, you need to make sure that FW-1 control connections are allowed to pass between the cluster members. Simply make a rule that allows the FW1 service from member to member.

After you have activated synchronization, you'll want to test it to make sure that it is working. There are a couple of different techniques. The quickest way is to check the size of the state tables on each machine. The command to do this is as follows:

```
fw tab -t connections -s
```

While this is quick, it is the least accurate. Remember, the state table is updated frequently, so there is a chance that the table on one machine could change before you can type the command.

The most accurate method (although we've seen it return false information) is the use of the *fw ctl* command. Using the *pstat* option will give you the info on the synchronization process (and other processes as well). A sample bit of the output is shown below.

```
sync new ver working
sync out: on   sync in: on
sync packets sent:
total: 2145 retransmitted: 0 retrans reqs:0 acks: 0
sync packets received:
total 2473 of which 1 queued and 31 dropped by net
also received 0 retrans reqs and 2 acks to 0 cb requests
```

Another way to check is to see that two or more firewalls are connected to one another via the *netstat −an* command (for example, *netstat −an | grep 256*). On Windows machines you can substitute the *findstr* command for *grep*.

The second line is the key to determining the operation of state synchronization. If synchronization is on, then both the *sync out* and *sync in* fields should be on.

What if you are working on a particularly busy boundary firewall cluster, where the vast majority of traffic consists of HTTP and SMTP connections? Each of these connections is relatively short-lived, and might not be the best candidates for synchronization. HTTP, for example, is totally stateless by design, so a fail-over probably wouldn't be noticed. Does the burden of synchronization outweigh the benefits? If so, you are in luck - you don't have to synchronize every protocol. You can selectively weed out those protocols that are hogging too many resources when compared to the necessity of their HA condition. This is done by editing the $FWIDR/lib/user.def file and inserting a line like this:

```
//Don't sync the web!
 non_sync_ports {<80, 6>};
```

The first line is a comment, which is always a wise thing to add. The second line supplies port numbers as arguments a port number (80) and a protocol number (6). After applying that change to all cluster members and restarting the firewall service, you'll no longer be synching HTTP, and perhaps will be saving CPU cycles.

Single Entry Point VPN Configurations (SEP)

SEP VPNs enable your enterprise to deploy a solution that protects what many consider an increasingly critical element of the network. VPNs enable you to extend your enterprise to the remote user, and as more companies look toward telecommuting, remote sales forces, and partner networks, their availability becomes increasingly important. Gone are the days when a VPN was a novelty or a convenience; today it's a necessity. Also, synchronized connections are a must. You wouldn't want users to notice that their VPN connection was just transferred to another gateway. Another nice feature is the support for SEP (and MEP) VPNs when dealing with both remote clients and with gateway-to-gateway VPNs.

Gateway Configuration

Before you go about configuring a SEP VPN solution, you need to make sure that Gateway Clusters are enabled on the management server. This is simply done from within the Global Properties in the Policy Editor. Figure 15.4 shows you the means of enabling HA on the Management server.

Figure 15.4 Enabling Gateway Clusters

In this section, you'll look at configuring an HA solution in depth. Figure 15.5 is presented here as a memory refresher. It shows you the General panel used for cluster configuration. This panel is used to initially identify the information about the cluster, such as the cluster name and IP address and also to specify the Check Point applications installed. Note that the IP address configured here is the cluster IP address. This will be the common IP of the cluster, and should be defined in the interface configuration of each cluster member.

Figure 15.5 Gateway Cluster: General Panel

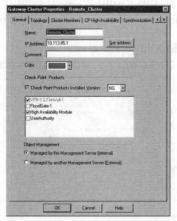

You also can specify, on the topology panel (Figure 15.7), which addresses reside behind this cluster. This is similar to the features on a workstation object's interface properties topology panel. One of the most common uses of a manually defined VPN domain is to define an overlapping encryption domain for the gateway cluster. Figure 15.6 shows a gateway cluster with an overlapping VPN domain. Note that the VPN domain contains the protected network and all of the cluster members.

Figure 15.6 Overlapping VPN Domain in an SEP Configuration

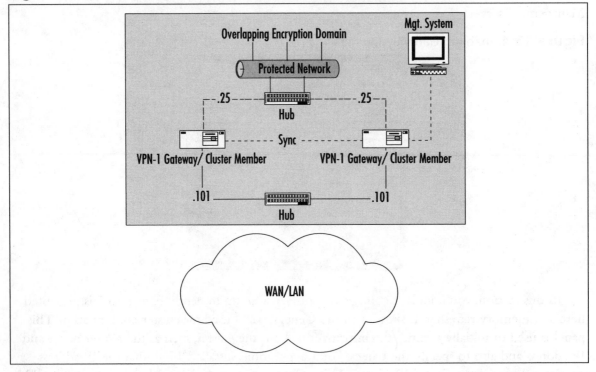

You'll first need to define a network object symbolizing the protected network. Then you'll want to define a group object containing each gateway cluster member, as well as the newly created network object. In Figure 15.7, this group is called Remote_VPN_Domain. Specifying this object on the Topology panel as shown is all you need to do to institute a full VPN domain overlap.

Figure 15.7 Gateway Cluster: Topology Panel

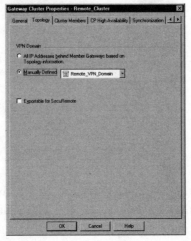

The next panel enables you to specify cluster members. This is your next task. Cluster members are the workstations previously defined for inclusion within the cluster. This configuration panel is illustrated in Figure 15.8. Here it is important to note that order is important, as the order in which the gateways are listed defines their priority. The order can be shuffled without much effort by the use of the familiar **Up** and **Down** sort buttons. Also, new gateways can be added and old ones simply removed, as well. In this case, the **Edit** button will take you to the Properties panels for the selected gateway, allowing very handy alteration of its settings information.

Figure 15.8 Gateway Cluster: Cluster Members

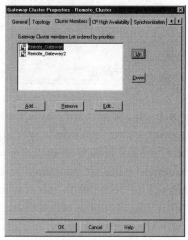

Figure 15.9 shows you how the High Availability settings are defined. The first option, High Availability Mode, tells the HA process how to react when a failed cluster member returns to service. There are two options, which are explained below:

- **Active Gateway Up** In this mode, when a primary gateway has failed and subsequently returned to service, it will not regain control of the cluster. Instead, it will assume the role of secondary. This is useful when you opt not to use state synchronization, as it causes the least interference in these cases.

- **Higher Priority Gateway Up** When the primary gateway in the cluster fails and subsequently returns to service, it will retake control of the cluster, assuming that it has been assigned a higher priority (as sorted in the cluster members panel).

Also defined on this panel is the action to take when a primary gateway fails:

- None
- Log
- Alert
- Mail

Figure 15.9 Gateway Cluster: High Availability Panel

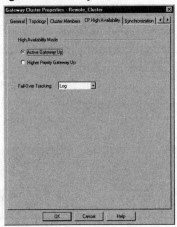

Figure 15.10 shows you the Synchronization panel. Synchronization is not required for a HA cluster to function, and is, in some cases, better excluded. Synchronization assures that no connections are lost when a primary cluster firewall fails. It does this by maintaining the state table across all cluster members. This table maintenance has an associated resource cost, which, depending on the size of the state table, can be large. The decision to use this feature is up to you. If you opt for its benefits, you'll need to define what Check Point calls a "synchronization ring," or, in common terms, a group of networks. Note that the network listed in this ring will be treated as trusted. The HA module will trust all messages coming from this network, and, as such, it should be segmented from normal user traffic. If you opt not to use synchronization, simply uncheck the **Use State Synchronization** field.

Recall from our earlier discussion of State Synchronization what the purpose of this mechanism is. Imagine if a user behind your firewall is getting a very large file via FTP, downloading the newest service pack from Microsoft, for example. If the primary firewall failed and synchronization was enabled, the secondary firewall would take over the connections and the user wouldn't notice the slightest difference. Without synchronization, the transfer would have to be restarted, perhaps with the loss of the already downloaded data.

Figure 15.10 Gateway Cluster: Synchronization

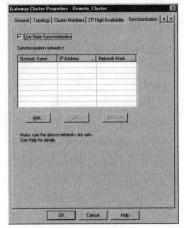

The remaining tabs of the Gateway Cluster are identical to their cousins in the workstation Properties. Hidden in the screenshots are VPN, Authentication, Masters, and Log Servers tabs (This is part of the workstation object). These allow the setting of the same information as for the individual member workstations, except that here the information is defined per cluster. This also means that the information will no longer be configurable on the individual cluster members.

Policy Configuration

When you have finished configuring the cluster and assigning all the proper members, you still need to allow the FW1 service to pass between the cluster members. As mentioned earlier in the High Availability section, it's best to make sure that the synchronization network is trusted completely. This is easily accomplished by simply not connecting that network to any other machines. You certainly wouldn't want others synching up with your firewalls—that could lead to very bad things. There's only one problem with making this rule. You can't use the cluster object as either a source or destination in the rule base. To work around this, you'll need to create a workstation object with the IP address of the interface on the synchronization network, and use that in the rule.

Multiple Entry Point VPN Configurations (MEP)

MEP VPN deployments make use of the VPN-1/FW-1 Backup Gateway feature. With this sort of implementation, gateways for logically separated networks can be used to connect to the same destination network, assuming that a link exists between those networks. A diagram of a MEP configuration is shown in Figure 15.11.

Figure 15.11 Simple MEP Illustration

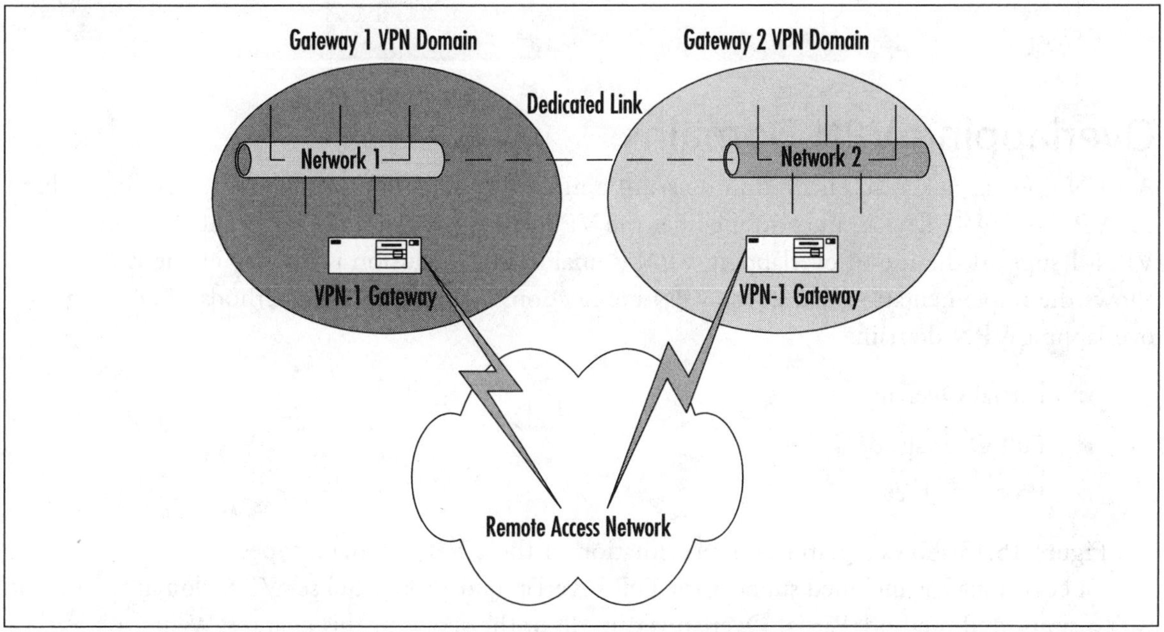

We consider MEP configurations to be more of a redundancy solution than a true HA solution. Since the networks are logically (and often geographically) separated, firewall synchronization is not possible. With this being the case, connections cannot be maintained as they can be with a SEP configuration. Instead, when the SecuRemote client's gateway fails, there is a brief pause before the backup gateway is connected. This will cause an interruption in the connection from a user's perspective. Usually this isn't a big deal. A user browsing the Web, for example, will simply click the browser's refresh button to continue as normal. Something like an SSL-secured Web page, however, would be more of a bother.

The first step toward setting up a MEP solution is to enable backup gateways on the Management server. This is done by altering the **Global Properties | Gateway High Availability** by placing a checkmark in the box labeled **Enable Backup Gateway**, as shown in Figure 15.12.

Figure 15.12 Enabling MEP

Overlapping VPN Domains

A VPN domain (a.k.a. an encryption domain) defines the entirety of the network residing behind the VPN-1/FW-1 device, and also includes the VPN-1/FW-1 gateway(s). Recent versions of VPN-1 support the use of overlapping VPN domains. This inclusion is the key element that allows the implementation of HA for VPN connections. There are three methods of creating an overlapping VPN domain:

- Partial Overlap
- Full Overlap
- Proper Subset

Figure 15.13 shows a graphical representation of these VPN domain types.

Check Point has included support for Full Overlap and Proper Subset VPN domains. Since it isn't a supported method, Partial Overlap is outside of the scope of this chapter. We'll look at the particulars of the two supported VPN domains over the next few paragraphs.

Figure 15.13 VPN Domain Types

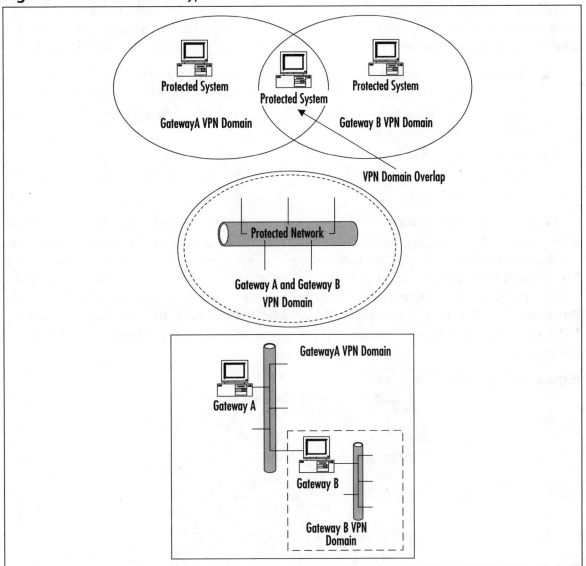

As we mentioned in the first paragraph of this section, a VPN domain consists of the network residing behind the gateway, including that gateway. What this means for you, as a firewall administrator, is that you define a network object consisting of the protected network and then point to that network object within the configuration of the workstation object that is the VPN gateway. Implementing a fully overlapping VPN domain isn't much more difficult. All you need to do is properly define the network object. Simply define a group of network objects containing all of the involved gateways and all of their protected networks, and then point to this new group object as the VPN domain for those gateways.

This type of VPN domain is very handy when dealing with critical connections. When a SecuRemote client attempts to communicate with a server residing within this overlapping domain, it will attempt to connect to all of the gateways, and will complete that connection with the first gateway to respond. This brings up a potential problem in that traffic that came in through one gateway could possibly be sent back out through a different gateway, which would result in that packet not being encrypted. To prevent this from happening, you have two choices.

- **The use of Network Address Translation**. Using NAT enables you to hide the connections passing through the gateway behind the gateway. This requires the use of a sensible hiding IP address (the hiding address, that is, for the SecuRemote client) that is routable to the issuing gateway.

- **The use of IP pools**. IP pools enable you to assign an address to the SecuRemote client from a previously configured source. This source can be either a network object or an address range.

Note that State Synchronization cannot be considered a solution to asymmetric routing. There is no way that you could hope two firewalls could synchronize fast enough to avoid this problem.

A popular solution to the problem of asymmetric routing is the use of IP pools. If you ever have to use a VPN solution that doesn't support pools, you'll quickly see why having them available is far superior to not having them. To enable pools, you need to modify the Global Properties to place a check in the field called **Enable IP Pool NAT for SecuRemote and VPN connections**. What to do when the pool evaporates is up to you. Figure 15.14 illustrates this panel.

Figure 15.14 Enabling IP Pool NAT

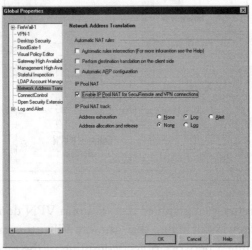

Address exhaustion, which has the familiar three options of None, Log, and Alert, defines what to do when the addresses allocated to your pool are all gone. It is not recommended that you select **None**. Address allocation and release is a must for logging. Equate this with DHCP lease information as far as function, and consider the gap in your security policy if you didn't have accountability here.

Gateway Configuration

The gateway configuration is much more simple than the SEP configuration. This is essentially because, as previously mentioned, this is more of a failover solution than a HA solution. The gateways aren't clustered and there's no way to synchronize. SecuRemote clients will connect to their primary gateway as normal. If that gateway fails, then the connections are reestablished with the backup gateway. This takes a few seconds, so there will be a momentary interruption in the user's connection. But momentary is a lot better than permanent, we think you'll agree. If, however, you don't want even a moment's interruption, SEP would be considered the best choice.

> **NOTE**
>
> So, you aren't sure if either SEP or MEP is the solution for you? Say, for example, that you have a really mission-critical connection, one that just cannot be down. But you also have a requirement for redundant connections. These redundant connections have to be available even if an entire site goes down.
>
> You have options. There's nothing that says you can't use both SEP and MEP in tandem. You could define a SEP group to handle the requirement for the highly available connection and then use MEP to define a redundant backup link!

Once you've enabled backup gateways in the Global Properties, you are able to define them within the Workstation object representing the gateways in your infrastructure. On the VPN tab of the Workstation Properties panel, you'll see a new checkbox called **Use Backup Gateways:** and an associated drop-down menu. Place a checkmark in this box and select the desired backup gateway from the list, and you're off to the races. The results will resemble the panel as shown in Figure 15.15.

Figure 15.15 Configuring a Backup Gateway

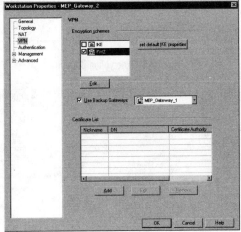

The next step is to define the VPN domain for this gateway. There are really no special tricks involved here. All you have to do is define the proper VPN domain for this gateway, just as you would if you were using a single gateway solution. Figure 15.16 illustrates this panel.

Figure 15.16 Selecting the VPN Domain

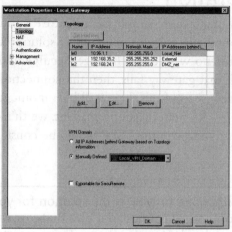

Overlapping VPN Domains

Establishing a MEP configuration using an overlapping VPN domain makes things about as easy as possible. In simple terms, an overlapping VPN domain makes the VPN domain of all partici-pating gateways identical. While a VPN domain usually contains a single gateway and the net-work that resides behind it, when establishing an overlap, the domain contains all of the gateways and their respective protected networks. Configuring a MEP configuration for a fully overlapping encryption setup isn't all that hard. Let's take a look at the steps. For these examples, we'll assume a dual gateway architecture protecting the following networks:

- 10.1.1.0/24

- 10.1.2.0/24

Figure 15.17 shows you a MEP configuration using a fully overlapping VPN domain.

Figure 15.17 Fully Overlapping VPN Domain

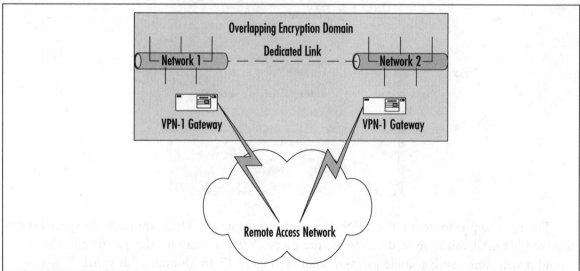

The first step is to define these networks for use within your rule base. By selecting **Manage | Network Objects | New | Network** from the Policy Editor, you'll be able to create the networks representing your VPN domain. You'll also need to create the workstation objects representing the gateways that you'll be using. After you have done that, you have to place them all into a group. Select **Manage | Network Objects | New | Group | Simple Group** from the Policy Manager menu, and create a group like the one shown in Figure 15.18.

Figure 15.18 Overlapping VPN Domain Group

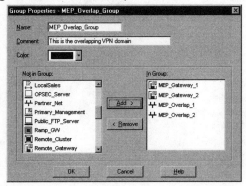

Next, you have to configure this new VPN domain on all of the firewalls that are participating within the configuration, and that's it. Shown in Figure 15.19 is what the Topology panel will look like. Note the Manually Defined VPN domain.

Figure 15.19 Overlapping VPN Domain

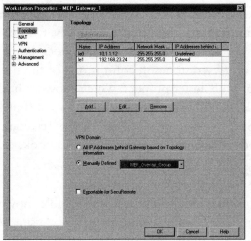

You also must use some means of avoiding the problem of asymmetric routing. Again, a popular choice is the use of IP pools. You'll also need to make sure that the routing within your network is properly configured to handle passing the traffic back to the network associated with the IP pool network. To associate an IP pool with the gateway, you first must define an address range that will be used as the pool. After you do that, access the Workstation Properties and select the NAT panel. Place a checkmark in the box marked **Use IP Pool NAT for SecuRemote and**

VPN connections, select the previously defined address range object, and you're ready to go. Figure 15.20 shows you this final configuration panel.

Figure 15.20 Using IP Pools

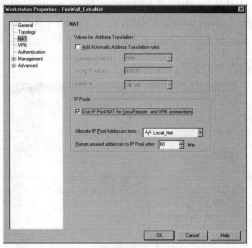

When your SecuRemote clients attempt to initiate a connection, the first gateway to respond will be selected. This is a pretty simple method and is one of the reasons that this configuration is so straightforward.

Other High Availability Methods

So far, we've been discussing some generic High Availability configurations, and we've only mentioned using the Check Point HA module. There are, however, other ways to accomplish the task of HA. Many vendors have developed HA solutions for Check Point VPN-1/FW-1, and some of them are very good. Stonesoft (www.stonesoft.com) is one of the more established players in this market with their StoneBeat FullCluster product, which provides both HA and load balancing. Another popular choice is RainWall from Rainfinity (www.rainfinity.com). You can see a full listing of Check Point OPSEC certified products at www.opsec.com. Discussion of the configuration for each of these products is beyond the scope of this book.

Routing Failover

Another failover method is to use a routing protocol to handle moving traffic around a downed firewall. The most popular method of implementing this is by using Virtual Router Redundancy Protocol (VRRP). We only know of one platform that currently supports VRRP, and that is the excellent Nokia appliance. For those readers with a networking background, think of VRRP as a takeoff on Hot Standby Routing Protocol (HSRP), or. The firewall software will have to take over the duties of synchronization, but that's not unusual to the HA solutions we've looked at.

Configuration of VRRP is outside the scope of this text, but we can discuss some of the more general points that you'll be dealing with. First, you need to decide which version of VRRP you want to implement. There are two versions in common use: VRRP v2 and VRRP

Monitored Circuit. Unless you have a pressing need to use VRRP v2 (address space exhaustion, backward compatibility, and so forth), you should opt for Monitored Circuit. In either of these configurations, you may experience problems with asymmetric routing. One of the main differences in v2 and Monitored Circuit is the convergence time, that is, the time it takes for a failure to be detected and corrected. In earlier versions of IPSO, convergence time could be over eight seconds. Using Monitored Circuit, the convergence time is less than one second. Like HSRP, VRRP uses HELO messages, sent at a default interval of one second, to a multicast destination (which must be allowed in the rule base) to announce their status. This HELO message includes a priority, which is used to determine which gateway should be the active member of the cluster. If the primary machine detects a failed interface, for example, it would decrement its priority, thus notifying the backup gateway to take over the cluster. Remember to include all of the firewall interfaces in the tracking list. It wouldn't do much good if the outside interface was down, but not tracked, and the inside interface was still taking traffic.

Hardware Options

A final method that we want to touch on briefly is the use of an external, hardware-based solution. Examples of these abound, and their usefulness varies… caveat emptor. One of the main disadvantages of hardware-based load balancers or HA solutions is that they generally introduce a single point of failure, which in essence is counter-productive. Generally, the meantime between failure (MTBF) of these units far exceeds that of the standard server machine, but we've rebooted far too many of these things to feel really comfortable with them. Also, most of these products don't really offer a true highly available solution. Load balancing with a health-checking option (which will direct packets around a downed unit) is the best you can expect, which is still pretty good.

One notable exception is the Foundry ServerIron XL content switch. This product was the first to be OPSEC-certified to provide full fail-over support, including the fail-over of active VPN sessions. ServerIron also supports clustering and synchronization of its load balancers, so that they are not a single point of failure. Also, the configuration commands for this switch are nearly identical to those of the Cisco IOS, which makes the learning curve simpler. You can get more information at www. opsec.com.

Summary

While you might not be using, or even considering, implementing a Highly Available solution within your network, it is a good idea to be aware of the capabilities that Check Point VPN-1/FW-1 offers you.

If you are currently using a High Availability solution, the coverage of some of the finer details in this chapter should have given you food for thought and perhaps some new configuration techniques. While most of the focus was on the VPN aspects of HA solutions, keep in mind that HA is also a valuable solution for any mission-critical network boundary.

## Chapter 16

Configuring Virtual Private Networks

Best Damn Topics in This Chapter:

- **Encryption Schemes**

- **Configuring an FWZ VPN**

- **Configuring an IKE VPN**

- **Configuring a SecuRemote VPN**

- **Installing SecuRemote Client Software**

- **Using SecuRemote Client Software**

Introduction

Many organizations are using virtual private networks (VPNs) over the Internet in order to have a secure channel for remote offices, business partners, and mobile users to access their internal networks. For many, the VPN is replacing dedicated Frame Relay circuits or dial-in VPN services for their organizational needs.

For example, your office headquarters may be in Hartford, Connecticut, but you have a small, remote office located in Tampa, Florida. You could set up a gateway-to-gateway VPN between these two offices so that they can share each other's resources on the network through an encrypted channel over the Internet. The communication between these two branches is secured by the endpoints of the connection, which are the firewalls at each location.

In this chapter, we discuss the different types of encryption available to you in VPN-1/FW-1 NG, and we'll explain this technology to you so that you'll understand how it is working. Check Point makes it easy to set up a VPN using their Policy Editor, and we show you how to configure VPNs between gateways and to mobile clients. Then we demonstrate how to install the SecuRemote client software. If you are interested in desktop security for the client, we will be covering that later in the book.

A bit of theory is necessary before beginning the process of describing how to set up VPNs with Check Point NG. You need to first understand the basics of encryption algorithms, key exchange, hash functions, digital signatures, and certificates before you can feel comfortable troubleshooting and deploying VPNs.

Encryption Schemes

Encryption is the process of transforming regular, readable data, or plaintext, into "scrambled" or unreadable form, called ciphertext. Decryption is the reverse process, the transforming of ciphertext into plaintext. The process of encryption can be used in various ways to ensure privacy, authenticity, and data integrity:

- **Privacy** No one should be able to view the plaintext message except the original sender and intended recipient.

- **Authenticity** The recipient of an encrypted message should be able to verify with certainty who the sender of the message is.

- **Data Integrity** The recipient of the message should be able to verify that it has not been tampered with or altered in any way while in transit.

Encryption is accomplished using an encryption algorithm, typically a pair of closely related mathematical functions that perform the actual encryption and decryption on the data provided to them. Modern encryption algorithms, including the ones used in Check Point NG, use what is called a *key* (or keys) to aid in the encryption or decryption process. There are two types of encryption algorithms: symmetric and asymmetric.

Encryption Algorithms; Symmetric versus Asymmetric Cryptography

In what is called *symmetric encryption*, the encryption algorithm itself is public, while the key is a secret. Anyone discovering the key, with knowledge of the algorithm, can decrypt any messages encrypted with that key. Since both the sender and recipient need to know the secret key before they can communicate, you must have a secure method of exchanging the key. Sometimes you will hear the term "Sneaker Net" used to describe this key exchange process, meaning that the exchange takes place via phone, fax, or in person, since an online exchange cannot be encrypted prior to the sharing of the key. Sometimes you will hear this key referred to as a "shared secret." Symmetric encryption is typically very fast, but has some disadvantages:

- As stated previously, anyone discovering the secret key can decrypt the messages.

- Since each sender-recipient pair (we will call them "users") needs a separate secret key, the number of separate keys that need to be managed increases rapidly as the number of users increases. Mathematically, we need $n(n-1)/2$ keys for a network of n users. Using this formula, a network of 500 users requires 124,750 unique keys.

Asymmetric encryption was developed to solve the problem of secure key exchange and to improve key management. It is called asymmetric because the encryption and decryption keys are different. In one form of asymmetric encryption, called "public key" encryption, both the sender and recipient each have two keys, one that is public and can be openly shared, and another that is private and is kept secret and never shared. If Alice wants to send an encrypted message to Bob, she and Bob only need to exchange public keys. The method used for the exchange need not be private in this case. Alice encrypts the plaintext message to Bob using Bob's public key. When Bob receives the message, he decrypts it using his private key. This method of public key encryption was invented in 1976 by Whitfield Diffie and Martin Hellman, and is sometimes called the "Diffie-Hellman" algorithm.

Another form of asymmetric encryption, called RSA encryption, is used by Check Point NG for generating digital signatures.

As we can see, asymmetric encryption solves the problem of key exchanges needing to be done in private. Users need only share their public keys to encrypt messages to one another. Asymmetric encryption does suffer one serious drawback, however: It is much, much slower than symmetric encryption (on the order of 1000 times slower). For this reason, real-life encryption schemes tend to use a *hybrid* form of public key exchange and private (symmetric) key encryption. Check Point NG is no different in this regard. A Diffie-Hellman key pair is used to generate and exchange a shared secret key, which is used for all encryption and decryption after the initial public key exchange. The shared secret key in this case is sometimes called a *session key*. The shared key can be regenerated at periodic intervals to lessen the chance of its compromise.

An encryption algorithm's security is completely dependent on its keys and how they are managed. Strong encryption that has a flawed key management algorithm is really weak encryption. You will often hear of an encryption algorithm described as using a 128-bit key, for example. What this means is that, if implemented properly, someone who tried to enumerate every possible key in order to break your encryption (called a *brute force* attack) would have to try 2^{128} different key combinations to be guaranteed success. This is not computationally feasible for the foreseeable future. In practice, cryptanalysts will typically attack an algorithm's key generation or key management scheme instead, attempting to find a flaw such as a predictable sequence of keys to exploit. The moral of all this is to pay attention to an algorithm's implementation, rather than to its key size exclusively. The latter will not guarantee your security. Note that asymmetric encryption schemes typically have key sizes that are much larger than symmetric ones (1024 bits, for example). The strength of these keys cannot be equated to the strength of symmetric keys, as they use different mathematical principles. The original Diffie–Hellman public key scheme, for example, was based on the difficulty of factoring very large prime numbers.

Check Point makes available several encryption algorithms. They are enumerated in Table 16.1, along with their shared key sizes and whether or not they are based on a public standard or are proprietary.

Table 16.1 Check Point Encryption Algorithms

Algorithm	Key-Length in Bits	Standard
FWZ-1	40-bits	Check Point proprietary
CAST	40-bits	Public
DES	56-bits	Public
3DES	168-bits	Public
AES	256-bits	Public

Key Exchange Methods: Tunneling versus In-Place Encryption

The previous encryption algorithms can be used in one of two key exchange schemes in FW-1: IKE (ISAKMP) or FWZ.

The Internet Security Association and Key Management Protocol (ISAKMP), or Internet Key Exchange (IKE), is an Internet encryption, authentication, and key exchange standard put forth by the IETF. It is widely used in today's Internet when implementing VPNs. Because it is a standard, a Check Point firewall using it will be able to interoperate with other third-party VPN products. We have tested or seen in production Check Point firewalls that interoperated with Linux gateways (Free/SWAN), OpenBSD, SonicWall, and Watchguard firewall products, as examples. The ISAKMP key exchange process is divided into two phases, and uses what are called *Security Associations* (SAs) to facilitate encryption and key generation. Keys and SAs are regenerated on a periodic basis.

IKE uses what is called *tunneling-mode encryption*. This means that each packet that is to be sent over a VPN is first encrypted (both header and data payload are encrypted), and then encapsulated with a new header. The new header will differ based on whether the packet is just being encrypted, just being authenticated, or both. This tunneling mode slightly degrades network performance, but is more secure.

FWZ is a Check Point proprietary key exchange scheme that uses another proprietary protocol, RDP (Reliable Datagram Protocol, not the same as the one described in RFC1151) to negotiate encryption and authentication methods between gateways.

FWZ uses what is called *in-place encryption*, in which packet bodies are encrypted, leaving the original TCP/IP headers in place. This method of encryption is faster than tunneling mode, but at the expense of security, since original header information is left in a readable state, including IP addresses, which are internal to an organization. Note that because FWZ does not encapsulate packets before sending them through a VPN, FWZ cannot be used in situations where any networks participating in the VPN domain have nonroutable addresses.

Hash Functions and Digital Signatures

A hash function, also known as a *one-way function*, is a mathematical function that takes a variable-length input and generates a fixed-length output, which is typically much smaller than the input. If we pass a plaintext message through a hash function, we produce what is called a *message digest*. A good hash function is one that, if we are given the message digest, it is impossible to *reverse* the function and deduce the original message. It is also one in which for any two different function inputs (two different messages in this context), the output should be unique to the input. To put it another way, the message digests for two different messages should also be different. As we will see in the following example, this principle can be used to ensure the integrity of a message. If a hash function generates the same message digest for two different inputs, we call this a *collision*. A good hash function will minimize collisions. When we talk about hash functions, we usually specify the length of the message digest in bits. This roughly corresponds (strengthwise) to the length of a symmetric encryption key. For example, a commonly used hash function, MD5, produces a 128-bit message digest for any size input it is given.

The output to a hash function is usually much smaller than the original message as well. MD4 and MD5 are good examples of hash functions. You may have heard of an MD5 checksum before. This checksum would be the result of sending a file through the MD5 hash algorithm.

Another important note about hash functions is that the output is unique to the message. If the original message was tampered with in any way, then a different message digest would result. Since you cannot "decrypt" a message digest, you run the algorithm against the message and compare the two digests to verify that the message is intact. This is how data integrity is achieved.

A *digital signature* is an attachment to a message that uses a hash function and enables the receiver to authenticate the sender and verify data integrity. Digital signatures can be attached to encrypted messages. Check Point NG generates digital signatures using an RSA private key and a hash function, as follows (assume that Alice wants to send a digitally signed message to Bob):

1. Alice sends the (unencrypted) message through a hash function, producing a fixed-length message digest.

2. Alice encrypts the message digest with her private RSA key, and sends it on its way, along with the encrypted message. The encrypted message is now "signed" by Alice.

3. Bob decrypts the message as usual, and passes it through the same hash function Alice used when it was sent. Bob compares this message digest he just generated with the decrypted message digest sent to him, making sure they match. Alice's public key is used to decrypt the message digest in this case.

A match in this case means that Bob can be sure that Alice sent the message, and that no one tampered with it in transit. We are assuming here that Bob trusts that he is using Alice's public key; this trust is usually provided by a certificate authority (CA) who will certify public keys.

The two hash functions offered by Check Point are *MD5* and *SHA-1*. MD5 is a 128-bit hash function, while SHA-1 is considered more secure with a 160-bit message digest length.

Certificates and Certificate Authorities

A CA is a trusted third party that we can obtain a public key from reliably. A certificate is issued by a CA, and contains reliable information about the entity wanting to be *certified* as authentic. This could be a person's or firewall's public key, or a secure Web-server host name and domain.

In the case of Check Point NG VPNs, certificates can be used by encrypting gateways to exchange public keys and to authenticate one another. Typically, the gateways themselves or (in the case of FWZ) the management consoles act as CAs in this regard.

Types of VPNs

There are logically two types of VPNs: *site-to-site* and *client-to-site*. Site-to-site VPNs are what we normally think of when we think VPN—two gateways separating an insecure network (usually the Internet), with encrypted traffic passing between them.

Client-to-site VPNs, on the other hand, have a fixed gateway at one end and a mobile client on the other, perhaps with a dynamic IP address. This type of VPN is implemented by Check Point's SecuRemote or Secure Client products.

VPN domains

We can define a *VPN domain* as a group of hosts and/or networks behind a firewalled gateway that participate in a VPN. In a site-to-site VPN, each gateway has its own VPN domain defined, and is also aware of the other gateway's VPN domain. Any traffic coming from one VPN domain and going to the other (behind the opposing gateway) will be encrypted outbound, and then decrypted inbound at the other end.

VPN domains are defined on each gateway's firewall object, and must be set up with certain rules in mind. We talk about this in more detail when we discuss VPN implementation.

Configuring an FWZ VPN

This section describes how to implement a site-to-site FWZ VPN. We discuss configuration of local and remote gateways first, and then add encryption rules to our rule base. We show configuration in the common situation of two gateway modules, with the local module acting as a management station for both modules. Since the management station manages both firewall modules, it will be a CA for both gateways. We must also decide which networks will participate in our VPN domain. For this example, we will use *Local_Net* and *Remote_Net*. Make sure these network objects are created prior to starting implementation of your VPN. It is worth noting that in order to install a policy with encryption rules, you will need to purchase an encryption license from Check Point. This can be added to an existing license, or included with an original software purchase.

NOTE

It is important not to include either peer's gateway object in their respective VPN domains, or else traffic to or from each gateway will be encrypted, which is not what we want, nor can it work, as key exchange has not yet taken place. Contrast this with SEP (Single Entry Point) configurations, in which gateways must be a member of each VPN domain. In addition, for nonroutable VPN domains, make sure opposing subnets are not identical. In large deployments, where you may have more than one gateway, each with a unique VPN tunnel, make sure the VPN domains don't "overlap" or include the same hosts/networks in both domains. Both gateways will want to encrypt traffic in cases where traffic passes through more than one gateway on the way to its destination. Better to use a SEP configuration for this, with some dynamic routing protocol inside your local network.

Defining Objects

For any site-to-site VPN, you will need to create and properly configure certain network objects, including both gateways and the networks or group objects representing your VPN domains.

Local Gateway

The first step in implementing your FWZ VPN is to configure your local gateway's encryption parameters. Under the **VPN** tab of your gateway's **Workstation Properties** window, select the FWZ encryption scheme and click **Edit**. The FWZ Properties dialog comes up (see Figure 16.1). Choose the management station (itself in this case) from the **Key manager management server** drop-down box, and generate a DH key if one is not present.

Figure 16.1 Local Gateway's FWZ Properties Dialog

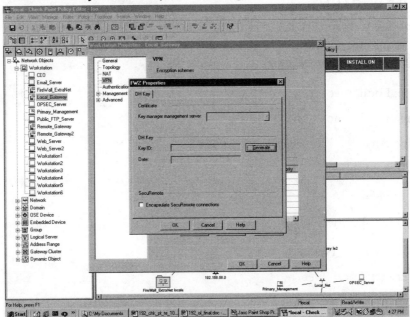

Next, open the **Topology** tab of the **Workstation Properties** window (see Figure 16.2). This is where you will define your VPN domain for the local gateway. Under **VPN Domain**, select **Manually Defined**, and then choose your local network from the drop-down list.

Figure 16.2 Topology Tab of the Workstation Properties Window

Remote Gateway

The remote gateway is set up exactly as the local gateway, with the distinction that your remote gateway's VPN domain is defined as *Remote_Net*, and your *Key manager management server* is still the local gateway object, since that is acting as the management station for both of your encrypting gateways.

Adding VPN Rules

You want to modify your rule base so that traffic between *Local_Net* and *Remote_Net* is encrypted. This is done rather simply with the addition of two rules to your rule base (see Figure 16.3).

One rule specifies the following:

- Source: Local_Net
- Destination: Remote_Net
- Service: Any
- Action: Encrypt
- Track: Log

While the other specifies the following:

- Source: Remote_Net
- Destination: Local_Net
- Service: Any

■ Action: Encrypt

■ Track: Log

Figure 16.3 Rule Base Encryption Rules

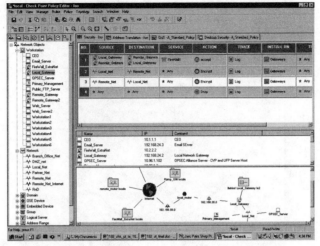

If you double-click on the **Encrypt** action in either encrypt rule, you will open the **Encryption Properties** dialog, from which you select **FWZ** and click **Edit** (see Figure 16.4). In the **FWZ Properties** dialog, you can choose your encryption method, allowed peer gateway (which gateway or gateways you are allowed to establish a VPN with), and a data integrity method. You are limited to MD5 data integrity with FWZ encryption.

Figure 16.4 FWZ Properties Window

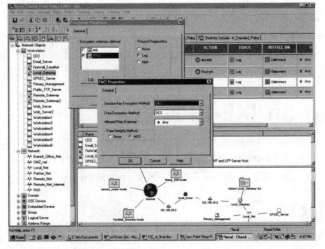

Note that in your encryption rule base, you have Rule 1 defined to allow the "FireWall1" group of services between both gateway endpoints. This rule is not always necessary, but must be added when you have **Accept VPN-1 & FireWall-1 control connections** unchecked in your security policy's **Global Properties** window (see Figure 16.5). This is checked by default after installation, so, in most cases you won't need a rule 1 as shown previously, but it is good to keep in mind, as this allows the key exchange between gateways.

Figure 16.5 FireWall-1 Implied Rules

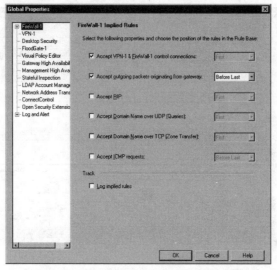

Once the gateway objects are properly configured and the VPN rules are added to the rule base, the security policy must be installed for the changes to take effect. Once the policy has been installed on both gateways, you can open your log viewer and begin testing your VPN.

FWZ Limitations

Because FWZ is a nonencapsulating protocol, you cannot use it in situations where the networks participating in your VPN domains have nonroutable addresses, or where both the source and destination IP addresses are being translated. FWZ will also not interoperate with other third-party VPN products, as it is a Check Point proprietary scheme. If you are in any of these situations, use IKE instead.

Configuring an IKE VPN

We will use the same assumptions that we have two gateways, both managed by the same management station. As before, be sure to define network objects for the networks that will be participating in your VPN domain. We will use Local_Net and Remote_Net again for these networks.

Defining Objects

For any site-to-site VPN, you will need to create and properly configure certain network objects, including both gateways and the networks or group objects representing your VPN domains.

Local Gateway

Under the **VPN** tab of your gateway's **Workstation Properties** window, select the **IKE encryption scheme** and click **Edit**. The IKE Properties dialog comes up (see Figure 16.6).

Notice that you have more encryption and data integrity choices with IKE than with FWZ. Select any and all of the encryption and data integrity methods you want your gateway to support, and check **Pre-Shared Secret** under **Support authentication methods** (you would check **Public Key Signatures** if you were using certificates). You will not be able to edit this secret until you define your remote gateway's encryption properties.

Figure 16.6 IKE Properties Dialog

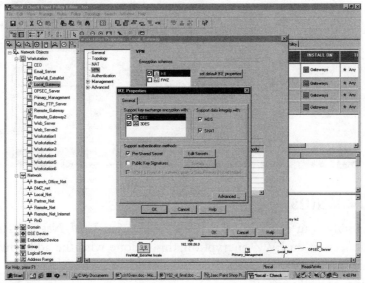

Next, open the **Topology** tab of the **Workstation Properties** window (see Figure 16.2). This is where you will define the VPN domain for your local gateway. Under **VPN Domain**, select **Manually Defined**, and choose your local network from the drop-down list.

Remote Gateway

Configuration of the remote gateway is nearly identical—you just need to make sure that you support the same methods of encryption and data integrity as you did on the local gateway. When you check **Pre-Shared Secret** this time, you can click on **Edit Secrets**, where you should see your peer, the local gateway, in the Shared Secrets List window (see Figure 16.7). You can edit the shared secret by highlighting the peer gateway in the list and clicking **Edit**. Enter the agreed-upon shared secret in the **Enter secret** text field, and click **Set** to define it. Don't forget to define your VPN domain under the Topology tab, by opening the **Topology** tab of the **Workstation Properties** window (see Figure 16.2). Under **VPN Domain**, select **Manually Defined**, and choose your remote network from the drop-down list.

Figure 16.7 Shared Secret Configuration

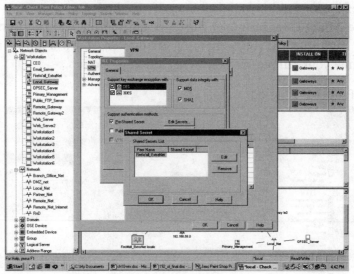

Adding VPN Rules

You will want to modify your rule base so that traffic between *Local_Net* and *Remote_Net* is encrypted. As in the section on FWZ encryption, this is done with the addition of two rules to your rule base (see Figure 16.8).

One rule specifies the following:

- Source: Local_Net
- Destination: Remote_Net
- Service: Any
- Action: Encrypt
- Track: Log

While the other specifies the following:

- Source: Remote_Net
- Destination: Local_Net
- Service: Any
- Action: Encrypt
- Track: Log

Figure 16.8 IKE Encryption Rules

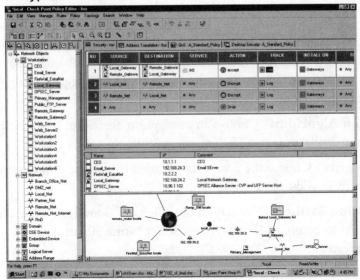

Rule 1 allows key exchange to occur between the two gateways by allowing the predefined service "IKE" to be accepted bidirectionally. This rule is only necessary if you have **Accept VPN-1 & FireWall-1 control connections** unchecked in your security policy's Global Properties window (see Figure 16.5). This is checked by default, so in most cases you won't need a rule 1 as shown previously. Note that the "IKE" service is included in the "FireWall1" service group, so you can use the same rules here that you used earlier, under FWZ encryption. Specifying only the IKE service here gives you more control over exactly what traffic you want to allow between gateways, and is especially important when your peer gateway is not managed by you. See the next section for more considerations of this sort.

If you double-click on the **Encrypt** action in either encrypt rule, you will open the **Encryption Properties** dialog, from which you select **IKE** and click **Edit** (see Figure 16.9).

Figure 16.9 IKE Properties Dialog

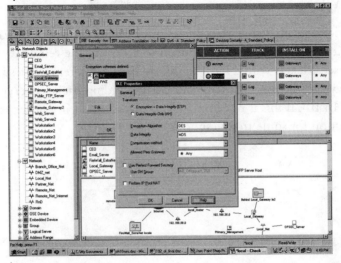

You have more choices here than you did when you used FWZ encryption. Go through the options given here one at a time:

- **Transform** Determines how each packet is encapsulated prior to being transmitted to the peer gateway. "Encryption + Data Integrity (ESP)" is the default, and is probably what you want in most cases. The other option, "Data Integrity Only (AH)," does not provide encryption, only authentication.

- **Encryption Algorithm** Choose an encryption algorithm from the list. Strong encryption is available with IKE (for example, Triple-DES or AES).

- **Data Integrity** Choose the hash method used to provide authentication. SHA1 is available here, in addition to MD5.

- **Compression Method** Normally, only "Deflate" is available here. This specifies the method used to compress IP datagrams. Select **None** if you do not want the added CPU overhead.

- **Allowed Peer Gateway** Specifies exactly which gateways this one is prepared to establish a VPN with. Defaults to "Any," meaning that you will allow VPN traffic from or to any gateway if the packets source or destination IP address is in the other gateway's VPN domain.

- **Use Perfect Forward Secrecy (PFS)** PFS adds an added measure of security to key exchanges, with some additional overhead.

- **Use DH Group** This enables you to select which Diffie-Hellman group you would like to use for encryption. Selecting a "longer" group means better key security.

- **Use IP Pooling** Allows the use of a predefined "Pool" of IP addresses that are assigned to incoming VPN connections. This is typically used to prevent or fix asymmetric routing conditions where inbound and outbound VPN traffic follow different routes.

Testing the VPN

Once the configuration is complete, install the security policy on both gateways. Try to establish a connection from a host in your local VPN domain to a host in the remote gateway's VPN domain. You should see packets with a local source address and a remote destination address being encrypted on the way out the local gateway, and corresponding packet decryptions on the remote gateway (see Figure 16.10). If this is not immediately apparent, or if you see errors in the log, then see the next section for some troubleshooting tips.

Figure 16.10 Log Viewer Showing Encrypts, Decrypts, and Key Exchanges

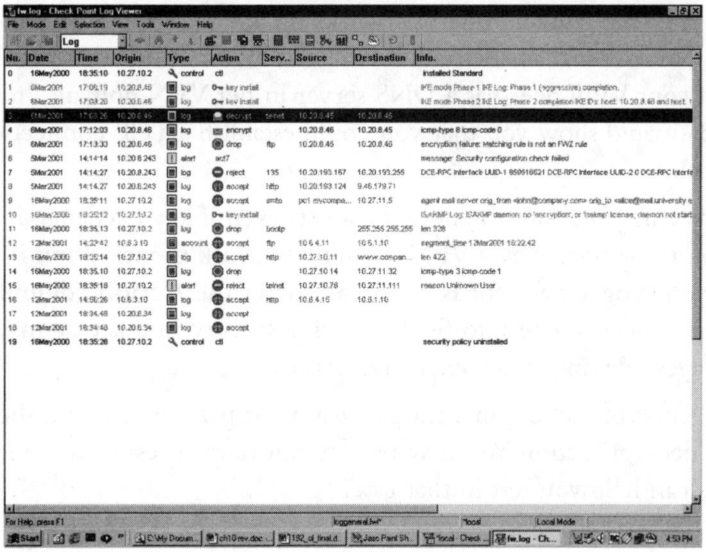

Debugging VPNs

Troubleshooting VPNs has traditionally been rather difficult. There are certain steps you can take to make troubleshooting and testing of VPN deployments easier:

1. Enable implied rule logging in the security policy **Global Properties** window.

2. Under the security policy **Log and Alert** tab in the **Global Properties** window, enable all the three encryption-specific log events: **VPN successful key exchange**, **VPN packet handling errors**, and **VPN configuration and key exchange errors**.

3. Disable NAT (Network Address Translation) by adding one or more manual rules to the NAT rule base that force traffic between opposing VPN domains to be "Original," or un-NATed. NAT can be used with VPNs; however, disabling it allows for cleaner testing (see Figure 16.11).

4. Be aware that the gateways participating in the VPN and perhaps the management stations need to communicate prior to the VPN tunnel being established (key exchange, protocol negotiation, etc.). You may need a rule in your rule base explicitly allowing this communication (see the previous FWZ and IKE encryption rule base examples). Be aware of where in your rule base your stealth rule is, and how this might impact such communication. Implied rule and VPN logging, discussed earlier, will show you such communication in a default installation.

5. Remember to test traffic from VPN domain to VPN domain, not from gateway to gateway. Normally, gateways are *not* included in VPN domains, and so they cannot provide a platform for reliable tests.

6. Be aware that using just ICMP (ping) tests may not tell whether a VPN is working correctly. This especially applies if you don't have control over the other VPN endpoint. Administrators are often leery of allowing ICMP through their firewall and/or border

routers, and may be dropping it with implicit or explicit rules before any encryption can take place. A better test, and one that works on any platform with a "telnet" binary, is to telnet to a port other than the traditional port 23, using one that you know is open. For example, if your VPN peer has a DNS server in her VPN domain, "telnet <IP of DNS server> 53" would show you that you could establish a TCP connection through your VPN tunnel.

7. Your gateway may attempt to encrypt packets even if key exchange is not complete, causing you to wonder why a VPN is failing to work if encryption is taking place. If you filter your Log Viewer for **Key Install** under the **Action** column, you will see key exchange as it occurs. The Info field of each log entry in this case may contain useful error messages relevant to key exchange errors.

8. For every "encrypt" action on your gateway, your partner's firewall should show a corresponding "decrypt" action. You may or may not have access to those logs, so the preceding tips can help you test in that case.

Figure 16.11 Address Translation Disabled between VPN Domains with Manual Rules

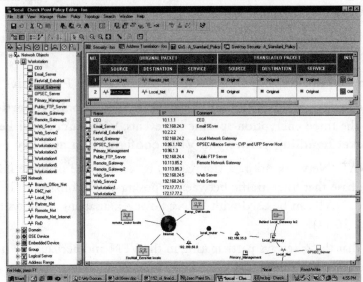

Considerations for External Networks

It is important that all encryption rules have the same exact parameters defined under their respective Encryption Properties dialog. Your VPN will fail if they do not. This is easy to check when you manage both the local and remote gateways, but can be harder to verify when the remote gateway is managed by another management station, or even another company. Typically, this coordination is done via telephone, agreed upon ahead of time as in "We will use IKE with 3DES encryption, SHA-1 data integrity, key exchange for subnets, and no perfect forward secrecy." Most VPN failures are a result of someone changing his or her respective VPN parameters, causing key exchange, encryption, or decryption to fail.

Configuring a SecuRemote VPN

In this section you will see how to configure your gateway for client encryption with SecuRemote, Check Point's client-to-site VPN tool. First, you will configure your gateway to act as a SecuRemote "Server," and then define the SecuRemote users, including their authentication methods. Finally, you will add the appropriate rules to your rule base to allow the encrypted communication.

Local Gateway Object

SecuRemote clients support both FWZ and IKE encryption schemes. From the **Workstation Properties** window on your local gateway (the gateway through which SecuRemote connections will pass), you need to make sure that the encryption scheme you are using is supported by checking it in the VPN tab. When using FWZ with SecuRemote, you have the option of encapsulating the packets prior to transmission—this option is available in the FWZ Properties dialog, which you saw earlier in the chapter (see Figure 16.1). This will enable SecuRemote clients to access nonroutable networks behind the SecuRemote server (gateway) once they are authenticated and a VPN tunnel is established.

Next, you must define your VPN domain, which in this case defines which networks your SecuRemote clients will have access to once they have been authenticated. Set this as usual in the **Topology** tab of the **Workstation Properties** window on your local gateway. For SecuRemote, you need to check **Exportable for SecuRemote** on the same tab (see Figure 16.2). This enables clients to download the networks that they will have access to after being authenticated.

Finally, you must choose which authentication methods your gateway will support; for these exercises, you will choose **VPN-1 & FireWall-1 Password** on the **Authentication** tab of the **Workstation Properties** window on your local gateway. If you neglect to check the appropriate authentication scheme here, your users will all get "Authentication not supported" errors when they attempt to log in.

Note that if you are using FWZ encryption, you must check off **Respond to Unauthenticated Topology Requests** in the **Desktop Security** page of the **Global Properties** window (see Figure 16.12).

Figure 16.12 Desktop Security Window from Policy | Global Properties

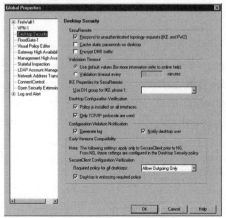

User Encryption Properties

Assume for this section that you have a preexisting set of users that you want to configure for client encryption.

Start by opening the Users window by choosing **Users** from the **Manage** menu in the Policy Editor. Select an existing user and click **Edit**. The User Properties window appears. Here, you have two choices. If you are using IKE, the user's authentication parameters are defined on the Encryption tab. If you are using FWZ, the user's authentication properties are defined on the Authentication tab.

FWZ

For FWZ, once you click on the **Authentication** tab, you can choose an authentication method from the drop-down list. Choosing **VPN-1 & FireWall-1 Password** will enable you to enter a password in the text box. On the user's **Encryption** tab, select **FWZ** and click **Edit**. This will present you with a dialog box, from which you can select encryption and data integrity methods (see Figure 16.13).

Figure 16.13 FWZ Properties

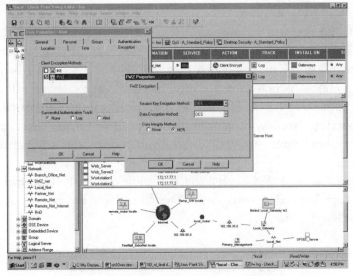

IKE

With IKE, you do all of your setup from the **Encryption** tab of the **User Properties** window. Choosing **IKE** and clicking **Edit** here brings up the **IKE Properties** window. On the **Authentication** tab, select **Password**, and enter the user's password. On the **Encryption** tab, select the encryption and data integrity methods you will use for the client VPN (see Figure 16.14).

Figure 16.14 IKE Properties

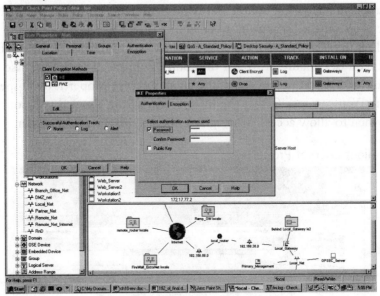

Client Encryption Rules

Your client encryption rule will look as follows (see Figure 16.15):

- **Source** AllUsers@Any

- **Destination** Local_Net

- **Service** Any

- **Action** Client Encrypt

- **Track** Log

Figure 16.15 SecuRemote Client Encrypt Rule

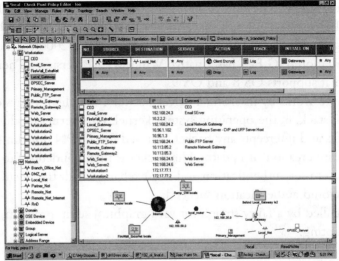

In this case, the Source column must specify a group of users and a location; the location can be "Any," or be a specific allowable source network. Destination must be the VPN domain defined for those users on the local gateway object.

Once the rule is in place, you can edit the Client Encrypt properties by double-clicking the **Client Encrypt** icon (see Figure 16.16). If the source column of your rule base conflicts with allowed sources in the user properties setup, the client encrypt properties will specify how to resolve the conflict. You can specify that the intersection of the allowed user sources and the rule base determine when to allow access, or to ignore the user database altogether.

Figure 16.16 Client Encrypt Properties

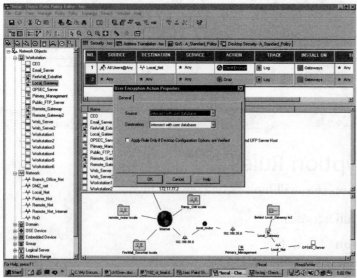

Installing SecuRemote Client Software

The SecuRemote client software must be installed on all the users' workstations or laptops to whom you as an administrator would like to give mobile access to your VPN domain. SecuRemote presently supports Windows 2000, NT, 98, and ME, and typically requires 32 to 64MB of RAM and about 6MB of disk space to install. It cannot be installed alongside Firewall-1. (As of this writing, SecuRemote version 4.1 SP5 for Windows 2000 can be installed on Windows XP. SecuRemote NG FP1 has a native Windows XP version.) There is also a Macintosh version that supports OS 8 and OS 9.

The client software works by inserting a driver between the client's physical network interface and the TCP/IP stack, in the operating system kernel. This kernel module monitors outbound TCP/IP traffic, and intercepts any packet destined for a VPN domain (from topology downloaded during site creation or update). The packet is then handed off to a user-space daemon, which handles user authentication and key exchange with the SecuRemote server, as well as encryption, should authentication succeed.

Installation is handled by a fairly straightforward graphical setup program; however, there are some points worth noting:

- You only need to install Desktop Security Support if you are using Secure Client (see Figure 16.17).

- If you do not install Desktop Security, you will be asked on which adapters to bind the SecuRemote kernel module (see Figure 16.18). You can choose from **Install on all network adapters**, (which would include Ethernet *and* dial-up adapters) or **Install on dialup adapters only**. The latter would be appropriate for remote users with a dial-up ISP who would never use their Ethernet interface to access the VPN domain from the outside. Mobile salespeople often fall into this category; they use dial-up access when on the road, and Ethernet to plug into the LAN when they are in the office.

- You can install over an older version of SecuRemote. You will be asked if you want to update the previous version, (which saves site and password information), or if you would like to overwrite the existing version.

- Although the client software is available for free download, a license is still required to use SecuRemote with Check Point NG.

Figure 16.17 SecuRemote Desktop Security Prompt During Installation

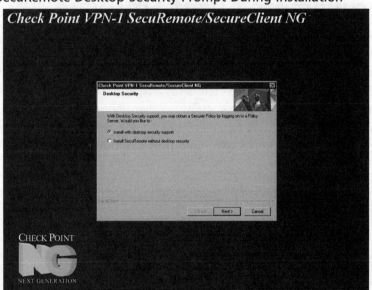

Figure 16.18 SecuRemote Adapter Configuration Screen During Installation

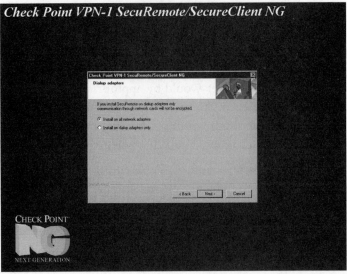

Using SecuRemote Client Software

Once the client software is installed, you can start the SecuRemote GUI by double-clicking in the **Envelope** icon in your taskbar. Before you can use SecuRemote, you must create a new site by choosing **Create New Site** from the **Sites** menu (see Figure 16.19). Enter the IP address or host name of your SecuRemote server (which is the gateway through which you will be connecting, or, in a distributed installation, that gateway's management console), and click **OK**. The site key information and topology will be downloaded automatically, and will be stored in a file called "userc.C" on the client, in the SecuRemote installation directory.

Figure 16.19 Creating a New Site

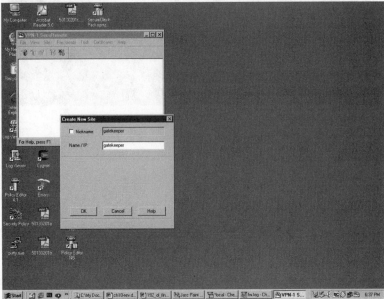

Once a site has been successfully created, you can attempt a connection to something in your VPN domain. You should see an authentication dialog box pop up (see Figure 16.20); here you would enter one of the previously defined usernames and passwords, after which you will be allowed access. Note that IKE encryption is the default, so if you are using FWZ, the client software needs to be reconfigured. Do this by choosing **Encryption Scheme** from the **Tools** menu, and then selecting **FWZ** instead of IKE.

Figure 16.20 SecureRemote Authentication Window

After a topology change, you will need to update the SecuRemote clients so that their topology is in sync with the SecuRemote server. Updating the site can be done manually by right-clicking on the **Site** icon and choosing **Update Site**. This works for a small number of clients, but if you have a large number of remote users, you can enable automatic update (in SecuRemote version 4.1 or NG) in one of three ways:

- Prompt the client to update its topology whenever SecuRemote is started by adding **:desktop_update_at_start (true)** to the :props section of the objects_5_0.C file on the management station. This can be refused by the client.

- Prompt for update of *all* defined site topologies whenever SecuRemote is started by adding **:update_topo_at_start (true)** to the :props section of the objects_5_0.C file on the management station. This can also be refused by the client.

- Force updating of the site topology every *n* seconds by adding **:desktop_update_frequency (*n*)** to the :props section of the objects_5_0.C file on the management station.

Making Changes to Objects_5_0.C Stick

Editing the objects_5_0.C file can be tricky—if not done correctly, your changes will be lost. You should follow these recommendations when making changes to the objects_5_0.C file on your management server. Note that this file is called "objects.C" on the firewall module, as it was in past versions of Check Point Firewall-1. Editing this file on the firewall module will have no effect, as it gets overwritten by the objects_5_0.C from the management station during policy installs.

1. Close all GUI clients.

2. Perform *fwstop* on the management console.

3. Delete or rename the files "objects_5_0.C.sav" and "objects_5_0.C.bak."

4. Back up the original objects_5_0.C.

5. Make the necessary changes to the objects_5_0.C file and save them.

6. Perform *fwstart* on the management console.

7. Install the security policy to all modules.

Secure Domain Login

Secure Domain Login (SDL) enables users to encrypt traffic to a Windows NT domain controller behind a FireWall-1 firewall. Normally, SecuRemote is activated *after* domain login, meaning that domain login is not encrypted. To enable SDL after installation, choose **Enable SDL** from the **Passwords** menu. This will take effect only after a reboot. Note that SDL over a dial-up connection is only supported when using the Windows 2000 or NT clients—the 98 or ME clients only support SDL over an Ethernet adapter.

In order to successfully log in to an NT domain, you need to make sure you have the following client settings:

- Your **Client for Microsoft Networks** has **Log on to Windows NT Domain** checked.

- Your dial-up profile is configured with your internal WINS server address OR.

- You need an LMHOSTS entry that points to your primary or backup domain controllers.

VPN Management

Easy VPN management is directly related to network topology choices. In general, one VPN endpoint with multiple small VPN domains behind it will be easier to manage than multiple distinct gateways, each with one VPN domain. The need for back-end security can be best solved by using gateways as needed, behind the sole VPN endpoint. Each smaller gateway must then be configured to pass encrypted traffic and key exchange traffic through untouched. You can use Table 16.2 to assist in this.

Table 16.2 VPN Ports and Protocols

Encryption Scheme	Ports/Protocols Used
FWZ	RDP (UDP port 259), FW1_topo (TCP port 264)
IKE	IKE (UDP port 500), ESP (IP protocol 50), AH (IP protocol 51), IKE over TCP (TCP port 500)*, UDP encapsulation (UDP port 2476)*,FW1_topo (TCP port 254) * Not always necessary

Summary

Virtual private networks (VPNs) can be used to provide authenticity, privacy, and data integrity. There are two types of VPNs: site-to-site and client-to-site; both provide two methods of key exchange (IKE and FWZ) and several encryption algorithms. Establishing a site-to-site VPN can be broken down into three steps: configuring the firewall and/or management stations, configuring the VPN domain, and adding encryption rules to the security policy rule base. Establishing a client-to-site VPN is similar, except that users are configured with the proper authentication method, and then the rule base is updated with a Client Encrypt rule. Remote users must install the SecuRemote software and download SecuRemote server topology before they can make use of a client-to-site VPN. Several methods exist for automatically updating site topology.

## Chapter 17

Overview of the Nokia Security Platform

Best Damn Topics in this Chapter:

- Introducing the Nokia IP Series Appliances
- Administration Made Easy

Introduction

In today's world, ensuring security and stability of the corporate network infrastructure is no longer an option. In a global economy, businesses demand 24x7 uptime and expect that communication with their peers will be both swift and secure. Previously, when contending with these requirements, network administrators were forced to install third-party firewall software (such as Check Point's FW-1) on standalone PCs or proprietary hardware. This necessity forced administrators to deal with details such as hardware selection, operating system configuration, and software installation and provided for inconsistent stability and security, even within the same organization. Even a formal, standardized corporate policy that specifies all of the above may be forced to differ in implementation by hardware vendors or will be implemented in slightly different ways by different administrators. Is the default installation of your operating system secure enough? Is the hardware adequate for the task at hand? Is the hardware optimized for high performance under conditions common to firewalls? Is secure, remote access or troubleshooting possible? Are remote operating system or firewall software upgrades possible?

Enter the Nokia Security Platform (NSP), a group of UNIX-based appliances that provide easy, integrated access to third-party software such as FW-1 or Internet Security Systems' (ISS) RealSecure intrusion detection platform. NSP applications provide a resounding "Yes" answer to all the questions we just asked. All the models have standardized on a common Web interface, called the Voyager, through which you can remotely administer and configure almost any aspect of the operating system or firewall. Serial console access is standard. The NSP consists of eight different hardware models, all part of the IP series. Two are for small office/home office (SOHO) implementations; the other six are for enterprise rollouts.

In this chapter, we discuss the enterprise IP series models, showing the hardware specifics of each and discussing where each would be appropriate in a business environment. Then we present an overview of the Voyager Web-based administrative interface and briefly discuss how Nokia has made the administrator's life easier in various ways.

Introducing the Nokia IP Series Appliances

In this chapter we look at the specifications and uses of the six enterprise models. Each model offers something that the others don't, although, of course, the higher-numbered models are considerably more expensive than the lower-numbered models.

You need to choose the model that is right for your network architecture based on your answers to the following questions. Where a model is specified, you can assume that all higher-numbered models support the desired feature, except for RAID-1, which is unique to the IP400 series. Now ask yourself these questions:

- **Do I need direct WAN connectivity?** If you do, you need at least an IP330.

- **Do I need VPN capability?** If you do, you need at least an IP71. The IP71 is part of Nokia's SOHO suite of appliances, which have varying user interfaces and are not discussed here.

- **Do I need Gigabit Ethernet capability?** If you do, you need at least an IP530.

- **Do I need hot-swappable or redundant components?** If you do, you need at least an IP650.

- **Do I need more than five Ethernet ports?** If you do, you need at least an IP410.

- **Do I have more than 50 network devices that need firewall protection?** If you do, you need at least an IP120.

- **Do I need VPN hardware acceleration?** If you do, you need at least an IP330.

- **Do I want SSH remote access capability?** If you do, you need at least an IP71.

- **Do I want hardware RAID-1 (mirroring) capability?** If you do, you need an IP440 or an IP410.

Enterprise Models

Nokia's Enterprise models all come bundled with full versions of Check Point's FW-1/VPN-1 software, as well as full versions of ISS's intrusion detection software, RealSecure. In addition, they all offer dynamic routing protocols and other routing configuration features (including VRRP for fail-over configurations), so firewall network integration does not have to include a separate router in most cases. Apart from the IP120, all in this series are upgradeable to varying degrees, since they are essentially PCs with off-the-shelf components and Nokia's IPSO operating system. Remember that although firewall and IDS software comes bundled with the Nokia, you still need to purchase a license from the vendor or a reseller prior to using the product. Both Check Point and ISS offer time-limited evaluation licenses for those who want to test implementations prior to purchase.

IP120

The IP120 strikes a good balance among features, performance, and cost for the small to medium-sized office. It is the first in the IP series of appliances to run on the IPSO operating system, and it is the first to support the full version of Check Point's FW-1. With 128MB of RAM, it is also able to handle full Check Point Next Generation (NG) installations. It is also the first appliance to support dynamic routing protocols through the IPSO routing daemon and has all the "standard" remote access protocols implemented, including File Transfer Protocol (FTP), Secure Shell (SSH), and Hypertext Transfer Protocol/Secure Hypertext Transfer Protocol (HTTP/HTTPS). As stated earlier, the IP120 is not upgradeable as the other models are; it has the small form factor of a SOHO appliance but with more features, including the following:

- Three on-board 10/100 Ethernet ports

- Two serial ports (AUX and console)

- 128MB RAM

- A National GX1, 300MHz CPU

- Static routing capability

- Dynamic routing, including RIP ng, OSPF, IGMP, VRRP, and optionally IGRP and DVMRP (the latter two require purchase of a license)

- BOOTP/DHCP relay capability

- IPv6 support

- SNMP v3 support

- Telnet, FTP, HTTP/HTTPS, and SSH servers

- Full version of Check Point FireWall-1, including full remote and site-to-site VPN capabilities

- Full version of ISS RealSecure

IP330

The IP330 is the first in the IP series that adds wide area network (WAN) support to its list of features. Supported protocols include Point-to-Point Protocol (PPP), Frame Relay, High-Level Data Link Control (HDLC), asynchronous transfer mode (ATM), Integrated Services Digital Network (ISDN), V.35/X.21, T1/E1, HSSI, and Fiber Distributed Data Interface (FDDI). A two-port Ethernet card can be added, giving the IP330 a maximum of five Ethernet interfaces. An analog modem can be added for remote, out-of-band management, and a virtual private network (VPN) hardware accelerator card is available. An internal analog modem is standard through the built-in RJ-11 port.

The IP330 has a small footprint and is rack-mountable in standard 19-inch racks, where it will only take up one unit of space. Along with the IP330's support for VRRP, this makes it ideal for stacked, fail-over implementations in small or medium-sized businesses where space is at a premium. Let's take a look at the specifications for the IP330:

- Three on-board 10/100 Ethernet ports

- 256MB RAM

- K6-2, 400MHz CPU

- Console port, RJ-11 port

- Static routing

- Dynamic routing, including RIP ng, OSPF, IGMP, VRRP, and optionally IGRP, BGPv4, and DVMRP (the latter three require purchase of a license)

- BOOTP/DHCP relay capability

- IPv6 support

- SNMP v3 support

- Telnet, FTP, HTTP/HTTPS, and SSH servers

- Full version of Check Point FireWall-1, including full remote and site-to-site VPN capabilities

- Full version of ISS RealSecure
- WAN support
- One compact PCI slot for add-ons
- 1U rack-mountable

IP400 Series

The IP400 series consists of three models: the IP440, the IP410, and the IP400. None of the appliances in the IP400 series is currently available for purchase from Nokia, although they were quite popular at one time and many 400 series deployments are still in use. Nokia will continue to support the existing IP400 series user base for the foreseeable future. The IP400 and the IP410 differ only in the processor they are built around—a high-end Pentium II or a low-end Pentium II, respectively. The latest IP440 models shipped with a Pentium III processor.

Both models come with a CD-ROM drive and a diskette drive. They are distinguishable from all of the other Nokia IP models in that they have no boot manager , meaning that certain upgrades must be done using a boot diskette.

> **NOTE**
>
> A *boot manager*, sometimes called a *boot loader*, is a small program that runs just after system startup but before the operating system kernel is loaded into memory. Its main function is to load the kernel from disk into memory, which then handles normal system startup and initialization. Nokia's boot manger has gone through several changes over the years and has been present on the system hard drive, a specially formatted diskette drive, or (most recently) in flash memory, the latter to ease upgrades and provide some measure of resiliency in the event of a hard disk crash. The boot manager will, if left unattended, simply bootstrap the system with the default kernel image, but the process can be interrupted and given options from a rudimentary command shell. This function-ality is typically useful, for example, to boot into "single-user" or non-networked mode for system maintenance.

No Ethernet interfaces come standard with the IP400 series; typically, at least one four-port Ethernet Quad Card is purchased, although the four PCI slots allow up to 16 Ethernet interfaces, if you choose to use that many. WAN options are the same as for the IP330: PPP, Frame Relay, HDLC, ATM, ISDN, V.35/X.21, T1/E1, HSSI, and FDDI protocols are supported.

An analog modem can be added for remote, out-of-band management, and a VPN hardware accelerator card is available. The IP400 series also provides for optional hardware RAID configu-ration, but only RAID Level 1 (disk mirroring) is available. Here are the specifications for the IP400 series:

- Console and auxiliary serial ports
- 256MB RAM standard, upgradeable to 768MB RAM
- PIII, 600MHz CPU

- Static routing

- Dynamic routing, including RIP ng, OSPF, IGMP, VRRP, and optionally IGRP, BGPv4, and DVMRP (the latter three require purchase of a license)

- BOOTP/DHCP relay capability

- IPv6 support

- SNMP v3 support

- Telnet, FTP, HTTP/HTTPS, and SSH servers

- Full version of Check Point FireWall-1, including full remote and site-to-site VPN capabilities

- Full version of ISS RealSecure

- WAN support

- Four PCI slots

- 3U rack-mountable

- CD-ROM and diskette drives

- Hardware RAID-1 available

IP530

The IP530 is the first in the IP series of appliances to support Gigabit Ethernet. As in the IP400 series, a maximum of 16 Ethernet interfaces are possible with the four on-board interfaces and the three PCI expansion slots. One internal PMC slot can be used for VPN hardware acceleration, leaving the PCI slots free for network interfaces if needed. WAN options are the same as for the IP330 and IP400 series: PPP, Frame Relay, HDLC, ATM, ISDN, V.35/X.21, T1/E1, HSSI, and FDDI protocols are supported. Two Type II PCMCIA slots have been added for analog modem support.

The IP530 is meant to be a *high-density* port device, meaning that it is useful in situations in which many network interfaces are required. The on-board Ethernet ports offer slightly more throughput than network interface devices added through the PCI bus (and consequently, the IP530 has a slightly higher interface throughput than the IP650); when coupled with Gigabit Ethernet support, this model is useful for large businesses with high throughput requirements but that do not need the carrier-class features of the 600 or 700 series. The specifications for the IP350 series are as follows:

- Four on-board 10/100 Ethernet ports

- Console and auxiliary serial ports

- 256MB RAM standard, upgradeable to 768MB RAM

- PIII, 700MHz CPU

- Static routing

- Dynamic routing, including RIP ng, OSPF, IGMP, VRRP, and optionally IGRP, BGPv4, and DVMRP (the latter three require purchase of a license)

- BOOTP/DHCP relay capability

- IPv6 support

- SNMP v3 support

- Telnet, FTP, HTTP/HTTPS, and SSH servers

- Full version of Check Point FireWall-1, including full remote and site-to-site VPN capabilities

- Full version of ISS RealSecure

- WAN support

- Three compact PCI slots (Gigabit Ethernet available)

- Two Type II PCMCIA slots

- 2U rack-mountable

IP650

The IP650 is one of Nokia's high-end firewall appliances, and is the first in the IP-series to offer carrier-class features such as hot-swappable PCI slots, fan trays, and power supplies. The IP650 does not have any on-board Ethernet ports, but has five PCI slots, and so can have a maximum of 20 Ethernet interfaces. Gigabit Ethernet is supported as well.

You can use an on-board Peripheral Component Interconnect (PCI) mezzanine card, or PMC, slot (see the sidebar "What Is a PMC slot?") for a VPN accelerator card, freeing PCI slots for network interfaces. WAN support is similar to previous models, with PPP, Frame Relay, HDLC, ATM, ISDN, V.35/X.21, T1/E1, HSSI, and FDDI protocols supported. Two Type II PCMCIA slots have been added for analog modem support.

> **NOTE**
>
> *PMC* is short for *PCI mezzanine card*, and the *PMC slots* that Nokia refers to in its documentation are simply PCI slots that allow an expansion card to be plugged in so that it is *parallel* rather than perpendicular to the motherboard. Because any PCI card you plug into a PMC slot is parallel to the board, it takes up less vertical space. For that reason, these slots are used frequently in high-density devices and smaller rack-mount devices in which space is at a premium. Nokia uses them in their 600 and 700 series devices.

According to Nokia, the IP530 has a slightly greater network interface throughput than the IP650, merely because the IP530 was designed with on-board Ethernet ports that do not need to access the PCI bus. This makes the IP650 suitable for large businesses that are more concerned about reliability than throughput. Organizations that want both will be satisfied with the 700 series, described in the following section. Here are the specifications for the IP650:

- Console and auxiliary serial ports

- 256MB RAM standard, upgradeable to 1GB RAM

- PIII, 700MHz CPU

- Static routing

- Dynamic routing, including RIP ng, OSPF, IGMP, VRRP, and optionally IGRP, BGPv4, and DVMRP (the latter three require purchase of a license)

- BOOTP/DHCP relay capability

- IPv6 support

- SNMP v3 support

- Telnet, FTP, HTTP/HTTPS, and SSH servers

- Full version of Check Point FireWall-1, including full remote and site-to-site VPN capabilities

- Full version of ISS RealSecure

- WAN support

- Five hot-swappable PCI slots (Gigabit Ethernet available)

- Hot-swappable fan trays

- Hot-swappable, redundant power supply optional

- Two Type II PCMCIA slots

- 2U rack-mountable

IP700

The IP700 series consists of the IP710 and the IP740. Both offer the IP650's carrier-class features such as hot-swappable PCI slots, fan trays, and power supplies.

The IP700 series has four on-board 10/100 Ethernet interfaces and four PCI slots, and so can have a maximum of 20 Ethernet interfaces. Gigabit Ethernet is supported as well. The main difference between the 700 models and the previous ones is firewall throughput; Nokia claims that speeds of over 2GB per second are possible with the IP740. (See Table 17.1 for more information.)

An on-board PMC slot can be used for a VPN accelerator card, freeing PCI slots for network interfaces. WAN support is similar to previous models, with PPP, Frame Relay, HDLC, ATM, ISDN, V.35/X.21, T1/E1, HSSI, and FDDI protocols supported. Two Type II PCMCIA slots have been added for analog modem support.

The IP700 series is designed for the largest businesses that demand both performance and reliability. Let's take a look at the IP700 series specifications:

- Four on-board 10/100 Ethernet ports

- Console and auxiliary serial ports

- 512MB RAM standard, upgradeable to 1GB RAM

- PIII, 866MHz CPU

- Static routing

- Dynamic routing, including RIP ng, OSPF, IGMP, VRRP, and optionally IGRP, BGPv4, and DVMRP (the latter three require purchase of a license)

- BOOTP/DHCP relay capability

- IPv6 support

- SNMP v3 support

- Telnet, FTP, HTTP/HTTPS, and SSH servers

- Full version of Check Point FireWall-1, including full remote and site-to-site VPN capabilities

- Full version of ISS RealSecure

- WAN support

- Four hot-swappable PCI slots (Gigabit Ethernet available)

- Hot-swappable fan trays

- Hot-swappable, redundant power supply optional

- Two Type II PCMCIA slots

- 2U rack-mountable

Administration Made Easy

You will need to configure your Nokia when you unpack and initially install it, and you should maintain that configuration throughout the life of the device, perhaps with updates and modifications. When you think about it, administering a production firewall or other network-critical device can be quite time consuming. You have to worry about security hotfixes, OS upgrades, software patches, and routing configuration changes—and that's just for starters. We're not mentioning the day-to-day problems that can arise and interfere with your plans. You will find that Nokia has made this process quite easy, relatively speaking.

The initial configuration of the NSP is even easier than it was in the past. Previously, you had to set up a console connection to the device for first-time boot, at which time you entered device hostname and interface information, allowing a network connection to be established so that you could complete the configuration. Starting with IPSO 3.5 FCS 6, the Nokia device has a built-in Dynamic Host Configuration Protocol (DHCP) client and will configure a network interface on its own when booted for the first time, assuming you have a DHCP server available. (Actually, any time the device boots and finds a missing or invalid global configuration file, it will initiate the first-time boot sequence.) Once you have an interface configured, Nokia's Web-based administrative interface, the Voyager, can be used for just about anything you need to do as an administrator, including point-and-click operating system and firewall software upgrades (see Figure 17.1).

Figure 17.1 Interface Configuration Through the Voyager Web Interface

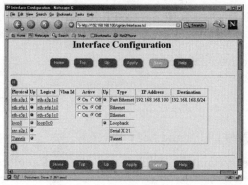

For administrators who don't like to maintain one device at a time, Nokia has a product called Horizon Manager that enables remote, centralized upgrades and maintenance of multiple devices simultaneously. Some of the things you can do with Horizon Manager include OS up-grades, hotfix applications, system backups, firewall configuration, and remote command execution.

If you only have a console connection to your Nokia device or you're someone who likes to live at a command prompt, you won't be disappointed. Voyager can be used over a console con-nection from the IPSO shell with the text-mode browser Lynx (see Figure 17.2).

Figure 17.2 Package Management Through the Lynx Interface

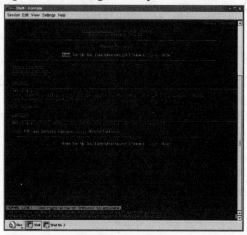

A command-line tool called *iclid* can be used to show and monitor various configuration set-tings. iclid has a syntax quite similar to that of Cisco's Internetworking Operating System (IOS) command shell and offers the nice feature of tabbed command completion and command history display present in most modern UNIX shells. See Figure 17.3 for more details.

Figure 17.3 Displaying VRRP Status Using iclid

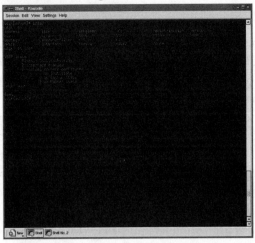

Because IPSO is based on UNIX and boots into a standard C-shell (csh), UNIX power users will feel quite at home here (see Figure 17.4). Beware, though, that changes made through standard command-line utilities such as *ifconfig* or *route* or edits to system configuration files will not normally persist across system reboots or even across changes made with Voyager. However, there are ways to use the standard tools to make permanent changes.

Figure 17.4 Output of Common Shell Commands

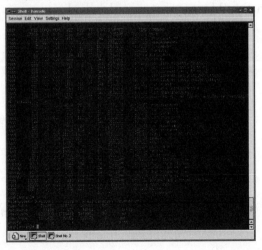

Finally, Nokia has gone to some effort to harden the IPSO operating system and provide a solid and secure basis from which to run a firewall, IDS sensor, or router. IPSO itself is based on FreeBSD UNIX and has been pared down in size to about 30MB. The root partition is mounted read-only; unnecessary network services have been turned off; no compiler, development tools or libraries are present (with the notable exception of GDB, the GNU debugger, which is useful for crash analysis); and the hard drive is partitioned for you in a sane and sensible fashion. There are very few UNIX manual pages, and, as you might expect from a 30MB OS, all but the most essential system binaries are gone.

Summary

The Nokia Security Platform consists of six enterprise models, from the IP120 to the IP740. All offer a wide range of features and hardware specifications, and it is easy to find something that fits the network architecture of both the small office and the largest ISP's or Telco's. The primary feature points that distinguish one model from another include direct WAN connectivity (IP330 and up), 16 or more network interfaces (IP400 series and up), Gigabit Ethernet (IP530 and up), and hot-swappable or redundant components (IP650 and up). All the devices are based on the Nokia IPSO operating system, and all of them can be almost entirely configured through Nokia's intuitive Voyager Web interface. These appliances' ability to function as full-fledged routers, with WAN support and support for many of the most common dynamic routing protocols, means that they can function as a drop-in replacement for the commonly seen "border router-firewall" configuration. The rack-mountable appliances are becoming very popular for use in high-availability VPN deployments, where they are configured in pairs with VRRP and Check Point's gateway clustering.

Nokia has implemented a feature called Firewall Flows, which works with FW-1 and can dramatically improve firewall throughput for most types of traffic.

Administration of the IP series devices can be easily accomplished several ways: using the Voyager tool through a graphical browser, using the Voyager tool through the text-mode browser Lynx, and through command-line utilities such as iclid or even the standard UNIX shell. Nokia has hardened the IPSO operating system, which is based on UNIX; as a result, these devices are ready to run out of the box (after network configuration, of course). Nokia also has a product called Horizon Manager that enables remote, centralized administration of multiple devices.

## Chapter 18

Configuring the
Check Point Firewall

Best Damn Topics in This Chapter:

- **Preparing for the Configuration**

- **Configuring the Firewall**

- **Testing the Configuration**

- **Upgrading the Firewall**

Introduction

The Nokia NSP is, above all else, a firewall platform. Nokia made the choice to bundle Check Point's FireWall-1 with its product both for its stateful and secure technology and for its ease of administration. Nokia developers have been working very closely with Check Point, and in their commitment to further this relationship Nokia platforms have some added features that enhance FireWall-1 performance and its ability to be easily maintained.

You can order a Nokia box with Check Point preinstalled or you can download the installation package from Check Point (with appropriate login ID) and install it yourself. If you need to upgrade your IPSO before installing NG, you need to obtain the IPSO image from Nokia support. It might be necessary to upgrade your boot manager prior to upgrading your IPSO image as well. Please read all release notes prior to installing new packages or images. Nokia recommends that you do not upgrade from 4.1 to NG if you have less than 128MB of memory; instead, do a fresh install.

Nokia's IPSO 3.6 supports Check Point FireWall-1 NG Feature Packs 2 and 3. This chapter shows how to enable and configure your Nokia/Check Point firewall for first-time use. Certain key differences in Nokia's branded version of FireWall-1—differences that make your life as an administrator easier—are discussed. Testing the firewall installation and upgrading the firewall version or service pack are also discussed.

Preparing for the Configuration

Since the Nokia appliance is already hardened, there is very little you need to do to prepare it for firewall installation. You must configure and test networking and DNS and set up the Host Address Assignment through the Voyager GUI, and you might need to upgrade your IPSO and boot manager.

Ensure that you have the following ready before you begin configuring Check Point FireWall-1:

- Get your Check Point licenses.
- Configure routing and test network interface cards (NICs).
- Ensure IP forwarding is enabled (*ipsofwd on admin*).
- Configure Host Address Assignment.
- Ensure you have at least 128MB of memory and 40MB of free disk space on /opt.
- Read the Release Notes.
- Verify that your IPSO is compatible with VPN-1/FireWall-1 (see Table 18.1).

Table 18.1 FireWall-1/IPSO Compatibility

IPSO Version	VPN-1/FireWall-1 Compatibility
IPSO 3.2.x	4.0 any service pack and 4.1 up to SP2
IPSO 3.3 FCS3	4.1 SP2 and SP3

Continued

Table 18.1 FireWall-1/IPSO Compatibility

IPSO Version	VPN-1/FireWall-1 Compatibility
IPSO 3.3 FCS6, FCS8 (not to be used with IP530)	4.1 SP3
IPSO 3.3E FCS4 (not to be used with IP530)	4.1 SP3
IPSO 3.3.1 FCS7 (IP530 only)	4.1 SP3
IPSO 3.4	4.1 SP4
IPSO 3.4.1 FCS5a	4.1 SP5
IPSO 3.4.1 FCS10-FCS12	4.1 SP5a and SP6
IPSO 3.4.2	NG FP1
IPSO 3.5 FCS3	4.1 SP5a
IPSO 3.5 FCS6-FCS8	4.1 SP5a, SP6 and NG FP2
IPSO 3.5 FCS10	4.1 SP5a, SP6, NG FP2 and FP3
IPSO 3.6	NG FP2 and FP3

For the most recent FireWall-1/IPSO compatibility matrix, look up Nokia Resolution 11253.

Obtaining Licenses

Check Point licenses have changed (again) with the Next Generation release. This means that you cannot use an old 4.1 license when installing NG. If you have 4.1 licenses, don't worry—you can get your 4.1 cert keys upgraded to NG for no additional charge. In order to obtain licenses, you can either go through your Check Point value-added reseller (VAR) or use the Check Point User Center to license your products at http://usercenter.checkpoint.com.

You have two options when it comes to licensing your firewall modules. You can either have them tied to their individual IP addresses (external interface recommended), as with previous versions, or you can tie them all to the management station's IP address. These licenses are called *local* or *central*, respectively. In NG, the SecureUpdate management tool can be used to maintain all licenses on the management console.

The management module itself must have a local license based on its own IP address. The nice thing about using central licenses for the enforcement modules is that you can change their IP addresses without needing to replace the license, and you can easily move a license from one module to another.

It is always best to obtain your licenses before you install the firewall software. The program will ask you for your license details during the configuration procedure. If you cannot obtain your permanent license prior to the install, you should ask for an evaluation license. Check Point's eval licenses have full functionality for almost all VPN-1/FireWall-1 features. They are usually valid for one month, and the product is not crippled in any way while running on eval.

Configuring Your Host Name

If you followed the instructions for initial configuration of your Nokia Security Platform, you should already have your host name configured for FireWall-1. If, however, you have jumped to this chapter, you need to know that your VPN-1/FireWall-1 configuration requires that you have your host name mapped to your external IP address in the **Host Address Assignment** configuration screen, which you can access from the Voyager main **Configuration** screen under the **System Configuration** section. If this function is not configured ahead of time, your license installation will fail.

To add a new host name, enter either the fully qualified domain name (FQDN) or the simple hostname in the field **Add new hostname**. We are using the name *gatekeeper*, which was the name assigned to this Nokia during initial system configuration. Next, click **Apply**, and then type in the IP address associated with gatekeeper. This should be the IP address that you will use if licensing the FireWall-1 product on your Nokia as well, and it is typically the external IP address of the firewall. Click **Apply** again and then click **Save** to complete the host address assignment. See Figure 18.1 for the completed configuration.

Figure 18.1 Host Address Assignment

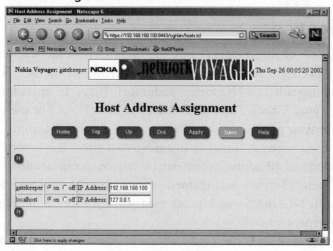

Understanding FireWall-1 Options

The following Check Point Next Generation packages are available:

- **VPN-1 & FireWall-1** Includes FireWall-1 Management module and enforcement point software along with the VPN-1 encryption component.

- **FloodGate-1** Provides an integrated QoS solution for VPN-1/FireWall-1.

- **UserAuthority** A user authentication tool that integrates with FireWall-1, FloodGate-1, and other e-business applications.

- **VPN-1 SecureClient Policy Server** Allows an enforcement module to install granular desktop policies on mobile users' SecureClient personal firewalls.

- **Reporting Module** An integrated reporting tool that can generate reports, graphs, and pie charts to display information obtained from the VPN-1/FireWall-1 logs.

- **Real Time Monitor** Allows an organization to monitor its VPN connections, Internet connections, and so on.

- **4.1 Backward Compatibility** Allows you to support version 4.1 firewalls from an NG management server.

The VPN-1/FireWall-1 component options are:

- **Enforcement Module** Select this to install an enforcement module only; the management server will be installed on a separate host.

- **Enterprise Management** Select this to install a management server only, which will be acting in either a primary or backup capacity.

- **Enterprise Management and Enforcement Module** Used to install both a VPN-1/FireWall-1 enforcement module and management module (stand-alone install).

- **Enterprise Log Server** Select this to install a management module that will be used as a log server only.

- **Enforcement Module and Enterprise Log Server** Use this option to install both a VPN-1/FireWall-1 enforcement module as well as a management module that will be used only as a log server.

After the Check Point cpconfig utility sets up the type of installation you have chosen, it will run through a number of configuration screens. The screens that you can prepare for in advance are:

- **Licenses** You should read the section on licenses if you need help getting licenses. You will fill in the following fields:

    - **Host/IP Address** The IP address associated with this license or eval.

    - **Expiration Date** The date that the license expires, which may be never.

    - **SKU/Features** The features this license enables (for example, management or 3DES).

    - **String/Signature Key** The license string provided by Check Point to validate the license. This key will be unique for each license and IP address.

NOTE

If you are installing just an enforcement module, you will have no administrators or GUI clients to configure.

- **Administrators** You will need to configure at least one administrator during install.

- **Administrator Name** Choose a login name for your admin. This field is case sensitive.

- **Password** Choose a good alphanumeric password. It must be at least four characters long.

- **Confirm Password** Repeat the same password entered in the previous step.

- **Management Clients** These are the IP addresses of the GUI clients that your administrators will use when connecting to this management module. You might need to configure static IP addresses for your administrators. You can add as many management clients as you'd like or you may enter none, it's up to you. See the following discussion for your Management Client options.

- **SIC Password** If you are installing an enforcement module only, you will be prompted for a password to initialize SIC. This password must also be entered in the configuration for the firewall object in the Policy Editor.

Configuring the Firewall

Next, we want to take you through the configuration of Check Point FireWall-1 on your Nokia and introduce you to the way FireWall-1 protects your Nokia during system bootstrap. Before you can start the firewall (*cpstart*) for the first time, you need to have the package enabled in Voyager and run through the Check Point Configuration tool (cpconfig). It is during this initial configuration that you determine the type of Check Point installation you want to run on your NSP. You can choose to install a management server and/or enforcement module during this time. This section walks you through each step of the initial configuration screens and gives you some tips for disabling the default and initial policies, which might be problematic when you're doing remote maintenance.

Installing the Package

If you are starting with a fresh Nokia installation and have no previous Check Point packages installed, you need to start by installing the Check Point packages in IPSO. Here we guide you through a package installation of NG FP2 on a Nokia using the *newpkg* command. If your Nokia was shipped with the appropriate Check Point packages preinstalled, you should skip to the next section. If you want to upgrade a Check Point package, read the section "Upgrading the Firewall."

Begin by downloading the FP2 wrapper file onto your Nokia into the /var/admin directory. You can download it from Check Point or from one of its resellers. The FP2 wrapper package is simply a .tgz file that installs NG FP1 (SVN Foundation and VPN-1/FireWall-1) and then upgrades you to NG FP2. Some other packages will be installed as well, including the version 4.1 Backward Compatibility package, Policy Server, FloodGate-1, and Real Time Monitor. When the install is complete, the NG FP2 SVN and FireWall-1 package will be the only ones enabled.

If you're starting with the NG FP3 wrapper package instead, you won't get the other Feature Packs like the FP2 wrapper—just the FP3 version will be installed. The other packages bundled in with the FP3 wrapper include the 4.1 Backward Compatibility package, Policy Server,

FloodGate-1, SmartView Monitor, and UserAuthority Server. Regardless of which wrapper package you choose, follow this procedure for installation:

1. Place the wrapper file in /var/admin. The filename will be something like CP_FP2_IPSO.tgz or CP_FP3_IPSO.tgz. Ensure that this is the only package in the /var/admin directory. Do not uncompress or untar the package.

2. From the /var/admin directory, type **newpkg –i**.

3. Choose **4** and press **Enter** at the prompt for installation method. This sequence will install the package from the local file system.

4. Next you will be prompted for the pathname to the package. Enter a single period (**.**) and press **Enter**. A single period or "dot" indicates the current working directory.

5. Now the install program will find the Check Point NG package and extract the necessary files for installation. You will be prompted with four options—to install, upgrade, skip, or exit. Enter **1** to install. At this time, the packages bundled in the wrapper will be installed. When the process is complete, you will again see the IPSO prompt. You can verify that the packages have been installed by logging in to Voyager and viewing the Manage Installed Packages configuration screen.

6. Now you need to log out and log back in to your IPSO session. This ensures that you get the new environment variables defined during the package installation. Without having these variables set, you cannot run cpconfig.

7. Run **cpconfig** and install a license. You can skip to the section on cpconfig later in this chapter for more help in this configuration tool.

8. Reboot your Nokia after running cpconfig by typing **reboot**.

Enabling the Package

Check Point packages are enabled just like any other packages on IPSO. In NG, you will always have at least two Check Point packages enabled at any time through the Manage Installed Packages configuration screen, the SVN Foundation, and the VPN-1/FireWall-1 NG package. Only one version of FireWall-1 can be active at any time. If all the Check Point packages are off, you should first enable the SVN Foundation (CPShared) package, then enable the Check Point VPN-1/FireWall-1 package, and then finally enable any other Check Point components (such as backward compatibility, Policy Server or FloodGate-1, and so on).

Follow these instructions to enable Check Point NG FP3 VPN-1/FireWall-1 in Nokia IPSO 3.6:

1. Log in to Voyager and click **Config**.

2. Click **Manage Installed Packages** under the System Configuration section.

3. Toggle the **Check Point SVN Foundation** package to **On**.

4. Click **Apply**.

5. Now, toggle the **Check Point VPN-1/FireWall-1** package to **On**.

6. Click **Apply** and then click **Save**.

If you need to disable Check Point packages at any time, follow the reverse procedure. Begin by disabling the Check Point VPN-1/FireWall-1 package and then the SVN Foundation. You cannot disable both of these packages simultaneously; you must turn them off one at a time.

Environment and Path

Check Point commands cannot be executed if you do not have the correct environment variables defined in your Nokia login session. Fortunately, during package installation these are configured for you in the file /var/etc/pm_profile. This profile is called from the .profile in your home directory, so whenever you log in you will always have the necessary environment to run Check Point commands for installed packages.

Some of the environment variables that are modified when Check Point packages are installed are CPDIR, FWDIR, and PATH. The CPDIR variable tells you where the base SVN Foundation (CPShared) installation directory is located. The FWDIR similarly contains the value of the base VPN-1/FireWall-1 installation directory. An easy way to change directories into the firewall software is to use this FWDIR variable, since the directory names are sometimes quite long and hard to type in without making a mistake. In NG FP3, the variables are defined as follows. You can display the value of any variable by using the *echo* command and including a dollar sign in front of the variable name. For instance, to display the value of the CPDIR variable, type **echo $CPDIR**. The dollar sign ($) in front of a variable means *the value of*:

- CPDIR = /opt/CPshared-50-03
- FWDIR = /opt/CPfw1-50-03
- PATH = /bin:/sbin:/usr/bin:/usr/sbin:/usr/libexec:/etc:/opt/CPshared-50-03/bin:/opt/CPfw1-50-03/bin

VPN-1 and FireWall-1 Directory Structure

Within the VPN-1/FireWall-1 package directories, you have several subdirectories, each with its own purpose. Here we would like to highlight some of the most important directories and explain the types of files that you will find in each of them.

$FWDIR directories:

- **bin** Binary files and scripts, such as the *fw*, *fwd*, and *fwm* binaries and *fwstop/fwstart* scripts, to name a few.
- **boot** Boot configuration files are stored here, including the compiled default filter file.
- **conf** Configuration files, including your objects, rules, and user database.
- **database** Database information.
- **lib** Library files.
- **log** Log files are stored in this directory. On Nokia devices, this is usually a symbolic link to /var/fw/log.
- **spool** SMTP Security Server default spool directory.

- **state** FireWall-1 state information.
- **tmp** Temporary directory where the daemon pid files are located.

Within the conf directory, you will find the objects_5_0.C file, which holds all your FireWall-1 objects and services. The rulebases_5_0.fws file contains all your rules, and the fwauth.NDB★ files contain your user database. You'll also find a gui-clients file here and either a masters or clients file if you have a distributed installation. The $FWDIR/conf directory is always the most important directory to back up.

Occasionally, you might make changes to the files in the database or lib directory, and you should have a good backup of those as well. Whenever you upgrade your Check Point software, these files will need to be modified again with those changes. Sometimes hot fixes that are applied simply replace some files in lib, such as table.def or base.def.

Your FireWall-1 log files should be maintained on a regular basis. Although the configuration in the Policy Editor allows you to schedule log switches in NG, certain log files will not be switched. Even if you are logging to a separate management server, some log files will be growing in your Nokia's $FWDIR/log directory. The security server logs such as ahttpd.elg, aftpd.elg, and asmtpd.elg will be in there, and you'll find that some daemons, such as fwd, will log there as well (for example, fwd.elg, mdq.elg, and fwm.elg). Most of the files that begin with fw.★ will be part of the active log files. You could find that if your firewalls have stopped logging to the management station and the management box isn't listening for incoming connections on TCP port 257 (verify with the command *netstat –an*), you might need to run *cpstop* on the management console, move the *$FWDIR/log/fw.★* files, and then run *cpstart* to get things moving again.

The state directory contains the current FireWall-1 state information, and the files here get updated whenever a policy is installed. At times you might need to clear out the state directory while the firewall is stopped, to clear a persistent setting. The files in here will be recreated on the next policy install.

IP Forwarding and Firewall Policies

During the Nokia's boot cycle, IP forwarding is disabled. Check Point FireWall-1 will control IP forwarding by enabling it once its services are started. During the boot process, the firewall loads a default filter, which blocks all inbound access to the Nokia but allows all outgoing and broadcast packets. This filter is loaded into the kernel before the interfaces of the Nokia are configured. This ensures that there is never a time during the boot process that the machine is unprotected.

When FireWall-1 services start for the first time, a policy cannot be loaded, because the firewall has no saved state. When this happens, it will load an initial policy, which allows a GUI client connection but blocks all other communication. You cannot even ping the device while the initial policy is loaded. If at any other time the system reboots and the firewall cannot fetch a policy either from a management console or from its locally saved state, it will load the initial policy filter. In order to remove either a default or initial filter, you need to type **fw unloadlocal** or **fw unload localhost**, the latter if you have a version of FireWall-1 prior to NG FP2. Use the command *fw stat* to display the current policy that is loaded:

```
gatekeeper[admin]# fw stat

HOST        POLICY       DATE

localhost InitialPolicy 25Sep2002 23:02:21 :  [>eth-s3p1c0]
```

When FireWall-1 is stopped via *cpstop*, IP forwarding is disabled as well. Run *ipsofwd list* to see the current state of IP forwarding. The value of net:ip:forwarding will be 0 if forwarding is disabled and 1 if it is enabled. A filter is not loaded if the firewall services are stopped, so your system could be at risk. Here are some commands you can use to control these settings, with brief descriptions:

- **fwstop –default** Kills all firewall processes and loads the default filter.
- **fwstop –proc** Stops all firewall processes but allows the policy to remain in the kernel for simple accept, drop, and reject inspection.
- **fwstart –f** Starts FireWall-1 services.
- **control_bootsec –r** Removes boot security.
- **control_bootsec –g** Enables boot security.
- **fwboot bootconf** Sets IP forwarding and configures the default filter.
- **comp_init_policy –u** Disables the initial policy.
- **comp_init_policy –g** Enables the initial policy.

The default filter is defined in the $FWDIR/lib directory. In NG FP3, the default filters listed in Table 18.2 are available to choose from in that directory on Nokia. The default default filter (pun intended) is the defaultfilter.boot file.

Table 18.2 Default Filters in $FWDIR/lib

Filter file	Description
defaultfilter.boot	Allows outbound communication (originating from the firewall) and broadcast traffic only.
defaultfilter.dag	Allows outbound communication (originating from the firewall), broadcast traffic, and DHCP.
defaultfilter.drop	Drops everything.
defaultfilter.ipso	Allows SSH, SSL (port 443), and ping inbound and all outbound communication originating from the firewall.
defaultfilter.ipso_ssh	Allows SSH and ping inbound and all outbound communication originating from the firewall.
defaultfilter.ipso_ssl	Allows SSL (port 443) and ping inbound and all outbound communication originating from the firewall.

We personally like the way that the defaultfilter.ipso looks, since it allows SSH and SSL connections to the Nokia while the filter is loaded. Follow this procedure to change the default filter to the defaultfilter.ipso file instead:

1. Log in to your Nokia and change directories to **$FWDIR/lib**. From here, copy the defaultfilter.ipso file to **$FWDIR/conf/defaultfilter.pf**.

2. Run **fw defaultgen** to compile the defaultfilter.pf file. The output file will be $FWDIR/state/default.bin. The output of this command is as follows:

```
gatekeeper[admin]# fw defaultgen
Generating default filter
defaultfilter:
Compiled OK.
Backing up default.bin as default.bin.bak
```

3. Copy the **$FWDIR/state/default.bin** file to the **$FWDIR/boot** directory. You can verify that the $FWDIR/boot directory is where the file belongs by printing the file path with the command **$FWDIR/boot/fwboot bootconf get_def**.

Unload InitialPolicy Script

If you are doing a remote upgrade or install, you could run into trouble when you reboot at the end of the installation. Before a security policy is loaded, the system will install a filter, called InitialPolicy, which will block all access to the VPN-1/FireWall-1 host computer (except GUI access). You can log in to the console and verify that the filter is loaded with the *fw stat* command:

```
gatekeeper[admin]# fw stat
HOST       POLICY      DATE
localhost InitialPolicy 25Sep2002 23:02:21 :  [>eth-s3p1c0]
```

If you have access to the console, log in as root and unload the filter with the following command:

```
# fw unloadlocal
```

If you do not have access to the console, you could write a shell script to unload the filter and enable it in cron. The various environment variables in /var/etc/pm_profile need to be defined. So, easily enough, we can call the pm_profile file from the unload.sh script. Even before you reboot, you can test that the script works by running it from the command line. Here's a sample unload.sh script that works for FireWall-1 NG FP3:

```
--------------------------------
#!/bin/sh

. /var/etc/pm_profile

$FWDIR/bin/fw unloadlocal
--------------------------------
```

To enter the script in cron, follow these steps.

1. Verify that you have enabled execute permissions on the file:

   ```
   chmod +x unload.sh
   ```

2. Edit cron with the following command:

   ```
   crontab -e
   ```

3. Finally, enter the following line into your crontab file (note this should be one line):

   ```
   0,5,10,15,20,25,30,35,40,45,50,55 * * * * /var/admin/unload.sh >
       /dev/null 2>&1
   ```

   This command tells the system to run the unload.sh script every five minutes and redirect all output to /dev/null.

Now you can safely reboot the system and log back in to it within a five-minute period from the time it is booted. Don't forget to remove (or at least comment out) the crontab entry once you are back in the firewall.

Running cpconfig

If VPN-1/FireWall-1 NG is installed on your Nokia appliance, but it hasn't been configured yet, you must run cpconfig before attempting to start the new package. If you just received your Nokia fresh from the factory and NG is installed, you still need to run cpconfig before the package will run properly. This is because you must accept the license agreement, choose the components you want to run (management and/or enforcement module), and configure licenses, administrators, GUI clients, and the like.

When you run cpconfig, you must be logged in either through the console or remote login, and your environment variables must be set as described earlier. Then, all you need to do to begin the configuration is to enter the command **cpconfig** and press **Enter**. The very first time the command is run, it will ask you to accept the licensing agreement and then take you through the configuration wizard, prompting you for input at each stage. The configuration options could be a little different depending on your choices along the way, such as whether you decide to install a management module and/or firewall module on the system.

Let's assume that we are installing both management and firewall modules on a stand-alone system. Here is a list of steps to configure your Nokia system:

1. Log in to your Nokia and run **cpconfig**.

2. Press **Enter** to read the license agreement, pressing **Spacebar** to continue until you reach the end, and then enter **y** to accept the terms and continue.

3. Next you are prompted for the type of installation you want on your NSP. To run both a management console and firewall module on this box, select option **3**.

4. If this is to be a primary management console (as opposed to a backup), press **Enter** to accept the default value of **1** at this next prompt. You will see some messages about the firewall controlling IP forwarding and loading a default filter (see Figure 18.2).

Figure 18.2 Initial Configuration

```
gatekeeper[admin]# cpconfig

Welcome to Check Point Configuration Program
====================================================
Please read the following license agreement.
Hit 'ENTER' to continue...

This End-user License Agreement (the "Agreement") is an agreement between
you (both the individual installing the Product and any legal entity on
whose behalf such individual is acting) (hereinafter "You" or " Your") and
 Check Point Software Technologies Ltd. (hereinafter "Check Point").
...

Do you accept all the terms of this license agreement (y/n) ? y

Select installation type:
------------------------


(1) Enforcement Module.
(2) Enterprise Management.
(3) Enterprise Management and Enforcement Module.
(4) Enterprise Log Server.
(5) Enforcement Module and Enterprise Log Server.

Enter your selection  (1-5/a-abort) [1]: 3
Please select Management type:
-----------------------------


(1) Enterprise Primary Management.
(2) Enterprise Secondary Management.

Enter your selection  (1-2/a-abort) [1]:
IP forwarding disabled
Hardening OS Security: IP forwarding will be disabled during boot.
Generating default filter
Default Filter installed
Hardening OS Security: Default Filter will be applied during boot.
This program will guide you through several steps where you
will define your Check Point products configuration.
```

Continued

Figure 18.2 Initial Configuration

```
At any later time, you can reconfigure these parameters by
running cpconfig
```

Licenses

The license configuration option will be displayed regardless of which modules you have installed. Since we have installed a primary management module, we should be installing a local license that was registered with the local management station's IP address. Follow this step-by-step procedure for adding your license(s). You can see the license configuration input and output outlined in Figure 18.3.

1. When prompted to add licenses, enter **y** for *yes* and press **Enter**.

2. Enter **m** to add the license manually and then press **Enter**. Now you will be prompted for each field of the license. Figure 18.3 shows the following license installed: cplic putlic eval 01Oct2002 dNrP4oprA-3MGjFUa69-PiNHuuHoa-4CyJa5yjk CPMP-EVAL-1-3DES-NG CK-CP. The license components are as follows:

    ■ **Host** The IP address or host ID associated with this license or the word *eval*.

    ■ **Date** The date that the license expires, which may be never.

    ■ **String** The license string provided by Check Point to validate the license. This key will be unique for each license and IP address/host.

    ■ **Features** The features this license will enable (for example, management and/or 3DES).

        As you can see in Figure 18.3, you also have the option of choosing **f** for [F]etch from file. If you select this option, the configuration will prompt you to enter the filename.

3. Enter the values for Host, Date, String, and Features, pressing **Enter** after each entry.

Figure 18.3 Configuring Licenses

```
Configuring Licenses...
=========================
Host             Expiration  Signature                    Features

Note: The recommended way of managing licenses is using SmartUpdate.
cpconfig can be used to manage local licenses only on this machine.

Do you want to add licenses (y/n) [y] ?

Do you want to add licenses [M]anually or [F]etch from file: m
IP Address: eval
```

Continued

Figure 18.3 Configuring Licenses

```
Expiration Date: 01Oct2002

Signature Key: dNrP4oprA-3MGjFUa69-PiNHuuHoa-4CyJa5yjk

SKU/Features: CPMP-EVAL-1-3DES-NG CK-CP


License was added successfully
```

Administrators

If you have installed a management module, as soon as you enter a license into the configuration program, it will move on to the next setting, which will be to add an administrator. You must define at least one administrator at this time. You can always come back later to add, edit, or delete your administrators. Figure 18.4 shows the steps involved to add your administrator.

NOTE

If you have installed an enforcement module only, you will not configure administrators.

It is best to use individual admin usernames instead of a generic username such ass *fwadmin*. The problem with using a generic login ID is that you cannot properly audit the activities of the firewall administrators. When you are troubleshooting a problem, it might be important for you to know who installed the last security policy. This becomes more and more important when there are several people administering a firewall system. The fields that you need to fill in are as follows:

- **Administrator Name** Choose a login name for your administrator. This field is case sensitive.

- **Password** Choose a good alphanumeric password. It must be at least four characters long and is also case sensitive.

- **Verify Password** Repeat the same password entered above.

- **Permissions for all Management Clients (Read/[W]rite All, [R]ead Only All, [C]ustomized)**

- **Permission to manage administrators (Yes or No)**

Figure 18.4 Adding an Administrator

```
Configuring Administrators...

=============================

No Check Point Administrators are currently

defined for this Management Station.

Do you want to add administrators (y/n) [y] ?
```

Continued

Figure 18.4 Adding an Administrator

```
Administrator name: Cherie

Password:

Verify Password:

Permissions for all Management Clients (Read/[W]rite All, [R]ead Only All,
    [C]ustomized) w

Permission to Manage Administrators ([Y]es, [N]o) y

Administrator Cherie was added successfully and has

Read/Write Permission for all Management Clients


Add another one (y/n) [n] ?
```

Setting permissions allows you to define the access level that you will require on an individual basis for each administrator. If you select Read/[**W**]rite All or [**R**]ead Only All, your admin will have access to all the available GUI client features with the ability to either make changes and updates or view the configuration and logs (perhaps for troubleshooting purposes), respectively. You may also choose to customize access so that administrators may be able to update some things and not others. To do this, select **Customized** and configure each of these options. Here are descriptions of each feature listed in Figure 18.5:

- **SmartUpdate** This GUI tool allows you to manage licenses and update remote modules.

- **Check Point Users Database** Allows you to manage users through the SmartDashboard.

- **LDAP Users Database** Allows you to manage LDAP users through SmartDashboard.

- **Security Policy** Allows you to manage the Security Policy tab in the SmartDashboard.

- **QoS Policy** Allows you to manage the QoS (FloodGate-1) bandwidth management policy in the SmartDashboard.

- **Monitoring** Enables access to the Log Viewer, System Status, and Traffic Monitoring GUI clients (a.k.a. SmartView Tracker, SmartView Status, and SmartView Monitor in FP3).

Figure 18.5 Setting Customized Permissions

```
Permissions for all Management Clients (Read/[W]rite All, [R]ead Only
```

```
    All, [C]ustomized) c
        Permission for SmartUpdate (Read/[W]rite, [R]ead Only, [N]one) r
        Permission for Check Point Users Database (Read/[W]rite, [R]ead
          Only) w
```

Continued

Figure 18.5 Setting Customized Permissions

```
        Permission for LDAP Users Database (Read/[W]rite, [R]ead Only,
           [N]one) r
        Permission for Security Policy (Read/[W]rite, [R]ead Only,
           [N]one) w
        Permission for QoS Policy (Read/[W]rite, [R]ead Only, [N]one) n
        Permission for Monitoring (Read/[W]rite, [R]ead Only, [N]one) w
Administrator Cherie was added successfully and has
Read Only Permission for SmartUpdate
Read/Write Permission for Check Point Users Database
Read Only Permission for LDAP Users Database
Read/Write Permission for Security Policy
Read/Write Permission for Monitoring
```

Management Clients

The management clients (also called *GUI clients*) are installed on either Windows or Solaris (X-Motif). These clients can be installed on as many desktops as you like, but before they can connect to the management server, you need to enter their IP addresses into the Management Clients configuration tool (see Figure 18.6). You can use this feature, for example, if you install the GUI clients on your own workstation to enable you to control the management server from your PC. This will allow you to connect remotely to manage the Security Policy and view your logs and system status. You do not need to configure any clients at all during the install, but if you are already prepared for this step, you may enter as many clients into this window as necessary. This client information will be saved in a file on your firewall under $FWDIR/conf and will be named *gui-clients*. This is a text file and can be edited directly, or you can bring up this Management Clients window at any time in the future by running cpconfig.

NOTE

If you have installed an enforcement module only, you will not configure GUI clients.

Figure 18.6 Configuring Management Clients

```
Configuring Management Clients...
====================================
Management clients are trusted hosts from which
Administrators are allowed to log on to this Management Station
using Windows/X-Motif GUI.


No Management clients defined
```

Continued

Figure 18.6 Configuring Management Clients

```
Do you want to add a Management client (y/n) [y] ?
Please enter the list hosts that will be Management clients.
Enter hostname or IP address, one per line, terminating with CTRL-D or
    your EOF character.
192.168.168.3
Is this correct (y/n) [y] ?
```

As you enter GUI clients into this configuration, you type their host name or IP address, one per line, pressing **Enter** at the end of each. When you are done editing the client list, press **Ctrl + D** to send an end-of-file (EOF) control character to the program to continue.

You are allowed to use wildcards in each GUI client host specification as follows:

- **Any** If you type in the word **Any**, you will allow anyone to connect without restriction (not recommended).

- **Asterisks** You may use asterisks in the host name, such as 10.10.20.*, which means any host in the 10.10.20.0/24 network; *.domainname.com means any host name within the domainname.com domain.

- **Ranges** You may use a dash (-) to represent a range of IP addresses, such as 1.1.1.3-1.1.1.7, which means the five hosts including 1.1.1.3 and 1.1.1.7 and every one in between.

- **DNS or WINS resolvable hostnames**

Figure 18.7 shows an example of the configured GUI clients window with various options that you can use for your GUI Client entries. We recommend staying away from using host names or domain names, however, since it requires DNS to be configured and working on the firewall. Specifying IP addresses is the best method since it doesn't rely on resolving and will continue to work even if you cannot reach your DNS name servers from the firewall.

Figure 18.7 Management Client Wildcards

```
Please enter the list hosts that will be Management clients.
Enter hostname or IP address, one per line, terminating with CTRL-D or
    your EOF character.
*.integralis.com
1.1.1.3-1.1.1.7
10.10.10.2
10.10.10.3
10.10.20.*
backwatcher.com
noc.activis.com
Is this correct (y/n) [y] ? y
```

Certificate Authority Initialization

Your management server will be a certificate authority (CA) for your firewall enforcement modules and will use certificates for Secure Internal Communication (SIC). This is the step in the installation process where the management server's CA is configured and a certificate is generated for the server and its components.

You will be presented with the Random Pool configuration option, where you are asked to input random text until you hear a beep. The timing latency between your key presses will be used to generate cryptographic data, so it is recommended that you enter the data at a random pace, so that some keystrokes are close together and others have a longer pause between them. The more random the key-press intervals, the more unlikely that the input could be duplicated. If the system determines that the keystrokes are not random enough, it will not take them as input and will display an asterisk to the right of the progression bar.

NOTE

The Random Pool configuration screen will also be presented to you if you have installed an enforcement module only so that you can generate an internal certificate for SIC.

Type random characters at random intervals into the Random Pool until the progress bar is full and the message "Thank you!" appears at the bottom of the window, as shown in Figure 18.8. The next step is to initialize the internal CA for SIC. It could take a minute for the CA to initialize. Figure 18.9 shows the messages you will receive on the console while configuring the CA. Press **Enter** to initialize the CA.

Figure 18.8 Random Pool

```
Configuring Random Pool...

===========================
You are now asked to perform a short random keystroke session.
The random data collected in this session will be used in
various cryptographic operations.


Please enter random text containing at least six different
characters. You will see the '*' symbol after keystrokes that
are too fast or too similar to preceding keystrokes. These
keystrokes will be ignored.


Please keep typing until you hear the beep and the bar is full.


    [..................]


Thank you.
```

Figure 18.9 Configuring Certificate Authority

```
Configuring Certificate Authority...

=======================================
The system uses an Internal Certificate Authority
to provide Secured Internal Communication (SIC) certificates
for the components in your system.


Note that your components will not be able to communicate
with each other until the Certificate Authority is initialized
and they have their SIC certificate.


Press 'Enter' to initialize the Certificate Authority...
Internal Certificate Authority created successfully
Certificate was created successfully
Certificate Authority initialization ended successfully
```

Once the CA is initialized successfully, you will be prompted to enter and send the FQDN of the management server to the internal CA (ICA). This name must be correct for the ICA to function properly and cannot be changed once it is input to the ICA. The following steps can be used to generate the FQDN shown in Figure 18.10 for this cpconfig setting:

1. Type **y** and press **Enter** to define the FQDN now.
2. The current FQDN obtained from the system is displayed. Enter **y** if you want to change it.
3. Enter the value of the FQDN (for example, gatekeeper.nokia.com).
4. Enter **y** if you are sure you typed the value correctly.
5. Now press **Enter** to send the FQDN to the CA.

Figure 18.10 Sending the FQDN to the ICA

```
The FQDN (Fully Qualified Domain Name) of this Management Server
is required for proper operation of the Internal Certificate Authority.


Would you like to define it now (y/n) [y] ?
The FQDN of this Management Server is gatekeeper
Do you want to change it (y/n) [n] ?


Warning: The FQDN might be incorrect!
Make sure it contains the host name and the domain name.
```

Continued

Figure 18.10 Sending the FQDN to the ICA

```
NOTE: If the FQDN is incorrect, the Internal CA cannot function properly,
and CRL retrieval will be impossible.


Are you sure gatekeeper is the FQDN of this machine (y/n) [n] ?
Do you want to change it (y/n) [n] ? y


Please enter the FQDN (Fully Qualified Domain Name) of this management:
    gatekeeper.nokia.com


Are you sure gatekeeper.nokia.com is the FQDN of this machine (y/n) [n] ? y


Press 'Enter' to send it to the Certificate Authority...


Trying to contact CA. It can take up to 4 seconds...
 FQDN initialized successfully


The FQDN was successfully sent to the CA
```

Finally, you will be presented with the fingerprint of the management server. This fingerprint is unique to your CA and the certificate on your server. The first time your GUI clients connect to the management server, they will receive the fingerprint so that they can match it to the string listed here and verify that they are connecting to the correct manager. After the first connection, every time the clients connect to the management server, the fingerprint is verified. If the fingerprints don't match, a warning message will be displayed, and the administrator can decide whether to continue with the connection. This transaction is shown in Figure 18.11.

1. When prompted by cpconfig, "Do you want to save it to a file?" as shown in Figure 18.11, type **y** and press **Enter** to save the fingerprint to a file.

2. Type the filename and press **Enter**. The file will be saved in $CPDIR/conf.

3. Enter **y** to confirm.

Figure 18.11 Saving the Certificate Fingerprint

```
Configuring Certificate's Fingerprint...

========================================
The following text is the fingerprint of this Management machine:
CARR HOST MEEK FORD ROOM MATH LAIN HOWE BOY SITU SLUM BALM


Do you want to save it to a file? (y/n) [y] ?
Please enter the file name [/opt/CPshared-50-03/conf]: fingerprint.txt
```

Continued

Figure 18.11 Saving the Certificate Fingerprint

```
The fingerprint will be saved as /opt/CPshared-50-03/conf/fingerprint.txt.

Are you sure? (y/n) [n] ? y


The fingerprint was successfully saved.
```

Installation Complete

When the configuration program ends, you might see on the screen a few messages such as "generating GUI-clients INSPECT code" as the system finishes the installation of the VPN-1/FireWall-1 package. Finally, you will receive the following question: "Would you like to reboot the machine [y/n]?" (shown in Figure 18.12). If you elect not to reboot, you will exit the installation and go back to a shell prompt. If you choose to reboot, the system will be restarted immediately.

> **WARNING**
>
> If you are remotely connected to this firewall, you will not have access after rebooting. The firewall loads a policy named InitialPolicy, which prevents all access after an install. See the sidebar "Unload InitialPolicy Script" for a workaround.

Figure 18.12 Installation Complete

```
generating GUI-clients INSPECT code
initial_management:
Compiled OK.


Hardening OS Security: Initial policy will be applied
until the first policy is installed


In order to complete the installation
you must reboot the machine.
Do you want to reboot? (y/n) [y] ?
```

Getting Back to Configuration

Now that installation is complete, you might need to get back into the configuration screens that you ran through with cpconfig. You can add, modify, or delete any of the previous configuration settings by running cpconfig at any time from the command line. Each screen that you ran through during the initial configuration will now be listed as a menu item, as shown in Figure 18.13.

Figure 18.13 cpconfig

```
gatekeeper[admin]# cpconfig
This program will let you re-configure
your Check Point products configuration.



Configuration Options:
---------------------

(1)   Licenses

(2)   Administrators

(3)   Management Clients

(4)   SNMP Extension

(5)   PKCS#11 Token

(6)   Random Pool

(7)   Certificate Authority

(8)   Automatic start of Check Point Products


(9) Exit


Enter your choice (1-9) :
```

Three options listed here did not come up during the initial installation process. Option 4 configures the SNMP Extension. By default, the Check Point module's SNMP daemon is disabled, but if you want to export SNMP MIBS to network monitors, you can use this option to enable SNMP in FireWall-1. Option 5 in the cpconfig output configures a PKCS#11 token that allows you to install an add-on card such as an accelerator card; option 8 allows you to configure the automatic start of Check Point modules at boot time. By default, the Check Point FireWall-1 product will start automatically on reboot.

If you installed an enforcement module only, the cpconfig screens will be a little different. There will be two new choices:

- **Secure Internal Communication** Enables a one-time password that will be used for authentication between this enforcement module and its management server as well as any other remote modules that it might communicate with.

- **High Availability** Allows you to enable this enforcement module to participate in a Check Point High Availability (CPHA) configuration with one or more other enforcement modules. This tab will not show up in your installation since you cannot have a management module installed on an enforcement module in a CPHA cluster.

Testing the Configuration

Now that the FireWall-1 package is configured and you have rebooted your Nokia, it's time to test access to the firewall so you can configure and install security policies. We want to make sure that our firewall is installed and configured correctly, and testing the basic administrative firewall tasks is an easy way to verify that fact. This is particularly important after we have performed an upgrade between major versions (such as 4.1 to NG). We will test GUI client access as well as defining and installing a basic policy. For the sake of completeness, we will test both the pushing and fetching of our security policy.

Testing GUI Client Access

After you have the Check Point packages installed, enabled, and configured, you can begin configuring a security policy for your Nokia firewall. Even if the InitialPolicy is loaded, you should be able to connect with a GUI client and push a policy. If you have any trouble with this process, unload the default filter with *fw unloadlocal* (prior to NG FP2, the command was *fw unload local-host*). You can run the management clients on the following operating systems:

- Windows 98/ME
- Windows XP (Home or Professional)
- Windows 2000 SP1 or SP2 (Professional, Server, or Advanced Server)
- Windows NT SP6a (Workstation or Server)
- Solaris 8 (32 or 64 bit—note that running the GUI on Solaris requires a Motif license)

If you are running a firewall prior to NG FP3, you will be logging in to the Check Point Policy Editor to manage security policies. In NG FP3, the name of the editor has been changed to *SmartDashboard*. The FP3 SmartDashboard doesn't look much different from the FP2 interface, so we will use the FP3 smart clients in our examples. On Windows, begin by going to **Start | Programs | Check Point SMART Clients | SmartDashboard NG FP3**. You will be presented with a login prompt like the one in Figure 18.14.

Figure 18.14 SmartDashboard Login

To log in the first time, enter your username, password, and management server IP address. If you are connecting to the Nokia as the management server, enter the IP address of the interface that is closest to you (it could be the internal IP or SSN IP) in the Management Server box. As the client connects, you will be presented with the management server's fingerprint that was generated during the initial configuration procedure. You should match the fingerprint in the client to the fingerprint on the management server to verify that you are connecting to the correct machine (see Figure 18.15). If it matches, click the **Approve** button to continue logging in to the management server.

NOTE

In NG FP2 and FP3, you can now select a check box to log in to your management clients in demo mode. Previously, you would need to log in with the management server field set to *local to run the demo. Also new in FP3 is the ability to select a management server from a pull-down list. This is a really nice feature if you normally manage multiple management servers, since each time you type in a new server, it is added to the list.

Figure 18.15 Fingerprint Identification

If the fingerprint changes because you reinstalled the management server software, put in new hardware as a replacement for the old management server, or regenerated the ICA certificate, you will receive a warning similar to the one shown in Figure 18.16. Again, you should verify the fingerprint before accepting the new one.

Figure 18.16 Fingerprint Warning

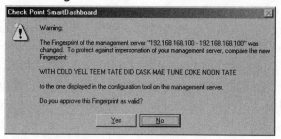

As long as the fingerprint remains the same, you will get no message after the first acceptance. Behind the scenes, Check Point will verify that the fingerprint matches. After you pass
authentication and accept the fingerprint, you will see the SmartDashboard window, as shown in
Figure 18.17. From here you can view and manage your network objects and policies. Initially,
you will have a single object configured to represent your firewall, which NG creates for you
during installation (see Figure 18.18).

Figure 18.17 Check Point SmartDashboard

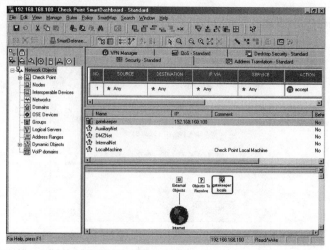

Figure 18.18 Check Point Gateway Object

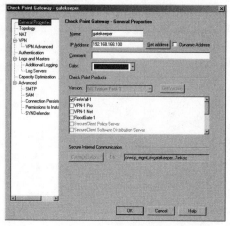

You should verify that your firewall object is configured properly before you try to push a policy. To edit your firewall object, click **Manage** in the main menu and select **Network Objects**. Highlight the firewall object and click **Edit**. Check that the correct IP address is entered in the General Properties tab. The IP entered here should correspond to the external IP address of your firewall, which is the same IP address that you use for a local license on the firewall. Modify the Check Point products installed to include the options that the installation didn't select for you, such as VPN-1, FloodGate-1, and so on. Also verify that the Topology tab is configured with the correct information about your firewall.

NOTE

If you have a distributed installation, you need to create the firewall object for you Nokia. It will not be created for you as it was in our previous example.

When you are finished editing your firewall object, click **OK**. Now you can begin creating all the other network objects that you will need to use in your Security Policy. Using these network objects, you will create a rule base in the Security tab of the SmartDashboard. Here we put in a simple "accept-all" policy to show you the procedure. Do not use an accept-all policy on your firewall, since a policy like this will provide you with no protection.

Begin by clicking the **Rules** menu option and select **Add Rule | Top**. This will enter the default rule, any source, destination, or service to drop without logging. Right-click the **Action** cell and select **Accept**. Then, right-click the Track cell and select **Log**.

Now choose the **File** menu and **Save** the policy. The policy is named *Standard* by default and is defined in Figure 18.17.

Pushing and Fetching Policy

Now you are ready to test pushing a policy to your Nokia firewall. From the SmartDashboard, click the **Policy** menu and choose **Install**. Your objects, rules, and users will be saved at this time. If this is the first time you are installing a policy, you will receive a warning message like the one shown in Figure 18.19 until you click the box to stop showing the message. This message simply informs you that there are some rules that are defined through the Global Properties that can be configured through the Policy menu. These rules are "implicit" rules and are not visible in your Security Policy window. You can make these rules visible by selecting **Implied Rules** from the **View** menu. Check the box so that you don't see this message again, and click **OK** to continue.

Figure 18.19 SmartDashboard Warning

Next you will receive a policy install window where you need to select the type of policy you will install on certain Check Point objects (see Figure 18.20). If you have multiple firewalls, they will all be displayed in this window. If you are installing to a stand-alone Nokia, accept the default values and click **OK** to begin the installation process. (By *stand-alone* we mean a VPN-1/FireWall-1 management server and enforcement module installed on a single platform—in other words, the opposite of a distributed installation.)

Figure 18.20 Policy Installation Targets

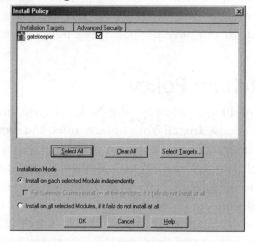

Now your management server will verify the rule base, compile the security policy, and push the policy to the firewall module. An installation process status window will be displayed, similar to the one in Figure 18.21. Now you must wait for the installation to complete. When the installation is done, the Close button will light up and the status will change to a green check mark if the install was successful. There could be warnings associated with the policy installation, and in that case a red exclamation point (!) will accompany the check mark, as shown in Figure 18.22. This installation window is new in NG FP3.

Figure 18.21 Installation Process

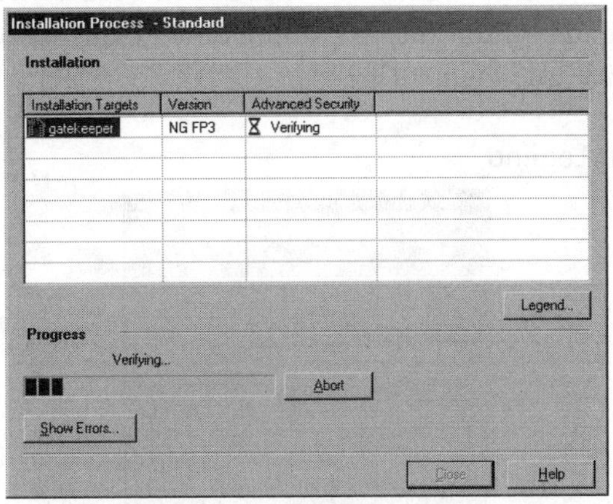

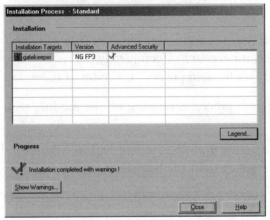

Figure 18.22 Installation Succeeded

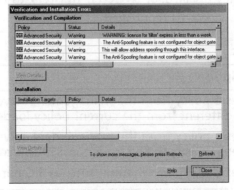

If you receive warnings or errors on the installation, you can view these messages by clicking the button labeled **Show Warnings**, as shown in Figure 18.22. If you have not yet configured antispoofing on your gateway's interfaces, you will always receive these warnings on a policy install. You could also have a warning about your license, if it will expire in less than a week. See the errors from the install in Figure 18.23.

Figure 18.23 Verification and Installation Errors

Other status options may be displayed in the Installation Process window. On this page Check Point provides a Legend button that pops up a quick explanation on each of the possible status icons you could receive (see Figure 18.24).

Figure 18.24 Status Icon Legend

If the policy installation was successful, you are done. You can continue to modify and install your policy as many times as is necessary to completely define a security policy for your organization. If policy installation fails for some reason, try some of these steps:

- Verify that the firewall process is running on the module with the command *ps −auxw | grep fw*.

- Try unloading the policy from the console with the command *fw unloadlocal*, and then try reinstalling the policy from the management server.

- Ensure that there is network connectivity between the management server and the module. Check cables and test with ping.

- Check that SIC is configured properly. Look at http://support.checkpoint.com/kb/docs/public/firewall1/5_0/pdf/sic.pdf for assistance.

Once you are set up to push a policy successfully, you will want to verify that the firewall can fetch a policy from the management station. The Nokia will attempt to fetch a policy on system startup or whenever the firewall module is restarted. To force the Nokia to fetch a policy, use the *fw fetch* command. Available switches for this command are listed in Table 18.3. Type **fw fetch localhost** to load the last policy installed, or **fw fetch master1** to fetch from the management host defined as master1 in the $FWDIR/conf/masters file.

Table 18.3 fw fetch Syntax

Switch	Description
-n	Fetches a policy from the management server and only loads the policy if it is different from the current policy loaded.
-f <filename>	Fetches a policy from the management server listed in <filename>. If no filename is specified, uses the $FWDIR/conf/masters file.
-i	Ignores the SIC information, such as SIC names.

FireWall-1 Command Line

The following are some other useful FireWall-1 commands that you might find handy while configuring Check Point on your Nokia firewall. Some of these have been discussed throughout the chapter:

- **cpstop** Stops all Check Point products and the SVN Foundation.

- **cpstart** Starts the SVN Foundation and all Check Point products.

- **cplic print** Prints the currently installed licenses.

- **cplic put** Adds a license.

- **fw tab –t connections –s** Lists the number of connections in the FireWall-1 connections table.

- **fw ver** Displays the version of VPN-1/FireWall-1. Use the –*k* switch to see the kernel version.

- **fw stat** Lists the currently loaded policy, date the policy was last installed, and the interface and direction that the security policy is enforcing.

- **fw unloadlocal** Unloads the current security policy so that no policy is loaded.

- **fw load** When run on the management console, this can push a policy from command line to a remote module.

- **fw lichosts** Displays the hosts that are protected by your firewall, when a limited license is installed.

- **fwstop –default** Stops all VPN-1/FireWall-1 services and loads the default filter into the kernel.

- **fwstop –proc** Stops all VPN-1/FireWall-1 services, but keeps the policy loaded in the kernel. Only simple accept, drop, and reject control decisions will be made.

- **fwstart –f** Starts the VPN-1/FireWall-1 services.

Upgrading the Firewall

This section is dedicated to upgrading your FireWall-1 software on your NSP. We'll start by assuming that you are running FireWall-1 4.1 SP-6 on IPSO 3.4.1 FCS10 or later. If you are on a prior version of FireWall-1 4.1, you should start by upgrading your IPSO to the latest 3.4.1 and then upgrading to SP-6. If you are on FireWall-1 4.0, you need to upgrade to 4.1 before upgrading to NG. Don't get overzealous; be careful and take small steps, and you will be better off in the long run. You can upgrade from 4.1 SP-6 to NG FP1, FP2, or FP3. We recommend that you first go to the FP2 bundle (which actually installs the FP1 packages as well) before moving on to newer Feature Packs.

The first thing you should do once you are on 4.1 SP-6 is to run your configuration through one of the upgrade verification tools that Check Point provides. This might catch errors that could cause the upgrade to fail or cause the resulting configuration to be unusable after the upgrade. There is a tarball named upgrade_verifiers_NG_FP2_nokia.tgz for IPSO 3.4.x and 3.5 and associated release notes. You should only run this on your Nokia if you have a management server installed. This script checks the $FWDIR/conf directory on your management console. Download this bundle to your Nokia management server and gunzip and untar it into its own directory. You can obtain this file from www.checkpoint.com/techsupport/downloadsng/utilities.html#upgrade_verify:

1. If the upgrade_verifiers_NG_FP2_Nokia.tgz file is in your /var/admin directory, create a subdirectory and put it in there: **mkdir upgrade_verifiers; mv upgrade_verifiers_* upgrade_verifiers; cd upgrade_verifiers**.

2. Now run **gunzip *** to uncompress the file.

3. Extract the tarball with the command **tar –xvf upgrade***.

4. Run the pre_upgrade_verifier script with the following syntax: **pre_upgrade_verifier –p $FWDIR –c 4.1 –t NG_FP2 –f upgrade.txt**.

5. Look in the upgrade.txt file to determine what you might need to change before beginning the upgrade process.

Remember to read any release notes before you begin the upgrade procedure. You could have certain configuration options that require special attention before you begin upgrading. Here's a brief list of some common configuration issues that you will need to resolve in 4.1 before you install NG FP2 or later:

- Disable all FWZ configurations. NG FP2 and later no longer support FWZ for VPNs.

- Disable objects that have certificates configured for Hybrid IKE. You might even be better off to delete these objects and recreate them once you've upgraded to NG.

- Disable any SKIP or manual IPSec VPN configurations. Only IKE is supported in NG FP2 and FP3.

- Ensure that your firewall object names match exactly the host name of the firewall modules. This name mapping should be in the hosts file on both the management and firewall modules as well. You cannot change the host name or object name once you have upgraded to NG due to the certificates' dependence on this information.

Upgrading from 4.1 SP6 to NG FP2

If you have a separate management server, always make sure that you upgrade that management server before you upgrade any firewall modules. Once you are confident that you are ready to upgrade to NG, download the NG FP2 or FP3 wrapper package to your Nokia and follow the instructions provided. Here we use the NG FP2 wrapper for demonstration, and we recommend that you go to FP2 before FP3 to ensure that your configuration is merged successfully at each step. You can follow this procedure whether your Nokia is a stand-alone or distributed installation:

1. Since you are on IPSO 3.4.1, the first thing you need to do is upgrade your IPSO image to the latest 3.6 release.

2. Start now with the wrapper package for NG FP2 named CP_FP2_IPSO.tgz. Ensure that this is the only package in your /var/admin directory before you begin. Then run **newpkg –i** from the /var/admin directory.

3. Press **4** and then press **Enter** to install from the local file system.

4. When asked to enter a pathname to the package, simply enter a single dot (.) and press **Enter**.

5. Now choose **2** and press **Enter** to upgrade from an old package.

6. Choose the **FireWall-1-strong.v4.1.SP-6 – Check Point FireWall-1 (Strong) Version 4.1 SP-6 (Wed May 15 16:10:58 IDT 2002 Build 41617)** package from the list of packages you can upgrade from. In our list it is number 1, so we choose **1** and press **Enter** to continue.

7. Next, the upgrade program will verify that you really want to perform this upgrade with the following question: "Do you want to upgrade from FireWall-1-strong.v4.1.SP-6 to CP_FP2_IPSO? [y/n]." Enter **y** for yes and press **Enter** to continue. As the packages are being upgraded and installed, you will receive a lot of messages on the console. There is no more text for you to input at this time. All you can do is sit patiently and wait for the upgrade to complete. You will see a message that the WebTheater service is no longer supported and that it will be deleted. You will also see a notice that the system failed to find an Internal CA in objects_5_0.C file, but it will be created after cpstart. You can safely ignore both messages. The following packages are installed while you wait:

   - NG FP1 SVN Foundation

   - NG FP1 VPN-1/FireWall-1

   - NG FP2 SVN Foundation

   - NG FP2 VPN-1/FireWall-1

   - NG FP2 Backward Compatibility with 4.1 package

   - NG FP2 Policy Server

   - NG FP2 FloodGate-1

   - NG FP2 Real Time Monitor

8. When the newpkg program exits, you will be brought back to a shell prompt. Both the SVN Foundation and VPN-1/FireWall-1 packages are already enabled in Voyager. You need to log out and log back in to the Nokia to obtain the latest environment variables. So, type **exit** and then log in again.

9. Run **cpconfig**. If you need help with any of the options here, read the section on cpconfig earlier in this chapter. You need to add a new license because 4.1 licenses will not function on NG.

10. **Reboot**. When the system comes back up it will not load the last policy you had installed in 4.1. It will load the defaultfilter policy instead. You need to push the policy to the firewall the first time after the upgrade.

11. Log into your management server from your NG FP2 Policy Editor Management Client. Accept the fingerprint and verify that your policy appears to be intact after the upgrade.

12. Select **Install** from the **Policy** menu to push a policy.

13. Test communication through your firewall. You might need to reconstruct VPN settings and set up Hybrid IKE again to get things working the way they were prior to the upgrade.

> **NOTE**
>
> If you receive a verification error that says "Missing IP protocol for user defined service MSExchange-DirectoryRef," simply delete this service from the **Manage | Services** window and restart the installation.
>
> If you upgraded from 4.1 directly to FP3, you might need to configure interfaces in the Topology tab on your Check Point Gateway object before you can install a policy.

Upgrading from NG FP2 to NG FP3

The upgrade procedure for FP3 is very simple. You begin as you did with the FP2 upgrade—by downloading the FP3 wrapper package called CP_FP3_IPSO.tgz. You can run this wrapper to upgrade from 4.1 SP-6, NG FP1, or NG FP2 or to install NG FP3 from scratch on your Nokia firewall. We took you through the procedure of a fresh install at the beginning of the chapter. To upgrade to FP3 instead, run *newpkg –i* as you normally do to install a new package, but when prompted whether to install or upgrade, select **2** and press **Enter** to upgrade from an old package.

After upgrading to FP3, the FP3 SVN Foundation and VPN-1/FireWall-1 packages will already be enabled in Voyager. All you need to do is exit your login session and log back in to obtain the correct environment variables. Run cpconfig and if there is nothing new to configure, exit cpconfig and reboot. When the system comes back up, the InitialPolicy will be loaded, which means that you need to push a policy after the upgrade.

Backing Out from NG to 4.1

If you need to back out from a recent upgrade for some reason, the procedure on a Nokia is quite simple. First, you need to disable any NG components such as Policy Server and FloodGate-1 and **Apply** and **Save** your changes. Next, disable NG VPN-1/FireWall-1 and **Apply** and **Save**, and then finally disable the NG SVN Foundation package and **Apply** and **Save**.

Now you can enable the old 4.1 package and **Apply** and **Save** your changes. Then you must reboot the box. When the box comes back up, the FireWall-1 services will not be started. You must log in to Voyager and go to the **Check Point FireWall-1** configuration screen found under the **Security and Access Configuration** heading. Click the option button next to **Start FireWall-1 automatically at reboot?** to **On**, then **Apply** and **Save**. Finally, log in to the Nokia and run **fwstart** from the command line. The firewall will load the last 4.1 policy you had configured, pick up where you left off before the upgrade, and start automatically on the next reboot. You can go back into Voyager and delete any disabled packages for cleanup if you don't want to save them for another try later.

Summary

All FireWall-1 administrators with Nokia firewalls need to know basic tasks such as installing and upgrading the Check Point FireWall-1 software packages. If you never upgraded your firewall, you could be at risk if there are known vulnerabilities in that release that have been resolved in newer patches. In this chapter we provided the tools necessary to complete these tasks so that you can continue to secure your organization with Check Point FireWall-1 on Nokia.

Preparation is always key to a successful upgrade or install. With FireWall-1, you need to obtain licenses, configure a hosts entry, and possibly upgrade the IPSO image on your Nokia before you can begin with Check Point. It's also very important to read all release notes available before you install new software.

Once you have the software installed on IPSO, you then need to enable it. If you are running Check Point NG, you will first need to enable the SVN Foundation, **Apply** and **Save** your configuration, and then enable the VPN-1/FireWall-1 packages. When you enable packages through the Manage Installed Packages configuration screen, the file /var/etc/pm_profile is updated with appropriate environment variables. This means that you will have to log in again to the Nokia after the packages are enabled to receive the correct shell environment. The next step to configuring the firewall is to run cpconfig. The first run of this utility will prompt you for the type of install (stand-alone or distributed), licenses, administrators, management clients, ICA initialization, SIC password (firewall module only), and then finally to reboot. You can always reconfigure your firewall at any time by running cpconfig again, which will provide you with a menu to choose the option you want to edit.

After configuring Check Point, you need to verify that you can log in with the management clients and push a policy. You should also test fetching a policy to ensure that the firewall will operate properly during a reboot. If you have any problem doing these things, verify that the firewall is running on the module with the command **ps –auxw | grep fw**, try unloading the policy from the console with the command **fw unloadlocal**, ensure that there is connectivity between the management server and the module by checking cables and testing with ping, and check that SIC is configured properly.

Once you have a running FireWall-1 installation, you eventually need to upgrade your firewall software to stay up to date. Whenever you are upgrading the firewall in IPSO, you must first upgrade your IPSO image to one compatible with the new software. The next step is to get the new firewall package downloaded to your Nokia, and then run *newpkg –i* to start the upgrade. Choose the option to upgrade from an old version (as opposed to install, which will not copy over your configuration), and then choose the old FireWall-1 package that you are upgrading from. If you're upgrading from 4.1 to NG, run your configuration through an upgrade verifier utility provided by Check Point to see if there are any configuration issues that you can sort out before you upgrade the management server. The recommended upgrade path is to go from 4.1 SP-6 to NG FP2 via the wrapper package (which installs FP1 first) and then to NG FP3.

## Chapter 19

Introducing the Voyager Web Interface

Solutions in this chapter:

- **Basic System Configuration, Out of the Box**

- **Configuring the System for Security**

- **Understanding Configuration Options**

Introduction

Administrators tasked with installing a firewall for the first time typically have to be very knowl-edgeable when it comes to configuring the underlying operating system to function efficiently as a firewalled router. The administrator must know how to configure interface IP addresses and speed/duplex settings, how to configure hostnames and Domain Name Service (DNS) properly, and how to configure static or dynamic routing, among many other things.

We have seen that the IPSO operating system that is at the core of the Nokia appliances is UNIX-based, but we don't need to have in-depth knowledge of UNIX to go through a first-time or even repeat configuration. The Nokia Voyager allows us to configure all of the previously mentioned features and much, much more through a simple, Web-based interface. The vast majority of changes we make do not require a system reboot, but take effect immediately (another helpful side-effect of IPSO's UNIX base).

In this chapter, we walk you through a very thorough initial configuration of your Nokia appliance, all done from within Voyager. The emphasis is on security, so when we talk about net-work access and services, we show you how to, for example, disable Telnet access and enable SSL for secure Web access through Voyager. We give you an alternative to FTP or show you how to make FTP more secure, if it must be used. We also go over each of the Voyager configuration options so that when you are done you will have a very good idea of just what can be accom-plished with this powerful interface.

Basic System Configuration, Out of the Box

Once the initial system is configured, your Nokia runs a minimal installation of Apache Web server, and the server runs on the standard port 80 by default. IPSO 3.3 through IPSO 3.6 FCS3 use Apache/1.3.6. You can view the Apache version on your Nokia by running the command */bin/httpd −v*. This server is running for the purpose of serving out the Web pages necessary for you to configure your Nokia Security Platform (NSP) using the Nokia Voyager Web interface.

You always have the option of running the Voyager interface using the lynx text browser through a console connection, but once you have assigned an IP address to your Nokia, you will be able to connect with any Web browser on the network to configure the system. Although Lynx is a useful tool, many administrators prefer the nicer Voyager GUI available through a graphical Web browser.

> **NOTE**
>
> Remember to save your configuration changes using the **Save** icon within your Voyager GUI if you want to save any changes you make to the system. At every configuration screen in the Voyager interface, you will see icons at the top and bottom of each page that give you the options to go **Home, Up, Top, Apply,** or **Save**. After every change that you apply to the system, the change takes effect immediately, but you must select **Save** to write your changes to the /config/active file if you want changes you make to be pre-served through a reboot of the system.

Front Screen

When you went through the initial configuration, you set up your internal interface with the Nokia. Now you can begin configuring your appliance by typing in the IP address of this interface in a Web browser such as http://10.10.10.10 or using a DNS-resolvable name instead of an IP address, if available. Next enter the admin username and password when prompted for authentication. This step brings you to the front screen of the Voyager interface, which should resemble the image in Figure 19.1.

Figure 19.1 The Voyager Front Screen Display

You should notice that some very important system information is listed on this initial screen, such as the Nokia's model, software release, and version, as well as the serial number, which you'll need when you call in a support or maintenance request. The information on this front screen is the same regardless of the Nokia model you possess. To continue from this initial screen, select **Config**, to enter the main configuration screen (see Figure 19.2). This screen gives you all the possible options for configuring your NSP. In versions previous to IPSO 3.6, this screen looks slightly different, but most of the options are the same. From the initial screen, select **Monitor** to enter a read-only area, which allows you to view system status and other interesting information about the system.

Figure 19.2 The Main Configuration Screen

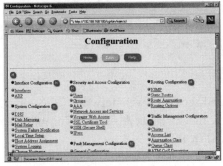

Navigating Voyager

When you are moving around within the Voyager interface, it is important that you do *not* use your browser's **Back** button to return to a previous screen. If you do this, you could end up getting cached pages that display incorrect information, which can cause confusion and possible misconfiguration. Instead, use the buttons that are provided for navigation across the top and bottom of each screen. These buttons and each of their functions are as follows:

- **Home** Displays the front screen.
- **Top** Displays the main Configuration screen or main Monitor screen, depending on which you are working under.
- **Up** Displays the previous page.
- **Apply** Applies changes entered on that page.
- **Save** Saves all changes that have been applied to the system, since either the last save or the last reboot.
- **Help** Displays help documentation relevant to the current page.

You will also see several small help buttons available throughout the various screens. You can identify these by the blue, circular icon with a white *H* displayed in the center. Each one gives you detailed help information for each section in which the button is displayed. This help feature pops up in a separate browser window, so you don't lose your current place within the Voyager interface.

If you installed the documentation package available for your version of IPSO, a **Doc** button is available along with the other navigation buttons on each page. This documentation provides even more help for each section of the configuration. In IPSO 3.6, there is even a *CLI Reference Guide* to assist you in using the new Command Line Interface Shell (CLISH) tool. In the documentation, select the **Content** button at any time to see a list of available topics.

Configuring Basic Interface Information

When configuring interfaces, you should know what IP address and netmask you will assign each interface in advance. For the examples that follow in this chapter, let's assume that you have a simple Nokia firewall with three interfaces: external (Internet facing, routable IP), internal (non-routable IP), and SSN (nonroutable IP). Assume an upstream router owned by the ISP that provides the Internet circuit as your default gateway.

In this section, we walk you through the process of configuring an Ethernet interface on your NSP. You will learn how to add or delete an IP address to an interface, manually set the speed and duplex, and check the status of your interfaces.

IP Addresses

When setting up the internal and secure server network (SSN or DMZ) interfaces, you should choose a network subnet within the Internet Assigned Numbers Authority (IANA) reserved IP address space, which are outlined in RFC 1918.

Adding an IP Address to an Interface

Follow these steps to configure an interface on your Nokia platform:

1. Bring up the Voyager Web interface via http in your Web browser.
2. Click **Config**.

3. Click **Interfaces**, the first link in the first column under the main Configuration screen. You will see the Interface Configuration page displayed as in Figure 19.3. This table shows you all your available interfaces along with their current status and configuration options.

Figure 19.3 The Interface Configuration Screen

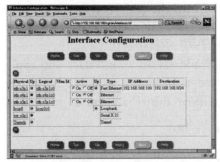

4. Select the logical interface to which you will assign an IP address. In our example, we'll select **eth–s4p1c0**, the second Ethernet interface listed in the table in Figure 19.3.

5. Click the toggle button to **On** to make the interface active, and type in the new IP address and mask length in your browser. All netmasks configured through Voyager will be in aggregate or bit mask format. For example, 255.255.0.0 is a 16-bit mask, so to set that mask on an interface, you would type **16** for the mask length. There is a good net-mask cheat sheet at http://noc.mwci.net/info/netmask.shtml, which might help you convert a netmask in dotted quad notation to the aggregate, and vice versa. Or, if you have *Check Point Next Generation Security Administration* by Syngress Publishing, Inc. (ISBN 1-928994-74-1), you'll find a cheat sheet in Appendix A.

6. Optionally, you can change the logical name of the interface from the default eth–s4p1c0 to a name that might make it easier to identify, such as either **internal** or **external**. The default name of the interface might not be easy to read, but it helps you identify the interface you are configuring on the Nokia. For example, eth-s4p1c0 is the Ethernet interface in slot 4, port 1. These numbers vary depending on how many inter-faces you have installed and which you are configuring. See Figure 19.4 for an example interface configuration before you go on to the next step.

Figure 19.4 Configuring IP Addresses

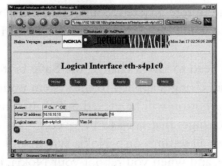

7. Click **Apply**. Once you apply your changes, they take effect immediately.

8. Click **Save**. You must save your configuration if you want your settings to be retained after a reboot. If you forget to save your changes, you need to start all over again after you reboot the system.

9. Click **Up** to return to the previous interface configuration screen. You should see your new interface entered into the table that we first saw in Figure 19.3.

Deleting an IP Address from an Interface

Once you have set the new IP address on an interface and apply the changes, you will see the Logical Interface page displayed, as in Figure 19.5. Notice that next to the IP address, you have a check box labeled *delete*. To remove this IP address from eth–s4p1, follow these three easy steps:

1. Click the **delete** check box.

2. Click **Apply**.

3. Click **Save**.

Figure 19.5 An Applied Interface Address

Voyager's /config/active File

The /config/active file contains all the system configuration information. Actually, /config/active is a symbolic link that points to the file /config/db/initial. If you attempt to make a change on the command line (for example, with *ifconfig*), these changes will be lost when the system is restarted. The safest way to make persistent modifications on your Nokia is to use either the Voyager Web interface or the CLISH, which is a new tool in IPSO 3.6. To use CLISH, simply type **clish** at the command prompt, and you will be presented with a *Nokia>* prompt.

You'll need to use one of these tools when you edit config files in /etc as well (for example, /etc/hosts), since these files are wiped out at each boot by the /config/active settings. If you keep a backup of this file, you could restore a system configuration this way, but any package-specific configuration would not be contained here (such as Check Point FW-1 rules, objects, licenses, and so on).

Notice how anytime you need to save a change, the **Save** button "lights up" in Voyager. Once this button is selected, all changes applied to the system until this time will be written to the /config/active file, and the button will be grayed out again. This button is a good indicator of whether you have made any changes that need to be saved.

Finally, if you want to erase all settings on a Nokia system and start from scratch, you can remove the file /config/active, and when you reboot your Nokia, it will begin to go through the initial configuration process all over again, prompting you to enter a hostname and so on. You need to have a direct console connection to perform this task.

Speed and Duplex

Most of the Ethernet interfaces that ship with the Nokia models are 10/100MB interfaces, unless you request a Gigabit Ethernet interface in your system. If you want to see the speed and duplex at which your interface is auto-negotiating, or if you want to force these settings manually, you can do so under the Physical Interface Configuration screen.

From the Interface Configuration screen, click the link under the physical interface column that you want to configure. For our example, let's select **eth-s3p1**. From here you have the option to disable the interface by toggling the **Active On/Off** button, as seen in Figure 19.6. The Physical Status table also informs you of the type, media, maximum transfer unit (MTU), and MAC address for this particular interface.

Figure 19.6 Physical Interface Configuration

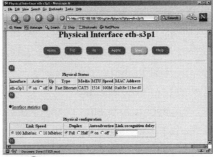

Confirming Interface Status

Now that you have the interfaces configured, how do you know if they have a link? There are a few ways that you can view your interface status within Voyager or from the command line. If you have just finished interface configuration, you can see the status displayed as either Up or Down with a green ball icon or a red ball icon, respectively, as shown in Figure 19.7. You can access this page in Voyager from the main configuration screen by clicking the **Interfaces** link.

In the Interface Configuration screen, there are two columns per interface that describe whether the interface is up or not. The first Up column relates to the physical interface. If there is a link, this icon is green; otherwise, it will be red. The second column refers to the logical state. This icon is red if the link is down, and it is green if the link is up. If you disable the interface by changing the active state to **Off**, no icon is displayed.

Figure 19.7 Interface Status Icons

Another way you can view interface status is via the Monitor link. If you are within Voyager Configuration already, click the **Home | Monitor** from the front screen. From here, you can click **Static Monitor | Interface** under the Static Monitor heading. You should now see a page

similar to the one in Figure 19.8. If you scroll down a little, you will see the interface information, which is the same information you would see if you were on the command line, typing in
ifconfig –a. Compare the following output with Figure 19.9:

```
gatekeeper[admin]# ifconfig -a
ser-s2p1:  flags=4126<UP,POINTOPOINT,MULTICAST,PRESENT> encaps none
eth-s3p1c0:  lname eth-s3p1c0 flags=e7<UP,PHYS_AVAIL,LINK_AVAIL,BROADCAST,
    MULTICAST,AUTOLINK>
        inet mtu 1500 192.168.168.100/24 broadcast 192.168.168.255
        phys eth-s3p1 flags=4133<UP,LINK,BROADCAST,MULTICAST,PRESENT>
        ether 0:a0:8e:11:be:d0 speed 100M full duplex
eth-s4p1c0:  lname eth-s4p1c0 flags=e7<UP,PHYS_AVAIL,LINK_AVAIL,BROADCAST,
    MULTICAST,AUTOLINK>
        inet mtu 1500 10.10.10.10/16 broadcast 10.10.255.255
        phys eth-s4p1 flags=4133<UP,LINK,BROADCAST,MULTICAST,PRESENT>
        ether 0:a0:8e:11:be:d4 speed 10M half duplex
eth-s5p1c0:  flags=e0<BROADCAST,MULTICAST,AUTOLINK>
        phys eth-s5p1 flags=4132<UP,BROADCAST,MULTICAST,PRESENT>
        ether 0:a0:8e:11:be:d8 speed 10M half duplex
loop0c0:  flags=57<UP,PHYS_AVAIL,LINK_AVAIL,LOOPBACK,MULTICAST>
        inet6 mtu 63000 ::1 --> ::1
        inet mtu 63000 127.0.0.1 --> 127.0.0.1
        phys loop0 flags=10b<UP,LINK,LOOPBACK,PRESENT>
soverf0:  flags=2923<UP,LINK,MULTICAST,PRESENT,IPV6ONLY>
stof0:  flags=2903<UP,LINK,PRESENT,IPV6ONLY>
tun0:  flags=107<UP,LINK,POINTOPOINT,PRESENT>
```

Figure 19.8 Monitoring Interfaces Screen 1

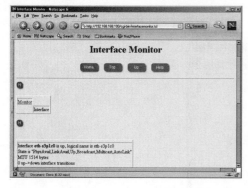

Figure 19.9 Monitoring Interfaces Screen 2

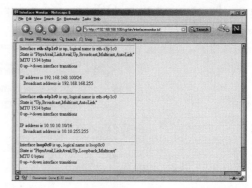

Adding a Default Gateway

If your Nokia firewall will be routing traffic to several networks, such as the Internet, you should configure a default gateway. The default gateway is typically the next-hop router closest to the Internet, which you point to by entering a default route into the routing table. You specifically tell the device that this gateway is the default, and if a packet does not match any other entry in the routing table, it will get sent to this gateway. Typically, there should be only one default gateway in the routing table. If you are doing load balancing or failover routing, you might have more than one, but often these will be dynamic routes and not static routes.

To configure a default gateway on your NSP, follow these instructions:

1. Bring up the Voyager Web interface using **http** in your Web browser.

2. Click **Config**.

3. Click **Static Routes** under the Routing Configuration heading.

4. Under the Static route, Default: Gateway column, select **On**. Leave the next-hop type as **normal**. You may also fill in a description if desired (see Figure 19.10). The other options in the next-hop type are **reject**, which drops all packets, sending an unreachable Internet control message back to the originator, or **blackhole**, which drops all packets quietly without notifying the sender.

Figure 19.10 Adding a Default Gateway: Gateway Column Options

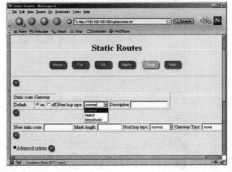

5. Click **Apply**.

6. For Gateway Type, select **address**, as shown in Figure 19.11.

7. Click **Apply** again.

Figure 19.11 Adding the Default Gateway: Address Screen

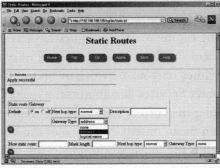

8. Enter the IP address of the gateway.

9. Click **Apply** one last time. At this point, the route is added into the system, and it will be functional, but don't forget the next step!

10. Click **Save**.

Now you have successfully added a default gateway to your Nokia. If you log in to the console of your Nokia and run a *netstat —rn* command, you should see an entry similar to the following. However, your default route might not be displayed if that interface is not physically up:

```
gatekeeper[admin]# netstat -rn | grep default
default              10.10.1.1          CU          0          0      eth-s4p1c0
default                                 RCU         1          0
```

As you can see in Figure 19.12, you have the option of setting a priority on your default route entry. This priority determines the route that will be used if there are multiple routes that are otherwise equivalent; lower-priority routes take precedence. You can enter a number between 1 and 8; however, you should know that the only time a lower-priority route will *not* be used is if that interface is down. So, it would not make sense to configure two routes with different priorities on the same interface. If the priorities are the same, the gateways will be treated with equal cost as multipath routes.

Figure 19.12 Setting Priorities on Default Gateway Route Entries

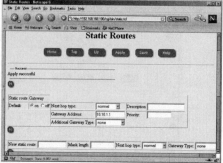

Setting the System Time, Date, and Time Zone

It's important that you set the correct time and date in your NSP so that your system and/or firewall logs will record the correct time that events have occurred and so any scheduled cron jobs will run at the time specified.

Time and Date

To manually configure the time and date, click the **Local Time Setup** option under the System Configuration heading on the main Configuration screen. Alternatively, you can configure Network Time Protocol (NTP), which allows you to synchronize your NSP time with the time from a NTP server, either on your network or on the Internet. The option to enable NTP is found under the Router Services heading on the main Configuration screen.

Let's start by setting the correct time zone for your region. The Nokia appliance will be configured for Greenwich mean time (GMT) out of the box. Many organizations with a global presence use GMT, which is the universal time standard. Others prefer to use a local time zone, such as Eastern standard time (EST) for those in the vicinity of New York in the United States. To select your time zone, choose a city from the list on the Time screen, displayed in Figure 19.13.

Figure 19.13 The Time Screen

Once you select the correct time zone, click **Apply** and then click **Save**. Then you can change the time, if needed, in the next section labeled Manually Set Date and Time. Simply enter the hour, minute, and/or second. If you leave any of these fields blank, the current value will not change. The current value is listed in parentheses next to each text entry box. Follow the same syntax when you change the date. Enter the month, day and/or year. The current value is displayed in parentheses next to each text box.

Configuring the Network Time Protocol

For security purposes, if you decide to set up NTP, it is probably best to synchronize to a server residing within your network. The Nokia can also be run as an NTP server. When you turn on NTP, it could take a while for the clock to update, so be patient. Bring up the NTP configuration screen, shown in Figure 19.14, by clicking **NTP** under the Router Services heading on the main Configuration screen.

Understanding NTP

NTP is a time protocol that allows administrators to synchronize local clocks over the Internet in a distributed client/server model. This protocol uses UDP 123 for communication, and you might need to allow UDP 123 through if you are trying to synchronize time through a firewall. NTP has been around since the mid-1980s and has had a few revisions since its inception. The current version of NTP is v3, but you can utilize any of the earlier versions on your NSP for flexibility. Version 3 code has been improved to remove minor bugs found in earlier versions, but the main advantage is that it has been enhanced for maximum stability and reliability over high-speed, gigabit networks. This means that even at lower speeds, the algorithms used will be more accurate.

Once NTP is enabled, it can begin to gather time data from other servers and calculate the offset needed to correct the local clock based on the remote server's time. It's also possible for the NTP server to communicate with other servers that are considered peers and compare all their clocks so that they can have the most accurate timekeeping between them. A great deal of hard work and effort have been put into keeping the time as accurate as possible in this protocol, and several other factors are taken into consideration, such as the time lag in receiving the data and errors that could affect the transmission, depending on how far from the time source your server is located. If you would like to know more about NTP, version 3 of the protocol is detailed in RFC 1305.

Figure 19.14 The NTP Configuration Screen

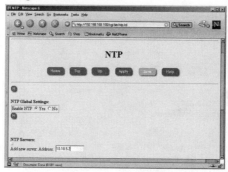

Configuring NTP

Once NTP is enabled, several settings are available on the Voyager configuration screens. As you can see in Figure 19.15, you can configure multiple NTP servers with which your Nokia can synchronize. If you want to specify that one server should be preferred over the rest, simply select **Yes** for that server in the Prefer section.

Another option is to set up NTP peers, which are other servers with which you want to compare your local time settings. Your local time is not used in the calculation with the NTP servers that were listed previously, but when you include peers in the configuration, your time is compared with the peer times to calculate a time that is most accurate between them.

Finally, if you want other servers to retrieve their time from you, click **Yes** at the bottom of the screen labeled NTP Reference Clock: NTP Master. You can enter a number from 0 to 8 in the Stratum field, which specifies the level of your NTP server in the hierarchy. Nokia recommends that you leave this at the default, 0. Your local clock will be the source of the data provided in the master state.

Figure 19.15 NTP Configuration Options

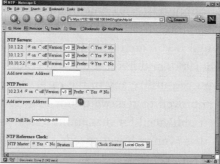

Configuring Domain Name System and Host Entries

Along with assigning IP addresses to all the hosts on your network, administrators will also configure DNS and host table entries on almost every PC. You might not want to set up name servers on a firewall, however, since you most likely will not be running user-facing applications directly on the box. There are some advantages to running a DNS resolver on a firewall, but there can be some major disadvantages to it as well. Configuring host entries, however, will be a necessary step on your Nokia firewall if you want to install an FW-1 license.

Since it is suggested to install your firewall while it is not plugged into any untrusted networks, it will be best to start with DNS disabled on the firewall. If you have DNS enabled and the system cannot reach its name servers, the system could become sluggish and system performance will be affected. It is important that when you do configure DNS, you configure it properly. Otherwise, if a primary name server goes down, all traffic, including your VPN connections, will be affected.

The firewall should be able to resolve its own external IP address to the name of the host computer. The Nokia platform must have the hostname associated with its external IP address for FW-1 licensing purposes as well; this is done through the Host Address Assignment link found under the System Configuration heading in the Voyager GUI. You must use this interface to configure host entries instead of editing a Hosts file. Here you should also add IP addresses for devices that your firewall might communicate with frequently, such as a management server and/or enforcement module.

Another DNS record that you should create is a pointer (PTR) record for your firewall's external IP address or any other address(es) that you will be using for Network Address Translation (NAT). Some Web sites and FTP servers require that you have a reverse resolvable IP address before they will grant you or your users access to download their files. If you have obtained a block of IP addresses from your ISP, chances are that the ISP controls the PTR records for your addresses. Sometimes they provide you with a Web site where you can administer these yourself. Other times you need to find the right person who can make the changes for you. If you have your own abstract syntax notation (ASN), you can set up your own in-addr.arpa domain and create your own PTR records.

If you will be running the FW-1 HTTP Security Server on your Nokia, enable DNS. Otherwise, the firewall will display "Unknown WWW Server" in users' Web browsers.

NOTE

You will not be able to apply your FW-1 license until you have configured the host address assignment for the Nokia's external interface. When you run through the initial configuration, you usually specify an internal IP address, which is set up in the host table for you. However, most FW-1 licenses are issued on external addresses, and you must configure this setting within Voyager before the license addition is successful.

DNS

DNS is used to resolve domain names to IP addresses, and vice versa. Behind the scenes, your PC uses DNS whenever you're using your Web browser or sending e-mail, among other things. Your Nokia device will not function as a domain name server, since the system was built as a high-performance security platform and running DNS servers on such a system doesn't make much sense. However, your device will operate as a DNS client. Most UNIX systems use an /etc/resolv.conf file to store their DNS settings, and the Nokia is no exception. However, you configure the NSP resolv.conf file via the Voyager GUI.

To configure DNS, click **System Configuration | DNS** on the main Configuration screen. Doing so displays the main DNS Configuration screen, similar to the one displayed in Figure 19.16.

Figure 19.16 The DNS Configuration Screen

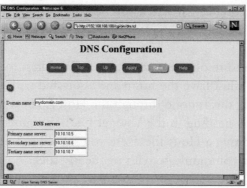

To enable DNS lookups, simply enter one or more name servers in the fields provided, then click **Apply** | **Save**. To disable DNS, delete the IP addresses listed, and then click **Apply** | **Save**. For obvious reasons, you should always use IP addresses rather than names for your name servers here. You can verify that your changes have been applied by looking at the /etc/resolv.conf file on the system:

```
gatekeeper[admin]# cat /etc/resolv.conf
#   This file was AUTOMATICALLY GENERATED
#   Generated by /bin/resolv_xlate on Sun Jun 23 22:51:24 2002
#
#   DO NOT EDIT
#
search mydomain.com
nameserver 10.10.10.5
nameserver 10.10.10.6
nameserver 10.10.10.7
```

The Hosts Table

As mentioned earlier, it is necessary to configure at least one static host entry on your Nokia in Voyager. To enter this configuration screen, displayed in Figure 19.17, click **Host Address Assignment** under the System Configuration heading on the main Voyager Configuration screen. Once the Static Host Entries configuration page is displayed, you should see an entry for the local host on IP address 127.0.0.1, also called the *loopback address*. You should never remove this host entry, because the system uses it for various local operations.

To add a new hostname, enter either the fully qualified domain name (FQDN) or a simple hostname in the Add new hostname field. We are using the name *gatekeeper*, which was the name assigned to this Nokia during initial system configuration. Next click **Apply**, and then enter the IP address associated with the gatekeeper. This should be the IP address that you will use if licensing the FW-1 product on your Nokia as well, and it is typically the firewall's external IP address. Click **Apply** | **Save** to complete the host address assignment.

Figure 19.17 Adding a New Hostname

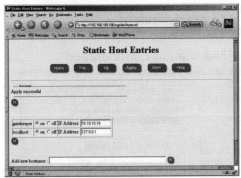

Configuring a Mail Relay

The Nokia Security Platform will not run a mail server, but you can configure it to deliver mail by setting up a mail relay within the system configuration in Voyager. This might be useful if you want to receive important system messages from syslog, configure mail alerts within your FW-1 Security Policy, or write some custom scripst that send mail.

When you configure your mail relay, you have the option of specifying a remote user on the mail relay server. This optional field allows you to choose a specific username on the remote system that will receive all mail that is meant for "admin" or "monitor" users on the Nokia system. The default username is *root*:

1. To enable a mail relay in Voyager, start by clicking **Mail Relay** under the System Configuration heading from the main Configuration screen.

2. In the empty box next to Mail Server:, enter the IP address of the mail server you will be using. This machine should be running an SMTP server and configured as a mail relay (see Figure 19.18).

3. Click **Apply**.

4. Click **Save**.

Figure 19.18 Mail Relay Configuration

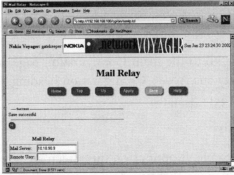

Configuring System Event Notification

If you click **System Failure Notification**, located on the main Configuration screen under the System Configuration heading, you will be able to turn the system event notification function on or off. If this function is enabled, an e-mail will be generated to whomever you specify. Note that the mail relay must be configured for this to function. The notification e-mail will contain information such as the system hostname, software version, the location of certain crash files, and a dump trace to help identify the problem. See Figure 19.19 for a sample notification configuration. Don't forget to click **Apply | Save**.

Figure 19.19 System Failure Notification Configuration

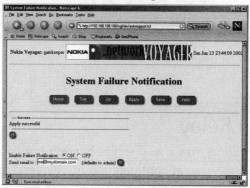

Configuring the System for Security

By default, Nokia takes a secure approach to network access by disabling most services. However, a couple insecure services such as Telnet and HTTP are enabled for functional purposes to help you get started. This section walks you through the configuration of Secure Shell (SSH) and disabling Telnet as well as changing from clear-text HTTP to SSL-encrypted Voyager access.

SSH is an encrypted Telnet provided in IPSO 3.4 and later as part of the operating system, so you aren't required to install any additional packages to use it, as in earlier versions. Nokia's implementation of SSH is OpenSSH version 2.1.1. All you need to do in order to get started with SSH is enable the server daemon, and then you are on your way to a more secure system. You need an SSH client to establish a connection to the Nokia to use it; several such clients are freely available for download. Some of the most common clients are Putty, TTSSH, OpenSSH, SecureCRT, and F-Secure. For a comprehensive list of both free and commercial clients for various operating systems, visit www.freessh.org.

Enabling SSH Access

Configuring SSH is a quick and easy three-step process:

1. To configure SSH access, go to the main Configuration page and click **Secure Shell (SSH)** under the Security and Access Configuration heading.

2. Click **Yes** to enable the SSH daemon.

3. Finally, click **Apply | Save**.

As shown in Figure 19.20, the default options on this screen are safe to accept. If you want to tighten access further, it is recommended that you do it in stages. Perhaps after you know that the default configuration works, you might want to disable admin login and set up a new user who can log in and *su* to the admin account.

Figure 19.20 The Main SSH Configuration Screen

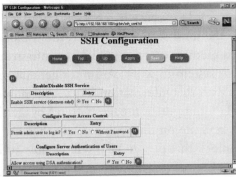

SSH Versions 1 and 2

You have the option of allowing SSH versions 1, 2, or both in the configuration settings. SSHv2 is generally believed to be more secure than v1 and should be your first choice. See Figure 19.21 for additional options.

Figure 19.21 Additional SSH Options

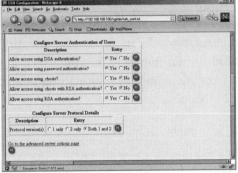

Be aware that if you check **1 only** under Configure Server Protocol Details, you will enable version 1 clients to connect to your firewall, but not version 2 clients, which are newer and becoming more common. The default setting is to allow both versions 1 and 2 SSH clients to connect so that you don't have to worry about which client you are using. A useful trick with newer (version 2-capable) clients is to specify **-1** on the SSH command line when connecting to an unknown host that seems to be rejecting your connection attempts. This forces the client to downgrade itself to version 1, perhaps allowing the connection. Similarly, **-2** forces the client to use protocol version 2. For the cautious, choose to allow only version 2, because it is considered to be more secure and the common free SSH clients now support protocol version 2.

Host Keys

A public/private host key pair is generated the first time you set up SSH and is displayed on this screen after you enable the SSH daemon. The host key is used to identify the host to the client during the connection. On the first connection attempt, the client receives the host's key and is asked whether to accept the key and save it or to reject it. SSH clients maintain a list of all known hosts in a file on the local system. If on a subsequent connection attempt the host key does not match the key obtained originally, the client will be warned that a possible man-in-the-middle attack could be occurring, giving them the option to terminate the connection and verify the new key. By default, the host key on IPSO is set to 1,024 bits.

Authorized Keys

You can configure SSH to be more or less secure by choosing from a few different types of authentication schemes. Probably the most secure method is the use of RSA and/or DSA (SSHv2 only) authentication. This method uses the public key infrastructure (PKI) to verify the user's authenticity. In order for this system to work, you must generate a unique public/private key pair and configure the client with this information. Then, you publish the public key to the Nokia by entering it into the SSH Configuration page within Voyager. This information is stored in the $HOME/.ssh/authorized_keys file on the system. Only the user with the associated private key (and the passphrase to unlock that private key) will be able to log in. Using authorized keys provides the ultimate security between client and server.

In order to configure authorized keys in Voyager, first log in to Voyager and click **Config**, then follow this procedure:

1. Click **SSH (Secure Shell)** under the Security and Access Configuration heading on the main Configuration screen.

2. Ensure that the SSH daemon is already enabled, and then scroll down to the bottom of the page, and click the link to **Go to the authorized keys page**.

3. From here, you can enter the client's RSA public key for version 1, which would be obtained from the SSH client, typically in a file called identity.pub. You can also enter the DSA key in OpenSSH format (typically in a file called id_dsa.pub on the ssh client) or in SSHv2 format (the key file could look something like id_KEYTYPE_KEYLEN_X.pub.

Starting the Daemon

Once you enable SSH in the Voyager configuration, the daemon is started automatically. You can verify whether the daemon is running or not by logging into the system locally and typing **ps -auxw | grep ssh**. If the daemon is running, you will see output similar to the following:

```
gatekeeper[admin]# ps -auxw | grep ssh
root      669  0.0  1.1   276  652  d0  S+   6:09PM   0:00.02 grep ssh
root      650  0.0  2.5   404 1476  ??  Is   6:06PM   0:00.62 /usr/sbin/
    sshd-x -D
```

If you try to kill the sshd process, the process monitor (pm) restarts sshd automatically. Available sshd options are listed in Table 19.1.

Table 19.1 SSHD Server Options

Switch	Option	Description
-f	Filename	Define the server configuration file. The default file is /var/etc/sshd_config.
-d	N/A	Turn on debugging.
-i	N/A	Run the server from inetd.
-q	N/A	Run in quiet mode, no logging.

Continued

Table 19.1 SSHD Server Options

Switch	Option	Description
-p	Port #	TCP port the server will listen on. The default port is 22.
-k	Number of seconds	How often to regenerate the server key. The default time interval is 3,600 seconds.
-g	Number of seconds	Authentication grace period. The default is 300 seconds.
-b	Bits	RSA key size. The default RSA server key is 768 bits.
-h	Filename	The file where the SSH host key is stored. The default file is /var/etc/ssh_host_key.
-4	N/A	Use IPv4 only.
-6	N/A	Use IPv6 only.
-D	N/A	Don't fork and detach on startup.

Disabling Telnet Access

If you followed the procedure to enable SSH access, and you have an SSH client installed and tested on your workstation, you should go back into Voyager and disable Telnet access. You will no longer need Telnet as long as you have SSH to access the system. Since you won't be using it, it is not wise to leave it open on the system as one more method for an attacker to attempt to gain access to the box. Figure 19.22 illustrates the default values of the network access services in IPSO 3.6.

To disable Telnet through Voyager, click the **Network Access and Services** link on the main Configuration screen under the heading Security and Access Configuration. From there, click the radio button for **No** in the table directly across from "Allow TELNET access." Finally, click **Apply | Save** to disable Telnet and commit the changes.

Figure 19.22 Default Network Access Settings

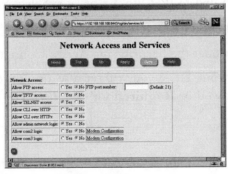

An Alternative to FTP

By default, FTP is disabled in your Nokia, as you saw in Figure 19.22, and the majority of boxes out there will not need this service running. Therefore, it would be prudent to leave FTP disabled within Voyager, and you can enable it only when necessary. FTP has been known to have several security vulnerabilities and transfers all data, including usernames and passwords in the clear. If you need to transfer files to or from your system, use Secure Copy (SCP) instead. This tool allows you to perform encrypted file transfers to or from your NSP (if you have SSH enabled), which is much more secure than the standard FTP protocol.

The only time that you might need to enable FTP on a Nokia is when you are performing remote file transfers of packages or IPSO images during system maintenance and you happen to have those packages on a local Nokia system already. You can use FTP on your local Nokia to retrieve the packages or images from all the other systems on your network when you use the automated tools within Voyager. Through the Voyager GUI, FTP and HTTP are your only options. This might be fine if your box is local and protected by a firewall, but you might want to simply SCP the files to each Nokia manually before you begin maintenance on them. For example, if you want to get the ipso.tgz file onto your Nokia using SCP, you could use a command like the one that follows:

```
gatekeeper[admin]# scp admin@192.168.200.8:ipso.tgz .
admin@192.168.200.8's password:
ipso.tgz          100% |*****************************|
```

Securing FTP

If you still want to use FTP on your Nokia, we can give you a couple of recommendations for making the use of this protocol more secure. First, you can require S/Key one-time passwords in IPSO 3.5 or later for Telnet and FTP authentication. You can also restrict FTP to local networks only by use of access lists or via your firewall policy. By implementing both of these actions together, you can use FTP in a secure fashion.

To configure the S/Key passwords, you first need to obtain a one-time password (OTP) generator. Most UNIX systems come with a generator on the command line called *key*, this is also available on IPSO. If this tool is not available to you, you need to find one to download. A Windows client called winkey32.exe, is available from Nokia Support in Resolution #1255. S/Key did not function properly in IPSO versions prior to 3.5, so if you want to use S/Key authentication, you first need to update IPSO to 3.5 or later. Select S/Key passwords as follows:

1. Log in to Voyager and click **Config**.

2. Select the link **Users** under the Security and Access Configuration heading.

3. Scroll down to the bottom. There you will see a section on configuring S/Key for each user. Select either **Allowed** or **Required** for each user. The default setting here is for S/Key to be disabled.

4. Click **Apply**.

5. Three new boxes will appear. Enter the current user password in the first box, and enter an S/Key secret password in the next two boxes that is between four and eight alphanumeric characters long (see Figure 19.23).

Figure 19.23 S/Key Configuration

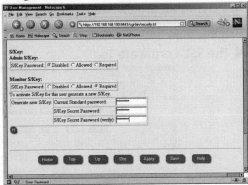

6. Click **Apply**. The sequence number (starting at 99 and decreasing each time S/Key is used) and the seed will be displayed. This information will also be displayed when you attempt to log in to the system. You will use this information as input to the S/Key OTP generator along with the original password you supplied to the system in order to begin using the S/Key authentication method.

7. Click **Save**.

Configuring Secure Socket Layer

Secure Socket Layer (SSL) allows you to view the Voyager Web interface through an encrypted tunnel. You can then use HTTPS instead of plain-text HTTP in the location window of your Web browser. Just as with ssh/scp, utilizing encryption for your connections to Voyager adds an extra layer of security to your session.

Creating the Self-Signed Certificate

The first step in configuring SSL is to create an SSL certificate for the Web server to use for authenticity. You can choose to generate a certificate request to send to a trusted third-party certificate authority (CA) for them to sign, which will cost you some money, or you can sign your own certificate, assuming that you trust yourself, and forgo the extra fee. We recommend generating a self-signed certificate through the Voyager interface. It is just as secure to use a self-signed certificate. The only difference is that your Web browser will ask you to verify that you want to accept the certificate that is not signed by a known CA. There is no difference in the quality of the encrypted connection, and you can begin using your certificate right away if you do it yourself.

To set up SSL in Voyager, follow this procedure:

1. Log in to Voyager and select **Config**.

2. Under the Security and Access Configuration heading, click **SSL Certificate Tool**.

3. The SSL Certificate Tool (Request) screen will be displayed (Figure 19.24). Select the private key size you want to use (the default of 1024 bits is recommended), and enter the passphrase that you will use to protect your private key. You need to enter this same passphrase on a later screen, so don't forget it.

4. Next you need to configure the distinguished name (DN) that identifies this certificate as unique and belonging to this machine. The values that are required are in bold, and they are Country Name (2-letter code), State or Providence Name, Organization Name,

and Common Name (FQDN). Finally, you must specify whether you want to create a self-signed X.509 certificate or generate a signing request. Select **A self-signed X.509 certificate** (see Figure 19.25).

Figure 19.24 The SSL Certificate Tool

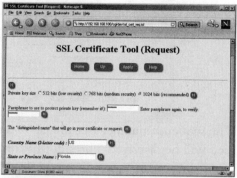

Figure 19.25 The SSL Certificate Tool, Continued

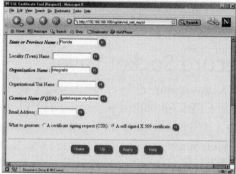

5. Click **Apply**, and the new X.509 certificate, private key, and fingerprint will be displayed.

6. Next, scroll down and click the **Voyager SSL Certificate** link at the bottom of the result page. This choice brings you to a new window where you need to cut and paste the certificate and private key from the result page. You might want to open this page in a separate window to complete the next step.

7. Copy the new X.509 certificate into the Voyager SSL Certificate screen, including the entire BEGIN and END line. This information should go in the first big text input area labeled New Server Certificate.

8. Now copy the new private key, including the entire BEGIN and END line, into the next text area labeled Associated private key.

9. Enter the passphrase that you used in Step 3.

10. Click **Apply | Save**.

11. Click **Up**. This displays the Voyager Web Access screen, which is discussed next (see Figure 19.26).

Enabling HTTPS for Voyager

Now that you have generated a self-signed certificate, as discussed in the previous section, you can enable encryption for secure Voyager access and configuration. If you are following along from the SSL configuration, you should already be at the screen displayed in Figure 19.26. If you are starting here, you can also get to this screen by clicking the **Voyager Web Access** link under the Security and Access Configuration heading on the main Configuration screen.

Figure 19.26 Enabling HTTPS

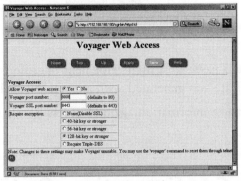

> **NOTE**
>
> When you enable SSL/HTTPS in the configuration for Voyager Web Access, you disable the unencrypted HTTP access that you had up to that point. If you cannot connect via HTTPS for some reason and you need to get remote Voyager access, you have these options to reset Voyager from the console or remote command line:
>
> 1. Restart Voyager with no encryption listening on port 80 with the *voyager -e 0 80* command.
> 2. Run *clish* and set the encryption level back to 0 on Voyager with the following options: *Nokia> set voyager ssl-level 0*
> 3. Run *lynx* to configure the system with a text-based Voyager interface locally, set the encryption level to **none**, and **Apply** the change.

To set up secure Voyager Access via SSL, enable it as follows:

1. Change the SSL port number to a value greater than 1024. The default port is 443, but since this is a well-known port for HTTPS connections, it would be wise to pick another port that is not as common.2. Next, select the minimum grade of encryption that you want to allow. By default, SSL is disabled and no encryption is required. Select **Require Triple-DES**, which gives you up to a 168-bit key if you have a Web browser that can support a key that size.

3. Click **Apply**.

4. If you try to click **Save** now, your connection will be refused. You must reconnect to Voyager using HTTPS and the port you choose for the connection—for example: *https://192.168.168.100:8443/cgi-bin/httpd.tcl*.

5. You will now be prompted to accept the self-signed certificate, which you generated previously. Choose to remember the certificate permanently and click **Continue** (see Figure 19.27).

Figure 19.27 Accepting the Certificate

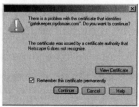

6. If you receive a domain name mismatch error next because you are connecting to an IP address but the certificate was generated with an FQDN, click **OK** to continue.

7. Enter your authentication information again to access Voyager.

8. Click **Save**.

Understanding Configuration Options

In this section, you are provided with an overview of all the configuration menu options found in Voyager. You should feel comfortable using this section of the chapter as a quick reference guide to each configuration link available on the main Configuration screen in Voyager. We'll be describing the highlights of each option so that you are aware of all the things you can do remotely through the Voyager Web interface.

Interface Configuration

Voyager provides a simple Web-based interface that you can access remotely to configure interface parameters and ARP settings:

- **Interfaces** Configuring physical and logical interfaces, including IP addresses, speed and duplex settings, and the like.

- **ARP** Address Resolution Protocol settings, adding static ARP entries, clearing the ARP table.

System Configuration

A wide variety of tools are available under the System Configuration heading. Each item in this section allows you to perform common system administration tasks, such as upgrading the IPSO images and scheduling jobs through crontab. Here is a description of each item:

- **DNS** Domain Name System—configure as a client only.

- **Disk Mirroring** Add or delete disk mirrors. This option is available for IP-500 and IP-700 series only. This is different from the RAID-1 available in the IP400 series, which was mentioned previously.

- **Mail Relay** Enter an IP address of a mail server that will accept mail from the Nokia for final delivery.

- **System Failure Notification** Enable or disable notification of system failures. Mail Relay must be configured for this option to function.

- **Local Time Setup** Manually set the date, time, and time zone of the system.

- **Host Address Assignment** Configure the Hosts table on the Nokia (/etc/hosts).

- **System Logging** Configure a remote syslog server or accept syslog from other devices.

- **Change Hostname** Change the hostname of the Nokia. If you have installed Check Point NG, *do not* change the hostname. The Secure Internal Communications certificate depends on the hostname.

- **Manage Configuration Sets** Save the current Voyager settings (/config/active) and toggle back and forth between various Voyager configurations.

- **Backup and Restore** Make a one-time backup or schedule a backup of the system. You may also use this screen to restore from a previous backup. You can even set it up to FTP the backup file off the server when complete.

- **Job Scheduler** Add scheduled cron jobs to the system.

- **Manage IPSO Images** Toggle between installed IPSO images and delete images.

- **Install New IPSO Image (Upgrade)** Download the IPSO image from a remote HTTP or FTP server and upgrade from an existing image.

- **Manage Installed Packages** Toggle packages (such as Check Point FireWall-1) off and on, FTP new packages, install new packages, and delete packages.

SNMP

Enable or disable Simple Network Management Protocol (SNMP), set community strings, and configure a server to receive traps. The default settings should be usable, but you can enable or disable many different trap options here.

IPv6

Configure the Nokia system to use IPv6 IP addressing instead of the more common IPv4. There are many options to select in this section, such as logical interfaces, IPv6 over IPv4, static routes, host address assignment, and network access and services, to name a few. Recent press releases state that Check Point NG FP3 will support IPv6. Note that prior to IPSO 3.6, the Apache server running on IPSO does not support IPv6 connections, meaning that you cannot use Voyager over IPv6 on earlier versions of IPSO.

Reboot, Shut Down System

This screen allows you to perform a system halt or reboot through Voyager and displays the currently selected image that will be used on the next boot.

Security and Access Configuration

The items located under the Security and Access Configuration heading allow you to perform access administration to your Nokia system by providing you with an interface for manipulating users and services available on the platform. Many of these are discussed in more detail throughout the book:

- **Users** Change passwords, add new users, and configure S/Key authentication.
- **Groups** Set up groups for file permissions and assign users to these groups.
- **AAA** Configure authentication, authorization, and accounting.
- **Network Access and Services** Enable or disable network protocols such as Telnet usually found in inetd.conf.
- **Voyager Web Access** Enable or disable Voyager Web access, configure the ports used to access Voyager, and determine if SSL encryption is required.
- **SSL Certificate Tool** Generate a request for a certificate or create your own self-signed X.509 certificate for SSL access.
- **SSH (Secure Shell)** Enable or disable SSH, make various configuration changes, and determine which version server you will run (1 or 2).
- **IPSec** IP Security; configure security associations (SA) to other IPSec-compliant devices in order to generate a VPN. This option supports native IPSec (without FW-1).
- **Check Point FireWall-1** Enable or disable Check Point FW-1 4.1 to start at boot time. Also configure FloodGate-1 v4.1 and ifwd. If you are running NG, this page only allows you to configure ifwd, since these options have moved to the cpconfig utility instead.

Fault Management Configuration

This section allows you to set certain alarm parameters for your NSP. You can have an active role in viewing and filtering alarms such as disk space, interface link, and temperature alarms.

- **General Configurations** Enable or disable Fault Management and configure general parameters such as log file size and the like.
- **Current Alarm List** View active alarms and cancel them.
- **Alarm Log** Display all past alarms, even if you cancelled them in the Current Alarm List.
- **Alarm Filtering** List all alarm types; allows you to suppress alarms.

Routing Configuration

You have a robust set of tools for routing configuration in the NSP. There are several network protocols to choose from, such as BGP, OSPF, and RIP:

- **BGP** Border Gateway Protocol. Configure your Nokia to participate in BGP exterior routing.

- **OSPF** Open Shortest Path First network protocol. Enable or disable OSPF on each interface.

- **RIP** Routing Information Protocol. Enable or disable RIP on each interface.

- **IGRP** Interior Gateway Routing Protocol. Enable or disable IGRP on each interface.

- **IGMP** Internet Group Management Protocol. Used in IP multicast routing, this protocol maintains the multicast group database.

- **PIM** Protocol-Independent Multicast. Enable or disable PIM on each interface.

- **DVMRP** Distance Vector Multicast Routing Protocol. Enable or disable DVMRP on each interface.

- **Static Routes** Add, edit, or delete routes and configure your default gateway.

- **Route Aggregation** Create new aggregates by lumping together similar routes into a more general route for route redistribution and advertisement.

- **Inbound Route Filters** Configure inbound route filters, set protocol rank, and determine which learned routes should be accepted.

- **Route Redistribution** Allows you to redistribute routes between static routes, aggregate routes, interface routes, BGP, OSPF, RIP, and IGRP.

- **Routing Options** Configure various routing options such as the next-hop selection algorithm and protocol rank and restart the routing subsystem.

Traffic Management

Use the tools provided in Voyager under the Traffic Management heading to customize your Nokia for your network environment. You can make the Nokia firewall a member of a cluster, configure your Nokia to behave like a firewall with access lists, or set up quality of service (QoS) for bandwidth management:

- **Cluster** Enable and configure firewall gateway clustering. This is a new feature in IPSO 3.6 and should prove to be a very popular high-availability option.

- **Access List** Configure access control lists (ACLs) on your Nokia.

- **Aggregation Class** Set up a maximum bandwidth rate, which you can use in the ACL config.

- **Queue Class** Create new queue classes, which are service definitions for setting precedence for certain types of traffic.

- **ATM QoS Descriptor** Create or delete an ATM QoS descriptor, which determines the traffic bandwidth parameters of an ATM.

- **Dial-On-Demand Routing** Allows you to use ACLs to determine if a packet should bring up an ISDN line.

- **DSCP-VLAN Priority** Enable or disable DSCP-to-VLAN or VLAN-to-DSCP priority mappings.

- **COPS** Configure the Nokia to utilize Common Open Policy Service (COPS). COPS is used in a client/server model where the server is a policy server or policy decision point (PDP) and the client is a policy enforcement point (PEP). The PEP will get control decisions from the PDP for things such as QoS policies, IPSec, or admission control. This protocol is described in RFC 2748.

Router Services

You don't pass broadcast traffic through a gateway without running some sort of relay. This section tells you how to configure a bootp relay on the gateway per interface and set up a relay for any UDP broadcast traffic. You may also advertise your NSP as a default gateway, configure fail-over routing, and set up NTP to synchronize system time:

- **BOOTP Relay** Enable or disable a bootp/DHCP relay on each interface.

- **IP Broadcast Helper** Enable or disable forwarding on any UDP broadcast traffic you determine on each interface.

- **Router Discovery** Enable the Nokia as an ICMP router discovery server so that it advertises itself as a default gateway.

- **VRRP** Virtual Router Redundancy Protocol allows you to share virtual IP and MAC addresses for fail-over routing. This is a popular fail-over mechanism with Check Point FW-1.

- **NTP** Network Time Protocol. You can run NTP as a client or a server.

NOTE

The remaining items do not provide enough information to warrant sections of their own; however they do offer you the following features:
- **Asset Management Summary** Asset Management Summary simply displays a summary of hardware information.
- **Licenses** You must apply licenses if you want to use certain routing protocols, such as DVMRP or IGRP. This is where those licenses are applied.
- **Show Configuration Summary** Shows a summary of network configuration, such as interface status, IP addresses, routing protocols, ARP, and routes.
- **Copyright Information** Displays all copyright information.

Summary

After you run through the initial configuration of your NSP, you will need to begin basic system configuration so that your NSP is usable. The remote administration GUI provided with the Nokia device is the network Voyager configuration tool. You connect to Voyager through a Web browser via HTTP, and the first thing you should do is to set up the network properties for your gateway. Start by configuring the interfaces with IP addresses, link speed, and duplex settings using the Interface Configuration screen. Then you might want to set up the default gateway on the system using the Static Routes configuration screen.

A few other basic system settings include the system date, time, and time zone, which can be configured using the Local Time Setup link under the System Configuration heading on the main Configuration screen, or you can synchronize with an NTP server via the NTP link. Do you want to be able to resolve Internet addresses from your Nokia? Then you need to configure name servers on the DNS configuration page. You also need to click the Host Address Assignment link to set up a host entry for the firewall's external IP address. This is particularly important if your Nokia will be running Check Point FireWall-1 software. You should configure your system to notify you if something is wrong. To accomplish this task, enter a mail server IP address under the Mail Relay link and enable the System Event Notification option.

Next, you will be concerned with securing the Nokia platform. Luckily, Nokia ships its products with security in mind. Most network protocols are already disabled, and the ones that are open by default have encryption alternatives, such as HTTPS instead of HTTP, SSH instead of Telnet, and SCP instead of FTP. The configuration parameters necessary to perform these substitutions were explained step by step in this chapter, allowing you to make your system as secure as possible from the start.

Finally, there is a large variety of configuration options available to you through Voyager's main Configuration screen. You have various tools under Interface Configuration, System Configuration, SNMP, IPv6, Reboot, Shutdown System, Security and Access Configuration, Fault Management Configuration, Routing Configuration, Traffic Management, Router Services, Asset Management, Licenses, Show Configuration Summary, and Copyright Information at your disposal in one location within Voyager.

Chapter 20

Basic System Administration

Best Damn Topics in This Chapter:

- **Rebooting the System**

- **Managing Packages**

- **Managing IPSO Images**

- **Managing Users and Groups**

- **Configuring Static Routes**

- **System Backup and Restore**

- **System Logging**

- **Scheduling Tasks Using cron**

Introduction

Once you have configured your Nokia so that it is up and functioning within your network environment, you might wonder how to accomplish the routine, day-to-day tasks that are part of a network administrator's job. Things such as package management and upgrades, performing system backups, and even replacing your IPSO operating system are often necessary to do at regular intervals.

Voyager was designed with the administrator in mind, and almost all the day-to-day tasks that you could think of can be handled through its interface. With each release of IPSO, Nokia adds more functionality to Voyager. For example, IPSO 3.5 and later allows you to schedule periodic tasks through cron with Voyager, something that could previously be done only from the command shell.

Rebooting the System

It is very important that you shut down your Nokia system cleanly so that any unsaved data is copied to the disk and the file systems are unmounted safely. To reboot your Nokia system from the command line, type **reboot** and press **Enter**. From Voyager, follow these steps:

1. Log in to Voyager.
2. Click **Config**.
3. Scroll down to the bottom of the main Configuration screen and select **Reboot, Shut Down System**.
4. Click either **Reboot** or **Halt**. Reboot will shut down the system and restart it again, and Halt will shut down the system for a power off (see Figure 20.1).

Figure 20.1 System Reboot

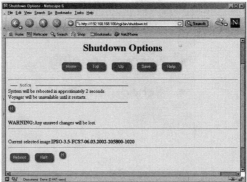

> **NOTE**
>
> If you are used to typing **sync; sync; reboot** to restart a UNIX system, you can certainly do that as well. However, the *reboot* command does flush the file system cache to disk, so it is no longer necessary to use the *sync* command.

If you do not shut down your system cleanly for whatever reason, perhaps due to a power outage or if you simply hit the power switch or there was a system crash, your Nokia will probably boot up fine on its own, but there could be a time when the system does not come up without some intervention. When the file systems are not cleanly unmounted, UNIX systems will perform an fsck (file system check) during the boot process to check blocks and sizes, pathnames, connectivity, reference counts, and cylinder groups for file system integrity. If there is an error that the system cannot fix during the automatic fsck process, it will stop booting and wait for you to press **Enter** on your keyboard. The following is the message you will see on the console:

```
Automatic file system check failed. Enter pathname of shell or RETURN for sh:
```

Follow these steps to run fsck manually:

1. Press **Enter**. You will then see an sh prompt (#). The system is in maintenance mode, so you have limited access to it at this stage.

2. Change directories to /sbin by typing #**cd /sbin**.

3. Run **fsck –y**. This command runs manually. Answer **yes** to any questions you are prompted with during the process. When the check is complete, you will return to the shell prompt.

4. Type **reboot** to restart the boot process, and the system should come up on its own this time.

NOTE

You can use the commands *reboot* or *halt* from within the CLISH tool as well. If you type **reboot save** or **halt save**, the system will shut down cleanly after saving any applied changes.

Managing Packages

Nokia *packages* are software bundles that are in a tarred, gzipped format ready to be installed on an IPSO system. You can get packages compatible with IPSO from Nokia, with the exception of Check Point FireWall-1, which must be obtained from Check Point or one of its resellers.

All Nokia packages are stored in the /opt file system. This is also the directory for administrators to put optional software.

Installing New Packages

When you download a new package to your NSP, you should not uncompress or extract the package files in any way prior to starting the installation. The IPSO tools provided expect to find most packages with a .tgz extension and will extract the files necessary as part of the package installation procedure.

Voyager

First, let's walk through the process of installing a new package using the Voyager Web interface. (If you want to use the command line instead, skip to the next section.) When installing packages through Voyager, you must specify an FTP server that you can use to download the package:

1. Log in to Voyager and click **Config**.

2. Select **Manage Installed Packages** from under the System Configuration section.

3. Click the link to **FTP and Install Packages** from the Manage Packages configuration page.

4. Fill in the required fields for the FTP session. This information includes the FTP server name or IP address, the directory where the packages are stored on that server, and a login name/password. You may leave the username and password fields blank if you want to use anonymous FTP. See the example illustrated in Figure 20.2. If you want to use the login directory, you might need to enter a single period (.) in the FTP dir box.

Figure 20.2 FTP Packages

5. Click **Apply**. The page will update once a connection has been made to the FTP server. A list of packages available on that server will be displayed in the Site Listing box.

6. Choose the packages that you want to download by highlighting them in the Site Listing box (see Figure 20.3).

Figure 20.3 Selecting a Package for Download

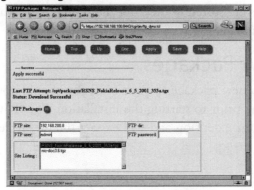

7. Click **Apply** again. This time, the Nokia device will begin to download the files. The page will update every 15 seconds during the download so you know that it is in progress. You will also see a message on the top of the screen similar to the following:

```
Last FTP Attempt: /opt/packages/RSNS_NokiaRelease_6_5_2001_353a.tgz
Status: Downloading
Status Can Be Refreshed By Either Waiting 15 Seconds or Clicking Apply
```

8. When the download is complete, you will see the message "Status: Download Successful" at the top of the page. Scroll down to the box now displayed that is labeled *Select a package to unpack*. You should see the package(s) that you retrieved in the previous step. Highlight the package you want to install.

9. Click **Apply**. Doing so will extract the package and list some package details on the screen, as shown in Figure 20.4.

Figure 20.4 Unpacked Package Details

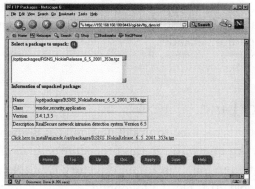

10. Select the link **Click here to install/upgrade**, which ends with the package name. In this example, the package used is /opt/packages/RSNS_NokiaRelease _6_5_2001_353a.tgz. You will see a page similar to the one shown in Figure 20.5.

11. Toggle the radio button to **Yes** to install a new package. If you want to upgrade the package from one already installed instead, choose **Yes** under the Upgrade option and from the list provided, select the software package that you want to upgrade.

12. Click **Apply**. The package is now installed and active. You can now view this package on the Manage Packages configuration screen along with all the other installed packages.

13. Click **Save**.

Figure 20.5 Installing the New Package in Voyager

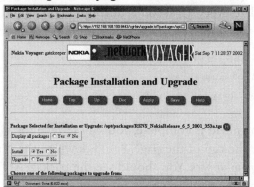

> ## WARNING
>
> If you are installing NG for the first time, you must install Check Point FireWall-1 NG FP2 using the bundled wrapper file named CP_FP2_IPSO.tgz instead of trying to install the individual packages. The wrapper will install NG FP1 and then update to FP2 automatically. If you are already running NG FP1, you shouldn't have any problem upgrading to FP2 using the separate packages.

The Command Line

The command-line tool that is used to install new images is *newpkg*. Follow these steps to install a package using the newpkg utility. To use this procedure, you should already have the package downloaded to the system in the /var/admin directory. Available command-line options for this tool are described in Table 20.1. Do the following:

1. From a command prompt on the Nokia device, type **newpkg –i**. The following options will be displayed:

   ```
   Load new package from:

   1. Install from CD-ROM.

   2. Install from anonymous FTP server.

   3. Install from FTP server with user and password.

   4. Install from local filesystem.

   5. Exit new package installation.
   ```

2. Type **4** at the *Choose an installation method (1-5):* prompt and press **Enter**.

3. Type a single period (.) and press **Enter** at the *Enter pathname to the packages [or 'exit' to exit]:* prompt. You will see the following output:

   ```
   Loading Package List


   Processing package nic-doc3.6.tgz ...
   ```

```
Package Description: Documentation for Nokia IPSO 3.6 07/08/02

Would you like to :

1. Install this as a new package
2. Skip this package
3. Exit new package installation


Choose (1-3):
```

4. Type **1** and press **Enter** to install the new package. You will then see the following output:

```
Installing nic-doc3.6.tgz

nic_doc36 does not exist previously. Proceeding with Installation.

Done installing nic_doc36


End of new package installation

cleaning up ..done

Use Voyager to activate packages
```

Table 20.1 newpkg Command-Line Arguments

Switch for newpkg	Description
-i	Installs the package but does not activate it. Prompts you for media type, new packages, and old packages that you want to install or upgrade.
-s <server>	Specifies the FTP server IP address.
-l <username>	Enter the FTP username. (You don't need to enter a username if you will be using anonymous FTP.)
-p <password>	Enter the FTP user's password.
-m <CDROM | AFTP | FTP | LOCAL>	Choose your media type. Your options are CDROM, AFTP, FTP or LOCAL.
-d	Prints debug messages.
-v	Verbose mode for FTP.
-n <new package>	Enter the full pathname to the new package you are installing.
-o <old package>	Enter the full pathname to the package from which you are upgrading.
-S	Sets the newpkg to install the package silently. If you enable silent mode, you must specify the following arguments: -o, -m, -n, and possibly –s and -l, –p if the media type is not LOCAL.
-h	Prints the usage for newpkg (help).

Enabling and Disabling Packages

Once you have installed packages, you might need to go into Voyager to enable them. Likewise, you can easily disable packages from the same screen:

1. Log in to Voyager and click **Config**.

2. Click **Manage Installed Packages** from the System Configuration heading (see Figure 20.6).

3. All the installed packages are listed with the option of being turned *Off* or *On*. Their current state is displayed. To enable a package that is disabled, toggle to the **On** position. Enabling a package will start any relevant processes so you can start using the software immediately.

4. To disable a package that is currently enabled, toggle the button to the **Off** position. You may enable or disable one or more packages at one time from this screen. Disabling a package will kill any running processes related to that package but will not uninstall it, so you may enable it again later.

5. Click **Apply** and then click **Save**.

NOTE

Using the Manage Installed Packages tool in Voyager, you have an easy method of toggling packages off and on, giving you the ability to disable one version of installed software and enable another. This tool is ideal for administrators since it provides a quick and simple way to back out of new package upgrades, if necessary.

For example, consider that you are running Check Point FireWall-1 4.1 SP-5 and you are planning an upgrade to FireWall-1 NG. As part of your upgrade procedure, it is always prudent to have a contingency plan in case the upgrade is not successful for any reason. With your Nokia system, you can simply toggle the new Check Point NG package to **Off** and toggle the Check Point 4.1 SP-5 package to **On**. Click **Apply** and then click **Save**, and the system will switch to running whatever package you have enabled at that time. The entire configuration will be saved in the old package. If you want to try NG again at a later time, just reverse the procedure.

After enabling a package, you will receive notification at the top of the Manage Packages configuration screen that the package has been registered and that the Voyager environment has been changed due to the new package. Any necessary environment variables have been updated within the login environment as well, but you might need to end your session and start a new one for these settings to take effect on the command line. This is because these settings are updated in the users' .cshrc or .profile and are run once at the beginning of each login session. You may also source these files to initiate the new variables into your current environment. To do this, simply type **source .cshrc** from the /var/admin directory.

Figure 20.6 Enabling and Disabling Packages

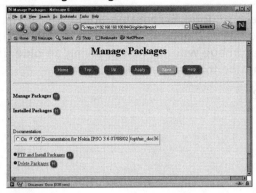

Removing Packages

To remove previously installed packages, follow these instructions after logging in to Voyager:

1. Click **Config**.

2. Click **Manage Installed Packages** from the System Configuration heading.

3. Click the link to **Delete Packages**.

4. Select the packages you want to delete by selecting the option button for **Delete** instead of Keep. You may choose any packages from the list that are not currently active, so you won't be able to accidentally remove a package you are using (see Figure 20.7).

5. Click **Apply** and then click **Save**.

Figure 20.7 Deleting Packages

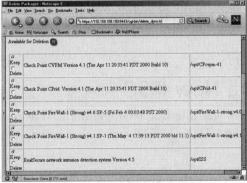

Managing IPSO Images

You may manage Nokia's IPSO images similarly to the way you manage packages. An IPSO image is the base operating system of your Nokia Security Platform. These images are located in the /image directory on your hard drive, and they contain a system kernel and system binaries. You should have at least one image on the system when you receive it, and you can add new images at any time.

WARNING

Please read all IPSO release notes before upgrading your system. You must take into account special considerations, depending on your Nokia model, and sometimes you cannot apply the latest image without first applying an older image. For example, IPSO 3.6 can be installed on the following model numbers:

- IP110 and IP120
- IP330
- IP440
- IP530
- IP650
- IP710 and IP740

Do not attempt to install 3.6 on any other models or you might leave the system in an unusable state, and the only way to make it usable again is to RMA the unit for Nokia to reimage the box. IPSO 3.6 can be upgraded on these models only if you are running one of the following previous versions of IPSO. Note that IPSO 3.5.1 is *not* supported:

- 3.3 or 3.3.1
- 3.4, 3.4.1 or 3.4.2
- 3.5

If you are running IPSO 3.2.1 or earlier and you want to upgrade to IPSO 3.4.*x* or later, you must do a manual boot manager upgrade. For that reason, we recommend that if you are on IPSO 3.2.1 or earlier, you first upgrade to IPSO 3.3 and then to 3.4.*x* or later. Nokia incorporated the boot manager update automatically into IPSO 3.4.*x* and later. Therefore, if you are on IPSO 3.3 or later and the boot manager needs to be updated during a new image install, it will happen automatically, or you can force a boot manager upgrade using the *newimage –b* option.

Upgrading to a New IPSO

If you want to use the Voyager interface to upgrade the IPSO image, you need to have the image file ipso.tgz available on an FTP or HTTP server that is accessible from your NSP. Upgrade IPSO image through Voyager:

1. Log in to Voyager and click **Config**.

2. Scroll down to the System Configuration heading and select **Install New IPSO Image (Upgrade)**.

3. Fill in the URL to the image and select **Test Boot New Image**. Fill in any of the other relevant information as shown in Figure 20.8:

    - Enter HTTP Realm (for HTTP URLs only). This is the name of the realm that you are authenticating to in a Web browser.

- Enter User Name (if applicable). If you are using HTTP or FTP, you might need to enter a username.

- Enter Password (if applicable). If you enter a username, enter the password here.

Figure 20.8 Updating Images through Voyager

4. Click **Apply**. You will receive the following message:

   ```
   "File download and image installation could take long time (depending
   upon  the network speed).
   Click Apply if you want to continue".
   ```

   This message is accurate; when writing this section, it took approximately 30 minutes for the installation to complete through Voyager.

5. Click **Apply** to begin the download and upgrade process.

NOTE

If you do not have a name server configured on your Nokia appliance, you need to enter the server's IP address instead of DNS resolvable name in step 3. You will know this is the case if you receive the following error messages: "Error: Invalid URL or server error" and "fetch: 'www.nokia.com': cannot resolve: Resolver Error."

6. Next you will see a screen that says, "New image installation has started…" and then you will be brought back to the New Image Installation (Upgrade) Status page, which displays the status of the download and installation. This page will continue to refresh. Be patient. If the download is not progressing for some reason, you will be notified. If you want to check the progress of the download, just log in to the NSP and run the **ls -al** command on /var/tmp. The ipso.tgz file will be there and the file size should continue to grow.

7. When the update is complete, you will see the message "Please reboot immediately," as shown in Figure 20.9. Reboot the system cleanly. Refer to the section "Rebooting the System" earlier in this chapter if you need help with rebooting.

8. When the system comes back up, log in and verify that the new image is running. If you did a test boot, you will want to set the new image as the active image through the Manage IPSO Images screen.

Figure 20.9 Voyager IPSO Upgrade Complete

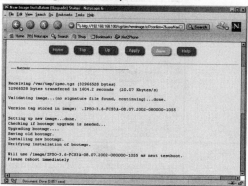

Installing with newimage

If you would prefer to update IPSO versions from the command line, you can use the *newimage* tool. Table 20.2 lists the various command-line options you can specify in running the command. If you have the ipso.tgz file loaded on the local system in /var/admin, use **newimage –k –R –l /var/admin** to update the operating system image. After the image is updated, you must reboot to load the new image. You will see the following output:

```
gatekeeper[admin]# newimage -k -R -l /var/admin
Enter ipso image file name [ipso.tgz]:
Validating image...(no signature file found, continuing)...done.


Version tag stored in image:   .IPSO-3.6-FCS3-08.01.2002-181200-1051


Setting up new image...done.
Checking if bootmgr upgrade is needed...


Will use /image/IPSO-3.6-FCS3-08.01.2002-181200-1051 as root for next boot.
To install/upgrade your packages run /etc/newpkg after REBOOT
Please reboot immediately


gatekeeper[admin]# sync; sync; reboot
```

Table 20.2 newimage Command-Line Arguments

Switch for newimage	Description
-k	Upgrades the IPSO image and keeps all currently active packages so they will be started upon reboot.
-r <image>	Specifies the image to use on the next boot.
-R	Sets the new image to be used on the next reboot.
-l <path to image>	Tells the *newimage* command where to find the ipso.tgz file, which contains the new image.
-t <image>	Specifies the image to use for a test boot.
-T	Enables you to perform a test boot with the new image.
-i	Sets the *newimage* command in interactive mode. Use this option if you need to FTP the file or use the CD-ROM drive (IP440 only) to upgrade the IPSO image.
-b	Forces upgrade of bootmgr.
-v	Verbose mode for FTP.

Deleting Images

If you don't have enough disk space in /image to load new images, you need to remove old images to make space. The process for deleting images is simply done through the Voyager Web interface. To delete old IPSO images:

1. Log in to Voyager.
2. Click **Config** to bring up the main Configuration window.
3. Click **Manage IPSO Images** under the System Configuration heading.
4. Click the link labeled **Delete IPSO images**.
5. Select the option button to **Delete** the old images. You may select one or more images to delete as shown in Figure 20.10.
6. Click **Apply** and then click **Save**.

Figure 20.10 Deleting IPSO Images

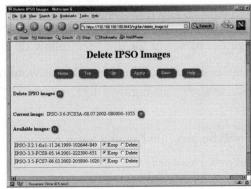

Managing Users and Groups

As with any operating system, one must administer users and groups. On most UNIX systems, the user with unlimited privilege and responsibility is the root user, also known as the *superuser*. In IPSO, the user *admin* takes the place of the root user but has all the same privileges. Whenever you need to make changes to your NSP, you log in as admin because this account has read/write capability to system configuration files and full system access. In this section, we show you how to change the password on your admin account, how to create and delete user accounts, and how to configure groups on your UNIX system.

Users

To manage users on your Nokia system, log in to Voyager and click **Config**. From here, click **Users** under the Security and Access Configuration heading. You should be presented with a screen like the one shown in Figure 20.11.

Figure 20.11 Managing Users

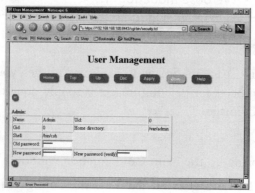

The admin User

As mentioned previously, the admin user is the superuser on the system. If you review some of the settings for admin in the User Management display, you will see that admin has a UID and a GID of 0. *UID* stands for *user ID*, and *GID* stands for *group ID*. These ID values determine that the admin user has superuser privileges on the system. These values mean the same thing on almost all UNIX systems. Other information listed on this page is the host directory, which is /var/admin, and the shell that admin uses—/bin/csh, pronounced "C-shell."

You configure a password for the admin user during the initial configuration of your Nokia platform. If you want to change the password for this user, follow this procedure:

1. From the User Management screen, fill in the Old password, New password, and New password (verify) fields, as shown in Figure 20.11.

2. Click **Apply**.

3. Click **Save** and you will be presented with a login prompt to reauthenticate.

4. Enter **admin** and the new password.

5. Click **Save** again, if the option is still available.

You have the option of accepting or requiring S/key authentication for the admin user on this screen as well.

> **NOTE**
>
> Using CLISH, you can change the admin user password with the following command:
> *Nokia>* **set user admin passwd**
> *Nokia>* **save config**

The monitor User

The monitor user is available in IPSO as a read-only user. Once this user is enabled, you can log in as monitor through Voyager to view system configuration and resources, but you cannot make any changes to the configuration. This account is predefined in Voyager with the following values:

- Name: Monitor
- UID: 102
- GID: 10
- Home Directory: */var/monitor*
- Shell: */bin/csh*
- Password: None (cannot log in)

By default, the monitor user has no password and cannot log in to the system. To enable the monitor user visible in Voyager, fill in the new password fields and click **Apply** and then click **Save**.

Other Users

You can create other users to log in to the IPSO system and Voyager. If you create a user with UID 0, that user will have read/write access through Voyager and the same permissions that the admin user has in IPSO. Other read-only user accounts can be created too. Simply use a new UID for each new account. To create another user from the User Manager configuration screen:

1. Scroll down to the **Add new user** section and type a username, UID, and home directory for the new user. For another superuser, enter a UID of **0**.

2. Click **Apply**.

3. Next, enter a password into the New password text boxes for the new user and click **Apply** again.

4. Click **Save**.

Users without admin access will not be able to run the new command-line shell CLISH, but they can log in to IPSO and run commands to view system resources and configuration settings. These users will not be able to make any changes that will affect the system. If you would like to give some of these users certain privileges, you could do so by setting up groups, which is discussed in the next section.

You can view the users who are logged in to your system with the command *w*. If you type **w** while logged in to your Nokia, you should see output similar to the following. This output includes the current time, the time that has passed since the system was last rebooted, the number of users logged in to the system, and the system CPU load average over 1-, 5-, and 15-minute intervals.

```
gatekeeper[cherie]# w
10:28PM  up 2 days, 11 mins, 4 users, load averages: 0.03, 0.05, 0.00

USER     TTY FROM             LOGIN@  IDLE WHAT
admin    d0  -                Thu10PM 11:09 -csh (csh)
monitor  p0  10.10.10.3       Fri07PM  1:26 -csh (csh)
fwadmin  p1  10.10.10.3        9:01PM     - -csh (csh)
cherie   p2  10.10.10.3       10:28PM     - w
```

NOTE

Use the following commands to add a new user using CLISH:
   Nokia> **add user camon uid 104 homedir /var/camon**
   Nokia> **set user camon passwd**
   Nokia> **save config**

Groups

One way that you can give privileges to users without giving them carte blanche access to your system is to create groups of users. Then you can assign certain permissions to these groups, so that any user who is a member of the group will have the ability to perform certain functions. For example, if you are running Check Point FireWall-1, only admin users can run the programs in $FWDIR/bin. However, if you want to allow a couple of other users the ability to log in and stop or start firewall services or add licenses to the firewall (FireWall-1 4.1 only), you could create an fwadmin group (see the Group Management screen in Voyager in Figure 20.12). After the group is created, you can go into the cpconfig utility and set group permissions on the $FWDIR directories. If you have Check Point FireWall-1 4.1 installed, follow these steps to set up group permissions on your Nokia firewall:

1. Log in to Voyager and click **Config**.

2. Click **Groups** under the Security and Access Configuration heading.

3. Fill in the Group Name: **fwadmin** under the Add Group Name heading and enter a new GID of **100**. See Figure 20.12 for an example.

Figure 20.12 Group Management

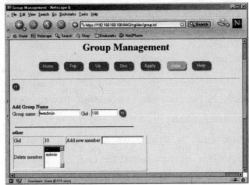

4. Click **Apply**. You will now see a new group listed along with the default groups *other* and *wheel*.

5. The next step is to add users to your fwadmin group. To do this, enter an existing user account into the field labeled *Add new member*. For our example, let's add a user called **sysadmin** that was created previously.

6. Click **Apply** and then click **Save**.

7. Now log in to IPSO as **admin** and run **cpconfig**. You will be presented with the following options:

```
gatekeeper[cherie]# cpconfig

This program will let you re-configure

your Check Point products configuration.



Configuration Options:
----------------------

(1)  Licenses

(2)  Administrators

(3)  GUI clients

(4)  SNMP Extension

(5)  Groups

(6)  PKCS#11 Token

(7)  Random Pool

(8)  Certificate Authority

(9)  Automatic start of Check Point Products


(10) Exit


Enter your choice (1-10) :
```

8.   Enter **5** to configure groups. You will be presented with the following output:

```
Configuring Groups...
======================
Check Point access and execution permissions
--------------------------------------------
Usually, a Check Point module is given group permission
for access and execution.
You may now name such a group or instruct the installation
procedure to give no group permissions to the Check Point module.
In the latter case, only the Super-User will
be able to access and execute the Check Point module.


Please specify group name [<RET> for no group permissions]:
```

9.   Type **fwadmin** and press **Enter**.

10.   The system will ask, "Group fwadmin will be used. Is this ok (y/n) [y]?" Press **Enter** to accept the default value *y* for *yes*.

11.   The group permissions will then be set on the $FWDIR directories, and you will see the confirmation message, "Setting Group Permissions... Done." on the screen. Then you will be presented with the cpconfig menu again, as in step 7. Type **10** to exit the configuration tool.

12.   You will now be presented with the option of restarting FireWall-1 services. Press **Enter** to accept the default setting *y* for *yes*.

WARNING

With Check Point FireWall-1 Next Generation, this process doesn't seem to work properly. Although the $FWDIR group permissions are changed, a user in the fwadmin group receives errors when trying to run *fw* commands.

In order to set group permissions on files and directories from the command line, use the *chgrp* tool. For example, if you want to set the fwadmin group on all files and directories under the $FWDIR/bin directory, you could change directories into the $FWDIR directory and issue the command *chgrp −R fwadmin bin*. The capital *R* will cause a recursive change on all files and directories under the bin directory, inclusive.

Two groups are created by default on your Nokia Security Platform: the *other* group and the *wheel* group. Any users without full system access, such as monitor, will be members of the *other* group by default. Your admin user will be a member of the *wheel* group. If you want your other users to have the ability to use the *su* command (this command, short for *superuser*, allows users with limited privileges to become the admin or superuser on the system), you will need to add them into the *wheel* group.

NOTE

Use the following syntax in CLISH to add a user to the wheel group:
Nokia> **add group wheel member camon**
Nokia> **show group wheel**
GID   Members
0   admin,camon,root

Configuring Static Routes

Almost all administrators need to add static routes into their network, unless they happen to have a very simplified LAN configuration. Nokia makes it very easy to add routes through the Voyager Web interface. Start by clicking **Config**, and then click **Static Routes** under the Routing Configuration heading. Here you have two options for adding routes:

- You can add routes one by one.
- You can compile a list of routes and aggregates to add one per line.

You should already have a default route in your Static Routes configuration if you set this up earlier. To add a single route to the system, fill in the destination network in the *New static route* text box. Also enter the Mask length, Next Hop Type, and Gateway Type fields. Click **Apply** and then fill in the Gateway Address (the next-hop router address), click **Apply**, and then click **Save**.

To add a list of routes at one time, enter routes in the large text box labeled *Quick-add static routes*. The syntax of the routes added here is to have one route per line with a new line at the end of each statement. The statement should include the destination network, mask length, and next-hop router. After you fill in the networks you want to add, click **Apply** and then click **Save**. The routes will be added as shown in Figure 20.13:

```
Example:<destination network>/<mask> <gateway>

172.16.0.0/16 10.10.10.1

172.18.0.0/16 10.10.10.1

192.168.100.0/23 10.10.10.1

192.168.103.0/24 10.10.10.1

10.0.0.0/8 10.10.10.1
```

NOTE

You can add and view routes in CLISH as follows:
Nokia> **set static-route 172.21.0.0/16 nexthop gateway address 10.10.10.1 on**
Nokia> **show route all**
To delete the route, use the same command, but change the last word to *off* instead of *on*.

Figure 20.13 Static Routes Display

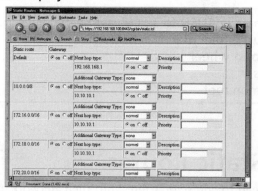

Once the routes are configured, you can perform maintenance on them through this same configuration screen. You can delete a route by clicking **off** next to the network address and then clicking **Apply** and **Save**. You can change a gateway address for a route by clicking **off** next to the gateway address, clicking **Apply**, then selecting **address** for the Gateway Type, then clicking **Apply** again. Finally, fill in the gateway IP address and click **Apply** and then **Save**. You also have the option of writing in a description and/or a priority for each route. To verify that the routing table on the system matches what you see in Voyager, log in and use one of the following options:

- Type **netstat –rn**.
- Type **iclid**, then type **show route** and press **Enter**.
- Type **clish**, then type **show route all** and press **Enter**.

System Backup and Restore

As a systems administrator, you already know the importance of having a good system backup procedure and disaster recovery plan in place should you need to restore important data for your organization. Your Nokias will most likely be some of the most important machines in your network since they are usually placed at key points, so you will want to ensure that you are getting backups regularly and that you know how to restore the system if you need to. In this chapter we show you the utilities available to back up and restore your NSP.

Configuration Sets

Using the Configuration Set Management tool in Voyager, you can make changes to the files that store your current Voyager configuration parameters. The default configuration database is stored in the file /config/db/initial, and a symbolic link file, /config/active, points to this database. Voyager always loads whichever file the /config/active link is associated with. You can use this tool to change that association or to simply make a backup of the current configuration. You also have the option of deleting past configuration sets from this screen.

Follow these steps to make a backup configuration database:

1. Log in to Voyager and click **Config**.

2. Click **Manage Configuration Sets** under the System Configuration heading.

3. In the **Save current state to new configuration database** field, type a new name for the current configuration set. In our example, we use the date so we can remember when we made this backup—**config09082002** (see Figure 20.14).

4. Click **Apply**.

5. Now your current config will be listed as *config09082002*, and the active file will now have a symbolic link to this new configuration file. If you only want to make a backup of your existing configuration and do not want it to be the active config, you need to change it back to *initial*. Do this by selecting the option button next to the **initial** database name.

6. Click **Apply**.

Figure 20.14 Managing Configuration Sets

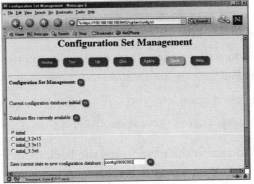

Making Backups

Using the option described in the preceding section, you can save the Voyager settings, but what about backing up the system? The Voyager configuration doesn't include anything from our /var/admin directory or package configuration, such as Check Point FireWall-1. Is there an option for making a full backup?

Yes, the Nokia has a Backup and Restore utility, which allows you to make a default system backup (system files only) and gives you the option to back up home directories and package configuration as well. This backup procedure simply creates a gzipped tarball of all the files you specify on the local system in /var/backup. Therefore, you will want to ensure that you have ample disk space on this partition before you begin the process:

1. Log in to Voyager and click **Config**.

2. Select the link for **Backup and Restore** under the System Configuration heading. This will bring you to the screen shown in Figure 20.15.

3. Enter a filename such as **backup** in the section marked *Backup file name*. The system will automatically add the current date to the filename, so if you include the date, the filename will be redundant.

4. System files will be backed up by default, including any IPsec files, cron config, and your /config directory. Now you must select from the list of other backup options. This list could be different for you depending on which packages you have in your active configuration. You need to toggle the option button next to each of these options to **Yes** if you want to back up any of the items in the list that follows. For our example, we select home directories and FireWall-1 NG FP2. These are all set to *No* by default:

   ■ Back up home directories (*/var/admin* and */var/monitor*) **Yes**

   ■ Back up log files (*/var/log*) **No**

   ■ Back up */opt/CPfw1-50-02* (Check Point VPN-1/FireWall-1 NG Feature Pack 2) **Yes**

   ■ Back up */opt/CPshared-50-02* (Check Point SVN Foundation NG Feature Pack 2) **No**

   ■ Back up */opt/ISS* (RealSecure network intrusion detection system Version 6.5) **No**

5. Click **Apply**. You will see the following message on the top of the Voyager screen: *Backup /var/backup/backup_20020908.tgz is running in the background.*

6. When the process is complete, you will see the file in /var/backup as follows:

   ```
   -rw-r--r-- 1 root wheel 136969567 Sep 8 12:19 backup_20020908.tgz
   ```

   You need to refresh the page to see the backup archive listed on the screen. Click **Up** and then click **Backup and Restore** under the System Configuration heading.

7. Click **Save**.

Figure 20.15 Backup Configuration

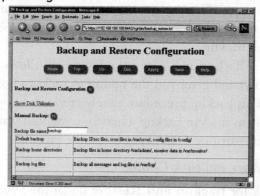

Now that you have a backup of system files, you might want to FTP or SCP it off the Nokia to another system for safekeeping. You can use FTP to accomplish this task from within this same screen in Voyager. Scroll down to where it says *Remote Transfer Archive File* and fill in the FTP site information, then choose the backup file that you want to transfer. When you're done, click **Apply** and you will see the following message:

```
Remote Transfer: the ftp is running in the background.
the file transfer might fail, please check /var/log/messages for
    the status of the transfer.
```

This process could take a while because the file is quite large, mostly because we backed up package configuration information. If we had backed up the default files only, the file size would be considerably smaller, as shown in the following output:

```
-rw-r--r--   1 root   wheel       67878 Sep  8 12:31 defaultonly_20020908.tgz
```

NOTE

When making a backup with CLISH, use the following commands:
> Nokia> **set backup manual filename backup**
> Nokia> **set backup manual homedirs off**
> Nokia> **set backup manual logfiles off**
> Nokia> **set backup manual on**

Now you might be asking, "can I schedule regular backups of my Nokia system?" The answer is yes. Starting with IPSO 3.5, the ability to schedule backups is built into Voyager with the use of *cron*, which is discussed in detail a little later in this chapter. To schedule a regular backup, scroll down to the section labeled *Scheduled Backup* on the **Backup and Restore Configuration** screen and select from the pull-down menu one of the following: None (default), Daily, Weekly, or Monthly. See Figure 20.16, where we selected **Monthly** and then clicked **Apply**. Now you are able to select the date, hour, minute, and filename for the monthly backup, as well as the files that you had to choose from when doing a manual backup earlier. When you are finished making your selections, click **Apply** and then click **Save**. The files will be backed up to /var/backup/sched and will be time-stamped. The configuration you specify will be entered into the /etc/crontab file.

Figure 20.16 Scheduling Backups

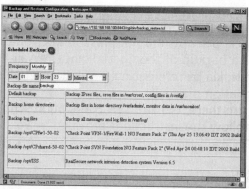

You might want to delete backup files from /var/backup occasionally as well, and you can do that by scrolling down to the very bottom of the Backup and Restore Configuration screen. Simply click the **delete** option button next to the backup filename that you want to remove, and then click **Apply** (see Figure 20.17).

Restoring Backups

You can restore a backup by either using a backup file on the local system in /var/backup or by using FTP to retrieve the backup file off a remote FTP server. If you are restoring a configuration from one Nokia to another, ensure that you have IPSO loaded and the software packages installed before you begin to restore the configuration files. You should also make sure that you are using the same version of IPSO and the same software package versions that you were using on the system from which you initially took the backup. Follow these steps to restore a backup from a local file:

1. Ensure that the file you want to restore from is in the /var/backup directory.
2. Log in to Voyager and click **Config**.
3. Click **Backup and Restore** under the System Configuration heading.
4. Scroll down to the Restore From Local: section (as shown in Figure 20.17) and select the backup file you want to restore from either the **Manual backup file**: or the **Scheduled backup file:** pull-down window.
5. Click **Apply** and then click **Save**.
6. Click the **Reboot** link on the same page.
7. Click the **Reboot** icon and the system will be rebooted with the new configuration.

Figure 20.17 Restore from Backup

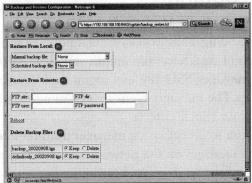

NOTE

To restore a backup through CLISH, use the following command:
Nokia> **set restore manual backup_20020922.tgz**

System Logging

Choose **System Logging** from the System Configuration heading under the main Configuration screen in Voyager. You will see the default Voyager configuration for system logging that is shown in Figure 20.18. By default, system logs are stored in a file named *messages* in the /var/log directory on your Nokia system. You can change the logging parameters so that you can accept syslog messages from remote machines, send local logs to a remote machine, and enable logging of Voyager changes through the System Logging configuration interface. If you decide to enable network logging, syslog will use UDP port 514 to transmit the messages. If your log data is traversing a firewall, you might need to open this port for remote logging to operate.

Figure 20.18 System Logging Configuration

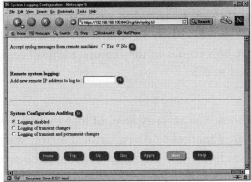

Local System Logging

To view local system logs, click the **Monitor** link in Voyager and select **System Message Log** under the System Logs heading. Here you have the option of searching through the messages file. To view an entire month of data, select the month and click **Apply**. Here you will see system boot messages, crontab messages, SSH key, user logins, and Voyager configuration change messages, among other things. The messages file is rotated monthly, and you can even select past messages files to include in your search criteria.

If you select the option to accept syslog messages from remote machines, your Nokia will begin listening for syslog messages on the network and will log any messages it receives locally, including the host name of the sending machine in the log entry.

NOTE

To turn on or off the option to accept syslog messages from remote machines through CLISH, use the following commands:

Nokia> **set syslog accept-remote-log on**
Nokia> **set syslog accept-remote-log off**

Remote Logging

Your Nokia can be configured to send syslog messages to a remote system. This functionality can be useful if you want to have a central syslog server that stores logs. This remote device might even be configured to search your logs for suspicious or unusual activities and generate alerts based on the system logs. Any logs that are sent to a remote syslog server will also be logged locally in the /var/log/messages file. To configure remote system logging in Voyager, follow these six easy steps:

1. Log in to Voyager and click **Config**.

2. Click **System Logging** under the System Configuration heading.

3. Enter the IP address of the remote syslog server in the box labeled *Add new remote IP address to log to:*. In Figure 20.19 we have added **10.10.10.1**. Note that Voyager in IPSO 3.4.*x* does not accept host names in the remote address box, only IP addresses. This is an IPSO bug that is fixed in 3.5.

4. Click **Apply**.

5. Now you need to choose the severity level of logs that you want to send to the remote server. Your choices are Emergency, Alert, Critical, Error, Warning, Notice, Info, Debug, and All. The level you choose and all higher levels will be sent to the syslog server.

6. Click **Apply** and then click **Save**. If you enter more than one severity level, the least severe level will be used.

NOTE

Use the following command to enable remote logging through CLISH:

Nokia> **add syslog log-remote-address 10.10.10.1 level crit**

Figure 20.19 Remote System Logging Configuration

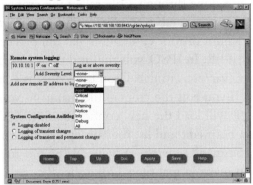

WARNING

Be careful not to configure two machines that send syslog data to each other. Doing so will create a logging loop, which is not desirable.

Audit Logs

Using the System Configuration Auditlog option within the System Logging Configuration screen allows you to track the changes that are made to the system configuration. By default, logging config changes is disabled, but you can choose to enable logging for either transient changes only (generated when the **Apply** button is selected) or for both transient and permanent changes (generated when the **Save** button is selected).

If you choose to enable configuration logging, you need to specify a file to send these logs to. The default filename is the standard system log file /var/log/messages. You can choose to create a separate file for configuration logs, however, such as /var/log/voyager. Keep in mind that you might need to maintain a new file by rotating it occasionally, especially if you are making a large number of changes to your system.

NOTE

To make changes to the Auditlog configuration through CLISH, use the following commands:

Nokia> **set syslog filename /var/log/messages**
Nokia> **set syslog auditlog permanent**

Scheduling Tasks Using cron

UNIX systems have a daemon named *cron* that is used to schedule tasks. If you are familiar with Windows scheduler or *at* commands, think of cron as a similar tool. You can use cron to run any executable file, including shell scripts and other commands, at any time of the day, week, or month, at regular intervals. For example, cron is used to rotate the /var/log/messages file on the first of every month. Tasks that are scheduled through cron are typically called jobs or cron jobs.

The configuration of cron is done through a file called the crontab. Typically, each user on the system can have his or her own crontab file, which will run with whatever privileges that user possesses. Of course, the admin or root crontab file has full privileges, and most system scheduling is done through that file. In IPSO, you can find the crontab file in /etc/crontab, which is actually a symlink to /var/etc/crontab. Cron then runs as a daemon and can be viewed with the **ps —aux** command. If you edit the crontab file manually, you need to restart cron (or send it a HUP signal) so that it will load the new configuration file. Alternatively, there is a *crontab* command that you can use to both edit and list the contents of the running crontab configuration. An *—e* switch with the command (*crontab —e*) will edit the file and update the running cron daemon with any changes you make in real time. Using the *—l* switch allows you to list the file. The syntax of the file is important; each line should have the following values: *minute hour day-of-month month day-of-week command*. Here's a clip of the default /etc/crontab file on IPSO 3.6:

```
#minute hour    mnthday month   weekday   user    command
#
5       *       *       *       *         root    /etc/hourly 2>&1 >>/var/
        log/hourly
30      0       *       *       7         root    /etc/weekly 2>&1 >>/var/
        log/weekly
45      23      1       *       *         admin   /etc/backup -f /var/etc/
        sched_backup_vars.sh
15      0       *       *       *         root    /etc/daily 2>&1 >>/var/
        log/daily
45      0       1       *       *         root    /etc/monthly 2>&1 >>/var/
        log/monthly
```

The *2>&1* after each command specifies what to do with standard output and standard error. Basically, this code says to send standard error to standard output and redirect all output to the file specified. The *>>* means to append to the specified file rather than overwrite it. If no particular action is specified, typically the system messages file will receive this output. It is often useful to redirect this output to /dev/null so that there are no logs generated from the output of the file. One example of this redirection is a FireWall-1 log export command, which would normally show the progression of the export on the command line 1%, 2%, and so on. You would end up with a very large log file if you logged all this output.

Prior to IPSO 3.5, you had to manually edit the crontab file on the system to make changes to cron, but in IPSO 3.5, 3.6 and later, you can schedule cron jobs through the Voyager Web interface (or via CLISH). Click **Job Scheduler** from the System Configuration heading in Voyager, and fill in the requested values to schedule a cron job. See Figure 20.20 for an example.

> **NOTE**
>
> To enable a new cron job through CLISH, use the following commands:
>
> *Nokia>* **add cron job newjob command /opt/local/bin/getfw1config.sh hour 23 minute 55**
>
> *Nokia>* **set cron job newjob on**
>
> Then to delete the job, type:
>
> *Nokia>* **delete cron job newjob**

Figure 20.20 Configuring Crontab

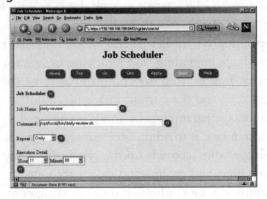

Summary

In this chapter, we presented common tasks performed by system administrators on a regular basis in the context of the Nokia Security Platform. It will be necessary for you to perform many if not all of these tasks throughout the duration of your NSP ownership.

Knowing how to properly shut down or reboot your Nokia is very important. If you don't shut down a Nokia system cleanly, you could boot up with a damaged file system, which will require a console connection so that you can run *fsck* to repair the file system. It's simple to reboot or halt your Nokia system properly through the Voyager Web interface.

Nokia packages are additional, optional software packages that run on IPSO, such as Check Point FireWall-1 or ISS RealSecure. A tool is available through Voyager to easily install, upgrade, or remove software packages. It is also easy to back out of new packages simply by toggling the package on or off; thus you can move from one package version to another in no time. If you don't like your latest upgrade to NG FP3, you can back down to NG FP2 without losing any configuration data.

IPSO images are the operating system kernel and binary files that run the system. Voyager provides an interface for installing, upgrading, and removing images for easy administration of the OS. If you prefer to install new images from the command line, use the newimage tool. Images are stored in the /image directory, and the current image is symlinked to the file /image/current. After making changes to the image parameters in Voyager, you need to reboot the NSP.

Another common sys admin task is to administer users and groups. Voyager provides you with a Web interface to manage your accounts on the system from any Web browser. You can change passwords, create new users and groups, and delete accounts through Voyager.

Maintaining network routes can be configured through Voyager as well. Using the Static Routes configuration screen, you can add or remove your default gateway or router and configure static route entries one by one or through an easy quick-add text box where you can enter multiple routes at one time.

Every administrator should plan on getting system backups and have recovery action plans in place in the event of a disaster. Even if you have a simple hardware failure, a backup can make a big difference if you need to rebuild from scratch on a new box. Since your Nokia will usually sit at key points in your network, it is an important box to back up. Voyager provides you with a Web interface for making backups of your system configuration, user home directories, log files, and package configuration. Using this interface, you can FTP the backup files off the Nokia or download them for a restore. Check Point NG FP1 and FP2 backup scripts are missing or corrupted, so if you have these packages, read the preceding section to find out how to back up these important software packages.

Every task covered in this chapter is very important, and system logging is no exception. Fortunately, Nokia's Network Voyager has an administration tool for configuring system logging; you can use this tool to enable remote logging, receive logs from the network, and enable an audit log of Voyager configuration changes. You can monitor system logs via the /var/log/messages file, which is available through the Voyager monitor area, under the System Logs heading.

The final topic we covered in this chapter was configuring cron. cron is used to schedule tasks for the system to run at specified times. Tasks could include running a custom written shell script to a system binary file. As long as the file is executable, the cron daemon will run the task. The /var/etc/crontab file holds the cron configuration, and it can be edited through Voyager's Job Scheduler link under the System Configuration heading. You can add or delete cron jobs through this interface, which is available in IPSO 3.5 and 3.6. Earlier IPSO releases would require that you manually edit the crontab file using the *crontab −e* command.

Chapter 21

High Availability and Clustering

Best Damn Topics in This Chapter:

- **Designing Your Cluster**
- **Installing FireWall-1 NG FP3**
- **Check Point ClusterXL**
- **Nokia IPSO Clustering**
- **Nokia IPSO VRRP Clusters**
- **Clustering and HA Performance Tuning**

Introduction

The key to a Single Entry Point (SEP) VPN is to use high-availability (HA) and clustering solutions. Of course, if you choose not to use the VPN features of FireWall-1, you can still use the HA and clustering features described in this chapter. Check Point, Nokia, and other third-party companies offer many methods for deploying HA solutions. Here we focus on the Check Point ClusterXL product, review the new Nokia IP clustering and VRRP solutions, and discuss the performance of these solutions. We also spend some time describing how each solution actually works and what the "life of a connection" is like through each clustering solution.

When you set up a cluster, one of the first things you want to do is test that it is working as expected. In this chapter, we cover a quick list of tests that you can do on each cluster to make sure you get the right responses. We also cover some of the command-line tools you can use to check the status of each node in the cluster.

Designing Your Cluster

There are a number of issues to be considered and decisions to be made when you're designing a cluster solution. It's worth keeping in mind that a resilient solution is worthless if poor design makes the clustering mechanism result in more downtime than would be expected with a single system.

Why Do You Need a Cluster?

It might be safe to say that the majority of this chapter's readers have already made the decision to install a clustered firewall, and so those readers know why this is a good idea. For readers who are not yet decided or aren't sure why they are installing a cluster, let's look at the reasons why a cluster might be a good option.

The concept of any cluster solution is that the cluster itself appears on the outside as a single system. In the case of a firewall cluster, this system is a secure gateway, possibly providing a VPN end point and other services. There are two key benefits of a cluster that consists of multiple physical hosts: resilience and increased capacity.

Resilience

A cluster of multiple hosts should have the advantage of being able to provide continuous service, irrespective of whether members of the cluster are available or not. Even the best cluster will struggle if every member is unavailable, but as long as one member is running, service should continue if other members have failed or are down for maintenance.

Increased Capacity

According to some pretty simple logic, if we have three active hosts in a cluster, we can push three times as much traffic through it. Things are not quite that simple, however; there can be significant overhead in operation of the cluster technology itself, which tends to increase in proportion to the number of members and could become a bottleneck. Other bottlenecks could be the network bandwidth available on either side of the cluster and the performance of servers protected by the cluster. This concept might appear obvious, but it could be overlooked during the calculations of the incredible throughput theoretically possible if a further five members are added to a cluster!

High Availability or Load Sharing?

There are two distinct models for clustering solutions: HA and load sharing. Let's take a brief look at each.

Load Sharing

In a load-sharing cluster, all available members are active and passing traffic. This setup provides both resilience and increased capacity due to the distribution of traffic between the members. Some load-sharing solutions can be described as load balancing because there is a degree of intelligence in the distribution of traffic between members. This intelligence might be in the form of a performance rating for each cluster member or even a dynamic rating based on current load.

High Availability

In an HA cluster, only one member is active and routing traffic at any one time. This solution provides resilience but no increased capacity. The choice of HA is often due to the simpler solution being easier to manage and troubleshoot and sometimes more reliable than a load-sharing solution due to the latter's additional complexity. The simplicity of these solutions often means that they are a cheaper option financially.

Clustering and Check Point

Let's now look at design issues that arise in planning Check Point firewall clusters.

Operating System Platform

Depending on the operating system platform, different options are available for clustering solutions, including Check Point solutions and those from Check Point OPSEC partners. Here we look at Check Point's ClusterXL solution, which is available on the usual NG platforms—Windows, Solaris, Linux, and SecurePlatform—with the exception of Nokia IPSO. The IPSO platform offers the IPSO clustering load-balancing solution and VRRP HA, both of which we also cover in this chapter. We do not cover OPSEC partner solutions other than references given toward the end of this chapter.

Clustering and Stateful Inspection

Key to the operation of FireWall-1 is the stateful inspection technology that tracks the state of connections. If a cluster solution is to provide true resilience, a connection should be preserved irrespective of which cluster member its packets are routed through. In order for stateful inspection to deal with connections "moving" between members, a method of sharing state information must be provided. This method is known as *state synchronization* and is an integral part of FireWall-1 clustering. A dedicated network, known as the *sync network* or *secured network,* is used for the state synchronization traffic. Note that it is possible to configure a cluster without state synchronization if no connection resilience is needed.

Desire for Stickiness

Although in theory state synchronization allows each packet of a given connection to pass through any one of the cluster members, it is far more desirable to ensure that each connection "sticks" to a specific cluster member where possible. This is due to timing issues; there is inevitably some delay between one cluster member seeing a packet and that member passing its updated state information to other members. This delay can cause a subsequent packet to be dropped because it appears to be invalid—out of state—to the other members. The problem is particularly likely to be an issue during connection establishment, where a quick exchange of packets must adhere to strict conditions—in the case of TCP connections, the three-way hand-shake. Fortunately, once a connection is established, it is more resilient to packet loss, and the state is not so strictly defined. This allows connection failover, where connections stuck to failed members can be moved to other cluster members with minimal disruption.

In an HA solution, stickiness is no problem; all connections naturally stick to the one active member. In a load-sharing environment, stickiness requires some intelligence from the clustering solution. It must ensure that there is stickiness, but the members should each have roughly equal numbers of connections stuck to them.

Location of Management Station

If you want a clustering solution, you must install an NG distributed management architecture, or in other words, your Check Point management station (also known as the *SmartCenter Server*) must be installed on a dedicated host, *not* on a cluster member.

Beware of upgrading FireWall 4.1 HA configurations that perform state synchronization but were not part of a cluster object. It was possible in version 4.1 to make one of the state synchro-nized firewalls a management station as well, but you cannot do this in FireWall-1 NG.

You must make a decision regarding which network the management station resides on. It is clearly desirable that each cluster member is reachable from the management station, irrespective of whether that member, and other members, are currently active in the cluster. Conversely, irre-spective of which cluster members are active, the management station requires normal network connectivity to allow remote management, access to DNS servers, and so on. This decision will depend largely on the type of clustering solution implemented. Let's now look at two options for location, with examples of a simplified network topology.

A Management Station on a Cluster-Secured Network

The traditional configuration for many HA solutions has been to place the management station on a dedicated, "secured" network (sometimes shared with cluster control and state synchroniza-tion traffic). The network topology is shown in Figure 21.1. Each cluster member is reachable over the secured network, whether the members are in Active or Standby mode. This configura-tion will be a requirement if members running in Standby mode are only contactable on this secured network interface; other interfaces are down while the member is in standby.

NOTE

This is the required configuration in which Check Point ClusterXL HA Legacy mode is implemented.

Figure 21.1 A Management Station on a Secured Network

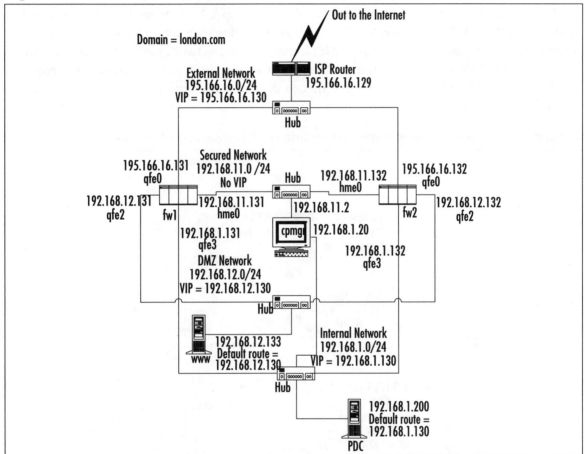

A limitation of this configuration is that the management station does not have reliable connectivity with any other networks, because its default gateway must be configured to one of the member's secured network IP addresses. Therefore, the management station relies on that member being active in order to "see" the outside world. To work around this problem, the management station can have a second interface that connects to an internal network. The management station default gateway can then be configured as the gateway on the internal network—possibly the internal IP address of the cluster itself. Alternatively, the second interface could be external facing, with a valid Internet address. This solution might be desirable if the management station manages remote firewall gateways. If the second interface is external facing, it *must* be firewalled in some way. A possible solution is to install a FireWall-1 enforcement module on the management station (at the time of install) and license it with a SecureServer (nonrouting module) license.

If you run a backup management station, it also needs to be on the secured network.

Management Station on Internal Network

The complications of placing the management station on a dedicated network can be avoided if the cluster solution allows members to be reachable on all interfaces, whether the member is active or not. This is achieved where members each have a unique IP address in addition to an IP address shared over the cluster.

Happily, all the other solutions we discuss—ClusterXL HA New mode, load sharing, IPSO clusters, and IPSO VRRP—behave in this way. These solutions can support a management station located behind any interface. Figure 21.2 shows a typical network topology, with the management station located internally. If the management station also manages a cluster at a remote site, it can do so by connecting via the Internet to the external interfaces of that remote cluster's members.

Figure 21.2 A Management Station on an Internal ("Nonsecure") Network

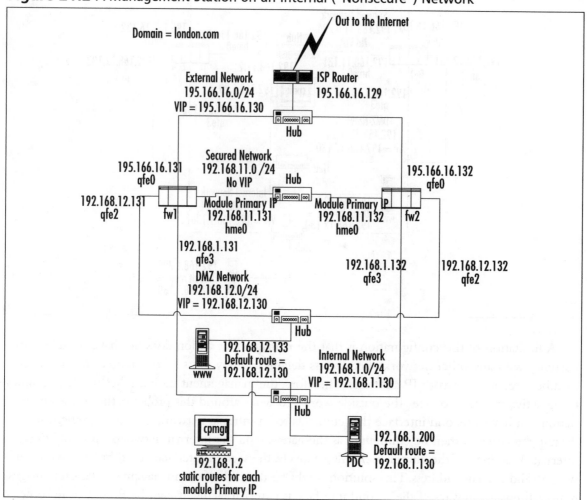

There are some routing factors to consider in using this topology. Some hosts on the internal network will often need to make connections to individual cluster members, including Check Point policy installs and administrative connections such as FTP or SSH. Where these connections are made to the "nearest" IP address, this is no problem. However, if an IP address other than the "nearest" is specified—for example, the external IP address of the member—the packet will probably be routed via the default route (the cluster virtual IP address). There is a good chance that the packet will route through a different member to the one we want to connect to, resulting in asynchronous routing at best and possibly no connection at all. To avoid this situation, static host routes are required on adjacent hosts/routers that ensure that packets destined for each member's unique addresses are routed via that member's nearest unique IP address.

Connecting the Cluster to Your Network : Hubs or Switches?

The nature of clustering—several devices trying to act as one—tends to throw up some unusual network traffic, which invariably upsets some other network devices in one way or another. The most vulnerable devices involved will be any network switches that are connected to cluster interfaces, because by their nature the switch wants to track which devices (with particular MAC addresses) are connected to each of their ports. If we have a number of cluster members, each connected to a different switch port, but each pretending to be the same device, it is no wonder that an unsuspecting switch might struggle. In addition, cluster solutions often use multicast IP and MAC addresses—something else that a switch might need advance warning of.

In summary, most switches can be persuaded to cope with cluster configurations, but some can't. More important, the cluster solution provider is likely to have a list of supported switch hardware—and if your switch is not on that list, you might find yourself in trouble. Always check to find out the supported switches for your chosen configuration.

Hubs, on the other hand, really don't care about any strange protocols that the cluster might be talking, so they make life a lot simpler. The downside is throughput; particularly in a load-sharing configuration, hubs can become a bottleneck. Even so, although switches are probably the best solution, a handful of spare hubs nearby are useful for troubleshooting. Do remember to disable full-duplex settings on network cards before dropping in a hub, though.

FireWall-1 Features, Single Gateways versus Clusters: The Same, But Different

The concept behind the cluster is that it replaces a single gateway but provides resilience and possibly increased capacity. In reality, some FireWall-1 features will behave differently or require different configuration in a cluster environment.

Network Address Translation

When you're configuring NAT, you always need to ensure that packets on a NATed connection are correctly routed to the firewall from adjacent routers. A typical single gateway configuration, with Static NAT performed on an internal server, has the firewall performing proxy ARP for the legal (virtual) IP address, advertising the gateway's own external MAC address. In a cluster environment, it is vital that these packets are routed to the cluster MAC address, not the MAC address of a cluster member. Similarly, if a static host route for the legal IP address is added on adjacent routers (for example, the ISP router), the destination gateway for the route must be the cluster IP address, not a cluster member IP address.

Security Servers

FireWall-1 uses security servers for user authentication and content scanning (in other words, where resources are used in rules). These servers run at the application level and are effectively transparent proxy servers (or mail relays, in the case of SMTP). These applications are not based on stateful inspection, and their state is not synchronized. Security servers can still be used in a clustered solution, but the clustering solution must maintain connection stickiness, and connections will not survive member failure. Whether this limitation is a problem will depend on the applications involved:

- **Relay-to-relay SMTP** Deals with connection failure cleanly, with the sending relay retrying the connection later.

- **Client-to-server SMTP** Shows the user an error if the mail client was in the process of sending a message at the time of failure—but the chances of this are fairly slim.

- **General HTTP Web browsing** Users are accustomed to the odd connection failure on the Internet from time to time, and one more when a cluster member fails should not be an issue.

- **Authenticated HTTP** Users (using user authentication and proxying *to the cluster*) throw up an additional complication. While each individual HTTP connection will stick to its cluster member, the browsing session consists of multiple HTTP connections, and each may stick to a different member. As the authentication takes place at the application level, users will need to authenticate against each member they connect to. Fortunately, Web browsers cache the proxy password that the user supplies, so this occurs transparently—unless a one-time password authentication method is in use (for example, RSA SecurID). The nature of one-time passwords means that a different password is required for each cluster member, and in the case of SecurID, this requires a delay of a minute between each attempt! In a load-sharing solution, this is unworkable.

- **File downloads over FTP (or HTTP)** Failures here are more likely to cause upset, particularly failure of long downloads that were 95-percent complete. A possible solution for FTP downloads is using client authentication (and not configuring a proxy for FTP).

NOTE

If the security server is used as a traditional proxy server or mail relay (in other words, connections are made directly to the gateway), the cluster IP address should be used as the target proxy address or mail relay address.

Remote Authentication Servers

Where the gateways must connect to a remote server to perform authentication—for example, RADIUS servers or RSA ACE servers—the remote server will often verify the request based on the source IP address of the connection. In some cluster environments, implicit address translation will occur so that this connection will appear to have come from the virtual cluster address. It might be that the remote server will be happy to treat the cluster as a single entity, but this will often cause problems—for example, authentication credentials might include one-time passwords that are maintained locally by the cluster members. In this scenario, we need each cluster member to communicate with the remote server as a separate client. In ClusterXL solutions, this can usually be achieved by creating explicit address translation rules that specify that the connections to remote authentication servers are translated to the real member addresses, as defined in the cluster member object. An example of NAT translation rules to avoid this problem is shown in Figure 21.3.

Figure 21.3 NAT Rules That Ensure No NAT for Authenticating Servers

ORIGINAL PACKET			TRANSLATED PACKET			INSTALL ON
SOURCE	DESTINATION	SERVICE	SOURCE	DESTINATION	SERVICE	
fw1	pdc.london.com	RADIUS	fw1	Original	Original	fwcluster
fw2	pdc.london.com	RADIUS	fw2	Original	Original	fwcluster

External VPN Partner Configuration

When participating in VPNs, the cluster appears as a single virtual gateway. External gateways should be configured appropriately, with references to the cluster address only, not member addresses.

Installing FireWall-1 NG FP3

We start the practical side of our clustering discussion by running through installation of the Check Point enforcement modules that will form our cluster. This process is not exceptionally different from installing on an ordinary module, but we highlight the areas of the installation that are relevant to clustering. It's also a good refresher to make sure that you have not forgotten to do something important! We are assuming that we have a healthy management station already running.

Checking the Installation Prerequisites

Follow these steps to check the installation prerequisites:

1. Ensure that your OS meets the requirements documented in the Check Point release notes. On the Windows 2000 platform, make sure that SP2 or SP3 is installed. On Solaris, make sure that the latest cluster patch its installed (for example, solaris8_Recommended.zip—about 80MB). Make sure that the SUNWter package is installed on Solaris. You need this package before you can run UnixInstallScript from the NG FP3 CD or wrapper.

2. On the Nokia platform, download the latest version of IPSO that is compatible with NG FP3.

3. It strongly recommended that you have all your interfaces configured and working on the firewall modules and your management server before you install FireWall-1 NG FP3. Make sure that you have tested that each interface is up and running.

4. Make sure that the member clocks are synchronized; see the sidebar "The Importance of Time."

5. Carefully read the Check Point NG FP3 release notes before proceeding. This is important!

WARNING

It is important to ensure that the correct time, date, and time zone are set on each of the cluster members and on the management module. The time on the cluster members needs to be synchronized as accurately as possible for the purposes of state synchronization and cluster control protocols. The time needs to be in step with the management module as the trust relationships between modules (SIC) is certificate based and time sensitive. The logs seen in SmartView Tracker are time-stamped with the local module's time, so these logs can be misleading if time settings are incorrect.

You should also take into account daylight savings time. If your platform does not automatically adjust for daylight savings (IPSO included), make sure that you set the time for the "unadjusted" time zone. This does mean that your local module time appears "wrong" by an hour during the summer months. SmartView Tracker will adjust the displayed time correctly, based on the time zone of the management station.

Given the importance of time synchronization, it should be automated using standard NTP. Obtain details of how to configure NTP on the platform chosen for your modules from your OS provider. (In the case of IPSO, this is configurable via Voyager.) When you're configuring NTP, it is recommended that only one of the cluster members synchronizes its time with an external source, whereas other members synchronize with that selected "master" member. This is because the priority is to ensure that all members are time synchronized with each other, rather than synchronized with an external source. Finally, don't forget to allow NTP as required in your FireWall-1 security policy.

Installation Options

Before installation, you need to be aware of some of the questions that you will be asked during the install. You need to have made a decision about the following points before starting the installation so that you answer correctly:

1. Each module needs to have VPN-1 SecureClient Policy Server installed if you want to use VPN-1 SecureClient later.

2. FloodGate-1 can be installed on the management and modules if required.

3. During installation of the enforcement module, you are asked if you would like to install a Check Point clustering product (CPHA, CPLS, or state synchronization). Answer **yes** to this option, even if you're installing a third-party clustering solution, because it is required for state synchronization.

Installation Procedure

The installation procedure is slightly different depending on which operating system you are running. With Windows, the installation procedure is a more visual experience, whereas with UNIX, it is a text-based installation. The UNIX installations are reasonably similar in the types of questions you will be asked and at what point you will be asked them.

To begin the installation:

- **Windows** Insert the FP3 CD. The installation wrapper should automatically launch. Alternatively, download the FP3 wrapper package and run **setup.exe**.

- **Solaris/Linux** Use the appropriate commands to mount the CD. Change directory to the mount point, and at the root of the CD, you should find a script called UnixInstallScript. Run this script: **./UnixInstallScript**.

- **IPSO** Use the *newpkg* command to install FP3 from an FTP server, CD, or the local file system.

- **SecurePlatform** Insert the FP3 CD and reboot.

In our example, we assume you are installing FireWall-1 NG FP3 on a Solaris host, but the screens are similar to what you would expect while installing on all platforms. On Windows the same procedure applies but via an installation GUI.

The first screen you will see when running the UNIX wrapper is shown in Figure 21.4.

Figure 21.4 Introduction Screen When Running UnixInstallScript

```
Check Point Software Technologies Ltd.

Welcome to Check Point Next Generation Feature Pack 3 Enterprise Suite!



We recommend that you close all other applications while running

this installation program.


This product is protected by copyright law and all unauthorized

reproduction is forbidden.


V-Evaluation Product U-Purchased Product N-Next H-Help E-Exit
```

Press **U** for purchased product. All this means is that you will be asked for the license during install, but you can install the license later on NG FP3. (It will work for 15 days with a fully featured evaluation license.)

Pressing **U** will display the next stage of installation, which is shown in Figure 21.5.

Figure 21.5 The Purchased Product Screen

```
Check Point Software Technologies Ltd.
Purchased Products.


 Before you continue, please ensure you have obtained a license.


 You can obtain license from your reseller or from
 www.Check Point.com/usercenter




              N-next B-go back C-contact information H-help E-exit
```

Press **N** to go to the next screen, shown in Figure 21.6, which will install the Secure Virtual Network (SVN) foundation. Note that just before the SVN foundation install, the installation scripts checks to make sure that the prerequisite patches are installed.

Figure 21.6 SVN Foundation Installation

```
Check Point Software Technologies Ltd.
Please wait while checking Check Point products installed...


 Installing Check Point SVN Foundation NG FP3...
                        Please wait!
```

Once the SVN installation is complete, the next screen will display (see Figure 21.7).

Figure 21.7 Selecting Products to Install

```
Check Point Software Technologies Ltd.
The following products are included on this CD.
Select product(s)

 1.[*] VPN-1 & FireWall-1.
 2.[*] FloodGate-1.
 3.[ ] SMART Clients.
 4.[*] VPN-1 SecureClient Policy Server.
 5.[*] UserAuthority.
 6.[ ] SmartView Monitor.
 7.[ ] Performance Pack.


    N-Next C-Contact information R-Review of products H-Help E-Exit
```

After the SVN has installed, select the packages that you would like to install (using the numeric keys) as shown in Figure 21.7. Option 1 is mandatory for a firewall module, but all the others are optional. Press **N** for the next screen.

The next screen asks if the installation will be a firewall module, a management station only, a management and module, and so on (see Figure 21.8).

Figure 21.8 Module or Management Installation Screen

```
Check Point Software Technologies Ltd.
Installation type



1.(*) Enforcement Module.
2.( ) Enterprise Management.
3.( ) Enterprise Management and Enforcement Module.
4.( ) Enterprise Log Server.
5.( ) Enforcement Module and Enterprise Log Server.




              N-next B-go Back H-help E-exit
```

Select **Enforcement module** only. The installation script will then display a validation screen to confirm the options you have selected before proceeding with the install. This process is shown in Figure 21.9.

Figure 21.9 Verifying Your Selections So Far

```
Check Point Software Technologies Ltd.
Validation

You have selected the following products for installation:
 * VPN-1 & FireWall-1 Enforcement Module
 * FloodGate-1 Enforcement Module
 * VPN-1 SecureClient Policy Server
 * UserAuthority




              N-next B-go Back H-help E-exit
```

Press **N** for the next screen. This will move you onto the screen shown in Figure 21.10. The installation script will then start installing the products you selected.

Figure 21.10 Products Installing...

```
Check Point Software Technologies Ltd.
Check Point Installation Program


 Installing VPN-1 & FireWall-1 NG FP3...



                            Please wait!
```

Wait while the installation completes (see Figure 21.11).

Figure 21.11 Initial Configuration

```
Welcome to Check Point Configuration Program
====================================================


**************** VPN-1 & FireWall-1 kernel module installation **********

Installing VPN-1 & FireWall-1 kernel module...
Done.



**************** Interface Configuration ****************

Scanning for unknown interfaces...
Would you like to install a Check Point clustering product (CPHA, CPLS or
     State Synchronisation)? (y/n) [n] ? y
```

When installation has completed, you will be prompted to choose whether you would like to install the Check Point Clustering product, as shown in Figure 21.11. Answer **y**. Following this screen, you'll see a number of configuration questions that you should be familiar with from a standard FireWall-1 installation.

You will be prompted to supply a secret key password that will be used to communicate with the firewall management station. This password will be used when you define the cluster object in SmartDashboard. Make a note of your chosen password! The installation will then complete, and you will be asked if you want to reboot. Answer **y**.

Now repeat the installation procedure for the other members of the cluster.

Check Point ClusterXL

We now take a look at the Check Point ClusterXL clustering solution. ClusterXL FP3 can actually be configured to work in three different modes. Each mode provides different functionality and has differences in the underlying clustering mechanisms:

- **HA New mode** New mode gateways maintain online, unique IP addresses in addition to Virtual IP (VIP) addresses that are shared over the cluster. Traffic for the VIP is handled by the master gateway only.

- **HA Legacy mode (as available in previous versions of ClusterXL)** Provides HA by providing standby gateways configured with the same addresses as the master gateway. The standby gateway interfaces remain disabled unless the master fails, and the gateway is promoted to master.

- **Load Sharing mode** As with HA New mode, all gateways have unique IPs and shared VIPs. However, all gateways are "live" and share the traffic load.

We begin by looking at HA New mode.

Configuring ClusterXL in HA New Mode

In this section, we describe how to configure Check Point FireWall-1 ClusterXL in HA New mode. In this example, we set up a two-member HA cluster using ClusterXL. Before we proceed with configuring the cluster, we need to make sure that we are starting from a point at which all the other essential tasks have already been completed.

Prerequisites for Installing ClusterXL in HA New Mode

Before configuring the cluster for HA New mode, you need to complete the following tasks:

- Design your cluster and know all the IP addresses and VIP addresses that your cluster will have. (You need one VIP per connected network other than the sync net. For details, see the "How Does ClusterXL HA New Mode Work?" section of this chapter).

- Plug all your multihomed hosts together using hubs (or switches) and checked IP connectivity between them.

- Make sure that your routers and adjacent hosts on either side of your cluster have default routes set to the adjacent VIP of the cluster (even though the IP address does not exist yet!).

- Make sure that you have added host names that resolve to IP addresses in the hosts files on all the hosts that will be part of the cluster—including the host that will be the management station.

- Your firewall modules should be installed and ready to communicate with your firewall management station (SmartCenter Server).

- Make sure that your management station is operating correctly. You can connect with the SmartDashboard GUI and see the object for your management station.

- If you're working on the Solaris platform, it is strongly recommended that you configure the network interfaces to use unique MAC addresses (they are the same by default). This can be done using the command:

```
eeprom local-mac-address?=true
```

- You would then need to reboot the Solaris host for the change to take effect. Type **ifconfig –a**. You should see that each interface now has a unique MAC address. This step will simplify testing and prevent problems that might occur if you are using switches.

Once this process is completed, you should have something similar to Figure 21.12. In our example, hubs have been used, so obviously no special switch configuration is required.

Figure 21.12 A Simple Topology for ClusterXL in HA New Mode

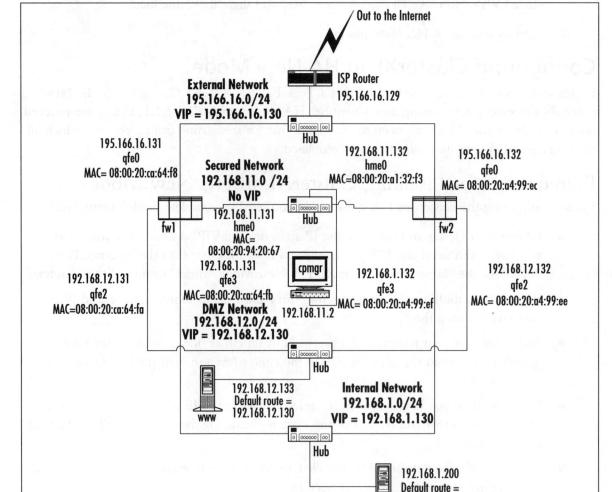

Configuration of ClusterXL HA New Mode

There are a number of ways in which you can create the cluster configuration and end up with the same results. When creating a new cluster in NG FP3, you can decide to create your firewall modules first and then add them to a cluster object, or you can create the cluster object first and define the firewall modules directly in the cluster object. Usually, if you are setting everything from scratch, it is probably quicker to create all your modules and trusts directly in the cluster object.

In this example, we create a cluster object first and define our first module (referred to as fw1 in this example) and make sure we can push a policy just to this new cluster object. We then configure the second module (referred to as fw2) as a stand-alone module, set up the trust, and push a policy to that. The final stage is to add the fw2 module to the cluster and then install the policy.

The following steps will enable us to achieve this goal.

Step 1: Creating a Gateway Cluster Object and Setting Up the Trust

Our first configuration steps aim to build a cluster consisting of just one enforcement module and test it by installing a policy:

1.   In SmartDashboard, create a Gateway Cluster object (**Manage | Network Objects | New | Check Point | Gateway Cluster**. You will see the Gateway Cluster Properties window pop up, as shown in Figure 21.13.

Figure 21.13 Gateway Cluster Properties Screen

2.   Fill in the name of the cluster. In our example, we called it *fwcluster*. We gave the object primary IP as the external VIP address—195.166.16.130. We then checked the boxes for **FireWall-1** (which is mandatory), **VPN-1 Pro** (because we plan to set up VPNs), **ClusterXL** (because we want to use the Check Point cluster solution), and **SecureClient Policy Server** (because we want to use SecureClients).

3.   Click **Cluster Members** on the left side of the screen. This is where we add the enforcement modules into our new cluster (see Figure 21.14).

Figure 21.14 The Cluster Members Screen Before Any Members Have Been Added

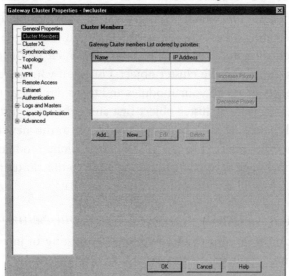

4. Clicking the **New** button will allow you to define a new firewall enforcement module that will be part of the cluster. In the **Name** field, enter the host name of this module. The IP address is the one chosen as the primary IP for that module, and the host name should resolve to this address consistently across all modules. Usually, the primary IP is that of the Internet-facing interface. In our example, the name is fw1 and the address is 195.166.16.131, as shown in Figure 21.15. Note that it would not be possible to use the external IP as the primary address if you were using HA Legacy mode, because the module's only unique address is that of the secured interface.

WARNING

Always use the member host name as the object name and then use the **Get address** button to test that the management station resolves the member host name correctly. If it does not, investigate this problem before proceeding further.

Figure 21.15 Defining the Cluster Member

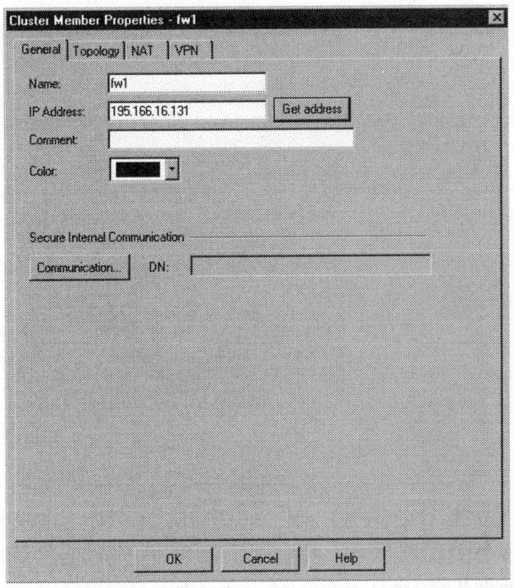

5. You now need to establish communication with the module. Click the **Communication** button. Clicking this button will pop up the window shown in Figure 21.16, in which you need to enter the secret password that you used when you installed this enforcement module. (Make sure that the module is started at this point.) Use this password in the **Activation Key** field and the **Confirm Activation Key** field. At first the trust state is *Uninitialized*. Click the **Initialize** button to set up the trust between the management station and the firewall enforcement module. Wait a short while, and then you should then see the window change to update the trust state to *Trust established*, as shown in Figure 21.17. Once trust has been established, click the **Close** button.

Figure 21.16 Uninitialized Trust between the Management Module and a Cluster Member

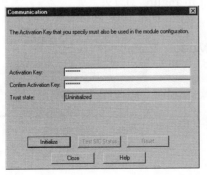

Figure 21.17 Trust Established between the Management Module and a }
Cluster Member

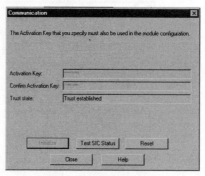

> **NOTE**
>
> It's a good idea to click the **Test SIC Status** button to ensure that the trust is working. When you click this button, you should get a pop-up window that reads, "SIC Status for fw1: Communicating." If you do not, you have a problem with the management station communicating with the firewall enforcement module and this situation will need to be rectified. Check routing and any intermediate firewall policies. If you manage intermediate firewalls from this management station, you should save the new cluster object without configuring communication, and then push a policy to those firewalls.

6. Click the **Topology** tab of the cluster, and click **Get topology**. This step should get the topology of your module, including IP addresses, netmasks, and IP addresses behind interfaces, where appropriate; an example is shown in Figure 21.18. Click the **Accept** button once you are happy with the topology obtained. Now select the interface that you are going to use as your *sync interface*—referred to as the Secured Network in the Check Point manuals. In our example, our sync network is on 192.168.11.131, on interface hme0. Double-click this interface. You will be presented with a new pop-up window, as shown in Figure 21.19.

Figure 21.18 Module Topology

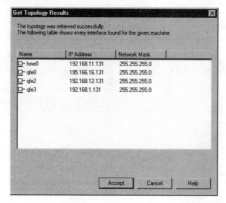

Figure 21.19 Defining the Secured Interface on One Member of the Cluster

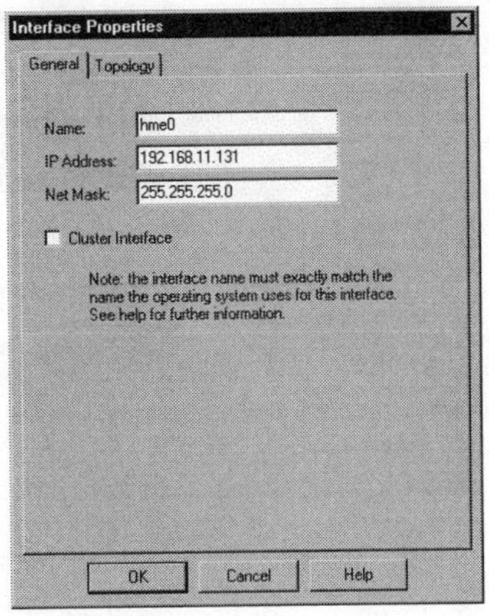

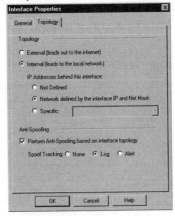

In the pop-up window, make sure that you uncheck the **Cluster Interface** check box so that the firewall module knows that this network will not have a VIP address. If you don't uncheck this box, you will receive a warning later in the configuration.

Click the **Topology** tab of this window. This allows you to define antispoofing for this interface. Select **Network Defined by the interface and netmask** for this example (see Figure 21.20).

Figure 21.20 Antispoofing Properties of the Secure Interface of a Module

Click **OK** when finished. You should now be on the Topology tab of the Cluster Members Properties window. Don't worry about the VPN and NAT details for now. Click **OK** again, and you should be looking at the Cluster Members screen (see Figure 21.21). You should see that the first cluster member has been defined.

At this stage, you could add further cluster members using the **New** button, but we will use the **Add** button later to add an existing firewall enforcement module to the cluster.

Figure 21.21 Cluster Members Screen After First Member Has Been Defined

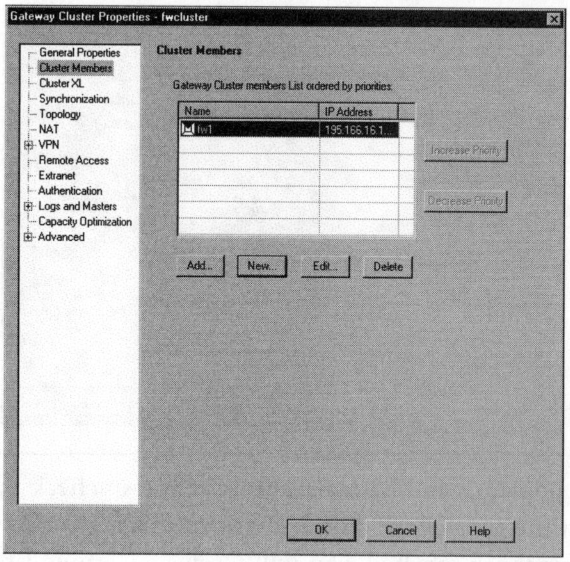

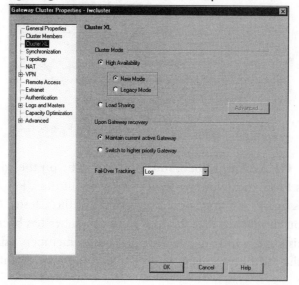

7. Click **ClusterXL** on the left side of the screen. This screen shows you the mode that ClusterXL will work in (see Figure 21.22). In this example, the defaults are High Availability in New mode, which we have selected. We have also left the "Upon Gateway recovery" setting at **Maintain current active gateway**. This means that when a member in the cluster fails and then the member returns, all the traffic will still go through the second firewall member. The effect of this choice is that failback is a manual process.

Figure 21.22 Configuring the ClusterXL Mode of Operation

8. Now click the **Synchronization** tree item. This screen, as shown in Figure 21.23, allows you to define the sync network. The cluster members should have interfaces on this network that are not cluster interfaces (defined in the cluster member interfaces details). It is possible to define multiple sync networks here in order to provide resilience. In our example, we define a sync network 192.168.11.0, subnet mask 255.255.255.0. To do so, click the **Add** button. A pop-up window will appear (see Figure 21.24). Enter the network name (of your choice), network address, and subnet mask. Click **OK** when you're done. Once this process is completed, you should see something similar to Figure 21.25.

WARNING

State synchronization must be used if connection resilience is required (in other words, connections are maintained during a cluster failover).

Figure 21.23 Defining the State Synchronization Network

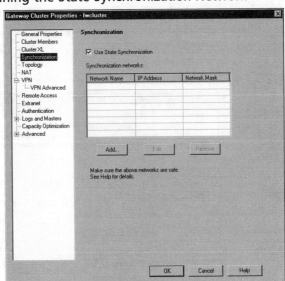

Figure 21.24 The State Synchronization Window

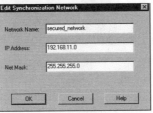

Figure 21.25 Our Completed Synchronization Network Definition

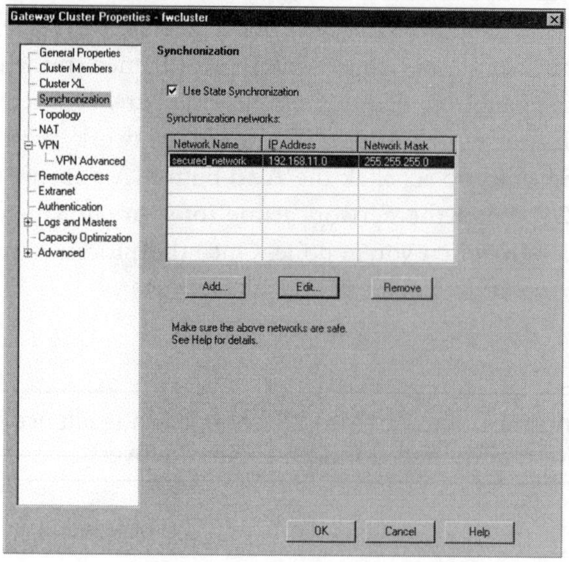

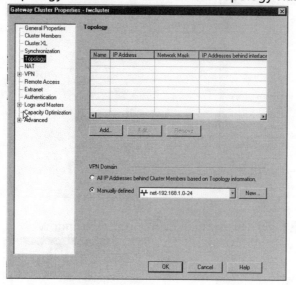

9. We now need to define the cluster's network topology. This is where you define the cluster's VIP addresses. Click the **Topology** item on the left side of the screen (see Figure 21.26). Click the **Add** button. A pop-up window (see Figure 21.27) will appear to allow you to create a VIP address and provide it with a netmask.

Figure 21.26 The Topology Screen of Cluster Before Topology Has Been Defined

Figure 21.27 Cluster Topology Definition: Defining the External Virtual IP Address

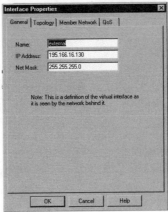

10. Next, click the **Topology** tab of the **Interface Properties** window (see Figure 21.28). Select this as the external interface because this is the Internet-facing VIP address on our cluster and we need to make sure that antispoofing is enabled.

Figure 21.28 Topology of Cluster: External Interface Definition of the Cluster

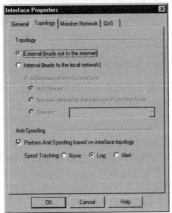

11. Select the **Member Network** tab of the **Interface Properties** window (see Figure 21.29). This tab determines which interfaces the VIP address will function on. By default, it picks up the network and subnet mask of any interfaces you have already defined in the same subnet. However, the VIP address and the physical interfaces that the VIP address will "listen" on do not have to be the same subnet. In our example, the VIP address is in the same subnet as our external interfaces.

Figure 21.29 The Member Network Tab of the Cluster's Interface Properties

12. Click **OK** when you have defined the network. Doing so brings you back to the screen in Figure 21.26, but this time, you will have the external VIP address of the cluster defined. You need to repeat steps 9–11 for all the interfaces of the cluster. In our example:

- DMZ, Virtual IP = 192.168.12.130, internal, network defined by this IP address and subnet, member network = 192.168.12.0, subnet = 255.255.255.0.

- Internal, Virtual IP = 192.168.1.130 , internal, network defined by this IP address and subnet, member network = 192.168.1.0, subnet = 255.255.255.0.

When this process is completed, the cluster topology screen should look like Figure 21.30.

Figure 21.30 The Completed ClusterXL Topology Definition

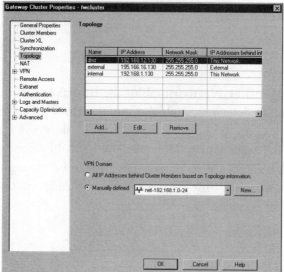

13. This completes the definition of the cluster module for just one cluster member. Click **OK** to complete the creation of the Cluster Gateway object. When you click OK, you will see the message shown in Figure 21.31. An IKE certificate is being created for the cluster object itself. Note that this would replace any IKE certificates that existed for any enforcement modules if we had added them to the cluster.

Figure 21.31 The IKE Certificate Message Displayed When You Click OK

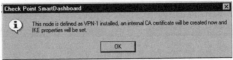

Step 2: Installing a Simple Security Policy to the New Cluster

Create a simple policy—perhaps even "Any source, any destination, any service, accept, log." At this point, we won't try any NAT or VPNs or otherwise run before walking. As we installed Policy Server on the module, we will also create a simple "open" desktop security policy. These policies are clearly insecure; don't connect the cluster to untrusted networks yet, but do keep all its interfaces "up." The idea here is to create a very simple rule base for testing the cluster:

1. Once the policies are ready, click the **Policy | Install** menu, as shown in Figure 21.32. The new cluster object should appear in the possible targets. Select the cluster object (only) and click **OK**. The FireWall-1 SmartCenter Server will then proceed to compile and install the policy to each cluster member (of which there is only one defined at present!).

Figure 21.32 Policy Install to the Cluster: Single Member Only

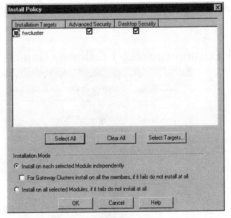

2. Hopefully the policy will install successfully. If it does not, possible causes could be a configuration error in the cluster object (although this is usually indicated at the time of configuration) or connectivity to the cluster. Assuming all went well, you now have configured a one-member ClusterXL HA New mode cluster. At this point, it is a good idea to check the cluster's health. You can start the SmartView Status client, and you should

be able to see the status, as shown in Figure 21.33. Check that the cluster member is active and that all the components in the cluster object show a green tick, which indicates that they are functioning correctly. You might see a warning against ClusterXL; possible causes are that an interface is down or HA is not enabled on the cluster member. In addition, take note of the working mode stated in the ClusterXL Details window. It should say *High availability*.

Figure 21.33 SmartView Status Showing Cluster with Single Member

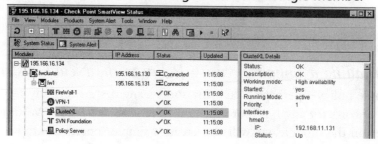

Step 3: Adding a Second Enforcement Module to the Cluster

We are now in a position where a Gateway Cluster object has been defined and has one member, and all appears to be working fine.

In our example, let's add an existing enforcement module to the cluster. If there were no existing module, we would add a new enforcement module to the cluster, following the same steps we used to add the first member. We will then push a policy to our newly expanded cluster.

Our existing enforcement module object is shown in Figure 21.34. Before proceeding, it is important to be happy that this module is working fine as a stand-alone gateway. Ensure that the Check Point products installed on this gateway (in reality and on the object!) match those of the new cluster object.

Figure 21.34 Existing FireWall-1 Gateway Object

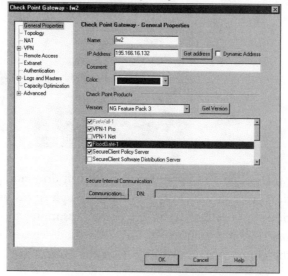

1. To start the process of adding the existing gateway into our cluster, edit the **Gateway Cluster** object. Click **Cluster Members** in the left side menu. Click the **Add** button to add an existing firewall module to the cluster. Select our existing **fw2** gateway module and click **OK** (see Figure 21.35).

Figure 21.35 Adding a Firewall Gateway to a Cluster Object

> **WARNING**
>
> You might not see an existing gateway object when you attempt to add a gateway into the cluster. This could be due to the gateway being a member of a VPN community. The procedure of adding the gateway to a cluster removes the gateway VPN configuration, so this is not allowed while the gateway is a community member. You must remove the gateway from the community using VPN Manager before adding the gateway to the cluster.

2. When you select OK, you will receive the warning shown in Figure 21.36. Click **Yes** to proceed.

Figure 21.36 fw2 Adding to Cluster Warning Message

> **WARNING**
>
> Adding the gateway to the cluster will remove the gateway VPN configuration. Restoring the VPNs will require configuration of the cluster VPN settings, but it could also require reconfiguration at the remote VPN end points. They will need to refer to your VPN gateway using the new VIP address of the cluster, and if the VPN is certificate based, the new IKE certificate must be distributed.

3. We need to identify which of this member's interfaces is on the secured network. Edit the member and click the **Topology** tab. Double-click the interface that is going to be

on your secured network (in this example, hme0, which is on 192.168.11.132). Make sure you uncheck the **Cluster Interface** check box (see Figure 21.37).

Figure 21.37 Selecting the Interface That Will Be the Secured Network

4. Your Cluster Members screen should now have two modules as members (fw1 and fw2), as shown in Figure 21.38. Note that if you click one, you can then promote or demote its priority in the cluster. This determines which one will be online initially.

Figure 21.38 A Cluster Gateway Showing Two Cluster Members

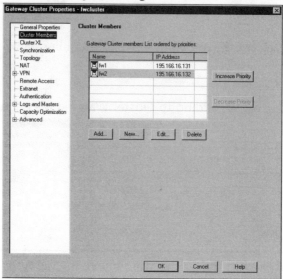

5. Click **OK**. You can now install the test policy to the cluster gateway module, which now has two members.

WARNING

It is recommended that you reboot the module that you have just added. After pushing a policy to a stand-alone module that requires that it becomes a cluster member, the ClusterXL module might not fully configure itself immediately. You could find that the active online member complains about the status of this new inactive member of the cluster (use the *cphaprob state* command on the online member or the SmartView Status GUI). Rebooting the offline member should remedy this situation.

NOTE

A new installation of an NG FP3 module inherits a full license for a 15-day trial period. It could well be that we have gotten this far in installation and configuration without actually adding a valid purchased license. Now is a good time to use the SmartUpdate management client to attach your purchased licenses to the cluster members, rather than forget and get a nasty surprise in 15 days.

Testing ClusterXL in HA New Mode

Once you have ClusterXL in HA New mode up and running, you will want to test it to ensure that it is functioning properly. There are many ways in which you can do this; we now look at three simple tests that you can perform.

Test 1: Pinging the Virtual IP Address of Each Interface

With ClusterXL in HA New mode, you should be able to ping the VIP address of each network from an adjacent host—providing that your security policy allows such an action. This is a useful test for a number of reasons:

- It tests that the VIP address is up and running.
- It identifies which of the members is replying to your ping. Look at the MAC address that you receive in your local workstation ARP cache. To view the ARP cache, use the command *arp −a*.

In our example (based on Figure 21.12), we log on to the host on IP 192.168.1.200 (PDC) and ping the VIP of 192.168.1.130. If host fw1 is active (therefore fw2 is on standby), we would expect to see the MAC address of 08:00:20:ca:64:fb in the ARP cache of 192.168.1.200. The reason why we know that fw1 is active is that the MAC address 08:00:20:ca:64:fb is the internal interface (qfe3) MAC address for fw1. If there was a failover to fw2, we would see the MAC address of the internal interface of member fw2 (08:00:20:a4:99:ef).

Test 2: Using SmartView Status to Examine the Status of the Cluster Members

When using ClusterXL, we use the SmartView Status GUI to monitor what each member in our cluster is doing. We are also able to stop and start the ClusterXL module on a member from this GUI. This tool can be used to manually fail over from the active member, perhaps before performing some maintenance. For example, in Figure 21.39, we can see that member fw2 is active. If we right-click fw2 and select **Stop Member**, we will force fw1 to switch to active. This assumes that fw1—or another cluster member—is available. Be sure to check this status before stopping the current active member!

Figure 21.39 SmartView Status GUI Showing ClusterXL HA New Mode with Member fw2 Active

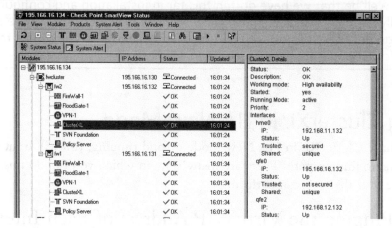

Take note of the Running Mode field, which states whether the member is active.

> **NOTE**
>
> Note that if a member has been disabled using "Stop member," the ClusterXL Details pane might still show the member as active. This is because we have lost contact with the ClusterXL module on that member, and the GUI is still displaying the last known status. It is worth checking the last updated time for the ClusterXL status and forcing an update (right-click **ClusterXL** and select **Update**).

A stopped member can be revived by right-clicking the member name and selecting **Start Member**. Note that it will stay in Standby mode irrespective of its priority if **Maintain Current Active gateway** is set in the cluster object.

Test 3: FTP Session Through the Cluster When an Interface Fails

As with all cluster solutions, the best tests are those simulating real-world failure. Physically damaging cluster members is probably the most challenging test but probably not a popular option, either. A more acceptable test is disconnecting a network cable from the current master member during a file download through the cluster.

In our example, we initiate a command-line FTP session from the internal host on 192.168.1.200 to 192.168.12.133 (refer to Figure 21.12). The default gateway of host 192.168.1.200 will be the cluster VIP address for that subnet (192.168.1.130). The default gateway for 192.168.12.133 will be VIP 192.168.12.130.

We will use the *ftp hash* command in order to display the blocks downloaded so we can see the download's progress. A large file should be chosen that will take at least a minute to download; that gives us time to test failover.

If you pull out the external interface of the active member (for example, if member fw1 were active, removing the Ethernet cable from qfe0 would cause a fail condition), you should see member fw2 become active and the FTP session should continue, probably after a pause of a few seconds. This particular test is useful because it tests the following things:

- The hosts communicating have the correct default gateway.

- The hubs and switches are working correctly in an HA environment.

- The firewall members are failing over correctly.

- The hosts on the local subnet respond to the failover gratuitous arp.

- The firewall members' state tables are fully synchronized.

Command-Line Diagnostics on ClusterXL

Let's take a look at some useful command-line tools that can be used to monitor ClusterXL.

fw hastat

The *fw hastat* command can be used to check the basic status of each cluster member locally or remotely. The *fw hastat* command has the following syntax:

```
fw hastat <hostname / or IP address>
```

A typical response if this command is run on a local firewall cluster member module is:

HOST	NUMBER	HIGH AVAILABILITY STATE	MACHINE STATUS
localhost1	1	active	OK

cphaprob

The *cphaprob* command is probably the most versatile command that can be used to monitor and manipulate ClusterXL. Here we cover just a few of the common syntaxes of this command, but it can do a lot more than merely show information about the cluster. This command can be used in order to integrate tailored status checking—maybe checking hardware health of a member.

The command can be used on either of the cluster members (not on the firewall management module). Running *cphaprob state* on either of the firewall cluster members should tell you the status of each of the cluster members from the point of view of the cluster member you are running the command on. Here is an example output:

```
Working mode: Active up (unique IPs)


Number          Unique Address          State


1               192.168.11.132          active
2 (local)           none*               standby
```

> **NOTE**
>
> If you see *none* in the unique address for one of the cluster members, you need to reboot the module, and then run the *cphaprob state* command again. It can also mean that the member is not correctly configured in the SmartDashboard GUI and that no secured interface exists on the member.

You can also use this command with different arguments to provide details of interfaces. The syntax for examining the interfaces on the local member is *cphaprob -a if.* The command will tell you the status of each interface and the virtual cluster IP addresses.

In this example, the local cluster member is in Standby mode:

```
Required interfaces: 3
Required secured interfaces: 1


hme0        UP                          (secured, unique)
qfe0        DOWN (2505.8 secs)          (non secured, unique)
qfe2        UP                          (non secured, unique)
qfe3        UP                          (non secured, unique)


Virtual cluster interfaces: 3


qfe0            195.166.16.130
qfe2            192.168.12.130
qfe3            192.168.1.130
```

In this example, we can see that the interface qfe0 is down—probably a cable or interface problem. Looking at the information further down, we see that qfe0 is associated with the VIP address of 195.166.16.130, the external interface, so that is where we should start looking for network problems. Until this problem is resolved, we expect this member to stay in Standby mode; hopefully another member in the cluster will be active.

cpstat ha

The *cpstat ha* command gives detailed status details from the local member—similar information to that displayed by the SmartView Status GUI. Run without arguments, the output to this command is something like:

```
Product name: High Availability
Version:      NG Feature Pack 3
Status:       OK
HA installed: 1
Working mode: High availability
HA started:   yes
```

More usefully, you can use the syntax *cpstat –f all ha* to get this:

```
Product name:        High Availability
Major version:       5
Minor version:       0
Service pack:        3
Version string:      NG Feature Pack 3
Status code:         0
Status short:        OK
Status long:         OK
HA installed:        1
Working mode:        High availability
HA protocol version: 2
HA started:          yes
HA state:            active
HA identifier:       1


Interface table
--------------------------------------------------
|Name|IP          |Status|Verified|Trusted|Shared|
--------------------------------------------------
|hme0|192.168.11.131|Up   |      0|      1|     0|
|qfe0|195.166.16.131|Up   |    500|      0|     0|
|qfe2|192.168.12.131|Up   |      0|      0|     0|
|qfe3| 192.168.1.131|Up   |      0|      0|     0|
--------------------------------------------------
```

```
Problem Notification table

---------------------------------------------------
|Name              |Status|Priority|Verified|Descr|
---------------------------------------------------
|Synchronization|OK    |      0|     198|    |
|Filter         |OK    |      0|     188|    |
|cphad          |OK    |      0|      0|    |
|fwd            |OK    |      0|      0|    |
```

How Does ClusterXL HA New Mode Work?

In HA New mode, on each member of the cluster, each interface that will share a VIP address will keep its existing MAC address. No additional shared MAC addresses are used. When a client that is on the nonsecured network ARPs for the virtual IP (which will be the client's default gateway IP address), the cluster member that is active will reply with its MAC address and so will receive the through routed traffic.

Note that a client should still be able to connect to any of the valid IP addresses of the cluster on the same local subnet, regardless of which member is active (assuming that the interface is not down, the OS hasn't crashed, or the local firewall policy does not prevent it).

Because all members are "live" but only one handles traffic, HA New mode could be seen as load sharing but with 100 percent of the traffic going through one member only and all other members on standby having 0 percent of the traffic. This is opposed to traditional HA solutions in which the standby members are "offline" and unreachable.

If we consider the diagram in Figure 21.40, we can see that member fw1 is active and fw2 is in Standby mode.

Figure 21.40 Active Traffic Routing Through the Active Cluster Member

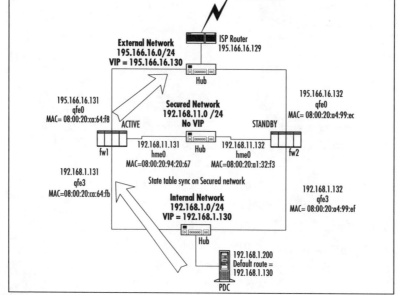

All network traffic should be routed through firewall member fw1—but only if its default gateway is set to the VIP address of 192.168.1.130.

If we take an example in which host 192.168.1.200 initiates a connection to a host out on the Internet and we are using Hide NAT behind the external cluster IP of 195.166.16.130, it will first ARP for the default gateway IP address. Host fw1 should respond because it is the active member in the cluster, with its internal interface MAC address of 08:00:20:ca:64:fb. This will be put in the ARP cache table of host 192.168.1.200, and a TCP connection—source IP 192.168.1.200, destination IP = 216.238.8.44, destination MAC 08:00:20:ca:64:fb—will originate from the host.

It is normal to use Hide NAT when internal hosts access the Internet, and this also makes it easy for replies to get back to your site. When the packet from host 192.168.1.200 leaves host fw1, the source IP will be address translated to 195.166.16.130 (and the source port will also change). The packet will then be routed out toward the ISP router (based on the default gateway of member fw1).

The reply packet will come back through the ISP router, which will ARP for a MAC address for 195.166.16.130. The fw-1 member is active and will respond with its external interface MAC of 08:00:20:ca:64:f8. The ISP router adds this into its ARP cache and sends the reply packet for the session back to 195.166.16.130, MAC address 08:00:20:ca:64:f8.

Member fw-1 then uses its stateful inspection to address translate the existing Hide NAT session so that the destination IP is changed from 195.166.16.130 to 192.168.1.200. The reply is then sent from interface qfe3 on fw1, source MAC address 08:00:20:ca:64:fb, to the host on 192.168.1.200.

ClusterXL HA New Mode Failover

On failover from the active cluster member to the standby member, adjacent routers and hosts still maintain the MAC address for the failed member in their ARP caches. Packets sent at this point arrive at the failed host and probably go no further. The cluster member that has just come active resolves this problem by issuing a "gratuitous ARP." The ARP is broadcast on the local subnet of all interfaces that have a VIP and will have the MAC address for the local interface of the new active member in the cluster. This should mean that adjacent routers will learn the new MAC addresses for the VIP addresses.

NOTE

Under some circumstances in NG FP3, there is a problem where the cluster member that comes online does not always issue a gratuitous ARP. This should be resolved in hotfix releases. It is a good idea to obtain and apply the latest released hotfix.

Let's now look in detail at what happens if the active member fails. If we consider the diagram in Figure 21.40, we can see that traffic is routing through the active member, and Hide NAT is being done to hide the internal host of 192.168.1.200 behind the cluster IP address of 195.166.16.130. Should an interface fail (as shown in Figure 21.41, for example), all traffic from

192.168.1.200 will not be able to get through to the qfe3 interface on member fw1, and traffic that is coming back will not get back to 192.168.1.200 because the interface is down.

Figure 21.41 Interface Failure on Active Member

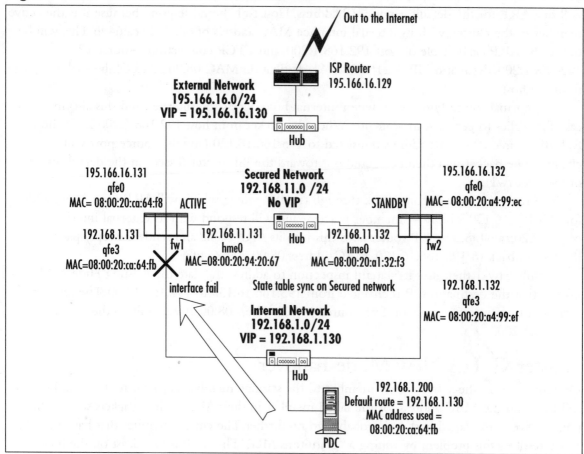

At this point, fw2 will notice that fw1 is not responding on the qfe3 interface and will take note of this situation. If the interface stays down for a period of time, fw2 will start running its pre-online tests. These pre-online tests allow fw2 to determine if it is healthy enough to take over from host fw1. (We discuss these tests in more detail in the "Nokia Failover Conditions" section of this chapter.) Once fw2 has determined that it is able to take over from fw1, it will issue a gratuitous ARP on all its interfaces that have a VIP address (see Figure 21.42).

This will be cached by all devices on the local subnet of the interfaces of the firewall cluster, and they will update their ARP tables appropriately. This means that host 192.168.1.200 will now have a MAC address of 08:00:20:a4:99:ef in its ARP cache for IP address 192.168.1.130, so current through connections—perhaps an FTP session—should be able to continue.

On the external interface of the cluster, the ISP router would also have received a gratuitous ARP, updating its ARP table for 195.166.16.130 with MAC address 08:00:20:a4:99:ec—the external MAC address of qfe0 of fw2. At this point, fw1 will have considered itself offline in the SmartView Status GUI, stating that interface qfe3 is down.

Figure 21.42 Gratuitous ARP by fw2 to Take Over from fw1 on Failure

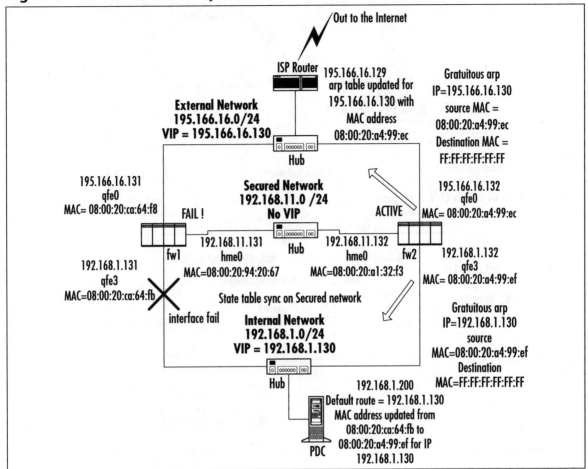

Once the FTP session recovers (which will only be the case if the gratuitous ARP is issued by fw2 and if state table sync is enabled between member fw1 and fw2), all traffic will continue to go through member fw2, as shown in Figure 21.43.

Should member fw1 recover, the cluster can be configured to either fail back to fw1 (which will have the highest priority) or continue working through fw2, which could have a lower priority. This can be configured in the **Cluster Gateway Object | Cluster XL Screen** (see Figure 21.22).

Figure 21.43 ClusterXL in HA New Mode, with Maintain Current Active Gateway Set After

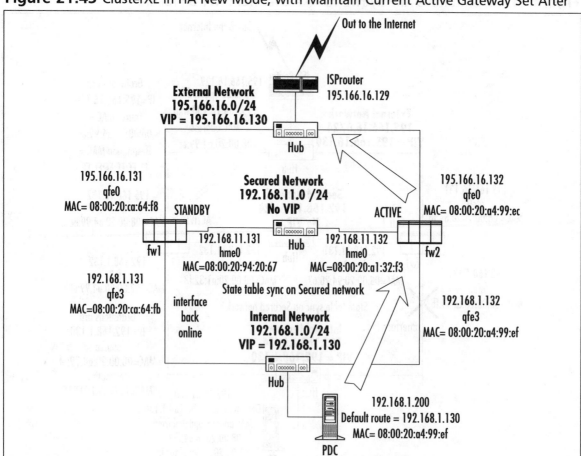

ClusterXL Failover Conditions

There are a number of conditions in which failover from one member to another will occur:

- An interface or cable fails.

- Security policy is uninstalled.

- The machine crashes.

- Any process or device that specified with the *cphaprob* command (such as the *fwd* process) fails.

These conditions can be listed using the command *cphaprob list*.

But how does fw2 know to take over from fw1 when one of these conditions is met? How does a member in the cluster know that it can take over? These questions are answered when you analyze the CPHA protocol packets that each member sends to other members on each interface that has a VIP address.

When a member of a cluster comes online, it issues an IGMP packet in order to advertise its membership of a multicast group. Connected switches with IGMP snooping ability can use this feature when deciding how to forward multicast traffic.

Status updates are sent from each member at regular intervals. Analysis shows the following properties of the update traffic for NG FP3, HA New mode:

- At the data link layer (Layer 2 of the OSI model), the originating MAC address is always *00:00:00:00:fe:<member number>*, where member 1 in the cluster would be 00 and member 2 in the cluster would be 01—*member number - 1* is the last digit in the source MAC address.

- The destination MAC address is the multicast MAC for that VIP. For example, 01:00:5e:26:10:82 is the destination MAC seen on the external interface of our example network. The last two digits represent the VIP address's last two octets (16.130 where the entire VIP is 195.166.16.130).

- At Layer 3, we see that the source IP is always 0.0.0.0 and the destination IP is the network address (195.166.16.0 in our example).

- Layer 4 shows that the transport is UDP with the source and destination port of 8116. The payload of the UDP packet is CPHA, which contains the following information:

  - Source machine ID is the same as last octet in the source MAC address of the packet.

  - Protocol version is 530 for NG FP3.

The rest of the UDP payload determines whether the member is sending out its status as a member on the cluster (there are other types). This includes each member's status as perceived by the member originating the packet and the last time it heard from the other members. This mechanism allows all members of the cluster to share their system status information.

WARNING

The multicast groups selected for intercluster communications are based on the last three octets of the VIP address. With this in mind, avoid using VIPs that end in the same three octets as other VIPs in the same broadcast domain.

> **NOTE**
>
> CPHA protocol in NG FP2 (HA Legacy mode) is different from NG FP3 HA New mode in a number of ways. For one, the destination MAC address is a broadcast, not a multicast.

Once an interface stops sending out status updates to the other members of the cluster, actions will start to be taken so that the highest-priority member that is active can then take over. When a member stops seeing status updates from the other member (or all the other members), it starts running a series of tests to determine the problem.

It will see if it can reach any other hosts that are valid on its subnet by ARPing for a selected range of IP addresses. A response suggests its own networking is good; no response could mean that it is disconnected from the network itself. It will attempt to ping the cluster IP address to see if it can receive any response from an active member; it will also attempt to ping the physical real IP of the other cluster member members. (For example, member 195.166.16.132 would ping 195.166.16.131 to see if it gets a response.) The member will also ping its default gateway.

Once these tests have completed, the member will make a decision as to whether it might be eligible for being a master and announces that it is active—and that the other member is dead—via the CPHA protocol.

The final step is that the member then issues a gratuitous ARP to the local subnets for the VIP (195.166.16.130 on qfe0 and 192.168.1.130 on qfe3 in our example)—and hopefully traffic resumes normally through this new active member.

> **NOTE**
>
> Now that you know that the firewall member that is in standby will issue ICMP echo requests to the default gateway—and other hosts on the local subnet as well as to the cluster IP and the other members in the cluster—it is a good idea to make sure that there are no access control lists (ACLs) on neighboring equipment on the same subnet that would block ICMP. The FireWall-1 policy on the cluster members themselves will not be a problem, because this CPHA module traffic bypasses the firewall filtering.

In Figure 21.44, we can see that the CPHA packet originated from the primary member. We can deduce this because the last octet in the MAC address source is 00. This is also confirmed in the CPHA protocol at a higher level, where the packet identifies the Source Machine ID as 0.

Figure 21.44 Breakdown of a CPHA Packet from Our Example

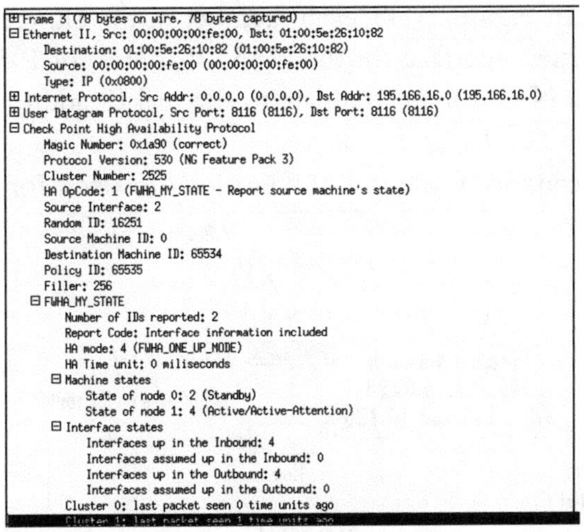

```
Frame 3 (78 bytes on wire, 78 bytes captured)
Ethernet II, Src: 00:00:00:00:fe:00, Dst: 01:00:5e:26:10:82
    Destination: 01:00:5e:26:10:82 (01:00:5e:26:10:82)
    Source: 00:00:00:00:fe:00 (00:00:00:00:fe:00)
    Type: IP (0x0800)
Internet Protocol, Src Addr: 0.0.0.0 (0.0.0.0), Dst Addr: 195.166.16.0 (195.166.16.0)
User Datagram Protocol, Src Port: 8116 (8116), Dst Port: 8116 (8116)
Check Point High Availability Protocol
    Magic Number: 0x1a90 (correct)
    Protocol Version: 530 (NG Feature Pack 3)
    Cluster Number: 2525
    HA OpCode: 1 (FWHA_MY_STATE - Report source machine's state)
    Source Interface: 2
    Random ID: 16251
    Source Machine ID: 0
    Destination Machine ID: 65534
    Policy ID: 65535
    Filler: 256
    FWHA_MY_STATE
        Number of IDs reported: 2
        Report Code: Interface information included
        HA mode: 4 (FWHA_ONE_UP_MODE)
        HA Time unit: 0 miliseconds
        Machine states
            State of node 0: 2 (Standby)
            State of node 1: 4 (Active/Active-Attention)
        Interface states
            Interfaces up in the Inbound: 4
            Interfaces assumed up in the Inbound: 0
            Interfaces up in the Outbound: 4
            Interfaces assumed up in the Outbound: 0
        Cluster 0: last packet seen 0 time units ago
        Cluster 1: last packet seen 1 time units ago
```

Other areas to take note of are the source and destination MAC addresses, the IP addresses, and the port numbers used by the CPHA protocol.

The "Machine states" field shows what member 0 in the cluster thinks the status of the other members in the cluster is. Of course, member 0 could be incorrect.

Special Considerations for ClusterXL in HA New Mode

As with all clustering solutions, ClusterXL requires that you must always take into account some special considerations. These are usually based on the way that the clustering solution functions and can cause limitations when attempting to use certain functions of the firewall.

Network Address Translation

When using NAT on a cluster, you have to consider carefully how you are address translating and how it will be affected by the way the cluster works—especially when failover to another member occurs.

In ClusterXL in HA New mode, the original MAC addresses of the physical interfaces are used. When using static destination NAT, this will cause a problem if you have *manual* proxy ARP entries for the NAT addresses. This causes a problem because each member in the HA cluster would be advertising its own physical MAC address, and all may respond when an adjacent router ARPs for the NAT address. There is no control over which of the members will receive traffic for the NAT address.

WARNING

Manual proxy ARP entries in the ARP table of a cluster member's operating system will not work with HA New mode.

In Figure 21.45, we can see the types of problems that manually added static ARP entries for Manual NAT might cause. In Figure 21.45, each member in the cluster is proxy ARPing its own local MAC address for the qfe0 interface for the NAT IP address of 195.166.16.133, which the firewall modules will have a NAT rule to translate to the real IP address of 192.168.12.133.

Figure 21.45 Possible Scenario If Manual ARP Entries Are Used for NAT

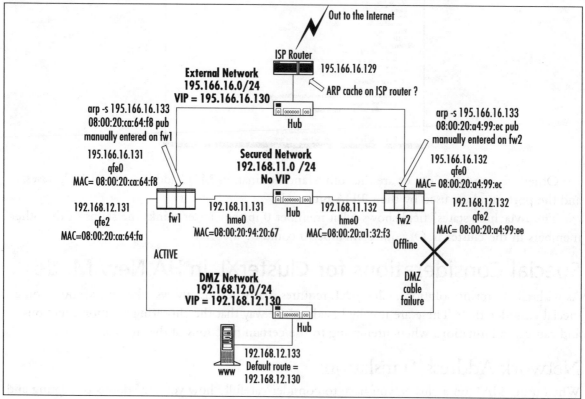

This will cause undesirable effects in an HA environment. You have no easy way of determining which MAC address the ISP router will have cached for the IP address 195.166.16.133. If you are unlucky, it could be the member that is in Standby mode.

In this scenario, and if the member in standby is "fit" and there are no faults, the packet will travel through the member as normal (even though it is on standby) and reach the internal host 192.168.12.133. However, because the default gateway of host 192.168.12.133 is the DMZ VIP of 192.168.12.130, the www host will have the MAC address of qfe2 of member fw1 in its ARP cache, so the reply packet would travel via member fw1. This means that you have asymmetric routing occurring.

If we take this scenario one step further, where qfe2 fails (as shown in Figure 21.45), the NATed packet would not get through at all. What are the alternatives to manual ARP entries?

With Manual NAT Rules

If you want to keep using Manual NAT rules, you only have one option, which is to enter routes on the adjacent router(s). This would be a static host route entry forcing the NAT IP address to forward to the cluster VIP. For example, in our ClusterXL example, if you had a manual static destination NAT rule to NAT 195.166.16.133 to 192.168.12.133, you would add a route on the ISP router that looks something like:

```
195.166.16.133 , netmask 255.255.255.255 gateway 195.166.16.130
```

This states that to get to IP address 195.166.16.133 as a host route, the next hop is the VIP address of the cluster (see Figure 21.46).

Figure 21.46 Using Static Routes on the ISP Router for NATed IP Addresses

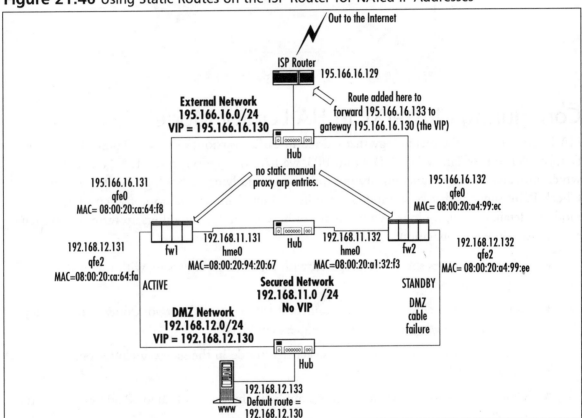

With Automatic NAT Rules

If you are using Automatic NAT, you have some options. You can still use static routes on the ISP router to get the packets onto the active member of the cluster, as described in the Manual NAT section, but you also have another useful alternative.

If you are using Automatic NAT and you have the Automatic ARP Configuration set in the SmartDashboard menu **Policy | Global Properties | NAT − Network Address Translation | Automatic Rules** section (see Figure 21.47), a firewall member switching to Active mode will issue a gratuitous ARP for all the Automatic NAT objects as well as the cluster VIP.

Figure 21.47 Automatic NAT Settings for Cluster Member to Issue a Gratuitous ARP on

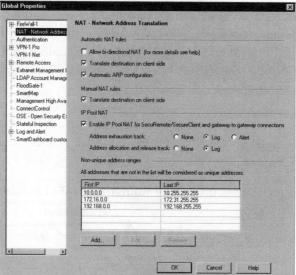

Configuring ClusterXL in HA Legacy Mode

HA Legacy mode is the technology that existed in earlier versions of Check Point NG (and, in fact, late versions of FireWall-1 4.1). From FP3, we have the option to use HA New mode, which provides the same functionality but improved underlying technology. For this reason, Check Point suggests that New mode is used in FP3 installations. We do not discuss Legacy mode in detail; instead, we look at a summary of how Legacy mode differs, in terms of configuration procedure and operation:

- Cluster members should be prepared with identical IP addresses, with the exception of the secured network.

- When adding a cluster member, connect it to the secured network only until a policy has been installed to it, to avoid IP address conflicts.

- To select Legacy mode operation, select that mode in the gateway cluster object ClusterXL tab.

- Cluster object topology is configured implicitly by the duplicated IP addresses over the members.

- Standby members are reachable via the secured network only, so the management station must be connected to that network.

- The ClusterXL module configures all cluster members to use the same MAC address on their connected interfaces, so a single MAC address is presented to adjacent network devices.

- The CPHA protocol uses a broadcast destination MAC address.

Configuring ClusterXL in Load-Sharing Mode

In this section, we configure and test ClusterXL in Load-Sharing mode. As you will see, ClusterXL in Load-Sharing mode has a lot in common with ClusterXL HA New mode—especially its configuration. For this reason, it is a good idea to digest the contents of the HA New mode section of this chapter first! This mode also has a great deal in common with Nokia clustering in terms of how the cluster operates and appears to adjacent network equipment. These similarities will become apparent as we proceed.

Prerequisites for Configuring ClusterXL in Load-Sharing Mode

The configuration of ClusterXL in Load-Sharing mode is so similar to ClusterXL in HA New mode that all the HA prerequisites apply. Our example network topology is also identical (refer back to Figure 21.12).

You must make sure that your ISP router (and any adjacent routing equipment that is physically connected to the load-sharing interfaces) will accept an ARP reply with a multicast MAC—even if the IP address is not a multicast IP address. There are various ways of doing this, depending on the specific networking equipment. The reason for doing so is that ClusterXL in Load-Sharing mode allocates a multicast MAC address to the VIP address. This means that for a specific VIP address, the MAC address will stay the same. This means that all members in the cluster receive the network traffic, but only one will route the traffic based on a load-sharing algorithm that takes into account which members are available and properties of the traffic.

Configuration of ClusterXL in Load-Sharing Mode

In order to configure load sharing, follow the steps as you would for HA New mode, but when you come to configuring the Gateway Cluster object ClusterXL mode, select the **Load Sharing** radio button (see Figure 21.22).

Installing the policy will then make the cluster behave as a load-sharing cluster as opposed to an HA cluster. If the cluster was previously operating in HA mode, it is wise to reboot each member after the new policy install, to ensure that the ClusterXL modules are configured correctly.

Testing ClusterXL in Load-Sharing Mode

Once you have configured your ClusterXL in Load-Sharing mode, you will want to perform some tests to determine that your load sharing is working properly and to make sure that it functions as you expect under failure conditions. We can use the same tests we used for HA New mode, but we should see some differences in results.

Test 1: Pinging the Virtual IP Address for Each Interface

You should be able to ping the VIP address for each network. The main difference between this test and the HA test is that the MAC address of the VIP address is a multicast MAC address. When you ping from a host that is on the same local subnet as a VIP of the cluster, you should receive an ARP reply from one of the members of the cluster (not necessarily the member that will take the traffic; this is based on the load-sharing algorithm). The MAC address that you receive in the ARP cache will be a multicast MAC address.

If you were to run a packet trace while pinging the VIP address of the cluster, in the ping echo response packet from the cluster you will see the *real* MAC address of the member that responds as the source MAC address.

Test 2: Using SmartView Status to Examine the Status of the Cluster Members

As with HA modes, the SmartView Status GUI allows detailed monitoring and manual stop and start of the cluster members.

Looking at Figure 21.48, you can see that ClusterXL on member fw1 has a problem. If you examine the ClusterXL Details on the right side of the screen, you can see that interface qfe3 (the internal interface) is down. In this particular case, because it is a test, this was the interface we unplugged, so this was the expected result.

Figure 21.48 SmartView Status Demonstrating a Problem with an Interface

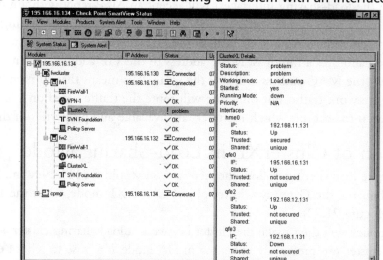

If you click **ClusterXL** for member fw2, you will see all the details of this member as well. You can see the details regarding the status of fwd and policy loaded if you scroll down a little further in the ClusterXL Details. The details show that the Working mode is Load Sharing and that the Running mode is *down* for member fw1. As with ClusterXL in HA New mode, you can right-click the **ClusterXL** icon and take that particular member down or start it up again. Be wary that if you do this, the SmartView Status will no longer receive updated information from the ClusterXL member, so it might still state that the member is up and running.

Test 3: FTPing through ClusterXL Load Sharing During Failover

This test applies to load sharing as it did for HA mode; we still want connection resilience, so if a member fails, the load-sharing algorithm reallocates those connections to other members, and they are preserved. One snag with performing this type of test on a load-sharing cluster is this: How do we know which member the FTP traffic is going through? If you have the Real Time Monitor package installed on the modules, you could use that, as demonstrated later in the "How Nokia Clustering Works" section of this chapter. Another alternative is to watch the SmartView Tracker firewall logs and note which member logs the Accept of the FTP connection. However, in NG FP3, logging from cluster members is identified by the cluster name only, not the member name, so this is no help. Your other—rather unpleasant—option is to run a packet trace while the FTP download is taking place, identify a packet on the FTP connection that has come from the cluster, and check the source MAC address. This process will tell you which member the traffic is going through. You can then pull an interface cable out of the correct member in the cluster to observe failover. Take care not to stop the FTP session after taking the packet trace, and then start the FTP session again, because the new connection could go through a different member in the cluster!

NOTE

Happily, by the time you read this, there should be an FP3 hotfix release that will result in logging with the origin of the member, not the cluster name.

Command-Line Diagnostics for ClusterXL

The command-line diagnostic tools for ClusterXL in Load-Sharing mode are the same as ClusterXL in HA New mode, but the responses are different. Here, we take a quick look at how they differ.

fw hastat

When you run the *fw hastat* command on the cluster members, they should all respond with a status of active. In our little example, you would see something like:

```
fw2 #fw hastat


HOST        NUMBER      HIGH AVAILABILITY STATE        MACHINE STATUS
localhost 2             active                         OK
fw2 #


fw1 # fw hastat


HOST        NUMBER      HIGH AVAILABILITY STATE        MACHINE STATUS
localhost 1             active                         OK
fw1 #
```

If there was a problem on a member, for example, and interface was down on member fw2, *fw hastat* would produce an output that looks something like:

```
HOST        NUMBER      HIGH AVAILABILITY STATE        MACHINE STATUS
localhost 2             not active                     problem
fw2 #
```

cphaprob

We explored two variations of this command when we looked at ClusterXL in HA New mode. The first was the *cphaprob state* command. On a load–sharing cluster, you would see an output such as:

```
fw1 # cphaprob state

Working mode:   Load Sharing

Number     Unique Address   State

1 (local)  192.168.11.131   active
2          192.168.11.132   active

fw1 #
```

Note that both members have a state of Active as opposed to Active/Standby in a ClusterXL HA New mode cluster. Should there be a failure on one of the members, you would see something like:

```
fw1 # cphaprob stat

Working mode:   Load Sharing

Number     Unique Address   State

1 (local)  192.168.11.131   active
2          192.168.11.132   down

fw1 #
```

In this example, member fw2 was taken down (an interface connection was removed), but the command was run on member fw1. All members in the cluster should report the same state for a member in a correctly working cluster.

cpstat ha

The information returned using the *cpstat ha* command is similar to the ClusterXL in HA New mode, but it reports on the load-sharing aspect of the cluster. The command *cpstat ha* will give you an output such as:

```
fw1 # cpstat ha

Product name: High Availability
Version:      NG Feature Pack 3
```

```
Status:        OK
HA installed: 1
Working mode: Load Sharing
HA started:   yes


fw1 #
```

The only differences here worthy of note are the working mode and the status. Predictably, if there is a problem, you will see the status change to:

```
Product name: High Availability
Version:        NG Feature Pack 3
Status:         problem
HA installed: 1
Working mode: Load Sharing
HA started:   yes
```

The other syntax of this command is *cpstat —f all ha*. An example of the output is as follows:

```
fw1 # cpstat -f all ha


Product name:          High Availability
Major version:         5
Minor version:         0
Service pack:          3
Version string:        NG Feature Pack 3
Status code:           2
Status short:          problem
Status long:           problem
HA installed:          1
Working mode:          Load Sharing
HA protocol version: 2
HA started:            yes
HA state:              down
HA identifier:         1



Interface table
--------------------------------------------------
|Name|IP                |Status|Verified|Trusted|Shared|
--------------------------------------------------
|hme0|192.168.11.131|Up    |       0|       1|      0|
|qfe0|195.166.16.131|Up    |       0|       0|      0|
```

```
|qfe2|192.168.12.131|Up       |          0|        0|        0|
|qfe3|  192.168.1.131|Down     |      32000|        0|        0|
---------------------------------------------------------------



Problem Notification table
---------------------------------------------------------------
|Name               |Status|Priority|Verified|Descr|
---------------------------------------------------------------
|Synchronization|OK     |          0|      1618|         |
|Filter         |OK     |          0|      1618|         |
|cphad          |OK     |          0|         0|         |
|fwd            |OK     |          0|         0|         |
---------------------------------------------------------------



fw1 #
```

From this output, we can see that there is a problem with the local member (fw1 in this example) and that the status of interface qfe3 is down.

How ClusterXL Works in Load-Sharing Mode

ClusterXL in Load-Sharing mode works in a very similar way to ClusterXL in HA New mode but with the following unique distinctions:

- The MAC address used for the VIP address is shared among cluster members for that subnet. This means that there is no MAC address change on failure of a member as far as the network equipment on the local subnet of the cluster is concerned.

- The MAC address of the VIP address is a multicast MAC address. (in other words, its first octet is an odd number).

- In a healthy load-sharing cluster, all members of the cluster should be active and routing a portion of the active traffic.

Connections through the cluster are managed on a per-connection basis. For example, if a host on 192.168.1.200 initiates a connection through the cluster to 195.166.16.129 and member fw1 takes the connection, the connection will just go through member fw1 unless a failure of member fw1 occurs. The connection will continue through member fw1 until the session has completed. No asymmetric routing should occur on this particular connection.

The member in the cluster a new connection will go through is based on a hash of specific parameters defined in the Advanced section for ClusterXL Load Sharing (see Figure 21.49).

Figure 21.49 A Load-Sharing Algorithm Hash Can Be Based on These Parameters

Assuming a "normal" connection passing through the cluster, all the packets involved will have the same hash value. For an Internet firewall, this means that, for a particular connection, a packet arriving from the internal network and a packet arriving from the Internet will have the same hash value. However, if the cluster is performing NAT or if VPNs are involved, we have a potential problem. The IP addresses and ports will be different on the "inside" and "outside" of the firewall. FireWall-1's stateful inspection helps us out here; because it understands what changes have been applied to connections, it can adjust the hashing accordingly.

As with ClusterXL in HA New mode, the members of the cluster still have their real IP addresses bound to their interfaces. This is particularly useful when the SmartCenter server is communicating with the cluster members, because it need not be located on the secured network. This makes it easier for the SmartCenter server to manage other firewall modules as well as the cluster.

Although all members are live and handling traffic, who should respond to ARP requests for the VIP address? The members in the ClusterXL cluster will agree on which member in the cluster will respond to the ARP request; however, that choice is not based on the member priority in the cluster, and even if a member is designated as having a problem but the interfaces on the member are active, the problem member may still respond to the ARP request. Within the ARP reply packets is the multicast MAC address for the VIP.

> **NOTE**
>
> You need to make sure that adjacent hosts and routers will accept a multicast MAC reply for a nonmulticast IP address. For example, host 192.168.1.200 would ARP for 192.168.1.130—the VIP address of the cluster—in order to route packets through the cluster. The ARP response would contain a multicast MAC address. Different systems respond in different ways: Windows is generally fine, but Cisco routers on the same subnet will not accept the ARP reply and will not cache the multicast MAC address, so steps need to be taken to circumvent this problem for Cisco routers. These steps usually involve entering a static entry into the ARP table of the router for the multicast MAC address.

ClusterXL Load-Sharing Mode Failover

As with ClusterXL in HA New mode, the key to how failover works is in the CPHA protocol that the members send to all the other members in the cluster, using multicasts.

There are many similarities between ClusterXL HA New mode and ClusterXL Load-Sharing mode CPHA protocol packets. In fact, they are identical in the way they work, apart from some details in the UDP data payload. The similarities include:

■ The source MAC address of the CPHA update packet is always 00:00:00:00:fe:<*member number*>, where member 1 would be 00, member 2 would be 01, and so on.

■ The destination MAC is always a multicast MAC address, ending with the VIP address in the last two octets of the MAC address.

■ The source IP of the CPHA update packet is always 0.0.0.0.

■ The destination IP address of the CPHA update packet is always the network IP address.

■ Layer 4 (the transport layer of the OSI model) is always UDP, source port 8116, destination port 8116.

■ The first part of the CPHA payload within the UDP header packet is the same as ClusterXL in HA New mode, and the format of an FW_HA_MYSTATE payload is the same parameters but *different data* for these parameters.

If we focus on the last point, we can see from Figure 21.50 how the data for the same parameters differ.

Figure 21.50 Packet Structure of a CPHA Packet When a Cluster Is in Load-Sharing Mode

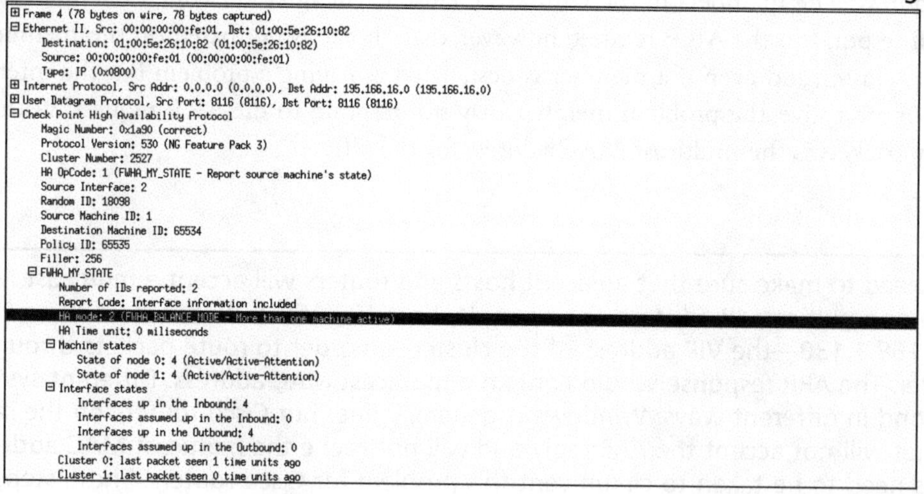

```
⊞ Frame 4 (78 bytes on wire, 78 bytes captured)
⊟ Ethernet II, Src: 00:00:00:00:fe:01, Dst: 01:00:5e:26:10:82
    Destination: 01:00:5e:26:10:82 (01:00:5e:26:10:82)
    Source: 00:00:00:00:fe:01 (00:00:00:00:fe:01)
    Type: IP (0x0800)
⊞ Internet Protocol, Src Addr: 0.0.0.0 (0.0.0.0), Dst Addr: 195.166.16.0 (195.166.16.0)
⊞ User Datagram Protocol, Src Port: 8116 (8116), Dst Port: 8116 (8116)
⊟ Check Point High Availability Protocol
    Magic Number: 0x1a90 (correct)
    Protocol Version: 530 (NG Feature Pack 3)
    Cluster Number: 2527
    HA OpCode: 1 (FWHA_MY_STATE - Report source machine's state)
    Source Interface: 2
    Random ID: 18098
    Source Machine ID: 1
    Destination Machine ID: 65534
    Policy ID: 65535
    Filler: 256
  ⊟ FWHA_MY_STATE
    Number of IDs reported: 2
    Report Code: Interface information included
    HA mode: 2 (FWHA_BALANCE_MODE - More than one machine active)
    HA Time unit: 0 miliseconds
  ⊟ Machine states
      State of node 0: 4 (Active/Active-Attention)
      State of node 1: 4 (Active/Active-Attention)
  ⊟ Interface states
      Interfaces up in the Inbound: 4
      Interfaces assumed up in the Inbound: 0
      Interfaces up in the Outbound: 4
      Interfaces assumed up in the Outbound: 0
    Cluster 0: last packet seen 1 time units ago
    Cluster 1: last packet seen 0 time units ago
```

The main areas of note here are the HA mode, which states that the mode is mode 4 FWHA_Balance_mode—more than one member active. ClusterXL in HA New mode is referred to as mode 2 in this field.

The other field of note is "Machine states." This field communicates what the member originating the CPHA packet thinks the status of all the other members is. As we can see in Figure 21.50, the sending member is aware that member 0 is active. This packet was originated from member 1, or fw2 from our example.

Under normal operation, these CPHA packets are multicast to all the other members in the cluster. Each member multicasts its perception of the state of the rest of the members in the cluster. This process occurs on each interface of a cluster member and is sent at regular intervals, several a second.

Examining the CPHA protocol between cluster members, we see that if there is a problem on the member, the other members will show a "Machine states" value for that the member as *down/dead*. The member that is taking over a particular connection will then ARP for the MAC address of the local host it needs to push a packet to, and on response, it will continue the session. Note that the hosts on the local subnet do not notice any change in MAC address or IP address on failover. You could notice a small glitch in the data transfer while the failure occurs and failover to another member takes place, but the period of disruption should always be less than three seconds and is usually just over one second.

Note that when a member in a load-sharing cluster takes over from another member, there is no gratuitous ARP broadcast, unlike HA mode. This is because it is unnecessary since there has been no MAC address change.

Special Considerations for ClusterXL in Load-Sharing Mode

We have covered the principles of how ClusterXL in Load-Sharing mode works. We now contrast and compare how the special considerations for ClusterXL in Load-Sharing mode differ relative to other cluster modes.

Network Address Translation

ClusterXL in Load-Sharing mode is actually quite forgiving with regard to NAT and how proxy ARP is performed, unlike HA mode. It will handle manual proxy ARP entries fine for NATed IP addresses, as long as you proxy ARP for the cluster multicast MAC address. You enter these static published ARP entries on all members in the cluster. Automatic ARP configuration can be selected in the **Policy | Global Properties | Network Address Translation** area of the SmartDashboard GUI. This works fine because the multicast MAC address is used for all the automatic ARPs that are required. Manual routes on the ISP router can also be used instead of using proxy ARPs.

To summarize, as long as the multicast MAC address is used in any manual proxy ARPs, there should be no issues with Load-Sharing mode and NAT.

User Authentication and One-Time Passcodes

Like all HA and Load-Sharing clustering solutions, if you are using the Check Point security servers (for SMTP, HTTP, or FTP services) and a failover occurs, you will lose the connection and have to start again through the new member that the traffic is now going through. The security server and remote authentication issues discussed earlier in this chapter (comparing single gateway and clustering functionality) apply particularly to Load-Sharing mode, because sessions—with multiple connections—are always likely to be shared between all cluster members, unlike HA, when problems only occur on failover.

Nokia IPSO Clustering

ClusterXL is not available for the Nokia platform. This is because Nokia provides its own HA and load-sharing solutions. In this section, we look at the load-sharing cluster solution that Nokia provides on IPSO 3.6-FCS4, how to configure it, and how to configure FireWall-1 NG FP3 so that you have a complete Nokia load-sharing solution. We then talk about how you can test the cluster and go over any special considerations for this solution.

Nokia Configuration

To configure a Nokia load-sharing cluster, you need to take the following steps:

1. Configure the interfaces of a Nokia.
2. Configure FireWall-1.
3. Configure clustering in Voyager.

We assume that you have installed IPSO 3.6 FCS-4 on your Nokia and that you have the Check Point FireWall-1 NG FP3 package installed and configured. As with setting up all clusters, it is recommended that you complete and test the physical connectivity first so that any problems that you encounter later aren't due to a misconfigured switch or interface, because these could be difficult to spot later.

In our example shown in Figure 21.51, you can see a sample Nokia cluster topology.

Figure 21.51 Our Example Nokia Clustering Topology Setup

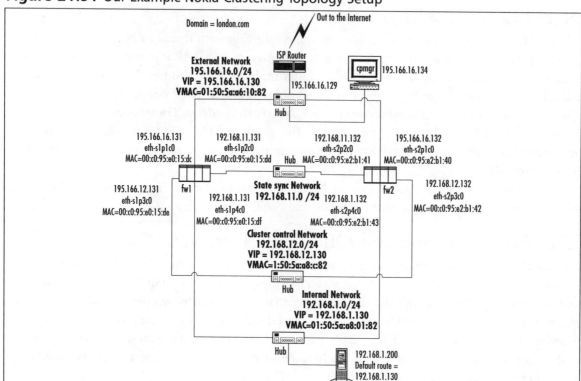

The main difference in network topology between Nokia clustering and using Check Point ClusterXL is that you require a dedicated network for Nokia cluster control communications. This is in addition to the Check Point state sync network.

As you can see from Figure 21.51, each network that has a VIP also has a virtual MAC address—a multicast MAC that is used for the VIP. From a network perspective of neighboring equipment on the same network as the cluster interfaces, it looks very similar to Check Point ClusterXL in Load-Sharing mode.

You should ensure that you have configured all of the following using Voyager on each of the cluster members:

- Make sure that interface speeds are consistent across host and switches on the subnet. Only use full-duplex where connected directly to full-duplex-enabled switches!

- Make sure you have entries in each hosts file for the FireWall-1 management station and the other modules in the cluster.

- Make sure you have the correct time and date and the correct default local for each member in the cluster and on the Check Point management station.

- Make sure that the FireWall-1 NG FP3 package is installed.

- Read the Nokia IPSO and Check Point NG FP3 release notes!

A Few Points about Installing an Initial Configuration of NG FP3 on Nokia IPSO

Installing software packages on the Nokia platform is very different compared to installing on other platforms. Packages are added to Nokia and "enabled" using the Voyager interface. However, that is not the end of the process of installing FireWall-1 NG FP3. You need to log out after the package install and run the *cpconfig* command on the Nokia console. The output you will see is fairly similar to the output you would see in the UNIX installation of a cluster, and the choices you would make are identical.

One section during the install is specific to clustering:

```
Would you like to install a Check Point clustering product (CPHA, CPLS or
    State Synchronization)? (y/n) [n] ? y
```

Even though you will be using the Nokia clustering solution, make sure you answer **y**. This will make sure that you have the state synchronization available when you set up your cluster. That is essential for ensuring that connections continue through another member when failover occurs.

Check Point FireWall-1 Configuration for a Nokia Cluster

We will run through the most direct method of configuring FireWall-1 objects and rules for a Nokia cluster. This means that we will create the cluster member objects via the gateway cluster object directly and set up the SIC trusts between the management station and the cluster members within the cluster gateway object. Once the cluster gateway object is configured, we will install a basic policy to the cluster. If you have not already done so, it's a good idea to look through the "Configuring FireWall-1 for ClusterXL in HA New Mode" configuration procedure described earlier in this chapter, because there are many similarities.

Configuring the Gateway Cluster Object

Within the NG FP3 SmartDashboard GUI, click **Manage | Network Objects** and click the **New** button. Select **Check Point | Gateway Cluster**. You will be presented with a pop-up window (see Figure 21.52).

Figure 21.52 Defining General Properties of the Nokia Cluster

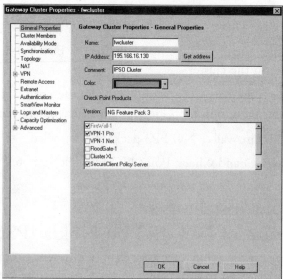

Particular areas of note here are that the IP address stated in the General tab is the external interface. The other important points to note are that the ClusterXL check box is *unchecked*.

Now click the **Cluster Members** menu option on the left side of this screen. Run through the steps for creating a new member, as we did when configuring Cluster XL HA New mode.

After the trust has been set up between the management module and enforcement module, click the **Topology** tab and click **Get Topology**. For each interface that is received, click it and set the topology for it. For example, the eth-s1p1c0 interface has IP address 195.166.16.131 assigned to it, and this is marked as our **External** interface in the topology. All the others are defined as **This Network** (see Figure 21.53).

Figure 21.53 Topology of a Cluster Member

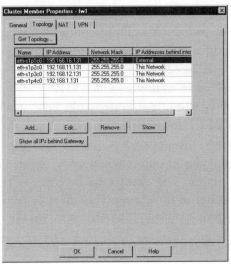

Click **OK**. You should now have the first member of the cluster defined and trusted. Repeat the procedure again in the **Cluster Members** menu to add the second cluster (and third, fourth, and so on). Use the **New** button each time. Once complete, you should have a list of cluster members defined.

Click **Availability Mode** on the left side of the screen to select which mode the Nokia cluster will operate in. Make sure you select **Load Sharing** (see Figure 21.54). Note that in Nokia clustering, this setting has no functional effect, but it is useful to select the correct one so that when you look at it again, you know what mode you are operating your Nokia cluster in! It is also useful to avoid any confusion if you need to seek technical support.

Figure 21.54 Availability Mode Configuration for a Nokia Cluster

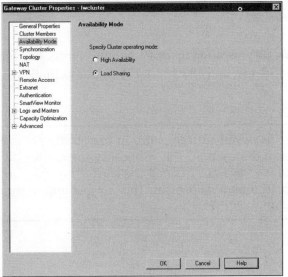

Click the **Synchronization** menu option on the left side of the screen. You need to add the network you are going to use for synchronizing the FireWall-1 state tables. Note that this network should not be the same as your Nokia cluster control network.

Click the **Add** button to add a synchronization network. In our example, the IP address is 192.168.11.0 , and the netmask is 255.255.255.0. (See step 8 and Figure 21.23 of "Configuring ClusterXL in HA New Mode" for an example.) Click **OK**.

It is possible to add backup synchronization networks here; it would be acceptable to include the Nokia control network as a backup sync network, but if you do, the cluster should be monitored carefully so that a failover to this network is quickly identified and addressed.

Configuring topology in the cluster object when using Nokia clustering is not mandatory—in fact, *it is not recommended*. Doing so will change the behavior of the cluster with regard to packets originating from a member in the cluster. The effect of configuring a topology is covered in "Special Considerations for Nokia Clusters" later in this chapter.

Once this process is complete, you are ready to click **OK** and start defining your security policy.

Configuring the Nokia Cluster Rule Base

You have some choices as to the rule base you want to install. You can either see if the configuration of your cluster object is going to work and install an open policy, or you can create a strict policy now. Remember, there is still one more step to do, which is to configure the clustering on Nokia using Voyager. This being the case, you might want to install an open policy now and then tighten it later once you are happy that your clustering is working correctly.

You need to allow IPSO cluster control protocols between each IP address of the Nokia cluster. This means you will have a rule, close to the top of your rule base, that will look something like Figure 21.55.

Figure 21.55 Rule Showing Communication between Cluster Members

The group *fwcluster-clusterips* is made up of node host objects, one for each VIP address (195.166.16.130, 192.168.12.130, and 192.168.1.130 in our example).

> **WARNING**
>
> It is vital to add the *fwcluster-clusterips* group to security policy rules wherever you use the cluster object as a destination. This is because the cluster object does not include the VIP addresses, since we have not defined the cluster topology information. However, it is possible to connect to the VIP addresses. This is most important when defining the "stealth" rule (see Figure 21.57).

The *ipso-cc* group is made up of two services that we will call IPSO Cluster Control Protocol 1 and IPSO Cluster Control Protocol 2. You define these by clicking **Manage | Services | New | TCP**. The definition of these services is shown in Figures 6.56 and 6.57, respectively.

Figure 21.56 Defining Service for IPSO Cluster Control Protocol 1

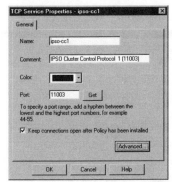

Figure 21.57 Defining Service for IPSO Cluster Control Protocol 2

Once defined, these services can be added to a service group (defined as *ipso-cc* in our example).

In addition to the *ipso-cc* services, we have also accepted the Network Time Protocol (NTP). Running NTP is a good idea to make sure that the time between the Nokia cluster members does not drift.

When you define the "stealth" rule in order to explicitly protect the cluster members, add the cluster object *and* the group of VIPs, *fwcluster-clusterips*, as shown in Figure 21.58.

Figure 21.58 A Stealth Rule on a Nokia Cluster Rule Base

Once you have configured your policy, install it to the cluster object. Note that in Figure 21.59, we can see that the policy will fail to install if it does not install to all members of the cluster. One thing to be acutely aware of here is that if a member in the cluster is down or switched off and later comes online and becomes functional, it will first look at other members of the cluster to compare the policy that it has against the policy that the other cluster members have. If the other cluster members have a more recent policy, the cluster member that has just come up will download the policy from one of the other cluster members—before it attempts to download the policy from the management module.

Figure 21.59 Installing the Security Policy for the Cluster

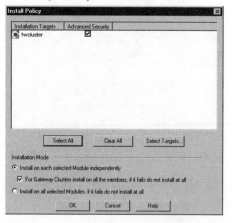

Once you have installed a policy, you have to complete the last step in configuring a Nokia load-sharing cluster: configuring the clustering on the Nokia appliances themselves.

Nokia Cluster Configuration on Voyager

When we configured the Gateway Cluster object in the SmartDashboard GUI, we did not configure the gateway cluster to have ClusterXL installed. This feature is not available on the Nokia platform; Nokia provides its own solution for load sharing. However, you have to configure it within the Voyager interface.

Note that you have to configure the cluster on each Nokia in the cluster, so you will have to repeat the procedure of configuring the cluster on each Nokia. This might sound obvious, but it is often something that is forgotten!

Voyager Configuration

Make sure that you have network connectivity from your browser to your Nokia FireWall-1 modules in your cluster, and make sure that the security policy you have installed on the Nokia appliances does not prevent you from accessing Voyager from your browser. Navigate to Voyager on the first member in your cluster. In our example, we do this by going to https://195.166.16.131 (see Figure 21.60).

Figure 21.60 Voyager's Main Screen

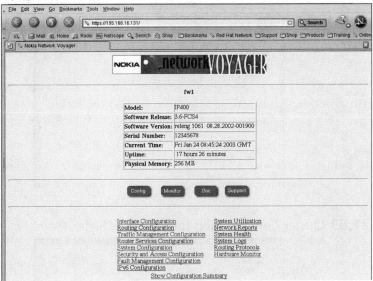

Here are the steps you need to follow after you have authenticated and are presented with the main screen:

1. From the main Voyager screen, click **Traffic Management Configuration**.

2. Click **Cluster**. The new screen will look something like Figure 21.61.

Figure 21.61 The Initial Cluster Configuration Screen

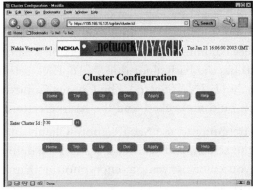

3. Enter a cluster ID. This can be any decimal number between 0 and 65,535. For simplicity, we chose 130 for our example. Once you've entered an ID, click **Apply** and then **Save**.

4. The cluster configuration screen will then expand to include more parameters that can be configured within the cluster.

5. The bottom half of the screen presented in Figure 21.62 is shown in Figure 21.63; it shows how to configure the clustering for member fw1 in our example.

Figure 21.62 Uninitialized Cluster in Voyager

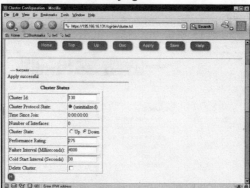

Figure 21.63 Cluster Configuration for the First Cluster Member

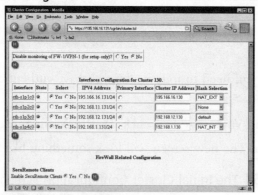

6. Set up your cluster information. Note that the sync interface, eth–s1p2c0, has parameter *No* for the Select column and the Hash Selection column has *None*. The external interface eth–s1p1c0 has the hash algorithm *NAT_EXT* selected, and the internal interface eth–s1p4c0 has *NAT_INT* selected. The Cluster Control network has the Primary Interface option button checked, and the hash selection is set to *default*.

7. Decide if you are going to use SecuRemote Clients and select **yes** or **no**. If you scroll further down the screen, you will see a section for defining VPN tunnel information. This is where you enter the remote encryption domain and remote gateway IP address so that this information is taken into account when the load-sharing algorithm is calculated. This ensures that the same member of the cluster participates in the VPN connection (as asymmetric routing would cause the VPN to fail).

> **WARNING**
>
> UDP encapsulation for secure remote connections is not taken into account for the Nokia IPSO cluster load-sharing algorithm, so it will therefore fail.

8. Make sure that you click **Apply** and **Save** to save the changes you have made.

9. You can now make the cluster active, even with just one member. Click the **Cluster State Up** option button, and then click **Apply** and **Save**, as shown in Figure 21.64. Once it is up and running, your cluster should route traffic through member fw1, if adjacent hosts are using the VIP address of the local subnet that they are connected to as their default gateway.

Figure 21.64 Bringing Up the First Cluster Member

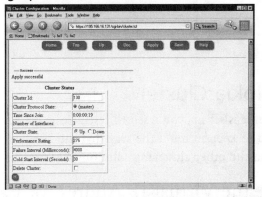

10. This completes member fw1 in the cluster configuration. You now need to point your browser to the second member and configure it to complement your configuration of member fw1. Note that the settings have to be correct and you have to use the equivalent interfaces on fw2 as fw1 and that the hashing algorithm you select must be identical to member fw1. When you change the **Cluster State** to **Up**, Voyager will inform you that the fw2 member is joining the cluster. This could take a little while (see Figure 21.65) and you will be informed as to whether the procedure succeeds or fails.

Figure 21.65 Member fw2 Joining the Cluster

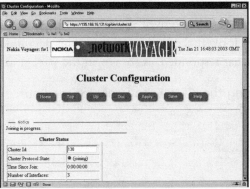

11. If joining the cluster is successful, the member will announce that it is now a member of the cluster (see Figure 21.66). Both members of the cluster are now up and running, and you are ready to test your Nokia cluster.

Figure 21.66 Second Member of a Nokia Cluster Is Now Online

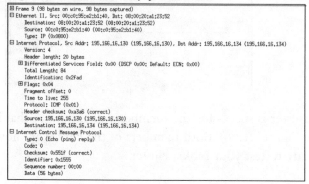

Testing the Nokia Cluster

Once your Nokia cluster is set up, you need to test it to make sure that it is functioning correctly. Again, you need to keep in mind the way that this particular clustering technology works and how it differs from the other clustering solutions we have covered so far.

Test 1: Pinging the Virtual IP Address of Each Interface

With Nokia clustering in load sharing, you should be able to ping the local VIP address of the cluster with a host that is on the same subnet as the cluster interfaces. You will receive a response if everything is working properly.

In the test we ran on our example network, a ping was initiated from the FireWall-1 management station (195.166.16.134) to the VIP of the cluster (195.166.16.130). A packet trace was run at the same time on the management station to analyze the packet for the ping session. If you look at the ARP cache of the local host initiating the ping, you should now have the multicast MAC address of the VIP. In our case, this is 01:50:5a:a6:10:82 (which you can check against Figure 21.51). This in itself does not tell you much—just that the VIP address is up and running and that a member in the cluster responded. But can we tell which member?

The answer is yes, we can, but only if we examine the packet trace we took when the ping session took place. If we look at the reply packet, in the data link layer, we can see the real MAC address of the member that responded, as shown in the packet analysis in Figure 21.67.

Figure 21.67 Analyzing the ICMP Echo Reply for the Source MAC Address

```
⊞ Frame 9 (98 bytes on wire, 98 bytes captured)
⊟ Ethernet II, Src: 00:c0:95:e2:b1:40, Dst: 08:00:20:a1:23:52
    Destination: 08:00:20:a1:23:52 (08:00:20:a1:23:52)
    Source: 00:c0:95:e2:b1:40 (00:c0:95:e2:b1:40)
    Type: IP (0x0800)
⊟ Internet Protocol, Src Addr: 195.166.16.130 (195.166.16.130), Dst Addr: 195.166.16.134 (195.166.16.134)
    Version: 4
    Header length: 20 bytes
  ⊞ Differentiated Services Field: 0x00 (DSCP 0x00: Default; ECN: 0x00)
    Total Length: 84
    Identification: 0x2fad
  ⊞ Flags: 0x04
    Fragment offset: 0
    Time to live: 255
    Protocol: ICMP (0x01)
    Header checksum: 0xa3a6 (correct)
    Source: 195.166.16.130 (195.166.16.130)
    Destination: 195.166.16.134 (195.166.16.134)
⊟ Internet Control Message Protocol
    Type: 0 (Echo (ping) reply)
    Code: 0
    Checksum: 0x551f (correct)
    Identifier: 0x1555
    Sequence number: 00:00
    Data (56 bytes)
```

In our example, we can see that the source MAC is 00:0c:95:e2:b1:40, which corresponds with member fw2 in the cluster (see Figure 21.51). Note that even though the real MAC address of the fw2 member was used, the source IP address for the ICMP echo reply was the virtual IP of 195.166.16.130.

Test 2: Determining the Status of Each Member in the Cluster

In a Nokia cluster, there are two tools you can use to monitor the status of the cluster and its members. One is the SmartView Status GUI, and the other is using Voyager monitoring.

The SmartView Status GUI shows you the health of each member and if it is in state table sync with other members of the cluster. What it won't show you is the correct status of each interface of each member. For this information, you have to use the Nokia Voyager screens on each member in the cluster.

Notice that in Figure 21.68, all the interfaces seem to be up; however, they would report this status even if one of the interfaces was unplugged. The giveaway that SmartView Status cannot monitor the interfaces is that the "Working mode" field says *Sync only*. This means that the only function ClusterXL is performing on a Nokia cluster is state table synchronization.

Figure 21.68 SmartView Status Does Not Show an Accurate Interface Status

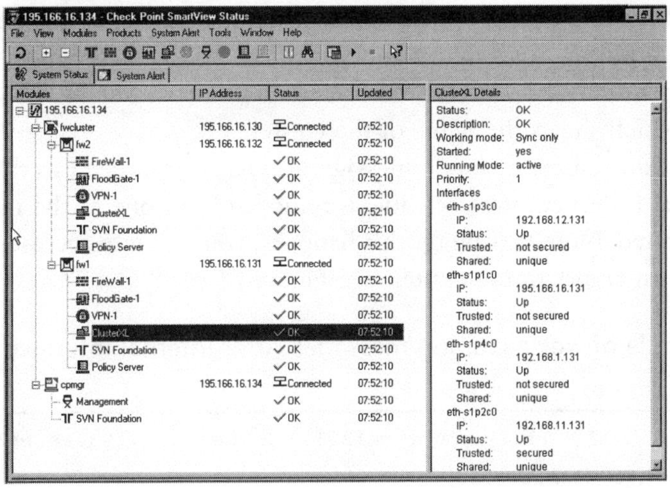

Checking the monitoring of the cluster through Voyager is straightforward. Connect your browser to one of the members, select the **Monitor** button, and then click **Cluster Monitor**. This will show you the main statistics of each member in the cluster (see Figure 21.69) from the point of view of the member you are connected to. If everything is working correctly, it should not matter which member you connect to with Voyager, because they should all report the same status.

Figure 21.69 Both Members Are Online as Part of the Cluster

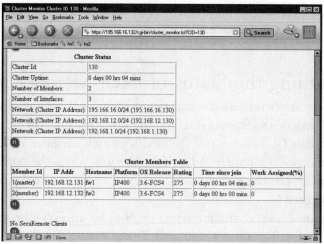

If a member in the cluster fails, you will see it removed from the cluster members table. If you only have one member left after a member fails (if you have a two-member cluster), the remaining member will also become master. Take note of the Time Since Join parameter in the cluster members table. This parameter tells you how long a particular member has been online.

One other place not to be forgotten when you're checking the health of your Nokia cluster is the system logs. These can be located in the /var/log/messages file. You should see entries from the *clusterd* process, which shows the status of the cluster.

In Figure 21.70, you can see a sample message of what will be seen in the /var/adm/message file when the internal Ethernet interface cable is removed from one of the members of the cluster, and then restored. Note that when this happens, you will also see the cluster members table show one fewer member in the cluster (see Figure 21.71).

Figure 21.70 Sample of Nokia /var/log/messages After Internal Interface Was Removed, Then Restored

```
Jan 27 07:29:35 fw1 [LOG_NOTICE] clusterd[251]: Member(192.168.12.132)
    member id (2) left cluster(130):
Jan 27 07:30:15 fw1 [LOG_NOTICE] clusterd[251]: New member(192.168.12.132)
    joined cluster(130) with member id(2).
```

Figure 21.71 One Member Only in Cluster

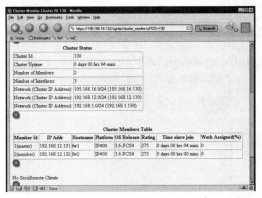

Test 3: FTPing through a Load-Sharing Nokia Cluster During Interface Failure

Like ClusterXL load sharing and HA New mode, the best test you can perform is a real-world test. In load sharing, a simple test consists of starting a connection through the cluster and monitoring the cluster to determine which member the connection has gone through. If the test connection is the only connection, you might be able to see this from the "Work assigned" value in the cluster monitoring facility in Voyager, or you could use the FireWall-1 NG FP3 SmartView Tracker (with a hotfix applied to show origin IP addresses of the member in the cluster), or you could use SmartView Monitor.

In this example, we have started an FTP session through the cluster, and we are using SmartView Monitor to monitor the traffic through the cluster. When we initiate the FTP session through the cluster and start downloading data, we can see that all the load is on member fw2 in the cluster (see Figure 21.72).

Figure 21.72 Display of Traffic through SmartView Monitor

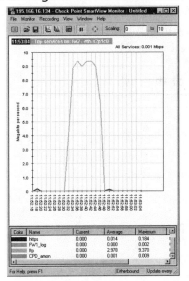

As we can see in Figure 21.72, the FTP session was started at 11:52:30, and failure occurred at 11:52:48 (actually, we pulled the internal interface connector out of member fw2). Figure 21.73 shows that member fw1 took over the session.

Figure 21.73 Display of Traffic through Member fw1 When fw2 Fails

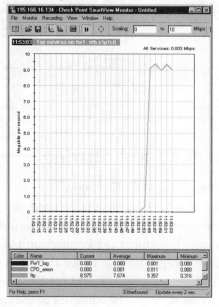

Note that the timeline shows that member fw1 did not take over the load for three seconds.

Command-Line Stats

We saw earlier that ClusterXL uses the *cphaprob* command to determine status of the cluster. We can use a similar Nokia command-line tool to check the status of a Nokia cluster.

On the Nokia platform, we use the Command Line Interface Shell (known as *clish*). This is an interactive command line, although a single command can be executed using the −*c* "command" option. Once in the shell, you can use the command *show clusters* to determine the status of the members in the cluster (see Figure 21.74).

Figure 21.74 Example of Use of the *clish* Command to Check the Cluster Status

```
fw2[admin]# clish
Nokia> show clusters
CID 130
    Cluster State up
    Member ID 1
    Protocol State master
    System Uptime At Join 1:02:58:57
    Performance Rating 275
    Failure Interval 4000
```

Figure 21.74 Example of Use of the *clish* Command to Check the Cluster Status

```
    Cold Start Delay 30

    Number of Interfaces 3

    Primary Interface eth-s2p3c0

    Interface eth-s2p1c0

        IP Address 195.166.16.132/24

        Cluster IP Address 195.166.16.130

        Hash NAT-external

    Interface eth-s2p3c0

        IP Address 192.168.12.132/24

        Cluster IP Address 192.168.12.130

        Hash default

    Interface eth-s2p4c0

        IP Address 192.168.1.132/24

        Cluster IP Address 192.168.1.130

        Hash NAT-internal


Member(s) information

    Number of Member(s) 2

    Member 1 (master)

        IP Address 192.168.12.132

        HostName(Platform) fw2(IP400)

        OS Release 3.6-FCS4

        Rating 275

        Time Since Join 0:19:20:57

        Cluster Uptime At Join 0:00:00:00

        Work Assigned 50%

    Member 2 (member)

        IP Address 192.168.12.131

        HostName(Platform) fw1(IP400)

        OS Release 3.6-FCS4

        Rating 275

        Time Since Join 0:19:14:34

        Cluster Uptime At Join 0:00:06:22

        Work Assigned 50%


Nokia> show cluster securemote

yes

Nokia> show cluster vpn-tunnels
```

Figure 21.74 Example of Use of the *clish* Command to Check the Cluster Status

```
VPN tunnel(s) configured

Network/Mask          Destination
192.168.254.0/24      194.155.13.33
Nokia> exit

Goodbye..
```

Many commands are variations of the *show cluster* command. See the *Nokia Command Line Reference Guide* for further information. You can use the *cphaprob* command on the Nokia platform if you like, but the information that it will tell you is limited. For example, it can't tell you which interfaces are up or down. It can tell you if the state table synchronization is working or not.

How Nokia Clustering Works

Nokia clustering has many similarities to the Check Point ClusterXL load-sharing solution, but because the clustering is not part of the Check Point product, you do get some differences that are significant. We can draw some parallels between ClusterXL load sharing and Nokia clustering as follows:

- Both ClusterXL load sharing and Nokia clustering use a VIP address and a multicast MAC address, so devices on the local subnet do not see any difference when initiating connections through the cluster. On a Nokia cluster, there is always a host that is assigned master in the cluster, and this member will respond to ARP requests.

- Both ClusterXL and Nokia clustering have a method for each member to tell the other members its status in the cluster. However, the ways that they do this are different. ClusterXL does this using the CPHA protocol, which is sent from each interface of the cluster member to all other cluster members. Nokia uses a dedicated network to communicate using its own protocols: IP protocol 0x90 (144 decimal), which is a multicast MAC destination and IP address, and two TCP services (ports 11003 and 11004). Note that the protocol 0x90 traffic bypasses the firewall, so no policy rules are required.

- Both systems have a load-sharing hashing method that can be altered by the user. On Nokia, this method is set up in Voyager, based on whether your interface is external or internal (or a VPN gateway); on Check Point ClusterXL, this is based on three choices: IP addresses, ports, and SPI (VPN negotiation); IP addresses and ports; or just IP addresses.

- Like ClusterXL, connections through the Nokia cluster are directed through one member in the cluster on a per-connection basis. Asymmetric routing is avoided by the load-sharing algorithm, and although this would still work if it does occur, you could get some sessions dropped when they initiate, due to the reply being received from the remote host before the state tables have an opportunity to synchronize between the cluster members.

■ Just like ClusterXL, the Nokia members still have valid IP addresses that you can connect to.

Let's walk through an example of how a connection would work through a Nokia cluster. In our example, host 192.168.1.200 will initiate a Telnet session through the Nokia cluster to our ISP router on IP address 195.166.16.129, and as before, in our ClusterXL HA New mode, we will hide the connection behind the cluster external IP address of 195.166.16.130, using a hide rule in our firewall NAT rule base.

When the Telnet session is initiated, the host 192.168.1.200 sends out an ARP request for 192.168.1.130, which is the default gateway on the network 192.168.1.0. The response in the ARP will be a multicast MAC address—a MAC address that applies to all members of our cluster for the internal interface. The Nokia member that is the master will always send the ARP response. (More on the master later.) In our example, the MAC address returned is 01:50:5a:a8:01:82. Our host on 192.168.1.200 then sends a SYN TCP packet, high source port, destination is to 195.166.16.129, destination MAC is 01:50:5a:a8:01:82 (the default gateway MAC address).

All members in the cluster will receive this packet, but only one of them will do anything with the packet—depending on which member in the cluster is meant to pick up the packet, which is based on the load-sharing algorithm. The member who will deal with the connection will pass the packet up through the IP stack to the Check Point FireWall-1 NG FP3 kernel for the incoming interface. The TCP SYN packet will pass through the rule base of the firewall and, providing everything is fine, it will then send the packet out of its external interface, with the source IP address of 195.166.16.130 (the external cluster IP address), with the source MAC address of the member that is taking the connection (in our example, the source MAC address is 00:c0:95:e2:b1:40, which corresponds with member fw2 external interface eth-s2p1c0), and the destination IP address will be 195.166.16.129 (see Figure 21.75).

Figure 21.75 Description of a Connection through a Nokia Load-Sharing Cluster

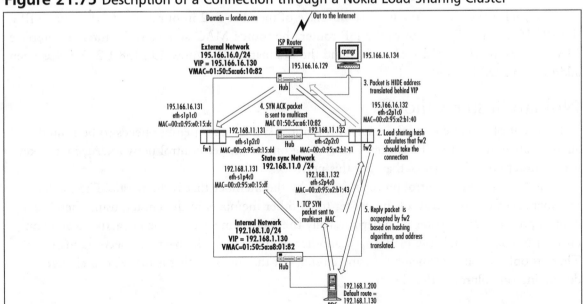

If the Telnet daemon is listening when the packet reaches the ISP router on 195.166.16.129, it will produce a response. Again, the ISP router will issue an ARP request for IP address 195.166.16.130, which is the VIP of the cluster. The master member will respond to the ARP request, sending the multicast MAC address as the MAC address associated with IP 195.166.16.130 (but it will keep the source MAC address of the ARP reply as its own physical external interface; this is one way to see which of your Nokia members is the master without using Voyager). Host 195.166.16.130 will then send a SYN,ACK TCP packet, the source IP will be 195.166.16.129, source port will be 23, and the destination MAC will be the multicast MAC address of the VIP 195,166.16.130, which is 01:50:5a:a6:10:82 in our example.

Again, the reply packet gets onto all members in the cluster, and the correct member that took the original SYN packet for the connection is selected by the hashing algorithm that was selected for that interface.

NOTE

It is important to understand the importance and meaning of the various hashing algorithms. The reply packets get sent back through the same member based on which hashing algorithms you select. For example, if you use Hide NAT when initiating a connection that leaves through the external interface, you have to pick hashing methods that take the NAT into account: NAT_EXT for the external interface, NAT_INT for the internal interface. Not doing this could cause the reply packets to be accepted by the wrong member in the cluster by the load-sharing algorithm, ending up with asymmetric routing. In some complex NAT configurations, there will be conflicts as to which hashing algorithms should be used—for example, where "double NAT" takes place. If these configurations cannot be avoided, other measures should be taken to avoid asynchronous routing, such as static routing via members. This could well lead to imbalances in load sharing and lack of resilience for some connections.

The packet then leaves the internal interface of member fw2 in our example; the source IP is the 195.166.16.129 IP address of the ISP router, the source MAC address is the internal interface MAC address 00:c0:95:e2:b1:43 of fw2, and the destination IP is now 192.168.1.200 (it has been address translated by FireWall-1).

Nokia Cluster Failover

In the event of a failure condition, network traffic taken by that member needs to be routed by an alternative member in the cluster. This is done on the cluster control network. Again, the key is the cluster control protocol that uses this network.

The Nokia cluster control protocol is used by the member that is the master. The master member sends out the status of the cluster to all other members in the cluster, using the cluster control protocol. The master member is usually the first member that is made active when you create a Nokia cluster. If the master fails, another member will take over and become master. There is only one master member in any cluster, but the member that is master can change depending on failures in the cluster.

When the master member in the cluster communicates with the other members in the cluster, it uses the Nokia cluster control protocol, which is IP protocol 0x90 (144 decimal). The cluster control network is used exclusively (unlike the CPHA protocol used in ClusterXL). When the master communicates with the other members in the cluster, it is from the real source MAC address of the master on the control network, the source is the real IP address of the master, the destination MAC address is a multicast MAC address, and the IP address is a multicast IP address. For example, if member fw1 were the master, it would send out a packet, source MAC 00:c0:95:e0:15:de, source IP 192.168.12.131, destination MAC 01:00:5e:00:01:90, destination IP address 224.0.1.144. All members that receive the packet will often respond, with their real source MAC and IP address, to the real destination MAC and IP address of the master.

In our example, if member fw1 were the master and member fw1 failed, fw2 would be the master. You would notice that fw2 would start to issue IP protocol 0x90 packets from its real IP, and the destination IP would be the multicast IP for the other members in the cluster. This is another method you can use to determine which member in the Nokia cluster thinks it is the master. Note that when a new master is chosen, it will stay the master until it fails and cannot be the master any longer. You will also see TCP ports 11003 and 11004 Nokia cluster control connections on the cluster control network.

Failover from the point of view of the networking devices on the same local subnet as the VIPs is transparent because the MAC address used by the cluster does not change. There will be a short delay during failover as the load-sharing algorithm determines which member in the cluster will take over the connections of the failed member. This process can take up to four seconds.

Nokia Failover Conditions

Failure of a Nokia cluster member is determined when one of the following occurs:

- IP forwarding fails or is stopped (for example, by *cpstop*).
- The FireWall-1 process *fwd* dies.
- An interface goes down.

All these scenarios are monitored by the *clusterd* process on each Nokia member. When a failover occurs, the *clusterd* process logs the event in the Nokia system logs (/var/log/messages file).

Special Considerations for Nokia Clusters

We have talked a little about how the Nokia clustering solution works, so based on how the technology in Nokia clustering works, we need to take into account its effects when setting up our cluster and the rule base we are likely to use.

Network Address Translation

As with all clusters, the way you decide to implement your NAT rules needs to be taken into account. In ClusterXL in HA New mode, we noticed that you cannot use manual proxy ARP entries into the OS. In ClusterXL in Load-Sharing mode, we stated that all methods of NAT and proxy ARP should work fine.

In a Nokia cluster, you cannot use Check Point's own Automatic ARP setting in the **Policy | Global Properties | NAT – Network Address Translation | Automatic Rules for Automatic ARP Configuration** menu.

The reason for this is that each member will proxy ARP for the real MAC address of the member in the cluster as opposed to proxy ARPing the multicast MAC address of the cluster. For this reason, you cannot use Automatic ARP Configuration.

You can enter proxy ARP entries into Voyager for NATed IP addresses, using the multicast MAC address of the cluster interface. You can also use static routes on the ISP router to route traffic to the VIP address of the cluster for the NATed IP address.

If you plan to use proxy ARPs for multicast MAC addresses on the Nokia platform, you need to enable **Accept Multicast reply to ARP** on the **ARP** page of the Voyager interface. You need to do this for all members that make up your cluster.

NOTE

Accept Multicast reply to ARP must be enabled for the cluster to work properly.

Defining the Cluster Object Topology

When defining the gateway cluster object for the Nokia cluster, it is possible to define the cluster topology, listing the VIPs. However, this apparently harmless change results in a significant change in FireWall-1 behavior. Connections that originate from individual cluster members are subject to implicit Hide NAT behind the outgoing cluster VIP. This will affect traffic such as DNS lookups and outgoing FTP connections originating from cluster members. This is the same behavior we saw under ClusterXL. As with ClusterXL, once FP3 Hot Fix 1 is applied, packets routed back to the wrong member will be routed onward via the sync link. Check Point ClusterXL makes allowances for this when handling this traffic, dealing with it gracefully. A Nokia clustering solution will not deal with it as well, and the traffic involved will not be reliable. This behavior will also cause a problem with traffic between external interfaces of members. For these reasons, defining the cluster topology is not recommended when you're using a Nokia solution. Possibly this configuration will be made workable in future releases of NG.

Nokia IPSO VRRP Clusters

If a simple HA cluster solution is required for the Nokia platform, a VRRP configuration should be considered. In this section, we provide an overview of the VRRP protocol, how to configure it on IPSO, and how to configure FireWall-1 NG FP3 for a VRRP cluster. We'll then talk about how you can test the cluster and go over any special considerations that you need to keep in mind when using a cluster.

Nokia Configuration

To configure a Nokia VRRP cluster, you need to take the following steps:

- Configure the interfaces of a Nokia.

- Configure FireWall-1.

- Configure VRRP in Voyager.

We assume that you have installed IPSO 3.6 FCS-4 on your Nokia and that you have the Check Point FireWall-1 NG FP3 package installed and configured. As with setting up all clusters, it is recommended that you complete and test the physical connectivity first so that any problems that you encounter later aren't due to a misconfigured switch or interface, because these could be difficult to spot later.

In Figure 21.76, you can see an example Nokia VRRP configuration. Plenty of the information shown won't make much sense yet, so just look at the topology and IP addresses for now.

Figure 21.76 Our Example Configuration: A Nokia VRRP Cluster

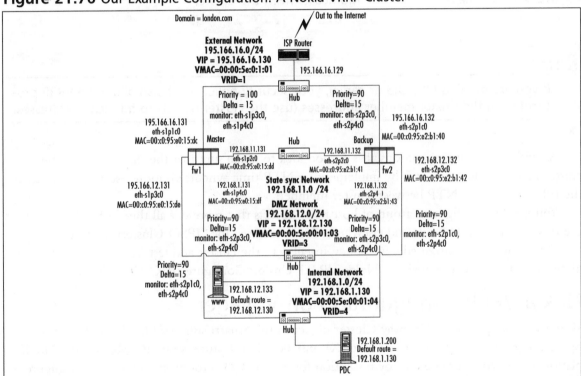

Unlike Nokia clustering, a VRRP configuration does not require a separate cluster control network. As you can see from Figure 21.76, each network that has a VIP also has a virtual MAC address—a unicast VRRP MAC that is used for the VIP. From a network perspective of neighboring equipment on the same network as the cluster interfaces, it looks the similar to Check Point ClusterXL in Load-Sharing mode, but with unicast MAC addresses involved rather than multicast.

You should be able to perform basic IPSO configuration, install Check Point NG FP3, and configure the Gateway Cluster object in the same way as you would for IPSO clustering, with one exception: When configuring the gateway cluster object Availability Mode, select **High Availability**.

Configuring the Nokia VRRP Rule Base

You have some choices as to the rule base you want to install. You can either see if the configuration of your cluster object is going to work and install an open policy, or you can create a strict policy now. Remember, there is still one more step to do, which is to configure VRRP using Voyager, so you might want to install an open policy now and then tighten it later once you are happy that your clustering is working correctly.

The VRRP protocol is multicast based. VRRP multicasts are sent by whichever member currently considers itself VRRP master. In IPSO 3.6, this traffic bypasses the firewall kernel, so no rules accepting the traffic are required in the security policy. If your switches are performing "IGMP snooping" to detect multicast group members, you need to allow the IGMP protocol from the cluster to multicast addresses, as shown in Figure 21.77.

Figure 21.77 Rule Allowing IGMP Multicasts from the Cluster

> **NOTE**
>
> If you are running IPSO 3.5 or earlier, your security policy must also allow the VRRP protocol from the cluster member addresses (use the cluster object) to multicast addresses.

As with other cluster solutions, it is a good idea to make sure that the time between the cluster members does not drift by implementing NTP time synchronization—so make sure that the rule base accepts NTP between cluster members.

You need to configure a group of host node objects that represent all the VRRP VIPs and use this in your "stealth" rule and elsewhere. For details, see the "IPSO Clustering" section.

Once you have configured your policy, install it to the cluster and test. You now have to complete the last step in configuring a Nokia VRRP cluster: Configure IPSO to use VRRP.

Nokia VRRP Configuration on Voyager

When we configured the Gateway Cluster object in the SmartDashboard GUI, we did not configure the gateway cluster to have ClusterXL installed. This feature is not available on the Nokia platform, but Nokia provides its own solution for HA: VRRP. However, you have to configure it within the Voyager interface.

> **NOTE**
>
> Remember that you have to configure VRRP on each Nokia in the cluster, so you will have to repeat the procedure on each Nokia.

In the section that follows, we deal with one particular VRRP configuration: VRRP monitored circuits with a single virtual router, and single virtual IP address, for each connected subnet, with two systems participating in the cluster. This is probably the most common and well-tested configuration, but VRRP provides many other possibilities. VRRP is a standard protocol for router redundancy and is well documented elsewhere, and brave readers might want to refer to RFC2338. For more details regarding IPSO VRRP configuration, refer to *Nokia Network Security Solutions Handbook* (Syngress Publishing, ISBN 1931836701).

Voyager Configuration

Make sure you have network connectivity from your browser to your Nokia FireWall-1 modules in your cluster, and make sure that the security policy you installed on the firewall does not prevent you from accessing Voyager from your browser. Navigate to Voyager on the system that you want to become the master member of the cluster. In our example, we would do this by going to https://195.166.16.131 (see Figure 21.78).

Figure 21.78 Voyager's Main Screen

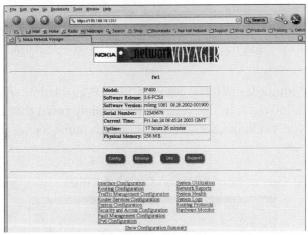

Here are the steps that you need to follow after you have authenticated and are presented with the main screen:

1. From the main Voyager screen, click **Router Services Configuration**.

2. Click **VRRP**. The initial configuration page appears.

3. Enter a cold start value. This introduces a delay after the VRRP system initializes, before it will consider itself a potential master router. A value of 30 seconds provides ample time for FireWall-1 to initialize (see Figure 21.79). Click **Apply**.

Figure 21.79 Initial VRRP Configuration Page in Voyager

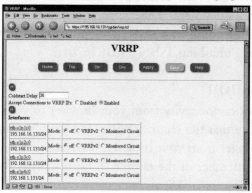

4. Select the VRRP mode for each interface on which redundancy is required. Typically, VRRP is enabled on all interfaces except the dedicated Check Point "sync" network. In this example, we use VRRP monitored circuits mode. The cluster configuration screen then expands to include more parameters that can be configured within the cluster. Click **Apply**.

5. Enter a virtual router ID (VRID) for each VRRP-enabled interface. Select a different VRID for each interface. In this case, we have simply based them on interface port numbers, but you could use, for example, network numbers (see Figure 21.80). Click **Apply**.

Figure 21.80 Cluster Configuration Defining VRIDs

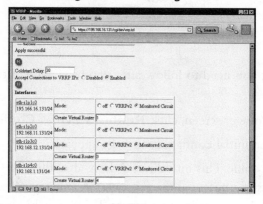

6. The next page allows you to configure VRRP for each interface. Supply values for each interface as follows:

-   **Priority** This should indicate your preference as to which member runs as master. In this example, we give a priority of 100 to our preferred member for each interface. When configuring the other member, we give a value of 90.

-   **Hello interval** The interval in seconds between each announcement from the current master. We are using a value of 1 second to give the quickest failover. If bursts of serious network congestion results in loss of some of these hello packets, a greater value might be specified, resulting in slow failover but less chance of "false" failover.

- **VMAC Mode** Choose VRRP for default VRRP behavior.

- **Backup Address** The virtual cluster IP address on this interface's subnet (see Figure 21.81).

  Once values have been specified for all the interfaces, click **Apply**.

Figure 21.81 Configuration for One of the Virtual Routers

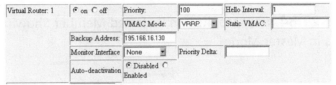

7. For each interface, we can now identify which other interfaces are monitored. This identification is key to the operation of Monitored Circuits mode. We want to ensure that if any one of the cluster interfaces fails on the current master, the backup system will become master and take over routing. To do this, each interface monitors all other VRRP enabled interfaces, with a priority delta of greater than the difference between the priority specified on the preferred master and the backup. In our example, the priority on our preferred master was 100 and on the backup, 90. We will use priority deltas of 15, ensuring that failure of any interface will reduce the effective priority of the current master to below that of the backup member (refer back to Figure 21.76 and see Figure 21.82).

Figure 21.82 A Virtual Router with Monitored Interfaces Enabled

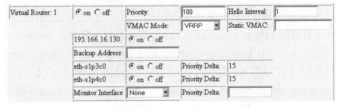

8. We will also configure authentication for each virtual router by enabling **Simple Authentication**, supplying a password, and clicking **Apply** (see Figure 21.83). This simple authentication is far from secure; the password given appears in Voyager after it is set and is transmitted in VRRP traffic as plaintext! It does, however, protect against simple attacks, or more likely, problems caused by other VRRP devices that have coincidentally been configured with the same VRID. Be aware that if the password (or lack of one) does not match that used by other members, this member will assume itself as master (there being no other devices with "correct" passwords enabled)—so always set the password correctly immediately on configuration of a new member's VRRP interfaces.

Figure 21.83 Configuring VRRP Interface Authentication

Authentication	○ None ⦿ Simple	Password	√22pp3ss

9. Finally, don't forget to click **Save**.

10. To verify that the members have correctly identified themselves as master and backup, click the link at the bottom of the page to VRRP Monitor (see Figure 21.84). The preferred member should indicate that all its virtual routers are in Master mode. The backup member should indicate that its virtual routers are in Backup mode.

Figure 21.84 VRRP Monitor on Preferred Member Showing All Three Virtual Routers in Master Mode

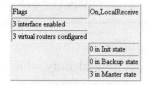

Flags	On,LocalReceive
3 interface enabled	
3 virtual routers configured	
	0 in Init state
	0 in Backup state
	3 in Master state

Testing the Nokia VRRP Cluster

Once your Nokia VRRP cluster is configured, you need to test it to make sure that it is functioning correctly. Again, keep in mind the way that this particular clustering technology works and how it differs from the other clustering solutions we have covered so far.

Test 1: Pinging the Virtual IP Address for Interface

You should be able to ping the local VIP addresses (VRRP backed-up addresses) from a host that is on the same subnet as the cluster interfaces.

You will receive a response if everything is working properly. If you do not receive a response, verify that your rule base allows echo-request to the cluster IPs and that **Accept Connections to VRRP IPs** is enabled in the Voyager VRRP page.

In the test we ran on our example network, a ping was initiated from the FireWall-1 management station (195.166.16.134) to the VIP of the cluster (195.166.16.130). A packet trace was run at the same time on the management station to analyze the packet for the ping session. If you look at the ARP cache of the local host initiating the ping, you should now have the VRRP MAC address of the VIP. In our case, this is 0:0:5e:0:1:1 (which you can check against Figure 21.76). This in itself does not tell you much—just that the VIP address is up and running, and that a member in the cluster responded—but can we tell which member?

Unlike other solutions, because the source MAC address of the echo reply is the VRRP MAC address, there is no indication of which member actually replied.

However, if we ping a host behind the cluster—as long as doing so is allowed by the firewall policy—the source MAC address of the reply packet will be the real MAC address of the member that passed the packet.

Test 2: Finding Which Member Responds to Administrative Connections to the VIPs

A rather unconventional test for the cluster is to attempt an administrative connection—in other words, Telnet, FTP, Voyager (HTTP or HTTPS) to a cluster VIP. The responding member will indicate its host name in its response, allowing you to deduce which member is the current master. If the connection fails, make sure that your rule base allows that type of connection to the cluster IP and that that type of access is supported by your IPSO configuration.

Test 3: Determining the Status of Each Member in the Cluster

In a VRRP configuration, there are two tools for monitoring the status of the cluster and its members. One is the SmartView Status GUI, and the other is Voyager monitoring.

The SmartView Status GUI shows you the health of each member and if it is in state table sync with other members of the cluster. What it won't show you is the correct status of each interface of each member. For this information, you have to use the Nokia Voyager screens on each member in the cluster.

Checking the monitoring of the cluster through Voyager is straightforward. Connect your browser to one of the members, and select **Monitor VRRP**. The summary information will indicate whether the member considers itself a master or backup (see Figures 6.85 and 6.86). More detailed information is available in the interface and stats pages (linked from this page).

Figure 21.85 The VRRP Monitor Interface Page

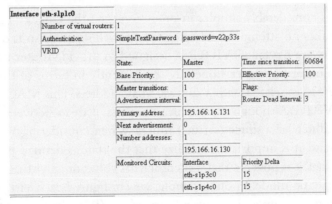

Figure 21.86 The VRRP Monitor Stats Page

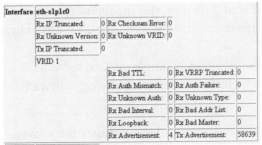

Test 4; FTPing through a VRRP Cluster During Interface Failure

We can follow the same steps as suggested for IPSO clustering configurations to perform a test. If SmartView Monitor is available, this provides a good method of observing the failover (or not).

Command–Line Stats

We can use the IPSO *clish* command to monitor VRRP from a console session. This command provides very similar information to that provided by Voyager but provides a useful alternative.

Once in the *clish* shell, you can use these commands:

- **show vrrp** Shows a summary of VRRP status.

- **show vrrp interface** *<interface name>* Provides for more details for a particular interface.

- **show vrrp interfaces** All interfaces.

- **show vrrp stats** Detailed VRRP statistics.

You can use the *cphaprob* command on the Nokia platform if you want, but the information that it will tell you is limited. For example, it can't tell you which interfaces are up or down, but it can tell you whether the state table synchronization is working or not.

How VRRP Works

The VRRP solution is considerably simpler in operation than the Check Point or Nokia cluster technology. VRRP makes no attempt to monitor the firewall software so it does not failover if the master firewall software has failed. VRRP is designed to provide router resilience, so if one physical router fails, another takes over, hopefully transparently in terms of through connectivity.

Each VRIP address is associated with a unicast MAC address. This MAC address comes from a range allocated for VRRP. Although it is a unicast address, it floats between members so that devices on the local subnet see a single (virtual) router. When considering whether a member is in master or backup state, it is important to realize that the state is defined per virtual router per interface. This means that it is possible that a member has some of its virtual routers in Master mode and others in Backup mode. In our example, we configured each virtual router on a member to use the same priority and monitor all its other VRRP enabled interfaces and associate those with the same delta; this should ensure that all virtual routers on a member are in a consistent state. In more advanced configurations, this flexibility can be used to advantage because it allows a member to be a preferred master for some routes but backup for others by using multiple virtual routers.

Communication between members is simple; in fact, there is no two-way communication as such. There are reasonably straightforward rules governing when members switch a VR between Master and Backup state:

- The member that believes itself to be the master for a given virtual router (VR) will send VRRP announcements for that VR at intervals as configure—in our example, every second—advertising its effective priority (that is, its base priority less the deltas of any failed interfaces). This concept is illustrated in Figure 21.87.

- If a member with a VR in master state sees an announcement with a higher effective priority than its own, it switches itself to backup state and stops sending announcements.

- If a member with a VR in backup state sees an announcement that has a higher effective priority, it will switch to master state itself and begin announcements.

- If a member with a VR in backup state does not see any advertisements for a given timeout period, it will switch to master state.

Figure 21.87 VRRP Announcements

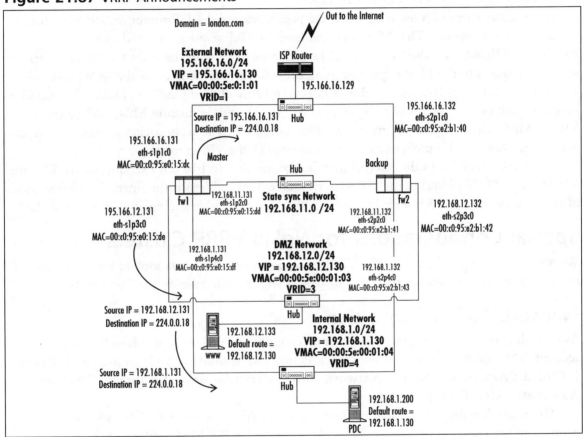

Let's walk through an example of how a connection would work through a VRRP cluster. In our example, host 192.168.1.200 initiates a Telnet session through the cluster to our ISP router on IP address 195.166.16.129, and we address hide the connection behind the cluster external IP address of 195.166.16.130, using a hide rule in our firewall NAT rule base.

When the Telnet session is initiated, the host 192.168.1.200 sends out an ARP request for 192.168.1.130, which is the default gateway on the network 192.168.1.0. The address in the ARP response will be the VRRP MAC address for the VR on that network. The member that has the

VR in master status will always send the ARP response. In our example, the MAC address returned is 0:0:5e:0:1:4. Our host on 192.168.1.200 then sends a SYN TCP packet, high source port, destination is to 195.166.16.129, destination MAC is 0:0:5e:0:1:4 (the default gateway MAC address).

Only one member of the cluster will do anything with the packet—the one with the VR in master state. This will pass the packet up through the IP stack to Check Point FireWall-1 for the incoming interface. The TCP SYN packet will pass through the rule base of the firewall and, providing that everything is fine, it will then send the packet out of its external interface, with the source IP address of 195.166.16.130 (the external cluster IP address), with the source MAC address of the member that has routed the packet (in our example, the source MAC address is 0:c0:95:e0:15:dc , which corresponds with member fw1 external interface eth-s1p1c0), and the destination IP address will be 195.166.16.129.

If the Telnet daemon is listening when the packet reaches the ISP router on 195.166.16.129, it will produce a response. The ISP router will issue an ARP request for IP address 195.166.16.130, which is the VIP of the cluster. The member with the external VR in master state will respond to the ARP request, sending the VRRP MAC address as the MAC address associated with IP 195.166.16.130. Host 195.166.16.129 will then send a SYN,ACK TCP packet, source IP will be 195.166.16.129, source port will be 23, and destination MAC will be the VRRP MAC address of the VR master for 195.166.16.130. The reply packet arrives at all members in the cluster and is processed by the member with the VR in master state.

The packet then leaves the internal interface of member fw1 in our example, source IP is the 195.166.16.129 (IP address of the ISP router), source MAC address is the internal interface MAC of fw1, and destination IP is now 192.168.1.200 (it has been address translated by FireWall-1).

Special Considerations for Nokia VRRP Clusters

We have talked a little about how the VRRP solution works. Now we look at issues that should be taken into account when setting up our cluster and the rule base we are likely to use.

Network Address Translation

As with all clusters, the way you decide to implement your NAT rules needs to be taken into account. With VRRP, you cannot use Check Point's own Automatic ARP setting in the **Policy | Global Properties | NAT – Network Address Translation | Automatic Rules** for **Automatic ARP Configuration**.

The reason for this is that each member will proxy ARP for the real MAC address of the member in the cluster as opposed to proxy ARPing the VRRP MAC address of the relevant cluster VR. For this reason, you cannot use Automatic ARP Configuration.

You can enter proxy ARP entries into Voyager for NATed IP addresses using the VRRP MAC address of the cluster VR. Alternatively, you could add static host routes on the ISP router to route traffic for the NATed IP address to the external VRIP address. Note: It is *not* recommended to add the NATed IP address as a VRIP address, because doing so could cause problems with FireWall-1 antispoofing configurations.

Connections Originating from a Single Member in the Cluster

When defining the CP cluster object for the IPSO cluster, the cluster topology could be defined using the VIPs. This results in the same behavior as ClusterXL on connections from members out of the external if they implicitly hide NAT behind cluster VIPs. As with ClusterXL, once FP3 Hotfix 1(or a more recent hotfix that includes Hotfix 1 features) is applied, packets routed back to the wrong member should be routed onward via the sync link, so this configuration will work—to a degree. However, in practice, there seems to be problems with this configuration in non-ClusterXL solutions that result in packet loss, and as such we recommend that the cluster topology *not* be defined when you're using a VRRP solution.

Third-Party Clustering Solutions

A range of solutions are available that provide HA and load-sharing functionality for FireWall-1. Some integrate with FireWall-1 on the cluster members themselves, while others are located adjacent to the cluster and allocate traffic between members from there. The most widely used third-party solutions are probably Stonesoft StoneBeat and Rainfinity Rainwall; both have HA and load-balancing variants. For information on other OPSEC partner HA solutions, and indeed more about OPSEC, refer to the OPSEC Web site. It is wise to check the OPSEC site to match product version with supported FireWall-1 version for any third-party solution:

- **Stonesoft** www.stonesoft.com

- **Rainfinity** www.rainfinity.com

- **Other OPSEC partners** www.opsec.com

Clustering and HA Performance Tuning

If you have gotten this far after configuring and testing your cluster, you'll want to know what you can do in terms of improving your cluster's performance. A great deal of performance tuning on firewalls depends on how well you know the type of traffic that goes through the firewall and then tuning the firewall to handle the most common type of traffic more efficiently. In a clustering environment, you need to expand on the concept of tuning considerations, all the way down to hardware, depending on the clustering solution you have implemented. In this section, we discuss the main considerations for optimizing your cluster solution.

Data Throughput or Large Number of Connections

Firewall load-sharing clustering solutions are very good at increasing the overall data throughput of your firewall; the higher the throughput you require, the more members you add in your cluster. However, you will soon reach a stage where adding more members to your cluster just doesn't make any performance difference, because the bottleneck moves somewhere else on the data path—either the line speed of connecting equipment or cables or routers. Furthermore, consider the fact that a two-member load sharing of fast machines with fast network cards for cluster members will probably scale better than slower machines with slower network cards but more cluster members. This is where the price that you pay for hardware is probably significantly lower than paying for an extra enterprise license FireWall-1 module. However, if you are looking for higher resilience, more members in the cluster might be the way to go.

In large numbers of connections, clustering is less help than you might think. The reason for this is that if you have 50,000 connections going through one member and 50,000 connections going through the other member, and you only have two members in the cluster, and one member fails, you will have 100,000 connections going through one member. However, both members will still have a connections table showing 100,000 connections (assuming that the connections are synchronized between members), even when both members were online. The point here is that the connections tables are going to be large the more connections that you push through the cluster, because every member in the cluster should have its connections table synchronized with every other member in the cluster in case of a member failure. The rate of change of new connections makes the situation worse because it has a strong impact on the amount of data that is synchronized between cluster members. High rates of change of connections need to be identified wherever possible because these are prime services that you would target for not synchronizing across the cluster members.

Based on these two definitions of load on a firewall cluster, let's look at each type of load and what can be done to improve performance.

Improving Data Throughput

Improving data throughput is probably the easiest of the two performance areas that can be addressed. It can be addressed in the following ways:

- Use good fast networking cards—100Mbps Ethernet full duplex or gigabit Ethernet cards—in the cluster members. Make sure that surrounding hubs and routers from the origin of the data through to the destination of the data have fast physical networking hardware. These are the key areas that will give you high throughput.

- Use fast single-processor members in the cluster, with lots of memory.

- Use a load-sharing cluster as opposed to an HA cluster. Traffic can be shared across the members in the cluster, which will give higher data rates of throughput.

- Keep your rule base short and compact. Larger numbers of rules will slow throughput. This applies to NAT rules and the security rule base.

You need good networking cards, and your hubs and routers—all the way from data source through the cluster to the data destination—need to be as good as you can get. This will define your maximum throughput, and it is this line speed that you will aim for.

Using fast single-processor members and plenty of memory is good practice. It enables the member in the cluster to deal with highly processor-intensive services, such as VPN connections, as quickly as possible. Different members in the load-sharing cluster will take different VPN connections between the cluster and the remote sites, so this means that one member will not be dealing with all the VPN traffic. If you just have one VPN set up between the cluster and the remote site, only one member in the cluster will take the load. If you have several VPNs set up, multiple members in the cluster will be dealing with the VPN connections. This will be based on the load-sharing algorithm used.

In addition, if you are using the security servers for passing traffic, such as FTP, HTTP, or Telnet, this is load shared across the cluster as well and will also give you efficiencies because it can also be CPU intensive. If you are using security servers, make sure that the DNS resolver on each member of the cluster is pointing at a high-speed DNS server or servers (which preferably have a very rich cache) so that DNS lookups do not hold up the performance.

Lots of memory will prevent your host from writing too much to the swap memory area, although some operating systems use their swap space regardless of how much physical memory you install.

If you are going for high throughput, you have to use a load-sharing clustering solution. This gives you scalability and allows big benefits for VPNs and security server connections. It gives big benefits for normal connections as well.

You can do many things with rule base tuning that will make a big difference to increasing the throughput of a member. Tuning the rule base will also give you some major connections-based performance as well. The types of things you need to do to a rule base to make it more efficient are as follows:

- Reduce the number of rules to a minimum.

- Try not to have rules that are sourced with group objects, destination group objects, because this will multiply out into individual rules when the policy is compiled. Instead, use network objects subnetted appropriately.

- Do not use group objects nested inside one another. Again, this causes the compiled rule base to have a large number of rules in it.

- Reduce the number of NAT rules to a minimum.

- Reduce the number of objects you reference in the rule base.

- Don't use resource rules or user authentication unless you need to. The throughput of the security servers is not as fast as a straight stateful connection through the FireWall-1 kernel.

- Place the most commonly accessed rules as close to the top of the rule base as you can get away with.

- Avoid using domain objects.

- Keep logging to a minimum on rules.

Tuning VPNs for throughput is a special case. You can always increase the overall performance of a VPN by making the member do less work to encrypt and decrypt packets, but this is usually at the price of security. For example, using weaker encryption strengths will reduce the security of encrypted packets, but it will mean that the firewall members have to do less work. Using perfect forwarding secrecy also causes a significant performance overhead, but changing this setting will reduce security.

If no compromise of security versus throughput is possible, you have two other options open to you. One is to use the Check Point Performance Pack, which will give you VPN acceleration. The other possibility is to use a hardware accelerator in each member of the cluster, which will aid DES and 3DES calculations for VPNs.

To summarize, anything that you can do on a single firewall member to improve performance is also true of a FireWall-1 member in a clustered environment.

Improving for Large Number of Connections

In many ways, improving for a large number of connections requires more thought than tweaking your cluster for maximum data throughput because it is less dependent on hardware. The first thing you need to be aware of that will reduce the performance of a cluster as far as a large number of connections is concerned is the rate of change of new connections. If this is very high, these particular types of connections are good candidates for not being synchronized between cluster members. On clusters, you need to reduce the number of connections in the connections state table, and you also need to reduce the number of connections that are synchronized statefully.

For example, DNS lookups through a member will be done often. These are small packets, which are often responded to very quickly, and most DNS resolvers are quite patient about waiting for a response. Many DNS lookups are done, especially by any HTTP clients, FTP clients, and the FireWall-1 management server itself if logging has been told to resolve host names.

DNS is a classic service for which you would turn off state table sync. It is a very transient UDP-based service, so synchronizing the state makes little sense. By default, the service is synchronized across the cluster members.

To do this, start the SmartDashboard GUI, log in, click **Manage | Services**, and select the service **domain-udp**, as shown in Figure 21.88. Click the **Edit** button, and then click the **Advanced** button. Uncheck the **Synchronize on cluster** check box, and then click **OK** and install the policy.

Figure 21.88 Turning Off State Synchronization for a Specific Service

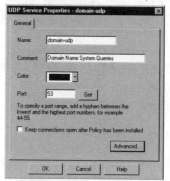

There are a large number of services to which you might want to do this. The more you reduce the state synchronization required, the better your members in your cluster will perform for connections.

The other weapon you have for reducing the number of connections in the state table is reducing the virtual session timeout for each service. This especially applies to UDP services, but it can also apply to many TCP-based services, such as HTTP.

Most HTTP sessions are short and transient, so unless you are hosting a Web site where it is vital that each HTTP session opened is longer than 3600 seconds (or 1 hour), it is a good idea to reduce this in the service itself. This means that if the session did not finish normally, the timeout will clear more quickly than the default of one hour. You can do this by clicking **Virtual Session Timeout** in the **Advanced** area of each service definition, as shown in Figure 21.89.

Figure 21.89 Advanced Settings of the DNS UDP Service

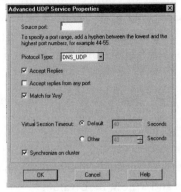

Once you have done as much as you can do to reduce the number of connections that each member will have and you have reduced the number of connections that will be synchronized across the cluster, you need to tune each member in the cluster to accept more than 25,000 connections and tune the kernel memory and NAT table sizes as well to cater for the increase in connections.

This process used to be a manual process of hacking text files previous to FireWall-1 NG FP3, but now it can all be done from the SmartDashboard GUI. Navigate to the **Manage** menu, choose **Network Objects**, then locate the **Cluster Gateway Object** of your cluster, and click **Edit**. On the left side of the pop-up window, select **Capacity Optimization**.

From Figure 21.90, you can see that you can modify all the parameters mentioned earlier. The automatic setting for memory pool size and connection hash table size is usually fine, but you might want to monitor these parameters (which we discuss next). If you need to manually tweak the hash table size and the memory pool size, you can also do this from this screen. Note that after policy install, the size of the connections table changes will take effect.

Figure 21.90 Configuring Capacity Optimization of Your Cluster

You'll want to monitor the connections table sizes, the memory pool size, and the table hash sizes. How can you do this? The best way is to get a console connection to one of your modules and run the diagnostic commands to reveal this information.

Monitoring the Connections Table

The first thing you will want to do is examine the connections table of a module to determine the current maximum limit for number of connections. This can be done with the *fw tab −t connections* command from one of the firewall modules in the cluster.

At the top of this command's output are the parameters of this table, which you need to take note of—including the maximum number of connections parameter.

```
-------- connections --------
dynamic, id 8158, attributes: keep, sync, expires 60, refresh, limit
    25000, hashsize 32768, kbuf 16 17 18 19 20 21 22 23 24 25 26 27 28
        29 30, free function 707138a0 0
```

Altering the number of connections up to 50,000 and then running the command will show the new table size for connections and a new hash value:

```
-------- connections --------
dynamic, id 8158, attributes: keep, sync, expires 60, refresh, limit
    50000, hashsize 262144, kbuf 16 17 18 19 20 21 22 23 24 25 26 27
        28 29 30, free function 707138a0 0
```

Note that when you change the connections size, you will also see that the SmartView Tracker logs show that the connections table has changed, the connections table hash has changed, and the memory pool size has been changed.

If you want to monitor the number of connections going through a member at any one time, use the command *fw tab −t connections −s*. This will give you statistics of the current number of connections in the table (#VALS column) and the peak number of connections (#PEAK column):

```
fw1 # fw tab -t connections -s
HOST                    NAME                      ID #VALS #PEAK #SLINKS
localhost               connections             8158     5    20       8
```

You could get to the stage where you would like to identify a specific connection on a module and check that you can see that connection synchronized to another module in the cluster. To look at the connections table to make sure that it makes sense, use the command *fw tab −t connections −f*:

```
10:49:12         192.168.11.131 >     ------------------------------------
(+); Direction: 0; Source: 192.168.1.100; SPort: 4990; Dest: 192.168.1.
130; DPort: telnet; Protocol: tcp; CPTFMT_sep: ;; Type: 114689; Flags:
8405120; Rule: 2; Timeout: 3600; Handler: 0; Uuid: 3e37b13c0c3a610837b6;
Ifncin: 4; Ifncout: 4; Ifnsin: -1; Ifnsout: -1; Bits: 0000000002000000;
```

```
NAT_VM_Dest: 192.168.1.131; NAT_VM_Flags: 100; NAT_Client_Dest: 192.168.1
.130; NAT_Client_Flags: 100; NAT_Server_Flags: 0; NAT_Xlate_Flags: 32836;
 SeqVerifier_Kbuf_ID: 1076676608; Expires: 3495/3600; product: VPN-1 &
FireWall-1;


10:49:12        192.168.11.131 >     ------------------------------------
(+); Direction: 1; Source: 192.168.1.131; SPort: telnet; Dest: 192.168.1.
100; DPort: 4990; Protocol: tcp; CPTFMT_sep_1: ->; Direction_1: 0;
Source_1: 192.168.1.100; SPort_1: 4990; Dest_1: 192.168.1.130; DPort_1:
telnet; Protocol_1: tcp; FW_symval: 5; product: VPN-1 & FireWall-1;
```

Normally, the *fw tab −t connections −f* command would show all connections, but you can filter it down by piping into the *grep* command (such as *fw tab −t connections −f | grep telnet*, which was done in the preceding example).

The connection we are interested in is the connection that has an *Expires:* parameter. This shows the TCP timeout of the connection and so is a good method to prove that your changes to a service's virtual session timeout are working (see Figure 21.86). The other connection we can see is present for the reply from the cluster IP address (as the session initiated was a Telnet from host 192.168.1.100 to the VIP address of 192.168.1.130).

The Telnet service is state synchronized, so we should see exactly the same connection in the connections table of fw2 in the cluster. State table synchronizes an update at least every 100ms to all members in the cluster.

Monitoring Pool Memory

Pool memory is fairly easy to monitor in FireWall-1 NG FP3. You need to make sure that kernel memory for the firewall kernel is not exhausted, or you could end up with *halloc* memory allocation error messages in the system logs of your operating system. This can lead to the host becoming unresponsive and intermittently locking up—including locking up console access to the member.

You can monitor the kernel memory situation using the command *fw ctl pstat* on the firewall module:

```
fw2 #fw ctl pstat


Hash kernel memory (hmem) statistics:
   Total memory allocated: 20971520 bytes in 5118 4KB blocks using 2 pools
   Initial memory allocated: 6291456 bytes (Hash memory extended by
       14680064 bytes)
   Memory allocation  limit: 83886080 bytes using 10 pools
   Total memory bytes  used:    348308   unused: 20623212 (98.34%)   peak:
       369584
   Total memory blocks used:        114   unused:     5004 (97%)   peak:
       126
```

```
        Allocations: 71973 alloc, 0 failed alloc, 66671 free

System kernel memory (smem) statistics:
   System   physical   memory: 255074304 bytes
   Available physical memory: 59908096 bytes
   Total memory  bytes  used: 31724112   peak: 31869120
      Blocking  memory  bytes   used: 1531912   peak:  1636904
      Non-Blocking memory bytes used: 30192200   peak: 30232216
   Allocations: 3645229 alloc, 0 failed alloc, 3644952 free, 0 failed free


Kernel memory (kmem) statistics:
   Total memory  bytes  used: 11088212   peak: 11826720
         Allocations: 81792 alloc, 0 failed alloc, 76215 free, 0 failed free


Kernel stacks:
         262144 bytes total, 16384 bytes stack size, 16 stacks,
         2 peak used, 4124 max stack bytes used, 1028 min stack bytes used,
         0 failed stack calls


INSPECT:
         13746 packets, 2698521 operations, 43174 lookups,
         0 record, 702731 extract


Cookies:
         2309961 total, 0 alloc, 0 free,
         21 dup, 863658 get, 1243 put,
         1458553 len, 0 cached len, 0 chain alloc,
         0 chain free


Connections:
         4019 total, 436 TCP, 3381 UDP, 201 ICMP,
         1 other, 5 anticipated, 7 recovered, 10 concurrent,
         26 peak concurrent, 861843 lookups


Fragments:
         0 fragments, 0 packets, 0 expired, 0 short,
         0 large, 0 duplicates, 0 failures


NAT:
         215/0 forw, 1021/0 bckw, 1214 tcpudp,
         22 icmp, 1268-1410 alloc
```

```
sync new ver working
sync out: on   sync in: on
sync packets sent:
total: 9302 retransmitted: 0 retrans reqs: 0 acks: 49
sync packets received:
total 4911 of which 0 queued and 0 dropped by net
also received 0 retrans reqs and 38 acks to 17 cb requests
callback average delay 1 max delay 6
```

The area for kernel memory you should keep an eye on is the total memory bytes used, unused, and the peak usage. The peak usage will tell you whether in the past there has not been enough kernel memory. You will get some statistical count in the *failed alloc* field of hash kernel memory and system kernel memory if there is a memory allocation problem for connection load.

The output of this command also gives you connections statistics, fragmented packets stats, and NAT stats. It provides the state synchronization statistics as well.

Final Tweaks to Get the Last Drop of Performance

We have by no means covered everything you can do to the members in your cluster to maximize their performance. One particular area of note is optimizing the operating system that the members use. This varies considerably from one operating system to another in terms of the types and extent to which you can do this, but it is thoroughly worth doing.

Summary

Most of the hard work and decision making you'll encounter will be at the design stage. Are you using existing modules to upgrade to NG FP3, what platforms are the modules on, and what hubs and switches do you have available are all questions you will have to consider. Many of these issues are based on the type of clustering solution you choose. In short, the pertinent points of each clustering solution are as follows:

- **ClusterXL in HA New mode** High availability with monitoring of system, cluster, and network state, integrated with FireWall-1. Unicast MAC addresses are used for the VIP address on each subnet. Can be fully managed from SmartView status GUI. SmartCenter Server (management station) can be located on the secured network or elsewhere. Interfaces of the members in the cluster also have real IP addresses as well as the VIP address.

- **ClusterXL in HA Legacy mode** High availability with monitoring of system, cluster, and network state, integrated with FireWall-1. Included for compatibility with older FireWall-1 versions, limited by technology that leaves standby nodes unreachable except from management network. Can be fully managed from SmartView Status GUI, depending on failover conditions and location of GUI client on network. Unicast MAC for the VIP address, which is shared across the cluster, as is the MAC address for a particular subnet. SmartCenter Server *must* be located on the secured network and should have a second interface onto an Internet-routable IP address if managing other FireWall-1 enforcement points outside of the local network. Interfaces of the members in the legacy cluster do not have unique IP addresses or MAC addresses, apart from the secured network.

- **ClusterXL in Load-Sharing mode** Load sharing with monitoring of system, cluster, and network state, integrated with FireWall-1. Can be fully managed from SmartView Status GUI. Multicast MAC address responses for an ARP of the VIP (which is not a multicast IP address). This means that each member in the cluster has the same MAC and VIP across the cluster for a particular subnet. The SmartCenter Server can be located on the secured network or elsewhere. Interfaces of the members in the cluster also have real IP addresses as well as the VIP address.

- **Nokia Load Sharing cluster** Load sharing with monitoring of system, cluster, and network state, limited integration with FireWall-1. Can be partially managed by SmartView Status GUI but also must use Voyager to find the status of the cluster. Multicast MAC address responses for an ARP of the VIP (which is not a multicast IP address). This means that each member in the cluster has the same MAC and VIP across the cluster for a particular subnet. The SmartCenter Server can be located on the secured network or elsewhere. Interfaces of the members in the cluster also have real IP addresses as well as the VIP address. The solution requires no license since it is part of the IPSO operating system.

- **Nokia VRRP cluster** Simple configuration but limited management. No monitoring of system or cluster state other than network interfaces. Unicast shared MAC for the VIP address, which is shared across the cluster. The SmartCenter Server can be located on the secured network or elsewhere. Interfaces of the members in the cluster also have real IP addresses as well as the VIP address. The solution requires no license since it is part of the IPSO operating system.

After you initially configure the cluster, make sure that you have the clustering solution working as you would expect before configuring a complex firewall rule base. The key here is to keep testing the functions of the cluster failover after each significant change to ensure that you have not done something to compromise the functionality of your cluster.

Once your cluster is configured and working and you have your security policy in place, take careful note of the configuration of your cluster and its members—and the settings of all the networking equipment on the same subnet as the VIP addresses of the cluster. This includes settings on routers, switches, and hosts. Taking note of these settings will be very useful if you ever need to troubleshoot the cluster. Sometimes configuration of adjacent devices has a habit of changing without advance warning to the firewall administrator.

The final step is to tune your cluster. Go through the procedure of examining your connections table to determine which services are most common in your connections table, and determine if you need to synchronize that service across the cluster. Is the service very transient? If so, it's a good candidate for switching off state table synchronization. Can you reduce the TCP or UDP timeout for a particular service? Additionally, make sure you increase the number of connections that your cluster will be able to handle and the kernel and hash allocation.

Part V

ISA Server

## Chapter 22

ISA Server Deployment Planning and Design

Best Damn Topics in This Chapter:

- **ISA Deployment: Planning and Designing Issues**

- **Active Directory Implementation**

- **Mission-Critical Considerations**

- **Planning the Appropriate Installation Mode**

Introduction

Planning your ISA Server installation before actually performing it is absolutely critical. As with any firewall, the amount of thought and analysis you put into your design will help optimize ISA performance and will minimize the chance of making a substantial error that will adversely affect your security or access schemes.

All traffic that moves between the Internet and your internal network should move through a firewall, which is your ISA server. It is the job of the bastion host to ensure that all packets sent to and received from the Internet are evaluated and assessed for their relevance and safety.

The ISA server is a firewall because it provides the demarcation point between a trusted and untrusted network. Moreover, the ISA server can provide DMZ services through additional network interfaces. Because of this, it is critical to make sure that the ISA server is set up as securely as possible.

ISA Deployment: Planning and Designing Issues

When you decide to put together an ISA Server solution for your organization, you should plan ahead. ISA Server is an integral part of your security configuration scheme, and you do not want to merely install the server and hope that everything works out right. Carpenters have an old saying: "Measure twice, cut once." If you thoroughly map out your design, you'll avoid pitfalls in your deployment and further down the line.

In this section, we focus on planning and design issues as they relate to the installation of ISA Server. The primary issues of concern are:

- Network and hardware specifications
- The edition of ISA Server to be installed
- The mode in which ISA Server will be installed
- Stand-alone versus array configurations
- Client configuration requirements
- ISA Server Internet connectivity

You should make firm decisions about each of these ISA Server design issues *before* you begin your installation. The conclusions you reach at this point will determine your choices when it comes time to install ISA Server.

Assessing Network and Hardware Requirements

Prior to installing ISA Server, you need to assess hardware requirements to meet the needs of your organization's ISA Server deployment plan. An organization that has 50 network clients and chooses to use only the Web proxy service will have very different requirements than an organization with 30,000 network clients that wants to avail itself of all the networking services ISA Server has to offer.

System Requirements

Whether you choose to install one or 100 ISA servers, each server must meet minimum hardware and software requirements. The minimum requirements for any ISA server—regardless of the role the machine might play on the network are:

- Windows 2000 Server or Windows Server 2003 family operating system with the latest service pack installed

- A Pentium II or K7 (Athlon) Processor running at 300MHz or faster

- A minimum of 256MB of RAM (Microsoft recommended)

- A minimum of 20MB for the program files

- A minimum of 2GB for the Web cache

- At least two network interfaces—one to the internal network and a second to an external network, such as the Internet or corporate backbone (the exception is an internal caching-only server)

- Partitions formatted as NTFS to store the program, log, and cache files

- A Windows 2000 domain if Enterprise Policies will be implemented

Each of these components requires thoughtful consideration before implementing the ISA Server on your network. Let's look at each in more detail.

Software Requirements

ISA Server must be installed on a Windows 2000 Server or Windows Server 2003. It will not install on Windows NT 4.0 or Windows 2000 Professional. If you try to install ISA Server on a Windows 2000 Server machine that does not have the latest service pack installed, you will get an error message during the installation, informing you that you must first install the service pack before the installation routine can continue.

ISA Server Standard Edition can be installed on any member of the Windows 2000 Server family. The Enterprise Edition of ISA Server must be installed on Windows 2000 Advanced Server, Datacenter Server, or Windows Server 2003. Therefore, if you organization has only the "Server" version of Windows 2000, not the Advanced or Datacenter versions, you need to upgrade before installing ISA Enterprise Edition.

Processor Requirements

Processor requirements are somewhat flexible. It is rather unusual to see a production server in a corporate environment running at 300MHz or less; such a server would be rather long in the tooth at this point. If your servers are even a year old, it's unlikely that they are slower than 500MHz. Because the address translation and rule processing performed by ISA Server is processor intensive, you will benefit from a more powerful processor or multiple processors.

If you configure a large number of packet filters or content and site rules, you'll want to maximize the processor configuration on your server. If you don't plan to implement a lot of rules on the server and will use it primarily for Web caching, a 300MHz machine should present no problems. Table 22.1 will help you assess your processor requirements.

> **NOTE**
>
> The rate-limiting factor when it comes to processor requirements can be boiled down to the number of rules per second that ISA Server needs to evaluate. An ISA server with a few rules but high throughput could have roughly the same requirements as a machine that has many rules but little throughput through its external interface. Note that we cannot make a decision based on throughput on the internal interface, because it is assumed that other types of traffic that are not processed by any ISA services could flow through this interface. Therefore, you can use the speed of the external interface as a guideline for the level of processor support your ISA server requires.

Table 22.1 ISA Server Processor Requirements

External Interface Data Rate	Processor Requirement	Type of Connection
Less than 10Mb/second	Pentium II or K6-2 300MHz	ISDN, cable, or DSL
10–50Mb/second	Pentium III or K7 500MHz	T3 or comparable
More than 50Mb/second	Pentium III or K7 500MHz; add a processor for each increment of 50Mb/second	Very Fast

We have included AMD processor offerings along with the Intel specifications that Microsoft includes in its documentation. Microsoft still doesn't like to talk too much about AMD because of Microsoft's long association with Intel. However, AMD has closed the gap, and its K7/Athlon processors provide superior performance at lower cost. The only reservation you might have regarding the K7 series is its multiprocessor support. At this juncture, it might be wise to go with Intel when designing a multiprocessor solution.

Multiprocessor Support

Keep in mind that ISA Server, Windows 2000, and Windows Server 2003 support multiprocessor system setups. If you are configuring the server as an integrated firewall and Web cache server, and if the server is performing any other duties (such as acting as a domain controller for a dedicated ISA Server domain), you'll want to strongly consider a multiprocessor machine. ISA Server has been certified as Windows 2000 compliant, and part of the certification process included its ability to take advantage of symmetric multiprocessing. Windows 2000 Server supports up to four processors. Windows 2000 Advanced Server supports up to eight processors, and Windows 2000 Datacenter Server and Windows Server 2003 support up to 32 processors.

The number of processors determines how much you'll pay for ISA Server, because the licensing fees are based on the number of processors on the server. Since the costs can increment outrageously for a multiprocessor machine, you should consider installing ISA Server on a system with a single processor, and then carry out performance monitoring to aid you in making a cost/benefit analysis of a multiple-processor solution.

If you do not qualify for the upgrade, you should consider the cost of purchasing Proxy Server 2.0, which is very reasonably priced, and then upgrade your version of Proxy Server to ISA Server. This is especially sound advice if you intend to purchase the Enterprise Version of ISA Server. Open license and select license plans are also available; these can dramatically reduce costs. You'll have to call your local Microsoft representative for the details on these types of licensing.

RAM Configuration

Microsoft recommends that any ISA server you deploy should have at least 256MB of RAM to take advantage of all the product's features. However, we have installed ISA Server on machines with 192MB of RAM without difficulty, and it performed reasonably well in a limited laboratory environment. If you do choose to install ISA Server on machines with less than 256MB of RAM, you should not run any other memory (or processor) intensive services on that machine and should limit such configurations to very small businesses.

> **NOTE**
>
> If you are "hardware challenged" and must use a minimal RAM configuration, you should dedicate the machine to ISA only and use it for no other services, not even file-sharing and Web services.

The Network Address Translation (NAT) tables maintained by ISA Server are stored in RAM. Even in a large network, the NAT tables should not consume much memory. However, ISA Server offers a new feature as part of the Web proxy service: the ability to hold a large portion of the Web cache in RAM. This capability greatly improves cache performance, but you must have a large chunk of RAM to dedicate to the cache in order to realize these benefits.

Hardware designs that include less than 256MB of RAM can experience bottlenecks in Web-caching performance. This is because the ISA Server Web-caching feature takes advantage of RAM to store the Web cache. When there isn't enough RAM to store a good portion of the Web cache in memory, the server must place the files in the disk-based cache. This results in URL retrieval times that are much longer than retrieval times from RAM cache.

The size of the Web cache you want to keep in RAM correlates with the number of users on your network. Table 22.2 provides some general guidelines regarding the relationship between number of users and RAM requirements.

Table 22.2 ISA Server RAM Requirements

Users Behind ISA Server	Total ISA Server RAM
Fewer than 250	192MB (Microsoft states128 MB)
250–2,000	256MB
More than 2,000	256MB plus an incremental increase of 256MB for every 2,000 users

Note that the Microsoft recommendation for fewer than 250 users correlates with our own recommendation for small, simple networks. However, we believe that the 128MB lower limit is set too low. RAM prices are quite volatile, but they continue to fall with time. We recommend that you get as much RAM as your hardware budget allows. You will notice considerable improvement in Web cache if the amount of RAM in the machine exceeds the size of your Web cache.

Disk Space Considerations

The amount of disk space you allot to your ISA Server configuration can be quite variable. The space required for the program files will always be about 20MB, which shouldn't be an issue on any mission-critical server on which you chose to install ISA Server. However, when you plan your disk space requirements, you must consider other important factors.

The most important issue is the amount of disk space you want to dedicate to the Web cache. Unlike that of Proxy Server 2.0, the ISA Server Web cache is stored in a single file. This single-file format is a lot more efficient than the file system–based storage used in Proxy Server 2.0.

The file system–based storage used in Proxy Server 2.0 also had some security problems because it allowed users with the appropriate permissions to easily view the contents of the cache by opening the individual files. The cache could also be indexed and searched for information that an organization might consider proprietary.

Even though SSL-protected pages were not cached on Proxy Server 2.0, most companies did not protect their internal network Web resources using SSL and used authentication-based access instead. Although access to internal Web servers was secured by requiring authentication, the contents of the interaction were cached and therefore could be made available to users without the users having to actually access the server itself.

The single-file storage system for the Web cache gets around this problem. The .CDAT file used to store cached objects on the ISA server is a database file. You cannot open this file with a text editor or Web browser. However, you can use a tool on the ISA Server CD-ROM called CacheDir.exe to view the contents of the cache and key information about the cache file entries.

Another major advantage of the single-file storage system is that the cache file is not dynamically resized. If you set the cache for a particular drive to 100MB, the .CDAT file will start as 100MB and will not change. Performance gains are realized by avoiding processor cycles required to dynamically resize the file.

Cache Size Considerations

In the past, Microsoft recommended that you begin with a Web cache of at least 100MB plus 0.5MB for each user on the network. These figures were included with the Proxy Server 2.0 documentation. The nature of the Internet and how people interact with the Internet has changed radically since the release of Proxy Server 2.0, and therefore these minimal guidelines no longer apply. To fully realize the advantages of Web caching, you need to create a much larger Web cache.

Table 22.3 provides guidelines for configuring your Web cache. *These Web cache recommendations are extremely conservative.* Even in small networks, you should plan for a much larger Web cache.

Table 22.3 ISA Server Disk Space Requirements

Number of Users	Disk Space for Web Cache
Fewer than 250	2GB to 4GB
250–2,000	10GB
More than 2,000	10GB plus another 10GB for every 2000 users

> **NOTE**
>
> The numbers given by Microsoft for disk space allocations are interesting because they represent disparate requirements per user, based on the number of users behind the ISA server. For example, suppose we have 200 users. Let's assume that we choose to use the top recommendation for that number of users, which is 4,000MB (4GB). The number of MB per user is therefore 4,000MB/200 users, which turns out to be 20MB per user. Now, if we have a network that has 2000 clients behind the ISA server, the number of MB per user is 10,000MB (10GB) ÷ 2,000, which equals only 5MB per user.

You need to plan for a larger amount of disk space per user in a larger environment because there will be a wider variation in the per-user statistics. The high-end users will typically throw your averages off and have a disproportional effect on your cache requirements. We therefore recommend that you plan for at least 20MB per user, and if your hardware can support it, try for 50MB per user.

Logging and Reporting

Another factor in determining ISA Server disk space requirements includes the log files and reports that will be stored on your ISA server. The log files can grow very quickly, depending on the level of logging you have configured on your server. If you enable packet filtering and detailed Web proxy service logging, even a small network can easily generate log files in the range of 5 to 10MB per day.

If you are working on larger networks, you can expect your log files to expand at the rate of 50 to 100MB per day if you carry out detailed logging. It is a good idea to dedicate a partition of *at least 1GB* to your log files if you plan to carry out even a moderate amount of logging. You might also want to compress the partition on which the log files are created. Since these are plain-text files, you should be able to get a compression ratio of 4:1 or greater. Be aware that compression does require additional processor cycles and increases the amount of fragmentation on the drive. If your monitoring sessions indicate a potential processor bottleneck, you should not implement file compression.

You need a month's worth of log files to create many of the more interesting reports that ISA Server can generate. Furthermore, you might want to create reports spanning multiple months, in which case you need all the log files available on disk.

Network Interface Configuration

You should have at least two network interfaces if you plan to use the ISA server as a firewall. However, if you want to use the machine as a Web-caching server only, you can use a computer with a single, internal network interface.

If you configure multihomed computers, at least one of those interfaces will be directly connected to the Internet or to a network backbone. If you connect directly to the Internet, the interface can be an Ethernet connection (for example, to a DSL or cable modem), ISDN, or analog modem connection. For the internal network interface, you will likely use an Ethernet connection.

If you plan to use a perimeter network, that network can be connected to a third interface connected to the ISA server. That interface will be considered an external interface and must be configured with public addresses on a different subnet from the external interface. Figure 22.1 shows the configuration of such a perimeter network.

Figure 22.1 A Trihomed Server with a DMZ Network on the Third Interface

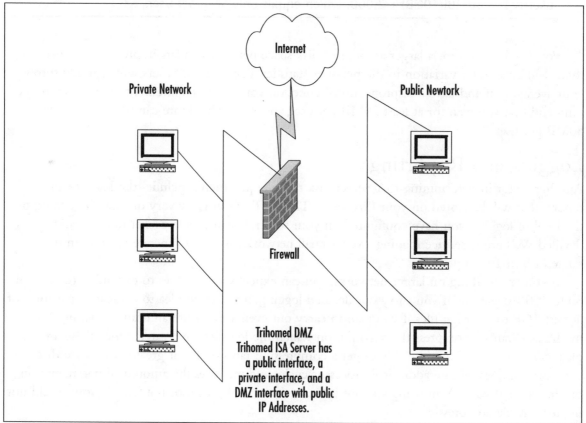

> **NOTE**
>
> You can also configure a DMZ network between a pair of ISA servers. In this case, the DMZ network interface would be considered an internal interface for the ISA machine because an ISA machine must have at least one internal interface.

A perimeter network can also be configured to lie between a pair of ISA servers. In this model, an ISA server lies on the edge of the network with an interface directly connected to the Internet, while a second interface is connected to a perimeter network. The second ISA server has one interface connected to the perimeter network; the second interface is connected to the internal network. Note that this intermediary network is a public network and should not be considered part of the internal network.

Figure 22.2 shows what such an intermediary DMZ network configuration might look like.

Figure 22.2 An Intermediary DMZ Network

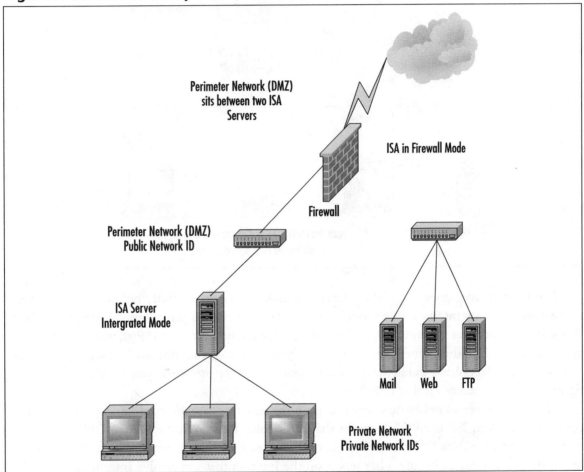

The ISA server that acts only as a Web-caching server can get by with a single internal network interface. Network clients send their requests to the ISA server's internal interface, and the ISA server forwards those requests to *its* gateway to the Internet. Responses from Internet servers are returned to the single-homed Web-caching server, which in turn returns data to the ISA clients.

Figure 22.3 shows what such a single-homed network configuration might look like.

Figure 22.3 A Single-Homed Web-Caching-Only Server

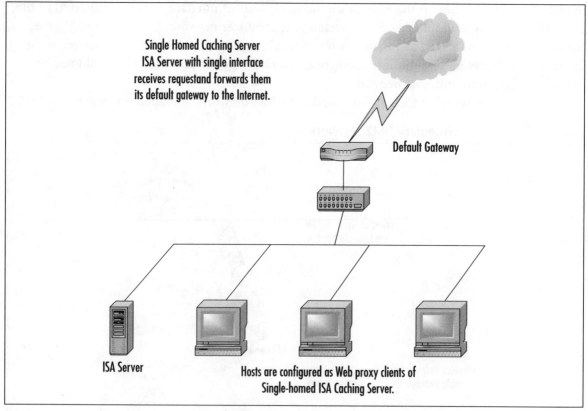

The TCP/IP configuration of the interfaces should be set up correctly before the ISA server is installed. The only interface that should have a default gateway is the external interface of the ISA server. If you have multiple external interfaces that connect to your ISP(s), you can put in gateways for each of those interfaces. However, if you are using multihomed ISA servers in which one of the interfaces has a public IP address for your perimeter network, you should not configure a default gateway on that interface.

The DNS server addresses vary depending on the interface you are configuring. The interfaces connecting to your ISP need DNS entries that can resolve Internet names. These DNS server entries can be your ISP's DNS servers (which is the most typical arrangement), or you can configure the DNS entry to be any other server on the Internet that can resolve Internet addresses.

For your internal interfaces, configure the DNS entry to a server that can resolve the names of the computers on your internal network. It is critically important that you have your DNS infrastructure in place and that it is functional prior to implementing ISA Server, because inbound requests will use your internal DNS server to resolve requests for machines on the internal network.

Securing the Network Interfaces

ISA Server includes features such as packet filtering that will protect your external interface, but there are some general measures you should take in order to prevent potential security breaches.

> **NOTE**
>
> The File and Printer Sharing for Microsoft Networks option allows you to turn off or on the Microsoft *Server Service*. This Server Service allows you to create shares that are accessible to other server message block (SMB) clients on the network. The flip side of the Server Service is the *Workstation Server* or *Redirector*. The Redirector (technically, the SMB Redirector) allows a machine to be a client to a machine running the Server Service. When you turn off the Redirector, it will not be able to access SMB shares on a Microsoft network.

You should always disable file and print sharing for Microsoft networks on the external interface and even for the internal interface of the ISA computer. Due to the inherently insecure nature of the file-sharing protocol (SMB) used on Microsoft systems, you should never expose the file system to SMB access. The ISA server should be a device dedicated to firewall and/or Web-caching functions and should not be used as a file or network application server.

To disable file and print sharing on a particular interface:

1. Open the **Interface Properties** dialog box.

2. Remove the check mark from the **File and Printer Sharing for Microsoft Networks** check box.

3. Remove the check mark from the **Client for Microsoft Networks** option.

4. If you are using a dial-up connection and it is up when you make the changes, hang up the connection and then redial for the new settings to take effect.

Figure 22.4 shows what this process looks like.

Figure 22.4 Disabling File and Print Sharing on the External Interface

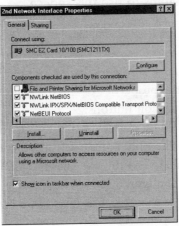

You should also disable the NetBIOS interface on the external interface. No machine on the Internet needs access to the ISA server via NetBIOS over TCP/IP; such access could provide an avenue for attackers to compromise your ISA server. To disable NetBIOS over TCP/IP:

1. Open the **Network Interface Properties** dialog box.

2. Click the **Advanced** button.

3. Click the **WINS** tab. You will see a screen like the one in Figure 22.5.

Figure 22.5 Disabling NetBIOS on the External Interface

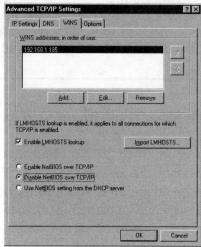

You might also want to disable NetBIOS on the internal interface. However, you must be careful about doing so, because certain services that you might want to enable, such as the Alerter service, remain dependent on NetBIOS to communicate with stations on the internal network.

> **NOTE**
>
> The Alerter service sends ISA messages through Windows networks, which uses NetBIOS. However, you may want to use NetBIOS only on your internal network because doing so will not allow untrusted systems to use this service.

Note that if your external interface is a dial-up connection such as an analog modem or ISDN terminal adapter, you will not be able to disable the NetBIOS interface via the methods described. In fact, if you go into the properties of the dial-up connection you've configured, you'll not even see the NetBIOS option buttons.

Keep in mind that a *dedicated* ISDN connection connects to its remote router in the same way that a "dial-up" connection does. The only configuration difference is that the dedicated connection will have a static IP address affixed to the external interface. Another thing to remember is that a dial-up connection can be configured only with a single IP address. ISA Server does not provide the address-pooling features that the Windows 2000 NAT Server provides.

Keep the External Interface Off the LAT

Although this is not an interface configuration option per se, it is related to the internal and external interfaces. The Local Address Table (LAT) keeps track of the internal IP address ranges (the IP addresses used in the internal, or trusted, network). The LAT is used by the ISA server's Firewall Service to determine which networks are internal and which are external. ISA Server does not apply policies to packets destined to an internal network location. If it receives such packets, it merely forwards them.

> **NOTE**
>
> The ISA server's LAT is a standard part of how a firewall functions. Many firewalls provide a form of NAT and the LAT is how the ISA server stores it. Linux firewalls call this *IP masquerading*.

You will run into problems if the external interface on your ISA server is included in the LAT. If the external interface is seen by ISA Server as local, it assumes that any packets it receives on that interface are from internal network hosts, and it does not apply security policy to those packets. In addition, keep in mind that packet filtering is applied only to *external* interfaces on the ISA server. If the external interface is on the LAT, no packet filtering rules will apply.

Incorrectly configuring the NAT is a one of the quickest ways to completely disable security provided by ISA Server. Prior to installation, be sure to write down and confirm all the internal network IDs your organization uses so that the LAT is configured properly. During setup, double-check your selections when the LAT Configuration dialog box appears.

Active Directory Implementation

If you plan to centralize configuration of your ISA servers or you want to install an array of ISA servers, you need an Active Directory domain.

ISA servers that have all network interfaces connected to the internal network can safely be configured as members of an internal Active Directory domain. Since these servers are not at risk for Internet intrusion, you can focus security concerns on internal network threats that affect all servers on the internal network.

However, if you plan to keep an array of ISA servers on the edge of the network, you should strongly consider creating a domain dedicated to the ISA array itself. For security reasons, you do not want to expose your internal network's Active Directory and user accounts database to the Internet. To prevent such exposure, you can create a dedicated ISA Server domain to interface with the Internet.

This dedicated ISA Server domain should be in a different forest from your internal Active Directory domain. The ISA Server domain can then be configured to trust the internal Active Directory domain but *without* a reciprocal trust. This is because you do not want your internal network to trust the accounts on the ISA Server domain. This setup helps minimize potential damage should an administrative account in the external domain become compromised.

This type of domain configuration is the ideal, but it might not fit the needs of organizations that have more than one domain as part of their internal networks. For example, if you have a root domain of isacorp.net and subdomains of west.isacorp.net and east.isacorp.net, and you then configure an external trust (also known as an *explicit trust*) from the ISA Server domain to the isacorp.net domain, you will run into problems with the lack of transitivity. The security accounts in the isacorp.net domain will be respected by the ISA Server domain, but the subdomains' accounts will not be trusted, because external trusts lack transitivity.

To solve this problem, you need to make the ISA domain a part of the same forest as the rest of your domains so that you can take advantage of trust transitivity. The ISA domain administrators do not have any automatic administrative privileges in the internal network domains. Just be sure *not* to delegate to ISA domain accounts any authority regarding resources in the internal network's domain.

Mission-Critical Considerations

Your ISA Server installation is likely to be a cornerstone of your Internet access scheme. Some businesses live or die by their ability to connect to and work via the Internet. Even a few minutes of downtime can lead to thousands or even tens of thousands of lost dollars. Therefore, before implementing your plan, if Internet access is a mission-critical service for any part of your organization, you need to consider fault tolerance.

Four key areas of fault tolerance and mission-critical availability are:

- Hard disk fault tolerance
- Network fault tolerance
- Server fault tolerance
- Bastion host configuration

Hard Disk Fault Tolerance

When considering disk fault-tolerance schemes, you need to pin down what it is that you want to accomplish. Right out of the box, Windows 2000 supports two forms of software-based disk fault tolerance:

- Mirrored volumes (mirror sets)
- RAID 5 volumes (stripe sets with parity)

Although Windows 2000 does include these methods of disk fault tolerance without requiring any added software or hardware, you might find that your situation requires a more high-performance solution. If you are implementing ISA Server in a large enterprise environment, you will find that the resource demands of software fault tolerance drain server resources to an unacceptable degree.

For high-load ISA Server environments, the better solution is hardware-based *Redundant Array of Independent Disks (RAID)*. In hardware-based RAID, the fault-tolerance mechanisms are built right into the hard disk controller and require no appreciable processor or memory overhead. We cover both software and hardware RAID implementations in this chapter.

> **NOTE**
>
> Before you can implement mirrored volumes or RAID 5 volumes on a Windows 2000 server, you must convert the disks on which the volumes will reside to *dynamic* disks.

Mirrored Volumes (Mirror Sets)

Mirrored volumes provide a method to allow all data written to one volume to be automatically copied to a second volume. Mirrored-volume configurations allow for real-time fault tolerance for the data stored on a mirrored volume.

The best use of the mirrored-volume configuration is found when the boot and system files are on the primary member of the mirrored volume and then mirrored on a secondary member of the mirror set, with the secondary volume located on a different disk and controller. This configuration, in which the secondary member of the mirrored volume is located on a different disk and controller than the primary member, is known as *disk duplexing*. Figure 22.6 characterizes this type of configuration.

NOTE

To the operating system, mirrored disks (both disks on the same controller) and duplexed disks (on different controllers) appear the same, and both are shown as mirrored volumes in the Windows 2000 disk management console. Duplexing is a hardware differentiation. Duplexing provides both fault-tolerance benefits and superior performance, since disk reads and writes can take place simultaneously across different controllers.

Figure 22.6 Mirrored Volumes Configured in a Duplex Arrangement

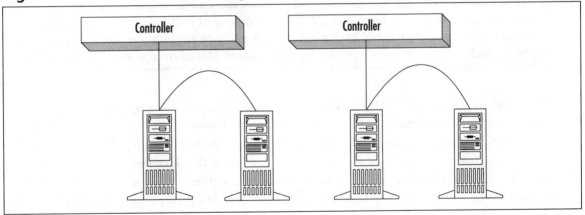

The primary member of the mirror set is the "live" part of the mirror set—the one that is actually being used by the user and operating system. However, everything that is copied or changed on the primary member is also updated on the secondary member of the mirror set. If the primary member should fail, the system will automatically fail-over and the secondary member of the mirror set will take over the duties once held by the primary member. There is no negative effect on performance. In fact, write performance should improve slightly because changes will not have to be written twice.

When either member of the mirror set fails, there will be no discernable change in terms of server availability, and users will be totally unaware that any changes have taken place. However, you should configure some type of notification mechanism so that an administrator is informed when a member of the mirror set fails so that it can be repaired quickly.

> **WARNING**
>
> Once a single member of the mirror set fails, there is no longer any fault tolerance until a new disk is configured as a secondary disk. Note that regardless of which disk fails, the remaining disk becomes the primary member and the new disk becomes the secondary member.

RAID 5 Volumes (Stripe Sets with Parity)

The other "out of the box" RAID solution that you can consider using in your ISA Server solution is the *RAID 5 volume*. RAID 5 volumes were known in the Windows NT world as *stripe sets with parity*. Because parity information is stored in the RAID 5 volume, you have fault tolerance in the event of a single disk failure, regardless of how many disks are included in the RAID 5 volume. The data on the failed disk can be regenerated from the parity information stored on the other disks in the set. You must have a minimum of three physical disks (and up to 32 disks) to create a RAID 5 volume.

> **WARNING**
>
> Unfortunately, a RAID 5 volume can tolerate the failure of only one disk. If two or more disks in a RAID 5 volume should fail either sequentially or simultaneously, the data cannot be regenerated and you must restore the information stored on the array from backup.

The major advantage of a RAID 5 volume over a mirrored volume is speed. Striped volumes have faster read/write performance than mirrored volumes. However, one disadvantage of the RAID 5 volume is that you cannot place the system or boot files on such a volume. This is a limitation of the software implementation of RAID 5, because the operating system must be able to load and access the fault-tolerance disk driver (ftdisk.sys) before it can mount the volume. Since you must be able to access the system files to load the disk drivers, you cannot include the system files on a RAID 5 volume.

The primary disadvantage of a RAID 5 volume compared with a RAID 1 volume is a higher cost of entry. You can create a RAID 1 volume with a single pair of disks, whereas the RAID 5 volume requires at least three physical disks. This could be a factor for very small shops that are highly cost constrained.

However, RAID 5 has a couple of advantages over RAID 1 in that the total cost of a RAID 5 solution per megabyte is lower when more disks are added to the array. The amount of "unusable" disk space on a mirror set equals 50 percent of the total disk space dedicated to the set, whereas the space required for storing parity information on a RAID 5 array equals $1 \div number\_of\_disks$. So, if you have a 10-disk array, you are only "wasting" one-tenth of your disk space for fault-tolerance information.

The second advantage of the RAID 5 array is the much larger volume size that can be created. The largest usable volume size on a RAID 1 array is equal to the size of one of the disks in the array. However, the size of a RAID 5 array is the sum of all the disks (up to 32) minus the fraction used for parity information.

> **NOTE**
>
> Initial hardware cost for implementing a mirrored volume is less to implement than implementing a RAID 5 volume. This is because you must buy only two disks for a mirrored volume, but you must have a minimum of three disks for RAID 5.
>
> However, the cost per megabyte of data is less for a RAID 5 configuration, and that cost decreases as the number of disks in the RAID array increases. For example, if you have three physical disks in the RAID 5 set, the equivalent of one physical disk (or one-third of the total disk space) is used for parity information, whereas the rest (two-thirds of the disk space) is available for data. If you increase that to 10 physical disks, only one-tenth of the total disk space must be used for storing the parity information, and nine-tenths is available for storing your data.
>
> Thus, over the long term, a RAID 5 volume is usually better in terms of pure cost effectiveness. You will want to weigh other factors, such as ease of recovery and need to provide fault tolerance for system and boot partitions, when selecting the best fault-tolerance method for your situation. Figure 22.7 characterizes a RAID 5 configuration.

Figure 22.7 A RAID 5 Volume

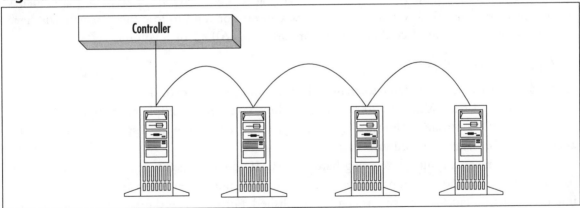

Optimizing a Software RAID Configuration

In your ISA Server configuration, you should include log files, cache files, and reports on the RAID 5 array. Doing so will significantly speed ISA server performance and allow for fault tolerance for these important files. *Keep in mind that your array is fault tolerant only when all disks are in working order.*

If a single disk in a RAID 5 fails, your array is no longer fault tolerant, and you need to replace the disk as soon as possible—not only for fault tolerance reasons, but also because the process of reconstructing the data from the parity information will slow performance significantly.

If you are running the Web proxy service's Web-caching feature, you want to be able to ensure the fastest read performance possible. This is because the Web cache is typically implemented to improve client-perceived performance. Write time to the cache isn't quite as important, since the Web-caching feature will store URLs in RAM for a certain period of time before writing them to cache. However, you do want to be able to retrieve cached Web objects as quickly as possible.

RAID 5, because it is striped, has better read performance than RAID 0; therefore, you should consider placing the cache files on a RAID 5 array if you require fault tolerance for your cache. In a production environment that is strapped for Internet bandwidth, you might consider this option. However, the Web cache itself is not generally a mission-critical component, and you might want to sacrifice fault tolerance for superior read performance. In this case, you should use the software-based RAID 0, or *striped volumes*. Although they do not provide fault tolerance, they do provide the best read performance of any RAID type.

The log files present a different set of requirements. If you plan to do extensive logging (which you would consider in a very secure environment), you need to place the log files on a volume that supports optimal *write* performance. Log files are read only occasionally, but they are written to constantly. Both RAID 1 and RAID 5 suffer from write latency because, in a RAID 1 configuration, the data must be written twice, and in a RAID 5 configuration, the parity information must be calculated and then written in addition to the data.

Unlike the situation with the Web cache, the log files are mission critical and do require placement on a fault-tolerant disk set. Given the choice between RAID 1 and 5, your best option is the mirror set.

Reports are rarely written and only occasionally accessed. Therefore, read/write performance is not a primary issue. However, like the log files, you do not want to lose these or you will have to recreate them. You can place these reports on either a RAID 1 or 5 volume.

Hardware-Based RAID

Although we have discussed fault-tolerant disk arrays in the context of the software-based schemes provided with Windows 2000 out of the box, you can also implement fault tolerance via hardware RAID controllers. Almost all organizations that require the highest level of fault tolerance and performance use hardware-based RAID.

There are many advantages to using hardware RAID controllers. These controllers allow you to mirror the boot and system partitions, because they are not dependent on the operating system initializing before fault-tolerance sets can be established. Furthermore, the hardware solutions are significantly faster on software-based RAID. A hardware implementation of RAID appears to the operating system as though the array were a single physical disk.

One type of hardware-based RAID that has gained widespread popularity is known either as RAID 10 or RAID 0+1. This RAID implementation creates a *striped volume* and then mirrors the striped volume to provide fault tolerance. This process gives you the best of both worlds: the performance of a striped volume and the fault tolerance of a mirror set.

For example, you could configure a three-disk set as part of a RAID 0 array. This set would be mirrored onto another three disks, so such an array would require a total of six disks. If any member of the RAID 0 array should fail, a corresponding disk from the mirror set would be brought into service. However, at this point you no longer have fault tolerance and you need to replace the disk as soon as possible.

More sophisticated (and expensive) RAID implementations allow you to keep "hot spares" online so that, in the event of a disk failure, a hot spare is introduced to the array automatically. Again, you have fault tolerance as long as you have one hot spare available. When there are no more spares, you need to add new disks.

Network Fault Tolerance

When implementing ISA Server, you must consider the level of availability you require for both your internal and external network interfaces. Your server configurations can be designed to be fully fault tolerant, but if your single interface to the Internet becomes unavailable, all your machine fault tolerance is moot.

The type of fault-tolerant configuration you design for your external interfaces depends on the type of interface and the arrangements you have with your ISP. For example, if you have a single ISDN connection via a single account with your ISP, there's not much you can do with such a configuration, as is, to allow for any level of fail-over.

The ideal network fault-tolerance solution for your external interface is to have multiple ISA Servers participating in an enterprise array on the edge of your network. You would then configure routing rules so that, in the event of an interface failure, the request can first be resolved within the array and then forwarded to another server within the array if it needs to be sent to the Internet for retrieval.

> **NOTE**
>
> The ability to configure ISA Server with routing rules in the event of an external interface failure is a powerful fault-tolerance mechanism built into ISA Server. However, this mechanism requires you to have made provisions for multiple connections to the Internet, which require purchasing and maintaining multiple access accounts.

Large organizations can more easily absorb the costs of multiple high-speed dedicated connections. If you are working in a smaller networking environment that is more sensitive to cost, you might consider an analog backup line in the event of failure of another low-cost solution such as cable, dial-up ISDN, or DSL.

Network load balancing, another important issue related to fault tolerance (as well as performance), is a way of dividing up the network load. This prevents one system from getting overused and another from getting underused.

Server Fault Tolerance

There are several ways to ensure fault tolerance for ISA servers in the event of a server crash or the necessity of taking a server offline for maintenance or upgrade. The best way to provide for server fault tolerance is to take advantage of arrays of ISA servers when you deploy the Enterprise Edition. An ISA Server array is a collection of ISA servers that share the same configuration information and Web cache content. An array provides a high degree of fault tolerance; if a single server becomes unavailable, the other servers can take over to service requests for the downed ISA server.

> **NOTE**
>
> All members of an array share the same Web cache policies and can access each other's cached Web content. However, the contents of the cache do *not* mirror in any way the contents of other servers in the array. In addition, the cache location settings must be set on the individual servers. The cache location is not part of the cache configuration shared by the array. However, this setting doesn't happen automatically. If your clients are configured to access a certain ISA server and that server becomes unavailable, the client will not necessarily be able to access the next server in the array. In order to provide a measure of fault tolerance for client access, you must devise some scheme that will allow the clients to fail-over to another ISA server.

DNS Round Robin

One way you can accomplish server fault tolerance is to configure a *DNS round robin* on your network. In your DNS, you assign the same host name to the IP addresses of your respective ISA servers. That is, your ISA servers will each have the same fully qualified domain name (FQDN).

If you are using Windows 2000 DNS servers, DNS round robin is enabled by default. However, you should never take it for granted that the settings on a particular server are at their defaults. To assess whether DNS round robin is available on your Windows 2000 DNS server:

1. Right-click the **server name** in the left pane of the DNS console.

2. Click **Properties**.

3. Click the **Advanced** tab.

You will see the screen that appears in Figure 22.8. Make sure that **Enable round robin** is checked if you want to take advantage of the DNS round-robin feature.

Figure 22.8 Configuring DNS Round Robin on a Windows 2000 DNS Server

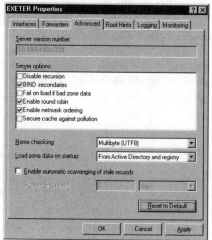

With DNS round robin enabled, when a network client queries DNS, it receives the IP address of one of the ISA servers. If that server is not available, the network client receives an error message. When a subsequent request is made, the ISA client receives another IP address after the expiration of the time-out period of the DNS response it received earlier. Since these addresses are assigned randomly, there's a good chance that it will receive the IP address of a different ISA server (one that is still up and running).

For example, suppose we create three DNS round-robin entries for the host name *isaserver* in the *tacteam.net* domain. The entries would look something like this:

```
isaserver.tacteam.net    A    222.222.222.222
isaserver.tacteam.net    A    222.222.222.223
isaserver.tacteam.net    A    222.222.222.224
```

We also set the time-out for these records so that the DNS clients wash the entries from their DNS caches after one minute. If a client makes a request for *isaserver.tacteam.net* and receives the IP address 222.222.222.222 and that machine is down, and then the client makes another request five seconds later, the IP address will be retrieved from the DNS cache and the DNS server will not be queried again. However, if the request is made 90 seconds later, the entry will have timed out of the cache, and the DNS server will be queried again to resolve the name *isaserver.tacteam.net*.

However, DNS round robin has some notable disadvantages when it comes to fault tolerance. Because the rotation of the IP addresses sent to DNS clients is random, there's the chance that the DNS client will receive the same IP address it got before and therefore will have to wait for the Time To Live (TTL) on that entry to expire before attempting to get another IP address.

WARNING

If you check Figure 22.8 again, you'll notice another option, **Enable netmask ordering**. When this option is enabled, *local subnet priority* has precedence over random round-robin assignments. Local subnet prioritization allows the DNS server to compare address records with the source IP address of the DNS query. If a host record in the DNS is located on the same or similar network ID as the DNS client, that record will always be delivered to the client and the client will not receive a random record. This could be an issue if you have array members on different network IDs and clients on the same networks as the array members. If all array members have the same network ID, DNS round robin will be applied to hosts on the same network as the array members.

You can help minimize this problem by configuring very short TTLs on your round-robin entries in the DNS. However, doing so reduces the efficacy of the client-side DNS cache and could have a negative impact on network performance on a loaded network.

Another thing that complicates this scheme is that the Windows 2000 DNS clients are configured with the ability to "negatively cache" failed DNS requests. By default, the negative cache entry stays in effect for five minutes. This means that if an ISA client receives the IP address of the downed ISA server, it will remain a negative cache entry for five minutes, and the client will not attempt to query the DNS server again until the negative cache entry has timed out.

You can change the time-out period for the negative cache entries by configuring the Registry. The key can be located at HKLM\System\CurrentControlSet\Services\Dnscache\ Parameters. The value to configure is the NegativeCacheTime, which, by default, is configured for 300 seconds.

Bastion Host Configuration

A *bastion host* is a computer that has an interface with an untrusted network. In the context of ISA Server, that untrusted network is typically the Internet. The bastion host can lie with an interface directly connected to the Internet, or it can be placed on a perimeter network behind a router but in front of the internal network.

Because of the central role the bastion host computer plays in your Internet access scheme, it is important that the operating system is hardened and made as stable as possible. System hardening can be performed via the ISA Server Security Configuration Wizard. This wizard applies security settings derived from a set of security templates that are installed with Windows 2000 Server family products.

In addition to applying strict security settings to the file system, Registry, and applications, you need to review the services running on the bastion host computer. Each service running on your bastion host provides a possible target for an attacker to exploit. Common operating system and network services that are installed by default can provide avenues of opportunity for attackers. Some of these services include:

- The Browser Service
- The IIS Admin Service
- The Indexing Service
- The Remote Registry Service
- The SMTP Service

Many more potentially hazardous services are started by default on Windows 2000 Server family products.

Planning the Appropriate Installation Mode

There are three types, or *modes*, of ISA Server installation. You must select one of the three modes when you install ISA. The selections are:

- Firewall mode
- Cache mode
- Integrated mode

The type of installation you choose determines which feature set will be available to you. Table 22.4 lists the features available in firewall and cache modes. *Integrated mode allows you to take advantages of both firewall and cache mode features.*

Table 22.4 Comparing Firewall and Cache Mode Features

ISA Server Feature	Firewall Mode	Cache Mode
Secure NAT client support	Yes	Yes
Web proxy client support	Yes	Yes
Reports	Yes	Yes
Alerts	Yes	Yes
Real-time service monitoring	Yes	Yes
Web site filtering	Yes	Yes
Web server publishing	Yes	Yes
Enterprise policy	Yes	Yes
Access policy—HTTP	Yes	Yes
Access policy—all protocols	Yes	No
Non-Web server publishing	Yes	No
Packet filtering	Yes	No
Application filters	Yes	No
Web caching	No	Yes

When we take a closer look at this table, it is relatively easy to digest. Let's look at a few factors you'll want to consider in deciding which mode to deploy.

Installing in Firewall Mode

Firewall mode ISA servers support virtually all ISA Server features, with the exception of the Web cache. The Web-caching feature is very memory and processor intensive; therefore, it makes sense to exclude this feature from a server for which the primary purpose is to act as a firewall. A firewall should not run extra services in order to minimize the risk of exposure.

In addition, you want to be able to harness all the available system resources in order to process packet-filtering rules, protocol rules, and site and content rules as quickly as possible on your firewall.

Installing in Cache Mode

When you install the server in cache mode, you intend that server to work as a Web proxy server only. The Web proxy service supports the HTTP, HTTPS, FTP, and Gopher protocols. If you want to support only these protocols and take advantage of the Web-caching features, but you don't want to implement a full-fledged, policy-based firewall, the Web cache option is a good one.

Another reason why you might want to implement a caching-only server is that you already have a firewall in place. Many organizations already have powerful firewall solutions such as Cisco PIX, Checkpoint Software's Firewall-1, and many others. You might even want to consider this scenario when you are using a second ISA server for a firewall on the edge of your network. In this way, you can take advantage of the powerful Web-caching features included with ISA Server and have the protection of a sophisticated firewall.

> **NOTE**
>
> You should consider the Web proxy mode a minimalist configuration. In fact, if all you want is a Web-caching server, we strongly recommend that for security reasons, you do not place this server at the edge of your network. The cache mode configuration is secure to the extent that it allows you to use private IP addresses on your internal network, but it does not allow the firewall features required for a server that is located on the edge of the network.

A cache mode server is best placed on the internal network, in which case you can use a single interface or multiple interfaces. *Be sure that you implement some type of firewall solution at the edge of your network to protect your internal computers from Internet intruders.*

Installing in Integrated Mode

The integrated mode ISA Server allows you to take advantage of all the features ISA Server has to offer. However, this configuration is probably best left to organizations that are testing ISA features or are cost contained and cannot bear the expense of purchasing separate caching servers and firewalls.

The reason why you would prefer not to have both the Web-caching services and the firewall services running on the same computer relates back to our discussion of bastion hosts. The more services running on a single computer, the more avenues of attack are open to intruders. Although ISA Server was tested thoroughly prior to its release, you must remain aware that all security software has potential holes that can be exploited. An attacker cannot exploit a hole in the Web proxy services on your mission-critical firewall if the hole is not there.

One exception to this general rule is when the ISA server is placed between a departmental LAN and the corporate backbone. In this case, you might want to avail yourself of some of the firewall features while also taking advantage of the Web-caching features. This is a reasonable configuration because the corporate backbone is less vulnerable to the type of attacks seen on the open Internet.

Table 22.5 shows some common placement scenarios for each configuration.

Table 22.5 Recommended Roles for ISA Server Modes

ISA Server Mode	Location
Firewall	1. Edge of the network 2. Server that interfaces with internal and DMZ networks
Cache	1. Single-homed or multihomed, with all interfaces connected to the internal network 2. Interfaces on the internal network and a DMZ network; DMZ is protected by a firewall
Integrated	1. Test network 2. Interface with corporate backbone

Prior to implementing your solution, be sure that all members of the network security team are aware of the implications of the various ISA Server modes. This is important when you are comparing the exposure and protection that each mode provides for the network.

Planning for a Stand-Alone or an Array Configuration

ISA Server Enterprise Edition can be installed as either an array member or as a stand-alone server. There are many advantages to installing the server as an array member. These advantages include:

- The ability to implement enterprise wide array policies via Active Directory
- The ability to easily implement a common configuration for multiple ISA Server computers
- The option to expand the scope of a single ISA server to multiple servers with a common configuration
- Fault tolerance

You must first prepare Active Directory prior to installing an ISA server as an array member. The procedure for preparing Active Directory, called *enterprise initialization*, is accomplished via the Installation Wizard included on the ISA Server CD. If you like, you can manually run the ISA Enterprise initialization and install ISA Server at a later time. If you choose to install ISA Server in an array configuration, the Setup program will check to see if the schema has been properly modified before it allows you to continue.

Once the array member is installed, a single enterprise array policy can be implemented on any array in your organization. All array members are able to access configuration information, because array configuration settings are stored in Active Directory. This is a nice fault-tolerance method for your configuration because Active Directory is replicated throughout your Active Directory domain controller network.

> **NOTE**
>
> You might want to implement an enterprise security policy before installing a single member of an array. You can do this by creating the array first in the ISA Management console. After the array is created, you can configure your enterprise policies. Once the policies are completed, you can begin to install ISA servers and join them to the array.

Even if you plan to implement just a single ISA server, you should consider the possibility that you will want to expand your configuration in the future. If you choose the stand-alone ISA Server configuration and later decide to deploy an array of ISA servers, you will need to run the enterprise initialization. Then you can *promote* the stand-alone server to array member.

> **NOTE**
>
> If you have the Standard Edition of ISA Server, you won't have the choice to deploy an array. The Standard Edition is a viable solution for small companies with relatively simple requirements, but it is not designed to scale to the needs of complex enterprise networks.

Planning ISA Client Configuration

A critical aspect of your ISA Server design is the ISA Server *client base* you expect to support. Proxy Server 2.0 supported what were known as the *Web proxy client*, *WinSock proxy client*, and *SOCKS proxy client*. The SOCKS service is no longer required, and the Winsock proxy client has changed its name.

The client types supported by ISA Server are:

- The Firewall Service client
- The Web proxy client
- The secure NAT client

Each client type offers it own advantages and disadvantages. Let's examine the features and capabilities of each client type and assess how they fit into an overall ISA design scheme.

The Firewall Service Client

Network computers configured as Firewall Service clients are able to access all Winsock protocols. When applications on the firewall client send a request to a host on a network ID not contained on the LAT (typically the Internet), the firewall client software installed on the firewall client will intercept the request and forward it to the Firewall Service on the ISA server.

The primary advantage of a configuring machine as a Firewall Service client is that you can control access to protocols, sites, and content on a per-user or per-group basis. This feature allows you more granular control over your access policies than you have compared with the secure NAT or Web proxy client. You cannot control access to specific protocols on a user or group basis with the secure NAT client, only via IP addresses, in a manner similar to the SOCKS Service in Proxy Server 2.0. The Web Proxy Service can be configured to require authentication, but you cannot limit access to the Web Proxy Service mediated protocols on a per-user or per-group basis.

Another significant advantage to the firewall client software is that it supports just about any application protocol it encounters. Some applications require that multiple connections be established between the client and the destination server. The Firewall Client supports these protocols; the NAT client might or might not be able to support them. However, since all NAT calls to the ISA server must be processed by the Firewall Service, almost all applications should be supported.

The disadvantage of configuring a host as a firewall client is that you must install the firewall client software. Not all operating systems support this software. The only operating systems that do support it are:

- Windows 95 OSR2
- Windows 98
- Windows ME
- Windows NT 4.0
- Windows 2000
- Windows XP
- Windows Server 2003

This represents a departure from the support offered by the firewall client's "older brother," the Winsock proxy client. The Winsock proxy client software included with Proxy Server 2.0 supported Windows 3.*x* machines using a 16-bit client software installation. The firewall client software does not include a 16-bit client. Keep this in mind if you have the ill fortune of needing to support Windows 3.*x* machines.

Firewall Client Support for Windows 3.x Machines

If you must support Win 3.*x* machines, one workaround is to use the Winsock proxy client provided with Proxy Server 2.0. Of course, you must have a copy of Proxy Server 2.0 to implement this solution. The reason why you can do this is that the firewall client and the Winsock client are interchangeable in terms of their functionality.

For this reason, you do not need to install the firewall client on your machines that already have the Winsock proxy client installed. You can also use the firewall client software to connect to the Winsock proxy service on a Proxy Server 2.0 server. The Firewall Service client on ISA Server is more sophisticated than the Winsock proxy service in Proxy Server 2.0, but the client side essentially works the same way.

Firewall Client Does Not Support IPX/SPX

Another feature that was supported by the old Winsock proxy client software was the IPX/SPX gateway. In Proxy Server 2.0, you could configure Winsock proxy clients to use the IPX/SPX protocol to gain access to the Internet via the WinSock Proxy Service. The Firewall Service does not provide this support. If you are still running IPX/SPX on your internal network, you'll have to take this factor into consideration.

In fact, prior to considering an ISA Server proxy solution, you need to convert your network to a TCP/IP-based infrastructure. This conversion is required in order to implement ISA Server, but there are many other compelling reasons to retire your IPX infrastructure. If yours has been a Novell shop for some time, you might need to retrain your administrators. The cost of investing in learning and implementing TCP/IP on your network will expand the possibilities of expansion for your network and allow you to more easily troubleshoot network problems because of the large number of tools available to investigate TCP/IP networks.

The Web Proxy Client

The Web Proxy Service provides access to a limited set of protocols:

- HTTP
- HTTPS (HTTP secured via SSL)
- FTP
- Gopher

Whereas we can safely dismiss Gopher from our consideration, the other protocols represent the bulk of typical Internet connectivity requirements for the majority of organizations that want to implement ISA Server solutions.

If all you require are these "Web" protocols, a Web proxy client/server configuration might best fit your organization. Even if you need to install the firewall client software to take advantage of other Winsock applications, you might still want to configure your machines as Web proxy clients due to a slight performance advantage you'll gain for Web access via HTTP 1.1 CERN-compliant browsers.

> **NOTE**
>
> Among the group of ISA Server application filters is the HTTP Redirector filter. If you configure this filter to redirect HTTP requests to the Web Proxy Service (so that firewall and secure NAT clients can take advantage of the Web cache), security information sent from the firewall client will be lost. This means that the firewall client might need to manually enter authentication information to access HTTP. You can circumvent this manual authentication process by making the firewall (and secure NAT) client a Web proxy client as well.

The Web proxy client has the advantage of not requiring installation of any dedicated client software and is compatible with all operating systems. If you have a browser that supports proxy client configuration, such as Internet Explorer, you can take direct advantage of the Web Proxy Service. You can even configure Netscape Navigator running on Linux to use the Web Proxy Service. The Web Proxy Service also supports user authentication, which gives it an advantage over the secure NAT client.

The Secure NAT Client

Secure NAT clients are the simplest type of ISA client to set up, because virtually no configuration is required. In order to create a secure NAT client, all you need to do is one or the other of these:

- Configure the client to use the ISA server as its default gateway.
- Point the secure NAT client to a gateway that will be able to route Internet-bound packets to an ISA server.

The secure NAT client is able to take advantage of the Web cache when the HTTP Redirector filter is enabled. However, even though the secure NAT client is able to use the Web cache portion of the Web Proxy Service, secure NAT clients cannot be authenticated against Active Directory or a server's local security accounts database. Access controls for secure NAT clients are implemented via IP addresses rather than user or group membership. If you want a secure NAT client to be authenticated before accessing "Web protocols," configure the secure NAT client as a Web proxy client.

Small organizations that do not have easy access to technical support assistance or those that do not want to install or configure client software will benefit most from the secure NAT client.

Assessing the Best Solution for Your Network

You should decide in advance what type of ISA client configuration you want to implement on your network before beginning the ISA Server rollout. Table 22.6 can be of some assistance when weighing your options.

Table 22.6 Comparing ISA Server Client Features

ISA Client Type	Best-Fit Scenarios
Secure NAT client	1. Organization has a simple setup. 2. Organization has no technical support in house. 3. Organization wants to avoid client software installation. 4. Organization does not require user or group authorization to access resources. 5. Organization has non-Windows clients or non-CERN-compliant browsers. 6. Organization wants to publish servers on the internal network or on a DMZ segment.
Firewall client	1. Client software installation is not an issue. 2. Organization requires user- or group-based authentication for access control on a per-protocol basis. 3. Organization requires access to all Winsock protocols. 4. Organization has administrative support for client installation, policy configuration, and client/server troubleshooting.
Web proxy client	1. Organization requires only HTTP, HTTPS, FTP, and Gopher access. 2. Organization uses HTTP 1.1 CERN-compliant browsers. 3. Organization does not require access to other Winsock protocols. 4. Organization requires authentication for Web protocols. 5. Organization does not want to configure a default gateway on network clients. 6. Organization has non-Windows clients.

Of course, you are not limited to implementing a single ISA client configuration. You can take advantage of various combinations of clients. For example, you can configure an ISA client as a Web proxy and firewall client to improve performance of Web protocol access, or you can configure a client to be a secure NAT and Web proxy client and take advantage of authentication for Web protocols.

The only mutually exclusive client configuration pair is the firewall client and the secure NAT client. That is because the firewall client will always be subject to the firewall client configuration parameters. The firewall client software will intercept all Winsock requests and forward them to the ISA server. This is in contrast to the secure NAT client, for which the native Winsock interface forwards packets to the machine's default gateway.

Internet Connectivity and DNS Considerations

ISA Server supports just about any interface you want to use to connect to the Internet. Your external interface can be:

- ISDN
- Analog
- DSL
- Cable
- T-Carrier
- X.25
- ATM

An important consideration is whether you want to implement a dedicated or a dial-up solution for Internet connectivity. The advantages of a dedicated connection are speed and reliability. The prime disadvantage of dedicated connections is often cost. However, even the cost of dedicated connections is coming down. In areas that support cable and DSL connections, you can have a dedicated connection to the Internet for well under $100 per month.

Level of Service

Consider the level of service you require before deciding on the type of connection you will use on the external interface. Many businesses seem almost hypnotized by the low prices and potential for high-speed access that DSL and cable connections offer. However, those businesses are often left grinding their teeth and cursing their providers later.

The problem lies in the fact that you are not guaranteed bandwidth or level of service with these types of connections. Although you typically purchase a certain level of service based on an agreement for minimum and maximum throughput, those numbers represent upper limits of service more often than they ever guarantee a minimum level of service. At this time, neither cable nor DSL should be considered reliable enough alternatives on which to base your corporate Internet solution.

If your business requires a reliable and dedicated connection to the Internet, you are best served by using established technologies such as T-carrier and ISDN. Although the cost of these connections is much higher, you won't find yourself worrying about when your connection might become unavailable.

However, it is important to keep in mind that your bandwidth is guaranteed for a couple of router hops. You have no guarantees to bandwidth once your request leaves the control of your service provider. Therefore, although you should be watchful of your average sustainable bandwidth parameters, your primary concern is uptime.

Finally, when researching ISPs, look for a provider that will be able to grow with your organization. Your company might have modest needs for access at this time, but you hope to grow, and your Internet requirements will likely grow with you. You can avoid a significant amount of stress and strain if you can avoid having to move a large and complex Web site in the future when your ISP can no longer handle the traffic.

External Interface Configuration

Regardless of your connection method, you need to configure the external interface's IP configuration. Depending on the design of your Internet access solution, you might have a single IP address or multiple IP addresses bound to the external network interface. You can also choose to use multiple external interfaces. ISA Server does support multiple external interfaces as well as multiple IP addresses bound to a single interface. In fact, it does not even differentiate between them.

If you plan to provide Internet users with access to internal network resources, you will probably want to get one or more static IP addresses to bind to the external interface. If your organization is exceptionally sensitive to cost issues, you can get around the problem of using dedicated IP addresses by taking advantage of third-party dynamic DNS hosting.

> ### WARNING
>
> Many companies use ISDN to access the Internet. ISPs sell ISDN corporate packages that often include a higher level of service and support. They also provide a subnetted block of IP addresses for your internal servers. Although you would not want to run a busy Web presence via an ISDN terminal connection, you can use multiple IP addresses and register different domain names to each one. However, you cannot do this with dial-up connections, which includes "dedicated" ISDN. The dial-up account interface only allows you to bind a single IP address to the ISDN terminal adapter.

Services such as www.tzo.com allow you to have a dynamically assigned IP address register in your own domain name on their servers. If you have a cable, ISDN, or DSL configuration that uses DHCP, you can get around changing IP addresses using such a service. You can even create publishing rules that will allow you to register a single domain name and redirect requests to multiple servers on your internal network without having to enter individual Host (A) records on the Tzo.com DNS servers. Larger organizations will foot the cost of dedicated addresses if Internet users must have access to internal network resources.

When configuring the external interface, be sure to include the IP address, subnet mask, and default gateway (remote router) used by that interface. Do *not* configure any internal interface on the ISA server with a default gateway. Since the ISA Server services handle all requests coming into the internal interfaces, you do not need to have a gateway configured on the internal interface. Finally, do not configure the external interface to use DHCP unless your ISP explicitly gives you instructions to do so. For most ISA Server installations on the edge of a network, you will use dedicated IP addresses, so it would be rare to use DHCP.

DNS Issues

ISA Server supports Web publishing and server publishing. By publishing servers, you are able to offer Internet clients services on your internal network. ISA Server Publishing allows you to publish services such as HTTP, NNTP, SMTP, and POP mail to users on the Internet in a secure context.

Most users want to connect to your published network resources via an FQDN rather than an IP address. Therefore, you need to obtain one or more domain names to implement a fully functional publishing solution. Once you have obtained these domain names, you can have your ISP's DNS server host your domain database, or you can manage your own DNS servers. If you choose to manage your own DNS, you need to provide the IP addresses of at least two publicly available DNS servers.

After registering your domain names, you need to populate your DNS database with Host (A) address records. Typically, you'll add a record for host names such as "www," "ftp," "mail" and "news" for the Web, FTP, SMTP, and NNTP access, respectively. ISA allows you to publish servers on your internal network or on a perimeter network, so you can use just a single IP address on the external interface and access multiple servers hosting these services.

> **NOTE**
>
> When users connect to an Internet or intranet resource via a Winsock application, they typically do so using a *fully qualified domain name*, or *FQDN*. The FQDN is actually a combination or two names: a *host name* and a *domain name*.
>
> For example, if you are managing the DNS for a domain such as *tacteam.net* and you have a host in that domain named *www*, the FQDN for that host is *www.tacteam.net*. An *unqualified* name would either not include the host name or, more frequently, would include an incomplete path for the domain name. If someone used the name *www.tacteam*, that would represent an unqualified request. Resolution of unqualified requests depends on the DNS client configuration of a particular machine.

For example, you have two machines on your internal network, one that will host your Web server, and a second that will host your mail server. You have registered your domain name, *isaserver.net*. You have one external IP address: 222.222.222.222. In the DNS, you enter a Host (A) address record for *www.isaserver.net* and *mail.isaserver.net*. Both of these Host (A) records will point to 222.222.222.222. When a user types *www.isaserver.net* into his or her browser address bar, the user will be connected to 222.222.222.222 Port 80. The server-publishing rule will forward the request to the internal Web server. In the same fashion, when an SMTP application attempts to connect to *mail.isaserver.net*, it will connect to 222.222.222.222 Port 25. The ISA server will forward the request to your published internal mail server.

DNS planning is pivotal to a successful server-publishing scheme. You must configure multiple DNS zones to account for machines located on the internal and external domains.

Summary

In this chapter, we covered key planning and design considerations you should undertake before beginning your ISA Server rollout. We highly recommend that you put a good deal of time into the planning phase before you begin to roll out your ISA Server solution. If you know what you need to accomplish prior to the actual execution of your task, you minimize the chances of security breaches during the implementation phase of your plan.

We discussed important issues related to preparing the computer software and hardware for ISA Server. The base requirements for ISA Server are not extreme, but they do need to match the requirements for the level of service you expect ISA Server to provide. The more users who will access the server, the higher the hardware requirements.

You learned about important planning issues regarding network configuration and what to consider when planning your internal and external interfaces. You need to be sure that all interfaces on the ISA server computers are as free from potential security holes as possible, since the ISA server will likely be one of the primary gateways into your internal network.

Internet access for your organization is a mission-critical concern. Therefore, you need to ensure that a high level of fault tolerance is built into your ISA Server solution. We discussed some methods you can put into play when building a fault-tolerant ISA Server deployment.

Finally, we covered some basic issues regarding Internet access and DNS issues. The DNS configuration will be one of your most challenging planning issues, and it must be set up correctly to make internal resources accessible to external hosts and external resources accessible to internal hosts.

## Chapter 23

ISA Server Installation

Best Damn Topics in this Chapter:

- **Installing ISA Server on a Windows 2000 Server**

- **Migrating from Microsoft Proxy Server 2.0**

- **Performing the Installation**

Introduction

Installing ISA Server is a relatively simple matter, but you should know what to expect before you run the Installation Wizard. When you are deploying ISA on a production network, it is very important that you have completed and approved your ISA network design before beginning the installation.

Only a few important decisions must be made during the installation. The installation is a software installation; even though a typical Install Shield type of install, this is the part that determines what type of firewall you're setting up on your ISA server. However, you do need to make sure you understand what your ISA server is doing as a firewall, to understand the installation process.

Putting Together Your Flight Plan

To ensure that your installation goes smoothly, have the answers to the following questions before you begin:

- Where are the installation files?

- Do you have appropriate permissions to install ISA Server?

- What is the CD key, and where is the product license?

- Will the Active Directory Schema need to be updated?

- What server mode will you use?

- Where will you store the program files, log files, and Web cache?

- What are the network IDs for the hosts on your internal network?

- What ISA features do you want to include in your installation?

- Will you be creating or joining an array?

Let's look at these points in a little more detail before beginning the installation.

Installation Files and Permissions

The installation files for ISA Server can be accessed via the product CD-ROM or from a network installation share point. If you are installing from a share point, make sure that the Share and NTFS permissions at the source allow you to install the program.

You must be logged on with an account that has permission to install the program. If you are installing a stand-alone ISA server, you must at least be a member of the Administrators group for that machine. If you want to install an enterprise array, you must be a member of the Domain Administrators group. If you have a multiple forest environment, you should be a member of the Enterprise Admins group, and if you are responsible for initializing Active Directory, you also have to be a member of the Schema Admins group.

Table 23.1 lists the required permissions for ISA Server installation.

Table 23.1 Permissions Required to Install ISA Server and Components

You Plan to Install:	Permissions Required:
Stand-alone ISA server	Local Administrators Group (Domain Administrators are automatically placed in this group)
An array member	Domain Administrator
An enterprise array	Enterprise Admin

NOTE

You must be a member of *all* the following groups to install the ISA schema to Active Directory: administrators group on the local computer, enterprise administrators group, and schema admins group.

CD Key and Product License

The *CD key* is located on the CD case. It is a 10-digit number. You might also find it on the product packaging. Be sure that you have the license readily available and that you photocopy it, scan it, and then put it in a safe place.

It is an important part of your fault-tolerance plan to have multiple copies of your product licenses and to store them in a safe, centralized location or locations. Doing so will help you avert unfortunate fines should your company be the subject of an audit.

NOTE

The CD key is a 10-digit number. You will be requested to supply the CD key during the installation process.

Active Directory Considerations

If you plan to install an enterprise array, the machine onto which you install ISA Server must be a member of a domain. You also need to connect to a domain controller during the installation. Confirm network connectivity to a domain controller prior to beginning the installation.

As mentioned earlier, when you perform an enterprise initialization, you will be altering Active Directory so that it can store array configuration information. Remember that alterations to the schema are a one-way process and that you cannot go back and restore the schema to its previous state.

NOTE

You must be able to communicate with a domain controller in your domain via a secure channel before performing the enterprise initialization. This is not the same as being able to access a file share on the domain controller. To confirm a secure channel between your computer and a domain controller, use the Netdom utility included with the Windows 2000 Resource Kit. Use the *netdom query /Verify server* command to obtain a screen print of the servers in your domain that have a verifiable secure channel.

Server Mode

Decide in advance the server mode you will assign to the ISA server. The server modes are cache mode, firewall mode, and integrated mode. This decision should be made after conferring with your security group and determining exactly what function(s) this ISA server will perform on your network. The security implications of the modes are quite different; these implications need to be addressed prior to implementation.

Disk Location for ISA Server Files

Decide where you want to install the ISA Server program files. These files require only about 20MB of disk space and do not incur much read/write activity, so you will usually be safe installing them to the default location, which is in the Program Files folder on the boot partition.

During installation, you need to decide where you want to place your Web cache files. It is best to place these on a RAID array, which must be formatted as NTFS. The RAID configuration should ensure the best performance possible.

NOTE

Web cache files can be placed only on an NTFS partition or volume. In fact, when you configure the Web cache, either during installation or via the ISA Management console, you will not be given the opportunity to place the cache on FAT formatted drives.

Although you won't need to decide where to put your log files during installation, you should have your server configured so that you can adjust the configuration to put the logs on their own volume, if possible. Log files are written to much more than they are read. Therefore, after the installation is complete, you should move the log file location to a volume that has the fastest write access.

NOTE

By default, the log files are placed on the boot partition, but after installation is complete, you will be able to change the location via the ISA Administration console. The path for the default location is <drive>:\Program Files\Microsoft ISA Server\ ISALogs.

Internal Network IDs and the Local Address Table

You will be asked to configure the local address table (LAT) during the installation routine. To prepare the LAT correctly, you need to know the network IDs that are in use inside your company. The LAT will be used to determine if requests should be sent directly to an internal server or if they should be subjected to ISA Server rules and policies.

It is paramount that you configure the LAT correctly because it defines the networks that are considered internal and those that are considered external. If for some reason an external network ID finds itself on the LAT, requests from that network ID will be treated as internal network clients and will not be subjected to the same access controls applied to external network hosts. This means that these external network hosts could have direct access to your internal network resources.

Optimal configuration of your LAT is based on the routing tables configured on your ISA servers. You'll have the option for ISA Server to configure the LAT based on the routing table on that server. The best way to have the LAT configured correctly and reliably is to have an accurate routing table on the machine. This can be done automatically via a routing protocol, such as RIP or OSPF, or you can create manual routing table entries via the Routing and Remote Access console GUI interface or via the *ROUTE* command using the command prompt interface.

ISA Server Features Installation

A few services are labeled "add-in" services by the ISA Server installation routine. Before you begin the installation, you should determine whether you want to include these services:

- The H.323 Gatekeeper Service
- The Message Screener
- The H.323 Gatekeeper Administration Tool

The H.323 Gatekeeper allows multiple inbound and outbound calls using a program such as NetMeeting to conduct voice, video, and data sessions. The H.323 Administration tool allows you to administer the service. Thus, if you install the service, you should install the tool as well.

The Message Screener is a tool you use together with secure Mail Server publishing. The Message Screener tool allows you to check incoming mail for a number of elements, such as keywords. If you plan to implement secure Mail Server publishing, you should install this tool.

NOTE

If you plan to use the Message Screen tool, you need an installation of the IIS 5.0 SMTP Service to act as a relay. The IIS SMTP service is used to relay messages to your internal mail server.

> **WARNING**
>
> As part of the installation routine, the ISA Server Setup program will change the TCP/IP driver's dynamic port range to 65,535. (The effect takes place when the computer is rebooted after installing ISA Server.)

Performing the Installation

We are now at the point where we can start installing ISA Server. The following walkthrough goes through each step required to install ISA Server as a stand-alone server on a Windows 2000 Advanced Server computer. Later, we will perform the enterprise initialization and upgrade the stand-alone server to an array member.

Installing ISA Server: A Walkthrough

These are the steps for performing a typical installation of a stand-alone ISA server:

1. We begin the installation by placing the installation CD into the CD-ROM drive. The autorun begins and we are presented with the installation options screen (see Figure 23.1). Note that you have six options:

   - **Review Release Notes (the README file)** Select this option to read the latest information about ISA Server that did not make it into the Help files. It is highly recommended that you read these notes before beginning. If you don't want to read the notes right away, you should at least open the file and print it for reference. It contains important information that you must know before beginning the configuration phase of the ISA Server installation.

   - **Read Installation Guide** The installation guide is a pared-down version of the Help files. This guide focuses on the concepts that are important to planning, installation, and basic configuration of ISA Server. You should also print this file and read it at your leisure.

   - **Register ISA Server** Use this link to register your server online.

   - **Run ISA Server Enterprise Initialization** Use this link to prepare Active Directory for configuring an ISA Server array. We cover how to perform the enterprise initialization later in this chapter.

   - **Install ISA Server** This option begins the installation of ISA Server.

   - **Read About Migrating to ISA Server** This link opens a document that provides information about how to upgrade from Proxy Server 2.0 and Windows NT 4.0 installations that have Proxy Server 2.0 installed on them. We cover important migration issues in this chapter.

     For the purposes of this walkthrough, click the **Install ISA Server** option.

Figure 23.1 The ISA Server Setup Dialog Box

2. After beginning the installation, you will see the information screen shown in Figure 23.2, which informs you that you can install the product on only one server if you have only one license. Be aware of the licensing guidelines for ISA Server Standard Edition and Enterprise Edition.

Figure 23.2 The Setup Welcome Screen

3. Click **Continue**.

4. Enter your **CD key** (see Figure 23.3) and click **OK**. Notice that ISA Server uses the old CD key format, similar to that used by Proxy Server and different from the format used by other 2000 Series BackOffice server products.

Figure 23.3 CD Key Dialog Box

5. After entering the CD key, you will get your product ID number (see Figure 23.4). This is the number that you must provide to Microsoft Product Support Services if you want to get technical assistance from them. Take a screen shot of this dialog box, write down the product ID number, and put it in a safe place. Make multiple copies so that they're always available. The time that you won't be able to find your product ID is when you can't get your ISA server started. Click **OK** to move to the next step.

Figure 23.4 The Product ID Dialog Box

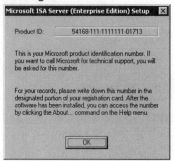

6. The ISA Server end-user license agreement (EULA) screen comes up (see Figure 23.5). You can scroll thought the license agreement, or you can right-click the body of the license agreement text, click the Select All command, right-click again and select the Copy command, and copy the whole thing to Notepad to read it at your leisure. Click **I Agree to continue the installation**. (If you were to click I Decline, the installation would stop and you would be returned to the Desktop.)

Figure 23.5 The ISA Server End-User License Agreement

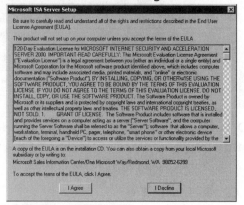

7. You now get to choose how you want to proceed with the installation (see Figure 23.6):

   ■ **Typical Installation**   Install all the components on the boot partition. This option does not include the "add-on" products. The add-ons can be installed later if you choose not to install them at this time.

   ■ **Full Installation**   The full installation includes all core program files and the add-on products. It installs these files to the boot partition.

- **Custom Installation** The custom installation allows you to choose which optional components to install.

- **Change Folder** The Change Folder button allows you to change the location of the core program files. If you do not want to install the program to the Program Files folder on the boot partition, click this button and change the location of the core program files.
  For this walkthrough, click the **Custom Installation** button.

Figure 23.6 The ISA Server Installation Options Dialog Box

8. When you select the custom installation, you get the dialog box shown in Figure 23.7, which allows you to choose the components to install. There are three options:

- ISA Services

- Add-in Services

- Administration Tools
  You *must* install the ISA Services. However, you can customize your selections for add-in services and administration tools. If you select Add-in Services and click the Change Option button, you will see the screen that appears in Figure 23.8. You have the choice of installing either or both the H.323 Gatekeeper Service and the Message screener. Now, if you click the Administrative Tools option, you will see the options shown in Figure 23.9.

Figure 23.7 The Custom Installation Dialog Box

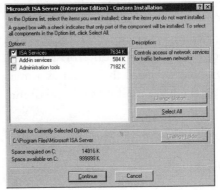

Figure 23.8 Add-in Services Change Option Dialog Box

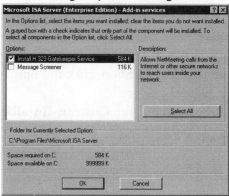

Figure 23.9 The Administrative Tools Options Dialog Box

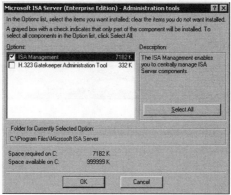

Here you have the choice of installing the ISA Management and/or the H.323 Gatekeeper administration tool. If you are installing the full product on the server, you will want to install the administrative tools. In addition, you can choose to install only the administrative tools on a Windows 2000 Professional computer and administer any server or array in your organization.

If you choose to install the H.323 Gatekeeper administration tool, it will place a node in your ISA Management console that will allow you to configure the H.323 Gatekeeper service.

In this walkthrough, select all the options and click **OK**.

9. We have not run the enterprise initialization tool yet, so we get the dialog box shown in Figure 23.10. Since the ISA Server Enterprise Initialization tool has not yet updated the schema, we are not able to install this server as a member of an enterprise array. However, we are allowed to install it as a stand-alone server. Click **Yes** to install a stand-alone ISA server.

10. Here you choose the server mode from the options shown in Figure 23.11 and reviewed here:

Figure 23.10 Deciding to Join an Array

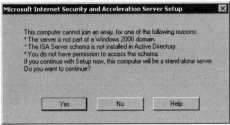

- **Firewall Mode** Choose this option if you want to install the server as a firewall only and do not want to use the Web proxy server. Keep in mind that if you do not install the Web Proxy Service, you will not be able to take advantage of either forward or reverse Web caching.

- **Cache Mode** Choose this option if you want to use only "Web" protocols. Cache mode supports only HTTP, HTTPS, FTP, and Gopher. If you want to use other protocols such as SMTP for e-mail or NNTP for newsgroups, you need to install either firewall mode or integrated mode. It is also recommended that you do not install a cache-mode-only server on the edge of your network, because the firewall features are especially important at the edge of the network.

- **Integrated Mode** Choose this mode if you want to take advantage of all the features of ISA Server. You will be able to support all Winsock applications and take advantage of the Web proxy server's Web caching feature.

Figure 23.11 Selecting the Server Installation Mode

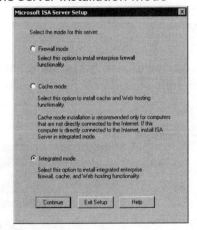

11. For this walkthrough, select **Integrated Mode** so that we can examine both the Cache Mode and the Firewall Mode components. After selecting the Integrated Mode option, click **Continue** to continue with the setup routine.

12. At this point, the ISA Server installation program will stop the IIS WWW service (W3SVC), as shown in Figure 23.12. However, the service will be restarted by the end of installation. It is important to understand the implications of running IIS on the same

computer as ISA Server. On a multihomed machine, ISA Server uses TCP port 80 on the external interface to listen for incoming Web requests for servers that have been published using the Web Publishing Wizard. If you have a Web site or sites that are using port 80 on the ISA server's external interface, they will no longer respond to requests. You need to either change the port number for those Web sites or use the Web Publishing Wizard to publish them via the internal interface on an alternate port number.

ISA Server listens for Web proxy server requests on port 8080 on the internal interface. This is a departure from the way Web proxy clients accessed the Proxy Server 2.0 Web Proxy Service, which they were able to access by connecting to port 80.

These changes point out an important fact: No component of ISA Server is dependent on IIS. In Proxy Server 2.0, the Web Proxy Service was an ISAPI plug-in to IIS; the management interface for the other services was dependent on IIS as well.

For this walkthrough, click **OK** to move on to the next step.

Figure 23.12 Warning Dialog Box about IIS Services

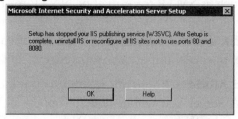

13. You now can configure the Web cache settings (see Figure 23.13). You are presented with a list of NTFS drives that can support the Web cache. You *must* place the cache on an NTFS drive. FAT partitions or volumes do not appear on the list. The default setting is to create a 100MB Web cache file on the partition that has the most free disk space. After you enter the size of the cache, you must click the **Set** button.

     For this walkthrough, configure a 100MB cache on the E: drive. To move to the next step, click the **OK** button.

Figure 23.13 Configuring Web Cache Size

14. The LAT configuration dialog box (see Figure 23.14) appears and provides you a chance to configure the LAT during setup. If you choose not to configure the LAT at

this time or if you change your mind regarding the configuration of the LAT, you can change the settings via the ISA Management console after the installation is complete. You can approach configuring the LAT in two ways. You can manually enter the start and end addresses in the Edit frame on the left side of the dialog box, or you can use the Table button:

■ When manually entering the information, you must include the entire range of your network IDs that are part of your internal network. Note that we have entered an illegal address for the start address for the LAT. This is OK and will not impair the functionality of the LAT.

■ If you choose to use the Construct Table button, ISA Server will try to create the LAT for you based on the network ID of your internal interface(s). In addition to the network ID of your internal interface, it will also add the three private network ranges:

192.168.0.0/24

172.16.0.0/12

10.0.0.0/8

■ If you choose to let ISA Server construct the table for you, you must be sure to check it very carefully. If you have a network with multiple logical IP segments, you need to include all these segment IDs in your LAT. Otherwise, requests for those internal network clients will be subjected to the rules created for requests for external network requests.

■ Always make sure that your ISA server can route to all your internal networks properly. The way to accomplish this task is to configure routing table entries that accurately reflect the configuration of your internal network. By configuring the routing table appropriately, you will ensure reliable communications within your network and prevent problems with incorrect LAT entries that can compromise the security of your internal network.

In this walkthrough, we have created an entry for our internal network ID, which falls within one of the private network address ranges. Click **OK** to continue to the next step.

Figure 23.14 Configuring the Local Address Table

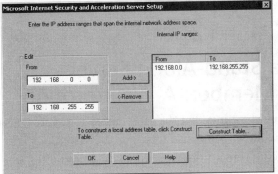

15. The installer copies the files to their target directories. After the file-copy phase is complete, you are offered the opportunity to have the Setup program open the ISA Management console and begin the Getting Started Wizard (see Figure 23.15). The wizard walks you through the configuration steps for ISA Server. We like to be obliging, so we'll click **OK** to allow the installation routine to start the wizard for us. However, we'll avoid the Getting Started Wizard because we're going to learn how to configure the server ourselves!

Figure 23.15 Launch the ISA Admin Tool Dialog Box

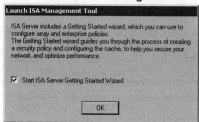

16. The Getting Started welcome screen (see Figure 23.16) is presented as the ISA Administration console is opened. You can use the wizard to help walk you through the steps of configuring the server. However, you should have a thorough understanding of ISA Server and all the implications of the settings you create *before* you work with the Getting Started Wizard. Once you have a firm understanding of ISA Server, the wizard can help you configure your server in an orderly fashion.

Figure 23.16 The ISA Server Management Console

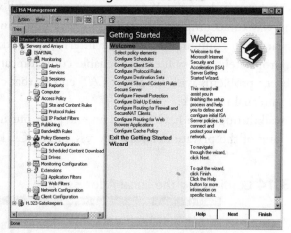

Upgrading a Stand-Alone Server to an Array Member: A Walkthrough

In the first walkthrough, we installed the ISA server as a stand-alone server. You might want to do this in your test lab while you're learning about the system, or you might like to put ISA Server into a limited production environment in order to get a better feel for how it fits into your organization. The chance is good that you'll like what you see, and later you'll want to take advantage of the additional features provided in an enterprise array configuration. The good news is that you don't have to reinstall ISA Server to make it an enterprise array member; you can *promote* the stand-alone server instead.

As we discussed earlier, you need to have Windows 2000 deployed and available if you want to make the server a member of an enterprise array. The computer on which you want to perform the upgrade also needs to be a member of the Windows 2000 domain. If the machine is a member of a Windows NT 4.0 domain, the enterprise upgrade will not work, because the Windows NT 4.0 domain controller does not have the Active Directory in which to store the enterprise array configuration information.

> **NOTE**
>
> When you install an add-in feature on one server in an array, it is not automatically installed on all the servers in the array. You must install the add-in on each server in the array individually.

Performing the Enterprise Initialization

Before you promote a stand-alone server to an array member, you need to complete the *enterprise initialization*. This is the process of updating Active Directory so that it will support the ISA Server array configuration information. There are two ways you can perform the initialization:

- From the Startup Installation screen
- From the ISA Server installation files in the i386 directory, run the msisaent.exe file

Both these methods walk you through the same process:

1. When you put the CD-ROM into the drive, the Autorun feature brings up a dialog box. You can also get it to run by clicking the **isaautorun.exe** file in the root of the installation files hierarchy.

2. To run the enterprise initialization, click the **Run ISA Server Enterprise Initialization** icon.

3. After starting the initialization process, you'll get a dialog box informing you that the Active Directory schema will be updated and that this is not a reversible process (see Figure 23.17). If you get an error message stating that the "the computer name is unacceptable," click **OK** to close the dialog box and restart the computer. The enterprise initialization will proceed normally after restarting. Click **Yes** to continue.

Figure 23.17 Warning about Irreversible Changes to the Active Directory

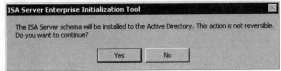

4. At this point, you need to decide how you want to apply enterprise policy (see Figure 23.18). Your choices are:

    ■ **Use Array Policy Only** When you choose to use Array Policy Only, an enterprise policy is created, but it will not be automatically applied to the array. You will have the opportunity to manually assign enterprise policy to the array after the initialization is completed by configuring it in the ISA Management console.

    ■ **Use This Enterprise Policy** When you choose Use This Enterprise Policy, a default policy is created with the name Enterprise Policy 1. You can change the name if you want. If you select this option and do not select the Also Allow Array Policy option, any array policies are replaced by the enterprise policy. If you are thinking of choosing this option, be sure to back up your existing array policy prior to the enterprise initialization in the event that you want to restore the existing array policy (stand-alone policy as well) on the server.

    ■ **Allow Array-Level Access Policy Rules That Restrict Enterprise Policy** If you choose this option, both the enterprise policy and the array policies will be applied. However, *array policies can only further limit the policies set for the enterprise*. What this means is that array policy cannot have any *allow rules*. The only allow rules are those determined by the enterprise policy.

    ■ **Allow Publishing Rules** This option does exactly that. Publishing rules must be created on each server of an array separately, because the IP address(es) listening for requests for published servers will be different for each server. If you do not choose this option now, you can do so later after the enterprise is initialized and you promote the stand-alone server to an array.

    ■ **Force Packet Filtering on the Array** This option enforces packet filtering on the array(s) to which this policy is applied. This forces packet filtering on each server in the array and cannot be overridden by array policy.

The default settings are shown in Figure 23.18. We will allow array policy, allow publishing rules to be configured on the array, and force packet filtering. Then, click **OK**.

Figure 23.18 Determining Policy

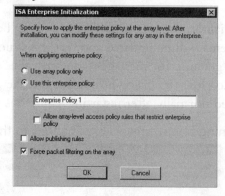

The schema is updated and shows the progression with a nice animated icon (see Figure 23.19).

Figure 23.19 Initializing the Active Directory for ISA Server

5. When the enterprise initialization is completed, you will see a dialog box informing you that everything worked (see Figure 23.20). If there were problems updating Active Directory, you will receive an error dialog box, and you will have to troubleshoot the problems with Active Directory and perhaps with connectivity. Note that if you have multiple domain controllers, you should wait before configuring ISA Server as an array member.

Figure 23.20 ISA Server Enterprise Initialization Tool Dialog Box

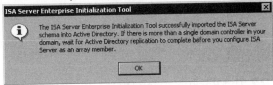

WARNING

We cannot stress too much the importance of the decision you make when deciding which policy or policies will be applied to the array. If you choose to allow enterprise policies, *only* enterprise policies will be applied and you will *not* be able to create any array policies. If you do allow for array policies, remember *that you cannot create any allow rules in the array policy.* Array policies can *only restrict* the policies you set in the enterprise policy.

Backing Up a Configuration and Promoting a Stand-Alone Server to an Array Member

After updating Active Directory to support your array, you can begin the process of promoting your stand-alone ISA server. Before promoting the server, confirm that you have connectivity with a domain controller in your Windows 2000 domain. You might also want to back up your configuration if you have not yet done so.

It's a good idea to back up your configuration when making changes of this kind. In fact, you should back up your stand-alone server or array configuration prior to making any changes to rules or filters. By backing up, you can easily roll back to a previous configuration that has worked for you. It is much easier, and much less error prone, to restore a backed-up configuration than to try to remember all the rules and configuration settings you made and hope that you enter them correctly a second time.

To back up an array or stand-alone configuration, perform the following steps:

1. Open the **ISA Management console** and right-click the name of your server or array (see Figure 23.21). Click the **Back Up** command.

Figure 23.21 Accessing the Back Up Command

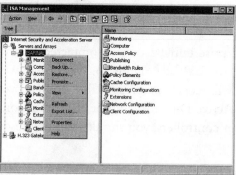

2. In the Backup Array dialog box, type the path where you can store the configuration backup file (see Figure 23.22). Be sure to include the name of the file to fully qualify the path. Then, click **OK**.

Figure 23.22 The Backup Array Dialog Box

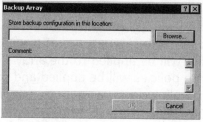

3. If the configuration backs up successfully, you will see a dialog box confirming that fact as seen in Figure 23.23. Note the warning in this dialog box. Although you have saved configuration settings specific to this array, it is not a complete backup of all system settings as they relate to ISA Server. This type of backup allows you to recover from errors you make in configuration settings in the ISA Management console, but it will not be enough to recover from a total system crash. For the purposes of disaster recovery, you should use the Windows Backup program or another backup program of your choice to back up the entire system, including the system state data. The system state data includes the Registry, the COM+ Class Registration database, and the system boot files. It also includes the Certificate Services database if the machine is acting as a Certificate server.

If the computer is a domain controller, the system state will include the Active Directory database (ntds.dit) and Sysvol directory.

Figure 23.23 Confirmation of a Successful Backup

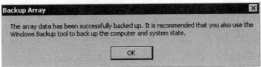

4. You can confirm the location of your backup files by opening Windows Explorer. Figure 23.24 shows these files in the root of the C: drive. Note that these are the names we chose for the backup files. The system does not provide a default name. However, the backup files for stand-alone servers will always have the .BIF file extension.

Figure 23.24 Backup Files Identified in the Root of Drive C:

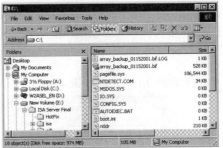

Now that we have backed up our stand-alone configuration, the next step is to back up the entire system. This way, we can roll back the system to a stand-alone server after the array promotion has been completed. There is no automatic mechanism for you to use to roll back from an array to a stand-alone server; you must restore from backup. After completing our backup duties, we can get to the process of promoting our server. Before we begin the promotion sequence, right-click the name of the server and click **Properties**. The Properties show that the server is a stand-alone server in integrated mode (see Figure 23.25). Note the tabs available when the server is a stand-alone server. There will be a new tab by the time we're finished with this walkthrough.

Figure 23.25 The General Tab in the Server's Properties Dialog Box

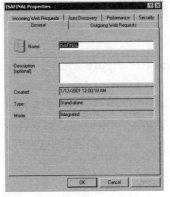

5. To begin the promotion, right-click the array node in the left pane, and then click the **Promote** command, as shown in Figure 23.26.

Figure 23.26 Beginning the Promotion Process

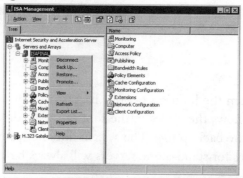

6. After clicking the Promote command, we get a dialog box that warns us that we can't go back to stand-alone server mode once the promotion to an array is completed (see Figure 23.27). Click **Yes** to continue the promotion.

Figure 23.27 Array Warning Dialog Box

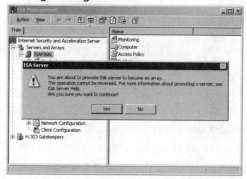

7. Before the promotion begins, you need to decide on the enterprise policy settings for the array (see Figure 23.28). We discussed the meaning of each of these choices earlier in this chapter. The default setting is Use Default Enterprise Policy Settings. However, for this walkthrough, choose **Use Custom Enterprise Policy Settings** and **Also Allow Array Policy**. **The Force Packet Filtering on the Array** option is also a default selection; select **Allow Publishing Rules to Be Created on the Array** as well. Then, click **OK**.

8. The promotion begins (see Figure 23.29). Several things happen during the promotion, and you'll be informed of these events in the Promoting Array dialog box. The first step is Converting Stand-alone Server to an Array. The subsequent steps are:

- Storing configuration in the Active Directory
- Stopping all services
- Committing changes

Figure 23.28 Setting Enterprise Policy Settings

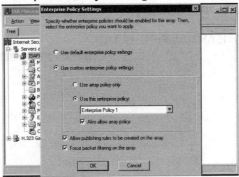

- Restarting all services
- Refreshing array list

If the promotion proceeds smoothly, note the instructions in the dialog box and click **OK**.

Figure 23.29 The Promotion of the Stand-Alone Server to an Array Begins

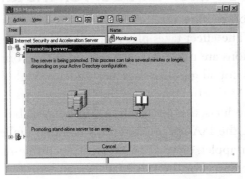

9. After clicking **OK**, you have to right-click the **Internet Security and Acceleration Server** node in the left pane of the ISA Management console and click the **Connect to** command. You then select the **Connect to Enterprise and Arrays** option button and click **OK**. Once connected, your console will have changed and look like what appears in Figure 23.30.

Figure 23.30 ISA Management Reflects After Promotion to Array Status

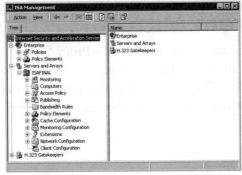

10. Right-click the array name and click **Properties**, and notice that there is a new tab in the dialog box, the Policies tab (see Figure 23.31). Note the options available.

Figure 23.31 ISAFINAL Policies Tab

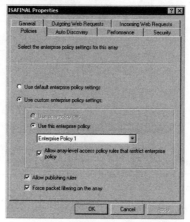

Changes Made After ISA Server Installation

As part of the installation routine, the ISA Server setup will change the TCP/IP driver's dynamic port range to 65,535. (The effect takes place when the computer is rebooted after installing.)

A number of additions are made in the Registry of the computer running ISA Server. Unfortunately, they are not all grouped together under a single Registry key, so you'll have to hunt around for them. At this time, none of the Registry keys has been documented. However, as with most Microsoft products, this information will be available in the future.

After installing ISA, the ISA-specific counters will be installed. You can access these counters via the System Monitor applet, or you can access a preconfigured ISA System Monitor console via the Start menu. The entry for the ISA Management console is also found in the Microsoft ISA Server entry in the Start menu.

ISA Server has its own management console and does not snap into the Internet Services Manager console the way Proxy Server 2.0 does. You can create your own console that includes the ISA Management stand-alone snap-in along with other snap-ins. In this way, you can stream-line management by including snap-ins such as the ISA Management, Internet Services Manager, and other network- and Internet-related snap-ins to provide a central interface for your Internet and intranet-based solutions.

Migrating from Microsoft Proxy Server 2.0

If you work in an organization that already has a Proxy Server 2.0 installation in place, you prob-ably don't want to redo all the configuration settings that you have so carefully applied to your three-year-old deployment. The good news is that just about every rule you created in Proxy Server 2.0 will be successfully migrated, depending on the type of migration you perform.

What Gets Migrated and What Doesn't

When you migrate your Proxy Server 2.0 configuration to Windows 2000, virtually all components of your configuration will be ferried over to ISA Server. These include:

- Proxy Server Domain Filters (ISA Server Rules)
- Proxy Server Network Settings (ISA Protocol Rules)
- Proxy Server Monitoring configuration (ISA Server Performance Monitor)
- Proxy Server Cache Configuration (ISA Cache Configuration)

All these elements will be brought over, depending on how you perform the migration in relation to your enterprise array configuration. The ways in which rules and other configuration elements are migrated depends on the user who performs the migration and the Enterprise Policy settings, if any, for that particular server or array.

Table 23.2 shows what happens during the migration from Proxy Server 2.0 to ISA Server when the enterprise array setting is set to Use Array Policy Only.

Table 23.2 The "Use Array Policy Only" Effect on Migration from Proxy Server 2.0

Enterprise Policy Setting	Enterprise Administrator Performing Upgrade	What Gets Migrated
Use Array Policy Only	Doesn't matter	All proxy server rules are migrated to the array policy

Note that when the enterprise policy is set to use the array policy only, it doesn't matter whether you are a domain admin or an enterprise admin. All the proxy server rules will be migrated to the array because, when only the local array policy is used, there are no interactions with the enterprise policy, so there's no impact on the permissions related to the enterprise policy and how it applies to a particular array.

Let's look at an example when the enterprise policy setting is configured to the Use Enterprise Policy Only setting (Table 23.3).

Table 23.3 The "Use Enterprise Policy Only" Effect on Migration from Proxy Server 2.0

Enterprise Policy Setting	Enterprise Administrator Performing Upgrade	What Gets Migrated
Use Enterprise Policy Only	Yes	All proxy server rules are migrated, and enterprise policy is set to Use Array Policy Only
Use Enterprise Policy Only	No	None of the Proxy Server rules are imported, and the new array uses the enterprise policy only

Note that when the user running the upgrade is an enterprise administrator, all the proxy server rules are migrated and the upgrade routine changes the enterprise policy to Use Array Policy Only to allow for the migration of the configuration settings from Proxy Server 2.0. It must do this in order to bring over the *allow rules* you have configured in Proxy Server 2.0.

This is not the case when the person performing the upgrade is *not* an enterprise administrator. Since the non-enterprise admin is not able to influence enterprise policy, none of the Proxy Server 2.0 rules will be imported. That's because the policy setting in this scenario is configured to use the enterprise policy only, and therefore the Setup program will not allow the domain admin or local admin security account to change the enterprise policy to Use Array Policy Only, if only temporarily for the upgrade process.

In the next scenario (see Table 23.4), we see what happens when the enterprise policy setting is configured to Use Enterprise and Array Policy.

Table 23.4 The "Use Enterprise and Array Policy" Effect on Migration from Proxy Server 2.0

Enterprise Policy Setting	Enterprise Administrator Permission	What Gets Migrated
Use Enterprise and Array Policy	Yes	All proxy server rules are migrated, and the enterprise policy configuration is set to Use Array Policy Only
Use Enterprise and Array Policy	No	Only deny rules are migrated to the array policy; allow rules are dropped

In this case, when the user performing the upgrade is an enterprise admin, the enterprise policy is changed to Use Array Policy Only so that the Proxy Server 2.0 rules can be migrated to the ISA array policy. You can then change the enterprise policy back to Use Enterprise and Array Policy after the migration is completed. Be sure to back up the migrated array policy after the upgrade and before the change policies settings to enterprise and array policy, because you won't be able to change back.

If the user performing the upgrade is not an enterprise admin, only deny rules are migrated. This puts you at a disadvantage in not migrating all your old settings and does not afford you the opportunity to use them in an array, should you decide *not* to use an enterprise policy.

Functional Differences between Proxy Server 2.0 and ISA Server

Proxy Server 2.0 and ISA Server have a good deal in common, but some of the things that you're used to doing in Proxy Server 2.0 are done a little differently with ISA Server. Some of the differences between the two include:

- IPX/SPX is *not* supported.
- The Web Proxy Service listens on Port 8080 and Web proxy client implications.
- The Winsock client is not required on published servers.
- The Web cache is stored as a single file.
- There is no SOCKS service.
- The firewall client doesn't support 16-bit operating systems.
- There are incompatibilities between ISA and IIS on same machine.

ISA Server Does Not Support IPX/SPX

Proxy Server 2.0 included the ability to access the Internet while network clients ran IPX/SPX as their transport protocol. This capability has not been extended to ISA Server. When Proxy Server 2.0 was released, Novell NetWare networks were not considered legacy. In order to successfully integrate into a mixed Windows NT/NetWare network, support for an IPX gateway was important. The versions of NetWare in use at that time required IPX/SPX.

However, NetWare's market share has profoundly diminished as Windows NT and now Windows 2000 have grown in popularity. Additionally, current versions of NetWare (5.0 and up) can run on pure IP. With the ascendance of TCP/IP as *the* networking protocol, Microsoft decided to drop IPX/SPX support in ISA Server.

If you are running Proxy Server 2.0 on an IPX network, you need to upgrade the networking infrastructure to support TCP/IP prior to installing ISA Server.

Web Proxy Service Users Port 8080

The Web Proxy Service in Proxy Server 2.0 listened for Web protocol requests on the server's internal interface port 80. It did so because the Web Proxy Service in Proxy Server 2.0 was actually an ISAPI plug-in to the WWW Service included with Internet Information Server, and the WWW service listened on port 80. This made the Web Proxy Service dependent on the WWW service configuration. The Web Proxy Service included with ISA Server is not dependent on IIS or WWW Service configuration parameters.

ISA Server Web proxy clients need to send their requests to TCP port 8080 on the internal interface of the ISA server (by default). This does have some advantages, because the Autodiscovery mechanism uses TCP port 80 on the internal interface of the ISA server. It is important to note that you should *not* host a Web site on the external interface of the ISA server on TCP port 80, because the Web Proxy Service's Listener, which is used to listen for requests made for servers on the internal network that have been published, uses this port number. However, you do have the option of publishing a Web site hosted on any other available port on the internal interface if you need to run a Web site on the ISA server.

> **WARNING**
>
> You cannot run Web sites off port 80 on the internal interface of the ISA server. Autodiscovery allows firewall and Web proxy clients to obtain valuable configuration information automatically. ISA Server allows firewall and Web proxy clients to obtain this information via port 80 on the internal interface.
>
> However, our advice is to run no Web services on the ISA server and instead take advantage of publishing internal servers or providing Web services via a perimeter network. If you must use the ISA server to provide Web services, bind to the Web site an alternative port number that is not being used by any other services.

Because of this change in the Web Proxy Services internal listening port, you have to change either the default internal Web proxy listener port number or the configuration of the Web proxy clients to send requests to port 8080 on the ISA server.

You can manually change this information on all the Web proxy clients, but that could be a time-consuming and administratively expensive proposition. A better approach is to configure your DNS and/or DHCP server to provide the address of the ISA server, and then allow the ISA server to provide configuration information automatically to the network clients.

Published Servers Do Not Require the Winsock Client

One of the sweetest features of ISA Server is that you do not need to configure servers that you want to publish to the Internet as Winsock proxy clients. In Proxy Server 2.0, you often had to monkey around with the wspclnt.ini settings on your published servers. Sometimes the configuration settings worked, but more often they didn't, at least not until after you spent an enormous amount of time trying to figure out what was wrong with your settings. When you publish a DNS server, a mail server, or a database server with ISA, you do not need to configure tiresome text files and cross your fingers. The only requirement to make server publishing work correctly with ISA Server is that you configure the published servers to be secure NAT clients. Since setting up a secure NAT client is a no-brainer, you'll find the task of publishing internal servers to Internet clients easier than you ever imagined.

The Web Cache Is a Single File

Proxy Server 2.0 saved the Web cache to the file system. That meant you could easily collect tens of thousands of discrete files that needed to be managed by the NTFS file system.

Even though the NTFS file system is quite efficient, the large number of files did cause a perceptible performance hit for Web cache access times. The excessive number of files became even more problematic when you performed routine maintenance duties such as a nightly virus check, disk defragmentation, or searches of the hard disk for particular files.

ISA Server has solved this problem by saving the Web cache to a single file. The file is saved with the .CDAT file extension stored in a folder named urlcache. One .CDAT file is created on each drive you configured to store the Web cache. More than one .CDAT file can be created on a drive if your cache size is larger than 10GB, since one .CDAT file is created for each 10GB of cache file size. For example, if you created a cache file of 15GB on drive D:, there would be one 10GB .CDAT file and one 5GB .CDAT file on that drive.

No More SOCKS Proxy Service

If you ran the SOCKS Proxy Service and configured access rules for SOCKS proxy clients on your Proxy Server 2.0, you won't be able to configure selective rules for those clients in ISA Server. This is because ISA Server does not have a SOCKS Proxy Service.

ISA does support SOCKS version 4 clients via the SOCKS application filter. Machines that ran as SOCKS proxy clients in Proxy Server 2.0 must be configured as secure NAT clients when connecting to ISA Server. The SOCKS Application Filter intercepts the SOCKS requests on port 1080 and forwards the requests to the Internet. You can control access for these clients as you would with any other secure NAT client.

Incompatibilities between ISA and IIS on the Same Machine

Proxy Server 2.0 was highly integrated into IIS, so you did not have to worry about any potential incompatibilities between the two. However, you have to make some changes to your IIS configuration prior to upgrading a Proxy Server 2.0 installation to ISA Server.

When you upgrade from Proxy Server 2.0, you must take into consideration the IIS configuration. As discussed earlier, the best course of action is to not run Web services on your ISA server and to uninstall IIS completely. However, you might not have this option.

If you must run a Web server from the same machine running ISA, make sure that no Web sites listen on port 80 of either the internal or external interface. As we said earlier, port 80 on the external interface is used by the Web Proxy Service Listener, and port 80 on the internal interface is used by the ISA Autoconfiguration publishing system.

Other IIS services could find themselves at issue with ISA Server if you plan on publishing internal servers to the Internet. If you want to publish internal mail servers, you cannot run the IIS SMTP Service on port 25 of the ISA server, because the publishing rule will use the external interface port 25 for publishing the internal SMTP server. In the same fashion, you cannot run the IIS NNTP Service on the external interface of the ISA server if you want to publish an internal NNTP site, because the published server needs to use the default port number for the service on the external interface, which is 119.

NOTE

When publishing internal servers to the Internet, you cannot configure ISA Server to remap ports. If a published server is configured to listen on a particular port number, the request will be forwarded to the same port number on the internal server. This setup prevents you from publishing internal servers by having them listen on alternate port numbers on the external interface.

An alternative is to change the listening ports on the IIS Services to an alternative number so that the published services can use the default port numbers. The changes to the listening ports can be made in the Internet Services Manager console.

Learn the ISA Server Vocabulary

If you are upgrading from Proxy Server 2.0 to ISA Server, you are probably already comfortable with the vocabulary of Proxy Server 2.0. It will be easier for you to make the transition if you learn the "new language" of ISA Server.

Table 23.5 includes some terms that mean the same thing in Proxy Server 2.0 and ISA Server.

Table 23.5 Translating Proxy Server 2.0 to ISA Server

Proxy Server Term	ISA Server Term
Web Proxy Service routing rules	Routing rules
Packet filters	Allow or block packet filters
Winsock permissions	Protocol rules
Publishing properties	Web publishing rules
Domain filters	Site and content rules

Upgrading Proxy 2.0 on the Windows 2000 Platform

Performing the actual migration from Proxy Server 2.0 to ISA Server is relatively easy. However, if you are going to install Proxy Server 2.0 directly onto a Windows 2000 machine, you must to use a special installation file called msp2wizi.exe that can be downloaded from the Microsoft Proxy Web site at www.microsoft.com/proxy.

However, there are a couple of things that you should do prior to beginning the migration:

- Back up your Proxy Server 2.0 settings.
- Stop all Proxy Server 2.0 services.

You should back up your Proxy Server 2.0 settings in case the ISA installation fails and you need to return to Proxy Server for some reason. You can back up the Proxy Server 2.0 configuration files from the Properties sheet of any of the Proxy Server 2.0 services. Perform the following actions to back up Proxy Server 2.0:

1. Start the Internet Services Manager.

2. Right-click one of the services, and click the **Properties** command. In the services' Properties dialog box, click the **Server Backup** button, as shown in Figure 23.32.

Figure 23.32 The Services Dialog Box

3. Type the complete path to the file that contains the backup information, as shown in Figure 23.33. Do not include the filename. The file will be saved with the name MSP*.mpc, where the wildcard will be replaced with the data. Click **OK**, and the text-based backup file will be saved to that location.

Figure 23.33 The Backup Dialog Box

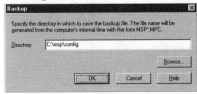

After the configuration, it's a good idea to copy the files to another location for safekeeping. You do not need to keep the backup on the same machine, because no utility will allow you to roll back from ISA Server to Proxy Server once the migration is completed. You would have to uninstall ISA Server, reinstall Proxy Server 2.0, and then restore your settings from the backup.

You also need to stop all Proxy Server-related services prior to the migration. Type the following commands to stop the services:

```
net stop wspsrv
net stop mspadmin
net stop mailalrt
net stop w3svc
```

If everything works the way it's supposed to, you should see something like the screen shown in Figure 23.34.

Figure 23.34 Stopping Proxy Server 2.0-Related Services

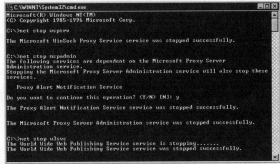

After stopping these services, you can begin the ISA Server installation process as we did earlier. Everything about the installation is the same, except for two dialog boxes related to the upgrade process itself. The first upgrade-related dialog box is shown in Figure 23.35.

Figure 23.35 Information Box Regarding Upgrading Proxy Server

When the ISA Server installation routine detects that Proxy Server 2.0 was installed on the same machine, it will tell you that an older version of ISA Server is on the machine. Well, this isn't *exactly* right, but you know what it's trying to say. When you are performing the upgrade, you want to install the files into the same folder.

NOTE

If you install the files into a different folder, you will be able to keep the original Proxy Server 2.0 files on your machine, although they won't be of much use to you because you can't run both Proxy Server 2.0 and ISA Server at the same time and you can't switch back and forth between the two.

The second upgrade-related dialog box is a little more accurate, as you see in Figure 23.36.

Figure 23.36 Proxy 2.0 Migration Dialog Box

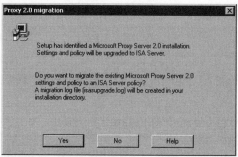

Since you want to migrate your Proxy Server 2.0 settings to the ISA Server, click **Yes** in this dialog box. If you want to install ISA Server without migrating your Proxy Server 2.0 settings, you can click **No** and the installation routine will ignore all settings from your old configuration. Keep in mind our earlier discussion regarding how the migration is affected by the group membership of the logged-on user and the enterprise policy settings.

Upgrading a Proxy 2.0 Installation on Windows NT 4.0

If you are planning to upgrade your Windows NT 4.0 Server that has Proxy Server 2.0 installed and then migrate your Proxy Server 2.0 settings to ISA Server, you'll need to know how to handle the upgrade to Windows 2000 while preserving your Proxy Server 2.0 settings.

If you are upgrading your Windows NT 4.0 Server with Proxy Server 2.0 installed, you are likely to run into one of two scenarios:

- You have planned the upgrade with the Proxy Server installation in mind.
- You forgot about Proxy Server and have already upgraded the Windows NT 4.0 machine to Windows 2000 without thinking about Proxy Server.

The following procedures will guide you in how to proceed in either situation.

A Planned Upgrade from Windows NT 4.0 Server to Windows 2000

The best way to approach an upgrade from Windows NT 4.0 to Windows 2000 is to plan the upgrade with Proxy Server 2.0 in mind. The following procedure will allow the upgrade from Windows NT 4.0 to Windows 2000 to go smoothly:

1. Use the Proxy Server configuration interface to back up your Proxy Server 2.0 settings as we did earlier in the chapter. To back up the Proxy Server 2.0 configuration, click the **Server Backup** button and select a location to store the proxy configuration files.

2. After backing up the Proxy Server 2.0 configuration, you need to uninstall the proxy server. Go to the **Start | Programs | Microsoft Proxy Server**, and click the **Uninstall** command. During the uninstall process, be sure to leave the proxy server log files, Web cache, and backup configuration files in place. The Uninstall program will ask if you want to save these components.

3. Perform the upgrade of the Windows NT 4.0 Server to Windows 2000 Server or Advanced Server.

4. After the machine has been upgraded, confirm that the upgrade was successful by letting the machine run for a short shakedown period. If the installation is stable, install Microsoft Proxy Server 2.0.

5. Once Proxy Server is installed, use the **Server Restore** button in the Proxy Server Properties dialog box to restore your previous configuration. *You must remember the location where you stored the configuration files!*

The key to this approach is that you've backed up the Proxy Server 2.0 configuration, uninstalled Proxy Server 2.0, reinstalled Proxy Server 2.0 after the upgrade to Windows 2000, and then restored the old Proxy Server 2.0 configuration from the backup you made before the upgrade.

What If You Forgot about Proxy Server?

It is possible that when you upgraded your Windows 2000 Server, you forgot about Proxy Server or realized during the upgrade that Proxy Server was installed, but you thought that you'd get around to dealing with it after the Windows 2000 upgrade was completed. If you find yourself in this position, perform the following procedure:

1. Run the Update Wizard (msp2wizi.exe) that you downloaded from the Microsoft Web site. Be sure that the Internet Information Server 5.0 Management console is closed before you start the update.

2. During the installation process, you won't be given the option to update the existing Proxy Server installation. You need to perform a fresh installation. Be sure to choose the same installation locations that you did when you first installed Proxy Server 2.0 on the Windows NT 4.0 Server. If you place the files in the same location, your previous configuration *should* remain intact.

Once the Microsoft Proxy Server 2.0 is installed on your Windows 2000 computer, you can access it via the Administrative Tools menu by clicking the Internet Services Manager command. You will see the Internet Information Services console as it appears in Figure 23.37.

Figure 23.37 The Internet Information Services Console

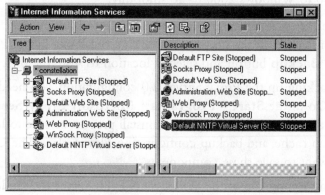

After you have installed Proxy Server 2.0, there will be three new nodes in the left pane of the Internet Information Services console: the Socks Proxy, the Web Proxy, and the WinSock Proxy. To access the configuration of any of these proxy services, just right-click any one of them and click the **Properties** command.

Realize that *all* upgrades place you in a delicate position. Even though everything should work correctly, experience tells us that whatever can go wrong with an upgrade *will* go wrong. Even when an upgrade appears to be successful, rarely will the program work like a fresh installation.

Summary

In this chapter, we focused on issues related to planning and implementing the installation of ISA Server. We emphasized the critical importance of planning your ISA Server design before beginning the installation in order to prevent unexpected and potentially harmful results after the ISA Server installation is complete.

The following checklist will help guide you through the installation process:

- Check system requirements and ensure that you have the proper hardware and operating system.

- Review key concepts about ISA Server:
    - Firewall and security functions
    - Publishing
    - Caching

- Determine if you will install ISA Server as a stand-alone or array member.

- Determine the mode in which you will install ISA Server.

- Confirm that the routing table on the machine reflects the internal network infrastructure and contains all routes to networks within your internal network.

- Secure the network interfaces by disabling NetBIOS over TCP, the Microsoft client, and file and printer sharing for Microsoft networks.

- Confirm that no "stray" ports are opened by using the *netstat –na* command. This command lists ports that are connected or listening on your computer.

- Make the appropriate changes to your IIS installation, if you have one on your server. Either move the IIS services to another machine or make the port configuration changes, as discussed in this chapter.

- If you are installing in cache or integrated mode, verify that the computer has a Windows 2000 NTFS (NTFS 5.0) partition.

- If you are installing the first array member, initialize the enterprise.

- Review the installation process and ensure that you have all the necessary information (CD key, domain membership information) that will be requested during installation.

- Confirm connectivity to a domain controller if you are creating an enterprise array.

- Ensure that you have the appropriate permissions.

- Start the ISA Server Setup program.

The ISA Server installation process is relatively straightforward, but you can help prevent any unexpected problems during installation by proper planning—which includes backing up your Proxy Server 2.0 files if you are upgrading.

## Chapter 24

Managing ISA Server

Best Damn Topics in this Chapter:

- **Understanding Integrated Administration**

- **Performing Common Management Tasks**

- **Using Monitoring, Alerting, Logging, and Reporting Functions**

- **Understanding Remote Administration**

Introduction

Flexibility, power, and features are important considerations in adopting any piece of software, especially an enterprise-level, mission-critical software package that is a vital part of your organization's security scheme. However, no matter how powerful and feature-rich a program, if its interface is not user friendly and it is difficult to configure and administer, you probably will not get the full benefits that it could offer.

In its efforts to make ISA Server as usable as it is powerful, Microsoft has equipped the product with the familiar Microsoft Management Console (MMC) interface used to give a standardized look and "feel" to all of Windows 2000's built-in administrative tools. The ISA Management Console is installed automatically as the interface to your ISA Server installation. It is also added to the list of stand-alone snap-in components that can be made part of a custom MMC.

In this chapter, we take a look at the ISA Management Console used to perform administration of ISA Server, the "how to's" of some specific management tasks, and ways of using the monitoring, alerting, logging, and reporting functionalities of ISA. We also discuss methods of administering your ISA server or array from a remote location. Let's start by examining the concept of *integrated administration*.

Understanding Integrated Administration

You already know that an ISA server or array can "wear more than one hat," or serve more than one function, on your network—as a firewall, as a caching server, or both. Unlike other solutions in which security and firewall functionality and caching and acceleration functionality require separate technologies, ISA's integrated administration enables you to manage both services using the same unified console and application of integrated policies.

An entire array of servers can be managed together as one entity. When the configuration of an array is changed, the desired modifications are made to every server in the array. Access policies and cache policies are all centrally managed. This system increases security as well, since it means that all configuration tasks can be performed at a single location.

Centralized administration is not limited to the array level. Enterprise policies can be used to control multiple arrays on your network. This integration allows an administrator to control all the ISA servers or server arrays in a large enterprise conveniently, even from a remote location.

In this section, you will learn to navigate the ISA Management Console, which is used to perform most management tasks, and you'll become familiar with the ISA wizards that make common administrative duties easier by walking you through the process step by step.

The ISA Management Console

When you install ISA Server on a Windows 2000 server, the ISA Server selection will be added to the Programs menu with two selections, ISA Management and ISA Server Performance Monitor, as shown in Figure 24.1.

Figure 24.1 The ISA Management Programs Are Added to the Windows 2000 Programs Menu

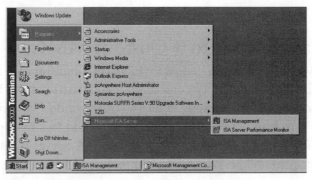

The console can also be opened by typing the full path for the msisa.msc file (for example, **C:\Program Files\Microsoft ISA Server\msisa.msc**) at the Run prompt or by navigating in Windows Explorer to the folder into which ISA Server was installed and double-clicking the **msisa.msc** icon. The ISA Management Console is shown in Figure 24.2.

Figure 24.2 The ISA Management Console Allows You to Administer Your ISA Servers and Arrays

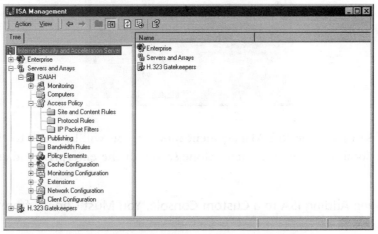

General procedures for working with the console are the same as with any MMC. You use the **View** menu at the top of the console to work with it. For example:

- You can choose the columns to be displayed in the right detail pane by selecting **View | Choose columns** and adding available columns to or removing them from the display.

- You can choose the display mode for the icons in the right detail pane by selecting **Large Icons, Small Icons, List,** or **Details** from the **View** menu.

- You can select either the **Taskpad** or the **Advanced** view.

- You can customize the console by selecting the elements that will be displayed or hidden.

A big advantage of the MMC interface is the ability to create custom MMCs that incorporate the specific snap-ins that you—or an assistant administrator to whom you delegate administrative duties—need to work with.

Adding ISA Management to a Custom MMC

To create a custom MMC to which you can add whichever administrative tools you desire as snap-in modules, you first create an empty console by typing **mmc** at the Run prompt. The new empty console root window will be encapsulated in a larger window for which the menu bar includes the **Console**, **Window**, and **Help** menus. You can add ISA management by selecting **Add/Remove Snap-in** from the **Console** menu. When ISA Server is installed on the machine, the ISA Management snap-in will be available to add to custom consoles, as shown in Figure 24.3.

Figure 24.3 ISA Management Can Be Added to a Custom MMC

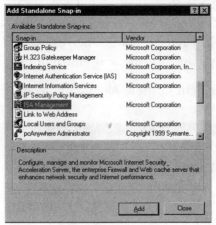

When you elect to add the ISA Management module, you will be asked to choose whether to connect to the local server, another stand-alone server, or the enterprise and arrays, as shown in Figure 24.4.

Figure 24.4 When Adding ISA to a Custom Console, You Must Choose from Three Connection Options

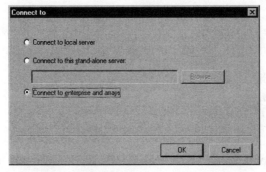

You will see the same console tree as in the preconfigured ISA Management tool. You can now add other snap-ins to allow you to perform a set of related administrative tasks, all from the

same MMC. For example, in the MMC shown in Figure 24.5, you can manage your ISA Server array, the local certificate authority (CA), and IIS, all from the same custom console.

Figure 24.5 ISA Management Can Be One of Several Components in a Custom MMC

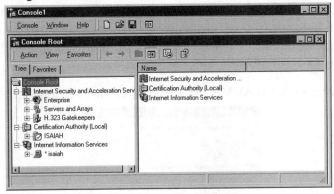

The custom console can now be saved with a unique name. By default, it will saved in the Administrative Tools folder in the Programs menu, in the profile of the currently logged-on administrator, and can subsequently be started from the **Start | Programs | Administrative Tools** menu.

Console Mode Options

Your custom console can be saved in one of four modes:

- **Author mode** Allows you to create new consoles or modify existing consoles.
- **User mode—full access** Provides full window management commands and full access to the console tree but prevents adding or removing snap-ins or changing console properties.
- **User mode—limited access, multiple window** Allows use of multiple windows.
- **User mode—limited access, single window** Limits access to a single window.

You specify the console mode by selecting **Options** from the **Console** menu. Regardless of the default mode in which the console is saved, it can be opened in author mode by typing the full MMC pathname with the **/a** switch at the **Run** prompt.

The Components of the ISA MMC

In this section, we look at the components of the ISA MMC and explain the function of each, including:

- The MMC window
- The menu bar
- The toolbar icons
- The console root and tree

The MMC Window

If you have created a custom console, you'll see a window within a window, as shown earlier in Figure 24.5. The outer window contains the main menu bar and the main toolbar common to all MMCs. The inner window is the *console window* and includes a menu bar, toolbar, description bar, and status bar. You can hide any of these elements by selecting **Customize** from the **View** menu and checking the check boxes of those elements you want displayed and unchecking those you want to hide, as shown in Figure 24.6.

Figure 24.6 You Can Select the MMC Elements You Want to Display or Hide

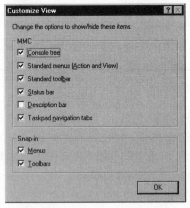

The console window of the ISA MMC contains a tab labeled **Tree**, which displays in the left console pane the hierarchy of your ISA management components. In the section "The Console Root and Tree," we look at these elements and how they are used in administering your ISA server or array.

The right console pane displays the details of the left pane element that is selected. For example, when you select **Policy Elements** in the left pane, those policy elements that appear under that container in the left console tree will be displayed in the right pane, as shown in Figure 24.7.

Figure 24.7 The Right Detail Pane Displays the Child Objects of the Selected Object in the Left Console Tree

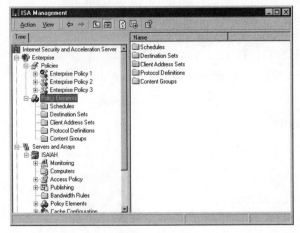

Note that in Figure 24.7, there are three containers under the root:

- Enterprise
- Servers and Arrays
- H.323 Gatekeepers

If the ISA server is a stand-alone server that is not a member of an array, only the last two objects will appear under the root; there will be no Enterprise object (as shown in Figure 24.8).

> **NOTE**
>
> The H.323 Gatekeepers object will appear here only if you specified that it be installed during the ISA Server installation process.

Figure 24.8 A Standalone ISA Server Has No Enterprise Object in the Left Pane

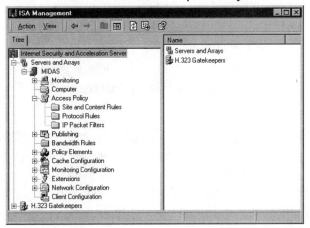

Observing the objects that appear in the left pane is one way to determine quickly, by a glance at the ISA MMC, whether the server is a stand-alone server or an array member.

The Menu Bar

The *menu bar* consists of two menus: **Action** and **View**. The contents of the **Action** menu depend on whether the ISA server is an array member and which object is highlighted in the console pane. The contents of the **Action** menu will be the same as the contents of the right context menu when you highlight the specified objects.

For example, the **Action** menu for an ISA server that belongs to an array provides the following options when the array or server object is highlighted:

1. The **Set Defaults** selection on an ISA server that is a member of an array allows you to elect to use the array policy only or to use an Enterprise policy. If you choose the latter, you can designate which Enterprise policy is to be used by selecting from a drop-down box. You can also choose whether to allow array-level access policy rules that will

restrict enterprise policy, whether to allow publishing rules, and whether to force packet filtering on the array.

2. Use the **Back Up** selection to select a location for backing up the ISA configuration information.

3. The **Restore** selection is used to restore the configuration from backup.

4. The **Refresh** selection refreshes the contents of the console window.

5. The **Export List** selection allows you to save the contents of the detail pane to a text file. You can choose from four formats: Text (tab delimited), Unicode Text (tab delimited), Text (Comma Delimited), and Unicode Text (Comma Delimited). The first two formats are saved with the .TXT extension; the last two are saved with the .CSV extension. The text files can be imported into a spreadsheet program such as Excel or a database program such as Access for data sorting and processing.

6. The **Properties** selection allows you to set the security (DACL permissions) on the object and specify whether to allow inheritable permissions from the parent object to propagate to this one. The **Advanced** button allows you to edit permission entries, set auditing on the object, and view or change ownership of the object. These are the standard Windows 2000 access control settings.

7. The **Help** selection invokes the ISA Help file, which is stored in the directory in which you installed ISA Server (**Program Files | Microsoft ISA Server** by default) as **ISA.CHM**.

If the ISA server you are managing is a stand-alone server instead of an array member, the **Action** menu will still include the **Refresh**, **Export List**, and **Help** selections, but it will include none of the others listed previously. It will have one additional selection, **Connect to**. This option is used to connect to another stand-alone server or to an enterprise or array, as shown in Figure 24.9. Note that you cannot connect to an array from a stand-alone server.

Figure 24.9 From a Stand-Alone ISA Server, You Can Connect to Another Stand-Alone Server

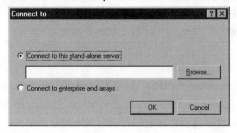

The **View** menu is identical for both stand-alone servers and array members. It contains the **Choose Columns** option that allows you to specify the column headers that will be displayed in the right detail pane. The choices available depend on which object you have highlighted in the left console tree. For example, if you have highlighted **Servers and Arrays** in the left pane, you will see a list of columns as shown in Figure 24.10.

Figure 24.10 You Can Choose the Columns to Display or Hide in the Right Detail Pane

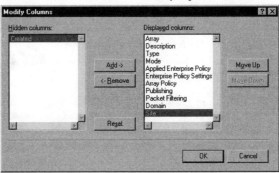

By default, all but one of the available columns is displayed. You can remove columns from the display by clicking the **Remove** button or add them by clicking **Add**. The **Reset** button will return the selection to the default setting.

You can select from the **View** menu the way you want the items in the right detail pane displayed, in keeping with the usual Windows Explorer views:

- Large icons
- Small icons
- List
- Detail

The Detail view is the default. You can also elect to use the Taskpad or Advanced view. The Taskpad view is the default, although many administrators are likely to opt for the Advanced view.

> **NOTE**
>
> The screenshots of the ISA Management Console in this book, except for those specifically illustrating the use of the Taskpad, are shown in the Advanced view.

The Taskpad view provides a more graphical interface for navigating the management options and configuring various elements of ISA Server. The Taskpad view uses a tabbed format that some administrators find more appealing than the standard detail pane. An example of the Taskpad view, with **Servers and Arrays** selected in the left pane, is shown in Figure 24.11.

The same element selected (Servers and Arrays) with the Advanced view is shown in Figure 24.12. As you can see, the Taskpad view offers a more intuitive interface, whereas the Advanced view is simpler and less cluttered. Each administrator will make the choice of view based on personal preference.

The last choice on the **View** menu is **Customize**, which allows you to customize the display by hiding certain MMC elements, as discussed earlier.

Figure 24.11 The Taskpad View Provides a More Graphical, Tabbed Interface

Figure 24.12 The Advanced View Provides a Simpler, Less Cluttered, Less Intuitive Interface

The Toolbar Icons

Seven icons appear on the ISA MMC main toolbar. These icons are standard navigation tools or items that mirror the functions of menu items. They include:

- **Back** and **Forward** buttons to return to previous locations in the console tree.

- The **Up One Level** button that takes the focus up a level in the console tree.

- The **Show/Hide Console Tree/Favorites** button that can be used to hide the left console pane, displaying only the right detail pane across the whole window.

- The **Refresh** button that, like the same choice on the **Action** menu, refreshes the display.

- The **Export List** button that performs the same function as the same selection on the **Action** menu.

- The **Help** button that invokes the ISA Server Help file.

Note that unlike the menu or toolbar for an application window, the MMC menu and toolbar cannot be customized.

The Console Root and Tree

The *console root* is the top-level object in the left pane of the ISA MMC. All objects under it are *child objects* of the root. Together, the root and its child objects make up the *console tree*. The console tree is the heart of the ISA Management Console, providing all the objects that can be configured.

The ISA Console Objects

If your ISA server belongs to an array, the first second-level object under the **Internet Security and Acceleration Server** root is the **Enterprise** container.

> **NOTE**
>
> If you have worked with Windows 2000's Active Directory, you'll remember that a *container object* is an object in the tree inside of which other objects can reside.

The Enterprise Object

The **Enterprise** container holds two child container objects:

■ Policies

■ Policy elements

The **Policies** object will hold any Enterprise policies that have been configured. By right-clicking an enterprise policy object in the left pane and selecting **Properties**, you can assign the policy to be explicitly applied to an array by checking the check box, as shown in Figure 24.13.

Figure 24.13 Enterprise Policies Are Explicitly Assigned to Arrays Via the Arrays Tab on Their Properties Boxes

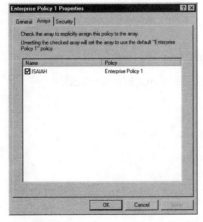

More information about the policy is shown in the right detail pane when you select the policy name in the left pane. As shown in Figure 24.14, this information includes the policy name, type, scope, action, protocol, schedule, source, destination, and content.

Figure 24.14 Information about Each Enterprise Policy Is Shown in the Right Detail Pane

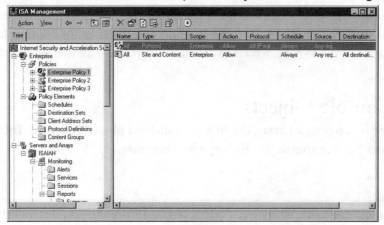

By right-clicking the policy row in the right detail pane and selecting **Properties**, you can configure the following:

- Enabling the policy
- The policy action (allow or deny requests)
- The protocol(s) to which the rule applies:
    - All IP traffic
    - Selected protocols
    - All IP traffic except selected protocols
- The schedule for applying the rule:
    - Always
    - Weekends
    - Work hours
    - A new, custom schedule
- Requests to which the rule should be applied:
    - Any request
    - Requests from specified client addresses
    - Requests from specified users and groups

You can determine which Enterprise policy has been applied by checking the icons in the right detail pane. The icon with a check mark indicates that the policy is applied. See Figure 24.15 for an illustration of this concept.

Note that in Figure 24.15, Enterprise Policy 1 displays the icon with the check mark and thus is the policy that is applied.

Figure 24.15 A Check Mark in the Right Detail Pane Indicates the Policy That Is Applied

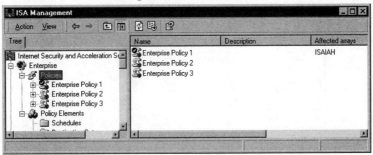

The enterprise **Policy Elements** container has five child objects:

- **Schedules** Specify when the rule will be in effect; can be applied to site and content rules, protocol rules, or bandwidth rules.

- **Destination Sets** One or more destinations (computer, IP address or IP range, path); can be applied to site and content rules, bandwidth rules, Web publishing rules, or routing rules.

- **Client Address Sets** One or more computers; can be applied to site and content rules, protocol rules, bandwidth rules, server publishing rules, or Web publishing rules.

- **Protocol Definitions** Used to create protocol rules or server publishing rules (inbound protocol definitions). Application filters can include protocol definitions as well.

- **Content Groups** Used to specify MIME types and filename extensions; apply only to HTTP and tunneled FTP traffic that goes through the Web proxy service.

The policy elements must be configured before the policies are configured. There are policy elements for both the enterprise policy and each array policy.

> **NOTE**
>
> Remember that when an enterprise policy is used in conjunction with array policies, the array policy can only impose further *restrictions*; it cannot be less restrictive than the enterprise policy.

When you use array and enterprise policies together, array-level rules can be applied to enterprise-level policy elements. This means that when you create a policy element at the enterprise level, it appears as a selection when you create a new rule at the array level. Let's look at how this works.

In Figure 24.16, you can see that we have created a custom schedule policy element at the enterprise level (displayed along with the two preconfigured schedule policy elements in the right detail pane).

Figure 24.16 An Enterprise-Level Policy Element Named Custom Has Been Created

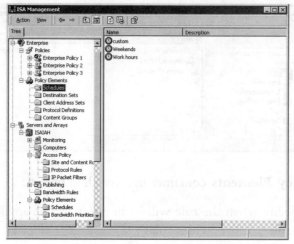

Now, if we go down to the array level (under the **Servers and Arrays** object) and, in the **Site and Content Rules** under **Access Policy**, we create a new rule, the wizard will walk us through the steps of creating our new rule. If we choose to apply the rule based on time ("Deny access only at certain times"), we will find in the drop-down box of schedule policy elements the custom schedule that we created back at the enterprise level (see Figure 24.17).

Figure 24.17 The Policy Element Created at the Enterprise Level Is Available to Be Applied to Rules at the Array Level

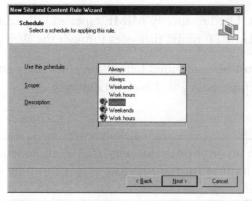

The Servers and Arrays Object

In the console tree, under **Servers and Arrays**, you will find a child object for each array, identified by the array name. By default, the array name is the same as the name of the first server that joins the array. However, you can change the array name (and you might want to do so, to avoid confusion) by right-clicking it, selecting **Properties**, and typing in the new array name, as shown in Figure 24.18.

The array's Properties sheet also provides, on the **General** tab, information regarding the date and time the array was created and the mode in which its servers are installed (firewall, caching, or integrated).

Figure 24.18 You Can Change the Array Name to Avoid Confusion with a Server by the Same Name

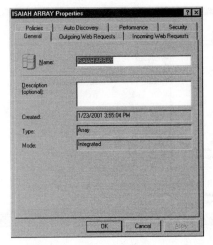

The other tabs are used for configuration of outgoing and incoming Web requests, publication of autodiscovery information, and performance tuning as well as incoming Web requests, selection of enterprise policy settings for the array, and setting security permissions on the array object. (Object permissions are discussed later in this chapter, in the section titled "Performing Common Management Tasks.")

Under the Array object, you will see the following child objects:

- Monitoring
- Computers
- Access Policy
- Publishing
- Bandwidth Rules
- Policy Elements
- Cache Configuration
- Monitoring Configuration
- Extensions
- Network Configuration
- Client Configuration

If you expand the **Monitoring** object, you will see four folders: Alerts, Services, Sessions, and Reports. Note that the **Alerts** object is used to *view* alerts; they are actually *configured* using the **Alerts** object, which is a child of the **Monitoring Configuration** object lower in the tree.

The **Services** child object contains ISA services on all servers in the array (the firewall service, Web proxy service, and scheduled content download service), indicating whether they are running or stopped, as shown in Figure 24.19.

Figure 24.19 The Services Folder Contains Information about ISA Services on All Servers in the Array

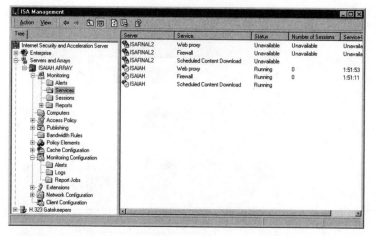

Note that, as shown in Figure 24.19, if a member of the array is offline, the status of its services will be displayed as "Unavailable."

The **Sessions** folder contains information about current sessions that are active for the Web proxy or firewall service, as shown in Figure 24.20.

Figure 24.20 Active Sessions Are Displayed in the Detail Pane When You Select the Sessions Folder

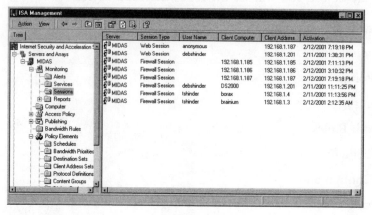

The **Reports** folder contains the results of report jobs that have been configured under the **Monitoring Configuration** object. These are further divided into five categories, or subfolders:

- Summary
- Web Usage
- Application Usage
- Traffic & Utilization
- Security

You can view a report by double-clicking it in the right detail pane (see Figure 24.21).

Figure 24.21 You Can View Reports by Double-Clicking the Report Name in the Right Detail Pane

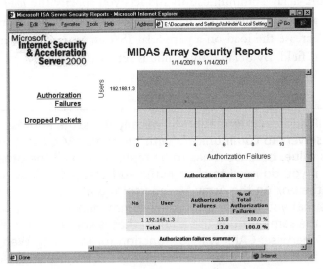

You will learn how to configure alerting, logging, and reporting later in this chapter, in the "Using Monitoring, Alerting, Logging, and Reporting Functions" section.

The next object in the console tree is the **Computers** folder, which contains an object for each computer that belongs to the array. By double-clicking a computer object in the right detail pane, you can display its Properties sheet, as shown in Figure 24.22.

Figure 24.22 Access the Properties Sheet for Each Array Member through the Computers Folder

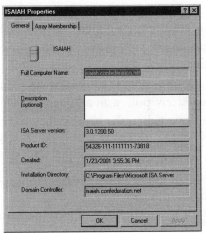

NOTE

Although the ISA Management Console allows you to change the name of an array, it does not support changing the name of an ISA Server computer.

In addition to general information such as the version number of ISA Server that is installed, the product ID, the date the ISA server was created, the installation directory path, and the domain controller, the Properties sheet has a tab labeled **Array Membership**. This tab shows the IP address used for intra-array communication and lets you specify the *load factor* for the server, which indicates its relative availability for caching in comparison to the other servers in the array. You can increase or decrease the load on a particular ISA server by increasing or decreasing the value in the load factor field. By default, this value is set to 100.

Continuing down the console tree, you will find the **Access Policy** object, which has three subfolders:

- Site and Content Rules
- Protocol Rules
- IP Packet Filters

If you have an array, you can create access policies at the enterprise level, the array level, or both. If the enterprise policy settings are configured to use enterprise policy only, you cannot add new rules at the array level. Conversely, if settings are configured to use array policy only, no enterprise policy will be applied to the array. If the enterprise administrator has configured settings for combined enterprise and array policy, an array policy will be added to the enterprise policy, with the enterprise policy overriding the array policy so that restrictions imposed by the enterprise policy will always apply. You can impose additional restrictions with the array policy but, as discussed previously, you cannot set an array policy that is less restrictive than the enterprise policy. If you configure settings to use enterprise policies only, you will not be able to use array policies without reinstalling ISA Server.

The next object in the tree is the **Publishing** object, containing two folders:

- Web Publishing Rules
- Server Publishing Rules

You can create a new rule of either type by right-clicking the appropriate folder and selecting **New** from the right context menu. This action invokes a wizard (see Figure 24.23), which will walk you through the steps required to create the new rule.

Figure 24.23 New Web Publishing or Server Publishing Rules Are Created with a Wizard

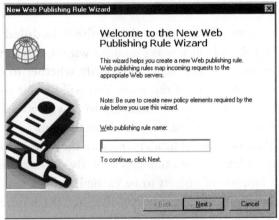

The **Bandwidth Rules** object is the next element in the console tree. Bandwidth rules let you specify which connections have priority over other connections.

> **NOTE**
>
> Don't confuse bandwidth priority rules with bandwidth limitation. ISA Server rules do not limit the amount of bandwidth that can be used by a connection; they specify how the QoS packet-scheduling service should prioritize the use of multiple network connections.

As with the creation of other rules, a New Bandwidth Rule Wizard assists you in creating bandwidth rules.

Policy elements come next in our journey down the left console pane. You will recognize most of these as the same as the policy elements available under the **Enterprise** object. However, there are two additional folders here: the Bandwidth Priorities element and the Dial-up Entries element.

Moving down the tree, we come to the **Cache Configuration** object. You will find two subfolders here:

- Scheduled Content Download
- Drives

The scheduled content service is **w3prefetch**, which lets you configure ISA to download cache content from specific URLs at specified times. This *prefetching* of regularly accessed pages speeds your users' access because the pages are already in the cache when users attempt to access them. For example, if users visit a particular news site daily, you could configure a scheduled download to occur on a daily basis so that the content in the cache would be updated each day.

WARNING

You cannot schedule a content download job if the Web server on which the Web objects reside requires client authentication. The job will fail because the Web server cannot authenticate the ISA server.

You create scheduled content jobs by right-clicking the **Scheduled Content Download** folder and selecting **New | Job**, which invokes another wizard. After giving the job a name, you can set the date and time to start the download and specify whether to download the content just once, daily, or weekly on a specified day of the week. You will be able to choose the URL from which the content should be downloaded and whether to download only content from the URL domain, not from sites to which it is linked. You also have the option of caching dynamic content, even when the HTTP cache control headers indicate they are not cacheable.

You can limit the depth of links to be cached as well. By default, there is no limit. You can also set a limit on the total number of objects to be cached, up to a maximum of 99,999.

When you have completed providing the information for the wizard, a summary of your selections will be presented, as shown in Figure 24.24.

Figure 24.24 The Scheduled Content Download Wizard Makes It Easy to Create a Job to Automatically Update the Cache of Specified URLs

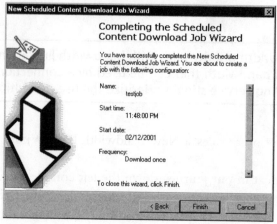

Now the job is displayed in the right detail pane along with other scheduled jobs, as shown in Figure 24.25.

The **Drives** folder displays NTFS logical drives on the ISA servers in the array, provides information on the total amount of disk space and the amount of free space on each drive, and allows you to set a limit on the cache size, in megabytes, for each drive. Right-click the drive in the right detail pane to access the Properties sheet shown in Figure 24.26.

Figure 24.25 Scheduled Content Download Jobs Appear in the Right Pane When the Folder Is Selected

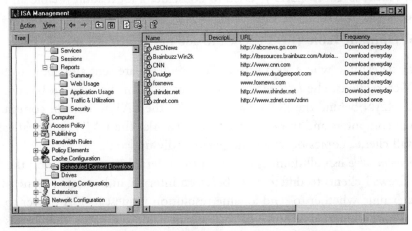

Figure 24.26 Configure the Amount of Disk Space on Each NTFS Drive to Be Allocated to the ISA Cache

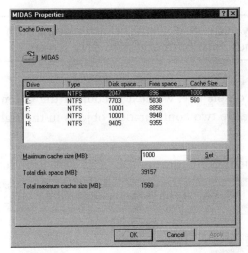

Continuing to move down the left console tree, you will see the **Monitoring Configuration** object that holds folders for Alerts, Logs, and Report Jobs. Later in this chapter, in the "Using Monitoring, Alerting, Logging and Reporting Functions" section, you will learn how to use each of these objects.

The next item in the tree is an object labeled **Extensions**. *Extensions* are filters that provide additional functionality for filtering applications and Web requests. Thus there are two types of filters: application filters and Web filters. Several filters of each type are installed with ISA Server, but additional filters can be developed by third parties to be used with ISA Server.

The **Network Configuration** object is used to set up a local or remote ISA VPN server and allow VPN client connections. These setups are done with a series of wizards that make it easy to configure ISA VPNs.

There are three subfolders under **Network Configuration**:

- **Routing** Used to create and configure routing rules (using the Routing Rule Wizard).

- **Local Address Table (LAT)** Used to construct a local address table and to add entries to the existing LAT.

- **Local Domain Table (LDT)** Used to add new entries to the LDT.

Routing rules determine where Web proxy client requests are sent and apply to both incoming and outgoing Web requests. The *local address table* keeps track of the internal IP address ranges that are in use by the LAN behind the ISA server. ISA users the LAT to control communication between internal computers and those on external networks; the LAT is automatically downloaded to firewall clients, copies of which are periodically updated.

The *local domain table* lists all domain names in the internal network behind the ISA server and is used by firewall clients to differentiate between internal and external names. Clients use the LDT to determine whether to send a name resolution request to ISA Server to handle the name resolution for an external resource or to perform name resolution themselves for a local resource.

> **NOTE**
>
> The LDT is not used by SecureNAT clients, which resolve both internal and external names via DNS and thus must have access to DNS servers.

As we move down the console tree, we next encounter the **Client Configuration** object. As shown in Figure 24.27, there are two configuration objects in the right detail pane: Web Browser and Firewall Client.

Figure 24.27 The Two Client Configuration Objects: Web Browser and Firewall Client

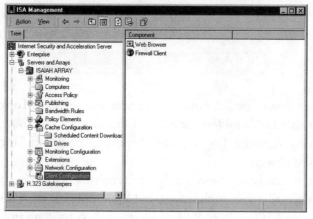

By double-clicking the configuration object name, you can access its Properties sheet, allowing you to view or change settings.

The *Web browser* Properties sheet allows you to choose whether to configure the Web browser during firewall client setup and whether to use automatic discovery and configuration. You can also choose to have the client bypass the proxy for local servers and/or directly access computers specified in the LDT, and you can specify the IP addresses, domain names, or computer names of specific computers that you want the client to be able to access directly, without going through ISA. You can also configure a backup route, designating how clients should access the Internet if the ISA server is unavailable.

> **NOTE**
>
> Like most firewalls, it is the gatekeeper of network traffic. You need to define what's trusted and not trusted to go through the ISA server. The LDT provides an interface for this.

The Properties sheet for the *firewall client* is less complex. It allows you to specify whether the firewall client will connect to the ISA computer or array by name or IP address (and enter the DNS name or IP address of the ISA server to be used), and you can enable or disable autodiscovery in the firewall client. The Application Settings tab is used to add client configuration information for specific applications, if necessary.

> **NOTE**
>
> The default firewall client configuration works for the majority of Winsock applications, but in some cases, custom client configuration information needs to be stored in the Mspclnt.ini or Wspcfg.ini file.

The H.323 Gatekeepers Object

The last second-level object in the console tree is the **H.323 Gatekeepers** object. By right-clicking this object, you can add a gatekeeper computer (either on the local machine or on a remote computer identified by fully qualified domain name) and view and configure active terminals, active calls, and call routing (see Figure 24.28).

Figure 24.28 Add and Configure H.323 Gatekeepers Via the Last Second-Level Object in the Console Tree

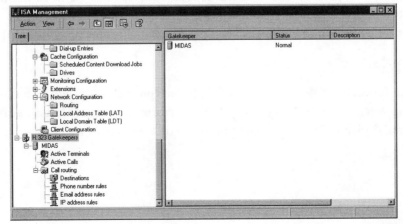

The H.323 Gatekeeper is used to allow clients to use NetMeeting and other H.323-compliant applications through the ISA server. The clients register a *well-known alias* (typically an e-mail address) with the gatekeeper, which allows others to contact them. The gatekeeper provides directory services and call routing for registered clients. All inbound calls to a well-known alias via these programs require registration with the gatekeeper. Outbound calls require only that clients are registered if they are using translation services; other outbound calls can be made without using the gatekeeper.

Understanding the H.32X Series Standards

The H.323 ITU standard for audio, video, and data communication across IP networks that do not provide QoS is part of a series of standards that all work to enable videoconferencing across disparate networks. The series is known collectively as the *H.32X standards.* H.320 provides specifications for using ISDN, and H.324 addresses the Public Switched Telephone Network (PSTN), also referred to in the industry as *POTS,* or *plain old telephone service.*

H.323 applies to both voice-only and full audio-videoconferencing. An advantage of the H.323 standard is that it allows communication over existing IP-based networks without any modifications to the network infrastructure. H.323 supports management of network bandwidth, allowing administrators to restrict the amount of bandwidth that can be used for conferencing or specify a maximum number of H.323 connections active on the network at any one time. H.323's support for multicasting also decreases bandwidth requirements. Platform independence means that users can communicate with one another using a variety of hardware platforms and operating systems.

The H.323 standard designates four major elements: terminals, gateways, gatekeepers, and multipoint control units (MCUs). The terminal is the endpoint for real-time two-way communication with another terminal or a gateway or MCU. H.323 terminals also must support H.245. The latter negotiates channel usage and capabilities. Gateways provide translation functions between the H.323 endpoints and other types of terminals. Gateways are optional components; if both endpoints are on the same LAN, they are not needed. Gatekeepers function as the central point for call control services to registered endpoints in their zones. Gatekeepers provide address translation from terminal or gateway aliases to IP addresses. Gatekeepers can also manage bandwidth and route H.323 calls. A gatekeeper's *zone* refers to all the terminals, gateways, and MCUs that are managed by that gatekeeper. An MCU enables conferencing between multiple (three or more) endpoints (as opposed to simple one-to-one communication). The MCU is made up of two components: the multipoint controller (MC) and the multipoint processor (MP).

ISA Wizards

Following in the footsteps of Windows 2000, ISA Server provides a variety of wizards to assist you in setting up services, configuring features, and performing other common tasks. A wizard is a series of "friendly" dialog boxes that walk you through a process in a step-by-step fashion.

The Getting Started Wizard

The Getting Started Wizard is available when you start ISA Server after installing the ISA software. The wizard is designed to help you configure your initial array and enterprise policies. Steps include:

- Configuring enterprise policy settings and enterprise-level policy elements, protocol rules, and site and content rules (if you have installed an array rather than a stand-alone ISA server)

- Creating array-level policy elements, protocol rules, and site and content rules

- Setting the system security level

- Configuring packet filtering

- Configuring routing and chaining

- Creating a cache policy

Rules Wizards

After ISA Server is installed, you can create and configure new rules (routing rules, protocol rules, site and content rules) using the Rules wizards that are invoked when you right-click the rule type under **Access Policy** or **Network Configuration** and select **New | Rule**.

One of the handiest aspects of the ISA wizards is the screen that appears after you finish entering the information requested by the wizard. This page summarizes the information you have entered, so you can double-check for accuracy *before* you click **Finish** to actually complete the process (see Figure 24.29).

Figure 24.29 The ISA Wizards Allow You to Check the Information Entered for Accuracy Before You Click Finish

These rules wizards make it easy for you to create a new rule, but you can change the properties of the rule later by accessing the rule's Properties sheet; double-clicking the rule in the right detail pane to do so.

VPN Wizards

ISA includes three wizards to help you perform tasks related to setting up VPN connections:

- **The Local ISA VPN Wizard** Used for configuring the ISA server that will receive inbound VPN connections (the VPN server) or to set up the local ISA server to initiate VPN connections.

- **The Remote ISA VPN Wizard** Used to set up a remote ISA server to initiate or receive connections.

- **The Set Up Clients to ISA Server VPN Wizard** Enables roaming clients to connect to a VPN server.

Performing Common Management Tasks

In this section, we look at some common management tasks. This includes setting Enterprise Policies and special object permissions, as well as managing arrays. It is important that your firewall has its security policies implemented properly, as the ISA Server has this defined in the Enterprise policy and Enterprise policy settings.

Configuring Object Permissions

ISA Server uses Windows 2000 discretionary access control lists (DACLs) to control access to objects and object properties. With Windows 2000, access is granted on a granular basis and can be granted to individual users or to groups (Microsoft's recommended approach).

The ISA Server objects for which you configure permissions are:

- Enterprise policy settings
- Enterprise policies
- Arrays
- Alerts
- Sessions
- The gatekeeper

Default Permissions

Depending on the type of object, certain permissions are assigned by default. You can view or change the object permissions by right-clicking on the object, selecting **Properties**, and selecting the **Security** tab, as shown in Figure 24.30.

The example in Figure 24.30 shows the permissions settings for the Array object. By default, the Administrator, Domain Admin, Enterprise Admin, and System accounts have full control, and the Authenticated Users group has read access. You can change the permissions or add other groups or individual user accounts in the same way you configure any NTFS permissions in Windows 2000.

Figure 24.30 Set Permissions on Objects Via the Security Tab on the Object's Properties Sheet

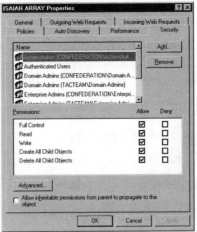

Special Object Permissions

You will find that some ISA objects have special permissions, accessed by clicking the **Advanced** button and then selecting **View/Edit** for permissions. For example, the Sessions object has the **Read Sessions Information** and the **Stop Sessions** permissions. By default, authenticated users have the **Read Sessions Information** permission, whereas Administrators, Domain Admins, and Enterprise Admins have full control, which encompasses both of these special permissions. Likewise, the **Alerts** object has special **Read Alerts Information** and **Reset Alerts** permissions. Again, authenticated users have the first, and Administrators, Domain Admins, and Enterprise Admins have full control, encompassing both (see Figure 24.31).

Figure 24.31 Some ISA Objects Have Special Advanced Permissions Such as the Read Alerts Information and Reset Alerts Permissions for the Alerts Object

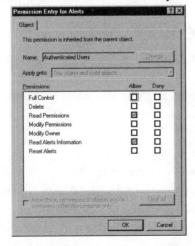

Permissions may be directly assigned to an object or they may be *inherited* from a parent object. Inheritance can be controlled by the administrator. At the bottom of an object's **Security** tab is a check box that, when checked, allows inheritable permissions to propagate to the object.

You can prevent inheritance of special permissions by checking the **Apply these permissions to objects and/or containers within this container only** check box when you elect to view/edit advanced permissions.

Similarly, you'll find that the Gatekeeper objects have several special permissions, including Read call routing info, Modify call routing, Read terminals, Create static user, Unregister terminal, Read active calls, and Terminate call. By default, these permissions are granted to the Everyone group, which has full control.

Setting Permissions on ISA Objects

To set the standard and special permissions on an ISA object, follow these steps:

1. Right-click the object for which you want to set permissions.
2. Select **Properties** from the right context menu.
3. On the Properties sheet, select the **Security** tab.
4. Here you can change standard permissions and add or remove users and groups.
5. To set special permissions, click the **Advanced** button.
6. Select the user or group for which you want to modify special permissions, and click the **View/Edit** button or add a new user or group by clicking the **Add** button.
7. Allow or deny the desired permissions.

NOTE

All ISA Server services run in the context of the user account named Local System. This account must have the appropriate permissions and user rights to run the services.

Managing Array Membership

Installing the first ISA server that is made a member of an array creates the array. There are several requirements for doing this: You must be a member of the local Administrators, Enterprise Admins, and Schema Admins groups, because you must first initialize the enterprise, which modifies the Active Directory schema.

Creating a New Array

Once an array has been created, you can create new arrays. Right-clicking the **Servers and Arrays** object in the left console pane and selecting **New | Array** invokes the New Array Wizard. You will be asked to supply information such as the site and domain name in which the new array will be located, as well as a name for the new array and the mode (caching, firewall, or integrated) in which the array will run.

When you add an array to or remove an array from the enterprise, the information is written to the Active Directory and replicated to all domain controllers in the domain.

Adding and Removing Computers

You can remove a server from an array by right-clicking its name in the right detail pane when you highlight the **Computers** folder. Select **Delete**, and you will be prompted by the dialog box shown in Figure 24.32.

Figure 24.32 Delete an ISA Server from an Array Via the ISA Management Console

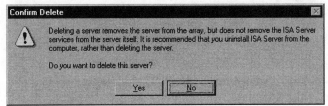

If a server was previously deleted from an array, you cannot use Add/Remove Programs in the Control Panel to uninstall ISA Server. Instead, you must use the rmisa.exe program on the ISA CD-ROM. Note that if you uninstall the only remaining computer in an array, the entire array will be removed.

To join a server to an existing array, you must install (or reinstall) ISA Server. If the enterprise has been initialized, you can select which array the server will join (see Figure 24.33). When you install ISA as a member of an existing array, you must install it in the same mode as the other array members (caching, firewall, or integrated).

Figure 24.33 When You Install ISA Server, If the Enterprise Has Been Initialized, You Have the Option of Joining an Existing Array

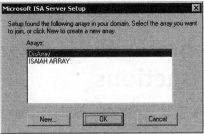

To move a server from one array to another, you must uninstall and reinstall ISA Server.

Promoting a Stand-Alone ISA Server

A stand-alone ISA server cannot be joined to an existing array; however, after you have initialized the enterprise, you can *promote* a stand-alone server to create a new array of which the promoted server will be a member. To promote a stand-alone server and create a new array, right-click the server name in the left console pane, and select **Promote** from the context menu. You will see the message shown in Figure 24.34.

Figure 24.34 Promoting a Stan-Alone Server to Become an Array—An Operation That Cannot Be Reversed

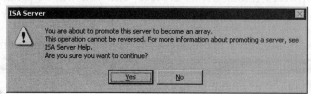

!

WARNING

Once you promote the stand-alone server to become an array member, the action cannot be reversed. You can remove the server from the array, but doing so will *not* return it to stand-alone server status. ISA Server will have to be reinstalled.

If you choose to promote the server, you will be asked to set global policy and choose how enterprise and array policies will be applied to the array. When you promote a stand-alone server to create an array, the configuration information for the array is stored in Active Directory.

Remember: Although a stand-alone ISA server is not required to be a member of a Windows 2000 domain, an array member must be a domain member. Thus, in order to promote a stand-alone server to an array, the server must belong to a Windows domain.

NOTE

After you promote a stand-alone server to array status, you need to reconfigure the ISA Server object permissions.

Using Monitoring, Alerting, Logging, and Reporting Functions

In this section, we discuss how you can monitor ISA Server alerts and logging and generate reports using the ISA Management Console.

Creating, Configuring, and Monitoring Alerts

ISA Server allows real-time monitoring of all alerts that occur on any of the servers in an array. This feature is useful in troubleshooting problems and assessing activity and usage.

Viewing Alerts

You can view the alerts by selecting **Monitoring | Alerts** under the Server or Array object and viewing the alerts in the right detail pane, as shown in Figure 24.35.

Figure 24.35 Viewing Alerts That Occurred on the ISA Server or Array

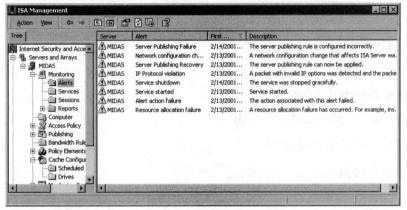

You will see, displayed in the detail pane, the server on which each event occurred, the alert type, the date and time of first occurrence, and a description of the event. Remember that this is where you *view* the alerts; they are configured using the **Alerts** object under the **Monitoring Configuration** object, further down in the tree.

Creating and Configuring Alerts

To create and configure a new alert, right-click the **Monitoring Configuration | Alerts** object, and select **New | Alert**. The New Alert Wizard will ask you for the following information:

- A name for the new alert
- An event or condition that will trigger the alert
- An action to be performed when the alert is triggered

Trigger Events

You can select from the following events to trigger the alert:

- Alert action failure
- Cache container initialization error
- Cache container recovery complete
- Cache file resize failure
- Cache initialization failure
- Cache restoration completed
- Cache write error

- Cached object ignored
- Client/server communication failure
- Component load failure
- Configuration error
- Dial-on-demand failure
- DNS intrusion
- Event log failure
- Intrusion detected
- Invalid dial-on-demand credentials
- Invalid ODBC log credentials
- IP packet dropped
- IP protocol violation
- IP spoofing
- Log failure
- Missing installation component
- Network configuration changed
- No available ports
- Operating system component conflict
- Oversize UDP packet
- POP intrusion
- Report summary generalization failure
- Resource allocation failure
- Routing (chaining) recovery
- Routing (chaining) failure
- RPC filter—connectivity changed
- Server publishing failure
- Server publishing recovery
- Service initialization failure
- Service not responding
- Service shutdown
- Service started
- SMTP filter event

- SOCKS configuration failure
- The server is not in the array's site
- Unregistered event
- Upstream chaining credentials
- WMT live stream-splitting failure

Additional Conditions

Some of these event triggers allow you to select an additional condition. For example, if you select intrusion detection as the event that will trigger the alert, you will also be asked to select whether the alert will be triggered by any intrusion or by a specific intrusion type (see Figure 24.36).

Figure 24.36 Some Events Allow You to Specify Additional Conditions to Trigger the Alert

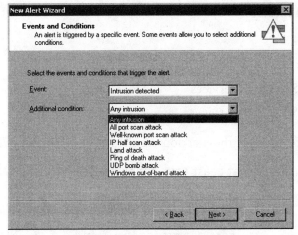

The ISA Server's alert service acts as an event filter, recognizing when events occur, determining whether configured conditions are met, and seeing that the chosen action(s) occurs in response.

NOTE

You can configure the alert for the entire array, or you can limit the event to a specific server in the array.

Once configured, you can enable or disable an alert by checking or unchecking the **Enable** check box on the **General** tab of its Properties sheet. To do so, you can right-click the alert name in the detail pane when you have selected **Alerts** under **Monitoring Configuration**, and choose **Properties** in the right context menu.

Additional Configuration Specifications

You can also specify the following:

- Event frequency threshold (how many times per second the event must occur in order to issue an alert)

- Number of events that must occur in order to issue an alert

- Length of time to wait before issuing an alert a second or subsequent time

To set these specifications, right-click the alert you want to configure, and select **Properties**, then select the **Events** tab.

Actions to Be Performed When an Alert Is Triggered

You can choose from the following actions to be performed when a triggering event occurs and the conditions are met for issuing an alert:

- Send an e-mail message

- Run a program

- Report the event to a Windows event log

- Stop selected ISA Server services

- Start selected ISA Server services

You can select one or more of these actions, as shown in Figure 24.37.

Figure 24.37 You Must Select at Least One Action to Be Performed When an Alert Is Triggered

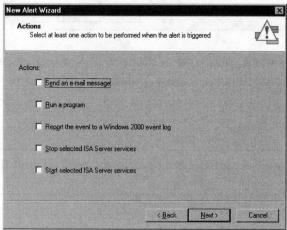

If you elect to send an e-mail message, you will be prompted to provide addressing information for sending the e-mail message, including the SMTP server and the From, To, and CC fields. You can send e-mail to multiple recipients by separating the addresses with semicolons in the To or CC field.

> **NOTE**
>
> If you want to send an e-mail message to a client using an external SMTP server (outside the local network) by specifying an external IP address, you need to create a static packet filter to allow the SMTP protocol. Another way to send a message to an external mailbox is to specify the internal IP address of an SMTP server on the local network that is capable of relaying to an external address.

If you elect to run a program, you will be prompted to enter the path to the program you want to run. You also need to specify whether the credentials of the Local System account or a different user account should be used. If you choose the latter, you must enter the user account name and password. Otherwise, you must run the program in the context of the system account.

If you elect to stop or start selected ISA Server services, you will be prompted to select the services that should be stopped or started. You can choose from one or more of the following: the firewall service, the scheduled content download, or the Web proxy service.

Refreshing the Display

The Alerts display is automatically refreshed on a periodic basis by default. (You will see the screen flicker when the display is updated.) You can force an immediate refresh or control the refresh rate by right-clicking the **Alerts** object under **Monitoring**. Select **Refresh** to immediately refresh the display, or select **Refresh Rate** to change the rate at which the display is updated. You can choose a high, normal, or low refresh rate. By default, this setting is Normal.

You can also elect to Pause the refresh if you do not want the display to be updated.

Event Messages

A number of event messages are related to ISA Server alerts. For example, message ID 14033 indicates that alert notification did not start and alerts are limited to event reporting. You will be advised to restart the ISA Server Control Service and to restart the firewall and Web proxy services because they are dependent on the Control Service.

A full listing of ISA event messages is available in the ISA Server Help files. (In the Help Index, search for Alerts, Alert event messages (list)).

Monitoring Sessions

You can view the sessions that are active by selecting the **Sessions** object in the left console pane of the ISA MMC; information about current sessions will appear in the right detail pane, as shown in Figure 24.38.

The Sessions display can be refreshed or the refresh rate set, in the same manner as that previously described for the Alerts display.

Figure 24.38 View the Current Active Sessions in the Right Detail Pane of the ISA MMC

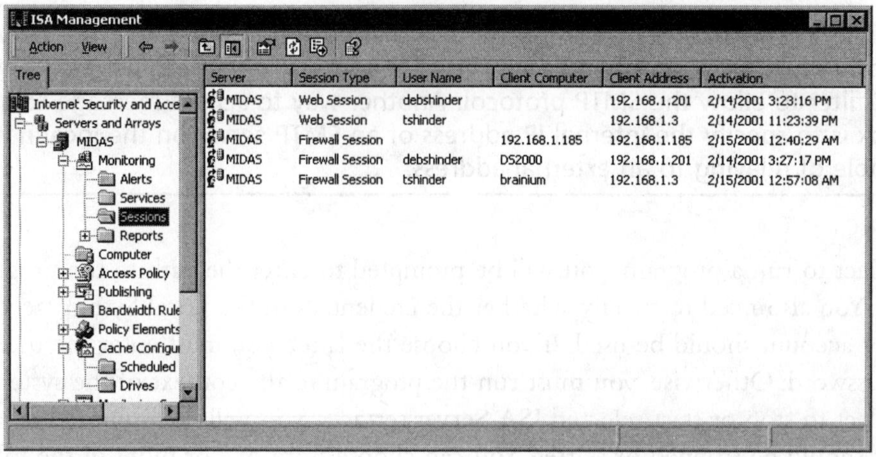

Session Information

Information available for each session includes:

- The server name
- The session type (Web or firewall)
- Username (for authenticated sessions; SecureNAT sessions are displayed as firewall sessions, with no username shown)
- Client computer (computer name for authenticated sessions or IP address for SecureNAT sessions)
- Client address
- Date and time of activation

> **NOTE**
>
> Web proxy sessions show the last minute of Web browser activity, even if the client is not browsing at the time you view the display.

Firewall sessions could be listed, even if no firewall clients are actually connected. The reason for this is that ISA shows a publishing server that is currently being published as a firewall session.

Disconnecting Sessions

You can disconnect a client session via the ISA Management Console. First, you must ensure that the **Advanced** option is checked in the **View** menu (by default, it is not).

To disconnect a session, right-click the session in the detail pane, and then from the right context menu, select **Abort Session**. This action disconnects the selected session, with no warning or notification to the client.

Using Logging

You can configure and generate logs in standard data formats for the following ISA Server components:

- Packet filters
- Firewall service
- Web proxy service

When your ISA servers belong to an array, logging is configured for the entire array, but log files are created on every ISA server that is a member of the array. The logs can be created on a daily, weekly, monthly, or yearly basis and saved to a file or logged directly to a database.

Firewall logging is critical if you are trying to establish any patterns of a break-in. For example, you can log access to who's trying to come in from the outside to your DMZ or even just scan your network. Moreover, some IT departments are more draconian than others—they not only care about who's coming in from the outside; but also, where people on the outside are going to (porn sites, and so forth).

Logging to a File

You can save ISA log data to a file in a directory that you specify. The files can be opened in a text editor or imported to a spreadsheet or database program.

Specifying a Log File Directory Location

There are two ways in which you can specify the directory to which the log file should be saved.

- **Save to a relative path** If you specify a relative path, the log will be saved in a folder named ISALogs in the ISA Server installation folder, which, by default, is named Microsoft ISA Server and is placed in the Program Files directory on the boot partition (the partition containing the system root folder in which the Windows 2000 operating system files reside, normally named WINNT).

- **Save to an absolute path** If you specify an absolute (full) path, that path must exist on every server that belongs to the array. If it does not, the ISA Server services will fail.

Selecting a Log File Format

When you choose to save ISA logs to a file, you can select one of the following formats:

- **W3C** Tab-delimited file that includes, along with the data itself, directives that describe the version, date, and logged fields (date and time are shown in GMT rather than local time). Unselected fields are not logged.

- **ISA** Comma-delimited file that contains only data. No directives are included, and all fields are always logged (unselected fields contain a dash to flag them as empty). Note that date and time in ISA format are shown in local time.

> **NOTE**
>
> Log files can be compressed to save disk space *if* they are saved on an NTFS-formatted partition. Microsoft recommends that you always store log files on an NTFS partition, which also allows you to configure NTFS permissions for the files.

Logging to a Database

A second way to save ISA log data is to log it to an Open Database Connectivity (ODBC) database. OBDC is a programming interface that allows various programs to access the data in systems using Structured Query Language (SQL). Programs use SQL to obtain information from or update information in a database, using command (query) language that allows users to locate, access, and insert data.

Database programs such as Access, dBase, and FoxPro support ODBC, and ODBC connectivity is provided by "back-end" client/server database solutions such as Microsoft SQL Server and Oracle.

In the context of this book, ODBC is a means for providing access, from an ODBC-compliant application such as Excel, to any data that is stored in an ODBC-compliant database server, such as SQL Server. The ODBC driver translates the application's queries into commands that can be understood by the target database application.

You can find a wealth of information about ODBC at the Microsoft Universal Data Access Web site at www.eu.microsoft.com/data/.

> **NOTE**
>
> Logging to a database is unnecessary when you have SQL's Data Transformation Services (DTS) to move the data from the log files into database tables on a scheduled, automated basis. Logging to a database is not the best practice from a performance standpoint.

Using Scripts

Several sample scripts are included with ISA Server; you can use these scripts as templates to create log databases. Scripts for logging to a SQL database file are contained in the \ISA folder on the ISA Server CD-ROM. The script files include the following:

- **Pf.sql** Used to define the packet filter log table (PacketFilterLog).
- **W3proxy.sql** Used to define the Web proxy service log table (WebProxyLog).
- **Fwsrv.sql** Used to define the firewall service log table (FirewallLog).

Configuring ISA Server for Database Logging

After you create the log table(s), follow these steps to configure the ISA server to use the data source name:

1. Select **Start | Programs | Administrative Tools | Data Sources (ODBC)** on the ISA server.

2. Select the **System DSN** tab. It is important to select the correct DSN, because choosing the wrong data source is a common mistake.

3. Click the **Add** button.

4. Select the applicable database driver in the Create New Data Source dialog box (for example, the Microsoft Access driver selected in Figure 24.39). You will be prompted for information needed to create the database.

Figure 24.39 Install the Appropriate ODBC Driver to Set Up a Data Source

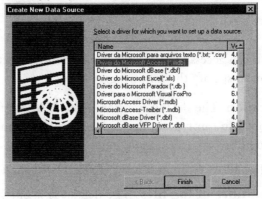

You will be required to enter a data source name, or DSN. Note that you cannot use spaces in the name. If you do so, the ISA Server services will stop.

Configuring Logging

To configure logging to either a file or a database, select **Logs** under the **Monitoring Configuration** object in the left console pane of the ISA MMC. The three ISA components for which logs can be generated (packet filters, firewall service, and Web proxy service) will appear in the right detail pane. Right-click the service for which you want to log data, and select **Properties**. You can configure logging using the Properties sheet, as shown in Figure 24.40.

Select whether to log to a file or a database, and then configure the parameters for the selected option. If you log to an ODBC database, you need to set the user account and password to be used, and these must have the appropriate permissions.

Figure 24.40 Logging Is Configured Via the Properties Sheet for the Service for Which Data Will Be Logged

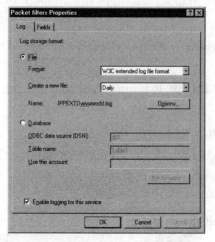

Logging Options

If you log to a file, you can access the Options configuration sheet by clicking the **Options** button. This allows you to specify the following:

- **Log file location** The default location is the ISALogs folder in the ISA Server installation folder, but you can type in the path or browse to another folder in which you want to save the log file.

- **Compress log files** Compression is enabled by default.

- **Limit the number of log files** The default is 7, but you can enter any number up to 999,999,999.

Selecting Fields to Be Logged

Click the **Fields** tab and select the fields that should be logged by checking the appropriate check boxes. For packet filter logging, you can choose to log the fields shown in Table 24.1. For firewall service logging, you can choose to log the fields shown in Table 24.2. For Web proxy service logging, fields available are generally the same as in Table 24.2, with the exceptions of the sessionid and connectionid fields.

Table 24.1 Log Field Options: Packet Filters

Field Name	Information in Field
PFlogDate	Date
PFlogTime	Time
SourceAddress	Source IP address
DestinationAddress	Destination IP address
Protocol	Protocol

Continued

Table 24.1 Log Field Options: Packet Filters

Field Name	Information in Field
Param#1	Source port, or protocol type if ICMP
Param#2	Destination port, or protocol code if ICMP
TcpFlags	TCP flags
Interface	IP address of interface
IPHeader	Header
Payload	Payload

Table 24.2 Log Field Options: Firewall Service

Field Name	Information in Field
c-ip	Client IP address
Cs-username	Client user account name
c-agent	Client agent
Sc-authenticated	Authorization status
Date	Date
Time	Time
s-svcname	Service name
s-computername	Computer name
Cs-referred	Referring server name
r-host	Destination host name
r-ip	Destination IP address
r-port	Destination port
Time-taken	Processing time
Cs-bytes	Number of bytes sent
Sc-bytes	Number of bytes received
Cs-protocol	Protocol name
Cs-transport	Transport used
s-operation	Operation
Cs-uri	Object name
Cs-mime-type	Object MIME
s-object-source	Object source
Sc-status	Result code
s-cache-info	Cache information
Rule#1	Rule #1
Rule#2	Rule #2
Sessionid	Session identification
Connectionid	Connection identification

Generating Reports

ISA Server's report functionality allows administrators to use the information recorded in the log files to create summary databases and combine relevant summary databases into a single report database. All of these databases are stored on the ISA server's hard disk. Reports can be generated on a periodic basis and saved to a specified folder.

> **NOTE**
>
> When you generate a report on an ISA server, it can be read only on that same computer. You cannot view it from another ISA Server computer's management console, even if the other server is in the same array.

Creating Report Jobs

You can create a report job by right-clicking **Report Jobs** under the **Monitoring Configuration** object, selecting **New**, and then selecting **Report Job**. This sequence displays the Report Job Properties sheet, shown in Figure 24.41.

Figure 24.41 A Name and Description for the Report Job Are Specified Via the General Tab

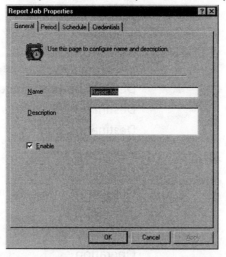

Configuring General Properties

On the **General** tab of the Properties sheet, you must specify a name for the report job. The default name is *Report Job*. The name must be unique; if it is not, you will receive a message from the ISA Report Generator informing you that the name already exists, and you will not be allowed to create the report job until you choose a new name. You can also provide a description of the job; this field is optional.

The report job is enabled by default when you create it. You can disable it later by accessing the **Properties** sheet (right-click on the report job name in the right detail pane) and unchecking the **Enabled** check box.

NOTE

The check box shown here enables reporting. You must also ensure that logging is enabled for the relevant ISA component(s), or there will be no meaningful data from which a report can be generated. A report job can still be created and a report will be generated, but it will contain no current data.

Configuring the Reporting Period

You can elect to have a report generated on a daily, weekly, monthly, or yearly basis or for a custom period. First, select a reporting period on the **Period** tab of the **Properties** sheet, shown in Figure 24.42. You also need to configure the **Schedule** tab, as shown in the next section, if you want the report to be generated on a recurring basis.

Figure 24.42 Configure the Reporting Interval by Selecting the Period Tab on the Properties Sheet

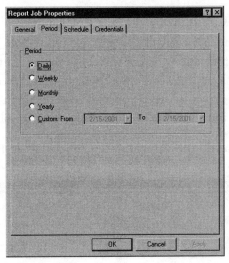

The report period configuration determines the period each report covers. The **Daily** option generates a report that covers the previous day's activity, the **Weekly** option covers the previous week's activity, and so forth. When you select the **Custom** option, you are prompted to choose a starting and ending date from a drop-down calendar.

Configuring the Reporting Schedule

Using the **Schedule** tab of the Properties sheet, you can specify when report generation should begin. By default, it is set to begin immediately on successful creation of the report job, but you can select a specific date and time using the drop-down boxes, as shown in Figure 24.43.

The **Schedule** tab is also used to specify the recurrence pattern for report generation. You can elect to have the report generated only one time or to recur every day, on specified days, or once per month on a specific day of the month.

Figure 24.43 The Schedule Tab Allows You to Set a Start Time and a Recurrence Pattern

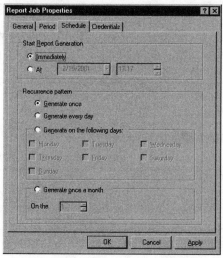

Configuring Report Job Credentials

You need to supply a username and password to run the report job. The user account must have permission to access report information for the server(s) relevant to the report job. You can create a report job on a local stand-alone ISA server without providing credentials. However, if you attempt to do so on a remote server or array, you will receive the message box shown in Figure 24.44, notifying you that you must provide credentials to run the job.

Figure 24.44 You Must Provide the Appropriate Credentials to Run a Report Job on a Report Computer or Array

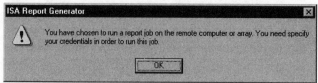

To provide credentials for running the report job, enter the user account name (or browse for it in the Directory by clicking the **Browse** button), the domain name to which the user account belongs, and the password on the **Credentials** tab of the Properties box shown in Figure 24.45.

> **NOTE**
>
> The user account must have the proper permissions to run reports. By default, Domain Administrators have this permission, as does any user who is a member of the local Administrators group on *every* ISA server computer in the array.

Figure 24.45 Enter a User Account Name, Domain, and Password to Run the Report Job

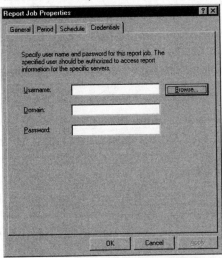

Viewing Report Job Information

Once the report jobs have been created, they appear in the right detail pane when you select the **Report Jobs** folder, as shown in Figure 24.46.

Figure 24.46 Information about Each Configured Report Job Appears in the Right Detail Pane

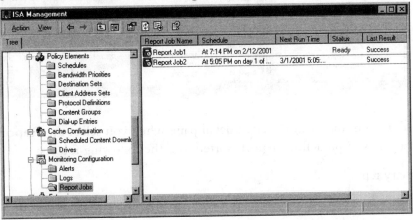

The following information about each report job will be displayed:

- The name of the job

- The scheduled start date and time

- The next run time (if it is a recurring job)

- The ready status

- The result of the last attempt to run the job

> **NOTE**
>
> When you select a start time other than "Immediately" on the Schedule tab of the Properties sheet, the time is shown in 24-hour clock format. However, in the detail pane, that information is shown in AM/PM format. Thus, if you choose 19:00 as the start time on the Schedule tab, it will be displayed in the detail pane as 7:00 PM.

You can go back and change the configuration properties of a report job by double-clicking it (or right-clicking it and selecting **Properties**) and accessing its Properties sheet.

Viewing Generated Reports

The reports themselves are accessed via the **Reports** folder under the **Monitoring** object near the top of the left console tree, as shown in Figure 24.47.

Figure 24.47 The Reports That Have Been Generated Are Accessed from the Reports Folder

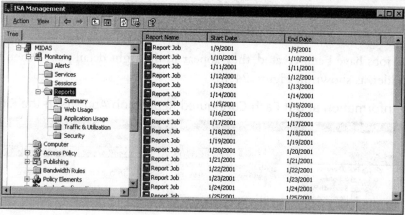

Note that all reports appear in the right detail pane when you select the **Reports** folder. You also see five categories of predefined reports sorted into the following folders:

- Summary reports
- Web usage reports
- Application usage reports
- Traffic and utilization reports
- Security reports

Reports are displayed in the Web browser and can be saved as .HTM (Web page) files. Let's take a look at what each of these includes.

Summary Reports

The summary reports network usage data that is sorted according to application. Network administrators can use these reports to plan or evaluate Internet connectivity issues. An example of a summary report for an array is shown in Figure 24.48.

Figure 24.48 Summary Reports Include Data from the Web Proxy and Firewall Service Logs
Pertaining to Network Usage

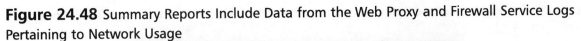

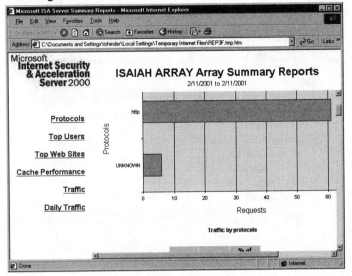

The information in the summary reports combines data collected from both the Web proxy service and firewall service logs. Logging for these services must be enabled to generate a meaningful summary report.

Web Usage Reports

Web usage reports use the Web proxy service logs to provide information about the following:

- Top Web users

- Web sites that have generated the greatest amount of traffic

- Protocols used for Web traffic

- Responses to HTTP requests (success, authorization failure, object not found, object moved, and other)

- Types of objects delivered by the ISA server (.DDL files, .HTML files, .EXE files, etc.)

- Web browser types used to connect to the Internet through the ISA server (browser name and version number)

- Operating systems used to access the Internet through ISA Server (Windows 2000, Windows NT 4.0, Windows 98, etc.)

An example of a Web usage report is shown in Figure 24.49.

The Web usage reports can be used to evaluate how the Web is used in your organization, which could be useful to network administrators in planning for Internet connectivity and capacity and for managers setting policies to govern use of the Web.

Figure 24.49 Web Usage Reports Contain Information Collected from the Web Proxy Service Log Files

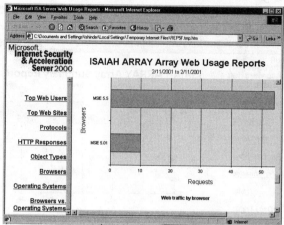

Application Usage Reports

Application usage reports are based on the information collected by firewall service logging. The following information is provided:

- Communications protocols used for network traffic going through the ISA server

- Top application users (by IP address)

- Client applications that have generated the largest amount of network traffic during the report period

- Operating systems used on computers that have accessed the Internet

- Top destination computers (by IP address) with which internal users have communicated through the ISA server

An example of an application usage report is shown in Figure 24.50.

Figure 24.50 Application Usage Reports Are Based on Information Collected in the Firewall Service Logs

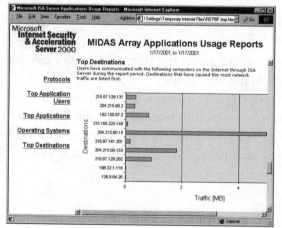

Application usage reports can help you plan for network and bandwidth capacity and determine the external network destinations that are creating the greatest amount of network traffic.

Traffic and Utilization Reports

The traffic and utilization reports use data from both the Web proxy and the firewall service logs to provide information such as the following:

- Communication protocols used
- Summary of traffic going through the ISA server, by date
- Cache performance data, showing the objects returned from the Internet, objects returned from cache with verification, objects returned from cache after verification that they had not changed, and objects returned from the Internet to update a file in cache
- Information on the peak number of simultaneous connections each day
- Information on the average request processing time each day
- Chart summarizing average network traffic flow through the ISA server each day
- Errors reported by ISA Server in attempting to communicate with other computers, broken into Web proxy and firewall service error categories

An example of a traffic and utilization report is shown in Figure 24.51.

Figure 24.51 The Traffic and Utilization Reports Combine Information from the Web Proxy and Firewall Service Logs

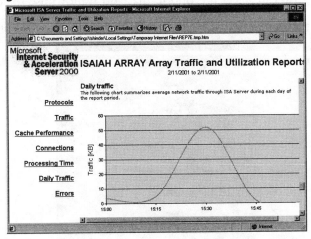

The traffic and utilization report information is useful for monitoring network capacity and planning bandwidth policies.

Security Reports

The security reports, as the name implies, provides information related to possible breaches of network security. Security reports use information from the Web proxy and firewall service logs as well as the packet filter log files. An example of a security report is shown in Figure 24.52.

Figure 24.52 Security Reports Can List Authorization Failures and Other Security-Related Events Recorded in the Web Proxy Service, Firewall Service, and Packet Filter Logs

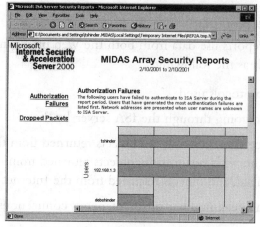

The security report shown in Figure 24.52 lists instances in which users or computers failed to authenticate to the ISA server and users for whom network packets were dropped.

Configuring Sort Order for Report Data

You can determine the order in which report data is sorted by right-clicking the report type (Summary, Web Usage, Application Usage, Traffic & Utilization, and Security) in the left console pane under **Reports** and selecting **Properties** from the context menu. On the Properties sheet shown in Figure 24.53, you can select the option that you want to use to sort the report data.

Figure 24.53 Select the Option to Use to Sort Report Data in the Report Type Properties Sheet

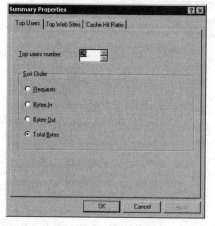

On the **Top Users** tab, you can select from the following: Requests, Bytes In, Bytes Out, or Total Bytes. On the **Top Web Sites** tab, you can sort by the same four options, and you have a fifth option: Users. On the **Cache Hit Ratio** tab, you have only two options for sorting order: Requests and Bytes.

After you configure the sort order, the data in the report will be sorted according to your criteria the next time you view the report.

Saving Reports

You can save reports in one of two file formats for later viewing or to a removable disk to be viewed on another machine.

- **Saving Reports in .HTM format** Reports can be saved as hypertext document files (.HTM) by selecting the report type under **Reports** in **Monitoring** in the left console pane, right-clicking the report name, and selecting **Save as** in the context menu.

- **Saving Reports in .XLS format** You can save a report as an Excel spreadsheet file (.XLS) by selecting **Reports** and right-clicking the report name in the right console pane, then selecting **Save as**.

- **Providing Information for Saving Reports** To save as .HTM, you access the report from the applicable report type folder; to save as .XLS, you access the report from the **Reports** folder. Either way, you will be asked to select a location in which to save the file and to enter a filename (the default filename is the name of the report displayed in the right detail pane).

> **NOTE**
>
> In order to save the report in .XLS format, you must have Excel installed on the ISA server computer. Otherwise, this option will not appear as an option.

Configuring the Location for Saving the Summary Database

You can specify the location in which the daily and monthly summaries database is to be stored. Right-click **Report Jobs** in the left console pane under **Monitoring Configuration**, and select **Properties** in the right context menu. On the **Log Summaries** tab, shown in Figure 24.54, check the box to enable daily and monthly summaries.

Figure 24.54 Set a Location for Saving Daily and Monthly Summaries, and Specify the Number of Each That Should Be Saved

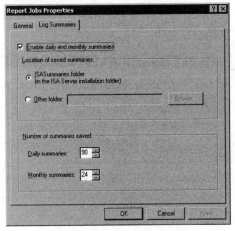

You can set the location for saving the summary database. You have two options:

■ Save the summaries in the ISA Summaries subdirectory, in the directory to which ISA Server is installed on the local computer (this is the default).

■ Save the summaries in a different location by choosing **Other folder** and typing a path or browsing for a folder by clicking the **Browse** button.

You can also specify how many daily summaries and how many monthly summaries are to be saved. You can specify a minimum of 35 and a maximum of 999 daily summaries, and a minimum of 13 and a maximum of 999 monthly summaries. Summary files are saved with the .ILS extension (see Figure 24.55).

Figure 24.55 Summary Files Are Saved by Default in the ISA Summaries Folder with an .ILS File Extension

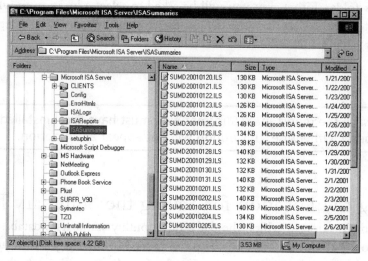

NOTE

The ISALogs, ISAReports, and ISASummaries directories are located on each server in the array in the Microsoft ISA Server installation folder.

Understanding Remote Administration

In this section of the chapter, we explore how you can administer an ISA server or array from a remote location, either using the ISA Management Console on a remote computer or by setting up the ISA server as a Terminal server and connecting to it via the Terminal Server client software. Remote administration allows you to perform management tasks and configure components for your ISA server or array when you are not at the same site as an ISA server computer.

You can connect to the network via a WAN link by dialing in to the remote access server or by connecting across the Internet through a VPN. Once the connection to the local network is established, you can remotely manage a stand-alone ISA server, an array, or the enterprise.

Installing the ISA Management Console

You can install ISA Management on a Windows 2000 Server that is not running ISA Server or on a Windows 2000 Professional computer. This is done as part of the setup process when you run the ISA Server installation CD.

> **NOTE**
>
> ISA Server or the ISA Management tools can also be installed on computers running Windows XP/Whistler, the next version of the Windows operating system.

When you run the setup program, select **Custom installation**, and check only the **Administration Tools** check box, as shown in Figure 24.56.

Figure 24.56 To Install ISA Management on a Computer from Which You Want to Administer ISA, Select Custom Installation and Check the Administration Tools Check Box

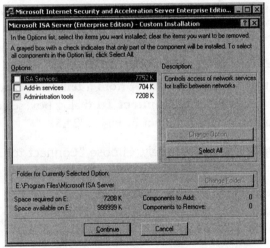

After you install the Administration tools, ISA Server Management is accessible through the **Programs** menu on the remote computer. You can then connect to an ISA server or an array that is in the same domain or a domain with which a trust relationship exists.

Managing a Remote Standalone Computer

To manage a stand-alone ISA server remotely, open the ISA Management Console and right-click the root object in the left pane (Internet Security and Acceleration Server). Select **Connect To** from the context menu, and type the name of the stand-alone server that you want to manage in the box, as shown in Figure 24.57, or click the **Browse** button to find a computer in the directory.

Figure 24.57 To Manage an ISA Server Remotely, You Must First Connect to It

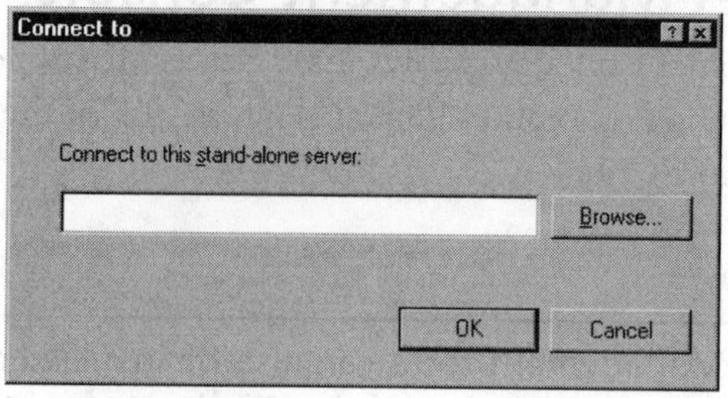

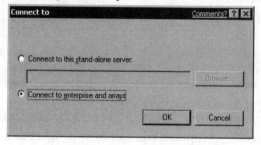

NOTE

You must be a member of the Administrators or Server Operators group on the remote computer that you want to manage.

After you are successfully connected to the remote ISA server, the ISA objects for that server appear in the management console, and you can administer the server as though you were logged on to it locally.

Remotely Managing an Array or Enterprise

To manage an ISA server that is an array member from a remote location, you must choose to manage the enterprise. In this case, in the **Connect To** dialog box, select the **Connect to enterprise and arrays** radio button, as shown in Figure 24.58.

Figure 24.58 To Manage an Array Remotely, Choose "Connect to Enterprise and Arrays"

You will be connected to the array and can administer it from the management console as though you were logged on locally to an ISA server belonging to the array.

Using Terminal Services for Remote Management of ISA

Another way to remotely administer your ISA servers and arrays without installing the ISA Management tools on the computer from which you want to manage ISA is to use Windows 2000 Terminal Services.

Windows 2000 Server family products (Server, Advanced Server, and Datacenter Server) include Terminal Services as a Windows component. Terminal Services provide remote access to a server desktop, using thin-client technology that serves as a terminal emulator. Processing is done on the server, so Terminal Services client software can be installed on low-powered machines running older operating systems such as Windows 3.*x*. With the Citrix MetaFrame client software, you can even connect to a Windows 2000 Terminal server from a machine running MS-DOS, UNIX, or Macintosh.

Terminal Services is the solution for remotely administering your ISA server if you need to do so from machines running these operating systems.

Installing Terminal Services on the ISA Server

Windows 2000 Terminal Services are installed from the **Add/Remove Programs** applet in Control Panel as a Windows component.

Terminal Server Mode

Terminal Services can be deployed in one of two modes: application server or remote administration. Application server mode is used to provide users a Windows 2000 desktop and applications via "thin-client" computing. By default, when you install Terminal Services, they are deployed in remote administration mode.

You should run Terminal Services in remote administration mode on the ISA server. This does not require Terminal Services client licenses and allows only two concurrent connections to the Terminal server. Additionally, only members of the Administrators group can connect to the Terminal server in remote administration mode.

Terminal Services Server Configuration

You can configure the Terminal server settings, including selection of the mode in which the Terminal Services will run, using the Terminal Services Configuration tool. This tool is installed in the **Start | Programs | Administrative Tools** menu when you install Terminal Services on the server. See Figure 24.59.

Figure 24.59 The Terminal Server Settings Are Configured Via the Terminal Services Configuration Tool

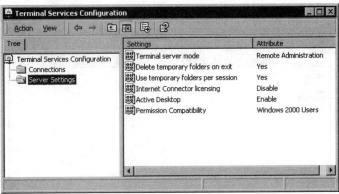

Another tool that is installed with Terminal Services on the server is the Terminal Services Manager, which is used to view and manage client connections to the Terminal server, as shown in Figure 24.60.

Figure 24.60 Use the Terminal Services Manager to View and Manage Client Sessions

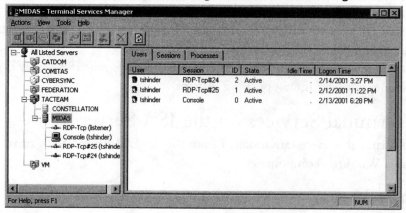

A Terminal server can be accessed from any other computer on the network running the terminal client software, including dial-in or VPN clients.

Installing Terminal Services Client Software

You can create installation disks containing the Terminal Services client software by running the Terminal Services Client Creator program on the Terminal server. The 16-bit client installation program for Windows 3.*x* requires four floppy disks; the 32-bit client installation program for Windows 9*x*/2000 computers requires only two floppy disks.

Run the appropriate client installation program to install the Terminal Services client to the computer(s) from which you want to access the ISA server running Terminal Services.

Creating a Connection Shortcut with the Client Connection Manager

Once the services are installed, you can access the Microsoft Terminal Services Client through the **Start | Programs** menu. The Client Connection Manager, shown in Figure 24.61, is used to create a new connection to the ISA server/Terminal server.

Figure 24.61 Use the Client Connection Manager to Create a Connection to a Terminal Server

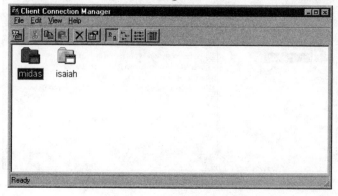

To create a new connection to a Terminal server, select **File | New Connection**. This sequence starts the Client Connection Wizard, which creates a shortcut for connecting to the

ISA server/Terminal server. You will be asked to provide a name for the connection and to enter the name or IP address of the Terminal server, as shown in Figure 24.62.

Figure 24.62 The Client Connection Wizard Creates a Shortcut to the Terminal Server

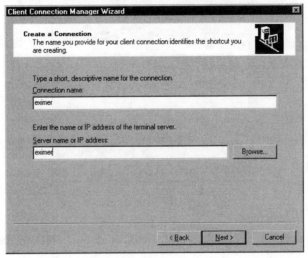

The wizard allows you to specify the user account name and password to use in logging on to the server. You can leave this blank if you want and type in the credentials each time you connect. If you enter the information, you will not have to provide it when you log on to a terminal session. You can also choose the screen resolution at which the terminal window should run, or you can elect to have the terminal connection displayed full screen instead of in a window. You can also choose to enable data compression and/or to cache frequently used bitmaps to speed access, and you can specify a program path to run a program automatically when you connect to the Terminal server.

The new connection shortcut will appear in the Client Connection Manager Wizard, and you can connect to the Terminal server by double-clicking it.

Connecting to a Terminal Server with the Terminal Services Client

If you have not created a shortcut to the Terminal server, you can still connect to it, using the Terminal Services Client, also accessed via the **Start | Programs | Terminal Services Client** menu. The Terminal Services Client is shown in Figure 24.63.

You can type a Terminal server name into the Server field, even if you have not created a shortcut connection to it using the Client Connection Manager. You can also use the Terminal Services Client when you want to connect to a Terminal server using a screen resolution or other parameters that are different from those specified in the shortcut connection. Just type in or select the Terminal server to which you want to connect, and click the **Connect** button.

Figure 24.63 You Can Use the Terminal Services Client to Connect to a Terminal Server

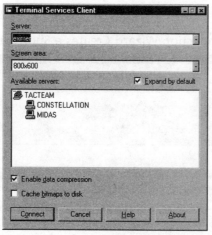

Using the Terminal Desktop

Once your connection to the Terminal server is established, you will see the server desktop, as shown in Figure 24.64.

Figure 24.64 Use the Terminal Server Desktop to Remotely Administer the ISA Server

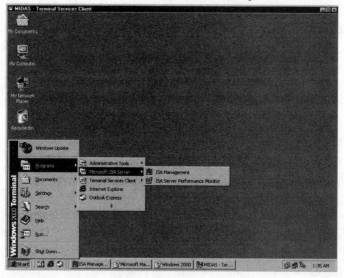

If the Terminal server is an ISA server, you can now open the ISA Management tool and perform all administrative tasks as you would if you were sitting at the ISA server.

Summary

This chapter has taken you through the concepts and practices involved in managing an ISA server—from the most basic use of the ISA MMC and wizards to remote administration, using either the ISA administrative tools on a non-ISA computer or running Windows 2000 Terminal Services on the ISA server and connecting to it using Terminal Services client software on a remote machine.

You learned that Microsoft's *integrated management* concept allows you to administer both of ISA Server's functions—caching and firewall—from a common interface and to manage an entire array of servers as one entity. You can even administer multiple arrays in an enterprise, from one centralized location.

We explored the ISA Management Console, and you learned to create a custom MMC and add the ISA Management snap-in for more convenient administration and easier delegation of selected administrative duties.

We examined each component of the ISA MMC, staring with the menu bar and main toolbar, describing the function of each icon or button and then looking at the console root and tree. You learned about each object in the left console pane and how to use the information in the right detail pane when various left-pane objects are selected.

Next, we looked at the many wizards provided with ISA Server to make configuration and creation of new objects simpler. Specifically, we addressed the Getting Started Wizard that helps you with the initial setup of your ISA server; the Rules wizards that walk you through the process of creating new routing, protocol, or site and content rules); and the three VPN wizards that assist you in performing tasks related to setting up virtual private networking connections.

You learned to perform some common management tasks such as configuring permissions on an ISA object and managing array membership. Then, we delved into the intricacies of using the monitoring, alerting, logging, and reporting functions of ISA. You learned to set up trigger events and conditions for issuing an alert and how to monitor and disconnect user sessions. We discussed logging of information relating to three ISA Server components: packet filters, the firewall service, and the Web proxy service. You learned that you can save log information to a file or to an ODBC database, and we showed you how to enable and configure logging. Next, you learned about generating reports from the data collected in the log files, how to create a report job, and how to view and save the reports that are generated.

Finally, we discussed remote administration of an ISA server or array, and you learned that you can manage either a stand-alone ISA server or an array or enterprise in one of two ways: by installing the ISA Management tools on a non-ISA Server computer and using the ISA MMC to connect, or by installing Windows 2000 Terminal Services on your ISA server, making it a Terminal server and connecting to it from another computer on the network that is running the Terminal Services Client software.

## Chapter 25

Optimizing, Customizing, Integrating, and Backing Up ISA Server

Best Damn Topics in this Chapter:

- Optimizing ISA Server Performance

- Customizing ISA Server

- Integrating ISA Server with Other Services

- Backing Up and Restoring the ISA Configuration

Introduction

With the information we've covered so far, you should be able to install and set up an ISA solution. However, you still might not be getting the best possible performance out of your ISA server(s). There is a difference between "getting it to work" and "getting it to work at peak efficiency." In this chapter, we turn to performance issues and explore ways of optimizing ISA Server to enjoy all its benefits without negatively impacting your overall network performance.

We'll talk about bandwidth, load balancing, and scalability issues as well as application compatibility and how you can use the ISA Server SDK to customize ISA to fit your network's needs or use third-party add-ons to provide even more functionality in specific areas.

This chapter also discusses how ISA "gets along" (or doesn't get along) with other services. You will learn how to ensure that ISA peacefully coexists with Active Directory, RRAS, IIS, and IPsec, along with how you can best integrate your ISA servers into an existing Windows XP, Windows 2000, or NT 4.0 network environment.

Optimizing ISA Server Performance

The word *performance* has different meanings to different people. To some, computer hardware or software performance refers solely to speed—how fast a computer can complete a specified task or operation, usually measured by some *benchmark test.*

Even though this is an ISA Server specific chapter, having good performance and benchmarks from any firewall is a good idea. Additionally, it may not strictly be the CPU you're benchmarking—you may also need to test the networking performance as well.

NOTE

A *benchmark* is a reference point or set of reference points against which something can be compared. This point or points can be a list of performance criteria a product is expected to meet, a set of conditions by which a product is measured, or a known product to which other products are compared.

A more generic definition of *performance* includes the total effectiveness of the computer's actions, taking into account such factors as availability, individual response time, cost effectiveness, and throughput.

NOTE

To understand the difference between *speed* and *throughput,* consider the task of downloading a file over a modem connection. The connection *speed* of 50Kbps refers to the rate at which a signal travels. The *throughput* refers to the actual amount of data that can be transferred across the link in a given time period. If many data packets are dropped or damaged, the throughput could be less than the speed. However, by using *data compression* technologies, you can achieve a throughput that is higher than the actual modem speed so that with a 50Kbps connection, you might be able to get a throughput of 100Kbps or more.

Optimizing performance involves finding a way to make all components of a system work together smoothly with the smallest possible amount of delay or downtime. As with any other computing component, the struggle to achieve and maintain optimum performance from your ISA server is a never-ending one.

Hardware specifications and condition, software configuration, and interaction with other networking components combine to determine the speed and efficiency with which your ISA servers do their jobs. In some cases, ISA's performance will be affected not only by the ISA Server software settings but also by other factors unique to your network's topology and configuration.

You should assess performance issues in the context of:

- The server's hardware resources (especially RAM and processor)
- Other services and applications running on the server
- The network's physical limitations (speed supported by NICs, hubs, switches, and cabling)
- Network protocols and services that could limit performance
- Actual performance needs of your network

Before you can optimize the performance of an ISA server—or any other system component—you must first be able to do two things:

- Establish criteria for what constitutes unsatisfactory, acceptable, or excellent performance.
- Have a way to objectively measure your system's performance to determine whether it meets your established criteria.

The process of defining acceptable criteria is referred to as *establishing a baseline*. Then, you measure your network's performance by *monitoring* over a set period of time, and you compare the results to your baseline.

In the next section, we examine how to establish a performance baseline and how to use performance-monitoring tools such as the ISA Server Performance Monitor to gather information about the performance of individual components.

Establishing a Baseline and Monitoring Performance

A key factor in any performance-monitoring program is to establish a baseline. This is done by collecting information at intervals, averaged over a period of time when the network is performing normally. If you gather this information at different times of day over a period of weeks or even months, you will be able to ascertain the characteristics of normal network traffic patterns.

How Baselines Are Used

Baseline measurements are used to perform *trend analysis*, which is a fancy term for comparing performance measurements to your historical values in order to spot patterns or trends from which you can project future performance expectations or determine future needs.

Baselining is an important element of performance management and performance tuning.

> **NOTE**
>
> It might seem logical to perform your data collections at a time when the network is experiencing low usage, such as at night or on weekends. However, if you limit your information gathering to these times, you will not be able to get an idea of accurate traffic patterns. You must gather your data at different times—low usage, peak usage, and average usage—in order to establish a true baseline.

The component values to be measured are sometimes referred to as *metrics*. A metric is a measurement of a specific characteristic or component of a system's or software program's performance or efficiency. A separate baseline will be associated with each metric.

Defining Threshold Values

Creating the baseline gives you a road map of the normal patterns for your network's performance. After you have this guideline, you can set *threshold values,* which are measured values at which performance becomes unacceptable. Depending on what component is being measured, you may set *rising threshold values*, *falling threshold values*, or both. A rising threshold indicates a measurable point that, when exceeded, indicates unsatisfactory performance. A falling threshold is the opposite; it indicates a value that, when measurements fall below it, indicates unsatisfactory performance. Threshold values should be set based on the baseline data.

ISA Server's performance alerts can be set to recognize when a threshold value is passed and do one or more of the following:

- Log an entry to the application event log
- Send a network message
- Start a performance data log
- Run a specified program

Threshold values might have to be adjusted on a periodic basis as you continue to collect and analyze data. It is important to set threshold values appropriately. If the values are set too high (for rising values) or low (for falling values), you will not be notified of performance events in time to prevent an impact on your network's productivity. If values are set too low (for rising values) or high (for falling values), there will be too many notifications; administrators could be overwhelmed with messages and, like the boy who cried "wolf" in the old fairy tale, the notifications could soon come to be ignored.

The first decision to make in creating a performance-monitoring and tuning program is how you plan to collect the necessary data. Although third-party monitoring tools are available, Microsoft has provided a built-in solution that will meet many of your needs in monitoring the performance of your system as a whole and your ISA Server installation in particular. In the next section, we look at the Windows 2000 Performance console, which includes the System Monitor tool and the Performance Logs and Alerts. Then we look at the special implementation of Performance that is installed with ISA Server.

Using the Performance Monitor Tools

Windows 2000 provides the Performance MMC with all versions of the operating system. Performance has two components:

- **System Monitor** This component is used to gather measurements of performance and activity in real time and view the data in graph, histogram, or report format.

- **Performance Logs and Alerts** This component is used to record collected data to be viewed later and to set alerts to notify you or perform a specified task when a particular performance counter falls above or below the threshold you have set.

The Windows 2000 Performance MMC is accessed via the **Start | Programs | Administrative Tools** menu or by typing **perfmon.exe** at the command line. When you install ISA Server, a new icon is placed in the **Start | Programs | Microsoft ISA Server** menu. This icon opens the ISA Server Performance Monitor, shown in Figure 25.1, which is an implementation of the Windows 2000 System Monitor that includes a set of ISA performance counters as default objects.

Figure 25.1 The ISA Server Performance Monitor Includes a Set of ISA Server-Specific Default Counters

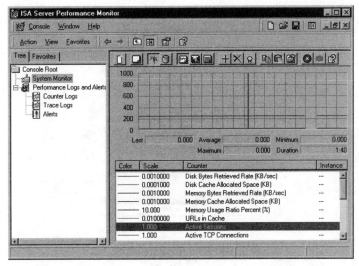

The ISA Server Performance Monitor also allows you to add monitoring of other Windows 2000 components included in System Monitor (such as processor, memory, server service, TCP, the browser service, and many more) along with the ISA object counters.

> **NOTE**
>
> When you install ISA Server on a Windows 2000 machine, the ISA Server object counters are also added to the Windows 2000 System Monitor's list of counters that can be monitored. The advantage of the ISA Performance Monitor is that ISA objects do not have to be individually added for monitoring but are monitored by default.

If you are familiar with the Windows 2000 System Monitor (which replaced the Performance Monitor tool in Windows NT 4.0), you will find the ISA Server Performance Monitor very easy to navigate. By default, measurements are shown in *graph view* (which can be changed, as we discuss in the next section), with the line graph for each counter shown in a different color.

Customizing the View and Appearance of the System Monitor

Data collected by the System Monitor can be presented in one of three ways:

- **Graph (also called a chart)** Data is shown as one or more line graphs, as shown in Figure 25.1.

- **Histogram** Data is presented as one or more bar charts.

- **Report** Data is summarized and presented as text information.

The line graph works best when you need to see immediate fluctuations in measurements in real time, because it traces the "peaks" and "valleys" over a period of time. The histogram is good for comparing the values of one counter to those of another at a given point in time. The report view gives you the exact numbers to work with in a form that is easy to understand at a glance. The histogram view is shown in Figure 25.2.

Figure 25.2 In a Histogram View, Data Is Presented as a Set of Bar Charts

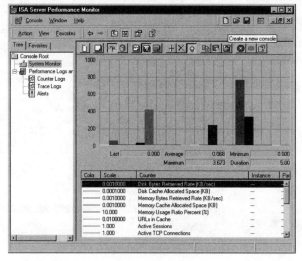

The report view is often the most useful for precise analysis of performance data, although perhaps less visually compelling. An example of the report view is shown in Figure 25.3.

NOTE

When you right-click **System Monitor** in the left console pane, you will see a selection called **Properties**; however, this choice will *not* open the System Monitor Properties sheet referenced here, nor will selecting **Properties** on the **Action** menu. Use the **Properties** icon in the toolbar to open the **Properties** sheet that allows you to configure these settings.

Figure 25.3 Report View Summarizes Data and Presents It in Text Format

You can change the view in one of two ways:

- Click the appropriate icon from the toolbar.

- Select the view in the **General** tab of the System Monitor **Properties** sheet. The **General** tab of the Properties sheet is shown in Figure 25.4.

Figure 25.4 The System Monitor Tool's Appearance Can Be Customized Using the Properties Sheet

In addition to changing the view for display of data, the **General** tab allows you to:

- Select the display elements that will be shown. (By default, the legend, value bar, and toolbar are all displayed. To hide one or more, uncheck its box.)

- Select the way data will be displayed in Report or Histogram view. (The Default value is the current value for activity being measured at that time, or the average for logged activity.) In Graph view, all these values are shown in the value bar beneath the chart.

- A 3D or flat appearance. (3D is the default.)

- Whether to show a fixed single border or no border. (None is the default.)

- Whether to update the display automatically, and if so, how often. (In seconds; default is one second.)

- Whether to allow duplicate counter instances to run simultaneously. (By default, this is allowed.)

Additional tabs on the Properties sheet allow you to do the following:

- **Source tab** Specify whether the source of the data displayed on the System Monitor is to be current (real-time) activity or data from a log file (for which you can enter the path or browse). If you select a log file, you can also specify a time range within the file if you don't want to display the data for the entire time over which the log was recorded.

- **Data tab** Allows you to add or remove counters from the display, specify the color assigned to each counter in the graph, and set the width and style of the graph line that represents each counter.

- **Graph tab** Allows you to create a customized graph with an identifying title, select which elements to show (vertical grid, horizontal grid, vertical scale numbers), and set maximum and minimum values for the vertical scale.

- **Colors tab** Allows you to customize the colors used for the grid, time bar, background, and foreground, as well as the system colors (menu bar, title bars, borders, scrollbars, and other system elements).

- **Fonts tab** Allows you to specify font style and size for the display. The selected font will be applied to all text in the System Monitor display and will be used for the text in the Report view.

System Monitor Components

The Windows 2000 System Monitor and the ISA Server Performance Monitor work in an identical manner, using the following components:

- **Performance object** This is a resource or service that can be monitored (for example, ISA Server Packet Filter and ISA Server Cache are two performance objects that can be monitored).

- **Performance counter** This is a collection of data items associated with a performance object, for which the monitor can measure a value that corresponds to a particular aspect of the object's performance (for example, Total Dropped Packets and Total Logging Packets Lost are two performance counters associated with the ISA Server Packet Filter performance object).

NOTE

It is possible for an object counter to have more than one *instance*. For example, if you are monitoring processor performance and the machine has multiple processors, you can have an instance of each processor object counter for each of the processors.

The Default Performance Counters

The ISA Server Performance Monitor console differs from the Windows 2000 System Monitor in that it already has a set of default performance counters configured. Monitoring of these counters starts when you open the Performance Monitor. Let's take a look at each of these default counters (descriptions of these counters are also found in the ISA Server Help files, which often provide more detailed information than is available using the **Explain** button).

The following are Firewall Service counters:

- **Active Sessions** This counter counts the number of active sessions for the Firewall Service. By comparing this counter at both peak and off-peak times, you can determine ISA Server usage patterns.

- **Active TCP Connections** This counts the total number of active TCP connections.

- **Active UDP Connections** This counts the total number of active UDP connections.

- **SecureNAT Mappings** This Firewall Service counter tracks the number of mappings created by secure network address translation (SecureNAT).

The following are Web Proxy Service counters:

- **Cache Hit Ratio (%)** This counter measures the relationship between two other Web proxy counters—**Total Cache Fetches** as a percentage of **Total Successful Requests**. This counter value, together with the value of **Cache Running Hit Ratio**, indicates how effectively the cache is performing. A high percentage for these counters indicates that a high level of requests is being serviced from the cache, meaning faster response times. A zero counter means caching is not enabled. A low counter can signal a configuration problem.

- **Cache Running Hit Ratio (%)** This counter measures the number of requests served from the cache as a percentage of total successful requests serviced. This is the same as the ratio measured by **Cache Hit Ratio (%)**. The difference between the two is that **Cache Running Hit Ratio (%)** measures the ratio for the last 10,000 requests serviced, and **Cache Hit Ratio (%)** measures the ratio since the last time that the Web proxy service was started.

- **Client Bytes Total/Sec** This counter presents the sum of two other counters, **Client Bytes Sent/Sec** and **Client Bytes Received/Sec**, for a total rate for all bytes transferred between the ISA Server computer and Web proxy clients.

- **Current Average Milliseconds/Request** This counter displays the average amount of time that it takes ISA Server to process a request. A low number indicates a faster response. A high number that remains high over a period of time indicates that ISA Server is working at maximum capacity, and you might need to add another server to the configuration.

- **Current Users** This counter shows how many clients are currently running the Web proxy service. You can monitor this counter at peak and off-peak times to determine server usage.

- **Requests/Sec** This counter indicates the rate of incoming requests made to the Web proxy service. A high value means that more ISA Server resources are required to service incoming requests.

The following are cache performance counters:

- **Disk Cache Allocated Space (KB)** This counter measures how much space is being used by the disk cache. (This will be equal to or less than the amount of space you have configured for the disk cache.)

- **Max URLs Cached** This counter presents the maximum number of URLs that have been stored in the cache.

- **Memory Cache Allocated Space (KB)** This counter measures how much space is being used by the memory cache.

- **Memory Usage Ratio Percent (%)** This counter calculates the ratio between the number of cache fetches from the memory cache and the total number of cache fetches. A high percentage could mean that you need to allocate more available memory resources to the cache. A low number could mean that some of the memory resources allocated to cache could be better used for other purposes.

- **URL Commit Rate (URL/Sec)** This counter measures the speed at which URLs are written to the cache. Note that if this rate is comparable to the value of another ISA Server cache counter, **Disk Failure Rate (Fail/Sec)**, a high proportion of attempts to write to the cache are failing, which might be due to a problem with cache configuration.

- **URLs in Cache** This counter measures the current number of URLs that are in the cache.

The following is a packet filter counter:

- **Total Dropped Packets** Displays the total number of packets that were dropped or filtered, for whatever reason.

Other ISA Performance Counters

The following performance objects are added to System Monitor when you install ISA Server:

- Bandwidth Control Performance Counters

- Cache Performance Counters

- Firewall Service Performance Counters

- Web Proxy Service Performance Counters

- Packet Filter Performance Counters

- H.323 Performance Counters

Let's take a look at the counters associated with each.

- **Bandwidth control performance counters** Five performance counters are associated with the bandwidth control object:

    - **Actual inbound bandwidth** Measures the actual inbound bandwidth in bytes per second.

    - **Actual outbound bandwidth** Measures the actual outbound bandwidth in bytes per second.

    - **Assigned connections** Counts the number of connections with an assigned bandwidth priority.

    - **Assigned inbound bandwidth** Measures the assigned inbound bandwidth in bytes per second.

    - **Assigned outbound bandwidth** Measures the assigned outbound bandwidth in bytes per second.

- **Cache performance counters** Twenty-two performance counters are associated with the ISA Cache performance object:

    - **Active Refresh Bytes Rate (KB/Sec)** Measures the rate at which bytes of data are retrieved from the Internet to actively refresh popular URLs in the cache. This will relate to the configuration set for active caching.

    - **Active URL Refresh Rate (URL/Sec)** Measures the rate at which popular cached URLs are actively refreshed from the Internet. This will relate to the configuration set for active caching.

    - **Disk Bytes Retrieve Rate (KB/Sec)** Measures the rate at which "bytes of data" are retrieved from the disk cache.

    - **Disk Cache Allocated Space (KB)** See the description under default counters.

    - **Disk Content Write Rate (Writes/Sec)** Measures the number of writes per second to the disk cache for the purpose of writing URL content to the cache disk.

    - **Disk Failure Rate (Fail/Sec)** Measures the number of input/output (I/O) failures per second. (An I/O failure occurs when ISA Server fails to read from or write to the disk cache.) A large number of I/O failures can indicate problems with disk cache.

- **Disk URL Retrieve Rate (URL/Sec)** Measures how many URLs are sent to clients from the disk cache in one second and can be used to evaluate the performance of the disk cache.

- **Max URLs Cached** See the description under default counters.

- **Memory Bytes Retrieved Rate (KB/Sec)** Measures the rate at which bytes of data are retrieved from the memory cache.

- **Memory Cache Allocated Space (KB)** See the description under default counters.

- **Memory URL Retrieve Rate (URL/Sec)** Measures how many URLs are sent to clients from the memory cache in one second.

- **Memory Usage Ratio Percent (%)** See the description under default counters.

- **Total Actively Refreshed URLs** Shows the cumulative number of popular URLs in the cache that have been actively refreshed from the Internet.

- **Total Bytes Actively Refreshed (KB)** Displays the total number of bytes that have been retrieved from the Internet to actively refresh popular URLs in the cache.

- **Total Disk Bytes Retrieved (KB)** Measures the cumulative number of disk bytes that have been retrieved from the disk cache. If you add the value of this counter to that of **Total Memory Bytes Retrieved (KB)**, you will have the total number of bytes retrieved from the cache.

- **Total Disk Failures** Measures the number of times that the Web proxy service failed to read from or write to the disk cache due to an I/O failure.

- **Total Disk URLs Retrieved** Measures the cumulative number of URLs that have been retrieved from the disk cache. You can calculate the total number of URLs retrieved from cache by adding the value of this counter to that of **Total Memory URLs Retrieved**.

- **Total Memory Bytes Retrieved** Measures the cumulative number of memory bytes that have been retrieved from the memory cache in response to client requests to the cache. A low value here could mean that memory resources allocated to the cache are not being used efficiently. A high number could mean that additional memory resources need to be allocated to the cache.

- **Total Memory URLs Retrieved** Measures the cumulative number of URLs that have been retrieved from the memory cache in response to client requests to the cache.

- **Total URLs Cached** Measures the cumulative number of URLs that have been stored in the cache. A low number might mean the cache size is too small.

- **URL Commit Rate (URL/Sec)** See the description under default counters.

- **URLs in Cache** See the description under default counters.

- **Firewall Service performance counters** Twenty-five performance counters are associated with the Firewall Service object:

  - **Accepting TCP Connections** Shows the number of connection objects that wait for a TCP connection from firewall clients.

  - **Active Sessions** See the description under default counters.

  - **Active TCP Connections** See the description under default counters.

  - **Active UDP Connections** See the description under default counters.

  - **Available Worker Threads** Shows the number of firewall work threads that are available or waiting in the completion port queue.

  - **Back-connecting TCP Connections** Shows the total number of TCP connections awaiting an inbound connect call to complete. These connections are placed by the Firewall Service to a client after accepting a connection from the Internet on a listening socket.

  - **Bytes Read/Sec** Shows the number of bytes per second read by the data pump.

  - **Bytes Written/Sec** Shows the number of bytes per second written to the data pump.

  - **Connecting TCP Connections** Shows the total number of TCP connections that are awaiting completion between the Firewall Service and remote computers.

  - **DNS Cache Entries** Displays the current number of DNS domain name entries that are cached because of Firewall Service activity.

  - **DNS Cache Flushes** Shows the total number of times the DNS cache has been cleared by the Firewall Service.

  - **DNS Cache Hits** Shows the total number of times a DNS domain name was located in the DNS cache by the Firewall Service.

  - **DNS Cache Hits %** Calculates the percentage of DNS names serviced by the DNS cache from the total number of DNS entries retrieved by the Firewall Service.

  - **DNS Retrievals** Shows the total number of DNS names that the Firewall Service has retrieved.

  - **Failed DNS Resolutions** Shows the number of failed **gethostbyname** and **gethostbyaddr** API calls from the Firewall Service.

  - **Kernel Mode Data Pumps** Displays the number of kernel mode data pumps that have been created by the Firewall Service.

  - **Listening TCP Connections** Shows the number of connection objects that are waiting for TCP connections from remote Internet computers.

  - **Memory Allocation Failures** Shows the number of memory allocation errors.

- **Non-connected UDP Mappings** Displays the number of mappings that are available for UDP connections.

- **Pending DNS Resolutions** Displays the number of **gethostbyname** and **gethostbyaddr** API calls that have been made by the Firewall Service and are awaiting resolution.

- **SecureNAT Mappings** See the description under default counters.

- **Successful DNS Resolutions** Displays the number of **gethostbyname** and **gethostbyaddr** API calls that have been successfully resolved.

- **TCP Bytes Transferred/Sec by Kernel Mode Data Pump** Shows the number of TCP bytes that have been transferred by the kernel mode data pump each second.

- **UDP Bytes Transferred/Sec by Kernel Mode Data Pump** Shows the number of UDP bytes that have been transferred by the kernel mode data pump each second.

- **Worker Threads** Displays the number of firewall worker threads that are currently active.

- **Web Proxy Service performance counters** Fifty-one performance counters are associated with the Web Proxy Service performance object:

  - **Array Bytes Received/Sec (Enterprise)** Monitors the rate at which bytes of data are received from other ISA servers within an array.

  - **Array Bytes Sent/Sec (Enterprise)** Monitors the rate at which bytes of data are sent to other ISA servers within an array.

  - **Array Bytes Total/Sec (Enterprise)** Displays the sum reached by adding the **Array Bytes Sent/Sec** and **Array Bytes Received/Sec**, to give you the total rate for all bytes of data that are transferred between this ISA server and other array members.

  - **Cache Hit Ratio (%)** See the description under default counters.

  - **Cache Running Hit Ratio (%)** See the description under default counters.

  - **Client Bytes Received/Sec** Calculates the rate at which bytes of data are received from Web proxy clients. If this rate is consistently slow, a delay could be occurring in the servicing of requests.

  - **Client Bytes Sent/Sec** Calculates the rate at which bytes of data are set to Web proxy clients. As previously stated, a consistently slow rate could signal a delay in request servicing.

  - **Client Bytes Total/Sec** See the description under default counters.

  - **Current Array Fetches Average (Milliseconds/Request)** Displays the mean number of milliseconds required for servicing a Web proxy client request that has to be fetched through another member of the array (not including SSL tunnel requests).

- **Current Average Milliseconds/Request:** See the description under default counters.

- **Current Cache Fetches Average (Milliseconds/Request)** Displays the time, in mean number of milliseconds, that it takes to service a Web proxy client request from the cache (not including SSL tunnel requests).

- **Current Direct Fetches Average (Milliseconds/Request)** Displays the time, in mean number of milliseconds, that it takes to service a Web proxy client request directly to the Web server or upstream proxy server (not including SSL tunnel requests).

- **Current Users** See the description under default counters.

- **DNS Cache Entries** Displays the number of DNS name entries cached by the Web Proxy Service (a high count usually means good performance, because the more entries in the cache, the fewer that require a DNS lookup, which takes additional time and resources).

- **DNS Cache Flushes** Displays the number of times the name cache has been cleared by the Web Proxy Service.

- **DNS Cache Hits** Displays the number of times a DNS name was found in the DNS cache by the Web Proxy Service. A low number of hits means that names must be looked up, which slows performance.

- **DNS Cache Hits (%)** Displays the percentage of DNS entries that have been resolved using cached data. A high value indicates better performance.

- **DNS Retrievals** Displays the number of DNS names that have been retrieved by the Web Proxy Service.

- **Failing Requests/Sec** Calculates the rate per second for Web proxy requests that result in an error. A high failure rate could mean that the connection settings for incoming Web requests are not configured properly or that there is not enough connection bandwidth to handle all the requests.

- **FTP Requests** Displays the number of FTP requests made to the Web Proxy Service.

- **Gopher Requests** Displays the number of Gopher requests made to the Web Proxy Service.

- **HTTP Requests** Displays the number of HTTP requests made to the Web Proxy Service.

- **HTTPS Sessions** Displays the number of Secure HTTP (HTTPS) sessions that have been serviced by the SSL tunnel.

- **Maximum Users** Displays the maximum number of users connected to the Web Proxy Service at the same time.

- **Requests/Sec** Calculates the rate of incoming requests to the Web Proxy Service. A high number could mean that you need to allocate additional ISA Server resources.

- **Reverse Bytes Received/Sec** Calculates the rate at which bytes of data are received by the Web Proxy Services from Web publishing servers in response to incoming requests.

- **Reverse Bytes Sent/Sec** Calculates the rate at which bytes of data are sent by the Web Proxy Services to Web publishing servers in response to incoming requests.

- **Reverse Bytes Total/Sec** Displays the sum resulting from the addition of the two preceding counters to provide a total rate of bytes transferred between the Web Proxy Service and the Web publishing servers in response to incoming requests.

- **Site Access Denied** Displays the number of Web sites to which the Web Proxy Service has denied access. If this number is high, you might want to re-evaluate your Web access policy.

- **Site Access Granted** Displays the number of Web sites to which the Web Proxy Service has granted access.

- **SNEWS Sessions** Displays the number of SNEWS sessions serviced by the SSL tunnel.

- **SSL Client Bytes Received/Sec** Displays the rate at which SSL data is received by the Web Proxy Service from secure Web proxy clients.

- **SSL Client Bytes Sent/Sec** Displays the rate at which SSL data is sent by the Web Proxy Service to secure Web proxy clients.

- **SSL Client Bytes Total/Sec** Calculates the sum resulting from adding the two preceding counters to provide a total rate for all SSL bytes transferred.

- **Thread Pool Active Sessions** Displays the number of sessions that are being actively serviced by thread pool threads.

- **Thread Pool Failures** Displays the number of requests that have been rejected because of a full thread pool.

- **Thread Pool Size** Displays the number of threads in the pool, representing the resources that are available for servicing client requests.

- **Total Array Fetches (Enterprise)** Displays the number of Web proxy client requests served by requesting data from another ISA server that is a member of the array, as a result of the CARP algorithm.

- **Total Cache Fetches** Displays the number of Web proxy client requests served from cached data.

- **Total Failed Requests** Displays the number of requests that the Web Proxy Service has failed to process because of errors. A high value could indicate configuration problems or that the connection is too slow.

- **Total Pending Connects** Displays the number of waiting Web Proxy Service connections.

- **Total Requests** Displays the number of requests made to the Web Proxy Service, the result of adding the **Total Successful Requests** and **Total Failed Requests** counters.

- **Total Reverse Fetches** Displays the number of incoming request that have been served by requesting data from Web publishing servers.

- **Total SSL Sessions** Displays the number of SSL sessions serviced by the SSL tunnel.

- **Total Successful Requests** Displays the number of requests made to the Web Proxy Service that have been successfully processed.

- **Total Upstream Fetches** Displays the number of requests serviced by getting the data from the Internet or from an upstream chained proxy server.

- **Total Users** Displays the total number of users that have connected to the Web Proxy Service over the history of the service.

- **Unknown SSL Sessions** Displays the number of unknown SSL sessions that have been serviced by the SSL tunnel.

- **Upstream Bytes Received/Sec** Calculates the rate at which bytes of data are received by the Web Proxy Service from servers across the Internet or upstream chained proxy servers.

- **Upstream Bytes Sent/Sec** Calculates the rate at which bytes of data are sent by the Web Proxy Service to servers across the Internet or upstream chained proxy servers.

- **Upstream Bytes Total/Sec** Displays the result of adding the two preceding counters to provide a total rate for bytes transferred between the Web Proxy Service and Internet or chained proxy servers.

- **Packet filter performance counters** Four performance counters are associated with the packet filter performance object:

  - **Packets Dropped Due to Filter Denial** Displays the number of packets that are dropped because the data was rejected due to dynamic packet filtering when the default "deny all" policy is set in the ISA Server configuration.

  - **Packets Dropped Due to Protocol Violations** Displays the number of packets that are dropped for reasons other than the default filtering rules (such as those rejected because of intrusion detection).

  - **Total Dropped Packets** Displays the total number of packets dropped, for whatever reasons.

  - **Total Lost Logging Packets** Displays the number of packets that cannot be logged.

- **H.323 performance counters** Only two performance counters are associated with the H.323 filter performance object:

  - **Active H.323 Calls** Shows the number of H.323 calls that are currently active.

  - **Total H.323 Calls** Displays the total number of H.323 calls that have been handled by the H.323 filter from the time the ISA server was started.

Understanding ISA Performance Logs

In addition to viewing the performance data in real time using the System Monitor component of the ISA Performance Monitor, you can record this data for later viewing using the Performance Logs functionality. Logs provide administrators with a permanent record and are useful for establishing and storing baseline data. You can create logs to record the data that is collected over time and analyze it to come up with your baseline values against which subsequent performance measurements will be compared.

NOTE

You can view the performance data in real time at the same time the data is being written to a log.

Logging runs as a service, so it is not necessary for a user to be logged on to the computer for the log to be written. Logged data can be saved as comma-delimited or tab-delimited text files, which can be imported into a spreadsheet program such as Excel or a database program such as Access. Logs can also be saved in binary format, which is used for *circular logging*. Circular logging is the action of writing the log continuously to a single file, overwriting the older data when the file reaches its maximum size.

You can configure two types of logs with the ISA Server Performance Monitor. In this section, we look at how to create and configure *counter logs,* which log data using the ISA performance counters discussed in the previous section.

The second type of log that the ISA Server Performance Monitor allows you to configure is called a *trace log.* Trace logs are triggered by specific system events. A trace log records data when the specified event occurs, rather than logging at specified intervals, as counter logs do. The trace log records data that is collected by the operating system or a program or service (called the *provider),* such as Kerberos, NetLogon, or the Active Directory Service. Trace logs are often used in troubleshooting situations.

Trace logs are configured similarly to counter logs. You will be asked to specify enabled providers and configure a filename, location, and maximum file size, as with counter logs. Trace logs can be saved as two types: sequential or circular. Sequential logging starts a new log when the maximum file size is reached (numbering the logs to distinguish them from one another). Circular logging overwrites the older data in the single log file when the maximum size is reached.

In trace logging, data is temporarily saved to memory buffers before being written to the log file. You can set a buffer size and minimum and maximum number of buffers, and you can specify that data be transferred from the buffers to the log file at specific intervals. (The default setting is to transfer the data to the file only when the buffers are full.)

Trace log output is interpreted by a parsing tool, which can be created by developers using the APIs available on the Microsoft Web site.

To create a counter log, follow these steps:

1. In the left console pane of the ISA Performance Monitor MMC, expand **Performance Logs and Alerts** and right-click **Counter Logs**, and then select **New Log Settings**.

2. You will be asked to provide a name for the new log. Type in your log name.

3. On the **General** tab of the New Log Properties sheet, you must add at least one counter to be logged. You can then set the interval at which the data should be sampled, as shown in Figure 25.5. (The default interval is every 15 seconds, but you can set intervals in seconds, minutes, hours, or days.)

Figure 25.5 Add at Least One Counter to Be Logged to the File

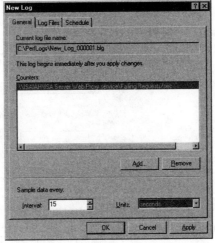

4. On the **Log Files** tab, you can set the location and filename for the log file, and if you want, you can specify that the log filename end with the date, selecting the date format (month/day/hour, month/day/hour/minute, year/day, year/month, year/month/day, or year/month/day/hour). You can also specify the use of a numeric sequence (default) and where to start numbering the log files (the default is 1). This is used to distinguish between multiple logs with the same name logged at different times or days.

5. Also on the **Log Files** tab, select the file type in which the file will be saved. Your choices are:

    ■   Text File CSV (comma-delimited text)

    ■   Text File TSV (tab-delimited text)

    ■   Binary File

    ■   Binary Circular File
        Binary files are saved with the .BLG extension.

6. Finally, at the bottom of the **Log Files** sheet, you can allow log files to grow to the maximum limit, or you can set a maximum size for the file in kilobytes (if you choose to set a specific limit, the default is 1,000KB), as shown in Figure 25.6.

> **NOTE**
>
> It is a good idea to specify a limit for the log file size; otherwise, the log file can grow until you run out of disk space, interfering with other operations.

Figure 25.6 Use the Log Files Tab to Set Filename, Location, and Other File Properties

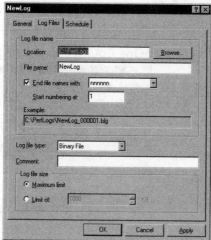

7. The last tab, labeled **Schedule,** is used to set the start and stop times for logging if you choose not to start and stop the logging manually (which is the default setting). If you set times, you can also specify what happens when a log file is closed—whether to start a new log file and whether to run a program (which you specify), as shown in Figure 25.7.

Figure 25.7 Use the Schedule Tab to Define Start and Stop Times for Logging

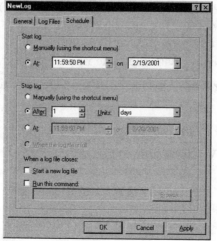

8. Click **OK** when you finish configuring the log file properties, and the new file will appear in the right detail pane when you select **Counter Logs** in the left console. You can change the configuration by right-clicking it and selecting **Properties,** or you can stop the logging activity by selecting **Stop** in the right context menu. To view the log, access it in the location you specified for it to be saved. (Use a text editor such as Notepad to view the raw data in the .CSV or .TSV files, or import the file into a spreadsheet or database for viewing.)

To create and use logging, you must have the appropriate permissions. In order to create a new log or make changes to an existing log configuration, you need to have Full Control permission to the Registry key **HKEY_LOCAL_MACHINE\SYSTEM\CurrentControlSet\Services\SysmonLog\Log\ Queries**. Members of the Administrators group have Full Control Permission for this key by default, but if you need to give a user permission to create or change log files and you do not want to grant other administrative privileges, you can use the **Security** menu in the Registry editing tool **Regedt32.exe** to do so. As always, exercise caution when editing the Registry.

You also need to have the right to start or configure services on the Windows 2000 or later release computer in order to run the service that runs in the background when you configure a log file. Again, members of the Administrators group already have this right by default. You can give users this right via Windows Group Policy.

Setting ISA Performance Alerts

Although you can monitor whether and when your performance thresholds are reached by enabling logging and reviewing the performance logs, in many instances it is important for an administrator to be made immediately aware when the threshold value has been reached. This is the case, for example, if a critical service fails or if free disk space reaches a low level that could threaten normal operations of the server. You can use alerts to notify administrators so that the problem can be addressed immediately and unpleasant consequences prevented.

Performance alerts can be set to perform a selected action when a performance counter reaches the defined threshold value.

> **WARNING**
>
> Don't confuse the performance alerts, which are configured on performance counters via the ISA Performance Monitor MMC, with the ISA Server alerts that are triggered by designated ISA events and conditions and are configured via the ISA Server Management Console.

To configure a performance alert, right-click **Alerts** under **Performance Logs and Alerts** in the left console pane of the ISA Server Performance Monitor MMC. The first step in creating a new alert is to assign it a name. You'll note that there is no wizard to walk you through the process, as there was when you configured ISA Server alerts. Instead, you will configure the performance alert via a three-page Properties sheet.

On the **General** tab, shown in Figure 25.8, you can optionally enter a comment to further identify the alert. You then must add one or more counters that will be monitored for triggering of the alert.

Figure 25.8 Counters to Be Monitored for Triggering of a Performance Alert Are Added Via the General Tab of the Alert Properties Sheet

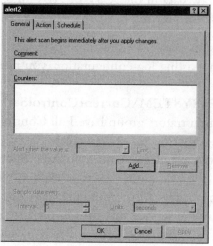

To add a counter, click the **Add** button, and select:

- Whether to use local computer counters or those on another computer (in which case, you must specify the UNC path for the computer to be monitored)
- The performance object to be monitored
- The counter(s) to be monitored (or you can select to monitor all counters for that object)

Once you have selected an object and counter(s) to be monitored, you need to configure the threshold value as well as how often data should be sampled, as shown in Figure 25.9.

Figure 25.9 After Adding Counters, You Must Define the Threshold and Data Sample Interval

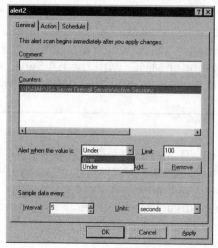

As you can see in Figure 25.9, you can set the alert to be triggered when the value is either over or under a specified limit. In our example, we have elected to monitor the Active Sessions counter for the ISA Server Firewall Service performance object. We have set the alert to be triggered when the threshold value (the number of active sessions) is *over* the limit of 100.

The data sample interval has been left at the default setting: sample data every 5 seconds. This value can be set in seconds, minutes, hours, or days.

Next, you must specify on the **Action** tab of the Properties sheet the action that should take place when the alert is triggered. As shown in Figure 25.10, you can select one or more of the following:

- Log an entry to the Application event log (accessed via Event Viewer).

- Send a network message to a specified computer or user account (you must enter the name of the account).

- Start a performance data log.

- Run a program, such as a script or batch file (you can enter the path or browse for the program file).

Figure 25.10 You Can Select One or More Actions to Be Taken When the Alert Is Triggered

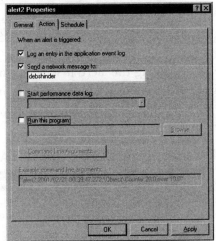

If you choose to run a program, you can specify one or more of the following command-line arguments:

- Single argument string
- Date/time
- Measured value
- Alert name
- Counter name

- Limit value
- Text message

On the **Schedule** tab, you can set a time to start and stop the scan, or you can choose to start and stop it manually using the shortcut menu. By checking the check box shown in Figure 25.11, you can also specify that when a scan finishes, a new scan should be started.

Figure 25.11 You Can Use the Schedule Tab to Schedule the Scan to Start and Stop at a Specified Time and Elect to Start a New Scan When One Finishes

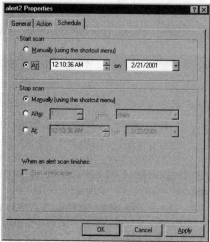

After you have finished configuring the alert, it will appear in the right detail pane in the ISA Server Performance Monitor MMC when you select **Alerts** in the left console pane. If you elect to send a message to your user account or computer account when the alert is triggered, you will receive a message, as shown in Figure 25.12.

Figure 25.12 A Network Message Is Sent to the Specified Account When the Alert Is Triggered

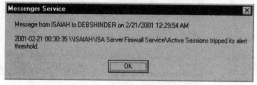

Note that the Windows Messenger Service is used for sending notifications. In order for alert notifications to be received, the Messenger Service must be running on the recipient's computer as well as the ISA server.

Addressing Common Performance Issues

In this section, we look at a few of the common performance issues related to ISA Server and what you can do to prevent them and/or to address them if they do occur on your network. Specifically, we discuss:

- Network bandwidth issues

- Load-balancing issues
- Cache configuration issues

We also show you how you can edit the Windows 2000 Registry to tune your ISA Server performance settings.

Addressing Network Bandwidth Issues

Network bandwidth usage is dependent on several factors: available bandwidth, number of users, type of usage, and timing of usage.

Performance Tuning for User Capacity

You can set the array properties to automatically optimize performance based on the number of users per day. To do so, right-click the name of the array in the left console pane of the ISA Management MMC, and select **Properties**. Select the **Performance** tab on the Properties sheet, as shown in Figure 25.13.

Figure 25.13 ISA Automatically Optimizes Performance Based on Number of Users Per Day

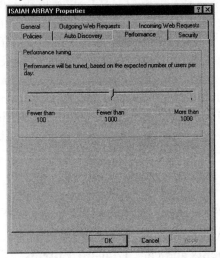

Set the slider to one of the following settings, as appropriate for your organization:

- Fewer than 100
- Fewer than 1000
- More than 1000

Performance will be tuned for all the servers in the array in accordance with the setting.

Determining Effective Bandwidth

The *effective bandwidth* is defined by Microsoft as the actual bandwidth for a specific connectivity device such as a modem or ISDN terminal adapter, or the total effective network bandwidth.

To determine the effective bandwidth, you should find out the maximum effective bandwidth for all the connections on the ISA server or array. For a dial-up device, the effective bandwidth will vary depending on several factors:

- Maximum rated speed of the device (for example, a 56K analog modem or a 128K ISDN terminal adapter).

- Maximum speed of the port to which the device is connected, for external modems and TAs; this speed is based on the UART chip and the limitations on port speed set in Windows (see the sidebar).

- Line condition; analog phone lines that are "dirty" (in other words, lines that have a high degree of noise or interference) will not support the top speeds attainable by your modem and port.

- Data compression allows actual throughput to exceed the top supported speed.

The *universal asynchronous receiver-transmitter (UART)* chip built into the motherboard or serial port card handles serial communications between the computer and an external modem or other serial device. Internal devices have their own UART chips built into their circuit boards. The UART chip limits the amount of data that can be transferred through the port. A high-speed UART (16650bps) will enable faster communications. Some manufacturers make super high-speed or enhanced serial ports (ESPs) that have a large buffer to increase data flow.

However, the speed of the hardware device doesn't matter if the software caps the speed at which the serial port can communicate. Windows 2000 and Windows Server 2003 allows you to set the port speed, using the **General** tab on the modem's Properties sheet. You can select a maximum port speed from 300bps to 115,200bps. In order to change this setting, you must be logged on with administrative privileges.

Setting Effective Bandwidth Limits

You can specify an effective bandwidth for a dial-up device by following these steps:

1. Under the server or array name in the left console pane of the ISA Management MMC, expand **Policy Elements** and click **Dial-up Entries**.

2. In the right detail pane, right-click the dial-up entry pane for which you want to specify an effective bandwidth.

3. Click **Enable bandwidth control** on the **Bandwidth** tab.

4. Enter the desired effective bandwidth in kilobits per second (for all devices in the array) in the **Effective Bandwidth** field, as shown in Figure 25.14.

Figure 25.14 Enable Bandwidth Control and Set Effective Bandwidth for a Dial-Up Entry

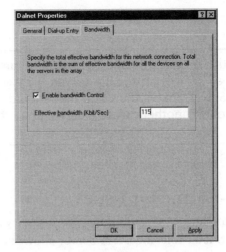

You can also set effective bandwidth for a network card in a similar way. To do so, right-click **Bandwidth rules** in the left console pane, select **Properties**, and choose **Enable bandwidth control** on the **General** tab. You can then enter the desired bandwidth in kilobits per second in the **Effective bandwidth** field.

The purpose of the bandwidth control feature in ISA Server can be confusing. The name might seem to imply that it allows you to allocate a specific amount of bandwidth to a specific user, group, or application. In fact, ISA bandwidth control does not limit how much bandwidth can be used; rather, it uses the Windows 2000 QoS packet-scheduling service to set *priorities* on network connections. Connections that have associated bandwidth rules will be scheduled ahead of those without associated rules (default priority connections).

In order to set bandwidth rules, bandwidth control must be enabled. Effective bandwidth is the actual bandwidth for the specified device. ISA uses your specifications in the effective bandwidth field on the **Bandwidth** tab of the Properties sheet to determine the actual bandwidth that will be assigned, taking into account the bandwidth priority that is specified for the rule.

When determining effective bandwidth for a modem, you must consider several factors:

- Speed of the modem
- Compression
- Phone-line condition

For Frame Relay connections, the ISP will determine the maximum effective bandwidth. Bandwidth is set in the same way as for a network card.

The steps in setting effective bandwidth are:

1. Determine the maximum bandwidth of all the connections on the ISA server.

2. Monitor performance for peak-hour activity and generate reports.

3. Analyze, based on the reports, how much bandwidth is actually allocated for all requests (on both the internal and external cards).

When ISA Server returns cached content to a computer on the internal LAN, bandwidth rules will not be applied.

> **NOTE**
>
> Configure the effective bandwidth, specifying the minimum bandwidth (the *lowest maximum*) available for all devices on the ISA server. For example, if the effective bandwidth for the modem is 56Kbps, that is the value that should be configured for the effective bandwidth, even though another device (such as the internal network card) has a higher effective bandwidth.

Addressing Load-Balancing Issues

Load balancing refers to a method of spreading the processing workload across multiple machines, for better performance and fault tolerance. ISA Server allows you to configure the load factor by dividing the ISA tasks among members of an array. Windows 2000 Advanced Server, Datacenter Server, and Windows Server 2003 include a feature called *Network Load Balancing*, or NLB, to enhance availability and performance for mission-critical servers. NLB is a means of *clustering* multiple computers running TCP/IP, allowing the group of computers to be addressed by the same cluster IP addresses. The NLB service distributes incoming client requests across the cluster of computers. You can configure the *load weight* of each server or distribute the load equally among all servers in the cluster.

In this section, we discuss:

- How to configure the load factor in an ISA Server using CARP
- Interaction between ISA Server and Windows NLB

> **NOTE**
>
> Prior to the release of Windows 2000, Microsoft called the Network Load Balancing service *Windows Load Balancing,* or WLB.

Configuring the Load Factor in an ISA Server Using CARP

When the Cache Array Routing Protocol (CARP) is enabled on an ISA Server computer, you can configure the servers in the array so that they have different loads by setting the *load factor.* Why would you want to do this? All servers are not created equal, and if some of your servers have larger hard disks, for example, you might want those servers to handle a larger amount of the cache load. Changing the load factor increases or decreases the proportion of the load for a specific ISA server.

To configure the load factor, select the **Computers** container object in the left console pane of the ISA Management MMC. In the right detail pane, you will see a list of the servers that belong to the array. Right-click the name of the server for which you want to configure the load factor, and select **Properties**. Select the **Array Membership** tab, as shown in Figure 25.15.

> **NOTE**
>
> By default, CARP is enabled for outgoing Web requests and is disabled for incoming requests. The load factor configuration is a global setting; that is, it cannot be set separately for incoming and outgoing requests but is applied to the requests for which CARP is enabled.

Figure 25.15 The Load Factor Is Configured on the Array Membership Tab of the Computer's Properties Sheet

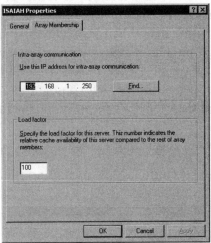

In the **Load Factor** field, specify a value relative to the other array members. The value should be between 0 and 100. A load factor of 0 would prevent this computer from handling any of the load.

ISA Server and Windows 2000 Network Load Balancing

If you are using Windows 2000 NLB on your network, you should not enable CARP on incoming Web requests. The reason for this is that the load-balancing driver will determine to which server the requests should be directed and route each request to one of the servers in the array.

External clients will not have the autoconfiguration script, so they can't perform resolution themselves. Thus, it is more efficient, from a performance standpoint, to have CARP disabled for external (incoming) requests, because it will result in the eventual caching of the Web objects on each of the servers.

Note that, for internal clients, the autoconfiguration script performs basically the same task as NLB; the Web proxy client has a list of all members of the array, and if the first doesn't respond, it tries another. This system provides fault tolerance. The firewall client, however, doesn't have the array information, so NLB is useful for fault tolerance.

ISA Server's load-balancing support enhances its scalability, making it especially suitable for use with large, high-traffic Web sites.

Cache Configuration Issues

Performance—specifically, Web performance—is the purpose of ISA Server's caching functionality. Performance can be improved by properly configuring the cache settings. In this section, we look at how you can improve performance by configuring RAM caching and how access to frequently used objects can be improved by configuring active caching. We also discuss how performance is impacted by the hard disk on which the cache is stored.

Improving Performance by Configuring RAM Caching

Because RAM is faster than hard disk speeds, objects that are cached in RAM can be retrieved faster than those that are cached on the disk. ISA Server caches objects in both locations; by default, objects that are less than 12,800 bytes in size are cached in RAM as well as being cached on the hard disk. If an object is larger than this, it is only cached to the disk.

If your ISA server has a large amount of RAM, you can improve performance by increasing the maximum size for objects that can be cached in RAM. To do so, right-click **Cache Configuration** in the ISA Management MMC left console pane, and select **Properties**.

Select the **Advanced** tab on the Properties sheet. In the field labeled **Maximum size of URL cached in memory**, enter a new size in bytes (see Figure 25.16). You can also change the percentage of free memory that can be used for caching.

Figure 25.16 You Can Increase Performance by Increasing the Size of Objects That Can Be Cached in RAM

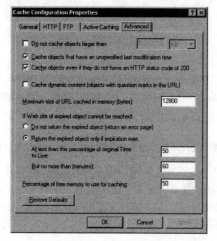

Improving Performance by Configuring Active Caching

Active caching is a means of speeding up access to files that are accessed frequently, by automatically refreshing the content of such objects when they are soon to expire. ISA automatically goes out onto the Internet and retrieves these objects based on the active caching settings. Active caching improves clients' Web performance, and because it works at off-peak hours when network activity is low, when properly configured it should not cause a hit on overall network performance. Microsoft allows you to configure settings in accordance with these factors that are most important in your situation.

One issue to consider is freshness of objects in cache. If an object is in cache and its TTL hasn't expired, the client will get the cached object and not the page on the Web site, which might have changed. The need for the most current content must be balanced against the desire for higher performance.

To enable active caching, select the **Active Caching** tab on the Cache Configuration Properties sheet and check the check box (by default, active caching is disabled), as shown in Figure 25.17.

Figure 25.17 Active Caching Balances Client Web Performance Against Network Traffic

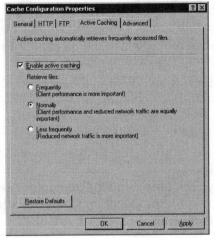

You can choose one of three settings:

■ **Frequently** All the most popular objects will be downloaded to the cache regularly, so they are not allowed to expire. This makes it more likely that a client request will be in the cache.

■ **Normally** Objects will be updated frequently, but network performance is also considered.

■ **Less Frequently** Some popular objects will be cached automatically; however, network load/performance will be given top priority.

If client Web performance is most important, choose the first setting. The second (Normally) is the default setting.

Performance Issues Associated with Passive Caching Settings

The settings on the **HTTP** tab control passive caching behavior. These settings allow you to control the expiration of objects in cache. You can select from three standard settings:

■ Frequently (objects expire immediately)

■ Normally

■ Less frequently

A fourth option is to set a specific TTL for objects in cache. The settings you select here can adversely impact performance in conjunction with the settings you have configured for active caching. For example, the worst possible combination of settings for cache performance would be to select **Less frequently** on the Active caching page and **Frequently** on the HTTP page. In this case, the TTL for objects in the cache will expire immediately, but the automatic update of objects by active caching will occur on a less frequent basis. Thus, ISA Server will have to go out on the Internet to retrieve objects requested by clients rather than being able to return them from cache.

Improving Performance by Cache Drive Configuration

You are prompted, during the installation of ISA Server in cache or integrated mode, to select the disk partition(s) on the local computer on which the cache will be stored. This partition must be formatted in NTFS.

For best performance, the cache should be stored on a physical disk that is fast and a different disk from those on which the Windows 2000 operating system and the ISA Server software are installed.

NOTE

Disk speed is indicated by *seek time* in milliseconds (for example, 9ms; a lower number indicates a faster disk) and *rpm* (for example, 7200rpm; a higher number indicates a faster disk). SCSI disks are generally faster than IDE disks.

By default, the installation program sets a default cache size of 100MB on the largest NTFS partition on the computer. You can cache the cache drive(s) by expanding the **Cache Configuration** object in the left console pane of the ISA Server Management MMC, selecting **Drives**, and double-clicking the server name in the right detail pane. This sequence displays the server's drives Properties sheet, shown in Figure 25.18.

Figure 25.18 You Can Change the Cache Drive Settings for Better Performance

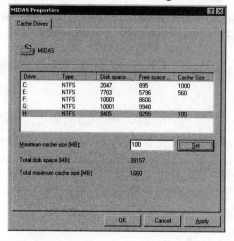

You need to know which drive letter represents a partition on which of your physical disks in order to choose the best location for the cache. You also need to know where your <system-root> directory is located and to which disk ISA Server was installed.

> **NOTE**
>
> The ISA Server cache can only be assigned to partitions that have designated drive letters, although Windows 2000 allows you to format a partition without a drive letter and mount it to an NTFS folder.

Editing the Windows 2000 Registry to Tune ISA Performance Settings

Several settings can be used to fine-tune performance that cannot be configured via the ISA interface. Changing these settings requires that you edit the Windows 2000 Registry.

> **WARNING**
>
> It is always imperative that you exercise caution when making any changes to the Registry. Incorrectly editing the Registry can create serious problems or even render your system unbootable. It is wise to back up valuable data prior to modifying the Registry.

To make these changes, you can use either of two Registry editing tools provided with Windows 2000: **Regedit** or **Regedt32**. You can start either one by typing its name at the **Run** prompt.

The Registry keys that you can edit to tune the performance of your ISA server are located in the HKEY_LOCAL_MACHINE\System\CurrentControlSet\Services path, shown in Figure 25.19.

Figure 25.19 The Registry Keys Used to Tune ISA Performance Are Found Under HKEY_LOCAL_MACHINE\System\CurrentControlSet\Services

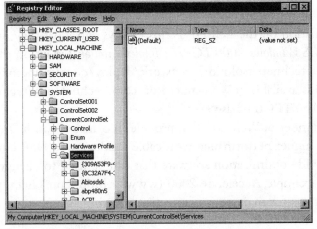

The following keys can be configured for ISA performance optimization:

- **\W3Proxy\Parameters\OutstandAccept** The value set for this key controls the number of accepted pending connections before new connection requests are rejected. A high value minimizes the number of rejected connection requests.

- **\Tcpip\Parameters\MaxUserPort** The value set in this key controls the number of TCP/IP ports that can be allocated by a client making a connection request. Setting the value to 0000ffff in hexadecimal (65,535 in decimal) sets the range for client port numbers to the maximum.

The following keys can be added (**Edit | New | Key** in the Registry Editor menu) and configured for optimum performance:

- **\W3PCache\Parameters\TZPersistIntervalThreshold** This key can be used to set a maximum time interval in minutes that will be lost when cache is recovered after the W3Proxy service is stopped unexpectedly.

- **\W3Cache\Parameters\RecoveryMruSizeThreshold** You can use this key to set a time interval in minutes in which the content cached will be recovered first from the time the W3Proxy service is stopped unexpectedly.

- **\W3Proxy\Parameters\MaxClientSession** You can use this key to control the size of the pool for the client session object. A client session object will be freed and its memory returned to system memory management only if the pool has a number of objects that exceeds this value. Freeing objects is time consuming, so you can cause objects to be freed less frequently by setting this key to a high value.

- **\Tcpip\Parameters\TcpTimedWaitDelay** This value sets a time interval in seconds that will pass before a socket is reused for a new connection.

NOTE

In most cases, after you make a change to Registry settings, you must restart the computer in order for the changes to be applied.

For general information on the TCP/IP Registry keys and what they do, see the Microsoft white paper entitled *MS Windows 2000 TCP/IP Implementation Details* on the Microsoft Web site at www.microsoft.com/technet/itsolutions/network/deploy/depovg/tcpip2k..asp. Information for Windows Server 2003 is available at www.microsoft.com/technet/prodtechnol/windowsserver2003/plan/TPCIP03.asp.

There are also a number of Web sites that provide information on how to tweak Registry settings to provide for higher performance with cable modems and DSL connections.

Some vendors provide optimization software that can be used to change these settings using a friendly interface. For example, Accelerate 2000 (www.webroot.com) helps you optimize MTU and other TCP/IP settings for maximum connection speed.

Customizing ISA Server

ISA Server's functionality can be enhanced in several ways. Microsoft provides the ISA Server Software Developer's Kit (SDK), which allows developers to extend ISA by creating components that are built on or that work with ISA Server. Several third-party software vendors have already developed add-on products that add flexibility to the ISA product. In this section, we take a look at the SDK and a few of the available third-party add-ons.

Using the ISA Server Software Developer's Kit

The ISA Server SDK is a comprehensive collection of development tools and sample scripts that can be used to build new, custom features that enhance ISA's firewall, caching, and management functionality.

The SDK comes with the ISA Server software. It includes full API documentation as well as useful sample extensions such as management tools, application and Web filters, and user interface extensions.

Administration Scripts

Administration scripts can simplify and automate administrative tasks. Developers can create custom administration scripts, or administrators can use the sample scripts included with the SDK.

Sample Administration Scripts

Sample administration scripts provided with the ISA SDK include:

- **Add_Dod** A VBScript sample that demonstrates how to add a new Dialup Entry and set the Dialup Entry Credentials.

- **AdditionalKey** A VBScript script that demonstrates how to change an additional key.

- **AddLATEntry** A VBScript script that demonstrates how to add an IP range to a LAT.

- **AddScheduledContentDownload** A VBScript that receives an array name, a URL, and a job name and adds a scheduled content download job.

- **ApplicationFilterList** A script that prompts the user to enter an array, then lists the application filters of the selected array.

- **CacheSettings** A script that prompts the user to enter the name of an array, then displays the cache settings of that array.

- **ConstructLAT** A script that demonstrates how to construct the LAT of an array based on its NICs.

- **DisableScheduledContentDownloads** A VBScript script that disables all prefetcher jobs on Monday and Wednesday on a given array.

- **Enterprise_Destination** A VBScript script that adds a new destination set to the Enterprise, sets the array policy to use Array and Enterprise Policies, and configures the new rule to use the Enterprise destination. (Can be run only by an enterprise administrator.)

- **FetchUrl** A VBScript script that causes the Web proxy to fetch an object and store it in the Web proxy's cache. The cached object can be stored under a different name than the source object.

- **ListServers** A script that lists all the servers in a given array through the name property of the FPCArray object.

- **FindScheduledContentDownload** A VBScript script that receives an array name and a URL and checks to see if any job includes that URL.

- **SetCache** A VBScript sample that configures cache settings.

- **SetUpstreamRouting** A VBScript script that demonstrates how to set up upstream routing to another server using the RoutingRules collection and the RouteEntity object.

- **ShowAllProtocolRules** A script that lists all the protocol rules of an array by looping through the PrxProtocolRules collection.

- **ShowAllRoutingRules** A VBScript script that lists all the routing rules of an array by looping through the RoutingRules collection. The script also lists whether or not each routing rule is enabled or disabled and the action that the rule follows.

- **StaticFilter** A VBScript script that demonstrates how to add a static packet filter that allows NTP communication from the ISA server to the Internet.

Running Administration Scripts

You can run the sample scripts simply by double-clicking the script name in the sdk\samples\admin\Scripts directory, located on the ISA Server CD. You can also run a script by typing its full path at the **Run** prompt.

Some scripts might prompt you to enter information before performing their tasks. For example, when you run the CacheSettings script, you will be asked to enter an array name (or you can leave the field blank and click **OK** to specify the first array listed in the ISA Server MMC), as shown in Figure 25.20.

Figure 25.20 The CacheSettings Script Prompts You to Specify an Array Name

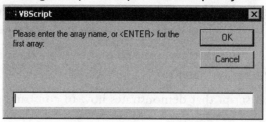

When you enter the information or click **OK**, the script will run and display its results, as shown in Figure 25.21.

Figure 25.21 The Script Runs and Displays the Results

Some of the sample admin scripts are provided in both Visual Basic Script (VBS) and Java Script (JS) versions; others are provided only in VBS.

Sample Filters

In addition to the sample scripts, Microsoft has provided in the SDK a number of sample filters to demonstrate how to create firewall, Web, and application filters. A readme.txt file is supplied with each sample filter, an example of which is shown in Figure 25.22.

Figure 25.22 Each Sample Filter Includes a Readme File That Provides More Information

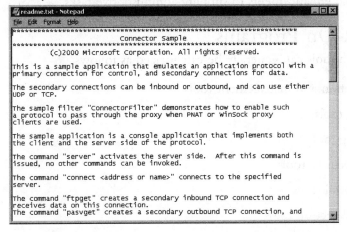

The readme.txt file provides additional information about the filter and the purpose of each file included in the sample. The following are descriptions of included sample filters:

- **Connector** A console application that emulates an application protocol with a primary connection for control and secondary connections for data. The secondary connections can be inbound or outbound and can use either UDP or TCP.

- **ConnectorFilter** Enables a complex protocol that requires secondary connections on random ports and makes it possible for the Connector sample to work through Microsoft Proxy for PNAT clients and Winsock clients.

- **DbgDump** Registers for notifications on all possible events and installs data filters on all connections, then outputs information about the events to the debugger.

- **ExeBlock** Demonstrates the use of data filters and hooking into the proxy thread pool.

- **ServerSplit** Demonstrates the use of connection emulation for inbound connections.

- **SMTPFltr** Captures and analyzes data sent by external clients using the SMTP protocol. The proxy attaches a new instance of the data filter to every inbound port 25 TCP session. The filter can be configured to look for a particular string in the SMTP message.

- **SOCKS 4/4a** Demonstrates the use of SOCKS protocol version 4/4A.

- **SOCKS 5** Demonstrates the use of the SOCKS 5 protocol.

Using Third-Party Add-Ons

Even before Microsoft released the final version of ISA Server, several third-party vendors had begun to develop solutions to customize and enhance ISA's features and functionality. In many cases, Microsoft has partnered with these companies to provide complementary products for ISA.

Third-party add-ons include tools to add security features such as virus scanning, additional intrusion detection filters, integrated access control solutions, more comprehensive reporting and monitoring tools, and enhancements to simplify administrative tasks.

Types of Add-On Programs

The available add-on tools can generally be categorized as follows:

- Administration and management tools

- Reporting tools

- Monitoring tools

- Content security tools

- Access control tools

- Intrusion detection tools

- Network protocol tools

In many cases, a vendor provides one tool that incorporates two or more of these functions. Most tools provide a user-friendly graphical interface. For example, GFI LANguard, shown in Figure 25.23, creates a custom console that includes the ISA Management snap-in along with the LANguard configuration tools. It links into ISA Server as an ISAPI extension so that alerting and reporting functions of ISA are integrated.

Figure 25.23 GFI LANguard Is a Third-Party Add-On That Creates a Custom Console, Which Includes the ISA Management Snap-In

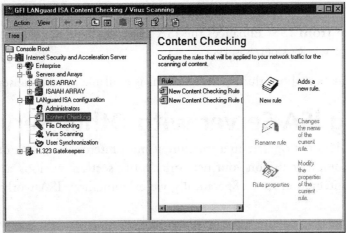

Some of the features of LANguard include virus protection (scanning of HTTP and FTP files) with automatic virus signature updates, and monitoring of Internet usage (including notification to administrators when users access undesirable sites or blocking users from accessing those sites) based on keywords in the URL or Web page. Word macros can be automatically removed from communications, and potentially dangerous file types (executables, Word documents, and the like) can be "quarantined." LANguard can even verify that a file is of the type that its extension indicates (for example, it can verify that a file with the .AVI extension is in fact a video file). LANguard offers very granular control; the program retrieves a list of users and groups from your network and allows you to specify particular users when you create a rule.

Overview of Available Add–On Programs

Other add-on programs provide functionalities similar to those of LANguard. Some of the add-ons that are available or will soon be available include:

- **btPatrol from Burst Technology** A real-time monitoring tool. More information is available at www.burstek.com/isaserver.

- **LANguard from GFI** Content filtering and antivirus protection. More information is available at www.gfi.com/isaserver.

- **WebTrends firewall suite** Analyzes ISA Server activity and generates custom reports. More information is available at www.webtrends.com/isaserver.

- **SmartFilter for ISA from Secure Computing** Allows you to control Internet access in a manner tailored to your network's needs. More information is available at www.securecomputing.com/isaserver.

- **AppManager for ISA Server from NetIQ** Monitors ISA modules and services. More information is available at www.netiq.com/isaserver.

- **SuperScout for ISA Server from SurfControl** Enhances management of Internet access in the corporate environment. More information is available at www.surfcontrol.com/products/web/ms_isa.

- **RealSecure from ISS** Enhances the ISA intrusion detection filters. More information is available at www.iss.net/isaserver.

Additional information about third-party add-ons is available at www.isaserver.org.

Integrating ISA Server with Other Services

ISA Server software does not operate in a vacuum; it must interoperate with other services and applications on the computer and on your network. In this section, we look at some common interoperability and integration issues. Specifically, we examine how ISA works in conjunction with:

- Windows Active Directory Services

- Windows Routing and Remote Access Services (RRAS)

- Internet Information Server (IIS)

- The IP Security protocol (IPsec)

- Windows NT 4.0 domains

It is also important to be aware of those services with which ISA Server *cannot* peacefully coexist. For example, you cannot use Internet Connection Sharing or the Windows 2000 Network Address Translation (NAT) functions to provide Internet connectivity on a computer that is running ISA Server. ISA replaces ICS/NAT, providing translation services along with security and caching.

Understanding Interoperability with Active Directory

The Windows 2000 Active Directory is a hierarchical database that is stored on Windows 2000 domain controllers. It holds information about objects on the network (users, groups, computers, printers, files, and other network resources). The Active Directory controls logon authentication, serving the same function as the Security Accounts Management (SAM) database in Windows NT. Active Directory Services provides for easy accessibility to network resources by authorized users.

Stand-Alone versus Array Member

The way in which ISA Server interacts with the Windows 2000 Active Directory is dependent on how ISA is installed: as a stand-alone server or as a member of an array.

When ISA is installed as a stand-alone system, its configuration information is saved to the Registry on the local machine. However, if you install ISA as an array member (or promote a stand-alone server to array membership status), the ISA configuration information is then stored in Active Directory. This means that information will be replicated to all domain controllers in the domain. This system obviously provides a measure of fault tolerance that a stand-alone server does not have.

The Active Directory Schema

Active Directory is governed by a set of rules called the *schema*, which define object classes and attributes (these are called *metadata* because they describe "data about data"). The content of the schema is controlled by a single domain controller that holds the role of *schema master.*

When Windows Active Directory is installed, the schema contains a basic set of metadata. However, the schema can be extended; members of the schema administrators group can define new classes or new attributes for existing classes. The schema is also extended by some programs, which need new object classes and/or attributes in order to function.

> **NOTE**
>
> Programmers use the Active Directory Service Interfaces (ADSI), available in the Windows 2000 SDK, to write programs that extend the schema.

When the first member of an ISA Server array is to be installed, you must first initialize the enterprise. This automatically makes the necessary extensions to the Active Directory schema.

ISA Server and Domain Controllers

Although the ISA configuration is stored on the Windows 2000 domain controllers, you do *not* have to install ISA Server on a domain controller. It is actually preferable that the ISA computer not be a domain controller, for a couple of reasons:

- Performance of the ISA server will be improved if the computer is not a domain controller, because domain controller tasks require significant resources.

- Security of the domain controller is improved if you place the domain controller (s) *behind* the ISA server on the local network, thus allowing the ISA server to protect the domain controller (s) from unauthorized access.

Because Active Directory is required in order to install ISA Server as an array member, ISA servers cannot be array members in a Window NT 4.0 domain.

Understanding Interoperability with Routing and Remote Access Services

Windows 2000 Routing and Remote Access Services (RRAS) provide a collection of services that allow a Windows 2000 server to function as a full-fledged software router, forwarding IP packets from one subnet or network to another, or as a dial-up server and to create and control dial-up networking policies and virtual private networking connections across WAN links.

RRAS Components

The RRAS console allows you to configure a number of components, including:

- Enabling IP Routing to allow the server to function as a router on the local network and as a demand-dial router
- Configuring the server to assign IP addresses via DHCP or a static address pool
- Enabling the remote access server service
- Enabling support for multilink PPP, Bandwidth Allocation Protocol (BAP), Link Control Protocol (LCP) extensions, and/or software compression
- Selecting an authentication method for remote access clients and demand-dial routers, using Windows authentication or RADIUS
- Selecting one or more authentication protocols (EAP, MS-CHAPv1 or v2, CHAP, SPAP, PAP) and allowing remote access without authentication
- Configure remote access logging properties
- Create demand-dial routing interfaces
- View remote access client connections
- Configure ports (modem, PPTP/L2TP, parallel routing)
- Add and configure routing protocols (IGMP, NAT, RIP, OSPF)
- Configure a DHCP relay agent
- Create remote access policies
- Configure static routes and view the Windows 2000 routing table

RRAS and ISA Server

RRAS can be enabled on an ISA Server computer. The ISA server can also function as a remote access server or VPN server.

However, there is one RRAS feature that is not compatible with the ISA Server software. You cannot use the NAT protocol on a server that is running ISA Server. The reason for this is that ISA Server provides its own translation service, which is more sophisticated and robust than the Windows NAT.

> **NOTE**
>
> Although the ISA address translation service provides sophisticated NAT functionality, some tasks that ISA's S-NAT cannot do, such as port mapping, can be done using Windows 2000's NAT.

If NAT is installed on a server on which you want to install ISA, you should delete it. The same is true of Internet Connection Sharing (ICS), a "light" form of NAT that is also included with Windows 2000 Server and is configured on a connection via the Network and Dialup Connections properties.

Understanding Interoperability with Internet Information Server

Microsoft Proxy Server required the presence of IIS in order to function. However, ISA does *not* require that IIS be installed on the ISA server, although you can install IIS on your ISA computer if you desire.

IIS Functionality

Windows 2000 Server includes IIS 5.0, and it is installed by default when you install the operating system. However, you can elect not to install it in a custom installation, or you can remove it later using the **Add/Remove Programs** applet in the Control Panel.

> **NOTE**
>
> IIS 5.0 will *not* be installed by default if you upgraded to Windows 2000 from Windows NT 4.0 and IIS 4.0 was not installed on the NT system.

IIS is Microsoft's Web server software, which also includes NNTP, FTP, and SMTP functionality. IIS 5.0 supports Active Server Pages (ASP); Windows Media Services (WMS), which is installed separately as a Windows component from **Add/Remove Programs**; distributed authoring and versioning; and other advanced features. IIS can be used to make documents and Web objects available over the Internet or on an intranet.

Publishing IIS to the Internet

If you do choose to install IIS on the ISA computer, there are two ways you can publish IIS to the Internet:

- Using Web publishing rules
- Using packet filters

Using Web Publishing Rules

The first way to publish the Web server that runs on the ISA Server computer is by configuring Web publishing rules. Note that you need to configure IIS not to use the ports that are used by ISA Server for outgoing and incoming Web requests (ports 8080 and 80, respectively, by default). You can also configure IIS to listen on a different IP address.

> **NOTE**
>
> When using Web publishing rules, you must associate the Web server with an internal IP address and change the port it uses to a different port number.

Using Packet Filters

You can allow IIS to continue using TCP port 80 to listen for Web requests if you configure an IP packet filter to map incoming requests on that port to IIS. In this case, you should ensure that ISA's autodiscovery is not set to listen on port 80. If you use this method, you should *not* create Web publishing rules to publish the Web server.

Note that this is *not* the preferred method of publishing, because it cannot take advantage of dynamic packet filtering.

> **NOTE**
>
> When you install ISA Server, the World Wide Web Publishing Service (w3svc) will be stopped. After you finish the installation, you should first change the port on which IIS will listen, and then restart the w3svc.

Understanding Interoperability with IPSecurity

The IP Security Protocol (IPsec) support is a new feature in Windows 2000 that was not included in Windows NT 4.0. IPsec is an Internet standard, developed by the Internet Engineering Task Force (IETF).

> **NOTE**
>
> IPsec specifications are defined in RFC2401.

IPsec provides security for data as it travels across a TCP/IP network. Although there are other methods of encrypting data, IPsec enjoys a distinct advantage: It operates at the Network layer (Layer 3) of the OSI model. This means that, unlike Application layer encryption protocol uses, there is no requirement for the network applications to be IPsec aware.

IPsec uses cryptographic security services to provide for confidentiality and integrity of transmitted data and authentication of the identity of the sender.

How IPsec Works

To secure and authenticate transmissions, IPsec uses two protocols:

- **Authentication Header (AH)** AH signs the entire data packet, providing authentication and integrity but not confidentiality, because it doesn't encrypt the data. AH can be used alone when it is not necessary that the message be kept secret—only that you ensure that it cannot be modified and that the sender's identity is verified.

■ **Encapsulating Security Payload (ESP)** ESP does not sign the entire packet (except in the case of tunneled data), but it does encrypt the data, providing confidentiality.

Both protocols support two modes: transport (which provides end-to-end security) and tunnel (which provides gateway-to-gateway security).

IPsec uses *Security Associations (SAs)* to establish a secure connection. An SA is a combination of policy and keys that define how data will be exchanged and protected. The Internet Security Association and Key Management Protocol (ISAKMP) is used in conjunction with the Oakley key generation protocol, in compliance with IETF standards. ISAKMP/Oakley uses a two-stage process that employs negotiated encryption and authentication algorithms, which are agreed on by the sending and receiving (or *source* and *destination)* computers.

In Windows 2000's implementation of IPsec, properties of security associations are governed by IPsec policies.

How IPsec Is Configured in Windows 2000

Windows 2000 allows you to set IPsec policies via Group Policy, which can be configured on a local machine via the **Local Security Settings** administrative tool or for a domain by editing the domain's Group Policy Object (GPO), as shown in Figure 25.24.

Figure 25.24 IPsec Policies Are Configured Via Windows 2000 Group Policy

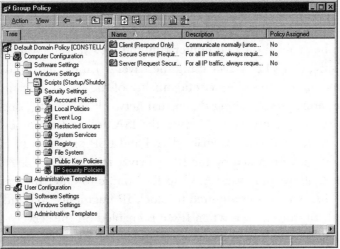

One option you have when editing the properties of an IPsec policy is to select which of the two IPsec protocols will be used. The Security Method Wizard allows you to configure the security method (Microsoft uses the term *security methods* to refer to the IPsec protocols), as shown in Figure 25.25.

You can use ESP and AH together to provide added security if you want the data encrypted and the entire packet signed. However, you cannot specify both protocols during the wizard process; you must edit the filter action afterward to add a second security method.

Figure 25.25 You Can Select the IPsec Protocol to Be Used Via the Security Method Wizard

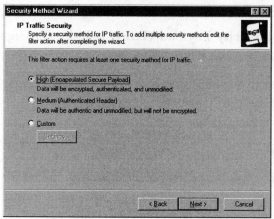

> **NOTE**
>
> IPsec is a complex topic; exploring all facets of its operation is beyond the scope of this book. For more information, see RFC2401 or *IP Security for Windows 2000 Server* at www.microsoft.com/windows2000/techinfo/howitworks/security/ip_security.

Microsoft implements IPsec in Windows 2000 via the *IPSec driver*. Let's take a look at this component.

IPsec and ISA Server

The IPsec driver can be enabled on a computer running ISA Server. Doing so is necessary if the ISA server is functioning as a VPN server using the Layer 2 Tunneling Protocol (L2TP). L2TP uses IPsec for data encryption, to ensure confidentiality of the communications sent across the internetwork via the tunnel, thus making the virtual network a "private" one.

When IPsec is not enabled on the ISA server, the ISA policy determines which packets are allowed or blocked. However, if IPsec is enabled, AH and ESP protocols (which are IP protocols 30 and 51, respectively) are controlled by the IPsec driver instead of the ISA Server packet filter driver. The IPsec driver allows only valid AH and ESP traffic to enter the network.

Note that when ISA Server is configured to block IP fragments, AH and ESP fragments will be blocked along with all others, even when IPsec is enabled on the server.

NAT is incompatible with protocols that use IP addresses in fields other than the standard TCP/IP header fields. IPsec encapsulates the TCP/IP headers; thus IPsec cannot be used *through* an ISA server. IPsec can only be used to encrypt L2TP traffic using the ISA Server machine as the endpoint for a VPN.

> **NOTE**
>
> When IPsec is used to encrypt data in an L2TP tunnel, public key computer certificates are used for authentication. At least one computer-level certificate must be configured on each computer (VPN client or server).

Integrating an ISA Server into a Windows NT 4.0 Domain

You can install Windows 2000 Server as a stand-alone or member server on a computer that is a member of a Windows NT 4.0 domain. (A Windows 2000 server *cannot* be a domain controller in an NT domain; when you promote a Windows 2000 computer to domain controller status, Active Directory is automatically installed and you must create or join a Windows 2000 domain.)

ISA Server can be installed *in stand-alone mode only* on a Windows 2000 server in an NT domain. The reason for this is that ISA arrays require Active Directory, and there is no Active Directory in an NT domain.

If you want to provide firewall protection to users who belong to an NT domain and you also want the benefits of ISA array membership (fault tolerance and distributed caching), you can set up a separate Windows 2000 domain on the same network and create a trust relationship between the new domain and the NT domain. Then, you can install an ISA Server array in the new domain.

Backing Up and Restoring the ISA Configuration

Backing up important system information is a vital part of any network administrator's routine, and ISA Server includes a backup and restore feature that allows you to save and reapply configuration information in the event of a failure.

Backup Principles

You should back up the configuration each time you make any major change to the ISA server or array settings. In particular, Microsoft recommends that you make a backup of the array configuration immediately after you do any of the following:

- Modify the installation mode (firewall, caching or integrated)
- Modify the enterprise policy settings in any way
- Add, remove, or rename an ISA server or array
- Change the location or size of the cache
- Add or remove Web filters

You should also back up server-specific information on a periodic basis. This is done on each ISA Server computer. The process includes:

- Passwords
- Local Registry parameters/settings
- Cache configuration information
- Cache contents

- The H.323 Gatekeeper configuration
- Local settings for application filters
- Performance-tuning parameters
- Reports
- Log files

Backing Up and Restoring Stand-Alone Server Configurations

You will recall that when an ISA server is installed in stand-alone mode, the ISA configuration settings are stored in the computer's local Registry. When you back up a stand-alone server, the configuration information is restored to the same stand-alone server.

To use the Backup feature, simply right-click the server name in the left console pane of the ISA Management MMC, and choose **Back Up** (or make the same choice on the **Action** menu while the server name is highlighted), as shown in Figure 25.26.

Figure 25.26 The ISA Management Console Provides a Tool for Backing Up Server Information

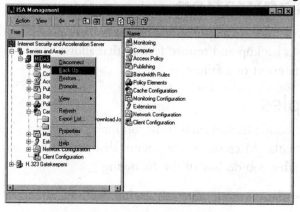

You will be prompted to enter a location where you want to store the backup confirmation information. You can type a path or browse for a location. The backup information file will be saved with a .BIF extension.

> **NOTE**
>
> Microsoft recommends that you always store the configuration backup on an NTFS partition for security purposes. Doing so will allow you to protect the files from unauthorized access, using NTFS permissions.

You can also enter a comment to provide more information about the backup file or to identify who made the backup, as shown in Figure 25.27.

Figure 25.27 You Can Provide an Identifying Comment for the Backup File

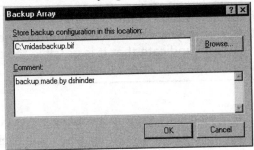

To restore the data, right-click the server name and select **Restore** from the context menu, and you will receive a warning message notifying you that the existing configuration will be replaced when you restore from a file. When you click **OK**, you will be asked to enter or browse for the path to a backup (.BIF) file.

> **WARNING**
>
> Be certain that the file you select is the most current backup of your ISA configuration. The existing configuration will be overwritten when you restore from backup. Restoring from the wrong file could have undesirable effects on your ISA server.

Backing Up and Restoring Array and Enterprise Configurations

When ISA Server is installed as an array member (even if the array has only one member), the configuration information is stored in Active Directory.

Backing Up and Restoring an Array Configuration

Backing up and restoring configuration information for an array is similar to the process for stand-alone devices. ISA Server backs up the array's general configuration information, including the following:

- Array policies
- Access policy rules
- Publishing rules
- Policy elements
- Alert configuration
- Cache configuration

The process for backing up the array is the same as shown for a stand-alone server; you right-click the array name in the left console pane, select **Back Up**, and follow the same steps.

NOTE

Microsoft's ISA Server documentation states that the backup files must be stored on the local computer—in other words, you cannot save them to a network location. The authors' experiments, however, indicate that it is possible to save the backups across the network and restore them from the remote location.

Some server-specific configuration information, including cache content, activity logs, reports, and effective enterprise policy, is not backed up when you back up the array. The restoration process, once again, involves selecting **Restore** from the context menu and entering a path or browsing for the backup file, as shown in Figure 25.28.

Figure 25.28 You Must Enter a Path to the File in Which You Backed Up the Array Configuration

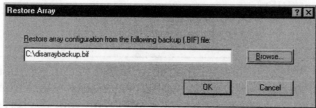

Backup file information will be displayed, as shown in Figure 25.29, so that you can ensure this is the correct file before you go ahead with the restoration process.

Figure 25.29 Backup File Information Is Displayed Prior to the Restoration

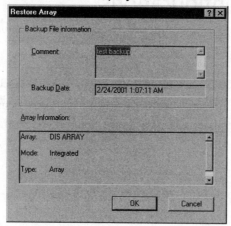

The restoration process might take a few moments. When it is completed, a message will be displayed notifying you that the array has been successfully restored.

NOTE

You cannot back up an array configuration and then restore that configuration to a different array or to a stand-alone server. You must restore to the same array.

Backing Up and Restoring an Enterprise Configuration

You can back up the enterprise configuration data to a separate file. Backing up the enterprise configuration saves all enterprise-specific information. This includes enterprise-level policy elements and policies as well as information regarding which arrays in the enterprise use specific enterprise policies.

NOTE

When you back up the enterprise configuration, array-specific data will *not* be saved. You must back up the array configuration separately, as described earlier.

The enterprise configuration is stored in a file with the .BEF extension (for *backup enterprise file*, to differentiate it from the .BIF array backup files). You should back up all arrays in the enterprise after you back up the enterprise configuration, and after restoring the enterprise, you should restore all arrays. This process ensures that arrays that use enterprise policies will have the policies applied correctly.

To back up the enterprise configuration, right-click the **Enterprise** object in the left console pane of the ISA Management MMC and select **Back Up**, then follow the same steps already discussed for backing up a stand-alone server or an array.

NOTE

A .BEF file cannot be restored to an array, nor can a .BIF file be used to restore the enterprise.

The restoration process is the same as for a stand-alone server or array: Right-click the object (in this case, **Enterprise**) and select **Restore**, then select the appropriate .BEF file.

Summary

In this chapter, we addressed ways of optimizing ISA Server's performance and customizing the product to better fit the needs of your network. We discussed how ISA Server interoperates with other Windows services and applications and how to integrate a stand-alone ISA server into a Windows domain. We also provided information on how to back up and restore the configuration of an ISA stand-alone server, an array, or the enterprise.

You learned some basic performance concepts, including how to establish and use a baseline in managing and tuning performance. We showed you how to define threshold values, and you learned that ISA Server can perform a specified action—such as logging an event, sending a network message, starting a performance data log, or running a specified program—when a threshold value is reached.

We demonstrated the use of the ISA Server Performance Monitor, which includes two components: the System Monitor and Performance Logs and Alerts. You learned to customize the view of the System Monitor and how to use the performance counters for various performance objects to determine how efficiently your ISA server is operating. You also learned to configure logs so that performance data can be saved and viewed at a later time and how to set performance alerts.

Next, we addressed some specific, common performance issues. You learned to set Performance properties based on user capacity as well as how to determine effective network bandwidth and set effective bandwidth limits for dial-up devices and network cards. We discussed load-balancing issues, and you learned how to configure the load factor in an ISA server using CARP. The interaction of ISA Server—particularly when CARP is enabled—with Windows 2000's Network Load Balancing (NLB) was discussed, and you learned that CARP should not be used for incoming Web requests when NLB is being used on the network. You then learned how to improve performance by configuring RAM caching and that you can speed up access by enabling and configuring active caching of frequently accessed files. We also discussed cache drive configuration and its impact on performance.

You discovered that some performance settings can be made only by editing the Windows Registry, and we showed you a few specific Registry keys that can be configured to fine-tune performance.

## Chapter 26

Troubleshooting ISA Server

Best Damn Topics in this Chapter:

- **Understanding Basic Troubleshooting Principles**

- **Troubleshooting ISA Installation and Configuration Problems**

- **Troubleshooting Authentication and Access Problems**

- **Troubleshooting ISA Client Problems**

- **Troubleshooting Caching, Publishing, and Services**

Introduction

As with any piece of computer software, many potential problems with ISA Server can be prevented—and time spent troubleshooting thus avoided—by careful deployment planning and attention to details during installation and configuration. A classic truism says that it's easier to get it right the first time than to go back and fix it later, and this is especially true when it comes to software. One incorrect setting made inadvertently because you were in a hurry or because you didn't understand how the setting works can result in hours or days of effort later as you search for the cause of the resulting problems.

Some network administrators enjoy the challenge of the hunt. Troubleshooting *can* be fun, especially when you can do it at your leisure. Unfortunately, in the real world, we often get those "Help! It isn't working!" calls at the most inconvenient times and are under pressure to figure out what's wrong and fix it *now*.

In this chapter, we address specific problems that commonly occur in conjunction with ISA Server. Even though these issues and diagnosis are specific to the ISA server, the methodologies used can help you troubleshoot any firewall. These problems are divided into logical categories so that you can more easily use this chapter as a reference in the field.

Troubleshooting Guidelines

Many professions exist for the purpose of solving problems of one sort or another. When people have legal problems, they call an attorney. When they have medical problems, they visit a doctor. When they have problems with their computers or the network, they turn to you—the administrator—to solve those problems. Doctors, lawyers, and other professionals learn, as part of their formal education and practical training, the importance of following a step-by-step procedure that can be applied to most problem-solving situations.

This basic process applies to troubleshooting problems with computer software programs such as ISA Server. In essence, you are the doctor of the ISA server. We have also another step, which the other professionals also practice but which is rarely mentioned in formal problem-solving models: documentation. Police officers file reports, doctors complete medical charts, and attorneys decimate entire forests to create the mass of paperwork that document every step of the legal process. IT professionals—although not required to do so by law, as those in the other professions are—should get into the habit of thoroughly documenting troubleshooting incidents. This practice will benefit you as well as others who encounter the same problem in the future.

The Five Steps of Troubleshooting

Our systematic approach to troubleshooting involves five basic steps:

1. Information gathering
2. Analysis and planning
3. Implementation of a solution
4. Assessment of the effectiveness of the solution
5. Documentation of the incident

In the following sections, we address each of these steps individually.

Information Gathering

Before we can determine how to address a problem—or even assess what the problem is—we must gather information. Doctors do it by asking questions of their patients, observing physical signs and symptoms, and conducting lab tests. Detectives do it by interviewing witnesses, personally examining the crime scene, and gathering evidence. Attorneys do it by taking depositions, researching the facts of the case, and studying prior court decisions.

An ISA Server administrator can gather information by observing the undesirable behavior of the software, questioning users who are experiencing problems, and using common tools and utilities to monitor the server's and network's activity (see Figure 26.1).

Figure 26.1 Information Gathering Can Take Many Forms

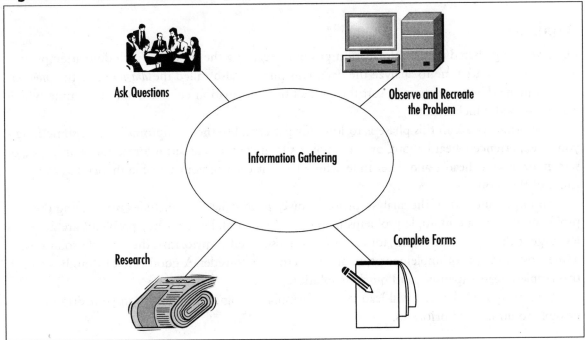

Log files comprise an important source of information you should consult during the data-gathering stage. Both the Windows Server logs (accessed via Event Viewer) and the ISA Server logs (by default, located in the ISA Server Installation folder, in the ISALogs subfolder) can provide valuable information and a starting point for troubleshooting problems. An example of an IP Packet Filter log is shown in Figure 26.2.

ISA logging can be configured for the Proxy Service, Firewall Service, and Web Proxy Service, in W3extended format or ISA Server format. Performance logs can also be useful in troubleshooting performance-related problems.

Figure 26.2 ISA Log Files Can Be Useful in Troubleshooting Various Problems

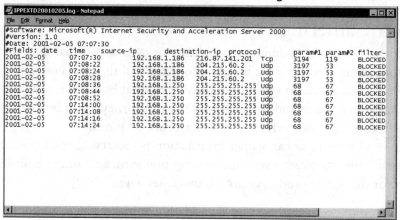

Analysis

Once you've gathered all the information possible regarding the problem (including attempting to reproduce it), it's time to analyze the data. This phase is also called the *diagnostic* or the *problem isolation* phase. The first step is to sort through all the information collected and determine which is relevant and which is not.

The primary task in this phase is to look for patterns. Do the "symptoms" match something you've experienced, heard about, or read about? Organize the relevant information—on paper, on screen, or in your head—and determine which facts fit each of your possible theories as to the cause of the problem.

An important part of the analysis phase involves *prioritizing*. This includes prioritizing the problems, if there are multiple problems (and often there are). Performance problems are generally less urgent than access problems, for example. You also need to prioritize the possible solutions. Time, cost, and ease of implementation are all factors to consider. A good rule of thumb is to try the simplest, least expensive, and quickest solutions first.

Your analysis of the data will lead you to formulate a logical *plan* based on your diagnoses, possible solutions, and priorities.

Solution Implementation

Although there could be several possible solutions to a problem, you should always implement *one change at a time*. Assess the results of that change before trying something else. This will save you much grief in the long run; there is nothing more frustrating than changing several different settings, discovering that the problem has been solved, and not knowing which of your actions solved it.

Assessment

This is also called the *follow-up* stage. It is vital that you assess the results of your actions and determine whether your "fix" worked, whether it was only a temporary workaround or actually solved the problem, whether it caused other problems while correcting the original one, and what can be done in the future to prevent the problem from recurring.

Documentation

After completing your assessment, you should develop a succinct summarization of the problem, which should include:

- The reported and observed symptoms of the problem
- Causation theories and the reasoning behind them
- Corrective actions taken
- Results of those actions
- Recommendations for prevention of a recurrence of the problem

This summarization should be in written form and kept in a permanent log. You might also want to distribute copies of the report to others, such as your superiors within the company, the affected users, other members of the IT department, and so forth. Documentation is a very important but often-overlooked step in the troubleshooting process.

ISA Server and Windows 2000 Diagnostic Tools

The Windows 2000 operating system and the ISA Server software include a number of tools and utilities that will help you gather information for troubleshooting purposes. These tools include:

- Event Viewer logs
- Performance Tool
- Network Monitor
- Various log files

In this section, we look briefly at the Event Viewer logs and the Network Monitor.

Event Viewer Logs

The Windows 2000 Event Viewer monitors application, security, and system events and records information to log files, which you can examine for clues to the causes of hardware and software problems. The Event Viewer is accessed via **Start | Programs | Administrative Tools | Event Viewer** or through the Computer Management MMC.

Three basic logs are available in the Event Viewer.

- The Application log contains information about events logged by programs (for example, ISA Server). Events logged by the application are determined by the developer of the application.

- The System log contains information about events that are logged by the Windows 2000 system components, such as driver failures, failure of a system service to load, and so forth.

- The Security log records security-related events. Auditing must be enabled in order for events to be logged to the Security log.

Depending on what other services you have installed on the Windows 2000 Server, there could be other logs in the Event Viewer (for example, the Directory Service log, DNS Server log, or the File Replication Service log).

The *event types* recorded depend on the log type. Event types are identified by special icons. For example, the Application log records three event types:

- **Error** Identified by a red circle with a white X, this event type indicates a significant problem that could result in loss of functionality or data.

- **Information** Identified by a white balloon with a blue *i*, this event type indicates successful completion of an operation.

- **Warning** Identified by a yellow triangle with a black exclamation point, this event type indicates a potential problem, although not as serious or imminent as events tagged as errors.

Events in the log are listed in the right detail pane of the Event Viewer. Additional information can be viewed in the event's Properties sheet, accessed by double-clicking the event. Each event is identified by an Event ID. In the Help files subsection of the next section, we discuss how to interpret ISA Server event IDs.

NOTE

When troubleshooting network problems, always start by checking the Event Viewer and other logs. In many cases, the information that will point you in the right direction is there waiting for you.

Network Monitor

The Windows 2000 Network Monitor is a built-in packet sniffer that can be used to capture and display frames (packets) that pass to or from the Windows 2000 server. Network Monitor can be invaluable in troubleshooting network-related problems.

The Network Monitor tool uses the Network Monitor driver to receive frames from a network adapter and display statistics relating to specified frames (which can be displayed according to protocol, sending/receiving computer, and other criteria).

Network Monitor's *capture filters* are configured by the administrator to specify the types of network information that should be monitored (for example, only the packets received from a particular IP address or using a specific protocol). Network Monitor's *display filters* allow you to sort data that has already been captured, to display only specified information.

Network Monitor can be used to view the packets that are sent to or from the ISA server. For example, you could monitor packets to determine what port is being used by a particular protocol or application.

NOTE

The version of Network Monitor included with Windows 2000 has limited functionality. It captures only frames sent to or from the computer on which Network Monitor is running, and it does not allow you to edit and transmit frames. Another version of Microsoft's Network Monitor provides these functions and will capture packets sent to and from all computers on the network segment. The full-featured version is included in Microsoft System Management Server (SMS).

ISA Server Troubleshooting Resources

As ISA Server is implemented on more and more networks, the amount of formal and informal documentation available is sure to increase. Meanwhile, there are already a number of resources (in addition to this book) to which you can turn when you need troubleshooting help. These include:

- ISA Server Help files

- Microsoft Tech Support

- Web resources

- Books and magazines

- Internet mailing lists and newsgroups

In the following sections, we discuss each of these resources in more detail.

ISA Server Help Files

The ISA Server Help files provide a wealth of information on both concepts and the how-to of configuration. The organization of the Help files makes them easy to navigate. You will find useful checklists to ensure that you don't omit important steps during installation, configuration, and other tasks. The "How To..." section guides you step by step through important procedures. In the "Concepts" section, you will find background information to help you understand how various ISA components operate and interoperate. Finally, a separate "Troubleshooting" section addresses specific reported problems and what to do about them (see Figure 26.3).

Figure 26.3 The ISA Server Help Files Contain a Special "Troubleshooting" Section

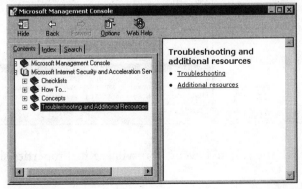

Under the "Additional Resources" heading in the Help files, you will find a glossary of terms relating to ISA Server. An especially important resource that is listed under "Additional Resources" is a list of event messages that will help you decipher those sometimes-mysterious ISA-related messages that appear in the Event Viewer logs.

Event messages are broken into the following categories:

- Alert event messages

- Bandwidth event messages

- Caching event messages

- Common service event messages

- Dial-up connection event messages

- Intrusion detection event messages

- ISA Server Control Service event messages

- ISA Server Firewall Service event messages

- ISA Server Web Proxy Service event messages

- Log event messages

- Packet filter event messages

- Server event messages

Within the categories, event messages are identified by the event ID. This ID number identifies the event type and is shown in the Event Properties sheet when you click the event (information, warning, or error) in the right pane of the Event Viewer in the Application log.

For example, in Figure 26.4, we can select an event from the right context pane. In this example, we have selected the Warning event recorded by the Microsoft Web Proxy Service at 3:01:46 P.M.

Figure 26.4 Select an Event from the Right Context Pane in the Application Log

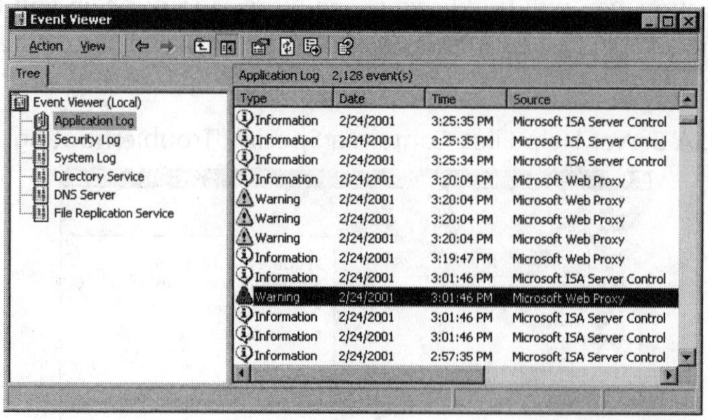

When you double-click the selected event, you will see its Properties sheet, as shown in Figure 26.5.

Figure 26.5 The Event's Properties Sheet Gives You a Great Deal of Information, Including the Event ID

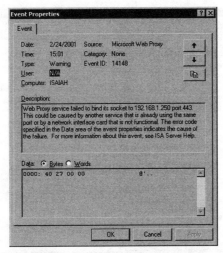

On the Properties sheet, you will see a summary of pertinent information about the event, including the date and time of occurrence, warning type, user or computer from which the event originated, source/service, category (if applicable), and the Event ID. There is also a description of the event, which refers you to the ISA Server Help file.

If we then go to the Help file and look under the event category (Web Proxy Service), we will find the ID (14148) in the list, as shown in Figure 26.6.

Figure 26.6 You Can Use the Event Category and ID to Locate the Event Message in the Help Files

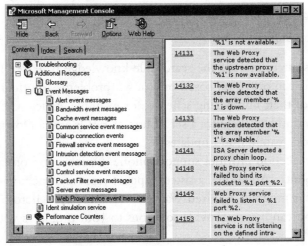

Clicking the Event ID will provide you with information about the event message, an explanation of the message, and suggested user action(s) to rectify the problem, as shown in Figure 26.7.

Figure 26.7 The Help File Provides Information about the Event Message, an Explanation, and Suggested User Action(s)

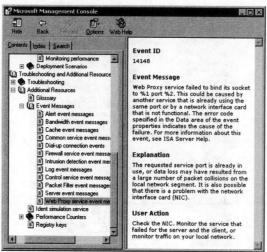

Another useful source of information included in the "Additional Resources" section is the list of all ISA performance counters and the descriptions and explanations of how each works. These are categorized according to the associated performance objects.

Finally, there is a list of Registry keys that can be modified to fine-tune ISA Server performance.

Microsoft Documentation and Technical Support

Microsoft provides a wealth of support resources on its Web site (http://support.microsoft.com/ directory), where you will find two categories of available support options:

- Self-support resources
- Assisted-support information

The self-support resources include the searchable knowledge base (see Figure 26.8), which provides technical support information based on known problems and their solutions (organized as "Q" articles because of their numbering scheme; for example, Article Q257218).

The self-support section also includes a set of lists of FAQs and a Download Center where you can find service packs, patches, and updates.

The assisted-support section provides support phone numbers and online support request forms for registered products. Additional assisted-support resources include the Microsoft Gold Certified Support Partner program, Expired Warranty options, and Microsoft Certified Partners (independent experts you can hire to provide solutions to your problems with Microsoft products).

NOTE

Professional support services do not come cheap. Telephone support from Microsoft costs $245 per incident if the product is not under warranty. Web-based support requests are $195 each. Pricing for certified partner support varies, ranging from $99 per incident and up.

Figure 26.8 The Searchable Knowledge Base Provides Technical Support Information and Self-Help Tools

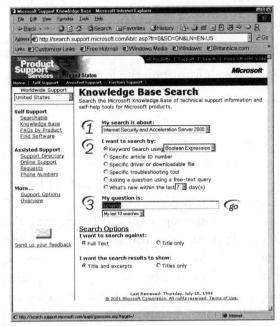

Premier and Alliance support packages are available to enterprise-level businesses. More information on these offerings can be found on the Microsoft Web site.

Another excellent source of support information is TechNet Online, at www.microsoft.com/technet. Here you will find security bulletins, planning and deployment guides, white papers, and announcements of upcoming professional and training events as well as evaluation kits for new software packages.

Microsoft maintains Web resources for each of its product lines. ISA Server is featured on its own Web site at www.microsoft.com/isaserver. Here you will find information and updates about ISA Server issues.

Third-Party Web Resources

Third-party Web sites can come and go, but a good search engine will turn up several sites that provide information on ISA Server or add-on products that work with it. One of the best third-party Web sites is www.isaserver.org. This site features current ISA Server-related news, tutorials and advice on deploying ISA Server, ISA Server FAQs, pointers to relevant articles and books, the newest bug fixes, white papers, and certification information. The site also provides message boards and instructions for joining an ISA Server discussion list (discussed in the "Internet Mailing Lists and Newsgroups" section of this chapter).

Books and Magazines

Specific issues (such as deploying ISA in a DMZ or perimeter network or configuring ISA servers in a chained hierarchy) could be the subject of articles in popular Windows 2000-oriented technical magazines. As the use of ISA Server becomes more widespread, you will see more information about it in both print publications and online "e-zines" and tech Web sites. Here are a few of the good online sources of technical articles on Microsoft products:

- **www.swynk.com** Microsoft-related articles and columns.

- **www.brainbuzz.com** IT career network, certification study aids, and IT resources.

- **www.techrepublic.com** Information site for IT professionals.

- **www.w2knews.com** The *Sunbelt Software W2K Electronic Newsletter*.

Internet Mailing Lists and Newsgroups

One of the most diverse sources of information for current and aspiring IT professionals is Internet mailing lists. There are literally hundreds of thousands of lists, powered by automated mailing list software such as Listserv, Majordomo, and Lyris, as well as those hosted through Web-based mailing list services such as Yahoogroups.com and Topica.com. There are mailing lists devoted to almost any IT (or other) topic imaginable, including ISA Server.

The premier ISA-specific mailing list is hosted by www.isaserver.org. It is a fairly high-volume list, membership is open, and list members share their experiences installing, configuring, and using ISA Server, posting their questions and problems and assisting one another with ISA-related issues.

Those who don't want to receive the large amount of mail generated by some mailing lists might find it more convenient to subscribe to Internet newsgroups. With a newsreader such as Outlook Express, you can subscribe to as many newsgroups as you like and read the messages only when you like. There are no mail messages to clutter up your inbox.

Microsoft hosts several public newsgroups devoted to discussions of ISA Server:

- ISA Server General Support group (microsoft.public.isa)

- ISA Server Enterprise (microsoft.public.isa.enterprise)

- ISA Server newsgroup (Microsoft.public.isaserver)

The newsgroups often generate a very high volume of posts. Most newsreaders allow you to sort posts by thread (subject line) to better organize the information, as shown in Figure 26.9.

Although Microsoft does not monitor the content of its public newsgroups, they are often populated by Microsoft Most Valuable Professionals (MVPs), who provide informal leadership.

Microsoft newsgroups can be downloaded from the msnews.microsoft.com news server. You can visit http://support.microsoft.com/default.aspx?scid=/support/news/howto/default.asp on the Web for information about how to view the newsgroups.

Figure 26.9 Microsoft's ISA Server Newsgroups Provide an Excellent Source of Troubleshooting Information

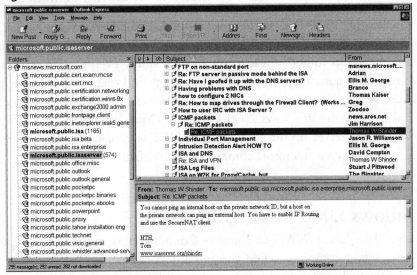

Troubleshooting ISA Server Installation and Configuration Problems

Installation of ISA Server usually proceeds in a straightforward fashion. Problems during or directly following installation are often related to one of three things:

- Hardware incompatibilities
- Software incompatibilities
- Improper initial configuration

Let's look briefly at each category in the following sections.

Hardware and Software Compatibility Problems

In most cases, ISA Server works with common hardware and software configurations. In some cases, however, hardware incompatibility causes a conflict or ISA does not run properly in conjunction with another software program that is installed on the server.

ISA Server Doesn't Meet Minimum System Requirements

In order for ISA Server to function properly, the computer on which it is installed must meet the minimum hardware specifications:

- Pentium II or compatible processor running at 300MHz or above
- A member of the Windows 2000 Server family with SP1 or later
- At least 192MB (256MB recommended) of RAM
- At least 20MB of free disk space

- At least one NTFS partition
- A Windows 2000-compatible NIC connected to the internal network

If you are installing ISA Server as an array member, Active Directory must be implemented on your network. In some cases, ISA could refuse to install if the proper hardware configuration is not present. In others, ISA might appear to install successfully, even though your machine does not meet the minimum requirements. However, you might find that unusual behavior results; for example, all ISA Server services might not start if you have an insufficient amount of RAM.

You should also check the Windows 2000 Hardware Compatibility List (HCL) prior to installing Windows 2000 Server on the machine. The HCL is available on the Microsoft Web site at the following location: www.microsoft.com/whdc/hcl/default.mspx.

ISA Server Exhibits Odd Behavior When Windows 2000 NAT Is Installed

If Network Address Translation (NAT) or Internet Connection Sharing (ICS) is being used on the Windows 2000 Server computer, when you install ISA Server, NAT/ICS will automatically be disabled. However, we have found that, in some cases, having NAT installed will cause continuing odd behavior on the part of the ISA server, resulting in intermittent loss of connectivity. The solution to this problem is to delete the NAT routing protocol from the **IP Routing** section of the RRAS console tree.

> **NOTE**
>
> ISA Server's address translation function is also incompatible with third-party NAT solutions such as Sygate or NAT32. You should install these programs from the Windows 2000 computer before installing ISA Server.

Internal Clients Are Unable to Access External Exchange Server

When you install ISA Server and your clients need to be able to use an external Exchange Server, you might find that using Outlook for e-mail does not work, although Web services function properly.

In this case, you need to add the IP address of the external Exchange Server to the LAT and install the firewall client software on the internal machines that are running Outlook. This will allow the clients' e-mail to go through.

Initial Configuration Problems

Many of the problems that occur following installation result from incorrect or incomplete configuration during the installation process or changes made to the ISA Server configuration following installation.

Unable to Renew DHCP Lease

You might find that, after upgrading from Microsoft Proxy Server or installing a fresh copy of ISA Server, you are unable to renew a lease from the DHCP Server using the *ipconfig /release* and *ipconfig /renew* commands. The only way to renew the lease is to reboot the server. This occurs even after adding a custom packet filter to allow UDP in both directions on local fixed port 68 and remote fixed port 67, as you might have done to solve this problem with Proxy Server.

> **NOTE**
>
> Knowing how ISA Server works—and how Windows 2000 services such as DHCP, with which it interacts, work—are the basis of solving problems of this type. For example, if you know that the lease is obtained before the packet filters are applied, you will understand why it is necessary to reboot the server to obtain a new DHCP lease.

The solution is to enable the DHCP client rule under Packet Filters, as shown in Figure 26.10. Once you enable the filter, you should be able to use the *ipconfig* switches to release and renew your DHCP lease.

Figure 26.10 Enable the DHCP Client Rule to Allow a Release and Renew of the DHCP Lease

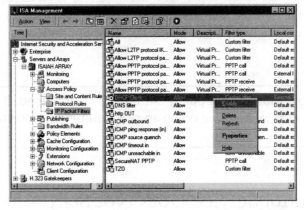

Failure of Services to Start After Completing Installation

For a couple of reasons, the ISA services might not start after installation has completed successfully. As always, check the Event Viewer for any relevant messages.

In some cases, we have noted that, if there is insufficient RAM in the server, the services might not start or might have to be started manually. Upgrading the physical memory will solve the problem if this is the cause.

If the LAT is not configured correctly and doesn't include the internal NIC (which communicates with Active Directory), the ISA Server services will not be able to start. In this case, you should first stop the ISA services (you can do this by typing **net stop mspfltext** at the command line) and then reconfigure the LAT using ISA Server Administration COM objects. An article in the ISA Server SDK, *Constructing the Local Address Table*, will instruct you in how to do this.

After you have added the appropriate entries to the LAT, you must reboot the ISA Server computer.

Inability to Join Array

You could find that it is possible to create a new array by right-clicking **Servers and Arrays** in the ISA Management MMC and selecting **New** and **Array**. This starts the New Array Wizard. You can enter a name, site, and domain location for the new array, and it will appear in the management console. However, when you install a new ISA server and attempt to join an array, you will not be able to join the new array you have created.

Our experience shows that during installation, you are given the option to join only those arrays that have at least one member. Because the array you created with the wizard contains no members, you cannot join it. You can create a new array during the installation of the first computer that will be a member of the new array, and then this array will be available to join when you install subsequent ISA servers.

Inability to Save LAT Entry

If you receive an error message: "ISA Server cannot save the properties. Error 0x80040340. The IP range already exists in the Local Address Table (LAT)," when you attempt to save a new LAT entry, this could be due to the fact that it is an exact duplicate of an already existing address.

It is possible to overlap IP ranges in the LAT. That is, a new entry can have either a "from" address or a "to" address that already exists in the LAT, but not both.

NOTE

Although Microsoft allows overlapping LAT entries as described, it is recommended that you *not* use such entries, because doing so can result in unpredictable behavior by the ISA server.

ISA Server Control Service Does Not Start

You could get the following error messages when you attempt to connect to an array in the ISA Management MMC:

```
ISA Error
The operation failed
Failed to connect
Error 0x8007203a
```

This happens when the LAT is not configured properly. If you have installed ISA Server Enterprise Edition as an array member and you include only the external interfaces in the LAT, the array will not be able to communicate with Active Directory on the internal Windows 2000 network. Array configuration information is stored in Active Directory when ISA Server is installed as an array member, and if ISA cannot contact Active Directory, it cannot determine its configuration.

The result is that the ISA Server Control (ISACTRL) service will not be able to start, and you will not be able to correct the LAT entries from any array member, because the ISA Management MMC will not display the current configuration.

This problem must be corrected from another computer or ISA array that is running the ISA Management MMC. The ISA management tools can be installed on any Windows 2000 computer (including Windows 2000 Professional) that is connected to the domain in which the ISA array resides.

Use the **Connect to** feature to connect to the array that has the misconfigured LAT. You will be able to access the configuration information that is stored in Active Directory and make the appropriate changes to the LAT. You need to restart the ISA servers in the array after you make the modifications to the LAT.

For detailed, step-by-step instructions and more information about this problem, see article Q282035 in the Microsoft Knowledge Base on the Microsoft Web site.

Troubleshooting Authentication and Access Problems

One of the purposes of ISA Server is to control unauthorized access; however, improper configuration or conflicts can result in the inability of authorized users to access the resources they need. In some cases, this could be due to authentication requirements and inability of clients to be authenticated; in other cases, it could be due to the ISA configuration, browser settings, or other reasons. In the following sections, we discuss some common authentication and access problems and what to do about them.

Authentication Problems

Authentication requirements depend on the client type making the request (firewall, Web proxy, or S-NAT) and whether rules have been configured that apply to specific users and groups. When a client makes a request for a Web object, authentication information is passed to the ISA server only if it is required, such as when the Web Proxy Service must identify the user in order for the request to be allowed.

With S-NAT clients, no authentication is involved (unless you are using the Web proxy client in conjunction with S-NAT). Only client address sets can be used to restrict outbound access.

> **NOTE**
>
> ISA Server can be configured to always require authentication for Web requests. To do so, you configure the array's **Outgoing Web Requests** properties by checking the option to ask unauthenticated users for identification.

HTTP requests that are made by firewall clients are treated as though they come from unauthenticated users if the filter to pass requests to the HTTP redirector is enabled. The ISA server will not ask for authentication information in this situation, so ISA is unable to pass the requests from unauthenticated users, and the request will be denied. A solution to this problem is to configure the Web proxy client.

User's HTTP Request Is Sometimes Allowed, Although a Site and Content Rule Denies Access

If you have configured a site and content rule that denies access to a specific user, you could find that the user's HTTP request is still allowed if the user's computer is set up as a Web proxy client and Web access is configured to allow anonymous access. If you have protocol rules that allow everyone to use all protocols, and you have site and content rules that allow everyone to access all sites, and you have an additional site and content rule that denies access to the specified user, the user might still be able to access the content.

If the computer is configured as a Web proxy client, no authentication will be required and the user will be allowed access.

If the computer is configured as a firewall client, the request will likewise be allowed because authentication will not be requested. (If non-HTTP content is requested, authentication will be required by the Firewall Service and the user's request will be denied.)

> **NOTE**
>
> Remember that access problems in general point to misconfiguration of permissions. This is true whether the problem is that users are unable to access resources to which they should have access or that users are being allowed to access resources that should be restricted.

If authentication is not requested, ISA Server will not know that this is the user who is supposed to be denied access. To make the rule that applies to the specific user work in these scenarios, configure the array to ask unauthenticated users for identification, as discussed previously.

Failure to Authenticate Users of Non-Microsoft Browsers

Users of Netscape or other non-Microsoft browsers might be unable to be authenticated by ISA Server. This happens because ISA can be configured to accept only Windows integrated authentication. If the client's browser cannot provide the user's credentials in NTLM format, those users will not be able to access the requested Web objects if authentication is required.

The supported authentication methods are configured in the array's incoming and outgoing Web request properties. In order to be authenticated, the client browsers must be able to use at least one of the authentication methods that ISA is configured to use.

To specify authentication methods, edit the listeners' properties, as shown in Figure 26.11.

Figure 26.11 The Authentication Method Is Configured Via the Listeners' Properties Sheet for Incoming and Outgoing Web Requests

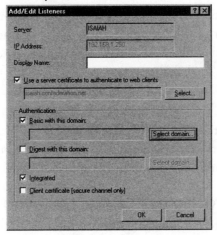

The following authentication methods can be used:

- Basic
- Digest
- Integrated Windows
- Client certificate

Microsoft Internet Explorer 5.*x* and later supports all of the preceding authentication methods. Some browsers might support only Basic or Digest authentication.

> **WARNING**
>
> Basic authentication transmits and receives the users' credentials as plain text. No encryption is used to protect the confidentiality of the information.

Error Message When Using Pass-Through Authentication with NTLM

Pass-through authentication could fail if you are attempting to use ISA pass-through authentication with NTLM authentication, using one of the following browsers:

- Microsoft Internet Explorer Versions 4.*x* or 5.*x* for Windows 95
- Microsoft Internet Explorer Versions 5.*x* for Windows 98 and 98 SE
- Microsoft Internet Explorer Versions 5.*x* for Windows 2000
- Microsoft Internet Explorer Versions 3.02, 4.*x*, and 5.*x* for Windows NT 4.0

This failure results in the following error message:

```
HTTP 401.2 unauthorized - Logon failed due to Authentication Failure Internet
Information Services
```

This is a problem identified with the Microsoft Internet Explorer browser software, which was corrected in MSIE version 5.5 with Service Pack 1. The solution is to install the latest version of MSIE, which you can download from the Microsoft Internet Explorer Web site at www.microsoft.com/windows/ie/default.asp.

Access Problems

Access problems include both the inability of authorized clients to access needed resources *and* the ability of unauthorized users to access resources that should not be available to them. Incorrect ISA Server configuration can result in both kinds of access problems.

Inability of Clients to Browse External Web Sites

When clients cannot access external Web sites, this can be related to one of two things:

- The ISA Server settings
- The client's browser settings

By default, ISA Server allows no communications to and from the Internet by internal clients. You must create rules to allow access. If you have just installed ISA Server and have not configured rules and your clients are unable to reach the external Web servers, this is normal ISA Server behavior. In this case, you can create protocol rules that will allow users (all users or selected users) to use the protocols and then create site and content rules to allow access to particular sites or all sites, using the protocols that are allowed by your protocol rules.

If the ISA Server settings are configured to allow client access and there is still a problem, it could be due to the client's browser settings. The proxy port must be set correctly (to 8080 if you are using the default port).

Problems with Specific Protocols or Protocol Definitions

If clients are unable to use specific protocols to communicate with the external network, you can allow the use of particular protocols in one of two ways:

- Configure IP packet filters to allow the protocols
- Configure protocol rules to allow the protocols

Protocol rules can be created to apply to all IP traffic, to only a specific set of protocol definitions, or to all *but* a selected set of protocols. A list of preconfigured commonly used protocol definitions is included with ISA Server, but you can also add protocol definitions.

> **NOTE**
>
> Protocol rules can only be applied to HTTP, Secure HTTP, Gopher, and FTP protocols when ISA Server is installed in caching mode.

Inability of Clients to PING External Hosts

A common complaint in regard to a new deployment of ISA Server is that internal clients are not able to ping computers on the external network. The *ping* command is often used to send an ICMP echo request message to a host on the Internet for the purpose of testing connectivity. By default, S-NAT clients do not pass ICMP messages between internal and external computers (a process called *ICMP proxying*).

To enable this feature, you must enable IP routing. Follow these steps:

1. In the ISA Server Management MMC, expand the array or server object node for the appropriate array or server.

2. Expand the **Access Policies** object.

3. Right-click **IP Packet Filters**.

4. Select **Properties**.

5. Switch to the **General** tab, and check the **Enable IP routing** check box.

In addition to having IP routing enabled, there must be a packet filter that allows ICMP packets to be transmitted and received by the external network interface. The default ISA Server installation package includes filters for outbound and inbound ICMP requests.

Redirection of URL Results in Loop Condition

A *redirection loop* can occur when URL redirection is specified in the site and content rules so that when you request the URL www.aaa.com, you are redirected to www.bbb.com, which in turns redirects you back to www.aaa.com, and so forth.

This can happen if the site and content rule you have created denies all destinations. When you select **Redirect the request to an alternate URL** and set the rule to apply to all requests, client browsers will continually try to reach the original destination and be redirected to the URL specified in the rule.

There are two ways to solve this problem:

- You can create a rule that denies all destinations *except* the destination to which you want to redirect the request.

- You can choose *not* to specify a URL to which requests will be redirected when you select **Redirect the request to an alternate URL**.

Ability of Clients to Continue Using a Specific Protocol After Disabling of Rule

You could find that even after you have disabled a protocol rule, clients are still using the protocol that was allowed by the rule. This happens because disabling a protocol rule does not terminate any of the existing client sessions. Until the session has been disconnected, clients can continue to use the protocol after you disable the rule.

Experienced administrators will recognize that this is the same thing that happens when you change the permissions on a file or folder; a user who is currently logged on must log off and log back on before the change applies, because the access token that specifies the users' permissions is issued at logon.

To solve this problem, you can disconnect the current client sessions that are using the protocol. To do so, expand the server or array name in the left console tree, expand the **Monitoring** object, and expand the **Sessions** object. Then, right-click the session that you want to disconnect and select **Abort Session**, as shown in Figure 26.12. Clients will not be able to use the protocols when they reconnect.

Figure 26.12 Disconnect the Sessions of Clients Who Are Using Protocols You Want to Disable

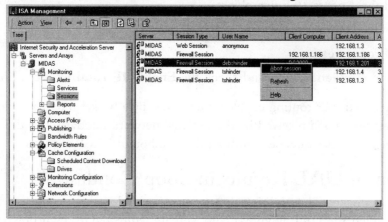

Dial-Up and VPN Problems

In the following sections, we look at some common troubleshooting scenarios that involve dial-up and VPN connections.

Inability of ISA Server to Dial Out to the Internet

If the ISA server is not able to dial out to connect to the ISP, but you can dial out manually, you should check the dial-up entry's credentials. If the incorrect username and password are entered (or if the credentials are not specified), the ISP's dial-up server will not authenticate the connection and it will disconnect before a logon is established.

The properties for the dial-up entry can be edited by expanding the server or array name in the left console pane, expanding **Policy Elements**, and selecting **Dialup Entries**. In the right detail pane, right-click the dial-up entry you want to edit, and select **Properties**.

Dial-Up Connection Is Dropped

A dial-up connection can be dropped because it was inadvertently disconnected. If you restart the ISA Server services, the connection should be automatically reestablished.

To restart the ISA Server services, expand the name of the server or array in the left console pane of the ISA Management MMC, expand **Monitoring**, and select **Services**. Right-click the service that you want to restart, and select **Start**.

Inability of PPTP Clients to Connect Through ISA Server

If internal clients are unable to create PPTP tunnels to a destination on an external network (on the other side of the ISA server), this could be due to the fact that you have not configured a PPTP pass-through in the ISA Management MMC. By default, this option is *not* configured.

To allow your internal clients to create PPTP connections through the ISA server, you need to do the following:

1. In the ISA Management MMC left console pane, expand **Access Policy** under the server or array name.

2. Right-click **Packet Filters**, and select **Properties**.

3. Ensure that **Enable IP Routing** is checked on the **General** tab.

4. On the **PPTP** tab, check the **PPTP through ISA firewall** check box.

PPTP sessions can now be established through the ISA server by S-NAT clients. Note that you cannot establish PPTP connections using the firewall client.

This is a very common problem and a good example of where one little check box can make all the difference.

Troubleshooting ISA Client Problems

Many ISA-related problems, even if they result from misconfiguration on the server side, manifest themselves on the client side. In the following sections, we discuss some common client problems and how you can resolve them. These problems include:

- Client performance problems
- Client connection problems

Client Performance Problems

Performance problems at the client end are often caused by configuration problems on the ISA server. The origin of the slow client connections might vary, depending on the client type. In the next sections, we look at possible causes and fixes for slow client connections involving SecureNAT clients and firewall clients.

Slow Client Connection: SecureNAT Clients

If Secure NAT (S-NAT) connections are slow, the cause could be the result of not enabling packet filtering.

You can solve this problem by enabling IP packet filtering. If IP routing is enabled (either in RRAS or in the ISA console), you should enable dynamic packet filtering.

> **NOTE**
>
> You will see the terms *IP routing* and *IP forwarding* used interchangeably in Microsoft and other documentation and even in different dialog boxes on Microsoft products. The meanings of the two terms are the same.

To enable packet filtering, expand the name of the server or array in the left console pane of the ISA Management MMC, expand **Access Policy**, and right-click **IP Packet Filters**; select **Properties**. Check the **Enable packet filtering** check box on the **General** tab of the Properties sheet. To enable IP routing, check the **Enable IP routing** check box on the same sheet, as shown in Figure 26.13.

Figure 26.13 You Can Enable IP Packet Filtering and IP Routing to Improve S-NAT Performance

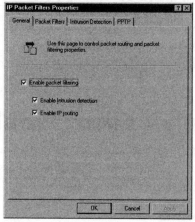

Note that if IP routing is enabled via the Windows 2000 RRAS console on the ISA server, IP forwarding will be enabled, even if the check box on the Packet Filters Properties sheet is unchecked.

Slow Internal Connections: Firewall Clients

If the internal connections are inordinately slow for firewall clients, it might be due to the fact that clients cannot resolve local names using an external DNS server that does not have the necessary records. When the client sends requests to the DNS server, it must wait for the requests to time out before attempting to resolve the names using some other method.

The solution is to configure an internal DNS server that has records for the names and addresses of all clients on the internal network. The clients using the Firewall Service should be configured with a DNS address; all client name resolution requests will be handled by the ISA Server computer, and clients will not be delayed by waiting for a response from a DNS server that cannot resolve the internal names.

If packet filtering is enabled, you should also create an IP packet filter to use DNS Lookup. This will allow the ISA server to send DNS queries for names of external hosts on the Internet. Note that if you are using internal DNS servers that are configured as forwarders, this might not be necessary.

Client Connection Problems

Client connection problems can take many forms. The inability of clients to connect can be caused by a variety of circumstances, including misconfiguration of the client or of the ISA server. In the following sections, we look at several scenarios in which clients are unable to connect, including:

- Inability of clients to connect via modem

- Inability of SecureNAT clients to connect to the Internet

- Inability of clients to connect to external SSL sites

- Inability of SecureNAT clients to connect using computer names

- Inability of SecureNAT clients to connect to specific port due to a timeout

Inability of Clients to Connect Via Modem

Client machines running the firewall client software cannot dial out directly to the Internet; this is a security feature.

To solve this problem, you must disable the firewall client. To do so, in **Start | Settings | Control Panel**, open the Firewall Client applet (shown in Figure 26.14). Uncheck the **Enable Firewall Client** check box to allow the client to dial out directly via the modem.

Figure 26.14 Disable the Firewall Client to Allow Direct Dial-Out from the Machine

Inability of SecureNAT Clients to Connect to the Internet

SecureNAT clients will not be able to connect to the Internet through the ISA server if the client is not properly configured with the default gateway and DNS server. Check the configuration settings in the client's TCP/IP properties.

Inability of Clients to Connect to External SSL Sites

If a client attempts to connect to a secure site via the Web Proxy Service, the data must be encrypted end to end. This means that ISA Server must create an SSL tunnel for the traffic to pass through. Because ISA Server only allows tunnel connections on ports 443 and 563 by default, if a client tries to connect to a secure site using a different port, the connection attempt will fail.

The solution is to modify the ISA Administration COM object to allow tunneling on additional ports. The correct object to be modified is FPCTunnelPortRange. A sample VBScript for adding ports to the tunnel port range is available in the ISA SDK.

Instructions on how to modify the COM objects are available in the ISA Server SDK Help files. To access the Help files, run **help.cmd** in the **sdk** folder on the ISA Server CD-ROM.

Component Object Model (COM) is an object-oriented programming architecture and includes a set of operating system services. COM is intended by Microsoft to allow developers to create applications in a modular, building-block process. New programs can be built by reusing existing components. Distributed COM (DCOM) adds interfaces to distribute various components of an application to different computers in a network.

The Administration COM objects in ISA Server can be used by developers working with any programming language that supports COM. Some of the objects are used for programmatic monitoring of currently running services; most are used for programmatic configuration of internal ISA settings.

Developers can extend ISA's functionality by using scripting to access and control ISA via the administration COM objects. The ISA Server SDK contains instructions on using the administration objects with Visual Basic and with C++.

Inability of SecureNAT Clients to Connect Using Computer Names

If an S-NAT client can connect to Internet sites using the IP address but is not able to connect using the "friendly" computer name, this is likely due to the fact that the client is configured to use an internal DNS server, which cannot resolve external Internet domain names.

The best solution is to configure the DNS server to forward requests to an external DNS server on the Internet. Another solution is to configure the clients to use a different DNS server that forwards name resolution requests to an external DNS server.

Inability of SecureNAT Clients to Connect to Specific Port Due to a Timeout

S-NAT clients could experience an inability to connect to specific ports because the connection times out, even though protocol rules are set to allow "any IP traffic."

This problem can occur if the application that is attempting to connect uses multiple ports. The solution in this case, if some of the ports are determined dynamically, is to use an application filter that specifies and defines the ports.

If the application does not use multiple ports, the problem might be that the protocol is not listed in the protocol definitions. In this case, you need to define a protocol in which the specific port is the primary port.

NOTE

You cannot edit protocol definitions that are installed with application filters (they can be deleted). You can neither modify nor delete protocol definitions included with ISA Server. You can edit protocol definitions that you have created (in other words, user-defined protocol definitions).

To create a new protocol definition, right-click **Protocol Definitions** in the left console pane of the ISA Management MMC, under the **Policy Elements** object for either the array or the enterprise. Select **New** and **Protocol Definition**. This invokes the Protocol Definition Wizard, which walks you through the steps. Specify the port (along with the protocol type and direction) for the primary connection on the **Primary Connection Information** page of the wizard.

Troubleshooting Caching and Publishing Problems

In this section, we examine some common problems involving two important ISA Server functions: caching and publishing.

Caching Problems

When ISA Server is installed in caching or integrated mode, it caches objects to accelerate client access. In some cases, you might encounter problems with the caching function. In this section, we look at some common cache-related problems.

All Web Objects Not Being Cached

You might find that client access to Internet objects does not seem to enjoy any noticeable improvement with ISA Server. This could be due to the fact that your clients are commonly requesting objects that are not in the cache. ISA Server caches only the objects that meet the caching criteria you have configured.

The solution could be to adjust the cache content specifications. You can determine which HTTP objects will be cached according to several factors. To configure which content should or should not be cached, right-click **Cache Configuration** in the left console pane of the ISA Management MMC under the name of the server or array. Select **Properties**.

Select the **Advanced** tab of the Properties sheet, shown in Figure 26.15. You can make adjustments here that result in caching of more (or fewer) objects.

Figure 26.15 You Can Configure Which Content Will Be Cached Using the Cache Configuration Properties Sheet

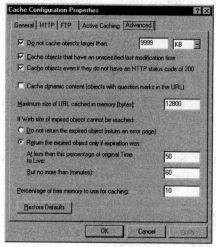

Web Proxy Service Does Not Start

If the Web Proxy Service will not start, this can be due to the fact that the cache contents file has become corrupted. The cache file is stored on a drive on which space has been allocated for this purpose. To correct this problem, you might need to reconfigure the cache drive(s). Remember that the cache drive(s) must be formatted in NTFS.

Publishing Problems

Publishing makes servers on the internal network available to users outside the LAN (on the other side of the ISA server). Publishing problems can involve the inability of authorized clients to access the published servers.

In this section, we look at some specific scenarios that involve publishing problems and how you can correct them.

Inability of Clients to Access Published Web Server

If clients are unable to access a published Web server and they receive a 403 ("Access Forbidden") error, this could be due to the fact that an access policy requires authentication. If no authentication method is configured for the listener, clients will not be able to authenticate, and thus access will be explicitly denied.

The solution is to configure one or more authentication methods for the listener. Clients' browsers will have to support one of the configured authentication methods in order to be authenticated. Authentication methods are configured on the **Incoming Web Requests** and **Outgoing Web Requests** tabs of the array's Properties sheet, as described earlier in this chapter.

Some of the more commonly encountered HTTP error codes include:

- **302** Redirection to a new URL. The resource has moved and the new URL is presented.

- **400** Bad request. The server did not understand the URL entered due to incorrect syntax.

- **401** Unauthorized. The user requested a document and did not provide authentication credentials.

- **403** Forbidden. Access is explicitly denied.

- **404** Not found. The document does not exist on this server.

- **500** Internal server error. The system administrator should check the error log.

- **8181** Certificate has expired (secure servers).

An HTTP 200 code indicates a successful transmission. All codes in the 3*xx* range indicate redirection messages; those in the 4*xx* range indicate client errors of some type; those in the 5*xx* range indicate server errors of some type. Messages in 1*xx* range are informational (for example, 101: switching protocols).

Inability of External Clients to Send E-Mail Via Exchange Server

If you have external clients who need to send e-mail via an internal Exchange Server and they are unable to do so, the cause and solution could depend on how the Exchange Server is set up, either as a firewall client or a SecureNAT client.

Exchange Server Set Up as Firewall Client

If the Exchange Server is a firewall client, there could be a conflict between a server publishing rule and a firewall client configuration file.

The solution is to remove the Wspclnt.ini file from the publishing server and run the Mail Server Security Wizard. The wizard allows you to host and secure a mail server behind the ISA server and easily configures ISA rules to publish the mail services to the external users.

To run the wizard, right-click **Server publishing rules** under the **Publishing** object for the server or array. Select **Secure Mail Server**, as shown in Figure 26.16.

Figure 26.16 Use the Secure Mail Server Option to Publish a Mail Server to External Clients

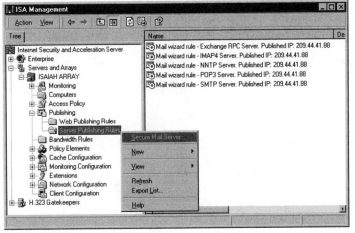

Another cause of this problem is the inability of the Exchange server to bind to the SMTP port on the ISA server due to another local or service or application on the ISA server that is binding to port 25 before the Exchange server has a chance to do so. Ensure that no other services or applications are using port 25 on the ISA server.

NOTE

If the connection between the ISA server and the Exchange server is broken momentarily, you need to restart the Exchange services in order for the Exchange server to bind to the appropriate ports on the ISA server.

Exchange Server Set Up as SecureNAT Client

If the Exchange server is a S-NAT client, this problem can be caused by incorrect configuration of the server publishing rules. The solution is to see that the publishing rules are configured to allow the external interface to pass SMTP traffic on port 25 and POP3 traffic on port 110 to the IP address and port of the internal Exchange server.

You should also check to ensure that the publishing rule is configured to apply to all Internet clients or that a client address set is specified that includes the addresses of the clients who need to use the server. Note that IP packet filtering must be enabled in order to use client address sets; if IP packet filtering is not enabled, the rule will apply to all clients.

Summary

In this chapter, we provided you with some guidelines to help you establish a troubleshooting "style" and routine that works for you. We discussed the common procedure that is most effective in approaching any problem-solving situation, in which you first gather information, then analyze the data and come up with possible "diagnoses" or causes, and then implement a solution and assess the success or failure of your actions (and if necessary, repeat the steps). Finally, you should fully document the incident to preserve what you learned from it for your own and for others' future reference.

We discussed some of the many resources that are available to help you solve problems involving ISA Server and the Windows 2000 Server operating system on which it runs. You learned about formal technical support venues; official and unofficial Web sites; where to find useful books, magazines, and online articles; and how to use mailing lists and newsgroups to cut down on the time spent "reinventing the wheel."

Next, we approached a sampling of real-life troubleshooting scenarios based on commonly reported ISA Server-related problems. You learned how to implement solutions to address problems involving ISA installation and configuration, authentication and access, client configuration, caching, publishing, and services.

## Chapter 27

Advanced Server Publishing with ISA Server

Best Damn Topics in this Chapter:

- Disabling Socket Pooling

- Server Publishing

- Web Publishing

Introduction

ISA Server allows you to control what internal network clients can access on the Internet and what external, Internet-based clients can access on the internal network. You are "publishing" servers when you configure the ISA server to allow external network clients access to resources on the internal network. ISA Server supports two types of publishing:

- Web publishing
- Server publishing

Web publishing rules publish HTTP and FTP servers located on the internal network, and give you the ability to do the following:

- Publish multiple Web servers using a single IP address on the external interface of the ISA server.

- Use an Incoming Web Requests listener to accept inbound HTTP requests.

- Authenticate with the ISA server at the Incoming Web Requests listener using basic, integrated, digest, or certificate authentication.

- Perform port redirection. Only the Web Proxy service can accept requests on a specific port on the external interface of the ISA server and forward it to an alternate port on an internal server.

- Examine the HTTP header and make decisions on how to redirect the request based on the destination URL.

- Bridge Secure Sockets Layer (SSL) requests as HTTP requests. This reduces processing overhead on the internal Web server and allows the ISA server to handle the SSL processing.

- Bridge SSL requests as SSL requests. This allows the ISA server to terminate an SSL connection on its external interface and then create a second SSL connection between its internal interface and the Web server on the internal network

- Extend the security features provided by the Web Proxy service by installing Web filters. Even the URLScan ISAPI filter can be installed on the ISA server to improve security for your Web publishing rules.

To get a better idea of how Web publishing rules work, consider the following scenario:

You have an ISA server with a single public IP address assigned to its external interface. You want to publish three Web servers on the internal network using one external network IP address. You also want to use the same public fully qualified domain name (FQDN) that users will type in to access the three servers on the internal network. The only difference is that the users will use a different path in the URL to access the servers; for example, /catalog, /specs, and /orders.

Note in this example that we used the path to determine what server the incoming request was redirected to. This is a very handy feature, but one limitation is that the request is redirected to the *same folder on the server on the internal network*. What you cannot do is have an incoming request to http://www.mydomain.com/server1 and redirect that request to http://server1. You can redirect to different servers based on the path, but you *cannot redirect to an alternate path*. This was something you could do with Proxy Server 2.0, but that functionality is not included with ISA Server.

Another feature of Web publishing rules is that requests handled by Web publishing rules pass the IP address of the internal interface of the ISA server to the internal Web server. The original IP address in the incoming client request is *not* included. The internal Web server's log files show all requests coming from the internal interface of the ISA server. This might create some problems for you if you want or need to analyze the Web server's log files for traffic patterns. You'll have to extract the information from the ISA server's Web Proxy logs.

NOTE

The only way you can get the original source IP address in the Web server's log files is to use server publishing rules. There is no way to pass the original source IP address to the internal Web server if you use Web publishing rules. There are a number of log analyzers you can run against the Web Proxy log that can assist you in site analysis. Check them out at www.isaserver.org/software/ISA/Reporting/.

Server publishing rules allow you to publish almost any type of server. However, server publishing rules lack the power and flexibility of Web publishing rules because a server publishing rule is essentially a reverse NAT mapping. Unlike Web publishing rules, server publishing rules do not have a service such as the Web Proxy service to examine application layer headers. Server publishing rules give you the ability to do the following:

- Map an IP address and port number on the external interface of the ISA server to an IP address on the *same* port number on an internal network server.

- Publish any protocol that has a primary connection as inbound. Server publishing rules use protocol definitions found in the **Protocol Definitions** node in the **ISA Server Management** console.

- Use client address sets to control what IP addresses on the external network can access a server publishing rule. For example, you can publish a Terminal Server on the internal network and allow only the IP address of your home computer access to that server publishing rule.

- Use "smart" application-layer filters that examine the application layer data as it moves through the ISA server. These application-layer filters perform a variety of functions to provide better security.

While server publishing rules do not automatically take advantage of application-layer data analysis, they will leverage the features of a number of application filters included with ISA Server. For example, you can publish SMTP, DNS, and POP3 servers on the internal network and have them protected against buffer overflows by enabling the SMTP, DNS, and POP3 application filters, respectively. The SMTP application filter can even go one step further and be used in conjunction with the SMTP message screener to filter out spam. The ISA Server SMTP Message Screener further extends the examination of the application-layer data by reviewing e-mail message content and blocking messages based on rules that you configure.

Server publishing rules can use application filters to help them publish complex protocols. A complex protocol is any protocol requiring one or more secondary connections. Only Firewall clients can use complex protocols. This creates a problem for servers published via server publishing rules because these servers need to be configured as SecureNAT clients. ISA Server comes with the FTP Access application filter, which allows you to publish FTP servers, even though these servers are configured as SecureNAT clients. Since FTP servers require secondary connections, the FTP access application filter manages the connection for the FTP server (which is configured as a SecureNAT client) on the internal network.

Server publishing rules allow you to publish almost any protocol, although you might have to create your own application filter to support servers requiring complex protocols. Another advantage that server publishing rules have over Web publishing rules is that you can record the actual source IP address in the publishing server's logs. The ISA server does not replace the source IP address when passing packets via server publishing rules.

> **NOTE**
>
> Some people refer to the situation in which the ISA server does not replace the source IP address in the packet as "half NAT." You can configure the ISA server to perform a "full NAT" and replace the source IP address with the IP address of the internal interface of the ISA server. This might be a preferred configuration when you want to avoid changing your network infrastructure just to support publishing servers. When you enable "full NAT," the only route required is one that allows the publishing server access to the network ID on which the internal interface of the ISA server is located. This allows you to avoid configuring a default gateway on the publishing server that routes packets to the Internet. Since the publishing server will not be responding to an Internet address, it will be responding to an internal network address (the address of the internal interface of the ISA server).

How do server publishing rules work? The ISA server's external IP address on TCP port 25 receives an incoming packet. The ISA server checks to see if there is a server publishing rule that matches packets arriving on the ISA server's external interface. If there is, the ISA server forwards the request to the internal network IP address listed in the server publishing rule.

Server publishing rules work well if there is only one server on the internal network that you want to publish for a particular service. For example, we have a single IP address on the external interface of the ISA server and we publish a single SMTP server on the internal network. This works without any problems. However, what if we have two SMTP servers on the internal network and we want to publish them both? You can do this, but not with a single IP address on the external interface of the ISA server. Unlike the situation with the Web Proxy service and its Web publishing rules, you cannot publish the *same service multiple times* using a single IP address on the external interface of the ISA server.

Publishing the same service multiple times with a single IP address on the external interface creates *port contention*. The ISA server realizes this and does not let you create two rules publishing the same service on the same external IP address. While the ISA server knows that you're trying to use the same socket twice on the external interface when you try to create two server publishing rules, you can still have problems with port contention if you run other services on the ISA server that listen on the same port as the service you want to publish.

Port contention created by non-ISA services on the ISA server is a common problem. This might happen if you are running any of the Internet Information Server (IIS) services on the ISA Server machine and then try to publish the same service located on an internal network server. You'll encounter the same problem if you try to publish Terminal Services and the Terminal server is running on the ISA server, or if you have Exchange 2000 installed on the ISA server and try to publish IMAP or POP3 services on the internal network (or even when those services are located on the ISA server itself).

Because port contention is a common problem for both Web and server publishing rules, let's look at how to handle the most common reason for this problem: IIS socket pooling. After you learn how to disable socket pooling, we'll get down to the details of publishing various services on the internal network using Web and server publishing rules.

Disabling Socket Pooling

Socket pooling is an IIS feature that allows IIS services to listen on all interfaces, regardless of the IP address you set the service to listen on. Socket pooling doesn't pose a problem for a unihomed server on the internal network. In fact, socket pooling helps to improve IIS performance by allowing all of the IP addresses on the server to share the same set of sockets, which can significantly reduce resource consumption by the services. The problem is that socket pooling is not a good thing when the server is connected to multiple networks and not all of those networks are trusted. This is exactly the situation we usually have with a multihomed ISA server.

The following IIS and Exchange services implement socket pooling:

- The IIS Web Publishing Service (W3SVC)
- The IIS FTP Publishing Service (MSFTPSVC)
- The IIS Simple Mail Transport Protocol (SMTP) Service (SMTPSVC)
- The IIS Network News Transport Protocol (NNTP) Service (NNTPSVC)
- The Exchange 2000 Post Office Protocol (POP3) Service (POP3SVC)
- The Exchange 2000 Internet Mail Access Protocol 4 (IMAP4) Service (IMAP4SVC)

If you run any of these services on the ISA Server machine, you should always disable socket pooling for that service and configure it to listen *only* on the ISA server's internal interface. Alternately, you can disable IIS services on the ISA.

> **NOTE**
>
> We recommend that you disable the IIS services on the ISA server. When properly config-
> ured, the ISA Server Firewall and Web Proxy services confer a high level of security
> against external network attacks. Adding services to the ISA server creates portals of
> attack that Internet criminals can use to compromise the ISA server and the internal net-
> work. Well-known exploits can be aimed against any of the IIS services and potentially
> disable security provided by the ISA Server software or create a denial-of-service (DoS)
> condition. The IIS Web Publishing Service is especially problematic in this regard.
> Although we will spend quite a bit of time discussing methods you can use to publish
> services on the ISA server itself, never do so unless budgetary constraints prevent you
> from purchasing a dedicated ISA Server computer. You obtain a level of security based
> on how much money you can spend.

How do you know if socket pooling is enabled on the ISA server? You can you the
netstat –na command to list all the active listening ports. Note that just because a port is listening doesn't mean that anyone can connect to it. If you enabled packet filtering on the ISA
server, none of the listeners on the external interface are available unless you explicitly create a
publishing rule or packet filter allowing access to the socket (a socket is a combination of a TCP
or UDP port number and an IP address).

Figure 27.1 shows the results of a **netstat –na** before disabling socket pooling. Notice in the
Local Address column the entries for IP address 0.0.0.0. Those entries indicate that the associated
port is listening on *all* IP addresses. A large number of services are listening on all IP addresses.
We need to disable socket pooling to prevent the server from listening on TCP ports 21 (FTP),
25 (SMTP), 80 (HTTP), and 119 (NNTP) for all interfaces.

Note that TCP 42 (WINS) and UDP 53 (DNS Query) are also listening on all interfaces.
The TCP 42 entry indicates that a WINS server is installed on this ISA server (something that we
should disable before bringing the server into production), and UDP 53 indicates that a DNS
server is installed on this machine. There aren't any contraindications to running a DNS server on
the ISA server, but you should configure the DNS service to listen on the internal interface only.
You can change the DNS service's listening address in the server's **Properties** dialog box in the
DNS console.

Figure 27.1 Results of netstat –na Before Disabling Socket Pooling

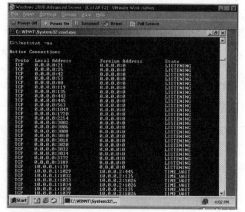

Disabling Web and FTP Service Socket Pooling

W3SVC and FTP service socket pooling is disabled using the same method. The only difference is the service name you enter in the command line. Perform the following steps to disable FTP and/or Web service socket pooling:

1. Open a **command prompt** and navigate to the **\Inetpub\Adminscripts** folder.

2. Type **net stop msftpsvc** and press **Enter**. Type **net stop w3svc** and press **Enter**.

3. Type in the following command: **cscript adsutil.vbs set msftpsvc/ disablesocketpooling true** (to disable FTP service socket pooling) or **cscript adsutil.vbs set w3svc/disablesocketpooling true** (to disable W3SVC service socket pooling), and then press **Enter**.

4. You should see what appears in Figure 27.2.

5. Restart the W3SVC by running **net start w3svc** at the command prompt. Restart the FTP service by running **net start MSFTPSVC** at the command prompt.

Figure 27.2 Disabling Socket Pooling

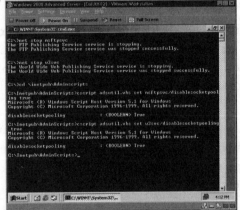

If you run a **netstat –na** again after disabling Web and FTP socket pooling, you'll see that they are still listening on *all IP addresses*. The reason for this is that the default setting for the built-in FTP and Web sites is to listen on all addresses. Keep in mind that a service can still listen on all IP addresses even if socket pooling is disabled. The difference is that after you disable socket pooling, you then have the option to configure the service to listen on only one IP address. You'll see the services listen only on the address you configure in the IIS console after you go into the IIS console and configure the sites to listen on the internal interface's address.

Figure 27.3 shows what you see after disabling socket pooling for FTP and WWW services, and what happens after configuring the services to use a specific IP address on the internal interface. Notice that immediately after disabling socket pooling, the FTP and Web services continue to listen on 0.0.0.0. You then see that both the FTP and Web services listen on 10.0.0.1 after configuring them to do so in the **Internet Information Services** console.

Figure 27.3 Running netstat –na After Disabling Socket Pooling

Disabling SMTP and NNTP Service Socket Pooling

You have to use a technique other than the one just discussed to disable socket pooling for the SMTP and NNTP services—why is unclear. In fact, no one seems to have any idea! We won't let this lack of understanding prevent us from disabling socket pooling for these services.

The first thing you need to do is get the **mdutil.exe** utility. You might be able to find it somewhere on the Microsoft Web site, but you'll always be able to download it at ftp:// ftp.tacteam.net/isaserver/mdutil.exe. Perform the following steps after downloading the **mdutil.exe** utility:

1. Put the **Mdutil.exe** executable in the **\Inetpub\Adminscripts** folder.

2. Open a **command prompt** window, change the focus to **\Inetpub\Adminscripts**, and run the following commands (Figure 27.4):

    ■ **mdutil set –path smtpsvc/1 –value 1 –dtype 1 –prop 1029 –attrib 1** (for the SMTP service)

    ■ **mdutil set –path nntpsvc/1 –value 1 –dtype 1 –prop 1029 –attrib 1** (for the NNTP service)

3. You will need to run these commands multiple times if you have more than one SMTP or NNTP virtual server. The difference is that you increment the value in **nntpsvc/1** and **smtpsvc/1** to the next higher value. If you have two SMTP and NNTP virtual servers, the second time you run the commands you would include **nntpsvc/2** and **smtpsvc/2**.

4. Go to the **Internet Information Services** console, right-click on the **Default SMTP Virtual Server**, and click **Properties**. Change the listening address to the internal interface of the ISA server. Do the same for the NNTP service so that it listens only on the internal IP address.

Figure 27.4 Disabling SMTP and NNTP Socket Pooling

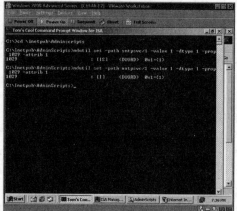

Disabling IIS Services on the ISA Server

Disabling socket pooling handles the port contention problem, but the real solution is to disable IIS services on the ISA server. We can't emphasize strongly enough how important it is to avoid running IIS services on the ISA server. In addition to increasing your security risks by running the IIS services, one of the most common reasons why publishing rules fail is that the ISA Server administrator has failed to disable socket pooling or the IIS services entirely. Even after almost two years and several hundreds of ISA Server installations, we continue to forget to disable IIS services on the ISA server. It's only after the publishing rules fail that we realize our error!

At one time, we recommended that you uninstall IIS from the ISA Server computer. While this fixes the IIS services problems, it introduces another. There have been several reliable reports of problems installing and uninstalling ISA Server after uninstalling IIS. The only way to install or uninstall ISA Server is to reinstall IIS. There is no compelling reason to uninstall IIS; all you need to do is disable the IIS services.

Perform the following steps to disable the IIS services:

1. Open the **Services** console from the **Administrative Tools** menu.

2. Double-click on the **FTP Publishing Service** in the right pane of the **Services** console.

3. In the **FTP Publishing Services Properties (Local Computer)** dialog box, change the **Startup** type to **Manual**. You'll still be able to start the service without having to restart the server. If you set the **Startup** type to **Disabled**, you will have to change the **Startup** type to **Automatic** or **Manual** and then restart the server to start up the service.

4. Click **Stop** to stop the service. Click **Apply**, and then click **OK**.

5. Repeat these steps with the NNTP, SMTP, and WWW publishing services.

You do not need to restart the ISA server for these changes to take effect.

Server Publishing

Server publishing rules allow you to publish almost any type of server protocol. As noted earlier, server publishing rules essentially perform a reverse NAT that allows the ISA server to accept packets on a certain IP address and port number and forward them to the same port number to an IP address on the internal network. While server publishing rules do not allow the ISA server to examine the data portion of the communication on their own, "smart" application filters can be applied to protect communications forwarded by server publishing rules.

In this section, look at how to publish the following services:

- Terminal Services
- Terminal Services Advanced Client (TSAC) Sites
- FTP Servers
- HTTP and HTTPS Servers
- VNC Servers
- pcAnywhere Servers

Publishing Terminal Services on the Internal Network

Publishing a Terminal server on the internal network is relatively straightforward. All you need is a protocol definition with Primary Connection set for Inbound TCP 3389, and a server publishing rule that uses this protocol definition. The only thing that can interfere with Terminal Server publishing rules is port contention. The best way to eliminate the Terminal Services port contention is to disable Terminal Services on the ISA server. However, most of us want to run Terminal Services on the ISA server to ease server administration, so we'll go over how to run Terminal Services on the ISA server and publish an internal network Terminal server at the same time later in this chapter.

Let's begin with how to publish Terminal Services on an internal network server when Terminal Services is not running on the ISA server. Perform the following steps to publish a Terminal server:

1. Open the **ISA Management** console. Expand your server name and then expand the **Policy Elements** node.

2. Right-click on the **Protocol Definitions** node, point to **New**, and click **Definition**.

3. On the Welcome to the New Protocol Definition Wizard page, type **RDP Server** for the **Protocol Definition name** and click **Next**.

4. On the Primary Connection Information page, type **3389** for the **Port number** and change the **Direction** to **Inbound**. Click **Next**.

5. The Remote Desktop Protocol (RDP) does not use secondary connections, so select **No** and click **Next**.

6. Click **Finish** on the Complete the New Protocol Definition Wizard page.

7. Expand the **Publishing** node in the left pane of the **ISA Management** console. Right-click on **Server Publishing Rules**, point to **New**, and click **Rule**.

8. On the Welcome to the New Server Publishing Rule Wizard page, type **Terminal Server 1** in the **Server publishing rule name** text box and click **Next**.

9. On the Address Mapping page, enter the IP address of the Terminal Server on the internal network in the **IP address of internal server** text box. Click **Browse** and select the IP address on the external interface of the ISA server you want to listen for Terminal Services requests. Click **Next**.

10. On the Protocol Settings page, select the **RDP Server** protocol definition. Note that protocol definitions with a primary connection as inbound are shown here. No protocol definitions with a primary connection as outbound will show up here. Click **Next**.

11. On the Client Type page, decide whether you want to allow all external hosts to connect to the Terminal server, or if you want to limit access to hosts contained in a client address set. You should limit the number of hosts that can connect to the Terminal server via the RDP server publishing rule. Note that you must enable packet filtering in order to apply a client address set to control what computers can access the server publishing rule. Packet filtering is enabled by default, but you might need to double check to

ensure that it's still enabled. Select the **Client address sets specified below** option and click **Next** (Figure 27.5).

Figure 27.5 Selecting the Client Address Sets Option on the Client Type Page

12. On the Add Client Sets page, click **Add**. Select the client address set you created for Terminal Services clients and click **Add**. The client address set will appear in the **Include these sets** frame. Click **OK** (Figure 27.6).

Figure 27.6 Selecting the Client Address Set

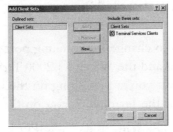

13. Click **Next** on the Client Sets page.

14. Click **Finish** on the Complete the New Server Publishing Rule Wizard page.

Now go to a machine configured as an external network client and connect to the Terminal server by using the external IP address on the ISA server used by the RDP publishing rule. After establishing the connection, check the name of the server you connected to by right-clicking on the **My Computer** icon and then clicking the **Properties** command. Click the **Network Identification** tab. If you see the name of the ISA server instead of the internal network server, you forgot to disable Terminal Services on the ISA server! Disable Terminal Services on the ISA server, restart the computer, and try again.

Publishing Terminal Services on an Alternate Port

You have to be careful about publishing Terminal Services. If intruders are able to connect to a Terminal server, they'll have a powerful launch point for subsequent attacks. You've already seen how you can limit access to a few selected Terminal Services clients on the Internet by applying a client address set to the RDP server publishing rule. Using client address sets is a good start, but there's more that you can do to secure your Terminal Services publishing rule.

Since TCP port 3389 is a well-known port, and Terminal Services is an attractive service to attack, you might want to impede Internet criminals by changing the port number used by Terminal Services. You can change the listening port number to any unused port number on the

ISA server's external interface, and then publish the Terminal Server on that alternate port. In order to do so, you'll have to make a Registry change at the Terminal Server and then change the port number that the Terminal Services client uses to call the Terminal Server.

If you use the new Remote Desktop Client software to connect to a Terminal Server, you don't need to make any changes on the client side. All you need to do is include the port number in the address you're calling. For example, if you want to call a published Terminal Server at **1.1.1.1** and that Terminal Server is listening on TCP port **58927**, just enter the address **1.1.1.1:58927** on the Remote Desktop Client and it will make the connection. It's not quite this easy with the original Windows 2000 or Windows NT 4.0 Terminal Services client software.

> **NOTE**
>
> You can obtain the Remote Desktop Client software for various operating systems at the following URLs:
>
> - **Windows** www.microsoft.com/windowsxp/pro/downloads/rdclinetdl.asp
> - **Macintosh** www.microsoft.com/mac/download/misc/rdc.asp
> - **Linux and UNIX** www.rdesktop.org

Perform the following steps to change the listening port for the Windows NT 4.0 Terminal Services Edition Terminal Server and the Windows 2000 Terminal Server. These steps should be performed on the Terminal Server you're publishing on the internal network. However, you can also change the listening port for the Terminal Server on the ISA server using the same procedure:

1. Click **Start** and then click **Run**. Type **regedt32** in the **Open** text box and click **OK**.

2. Navigate to the following key:
   HKEY_LOCAL_MACHINE\System\CurrentControlSet\Control\TerminalServer\ WinStations\RDP-Tcp

3. Find the **PortNumber** value in the right pane and double-click it.

4. In the **DWORD Editor** dialog box, select the **Decimal** option. Change the port number to something else. In this example, we'll change it to **64646**. Click **OK**.

5. Restart the Terminal Server computer.

Perform the following steps to create the new RDP server protocol definition:

1. Open the **ISA Management** console. Expand your server name and then expand the **Policy Elements** node.

2. Right-click on the **Protocol Definitions** node, point to **New**, and click **Definition**.

3. On the Welcome to the New Protocol Definition Wizard page, type **RDP Server 64646** for the Protocol Definition name and click **Next**.

4. On the Primary Connection Information page, type **64646** for the Port number and change the Direction to **Inbound**. Click **Next**.

5. RDP does not use secondary connections, so select **No** and click **Next**.

6. Click **Finish** on the Complete the New Protocol Definition Wizard page.

Perform the following steps to create the server publishing rule to publish the Terminal Server on the alternate port:

1. Expand the **Publishing** node in the left pane of the **ISA Management** console. Right-click on **Server Publishing Rules**, point to **New**, and click **Rule**.

2. On the Welcome to the New Server Publishing Rule Wizard page, type **Terminal Server 2** in the Server publishing rule name text box and click **Next**.

3. On the **Address Mapping** page, type in the IP address of the Terminal Server on the internal network in the **IP address of internal server** text box. Click **Browse** and select the IP address on the external interface of the ISA server that you want it to listen on for Terminal Services requests. Click **Next**.

4. On the **Protocol Settings** page, select the **RDP Server 64646** protocol definition. Click **Next**.

5. On the **Client Type** page, select the appropriate client type. In this example, we'll select **Any request**, but you should use a client address set in your production environment.

6. Click **Finish** on the Complete the New Server Publishing Rule Wizard page.

The last step is to configure the Terminal Services client to use the alternate port number:

1. Click **Start | Programs**. Point to **Terminal Services Client** and click **Client Connection Manager**.

2. In the Client Connection Manager, click **File | New Connection**. Go through the steps in the wizard to create a connection object for your published Terminal Server. Remember to use the IP address or FQDN that resolves to the external IP address on the ISA server that's publishing the Terminal Server.

3. Click on the icon for the connection in the Client Connection Manager window, and then click **File | Export**. Give the connection a name and save it on your desktop.

4. Right-click the **Terminal Services client** connection object on the desktop and click the **Open With** command. Select **Notepad** from the list of applications. If you are using a Win9x client, you'll have to open Notepad and open the connection object within Notepad.

5. In Notepad, find the Server Port= entry and change it to the port number you're using to publish your Terminal Server. Save the file and close Notepad.

6. Drag the icon on the desktop onto the Client Connection Manager window. A Client Connection Manager dialog box will appear and ask if you want to replace the connection object with the new one. Click **Yes**. A Client Connection Manager dialog box appears and asks if you want to replace the connection settings for all duplicates. Click **No**.

7. Double-click on the connection object in the Client Connection Manager window. Log on and confirm that you're connected to the correct server. Go to the ISA Server com-

puter and run **netstat −na**. You'll see an active connection to the alternate RDP server port used in the new server publishing rule.

Publishing Terminal Services on the ISA Server

Publishing services on the ISA server is always problematic. Your goal should be to run as few services as possible on the ISA Server computer. However, running Terminal Services on the ISA server is acceptable because you can create secure connections to the Terminal Server, and Terminal Services provides the best way to remotely manage an ISA server. We consider Terminal Services as secure as an SSL Web-based remote management solution.

You almost always have two options when publishing services on the ISA server itself. The easiest method is to create a packet filter so that external network clients can connect directly to the services via the external interface. The other way is to use a server publishing rule. The latter option can be used if you can configure the service to listen *only* on an IP address or set of addresses on the internal interface.

> **NOTE**
>
> Although you can always "publish" services that are on the ISA server itself by creating packet filters, the packet filter approach prevents you from using server publishing rules to publish services on the internal network using the same socket. Remember that a socket is the combination of an IP address, a protocol (TCP or UDP), and a port number. For example, if you create a packet filter to publish the Terminal server on the ISA server on 1.1.1.1 TCP port 3389, you will not be able to use 1.1.1.1 TCP port 3389 to publish a Terminal server on the internal network.

The Windows Terminal Server listens on all interfaces by default. This is similar to how the IIS socket-pooling feature works. Like the IIS socket pooling feature, you can configure it so that Terminal Services does not listen on all interfaces. Although you can choose what interface Terminal Services listens on, you cannot choose a specific IP address on the interface. If there are multiple IP addresses bound to the interface, Terminal Services will listen on all of them. This is an important consideration when you bind multiple addresses to the internal or external interface of the ISA server.

Publishing Terminal Services on the ISA Server Using Packet Filters

Let's look at how to publish Terminal Services using simple ISA Server packet filters:

1. Click **Start | Programs Administrative Tools | Terminal Services Configuration**.

2. In the Terminal Services Configuration console, click on the **Connections** node in the left pane of the console. In the right pane of the console, Double-click on the **RDP-T**cp entry.

3. Click on the **Network Adapter** tab. Click the **Down** arrow in the Network adapter drop-down list box. Notice that the default is **All network adapters configured with this protocol**. You can also choose a specific adapter. The adapters are listed by the adapter manufacturer's name rather than the name you give to the interface in the Network and Dial-up Connections window. When publishing the Terminal Server on the ISA server using packet filters, you can allow the Terminal Server to listen on all interfaces. By doing it this way, you won't have to loop back through the external interface to access the Terminal Server from an internal network client. However, if you plan to publish the Terminal Server by using server publishing rules, you'll need to configure Terminal Services to listen only on the internal interface (Figure 27.7).

Figure 27.7 Configuring Terminal Services to Listen on the Internal Interface

4. Open the **ISA Management** console. Expand your server name, and then expand the **Access Policy** node.

5. Right-click on the **IP Packet Filters** node, point to **New | Filter**.

6. On the Welcome to the New IP Packet Filter Wizard page, type **RDP (in)** in the **IP packet filter name** text box and click **Next**.

7. On the Filter Mode page, select the **Allow packet transmission** option and click **Next**.

8. On the Filter Type page, select the **Custom** option and click **Next**.

9. On the Filter Settings page, choose **TCP** for the **IP protocol**. Choose **Inbound** for the **Direction**. Choose **Fixed port** for the **Local port** and make the **Port number** value **3389**. For the **Remote port**, select **All ports** (Figure 27.8). Click **Next**.

Figure 27.8 Configuring the RDP Packet Filter

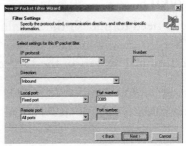

10. On the Local Computer page, select the option that best fits your situation. The **Default IP addresses for each external interface on the ISA Server computer** sets the filter to listen on the external interface's primary IP address. If you have multiple IP addresses bound to the external interface, you can choose the **This ISA Server's external IP address** option and type in the IP address to which you want the filter to apply. Make a selection and click **Next**.

11. On the Remote Computers page, select the **All remote computers** option and click **Next**.

12. Click **Finish** on the Completing the New IP Packet Wizard page.

Now try to connect to the Terminal Server from an external network client. You'll be able to connect directly to the external interface of the ISA server.

> **NOTE**
>
> You might be concerned about allowing a direct connection using a packet filter. As a result, you might believe that you will achieve a higher level of security by using a server publishing rule. However, this is misleading. Remember that server publishing rules do not expose the application-layer data to the Firewall service, unlike when using Web publishing rules. Since there are no application filters that will examine the RDP connections, a server publishing rule doesn't necessarily provide a higher level of security

Some of you might be concerned about allowing a direct connection using a packet filter. You might believe that you will achieve a higher level of security by using a server publishing rule—which is incorrect. Remember that server publishing rules do not expose the application-layer data to the Firewall service, unlike when using Web publishing rules. Since there are no application filters that will examine the RDP connections, a server publishing rule doesn't necessarily provide a higher level of security

The primary advantage of using a server publishing rule to publish Terminal Services on the ISA server is that it allows you to apply a client address set to control inbound access to the rule. While this doesn't protect the data stream, it's important that you limit who can connect to the Terminal server. For this reason, we recommend using server publishing rules to publish the Terminal server on the ISA server.

Publishing Terminal Services on Both the ISA Server and Internal Network

Many ISA Server administrators need to publish the Terminal Server on the ISA Server machine and allow access to Terminal Servers on the internal network. There are several methods that you can use to allow access to the Terminal Server on the ISA server and to machines on the internal network:

■ Use server publishing rules to publish all Terminal Servers.

- Use packet filters to publish the Terminal Server on the ISA server, and server publishing rules to publish the servers on the internal network.

- Publish the Terminal Server on the ISA server using server publishing rules or packet filters, and then access the other Terminal Servers on the internal network by running the Terminal Services client inside the Terminal Services session on the ISA server.

Any of these techniques will work. If you have a single IP address bound to the external interface of the ISA server, then you can create only *one* server publishing rule or packet filter. Other Terminal Services sessions will have to use alternate port numbers, using the methods described earlier in this chapter.

For example, suppose you have two Terminal Servers on the internal network and you are also running Terminal Services on the ISA server. You want to be able to access all of these Terminal Servers from the Internet. If you need Terminal Services access for only administrative purposes, you can publish the Terminal Server on the ISA server with the default port number (TCP 3389) and then use alternate port numbers for the other servers on the internal network.

No matter what method you choose, keep in mind that the limiting factor is port contention. You can publish as many Terminal Servers as you like, as long as you don't create a port contention condition on the external interface of the ISA server.

Publishing TSAC Sites

The Terminal Services Advanced Client (TSAC) provides a way for your users to access a Terminal Server using a Web browser interface. The Web interface allows you to connect to a Terminal Server without already having the Terminal Services or Remote Desktop Client already installed on the client machine. This allows users who haven't installed the client software to access the Terminal Server.

The TSAC software must first be installed on a Web server on the internal network. You can install the software on any Web server on your internal or external network (DMZ). There is no relationship between the physical location of the Web server hosting the TSAC site and the Terminal Server or servers to which users connect. After users connect to the TSAC Web site, they are offered the opportunity to install the TSAC ActiveX control. After installing the ActiveX control, the user enters the name of the Terminal Server to which he or she wants to connect.

NOTE

This brings up a common area of confusion for ISA Server administrators. When users enter the name of the Terminal Server in the TSAC logon form, they must enter a name or IP address that is valid on the *external* network. The Terminal Services client connection is established via the IP address on the external interface of the ISA server used by the RDP server publishing rule publishing the Terminal Server. Users and administrators often enter the *internal* name of the Terminal Server and discover that the connection fails. You must use a name or IP address that resolves to the public IP address on the external interface of the ISA server that matches the address used in the RDP server publishing rule.

Do the following to publish a TSAC site:

1. Install the TSAC software on the Web server.

2. Publish the TSAC Web server.

3. Publish the Terminal Server(s).

4. Connect to the TSAC Web site and then connect to the Terminal Server.

Installing the TSAC Software on the Web Server

Perform the following steps to install the TSAC Web software on a server on the internal network:

1. Open **Internet Explorer** and go to **www.microsoft.com/windowsxp/pro/ downloads/rdwebconn.asp**. Select the appropriate language for your site and click **GO**.

2. On the **File Download** page, select the **Save this program to disk** option, and click **OK**.

3. Save the **tswebsetup** file to the desktop, and click **Save** in the **Save As** dialog box.

4. Click **Open** in the **Download Complete** dialog box.

5. On the **Remote Desktop Web Connection Setup** dialog box, click **Yes** to install the package.

6. Read the license information and then click **Yes** to agree to the license.

7. A dialog box appears showing the default path in the **wwwroot** folder where the TSAC Web connection files are stored. You can change the path here. Click **OK** to continue.

8. An information dialog box appears asking if you want to read the release notes. Click **Yes** to read the notes. You'll notice that this is the TSAC Web package that's included with Windows XP.

Publishing the TSAC Web Server

You publish the TSAC Web server in the same way you publish any other Web server. You can even publish the TSAC site as an SSL site to make the connection secure. You'll want to use SSL if you require authentication to access the TSAC Web site. If you do publish the TSAC Web site as an SSL site, we recommend that you use only basic authentication to allow the widest range of clients to access the site and have fewer compatibility issues. You don't have to worry about credentials being passed in clear-text over the Internet, because SSL encryption hides the username and passwords. In this example, we'll publish a TSAC site that allows access to domain admins over a plain HTTP connection. Later in this chapter, we'll review procedures for publishing SSL sites.

The TSAC site can be published using either Web or server publishing rules. In this example, we'll use Web publishing rules because they allow a higher level of security than server publishing rules do.

Perform the following steps to publish the TSAC site:

1. Open the **ISA Management** console. Expand your server name and then expand the **Policy Elements** node. Right-click on the **Destination Sets** node, point to **New**, and click **Set**.

2. In the **New Destination Set** dialog box (Figure 27.9), type **TSAC Web** in the **Name** text box. Type in a description—for example, **Destination Set for the TSAC Web site**—in the **Description** text box. Click **Add**.

Figure 27.9 Creating the TSAC Destination Set

3. In the **Add/Edit Destination** dialog box, enter the **FQDN** that *external network users* will use to access the TSAC Web site (Figure 27.10). This FQDN must resolve to the IP address you are using for the Incoming Web Requests listener that will accept requests for the TSAC Web site. This is *not* the name of the server on the internal network. In the **Path** text box, enter **/tsweb★**. The Web Proxy service uses this path to redirect the request to the appropriate Web server on the internal network. The wildcard at the end of the path indicates that requests for the tsweb folder and all subfolders of the tsweb folder will be accessible via this set. Be aware that users will need to type in the full path, including **/tsweb**. ISA Server will not allow you to redirect from one path to another. Whatever path is included in the URL the external users send in the request must be available on the destination TSAC server on the internal network. Click **OK**.

Figure 27.10 Entering the FQDN and Path for the Destination Set

4. Click **OK** in the **New Destination Set** dialog box.

As is the case for all publishing rules, you must be sure to include an entry in your public DNS that resolves the FQDN used in the destination set. In our current example, we would put an entry for **tsweb.internal.net** in our public DNS. You should also consider putting the same entry in your private DNS if you want the site accessible to internal and external network clients. If you do, make sure you have configured a split DNS infrastructure. You can get more information on configuring a split DNS infrastructure at www.isaserver.org/pages/article.asp?id=995.

Now that the destination set is in place, you can create the Web publishing rule:

6. Open the **ISA Management** console and expand your server name. Expand the **Publishing** node and right-click on the **Web Publishing Rules** node. Point to **New** and click **Rule**.

7. On the **Welcome to the New Web Publishing Rule Wizard** page, type in the name of the rule in the **Web Publishing rule name** text box. In this example, we'll call the rule **TSAC Web site**. Click **Next**.

8. On the **Destination Sets** page (Figure 27.11), select the destination set you created for the TSAC Web site. Click **Next**.

Figure 27.11 Selecting the TSAC Site Destination Set

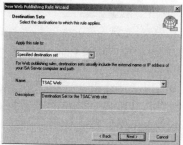

9. On the **Client Type** page, select the client type appropriate for your organization. If you want everyone to access the site, select **Any request**. You can limit access to specific computers using a client address set by selecting **Specific computer (client address sets)** and assigning a client address set. This would be most useful if you wanted to restrict access to a particular partner, or limit access to a group of administrators. You can also control access to this site with user/group-based authentication by selecting the **Specific users and groups** option. Users will need to enter credentials and authenticate with the ISA server before they access the site when you select this option. The users do not authenticate with the TSAC Web server. This allows you to offload authentication processing from the Web server to the ISA server. In this example, we'll enforce security by limiting access to the rule by specific users and groups. Select the **Specific users and groups** option and click **Next**.

10. In the **Users and Group** dialog box (Figure 27.12), click **Add**. Select the user or group you want to have access to this Web publishing rule. In this example, we'll select the **Domain Admins** group. Click **OK** and then click **Next** in the **Users and Groups** dialog box.

Figure 27.12 Configuring Authentication Requirements for the Web Publishing Rule

11. In the **Rule Action** dialog box, select the **Redirect the request to this internal Web server (name or IP address)** option. Then, type in the name of the server on the internal network. In this example, we will use the same name the user on the external network uses to access the server. This allows the same name to appear in the Web Proxy logs and makes analysis of the Web Proxy logs much easier, as the redirect is to the same name the user is accessing via the browser. If you use the same domain name for internal and external resources, you can create a split DNS infrastructure. If you do not want to, or cannot, create a split DNS infrastructure, you can use a HOSTS file on the ISA server and map the name you use for the redirect to the server on the internal network. For example, we will redirect the request to tsac.internal.net. This is the same name the external users use to access the server and in this example it resolves to 192.168.1.33 on the external interface of the ISA server. When the ISA server redirects the request, it will resolve tsac.internal.net to 10.0.0.2 because we put an entry in the HOSTS file on the ISA server to map tsac.internal.net to the internal IP address for the server. When you do it this way, you don't have to worry about sending the original host header to the server, because the host header won't be changed! Click **Next** to continue.

12. Click **Finish** on the final page of the wizard to complete the rule.

When users access the published TSAC Web site, they'll be asked for credentials.

Publishing the Terminal Server

The next step is to publish the Terminal Server. Remember that if you are running Terminal Services on the ISA server, you need to either disable Terminal Services, or configure the Terminal server to listen only on the internal interface. If you don't, you'll end up with port contention after creating the server publishing rule.

Perform the following steps to publish a Terminal Server:

1. Open the **ISA Management** console. Expand your server name and then expand the **Policy Elements** node.

2. Right-click on the **Protocol Definitions** node, point to **New**, and click **Definition**.

3. On the **Welcome to the New Protocol Definition Wizard** page, type **RDP Server** for the **Protocol Definition name** and click **Next**.

4. On the **Primary Connection Information** page, type **3389** for the **Port number** and change the **Direction** to **Inbound**. Click **Next**.

5. The RDP does not use secondary connections, so select **No** and click **Next**.

6. Click **Finish** on the **Complete the New Protocol Definition Wizard** page.

7. Expand the **Publishing** node in the left pane of the **ISA Management** console. Right-click on **Server Publishing Rules**, point to **New**, and click **Rule**.

8. On the **Welcome to the New Server Publishing Rule Wizard** page, type **TSAC Terminal Server** in the **Server publishing rule name** text box and click **Next**.

9. On the **Address Mapping** page, type in the IP address of the Terminal server on the internal network in the **IP address of internal server** text box. Click **Browse** and select the IP address on the external interface of the ISA server that you want it to listen on for Terminal Services requests. Note that the external IP address does not have to be the same as the one you used for your Incoming Web Requests listener, and the internal server does not have to be the same server as the Web server publishing the TSAC Web site. The TSAC Web site connection and the Terminal Services client connection are two completely different sessions. Click **Next**.

10. On the **Protocol Settings** page, select the **RDP Server** protocol definition. Note that protocol definitions with a primary connection set as inbound are shown here. No protocol definitions with a primary connection as outbound will show up. Click **Next**.

11. On the **Client Type** page, decide whether you want to allow all external hosts to connect to the Terminal Server, or if you want to limit access to hosts contained in a client address set. For security reasons, you should limit which hosts can connect to the Terminal Server via the RDP server publishing rule. Note that in order to control what computer can access the server publishing rule, you'll have to enable packet filtering. Packet filtering is enabled by default, but you should double check to ensure that it hasn't been disabled. Select the **Client address sets specified below** option and click **Next**.

12. On the **Client Sets** page, click **Add**. Select the client address set you created for the Terminal Services clients and click **Add**. If you haven't created a client address set for users who need access to the Terminal Server, you'll need to back out of the Server Publishing Rule Wizard and create the client address set. If the Terminal Server you're publishing will be accessed by users with dynamic addresses assigned to them, you will not be able to use client address sets for access control. The client address set will appear in the **Include these sets** frame. Click **OK**.

13. Click **Next** on the **Client Sets** page.

14. Click Finish on the Completing the New Server Publishing Rule Wizard page.

Connecting to the TSAC Web Site and the Terminal Server

You can now connect to the TSAC Site and Terminal Server using Internet Explorer. Go to an external network client and perform the following steps:

1. On the external network client, open **Internet Explorer**. Type the FQDN and path to the Terminal Services Web site. In our example, we'll type **http://tsac.internal.net**.

2. You will need to authenticate against the ISA server to access the TSAC Web site. We configured the Web publishing rule so that only authenticated users can access the TSAC Web site. Enter your credentials into the logon dialog box (Figure 27.13), and click **OK**.

Figure 27.13 Entering Credentials to Access the TSAC Web Site

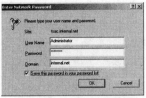

3. After you successfully authenticate, the TSAC Web page appears and then the **Security Warning** dialog box pops up asking if you want to install the **Remote Desktop ActiveX Control** (Figure 27.14). Note that if the Web browser is configured to block ActiveX controls, the TSAC client software will not work. Click **Yes** to install the client software.

Figure 27.14 The Security Warning Dialog Box

4. The client software installs, but it won't give you any indication of when installation was complete. Give it a few seconds to finish installation, and then type in an FQDN that resolves to the IP address on the external interface of the ISA server you used in the TSAC Web server publishing rule. You can also enter the public IP address. If the external IP address you used in the server publishing rule is the same IP address used by the Incoming Web Requests listener for the Web publishing rule used to access the TSAC Web site, users can type in the same FQDN they used to access the Web site in the **Server** text box. Select the size of the display and click **Connect** (Figure 27.15).

Figure 27.15 The Remote Desktop Web Connection Page

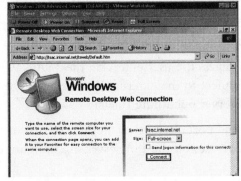

5. Once you connect, a Terminal Service session runs within the browser window. If you connected using the **Full Screen** option, you'll see something like what appears in Figure 27.16. Figure 27.17 shows the Terminal Services session as it appears in the browser window.

Figure 27.16 The TSAC Terminal Services Session Running in Full Screen Mode

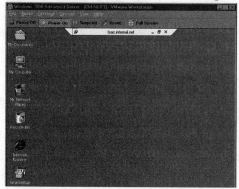

Figure 27.17 The Terminal Services Session as It Appears in the Browser

Some things to keep in mind when publishing TSAC sites:

- You can publish multiple Terminal Servers and allow users to access all of them from the same TSAC Web page.

- If you want to publish multiple Terminal Servers, you will need a separate IP address for each. Each Terminal Services publishing rule uses one IP address.

- The Terminal Server does not need to be on the same machine as the TSAC Web site.

- The name or IP address the user enters on the TSAC Web page is the name or IP address used to connect to the external IP address on the ISA server used in the Terminal Server's server publishing rule(s).

- Make sure you avoid port contention on the external interface of the ISA server. Either disable Terminal Services on the ISA server or configure it to listen only on the internal interface.

Publishing TSAC Sites on an Alternate Port

As you learned earlier in this chapter, it might be a good security measure to publish the Terminal Server on an alternate port. In the same way, it might be a good security move to publish the Terminal Servers that users access via the TSAC Web site on alternate ports.

The problem is that if you publish the Terminal Server on an alternate port, you cannot enter the port number in the **Server** text box on the TSAC Web page. For example, you might think that if you enter **tsac.internal.net:12345** into the **Server** text box, the RDP request would be directed to TCP port 12345. Unfortunately, this is not the case. The TSAC RDP client ActiveX control will sends requests to TCP port 3389, which is the default RDP server port number.

There is a hack you can use if you don't use the latest TSAC Web software. This requires you to copy the TSWeb files from a Windows XP computer that is pre-Windows XP Service Pack 1. After you copy those files to the Windows Terminal Server, you can then make a change to the **connect.asp** file in the **TSWeb** folder. This change allows the TSAC Web client ActiveX control to send requests to the alternate port number.

While this does work, you might run into major problems if you implement this solution. Microsoft issued a Security Alert regarding a buffer overflow problem with the old TSAC Web client ActiveX control. The fix was to install the patch noted in MS02-046 (www.microsoft.com/technet/treeview/default.asp?url=/technet/security/bulletin/MS02-046.asp). After installing the patch, users could no longer connect to the old TSAC Web site. You have to upgrade to the current TSAC Web site software to allow the post-fix clients to connect. After you upgrade the TSAC Web server files, your alternate port settings disappear and you cannot regain them.

Until this situation is changed, using an alternate port to connect to a Terminal Server via the TSAC Web site is a moot point. We'll keep you updated on this situation if it changes. Make sure to check www.isaserver.org/shinder on a regular basis to read up on ISA Server updates.

Publishing FTP Servers on the Internal Network

We get many questions at ISAServer.org regarding FTP server publishing. FTP server publishing is done the same way as other forms of server publishing. There is one important difference between publishing FTP servers and publishing another protocol, such as SMTP. That is that in order to fully support the FTP protocol, the FTP server publishing rules must be able to leverage the FTP protocol definitions created by the ISA server's FTP access application filter.

SMTP is a simple protocol that only requires access to a single TCP port. PORT mode FTP, however, is a complex protocol, where the FTP server must be able to create new outbound connections to the FTP client. Information about the new connection must be tracked by the firewall, and the only way the ISA server can track these secondary connections is with the help of the FTP access application filter.

The FTP access application filter monitors communication between the publishing FTP server and the FTP client on the Internet. When the FTP client on the Internet sends a PORT command to the publishing FTP server, the ISA server intercepts this information and manages opening and closing the appropriate ports. However, in order to do its job correctly, the ISA server needs to use the FTP server protocol definitions created by the application filter. This protocol definition "hooks into" the FTP access application filter and allows the rule to leverage the intelligence built into the filter.

Perform the following steps to publish an FTP server on the internal network:

1. Open the **ISA Management** console. Expand your server name and then expand the **Publishing** node. Right-click the **Server Publishing** node, point to **New**, and click **Rule**.

2. On the **Welcome to the New Server Publishing Rule Wizard** page, type in a name for the rule in the **Server publishing rule name** text box. Click **Next**.

3. On the **Address Mapping** page (Figure 27.18), type in the IP address of the internal network FTP server in the **IP address of the internal server** text box. Type the IP address on the external interface of the ISA server that you want to listen for the FTP requests in the **External IP address on ISA Server** text box. Click **Next**.

Figure 27.18 The Address Mapping Page

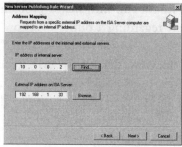

4. On the **Protocol Settings** page, select the **FTP Server** protocol in the **Apply the rule to this protocol** drop-down list box. Click **Next**.

5. On the **Client Type** page, select either **Any request** or **Specific computers** depending on your requirement. Click **Next**.

6. Click **Finish** on the **Complete the New Server Publishing Rule Wizard**.

7. The FTP server needs access to all sites because it needs to make a new outbound connection to the FTP clients sending the inbound request. Create a client address set that contains the IP address of the FTP server, and then create a site and content rule that allows the FTP server access to all sites and content.

8. Make sure the FTP server is configured as a SecureNAT client. The most common reason for the publishing rule to fail is that the administrator forgot to configure the server as a SecureNAT client.

You will be able to connect to the FTP server after you complete the FTP server publishing rule. The publishing server supports both PORT and PASV mode connections because the **FTP Server** protocol definition plugs into the FTP access application filter. Go to the **Protocol Definitions** node in the **ISA Management** console and you'll see that the **FTP Server** protocol definition is defined by an **Application Filter**. If you disable the **FTP Access** application filter, these FTP protocol definitions won't work.

It's difficult to make a mistake when publishing FTP sites. However, there do appear to be problems with publishing FTP sites on secondary IP addresses on the external interface of the ISA server. For example, if you have two IP addresses bound to the external interface of the ISA server, and you publish an FTP site on the internal network using a secondary IP address bound to the external interface, the publishing rule might not work.

However, this problem was corrected with ISA Server Service Pack 1, and you should not have this issue after installing the service pack. If you have problems publishing FTP sites on secondary addresses, make sure that ISA Server Service Pack 1 is installed. If it isn't, reinstall the service pack.

NOTE

Although not directly connected to FTP server publishing, there is a problem with PASV mode FTP access from internal network clients when you have multiple IP addresses bound to the external interface of the ISA server. There is an issue with PASV FTP downloads when using Internet Explorer from SecureNAT clients, when the ISA server has multiple addresses bound to the external interface. The workaround for this problem is to disable IP routing in the ISA Server Management console and enable the Routing and Remote Access Service (RRAS). This issue should be addressed with ISA Server Service Pack 2.

Publishing FTP Servers on Alternate Ports

Publishing an FTP server on the default port (TCP 21) is easy because the FTP access application filter does the footwork for you. However, when you want to publish an FTP site on an alternate port, the FTP access application filter isn't going to help you at all. You need to use the Firewall client on the publishing FTP server to make it work. The publishing server needs to be a Firewall client so that the Firewall client software can work with the firewall service to manage the connections. When the FTP access application filter manages the connections, the client can be a SecureNAT client. The problem is that the FTP access application filter only supports standard FTP port numbers.

Do the following to publish an FTP server on an alternate port:

1. Disable the FTP access application filter.

2. Change the listening port on the internal FTP server.

3. Install the Firewall client on the FTP server.

4. Place a **wspcfg.ini** file in the appropriate folder.

5. Use the **credtool.exe** file to provide credentials to the Firewall service.

6. Create an "All Open" protocol rule and site and content rule that can be used by the account.

The only reason we can see for publishing FTP sites on alternate ports is for "security through obscurity." This keeps out the weakest of hackers, but a simple port scan by a more sophisticated hacker will allow him to access your FTP site through the alternate port. Another reason to publish an FTP site on an alternate port is to violate the terms of service on your Internet account that prevents you from publishing servers.

Disable the FTP Access Application Filter

First, disable the FTP access application filter:

1. Open the **ISA Management** console, expand your server or array name, and then expand the **Extensions** node in the left pane of the console.

2. Click on the **Application Filters** node in the left pane of the console.

3. In the right pane of the console, right-click the **Ftp Access Filter** entry and click **Disable**. Choose the option to restart the **Firewall Service** and click **OK**.

It might take a few moments for the Firewall service to restart. That's not a problem because you have a few more things to do before publishing starts to work.

Change the FTP Site's Listening Port

The next step is to change the port number the FTP site listens on.

1. On the FTP server, open the **Internet Information Services** console from the **Administrative Tools** menu.

2. Expand your server name and right-click on **Default FTP Site**. Click the **Properties** command.

3. On the **FTP Site** tab (Figure 27.19), type the alternate port number you want to use for the site in the **TCP Port** text box. In this example, we'll use port number **12345**. Click **Apply** and then click **OK**.

Figure 27.19 Change the FTP Site Listening Port

4. Stop and restart the FTP service by clicking on the **Stop** and **Start** control buttons on the **Internet Information Services** button bar.

At this point, the FTP server listens on TCP port 12345. You can confirm this by opening a command prompt on the FTP server and doing a **netstat –na | find ":12345"**.

Install the Firewall Client

Proxy Server 2.0 used the Winsock Proxy client. Since ISA Server is new, they decided to rename the Winsock Proxy client and call it the Firewall client. The Winsock Proxy client and the Firewall client are interchangeable, and you can use either to access both an ISA server and a Proxy Server 2.0 machine.

1. Log on as an Administrator at the FTP server.

2. Click **Start** and then click the **Run** command.

3. At the **Run** dialog box, type **\\<ISAServerName>\mspclnt\setup.exe**. Be sure to enter the appropriate name for your ISA server. Click **OK**.

4. Follow the instructions to install the Firewall client.

5. After installing the Firewall client, restart the FTP server.

You don't have to restart the FTP server after the Firewall client software is installed, but we always feel better when we do.

Place a wspcfg.ini File in the Appropriate Folder

You must create a **wspcfg.ini** file if you want to bind the appropriate ports on the external interface of the ISA server. Creating Firewall client configuration files is somewhat of a black art. If you have a hard time understanding the entries in these Firewall client configuration files, check out Jim Harrison's article on the subject. Jim has gone a long way at providing insight into exactly how these Firewall client configuration files work. You can find Jim's fantastic article on this subject at www.isaserver.org/pages/article.asp?id=236.

1. Open the Windows Explorer and navigate to \WINNT\System32\inetsrv folder.

2. Right-click on an empty area in the right pane of the Explorer, point to **New**, and click **Text Document**.

3. Double-click on the **New Text Document.txt** file.

4. Type into **Notepad** the text appearing in Figure 27.20. Replace the **12345** entry with the alternate port number you want to use.

Figure 27.20 Creating the wspcfg.ini File

5. Save the file with the name **wspcfg.ini** as seen in Figure 27.21. It's important that you put the quotes around the name. If you don't, Notepad will append the ".txt" file extension to the filename. Click **Save**.

Figure 27.21 Saving the wspcfg.ini File

Use the credtool.exe Utility to Send Credentials

If you're using outbound access controls based on user/group membership, you need a way to send credentials to the ISA Server Firewall Service. This is an issue because a server is usually not going to have a logged-on user. You need a way for the FTP service (**inetinfo.exe**) to send credentials to the ISA server without a logged-on user. You could use client address sets to do this, but the **credtool** method is a bit cleaner, since you're going to have to create an "All Open" protocol rule to make this work.

First, create an account with a complex password that can be used by the FTP server to authenticate against the ISA server. After you create the account using the **Active Directory Users and Computer** console, open a command prompt and enter the following information:

```
C:>\Program Files\Microsoft Firewall Client\credtool.exe -w -n inetinfo
     -c ftpservice INTERNAL mypassword
```

Make sure you replace **ftpservice** with the name of an account you created for the FTP service to use. Replace the **INTERNAL** entry with the NetBIOS name of your Active Directory domain. Replace **mypassword** with the password you gave to the FTP service's domain account. If you entered everything correctly, you should see something like what you see in Figure 27.22.

Figure 27.22 Using the CREDTOOL

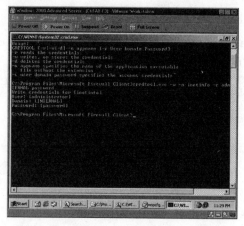

Create an "All Open" Protocol Rule

The FTP service's user account must have access to all protocols and all sites and content. For the site and content rule, you can use the built-in default. However, if you disable or change the default rule, make sure the account you created for the FTP service on the publishing server has access to all sites and content. This is just part of how the FTP protocol works. This allows outbound access to all outbound port numbers to the FTP service when creating secondary connections.

1. Open the **ISA Management** console, expand your server or array name, and expand the **Access Policy** node.

2. Right-click on **Protocol Rules**, point to **New**, and click **Rule**.

3. On the first page of the wizard, type in the name of the rule—we usually call it **All Open**. Click **Next**.

4. Set the **Rule Action** as **Allow** and click **Next**.

5. Set the **Protocols** for **All IP traffic** and click **Next**.

6. Set the **Schedule** for **Always** and click **Next**.

7. For the client type, select the **Specific users and groups** and click **Next**.

8. In the **Users and Groups** page, click **Add**.

9. Select your domain name in the **Look in** drop-down list box. Then, double-click on the username in the list box (Figure 27.23). Click **OK**, and then click **Next**.

Figure 27.23 Adding the User Account

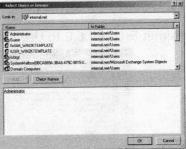

10. Click **Finish** on the last page of the wizard.

That's it! Restart the FTP server and let's have some fun.

Testing the Configuration

After restarting the FTP server, go to the ISA server, open a command prompt, and run a **netstat –na | find ":12345"**. You should see something like Figure 27.24.

Figure 27.24 The FTP Server Listening on the Alternate Port

Now we know that the FTP server was able to bind TCP 12345 on the ISA server. It looks like it has bound that port on all interfaces. This is the socket pooling issue raising its head again. This isn't a problem, since the FTP server is a unihomed server. Note that this does not pose a problem, because we're not creating a server publishing rule. If we needed to create a server publishing rule, we would end up with a port contention problem.

Go to an external network client and open an FTP session using the Windows 2000 command-line ftp application. You should be able to connect using PORT mode and get a directory listing (Figure 27.25).

Figure 27.25 Testing the FTP Server

How about some big fun? Configure Internet Explorer to use PASV mode. In IE 6.0, you have to configure the browser's Advanced Properties to use PASV mode (Figure 27.26).

Figure 27.26 Configure Internet Explorer 6.0 to Use PASV Mode

Now enter the FTP site information into the address bar (Figure 27.27), and you should be able to access the site using PASV.

Figure 27.27 Connecting to the FTP Using PASV Mode

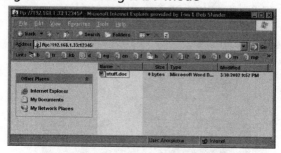

Tips on Configuring FTP Publishing

Publishing an FTP server on an alternate port might sound easy. It is in a way, but nothing comes both fast *and* easy in this business. When testing your configuration, you might want to reset the communication between the FTP server and the ISA server if you find you're having problems. You don't need to restart the FTP server to reset the Firewall client connection. Try this:

1. Stop the Firewall service.
2. Restart the Firewall service.
3. Stop the FTP service on the FTP server.
4. Restart the FTP service on the FTP server.

Confirm that the FTP server is communicating with the ISA server by using the ISA Management console's **Sessions** node (Figure 27.28).

Figure 27.28 Confirming the FTP Server's Link with the ISA Server

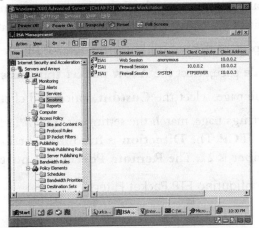

You should see **SYSTEM** as the account name and the name of the computer in the **Firewall Session** entry. Note that the **User Name** isn't correct. The User Name is listed as **SYSTEM** instead of the actual user name you configured in the CREDTOOL. However, when you see that SYSTEM is connected to the ISA server, the FTP server publishing rule using the Firewall client and the wspcfg.ini file is working.

Publishing FTP Servers Co-Located on the ISA Server

Cash-strapped organizations often need to run server services on the ISA server itself. As you know, this isn't the optimal way to make services available to Internet users because you expose the ISA Server machine to exploits carried out against services running on the ISA Server computer. However, if you have just a single server to do all the work, then you must put your public services on the ISA server.

FTP is probably the least secure of all Internet protocols, and it's the server that we would least like to put on the ISA server. However, if you want to run an FTP server on the ISA server, you can publish it as you do any other service on the ISA server, by using packet filters or server publishing rules.

Packet filters open the required port directly to the Internet, while server publishing rules allow you to leverage the FTP access application filter to publish the FTP site. Let's go over the packet filter method first, and then discuss the server publishing method.

Method One: Creating Packet Filters

Packet filtering should always be enabled. The only time where packet filtering might be disabled is when the ISA server is acting as a unihomed Web caching server on the internal network, or when the ISA server is on the edge of a departmental LAN that connects to a trusted corporate backbone. Packet filtering is the cornerstone of ISA Server's firewall security. If you have an interface directly exposed to the Internet, you *must* have packet filtering enabled.

You can create packet filters to allow external network users access to an FTP server located on the ISA server itself. This method doesn't require server publishing rules. The packet filters open ports required for PORT and PASV mode FTP clients.

To create the packet filters:

1. Open the **ISA Management** console. Expand your server and then expand **Access Policies**. Right-click **IP Packet Filters**, click **New**, and then click **Filter**.

2. In the **Welcome** page of the wizard, name the filter **FTP Port 21** and click **Next**.

3. On the **Filter Mode** page, select the **Allow packet transmission** option and click **Next**.

4. On the **Filter Type** page, select the **Custom** option and click **Next**.

5. On the **Filter Settings** page, match the settings as shown in Figure 27.29. The **IP Protocol** is set for **TCP**. The **Direction** is **Inbound**. The **Local Port** is **Fixed Port**, and the **Port number** is **21**. The **Remote Port** is **All ports**. Click **Next**.

Figure 27.29 Configuring FTP Packet Filters

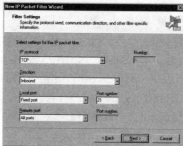

6. On the **Local Computer** page, select either the **Default IP addresses for each external interface on the ISA Server computer** option, or the **This ISA Server's external IP address** option, depending on whether you have more than one IP address bound to the external interface of the ISA server. Click **Next**.

7. On the **Remote Computers** page, select the **All remote computers** option if you want all computers to be able to access the FTP server, or select the **Only this remote computer** option if you want only a single external computer to access the FTP server. Click **Next**.

8. Confirm your settings on the final page of the wizard. If everything looks good, click **Finish**.

9. Repeat the process. However, for step 1 call it **FTP Port 20**, and for step 5, you should make the selections as shown in Figure 27.30. The **Direction** is **Outbound** and the **Local Port** is **20**.

Figure 27.30 Configuring the FTP Server Packet Filter

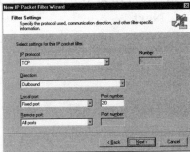

These packet filters only support PORT mode FTP clients. The reason is that PASV mode requires that the FTP client be able to connect to *any* ephemeral port on the ISA server. This would obviate your packet-filtering security mechanism. PASV mode FTP servers managed with packet filters are a special problem and they should be located only on DMZ segments, where the low security based on packet filtering is acceptable.

To see how what happens with PASV mode packet filters, perform the following steps to create packet filters to support PASV mode clients:

1. Open the **ISA Management** console, expand your server name, and expand the **Access Policies** node. Right-click on **IP Packet Filters**, point to **New**, and click **Filter**.

2. On the **Welcome to the New IP Packet Filter Wizard** page, type in **PASV Command Channel** in the **IP packet filter name** text box. Click **Next**.

3. On the **Filter Mode** page, select **Allow packet transmission** and check **Next**.

4. On the **Filter Type** page, click the **Custom** option and click **Next**.

5. On the **Filter Settings** page, the **IP Protocol** is set for **TCP**. The **Direction** is **Inbound**. The **Local Port** is **Fixed Port** and the **Port number** is **21**. The **Remote Port** is **All ports**. Click **Next**.

6. On the **Local Computer** page, select the appropriate entry. In this example, we'll select **Default IP addresses for each external interface on the ISA Server computer**, and click **Next**.

7. On the **Remote Computers** page, select **All remote computers** and click **Next**.

8. Review your settings and click **Finish** on the **Completing the New IP Packet Filter Wizard** page. This completes the packet filter for the FTP command channel.

9. You now need a packet filter to support the data connection. PASV mode clients must establish a second connection to the FTP server on a high port number, and the FTP client must be able to receive the data on a high port. Right-click on the **IP Packet Filters** node, point to **New**, and click **Filter**.

10. On the **Welcome to the New IP Packet Filter Wizard** page, type **PASV Data Channel** in the **IP packet filter name** text box and click **Next**.

11. On the **Filter Mode** page, select the **Allow packet transmission** option and click **Next**.

12. On the **Filter Type** page, select the **Custom** option and click **Next**.

13. On the **Filter Settings** page (Figure 27.31), make the **IP protocol TCP**. The **Direction** is **Inbound**. The **Local port** is set for **Dynamic** and the **Remote port** is set to **All ports**. Click **Next**.

Figure 27.31 The PASV Mode Data Channel Packet Filter

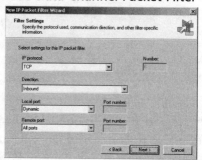

14. On the **Local Computer** page, select the **Default IP addresses** option and click **Next**.

15. On the **Remote Computers** page, select the **All remote computers** option and click **Next**.

16. Review your settings and click **Finish** on the **New IP Packet Filter Wizard** page.

The PASV mode data channel filter leaves the ISA server wide open. You're allowing inbound access to all high-number ports and allowing the ISA server to accept those requests to high-number ports from all port numbers. This is what we're referring to when we say that the FTP protocol is inherently unsecure. If you must run an FTP server on the ISA server, you should limit access to PORT mode FTP clients only.

Method Two: Server and Web Publishing Rules

The second method you can use to publish an FTP server is server publishing or Web publishing rules. The nice thing about doing it this way is that you can have PASV mode clients connect to the FTP server; the FTP access application filter takes care of connection management. Using a server publishing rule that leverages the FTP access application filter allows you to avoid creating wide-open packet filters that put your ISA server at significant risk.

Step 1: Disable Socket Pooling for the FTP Service

First, you need to disable FTP service socket pooling. The FTP service listens on all IP addresses when socket pooling is enabled, even if you configured the service to listen on a single IP address in the **Internet Information Service** console. While socket pooling is a good thing on a uni-homed server on the internal network, it's a very bad thing on a multihomed firewall.

Perform these steps to disable socket pooling for the FTP service:

1. Open a command prompt and navigate to the **\Inetpub\Adminscripts** folder.

2. Type **net stop msftpsvc** and press **Enter**.

3. Type in the following command and press **Enter**:

```
cscript adsutil.vbs set msftpsvc /disablesocketpooling true
```

You should see what appears in Figure 27.32.

Figure 27.32 Disabling FTP Service Socket Pooling

4. At the command prompt, type **net start msftpsvc** and press **Enter**.

5. Now let's run **netstat –na** again. You should see what appears in Figure 27.33.

Figure 27.33 The FTP Service Listens on a Dedicated Address

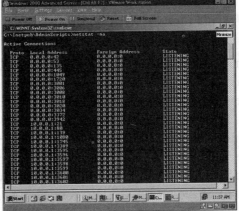

6. Notice that TCP port 21 is now listening on 10.0.0.1 and *not* on 0.0.0.0. No more socket pooling for Port 21! We're almost ready to publish the FTP service using a server publishing rule and pointing to the internal IP address of the ISA server (which in this case is 10.0.0.1).

Step 2: Configure the FTP Service to Listen Only on the Internal Interface

The default setting for the FTP service is to listen on all IP addresses, even after socket pooling is disabled. You need to go into the **Internet Information Services** console and configure the service to listen on the internal IP address *only*. You use this interface in your server publishing rule.

1. Open the **Internet Information Services** console from the **Administrative Tools** menu.

2. Right-click on the default FTP Site and click **Properties**.

3. In the Default FTP Site Properties dialog box, you will see what appears in Figure 27.34. Actually, you won't see what appears until you click the Down arrow in the TCP Port drop-down list box. Note that there are two IP addresses on this particular computer, one for the internal and one for the external interface. We'll select 10.0.0.1 to have the FTP service listen on that IP address only. After making the selection, click **Apply** and then click **OK**.

Figure 27.34 The FTP Service Listens on a Dedicated Address

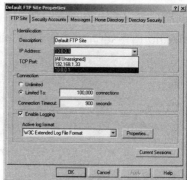

4. After making these changes, stop the FTP service and restart it.

Step 3: Disabling the FTP Port Attack Setting

Some FTP server implementations allow a PORT command to open a connection between the FTP server and an arbitrary port on another machine. This allows the attacker to establish connections to arbitrary ports on machines other than the actual source machine. By default, IIS 5.0 prevents this from happening and blocks connections from machines other than the client that initiated the connection. However, since the ISA server needs to act on behalf of the source host, we have to disable this mechanism. Disabling this IIS mechanism does not open the server to attack, because the ISA server publishing rule protects the server.

For more information on the "bounce" attack, check out www.cert.org/advisories/CA-1997-27.html. The link at the CERT site also contains more detailed information on how IIS blocks this type of attack.

We need to disable the Port Attack protection provided by the IIS to make the FTP server publishing rule work. Perform the following steps to disable the Port Attack setting:

1. Open **Regedt32** and drill down to the following key (Figure 27.35):

   `HKEY_LOCAL_MACHINE\System\CurrentControlSet\Services\Msftpsvc\Parameters\`

   Note that the default setting is **0**.

Figure 27.35 Disabling the EnablePortAttack Entry

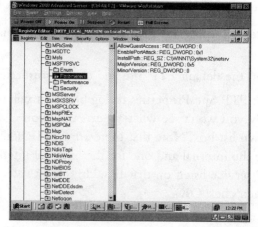

2. Change the **EnablePortAttack** value to **1**.

3. Close **Regedt32** and restart the FTP service.

Step 4: Create the Publishing Rule

The last step is creating the server publishing rule. You can use either the Web Publishing Wizard or the Server Publishing Wizard. The advantage of the Web Publishing Wizard is that you can publish multiple FTP servers using a single IP address on the external interface of the ISA server. If you use the Server Publishing Wizard, you can only publish a single FTP server (using TCP port 21) per IP address. We'll look at how to use the Web Publishing Wizard to securely publish an FTP site later in this chapter.

In this example, we'll use the Server Publishing Wizard.

1. Open the **ISA Management** console, expand your server, and then expand the **Publishing** node. Right-click on **Server Publishing Rules**, point to **New**, and then click **Rule**.

2. On the **Welcome** page, type a name for the FTP server publishing rule and then click **Next**.

3. On the **Address Mapping** page, type in the IP address of the internal interface of the ISA server in the **IP address of internal server** text box, and the IP address of the external interface in the **External IP address on ISA Server** text box, as shown in Figure 27.36. Then, click **Next**.

Figure 27.36 The Address Mapping Page

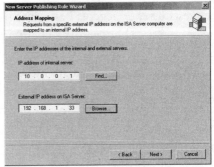

4. On the **Protocol Settings** page, select the **FTP Server** protocol. Click **Next**.

5. On the **Client Type** page, select either the **Any request** or the **Specific computers** option, depending on whether you want to limit access to a specific set of computers. In this example, we'll choose the **Any request** option. Click **Next**.

6. On the last page of the wizard, confirm your settings and click **Finish**.

Your FTP server is now ready to accept connections. If things don't work, check the status of the FTP access application filter. This filter is enabled by default. However, you might have disabled it and forgot to re-enable it. If it is disabled, enable it. The FTP access application filter is required to publish an FTP server.

> **NOTE**
>
> There is an interesting limitation you'll notice when publishing an FTP server on the ISA server. Server publishing rules are often used instead of Web publishing rules in order to preserve the original IP address of the client making the request in the FTP log. When you publish the FTP server located on the ISA server using server publishing rules, you'll always see the source IP address as 127.0.0.1. There is no way to change this behavior. If you need the source IP address in the FTP service logs, you'll have to use packet filters to publish the FTP server.

Using Web Publishing Rules to Allow Secure FTP Access

One limitation to FTP service publishing is that you must use basic authentication. There is no option to allow integrated or certificate authentication with the FTP site. Another limitation is that you can't secure the information contained in the data stream. The information transferred from the FTP server to the FTP client is sent in the clear. While there is an implementation of FTP referred to as "secure FTP," it requires third-party software and is very difficult to make work across a firewall.

You can get around the FTP server's security limitations by using Web publishing rules to publish FTP servers. ISA Server allows you to publish FTP servers on the internal network using Web publishing rules and protocol redirection. The incoming requests are made to the Web Proxy service as HTTP requests, and are then forwarded to the published server as FTP requests. The Web Proxy service receives the information from the FTP server and returns the data via HTTP to the requesting host.

The Incoming Web Requests listener accepts basic, integrated, and digest authentication. You can also require SSL for the connection between the client and the ISA server. When the external network client makes the request to the FTP server via HTTP, you can require integrated authentication and use SSL to protect the data moving between the client and server. Alternatively, you can use basic authentication and increase compatibility. You remain secure as long as the basic authentication credentials are protected by an SSL tunnel.

You need to address the following issues when using Web publishing rules to securely publish an FTP server on the internal network,:

- Configure the Incoming Web Requests listener to support your preferred authentication method
- Configure the Incoming Web Requests listener to support SSL connections
- Create the destination set for the FTP server
- Create the Web publishing rule

Configuring the Incoming Web Requests Listener

Web publishing rules depend on an Incoming Web Requests listener. The Web Proxy service accepts incoming requests for Web publishing rules on the port on the external interface of the

ISA server used by the Incoming Web Requests listener. The default setting for the Incoming Web Requests listener is TCP port 80.

The first thing you need to do is configure the Incoming Web Requests listener to support the type of authentication you require, and enable the SSL port on the listener.

Perform the following steps to configure the Incoming Web Requests listener:

1. Open the **ISA Management** console and right-click on your server name. Click the **Properties** command.

2. In the server **Properties** dialog box, click on the **Incoming Web Requests** tab. Select the **Configure listeners individually per IP address** option. Click **Add**.

3. In the **Add/Edit Listeners** dialog box (Figure 27.37), select your server name in the **Server** drop-down list box. Select an external IP address in the **IP Address** drop-down list box. Type a name for the listener in the **Display Name** text box. In the **Authentication** frame, you have a choice of authentication protocols. Put a check mark in the check box for the protocol you want to support. If you choose to support basic or digest authentication, make sure you click the **Select domain** button and enter the default domain. This greatly simplifies things for your users who might not know what domain they belong to. Just make sure that the default domain is your user domain and your users will never need to enter a domain name. If your user domain is a trusted domain, then check out Microsoft KB article Q319367 "How to Automatically Authenticate Users Against Trusted Domains." You also enter the certificate information used by this listener if you want to enable SSL on this specific listener. Each Incoming Web Requests listener supports one certificate. We cover details of SSL communications later in this chapter. Click **OK**.

Figure 27.37 Configuring Authentication Methods on the Web Requests Listener

4. On the Server **Properties** dialog box, click on the **Incoming Web Requests** tab (Figure 27.38) and put a check mark in the **Enable SSL listeners** check box. This causes the Incoming Web Requests listener to start listening for SSL requests on TCP port 443. Note that you might run into an issue with port contention if the W3SVC is enabled on the ISA server and you have assigned a certificate to the default Web site and configured it to use TCP port 443 to accept SSL connections. To prevent socket pooling for these SSL connections, you will need to disable socket pooling for "securebindings." We cover this issue later in this chapter. Click **Apply**. You'll see the **ISA Server Warning** dialog box. Select the option that works best for you, and click **OK**.

Figure 27.38 Configuring an SSL Listener

Creating the Destination Set for the FTP Site

As is true for all Web publishing rules, you need to create a destination set to use in the Web publishing rule. Perform the following steps to create the destination set:

1. Open the **ISA Management** console, expand your server name, and then expand the **Policy Elements** node. Right-click on **Destination Sets**, point to **New**, and click **Set**.

2. In the **New Destination Set** dialog box, type in a name for the set in the **Name** text box. Type in a description for the set and then click **Add**.

3. Select the **Destination** option button and type in the FQDN external users type into their browser to access the FTP site. Keep in mind that external users access the FTP site using HTTP, so they will *not* use an FTP client application to access the FTP site. You do not need to enter a path. Click **OK**.

4. Click **OK** in the **New Destination Set** dialog box.

Publishing the FTP Site with a Web Publishing Rule

The Web publishing rule uses the destination set you configured for the FTP site. We will first go through the **Web Publishing Wizard** to create the rule, and then we'll go through the Rule's **Properties** dialog box to fine-tune the redirection.

1. In the **ISA Management** console, expand your server name and then expand the **Publishing** node. Right-click on **Web Publishing Rules**, point to **New**, and click **Rule**.

2. On the **Welcome to the New Web Publishing Rule Wizard** page, type in the name for the rule. In this example, we'll call it **FTP Server**. Click **Next**.

3. On the **Destination Sets** page, select the **Specified Destination Set** option from the drop-down list box. Select the name of the destination set you created for the FTP server publishing rule in the **Name** drop-down list box. Click **Next**.

4. On the **Client Type** page, select the option that applies to the clients you want to support. In this example, we want to securely publish the FTP site, so we'll select the **Specific users and group** option. Click **Next**.

5. On the **Users and Group** page, click **Add**. In the **Select Users or Groups** dialog box, select the users or groups that you want to allow access to the site. Click **OK**. Click **Next** in the **Users and Groups** dialog box.

6. On the **Rule Action** page (Figure 27.39), select the **Redirect the request to this internal Web server (name or IP address)** option. Type in the IP address of the internal Web server. If you want to improve the relevance of your log file's information, you should create an entry in your internal DNS or on a HOSTS file on the ISA server. This entry resolves the name external users use to access the site to the IP address of the internal FTP server. For example, if external users type in **ftp.internal.net** to access the external IP address of the ISA server, create a HOSTS file entry on the ISA server that matches ftp.internal.net to the FTP server's internal IP address. Note that in this dialog box you have the option to redirect the request to an alternate port. This is very handy if you're publishing multiple FTP servers on the same machine, and you want to use the same IP address on the internal network for all your FTP sites. Just assign each FTP site on the internal server a different port number. Click **Next**.

Figure 27.39 Configuring the Redirect on the Rule Action Page

7. Review your settings and click **Finish** on the **Completing the New Web Publishing Rule Wizard** page.

8. Double-click on the Web publishing rule you just created. Click on the **Bridging** tab in the rule's **Properties** dialog box. In the **Redirect HTTP requests as** frame, select the **FTP** requests option. This will allow the ISA server to redirect the HTTP requests it receives that matches the destination set used by this rule to be forwarded as FTP requests to the internal network FTP server. Click **Apply** and then click **OK**.

Now, go to an external network client, open Internet Explorer, and type in the URL to access your published FTP site. You'll be welcomed by a dialog box where you can enter your credentials (Figure 27.40).

Figure 27.40 Logging on to the FTP Site

Enter your credentials, click **OK**, and you get into the FTP site (Figure 27.41). Not the most exciting FTP site to hit the Internet, but it does demonstrate that you can access the FTP site files via HTTP. Note that the Web Proxy service supports only FTP downloads. You will not be able to upload files to the FTP site when you publish the site using a Web publishing rule.

Later in this chapter, we'll go over how to attach a certificate to the Incoming Web Requests listener and secure the data stream using SSL.

Figure 27.41 The Published FTP Site

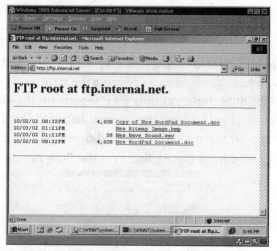

Publishing HTTP and HTTPS (SSL) Servers with Server Publishing Rules

One of the main failings of Web publishing rules is that the source IP address is changed to the IP address of the internal interface of the ISA server when the Web Proxy service forwards the request to the publishing server on the internal network. This causes a problem if you need the requesting host's original IP address recorded in Web or FTP server's log files. You can solve this problem by using server publishing rules instead of Web publishing rules.

You can publish Web servers with server publishing rules. While you won't have the features provided by the Web Proxy service, you can still publish TCP port 80 like any other port. You can also publish SSL sites on the internal network using server publishing rules.

When you use server publishing rules, you can only publish a service one time per IP address. If you choose to publish Web sites using server publishing rules, you will need an IP address on the external interface for each site. The same rule applies to SSL sites.

The procedure for using server publishing rules to publish Web sites includes:

- Configuring the Incoming Web Requests listener to prevent port contention

- Creating an HTTP server protocol definition (an HTTPS server protocol definition is included with the default ISA Server installation)

- Creating the server publishing rule to publish the Web site

Configuring the Incoming Web Requests Listener to Prevent Port Contention

You can use a server publishing rule to publish Web servers on the internal network via TCP port 80, but you have to avoid port contention on the external interface. Running the IIS W3SVC on the ISA server can cause port contention on the external interface if you don't disable socket pooling. The Incoming Web Requests listener can also cause port contention if it's listening on the same port number and IP address you want to use for a server publishing rule.

Take a look at the **Incoming Web Requests** listener interface (Figure 27.42). You have two choices: **Use the same listener configuration for all IP addresses** and **Configure listener individually per IP address**. If you choose **Use the same listener configuration for all IP addresses**, the Incoming Web Requests listener listens on TCP port 80 on all addresses bound to the external interface of the ISA server.

Figure 27.42 The Incoming Web Requests Listener Interface

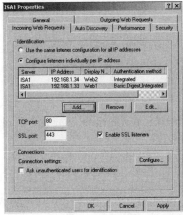

Select the **Use the same listener configuration for all IP addresses** option, and then run **netstat –na | find ":80"** at the command prompt. You'll see something like what appears in Figure 27.43. Notice that 192.168.1.33, 192.168.1.34, and 192.168.1.35 are all listening on TCP port 80. These three IP addresses represent the IP addresses bound to the external interface of the ISA server. Socket pooling has been disabled; that's why you don't see the machine listening on 0.0.0.0 port 80.

There's no problem allowing the listener to listen on all IP address bounds to the external interface if you're not using server publishing rules to publish Web sites. However, if you want to use server publishing rules to publish Web sites, you'll need to choose the **Configure listeners individually per IP address** option. When you choose this option, only the IP addresses you explicitly configure as listeners will listen on TCP 80 on the external interface. All other IP addresses will be available for publishing TCP port 80 using server publishing rules.

You will run into problems if you have only a single IP address bound to the external interface of the ISA server. If the Incoming Web Requests listener is enabled, it will use the only IP address on the external interface of the ISA server to listen on TCP port 80. You won't be able to create a server publishing rule for a Web site because if you do, you'll end up with port contention.

Figure 27.43 TCP Port 80 Listening on All External IP Addresses

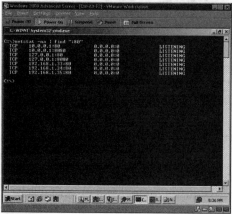

One option you have is to change the port number that the Incoming Web Requests listener uses. If you change the listener port to TCP port 8888, then TCP port 80 will be free to use for the server publishing rule. The drawback to this approach is that external network users will need to be told what port number you're using for the listener so that they can enter it in their requests.

Another option is to disable all listeners. If you select the **Configure listeners individually per IP address** option and remove all listeners using the **Remove** button (or just don't add any, since by default there are no listeners), then the Incoming Web Request listener won't listen on any IP addresses.

No matter what decision you make, remember that the goal is to prevent port contention on the external interface of the ISA server.

Create an HTTP Server Protocol Definition

ISA Server comes preloaded with many protocol definitions that you can use to create protocol rules. These definitions include those that allow inbound and outbound access. Protocol definitions that have their primary connection set as inbound can be used in server publishing rules. There is a built-in protocol definition for HTTPS server publishing, but there isn't one for HTTP server publishing. Microsoft didn't include this protocol definition because they expected you to use Web publishing rules to publish Web sites.

You need to create your own HTTP server protocol definition. Perform the following steps to create the HTTP server protocol definition:

1. Expand you server name and then expand the **Policy Elements** node. Right-click on **Protocol Definitions**, point to **New**, and click **Definition**.

2. On the **Welcome to the New Protocol Definition Wizard** page, type in the name of the protocol definition in the **Protocol definition name** text box. In this example, we'll call it **HTTP (Server)**. Click **Next**.

3. On the **Primary Connection Information** page, type **80** in the **Port number** text box. Leave the **Protocol type** as **TCP** and change the **Direction** to **Inbound**. Click **Next**.

4. Select **No** on the **Secondary Connections** page, and click **Next**.

5. Review your selections and then click **Finish** on the **Completing the New Protocol Definition Wizard** page.

Create the HTTP Server Publishing Rule

You can now create the server publishing rule to publish the Web site now that the Incoming Web Requests listener is configured and you have a protocol definition to support Web publishing using a server publishing rule.

1. Open the **ISA Management** console, expand your server name, and then expand the **Publishing** node. Right-click on **Server Publishing Rules**, point to **New**, and click **Rule**.

2. On the **Welcome to the New Server Publishing Rule Wizard** page, type in the name of the rule in the **Server publishing rule name** text box. In this example, we'll call it **Web Server**. Click **Next**.

3. On the **Address Mapping** page, type in the IP address of the internal network server in the **IP address of internal server** text box. Click **Browse** and select the IP address on the external interface of the ISA server that you want to accept connection to the Web server. Click **Next**.

4. On the **Protocol Settings** page, select the **HTTP (Server)** protocol definition in the **Apply the rule to this protocol** drop-down list box. Click **Next**.

5. On the client type page, select the client type appropriate for your environment. In this example, we'll select the **Any request** option. Click **Next**.

6. Review your settings and click **Finish** on the Complete the New Server Publishing Rule Wizard page.

Now, go to an external network client and connect to the Web site. The server publishing rule should start working immediately. If it doesn't, try restarting the Firewall service. If doing so doesn't fix the problem, check the **Event Viewer**. The Event Viewer reports problems with server publishing rules.

The most common reason for a server publishing rule to fail is port contention on the external interface. Always double check that the IIS W3SVC isn't trying to use the same port, and that you have configured the Incoming Web Requests listener in a way to avoid port contention.

Publishing pcAnywhere on the Internal Network

You can publish pcAnywhere hosts on the internal network using server publishing rules. There are a lot of questions and problems with pcAnywhere publishing on the www.isaserver.org Web boards and mailing list. Most of the time, the problems are easy to correct. You just need to follow the instructions in this section.

The procedure for publishing a pcAnywhere host on the internal network includes:

- Creating protocol definitions used by pcAnywhere
- Creating publishing rules used by pcAnywhere

■ Configuring the pcAnywhere client and server

Let's go through the process of publishing a pcAnywhere server on the internal network, and then we'll discuss areas where you might have problems and how to solve those problems. Keep in mind that when we speak of a "pcAnywhere server," we're talking about a machine that's set up to take calls. You'll be able to connect to the machine from the Internet when we successfully publish the pcAnywhere server.

> **NOTE**
>
> PCAnywhere allows remote control of a computer with a different means of authentication than Windows. Be aware that this can increase your security risks.

Creating the pcAnywhere Protocol Definitions

pcAnywhere versions 9.*x* and 10.*x* use the following protocols for server publishing:

■ TCP port 5631 inbound

■ UDP port 5631 receive send

■ TCP port 5632 inbound

■ UDP port 5632 receive send

These protocol definitions all have their primary connections set to inbound. Note that the UDP protocols use "receive" to indicate a primary inbound connection.

Perform the following steps to create the pcAnywhere server protocol definitions:

1. Open the **ISA Management** console, expand your server name, and then expand the **Policy Elements** node. Right-click on the **Protocol Definitions** node, point to **New**, and click **Definition**.

2. On the **Welcome to the New Protocol Definition** page, type **pcAnywhere 1** in the **Protocol definition name** text box. Click **Next**.

3. On the **Primary Connection Information** page, type **5631** in the **Port number** text box. Set the **Protocol type** to **TCP** and the **Direction** as **Inbound**. Click **Next**.

4. On the **Secondary Connections** page, select **No** and click **Next**.

5. On the last page of the wizard, review your settings and click **Finish**.

6. Repeat steps 1 through 5. Name the rule **pcAnywhere 2**. On the **Primary Connection Information** page, type **5631** in the **Port number** text box. Set the **Protocol Type** to **UDP** and the **Direction** as **Receive/Send**.

7. Repeat steps 1 through 5. Name the rule **pcAnywhere 3**. On the **Primary Connection Information** page, type **5632** in the **Port number** text box. Set the **Protocol Type** to **TCP** and the **Direction** as **Inbound**.

8. Repeat steps 1 through 5. Name the rule **pcAnywhere 4**. On the **Primary Connection Information** page, type **5632** in the **Port number** text box. Set the **Protocol Type** to **UDP** and the **Direction** as **Receive/Send**.

Creating the pcAnywhere Server Publishing Rules

You can now use the pcAnywhere protocol definitions to create the pcAnywhere server publishing rules. You will need four rules, one for each pcAnywhere protocol Definition.

Perform the following steps to create the pcAnywhere server publishing rules:

1. Open the **ISA Server** Management console, expand your server name, and then expand the **Publishing** node. Right-click on the **Server Publishing Rules** node, point to **New**, and click **Rule**.

2. On the **Welcome to the New Server Publishing Rule Wizard** page, type **pcAnywhere 1** in the **Server publishing rule name** text box. If you plan to publish multiple pcAnywhere servers on the internal network, you might want to append the name or IP address of the host on the internal network. Note that the pcAnywhere host on the internal network needs to have a static IP address. Server publishing rules do not support using computer names for redirecting requests to internal network servers. Click **Next**.

3. On the **Address Mapping** page, type in the IP address of the internal network pcAnywhere server in the **IP address of internal server** text box. Click **Browse** and select the IP address on the external interface of the ISA server that you want to accept calls for the pcAnywhere server on the internal network. Click **Next**.

4. On the **Protocol Settings** page, select the **pcAnywhere 1** protocol definition in the **Apply the rule to this protocol** drop-down list box. Click **Next**.

5. On the **Client Type** page, select the option that best fits your environment. Keep in mind that if they successfully authenticate, external users will have full access to the pcAnywhere server on the internal network. You should consider using a client address set to control inbound access to this server publishing rule. Note that you can't limit access to server publishing rules using users and groups. Only Web publishing rules can leverage users and groups. In this example, we'll use the **Any request** option and click **Next**.

6. Review your settings and click **Finish**.

7. Repeat steps 1 through 6. Name the rule **pcAnywhere 2**. On the **Protocol Settings** page, select the **pcAnywhere 2** protocol definition.

8. Repeat steps 1 through 6. Name the rule **pcAnywhere 3**. On the **Protocol Settings** page, select the **pcAnywhere 3** protocol definition.

9. Repeat steps 1 through 6. Name the rule **pcAnywhere 4**. On the **Protocol Settings** page, select the **pcAnywhere 4** protocol definition.

You should be able to connect to the internal network pcAnywhere server soon after creating the last server publishing rule. You can force the new rules to be active by restarting the Firewall service.

We've tested this configuration using both pcAnywhere and Windows authentication and they both work. You can also use compatibility mode and the default (accelerator enabled) mode. Performance is quite good, but it depends on the speed of the link. File transfer and chat functions also work between the external client and the internal network pcAnywhere server.

If you have problems connecting to the pcAnywhere server on the internal network, consider the following:

- Publishing pcAnywhere servers on the internal network requires you to configure the pcAnywhere host on the internal network. If the pcAnywhere host on the internal network isn't answering, make sure the machine on the internal network is set to host mode.

- Make sure you've configured the pcAnywhere server on the internal network as a SecureNAT client. This is the most common reason for server publishing rule failures.

- You need one IP address on the external interface of the ISA server for each pcAnywhere server on the internal network. You cannot publish multiple pcAnywhere servers on the internal network with a single IP address on the external interface of the ISA server.

- Recheck your pcAnywhere protocol definitions. It's very easy to make a mistake when typing in the port numbers. Make sure the direction of each protocol definition is correctly configured.

- Recheck your pcAnywhere server publishing rules. You have to create four server publishing rules, and it's very easy to select the wrong protocol definition when configuring the server publishing rules.

If you have a problem with your pcAnywhere server publishing rules, check for these issues and you'll likely find the cause of the problem.

Web Publishing

Web publishing rules allow you to take advantage of the Web Proxy service's ability to look at application-layer information in HTTP requests to make decisions on how to handle packets. At the beginning of this chapter, we discussed many features provided by Web publishing rules that aren't available with server publishing rules. Web publishing rules are the preferred method of publishing HTTP and FTP content on the internal network because they provide a higher level of security.

Several things need to be configured before you create a Web publishing rule. These include:

- The Incoming Web Requests listener
- Destination sets
- Public DNS entries
- Private DNS entries

Incoming Web Request Listeners

You must configure an Incoming Web Requests listener before a Web publishing rule can work. While you can create a Web publishing rule without configuring an Incoming Web Requests listener, the rule won't accept requests. You can configure listeners separately, or you can apply the same configuration to all listeners.

Each Incoming Web Request listener listens on a specific IP address on the external interface of the ISA server. By default, there are no incoming Web Requests listeners. As you learned earlier in the chapter, you have the choice to configure all IP addresses on the external interface of the ISA server to use the same settings, or you can configure listeners separately.

There are some situations where you must configure listeners separately:

- Only one certificate can be bound to a particular listener. If you need to support multiple certificates, you will need to create multiple listeners.

- If you want to support different authentication methods for different publishing rules, you will need to create separate listeners.

- If you want to use server publishing rules to publish some Web sites, and Web publishing rules to publish other Web sites, you'll need to create separate listeners

Keep in mind that when you create Web publishing rules, you are not asked what listener you want the rule to use. The listener used by a particular Web publishing rule is determined by the FQDN used in the destination set. When a user types in the URL to access a published Web site, the FQDN in the request resolves to the IP address of a specific Incoming Web Requests listener. The listener accepts the request, and then the Web Proxy service checks for rules containing a destination set entry matching the request.

The second most common reason why Web publishing rules will not work is that the Incoming Web Requests listener(s) have not been configured properly.

Destination Sets

The most common reason for Web publishing rule failure is that the destination set used in the Web publishing rule is configured incorrectly. The Web publishing rule uses the entries in the destination set and compares them against the URL in the incoming request. The Web Proxy service passes the URL information for the incoming request to the Web publishing rules, and if one of the rules uses a destination set containing matches for the incoming request, the Web publishing rule is activated.

Destination sets for Web publishing rules need to contain the FQDN (and perhaps that path) that the users on the external network use to access your published Web site. For example, if the user types in **http://www.mywebsite.com** to access your publishing server, then the destination set must contain an entry for www.mywebsite.com.

It's very common for ISA Server administrators to include the private name of the publishing server in the destination set. For example, suppose the external user needs to type in **http://www.mywebsite.com** to access the external IP address on the ISA server you're using for the Incoming Web Requests listener. The name of the server on the internal network is web1.internal.net. The ISA Server administrator enters **web1.internal.net** into the destination set and uses the destination set in the Web publishing rule. When the incoming request for www.mywebsite.com comes into the Incoming Web Requests listener, the Web Proxy service won't find a match because the destination set used doesn't contain www.mywebsite.com; it contains web1.internal.net.

You need to create destination sets before you create Web publishing rules. You'll find when you go through the Web Publishing Wizard that you are not allowed to create a destination set "on the fly." This would be a fine addition to the next version of ISA Server, and we hope to see this change.

Remember that a destination set can contain multiple entries. For example, suppose you run a Web server on the internal network and it houses multiple Web sites. All the sites listen on the same socket (IP address and port number). You configure the Web server to route the requests to the appropriate site using host headers. You can put all the sites in the same destination set and create a single Web publishing rule that forwards requests to all these sites to the same IP address and port number. Just configure the Web publishing rule to send *the original host header*, and the same header contained in the original request (the one sent by the user) will be sent to the publishing server on the internal network. The publishing server then forwards the request to the appropriate Web site based on host header information.

Public DNS Entries

External network users must use FQDNs to access your published Web sites. Destination sets used by the Web publishing rules have FQDNs and sometimes path statements in them. External users won't be able to access your site if your servers aren't registered in the public DNS.

You might be thinking, "I'll just put IP addresses in my destination set; then I won't have to worry about entries in the public DNS." While you can put IP addresses in the destination set and avoid placing entries in the public DNS, we highly advise against doing so. You lose a great deal of security when you publish using IP addresses, because many Internet worms take advantage of this configuration.

For example, if you published by IP address, your servers would not have been protected against the Code Red Worm and many of its variants. Those of us who use only FQDNs in our destination sets never had to worry about Code Red because ISA Server protected us via Web publishing rules and FQDNs in the destination sets.

> **NOTE**
>
> Always use FQDNs in your destination sets. Microsoft designed Web publishing rules with the idea that you would use FQDNs in your destination sets. They do not recommend, and do not support, using IP addresses in the destination sets used in Web publishing rules. In addition to the security issues with IP addresses in destination sets, there is a problem with mixing FQDNs and IP addresses in the same destination set. You can avoid this problem by never using IP addresses in your destination sets. You can use a dynamic DNS service such as www.tzo.com if you have a dynamic IP address assigned to your external interface.

The public DNS server can be on your internal network, on your DMZ segment, or be hosted by your ISP or other third parties. It doesn't matter where the DNS records are located; it just matters that they are available to external network users. Make sure there is a DNS Host (A) record allowing external network users to resolve the name of each server you publish with Web publishing rules, and that the DNS Host (A) entry matches the name included in the destination set used by the Web publishing rule.

Private DNS Entries

Internal network users often need to access the same servers that external network users access. While external network users need to access your sites via ISA Server and Web publishing rules, the internal network users should never "loop back" through the external interface of the ISA server.

Web Proxy clients allow the Web Proxy service to resolve names for them. If you configure the ISA server to use a DNS server that resolves the FQDN of the server to the external interface of the ISA server, the client ends up looping back through the external interface. You can get around this problem by configuring the ISA server to use a DNS server on the internal network. This internal network DNS server contains the private IP addresses of the servers you're publishing instead of the public IP addresses.

For example, if you're publishing a server that external network users access via the URL http://www.mystuff.com, you want the DNS server that the ISA server uses to resolve www.mystuff.com to the *internal* IP address of the server on the *internal* network. This means that you need to create two DNS zones for the same domain name: one zone used by external network users, and a second zone for internal network users. The zone used by internal network users allows internal network clients to access the server through its internal network address.

This works great for SecureNAT and Firewall clients; SecureNAT clients directly connect to the server on the internal network, and the Firewall clients see the destination IP address as being on the LAT and send the request directly to the Web server on the internal network. Web Proxy clients don't use the LAT. You have to use other methods to prevent the Web Proxy clients from looping back through the ISA server to access internal network resources.

> **NOTE**
>
> The Local Domain Table (LDT) is used to control how clients resolve names contained in the table. Firewall and Web Proxy clients typically allow the ISA server to resolve names on their behalf. The client resolves the name instead of the ISA server if the resource is located on the domain in the LDT. It's important that you configure all internal network clients with the address of an internal network DNS server that can resolve addresses of internal network servers.

One thing you need to do is configure the LDT. The LDT can be used by Web Proxy clients to allow them to resolve names locally instead of allowing the ISA server to resolve the name. Local name resolution only takes place for those servers or domains contained in the LDT. The ability to allow Web Proxy clients to resolve names locally isn't as important as the ability to configure the Web Proxy client to use direct access for domains on the LDT. Figure 27.44 shows how you configure Web Proxy clients to use direct access to access resources located in domains in the LDT.

Figure 27.44 Configuring Direct Access to Internal Site for Web Proxy Clients

Direct access means that the client bypasses the Web Proxy service to access resources configured for direct access. Since the resources are on the internal network, the machine will be able to directly access these resources.

While we're on the topic of direct access, note that when you configure external domains for direct access, the Web Proxy client will try to use the Firewall client or SecureNAT client configuration to access the resource. It will *not* use the Web Proxy client configuration; sites configured for direct access bypass the Web Proxy service.

Terminating an SSL Connection at the ISA Server

You can publish SSL sites using Web publishing rules. The ISA server terminates the SSL connection at the Incoming Web Requests listener when you use Web publishing rules to publish SSL sites,. The ISA server impersonates the secure server on the internal network.

The first thing you need to do is get a certificate for the site when you run secure Web sites. You can obtain a Web site certificate from commercial entities such as VeriSign and Thawte, or you can use the Microsoft Certificate Server included with Windows 2000 Server and Windows Server 2003. If you want to run a public site, you should use a commercial certificate. Commercial certificates are much easier to work with on public sites because most machines already include the major commercial sites' enterprise root certificates in their Enterprise Trust List. You should use the Windows 2000 Certificate Server if the secure site is for your own users only.

The ISA server needs to be able to impersonate the Web site on the internal network. The ISA server is able to impersonate the secure site on the internal network by presenting the Web site's certificate to external network clients. In order for the ISA server to do so, you will need to install the secure site's certificate into the ISA server's certificate store. You can attach the certificate to an Incoming Web Requests listener once you install the certificate in the machine's certificate store.

Installing the Web site certificate into the ISA server's certificate store is very easy to do. However, there seems to be a lot of misunderstanding on how to bring a certificate server online and how to request and assign certificates. To help you implement a simple certificate infrastructure for your published Web sites, we'll go over how to install a stand-alone root certificate server, an enterprise root certificate server, and how to request a certificate for your Web site from each of these certificate servers. Then, we'll go over how to export the Web site's certificate and how to import the root server's certificate into the enterprise trust list of the Web clients that access your Web site.

Creating a Stand-Alone Root Certificate Server

A stand-alone root certificate server is a good choice when you need to assign certificates to machines that are not members of the internal network domain. One of the big advantages of the stand-alone root certificate server is there are a number of certificate templates available via the Web-based enrollment site that are not available when you roll out an enterprise root certificate server. Another reason to implement a stand-alone certificate server is that you don't have an Active Directory domain in place.

Perform the following steps to install the stand-alone root certificate server:

1. Click **Start**, point to **Settings**, and click on **Control Panel**.

2. In the **Control Panel**, open the **Add/Remove Programs** applet.

3. In the **Add/Remove Programs** applet, click **Add/Remove Windows Components** in the left pane of the dialog box.

4. In the **Windows Components Wizard** dialog box, put a check mark in the **Certificate Services** checkbox. Click **Yes** in the dialog box that explains that you cannot rename the computer, or join or remove it from a domain, after installing certificate services. Click **Next** in the **Windows Components** dialog box.

5. On the **Certification Authority Type** page (Figure 27.45), select the **Stand-alone root CA** option. You do not need to select the **Advanced options** check box unless you want to use a custom Cryptographic Service Provider (CSP) and specific settings to be used in generating a key pair, or if you want to use an existing key pair. We will not cover those options in this exercise. Click **Next**.

Figure 27.45 Setting the Certification Authority Type

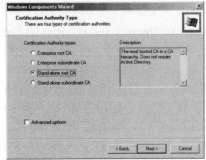

6. On the **CA Identifying Information** page (Figure 27.46), type in the information requested for each field. The only field required is the **CA name**. It's considered good practice to use the computer name (NetBIOS name) of the server in the **CA name** field. However, if you want to do certificate mappings and matching based on fields, you should enter the correct information in all fields. In our examples, we won't be doing any certificate mapping. However, keep in mind that if you want to use client certifi-

cates in SSL bridging scenarios, you will need to perform certificate mapping. After entering the information on the **CA Identifying Information** page, click **Next**.

Figure 27.46 The CA Identifying Information Page

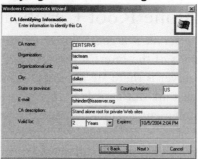

7. On the **Data Storage Location** page, select the locations where you want to store the **Certificate database** and **Certificate database log**. You also have the option to store configuration information in a shared folder. In this example, we'll use the default locations. Click **Next**. Click **OK** in the dialog box warning you that the IIS services must be stopped before continuing.

8. The Certificate Services files are installed. You might be asked for the Windows 2000 CD during the installation, so make sure you have it handy or have the installation files on a network share.

9. Click **Finish** on the **Completing the Windows Components Wizard** page.

Requesting a Web Site Certificate from a Stand-Alone Root Certificate Server

The Web site can now request a certificate from the stand-alone root certificate server. The Certificate Request Wizard on the Web server won't be able to directly communicate with the certificate server, so you'll have to create a certificate request file and then use the Web-based certificate enrollment system to send your certificate request.

Perform the following steps to begin the certificate request for your Web site:

1. Click **Start** and point to **Programs**. Point to **Administrative Tools** and click on **Internet Services Manager**.

2. Expand your server name in the Internet Information Services dialog box. Right-click on the Web site and click the **Properties** command.

3. In the Web site's Properties dialog box, click on the **Directory Security** tab. In the Secure communications frame, click **Server Certificate**.

4. Click **Next** on the **Welcome to the Web Server Certificate Wizard** page.

5. On the Server Certificate page, select the Create a new certificate option and click Next.

6. On the **Delayed** or **Immediate Request** page, select the **Prepare the request now, but send it later** option. This might be the only option available if there are no enterprise root certificate servers in your organization. Click **Next**.

7. On the **Name and Security Settings** page (Figure 27.47), give the certificate a friendly name. The friendly name doesn't matter in terms of the functionality of the certificate, but it does help you identify what the certificate is used for. Select a **Bit length** for the certificate. The more bits, the lower the performance. The required number of bits depends on the level of security you desire balanced by the required performance levels. Click **Next**.

Figure 27.47 The Name and Security Settings Page

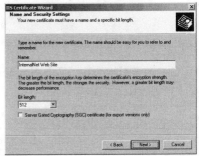

8. On the **Organization Information** page, enter your **Organization** and **Organizational unit** information. This information is not required. Click **Next**.

9. On the **Your Site's Common Name** page (Figure 27.48), type in the FQDN that users on the external network use to access your published Web server. This is an extremely important entry. The common name must be the same as the one you want external users to use to access the site; this is the same name you include in the destination set in the Web publishing rule you use to publish the site. Click **Next**.

Figure 27.48 The Site's Common Name Page

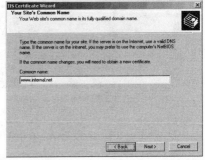

10. On the **Geographical Information** page, enter the **State/province** and **City/ locality** information. This information isn't required, but you should enter the information just in case you want to leverage this information for certificate mapping in the future. Click **Next**.

11. On the **Certificate Request File Name** page, note the default name and location of the certificate request file. You can use this default setting (c:\certreq.txt) in the majority of cases. Make a change if you need to, and click **Next**.

12. On the **Request File Summary** page (Figure 27.49), review the settings and click **Next**.

Figure 27.49 The Request File Summary Page

13. Click **Finish** on the **Completing the Web Server Certificate Wizard** page. Click **OK** in the Web site **Properties** dialog box.

The next step is to take the contents of the **certreq.txt** file and paste them into the Web enrollment form provided by the stand-alone certificate server.

Perform the following steps to obtain the Web server certificate:

1. Open the **certreq.txt** file you created when you ran the Web Server Certificate Wizard. Select the certificate request information that is highlighted in Figure 27.50. Right-click the highlighted area and click the **copy** command to copy it to the clipboard. Note that selecting the information the way we did in Figure 27.50 works with the Windows 2000/2003 Certificate Server. If you were to send information to a third-

Figure 27.50 Selecting the Certificate Request Information

party certificate authority, you should send the *entire contents* of the file, including the **BEGIN** and **END** entries at the beginning and end of the certificate request.

2. Open **Internet Explorer** and type in the URL to the stand-alone certificate server Web site. The URL is http://<certservername>/certsrv. In our example, the URL is http://webserver/certsrv.

3. On the **Welcome** page (Figure 27.51), select the **Request a certificate** option and click **Next**.

4. On the **Choose Request Type** page, select the **Advanced Request** option and click **Next**.

Figure 27.51 The Certificate Server Web Site Welcome Page

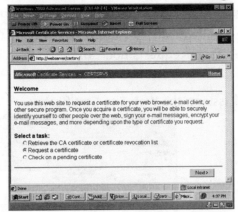

5.   On the **Advanced Certificate Requests** page (Figure 27.52), select the **Submit a certificate request using a base64 encoded PKCS #10 file or a renewal request using a base64 encoded PKCS #7 file** option. Click **Next**.

Figure 27.52 The Advanced Certificate Requests Page

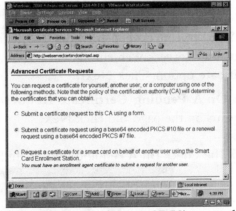

6.   On the **Submit A Saved Request** page (Figure 27.53), paste the certificate request information in the text box. Click **Submit**.

Figure 27.53 The Submit A Saved Request Page

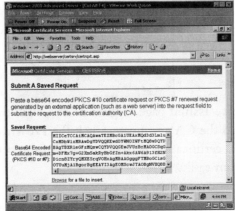

7. Go to the stand-alone certificate server machine. Click **Start** and point to **Programs**. Point to **Administrative Tools** and click **Certification Authority**.

8. In the **Certification Authority** console (Figure 27.54), expand your server name and click on the **Pending Requests** node. In the right pane, right-click on the submitted request, point to **All Tasks**, and click **Issue**.

Figure 27.54 Issuing the Web Site Certificate

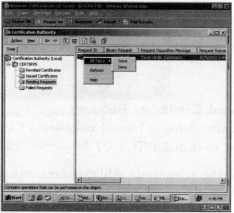

9. Return to the Web server and open **Internet Explorer**. Type in the URL for your stand-alone certificate server's Web enrollment page. Click on the **Check on a pending certificate** option. Click **Next**.

10. On the **Check On A Pending Certificate Request** page (Figure 27.55), select the request that appears on the page and click **Next**.

Figure 27.55 The Check On A Pending Certificate Request Page

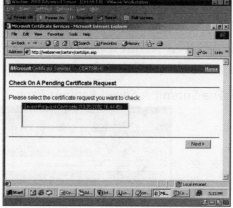

11. In the **Certificate Issued** page (Figure 27.56), click the **Download CA certificate** link to download the CA certificate. Click the **Download CA certification path** link to download the certification path. Save each of the certificates to the desktop so that you can find them easily.

Figure 27.56 Downloading and Installing the Certificate

12. Close Internet Explorer.

The final step is to install the Web server certificate:

1. Open the **Internet Information Services** console, right-click the Web site, and click **Properties**.

2. In the Web site's **Properties** dialog box, click on the **Directory Security** tab. In the **Secure Communications** frame, click **Server Certificate**.

3. On the **Welcome to the Web Server Certificate Wizard** page, read the **Status of your Web Server** information. You'll see that you have a pending request. Click **Next**.

Figure 27.57 Processing the Pending Request

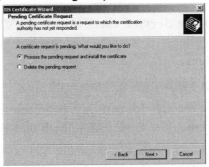

4. On the **Pending Certificate Request** page (Figure 27.57), select the **Process the request and install the certificate** option. Click **Next**.

5. On the **Process a Pending Request** page, click **Browse** and locate the certificate you saved to your desktop. You should see the **certnew.cer** certificate. Select that one and click **Open**. Click **Next**.

6. On the **Certificate Summary** page (Figure 27.58), review the settings and click **Next**.

Figure 27.58 Reviewing the Settings

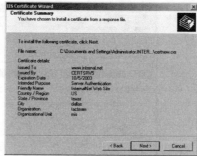

7. Click **Finish** on the **Completing the Web Server Certificate Wizard** page.

The Web server certificate is now installed on the Web server. Later we'll see how to export the Web site's certificate and import the certificate into the ISA server's machine store.

Creating an Enterprise Root Certificate Server

You can create an enterprise root certificate server if you have an Active Directory domain. The advantage of using an enterprise root certificate server is that when your Web server belongs to the same domain as the certificate server, it can send the certificate request directly to the certificate server. You don't have to save the certificate request to a text file and submit it via the Web interface.

Installing the enterprise root certificate server works just about the same as installing the stand-alone certificate server. Perform the following steps to install an enterprise root certificate server:

1. Open the **Control Panel** and double-click on the **Add/Remove Programs** applet.

2. Click **Add/Remove Windows Components** on the left side of the **Add/Remove Programs** window.

3. Select the **Certificate Service** check box in the **Windows Components** window. Click **Yes** in the dialog box warning you that you can't rename the server or leave/join a domain. Click **Next**.

4. Select the **Enterprise root CA** option and click **Next**.

5. Fill in the fields in the **CA Identifying Information** page. Although the only required field is the **CA name**, you should fill in each text box. Click **Next**.

6. On the **Data Storage Location** page, choose where you want to store the **Certificate database** and **Certificate database log**. In this example, we'll select the default locations and click **Next**. Click **OK** in the dialog box warning you that the IIS services must be stopped.

7. Click **Finish** on the last page of the wizard.

Requesting a Web Site Certificate from a Enterprise Root Certificate Server

Requesting a certificate from an enterprise root CA is much easier than from a stand-alone CA. If the Web server belongs to the same domain as the enterprise root CA, information about the

CA is stored in the Active Directory, and the Web server will be able to find the CA and request the certificate directly from the enterprise root CA.

Perform the following steps to have the Web site request a certificate from the enterprise root CA:

1. Open the **Internet Information Services** console and expand your server name. Right-click on your Web site and click the **Properties** command.

2. In the Web site **Properties** dialog box, click on the **Directory Security** tab. Click **Server Certificate** in the **Secure communications** frame.

3. Click **Next** in the **Welcome to the Web Server Certificate Wizard** page.

4. Select the **Create a new certificate** on the **Server Certificate** page.

5. Select the **Send the request immediately to an online certification authority** on the **Delayed or Immediate Request** page (Figure 27.59). Click **Next**.

Figure 27.59 Sending the Certificate Request Directly to the Certificate Server

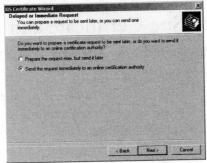

6. On the **Name and Security Settings** page, type a friendly name for the certificate in the **Name** text box. Select a bit length appropriate for the level of security required for your site. Click **Next**.

7. On the **Organization Information** page, type in the name of your organization and organizational unit in the **Organization** and **Organizational unit** text boxes. Click **Next**.

8. On the **Your Site's Common Name** page, type in the FQDN external users use to access the site. This is the name you will use in the destination set in the Web publishing rule you'll use to publish the site. Click **Next**.

9. On the **Geographical Information** page, type in the State/province and City/locality. Click **Next**.

10. On the **Choose a Certification Authority** page (Figure 27.60), click the **Down arrow** in the Certification authorities drop-down list box and select the enterprise CA from which you want to obtain the certificate. If you have a single enterprise CA, that name will appear automatically. Click **Next**.

Figure 27.60 Choosing a Certification Authority

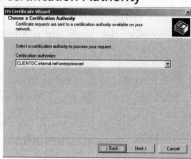

11. Review the information on the **Certificate Request Submission** page and click **Next**.

12. Click **Finish** on the **Completing the Web Server Certificate Wizard** page, and click **Finish**.

The certificate is now installed on the Web server.

Exporting the Web Site Certificate and Importing the Certificate into the ISA Server Certificate Store

You need to install the Web site certificate on the ISA server so that the ISA server can impersonate the secure Web site. The Web site's certificate is installed into the ISA server's *machine* certificate store. You can attach the certificate to an Incoming Web Requests listener once the certificate is in the ISA server's machine store.

Getting the certificate into the ISA server's machine store is a two-step process: first, export the Web site certificate from the Web server, and then import the exported certificate into the ISA server's machine certificate store. Perform the following steps to export the Web site's certificate:

1. Open the **Internet Services Manager** from the **Administrative Tools** menu.

2. In the Internet Information Services console, right-click on the Web site that contains the certificate you want to export, and then click **Properties**.

3. In the Web site's **Properties** dialog box, click on the **Directory Security** tab.

4. On the Directory Security tab, click **View Certificate**. Click on the **Details** tab. Click **Copy to File**. This opens the Certificate Export Wizard.

5. On the **Welcome to the Certificate Export Wizard** page, read the description of the wizard and what it does, and then click **Next**.

6. On the **Export Private Key** page, select the **Yes, export the private key** option, and click **Next**.

7. On the **Export File Format** page, remove the check mark from the **Enable strong protection** option. If you leave this option checked, you will have to enter information to confirm the certificate usage. Since the Web Proxy service needs to use the certificate in the background, you need to remove the strong protection option. Click **Next**.

8. On the **Password** page, type in a password to secure the certificate, and then confirm the password. Don't forget the password! You'll be asked for it when you import the certificate into the ISA server's certificate store. Click **Next**.

9. On the **File to Export** page, type in a name for the certificate, such as c:\webservercert in the File name text box. The wizard automatically adds the correct file extension (.pfx). Click **Next**.

10. On the **Completing the Certificate Export Wizard** page, confirm that the information is correct and then click **Finish**. If there are no problems, you'll see a dialog box informing you that the certificate export was successful. Click **OK** to dispatch the dialog box.

11. Close the Certificate dialog box and click **Cancel** in the Web server **Properties** dialog box.

Now we're ready to import the certificate into the ISA server's machine store:

1. Copy the exported certificate to the ISA server.

2. Click **Start** and then click the **Run** command. Type **mmc** in the **Open** text box and click **OK**.

3. Click the **Console** menu and then click the **Add/Remove Snap-in** command.

4. On the **Stand-alone** tab, click **Add** in the **Add/Remove Snap-in** dialog box.

5. In the **Add Stand-alone Snap-in** dialog box, select the **Certificates** entry and then click **Add**.

6. On the **Certificates snap-in** dialog box, select the **Computer account** option. It's important that you select the **Computer account** option because you want the certificate in the machine's certificate store. The most common error ISA Server administrators make is to select the wrong option and import the certificate into the user account's certificate store. Select the **Computer account** option and click **Next**.

7. On the **Select Computer** page, select the **Local computer: (the computer this console is running on)** option and click **Finish**.

8. Click **Close** in the **Add Stand-alone Snap-in** dialog box, and then click **OK** in the **Add/Remove Snap-in** dialog box.

9. Expand the **Certificates (Local Computers)** node and then right-click on the **Personal** node. Point to **All Tasks** and then click on the **Import** command.

10. On the **Welcome to the Certificate Import Wizard**, read the description of what the wizard does, and click **Next**.

11. On the **File to Import** page, click **Browse** to find the Web server certificate that you copied to the ISA server. Click **Next** after selecting the certificate.

12. On the **Password** page, type in the **Password** you assigned to the certificate. Put a check mark in the **Mark the private key as exportable** check box. This will make your life a bit easier if you need to export the key and use it on another machine. Click **Next**.

13. On the **Certificate Store** page (Figure 27.61), select the **Place all the certificates in the following store** option. The **Certificate store** should read as **Personal**. Click **Next**.

Figure 27.61 The Certificate Store Page

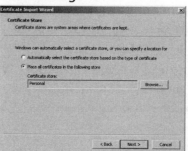

14. Read the settings on the **Completing the Certificate Import Wizard** page and then click **Finish**. If all goes well, you'll see a dialog box confirming that the import was successful. Click **OK** to dispatch the dialog box.

15. Refresh the display. You should now see the certificate in the list of certificates in the machine's certificate store (Figure 27.62).

Figure 27.62 Certificates Contained in the ISA Server's Machine Store

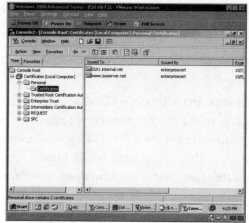

16. Minimize the Certificates console and open the **ISA Management** console. Right-click on your server name and click **Properties**.

17. On the server's **Properties** dialog box, click on the **Incoming Web Requests** tab. On the **Incoming Web Requests** tab, select the **Configure listeners individually per IP address** option, and then click **Add**.

18. On the **Add/Edit Listeners** dialog box (Figure 27.63), select your server name in the **Server** drop-down list box. Select an IP address on the external interface of the ISA server in the **IP Address** drop-down list box. Type in a short name for the listener in the **Display Name** text box. Put a check mark in the **Use a server certificate to authenticate to web clients** check box.

Figure 27.63 Selecting the Web Site Server Certificate

19. On the **Add/Edit Listeners** dialog box, click **Select**. In the **Select Certificate** dialog box (Figure 27.64), select the Web server certificate and click **OK**. The certificate will show up in the **Add/Edit Listeners** dialog box. Click **OK** in the **Add/Edit Listeners** dialog box.

Figure 27.64 Selecting the Web Site Server Certificate

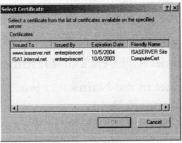

20. Click **Apply** in the server **Properties** dialog box. A warning dialog box appears and informs you that the Web Proxy service will need to be restarted. Select the option that works best for you, and click **OK**.

Now with the certificate attached to the Incoming Web Request listener, you are in the position to securely publish the Web site. You can publish the Web site so that the SSL connection terminates at the ISA server's external interface, or you can protect the information using SSL from the client to the internal Web server by forcing an SSL connection between the ISA server and the internal Web site. This is called *SSL bridging*, which we discuss in the next section.

Bridging SSL Connections

ISA Server supports SSL bridging, and can bridge incoming SSL requests in two ways:

- The incoming SSL request can be bridged as an HTTP request.
- The incoming SSL request can be bridged as an SSL request.

When ISA Server bridges an SSL request as an HTTP request, the SSL connection is terminated at the Incoming Web Requests listener. The ISA server receives SSL packets, decrypts the packets, and forwards them to the Web server on the internal network as HTTP. SSL protects data between the client and the external interface of the ISA server; the data is sent "in the clear" between the internal interface of the ISA server and the Web server on the internal network.

You might think its safe to send the data between the internal interface of the ISA server and the internal network Web server unencrypted if you trust the internal network,. However, if you don't completely trust the transit network between the ISA server and the Web server, you should protect that data as well.

You can protect data moving between the ISA server and the publishing Web server by bridging SSL requests *as* SSL requests. In this scenario, the Internet client establishes an SSL link with the ISA server's Incoming Web Requests listener. The data is decrypted by the ISA server after it is received by the listener. Then, the ISA server creates a second SSL connection between the internal interface of the ISA server and the publishing Web server. The data is re-encrypted and sent to the Web server over the secure SSL link.

In the following sections, we look at how to bridge the SSL connection as HTTP, and then how to bridge the connection as SSL.

Bridging SSL Connections as HTTP

You're ready to create a Web publishing rule that bridges an SSL connection as HTTP when the Web server's certificate is bound to the incoming Web Requests listener. Now all that's left to do is create the Web publishing rule:

1. Open the **ISA Management** console, expand your server name, and then expand the **Policy Elements** node. Right-click on **Destination Sets**, point to **New**, and click **Set**.

2. Type a name for the set in the **Name** text box. Type a description for it in the **Description** text box. Click **Add**.

3. In the **Add/Edit Destination** text box, select the **Destination** option and type in the FQDN for the Web site in the text box. Remember that this is the FQDN the external network users use to access your site. This FQDN must also match the name on the Web site certificate you bound to the Incoming Web Requests listener. Click **OK**. You'll see the completed destination set information in Figure 27.65. Click **OK** to complete the set.

Figure 27.65 A Completed Destination Set

Now that the destination set is completed, you're ready to create the Web publishing rule. To do so, perform the following steps:

1. Expand the **Publishing** node and right-click on the **Web Publishing Rule** node. Point to **New** and point to **Rule**.

2. On the **Welcome to the New Web Publishing Rule Wizard** page, type in a name for the publishing rule in the **Web publishing rule name** text box. Click **Next**.

3. On the **Destination Sets** page, select the **Specified destination set** option in the **Apply this rule to** drop-down list box. Select the name of your destination set in the **Name** drop-down list box. Click **Next**.

4. On the **Client Type** page, select the **Any request** option. Click **Next**.

5. On the **Rule Action** page, select the **Redirect the request to this internal Web server (name or IP address)** option. Enter either the IP address or the name of the server on the internal network. We recommend that you create a split DNS infrastructure, or put a HOSTS file entry for the FQDN used in the destination set. Enter that FQDN in the redirect. Using the FQDN in the redirect will make your log files cleaner and prevent the dreaded 14120 error from littering your application log in the Event Viewer. You can choose to send the original host header if you like; it won't matter if you're using the same name in the redirect as that contained in the original host header. Click **Next**.

Figure 27.66 The Rule Action Page

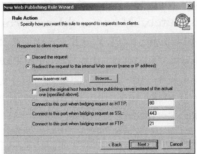

6. Review the settings on the **Completing the New Web Publishing Rule Wizard** page, and then click **Finish**.

7. In the right pane of the console, right-click on the Web publishing rule you just created and click **Properties**. Click on the **Bridging** tab. In the **Redirect HTTP requests as** frame, make sure the **HTTP requests** option is selected. Of course, this selection won't matter, because we're going to force SSL connections in this rule. In the **Redirect SSL requests as** frame, select the **HTTP requests (terminate the secure channel at the proxy)** option. This allows you to bridge incoming SSL requests as HTTP requests. Put a check mark in the **Require secure channel (SSL) for published site** check box. This check box forces users to use SSL to connect to the Web site. You can select the **Require 128-bit encryption** option if your clients support it. Click **Apply** and then click **OK**.

Go to an external network client and make the connection. If the external network client has a certificate from your CA, and the CA that issued the Web site certificate is in your enterprise trust list, you won't see anything unusual, and you'll make the connection with the ISA server without incident. You won't see any warning dialog boxes regarding the nature of the certificate.

You'll see what appears in Figure 27.67 if the client doesn't have the CA that issued the Web server's certificate in its enterprise trust list, . The error indicates that you don't trust the CA that issued the Web site's certificate. This is most commonly seen when you "roll your own" certificate server solution. You can avoid this by assigning user or machine certificates. In the process of obtaining the certificate from the certificate server, the CA you receive the certificate from will be placed in the **Trusted Root Certificate Authorities** list. If you don't want to assign certificates to the users or machines, you can copy the certificate server's certificate into your clients' Trusted Root Authorities list manually.

Figure 27.67 Security Alert Dialog Box Warning of an Untrusted Root Authority

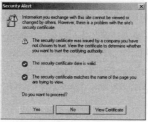

Another problem you might have is with the name of the certificate. In Figure 27.68, note that everything is okay except that **The name on the security certificate does not match the name of the site**. This is probably one of the most common errors we encounter when troubleshooting SSL Web publishing rules. You'll see this if the name on the certificate is not the same as the FQDN used by users to access the Web site. The only fix for this problem is to obtain a new certificate that has a name that matches the FQDN used to access the site. This is why it's so important that you make the proper entry for the "common name" of the Web site when you make the Web site's certificate requests.

Figure 27.68 Security Alert Dialog Box Warning of a Certificate Mismatch

Bridging SSL Connections as SSL

What if you need to protect the data end to end? You might not trust your internal network, so you need to protect the data on the Internet and you need to protect it from the internal interface of the ISA server to the Web site on the internal network. This might be the case when the internal network is actually a private address DMZ segment. In this scenario, the Web publishing rule is configured in very much the same way, except for the choice in the SSL bridging frame.

You also have to be mindful of how the Web site is configured, because if it is configured incorrectly, the ISA server will not be able to bridge the request. To successfully bridge SSL connections as SSL connections, you need to do the following:

■ Prepare the Web site for SSL

- Configure the Web publishing rule

Let's first look at how to prepare the Web site. If you're already expert at configuring SSL Web sites, you can skip to the section on how to configure the Web publishing rule. In this example, we'll assume that you've already bound a certificate to the Web site and exported that certificate and bound it to the external interface of the ISA server.

1. From the **Administrative Tools** menu, click on the **Internet Services Manager** link.

2. In the **Internet Information Services** console, right-click on the Web site you're publishing and click the **Properties** command.

3. In the Web site's **Properties** dialog box, click on the **Directory Security** tab.

4. On the **Directory Security** tab, click **Edit**. This brings up the **Secure Communications** dialog box (Figure 27.69). Put a check mark in the **Require secure channel (SSL)** check box. This requires the ISA server to establish an SSL connection with the Web site. Put a check mark in the **Require 128-bit encryption** check box if you want to force strong encryption (the ISA server will support it). You can also force the ISA server to use a client certificate to authenticate with the Web site, although this is *not* required. If you want to force the use of a client certificate, select the **Require client certificates** option. If you want the option to use a certificate, but allow non-client certificate connections too, select the **Accept client certificates** option. This option allows you to use other means of authentication (other than client certificates). We won't cover client certificate mapping for Web sites in this chapter, but check www.isaserver.org/shinder for an article on how to do this. For the greatest flexibility, select the **Accept client certificates** option. Click **OK**.

Figure 27.69 Forcing a Secure Channel to the Web Site

5. Click **Apply** and then click **OK** in the Web site **Properties** dialog box. Click **Stop** in the MMC button bar, and then click **Start** in the button bar.

If you want to use client certificates to authenticate against the Web server, you'll need to assign a certificate to the Web Proxy service. The Web Proxy service will act as the client of the internal network Web server. The funny thing about assigning a certificate to the Web Proxy service is that the service can't directly request a client certificate. What you can do is use the machine certificate by copying it to the Web Proxy service's machine store.

Perform the following steps to assign the machine's certificate to the Web Proxy service:

1. Click **Start** and then click **Run**. In the **Run** dialog box, type **mmc** and click **OK**.

2. In the console window, click the **Console** menu and click the **Add/Remove Snap-in** command. In the **Add/Remove Snap-in** dialog box, click **Add**.

3. In the **Add Stand-alone Snap-in** dialog box, select the **Certificates** entry and click **Add**. In the **Certificates snap-in** dialog box, click the **Service account** option and click **Next**.

4. On the **Select Computer** page, select the **Local computer** option and click **Next**.

5. On the **Select a service account to manage on the local computer** page, select the **Microsoft Web Proxy** entry and click **Finish**.

6. We need to add a second instance of the **Certificates** snap-in. Select the **Certificates** entry and click **Add**. On the **Certificates snap-in** page, select the **Computer account** option and click **Next**.

7. On the **Select Computer** page, select the **Local Computer** option and click **Finish**.

8. Click **Close** in the **Add Stand-alone Snap-in** dialog box. Click **OK** in the **Add/Remove Snap-in** dialog box.

9. Expand both of the **Certificates** nodes in the left pane of the console. Expand the **Personal** node for both the **Local Computer** and the **W3Proxy** services (Figure 27.70).

Figure 27.70 The Web Proxy Service Certificate List

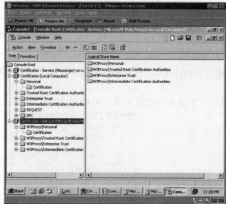

10. Click on the **Local Computer\Personal\Certificates** node. In the right pane of the console, you'll see the computer certificate. Right-click on your computer certificate and click the **Copy** command.

11. Click on the **Microsoft Web Proxy Service\W3Proxy\Personal\Certificates** node. Click in the right pane of the console. Next, right-click on the right pane of the console and click the **Paste** command. This pastes the computer certificate into the Web Proxy service's personal store.

The Web Proxy service now has a certificate it can present to the internal Web server in the event that you configure the Web server on the internal network to require client certificate authentication.

The last step is to configure the Web publishing rule to support SSL-to-SSL bridging:

1. In the **ISA Management** console, expand your server name and then expand the **Publishing** node. Right-click on the **Web Publishing Rules** node, point to **New**, and click **New**.

2. Type in a name for the rule on the **Welcome to the New Web Publishing Rule Wizard** page and click **Next**.

3. On the **Destination Sets** page, select the **Specified destination set** option and then select the destination set for your site. Click **Next**.

4. On the **Client Type** page, select **Any request** and click **Next**.

5. On the **Rule Action** page, select the **Redirect the request to this internal Web server (name or IP address)** option. Type in the name of the site, which is the same name on the site certificate and the same name used in the destination set (Figure 27.71).

Figure 27.71 Configuring the Rule Action

6. Click **Finish** on the last page of the wizard.

7. In the right pane of the **ISA Management** console, double-click on the new rule. Click on the **Bridging** tab.

8. In the **Redirect SSL requests as** frame, select the **SSL requests (establish a new secure channel to this site)** option. Select the **Require secure channel (SSL) for published site** check box. If you want the ISA server to use a client certificate to authenticate with the Web server, select the **Use a certificate to authentication to the SSL Web Server** check box. Click **Select**. You'll be presented with the **Select Certificate** dialog box (Figure 27.72). The certificates you see listed in this dialog box are those included in the Web Proxy service's personal certificate store. Select the certificate and click **OK**.

Figure 27.72 Assigning a Client Certificate for the SSL Bridge

9. The name of the client certificate will appear in the rule's **Properties** dialog box. Click **Apply** and then click **OK**. Note that you *do not* need to perform certificate mapping

for this to work. You do not need to create a one-to-one or many-to-one certificate mapping; the Web Proxy service will be able present the ISA server's machine certificate in order to authenticate to the Web site automatically.

Go to an external network client and connect to the published Web site. You'll be able to connect just as you did when you create the SSL-to-HTTP bridging. If everything is configured correctly, you won't see any warning dialog boxes and you'll have direct access to the site.

Just for fun, you might want to confirm that the ISA server is indeed sending a client certificate to authenticate with the Web site. If so, do the following:

1. Configure the Web site to require certificate authentication. Next, go to a client on the internal network that doesn't have a user certificate installed. What we want to determine is whether the Web site will accept requests from browsers without a certificate.

2. Type **http://IPADDRESS** of the Web site that requires certificate authentication. The Security Warning dialog box should appear, telling you that the name on the certificate doesn't match the request (see Figure 27.73). This is expected, since the Web site's certificate has the FQDN of the site, not its IP address. Click **Yes** to get past that dialog box.

Figure 27.73 Security Alert Dialog Box Warning of a Name Mismatch

3. Internet Explorer pops up a **Client Authentication** dialog box because the Web site is configured to require client certificates for authentication (Figure 27.74),. If your browser had a certificate configured on it, you would see the name of the certificate in this dialog box. Click **OK** to close the **Client Authentication** dialog box.

Figure 27.74 The Client Authentication Dialog Box

4. After closing the authentication dialog box, you'll see the **The page requires a client certificate** Web page (Figure 27.75). HTTP error 403.7 indicates that you need a client certificate to access the site and that you did not present a certificate and therefore are denied access.

Figure 27.75 Error Page Indicating that a Client Certificate Is Required

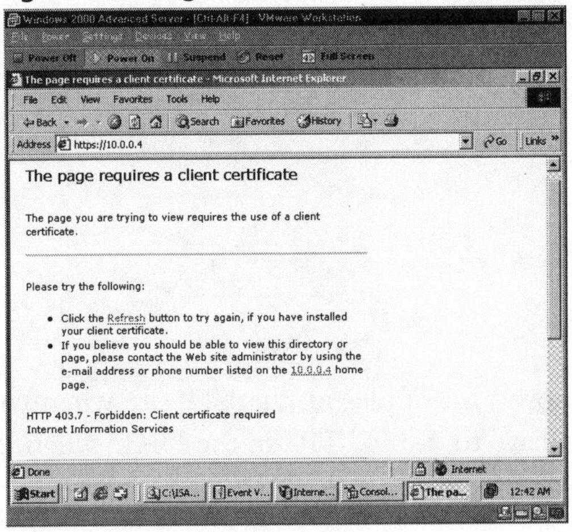

Secure FTP Connections Using SSL

Secure publishing of FTP requires you use Web publishing rules. You can only use the basic authentication protocol when you publish an FTP site using a server publishing rule. In addition, you can't protect the data using the FTP protocol.

The solution is to publish the FTP site using a Web publishing rule. You can configure the Web publishing rule to require an SSL connection and then redirect the SSL link as an FTP request. The FTP server on the internal network receives the request from the ISA server and returns the FTP data to the internal interface of the ISA server. The ISA server encrypts the data and returns it to the client. Note that the client must use a Web browser and the HTTPS protocol to access the secure FTP site via the Incoming Web Requests listener.

We have already reviewed most of the procedures required to make secure FTP server publishing work:

- Bind a certificate to the Incoming Web Requests listener that matches the name users use to access the site.

- Configure the Web publishing rule to redirect SSL requests as FTP requests.

- Train the users to use HTTPS to access the site, or create a Web page that redirects FTP downloads to HTTPS requests.

You saw how to bind the certificate to the external interface earlier in this chapter. For more information on how to bind certificates to the Incoming Web Requests listener, review the section on SSL bridging.

Creating a Web publishing rule to forward SSL requests as FTP requests is very similar to the rules you created in the SSL bridging scenarios covered earlier. The only difference is the setting on the **Bridging** tab of the rule (Figure 27.76). You need to enable the **Require secure channel (SSL) for published site** check box, and you can choose the **Require 128-bit encryption** check box if your clients support this option. Note that the client certificate check box is disabled and the **Select** button is grayed out. The reason for this is that you can't use certificates to authenticate with an FTP site.

Figure 27.76 Redirecting SSL Requests as FTP Requests

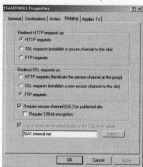

The browser will show a list of files on the FTP site when you connect to the site (Figure 27.77). Notice that you have to use HTTPS in the URL; when the connection is established, a "lock" icon appears in the status bar of the browser.

Figure 27.77 Connecting to the FTP Site

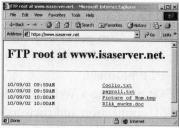

Publishing a Certificate Server

You might want to publish your certificate server. This is a good idea for two reasons:

- External network clients can access the certificate server's Web enrollment site from the Internet.

- The certificate revocation list (CRL) is available to Web clients.

You might want to publish the certificate server if you want users to access the Web enrollment site to obtain a client certificate from the certificate server. The user must be a member of the domain to request a user certificate from an enterprise certificate server. If the request is made to a stand-alone root certificate server, the user will have to wait for you to approve the certificate request (this is the default setting).

Another reason why you might want to publish the certificate server is to make the CRL available to external network users. One reason for poor SSL performance is that the client can't access the CRL. You can fix this problem by publishing the CRL.

Perform the following steps to make the CRL available to external network clients:

1. Open the **Internet Services Manager** from the **Administrative Tools** menu.

2. In the **Internet Information Services** console, expand the Default Web site node and right-click on the **CertEnroll** virtual directory. Click **Properties**.

3. Click on the **Virtual Directory** tab and put a check mark in the **Directory browsing** check box. Click **Apply** and then click **OK**.

4. Now let's check what the default URL is for the CRL. On the certificate server, click Start and then click Run. Type mmc in the Open text box and click OK. In the console, click on the Console menu and click the Add/Remove Snap-in command.

5. In the Add/Remove Snap-in dialog box, click Add. In the **Add Stand-alone Snap-in** dialog box, click the **Certificates** entry and click **Add**. On the **Certificates** snap-in page, select the **Computer account** option and click **Next**.

6. On the **Select Computer** page, select the **Local computer option** and click **Finish**. Click **Close** in the **Add Stand-alone Snap-in** dialog box. Click **OK** in the **Add/Remove Snap-in** dialog box.

7. In the left pane of the console, expand the **Certificates** node and then expand the **Personal** node (Figure 27.78). Click on the **Certificates** node. In the right pane of the console, double-click on the certificate that lists **<All> for Intended Purposes**.

Figure 27.78 The Certificates List

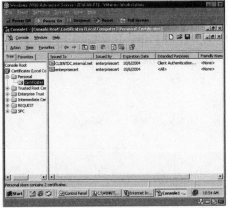

8. In the **Certificate** dialog box, click on the **Details** tab. Scroll through the list of fields and find the **CRL Distribution Points** entry (Figure 27.79). This is the URL you need to make available to external network users. In this example, the URL is http://clientdc.internal.net/CertEnroll/enterprisecert.crl. The FQDN in this URL must be accessible to external network clients; therefore, you need to enter this information into the public DNS. Close the **Certificate** dialog box.

Figure 27.79 CRL Distribution Point Information

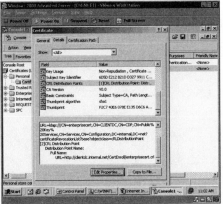

9. Go to the ISA Server machine. Create a destination set for the FQDN listed in the CRL. You also must create an entry in the public DNS that resolves the FQDN listed in the CRL to the external IP address of the ISA server used by the Incoming Web Requests listener. If you want to further limit access, you can enter the path **/CertEnroll** to the destination set.

10. Create a Web publishing rule to publish the CRL using the destination set you created in step 9.

11. You also need to make the certificate chain information available to the external network clients. The certificate chain is contained in the same folder as the CRL, so you shouldn't have to create a separate Web publishing rule to support this.

Your biggest challenge in publishing the CRL and the certificate chain information (contained in the root certificate) is to match the URL information in the certificate to that which is accessible to external network clients. You will need to create a split DNS infrastructure if the certificate server is an enterprise root or enterprise subordinate server. If the certificate server is a stand-alone root, you will have problems if only the NetBIOS name is contained in the URL.

You can add CRL Distribution Point and Authority Information Access (used to confirm the certificate chain) URLs in the **Certificate Authority** console.

Summary

Server publishing rules allow you to publish almost any protocol. This is the primary advantage of server publishing over Web publishing. The server publishing rule essentially performs a reverse NAT function. The ISA server does not replace the source IP address on the packet unless you implement the changes noted in Microsoft KB article Q311777. An important consideration when implementing server publishing rules is that you need to avoid port contention on the external interface. No two services can listen on the same port on the same IP address on the external interface of the ISA server. For this reason, you typically need to disable the IIS services on the ISA server. You can also use server publishing rules to publish Web sites. The most common reason for doing this is so that the original client IP address appears in the Web server's log files.

Web publishing rules allow you to publish Web and FTP sites. Web publishing rules are handled by the Web Proxy service. The Web Proxy service is able to examine the application-layer data and make decisions on how to handle requests based on information such as the destination URL. Web publishing rules also allow you to perform port and protocol redirection. Protocol redirection allows you to bridge HTTP requests as SSL or FTP requests. Port redirection allows you to accept requests on the port number on the external interface and then forward them to another port on an internal network Web server. The main drawback of Web publishing rules is that the client's source IP address is always changed to the internal IP address on the ISA server.

## Chapter 28

Protecting Mail Services with ISA Server

Best Damn Topics in this Chapter:

- Configuring Mail Services on the ISA Server

- Configuring Mail Services on the Internal Network

- GFI's Mail Security and Mail Essentials for SMTP Servers

Introduction

Mail services publishing is the most popular type of server publishing. Both small and large organizations prefer to have a higher level of control over their mail services than any other type of service. Why? Since most businesses are highly dependent on their mail services, they can little afford the foibles and inconsistent levels of service provided by third parties. If mail services go down, they might take the business with them!

The good news is that Microsoft's Internet Security and Acceleration (ISA) Server makes publishing mail services very simple. If you have your own third-party Simple Mail Transfer Protocol (SMTP)/Post Office Protocol 3 (POP3) mail server, you can use the Microsoft Internet Information server (IIS) SMTP service for a mail relay, and you can even leverage the IIS SMTP service and the ISA Server Message Screener to protect your third-party SMTP/POP3 mail server from spam. If you run Windows 2003, you already have a POP3 server available to you. Just put an IIS SMTP service in front of your Windows 2003 SMTP/POP3 server and you'll be protected against attackers and spam.

Even more impressive than support for simple IIS SMTP services is ISA Server's ability to make Exchange 2000 services available to Internet users. You can publish all the Exchange Server's mail services, or just certain ones. ISA Server integrates with Exchange 2000 by making it easy to securely publish Exchange Remote Procedure Call (RPC) and Outlook Web access (OWA). No other firewall on the market provides this level of integration and compatibility with Microsoft Exchange 2000.

This chapter is broken down into three main sections: publishing mail services on the ISA server, publishing mail services on a computer somewhere on the internal network, and using GFI Software's MailSecurity application to block out spam. If you're not publishing mail services on the ISA server, you might want to skip down to the publishing services on the internal network section. However, we advise against this, as we'll be going over many important principles early in the chapter that you should understand before trying to publish services on the internal network. If you have a single Windows 2000 server and need to publish everything on it, then you should focus on the section entitled "Configuring Mail Services on the ISA Server" section. Again, we recommend that you read the entire chapter, as we'll be including helpful tips and tricks throughout!

> **NOTE**
>
> Small Business Server (SBS) isn't explicitly covered in this book because of time and size considerations. Although we can't cover the specifics of SBS, the good news is that the same principles that we apply on the "Configuring Mail Services on the ISA Server" section apply to SBS. The major difference is we don't cover any of the SBS built-in wizards to accomplish the configuration. If you want to run ISA Server and Exchange on the same computer, you'll have to carry out the manual configuration steps detailed in this chapter.

We'll start with configuring and publishing mail services on the ISA server, and then move to the higher security option of putting them on the internal network. Pay very close attention to the steps outlined in the following sections. Many details must be covered. Missing even one step could prevent something from working and it may be very difficult to troubleshoot the problem. Be patient, be careful, and you won't find yourself reformatting and reinstalling because of an obscure misconfiguration issue.

Configuring Mail Services on the ISA Server

We get a tremendous number of questions on ISAServer.org and in the Microsoft newsgroups regarding how to configure and publish mail services on the ISA server. In the vast majority of cases we're not able to give any detailed level of information because of the number of factors you have to take into consideration when running mail services on the ISA server. We're usually able to throw out a quick tip, but not much more.

At the time of this writing, there is little or no documentation on the specific procedures you must carry out to install mail services on the ISA server. There is isolated information here and there, but nothing you can really use to create an integrated and working solution. This chapter solves this problem by giving you complete step-by-step working examples of how to carry out mail services publishing on the ISA server. You'll also learn about both common and obscure issues that might cause your mail services to perform poorly.

In this section we'll cover the following topics:

- Publishing the IIS SMTP Service on the ISA server
- Configuring the Message Screener on the ISA server
- Publishing Exchange Server services on the ISA server
- Publishing Outlook Web Access on the ISA server

If you've been wondering about the secrets of mail services publishing on the ISA server, then move ahead and see that veil of secrecy removed!

Publishing the IIS SMTP Service on the ISA Server

Many ISA Server administrators would like to take advantage of the IIS SMTP service on the ISA server for a number of reasons:

- They want to use the IIS SMTP service as a plain mail relay.
- They want to use the IIS SMTP service as a mail and spam-whacking relay using the ISA Server Message Screener.
- They are running Web sites on the ISA server that depend on a local SMTP service.
- They want to use the SMTP service on the ISA server to stop outgoing mail from containing attachments or keywords by using the SMTP Message Screener.
- They want to use the SMTP service on the ISA server as your smart host to take the burden of name resolution off your internal network mail server.

Should you publish the SMTP service on the ISA server? Again, it depends on the level of security you require. There is no problem with putting the SMTP services on the ISA server if you have light security requirements. You might want to consider removing all extraneous services from the ISA server if you have high security requirements,

Configuring the SMTP Service

Let's go through the steps required for configuring the SMTP services on the ISA server. In this scenario, ISA Server is already installed on the computer. The machine is a member of the internal network domain and it sits at the edge of the network. No Windows Internet Naming Service (WINS) or Domain Name Service (DNS) services are installed on the machine. It will function as an SMTP relay for the Exchange 2000 server setting on the internal network.

Perform the following steps to configure the IIS SMTP service on the ISA server:

1. Open a command prompt and type **netstat –na | find ":25"**. If socket pooling for the SMTP service is enabled, you'll see an entry for TCP 0.0.0.0:25. You'll have to disable socket pooling before you can publish the SMTP server (Figure 28.1).

Figure 28.1 Checking for SMTP Service Socket Pooling

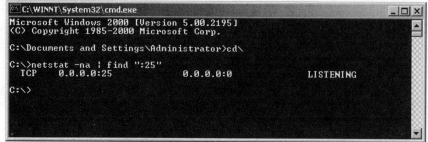

2. There are two ways to disable socket pooling on the ISA server. You can use the *mdutil* utility or the *metaedit* utility. The mdutil utility can be found at the www.isaserver.org site or at ftp.tacteam.net/isaserver. The metaedit utility can be found at the Microsoft Web site (Q232068). The metaedit utility provides a nice GUI interface, and the Q article gives detailed instructions on how to use the metaedit program. We'll go over using the mdutil utility is this section because we have the most experience with this utility and know that it works flawlessly.

3. Stop the SMTP service. At the command prompt, type **net stop smtpsvc** and press **Enter**.

4. Download the mdutil utility and place it in the root of the **C:** drive (actually, you can put it anywhere you want; we are placing it in the root of C: to make this example easier to follow). Type the following command at the command prompt:

```
mdutil set -path smtpsvc/1 -value 1 -dtype 1 -prop 1029 -attrib 1
```

Now press **Enter**. The /1 indicates that socket pooling is disabled for the first virtual SMTP server. In this example, we're only covering a single virtual server. If you plan to run multiple virtual SMTP servers, you'll need to repeat the command with the /2, /3, and so on.

5. From the Administrative Tools menu, open the **Internet Services Manager**. Expand your server name. Right-click on the **Default SMTP Virtual Server (Stopped) entry** and click **Properties**.

6. On the **General** tab, use the IP address drop-down list to select the address on the internal interface. Place a check mark in the **Enable logging** check box.

   If you select the **W3C Extended Log File Format** option, then click **Properties** and click on the **Extended Properties** tab. We recommend selecting all options for the highest level of logging, because SMTP security issues tend to be quite common. Make sure you have plenty of disk space on the drive on which you're storing the log files, and that you archive those log files on a regular basis. You can configure where the log files are stored by clicking on the **General Properties** tab and changing the **Log file directory** entry. Leave the **Log Files** dialog box and click on the **Access** tab.

7. On the **Access** tab, click **Authentication** in the **Access control** frame. You want to allow for anonymous access because this machine is acting as an SMTP relay. Internet SMTP servers will not be able to forward mail to your SMTP relay if you force authentication.

   You can force Transport Layer Security (TLS) encryption between an external SMTP client and the SMTP service by binding a certificate to the SMTP service and forcing TLS. This will not work in our current scenario, because the SMTP relay must be able to accept mail from all hosts, and most of those hosts don't support TLS sessions. The Connection control button allows you to control which hosts are able to connect to the SMTP service. Again, because this machine is configured as an SMTP relay, you can't set IP address restrictions; you want *all* SMTP servers on the Internet to be able to forward mail to your SMTP service. However, you do *not* want all servers on the Internet to use your SMTP server as an open relay. Click **Relay** in the Relay restrictions frame to begin solving this problem.

8. It's very important to tightly restrict which domains can be relayed through your SMTP service. You will be quickly blacklisted if you run an open mail relay. Unlike services such as SpamCop, legitimate Real-time Black Hole Lists (RBLs) search for open mail relays. Spammers can hijack an open mail relay and forward literally gigabytes of spam. Select the **Only the list below** option in the Relay Restrictions dialog box. The default setting has no entries in the list. Leave it this way so that no one is able to use the SMTP server as a generic mail relay server.

   If you want to use the SMTP server as a generic *outbound* mail relay, you can add the IP address of your internal network's mail server to the list of addresses that can relay through the default SMTP virtual server. Click **Add** to add the internal network mail server. In the Computer dialog box, select the **Single computer** option and add the IP address of your internal network's mail server. Click **OK**. You'll see that the computer is granted permission to relay through the SMTP server (Figure 28.2). Note that the **Allow all computers which successfully authenticate to relay, regardless of the**

list above option is checked. This isn't much use to us in the SMTP relay configuration we're using here. Click **OK** to complete the Relay Restrictions section.

Figure 28.2 Allowing the Internal Network Mail Server to Relay through the SMTP Service on the ISA Server

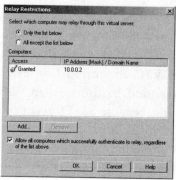

9. Click the **Messages** tab. Note the defaults enforced by the SMTP server. We've received many questions regarding the SMTP server "blocking" messages that were too large, or a user's mail not going out in a timely manner. The most likely reason for the problem is related to the setting in this dialog box. Review the options on this tab and make sure they fit your organizational requirements.

10. Click the **Delivery** tab. Set the **Retry Intervals** to a value that works best for you. We like to set a long expiration timeout, just in case something goes wrong with our SMTP server on the internal network; that way, we don't have to worry about lost mail because it's being held at the SMTP relay. Set the expiration timeout to **7 days**.

We also change the Subsequent retry interval (minutes) to **60**. We don't see the need to wait six hours after the third retry. Click **Advanced**. In the Advanced Delivery dialog box (Figure 28.3), make sure that the Fully Qualified Domain Name (FQDN) entry is resolvable by external network SMTP servers if you plan to use this server as an outbound SMTP mail relay. Many administrators perform reverse lookups at their SMTP servers, and if the name here doesn't match the reverse lookup on the primary IP address on the external interface of the ISA server, your mail might be dropped.

The Smart host entry allows the SMTP server to forward mail to another mail server with the goal of offloading MX domain name resolution. You might want to configure your Internet Service Provider's (ISP's) mail server here if you have a reliable ISP that knows how to maintain quality mail servers. You can use an FQDN or IP address in the Smart host text box. If you use an FQDN, make sure that the ISA server can resolve the name by using the *nslookup* command. If you use an IP address, make sure you use straight brackets [ ] around the IP address. We don't recommend using the **Attempt direct delivery before sending to smart host** and **Perform reverse DNS lookup on incoming messages** options. Click **OK** to save the settings in the Advanced Delivery dialog box.

Figure 28.3 Configuring Advanced Delivery Options

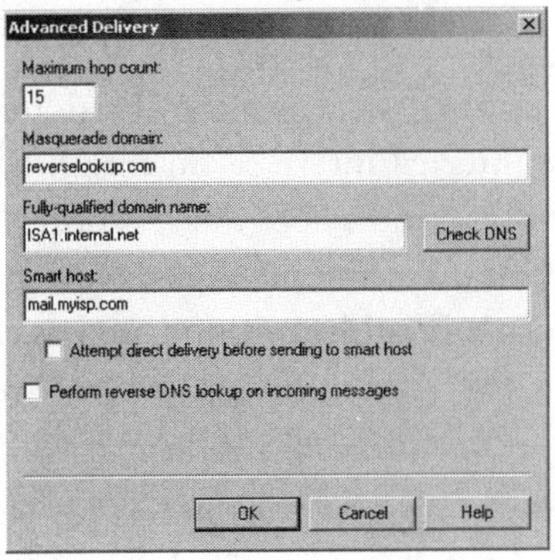

11. Click **Apply**, then click **OK** in the SMTP server's Properties dialog box.

12. Now you need to configure a remote domain for your own mail domain. The only mail you want to accept for inbound relay is mail destined for users in the mail domains under your administrative control. You allow this type of selective relay by using remote domains. Expand the Default SMTP Virtual Server node and right-click the Domains node. Select **New | Domain**.

13. On the **Welcome to the New SMTP Domain Wizard** page, select the **Remote** option and click **Next**.

14. On the **Select Domain Name** page, type in the name of the domain for which you want to receive mail. For example, if you're responsible for mail for the internal.net domain, type **internal.net** in the Name text box. Click **Finish**.

15. Double-click the **internal.net** remote domain entry in the right pane of the console. In the Properties dialog box, enable the **Allow incoming mail to be relayed to this domain** option. Select the **Forward all mail to smart host** option and enter in the IP address (surrounded by straight brackets) of your internal network SMTP server in the text box. Click **Apply**, then click **OK**. Note that relay for incoming mail is handled by the Remote Domain configuration. Outgoing mail relay is handled by the Relay configuration dialog box for the default SMTP virtual server. If you want the internal mail server to use the SMTP service on the ISA server as a relay, you need to allow the internal server to be able to relay to *all* mail domains.

16. Now restart the SMTP service. At the command prompt, type **net start smtpsvc** and press **Enter**. After the SMTP service starts, type the command **netstat –na | find ":25"** and press **Enter** . You should find that the SMTP service is now listening on the internal interface only.

Configuring the SMTP Server Publishing Rule

Now that SMTP services socket pooling is disabled, let's create the SMTP server publishing rule.

1. Open the **ISA Management** console, expand the server name, then expand the Publishing node. Right-click **Server Publishing Rules** and select **New | Rule**.

2. Give the rule a name on the Welcome to the New Server Publishing Rule Wizard page and click **Next**.

3. On the **Address Mapping** page, use the IP address of internal server text box to enter the IP address of the internal interface on the ISA server that the SMTP service is listening on.. Click **Browse** and select the IP address on the external interface on which the SMTP service should receive messages. Note that if you also use this server for outbound relay, this internal IP address is not used as the source IP address for outbound messages. The primary IP address on the external interface of the ISA server is used for the source IP address for outbound messages. Click **Next**.

4. On the Protocol Settings page, select the SMTP Server protocol from the Apply the rule to this protocol drop-down list. Click **Next**.

5. On the Client Type page, select the **Any request** option and click **Next**.

6. Review your settings and click **Finish**.

Now try sending a message from a mail client on the external network to the ISA server. Make sure that you send it to a user who belongs to one of your remote domains. The ISA server publishing rule will pass the message from the external interface to the SMTP server on the internal network. The SMTP service forwards the message to the smart host you configured in the Remote Domain Properties dialog box, which in most cases is your Exchange server (although it can also be a third-party SMTP server or even another SMTP relay).

It's important to note that relay works differently for incoming and outgoing messages. Although the SMTP service doesn't really know which messages are incoming and outgoing, it does evaluate messages in terms of their relay requirements. If the message is destined for one of your remote domains, the remote domain configuration determines how the message is handled. If the message is destined for a domain other than one of your remote domains, the message is handled by the relay properties configured for the virtual server.

For example, in the previous example we configured a remote domain for *internal.net* and set the smart host for the internal mail server. We also configured the default SMTP virtual server to deny mail relay for all hosts except the SMTP server on the internal network. If a message is sent from any host except the SMTP server on the internal network to a domain that is not one of your remote domains, the message will be dropped. The only exception is when that message comes from the IP address of the internal server that we configured to allow relay. This prevents spammers from abusing your mail server.

Something you need to be aware of is how the publishing rule affects the SMTP headers on the incoming messages. Look at the following example:

```
Received: from ISA1.internal.net ([10.0.0.1]) by CLIENTDC.internal.net
    with Microsoft SMTPSVC(5.0.2195.2966);
        Sat, 12 Oct 2002 14:22:40 -0500
Received: from EXTCLIENT ([127.0.0.1]) by ISA1.internal.net with Microsoft
    SMTPSVC(5.0.2195.2966);
        Sat, 12 Oct 2002 14:22:40 -0500
```

```
Message-ID: <001e01c27224$b4c89ab0$dc01a8c0@EXTCLIENT>

From: "Bob" <john@external.com>

To: <joe@internal.net>

Subject: test

Date: Sat, 12 Oct 2002 14:22:29 -0500

MIME-Version: 1.0

Content-Type: multipart/alternative;

        boundary="----=_NextPart_000_001B_01C271FA.CBE1C9D0"

X-Priority: 3

X-MSMail-Priority: Normal

X-Mailer: Microsoft Outlook Express 5.50.4522.1200

X-MimeOLE: Produced By Microsoft MimeOLE V5.50.4522.1200

Return-Path: john@dumbass.com

X-OriginalArrivalTime: 12 Oct 2002 19:22:40.0116 (UTC) FILETIME=[BAFA7340

    :01C27224]
```

Notice that the line for *Received:* shows the name of the external SMTP client sending the message and the IP address *127.0.0.1.* This will always be the case when you use server publishing rules to publish services on the ISA server. The incoming message will appear to be from the loopback address instead of the actual host's IP address. We can confirm this by looking at the SMTP service log file on the ISA server:

```
#Software: Microsoft Internet Information Services 5.0

#Version: 1.0

#Date: 2002-10-12 22:36:18

#Fields: time c-ip cs-method cs-uri-stem sc-status

22:36:18 127.0.0.1 HELO - 250

22:36:18 127.0.0.1 MAIL - 250

22:36:18 127.0.0.1 RCPT - 250

22:36:18 127.0.0.1 DATA - 250

22:36:18 127.0.0.1 QUIT - 0

22:36:18 - - - 0

22:36:18 CLIENTDC.internal.net EHLO - 0

22:36:18 CLIENTDC.internal.net - - 0

22:36:18 CLIENTDC.internal.net MAIL - 0

22:36:18 CLIENTDC.internal.net - - 0

22:36:18 CLIENTDC.internal.net RCPT - 0

22:36:18 CLIENTDC.internal.net - - 0

22:36:18 CLIENTDC.internal.net BDAT - 0

22:36:18 CLIENTDC.internal.net - - 0

22:36:18 CLIENTDC.internal.net QUIT - 0

22:36:18 CLIENTDC.internal.net - - 0
```

This makes forensic analysis of e-mail headers problematic because you never get the source IP addresses for incoming messages. There is no workaround for this problem other than putting the SMTP relay on an internal network client or using packet filters to publish the SMTP service. This is just one of the many reasons why we don't recommend putting network services on the ISA server.

Message Screener on the ISA Server

The ISA Server Message Screener works together with the SMTP filter and allows you to:

- Block mail from specific e-mail domains
- Block mail from specific e-mail addresses
- Block mail containing specific text strings in the e-mail header or body
- Block mail containing specific attachments

There is nothing to prevent you from running the Message Screener on the ISA server. However, it's very important to configure the SMTP server carefully, as you could end up with an open relay that any spammer could take advantage of. If you configure the SMTP service and publish it in the way we recommended in the previous section, you'll be in good shape.

One of the advantages of installing the SMTP Message Screener on the ISA server is that you don't have to configure permissions that allow the Message Screener to contact the ISA server using the SMTPCred tool, and you don't need to configure Distributed Component Object Model (DCOM) permissions. It's okay if you aren't familiar with the SMTPCred tool and DCOM permissions; you'll learn about them later in the chapter.

The SMTP Message Screener was automatically installed if you did a full installation of ISA Server; otherwise, it may or may not be installed. If you're not sure, check the Registry to see if the service is installed (Figure 28.4). Open the Registry Editor and look for:

```
HKEY_CLASSES_ROOT\CLSID\{4F2AC0A5-300F-4DE9-821F-4D5706DC5B32}
```

Figure 28.4 Checking Registry Entries for the SMTP Message Screener

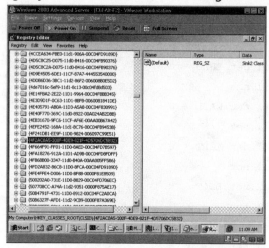

If the Message Screener is not installed, run the **Add/Remove Programs** applet in the **Control Panel**.

The Message Screener can be used to screen both inbound and outbound messages. Most organizations are more interested in controlling inbound SMTP messages. If that describes your organization, all you need to do is configure the remote domains for your organization on the SMTP server and configure those domains to relay to your internal network's mail server.

You'll need to configure the **Default SMTP Virtual Server** in the **Internet Services Manager** to allow *only* the internal mail server to relay if you also want to screen outgoing SMTP messages. You saw how to configure the relay to allow only the internal server to relay in the previous section.

Configure the SMTP Message Screener after you have the SMTP service configured. Perform the following steps to configure the SMTP Message Screener:

1. The Message Screener depends on the SMTP Filter, which is disabled by default. Open the ISA Management console, expand the server name, then expand the Extensions node. Right-click the SMTP Filter entry and click **Enable**. The ISA Server Warning dialog box will appear, telling you that it needs to restart the firewall service. Select the **Save the changes and restart the service(s)** option and click **OK**.

2. Double-click the SMTP Filter and click the SMTP Commands tab (Figure 28.5). This part of the SMTP filter does *not* depend on the Message Screener. What you see here is a list of SMTP commands and the maximum length allowed for each. The goal of this list is to prevent SMTP command buffer overflow exploits. There is a small problem with some of the commands, such as the *NOOP* command. The size is set to 6 by default. This can cause you to see a number of spurious SMTP Filter Event warnings in the Event Viewer. Click the **NOOP** command, then click **Edit**. Change the value to **1024** and click **OK**.

Figure 28.5 The SMTP Commands Tab

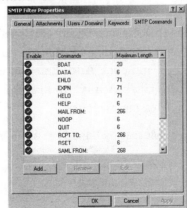

3. Click the **Keywords** tab. Here you can create a list of keywords for the Message Screener to check. Make sure that the **Enable keyword rule** check box is checked and click **Add**. Enter a keyword in the Keyword text box (Figure 28.6). In the **Apply**

action if keyword is found in frame, select the option that specifies where you want the Message Screener to check for keywords. It takes more processor cycles to check for the keyword in the message header or body than it takes to just check the message body. The Message Header option requires the fewest processor cycles. Select one of the following options from the **Action** drop-down list and click **OK**:

- **Delete message** The message will be deleted

- **Hold Message** The message will be saved to the \Inetpub\mailroot\Badmail folder and you can view the message later by opening it from that folder.

- **Forward message to** Enter an e-mail address to which the message can be forwarded. If you choose to forward the mail, make sure that you forward it to an SMTP server that the ISA server can reach. The easiest way to do this is to forward it to an SMTP server on the internal network. Make sure that the ISA server can resolve the MX record for mail domain in the e-mail address. You will need to create a packet filter allowing outbound access to TCP port 25 from any local port on the ISA server if you forward messages to an external SMTP server.

Figure 28.6 Adding a Keyword to the Message Screener

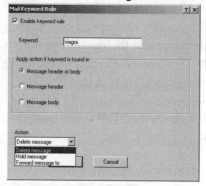

4. Click on the **Users/Domains** tab (Figure 28.7). Here you can block messages based on a user account name or an entire SMTP domain name. Enter an e-mail address in the **Sender's name** text box and click **Add**. Enter an e-mail domain name in the **Domain text box** and click **Add**. Click **Apply**. All mail from these users and/or mail domains will be blocked by the Message Screener.

Figure 28.7 Blocking Messages Based on an E-Mail Address or Domain Name

5. Click the Attachments tab (Figure 28.8). Here you can configure a list of attachments that you want the Message Screener to block. If you select the **Attachment name** option, you must enter the exact name of the attachment. For example, a common attachment name is joke.exe. If you enter **joke.exe,** the Message Screener will block messages with that attachment. If you select the **Attachment extension** option, you enter the name of the file extension you want blocked. For example, if you want to block all executable files, enter the **.exe** extension in the text box. Note that there's no option allowing you to block *all* attachments. If you want to block attachments over a certain size, select the **Attachment size limit** option and then the size in bytes. For example, if you want to limit attachments to less than 1MB, type **1024000**. Click **OK**. The Message Screener will block the attachments you've configured in this dialog box. Click **Apply** to set the rule.

Figure 28.8 Blocking E-Mail Attachments

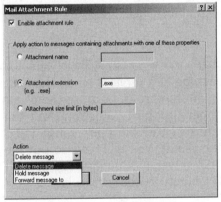

6. Click **OK** to close the **SMTP Filter Properties** dialog box.

Be patient when configuring the Message Screener rules. Many times, we've thought that the Message Screener wasn't doing its job because we began testing the rule too quickly. It might take a few minutes for the rule to take effect. However, if you configured the rules correctly, they will work.

Publishing Exchange Server on the ISA Server

Many people want to place their Exchange 2000 server on the ISA server. We generally recommend against this because each service you place on the ISA server provides a portal of attack for Internet criminals. However, not all users have the resources to purchase multiple Windows 2000 servers, which would allow you to put the Exchange server on a machine other than the ISA server.

You'll encounter a number of challenges when making an Exchange 2000 server work on the ISA server computer. First, you have to make the ISA server a domain controller (DC) because Exchange 2000 requires Active Directory. If you only have one Windows 2000 Server machine, that machine will also have to be a domain controller. You have to be very careful about how you configure DNS on the machine when you make the ISA server a domain controller. If

DNS is not configured correctly, the machine won't work properly as an ISA server, domain controller, or mail server.

The second major challenge is socket pooling. You have to disable socket pooling for all of the Exchange Services if you want to use server publishing rules to publish the Exchange services. Socket pooling causes a service to listen on all interfaces and IP addresses, which can cause port contention when creating server publishing rules. There are two ways to get around this problem: you can disable socket pooling for the services, or you can use packet filters to make the services available to Internet users.

Packet filters are the easiest way to publish Exchange services on the ISA server. This is why the Secure SMTP Server Publishing Wizard creates packet filters instead of server publishing rules. The problem with combining publishing services with packet filters is that you can't leverage any application filters to protect the Exchange 2000 mail services.

Again, note that running a mail server (be it Exchange or any other mail server) directly on a firewall adds complexity to your firewall. You'll want to be very careful doing this and give serious consideration to running your mail server on the DMZ or on the internal network.

NOTE

You can't publish Exchange RPC services when the Exchange server is on the ISA server. You can't use server publishing rules because there's no way to disable socket pooling for RPC endpoint mapper (TCP port 135). You can't use packet filters because you would need to statically open the entire high port range (1024–65535) to allow the dynamic port assignment to the clients. You will have to put the Exchange server on the internal network, not on the ISA server, if you want to publish Exchange RPC services and allow external Outlook MAPI clients to connect to it.

To publish Exchange 2000 services on the ISA server:

1. Install Windows 2000.
2. Configure DNS.
3. Make the server a domain controller.
4. Install ISA Server.
5. Install Exchange Server 2000.
6. Disable socket pooling.
7. Configure server publishing rules for the services you want to publish.
8. Optional: Obtain certificates for services you want to publish, and create server publishing rules for these secure services.

Let's look at these steps in detail. Make sure you follow them closely and understand why we're performing each step. Doing so will help you troubleshoot problems if and when they occur.

NOTE

The procedures we cover in this chapter apply to stand-alone versions of ISA Server, Windows 2000, and Exchange 2000 Server. You might be forced to use certain wizards to install services if you have Small Business Server. However, the same principles apply to all Windows 2000, ISA, and Exchange 2000 Server installations. The only difference is that some of the steps you take to get to the same result might differ. You will be able to replicate the steps described here if you avoid the wizards and install the services and server separately.

Installing Windows 2000

The first step in publishing Exchange services on the ISA server is to install Windows 2000. You might want to consider reinstalling if you already have Windows 2000 installed. A clean installation prevents problems that might occur on a machine that has already been installed on and may have a variety of known and unknown configuration changes. Requirements for installing Windows 2000 and ISA Server for a DC are:

- Windows 2000 Server, Advanced Server, or Datacenter Server.

- A generous amount of RAM. To support all these services, we recommend at least 1GB of RAM, and more would be better.

- Make sure that all network interface cards (NICs) you plan to use are *already installed and plugged into a hub or switch*. Domain controllers will run into problems if you multi-home them after you run *dcpromo*.

- Do not plug the external interface into the Internet during installation. Many ISA server administrators have been successfully hacked either during installation or after installation but before ISA Server is installed.

Keep in mind that you should use hardware that is on the hardware compatibility list (HCL), or that at least has Windows 2000 drivers.

1. Boot the from the installation CD-ROM. Format the partitions if required and perform the remaining steps in the text mode phase. There are no special installation requirements to make a DC work during the text mode phase of the installation.

2. Reboot in GUI mode. On the Regional Settings page, make any required changes and click Next.

3. On the Personalize Your Software page, enter your Name and Organization and click Next.

4. Enter your key on the Your Product Key page and click Next.

5. On the Licensing Mode page, select the appropriate licensing mode for your server and click Next.

6. On the Computer Name and Administrator password page, enter the computer (NetBIOS) name for your computer and a complex password for the administrator

account. You might want to rename the administrator account after installation is complete. If you do, make sure to do it immediately after installation. You might run into problems with ISA Server or Exchange Server if you rename the administrator account after installing those services. Click Next.

7. On the Windows Components page, double-click the Internet Information Services entry. If you need to support File Transfer Protocol (FTP) and Network New Transfer Protocol (NNTP), make the appropriate selections on the Internet Information Services page. We recommend that you minimize the number of IIS servers running on the ISA server, but since this is your only Windows 2000 server, you'll need to put all the services you require on this machine. Click OK.

8. Back in the Windows 2000 Components page, double-click the Management and Monitoring Tools node and select the Network Monitor Tools option. Click OK in the Management and Monitoring Tools dialog box.

9. Double-click the Networking Services entry. At the very least, you need to install DNS and WINS. Scroll through the list of networking services and make those selections. Then, click OK in the Network Services dialog box.

NOTE

If you install WINS, you *must* disable NetBIOS on the external interface of the ISA/DC computer. If you don't disable NetBIOS, the external IP address of the ISA/DC will be registered for all sorts of things that you don't want registered in WINS. Don't disable NetBIOS until you're finished with *everything*. Before disabling NetBIOS, check out the entries in the WINS database for the external IP address of the ISA/DC computer, and delete any you find. Make sure that you don't enter a WINS address in the TCP/IP Properties of the external interface. If you do install a WINS server on the ISA server, make sure you delete any entries in the WINS database that match the IP address of the ISA server's external interface. It is imperative that no external IP addresses are in the WINS database when you run *dcpromo* and afterward. Note that WINS is not required, but it is helpful for administrators who are still learning the details of DNS.

---

10. Double-click the Terminal Services option. Select the Client Creator Files option if you need to install the client, then click OK. Click Next.

11. On the Date and Time Settings page, set the correct date, time, and time zone. Click Next.

12. On the Terminal Services Setup page, select the Remote administration mode option and click Next.

13. On the Networking Settings page, select the Custom Settings option. Click Next.

14. On the Networking Components page, you are presented with the Configuration Settings dialog box for the external interface of the ISA server. We refer to this adapter as the external interface because this interface should be listed as second on the list of adapters in the advanced network adapter settings. If you don't want this to be the external interface,

you'll have to manually change the adapter's priority after completing the installation. Remove the check marks for the Client for Microsoft Networks and File and Printer Sharing options. Double-click the Internet Protocol (TCP/IP) entry and enter the IP addressing information appropriate for your external interface. If you don't want to configure your own DNS server to resolve Internet host names, enter your ISP's DNS server address in the Preferred DNS server text. DNS server configuration is explained later in this section. If you will be using your DNS server to resolve Internet host names, enter the *internal* IP address of the ISA/DC/Exchange server in this text box. The Default gateway will either be assigned by your ISP or it will be the LAN interface of the upstream Internet connection device. Click **Advanced**, then click the DNS tab. Disable the **Append parent suffixes of the primary DNS suffix** option; there is no reason for your external interface to resolve queries. Disable the **Register this connection's addresses in DNS** option; you do not want this interface to register with the DNS server installed on this computer. Click **OK**. You will see an informational message telling you that your WINS address is empty. Click **Yes**. Click **OK** to close the Internet Protocol (TCP/IP) Properties dialog box, then click **Next** in the Network Components page.

NOTE

After the Windows 2000 installation is complete, you should rename the interfaces to make them easier to work with. Give them names like *InternalNIC* and *ExternalNIC*. Do not use names like *internal* and *external*, because the name *internal* is also used by the RRAS console to represent an interface created and used by RRAS only, so it could cause some confusion.

15. Here you see the Networking Components page for the *internal* interface of the ISA/DC/Exchange computer. Double-click the Internet Protocol (TCP/IP) entry and enter the internal IP address and subnet mask. Make sure you make the Preferred DNS server the IP address of the internal interface. This is vitally important because this machine is the DNS server for your Active Directory domain and you want clients to identify the domain controller using the internal IP address. Click **Advanced**. Click the **WINS** tab, then click **Add**. and add the IP address of the internal interface of this ISA/DC/Exchange computer. You want this IP address to register with WINS. You do *not* want the external interface to register with WINS. Click **OK** in the Advanced TCP/IP Settings dialog box after you have added the WINS server address. Click **OK** in the Internet Protocol (TCP/IP) Properties dialog box and click **Next** on the Networking Components page.

16. Click **Next** on the Workgroup or Computer Domain page.

17. The Installation Wizard now installs and configures the services you selected. Click **Finish** to restart the computer when the wizard tells you to do so.

WARNING

You should disable NetBIOS on the external interface of the DC/ISA Server computer to prevent problems with the browser service and prevent browser announcements from trying leave the external interface. All they will do is fill up your logs because later you will enable packet filtering to block NetBIOS communications on the external interface. Leave this until the very last step—disable NetBIOS after you've installed Service Pack 3.

18. After the system restarts, confirm that the NIC binding order is correct. You want the internal interface to be at the top of the list, and the external interface to be *under* the internal interface. Right-click **My Network Places** and select **Properties**. In the Network and dial-up Connections window, select **Advanced | Advanced Settings**. In the Connections frame, ensure the internal interface is at the top o the list and that the Remote Access connections option is at the bottom.

19. After confirming that the interface order is correct, install Service Pack 3.

Configuring DNS Server Forward and Reverse Lookup Zones

Configuring the DNS server properly *before* you run *dcpromo* is important because you want the Active Directory to dynamically register Active Directory-related resource records into the DNS. Many ISA Server administrators unwittingly sabotage themselves because they've promoted the machine to a domain controller before configuring DNS.

Perform the following steps to configure your DNS server:

1. Select Start | Administrative Tools | DNS.

2. Expand all the nodes in the left pane. Right click **Forward Lookup Zone** and select **View | Advanced**.

3. Right-click **Reverse Look Zone** and select **New Zone**. Click **Next** on the Welcome page.

4. On the Zone Type page, select the **Standard Primary** option and click **Next**.

5. On the Reverse Lookup Zone page, type in the network ID for the segment connected to the *internal* interface of this DC/ISA Server computer. You might have to create additional reverse lookup zones if you have multiple network IDs on your internal network, but you need at least this first network to get started. You want to be able to create a Pointer resource record for the internal IP address of this ISA/DC computer. Click **Next**.

6. On the Zone file page, accept the default name for the DNS zone file and click **Next**.

7. On the Completing the New Zone Wizard page, click **Finish**.

8. In the left pane of the console, right-click the reverse lookup zone you just created and click **Properties**.

9. In the reverse lookup zone Properties dialog box, click the General tab. Select **Yes** in the Allow dynamic updates drop-down list box. Click **Apply**, then click **OK**.

The next step is to configure the forward lookup zone:

1. Right-click the **Forward Lookup Zone** node and click **New Zone**. Click **Next** on the Welcome page.

2. On the Zone Type page, select **Standard Primary** and click **Next**.

3. On the Zone Name page (Figure 28.9), type in the name you want to use for your Active Directory domain. In this example, the internal network's domain name is internal.net, so we'll type in **internal.net** in the Name text box. Click **Next**.

Figure 28.9 Entering Your Active Directory Domain Name

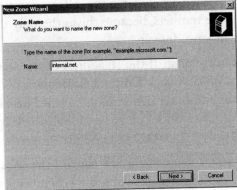

4. On the Zone File page, accept the default name for the DNS zone file and click **Next**.

5. Click **Finish** on the Completing the New Zone Wizard page.

6. Right-click on the zone you just created and select the **New Host** command.

7. In the New Host dialog box, type in the host name of this computer, the IP address of the internal interface, and select **Create associated pointer (PTR) record**. Click **Add Host**. An information message appears telling you the record was created. Click **OK**. Click **Done** in the New Host dialog box.

8. Check both the forward and reverse lookup zones to confirm that the records were created for this computer. Click **Refresh** if you don't see the records. Make sure the Host (A) and Pointer (PTR) records are there before you promote the machine to a domain controller. The domain controller requires these records to properly populate the DNS with Active Directory related entries.

Now configure the DNS server and the forward lookup zone properties:

1. Right-click you're the DNS server name in the left pane of the DNS console and click **Properties**.

2. In the server Properties dialog box, click the Interfaces tab. Select the **Only the following IP addresses** option. Click on the *external* IP address of this computer and

click **Remove**, then click **Apply**. The goal here is to remove the external IP address from the list to prevent the DNS server from listening on the external IP address. You want the DNS server to listen *only* on the internal IP address of this computer.

3. Click the Root Hints tab and confirm that the Root Hints file has been primed. You should see addresses and names for the Internet root servers there. Click **OK**.

4. Right-click the forward lookup zone you just created for your domain and click **Properties**.

5. Click the **General** tab. Change the Allow Dynamic Updates setting to **Yes**.

6. Click the WINS tab. Select the **Use WINS forward lookup** option.

7. Type in the IP address of the internal interface of this computer and click **Add**.

8. Click the Zone Transfers tab. Disable the **Allow zone transfers** option; There is no reason to allow zone transfers, because this is the only domain controller and authoritative DNS server in your domain.

9. Click the Name Servers tab. If the IP address of this server is listed as *unknown*, select your computer name and click **Edit**. Click **Browse** in the Edit Record dialog box. Double-click your computer name, double-click **Forward Lookup Zones**, then double-click your forward lookup zone. Double-click your computer name. Click **OK** and then click **Apply**. Click **OK** to close the Properties dialog box.

10. Right-click the server name in the left pane of the console and select **Tasks | Restart**. Close the DNS console after restarting the DNS server service.

Promoting the Machine to a Domain Controller

Now you're ready to promote the machine to a domain controller. This should go smoothly if the interfaces are configured correctly and you have the DNS server set up properly. If you run into problems, first make sure that DNS is configured correctly. If it looks right to you, check the interface configuration. Make sure that the IP addressing information is correct and that the interface order has the internal interface on top.

1. On the Windows desktop, select **Start | Run**.

2. Type **dcpromo** in the Open text box and click **OK**.

3. Click **Next** on the Welcome page.

4. Select the **Domain Controller for a new domain** option and click **Next**.

5. Select **Create a new domain tree** and click **Next**.

6. Select **Create a new forest of domain trees** and click **Next**.

7. In the New Domain Name text box, enter the full domain name. For example, if your domain name is *internal.net*, type **internal.net** in the text box. Remember that this is the same domain name that you just configured on the DNS server. Click **Next**.

8. On the NetBIOS Domain Name page, select **Next** to keep the default settings. Note that if you made your domain name too long, the NetBIOS name might be truncated. If so, you should change your domain name to one with 15 characters or less. This character limit only applies to the leftmost label and not to the top-level domain.

9. On the Database and Log Locations page, make any required changes and click **Next**.

10. On the Shared System Volume page, make any required changes and click **Next**.

11. You might see an information dialog box informing you that the wizard can't contact a server authoritative for the Active Directory domain. That's okay; click **OK** to continue.

12. On the Configure DNS page, select **No, I will install and configure DNS myself**. Don't allow the Active Directory DNS Wizard to configure the DNS because you've already created the zone. Click **Next**.

13. Select the appropriate permissions for your environment. Since this is the only domain controller and Windows 2000 server on your network, you should select the **Permissions compatible only with Windows 2000 Servers option** and click **Next**.

14. Enter your Directory Services Restore Mode password and confirm. Click **Next**.

15. Review your settings to make sure everything is correct, then click **Next**.

16. It should take less than five minutes to complete the Active Directory configuration if everything is configured correctly,. If the DNS zone wasn't configured correctly or if the interface IP addressing information wasn't entered correctly, it can take a very long time for Active Directory to be configured. When Active Directory creation and configuration is complete, click **Finish** on the Completing the Active Directory Installation Wizard page.

17. In the Active Directory Installation Wizard dialog box, select **Restart Now**.

18. It might take awhile before you can log on to the server after the restart because it's populating the DNS server zone file with Active Directory-related records and doing some last-minute configuration and cleanup tasks. Log on to the domain when the logon dialog box becomes available.

19. Wait about five minutes, then open the DNS console. Expand the forward lookup zone for your domain and you should see the Active Directory-related records. If you see the external IP address listed with a Host (A) address record, remove it by right-clicking the record with the external IP address and clicking **Delete**.

20. Right-click the forward look zone for your domain and click **Properties**. Click the General tab. Change the Allow dynamic updates setting to **No**. This prevents the external interface from registering with the DNS. It's interesting that even when you configure the external interface to *not* register with the DNS, it continues to do so anyway. Disabling dynamic updates should not pose a problem for a small network that has a single Windows 2000 server and domain controller. You will need to manually enter the names of your internal network clients in the DNS because dynamic update is now disabled. Click **Apply | OK**.

> **NOTE**
>
> While disabling dynamic updates causes few problems for small networks with a single domain controller, it can be a big problem on larger networks. Dynamic DNS (DDNS) is a powerful tool and it allows DNS to pick up where WINS leaves off. Multi-homed domain controllers cause quite a few problems related to name resolution and DDNS. There are several Microsoft Q articles you should refer to if you must enable DDNS. The first is Q292822, which deals with name resolution issues on Windows domain controllers with DDNS and RRAS installed (which is what your ISA server will be if you allow inbound Virtual Private Network [VPN] connections). The second is Q289735, which deals with similar issues and contains a registry entry to prevent VPN clients from shutting down Internet access for your internal network users.

At this point, decide if you want to use a forwarder to resolve Internet host names. As mentioned earlier, you don't need to use a forwarder; the DNS server can use the root hints file and perform recursion. However, you might want to consider using your ISP's DNS server as a forwarder if you have a good ISP that maintains its DNS servers. Perform the following steps if you have a lot of confidence in your ISP's DNS servers:

1. Right-click the server name and click **Properties**.

2. Select the **Forwarders** tab.

3. Select the **Enable forwarders** option. Enter the IP address(es) of your ISP's DNS server(s) and click **Add**. Enable the **Do not use recursion** option—this improves performance significantly. Click **Apply | OK**.

4. Right-click you're the server name and select **All Tasks | Restart**. This will restart the DNS server service and force the DNS server to use the forwarder.

You should test the DNS server now that it's configured to use a forwarder. The tests should include queries for local and Internet domains. Perform the following steps to complete the tests:

1. In the DNS console, right-click you're the server name and select **Properties**.

2. Select the Monitoring tab.

3. Enable the **A simple query against a DNS server** option and click **Test Now**. You should see a *PASS* entry in the Simple Query column. This indicates that the DNS server was able to query itself and resolve a name in one of its authoritative domains. In this case, the domain for which this DNS server is authoritative is your Active Directory domain.

4. Disable the **A simple query against this DNS server** option and enable the **A recursive query to other DNS servers** option. Click **Test Now**. You should see a *PASS* in the Recursive Query column. This indicates that the DNS server was able to accept a recursive query and respond with a definitive answer. In this case, the query was for a domain for which this DNS was not authoritative.

Installing ISA Server

The next step is to install the ISA Server software. We're often asked whether you should install the ISA Server or the Exchange Server first. From our experience, it doesn't seem to make much difference. Some people say that you should install Microsoft Server applications in the order in which they were released. If that was true, then you should install Exchange 2000 first and ISA Server second. However, Service Pack 3 for Exchange came out after Service Pack 1 for ISA Server.

There aren't any special steps required when installing ISA Server on the domain controller. However, we'll go through the procedure just to be thorough:

1. Put the ISA Server CD-ROM into the tray and when the autoplay dialog box appears, click the **Install ISA Server** button.

2. On the Welcome page, click **Continue**.

3. On the **CD Key** page, enter your CD Key and click **OK**. Click **OK** on the Product ID page.

4. Click **I Agree** on the license agreement page.

5. Click **Full Installation** on the setup page to install all features. Later on, you can disable services you don't plan to use, and by performing the full installation, you ensure that you won't have to come back to install other services that you *do* decide to use.

6. Since we haven't initialized the Active Directory, we can't join an array. If you're running SBS, you probably have a single server, so this isn't an issue. In this example, we'll run a stand-alone ISA server. Click **Yes** in the dialog box that appears.

7. On the Mode page, select the **Integrated mode** option and click **Continue**.

8. Click **OK** in the dialog box informing you that IIS services will be stopped. Note that the dialog box says that you will need to uninstall IIS or reconfigure the WWW service so it does not use TCP port 80. The reason for this is that the Outgoing Web Requests listener uses TCP port 8080 on the internal interface, and Autodiscovery information is published on TCP port 80 (also on the internal interface). You don't have to worry about ISA Server using TCP port 80 on the internal interface if you won't be publishing Autodiscovery information. However, the Incoming Web Requests listener will use TCP port 80 if you decide to configure Web publishing rules. We'll go into more detail on this issue when we configure IIS to publish Outlook Web Access.

9. On the Cache Size page, set the cache size and click **Set**. Remember, the cache must be placed on an NTFS drive. Optimal cache size varies—we generally start with 100MB and add 10MB per user. Click **OK** after setting the cache size.

10. On the LAT configuration page, click **Construct Table**. Note how we've configured the options in the Local Address Table dialog box (Figure 28.10). Disable the *Add the following private ranges* option and enable the *Add address ranges based on the Windows 2000 Routing Table* option. Enable the NIC connected to the *internal* network. Click **OK**. Click **OK** in the dialog box that warns you that your LAT is based on the routing table. Click **OK**, then click **OK** again.

Figure 28.10 Configuring the LAT

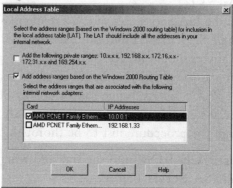

11. When the setup is finished, click **OK** to open the ISA Management console. Click **OK** again to finish.

12. Right-click the Servers and Arrays node and select **View | Advanced**. The advanced view provides you with a cleaner interface and makes it much easier to work with the ISA Server console.

13. Install ISA Server Service Pack 1 or later as soon as you complete the basic ISA Server installation. Restart the server after installing the ISA Server Service Pack.

Packet filtering is enabled by default. You don't need to worry about DNS query problems because there is a preconfigured DNS packet filter. You can run the DNS query tests again to confirm that the DNS server is still working.

Installing Exchange Server

The next step is to install Exchange Server 2000. It might be possible to install Exchange Server 5.5 on the ISA server, but there is no documentation on this issue and we've never been called upon to do this type of installation. A compelling reason to use Exchange Server 2000 instead of Exchange 5.5 is that Microsoft plans to stop supporting Exchange 5.5 in the near future. This probably explains why there is no documentation on how to make Exchange 5.5 work on an ISA server machine.

The good news is that installing Exchange 2000 on the ISA server is very easy. It's even easier when the Exchange server is installed on the only domain controller in the domain. You should refer to a good Exchange server book for documentation on how to install and configure Exchange 2000 if you have other Exchange servers or domain controllers in your organization. We won't go into the details of more advanced installation considerations in this discussion because we assume that you are installing Exchange on the ISA server because you don't have any other Windows 2000 servers on the network. .

Perform the following steps to install Exchange 2000 on the ISA server/domain controller:

1. Put the Exchange 2000 server CD-ROM into the tray. In the Setup dialog box, click the **Exchange Server Setup** icon.

2. Click **Next** on the Welcome to the Microsoft Exchange 2000 Installation Wizard page.

3. Select the **I agree** option and click **Next**.

4. Enter the CD key and click **Next**.

5. On the Component Selection page, set the Action to **Typical** for the **Microsoft Exchange 2000** component. If you need other services, you can install them later. Select **Change Folder** and select different drive to install to. Click **Next**. Select the **Create a new Exchange Organization** option and click **Next**.

6. On the Organization Name page, enter an organization name for your Exchange server organization. In this example, we have only one server, so we'll keep the default name, **First Organization**. Click **Next**.

7. Select **I agree that I have read and agree to be bound by the license agreement for this product** and click **Next**.

8. Review your choices on the Component Summary page and click **Next**. This begins the very long Exchange Server installation process. Once the installation finishes, click **Finish**.

9. Click the **Exit** link on the Exchange 2000 installation page and restart the server.

10. After the server restarts, install Exchange Server Service Pack 3. 15. Restart the server after the service pack is installed.

Disabling Socket Pooling for the Exchange Services

As you've probably realized by this time, socket pooling is the bane of the ISA Server administrator's existence. This is especially true when you want to install Exchange 2000 on the ISA Server computer and publish the Exchange 2000 Server services. The good news is that although it takes a little work, you can disable socket pooling for almost all of the Exchange 2000 services.

You will need the mdutil utility to disable socket pooling. If you don't have it, you can download it ftp.tacteam.net/isaserver. After you download the utility, move it to the root directory of the C: drive (it doesn't have to be placed there, it's just a convenient place to put it).

Perform the following steps to disable socket pooling for all of the Exchange services that we'll be publishing:

1. Stop the mail services before disabling socket pooling. Open a command prompt and enter the following commands:

   ```
   net stop w3svc
   net stop msftpsvc
   net stop smtpsvc
   net stop nntpsvc
   net stop pop3svc
   net stop imap4svc
   ```

2. We can get to the work of disabling socket pooling now that the mail services are stopped. As you learned earlier, there are two methods used to disable socket pooling:

scripts and the mdutil utility. To stop the WWW service, access a command prompt and go to the \Inetpub\AdminScripts directory. Once in that directory, run the following command:

```
cscript adsutil.vbs set w3svc/disablesocketpooling true
```

3. To disable the FTP service, run the following command:

```
cscript adsutil.vbs set msftpsvc/disablesocketpooling true
```

4. While still in the command prompt window, change the focus to the C: drive. Then, run the following commands:

```
mdutil set -path smtpsvc/1 -value 1 -dtype 1 -prop 1029 -attrib 1
mdutil set -path nntpsvc/1 -value 1 -dtype 1 -prop 1029 -attrib 1
mdutil set -path pop3svc/1 -value 1 -dtype 1 -prop 1029 -attrib 1
mdutil set -path imap4svc/1 -value 1 -dtype 1 -prop 1029 -attrib 1
```

5. The last service you need to disable socket pooling for is secure Web services (SSL listener). Go to the \Inetpub\Adminscripts folder and run the following command:

```
adsutil set w3svc/1/securebindings ""
```

6. You will see a dialog box that says "This script does not work with Wscript". Click **OK**.

7. The next dialog box will ask if you want to register CScript as your default host for VBscript. Click **Yes**.

8. Click **OK** in the Successfully registered CScript dialog box.

9. Now run the adsutil set w3svc/1/securebindings "" script again.

The services continue to run on all interfaces and all IP addresses, even though we have disabled socket pooling. The reason is that the services' default configuration is to listen on all interfaces. We need to change those default settings in the Internet Services Manager and the Exchange System Manager.

Perform the following steps to configure the listeners for the WWW and FTP services:

1. Select **Internet Services Manager** from the Administrative Tools menu.

2. Right-click the Default FTP Site entry in the left pane of the console and click **Properties**.

3. Change the IP Address from (All Unassigned) to the IP address on the internal interface of the ISA server. Click **Apply**, then click **OK**.

4. Right-click the Default Web Site entry in the left pane of the console and click **Properties**.

5. Change the IP address from (All Unassigned) to the IP address on the internal interface of the ISA server. Click **Apply**, then **OK**.

6. Click the Administration Web Site entry in the left pane of the console and click **Properties**.

7. Change the IP Address from (All Unassigned) to the internal IP address on the ISA server. Click **Apply**, then **OK**.

That takes care of the FTP and Web sites. If you want to run other Web sites, make sure that when you create the new Web site that it listens only on the internal interface of the ISA server.

We also need to configure the NNTP, SMTP, POP3, and Internet Message Access Protocol (IMAP)4 services. These services are configured in the Exchange System Manager. Remember that you won't be able to publish Exchange RPC services because you can't disable socket pooling for the RPC endpoint mapper.

Perform the following steps to configure the remainder of the Exchange services:

1. On the Windows desktop, select Start | Programs | Microsoft Exchange | System Manager.

2. Expand the Servers node, the server name, the Protocols node and the IMAP4 node. Right-click the entry and click **Properties**.

3. In the Default IMAP4 Virtual Server Properties dialog box, change the IP Address from (All Unassigned) to the IP address of the internal interface of the ISA server. Click **Apply**, then click **OK**.

4. Expand the NNTP node in the left pane of the console. Right-click the Default NNTP Virtual Server entry and click **Properties**.

5. In the Default NNTP Virtual Server Properties dialog box, change the IP address from (All Unassigned) to the IP address on the internal interface of the ISA server. Click **Apply**, then **OK**.

6. Expand the POP3 node. Right-click the **Default POP3 Virtual Server** entry and click the **Properties** command.

7. Change the IP address from (All Unassigned) to the internal IP address on the ISA server. Click **Apply**, then **OK**.

8. Expand the SMTP node. Right-click on the Default SMTP Virtual Server entry and click the **Properties** command.

9. In the Default SMTP Virtual Server Properties dialog box, change the IP address from (All Unassigned) to the internal IP address on the ISA server. Click **Apply**, then **OK**.

All the services are now configured to listen only on the internal interface. From the command prompt, run each of the following commands to restart all the services:

```
Net start w3svc
Net start msftpsvc
Net start nntpsvc
Net start smtpsvc
Net start pop3svc
```

```
Net start imap4svc
```

To confirm that the services are listening only on the internal interface, run the following commands:

```
Netstat -na | find ":21"
Netstat -na | find ":25"
Netstat -na | find ":80"
Netstat -na | find ":110"
Netstat -na | find ":119"
Netstat -na | find "143"
```

Configure Server Publishing Rules to Publish the Exchange Services

With socket pooling disabled and the services configured to listen only on the internal interface, you're now ready to create the server publishing rules. The following services on the ISA server are candidates for publishing:

- FTP server
- Web server
- POP3 server
- SMTP server
- NNTP server
- IMAP4 server

This chapter doesn't cover FTP server publishing, since it has nothing to do with Exchange mail services. Web server publishing is covered later, in the section "Publishing Outlook Web Access on the ISA Server". That leaves POP3, SMTP, NNTP, and IMAP4 publishing. Let's go through the procedure for publishing each of these services.

SMTP Server Publishing Rule

Publishing the Exchange 2000 SMTP server works the same as publishing the IIS 5.0 SMTP server discussed earlier in this chapter. You need to configure remote domains for the mail domains under your administrative control, and you need to configure the relay characteristics so that you're not running an open relay. Make sure you review the material on publishing the IIS 5.0 SMTP earlier in this chapter before publishing the Exchange 2000 SMTP service.

Perform the following steps to publish the Exchange 2000 SMTP service:

1. Open the ISA Management console, expand you're the server name, and expand the Publishing node. Right-click **Server Publishing Rules**, and select **New** | **Rule**.

2. On the Welcome to the New Server Publishing Rule Wizard page, enter a name for the rule. Click **Next**.

3. Enter the IP address of the internal interface of the ISA server in the IP address of internal server text box. Click **Browse** and select the external IP address on the ISA server on which you want to accept SMTP requests. Click **Next**.

4. Select the **SMTP Server** protocol definition and click **Next**.

5. Select the client type you want to support. The typical selection is **Any request**, since anonymous SMTP servers on the Internet will need to forward mail to your mail domains. Make your selection and click **Next**.

6. Review you settings on the Complete the New Server Publishing Rule Wizard page and click **Finish**.

We always like to do a quick check on our server publishing rules by using Telnet from an external network client. If you have a Windows 2000 client on the external network, access a command prompt and type **telnet <IP_Address> 25**. You should see an output similar to that in Figure 28.11. Type **help** to see the list of commands supported by the SMTP server and type **quit** to exit the Telnet session.

Figure 28.11 Telnet to the Publishing SMTP Server

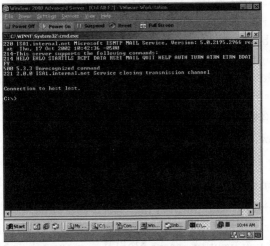

POP3 Server Publishing Rule

The POP3 server publishing rule allows external network users access to the Exchange 2000 server's POP3 Server component. This is useful when external users need to get e-mail from their message store and they don't have access to an Outlook Message Application Programming Interface (MAPI) connection. Users can configure Outlook 2000/XP, Outlook Express, or any other e-mail client to access POP mail services on the Exchange 2000 server.

There are some disadvantages to using POP3 to receive e-mail. The POP3 client will pull all mail out of the Inbox store *if* the POP3 client isn't configured to leave the mail on the server. We've seen many occasions where the user was shocked when he returned to the office and found that there was no mail in his inbox after opening Outlook 2000/XP. Another consideration is that username and password information is passed as clear text. You can resolve this problem by requiring Secure Socket Layer (SSL) to connect to the POP3 server.

Perform the following steps to publish the POP3 server:

1. Open the ISA Management console, expand you the server name, then expand the Publishing node. Right-click **Server Publishing Rules** and select **New | Rule**.

2. Enter a name for the rule and click **Next**.

3. Enter the IP address of the internal interface of the ISA server in the text box. Click **Browse** and select the external IP address on the ISA server on which you want to accept POP3 requests. Click **Next**.

4. Select the **POP3 Server** protocol definition and click **Next**.

5. Select the client type you want to support. The typical selection is **Any request**, since you usually can't tell where the external users are located in advance. Make your selection and click **Next**.

6. Review your settings on the Complete the New Server Publishing Rule Wizard page and click **Finish**.

Use Telnet to ensure that the server publishing rule worked.

NNTP Server Publishing Rule

The Exchange NNTP server can be used to host your organization's newsgroups. While the NNTP service provided by Exchange 2000 isn't a full-featured NNTP server, it does provide an excellent platform for sharing information in a threaded environment. Newsgroups are fast and they're easy to search. While many sites now offer newsgroup-like features in a Web-based format, they'll never be as fast or as efficient as the traditional News server.

Perform the following steps to publish the NNTP service:

1. Open the ISA Management console, expand the server name, then expand the Publishing node. Right-click **Server Publishing Rules** and select **New | Rule**.

2. Enter a name for the rule and click **Next**.

3. Enter the IP address of the internal interface of the ISA server in the IP address of internal server text box. Click **Browse** and select the external IP address on the ISA server on which you want to accept NNTP requests. Click **Next**.

4. Select the **NNTP Server** protocol definition and click **Next**.

5. Select the client type you want to support. The typical selection is **Any request**, since you probably don't know the IP addresses of your NNTP clients. Make your selection and click **Next**.

6. Review your settings on the Complete the New Server Publishing Rule Wizard page and click **Finish**.

Use Telnet to confirm that the server publishing rule worked.

IMAP4 Server Publishing Rule

The IMAP4 service allows you to connect IMAP4 clients to the Exchange 2000 message store. IMAP4 clients can download a list of mail headers without downloading the entire e-mail message. This is an ideal solution for users with low bandwidth connections. Another advantage of IMAP is that if you use Outlook 2000/XP to create subfolders off the main Inbox folder, you can use the IMAP4 protocol to access information in those folders. This is a great advantage over POP3 access because POP3 clients can only download mail contained in the Inbox; POP3 clients cannot download mail contained in subfolders under the main Inbox folder. If you use filtering rules to move mail automatically from the Inbox to subfolders, the POP3 client will not be able to retrieve sorted mail. Outlook Express provides basic IMAP4 support.

Perform the following steps to publish the IMAP4 service:

1. Open the ISA Management console, expand the server name, then expand the Publishing node. Right-click **Server Publishing Rules** and select **New | Rule**.

2. Enter a name for the rule and click **Next**.

3. Enter the IP address of the internal interface of the ISA server in the IP address of internal server text box. Click **Browse** and select the external IP address on the ISA server on which you want to accept IMAP4 requests. Click **Next**.

4. Select the **IMAP4 Server** protocol definition and click **Next**.

5. Select the client type you want to support. The typical selection is **Any request**, since it's unlikely that you'll know the IP addresses of your IMAP4 clients in advance. Make your selection and click **Next**.

6. Review your settings on the Complete the New Server Publishing Rule Wizard page and click **Finish**.

Use Telnet to confirm that the server publishing rule worked.

Secure Services Publishing

The publishing rules we created so far work fine, but they all suffer from the same major drawback: all information is sent "in the clear." When users access NNTP, IMAP4, SMTP, and POP3 resources, anyone with a packet sniffer will be able to see the contents of the communications. You won't want to allow this if you keep secure information on your Exchange server.

You can solve this problem by allowing only secure communications with the POP3, NNTP, and IMAP4 services. You could even configure SMTP access to be secure, but if you're publishing your SMTP server to allow Internet SMTP servers to send mail for your mail domains, you won't be able to enforce secure communications. Internet mail servers aren't configured to enforce secure communications, so any attempt to secure SMTP communications at the mail server level will fail for anonymously accessible SMTP servers. However, if you create a second SMTP virtual server for your employees to send mail to, you can enforce secure communications on that server. You can enforce secure communications with the SMTP server when you have administrative control over the users. .

We'll assume that you've secured your perimeter, so you don't have to worry about someone planting a packet sniffer there. What about your remote users? Suppose your salespeople call the mail server to retrieve mail via POP3 or SMTP from a hotel room that has broadband access. Or maybe they need to obtain private company information from your NNTP server. While your own perimeter might be secure, you have no assurances that the networks external users are connecting from are secure.

You'll need to assign certificates to the services you want to make secure. You can create your own certificates or use a third-party certificate provider. Since the services are meant for your own employees and not for Internet users at large, in most cases you'll want to create your own certificates.

You can install the Microsoft Certificate Server in enterprise or stand-alone mode. One of the advantages of enterprise mode is you can use the MMC to obtain certificates from the certificate server. The disadvantage is that not all certificate templates are available via the Web-based enrollment site. The stand-alone Certificate Server supports all templates, but you can't use the Microsoft Management Console (MMC) to obtain certificates.

We are assuming that you have a single Windows 2000 server, since you're installing Exchange 2000 on the ISA server. In this case, you'll need to install the certificate server on the ISA/Exchange server. Perform the following steps to install the enterprise root certificate server on the ISA server computer:

1. Access the Windows Control Panel and open the Add/Remove Programs applet.

2. Click **Add/Remove Windows Components**.

3. Enable the Certificate Services option. Click **Yes** in the dialog box that informs you that you can't change the name of the server while certificate services is installed. Click **Next**.

4. Select the **Remote Administration mode** option and click **Next**.

5. Select the **Enterprise root CA** option and click **Next**.

6. On the CA Identifying Information page (Figure 28.12), enter the necessary information for each field. While only the CA name field is required, you should enter valid information in each field just in case you want to perform certificate mapping based on this certificate in the future. Click **Next**.

Figure 28.12 The CA Identifying Information Page

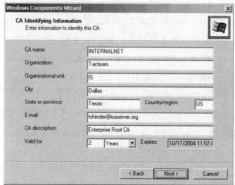

7. On the Data Storage Location page, leave the default settings as they are unless you have a compelling reason to change them. One reason to do so would be that your C: drive is lacking in space. Click **Next** to continue.

8. Click **OK** in the dialog box informing you that IIS must be stopped.

9. You might be asked for the Windows 2000 CD. If so, put the CD into the drive and follow the installer's instructions.

10. Click **Finish**. Restart the server after installing certificate services.

Assign Certificates to the Exchange Services

You can enforce secure communications with the SMTP, POP3, Web, and IMAP4 services. You can't enforce secure communications with the FTP service using server publishing rules (although you can do so using Web publishing rules and then using protocol redirection within those rules). You'll need to assign certificates to each of the services to allow secure links with the external clients.

The Web server is assigned a certificate via the Internet Information Services console. The remaining services are assigned certificates via the Exchange Management console. Let's start with assigning a certificate to the Web site. You'll use this Web site certificate later when configuring secure access to the Outlook Web Access (OWA) site.

1. Select **Internet Services Manager** from the Administrative Tools menu.

2. In the Internet Information Services console, expand the server name. Right-click **Default Web Site** and click **Properties**.

3. Select the Directory Security tab. In the Secure Communications frame, click **Server Certificate**.

4. Read the text on the Welcome to the Web Server Certificate Wizard page and click **Next**.

5. Select the **Create a new certificate** option and click **Next**.

6. Select the **Send the request immediately to an online certification authority option** and click **Next**. You have the option to send the request immediately to an online certificate authority because you have an enterprise root certificate server in your domain. You would not have this option if your only certificate server was a stand-alone certificate server.

7. Enter a "friendly" name for the Web site certificate in the Name text box and click **Next**. The default name is good to use here, and it will set this certificate apart from other Web sites you configure on this server. The bit length is set to 512 by default. Leave the default unless you have reasons to enforce a higher level of encryption.

8. Enter your Organization name and Organizational unit name.

9. Enter the name that external users will use to access your Web site. If you don't type in the exact name, error dialog boxes will appear when clients attempt to access the site. Type in the name for your Web site and click **Next**.

10. Select your Country/Region, and then type in your State/province and City/locally in the text boxes. Click **Next**.

11. Your certificate authority will appear in the drop-down list on the Choose a Certification Authority page. Click **Next**.

12. Review the settings on the Certificate Request Submission page and click **Next**.

13. Read the text on the Completing the Web Server Certificate Wizard page and click **Finish**.

14. When you return to the Default Web Site Properties page, you'll see that the View Certificate and Edit buttons are available. This confirms that the certificate has been assigned to the Web site. Click **OK** to close the dialog box.

The remainder of the services are assigned certificates via the Exchange System Manager. Assign certificates for the IMAP4, NNTP, POP3, and SMTP services here.

Perform the following steps to install a certificate on to the IMAP4 service:

1. Open the Exchange System Manager. Expand the server name, then expand the IMAP4 node. Right-click the **Default IMAP4 Virtual Server** and select **Properties**.

2. Select the Access tab, then click **Certificate** in the Secure communication frame.

3. Read the text on the Welcome to the Web Server Certificate Wizard page and click **Next**.

4. Select **create a new certificate** and click **Next**. . You have the option to assign an existing certificate, but you have more options available to you if you assign each service a separate certificate. There's no negative effect on the clients, since they'll all have the same certificate authority in their trust list.

5. Select the **Send the request immediately to an online certificate authority** option and click **Next**.

6. Enter a friendly name for the IMAP4 server certificate or accept the default settings. The default setting should work fine if you're running a single IMAP4 server on this machine. Click **Next**.

7. On the Organization Information page, the settings that you entered during the Web site certificate enrollment will be displayed. You can keep this information unless you have a reason to do otherwise. Click **Next**.

8. On the Your Site's Common Name page, type in the name of the site. For example, here we'll use the name **imap4.internal.net**. After entering the name of the site, click **Next**. The site's name is important. You need to configure the IMAP4 clients to use the common name of the IMAP4 server and not the IP address. You will see an error on the IMAP4 client if you configure the client to use the IP address of the server in the Client Configuration dialog box. You need to use an FQDN that is the same as the common name you enter on this page.

9. On the Geographical Information page, the information you entered during Web site enrollment is already entered. To keep this information, click **Next**.

10. Your certificate server will appear on the Choose a Certificate Authority page. Click **Next**.

11. Review the settings on the Certificate Request Submission page, and click **Next**.

12. Click **Finish**.

13. Click **OK**.

Repeat these steps to obtain certificates for the default NNTP, POP3, and SMTP virtual servers.

While you can obtain a certificate for the default SMTP virtual server, you should not use the certificate for that server if it is being used to accept incoming messages from public SMTP servers. However, you might want to use an SMTP service certificate to create a second SMTP virtual server on the Exchange server for your external users to use for their outbound mail server.

All of these Exchange service certificates are stored in the ISA/Exchange server's machine certificate store. You can open a Certificates MMC for the local machine store and you'll see all of the Exchange service certificates there.

Creating Server Publishing Rules for Secure Communications with Exchange Services

You can configure secure communications with the Exchange services after the certificates are installed. The default settings on the services allow both secure and non-secure communications. You can configure the services to force SSL connections. It 'is good practice to force secure communications at the server; if you don't, you're leaving it up to the clients to force the secure channel.

You can force a secure channel for the POP3, SMTP, and IMAP4 services. The NNTP service allows secure communications, but you *cannot force* a secure channel at the server. You have to depend on the client to use a secure channel.

Perform the following steps to force a secure channel with the Exchange POP3 server:

1. Open the Exchange System Manager. Expand the Servers node, then expand your server name. Expand the Protocols node, then expand the POP3 node. Right-click the **Default POP3 Virtual Server** node and click **Properties**.

2. Click the Access tab.

3. Click **Communication** in the Secure communication frame.

4. In the Security dialog box (Figure 28.13), enable the **Require secure channel** option. Enable **Require 128-bit encryption** if your clients support 128-bit encryption.

5. Click **OK**.

Figure 28.13 Forcing a Secure Channel to the POP3 Service

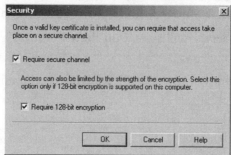

6. Click **Apply**, then click **OK** in the Default POP3 Virtual Server Properties dialog box.

Follow the same procedure for the default IMAP4 and SMTP virtual servers. You don't have the option to force a secure channel with the NNTP server. However, you can create a server publishing rule that only allows access via the secure channel. If users try to connect to the server via an open channel (i.e., non-SSL), the connection attempt will fail because there won't be a server publishing rule to support it. .

> **WARNING**
>
> Secure SMTP server publishing does not require a separate server publishing rule. If you have a regular SMTP server publishing rule enabled, external network clients will be able to use that rule for both open and secure SMTP communications. The Exchange 2000 SMTP service employs an *in-band* security subsystem, allowing it to service SSL connections at the default SMTP service port, TCP 25. All other Exchange services (HTTP, POP3, NNTP, and IMAP4) require a dedicated port for SSL communications. Create *only* secure server publishing rules for those protocols you want to use secure communications only. For example, if you want to allow only secure POP3 access, do *not* create a server publishing rule that allows non-secure POP3 access.

Configure Services "Publishing" with Packet Filters

You can also publish Exchange Server services on the ISA server by using packet filters instead of server publishing rules. The advantage of using packet filters is that you don't have to disable socket pooling; the only requirement is a simple packet filter. The disadvantage of packet filters is that you can't leverage features provided by application filters. This lessens the security provided by publishing servers, since the ISA server does not examine the incoming packets for anything more than source and destination IP address and port number.

Create the packet filters listed in Table 28.1 on the ISA/Exchange server to support Exchange Server services publishing if you want to avoid creating server publishing rules.

Table 28.1 Packet Filters for Exchange Services Publishing

Protocol	IP Protocol Number	Protocol	Direction	Local Port Number	Local Port	Remote Port
NNTP	TCP	6	Inbound	119	Fixed Port	All ports
IMAP4	TCP	6	Inbound	143	Fixed Port	All ports
SMTP	TCP	6	Inbound	25	Fixed Port	All ports
POP3	TCP	6	Inbound	110	Fixed Port	All ports
Secure NNTP	TCP	6	Inbound	563	Fixed Port	All ports
Secure POP3	TCP	6	Inbound	995	Fixed Port	All ports
Secure IMAP	TCP	6	Inbound	993	Fixed Port	All ports

Although you can use packet filters, we recommend that you use the server publishing rule method. Server publishing rules work, and they provide a higher level of security—and isn't a higher level of security the reason why you purchased ISA Server?

NOTE

You don't have manually create all of these packet filters. The Secure Mail Publishing Wizard will automatically create all of these packet filters for you. You need to tell the wizard that the server is on the ISA server. The server creates packet filters instead of server publishing rules when it knows that the Exchange server is on the ISA server.

Publishing Outlook Web Access on the ISA Server

If there's one issue that generates questions regarding ISA Server configuration, it's how to configure Outlook Web Access to work on the ISA server. The fact is that it's not that hard to get OWA to work; the problem is that there are many details to take care of in order to make it work correctly.

Many of the problems people have with OWA on the ISA server are related to issues with the Exchange server prior to Exchange Service Pack 3. Once you install Exchange Service Pack 3, the procedure is straightforward.

You need to address the following issues when publishing OWA:

- Assign a certificate to the Web site
- Configure the SSL listening port on the default Web site
- Configure authentication properties on the OWA folders
- Force a secure channel on the OWA folders
- Create the OWA Web publishing rule that forces a secure connection
- Configure user rights on the domain controller

We already assigned a certificate to the Web site when we ran the Web Publishing Wizard for the default Web site. Let's look at the rest of the OWA Web publishing details:

Configure the SSL Listening Port on the Default Web Site

The default Web site has a certificate. The problem is that you won't be able to use that certificate for secure communications until you configure the Web site with a port number to listen for secure requests. Perform the following steps to create the secure services listening port:

1. Select **Internet Services Manager** from the Administrative Tools menu.

2. In the Internet Information Services console, expand the server name. Right-click the Default Web Site and select **Properties**.

3. In the Default Web Site Properties dialog box, type **443** in the SSL Port text box. Click **Apply**, then click **OK**.

Now access a command prompt and type **netstat –na | find ":443"**. You should see that only the internal interface is listening on TCP port 443. The incoming Web Requests listener will need to use TCP 443 on the external interface.

Configure Authentication Methods on the OWA Folders

You can use either basic or integrated authentication to authenticate against the OWA Web site. The problem with integrated authentication is that Internet Explorer 5.0x cannot use integrated authentication when accessing Web sites through the ISA server, and there are various problems with pre-SP1 versions of Internet Explorer 6.0. There might be reasons why your organization wants to run Internet Explorer 5.0x and pre-Service Pack 1 Internet Explorer 6.0. You could go ahead and upgrade all the browsers in your organization to Internet Explorer 6.0 Service Pack 1, or you can forego integrated authentication and use basic authentication instead.

The primary concern with basic authentication is that username and password information is sent in the clear. We can get around that problem by using secure SSL links. The secure channel is created before any credentials are sent over the wire when you force SSL connections to the OWA site. This obviates the security weakness inherent in using basic authentication over a public network.

Perform the following steps to configure authentication for the OWA sites:

1. Return to the Internet Information Services console. Make sure that the server name and the Default Web Site are expanded. The first thing you might notice is that several of the folders have red STOP signs on them. For some reason, the Exchange virtual folders don't initialize properly during system startup. We'll leave that to the Exchange gurus to explain why this happens, but all we're concerned with is getting them to work.

2. Click **Stop** in the MMC button bar and then click **Start**.

3. Click **Refresh**. You will see the STOP signs change into virtual directory icons.

4. Right-click the Exchweb virtual directory and select **Properties**.

5. Click **Edit** in the Anonymous access and authentication control frame.

6. Disable the **Anonymous access** option.

7. Disable the **Integrated Windows authentication** Option.

8. Enable the **Basic authentication (password is sent in clear text)** option.

9. Click **Yes** in the dialog box explaining that usernames and passwords are passed in clear text if you don't use SSL.

10. Click **Edit**.

11. In the Basic Authentication Domain dialog box, click **Browse**.

12. In the Browse for Folder dialog box, expand the Entire Network entry and the Microsoft Windows Network icon.

13. Click the Domain name for your domain and click **OK**.

14. Click **OK** in the Basic Authentication Domain dialog box.

15. Click **OK** in the Authentication Methods dialog box.

16. Click **Apply** in the Exchweb Properties dialog box.

17. In the Inheritance Overrides dialog box, click **Select All**, then click **OK**.

18. Click **OK** in the Exchweb Properties dialog box.

Perform steps 2 and 3 above for the following virtual directories:

- Public

- Exchange

- Exadmin

A very common problem is the inability to change passwords via the OWA browser interface, the reason being that this feature is not enabled by default when you install Exchange 2000. In order to change passwords, you need to create a virtual directory for the IISADMPWD physical directory. Another requirement is that all communications with the IISADMPWD virtual directory must be done using SSL. We'll take care of those issues by forcing the Web Proxy service to use SSL to connect to *all* virtual folders.

Perform the following steps to create the virtual directory:

1. Right-click the Default Web Site and select **New | Virtual Directory**.

2. Click **Next** on the Welcome to the Virtual Directory Creation Wizard page.

3. Enter **IISADMPWD** in the Alias text box and click **Next**.

4. On the Web Site Content Directory page, enter the path **DRIVE:\SYSTEMROOT\system32\inetsrv\iisadmpwd**. Replace DRIVE with the drive your system root directory is located on, and replace SYSTEMROOT with the name of the root directory for your system files. The default for Windows 2000 is **WINNT**. Click **Next**.

5. On the Access Permissions page, enable the following options: **Read, Run scripts (such as ASP),** and **Execute (such as ISAPI applications or CGI)**. Click **Next**.

6. Click **Finish** on the You have successfully completed the Virtual Directory Creation Wizard page.

7. Change the authentication method for this virtual directory to match the permissions you set on the other OWA directories.

Force a Secure Channel to the OWA Folders

You don't have to force a secure channel to all of the OWA Web folders. The only folder requiring a secure channel from the Web Proxy service to the Web site is the IISADMPWD virtual directory. Access to the other OWA directories can be bridged as HyperText Transfer Protocol (HTTP). The steps are the same for each virtual directory.

Perform the following steps to force a secure channel to the IISADMPWD virtual directory:

1. Right-click the IISADMPWD folder and select **Properties**.

2. Click the Directory Security tab in the IISADMPWD Properties dialog box.

3. Click **Edit** in the Secure Communications frame.

4. Enable the **Require secure channel (SSL)** option.

5. Click **OK** in the Secure Communications dialog box.

6. Click **Apply**, then click **OK** in the IISADMPWD dialog box.

You can use the same procedure to enforce secure communications with other OWA virtual directories. You might want to do this when the OWA site is on the internal network and you don't completely trust your internal network. We'll cover that scenario later in the chapter.

Configuring the Incoming Web Requests Listener and the Web Publishing Rule

We want to use an SSL link to the Incoming Web Requests listener on the external interface of the ISA server in order to ensure a high level of security. The first thing you need to do is bind the Web server certificate to the Incoming Web Requests listener. This allows the listener to impersonate the Web site and create a secure channel with the browser client.

Perform the following steps to create the Incoming Web Requests listener and bind the certificate to the listener:

1. Open the ISA Management console

2. Right-click the server name and select **Properties**.

3. Click on the Incoming Web Requests listener tab.

4. Select the **Configure listeners individually per IP address** option and click **Add**.

5. Select the server name from the Server drop-down list.

6. Select the external IP address on the ISA server in the IP Address drop-down list.

7. Enable the **Use a server certificate to authenticate to web clients** option.

8. Click **Select**. You'll see a number of certificates in the Select Certificate dialog box if you obtained certificates for several of the Exchange mail services.

9. Select the certificate that you created for the Web site and click **OK**.

10. Click **OK** in the Add/Edit Listeners dialog box.

11. Enable the **Enable SSL listeners** option and click **OK**.

12. Click **Apply** in the server Properties dialog box.

13. Select the **Save the changes and restart the services(s)** option and click **OK**.

14. Click **OK** in the server Properties dialog box.

Access a command prompt and enter **netstat –na | find ":443"**. You'll find that now both internal and external IP addresses are listening on TCP port 443 (Figure 28.14). Note that this is not the same as socket pooling; different sockets are being used by the listener and the Web site.

Figure 28.14 Internal and External IP Addresses Listen for Secure Communications

You can create the secure Web Publishing rule now that the Incoming Web Requests listener is configured. The first decision you have to make before creating the rule is what type of destination set you want to use. The easiest approach is to create a destination set for the FQDN of the server and apply this destination set to the OWA Web publishing rule. This destination set does not use paths.

A destination set without any paths works fine if you don't plan on publishing any other Web sites on the same server. However, if you want to make other content available on the same server, and you do *not* want to require an SSL connection to that content, then this approach won't work. In that scenario, you'll have to create a destination set for OWA that contains only the OWA directories.

If you want to create a destination set that applies only to the OWA directories, the destination set includes your FQDN and the following paths:

- /exchweb/*
- /exchange/*
- /public/*
- /iisadmpwd*
- /_AuthChangeUrl*

The /_AuthChangeUrl* entry allows you to change your password via the OWA interface. Note that there is no slash at the end of the path, as there are a number of characters after this string. This isn't a virtual directory, so don't worry about trying to find it. It is something that appears in the Web Proxy logs, so you need to allow access to it. If you just include the /_AuthChangeUrl* entry with an asterisk, it will allow us to access files used for OWA online password changes.

Perform the following steps to create the destination set:

1. In the ISA Management console, expand the server name and the Policy Elements node.

2. Right-click **Destination Sets** and select **New | Set**.

3. Type **OWA** for the name of the destination set and click **Add**.

4. In the Add/Edit Destination dialog box, select the **Destination** option. Enter the FQDN for your site in the text box. In the Path text box, type **/exchweb***.

5. Click **OK**. Repeat steps 3 and 4 four more times, adding the **/exchange***, **/public***, **/iisadmpwd***, and **/_AuthChangeUrl*** paths, respectively.

6. Click **OK** in the New Destination Set dialog box.

You can create Web publishing rules now that you have the destination set:

1. In the ISA Management console, expand the server name and the Publishing Rule node. Right-click **Web Publishing Rules** and select **New | Rule**.

2. On the Welcome to the New Web Publishing Rule Wizard page, type in the name of the rule and click **Next**.

3. Select the **Specified destination set** option from the Apply this rule to drop-down list and select the **OWA destination set** from the Name drop-down list box. Click **Next**.

4. Select **Any request**. Users will authenticate with the Web site, so you don't need to authenticate against the Incoming Web Requests listener as well. In fact, it will not work if you try to authenticate with both the Incoming Web Requests listener *and* the Web site. Click **Next**.

5. On the **Rule Action** page, select the **Redirect the request to this internal Web server (name or IP address)** option.

6. Enter the name of the Web site in available text box. You must use the same name the user uses to access the site. If you have your DNS servers set up to handle this FQDN, you can allow the ISA server to resolve the name. If you don't, you must put the

FQDN for the site in the HOSTS file and match it up with the IP address of the *internal interface* of the ISA server. For example, in this rule, the external user types in the FQDN **www.internal.net**. We'll also put **www.internal.net** in the text box for the redirection. Then we'll create a HOSTS file entry for **www.internal.net** that resolves to the *internal IP address* of the ISA server.

7. Enable the **original host header** option and click **Next**.

8. Click **OK**.

9. Double-click the Web publishing rule you just created.

10. In the rule's Properties dialog box, click the Bridging tab.

11. Enable the **Require secure channel (SSL) for published site** option.

12. Enable the **Require 128-bit encryption** option if all of your clients support 128-bit encryption.

13. Click **Apply**, then click **OK**.

14. Return to the Internet Information Services console and restart the default Web site.

Configuring User Rights on the Domain Controller

You might wonder why we need to cover the issue of user rights in a discussion of OWA. Can't all users access the OWA machine? In most cases, you don't have to address this issue because the users can access OWA as soon as you complete the Web publishing rules. We run into problems when the OWA machine is also a domain controller. Not all users are allowed to log on to a domain controller.

A user should have the *log on locally* right to access resources on a Web site. Usually, the IUSR_MACHINE account has the *log on locally* right required to access any Web site. The problem is that you're not depending on the IUSR account; your users need to log on with their own user accounts. The default domain controller security policy does not allow all users to log on locally. If the OWA user can't log on locally, he or she will not be able to access the OWA site on the ISA Server machine.

> **NOTE**
>
> There is conflicting documentation regarding whether the *log on locally* right is required to access Exchange 2000 OWA sites. Article Q319888 "Access Is Denied Error Message Logging On to OWA" indicates that you must assign users who intend to connect to OWA sites the *log on locally* right. However, Q311422 "Log On Locally Right Not Required for Exchange 2000 OWA" says that you only need to allow users the *access this computer from the network* right. There are some variables that Q311422 doesn't take into account, so we recommend allowing OWA users the *log on locally* right. It is important to point out that it is not good general security practice to allow non-administrative users the *log on locally* right to the domain controller. However, in our "all but the kitchen sink on the ISA server" scenario, we have to deal with a number of security compromises.

You can fix this problem by changing the domain controller security policy. It's usually not a good idea to allow everyone to log on to a domain controller. Under normal circumstances, only administrators should be able to log on locally to a domain controller. When OWA is installed on the DC, you don't have a choice; the users must be able to log on locally. You can give all domain users permissions to log on locally, or you can create a separate group of users who need access to OWA, and grant that group the right to log on locally.

Perform the following steps to grant the *log on locally* right:

Select **Active Directory Users and Computers** from the **Administrative Tools** menu.

1. Expand the domain name. Right-click the node and select **Properties**.
2. Click the Group Policy tab.
3. Click the **Default Domain Controllers Policy** and click **Edit**.
4. Expand the Computer Configuration node and the Windows Settings node.
5. Expand the Security Settings node and the Local Policies node.
6. Click the User Rights Assignment node.
7. In the right pane of the User Rights Assignment node, find the **Log on Locally** right.
8. Double-click **Log on Locally**.
9. In the Security Policy Setting dialog box, click **Add**.
10. Enter the Group name in the Add user or group dialog box, or click **Browse** to find the user or group. Once the user or group is entered, click **OK**.
11. Click **OK** in the Security Policy Setting dialog box.
12. Close the Group Policy window.
13. Click **OK** in the Domain Controllers Properties dialog box and close the Active Directory Users and Computers window.
14. Access a command prompt and type **secedit /refreshpolicy machine_policy** and press **Enter**. You will see a message telling you that there will be a slight delay before machine security policy is updated.
15. At the command prompt, type **secedit /refreshpolicy user_policy** and press **Enter**. This will update the user policy.
16. Close the command prompt window.

That's it! Your configuration is now complete. The next step will test the configuration to see if it works.

Connecting to the OWA Site

The moment of truth is when you test the OWA site; it's so easy to miss just a single step. You're never sure if every configuration step has been done correctly. However, if you followed each step, and understood the reason for carrying out each step, chances are that everything will work nicely.

One thing you can do to speed up your OWA connections from Internet Explorer is to install a client certificate on the OWA client machines. This adds your CA to the Trusted Root Authorities on the client. This speeds up certificate processing quite a bit. You will also avoid an error dialog box on connecting, saying that your computer doesn't trust the CA that granted the server certificate.

Open Internet Explorer and type access the URL https://FQDN/exchange. It will take a few moments to establish the link. Type in your username and password. Note that you do not need to type in a domain name when you log in because you've configured a default domain name in the OWA folder's Authentication Properties dialog boxes. You should not be presented with a second or third dialog box; if you configured everything correctly, you will see only one.

If you received a Certificate Warning dialog box, it's probably because the name on the certificate doesn't match the FQDN you used to access the Web site. The other reason why you might get a Certificate Error dialog box is that your machine doesn't trust your certificate server's root authority. Just install a client certificate on the client and you'll fix that problem right away.

The OWA connection should not be slow if you have a decent speed link. If you're using a client with a 56K modem, performance will not be good, no matter what you do. If you find you have to wait several minutes to get a connection, or if the connection does not work at all, make sure that you have *disabled integrated authentication* on all of the OWA folders. If you're using the wrong version of Internet Explorer, you'll waste a lot of time trying to negotiate integrated authentication, and that won't work! You only need to support basic authentication as long as SSL is working correctly.

OWA users can change their passwords using the OWA interface; However, they must have permission to do so. If the user account properties do not allow the user to change his password, he will not be able to change his password via the OWA interface. Remember that you must also configure the /IISADMPWD directory to force SSL on connections to it by the Web Proxy service.

Troubleshooting Notes on Publishing OWA on the ISA Server

Are you having problems with your OWA configuration? There are so many steps, so many details, it's easy to miss a click here or there. Here's a list of things you should check for if you're having problems getting OWA to work:

- Make sure that the OWA folders are using basic authentication *only*. Sometimes the permissions on the folders change when you restart the server. If you restart the server, recheck all of the OWA folders and make sure only basic authentication is enabled.

- Install client certificates on the OWA clients. This is not required, but it will speed up communications a lot during the SSL negotiation phase.

- Make sure you configure a default domain in the Authentication Properties dialog box for each OWA folder.

- Remember to configure an SSL listener on the default Web site; IIS does not automatically enter the port for you.

- Make sure you configure an Incoming Web Requests listener and bind the Web site certificate to the listener; make sure that you haven't mistakenly used the ISA server's machine certificate.

- If you don't need to publish Web sites outside of the OWA site, you should just use the FQDN in the OWA destination set.

Message Screener on the ISA Server and Exchange Server

You can install the SMTP Message Screener on the ISA/Exchange/DC machine and filter both incoming and outgoing messages. The installation and configuration routine is almost the same as when you install the Message Screener on the ISA server using just the IIS 5.0 SMTP service (without Exchange Server installed). The primary difference is how messages arrive and are processed by the SMTP service.

When the Exchange server isn't installed, the IIS 5.0 SMTP service acts only as an intermediary relay server in the SMTP communication. The IIS 5.0 SMTP service always forwards the message to another SMTP server. This isn't the case when you install Exchange on the ISA server. While it's true that the Exchange server uses the IIS 5.0 SMTP service to send and receive SMTP messages, the situation is different because the Exchange server is the endpoint of the SMTP communications for incoming SMTP message. The Exchange SMTP server doesn't forward the message to another SMTP server.

The difference is subtle, but it does have practical importance. For example, if you use an SMTP client (remember that other SMTP can be SMTP clients) to send messages to the Exchange server's SMTP service, the messages will be exposed to the Message Screener. Therefore, if an SMTP server on the external network or Outlook Express on the external network tries to send an SMTP message to the Exchange server's SMTP service, the message would be exposed to the SMTP Message Screener and be filtered according to the rules you've configured for the Message Screener.

However, not all Exchange clients use SMTP to send messages to the Exchange server. Outlook 2000/XP uses MAPI to communicate with the Exchange server. When the Outlook 2000/XP client sends a message to the Exchange server, the message is not exposed to the SMTP Message Screener because SMTP was not used to send the message.

What if the message the Outlook user sent to the Exchange server is destined for an e-mail address on the Internet? For example, suppose we're using Outlook XP to connect to our Exchange 2000 server and we send an e-mail message to tshinder@isaserver.org. The Exchange server must use SMTP to send an outbound message to the SMTP server responsible for isaserver.org mail. You would expect that the outgoing messages would be exposed to the SMTP Message Screener on the way out.

The fact is that the messages are only *sometimes* exposed to the Message Screener when they leave the Exchange SMTP service. During our testing, it turned out that only the keyword *rule* on top of the list was triggered, and even then it didn't appear to be a consistent finding. It's clear that the SMTP message filter was not designed to be used in this way.

The solution to this problem is to create a second SMTP virtual server on the Exchange server machine. After you create the second virtual SMTP virtual server, configure the default SMTP virtual server to relay to the new virtual SMTP virtual server. When the message is relayed to the second SMTP virtual server, it is formatted as an SMTP message and exposes the message to the SMTP Message Screener. At this point, the outgoing messages will be filtered according to the rules you configured in the SMTP Application Filter dialog box.

The configuration is somewhat complex, but doable. You need to perform the following steps:

1. Disable the SMTP service.

2. Disable the ISA Server services.

3. Configure the new SMTP virtual server.

4. Configure the default SMTP virtual server to use the new SMTP virtual server as its smart host.

5. Restart the ISA Server services.

6. Restart the SMTP service.

Let's look at the details of this configuration:

Disable the SMTP Service

Perform the following steps to disable the SMTP service:

1. Access a command prompt. Type **net stop smtpsvc** and press **Enter**.

2. At the command prompt, type **netstat –na | find ":25"** and press **Enter**. You should see no data returned after issuing the command.

Disable the ISA Server Services

Perform the following steps to disable the ISA Server services:

1. Make sure that the ISA server is disconnected from the Internet before disabling the ISA Server services. Your machine is unprotected during this period and is open to Internet criminals while the ISA Server services are disabled.

2. At the command prompt, type **net stop mspfltex** and press **Enter**. The command will return information regarding the services that will be stopped. Press **Y** and press **Enter**.

3. At the command prompt, type **net stop ipnat** and press **Enter**. The command will return information telling you that the IPNAT service will be disabled. Press **Y** and press **Enter**.

Configure the New SMTP Virtual Server

Now that the ISA Server and SMTP services are disabled, the next step is to create the new SMTP virtual server. Perform the following steps to create the new SMTP virtual server:

1. You will need to add a second IP address on the internal interface of the ISA server. You will then bind the second SMTP virtual server to this second IP address. Right-click the My Network Places icon on the desktop and click **Properties**.

2. Right-click the internal interface and click **Properties**.

3. In the internal interface's Properties dialog box, select the **Internet Protocol (TCP/IP)** entry and click **Properties**.

4. In the Internet Protocol (TCP/IP) Properties dialog box, click **Advanced**.

5. In the Advanced TCP/IP Settings dialog box, click **Add**.

6. Enter a valid IP address for the internal network in the IP Address text box.

7. Enter a valid subnet mask in the Subnet mask text box.

8. Click **Add**.

9. Click **OK**.

10. Click **OK** in the Internet Protocol (TCP/IP) Properties dialog box and in the internal interface's Properties dialog box.

11. Open the Exchange System Manager. Expand the organization name and the Servers node. Expand the server name and the Protocols node. Expand the SMTP node.

12. You should see a red "x" on the **Default SMTP virtual server** entry, which is there because you disabled the SMTP service. If you don't see the red "x", click **Refresh** in the MMC button bar.

13. Right-click the SMTP node and select **New | SMTP Virtual Server**.

14. On the Welcome to the New SMTP Virtual Server Wizard page, enter a name for the SMTP virtual server. In this example we'll call it **Relay**. Click **Next**.

15. On the Select IP Address page, use the drop-down list to select the new internal IP address you previously configured. Click **Finish**.

16. The Relay virtual server will have a question mark on its icon. This will go away after you restart the SMTP service on the ISA/Exchange server. Right-click the new virtual SMTP server's icon and select **Properties**.

17. Click the Access tab. In the Relay restrictions frame, click **Relay**.

18. In the Relay Restrictions dialog box, select the **All except the list below** option. The reason why you want to select this option is that this virtual SMTP server is used by internal network clients to send outgoing mail. If you don't allow this virtual server to relay to all domains, outgoing mail to the Internet won't be relayed, and the mail won't be forwarded. External SMTP clients and servers won't be able to use this server as an open relay, because this server is not published via server publishing rules and therefore isn't directly available to external network hosts.

19. Click **OK** in the Relay Restrictions dialog box.

20. Click the Delivery tab.

21. On the Delivery tab, click **Advanced**.

22. Enter the IP address (surround by straight brackets) or the FQDN of your ISP's SMTP server in the Smart host text box. You should use your ISP's SMTP server because your machine is already overloaded running Exchange and ISA Server. There's no reason to add the burden of name resolution to your machine. Let your ISP's SMTP server handle name resolution by configuring it to be your Smart host.

23. Click **OK**.

24. Click **Apply**, then click **OK** in the SMTP virtual server's Properties dialog box.

25. Now we need to configure the Default SMTP Virtual Server. Right-click the Default SMTP Virtual Server and select **Properties**.

26. In the Default SMTP Virtual Server Properties dialog box, click the Delivery tab.

27. On the Delivery tab, click **Advanced**.

28. In the Advanced Delivery dialog box, enter the IP address of the new SMTP virtual server in the Smart host text box. Make sure that the IP address is surrounded by straight brackets!

29. Click **OK** in the Advanced Delivery dialog box.

30. Click **Apply**, then click **OK** in the Default SMTP Virtual Server Properties dialog box.

Restart the ISA Server Services

Perform the following steps to restart the ISA Server services:

1. Access a command prompt. Type **net start IPNAT** and press **Enter**. You will see that the IP Network Address Translator service was started successfully.

2. At the command prompt, type **net start mspfltex** and press **Enter**. You will either see the service start successfully, or you will see that the service has already been started.

3. At the command prompt, type **net start isactrl** and press **Enter**. You will either see that that the service was started successfully, or that the service has already been started.

4. Open the ISA Management console, expand the server name, then expand the Monitoring node. Click the Services node. Right-click the **Web Proxy** service and click **Start**. Repeat step #5 for the **Firewall** and **Scheduled Content Download** services.

Restart the SMTP Service

Perform the following steps to restart the SMTP service:

1. At the command prompt, type **net start smtpsvc** and press **Enter**.

2. At the command prompt, type in the following command:
```
mdutil set -path smtpsvc/2 -value 1 -dtype 1 -prop 1029 -attrib 1
```

3. The mdutil command has to be entered a second time in order to disable socket pooling for the second SMTP virtual server.

4. Return to the Exchange System Manager. Stop, then start the **Default SMTP Virtual Server** and the new SMTP virtual server using the **Stop** and **Start** buttons in the MMC console.

Notes on the SMTP Message Screener on the Exchange Server Configuration

Getting the SMTP Message Screener to work on the Exchange server takes a lot of steps, but it does work, and it works nicely with your Outlook 2000/XP clients on the internal network as well. We think you'll be very pleased with the results.

There are a couple of issues of which you do need to be aware. At the time of this writing, the SMTP application filter has a couple of flaws in it. First, you cannot send an *AUTH* command to the SMTP service through the SMTP application filter. This prevents users from authenticating with your SMTP service. This can and does pose a real problem for organizations that want to make their SMTP servers available to external users, but also want to prevent their servers from becoming open relays.

For example, the way we have the Exchange SMTP server set up now allows external users to send e-mail to users configured on the Exchange server. However, if the external user wants to send mail to a user outside of your Exchange organization, it won't work because the SMTP service needs to be able to relay the SMTP message to another SMTP server to deliver the message. You do not want to open your published SMTP server as an open relay, so there is no way around this problem if the user must send SMTP messages to the published Exchange SMTP server and the SMTP application filter is enabled (which it must be if you want the SMTP Message Screener to work properly). The only way around this is to send mail via another protocol. You can use OWA to send mail to outside mail domains, but you won't be able to use applications such as Outlook Express to send SMTP messages to outside domains. You could also use Exchange RPC publishing rules to solve this problem too, but these rules do not work when the Exchange server is on the ISA server.

The good news is that it's likely that the SMTP application filter will be fixed by the time you read this book. Make sure to check the news page at www.isaserver.org/shinder for details on an updated SMTP application filter.

The other problem with the SMTP application filter is that it does not support the *STARTTLS* command. This command is sent by SMTP clients when they negotiate a secure SSL connection with the SMTP server. This is an issue if you want to publish an SMTP server for external network users to use to send mail to a published SMTP server. Again, an updated SMTP application filter might be available by the time you read this book, so be sure to check www.isaserver.org/shinder early and often!

Finally, we encourage you to be patient with your configuration. There are a great number of steps to perform. There's a good chance that things won't work if you miss any of the details of the configuration. We know that this can become extremely frustrating! However, if you persevere and check and recheck your configuration, we can assure you that it works consistently and reliably.

Configuring Mail Services on the Internal Network

Configuring Mail services Exchange Server publishing configuration on the internal network is much easier than trying to get it to work on the ISA server. Many of the same principles we applied when publishing the Exchange server on the ISA server will work when publishing an Exchange server that sit on the internal network.

In this section, we'll cover the steps required to publish an Exchange server on the internal network. You'll find that almost all of the details are the same as those when you publish the Exchange server on the ISA server, except that you won't run into so many problematic IIS, ISA, and Exchange Server interactions. There is one major difference between publishing an Exchange server on the internal network and publishing an Exchange server on the ISA server: you can use Exchange RPC publishing rules to allow external network clients to connect to the Exchange server on the internal network.

In the section, we'll cover the following topics:

- Publishing Exchange Server services

- Exchange RPC publishing rules

- Publishing Outlook Web access

- Using the Message Screener on the Exchange server and configuring the Message Screener on an SMTP relay

- Using GFI Software's MailSecurity instead of or in addition to the SMTP Message Screener

---

NOTE

You may want run your mail server on the DMZ instead of on your internal network. This buys you a bit more protection for your internal network by not allowing anyone on an untrusted network to access anything internally.

Publishing Exchange Server on the Internal Network

In the first part of this chapter, we went through the procedures required to publish Exchange Server services on the ISA server. Here we will look at how to publish Exchange Server services when the Exchange server is on the internal network. There are ways to publish Exchange Server services: you can manually create server publishing rules, or use the Secure Server Publishing Wizard.

We wanted you to get a better understand of how publishing rules work by walking you through manually creating publishing rules in the first part of this chapter. You can accomplish the same tasks, and get them done faster, by leveraging the automation provided by the Secure Mail Server Publishing Wizard. The Secure Mail Server Publishing Wizard is an ideal way to publish an internal Exchange server.

The Secure Mail Server Publishing Wizard automatically creates the NNTP, SMTP, POP3, IMAP4, and RPC publishing rules for you. It will also enable the SMTP filter on the ISA server so that you can screen messages on the ISA server before they reach the Exchange server on the internal network. Note that while the wizard will enable the SMTP filter for you, you must install the Message Screener if you want the Message Screener to run on the ISA server. The Message Screener on the ISA server would work together with an SMTP relay on the ISA server when you have an Exchange server on the internal network.

The first step is to install the Exchange server on the internal network. You can install Exchange on a domain controller, or you can install it on a member server in your domain. If you install the Exchange Server on a member server, make sure you install the Exchange System Manager on the domain controller so that you get the Exchange 2000 related tabs and features included in your Active Directory Users and Computers console.

In this discussion, we will assume that the Exchange server is on the domain controller. There are no differences in the configuration when the Exchange server is on a domain controller or a member server, except for the *log on locally* requirement for OWA, so you don't have to do anything different in terms of publishing rules or ISA Server configuration. Just remember that if you do put the Exchange server on the ISA server, you will need to change the *log on locally* user right if you want to publish its OWA site.

Perform the following steps to publish Exchange Server services on the internal network using the Secure Mail Server Publishing Wizard:

1. First, you have to disable socket pooling on the ISA server, or disable the IIS services on the ISA server. Follow the instructions provided earlier in the chapter on how to disable IIS services or disable socket pooling. If you do disable socket pooling, make sure that you configure IIS services to listen *only* on the internal interface, and then restart the IIS services.

2. Open the ISA Management console, expand the server name, then expand the **Publishing** node.

3. Right-click the Server Publishing Rules node and select **Secure Mail Server**.

4. Click **Next**.

5. Select the protocols you want to publish on the Mail Services Selection page (Figure 28.15). The Default Authentication column creates publishing rules that do not support secure SSL connections. The SSL Authentication column creates server publishing rules that support secure SSL connections. Note that when you select the **Incoming SMTP** option, it enables the Apply content filtering dialog box. If you have already enabled the SMTP filter, this dialog will be checked, but grayed out. In this example, we'll select all of the options except the **Apply content filtering** and **Incoming Microsoft Exchange/Outlook** options. We'll cover secure Exchange RPC publishing and using the SMTP Message Screener later in this chapter. Make your selections and click **Next** to continue.

Figure 28.15 The Mail Service Selection Page

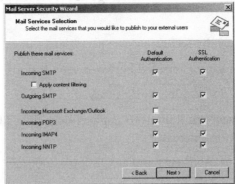

6. On the ISA Server's External IP Address page, click **Browse** and select the IP address on the external interface of the ISA server you want to listen to incoming messages for your internal Exchange server. Click **Next**.

7. On the **Internal Mail Server** page, enter the IP address of the internal network Exchange server in the **At this IP address** text box. Note that if you select the **On the local host** option, the wizard will create packet filters instead of publishing rules. This is why we did not use the Secure Mail Server Publishing Wizard when configuring Exchange services publishing on the ISA server. Click **Next** to continue.

8. Click **Finish**.

9. Click the Server Publishing Rules node and you'll see a number of server publishing rules created by the wizard. Click the **Protocol Rules** node and you'll see that an SMTP and SMTPS protocol rule has been created for the SMTP server so that it can communicate with external network SMTP servers

The wizard works almost perfectly except for one problem. Your SMTP server will probably need to resolve MX domain names using DNS queries. If you use an internal DNS server for MX domain name resolution, you don't have to create a DNS protocol rule for the Exchange server. If you want the Exchange server to resolve MX domain name records, then you should create a DNS Query and a DNS Zone Transfer protocol rule that allows the Exchange server to resolve Internet mail domain names.

The non-SSL publishing rules work right away. You'll need to follow the instructions provided earlier in this chapter regarding certificate assignment and secure connection configuration for the Exchange services if you want to users to connect to the Exchange server using secure SSL connections.

Exchange RPC Publishing

You have the option to publish Exchange RPC services when the Exchange server is on the internal network. This is one of the most compelling reasons for getting the Exchange server off the ISA server and onto an internal network server.

Why would you want to create an Exchange RPC server publishing rule? Here are some advantages:

- The RPC link can be secure.

- Data encryption can be enabled between the Outlook client and the Exchange server.

- Exchange RPC server publishing is easy.

- External client access is limited to mail services only. The client has no access to any other services on the network.

- Users continue to use their familiar Outlook 2000/XP client.

There is an impression that RPC connections are not secure. While in many circumstances this might be the case, it is not true when you use the Exchange RPC filter to publish Exchange servers. The RPC filter handles connections between the Internet Outlook client and the internal Exchange server; it creates dynamic packet filters that can be used *only* by specific Outlook clients that establish the connection. Only Exchange RPC UUIDs are available, so you don't have to worry about other RPC services being exposed to the Internet.

You can configure Outlook to encrypt data over the RPC link. If you do a Network Monitor trace, you'll find that even when the data isn't encrypted, there is *nothing* meaningful in the ASCII decode (in Network Monitor). You are assured a very high level of security for data transferred between the Outlook client and the internal Exchange server when you add data encryption to the connection

Exchange RPC publishing is easy. A single server publishing rule allows your Outlook MAPI clients to access the internal Exchange server. There are no special configuration requirements on the Exchange server, and when the network infrastructure is configured correctly, no configuration changes are required on the Outlook client.

The only other way to connect your external Outlook MAPI clients to an internal network Exchange server is to allow them to establish a VPN link into the internal network. While this option is a viable one for your network administrators and other trusted accounts, you do not necessarily want all of your users (which might include contractors and temps) to have free reign over the corporate network from remote locations. VPN connections are wholly inappropriate for Exchange hosting scenarios. Exchange RPC server publishing gets around this problem by allowing users access only to the Exchange server and nothing more.

End users balk when they have to switch applications to get the same job done. This is especially the case with mail client software. If you have standardized users on Outlook 2000/XP, those users want to use Outlook while at home or on the road. Exchange RPC publishing allows them to use the same familiar interface they use at work, at home, or on the road.

How Exchange RPC Publishing Works

The typical "on the road" Outlook client first establishes a connection to the Internet through a local ISP. The client might also be on a remote network and connects to the Exchange server via a Network Address Translation (NAT) server on the remote network. When the user opens Outlook, the following communications take place:

1. Outlook establishes a connection to TCP port 135 on the external interface of the ISA server.

2. The ISA server's Exchange RPC filter intercepts the request and forwards the request to the internal network Exchange server. The internal network Exchange server responds to the request by sending a port number on which the Outlook client can send its messages. The Exchange RPC filter on the ISA server intercepts this response and opens a dynamic packet filter on its external interface. The dynamic packet filter assigns a port on the external interface of the ISA server on which only this particular Outlook client can communicate. Any other Internet host will not be able to use that port for inbound access. The ISA server maps this port on its external interface to the port number the Exchange server expects to receive messages from the Internet Outlook client. In addition, when the Outlook client logs on, it registers a port on which it can receive new mail notification messages from the Exchange server. The ISA server RPC filter also registers this port number, creates a dynamic packet filter, and passes the new mail notification messages from the Exchange server to the Internet Outlook client.

3. The ISA server forwards the response from the Exchange server. The Outlook client receives the port number on the external interface of the ISA server to which it can send its messages to the Exchange server.

4. The Outlook client establishes a connection to the mapped port on the external interface of the ISA server and through that port connects to the internal network Exchange server.

Figure 28.16 depicts this sequence of events.

Figure 28.16 Establishing an Exchange RPC Connection

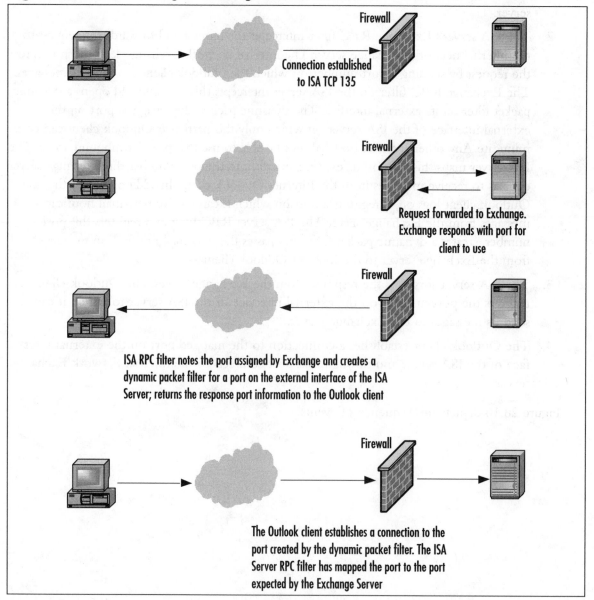

Connection established
to ISA TCP 135

Request forwarded to Exchange.
Exchange responds with port for
client to use

ISA RPC filter notes the port assigned by Exchange and creates a
dynamic packet filter for a port on the external interface of the ISA
Server; returns the response port information to the Outlook client

The Outlook client establishes a connection to the
port created by the dynamic packet filter. The ISA
Server RPC filter has mapped the port to the port
expected by the Exchange Server

Preparing the Infrastructure for Exchange RPC Publishing

You need to take care of a few things before your RPC server publishing rule works correctly:

- Creating the supporting DNS infrastructure
- Creating the DNS and SMTP protocol rules
- Configuring the Authentication method
- Supporting clients behind NAT servers/ISA servers

Creating the Supporting DNS Infrastructure

DNS issues crop up constantly on the ISAserver.org message boards and newsgroups. If your DNS infrastructure isn't in place and working properly, the ISA server rules won't do what you want them to do. If your DNS infrastructure is already set up and working, great! If it's not, you need to come to terms with it and get it fixed.

The ideal DNS configuration is referred to as a *split DNS*. In the split DNS configuration, you maintain two separate zones, one for *internal* network clients to use and one for *external* network clients to use. These two zones service the same domains, but the resource records on the *internal* DNS server have the private IP addresses for your network clients, and the *external* DNS server has the public IP address for your published network resources.

> **WARNING**
>
> Note that when we use the terms *internal* and *external DNS server*, we're not referring to the physical location of these DNS servers. The internal and external DNS server can be located on the internal network. The external DNS server on the internal network is published using a server publishing rule, allowing external network clients to resolve your public domain resources to the external interface of the ISA server. The internal network DNS is always on the internal network because only internal network clients use this server.

For example, a common problem is that users can access the published Web server www.domain.com from external network hosts, but can't access the site when they're on the internal network. The problem is that internal network clients are trying to connect to the published server via the *external interface of the ISA server* because internal network clients are using the same host records as the external network clients for name resolution. When you create an internal DNS server that internal network clients use, the internal network clients receive the private IP address of the published server and therefore connect directly to the server.

Now, in regard to our Exchange RPC publishing situation, you need to make sure that the host name of the internal network Exchange server is the same as the host name used to access the server from the Internet. This requirement makes the split DNS configuration even more important, since the split DNS allows the transition between the internal and external network to be transparent to the users.

For example, if the server name is exchange.domain.com on the internal network, you need to ensure that exchange.domain.com is also accessible from the external network. You can accomplish this with a split DNS configuration by creating a Host (A) record on your *external* DNS server for exchange.domain.com to point to the external interface address on the ISA server that you are using in the Exchange RPC publishing rule.

The reason why you must configure the Host (A) record is that the name of the Exchange server is returned to the Outlook client when it makes the RPC connection. The Outlook client must be able to communicate with the name received from the Exchange server, which is the Exchange server's NetBIOS name. Note that only the host name portion of the FQDN will appear in the Outlook configuration dialog box after the name is resolved. For example, when you configure Outlook to use the Exchange server, you type in the name of the Exchange server as **exchange.domain.com**. When the client successfully connects to the internal network Exchange server via the RPC publishing rule, the name in the configuration dialog box will change to **EXCHANGE**.

If your organization does not use the same naming conventions for internally and externally accessible resources, you can still access the Exchange server via the RPC publishing rule. In this case, all you need to do is create a HOSTS file entry with the NetBIOS name of the computer. You do not need to include the FQDN of the Exchange server in the HOSTS file; just the NetBIOS name is required to make it work.

> **NOTE**
>
> It is best practice to use the same name for both the computer DNS host name and NetBIOS name. We have not tested the configuration with a disjoint NetBIOS and DNS host name configuration, so we cannot guarantee that it will work if you maintain a disjoint NetBIOS/DNS namespace.

Creating the DNS and SMTP Protocol Rules

The Exchange server needs to forward mail it receives from the Outlook client to SMTP servers on the Internet. You need to create two protocol rules:

- A DNS Query and DNS Zone Transfer protocol rule
- An SMTP protocol rule

The DNS Query and Zone Transfer protocol rules allow the Exchange IIS SMTP service to resolve the MX domain name records for the outgoing mail. You can configure the protocol rule to allow only the Exchange server access, or you can configure it to allow all machines on the network to use it. Access control on the DNS Zone Transfer protocol rule depends on which machine is resolving the MX domain names. You might want to forward the queries to an internal DNS server and let it take care of name resolution.

Make sure you create a client address set for the servers that you want to have access to this DNS protocol rule. The servers, whether Exchange or DNS servers, will not have logged-on users, or will not have the Firewall client installed on them. The only way to allow outbound access control for SecureNAT clients is via client address sets. Create a client address set for all servers that need access to the rule, and assign the client address set to the rule.

The SMTP protocol rule is required for the Exchange server to send out mail to external mail domains. Access controls on the SMTP protocol rule depend on what machine actually sends mail to external SMTP servers. Allow only the Exchange server access to the SMTP protocol rule if the Exchange server sends mail directly to Internet SMTP servers. Allow the SMTP relay access to the SMTP protocol rule if you use an SMTP relay server for outbound mail. If you are using a mail relay, make sure that the SMTP relay server has access to the DNS protocol rule as well. The exception would be when you are allowing an internal DNS server to resolve Internet mail domains for the relay.

Configuring the Authentication Method

When Outlook logs on to the Exchange server, the Exchange server instructs the Outlook client to authenticate with an Active Directory domain controller. The problem is you do not want to open the ports responsible for authentication through the ISA server. To get around this problem, you can configure the Exchange server to perform authentication on the behalf of the Outlook client.

To configure the Exchange server to proxy authentication requests for the Outlook client, navigate to the following Registry key:

`HKLM\System\CurrentControlSet\Services\MSExchangeSA\Parameters`

Add the following:

- **Value** No RFR Service
- **Type** REG_DWORD
- **Data** 1

Note that the value *does* have spaces in it. At first we thought that this might have been a typo, but we confirmed that the spaces should be included. After adding the value, restart the Exchange server. Note that you do not need to add this value if the Exchange server is also a domain controller.

Clients Behind NAT Servers/ISA Servers

If the Outlook client is behind a NAT server or an ISA server, it will not be able to receive new mail notification requests. The reason is that these new mail notification requests are not part of the existing RPC connection between Outlook and the Exchange server. The NAT server and ISA server drop the packet because the new mail notification message is seen as an unsolicited inbound request.

This doesn't mean that you won't ever get any new mail. If you send mail to the Exchange server, a new mail notification message is sent through the active RPC channel between the Outlook client and the Exchange server when the message is sent. However, RPC wasn't designed for use over the Internet. If there is an error in any of the RPC packets carrying the new mail notification, the notification message will not go through. You can get around this by forcing synchronization with the F9 key in Outlook 2000, or set up the Exchange account to carry out an automatic send/receive every few minutes in Outlook 2002. The exception to this is when you encrypt the data connection between Outlook and the Exchange server. In that case, e-mail notification never works, and you have to click on a folder to initiate the connection.

The good news is that everything else works fine when Outlook is behind the NAT server. If you use the Windows 2000 RRAS NAT, no further configuration is required for the NAT routing protocol. If there is an ISA server in front of the Outlook client, you will need to configure an RPC protocol definition and configure the client as a Firewall client. You must use the Firewall client configuration because SecureNAT clients do not support secondary connections.

You need to create the following protocol definition (Figure 28.17):

- **Primary connection** TCP 135 Outbound
- **Secondary connections** TCP 1025-65534 Outbound

The initial connection takes place on TCP 135. The remote ISA server (the one publishing the Exchange server) sends back to the local ISA server (the one in front of the Outlook client) the port number on which the Outlook client needs for subsequent requests. Since this new outgoing connection is part of the original RPC conversation, a secondary connection to an ephemeral (high number) port is required outbound from the local ISA server to the remote ISA server. Once you create the RPC protocol definition, create a protocol rule using this protocol definition.

Figure 28.17 Outbound RPC Protocol Definition

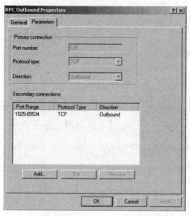

Creating the Exchange RPC Server Publishing Rule

The Exchange RPC server publishing rule uses a protocol definition provided by the RPC application filter. If you disable the application filter, you lose the protocol definition. Perform the following steps to create the server publishing rule:

1. In the ISA Management Console, expand the server or array name and the Publishing node.

2. Right-click the Server Publishing Rules node and select **New | Rule**.

3. On the page, enter a name for the rule and click **Next**.

4. On the Address Mapping page, enter the IP address of the internal Exchange server and the IP address on the external interface you want external network clients to use to access the Exchange server. Click **Next**.

5. On the Protocol Settings page, select the **Exchange RPC Server** rule and click **Next**.

6. On the Client Type page, select **Any Request** and click **Next** (it's unlikely you'll be able to identify a client address set to assign the external Outlook clients).

7. On the final page of the wizard, click **Finish**.

The rule will take effect soon after you click **Finish**. If you want the rule to apply right away, restart the Firewall service.

WARNING

Configuring the Outlook client is beyond the scope of this book, and the procedures vary depending on the version of Outlook you're configuring. Both Outlook 2000 and Outlook 2002 (XP) can use the Exchange RPC publishing rule to access the Exchange server on the internal network. It is important to note that you can force the client to use an encrypted RPC connection when connecting to the ISA server.

There is one drawback to using an encrypted channel: you will never receive notifications of new e-mail. In fact, you won't receive notification of new e-mail even if you schedule an automatic Send/Receive or press F9, depending on the version of Outlook. To receive new e-mail notification messages, you must click on an existing message or folder to initiate a connection with the Exchange server .

If you are using Outlook 2000, do *not* install Office Service Pack 2. There appears to be an undocumented issue preventing Outlook 2000 SP2 clients from connecting to an Exchange 2000 server published using the RPC server publishing rule. This problem appears to be specific to the server publishing rule, because if you bring the client onto the internal network, you can log on to the Exchange server without problems.

Publishing Outlook Web Access on the Internal Network Exchange Server

The same procedures used to publish OWA on the ISA server are used when you publish OWA on the internal network Exchange server. The only difference is that you don't need to worry about disabling socket pooling on the ISA server because you'll choose to disable the IIS W3SVC on the ISA server for security purposes.

As a review, here are the basic procedures required to publish the OWA site on the internal network Exchange server:

- **Configure the OWA Web site on the Exchange server** Configure folder permissions, obtain and assigning a certificate for the Web site, configure a port for SSL connections on the default Web site, and configure the sites to require an SSL connection.

- **Configure the Incoming Web Requests listener on the ISA server** Create the individual listener, export the OWA Web site certificate and import it into the ISA Server's machine certificate store, and bind the certificate to the Incoming Web Requests listener.

- **Create the Web publishing rule** Create the destination set used for the OWA Web publishing rule, create the Web publishing rule, and configure the rule to bridge SSL connections as SSL.

- **Configure the OWA client Web browser** Improve performance for the OWA client by installing a client certificate on all browser clients.

For details of this configuration, check the relevant sections on how to publish OWA on the ISA server. The only difference is that you use the internal IP address of the Exchange server rather than the IP address of the internal interface of the ISA server for the redirect.

> **NOTE**
>
> There is a good chance that by the time you read this book, Microsoft will have released the ISA Server Feature Pack. One of the features included in the major update to ISA Server is an Outlook Web Access Publishing Wizard. The wizard will greatly simplify publishing of OWA sites. However, like all wizards, it will have its limitations. Check www.isaserver.org/shinder for updates on this feature of the ISA Server Feature Pack and other important ISA Server news and articles.

Message Screener on the Internal Network Exchange Server

You can install the Message Screener on the internal network Exchange server. The difference between the installations is that when the Message Screener is on the ISA server, the entire ISA Server software package is installed on the ISA/Exchange Server computer. In contrast to the "all but the kitchen sink" approach we covered earlier, when the Exchange server is on a dedicated server, all you need to install is the SMTP Message Screener. You don't need to install any other component of the ISA Server software.

Run the ISA Server installation program as you usually would to install only the Message Screener component on the internal network Exchange server. Select the **Custom** installation option and then deselect the **ISA Services** and **Administration tools** options in the **Custom Installation** dialog box (Figure 28.18).

Figure 28.18 The Custom Installation Dialog Box

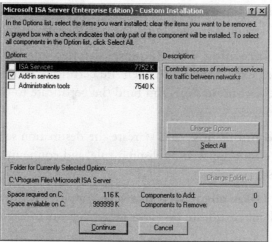

Select the **Add-in services** option and click **Change Option**. Remove the **Install H.323 Gatekeeper Service** option (Figure 28.19). The only component you want is the **Message**

Screener. Make sure that the **Message Screener** option is selected and complete the installation on the Exchange server computer. You won't see any new configuration interfaces or Start menu items related to the Message Screener on the Exchange server. Configuration of the Message Screener is done via the SMTP filter on the ISA server.

Figure 28.19 Selecting the Message Screener

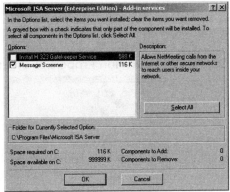

The next step is to configure credentials that the Message Screener software will use to communicate with the SMTP application filter on the ISA server. Credentials are configured using the SMTPCRED tool, which is installed in the Program Files\Microsoft ISA Server folder on the Exchange server's hard disk after running the Message Screener installation.

Open the SMTPCRED tool by double-clicking it. In the Message Screener Credentials dialog box (Figure 28.20), enter your ISA server name, the Username of the person who installed the ISA server, the Domain to which that user account belongs, and the Password of that user. Note that you do not need to use the credentials of the user who installed the ISA server, but it does streamline the process and reduces troubleshooting issues encountered with the Message Screener by an order of magnitude. Click **OK** after entering the information.

Figure 28.20 The SMTPCRED Tool

The last thing is to configure DCOM permissions. The Message Screener communicates with the SMTP application filter via DCOM. While this isn't an issue when the ISA server and the Exchange server are on the same machine, it does become an issue when they are on different machines.

Perform the following steps to configure the DCOM permissions:

1. Select **Start | Run** and type **dcomcnfg.exe** in the Open text box. Click **OK**.

2. Click the Applications tab and select **VendorData class | Properties** (Figure 28.21).

Figure 28.21 The DCOM Configuration Properties Dialog Box

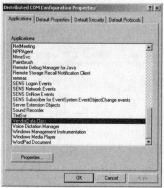

3. On the VendorData Class Properties dialog box, click the Security tab (Figure 28.22). Select the **Use custom access permissions** and click **Edit**. Figure 28.22 The VendorData Class Properties Dialog Box

4. Add the Everyone group by clicking **Add** and selecting the **Everyone** group (Figure 28.23). Click **OK**.

5. Repeat steps #3 and #4 to edit the **Use custom launch permissions** and **Use custom configuration permissions** options.

6. Click **OK**.

Figure 28.23 Adding the Everyone Group

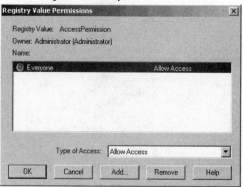

7. Restart both the ISA server and the Exchange server. We suggest restarting the ISA server first.

The remainder of the configuration is the same as when you run the Message Screener on the ISA/Exchange server computer. You will be able to screen for incoming and outgoing messages, but you will have the same limitations regarding Outlook MAPI clients sending SMTP messages to the Internet. The solution is the same: create a second virtual SMTP server and have the default SMTP virtual server forward mail to the second SMTP virtual server. The Internet-bound messages sent by Outlook clients will be exposed to the SMTP Message Screener when they are forwarded to the second SMTP virtual server.

GFI's Mail Security and Mail Essentials for SMTP Servers

It's estimated that spam makes up as much as 20 percent of the total traffic moving through the Internet. Spam clogs e-mail boxes, and contains viruses, worms, and offensive language. Spam fills the massive disks on today's mail servers and is a public nuisance. Spam can negatively impact your personal and professional life: just think about how many times you've accidentally ignored an important message because it got lost in a sea of spam in your inbox.

We don't have to convince you that something needs to be done about spam. Many network administrators use Real-time Black Hole Lists to automate spam blocking on their networks. The problem with RBLs is they are maintained by third parties. If there is one thing we learned during the dot com bomb, it's that inappropriate trust in third parties can put your business in jeopardy.

There are several types of RBLs. Legitimate RBLs look for open mail relays on the Internet and blacklist the IP addresses of the open relays. The blacklisting is based on the assumption that eventually, a spammer will find the open relay and use it to send spam. The problem with this approach is that the open relay will be blacklisted even if no spam has ever been sent through it. It's sort of like the police taking you into custody for a shooting because you have two hands, one of which *might* have held a gun.

The other type of RBL is based on user reports. One user of the service reports that he received mail that he thinks is spam. That user tells three of his friends to make the same report. BANG! The domain from which the alleged spam is sent is blocked by the RBL. Suppose you send someone an e-mail message inviting him to your birthday party. He didn't ask for that message, so he reports you as a spammer, and he gets three of his antisocial friends to send in the same report. A couple of days later, you find that some people aren't getting mail from you. Why? Your domain or account has been blocked by the RBLs that blindly trust user reports.

This type of spam blocking has to be the most egregious form of censorship we've seen in decades. Everyone hates spam, we really hate spam, but we hate the idea of a third party censoring what should be sent to *our* network. That's our job, our responsibility, and our mail. It's not the job of some anonymous RBL to decide what's legitimate.

The SMTP Message Screener goes a long way to resolving the spam problem. You can block mail based on text strings. The problem is that you don't have much flexibility with the SMTP Message Screener. For example, you can't:

- Easily save the keyword entries in the Message Screener
- Check for e-mail viruses using the Message Screener

- Check for viruses in e-mail attachments using the Message Screener
- Import a list of keywords from a text file into the Message Screener
- Check for non-virus-related e-mail exploits with the Message Screener
- Check for whole words in the Message Screener (you can only check for text strings)
- Creating conditional content checking rules for e-mail

It's our opinion that the only *valid* way to control spam is by using a keyword method. We've found that the most effective way to prevent spam from getting to user mailboxes is to create a list of keywords that don't apply to the legitimate business or personal communications. Using this method, you can control over 99 percent of the spam entering your network.

While the ISA Server SMTP Message Screener is better than nothing, we've found that the best tool for this job is GFI Software's MailSecurity, which can be used to block spam in both small and large organizations. MailSecurity is easy to set up, and you can import your spam filter list easily from a text file. It also detects e-mail viruses and attachments, and auto-updates its virus definition list on a daily basis.

MailSecurity Versions

There are two versions of MailSecurity. One plugs into your Exchange 2000 server and inspects the contents of the message store. The other version is for SMTP mail gateways and inspects mail as it moves through the gateway. The main advantage of the Exchange Server version is that it can inspect mail sent between internal users. The main advantage of the SMTP relay version is that it has more information about each e-mail and can decide better what mail is considered inbound and outbound. MailSecurity can be configured to inspect only inbound, only outbound, or both inbound and outbound e-mail.

We typically install an SMTP relay on all networks that have an Exchange 2000 server. For that reason we consider the SMTP gateway version the best choice. Note that you can use both versions. You can install the SMTP gateway version on your SMTP relay, and you can install the Exchange Server 2000 version on your Exchange server and you don't have to buy any more licenses for filtering based on keyword, user, or domain. You do need to pay extra for a maintenance contract and automatic anti-virus updates.

Installing MailSecurity for SMTP Gateways

Installing MailSecurity for SMTP gateways is straightforward:

1. Download the installation file from www.gfi.com/mailsecurity/index.html and run the **mailsecurity.exe** installation package. The Welcome to the GFI MailSecurity for Exchange/SMTP Installation Wizard page will be displayed (Figure 28.24). Click **Next** to continue.

Figure 28.24 The Welcome Page

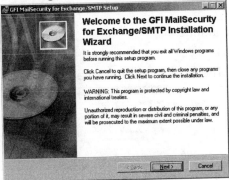

2. The License Agreement page appears. Select the **I accept the license agreement** option and click **Next**.

3. On the User Information page, enter your name, company name, and serial number (if you have one; otherwise, use **Evaluation** as your key). Click **Next**.

4. On the **Administrator Email** page (Figure 28.25), enter the MailSecurity administrator e-mail address. Notification messages can be sent to the administrator e-mail account you enter here. You can add more administrators or change the one you enter here later. Click **Next**.

Figure 28.25 The Administrator Email Dialog Box

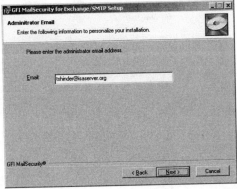

5. On the Destination Folder page, select the location of the program files and click **Next**.

6. This brings you to the Mail Server page shown in Figure 28.26. If your SMTP relay is on a DMZ segment, enter the IP address on the external interface of the ISA server used by the SMTP server publishing rule that's publishing the internal network Exchange server.

7. If the SMTP relay is on your internal network, enter the IP address of your Exchange server. The default port TCP 25 will work in the majority of cases. However, if you want MailSecurity to send to an alternate port, just type the alternate port number in the **on port** text box. The setup program will create a remote domain in the IIS SMTP service for the domain you enter in the **Local domain** text box. If you are managing multiple

mail domains, you should manually create those remote domains after the installation is complete.

7. Click **Next** to continue.

Figure 28.26 The Mail Server Information Page

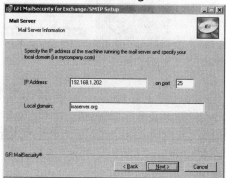

8. Identify the type of mail server that is running MailSecurity (see Figure 28.27). In this example, we're installing MailSecurity on an SMTP relay, so the **second** option is correct. Click **Next** to continue, and click **Next** one more time to start installing the application.

9. Click **Finish** when you get notification that the application has been installed successfully.

Figure 28.27 Choosing the Mail Server Type

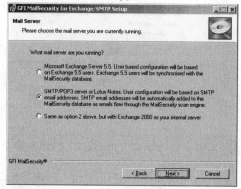

10. Open the Internet Information Services console after you're finished installing MailSecurity. Expand the Default SMTP Virtual Server node and click the **Domains** node. You'll see that a new remote domain was created and configured to use your internal mail server as a smart host. If you configure MailSecurity on a DMZ SMTP relay, you'll see the IP address used on the external interface of the ISA server in your SMTP server publishing rule. If you host multiple mail domains, create a remote domain for each domain you host and have them use your mail server as a smart host. Make sure that your server is not configured as an open relay by setting the appropriate relay settings on the Default SMTP Virtual Server (Figure 28.28).

Figure 28.28 Remote Domain Configuration

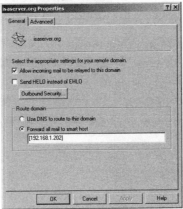

Configuring MailSecurity

1. Select **Start | Programs | GFI MailSecurity | MailSecurity Configuration**. Figure 28.29 shows all the features in an MMC console.

Figure 28.29 MailSecurity Configuration

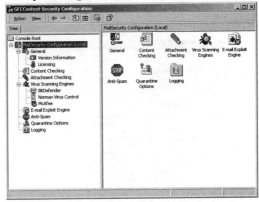

2. Click the Content Checking node in the left pane, then double-click the Default Content Checking Rule. This is where you create your e-mail content checking rules. You can create rules that look for a particular keyword, or you can create rules based on keywords with conditions. In Figure 28.30, you'll see some keyword rules that have conditions. For example, we want to block all mail that has the keywords "special offer." However, we don't want to block special offers from GFI.

3. Notice that you have the option to check inbound and outbound mails. You can also block PGP encrypted mail. This will prevent mail encrypted with PGP from bypassing your content checking rules. This is a valuable feature, as users might try to use PGP to send out proprietary information about corporate projects. For example, you might be working on a project and use an internal code name for that project. No one on the outside should know the project or its code name. If users sent mail encrypted by PGP,

they would get around your keyword filters. You can also check the attachment content. This prevents attachments with forbidden content from reaching users' mailboxes.

Figure 28.30 Configuring Keywords

4. You can monitor incoming mail in real time and see what mail was allowed and which ones where caught by the content checking rules. The **GFI Monitor** (Figure 28.31) shows you mail as it's being processed.

Figure 28.31 GFI Monitor Displaying Actions in Real Time

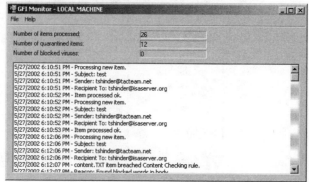

5. The **Moderator Client** (Figure 28.32) allows you to see the actual messages caught by the content checking rules. When you double-click the blocked message, you'll see the reason why the message was caught, some details about the message, and files associated with the message. You can right-click the **content** file and open the message. Plain text messages are saved as text files, and HTML messages are saved as HTML files. The HTML files are safe to open because dangerous scripts and viruses are removed.

Figure 28.32 The Moderator Client

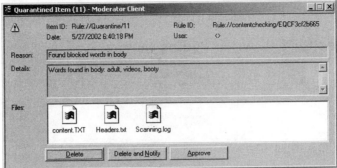

6. Click the Attachment Checking node in the left pane, and then double-click on the Default Attachment Checking Rule (Figure 28.33) in the right pane. This option allows you to block attachments for inbound or outbound mail (or both). There's a built-in list of attachments that can be blocked, and you can easily add your own custom attachments.

Figure 28.33 Attachment Checking Options

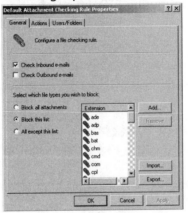

7. Now for the best feature of MailSecurity: the virus scanning engines. MailSecurity allows you to scan mail for viruses using multiple scanning engines. If one of the virus scanning engines doesn't catch a virus, it'll try again with another scan engine. This provides a high level of security for both incoming and outgoing e-mail. This redundant virus scanning method unique to MailSecurity.

8. Notice that you have the option to scan inbound mail, outbound mail, or both. You also can block Word documents that have macros. Word macro viruses are a big problem, so blocking them can go a long way toward protecting your users from Word macro exploits. In Figure 28.34, you see the options for automatically downloading and installing virus definition updates.

9. The system automatically downloads virus definitions, and we've never had a problem getting them to download from behind the ISA server. The system uses FTP to download the updates, so you need to create an FTP protocol rule to allow the mail server to download the updates. If you run MailSecurity on the ISA server, you'll need to create

packet filters to allow for PORT mode FTP communications between the ISA server and the GFI FTP server (Figure 28.35).

Figure 28.34 The Virus Checking Engines

Figure 28.35 Configuring FTP Virus Definitions Download Options

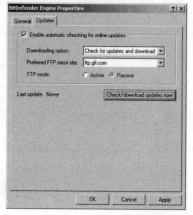

10.   Click the E-mail Exploit Engine node in the left pane of the console. In the right pane (Figure 28.36), you'll see an impressive list of e-mail exploits MailSecurity checks for. The e-mail exploit engine is disabled by default, so you have to right-click the node in the left pane of the console and click **Enable**. We don't see any reason not to run the e-mail exploit engine, so we recommend that you always enable it and allow MailSecurity to check for all of the included exploits. If for some reason you need to disable checking for a particular exploit, you can right-click it and click **Disable**.

Figure 28.36 Checking for E-Mail Exploits

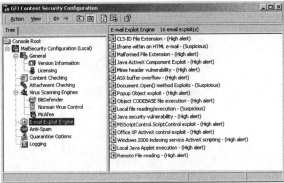

11. Some e-mails are so obviously spam that you don't need to ever look at them. This type of blatant spam can be deleted without you ever needing to review it in the Moderator Client console. The **Anti-spam** feature allows you to enter keywords that are never included in legitimate e-mails. As with the content checking feature mentioned earlier, you can have MailSecurity check the mail body or subject line for these uniquely inappropriate or offensive keywords. When a message matches the keywords in the Anti-Spam dialog box, the mail can be deleted immediately or put in a folder for later checking (Figure 28.37).

Figure 28.37 Whacking Spam with the Anti-Spam Feature

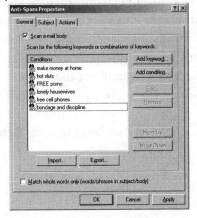

For both content checking and anti-spam rules, you can choose what action to take on the e-mail (See Figure 28.38). For the content checking option, you can quarantine the mail, delete it, or move it to a particular folder for evidence collection. You also have the option to notify users that they sent or received a forbidden mail. You can also inform the user's manager. The manager is defined in the user account properties in the Active Directory.

Figure 28.38 Deciding What Action to Take with Filtered Mail

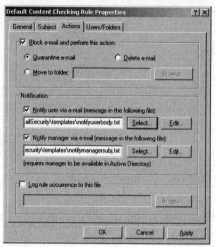

We have found the performance of MailSecurity acceptable. If you have a large number of rules and enable all the virus engines and exploit checking, it might take a few seconds to evaluate a single e-mail. If you have a busy mail server, you'll want to make sure to load it up with RAM and a fast processor. However, if you don't require instantaneous delivery of e-mail from the relay to the main mail server, you're in good shape. The engine doesn't choke or die when it's busy, it just slows. However, all the mail gets checked and cleaned before making its way to your server.

You need to put together a list of keywords that are specific for your organization in order to see the best results with your e-mail checking rules. This can take a week or two. One thing that we find useful is to create a Hotmail account and then subscribe that Hotmail account to a number of different Web sites. You can also post messages to USENET message boards and put that account in the return address. This will get the account quickly subscribed to a large number of spammer lists. You can use the spam sent to your Hotmail inbox for ideas on what keywords to put into the MailSecurity keyword database. If you want to get a head start on your list, check out our list of keywords, which we update weekly, at ftp.tacteam.net/isaserver/spamlist.tx_.

Summary

In this chapter, we reviewed the techniques used to publish SMTP and Exchange mail services. In the first part, you learned how to publish SMTP and Exchange mail services on the ISA server. Publishing Exchange 2000 services on the ISA server has been a long misunderstood subject that has never, until the publication of this book, been adequately explained to the public. There are a number of procedures you must go through in order to prevent conflict so you'll be able to get all the services to work together and publish the Exchange services among the Exchange services, the ISA server, and the Internet Information server.

We also covered how to publish Exchange mail services on the internal network. The procedures are very similar and in many ways much easier because you don't need to run IIS services on the ISA server. You can also leverage the automation provided by the Secure Mail Services Wizard to make your server publishing rules and protocol rules. Publishing mail services on the internal network is the preferred configuration because you don't have to worry about weaknesses in any of the Exchange services compromising your firewall.

Part VI

Intrusion Detection

## Chapter 29

Introducing Snort

Best Damn Topics in this Chapter:

- **What Is Snort?**
- **Snort System Requirements**
- **Exploring Snort's Features**
- **Using Snort on Your Network**
- **Security Considerations with Snort**

Introduction

Snort is a full-fledged open-source Network-based Intrusion Detection System (NIDS) that has many capabilities. These capabilities include packet sniffing and packet logging in addition to intrusion detection. In addition to all of the basic Snort Features, you can set up Snort to send real-time alerts. This provides you with the ability to receive alerts in real time, rather than having to continuously monitor your Snort system.

An Intrusion Detection System (IDS) is used as a "burglar alarm" for your network or host. If there is an anomaly detected (in the case of Snort, by using signatures), the system administrator is notified in various ways. Those ways include e-mail, network messages (like Windows pop-ups or UNIX write), or the syslog facility.

Snort is like a vacuum that takes particular items (in this case, packets) and allows you to perform different tasks, such as watching the items as they get sucked up (packet sniffer), putting the items into a container (packet logger), or sorting them and determining when a particular item has gone through your NIDS.

So why is Snort so popular? Providing packet sniffing and logging functions is an elementary part of Snort, but Snort's beefiness comes from its intrusion detection capabilities—which matches packet contents to an intrusion rule. Snort might be considered a *lightweight* NIDS. A lightweight IDS is one that has a small footprint and can run on various operating systems (OSs). Additionally, Snort provides functionality only before found in commercial-grade network IDSs such as Network Flight Recorder (NFR) and ISS RealSecure.

Snort's popularity runs parallel to the increasing popularity of Linux and other free OSs such as the BSD-based OSs, NetBSD, OpenBSD, and FreeBSD. Just because Snort's roots are in open source does not mean that it's not available for other commercial OSs. On the contrary, you can find ports of Snort available for Solaris, HP-UX, IRIX, and even Windows.

Snort is a signature-based IDS, and uses rules to check for errant packets in your network. A rule is a set of requirements that would trigger an alert. For example, one snort rule to check for peer-to-peer file sharing services checks for the string "GET" not connecting to a service running on port 80. If a packet matches that rule, that packet creates an alert. Once an alert is triggered, the alert can go a number of places, such as a log file, a database, or to an SNMP trap.

NOTE

Snort's logo is a pig, and many references are piggish in nature.

In this chapter, you'll get an understanding of what Snort is, what its features are, and how to use it on your network. Additionally, you'll learn about the history of Snort, and how it came to be such a popular IDS. You'll also learn the importance of securing your Snort system, and some of the pitfalls of Snort. However, as you will see, Snort's advantages far exceed its pitfalls.

NOTE

There are commercial solutions for Snort as well, but they are out of scope for this chapter. Although Snort is available for free under the GNU Public License (GPL), there are commercial solutions available for Snort through Sourcefire.

What Is Snort?

In short, Snort is a packet sniffer/packet logger/network IDS. Snort has an interesting history that began with a man named Marty Roesch. In November 1998, Roesch wrote a Linux-only packet sniffer called APE. Despite the great features of APE, Roesch also wanted a sniffer that would do the following:

- Work on multiple OSs.

- Use a hexdump payload dump (TCPDump later had this functionality).

- Display all the different network packets the same way (TCPDump did not have this).

With these goals in mind, Roesch developed Snort. Snort was written as a libcap application to provide system administrators with an alternative to TCPDump (the only other sniffer using libcap at the time—Libcap allows Snort to be portable from a network filtering and sniffing standpoint).

Snort became available at Packet Storm (www.packetstormsecurity.com) on December 22, 1998. At that time, Snort was only about 1,600 lines of code and had a total of two files. Roesch's first uses of Snort included monitoring his cable modem connection and debugging network applications that he coded.

NOTE

The name Snort came from the fact that the application is a "sniffer and more." In addition, Roesch said that he has too many programs called a.out, and all the popular names for sniffers called "TCP-something" were already taken.

Snort's first signature-based analysis (also known as rules-based within the Snort community) became a feature in late January 1999. This was Snort's initial foray down the path of intrusion detection, and Snort could be used as a lightweight IDS at the time.

By the time Snort version 1.5 came out in December 1999, Roesch had decided on the Snort architecture that is currently employed in versions up to 2.0. After version 1.5 was released, Snort was able to use all the different plug-ins that are available today. Because of Snort's increasing popularity, Roesch worked to make it easier to configure and get it working in an enterprise environment so that it would be useful to a greater number of people.

What started as a pastime for Roesch quickly became a full-time job. In an attempt to devote a full effort to the development of Snort, Roesch started a company named Sourcefire and hired most of the core team who developed Snort. However, Snort is still open source and will always be open source. Sourcefire has put a lot of work into Snort, but it's not Sourcefire's 2.0—it's Snort 2.0. The current version of Snort is 2.0.1, which is a rework of the architecture and at press time contains approximately 75,000 lines of code.

Even though Snort 2.0 is a complete rewrite and an improvement over the current Snort implementation, Snort has gone though a more in-depth evolution. Snort did not start out with preprocessing ability, nor did it start out with plug-ins. Over time, Snort grew to have improved network flow, plug-ins for databases such as MySQL and Postgres, and preprocessor plug-ins that check RPC calls and port scanning *before* the packets are sent to the rules to check for alerts.

NOTE

By supporting only the latest rules of the latest application, Snort ensures that users are using only the most recent version. As of press time, the latest revision is 2.0.1, so the rules only work with that version.

Speaking of rules, as time progressed, so did the number of rules. The size of the latest rules is increasing with the number of exploits available. To keep the rules organized, they have been categorized into several types including P2P, backdoor, distributed denial of service (DDoS) attacks, Web attacks, viruses, and many others. These rules are mapped to a number that is recognized as a type of attack or exploit known as a Sensor ID (SID). For example, the SID for the SSH banner attack is 1838.

Because of Snort's increasing popularity, other IDS vendors are adopting a Snort rule format. TCPDump adopted the hex encoding for packets, and community support is ever increasing. There are at least two mailing lists for Snort:

- One on Snort's usage and application http://lists.sourceforge.net/lists/listinfo/snort-users

- One dedicated entirely to the Snort rules http://lists.sourceforge.net/lists/listinfo/snort-sigs

Snort System Requirements

Before getting a system together, you need to know a few things. First, Snort data can take up a lot of disk space, and second, you may need to be able to monitor the system remotely. For Linux and UNIX, this means including Secure Shell (SSH) and Apache with Secure Sockets Layer (SSL). For Windows, this would mean Terminal Services (with limitation on which users and machines can connect, and Internet Information Servers [IIS]).

Hardware

One of the most important things you'll need, especially if you're running Snort in Network-based Intrusion Detection System (NIDS) mode, is a really big hard drive. If you're storing the data as either syslog files or in a database, you'll need a lot of space to store all the data that the Snort's detection engine uses to check for rule violations.

Another highly recommended hardware component for Snort is a second Ethernet interface. One of the interfaces is necessary for typical network connectivity (SSH, Web services, and so forth), and the other interface is for Snorting. This sensing interface that does the "snorting" is your "Snort sensor."

Snort does not have any particular hardware requirements that your OS doesn't already require to run. Running any application with a faster processor usually makes the application work faster. However, you will be limited in the amount of data you collect by your network connection and by your hard drive.

To run Snort, you will need to have a reasonable-sized network interface card (NIC) to collect the correct amount of network packets. For example, if you are on a 100MB network, you will need a 100MB NIC to collect the correct amount of packets. Otherwise, you will miss packets and be unable to accurately collect alerts.

In addition, you will need a good-sized hard drive to store your data. If your hard drive is too small, there is a good chance that you will be unable to write alerts to either your database or log files. A good setup for a single Snort sensor may be a 9GB partition for /var.

Operating System

As stated earlier, Snort was designed to be a lightweight NIS. Currently, Snort can run on x86 systems Linux, FreeBSD, NetBSD, OpenBSD, and Windows. Other supported systems include Sparc Solaris, PowerPC MacOS X and MkLinux, and PA-RISC HP-UX. Snort will run on just about any modern OS today.

NOTE

People can get into heated debates as to which OS is best, but *you* have to be the one to administer the system, so you pick the OS.

There is an ongoing argument regarding the best OS on which to run Snort. A while back, the *BSDs had the better IP stack, but since Linux has gone to the 2.4 kernel, the IP stacks are comparable. Our favorite is NetBSD, but your mileage might vary.

Other Software

Once you have the basic OS installed, you're ready to go. Make sure that you have the following prerequisites before you install Snort:

- autoconf and automake*
- gcc*
- lex and yacc (or the GNU implementations flex and bison, respectively)
- The latest libcap from tcpdump.org

> **NOTE**
>
> The package in this section are only necessary if you are compiling Snort using source code. If you are using Linux RPMs or Debian packages, you do not need these.

Optional software that you can install includes:

- MySQL, Postgres, or Oracle (SQL databases)
- smbclient if using WinPopup messages
- Apache or another Web server
- PHP or Perl, if you have plug-ins that require them
- SSH for remote access (or Terminal Server with Windows)
- Apache with SSL capabilities for monitoring (or IIS for Windows)

Exploring Snort's Features

Snort has several features that make it very powerful: packet sniffing, packet logging, and intrusion detection. Before getting into Snort's features, you should understand Snort's architecture. Snort has several important components, most of which are enabled through the use of plug-ins to customize your Snort implementation. These components include preprocessors, alert plug-ins (which enable Snort to manipulate a packet to make the contents more manageable by the detection engine), and the alert system, which can send its output to different destinations.

Snort consists of four basic components:

- The sniffer
- The preprocessor
- The detection engine
- The output

In its most basic form, Snort is a packet sniffer. However, it is designed to take packets and process them through the preprocessor, and then check those packets against a series of rules (through the detection engine). Figure 29.1 offers a high-level view of the Snort architecture. In its simplest form, Snort's architecture can be likened to a mechanical coin sorter:

1. It collects all the coins (packets from the network backbone).
2. The coins are sent through a chute to determine if they *are* coins, and how they should roll (the preprocessor performs this function on the IDS).
3. Next, the coins are sorted according to the coin type. This is for storage of quarters, nickels, dimes, and pennies (the detection engine performs this function on the IDS).
4. Finally, it is the administrator's task to decide what to do with the coins—usually you'll roll them and store them (logging and database storage).

Figure 29.1 Snort Architecture

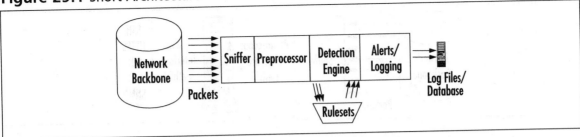

The preprocessor, the detection engine, and the alert components of Snort are all plug-ins. Plug-ins are programs that are written to conform to Snort's plug-in API. These programs used to be part of the core Snort code, but were separated out to make modifications to the core source code easier and more reliable.

Packet Sniffer

A packet sniffer is a device (either hardware or software) used to tap into networks. It works in a similar fashion to a telephone wiretap, but it is used for data networks instead of voice networks. A network sniffer allows an application or a hardware device to eavesdrop on data network traffic. In the case of the Internet, this usually consists of IP traffic, but it can be other traffic such as IPX and AppleTalk network protocols.

Because IP traffic consists of many different types of network traffic, including TCP, UDP, ICMP, routing protocols and IPSec, many sniffers analyze the various network protocols to interpret the packets into something human-readable.

Packet sniffers have various uses:

■ Network analysis and troubleshooting

■ Performance analysis and benchmarking

■ Eavesdropping for clear-text passwords and other interesting tidbits of data

Encrypting your network traffic can prevent people from being able to sniff your packets into something readable. Like any network tool, packet sniffers can be used for good and evil.

As Marty Roesch said, he named the application because it does more than sniffing—it snorts. The sniffer needs to be set up to obtain as many packets as possible. As a sniffer, Snort can save the packets to be processed and viewed later as a packet logger. Figure 29.2 illustrates Snort's packet sniffing ability.

Figure 29.2 Snort's Packet Sniffing Functionality

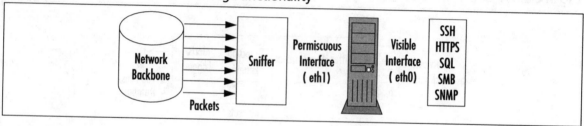

Preprocessor

At this point, our coin sorter has obtained all the coins it can (packets from the network), and is ready to send the packets through the chute. Before rolling the coins (the detection engine), the coin sorter needs to determine if they are coins.

This is done through the preprocessor. The preprocessor takes the raw packets and checks them against certain plug-ins (like an RPC plug-in and a port scanner plug-in). These plug-ins check for a certain type of behavior from the packet. Once the packet is determined to have a particular type of behavior, it is then sent to the detection engine. From Figure 29.3, you can see how the preprocessor uses its plug-ins to check a packet.

This is such a great feature for an IDS because other plug-ins can be enabled and disabled as they are needed at the preprocessor level. For example, if you are not interested in the RPC traffic coming into your network, you can disable this plug-in and use the others.

Figure 29.3 Snort's Preprocessor

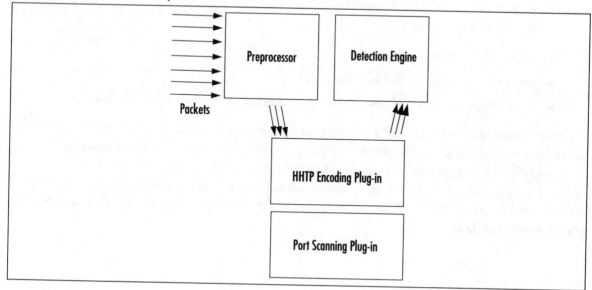

Detection Engine

The detection engine is the meat of the IDS in Snort. The detection engine takes the data that comes from the preprocessor and its plug-ins, and that data is checked through a set of rules. If the rules match the data in the packet, then they are sent to the alert processor.

Earlier in this chapter, we described Snort as a signature-based IDS. The signature-based IDS function is accomplished by using various rule sets. The rule sets are grouped by category (Trojan horses, buffer overflows, access to various applications), and are updated regularly.

The rules themselves consist of two parts:

- **The rule header** The rule header is basically the action to take (log or alert), type of network packet (TCP, UDP, ICMP, and so forth), source and destination IP addresses, and ports.

- **The rule option** The option is the content in the packet that should make the packet match the rule.

The detection engine and its rules are the largest portion (and steepest learning curve) to learn and understand with Snort. Snort employs a specific syntax with its rules. Rule syntax can involve the type of protocol, the content, the length, the header, and other various elements, including garbage characters for defining buffer overflow rules.

Once you learn how to write Snort rules, you can fine tune and customize Snort's IDS functionality. You can define rules that are particular to your environment and customize however you want.

The detection engine is the part of the coin sorter that actually rolls the coins based on the type. The most common American coins are the quarter, dime, nickel, and penny. However, you might get a coin that doesn't match, like the Kennedy half-dollar, and discard it. This is illustrated in Figure 29.4.

Figure 29.4 Snort's Detection Engine

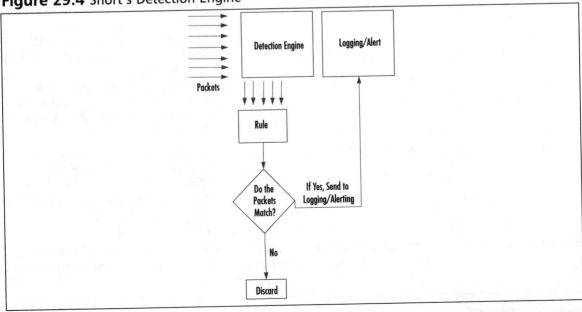

Alerting/Logging Component

After the Snort data goes through the detection engine, it must be output somewhere. If the data matches a rule in the detection engine, then an alert is triggered. Alerts can be sent to a log file, through a network connection, through UNIX sockets or Windows pop-up (Server Message Block [SMB]), or SNMP traps. The alerts can also be stored in an SQL database such as MySQL and Postgres.

Additionally, there are all sorts of other tools you can use with Snort, including various plug-ins for Perl, PHP, and Web servers to display the logs through a Web interface. Logs are stored in either text files (by default in /var/log/snort) or in a database such as MySQL and Postgres.

Like the detection engine and the preprocessor, the alert component uses plug-ins to send the alerts to databases and through networking protocols such as SNMP traps and WinPopup messages. See Figure 29.5 for an illustration of how this works.

Additionally, with syslog tools such as Swatch, Snort alert messages can be sent via e-mail to notify a system administrator in real time so no one has to monitor the Snort output all day and night. Table 29.1 lists a few examples of various useful third-party programs and tools.

Table 29.1 Useful Snort Add-Ons

Output Viewer	URL	Description
SnortSnarf	www.silicondefense.com/ software/snortsnarf	A Snort analyzer by Silicon Defense used for diagnostics. The output is in HTML.
Snortplot.php	www.snort.org/dl/contrib/data_ analysis/snortplot.pl	A Perl script that will graphically plot your attacks.
Swatch	http://swatch.sourceforge.net	A real-time syslog monitor that also provides real-time alerts via e-mail.
ACID	http://acidlab.sourceforge.net	The Analysis Console for Intrusion Databases. Provides logging analysis for Snort. Requires PHP, Apache, and the Snort database plug-in. Since this information is usually sensitive, it is strongly recommended that you encrypt this information by using mod_ssl with Apache or Apache-SSL.
Demarc	www.demarc.com	A commercial application that provides an interface similar to ACID's. It also requires Perl, and it is also strongly recommended that you encrypt the Demarc sessions as well.
Razorback	www.intersectalliance.com/ projects/RazorBack/index.html	A GNOME/X11-based real-time log analysis program for Linux.

Continued

Table 29.1 Useful Snort Add-Ons

Output Viewer	URL	Description
Incident.pl	www.cse.fau.edu/~valankar/ incident	A Perl script used for creating incident reports from a Snort log file.
Loghog	http://sourceforge.net/projects/ loghog	A proactive Snort log analyzer that takes the output and can e-mail alerts or block traffic by configuring IPTables rules.
Oinkmaster	www.algonet.se/~nitzer/ oinkmaster	A tool used to keep your rules up to date.
SneakyMan	http://sneak.sourceforge.net	A GNOME-based Snort rules configuration tool.
SnortReport	www.circuitsmaximus.com/ download.html	An add-on module that generates real-time intrusion detection reports.

Figure 29.5 Snort's Alerting Component

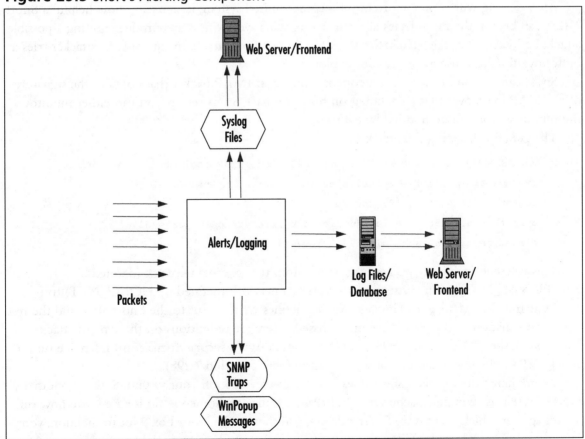

Using Snort on Your Network

Your IDS can use just one Snort system, or more than one if you need redundancy. For example, it is possible to divide the task of network monitoring across multiple hosts. The chief benefit of redundancy is that if one element of the system goes down, the network can still be monitored and protected.

The previously outlined network structure can be used for *passive monitoring* or *active monitoring*. Passive monitoring is simply the ability to listen to network traffic and log it. Active monitoring involves the ability to:

- Monitor traffic and send alerts concerning the traffic that is discovered
- Intercept and block traffic

Snort is primarily used for active auditing and can perform signature-based and anomaly-based detection. Signature-based detection means that you predefine what an attack looks like, and then configure your network monitoring software to look for that signature. Anomaly-based detection requires the IDS to actually listen to the network and gather evidence about "normal" traffic. Then, if any traffic occurs that seems different, the IDS will respond by, for example, sending out an alert to the network administrator.

After dealing with a post-mortem on a compromised system, it's amazing how helpful a Snort NIDS can be. On the flip side, it's also frustrating when your Snort system does not log a possible attack. Let's take a possible attack: the IMAP login overflow attack. In this case, an attacker tries a buffer overflow to cause a remote root exploit.

Snort can let you know that someone is sending an IMAP packet that contains the signature of an IMAP login overflow. Depending on how you have Snort set up, you can either monitor the output or you can be notified by e-mail.

The rule for detecting this attack is:

```
alert tcp $EXTERNAL_NET any -> $HOME_NET 143 (msg:"IMAP login buffer \
    overflow attempt"; flow:established,to_server; content:"LOGIN";     \
    content:"{"; distance:0; nocase;                                    \
    byte_test:5,>,256,0,string,dec,relative; reference:bugtraq,6298;  \
    classtype:misc-attack; sid:1993; rev:1;)
```

This rule checks for any packet originating from the external network (defined by EXTERNAL_NET) to any system on the internal network (defined by HOME_NET) to port 143, which is the IMAP port. The *msg* variable defines what is sent to the Snort alert, and the rest of the information of the packet is content based. There are definitions on the type of attack (*misc-attack*), the SID number (1993), and the Bugtraq (www.securityfocus.com) reference on the attack *6298* (which you can find at www.securityfocus.com/bid/6298).

Then, there's the flip side: Snort does not detect an attack on your system. Suppose another UNIX system is running Apache with FrontPage extensions. Someone finds a new overflow on FrontPage for which there is no Snort rule yet, and then he has your box. Not to mention, your security solution did not provide any assistance with the attack.

Snort's Uses

Snort has three major uses:

- A packet sniffer
- A packet logger
- A NIDS

All the uses relate to each other in a way that builds on each other. However, it's easiest to put the packet sniffer and the packet logger together in the same category—basically, it's the same functionality. The difference is that with the logging functionality; you can save the packets into a file. Conversely, you can read the packet logs with Snort as well.

Using Snort as a Packet Sniffer and Logger

In its simplest form, Snort is a packet sniffer. That said, it's the easiest way to start. The command-line interface for packet sniffing is very easy to remember:

```
# snort -d -e -v
```

Note that the *-v* option is required. If you run Snort on a command line without any options, it looks for the configuration file (.snortrc) in your home directory. **Table 29.2 lists Snort options and their function.**

Table 29.2 Basic Snort Options for Packet Sniffing and Logging

Option	What It Does
-v	Put Snort in packet sniffing mode (TCP headers only)
-d	Include all network layer headers (TCP, UDP, and ICMP)
-e	Include the data link layer headers

You cannot use options *−d* and *−e* together without also using the *−v* option. If you do, you get the same output if you use *snort* without any options:

```
florida:/usr/share/doc/snort-doc# snort -de
Log directory = /var/log/snort


Initializing Network Interface eth0
using config file /root/.snortrc
Parsing Rules file /root/.snortrc


++++++++++++++++++++++++++++++++++++++++++++++++++++
Initializing rule chains...
ERROR: Unable to open rules file: /root/.snortrc or /root//root/.snortrc
Fatal Error, Quitting..
```

Now, if you run snort with the −*v* option, you get this:

```
florida:/usr/share/doc/snort-doc# snort -v
Log directory = /var/log/snort

Initializing Network Interface eth0

    —== Initializing Snort ==—
Decoding Ethernet on interface eth0

    —== Initialization Complete ==—

-*> Snort! <*-
Version 2.0.1 (Build 88)
By Martin Roesch (roesch@sourcefire.com, www.snort.org)
01/22-20:27:44.272934 192.168.1.1:1901 -> 239.255.255.250:1900
UDP TTL:150 TOS:0x0 ID:0 IpLen:20 DgmLen:297
Len: 277
=+=+=+=+=+=+=+=+=+=+=+=+=+=+=+=+=+=+=+=+=+=+=+=+=+=+=+=+=+=+=+=+

01/22-20:27:44.273807 192.168.1.1:1901 -> 239.255.255.250:1900
UDP TTL:150 TOS:0x0 ID:1 IpLen:20 DgmLen:353
Len: 333
=+=+=+=+=+=+=+=+=+=+=+=+=+=+=+=+=+=+=+=+=+=+=+=+=+=+=+=+=+=+=+=+
[]
```

After a while, the text scrolls off your screen. Once you press Ctrl-C, you get an output summary that summarizes the packets that Snort picked up, by network type (TCP, UDP, ICMP, IPX), data link information (including ARP), wireless packets, and any packet fragments:

```
Snort analyzed 56 out of 56 packets, dropping 0(0.000%) packets
Breakdown by protocol:        Action Stats:
     TCP: 0      (0.000%)        ALERTS: 0
     UDP: 44     (78.571%)       LOGGED: 0
    ICMP: 0      (0.000%)        PASSED: 0
     ARP: 1      (1.786%)
   EAPOL: 0      (0.000%)
    IPv6: 0      (0.000%)
     IPX: 0      (0.000%)
   OTHER: 11     (19.643%)
 DISCARD: 0      (0.000%)
================================================================
```

```
Wireless Stats:
Breakdown by type:
    Management Packets: 0    (0.000%)
    Control Packets:    0    (0.000%)
    Data Packets:       0    (0.000%)
============================================================================
Fragmentation Stats:
Fragmented IP Packets: 0   (0.000%)
    Fragment Trackers: 0
    Rebuilt IP Packets: 0
    Frag elements used: 0
Discarded(incomplete): 0
    Discarded(timeout): 0
  Frag2 memory faults: 0
============================================================================
TCP Stream Reassembly Stats:
    TCP Packets Used: 0       (0.000%)
    Stream Trackers:  0
    Stream flushes:   0
    Segments used:    0
    Stream4 Memory Faults: 0
============================================================================
Snort received signal 2, exiting
```

Since this isn't very useful for checking the data of the packets, we'll run snort with the *–dev* option to give us the most information:

```
florida:/usr/share/doc/snort-doc# snort -dev
Log directory = /var/log/snort


Initializing Network Interface eth0


    —== Initializing Snort ==—
Decoding Ethernet on interface eth0


    —== Initialization Complete ==—


-*> Snort! <*-
Verions 2.0.1 (Build 88)


By Martin Roesch (roesch@sourcefire.com, www.snort.org)
01/22-20:28:16.732371 0:4:5A:F2:F7:84 -> 1:0:5E:7F:FF:FD type:0x800 len:0x5B
```

```
131.215.183.30:57535 -> 239.255.255.253:427 UDP TTL:254 TOS:0x0 ID:26121 IpLen:20
DgmLen:77
Len: 57
02 01 00 00 31 20 00 00 00 00 73 70 00 02 65 6E   ....1 ....sp..en
00 00 00 17 73 65 72 76 69 63 65 3A 64 69 72 65   ....service:dire
63 74 6F 72 79 2D 61 67 65 6E 74 00 00 00 00 00   ctory-agent.....
00

=+=+=+=+=+=+=+=+=+=+=+=+=+=+=+=+=+=+=+=+=+=+=+=+=+=+=+=+=+=+=+=+=+=+=+=+

01/22-20:28:18.354830 0:4:5A:F2:F7:84 -> 1:0:5E:0:0:2 type:0x800 len:0x3E
131.215.184.253:1985 -> 224.0.0.2:1985 UDP TTL:2 TOS:0x0 ID:0 IpLen:20 DgmLen:48
Len: 28
00 00 10 03 0A 78 01 00 63 69 73 63 6F 00 00 00   .....x..cisco...
83 D7 B8 FE                                        ....

=+=+=+=+=+=+=+=+=+=+=+=+=+=+=+=+=+=+=+=+=+=+=+=+=+=+=+=+=+=+=+=+=+=+=+=+
```

If you've used TCPDump before, you will see that Snort's output in this mode looks very similar. It looks very typical of a packet sniffer in general.

```
{date}-{time} {source-hw-address} -> {dest-hw-address} {type}
{length} {source-ip-address:port} -> {destination-ip-address:port} {protocol} {TTL}
{TOS} {ID} {IP-length} {datagram-length} {payload-length} {hex-dump} {ASCII-dump}
```

This is all great information you're gathering, and Snort can collect it into a file as well as display it to standard output. Snort has built-in packet logging mechanisms that you can use to collect the data as a file, sort it into directories, or store the data as a binary file.

To use the packet logging features, the command format is simple:

```
# snort -dev -l {logging-directory} -h {home-subnet-slash-notation}
```

If you wanted to log the data into the directory /var/adm/snort/logs with the home subnet 10.1.0.0/24, you would use the following:

```
# snort -dev -l /var/adm/snort/logs -h 10.1.0.0/24
```

However, if you log the data in binary format, you don't need all the options. The binary format is also known as the TCPDump formatted data file. Several packet sniffers use the TCPDump data format, including Snort.

The binary format for Snort makes the packet collection much faster because Snort doesn't have to translate the data into a human readable format immediately. You only need two options: the binary log file option −L and the binary option -b.

For binary packet logging, just run the following:

```
# snort -b -L {log-file}
```

For each log file, Snort appends a timestamp to the specified filename.

It's great that you're able to collect the data. Now, how do you read it? You need to parse it back through Snort with filtering options. You also have the option to look at the data through TCPDump and Ethereal, as they use the same type of format for the data.

```
# snort [-d|e] -r {log-file} [tcp|udp|icmp]
```

The last item on the line is optional if you want to filter the packets based on packet type (for example, TCP). To take further advantage of Snort's packet logging features, you can use Snort in conjunction with the Berkeley Packet Filter (BPF).

```
# snort -vd -r <file> <bpf_filter>
```

The BPF allows packets to be filtered at the kernel level. This can optimize performance of network sniffers and loggers by eliminating packets with the best performance because it happens at such a low level in the operating system.

The following are some examples of BPF filters. They are commonly used for ignoring packets, and work with expressions (and, or, not).

If you want to ignore all traffic to one IP address:

```
# snort -vd -r <file> not host 10.1.1.254
```

If you want to ignore all traffic from the 10.1.1.0 network to destination port 80:

```
# snort -vd -r <file> src net 10.1.1 and dst port 80
```

If you want to ignore all traffic coming from host 10.1.1.20 on port 22:

```
# snort -vd -r <file> not host 10.1.1.20 and src port 22
```

Using Snort as an NIDS

Now that you understand the basic options of Snort, you can see where the IDS comes into play. To make Snort an IDS, just add one thing to the packet logging function: the configuration file.

```
# snort -dev -l /var/adm/snort/logs -h 10.1.0.0/24 -c /root/mysnort.conf
```

Your rules are in the configuration file, and they are what trigger the alerts.

Snort and Your Network Architecture

So, how do you make Snort as useful as possible? You put the Snort system(s) on your network where it (they) will be most useful. Where this is depends on factors such as the size of your network and how much money you have to spend on Snort systems.

If you cannot afford to acquire enough Snort systems to achieve the optimal designs shown in Figure 29.6, you'll need to see what you can use from a practical sense. If you need to limit your spending, forego the system inside the router and just make sure you have the Snort systems inside the subnets you want to protect.

Many network administrators set up a screening router. This enables the router to act as a poor-man's firewall and stop packets at the network level, usually by their well-known ports. The problem with this is that many packets can be rerouted through other ports.

However, if a packet gets past your screening router, this might be a good place to put your IDS. This enables you to detect what you deem as attacks while enabling some filtering to hopefully catch some of the problems with the router. Figure 29.6 shows the IDS network architecture with a screening router.

Figure 29.6 An IDS Network Architecture with a Screening Router

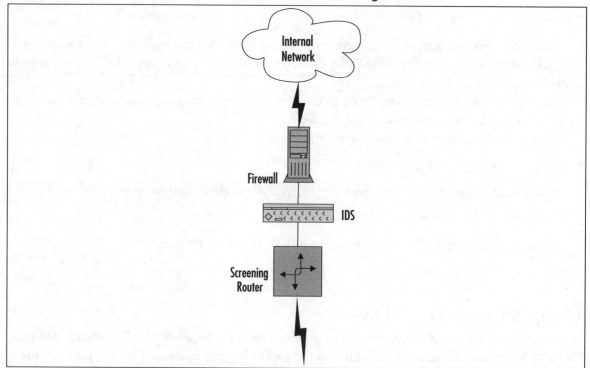

In this case, you would want to put an IDS system on the inside of your firewall and another in between your outside router and your firewall. Here we're also assuming that your router is filtering some traffic through the access lists as well. You do not want your Snort system on the outside of your network because it will increase your false positive rate, and it leaves your Snort system more vulnerable to attack. This is illustrated in Figure 29.7. Most important is the Snort system inside your firewall. This is the one you should monitor frequently for attacks. This system should only trigger alerts from possible legitimate attacks, and produce much fewer false alerts, or a false positive. However, the Snort system between your router and your firewall will also provide you with useful information—especially for a postmortem on a compromised system.

Figure 29.7 A Firewalled Network with Snort Systems

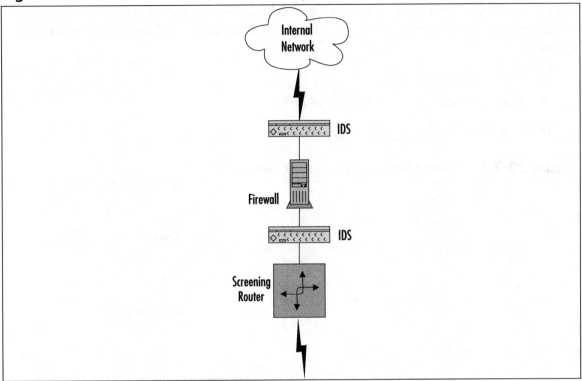

Many network architectures have a Demilitarized Zone (DMZ) for providing public services such as Web servers, FTP servers, and application servers. DMZs can also be used for an extranet (which is a semi-trusted connection to another organization), but we'll stick to the public server DMZ architecture in this example. This is illustrated in Figure 29.8.

Figure 29.8 A Firewalled Network with a DMZ

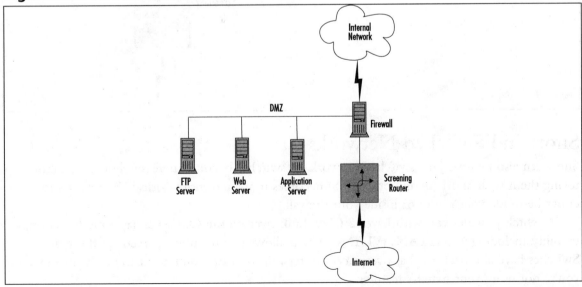

In this case, you would want three Snort systems: one inside the router, one inside the DMZ, and one inside the firewall. The reason for the additional IDS machine is that you have an additional subnet to defend. Therefore, a good rule of thumb for an optimal situation for your Snort systems is:

- One inside the router
- One inside each subnet you want to protect

This is illustrated in Figure 29.9.

Figure 29.9 A Firewalled Network with a DMZ and Snort

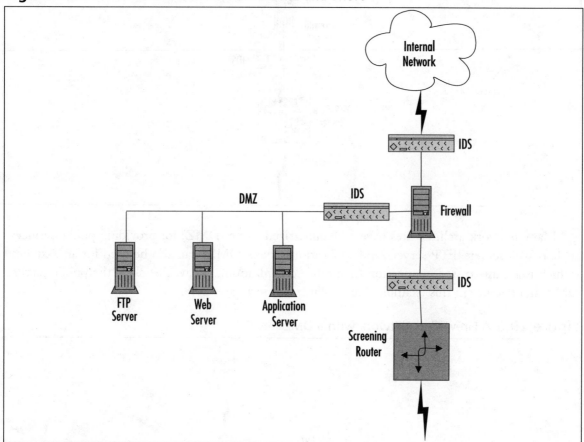

Snort and Switched Networks

Snort can also be used on a switched network. As switches become increasingly popular, monitoring them with Snort (or any other IDS) becomes more and more critical. Your switch can either be inside your router or inside your firewall.

A switch provides you with Layer 2 (Data Link layer on the OSI seven layer model) configurability, including virtual LANs (VLANs), which allows you to subnet directly at the switch. Switches have also been used as overpriced routers. In this case, you'll want to save your money if you're not using your switch's features.

You can connect the Snort system directly to the switch. The switch has a Switch Port ANalyser (SPAN) port, which is where the Snort system will be connected. The Snort system then takes copies of the packets to be analyzed. This is illustrated in Figure 29.10.

Figure 29.10 A Switched Network

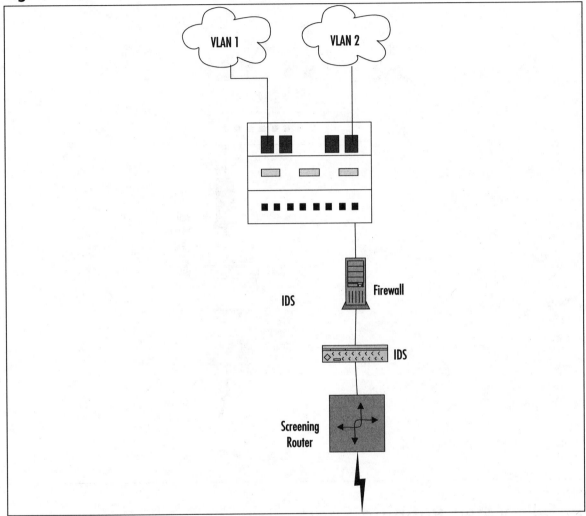

In this case, you'll have to decide which other ports on your switch you want to monitor with the SPAN port. Usually, you will monitor just one port; otherwise, you can flood the SPAN port. This might kill the performance of both your switch and your IDS. This is illustrated in Figure 29.11.

Figure 29.11 A Switched Network with Snort Systems

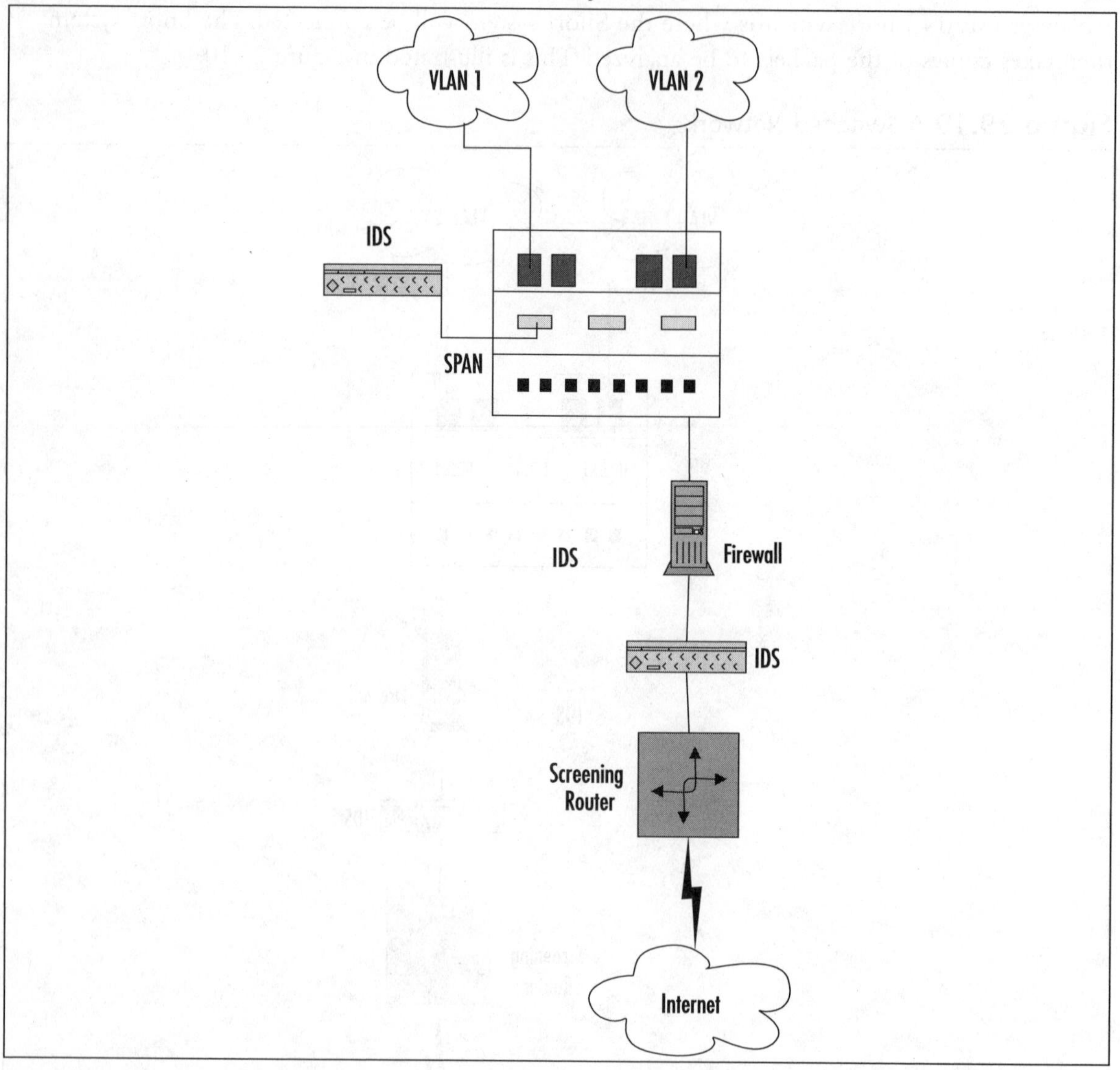

Pitfalls When Running Snort

Snort is a wonderful tool; however, like all tools, it has its disadvantages. Snort has three major pitfalls:

- Not picking up all the packets
- False positive alerts
- False negative alerts.

Snort might not pick up all packets because of the speed of the network and the speed of the promiscuous interface. This can also be dependent on the network stack implementation of the operating system.

False Alerts

False positives occur when Snort gives you a warning when it shouldn't. Basically, a false positive is a false alarm. If you go with a default rule set with Snort, then you will definitely get many false alarms. This can trigger a lot of alerts until you decide what is relevant to your network. The more open your network is, the more alarms you'll want to monitor.

On the opposite end, you can get false negatives. In other words, someone compromises a Snort- monitored system and your Snort system doesn't detect it. You might think that this doesn't happen, but this is a very real scenario. Make sure you keep your Snort rule sets up to date, and your continually evaluate your expectations as to what to expect from your Snort system.

Upgrading Snort

Upgrading Snort can be quite painful for two reasons: the rule set syntax might change, and the interface to the alert logs. We have found both to be obstacles when trying to upgrade Snort systems, and can be quite tedious to deal with. Any upgrade could mean a significant change with your local rule sets, so you need to be aware of this when you upgrade.

Security Considerations with Snort

Even though you are using Snort to improve your security, making sure that your Snort system is as secure as possible will make the data trustworthy. If someone breaks into your Snort system, there is no reason to trust the alerts it sends, thereby making the system completely useless until you wipe the disks and reinstall everything.

Snort Is Susceptible to Attacks

With that said, a typical Snort installation is subject to attacks. Why? You'll want to get in remotely (SSH) and you'll probably want to store the alerts in a database (MySQL or Postgres). In addition, you'll probably want to view the alerts with a spiffy interface that might require a Web server (Apache or IIS).

Based on this scenario, you will have several ports open on your Snort system: SSH (port 22), HTTP (port 80), HTTPS (port 443), and possibly MySQL (port 3306) or Postgres (port 5432). Now, anyone with access to a network can use NMAP and portscan your sniffer directly on its non-promiscuous interface. This makes your Snort system just like any other application, so stay on top of security vulnerability announcements and OS security announcements.

This is something that needs to be addressed because all of the preceding applications have had quite a few serious security issues, even as recently as last year (2002). In addition to making sure that your applications are up to date, you need to make sure that your kernel is configured properly and also up to date. You didn't think that running Snort allows you to disregard basic system administration practices, did you?

> **NOTE**
>
> All applications end up with some discovered vulnerability; however, Snort's are minimal. For a security application, SSH seems to have the lead on the amount of security vulnerabilities discovered.
>
> Snort, however, has very few in its few years of existence. It's nice to see a security application practice good security. The Snort core has never had a network-based vulnerability, excluding a DoS attack if Snort was configured in a nonstandard manner. Third party plug-ins can be vulnerable, but they aren't part of the Snort core, which helps keep Snort itself secure. Table 29.2 lists Snort's vulnerabilities to date.

Table 29.2 Snort's Vulnerabilities to Date

Version	Vulnerability	Fixed
1.8	Snort dumps core. This was a bug in the stream preprocessing.	1.8.1
Prior to 1.8.1	Unicode HTTP encoding to IIS can be used to bypass Snort.	1.8.1
1.8.3	DoS attack from incorrect ICMP handling.	1.8.4
1.8.6	State problems were generated by fragroute.	1.8.7 beta1
1.9.0 and earlier	Buffer overflow in the RPC preprocessor plug1.9.1	2.0

Securing Your Snort System

Even though your Snort implementation is locked down, your system itself might not be. Make sure you do the basics. There are some things you need to do; no excuses:

- **Turn off services you don't need.** Services like Telnet, the Berkeley R services, FTP, NFS, and NIS should not be running on your system. In addition, make sure you don't have any unnecessary services running, for example, echo, discard, and chargen.

- **Maintain system integrity.** Tripwire is a freeware application that checks for those backdoors and Trojans you don't suspect. There are plenty of other freeware applications like Tripwire—AIDE and Samheim are two worth mentioning.

- **Firewall or TCP Wrap the services you do use.** Services like SSH and MySQL should be TCP wrapped or firewalled, as they have their own security holes as well. For services that you can't TCP Wrap, such as Apache, make sure you have it configured as securely as possible. IPTables is the latest version of the Linux firewall, and there are plenty of references on how to implement it.

- **Encrypt and use public key authentication as much as you can.** You should enable public key authentication only for OpenSSH. You might want to consider using Apache-SSL for viewing Apache logs and using digital certificates for client-side authentication. This helps keep the obvious people out of your system through the usual vulnerable channels.

- **Patch, patch, patch.** We cannot stress this enough. Make sure you keep your patches and packages up to date as much as possible. Stay on top of applications you use and their security announcements—the same goes for any operating system you use. For FreeBSD/NetBSD/OpenBSD, make sure you keep your ports and packages up to date. For Red Hat Linux, make sure you stay on top of the updated RPMs. For those of you who are using Debian, you'll have the easiest time as long as you remember to run *apt-get update && apt-get upgrade* on a regular basis.

Summary

This chapter provided practical knowledge of the open-source IDS Snort, and how it can help you with your security concerns. You learned about the history of Snort, how the Snort architecture works, and system requirements.

Additionally, you learned about Snort's different uses. These include using Snort as a packet sniffer, a packet logger, and an IDS. You also learned about some pitfalls with Snort, including false positives.

Finally, this chapter touched on some security considerations you should have when running a Snort system. It's critical to keep the system as secure as possible, especially as an active packet logger or IDS.

## Chapter 30

Installing Snort

Best Damn Topics in this Chapter:

- A Brief Word on Linux Distributions
- Installing PCAP
- Installing Snort

Introduction

In this chapter, we cover all of the steps necessary to complete a functioning Snort Intrusion Detection System (IDS) install. Due to the overwhelming amount of Linux distributions available today, installation instructions can vary from distribution to distribution, and are beyond the scope of this chapter. For this reason, we will cover the information specific to installation on the Red Hat 8.0 platform for the Linux portions of the documentation. We have chosen Red Hat because it is the most commonly used Linux distribution in the world, and serves as a good starting point on which to base further installations. Most of what we cover here should apply to most other popular distributions without a huge amount of modification; if the instructions do vary, it will be minimal. We will go into a bit more detail later in this introduction. As a side note, if you would like to acquire Red Hat Linux to use as a test bed for the exercises in this book, you can download it from one of their mirrors free of charge at www.redhat.com/download/mirror.html. Alternately, you can purchase the full package, complete with support, from most computer software retailers. As advocates of Linux and free software, we recommend the latter if you really enjoy the product. Your contributions help to keep the whole thing going, and at a less than $40.00 USD, you can't go wrong.

Let's take a moment to introduce you to the way we approached this chapter. We know that not everyone is a Linux guru, and we do not expect you to understand everything (*we* don't even understand everything), so we tried to approach almost every subject as if we were learning it for the first time. Our only assumption is that you do have a basic understanding of the operating system (OS) and the basic operation of it. Knowing that this can be redundant information for those of you who are already comfortable with the terminology and procedures, we made the step-by-step instructions for each install easy to find and read. This chapter will serve as an excellent *skimming* reference for that crowd. The only time we get wordy with the procedures is when there is possibly some pitfall to watch for, or maybe some side notes that might be helpful. We keep all of our lengthy descriptions and discussions *outside* of the documentation.

As with any other common package installation, it is best to start with a solid OS installation. Please make sure that your OS is current and error free. For this installation, you must first verify that your networking setup on the target machine is up to date and functioning properly.

The packages you will need for installing Snort IDS are all available free of charge on the Internet at their respective Web sites.

A Brief Word about Linux Distributions

As stated earlier, we will be focusing, for the most part, on the Red Hat 8.0 Linux platform for all of our examples and walk-throughs. Many of you might not use Red Hat as your preferred distribution, so we would like to stop and acknowledge a few of the more prevalent versions out there and some variations you will find in the documentation you are about to read. We are going to look at just a few of the distros not based on the Red Hat Package Manager (RPM) management system. The following distributions rely on either source-based distribution, or proprietary methods of package management. Other releases that use RPM as their system of choice include SuSE, Mandrake, Turbolinux, and Conectiva.

Debian

Debian GNU/Linux (currently in stable version 3.0) has been around forever and is known to many as the most secure and stable version of Linux available. apt-get, the package management system on Debian, is second to none in terms of ease of use. The apt-get syntax goes something like this

- **apt-get install** *packagename* (where *packagename* is the name of the software package) installs new packages. These packages can come from the Debian CD, an NFS share, or straight from the Debian mirrors on the Internet, and download and install in one simple step.

- **apt-get remove** *packagename* uninstalls software already on the machine.

Slackware

Slackware Linux (currently in stable version 9.0) is a favorite among hardcore Linux users, and understandably so. The support base for it is huge, and the system itself is stable, fast, and secure. Although this distribution is not for the faint of heart, we recommend it to anyone ready for the challenge. Slackware Linux also has a package management system based on the compile-from-source tarball model. Its packages can be easily identified by their .tgz extension. There is a built-in utility called pkgtool that allows for easy package management, or you can simply add/remove/edit packages right from the command line. For example:

- **installpkg** *packagename* will install the package you choose onto your system.

- **removepkg** *packagename* will uninstall the package of your choice.

- **upgradepkg oldpackage%newpackage** is the quick-and-dirty way to upgrade your packages on-the-fly.

One other thing we would like to point out about the Slackware distro is the rpm2targz utility. This program converts RPM files to a format usable on a system without RPMs. The syntax for rpm2targz is:

```
rpm2targz packagename.rpm.
```

Gentoo

Gentoo Linux (currently in pre-release 1.4rc3) is an interesting distribution unlike any other available today. The only thing close that we are aware of is the *Linux From Scratch* (LFS) project. The idea behind Gentoo Linux is to provide users with a minimal (45.3MB according to their FTP mirrors) CD that you boot to and connect to the Internet to download the rest of the distribution. Gentoo then builds the entire OS to be optimized for your specific hardware. For package management, Gentoo uses the emerge system. emerge works much like apt-get, but is slower because it builds and compiles each package optimized for your system. The way in which emerge works is fairly straightforward: It downloads the source code for the software package you request, compiles it, and installs it into the running system. Like we said, it's a close cousin of apt-get, and the only noticeable difference is that apt-get doesn't compile the software it downloads. Emerge, like apt-get, pulls its software index from what is called the *Portage tree*. The Portage tree is basically a database containing information about every package ready to run on Gentoo Linux. To give you an idea of how emerge works, including syntax, we have included an example shown next. In this example, we will download and install the Snort package. (Sounds like a proper choice considering the material we are going over, doesn't it?)

First, we will find out if Snort is available in the Portage tree by querying it with the following syntax:

```
emerge -p snort
```

This tells emerge that we want to pretend to install Snort (you guessed it... –*p* means pretend). emerge will then present us with a list of software that will be downloaded to satisfy Snort and its dependencies. It will look something like this (this is not actual output... it's fictitious, but you get the idea):

```
Calculating dependencies........ done!
[ebuild    U] sys-libs/lib-1.1.3-r2 to /
[ebuild    U] sys-libs/glib_not-1.2.9 to /
[ebuild N  ] snort-libs/fakelibs-1-a2 to /
[ebuild N  ] snort-base/snort-1.9.1 to /
```

If we are satisfied with the output, simply enter the command `emerge snort`, and Gentoo will gladly install Snort for you. To uninstall a package, the command is `unmerge snort`. Enough said—emerge is that simple, and an excellent package tool.

Installing PCAP

libpcap is a packet capture library for Linux systems. What is unique about this library is that it can capture packets destined for the local hosts, and can also pick up packets destined for other hosts on the network. This, in essence, means that you can place a machine in a strategic location on your network and have it analyze the packets that travel through (for a quick example, see Figures 30.1 and 30.2). Snort requires this library to function, and it is best to download the newest version of it every time you install or upgrade Snort. The benefits of getting the newest release are twofold: You will realize increased stability *and* speed running the program. Even if your system already has a version of PCAP (such as Red Hat Linux) you should follow this advice. The current version of libpcap can be found at www.tcpdump.org.

NOTE

Some operating systems (such as Red Hat) include a modified PCAP library. It is usually worth the effort to install the latest version of libpcap every time you install a new version of Snort. Installing the latest version of libpcap provides two major benefits: Increased stability and speed.

Figure 30.1 Snort IDS Monitoring Internal Traffic

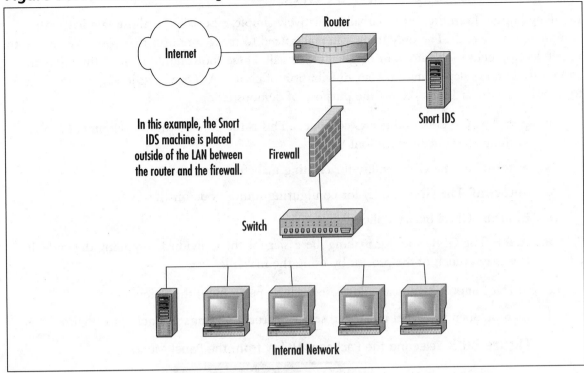

Figure 30.2 Snort IDS Monitoring External Traffic

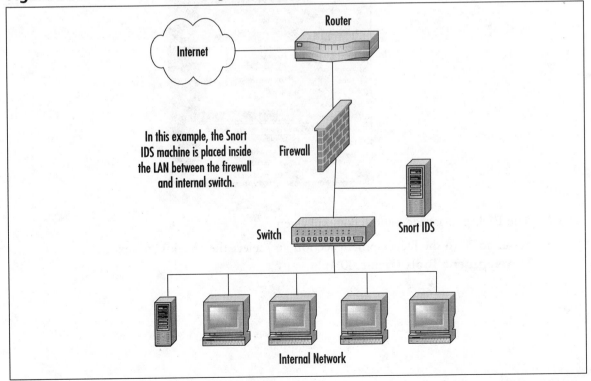

Installing libpcap from Source

Installing libpcap from the source tarball is relatively simple, especially for those familiar with compiling source code. The only thing you really need to make sure of is that you have chosen to install development tools into your original OS install. These tools should include the following, and probably more depending on your distribution of choice. As noted previously, we are going to be using Red Hat Linux 8.0 for the purpose of demonstration.

- **gcc** The GNU cc and gcc C compilers. This is the core of your development tools; nothing else functions without it.

- **automake** The GNU utility for creating makefiles on-the-fly.

- **autoconf** The GNU utility for configuring source code on-the-fly.

- **binutils** GNU binary utilities.

- **make** The GNU tool for making life easier for the individual compiling the code. It automates much of the process by using the makefile.

In Red Hat Linux 9.0, you can add these tools by performing the following:

1. As root, open the Panel menu and select **System Settings | Packages** (Figure 30.3).

Figure 30.3 Selecting the Packages Utility from the Panel Menu

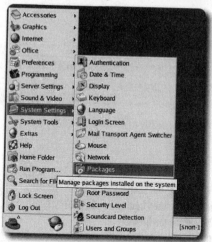

2. The Package Management dialog will open.

3. Scroll down to the Development section and select the check box next to **Development Tools** (Figure 30.4).

Figure 30.4 The Package Management System

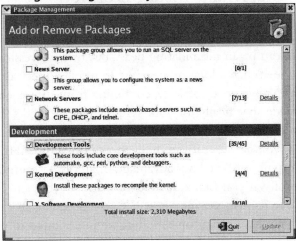

4. Click **Update** in the bottom-right corner of the window.

5. The OS will calculate the required packages and dependencies.

6. When it is complete, it will present you with a dialog confirming your package selection choices (Figure 30.5). You can always double-check your selections by clicking **Show Details** in this dialog.

7. Simply click **Continue** and the system will proceed with the installation. This is the last dialog you will see, unless you are prompted for CD-ROM media, or if there are errors during the install. On a successful operation, there are no further visual or audible prompts.

Figure 30.5 Completing the Package Install

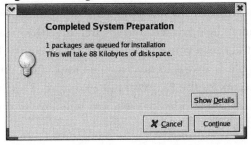

Now that your system is complete with all of the tools necessary for package compilation, we will continue with the configuration and build stages. Again, if you have any experience compiling software on Linux, you will be able to get through this section fairly quickly. We will be following the common **configure | make | make install** format for building the package into the system. For those of you who are new at this, don't be afraid; this is pretty simple as long as your system has the tools described in the last section.

For those of you who are not familiar with the source code compilation/installation of packages from tarballs (a tarball is a compressed set of files similar to a zip file created in Windows using WinZip or PKZip), we have given you a little history on the subject in the subsequent section.

Configure, Make, Make Install Defined

Most of you might already be familiar with this time-tested method of software installation on Linux, but we think it might be a good idea for those new to the scene to cover the definition. At first glance, Linux can be an intimidating beast, but first impressions are not always accurate. Although this might seem like a long process just to install a piece of software, it really is worth the effort. Unlike shrink-wrapped software, compiling from source code is almost always better because it is being made specifically for your system. Prepackaged software is always built for the lowest common denominator, so if the programmer's target *lowest* machine is a 100MHz Pentium, that is what you get … software built to run on a 100MHz Pentium. If you have a 2GHz processor, you will not be taking advantage of all of the optimizations for your processor. When you compile software on Linux, it is being made by you, and for you. Each machine you compile it on will have its own unique setup. We are not saying that all prepackaged software is bad, because it's not. We have run a ton of it, but we just wanted to point out the benefits of doing it the Linux way.

Most software developed for Linux is distributed in what is known as a *tarball*. A tarball is nothing more than a compressed file containing other files and/or directory structures. We like to equate it to a zip file created with WinZip (for those of us familiar with the Windows OS). Tarballs can come in several formats, the most popular end with the extensions tgz, tar.gz, or tar.bz2. Each extension signifies a specific compression algorithm that was used to create the file. Depending on the source, the extensions might differ, but they are all capable of being extracted by modern versions of the *tar* program. Tar is a console program designed to create and extract compressed archives. You can read more about tar and its features at www.gnu.org/software/tar/. It comes as a standard package with almost every Linux distro, but you can get the latest version at that address as well.

When you receive a tarball, the first step is to extract it into a temporary directory where you can work with it; /tmp is usually a good place to accomplish this task. Once the tarball is extracted, verify that the archive created a new directory (they usually do) with its contents. In some cases, it might extract into your current working directory. In any case, locate a file named *configure*. The configure file is always located in the "root" (this directory is usually named after the package name) directory of the files you just extracted. This is the main directory you will be working from to install your software package. You will almost always use these three commands successively:

- **./configure** The configure file is a script that contains code designed to essentially "figure out" the machine on which it is running. It looks at environment variables, dependencies, and verifies what software, if any, is missing. If you watch the screen when it is running, you will see a lot of questions and answers flying by. This is exactly what is going on. It is checking to make sure that everything is where it is supposed to be. The configure script is responsible for generating the makefile, which will become important in the next step. If you see any errors here, you will need to tend to them before continuing. Most issues will be cleared up by installing whatever dependency the configure script was missing. When all dependencies are fulfilled, you can run configure again.

- ■ *make* The *make* command is a part of almost every UNIX/Linux installations in existence today. It is not a script like configure is, but an actual utility. *make* will use the makefile created by the configure script in the last step. The primary function of make is to compile the code to be used during the final install. It accomplishes this by reading and executing the code in the makefile in a specific order determined by the configure script. The makefile is similar in layout to an initialization file in that it has "headings" or categories for each step of the make process. One of these headings is install, which is used in the next step by make install. Again, it is important to note any errors during the compilation process to make sure you take care of them before continuing.

- ■ *make install* This is the final step of the installation process. What make install does is fairly simple: it reads the information from the install section of the makefile and distributes the executables and other files created by make to the proper locations in the machine's directory structure. Once this step is complete (without error), the software is installed and ready to use.

Now when you are ready to tackle your next big software installation, you will be armed with the knowledge of what all of the syntax and commands actually mean. This has always been helpful to us … to be able to understand the meaning behind what we're doing, and not just going through the motions presented to us via documentation.

Installing libpcap from RPM

You can also install libpcap from an RPM package if your distribution supports it. At the time of writing, www.rpmfind.net returned 57 results (spanning 11 Linux distributions) when presented with a query for libpcap. Frankly, we believe that this is the best place to find custom-compiled RPMs for your distribution of choice.

- ■ **Mandrake** Version 9.0 (RPM), version 9.1 (RPM and SRPM)
- ■ **Red Hat (7.2, 7.3, 8.0, 8.1)** Version 6.2 (RPM only)
- ■ **SuSE Linux** Version 7.1 (RPM only)

The procedures involved in installation via RPM are, more often than not, much easier than an installation that uses source code—if there are no dependency problems. The RPM system, while an excellent package management tool, is fraught with problems regarding dependencies. It understands and reports what the specific package requires to install, but is not yet capable of acquiring and installing the packages necessary to fulfill its requirements.

If you are not familiar with the term, *dependencies* are packages and/or libraries required by other packages. The Linux operating system is built on dependencies, which you can visualize as an upside-down tree structure. At the top of the tree are your basic user-installed programs, such as Snort. Snort depends on libpcap to operate, and libpcap requires other libraries to function.

Installing Snort

Now we can get into the actual installation of Snort. So far, we have covered the basics of Linux package management, including RPM installs, source compilation, and installing libpcap, so this next section should be fairly easy for us to get through. Luck for us, the installation of Snort is painless, so we can save all of our energy for the setup, configuration, and rules management.

First, you need to get Snort. The latest version as of press time is 2.0.1, so we will use it in our example install. This is the most current stable version available at press time. Please note that we strongly recommend going to www.snort.org and downloading the very newest stable release, as you will benefit from new functionality, bug fixes, stability, and speed enhancements. This software is constantly changing, growing, and getting better every day.

Installing Snort from Source

There is something to be said about installing software from source code. In our opinion, it is the easiest and best way to install a properly functioning software package. In this section, we will be installing the Snort 2.0.1 package from a source tarball located at the Snort Web site (www.snort .org). To install Snort, follow these simple steps:

1. As root, download the latest version of snort from www.snort.org/dl. The latest version at press time is Snort 2.0.1.

2. Change directories to /tmp by typing **cd /tmp** at the command line.

3. Copy the tarball to the /tmp directory by typing **wget http://www.snort.org/dl/ snort-2.0.1.tar.gz** at the command line.

4. Extract the tar archive by issuing the command tar **–zxvf snort-2.0.1.tar.gz**.

5. Change directories into the newly created Snort directory by typing **cd snort-2.0.1**.

6. At the command line, type **./configure** to configure the package. You should see text start to scroll by (similar to the example in Figure 30.6)

Figure 30.6 Running the Snort *configure* Script

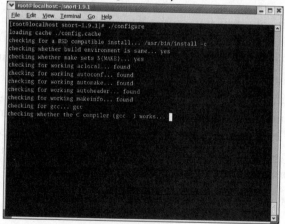

7. Next, type **make** at the command line. This will create the makefile.

This might take some time depending on the speed of the target machine.

8. As the final step in the build process, type **make install** at the command prompt. This action will deliver the package and its files to where they belong in the system. The Snort install is now officially complete. We can now move on to basic customization.

Customizing Your Installation: Editing the snort.conf File

The first order of business after completing the Snort install is to customize it to your needs. We are going to begin with the snort.conf file located in the /etc/snort directory. This file contains the configuration settings that Snort will use every time it is invoked. This configuration file is lengthy, but the sample file that the developers provided us is complete with basic instructions on syntax and use. Although it is very thorough in its descriptions, we would still like to cover a few basic settings that will allow Snort to function properly.

First, we will need to change the *var HOME_NET* variable in the snort.conf file. What this variable signifies is the internal network address of your LAN. In most textbook cases, this value will be an entire subnet, but it can also be in the form of a single IP address. In this example, we are going to use the subnet of our internal network card. In this case, it will be 192.168.0.0/24, which means that the address space of 192.168.0.1–192.168.0.254 will be represented, using a subnet mask of 255.255.255.0 (Figure 30.7).

The next variable we need to look at is *var EXTERNAL_NET*. You can set this to whatever subnet your external network adapter is answering requests (or in this case, listening) on. In this example, we will use *var EXTERNAL_NET any*. This tells Snort to listen for all addresses on the external network. In our opinion, this value should be left at the default state of *any*.

Figure 30.7 Editing the snort.conf File in gedit

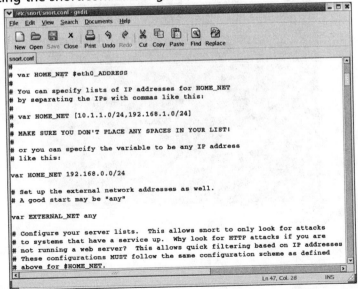

If you scroll down further into the config file, you will see a section dedicated to server-specific variables. These variables will look similar to *var HTTP_PORTS 80* or *var ORACLE_PORTS 1521*. These variables (or vars) specify specific ports on which Snort should watch for attacks. The only downside to the current implementation is that you either have to list ports in succession (for example, 80:82, which means 80 through 82 inclusive) or on separate lines. Work is underway to add support for port lists.

Other areas of initial interest should include the preprocessors, output plug-in, and ruleset sections. Preprocesses are the filters that Snort puts the incoming data stream through before it actually processes the data. In the example snort.conf file, notice that IP defragmentation is turned on. This helps to detect fragmentation and denial-of-service (DoS) attacks. You can also enable other preprocessors in this section to fit your particular scenario.

The output plug-ins section defines whether Snort will use various logging and alert features, and tells it what format to use to dump the data. The ruleset section defines what the system will consider "suspicious" activity. Based on this alone, you should visit www.snort.org *frequently* to download the latest rulesets to ensure that your IDS is doing the job you meant for it to do—without an up-to-date ruleset, you machine will be nothing more than an expensive paperweight. It is also a good practice to comment out rules that do not apply to your organization and/or needs. Unnecessary and extra rules can lead to false positive alerts from the system.

Also make note that you can alter the path to your rulesets here as well, by changing the *include $RULE_PATH/rule.rules* line to reflect the location of your updated rules.

The final step in this section is to simply verify that Snort will actually run without error. To accomplish this, we will run Snort with a generic configuration/ruleset and no options. To do this, open a terminal window, type **snort −v**, and verify that the program loads without error. You will see a screen similar to the one in Figure 30.8. All we are doing here is running Snort in *verbose* mode (hence the *−v* flag). Since everything looks good, let's move on to the next section.

Figure 30.8 Running Snort with the Verbose Option Enabled

Enabling Features via configure

During the build process (more specifically, during the *configure* script portion), we can pass options to the installer to customize it to whatever specific situation or needs we might have. These were harvested from the INSTALL file in the Snort 2.0.1 tarball.

- **--enable-debug** Enable debugging options (bug reports and developers only).

- **--with-snmp** Enable SNMP alerting code.

- **--enable-smbalerts** Enable the SMB alerting code, which is somewhat unsafe because it executes a popen() call from within the program (which runs at root privs). You've been warned, use it with caution!

- **--enable-flexresp** Enable the "Flexible Response" code, which allows you to cancel hostile connections on IP-level when a rule matches. When you enable this feature, you also need the libnet-library that can be found at www.packetfactory.net/libnet. See README.FLEXRESP for details. This function is still alpha, so use with caution.

- **--with-mysql**=DIR Support for MySQL; turn this on if you want to use ACID with MySQL.

- **--with-odbc=DIR** Support for ODBC databases; turn this on if you want to use ACID with a nonlisted DB.

- **--with-postgresql=DIR** Support for PostgreSQL databases; turn this on if you want to use ACID with PostgreSQL.

- **--with-oracle=DIR** Support for Oracle databases; turn this on if you want to use ACID with Oracle.

- **--with-openssl=DIR** Support for OpenSSL (used by the XML output plug-in).

- **--with-libpq-includes=DIR** Set the include directories for PostgresSQL database support to DIR.

- **--with-libpq-libraries=DIR** Set the library directories for PostgresSQL database support to DIR. Setting both of these values enables the Postgres output plug-in module.

- **--with-libpcap-includes=DIR** If the configuration script can't find the libpcap include files on its own, the path can be set manually with this switch.

- **--with-libpcap-libraries=DIR** If the configuration script can't find the libpcap library files on its own, the path can be set manually with this switch.

Installing Snort from RPM

Depending on your distribution and release number, there might not be RPMs available. In most cases, you can probably find contributed source RPMs from a Web site such as www.rpmfind .net, and then you can build your own. We recommend building your own because all systems are inherently different and have their own file system structure and environments. We cover installation via RPM and source RPM in this section. This should seem pretty easy to you in comparison to installation by tar archives.

Let's start with the RPM installation. The installation is simple, just follow one of two things after you download the RPM:

- **In console mode** At a console prompt, just enter the command **rpm –Uvh snort-1.9.1-snort.i386.rpm**. This will complete the installation routine for you. Note that we used the *–U* (upgrade) option versus *–i* (install)—it will install with either. We are always concerned that if we use *–i*, the installer will not upgrade files properly (if there are any files to upgrade to newer versions), but if we use the *–U* flag, it will do a more thorough job of installing the software. What we're trying to say is that you can install the software simply by typing **rpm –i snort-1.9.1-1snort.i386.rpm**.

- **Inside X Windows** If you are using KDE, GNOME, or one of the many X Windows systems out there, this set of instructions is for you. Under Red Hat Linux 8, you will be prompted with a dialog asking if you would like to proceed. All you have to do is click **Continue** and RPM will install the package. As stated earlier, depending on your distribution instructions might vary; so make sure to consult the documentation or man files that came with your distribution. Most of the RPM-based distributions are not much different from what we have witnessed here. Another point that is distribution dependent is that you might not get a confirmation that the package was successfully installed onto the system. In true UNIX/Linux fashion, some distributions do not waste time displaying unnecessary information to the screen. The only time you might ever hear Linux speak is when something went dreadfully wrong (and we all hope that day never comes).

Now we will look at the source RPM (or SRPM) as a means of a more solid installation. This is the preferable way to install packages if you use RPM-based distributions such as Red Hat, and the SRPMs are readily available to you. Usually, sites such as www.freshrpms.net and www.rpmfind.net will have these available for most packages and almost all RPM-based distros.

Recompiling a source RPM is not as daunting as it might sound. RPM takes care of all the minute details involved in a recompile and rebuild. Depending on the version of RPM you are using, the syntax can vary slightly. The first example we will give you will run on RPM version 4.1 or higher (Red Hat 8.0 includes this version). At a console prompt, all you have to do is download the source rpm (which ends in .src.rpm) folder and enter **rpmbuild —rebuild snort-2.0.10-1snort.src.rpm**. This will prompt RPM to rebuild the file into a regular RPM specifically designed for your system.

The second example is for versions lower than 4.1. For these systems, just enter **rpm —rebuild snort-2.0.1-1snort.src.rpm**. This command will do exactly the same thing as in the previous example, but in a slightly different syntax. Both versions will place the completed RPM package in a subfolder under the **/usr/src/** directory. On a Red Hat 8.0 system, the completed builds are located under **/usr/src/redhat/RPMS/i386**.

> **NOTE**
>
> The only drawback to building a package from an SRPM is that all of the package's dependencies must be met, even though you are not *actually* installing the program. In the case of Snort, you must have MySQL, PostgreSQL, and UCD-SNMP installed (including devels and libraries). The reason for this is simple: With Snort, the developers have coded the software to support a variety of databases. When you attempt to rebuild the SRPM, it looks for all of the various dependencies required for *all* database systems it was built to run with. This is true even if you don't ever intend to use all of the options. The fact of the matter is that they are present and must be rebuilt into the final package for it to function properly. If you do not satisfy all of the program's dependencies, the rebuild will fail. One good thing is that it will explain what components it is missing to allow you to install them and try the rebuild again.

Installation on the MS Windows Platform

All you Microsoft users were probably wondering when we were going to get to the section designated for you. Well, we are here. Sorry for the delay. Please keep in mind that we have not pushed the Microsoft portion to the end for any reason other than for the simple fact that it is an easier task installing on this system than on its Linux counterparts. This is going to be much shorter in terms of installation steps. Configuration should be a breeze as well. As a personal opinion, we always recommend installing on Linux (rather than Windows) if you have the resources to do so—for reasons of stability and pure speed. Linux is also far superior at performing network-related tasks.

Let's get started with the installation. First, we'll need to install the packet capture library for Windows, WinPcap, which is available at winpcap.polito.it/install/default.htm.

1. Download WinPcap.exe.

2. Double-click **WinPcap.exe** to launch the installer.

3. The installer will present you with a Welcome dialog as in Figure 30.9. Click **Next**.

Figure 30.9 The Snort Installer Welcome Screen

4. The next dialog is a simple notification that lets you know that the installation was completed successfully (Figure 30.10). Click **OK**.

Figure 30.10 Confirming a Successful WinPcap Installation

5. The next screen is another confirmation that the installation has finished on your computer (Figure 30.11). Click **Finish**.

Figure 30.11 Completing the WinPcap Install

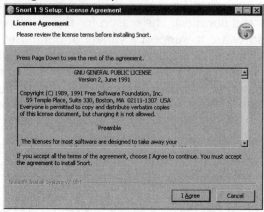

Congratulations! The WinPcap installation was a success. Although it is not noted during the installation, we recommend rebooting the machine for any changes to take effect, as Windows always seems to need a little extra coaxing. If you ever need to uninstall WinPcap, it places an entry in the Add/Remove Programs applet in the Windows Control Panel. Simply remove it from there if something goes wrong.

The latest version of Snort is available at www.snort.org/dl/binaries/win32 to download the latest and greatest version.

1. Download snort-2.0.1.exe and double-click on it. This will start the installer.

2. Once the installer launches, you will be presented with the GNU General Public License (GPL). We strongly recommend reading this in its entirety if you have the patience and the time. It is a wonderful piece of literature and has remained unchanged since its inception in 1991. This is the license under which most open-source software is distributed, including Linux. When you have finished reading the license, click **I Accept**.

3. The next screen to appear is the Installation Options dialog. Here, you will be able to select optional components to fit your unique situation. As the software states, if you choose the SQL option, make sure that the SQL client software is already installed on the target machine. Click **Next** when you are ready to continue.

4. Next, you are presented with a list of components to install. Again, you can choose what you would like to install here to fit your needs. Please note that it is pretty important to make sure that Snort is one of your choices—it might make for an interesting installation without it. Your component options are as follows:

   ■ **Snort** Installs Snort, configuration files, and rules.

   ■ **Documentation** Installs the Snort documentation.

   ■ **Contrib** Copies additional user-contributed add-on modules and tools.

5. Click **Next** when you are satisfied with your choices.

6. You should be prompted for an installation location. The default is fine unless you're feeling creative. Click **Install**.

7. The installer will start copying files to your hard drive. It doesn't take long, so don't go anywhere.

8. The installation is now complete. Just click **Close** and consider Snort to be ready to use! Optionally, you can click **Show Details** to view the output of the installer. This is especially helpful if something goes wrong.

Detailed Component Selection Options

During the install of the Win32 version of Snort (when the custom install option is chosen), we are presented with more a detailed selection of choices. Here, we will attempt to discuss, in general terms, what each option does and how it will affect your installation.

- **Snort-Barebones** This is the installation we are performing in this chapter, and is subsequently the base, or "bare," version of Snort.

- **Snort-Flexresp** This will install Snort with flexible response (session sniping) activated.

- **Snort-MySQL-Flexresp** This will install Snort with added support for MySQL and Flexresp.

- **Snort-MSSQL-MySQL-Flexresp** This will install Snort with added support for Microsoft SQL, MySQL, and Flexresp.

- **Snort-MSSQL-MySQL** This will install Snort with added support for Microsoft SQL and MySQL.

- **Snort-MySQL** This will install Snort with added support for MySQL.

Please note that in order to install most of these custom options with Snort, you will need to have a fully functioning dependency tree. For example, if you want to install Snort with MySQL support, you must have a functioning MySQL database server before you attempt to install Snort. If you don't, Snort will fail miserably and your network security needs will go unattended.

Installing Bleeding-Edge Versions of Snort

If you are one of those types who like to live life to the fullest, you might want to just go out and get the latest version of the software directly from the developers, and they are always happy to provide you with what you need and crave. For this reason, they make their daily Concurrent Version System (CVS) (see the following section) snapshots available for download. You can find them at www.snort.org/dl/snapshots if you would like to try them out. Keep in mind that CVS builds are the equivalent to beta builds and must be approached as such. They can contain bugs, and there is not a reasonable amount of support for that type of installation.

The CVS System

The CVS is a versioning system that allows many developers to work on the same project simultaneously, while keeping track of what changes have been made, who made them, and most importantly, what versions exist and keeping them separated. You will generally find many versions of a project in a CVS tree.

You will find that CVSs exist on many Web sites for almost every open-source project. For example, SourceForge (www.sourceforge.net) has CVS repositories for all of the projects it contains. To browse most CVS trees, you will need a CVS client application. However, SourceForge has a Web interface for browsing as well, which is a nice feature if you need to quickly get some information or code from a CVS tree. Here are a couple of GUI applications for CVS:

- If you would like a CVS front-end app for Linux, VisualCVS (www.scentech.ch/products/visualcvs) is a client worth checking out.

- If you would like a CVS application for Windows, WinCVS (www.wincvs.org) is a pretty good client.

Summary

In this chapter, we covered the basics of package management, including RPM and source code packages. We also covered complete installs of the PCAP libraries for Linux and Windows systems, Snort IDS for Linux and Windows. You are now armed with the knowledge and software necessary to continue with this book.

As stated several times in this chapter, it is important to keep your Snort installation up to date. This includes the packet capture libraries and the Snort system itself. You should also visit the Snort site frequently for updated rulesets. Computer security is a fast-paced sector, and it is necessary to keep on top of things so that your systems are not easily compromised.

We also strongly recommend that you keep your OS up to date as well, especially when it comes to security updates and patches. Windows makes this easy through the Windows Update interface. Red Hat Linux has the option for Red Hat Network, which, in our opinion, is far better than its Windows counterpart.

All of these parts will come together to form a solid IDS that will serve you well for years to come.

## Chapter 31

Combining Firewalls and IDS

Best Damn Topics in this chapter:

- Policy-Based IDS

- Inline IDS

- IDS Functionality on the PIX Firewall

Introduction

So far, we've discussed the concepts behind Intrusion Detection Systems (IDSs) and their basic configuration. While many of these topics covered some very basic functions of IDS, this chapter is dedicated to the more advanced features of IDS and how it can be very powerful when combined with firewall technologies.

Both Snort (combined with various firewalls) and the Cisco PIX can perform the same extensive intrusion detection tasks. In this chapter, we discuss *policy-based intrusion detection* and *inline intrusion detection*. These are additional functions that Snort (combined with Iptables or Sun's firewalling capabilities) and the PIX are able to provide that work alongside its normal intrusion detection capabilities. By using some or all of these functions, you can leverage the capabilities of IDS and firewalls to help make your systems even more secure.

Policy-based intrusion detection and inline intrusion detection are simply variants of normal intrusion detection and differ only in their implementation. As always, intrusion detection is the concept of detecting intrusions on your systems or networks. Whether you're using standard *signature-based* intrusion detection techniques or *anomaly-based* intrusion detection, the result is the same—a more secure network environment.

Policy-Based IDS

When defining rules or attack signatures for an IDS operating normally, you define which attack signatures you *don't* want to see on your network. For example, if a new attack comes out, you would add its signature to your IDS because you want to be alerted if a packet containing that signature is seen on your network. In other words, you don't want to see a packet with this signature on your network because it indicates that an attack of a specific type is being performed. Following this process and performing frequent rule updates allows your IDS to constantly watch for the latest attacks.

By operating in this fashion, your IDS is constantly playing catch-up with intruders. When a new attack is performed somewhere in the world, you have to wait for a signature for the attack to be determined, and then add it to the rules for your IDS. During this time, the attack could conceivably happen to your network and you wouldn't be aware of it. This is one of the principal problems with normal intrusion detection.

Policy-based IDS is almost a complete reversal of normal intrusion detection. With policy-based IDS, the IDS administrator defines what is normal and acceptable behavior for the network. This can include communication of specific types between specific hosts, specific protocols, and so forth. The benefit of defining this policy is that the administrator is able to set baselines of what "normal" operations for the network should look like. This information can then be used to determine what unusual behavior is.

The concept behind policy-based IDS is that whatever is not included as part of the list of acceptable behavior is potentially an intrusion. The IDS administrator goes through the often long and arduous process of determining what should *not* trigger an alert. Then, the IDS sends an alert on anything not previously defined by the administrator as acceptable traffic.

Using a policy-based IDS has several advantages over normal IDSs. A policy-based IDS can be used to determine whether your firewall is performing properly by checking the network to see if traffic that should have been blocked at the firewall has made it to the internal network. This provides an added layer of redundancy to your existing security system by allowing you to be notified in the event of an unexpected failure. This also works with other security systems in place besides firewalls, such as ensuring that switches have not become susceptible to an Address Resolution Protocol (ARP) spoofing attack, and so forth.

Another very beneficial aspect of using a policy-based IDS is that it can be used to detect new and previously undocumented attacks. Whereas a normal IDS is reactive based on its predefined rules, a properly configured policy-based IDS is proactive in that it will alert you to *any* unexpected activities on the network. This can allow you to diagnose a new form of attack that might not have been detected by a standard or typical IDS.

In many cases, a policy-based IDS can make you aware of an attack faster than a typical IDS can. Since there are typically fewer rules involved in defining acceptable traffic compared to the number of rules necessary to define all known attack signatures, a policy-based IDS can sometimes outperform a normal IDS. Additionally, sometimes the start of an attack might not necessarily match a known attack signature, but it might be flagged as unusual behavior to a policy-based IDS. This can allow you to head off an attack before it occurs.

Defining a Network Policy for the IDS

The first step in setting up a policy-based IDS is to define your network policy. This should be a *very* detailed policy specifying exactly what is allowable on the network. This can include communication between specific systems, the use of specific protocols on the network, and so forth. The main point to keep in mind when defining this policy is that *any* traffic that does not conform to your policy of allowable behavior will be considered suspicious and will trigger an alert. You don't want your policy to be so stringent that you get alerts every few minutes, nor so lax that you miss an actual attack. Getting this policy defined properly is the most difficult task in setting up your policy-based IDS.

When defining your policy, you can determine your allowable traffic based on IPs, protocols, ports, and so forth. As the first part of your policy definition, you need to be aware of what devices are communicating on your network and how they are communicating. For example, if you have a Web server communicating on your network, you will need to know what its IP is and the ports on which it is publishing. The best way to start this process is to inventory your systems and determine what their purposes are. In a large enterprise, this is a *huge* task, but it can be fairly easy in smaller networks. For example purposes, we will create a fictional network with a number of servers and clients to demonstrate the definition of a network policy. Figure 31.1 is the network diagram illustrating our environment.

While the diagram in Figure 31.1 is fairly complex, it shows a very basic, well-designed network for a small office with a public Web presence and plans for future growth. The clients are connected to a dedicated switch, which is in turn connected to a router and another dedicated switch used for the environment's servers. A system functioning as a policy-based IDS is connected to SPAN ports on each of these switches, using two interfaces to perform IDS functions for both networks. The dedicated server switch has a few servers attached to it and a connection to the internal firewall. This firewall separates the DMZ from the internal network and functions as a router.

Figure 31.1 Network Diagram

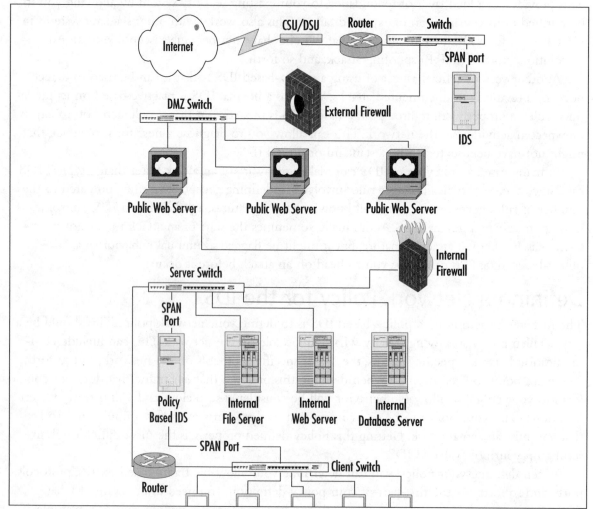

Within the DMZ, there are three publicly accessible Web servers. These servers and the externally facing port on the internal firewall are connected to a switch for the DMZ network. Also attached to this switch is the internally facing port on the external firewall. The externally facing port of the external firewall is connected to yet another switch that also has connections to the router for the CSU/DSU and a normal IDS.

Many modifications can be made to this design to improve security, such as adding another firewall situated between the CSU/DSU and the switch; however, this design is fairly typical in most small organizations. Additional security usually involves additional funds that are not always available. For the purpose of example in this section, we will be referring back to this diagram regularly.

To design our policy, we'll assume that this diagram shows every entity connected to our network. In reality, there are usually a few rogue systems of which the administrators are not aware, but we'll discuss how to find those later in this section.

The next step in defining our network policy is to determine what traffic is acceptable between these known hosts. We'll start with the client/server communications. First, there is the internal network's file server. In this network, we'll assume that this is a standard Microsoft Windows 2000 server hosting a file share for the network. It is probably also performing authentication for the network to grant access to its files. Table 31.1 lists the ports used by a Windows 2000 server based on Microsoft Knowledge Base article 150543.

Table 31.1 Windows 2000 Server Ports

Function	Static Ports
Browsing	UDP:137,138
DHCP Lease	UDP:67,68
DHCP Manager	TCP: 135
Directory Replication	UDP:138 TCP:139
DNS Administration	TCP: 135
DNS Resolution	UDP: 53
Event Viewer	TCP: 139
File Sharing	TCP: 139
Logon Sequence	UDP:137,138 TCP:139
NetLogon	UDP: 138
Pass Through Validation	UDP:137,138 TCP:139
Performance Monitor	TCP: 139
PPTP	TCP: 1723 IP:47
Printing	UDP: 137,138 TCP:139
Registry Editor	TCP: 139
Server Manager	TCP: 139
Trusts	UDP: 137,138 TCP:139
User Manager	TCP: 139
WinNT Diagnostics	TCP: 139
WinNT Secure Channel	UDP: 137,138 TCP:139
WINS Replication	TCP: 42
WINS Manager	TCP: 135
WINS Registration	TCP: 137
SMB	TCP,UDP: 445
ISAKMP (IPSec)	UDP: 500
ESP (IPSec)	IP: 50
AH (IPSec)	IP: 51
Kerberos	TCP,UDP: 88
RSVP	IP: 46

Based on the port information shown in Table 31.1, we can determine that the clients will need to be able to communicate to this server on a number of these ports. Now, let's assume that all of these services might be needed at some point. That leads us to the conclusion that the clients will need to communicate with the file server on the ports listed in Table 31.2.

Table 31.2 File Server Communication Ports

IP	TCP	UDP
46	42	53
47	88	67
50	135	68
51	137	88
	139	137
	445	138
	1723	445
		500

Now that we have determined the communication needs of the clients for connecting to the file server, let's work on the remaining servers. The next server in our diagram is an internal Web server. Assuming that all traffic to this server is using either HTTP or HTTPS on their standard ports, we'll simply need to allow traffic to TCP ports 80 and 443 on this server. Our last server is an internal database server, and we'll assume that it is running Microsoft SQL Server. If this is the case, communication to the server will take place over TCP port 1433 by default. Allowing traffic to this server on TCP port 1433 will take care of the client communication needs.

It looks like we have a handle on the communication from the clients to the servers, so let's look at communication from the servers back to the clients. In most cases when using Microsoft Windows, a client system will open a TCP or UDP connection to a remote system using a port between 1024 and 5000. This can be changed by modifying the Registry of the Windows client. Other operating systems use different standards, but for this example we'll assume that non–modified Windows clients are in use. Based on this, we will assume that any traffic between the server subnet and the client subnet on these ports is acceptable. In addition, some of the clients might be running some Windows services, so we'll also apply the port list from Table 31.2 to the client systems and the servers.

At this point, we have basically defined our network policy and just need to put it all together. We've defined communication with each device, so let's see what we have determined to be acceptable traffic:

- Clients to file server on ports defined in Table 31.2
  - Clients to Web server on TCP ports 80 and 443
  - Clients to database server on TCP port 1433
  - Servers to clients on TCP and UDP ports 1024 through 5000
- Servers to clients on ports defined in Table 31.2

Anything outside this list will be deemed unacceptable traffic when we define the rules for our policy-based IDS. In truth, we certainly have not captured every port that will be used, but this will give us a baseline for determining what else is acceptable. We'll discuss the process of fine-tuning in the section "Policy-Based IDS in Production".

An Example of Policy-Based IDS

Since we have now defined our basic network policy, we'll move on to how to actually use this information. Our first step is to translate this policy into actual Snort rules. As previously mentioned, using a policy-based IDS is really the reverse of normally running an IDS. Therefore, we have to pass a parameter to Snort to cause it to process the rules in a different order.

By default, Snort processes alert rules first, followed by pass rules. For our needs, we will have to force Snort to process pass rules before alert rules. Otherwise, we would receive an alert on all traffic, as Snort would not even check to see if it was acceptable based on our pass rules. Using the -o command-line parameter when starting Snort will cause it to process the pass rules before the alert rules. For example, you could start Snort using the following command:

```
./snort -c /etc/snort/snort.conf -o
```

We also need to add an entry to our snort.conf file to point to a new rule file. This is simply another *include* statement in the rules section of the snort.conf file. Add the following line to the file:

```
include $RULE_PATH/policy-based.rules
```

The policy-based.rules file will hold all of the rules we define for our policy-based IDS. The first step in defining this set of rules is to set up the alert rules. In this case, we want to generate alerts on any TCP, UDP, or IP-based traffic that is not explicitly defined in a pass rule. The following code shows how we would configure these alert rules in the policy-based.rules file:

```
# $Id: policy-based.rules,v 1.0 2003/02/08 16:00:00 jeremyfaircloth Exp $
# ---------
# POLICY BASED RULES
# ---------
# These rules are defined for policy based intrusion detection.
#
# Alert Rules
# This will alert on ANY TCP connections on these subnets
alert tcp any any <> [10.10.10.0/24,10.10.11.0/24] any
# This will alert on ANY UDP connections on these subnets
alert udp any any <> [10.10.10.0/24,10.10.11.0/24] any
# This will alery on ANY IP connections on these subnets
alert ip any any <> [10.10.10.0/24,10.10.11.0/24] any
```

In this rules file, we first define an alert for TCP traffic from any IP and any port going to or from two subnets on any port. These two subnets, 10.10.10.0/24 and 10.10.11.0/24, are our client and server subnets, respectively. We then duplicate the rule to cover the UDP and IP protocols. With the alert rules defined in this manner, we will receive an alert on every connection attempt in these two subnets.

Next, we have to transform our previously defined network policy into Snort rules. Let's go over our network policy again. There are five specific directives in our policy on which traffic is permissible:

- Clients to file server on ports defined in Table 31.2
    - Clients to Web server on TCP ports 80 and 443
    - Clients to database server on TCP port 1433
    - Servers to clients on TCP and UDP ports 1024 through 5000
- Servers to clients on ports defined in Table 31.2

The first order of business is to define rules that allow the systems on the client subnet (10.10.10.0/24) to communicate with the file server (10.10.11.1) on the specific ports defined in Table 31.2. We'll begin with IP traffic, and then move on to TCP and UDP. For IP ports 46, 47, 50, and 51, we can define the pass rules in two lines and cover only these specific ports. We could cover the range of ports 46 through 50 in a single rule, but we want to be as restrictive as possible.

```
pass ip 10.10.10.0/24 any -> 10.10.11.1 46:47
pass ip 10.10.10.0/24 any -> 10.10.11.1 50:51
```

These rules tell Snort to allow any traffic from the 10.10.10.0/24 subnet from any port to 10.10.11.1 ports 46, 47, 50, and 51 to pass and not signal an alert. From here, we'll move on to defining the rules for TCP communication to the file server. We'll define the rules in the same manner, but use TCP rather than IP. These rules should look like the following:

```
pass tcp 10.10.10.0/24 any -> 10.10.11.1 42
pass tcp 10.10.10.0/24 any -> 10.10.11.1 88
pass tcp 10.10.10.0/24 any -> 10.10.11.1 135
pass tcp 10.10.10.0/24 any -> 10.10.11.1 137
pass tcp 10.10.10.0/24 any -> 10.10.11.1 139
pass tcp 10.10.10.0/24 any -> 10.10.11.1 445
pass tcp 10.10.10.0/24 any -> 10.10.11.1 1723
```

Again, these rules simply tell Snort to allow any traffic from the 10.10.10.0/24 subnet from any port to 10.10.11.1 on the specific ports defined to pass without generating an alert. We'll do the same for the UDP ports shown in Table 31.2:

```
pass udp 10.10.10.0/24 any -> 10.10.11.1 53
pass udp 10.10.10.0/24 any -> 10.10.11.1 67:68
pass udp 10.10.10.0/24 any -> 10.10.11.1 88
pass udp 10.10.10.0/24 any -> 10.10.11.1 137:138
pass udp 10.10.10.0/24 any -> 10.10.11.1 445
pass udp 10.10.10.0/24 any -> 10.10.11.1 500
```

We've now defined all of the rules necessary to achieve objective one of our network policy. The following code shows all of these rules.

```
# Rules for Network Policy Objective One
pass ip 10.10.10.0/24 any -> 10.10.11.1 46:47
pass ip 10.10.10.0/24 any -> 10.10.11.1 50:51
pass tcp 10.10.10.0/24 any -> 10.10.11.1 42
pass tcp 10.10.10.0/24 any -> 10.10.11.1 88
pass tcp 10.10.10.0/24 any -> 10.10.11.1 135
pass tcp 10.10.10.0/24 any -> 10.10.11.1 137
pass tcp 10.10.10.0/24 any -> 10.10.11.1 139
pass tcp 10.10.10.0/24 any -> 10.10.11.1 445
pass tcp 10.10.10.0/24 any -> 10.10.11.1 1723
pass udp 10.10.10.0/24 any -> 10.10.11.1 53
pass udp 10.10.10.0/24 any -> 10.10.11.1 67:68
pass udp 10.10.10.0/24 any -> 10.10.11.1 88
pass udp 10.10.10.0/24 any -> 10.10.11.1 137:138
pass udp 10.10.10.0/24 any -> 10.10.11.1 445
pass udp 10.10.10.0/24 any -> 10.10.11.1 500
```

Now, let's move on to the second objective in our network policy. We need to define rules that allow the client systems to communicate with the internal Web server. We'll set the internal Web server IP as 10.10.11.11, and the client systems are still on subnet 10.10.10.0/24. Based on this information, these rules are very simple to define. Since we're just using TCP, we define the rules as follows:

```
pass tcp 10.10.10.0/24 any -> 10.10.11.11 80
pass tcp 10.10.10.0/24 any -> 10.10.11.11 443
```

Those two simple rules cover the second objective of the network policy and allow traffic originating from any port on the 10.10.10.0/24 subnet directed to ports 80 or 443 to pass without generating an alert. The third objective is just as easy and only requires one rule. We need to allow the clients to communicate with the database server on TCP port 1433. In this fictitious network, we'll put our database server at IP 10.10.11.21.

```
pass tcp 10.10.10.0/24 any -> 10.10.11.21 1433
```

Objective four of our network policy defines traffic going in the other direction, from the servers to the clients. For this objective, we need to allow the servers to connect back to the clients on TCP and UDP ports 1024 through 5000. These rules are fairly simple to define, as we can easily specify more than one source IP address.

```
pass tcp [10.10.11.1,10.10.11.11,10.10.11.21] any -> 10.10.10.0/24 1024:5000
pass udp [10.10.11.1,10.10.11.11,10.10.11.21] any -> 10.10.10.0/24 1024:5000
```

The rules we've defined now meet the first four objectives of the network policy. The fifth objective is a little trickier—we must allow the servers to communicate back to the clients on the ports defined in Table 31.2. We can do this in a number of ways. We could simply allow all communication between the server subnet and the client subnet on these ports to be allowed. Alternatively, we could define the specific server IPs and allow any traffic from the servers to the client subnet on these ports to pass. Finally, we could define the IPs of the servers and the clients and allow traffic from the specific server IPs to the specific client IPs on these ports to pass.

Since in our previous rules we allowed traffic from the entire client subnet to pass to the servers, we'll do the same here and take the second option. This allows for easier rule definition, yet gives us a good level of security. In addition, this allows for future growth in the number of client systems that is typically more likely than growth in server systems. The following shows the five rules that we defined to meet this objective:

```
# Rules for Network Policy Objective Five
pass ip  [10.10.11.1,10.10.11.11,10.10.11.21] any -> 10.10.10.0/24 46:47
pass ip  [10.10.11.1,10.10.11.11,10.10.11.21] any -> 10.10.10.0/24 50:51
pass tcp [10.10.11.1,10.10.11.11,10.10.11.21] any -> 10.10.10.0/24 42
pass tcp [10.10.11.1,10.10.11.11,10.10.11.21] any -> 10.10.10.0/24 88
pass tcp [10.10.11.1,10.10.11.11,10.10.11.21] any -> 10.10.10.0/24 135
pass tcp [10.10.11.1,10.10.11.11,10.10.11.21] any -> 10.10.10.0/24 137
pass tcp [10.10.11.1,10.10.11.11,10.10.11.21] any -> 10.10.10.0/24 139
pass tcp [10.10.11.1,10.10.11.11,10.10.11.21] any -> 10.10.10.0/24 445
pass tcp [10.10.11.1,10.10.11.11,10.10.11.21] any -> 10.10.10.0/24 1723
pass udp [10.10.11.1,10.10.11.11,10.10.11.21] any -> 10.10.10.0/24 53
pass udp [10.10.11.1,10.10.11.11,10.10.11.21] any -> 10.10.10.0/24 67:68
pass udp [10.10.11.1,10.10.11.11,10.10.11.21] any -> 10.10.10.0/24 88
pass udp [10.10.11.1,10.10.11.11,10.10.11.21] any -> 10.10.10.0/24 137:138
pass udp [10.10.11.1,10.10.11.11,10.10.11.21] any -> 10.10.10.0/24 445
pass udp [10.10.11.1,10.10.11.11,10.10.11.21] any -> 10.10.10.0/24 500
```

The rules defined here are similar to the rules we defined for traffic coming from the client subnet to the file server. The main difference is that these rules define the source IPs of all of the servers and a destination IP of the client subnet. Otherwise, the port definitions are identical and the functionality of the rules is the same.

We've now covered all of the objectives of our network policy. Each of the five objectives has been translated into Snort rules and defined in our *policy-based.rules* file. The contents of this file are shown in the following output:

```
# $Id: policy-based.rules,v 1.0 2003/02/08 16:00:00 jeremyfaircloth Exp $
# ----------
# POLICY BASED RULES
# ----------
# These rules are defined for policy based intrusion detection.
```

```
#
# Alert Rules
# This will alert on ANY TCP connections on these subnets
# alert tcp any any <> [10.10.10.0/24,10.10.11.0/24] any
# This will alert on ANY UDP connections on these subnets
# alert udp any any <> [10.10.10.0/24,10.10.11.0/24] any
# This will alery on ANY IP connections on these subnets
alert ip any any <> [10.10.10.0/24,10.10.11.0/24] any
#
#
# Pass Rules
# These rules define acceptable network traffic
# Rules for Network Policy Objective One
pass ip 10.10.10.0/24 any -> 10.10.11.1 46:47
pass ip 10.10.10.0/24 any -> 10.10.11.1 50:51
pass tcp 10.10.10.0/24 any -> 10.10.11.1 42
pass tcp 10.10.10.0/24 any -> 10.10.11.1 88
pass tcp 10.10.10.0/24 any -> 10.10.11.1 135
pass tcp 10.10.10.0/24 any -> 10.10.11.1 137
pass tcp 10.10.10.0/24 any -> 10.10.11.1 139
pass tcp 10.10.10.0/24 any -> 10.10.11.1 445
pass tcp 10.10.10.0/24 any -> 10.10.11.1 1723
pass udp 10.10.10.0/24 any -> 10.10.11.1 53
pass udp 10.10.10.0/24 any -> 10.10.11.1 67:68
pass udp 10.10.10.0/24 any -> 10.10.11.1 88
pass udp 10.10.10.0/24 any -> 10.10.11.1 137:138
pass udp 10.10.10.0/24 any -> 10.10.11.1 445
pass udp 10.10.10.0/24 any -> 10.10.11.1 500
# Rules for Network Policy Objective Two
pass tcp 10.10.10.0/24 any -> 10.10.11.11 80
pass tcp 10.10.10.0/24 any -> 10.10.11.11 443
# Rules for Network Policy Objective Three
pass tcp 10.10.10.0/24 any -> 10.10.11.21 1433
# Rules for Network Policy Objective Four
pass tcp [10.10.11.1,10.10.11.11,10.10.11.21] any -> 10.10.10.0/24 1024:5000
pass udp [10.10.11.1,10.10.11.11,10.10.11.21] any -> 10.10.10.0/24 1024:5000
# Rules for Network Policy Objective Five
pass ip [10.10.11.1,10.10.11.11,10.10.11.21] any -> 10.10.10.0/24 46:47
pass ip [10.10.11.1,10.10.11.11,10.10.11.21] any -> 10.10.10.0/24 50:51
pass tcp [10.10.11.1,10.10.11.11,10.10.11.21] any -> 10.10.10.0/24 42
```

```
pass tcp [10.10.11.1,10.10.11.11,10.10.11.21] any -> 10.10.10.0/24 88
pass tcp [10.10.11.1,10.10.11.11,10.10.11.21] any -> 10.10.10.0/24 135
pass tcp [10.10.11.1,10.10.11.11,10.10.11.21] any -> 10.10.10.0/24 137
pass tcp [10.10.11.1,10.10.11.11,10.10.11.21] any -> 10.10.10.0/24 139
pass tcp [10.10.11.1,10.10.11.11,10.10.11.21] any -> 10.10.10.0/24 445
pass tcp [10.10.11.1,10.10.11.11,10.10.11.21] any -> 10.10.10.0/24 1723
pass udp [10.10.11.1,10.10.11.11,10.10.11.21] any -> 10.10.10.0/24 53
pass udp [10.10.11.1,10.10.11.11,10.10.11.21] any -> 10.10.10.0/24 67:68
pass udp [10.10.11.1,10.10.11.11,10.10.11.21] any -> 10.10.10.0/24 88
pass udp [10.10.11.1,10.10.11.11,10.10.11.21] any -> 10.10.10.0/24 137:138
pass udp [10.10.11.1,10.10.11.11,10.10.11.21] any -> 10.10.10.0/24 445
pass udp [10.10.11.1,10.10.11.11,10.10.11.21] any -> 10.10.10.0/24 500
```

Policy-Based IDS in Production

At this point, you've modified the snort.conf file to include the new policy-based.rules file. You've also created the policy-based.rules file and the rules to implement our network policy. Now it's time to start Snort and put the rules into action.

We discussed previously that Snort has to be started with the *-o* parameter to cause the pass rules to be processed before the alert rules. Assuming that the snort.conf file is in /etc/snort, start Snort using this syntax:

```
# snort -c /etc/snort/snort.conf -o
```

If your configuration is correct and there are no errors in the new rules, Snort should successfully start and begin scanning. It should be noted from the start screen (unless you're running in daemon mode) that Snort is indeed processing the pass rules before the alert rules, as shown in the following output.

```
Running in IDS mode
Log directory = /var/log/snort


Initializing Network Interface any


        --== Initializing Snort ==--
Rule application order changed to Pass->Alert->Log
Initializing Output Plugins!
Decoding 'ANY' on interface any
Initializing Preprocessors!
Initializing Plug-ins!
Parsing Rules file /etc/snort/snort.conf
```

With Snort now actively scanning, you can refine your rules based on the *reality* of the traffic on your network. While the rules that we have defined cover the expected traffic on your network, there is always unexpected traffic that is probably acceptable. The process of actively monitoring your alert log during this burn-in period allows you to fine-tune your rules.

For example, during a review of your alert log, you see the following entries:

```
[**] Snort Alert! [**]
[Priority: 0]
02/09-15:49:03.042888 10.10.10.1:3137 -> 10.10.11.21:21
TCP TTL:128 TOS:0x0 ID:33435 IpLen:20 DgmLen:48 DF
******S* Seq: 0x57E7A50F  Ack: 0x0  Win: 0x4000  TcpLen: 28
TCP Options (4) => MSS: 1460 NOP NOP SackOK


[**] Snort Alert! [**]
[Priority: 0]
02/09-15:49:05.946778 10.10.10.1:3137 -> 10.10.11.21:21
TCP TTL:128 TOS:0x0 ID:33572 IpLen:20 DgmLen:48 DF
******S* Seq: 0x57E7A50F  Ack: 0x0  Win: 0x4000  TcpLen: 28
TCP Options (4) => MSS: 1460 NOP NOP SackOK


[**] Snort Alert! [**]
[Priority: 0]
02/09-15:49:11.963321 10.10.10.1:3137 -> 10.10.11.21:21
TCP TTL:128 TOS:0x0 ID:33848 IpLen:20 DgmLen:48 DF
******S* Seq: 0x57E7A50F  Ack: 0x0  Win: 0x4000  TcpLen: 28
TCP Options (4) => MSS: 1460 NOP NOP SackOK
```

These log entries indicate that one of the client systems is attempting to connect to the Web server using port 21. This is the well-known port used for FTP, so apparently someone is trying to use FTP to connect to the Web server. Following up on this, you might find that the Web content developer uses FTP to upload new content to the Web server. If management approves this operation, you'll need to modify your network policy to include this objective. In addition, you'll need to create a new rule to indicate that this is acceptable traffic for Snort. This rule could be defined as:

```
# Rules for Network Policy Objective Six
pass tcp 10.10.10.1 any -> 10.10.11.21 21
```

You will run into many of these exceptions during the burn-in period of your policy-based IDS. Tuning your IDS might take quite a while, depending on the number of systems on the network, the type of work being performed, and many other factors. Moreover, adding and modifying rules is a nonstop administrative effort. There will always be something new added to the network or some new service added to an existing system. The ongoing modifications of this system might be tedious, but they do offer a high level of security to your environment.

It should be noted that we did not remove any of the existing rules from Snort when we configured the system to operate as a policy-based IDS. When you are using a policy-based IDS, it is still important to process normal IDS rules as well. Many attacks could easily slip by the policy-based rules that we defined, but the normal IDS rules would catch these attacks. For example, our policy-based rules do not define any restrictions on ICMP traffic. That leaves the door open for an ICMP (ping) flood attack.

In addition, we are allowing traffic to port 80 on the Web server, but the policy-based rules are not scanning the content of those packets. There is a problem here in that the IDS is now configured to process pass rules before alert rules. That means that even if there is malicious content inside a packet destined for the Web server, the IDS will not generate an alert.

The only real solution to this problem is to run one IDS in policy-based mode and the other normally, or creating a new rule action. In our fictitious network design, we haven't done this because it's unlikely that someone would attack the internal Web servers from the internal network, but it could happen. To add an additional layer of security, you can simply add another IDS into the mix or create a new rule action in your rules file:

```
#####
ruletype passgood
{
    type alert
    output log_null
}

ruletype everything
{
    type log
    output log_tcpdump: suspicious.log
}

config order: alert passgood everything

# insert all your normal rules here

passgood tcp any any <> $HTTP_SERVERS $HTTP_PORTS
passgood tcp any any <> $SMTP_SERVERS 25
passgood tcp any any <> $DNS_SERVERS 53
passgood udp any any <> $DNS_SERVERS 53
everything ip any any <> any any
```

The primary disadvantage to implementing a policy based IDS is the amount of time and effort necessary to define the policy as to what behavior is acceptable. This is fairly simple in a small network, but in a large enterprise, it can be a very daunting task. Sometimes using a policy-based IDS isn't feasible due to the size of the network or the amount of administrative effort required to maintain the IDS. Keep in mind that the combination of a policy-based IDS and a normal IDS can provide for an incredibly high level of security, but it's not always possible to implement this strategy.

Inline IDS

An inline IDS is the latest technology in use within the *intrusion prevention* genre. Intrusion prevention is the next step in the evolution of intrusion detection. Whereas intrusion detection is designed to make the security administrator aware of potential attacks, intrusion prevention goes one step farther and works actively to prevent the intrusion.

The basic concept of intrusion prevention is to take the data gathered during intrusion detection and act upon it through an automated process. This provides for faster response than what could be provided by an on-call administrator. An example of intrusion prevention would be an active firewall that stops communication from a specific IP address when an attack is detected from that address.

Inline IDS acts in a manner similar to that of an active firewall, but does offer several advantages. First, as an IDS, it can be configured to respond to the latest available attack signatures. It also acts more intelligently than a firewall in that it does not simply block communication from a specific IP address or port. Inline IDS has the ability to drop the packets that contain the attack and allow normal traffic to go through.

> **WARNING**
>
> One major problem with "intelligent" firewalls is their ability to automatically react to attacks without administrative intervention. While this might seem like a very useful feature of the firewall, it can easily be abused. For example, let's say that you have a firewall set up and configured to block access to a specific IP address if a portscan is detected from that IP. An intruder starts probing your network and performs a portscan from one of his systems. After a few moments, the intruder sees that he is no longer able to connect to your network from that IP. This makes it obvious that you are blocking his IP by using a firewall configured to block portscans. The next step for the intruder if they want to wreak havoc on your network would be to simply spoof the IP address of your upstream router and perform a portscan using this spoofed address. The firewall will detect the portscan and believe that it is coming directly from the upstream router. Therefore, the firewall does its job and blocks access to the IP address of your network's upstream router. Now your network can no longer send or receive data from your upstream router. External communications are now down for the network, and all because your firewall reacted "intelligently" to an attack.

Using an inline IDS affords you the capabilities of a good IDS and allows you to incorporate the data gathered from this system into an intelligent firewall. This gives you a great method of securing your network from intrusion.

Where Did the Inline IDS for Snort Come From?

Snort first had the capability of being an inline IDS because of a project called *Hogwash*. Hogwash is based on the Snort engine and was designed to operate inline with your Internet connection similar to a firewall. Rather than functioning like a firewall, Hogwash provides the ability to drop individual packets based on a set of rules similar to Snort's. These rules define the behavior of Hogwash and instruct it on which packets should be passed, dropped, or alerted upon.

The Hogwash implementation was designed to work at the data link layer of the OSI model (Layer 2) to offer a higher level of security to the system on which Hogwash is running. Because of this design, the machine running Hogwash does not even necessarily have to have an IP stack; therefore, it is invulnerable to IP-based attacks. This feature makes the system almost invisible to intruders.

There is now an effort underway to merge Hogwash back into the original Snort system, primarily because of the difficulties of keeping Hogwash up to date with changes in Snort. It makes more sense from a development point of view to integrate the advanced features available with Hogwash back into the base Snort application. This allows for Snort and Hogwash to be kept at the same build level without the requirement of a large maintenance effort.

This effort has led to the release of a Snort inline mode patch by Jed Haile. This patch is designed to merge the efforts of the Hogwash project back into Snort. It is currently available at www.snort.org/dl/contrib/patches/inline. More information about Hogwash is also available at http://hogwash.sourceforge.net.

Installation of Snort in Inline Mode

Before installing Snort in inline mode, you need to be aware of a few requirements. First, to run Snort in inline mode, you must give your system the ability to be inline with a network connection. This means that you'll be running your IDS as a bridge in one form or another. There are two options for this. You can either run your system as a normal network bridge, or you can bridge traffic and provide for network address translation (NAT) at the same time. For this example, we will be running our system as a normal bridge. Figure 31.2 shows a simple network with our system placed inline with a network connection to the Internet. Table 31.3 lists all of the software we'll need to install Snort in inline mode.

Figure 31.2 Inline Network Diagram

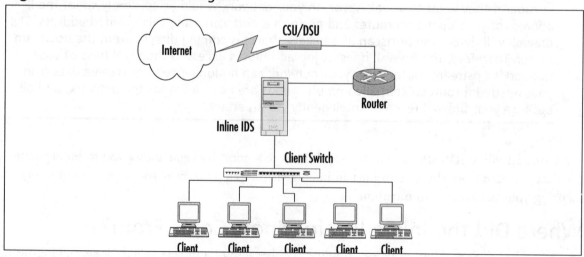

Table 31.3 Software Required for an Inline Mode Installation of Snort

Name	Location
Red Hat 8.0 Linux Distribution	ftp://ftp.redhat.com/pub/redhat/linux/8.0/en/iso/i386
IPTables	www.netfilter.org/downloads.html#1.2.8
libpcap	http://freshmeat.net/projects/libpcap
Linux bridge patch	http://bridge.sourceforge.net/devel/bridge-nf/ bridge-nf-0.0.7-against-2.4.19.diff
bridge-utils	http://bridge.sourceforge.net/download.html
Snort Inline Patch	www.snort.org/dl/contrib/patches/inline
Snort Rules	www.snort.org/dl/rules/snortrules-current.tar.gz
rc.firewall Script	www.honeynet.org/papers/honeynet/tools

Keeping with that, we will be performing our examples in this chapter on the Red Hat 9.0 distribution of Linux. One of the features of the Linux 2.4 kernel build is that *IPtables* is included. This is an open-source stateful (or stateless) firewalling subsystem and replaces its predecessor, *IPchains*. IPtables is used for examining each packet based on a series of *chains* that you define. We'll discuss the specific IPchains functionality that we'll be using a little later in this chapter.

Unfortunately, the Snort inline patch requires some additional library and header files for IPtables that are not included with the distribution. Therefore, you'll need to download IPtables 1.2.7a from the location listed in Table 31.3. Once downloaded, extract this file into a temporary directory. Installation is a little different and requires that you have the Linux kernel source files available. Perform the install by issuing the following commands:

```
make KERNEL_DIR=/usr/src/linux-2.4.18-14
make install KERNEL_DIR=/usr/src/linux-2.4.18-14
make install-devel
```

These commands direct the compiler to your kernel source directory, install IPtables, and install the *libipq* libraries required by the Snort inline patch.

> **NOTE**
>
> Keep in mind that if you performed an upgrade to get to Red Hat 8, you might still have IPchains on your system. IPchains and IPtables are not compatible and will not run together. If you have any problems starting this IPtables service, you might have to stop the IPchains service.

Another requirement to running Snort in inline mode is *libpcap*. By default, the kernel included with Red Hat 8 includes the ability to do bridging and firewalling, but not to do both at the same time. To do this, we're going to need to patch the kernel and recompile it. The Linux bridge patch can be found at the location shown in Table 31.3. Download this patch and place it in a temporary directory. Then, apply the patch using the following command:

```
patch -p1 < bridge-nf-0.0.7-against-2.4.18.diff
```

While the specific methods available to configure and recompile the kernel are beyond the scope of this book, we will cover the specific changes that you need to make to enable the features that we need on the system. After applying the bridge patch, we'll need to configure the kernel. You can do this by issuing *one* of the following commands in your kernel source directory:

```
make menuconfig
make xconfig
```

Your choice of configuration utilities will vary based on your preference for using the X Window system or a menu-based command-line tool. For our example, we'll be using *xconfig*, which is shown in Figure 31.3.

Figure 31.3 xconfig Linux Kernel Configuration

Go through the various menu options and ensure that the specific kernel options required for your system are enabled. In addition, the following options must be enabled and compiled into the kernel for our bridging firewall to work:

- Code Maturity Level Options
  - Prompt for Development and/or incomplete code/drivers
- Networking Options

  - Network packet filtering (replaces ipchains)
  - IP: Netfilter Configuration
  - All options
  - 802.1d Ethernet Bridging
  - Netfilter (firewalling) support

Figure 31.4 shows how the Networking options section of xconfig should look when configured for Snort in inline mode. It is very important to go through these configuration options and confirm that the additional options required for Linux to run on your system are selected.

Figure 31.4 xconfig Networking Options Dialog

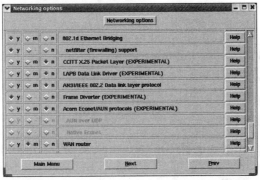

Your next step will be to recompile the kernel using the new patch and options. Again, this process is beyond the scope of this book, but the following syntax worked well for us and automatically placed a new entry into the grub.conf file for the new kernel:

```
make dep clean bzImage install modules modules_install
```

You'll also need the bridge-utils software to control the bridging features of your system. This software can be found at the location shown in Table 31.3. Extract the files from the source tarball into a temporary directory, and then install them using the following commands:

```
./configure
make
make install
```

Next, you'll need the Snort inline patch. Download this from the location shown in Table 31.3. Next, decompress this patch into a temporary directory. If you have Snort running on the system on which you are installing the patch, it is best to stop Snort first. Keep in mind that although this is labeled as a patch, it is a full Snort install; therefore, having the normal version of Snort installed is not a prerequisite. Perform the patch installation by issuing the following commands in the directory to which you extracted the patch:

```
./configure --enable-inline
make
make install
```

One error you might run into is the Snort inline patch being unable to find your libpcap files. If this occurs, simply copy the files extracted from the libpcap archive into a directory called *pcap* within your Snort inline patch temporary directory.

If you don't already have them, you'll certainly want the latest Snort rules. These can be found at the location specified in Table 31.3 and must be placed in your Snort rules directory. You'll also need Rob McMillen's rc.firewall script. This is an IPtables script used for counting and controlling outbound connections and is available at the location listed in Table 31.3. To make the best use of this script, you should configure it to start with the system, so copy the rc.firewall script to your /etc/rc.d directory and modify it using the following commands:

```
cp rc.firewall /etc/rc.d
chmod 700 /etc/rc.d/rc.firewall
```

After the file has been copied, you'll need to edit your /etc/rc.d/rc.local file using your favorite text editor and add the following lines at the bottom of the file:

```
if [ -x /etc/rc.d/rc.firewall ]; then
      /etc/rc.d/rc.firewall
fi
```

Now we need to start configuring all the software we've installed. The Snort inline installation will have to have the snort.conf file configured to suit your environment.

Next, configure the rc.firewall script. Load the script with *vi* or your favorite text editor. Many changes are necessary to make this script work for a normal firewall rather than a honeynet firewall. First, note any systems that should be able to access the external interface and add them to the line that reads *PUBLIC_IP="192.168.1.144"*. Multiple addresses can be added by placing a space between each. Next, ensure that the *INET_IFACE="eth0"* corresponds with the network interface that is facing externally. The three variables shown below should be changed to reflect your internal network. For example, if your internal network is 10.10.10.*, then you should change the variables as shown here:

```
LAN_IFACE="eth1"                        # Firewall interface on internal network
LAN_IP_RANGE="10.10.10.0/24"            # IP Range of internal network
LAN_BCAST_ADRESS="10.10.10.255"         # IP Broadcast range for internal network
```

The next configuration change in the rc.firewall script will allow it to interface with Snort. Change the following setting as shown here:

```
QUEUE="yes"             # Use experimental QUEUE support
#QUEUE="no"             # Do not use experimental QUEUE support
```

The *Location of Programs Used by This Script* section lower in the file will have to be changed to suit your environment. For our installation, the following changes were necessary:

```
###########################################
# LOCATION OF PROGRAMS USED BY THIS SCRIPT #
###########################################
IPTABLES="/usr/local/sbin/iptables"
BRIDGE="/usr/local/sbin/brctl"
IFCONFIG="/sbin/ifconfig"
ROUTE="/sbin/route"
MODPROBE="/sbin/modprobe"
```

It is very important that you use the correct location for each of these, as you might have different versions loaded in different locations. For example, the Red Hat 8.0 Linux install has a binary for *iptables* located in /sbin, but this is an older version.

We also need to change the way in which the rc.firewall script uses IPtables. We will be using one simple IPtables command to cause Snort to be in charge of all packets being forwarded through the system. This command has to used instead of all of the current rc.firewall IPtables commands:

```
$IPTABLES -A FORWARD -j QUEUE
```

If you want to see what the script is doing when you start it, simply go back to the beginning of the file and remove the # symbol from the beginning of the *#set −x* line. This should complete the modifications necessary to the rc.firewall script, but you can also do some optional things such as auto-starting Snort. The following code shows what the completely modified rc.firewall script should look like and includes commands to start Snort automatically (based on the snort.sh script from www.honeynet.org):

```
#!/bin/bash
#
# rc.firewall, ver 0.6.1
# http://www.honeynet.org/papers/honeynet/tools/
# Rob McMillen <rvmcmil@cablespeed.com>
#
# CHANGES:
# 14 Feb 2003: Modified extensively to support Snort Inline mode for
#                 a bridging firewall.  Snort controls all packet decisions
#                 and IPTABLES simply queues everything. - J. Faircloth


#### If you want to see all the commands or which command is giving your
#         problems, remove the comment below.
set -x



#****************************************************************************
# USER VARIABLE SECTION
#****************************************************************************


##############
# COMMON VARS #
##############


# The MODE variable tells the script to #setup a bridge HoneyWall
# or a NATing HoneyWall.
#MODE="nat"
MODE="bridge"
```

```
# A space delimited list of honeypots IPs (public IP)
# If you are in "bridge" mode, this is the list of your
# honeypot IP's that will be behind the bridge.  If you are
# in "nat" mode, this is the list of public IPs you will
# be using for IP address translation.  Still confused?  Its
# the list of IPs the hackers will attack.
PUBLIC_IP="10.10.11.100"


### Variable for external network
INET_IFACE="eth0"                          # Firewall Public interface


### Variables for internal network
LAN_IFACE="eth1"                           # Firewall interface on internal network
LAN_IP_RANGE="10.10.11.0/24"        # IP Range of internal network
LAN_BCAST_ADRESS="10.10.11.255"     # IP Broadcast range for internal network


### IPTables script can be used with the Snort-Inline filter
### You can find the current release at
###   http://www.snort.org/dl/contrib/patches/inline/
QUEUE="yes"                 # Use experimental QUEUE support
#QUEUE="no"                   # Do not use experimental QUEUE support


PID=/var/run/snort_eth0.pid # Location for Snort's PID
DIR=/var/log/snort # Logging Directory
DATE=`date +%b_%d` # Date for creating log directories


####################
# END OF COMMON VARS #
####################


#########################
# VARIABLES FOR NAT MODE #
#########################
#  You use these variables ONLY if you are using NAT mode.
#  If you are in bridging mode, then these variables will
#  not be used.
#


ALIAS_MASK="255.255.255.0"              # Network mask to be used alias
```

```
HPOT_IP="192.168.0.144"              # Space delimited list of Honeypot ips
                                         # NOTE: MUST HAVE SAME NUMBER OF IPS AS
                                         # PUBLIC_IP VARIABLE.


############################
# END OF NAT MODE VARIABLES #
############################


######################################
# VARIABLES FOR MANAGEMENT INTERFACE #
######################################



# Interface for remote management.  If set to br0, it will assign
# MANAGE_IP to the bridge logical interface and allow its use
# as a management interface.  If you do not want to use a
#  management interface, set it to "none"
#MANAGE_IFACE="br0"
#MANAGE_IFACE="eth2"
MANAGE_IFACE="none"


MANAGE_IP="192.168.0.104"          # IP of management Interface
MANAGE_NETMASK="255.255.255.0"     # Netmask of management Interface


# Space delimited list of tcp ports allowed into the management interface
ALLOWED_TCP_IN="22"


# IP allowed to connect to the management interface
# If set to "any", it will allow anyone to attempt to connect.
# The notation ip/mask or a space delimited list of ips are
# allowed.
#MANAGER="any"
MANAGER="10.1.1.1 172.16.1.0/24"



###################
# END OF MANAGE VARS
###################


#########################################################
# VARIABLES THAT RESTRICT WHAT THE FIREWALL CAN SEND OUT #
#########################################################
```

```
# This variable will limit outbound Firewall connections
# to ports identified in the ALLOWED_TCP_OUT and
# ALLOWED_UDP_OUT variables.  If set to yes, it will
# restrict the firewall.  If set to no, it will allow all
# outbound connections generated by the firewall.
# NOTE:   There must be a management interface in bridge
# mode in order to have a firewall interface to restrict.

#RESTRICT="yes"
RESTRICT="no"

ALLOWED_UDP_OUT="53 123"
ALLOWED_TCP_OUT="22"

#########################
# END RESTRICT VARIABLES #
#########################

###########################################
# LOCATION OF PROGRAMS USED BY THIS SCRIPT #
###########################################
IPTABLES="/usr/local/sbin/iptables"
BRIDGE="/usr/local/sbin/brctl"
IFCONFIG="/sbin/ifconfig"
ROUTE="/sbin/route"
MODPROBE="/sbin/modprobe"
SNORT="/usr/local/bin/snort"

###################
# END OF PROG VARS #
###################

#************************************************************************
# END OF USER VARIABLE SECTION (DO NOT EDIT BEYOND THIS POINT)
#************************************************************************

#########
# First, confirm that IPChains is NOT running.  If
# it is running, clear the IPChains rules, remove the kernel
# module, and warn the end user.
```

```
lsmod | grep ipchain
IPCHAINS=$?

if [ "$IPCHAINS" = 0 ]; then
    echo ""
    echo "Dooh, IPChains is currently running! IPTables is required by"
    echo "the rc.firewall script. IPChains will be unloaded to allow"
    echo "IPTables to run.  It is recommened that you permanently"
    echo "disable IPChains in the /etc/rc.d startup scripts and enable"
    echo "IPTables instead."
    ipchains -F
    rmmod ipchains
fi


#########
# Flush rules
#
$IPTABLES -F
$IPTABLES -F -t nat
$IPTABLES -F -t mangle
$IPTABLES -X

echo ""


##########
# Let's setup the firewall according to the Mode selected: bridge or nat
#
if [ $MODE = "bridge" ]
then

    echo "Starting up Bridging mode."

    #########
    # Let's clean up the bridge.  This will only work if this script
    #    started the bridge.
    #
    $BRIDGE delif br0 ${INET_IFACE} 2> /dev/null
    $BRIDGE delif br0 ${LAN_IFACE} 2> /dev/null
    $IFCONFIG br0 down 2> /dev/null
    $BRIDGE delbr br0 2> /dev/null
```

```
#########
# Let's make sure our interfaces don't have ip information
#
$IFCONFIG $INET_IFACE 0.0.0.0 up -arp
$IFCONFIG $LAN_IFACE 0.0.0.0 up -arp


#########
# Let's start the bridge
#
$BRIDGE addbr br0
$BRIDGE addif br0 ${LAN_IFACE}
$BRIDGE addif br0 ${INET_IFACE}

# Let's make sure our bridge is not sending out
#   BPDUs (part of the spanning tree protocol).
$BRIDGE stp br0 off

if [ "$MANAGE_IFACE" = "br0" ]
then
    $IFCONFIG br0 $MANAGE_IP netmask $MANAGE_NETMASK up
else
    $IFCONFIG br0 0.0.0.0 up -arp
fi

elif [ $MODE = "nat" ]
then

    echo "Starting up Routing mode and enabling Network Address Translation."

    i=0
    z=1
    tempPub=( $PUBLIC_IP )

    for host in $HPOT_IP; do

        # Bring up eth aliases
        $IFCONFIG $INET_IFACE:${z} ${tempPub[$i]} netmask ${ALIAS_MASK} up

        # Ensure proper NATing is performed for all honeypots
```

```
        $IPTABLES -t nat -A POSTROUTING -s ${host} -j SNAT --to-source ${tempPub[$i]}
        $IPTABLES -t nat -A PREROUTING -d ${tempPub[$i]} -j DNAT --to-destination
${host}
        let "i += 1"
        let "z += 1"
    done
fi


# Let's figure out dns
if [ $DNS_HOST -z ]
then
    if [ $MODE = "bridge" ]
    then
        DNS_HOST=$PUBLIC_IP
    else
        DNS_HOST=$HPOT_IP
    fi
fi



#########
# Load all required IPTables modules
#

### Needed to initially load modules
/sbin/depmod -a

### Add iptables target LOG.
$MODPROBE ipt_LOG

### Add iptables QUEUE support (Experimental)
if test $QUEUE = "yes"
then
    # Insert kernel mod
    $MODPROBE ip_queue

  # check to see if it worked, if not exit with error
  lsmod | grep ip_queue
  IPQUEUE=$?

  if [ "$IPQUEUE" = 1 ]; then
```

```
        echo ""
        echo "It appears you do not have the ip_queue kernel module compiled"
        echo "for your kernel.  This module is required for Snort-Inline and"
        echo "QUEUE capabilities.  You either have to disable QUEUE, or compile"
        echo "the ip_queue kernel module for your kernel.  This module is part"
        echo "of the kernel source."
        exit
    fi



        echo "Enabling Snort-Inline capabilities, make sure Snort-Inline is"
        echo "running in -Q mode, or all outbound traffic will be blocked"
fi


### Support for connection tracking of FTP and IRC.
$MODPROBE ip_conntrack_ftp
$MODPROBE ip_conntrack_irc


### Enable ip_forward
echo "1" > /proc/sys/net/ipv4/ip_forward


### Queue everything and let Snort figure out what to do with each packet.


$IPTABLES -A FORWARD -j QUEUE


#########
# Kill off old Snort and start a new instance

### Kill snort
if [ -s $PID ]; then
  PRO=`cat $PID`
  echo ""
  echo "Previous version of Snort running"
  echo "Killing Snort, PID $PRO"
  echo ""
  kill -9 $PRO
fi


# Make directory based on date, if already exists do nothing.
if [ -d $DIR/$DATE ]; then
```

```
            :
else
        mkdir $DIR/$DATE

fi


# Snort options explanation
# -c configuration file
# -d log packet details
# -D daemon mode
# -l log directory
# -i interface in our case eth0, this option is required when using
#    the -Q option.
# -Q (used ONLY with Snort-Inline for QUEUE mode)


### Start snort for the Honeynet
$SNORT -D -d -c /etc/snort/snort.conf -Q -l $DIR/$DATE
```

Now, change to the /etc/rc.d directory and run the script by issuing the following
commands:

```
cd /etc/rc.d
./rc.firewall
```

You'll see a lot of data scroll across the screen as the script sets up the bridging functions and
configures the firewall if you enabled *set −x* in your rc.firewall file. You'll probably want to scroll
through this data just to make sure everything worked properly. At this point, you should have a
functioning firewalling bridge.

If everything appears to be functioning correctly, it's time to reconfigure Snort. The primary
change we're going to make is in the rules files. All of the default rules are set to *Alert*. For our
inline IDS to function, we'll need to change the actions on some or all of the Alert rules to Drop
rules, depending on your needs. This will cause Snort to drop the packet rather than issue an
alert. Which rules you set to drop will differ based on the purpose of your IDS and the structure
of your network. If you are running a honeynet, a good list of drop rules can be found at
www.honeynet.org.

Modifying your rules files can be done manually by editing each rule file using *vi* or your
favorite text editor. This will have to be done for any rules that you want to use as drop rules.
The rules that you modify will depend on the needs of your network environment. If you use *vi*,
you can issue the following command to quickly replace all instances of Alert with Drop:

```
:%s/alert/drop/
```

At this point, you should be ready to run Snort in inline mode. We'll need to restart Snort
for the rules to take effect, so simply rerun the rc.firewall script using the following command:

`/etc/rc.d/rc.firewall`

Snort should successfully start and begin monitoring the network traffic going across the bridge. Hopefully, you have an operational Snort inline installation at this point. If you run into any problems with the installation of software or their configuration, refer to the Web site from which the software was gathered. Moreover, don't forget some of the invaluable resources available on the Web for specific help in setting up an IDS or Snort. Table 31.4 lists some of the Web sites that we found to be very helpful in setting up Snort in inline mode.

Table 31.4 Web Resources

URL	Description
www.snort.org	The main source for Snort information and documentation.
http://groups.google.com	A search engine for newsgroups that can help you find a great deal of help on any subject.
www.honeynet.org	Information on honeynets and the configuration of an IDS for honeynets.
www.redhat.com	Information on the Red Hat Linux distribution.

Using Inline IDS to Protect Your Network

Now that we have a functioning inline IDS, we need to test it and see how it can be used to protect our network. We will continue to use the network diagram shown in Figure 31.2 for example purposes. This will allow us to configure some basic rules and see how the IDS reacts to them.

To recap, we have configured the Linux system to function as a bridge. The system has two network cards, with one facing the external network and the other facing the internal network. IPtables is being used to bridge between the network cards and route the traffic to a queue for processing. The Snort inline patch has been installed and configured to monitor this queue and determine the fate of all packets crossing the bridge. By configuring the rules files with *drop* statements, we can set specific packets to be dropped and not routed between the interfaces.

For our first test, we will set up a Web server on one of our client systems. This Web server will be configured without SSL and will be listening on port 80. To test this, we will need access to a system outside the protected network. For the purposes of this test, we will be using a freely available online port scanning site at www.securitymetrics.com/portscan.adp. If you run this test from the system hosting the Web server, you will receive a response similar to the one shown in Figure 31.5.

Figure 31.5 Portscan from Web Server

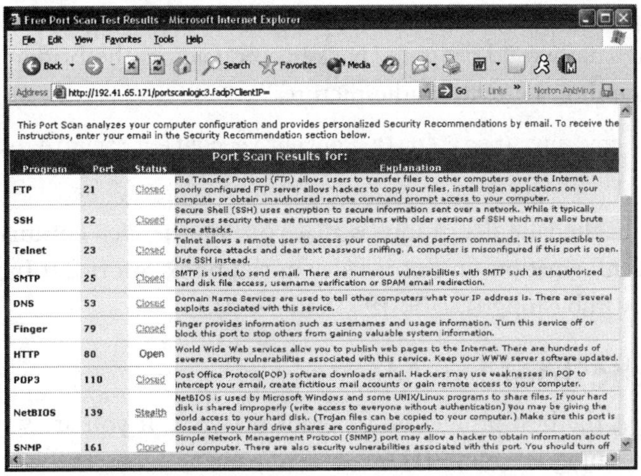

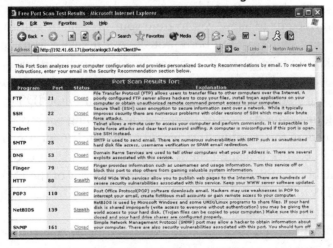

As you can see in Figure 31.5, port 80 has been detected as Open, which means that this port can be detected from an outside system. To prevent this, we're going to add a rule for Snort to drop packets destined for port 80 on the internal network.

Open the file local.rules in your rules directory using your favorite text editor. Add a rule similar to the following to configure Snort to drop traffic destined for this port:

```
drop tcp any any -> 10.10.10.0/24 80
```

This simple rule will make your IDS drop any traffic destined for port 80 on your internal network. Ensure that the local.rules line has been uncommented in your snort.conf file, and then restart Snort to make this rule take effect. If you repeat the portscan from the remote system, you should receive the result shown in Figure 31.6.

Figure 31.6 Portscan from Web Server with Snort Filtering

As you can see, it is extremely easy to configure Snort to drop packets after the software has been properly configured. A more complex example would be to make Snort drop packets based on both their port and their content. This is just as easy to do and, as previously mentioned, can be accomplished by simply changing the current Snort rules to Drop instead of Alert. For example, the following rule would drop *any* packet going across the bridge via an established TCP connection containing the text "nudie pictures":

```
drop tcp any any -> any any (msg:"Adult Content"; content:"nudie pictures"; nocase;
flow:to_client,established;)
```

The basic change in the rule definitions is that you use the *drop* command instead of *alert*. There's more detailed information on Snort rules in the book Snort 2.0 Intrusion Detection available from Syngress Publishing (ISBN: 1931836-74-4).

Is Inline IDS the Tool for Me?

Inline IDS is not always the best protection for your network. If you are working in a large corporate environment, running an inline IDS can slow your network traffic to an unacceptable level. In addition, if the IDS has not been configured properly or is malfunctioning, the possibility exists that the IDS could interrupt normal network functionality. Valid traffic could be mistakenly dropped, or communications in their entirety could be stopped. The proper use of tools such as this is an important skill for a security administrator to learn.

If you are running a typical corporate network, chances are that you have one or more high-speed Internet connections going into your network. These are typically protected by a powerful firewall that is designed to handle the amount of data received from these high-speed connections. To provide an acceptable quality of service to the users on the network, these firewalls are typically configured with rules that process traffic quickly and efficiently. In the case of inline IDS, the rules can be very complex, and the actions performed by the IDS might take longer than what is acceptable for your network.

One option to consider with the use of an inline IDS is a honeynet implementation. A great deal of information on honeynets can be found at www.honeynet.org. There are occasions when you might want to set up a honeynet beside your normal network connection to see what new attacks are being performed or to allow you to tune your firewall. In a situation such as this, an inline IDS would be very appropriate to both protect your network from devastating attacks and to keep your network from being used as a staging area to launch further attacks.

There is a great deal of liability in setting up a honeynet, and you need to ensure that an intruder cannot use your honeynet to attack other systems. An inline IDS can help to prevent this by blocking outgoing malicious packets or by rewriting outgoing packets.

Another useful purpose for an inline IDS would be to implement it in a position where only a specific portion of a network is behind the IDS. This can provide an extra layer of security to systems containing highly confidential data. By using the content of the packets as a guide, you can configure your IDS to ensure that confidential data can only be accessed by specific entities that are explicitly granted access to the data.

Whatever your intentions, put some thought into both the advantages and disadvantages of installing an inline IDS onto your network. There are many situations in which this type of security device can be very useful, but just as many where it can be devastating to your user community.

IDS Functionality on the PIX Firewall

One of important features of the PIX firewall is its intrusion detection capability. Cisco has a dedicated IDS product called Cisco Secure IDS (former NetRanger appliance), but a limited part of its functionality is implemented in both Cisco IOS and Cisco PIX. Because the PIX is basically an OSI Layers 3 and 4 filtering device, it supports detection of only simpler attacks that happen on these layers of network communication and can be detected by inspecting a single packet in the traffic. The IDS signatures (that is, descriptions of attacks) that the PIX supports are a subset of the Cisco Secure IDS signature set and are embedded in PIX software. In order to upgrade this set of signatures, you need to upgrade the entire PIX firmware using a general upgrade procedure. Doing so does not pose a big problem, though, because these signatures describe very general and simple attacks, which are not invented often. Intrusion detection can be configured on each interface in inbound and outbound directions. When the PIX detects each signature, the device produces an alert (the alert can be of two types, *information* or *attack*, depending on the severity of the attack) and sends it via syslog to the configured destination.

Supported Signatures

Unfortunately, Cisco's own documentation is not quite clear about signatures supported in each specific version. The best way to check what your PIX can do in the area of intrusion detection is to browse a list of syslog messages produced by the specific version (for example, see the *Cisco PIX Firewall System Log Messages* guide). For version 6.2, syslog messages numbered from 400 000 to 400 050 are reserved for IDS messages. Their format is shown here:

```
%PIX-4-4000<nn>: : <sig_num> <sig_msg> from <IP_addr> to <IP_addr> on interface
<int_name>
```

This syslog message means that PIX has detected an attack with number *sig_num* and name *sig_msg*. The two IP addresses show the origin and the destination of this attack. Finally, the interface on which the attack was detected is mentioned. For example:

```
%PIX-4-400013 IDS:2003 ICMP redirect from 1.2.3.4 to 10.2.3.1 on interface dmz
```

Table 31.5 lists all signatures detected by PIX, with short descriptions.

Table 31.5 PIX IDS Signatures

Message Number	Signature ID	Signature Title	Signature Type
400000	1000	IP options-Bad Option List	Informational
400001	1001	IP options-Record Packet Route	Informational
400002	1002	IP options-Timestamp	Informational
400003	1003	IP options-Security	Informational
400004	1004	IP options-Loose Source Route	Informational
400005	1005	IP options-SATNET ID	Informational
400006	1006	IP options-Strict Source Route	Informational
400007	1100	IP Fragment Attack	Attack

Continued

Table 31.5 PIX IDS Signatures

Message Number	Signature ID	Signature Title	Signature Type
400008	1102	IP Impossible Packet	Attack
400009	1103	IP Fragments Overlap	Attack
400010	2000	ICMP Echo Reply	Informational
400011	2001	ICMP Host Unreachable	Informational
400012	2002	ICMP Source Quench	Informational
400013	2003	ICMP Redirect	Informational
400014	2004	ICMP Echo Request	Informational
400015	2005	ICMP Time Exceeded for a Datagram	Informational
400016	2006	ICMP Parameter Problem on Datagram	Informational
400017	2007	ICMP Timestamp Request	Informational
400018	2008	ICMP Timestamp Reply	Informational
400019	2009	ICMP Information Request	Informational
400020	2010	ICMP Information Reply	Informational
400021	2011	ICMP Address Mask Request	Informational
400022	2012	ICMP Address Mask Reply	Informational
400023	2150	Fragmented ICMP Traffic	Attack
400024	2151	Large ICMP Traffic	Attack
400025	2154	Ping of Death Attack	Attack
400026	3040	TCP NULL flags	Attack
400027	3041	TCP SYN+FIN flags	Attack
400028	3042	TCP FIN only flags	Attack
400029	3153	FTP Improper Address Specified	Informational
400030	3154	FTP Improper Port Specified	Informational
400031	4050	UDP Bomb attack	Attack
400032	4051	UDP Snork attack	Attack
400033	4052	UDP Chargen DoS attack	Attack
400034	6050	DNS HINFO Request	Attack
400035	6051	DNS Zone Transfer	Attack
400036	6052	DNS Zone Transfer from High Port	Attack
400037	6053	DNS Request for All Records	Attack
400038	6100	RPC Port Registration	Informational
400039	6101	RPC Port Unregistration	Informational
400040	6102	RPC Dump	Informational
400041	6103	Proxied RPC Request	Attack

Continued

Table 31.5 PIX IDS Signatures

Message Number	Signature ID	Signature Title	Signature Type
400042	6150	ypserv (YP server daemon) Portmap Request	Informational
400043	6151	ypbind (YP bind daemon) Portmap Request	Informational
400044	6152	yppasswdd (YP password daemon) Portmap Request	Informational
400045	6153	ypupdated (YP update daemon) Portmap Request	Informational
400046	6154	ypxfrd (YP transfer daemon) Portmap Request	Informational
400047	6155	mountd (mount daemon) Portmap Request	Informational
400048	6175	rexd (remote execution daemon) Portmap Request	Informational
400049	6180	rexd (remote execution daemon) Attempt	Informational
400050	6190	statd Buffer Overflow	Attack

The signature IDs listed in the table correspond to signature numbers on the Cisco Secure IDS appliance. See www.cisco.com/univercd/cc/td/doc/product/iaabu/csids/csids1/csidsug/ sigs.htm (*Cisco Secure Intrusion Detection System Version 2.2.1 User Guide*) for a complete reference. All signatures are divided into two classes: informational and attack. The division is rather deliberate and cannot be changed, but it makes sense most of the time. For example, all Denial of Service (DoS) attacks are listed as attacks, and all information requests only have informational status. You might feel that if somebody tries to obtain information on RPC services on one of your hosts, this constitutes an attack, but it is still listed as informational by Cisco. Generalizing a little, it is possible to suggest the following reasoning on attack classification (from top to bottom in the table):

- Packets with IP options will not do any harm because they are always dropped by the PIX, so if these packets are detected, send only an informational message.

- Fragmented packets can pass through the firewall and are generally difficult to inspect, so they constitute an attack attempt.

- Legitimate ICMP traffic, although unwanted and maybe revealing some information about your network (for example, ICMP Information Request), is not classified as an attack.

- Fragmented ICMP, Ping of Death, and so on are considered attacks.

- Impossible TCP flag combinations are considered attacks because they are sometimes used for stealth scanning of networks.

- All floods/DoS attempts (including the UDP Snork attack) are classified as attacks.

- DNS transfers are classified as attacks; they reveal too much about the network.

- General RPC requests and all information requests for various RPC services are not considered that harmful and are classified as informational.

- Some specific one-packet attacks on RPC services are recognized separately.

Configuring Auditing for the PIX with an IDS

Auditing is configured using the *ip audit* command. Auditing can be turned on or off, different auditing policies can be created, the policies can be applied to specific interfaces, and specific signatures can be turned on or off. The easiest configuration requires you to assign a name for the auditing policy, specify actions (one for informational signatures and one for attack signatures) to be taken, and apply the policy to an interface. The actions that can be taken are:

- **Alarm** When PIX detects a signature in the packet, it reports with the message described previously to all configured syslog servers.

- **Drop** When this action is configured, PIX drops the offending packet.

- **Reset** This action means that PIX should drop the packet and close the connection if this packet was a part of an open connection.

The default action is alarm. Policy configuration usually takes no more than two commands:

```
ip audit name <audit_name> info action [drop | alarm | reset ]
ip audit name <audit_name> attack action [drop | alarm | reset ]
```

For example, the following commands create a policy with the name *myaudit* and specify that when an informational signature is matched, the PIX should send an alarm to syslog, and when an attack signature is matched, the PIX should drop the packet:

```
PIX1(config)# ip audit name myaudit info action alarm
PIX1(config)# ip audit name myaudit attack action drop
```

It is possible to omit the *action* in the configuration. In this case, the default action is applied. Default actions are configured via these commands:

```
ip audit info action [drop | alarm | reset ]
ip audit attack action [drop | alarm | reset ]
```

If not changed, the default action is *alarm*. Note that if you issue only the following command but not the corresponding *attack* command, no attack signatures will be matched:

```
PIX1(config)# ip audit name myaudit info action alarm
```

On the other hand, if you configure the policy in the following manner, omitting the action for informational signatures, both informational and attack signatures will be matched, and the default action (alarm) will be applied when a packet is matched with an informational signature:

```
PIX1(config)# ip audit name myaudit info
PIX1(config)# ip audit name myaudit attack action drop
```

After creating a policy, you need to apply it to an interface in order to activate IDS on the interface. For example:

```
PIX1(config)# ip audit interface outside myaudit
```

This means that all signatures and actions configured should be matched on the outside interface. The general form of this command is:

```
ip audit interface <if_name> <audit_name>
```

- *if_name* is the name of an interface where the IDS has to check for packets.
- *audit_name* is a name of the policy that describes which actions to take.

As an example, let's configure a simple IDS on the outside interface, which will send an alarm when an informational signature is matched and drop the connection when an attack is noticed:

```
PIX1(config)# ip audit name myaudit info alarm
PIX1(config)# ip audit name myaudit attack action drop
PIX1(config)# ip audit interface outside myaudit
```

Each command has its *no* equivalent, which removes the command from the configuration. For example:

```
PIX1(config)# no ip audit interface outside myaudit
PIX1(config)# no ip audit name myaudit info
```

Another command allows easy clearing of all IDS configuration related to an interface, policy, or default action:

```
clear ip audit [name | signature| interface | audit | info | attack ]
```

The following set of commands displays the corresponding configuration of IDS related to the interface, audit, or default action. This code simply shows the commands you entered when configuring these parameters:

```
show ip audit interface <if_name>
show ip audit info
show ip audit attack
show ip audit name <audit_name>
```

Disabling Signatures

Imagine the following situation: You are interested in being alarmed on the informational signature 6102, "RPC Dump." This means that you have to include all informational signatures in your policy with a command such as:

```
PIX1(config)# ip audit name myaudit info action alarm
```

Here comes the problem: Many other signatures are listed as informational, and some of them are very "noisy"—generating lots of alarms—for example, number 2000, "ICMP echo reply," which is simply a response to a ping. Chances are, you will be flooded with alarms on this latter signature and will not notice the former one, which is the one in which you are actually interested. One way to get around this issue is to disable the noisy signatures with the following command, which disables the detection of the signature with number *sig_number*:

```
ip audit signature <sig_number> disable
```

In our case, to disable the "ICMP echo reply" signature, use the following command:

PIX1(config)# **ip audit signature 2000 disable**

After this command is entered, signature number 2000 ("ICMP echo reply") will not be detected by the PIX at all. Note that disabling a signature means disabling it globally, not for a specific interface or audit.

It is possible to see the list of all disabled signatures with the command:

PIX1(config)# **show ip audit signature**

You can enable a disabled signature with a *no* command in configuration mode:

```
no ip audit signature <sig_number> disable
```

Configuring Shunning

Shunning is a term used in the IDS context to describe blocking traffic from an attacking host. Shunning it is configured on the PIX using the following command:

shun <src_ip> [<dst_ip> <sport> <dport> [<protocol>]]

This technique temporarily blocks all traffic from the specified source IP address. To block all traffic, the source IP address of 10.0.1.1, use the following command:

PIX1(config)# **shun 10.0.1.1**

You can also deny specific traffic from the source IP by specifying a source port, destination IP address, and destination port number. After the *shun* command is entered, the PIX deletes all matching connections from its internal connection table and drops all further packets that match the command's parameters. The action of this command takes priority over access list entries and even security levels on interfaces; all specified traffic is blocked, whether the offending host is on the inside or outside of the interface. In order to remove this blocking action, use the corresponding *no* command. For example:

PIX1(config)# **no shun 10.0.1.1**

This command is dynamic and is not displayed or stored in the configuration. If you want to view active shuns, use the *show shun* command. The *clear shun* command deletes all shun entries.

Summary

In this chapter, we covered some of the more advanced features of Snort. We began by discussing policy-based intrusion detection. With policy-based intrusion detection, all acceptable traffic on the network is defined in advance by the security administrator, and a network policy is developed. This network policy is then translated into Snort rules, and Snort is configured to monitor the network for traffic that does not comply with the network policy. Policy-based intrusion detection can be used in smaller networks or in very high security environments to ensure that all traffic flowing across the network complies with the approved network policy.

Next, we reviewed the concepts behind an inline IDS. An inline IDS is an IDS that functions between two portions of the network by bridging traffic between two interfaces. This allows the IDS to take action on traffic flowing between its interfaces before the traffic gets to its destination. Using Snort in inline mode allows you to selectively drop individual packets based on their intended host, port, or content. By using a combination of several different pieces of software working together, Snort can actively protect your network from attack rather than just alert you to attacks in progress.

The PIX firewall supports the same set of atomic intrusion detection signatures as the Cisco IOS firewall. This set is a subset of signatures supported by the Cisco Secure IDS product. These signatures are divided into two sets: informational and attack. It is possible to configure different response options for each set of signatures. The responses range from simple alerting via syslog to blocking the connection in which a signature was detected.

Summary

Index

Syngress: *The Definition of a Serious Security Library*

Syn·gress (sin-gres): *noun, sing.* Freedom from risk or danger; safety. See *security*.

Snort 2.0 Intrusion Detection
Jay Beale and Brian Caswell, Snort.org

Written by Snort gurus, including Brian Caswell, the Snort.org webmaster, this bestselling title will put you on solid training ground with Snort intrusion detection. It guides you through IDS concepts, Snort installation, configuration, and optimization.

ISBN: 1-931836-74-4
Price: $49.95 USA $59.95 CAN

Special Ops: Host and Network Security for Microsoft, UNIX, and Oracle
Erik Pace Birkholz

"Strap on the night vision goggles, apply the camo paint, then lock and load. Special Ops is an adrenaline-pumping tour of the most critical security weaknesses present on most any corporate network today, with some of the world's best drill sergeants leading the way."

—*Joel Scambray, Senior Director, Microsoft's MSN*

"Special Ops has brought some of the best speakers and researchers of computer security together to cover what you need to know to survive in today's net."

—*Jeff Moss, President & CEO, Black Hat, inc.*

ISBN: 1-928994-74-1
Price: $69.95 USA $108.95 CAN

Stealing the Network: How to "Own the Box"
Ryan Russell, FX, Kingpin, and Ken Pfiel

"*Stealing the Network: How to Own the Box* is a unique book in the fiction department. It combines stories that are false, with technology that is real. While none of the stories have happened, there is no reason why they could not. You could argue it provides a road map for criminal hackers, but I say it does something else; it provides a glimpse into the creative minds of some of today's best hackers, and even the best hackers will tell you that the game is a mental one."

—*from the foreword by Jeff Moss, President & CEO, Black Hat, Inc.*

ISBN: 1-931836-87-6
Price: $49.95 USA $69.95 CAN

SYNGRESS®